Revised Second Edition

Masterplots

1,801 Plot Stories and Critical Evaluations of the World's Finest Literature

Revised Second Edition

Volume 8
Mys – Per
4357 – 4978

Edited by
FRANK N. MAGILL

Story Editor, Revised Edition
DAYTON KOHLER

Consulting Editor, Revised Second Edition
LAURENCE W. MAZZENO

SALEM PRESS

Pasadena, California   Englewood Cliffs, New Jersey

Editor in Chief: Dawn P. Dawson

Consulting Editor: Laurence W. Mazzeno

Project Editors: Eric Howard
Juliane Brand

Acquisitions Editor: Mark Rehn

Production Editor: Cynthia Breslin Beres

Managing Editor: Christina J. Moose

Research Supervisor: Jeffry Jensen

Research: Irene McDermott

Proofreading Supervisor: Yasmine A. Cordoba

Layout: William Zimmerman

Library of Congress Cataloging-in-Publication Data

Masterplots / edited by Frank N. Magill; consulting editor, Laurence W. Mazzeno. — Rev. 2nd ed.

    p.   cm.

Expanded and updated version of the 1976 rev. ed.

Includes bibliographical references and indexes.

1. Literature—Stories, plots, etc. 2. Literature—History and criticism. I. Magill, Frank Northen, 1907-1997. II. Mazzeno, Laurence W.

PN44.M33   1996

809—dc20

ISBN 0-89356-084-7 (set)

ISBN 0-89356-092-8 (volume 8)

96-23382

CIP

Revised Second Edition
Third Printing

PRINTED IN THE UNITED STATES OF AMERICA

LIST OF TITLES IN VOLUME 8

MASTERPLOTS

Revised Second Edition

THE MYSTERIES OF PARIS

Type of work: Novel
Author: Eugène Sue (1804-1857)
Type of plot: Melodrama
Time of plot: Mid-nineteenth century
Locale: France and Germany
First published: Les Mystères de Paris, 1842-1843 (English translation, 1843)

Principal characters:
    RODOLPH, the Grand Duke of Gerolstein
    LADY SARAH MACGREGOR, his wife
    FLEUR-DE-MARIE, their daughter
    CLÉMENCE D'HARVILLE, the wife of one of Rodolph's friends
    LA CHOUETTE and
    SCHOOLMASTER, two Paris criminals
    JACQUES FERRAND, a hypocritical and cruel lawyer
    MADAME GEORGES, a woman befriended by Rodolph
    RIGOLETTE, Fleur-de-Marie's friend

The Story:

Rodolph, the Grand Duke of Gerolstein, a small German state, was a handsome young man in his thirties in 1838. Behind him lay a strange past. As a youth, he had been brought up in his father's court by an evil tutor named Polidori, who had done his best to warp and confuse the young prince's mind. Polidori had been urged on by the beautiful but sinister Lady Sarah Macgregor, who had been told in her youth that she was destined someday to be a queen.

Sarah had decided that Rodolph, heir to a duchy, would be the perfect husband for her, and, with the aid of Polidori, she had forced Rodolph into a secret morganatic marriage. In England, where she had fled, she gave birth to a daughter. Rodolph's father was furious, and he had the marriage annulled. One day, after he had threatened to kill his father, Rodolph was sent into exile. Before long, Sarah lost all interest in her child and paid her Paris lawyer, Jacques Ferrand, to find a home for the girl. Ferrand gave the child into the care of some unscrupulous child takers and, after a few years, falsely wrote to Sarah that the child had died. Sarah forwarded the letter to Rodolph.

Rodolph moved to Paris, where he amused himself by roaming through the slums in disguise. Although he was strong, agile, and a fine fighter, the young duke was always followed by his faithful servant, Sir Walter Murphy. Together they ferreted out the secrets and mysteries of Paris streets. One night, Rodolph chanced to save a young girl who was being attacked. When he had heard her story, he was so touched by it that he decided to help her. Fleur-de-Marie, as she was called, was an orphan who had been brought up by criminals and had been in prison. Freed, she was recognized by her old tormentors and captured by them, drugged, made a prisoner, and compelled to suffer great indignities. Feeling that she was really innocent of the crimes into which she had been forced, Rodolph took her to the farm of Madame Georges. The girl's beauty, her sad plight, and the fact that she was the age his dead daughter would have been, aroused his interest and pity.

Madame Georges was likewise a woman whom the duke had befriended. Her criminal husband had deserted her, taking their son with him. Rodolph had searched the streets of Paris for a clue to the whereabouts of Madame Georges' son. At the farm, Fleur-de-Marie soon developed into a devout and delightful young woman.

Rodolph continued to live his double life. He attended diplomatic balls and the parties of thieves, and on both planes he found much to do to help people to live better lives. At last, in order to learn better the secrets of Paris, he took lodgings in a boardinghouse in one of the poorer sections of town. There he met many needy families, and in countless ways he helped them all. One of the occupants of the house was a girl named Rigolette, who had been Fleur-de-Marie's friend in prison. Rigolette was hardworking and kind, and Rodolph learned a great deal about the people of the house from her.

One day he learned that Clémence d'Harville, the wife of one of his good friends, was involved in an affair with a lodger in the house. It did not take him long to discover that the person behind this affair, plotting the destruction of d'Harville and his wife, was Lady Sarah Macgregor. As soon as he could, Rodolph warned Clémence and saved her from her folly. Clémence was unfortunate in that she had been forced into marriage with d'Harville by her mother-in-law, for she did not love her husband. Because he and their daughter were subject to epileptic fits, her life was an unhappy one. By chance, d'Harville learned of his wife's unhappiness and contrived to commit suicide in such a way that everyone thought his death accidental. By this act, he saved Clémence from greater unhappiness and atoned for the evil he had committed in marrying her.

While staying at the lodging house, Rodolph had learned of the numerous evil deeds of the hypocritical lawyer, Jacques Ferrand. When Rodolph learned that Ferrand was planning the murder of Clémence's father, he and Sir Walter Murphy succeeded in thwarting the lawyer's evil scheme. Ferrand was also responsible for the imprisonment of Rigolette's lover. In order to get to the bottom of Ferrand's plans, Rodolph remembered Cecily, a beautiful woman who had once been married to his private doctor, but who later became a depraved creature. Rodolph secured her release from prison and had her introduced into Ferrand's household, where she could spy on his activities and learn his secrets.

Meanwhile, Sarah had asked Ferrand to find a young girl whom she could claim was really her child by Rodolph, for she hoped that if she could produce the dead girl she could effect a reconciliation, now that Rodolph was the reigning duke of Gerolstein. Ferrand, learning the whereabouts of Fleur-de-Marie, hired La Chouette, an ugly one-eyed woman, and a criminal called the Schoolmaster to kidnap the girl from the farm of Madame Georges. When the Schoolmaster arrived at the farm, he discovered that Madame Georges was his wife, the woman he had deserted. He did not succeed in getting Fleur-de-Marie. Instead, she was put in jail for failing to give testimony concerning a crime she had witnessed before Rodolph had saved her from the slums. By chance, Clémence found the girl while on a charitable errand. Not knowing that Fleur-de-Marie knew Rodolph, she tried to make the girl's life more pleasant in prison.

When Sarah learned that Fleur-de-Marie had been under the care of Rodolph's friends, she became jealous and made arrangements to have her killed as soon as she could be released from the prison. Ferrand, entrusted with plans for her death, had her released from prison by an accomplice who pretended to be an agent of Clémence d'Harville. On leaving the prison, Fleur-de-Marie met Rigolette and told her old friend of her fortune. Rigolette, who knew Clémence through Rodolph, was pleased. After they parted, Fleur-de-Marie was seized by Ferrand's hirelings and taken into the country, where she was thrown into the river. Some passersby, however, saw her in the water and pulled her ashore in time to save her life.

Meanwhile, La Chouette, learning that Fleur-de-Marie was really the daughter of Rodolph and Sarah, had hurried to Sarah with her information. Sarah was shocked at the discovery. La Chouette, seeing a chance to make more money by killing Sarah and stealing her jewels, stabbed her protector. The attacker escaped with the jewels and returned to the Schoolmaster to taunt him with her success. The two got into a fight, and the Schoolmaster killed La Chouette. He was captured and put into prison.

Through Cecily, Rodolph had also learned that his daughter was not really dead. Cecily had had little difficulty in uncovering Ferrand's past. As soon as he knew what Sarah had done, Rodolph went to see her; despite her terrible wound, he accused her violently of the shameful and criminal neglect of her daughter.

Returning home, Rodolph was surprised to hear that Clémence had visited him. Clémence had had the fortune to find Fleur-de-Marie in the home where she had been cared for after her escape from drowning, and she had brought the girl to Rodolph. Clémence did not know that events had proved that Fleur-de-Marie was Rodolph's daughter, and so the reunion of father and child was not without pain as well as pleasure, for Clémence and Rodolph had long secretly known that they loved each other. Rodolph begged Clémence to marry him and to be a mother to his child. He felt sure that Sarah would die and the way would thus be clear for their happy life together.

Rodolph remarried Sarah on her deathbed so that their daughter could be called truly legitimate. Information that Rodolph had received from Cecily also made it possible for him to free Rigolette's lover from prison, and it turned out that he was the long-lost son of Madame Georges. With these problems solved, Rodolph planned to return to Germany. First, however, he used his knowledge of Ferrand's activities to force the lawyer to establish many worthy charities. His money gone, Ferrand went into a decline and died soon afterward. Rigolette's lover became administrator for one of the charities, and, after their marriage, he and Rigolette lived happily with Madame Georges.

Rodolph returned to Germany with Fleur-de-Marie as his legitimate daughter and Clémence as his wife. For a time the three lived together with great happiness. Then Rodolph noticed that Fleur-de-Marie seemed to have moods of depression. One day, she explained, weeping, that his goodness to her was without compare but that the evil life that she had led before he had rescued her from the slums preyed constantly on her mind. She begged to be allowed to enter a convent. Rodolph, realizing that nothing he could say would change her mind, gave his permission.

While serving as a novice at the convent. Fleur-de-Marie's conduct was so perfect that when she was admitted to the order, she immediately became the abbess. This honor was too much for her gentle soul to bear, or for her weak, sick body to withstand, and that very night she died. Rodolph, noting that the day of her death was the anniversary of the day on which he had tried to kill his father, felt that the ways of fate are strange.

Critical Evaluation:

One of the legacies of the French Revolution of 1789 was that the movement toward universal literacy proceeded more rapidly in France than anywhere else in Europe. A circulation war developed among French daily newspapers, and one of the weapons with which the war was fought was serial fiction of a melodramatic kind, whose relentless narrative thrust made readers anxious to acquire every episode. *The Mysteries of Paris* was the breakthrough work which demonstrated the potential of this curious new medium, revealing the remarkable truth which is responsible for the seemingly paradoxical face of modern journalism: that most newspaper readers are not much interested in news of political and economic significance; they prefer "human interest stories," the more sensational and scandalous the better, preferably spiced with a little local interest and some connection to royalty. Eugène Sue imported this idea into his fiction with great enthusiasm.

The plot of *The Mysteries of Paris* is firmly located in the well-known streets, prisons, hospitals, and asylums of contemporary Paris. It features a host of nasty villains who add to the cruel blows inflicted by ill-fortune and bad laws upon honest working folk. The desperate attempts made by humbly virtuous individuals to get by in life are here aided by the charitable efforts of a princely paragon of nobility who goes among them in disguise (as some princes have been reputed by legend to do). The multistranded story moves from drinking dens and dungeons to grand houses and palaces but is careful to bind its disparate elements together with a series of careful contrivances. As the plot unwinds, everyone eventually turns out to be related to everyone else, either by blood or by virtue of being unluckily enmeshed in the same evil conspiracies. No previous work had ever offered the poor such a sense of being a part of the affairs of the world or such wild fantasies of salvation from their most desperate plights. Nor had any previous work of popular fiction addressed the rich with such frankness on the subject of the desperate plight of the poor and the practical possibilities of its alleviation.

Such scenes as the deliberate blinding of the Schoolmaster and the death of La Chouette led Sue's detractors to accuse him of sadism, but the charge is mistaken. What such scenes actually attempt to give is an appropriate expression of an outrage so profound that nothing but extremes of horror can possibly contain it. There is a key scene set in La Force (the main prison of Paris at the time) in which a petty thief must unwittingly play Scheherazade, spinning out a story to frustrate the planned murder of the unjustly imprisoned Germain. The thief points out— presumably echoing the author's fascination with an equivalent discovery—that, although the criminals who constitute his audience have no liking for tales in which men like themselves go to the guillotine, they retain a more profound sense of morality which gladly and greatly rejoices in the unusual punishment of the unusually wicked.

Pursuing this aim, Sue distinguishes between those criminals who retain a certain essential "heart" and "honour" and those who give themselves over entirely to predatory cruelty. For the latter, fates as hideous as he can contrive are carefully and fervently designed. The worst of crimes inflamed such indignation in Sue that nothing within the law would serve as recompense, and for him the worst crimes of all were crimes of greed and ambition masked by respectable appearances: the crimes of crooked lawyers, corrupt bailiffs, and poison-supplying doctors. There were many readers ready to agree with him.

In the end, though, Sue could not contrive a wholehearted escape from the prison of contemporary morality, and his failure to carry through the bold thrust of his own ideals is evident in the concluding passage, in which the happy ending he has so cunningly contrived is eaten away as if by a cancer. Sue does not allow Fleur-de-Marie to forget that, no matter how little choice she had in the matter, she had briefly been a whore. That her true place in the world is that of a princess there is not a shadow of doubt, and her saintliness continues to increase when she belatedly comes into that inheritance, but her sense of guilt and shame poisons her peace of mind.

"Critical Evaluation" by Brian Stableford

Bibliography:
Atkinson, Nora. *Eugène Sue et le roman-feuilleton.* Paris: A. Nizet & M. Bastard, 1929. In the absence of any in-depth study in English, this is perhaps the most useful French source.
Chaunu, Pierre. *Eugène Sue et la seconde république.* Paris: Presses Universitaires de France, 1948. A compact study of Sue's life and works.

James, Louis. *Fiction for the Working Man 1830-1850*. New York: Oxford University Press, 1963. *The Mysteries of Paris* and other Sue works are discussed in chapter 8, "Fiction from America and France."

Palmer, Jerry. *Thrillers: Genesis and Structure of a Popular Genre*. London: Edward Arnold, 1978. *The Mysteries of Paris* is discussed in part 3, subsection 3, in "The Literary Origins of the Thriller."

THE MYSTERIES OF UDOLPHO

Type of work: Novel
Author: Ann Radcliffe (1764-1823)
Type of plot: Gothic
Time of plot: 1584
Locale: France and Italy
First published: 1794

Principal characters:
> EMILY ST. AUBERT, a young French aristocrat
> SIGNOR MONTONI, a villainous Italian who is married to Emily's aunt
> VALANCOURT, Emily's sweetheart
> COUNT MORANO, a Venetian nobleman who is in love with Emily
> MADAME MONTONI, Emily's aunt

The Story:

After the death of his wife, Monsieur St. Aubert, a French aristocrat, took his daughter on a trip in the Pyrenees. High on a mountain road, the St. Auberts met a young nobleman dressed in hunting clothes. He was Valancourt, the younger son of a family with which Monsieur St. Aubert was acquainted. Joining the St. Auberts on their journey, the young man soon fell in love with eighteen-year-old Emily St. Aubert, and the girl felt that she, too, might lose her heart to him.

St. Aubert became gravely ill and died in a cottage near the Chateau-le-Blanc, ancestral seat of the noble Villeroi family. After her father's burial at the nearby convent of St. Clair, Emily returned to her home at La Vallée and, as her father had requested, promptly burned some mysterious letters. She found a miniature portrait of a beautiful unknown woman among the letters. Since she had not been told to destroy the portrait, she took it with her when she left La Vallée to stay with her aunt in Toulouse.

Valancourt followed Emily to Toulouse to press his suit. After some remonstrance, the aunt gave her permission for the young couple to marry. A few days before the ceremony, the aunt herself married Signor Montoni, a sinister Italian, who immediately forbade Emily's nuptials. To make his refusal doubly positive, he took Emily and her aunt to his mansion in Venice.

There Emily and Madame Montoni found themselves in unhappy circumstances, for it soon became apparent that Montoni had married in order to secure the estates of his new wife and her niece for himself. When he tried to force Emily to marry a Venetian nobleman, Count Morano, Emily was in despair. On the night before the wedding, Montoni suddenly ordered his household to pack and leave for his castle at Udolpho, high in the Apennines.

When the party arrived at Udolpho, Montoni immediately began to repair the fortifications of the castle. Emily did not like the dark, cold castle from which the previous owner, Lady Laurentini, had disappeared under mysterious circumstances. Superstitious servants claimed that apparitions flitted about the halls and galleries of the ancient fortress.

Shortly after Montoni and his household had settled there, Count Morano attempted to kidnap Emily. Foiled by Montoni, who wounded him severely in a sword fight, Morano threatened revenge. A few days later, Montoni tried to force his wife to sign over her estates to him. When she refused, he locked her up in a tower of the castle. Emily tried to visit her aunt that night.

Terrified to find fresh blood on the tower stairs, she concluded that her aunt had been murdered.

Ghostly sounds and shadows about Udolpho began to make everyone uneasy. Even Montoni, who had organized a band of marauders to terrorize and pillage the neighborhood, began to believe the castle was haunted. Emily heard that several hostages had been taken. She was sure that Valancourt was a prisoner, for she had heard someone singing a song he had taught her, and one night a mysterious shadow had called her by name. Her life was tormented by Montoni's threats that unless she sign away her estates to him she would suffer the same fate as her aunt. As Emily discovered from her maid, her aunt had not been murdered except indirectly, for she had become so ill from the harsh treatment that she had died. She had been buried in the chapel of the castle.

Morano made another attempt to steal Emily away from the castle, this time with her assistance, as she was now afraid for her life. Montoni and his men, however, discovered the attempt in time to seize the abductors outside the castle walls. Shortly afterward, Montoni sent Emily away after forcing her to sign the papers that gave him control of her estates in France. At first, she thought she was being sent to her death, but Montoni sent her to a cottage in Tuscany because he had heard that Venetian authorities were sending a small army to attack Udolpho and seize him and his bandits after the villas of several rich Venetians had been robbed.

When Emily returned to the castle, she saw evidence of a terrible battle. Emily's maid and Ludovico, another servant, disclosed to Emily that a prisoner who knew her was in the dungeons below. Emily immediately guessed that it was Valancourt, and she made arrangements to escape with him. The prisoner, however, turned out to be Monsieur Du Pont, an old friend of her father. Emily, Monsieur Du Pont, the girl's maid, and Ludovico made their escape and reached Leghorn safely. There they took ship for France. Then a great storm drove the ship ashore close to the Chateau-le-Blanc, near which Emily's father had been buried.

Emily and her friends were rescued by Monsieur Villefort and his family. The Villeforts had inherited the chateau and were attempting to live in it, although it was in disrepair and said to be haunted. While at the chateau, Emily decided to spend several days at the convent where her father was buried. There she found a nun who closely resembled the mysteriously missing Lady Laurentini, whose portrait Emily had seen at the castle of Udolpho.

When Emily returned to the chateau, she found it in a state of turmoil because of weird noises that seemed to come from the apartments of the former mistress of the chateau. Ludovico volunteered to spend a night in the apartment. Although all the windows and doors were locked, he was not in the rooms the next morning. When the old caretaker came to tell Emily this news, she noticed the miniature portrait that Emily had found at La Vallée. The miniature, said the servant, was a portrait of her former mistress, the Marquise de Villeroi. She also pointed out that Emily closely resembled the portrait.

Valancourt reappeared and once again made plans to marry Emily, but Monsieur Villefort told her of gambling debts the young man had incurred and of the wild life he had led in Paris while she had been a prisoner in Italy. Emily thereupon refused to marry him and returned in distress to her home at La Vallée, where she learned that Montoni had been captured by the Venetian authorities. Since he had secured the deeds to her lands by criminal means, the court now restored them to her. She was once again a young woman of wealth and position.

While Emily was at La Vallée, the Villefort family made a trip high into the Pyrenees to hunt. They were almost captured by bandits, but Ludovico, who had inexplicably disappeared from the chateau, rescued them. He had been kidnaped by smugglers who had used the vaults of the chateau to store their treasure. He disclosed that the noises in the chateau had been caused by the outlaws in an effort to frighten away the rightful owners.

When she heard this, Emily returned to the chateau to see her friends. While there, she again visited the convent of St. Clair. The nun whom she had seen before and who resembled the former mistress of Udolpho, was taken mortally ill while Emily was at the convent. On her deathbed, the nun confessed that she was Lady Laurentini, who had left Udolpho to go to her former lover, the Marquis de Villeroi. Finding him married to Monsieur St. Aubert's sister, she ensnared him once more and made him an accomplice in her plot to poison his wife. When the Marquis, overcome by remorse, fled to a distant country and died there, she had retired to the convent to expiate her sins.

Emily's happiness was complete when Monsieur Du Pont, who had escaped with her from Udolpho, proved that Valancourt had gambled only to secure money to aid some friends who were on the brink of misfortune. Reunited, they were married and went to La Vallée, where they lived a happy, tranquil life in contrast to the many strange adventures that had separated them for so long.

Critical Evaluation:

Christmas Eve of 1764 saw the issuance of Horace Walpole's *The Castle of Otranto*, a story of supernatural terror set in a vaguely medieval past and complete with a gloomy castle, knights both chivalrous and wicked, and virtuous fair maidens in distress—the first English gothic novel. During the preceding summer, while Walpole was transforming a nightmarish dream into a gothic novel at Strawberry Hill, Ann Ward was born in London. By the time she married the law student William Radcliffe twenty-three years later, the era of the gothic novel was under way, having begun to flourish with Clara Reeve's professed imitation of *The Castle of Otranto* in *The Old English Baron* (1777). Ann Radcliffe, born in the same year as the genre itself, was to be supreme among the gothic novelists, whose works were so popular in the last decades of the eighteenth century.

Apart from one posthumously published novel, Radcliffe's total output as a novelist consists of five immensely successful gothic novels. *The Mysteries of Udolpho* was her fourth and most popular. Anna Laetitia Barbauld in her preface to this novel for *British Novelists* (1810), noted that a "greater distinction is due to those which stand at the head of a class," and she asserts that "such are undoubtedly the novels of Mrs. Radcliffe." This estimate continues to be valid.

Yet Radcliffe might have been relegated entirely to the pages of literary history had it not been for Jane Austen's delightful burlesque of gothic novels, *Northanger Abbey* (1818), in which a sentimental heroine under the inspiration of *The Mysteries of Udolpho* fancies herself involved in gothic adventures. Through the exaggerated sentiment of her heroine, Jane Austen ridicules a major element in gothic novels in general—sensibility. A reliance on feeling, in contradiction to the dominant rationalism of the eighteenth century, the cult of sensibility was nonetheless a vital part of the age. Individuals of sensibility were peculiarly receptive to the simple joys of country life, to the "sublime" and "beautiful" aspects of nature, and, above all, to benevolence; their own depth of feeling compelled sympathy, and it was considered proper to manifest sensibility through such traits as a readiness to weep or faint and a touch of melancholia.

In *The Mysteries of Udolpho*, the good characters are endowed with sensibility, the bad are not. Emily St. Aubert, her father, and her lover Valancourt are exemplars of a highly refined capacity for feeling. St. Aubert scorns worldly ambition and is retired from the world, represented by the city of Paris, to his rural estate, La Vallée, where his days are spent in literary, musical, and botanical pursuits; these pleasures are heightened by a pensive melancholy. The villainous Montoni, by contrast, loves power, and he responds to the idea of any daring exploit with eyes that appeared to gleam instantaneously with fire. At home in cities, with their atmosphere of fashionable dissipation and political intrigue, he thrives in the solitary Castle of Udolpho only when he has made it a bustling military fortress. Cold, haughty, and brooding, he is—unlike the ingenuous St. Aubert—adept at dissimulation.

Much of Emily's anguish is caused by the lack of sensibility in Montoni's world; her own ingenuousness and benevolence is misinterpreted as mere policy, spurring her enemies to further mischief. Emily's sensibility, however, sometimes functions as an effective defense, for her profuse tears and spells of fainting postpone immediate confrontations. Sometimes, too, sensibility assists discovery, as when Emily, shutting herself away to read, play her lute, sketch, or simply meditate and gaze rapturously upon the landscape at hand, could become vulnerable to mystery.

In this novel, the conventionally spurious medieval setting serves well the solitude of sensibility and gives scope for a range of feelings as the heroine is forced to travel about France and Italy, inhabit gloomy, ruined castles, and encounter chevaliers, noble ladies, courtesans, mercenary soldiers, bandits, peasants, monks, nuns, war, and murder. She encounters deaths by poisoning, stiletto, sword, torture, pistol, and cannon fire. Emily's wide-ranging adventures in a remote, dark age are the fit trials of her sensibility, foreshadowed in her dying father's lecture on the danger of uncontrolled sensibility; and if later readers are overwhelmed by evidence of her frequent trembling, weeping, and fainting, Emily herself is more conscious of her constant endeavor to be resolute, her ultimate survival with honor unscathed being sufficient proof of her strength of sensibility.

Although Jane Austen ridicules excessive sensibility, she also allows Henry Tilney, her spokesman for reason in *Northanger Abbey*, to praise Mrs. Radcliffe's novel, however face-tiously, by claiming that he could hardly put down *The Mysteries of Udolpho* once he had begun reading it and, in fact, had finished the novel, hair standing on end, in two days. Henry's count of two entire days accurately indicates average reading time; even more important, his appreciation of the suspense that is maintained throughout the book pays tribute to Radcliffe's narrative powers.

The essential quality that sustains gothic suspense is a pervasive sense of the irrational elements in life. Emily herself provides the appropriate image when she describes her life as appearing to be like the dream of a distempered imagination. Although basically a straightforward, chronological narrative, *The Mysteries of Udolpho* seems timeless and dreamlike, the sweeping length of the story suggesting the cinematic technique of slow-motion photography. The novel accomplishes shifts in scenery with the rapidity peculiar to dreams: Now Emily is in Leghorn; now she is in a ship tossed amid white foam in a dark and stormy sea, incredibly, upon the very shores where lies the mysterious Chateau-le-Blanc. Written in the generalizing poetic diction of the eighteenth century, the vast amount of scenic description contributes to the unreal atmosphere and is suggestive of a dream world where forms are vague and time and space ignore ordinary delimitations. Therefore, the Castle of Udolpho seems limitless in size; its actual shape and substance, typically viewed in the solemn evening dusk, seems indefinite, gloomy, and sublime with clustered towers. Other scenes call up boundless space, as in the recurrent images of blue-tinged views of distant mountaintops.

The repetitive pattern of Emily's adventures is also dreamlike: She is repeatedly trapped in a room with no light, and again and again she flees down dark, labyrinthine passages or seemingly endless staircases. People who are rationally assumed to be far away suddenly materialize, often in shadowy forms; their features are obscure and are known to Emily only intuitively. Disembodied voices and music from unseen instruments are commonplace. Continually beset with a dread of undefined evil, she recurrently experiences a paralysis of body and will before an imminent yet concealed danger.

In post-Freudian times, readers detect the realm of the subconscious emerging in Emily's nightmare world, not only in the repetitious, dreamlike patterns but also in the very nature of her predicament—that of the pure, innocent "orphan child" whose physical attractions precipitate sword fights, subject her to would-be rapists who pursue her down the dark corridors, and render her helpless before the cold, cruel Montoni, whose so-called preposterous depravity holds for her the fascination of the abomination.

Mrs. Radcliffe, however, is too much a part of the Age of Reason to permit irrationality to rule. Emily is preserved by her innate strength of sensibility from assaults on her person and her mind. In all of her melancholy meditations, once her ordeal has ended, she is never required to wonder why Montoni appealed to her as he did when he was triumphant, bold, spirited, and commanding. Instead, her mind dismisses him as one who was insignificant, and she settles down to a secure life with Valancourt, a candid and openhanded man. In her retirement to La Vallée, Emily may never be able to avoid counterparts of Madame Montoni, whose fashionable repartee recalls the comedy of manners in which Jane Austen was to excel, but she will be safe from such men as Montoni.

In the spirit of reason, the author also banishes the mystery of the supernatural happenings that provide so much suspense. Every inexplicable occurrence finally has its rational explanation. Mrs. Barbauld, herself a rationalist, complains with some justice about the protracted suspense and the high expectations that defuse Mrs. Radcliffe's increment of horrors and nebulous challenges to the imagination. Nevertheless, when a reader, like Henry Tilney, has kept pace with this lengthy novel, the impression of Emily St. Aubert's nightmare world is more vivid than the skepticism of reason that explains away all the dark secrets. Ultimately, the vague shapings of the imagination triumph.

"Critical Evaluation" by Catherine E. Moore

Bibliography:
Castle, Terry. "The Spectralization of the Other in *The Mysteries of Udolpho*." In *The New Eighteenth Century: Theory, Politics, English Literature*, edited by Felicity Nussbaum and Laura Brown. New York: Methuen, 1987. Examines the neglected segments of *The Mysteries of Udolpho* and asserts that the supernatural is "rerouted" rather than explained.

Freeman, R. Austin. Introduction to *The Mysteries of Udolpho*, by Ann Radcliffe. London: J. M. Dent & Sons, 1931. Freeman shows that the denouement of *The Mysteries of Udolpho* qualifies it as one of the earliest detective novels.

Graham, Kenneth W. "Emily's Demon-Lover: The Gothic Revolution and *The Mysteries of Udolpho*." In *Gothic Fictions: Prohibition/Transgression*, edited by Kenneth W. Graham. New York: AMS Press, 1989. Places Radcliffe's works in the historical moment of revolution.

Howells, Coral Ann. *Love, Mystery, and Misery: Feeling in Gothic Fiction*. London: Athlone Press, 1978. Analyzes Emily St. Aubert as a character through whom Radcliffe experiments with subjectivity and points of view.

Kiely, Robert. *The Romantic Novel in England*. Cambridge, Mass.: Harvard University Press, 1972. Kiely observes innovative aspects in the character of Emily St. Aubert, including the fact that she is aware of her own thinking and that she is astute rather than helpless in finding her way in her gothic situation.

Roberts, Bette B. "The Horrid Novels: *The Mysteries of Udolpho* and *Northanger Abbey*." In *Gothic Fictions: Prohibition/Transgression*, edited by Kenneth W. Graham. New York: AMS Press, 1989. Challenges conventional notions of Jane Austen's evaluation of Radcliffe's art by examining Austen's treatment in *Northanger Abbey* of both Radcliffe's *Mysteries of Udolpho* and other contemporary "horrids."

THE MYSTERIOUS ISLAND

Type of work: Novel
Author: Jules Verne (1828-1905)
Type of plot: Adventure
Time of plot: 1865-1869
Locale: An island in the South Pacific
First published: L'Île mystérieuse, 1874-1875 (English translation, 1875)

Principal characters:
   CAPTAIN CYRUS HARDING, an engineer
   NEBUCHADNEZZAR, his black servant
   GIDEON SPILETT, a reporter
   JACK PENCROFT, a sailor
   HERBERT BROWN, an orphan
   AYRTON, a mutineer
   CAPTAIN NEMO, the captain of the *Nautilus*

The Story:

On March 24, 1865, a balloon carrying five persons who were escaping from Richmond, capital of the Confederacy during the Civil War, fell into the sea. Caught in a storm, the balloon had flown some seven thousand miles in five days. The five passengers were Captain Cyrus Harding, an engineer in General Grant's army; his black servant, Nebuchadnezzar, known as Neb; Gideon Spilett, a reporter; Jack Pencroft, a sailor; and Herbert Brown, the fifteen-year-old orphan son of one of Pencroft's former sea captains.

The balloon fell near an uncharted island, and Harding, together with his dog Top, was washed overboard. Once its load was lightened, the balloon then deposited the other travelers on the shore of the island. The next morning, Neb went to look for his master while the others explored the island. The next day Herbert, Pencroft, and Spilett took stock of their resources, which consisted of the clothes they wore, a notebook, and a watch. They suddenly heard Top barking. The dog led them to Captain Harding who, having been unconscious, was at a loss to explain how he had arrived at a place more than a mile away from the shore.

When Harding was stronger, the group decided to consider themselves colonists rather than castaways, and they called their new home Lincoln Island. Harding found on the island samples of iron, pyrite, clay, lime, coal, and other useful minerals. The colonists made bricks, which they used to construct an oven in which to make pottery. From Top's collar, they were able to make two knives, which enabled them to cut bows and arrows. Eventually, they were able to make iron and steel tools.

Under the brilliant direction of Harding, who seemed to know a great deal about everything, the colonists worked constantly to improve their lot. After discovering a cave within a cliff wall, they planned to make this their permanent residence; they called it Granite House. They made a rope ladder up the side of the cliff to the door of the cavern, which they equipped with brick walls, furniture, and candles made from seal fat.

One day Pencroft found washed up on the beach a large chest containing many useful items, including books, clothes, instruments, and weapons. On another occasion, the colonists returned to Granite House to find that their home had been invaded by orangutans, who suddenly became terrified by something and began to flee. The colonists killed all but one, which they domesticated and called Jup.

The colony prospered. They domesticated various animals, used a stream to power an elevator to Granite House, and made glass windows. They built a boat designed by Harding and named it the *Bonadventure*. As they were sailing it, they found a bottle with a message, saying that there was a castaway on nearby Tabor Island. Pencroft, Spilett, and Herbert sailed to Tabor Island, where Herbert was attacked by a strange wild man. Pencroft and Spilett succeeded in capturing the creature and took him back to Lincoln Island, where he began to become civilized again. One day he confessed with shame that his name was Ayrton, that he had attempted mutiny on one ship, had tried to seize another, and had finally been put ashore on Tabor Island by Captain Grant, of the *Duncan*. Ayrton, who repented his past life, was accepted by the colonists as one of them. He lived at a corral that the colonists had built some distance from Granite House.

One day the colonists sighted a pirate ship. A battle between the pirates and the colonists developed, and just when things were going badly for the colonists, the pirate ship seemed to explode. Later, the colonists found the remains of a strange torpedo that had destroyed the ship. A short time later, the colonists discovered that the telegraph system that Harding had built to the corral had broken down. When they went to the corral to investigate, they were attacked by some of the pirates who had not perished with their ship, and Herbert was seriously wounded. Ayrton, moreover, was gone. While the colonists were trying desperately to keep Herbert alive, the pirates set fire to the mill and sheds close by Granite House and destroyed the plantation. By the time the colonists were able to make their way back to Granite House, Herbert had weakened seriously. The one thing needed for his recovery, sulphate of quinine, was lacking on the island, but on the crucial night that might have been Herbert's last, the colonists found a box of quinine beside Herbert's bed, and the medicine enabled him to recover.

The colonists set out to find their mysterious benefactor and to exterminate the pirates. When the expedition arrived at the corral, they found Ayrton, who had been tortured by the pirates but who was still alive. Top then discovered the corpses of all the remaining pirates, who had been killed in a mysterious way. The colonists made plans to build a ship large enough to carry them back to civilization. When they discovered smoke rising from the crater of the volcano, they redoubled their efforts to complete the boat.

One day the colonists received a call on the telegraph telling them to go to the corral immediately. There they found a note that told them to follow the wire that had been attached to the telegraph line. They followed the wire into a hidden cove, where they found the fantastic submarine *Nautilus* and its captain, their benefactor, Captain Nemo. He told them how he had been a rich nobleman in India, how he had been defeated in his fight for the independence of his country, and how he and his followers, disgusted with the ways of humanity, had built a gigantic undersea craft. His followers had died, and Nemo, old and alone, had taken the *Nautilus* to Lincoln Island, where he had lived for the past six years, giving aid to the colonists because he believed them to be good people. After presenting Harding with a box of jewels and pearls and making a last request that he be buried in his ship, he died. The colonists sealed the *Nautilus* with Captain Nemo's body inside and then opened the flood valves to sink the ship.

Following advice Captain Nemo had given him, Harding investigated the caverns beneath the island and saw that, as soon as the seawater penetrated to the shaft of the volcano, the entire island would explode.

The colonists worked with all haste to complete work on the boat. By March of their fourth year on the island, the hull had been built; but on the night before the launching, the entire island was shattered with a tremendous roar. All that was left of Lincoln Island was a small rock formation. The colonists had all been able to reach safety there, but their ship had vanished. The colonists stayed on the rock formation for nine days.

On March 24, they sighted a ship. It was the *Duncan*, which had come to rescue Ayrton after his twelve-year exile on Tabor Island. The colonists went to the United States. With the treasure Captain Nemo had given them, they bought land in Iowa. They prospered in their new home.

Critical Evaluation:

The Mysterious Island is, in a sense, a sequel to Jules Verne's famous *Twenty Thousand Leagues Under the Sea* (1870), for in this work, Verne describes the death of Captain Nemo. Primarily, however, it is a story of survival and a celebration of the adaptability and ingenuity of intelligent, hardworking people. Verne shows the great satisfaction that can be derived from personal accomplishment. The wealth of detail and description and the valid explanations of mysterious happenings create a sense of realism. At the urging of his publisher, Pierre-Jules Hetzel, Verne turned an early, rather unpromising manuscript into *The Mysterious Island* by adding scientific data, mystery, dramatic complications, and a startling, original conclusion.

Apart from its interest as a story, *The Mysterious Island* is significant for its technological detail. Unlike many tales of the shipwreck variety, unlike even many science-fiction stories of the twentieth century, there are not merely the trappings of science; there is much scientific substance as well. Verne goes into the most detailed accounts of the ways in which tools, chemicals, and communications equipment can be manufactured from elementary materials. All of this description, which may appear to be unrelated to the plot, is significant because it reflects the optimism of nineteenth century European society and especially the widespread confidence placed in technology. Although in some stories, Verne suggests the danger of this new power, for the most part, he is the celebrator of industrialism and especially the revolutionary technology that gives birth to it. Industrialization and technology, however, were also massively abused during this period, largely for reasons of profit; so Verne's celebration was generally placed either in the future or in some imaginary place, as in *The Mysterious Island*. The novel's technological descriptions show, in effect, technical history from the most primitive beginnings to a reasonably advanced state; these descriptions may be said to recapitulate, in capsule form, the progress of humanity. Thus it is significant that the heroes are from the United States, because it was seen, at the time, as a rising, dynamic industrial power, leading the world into a new age.

Although Verne's ideas, and his enthusiasm for his ideas, are a pleasure in the novel, there are serious literary flaws in the work. The most damaging of these is probably Verne's shallow characterizations; although his characters are generally adequate, they are never wholly successful or convincing. Nebuchadnezzar, for example, is little more than a stereotype. Verne is not interested in exploring the depths of people's characters, although he is vitally interested in their achievements.

Bibliography:

Angenot, Marc. "Jules Verne: The Last Happy Utopianist." In *Science Fiction: A Critical Guide*, edited by Patrick Parrinder. New York: Longmans, 1979. Focuses on a concept of circulation, seen as underlying the mainstays of the author's narratives: characters, forces of nature, and scientific innovation. Describes Verne as happy in that mobility; views the knowledge that accompanies it as continual and positive.

Costello, Peter. *Jules Verne: Inventor of Science Fiction*. New York: Charles Scribner's Sons, 1978. A detailed and lucid study of Verne's life and works. Includes a thoughtful review and commentary of *The Mysterious Island*'s events and character significance.

Evans, Arthur B. *Jules Verne Rediscovered: Didacticism and the Scientific Novel*. Westport,

Conn.: Greenwood Press, 1988. Scholarly, forthright discussion explores and clarifies myths and misunderstandings about Verne's literary reputation and achievements. Perceives the author not as the father of science fiction but of scientific fiction and examines its social benefits.

Jules-Verne, Jean. *Jules Verne: A Biography*. Translated and adapted by Roger Greaves. New York: Taplinger, 1976. Readable volume by Verne's grandson, with illustrations and quotations adding to intimate flavor. Recounts highlights of the novel and circumstances related to its development.

Lynch, Lawrence. *Jules Verne*. New York: Twayne, 1992. The first critical assessment of the complete works by the author. Includes generous synopsis of the novel and analysis of major themes, such as the island itself, and its interconnection with themes from other of Verne's epics. Excellent introductory resource.

THE MYSTERY OF EDWIN DROOD

Type of work: Novel
Author: Charles Dickens (1812-1870)
Type of plot: Detective and mystery
Time of plot: Mid-nineteenth century
Locale: England
First published: 1870

Principal characters:

> EDWIN DROOD, a young engineer
> JACK JASPER, Edwin's young uncle and guardian
> ROSA BUD, Edwin's fiancée
> NEVILLE LANDLESS, an orphaned young man
> HELENA LANDLESS, his sister and Rosa Bud's schoolmate
> DURDLES, a stonemason and acquaintance of Jack Jasper
> MR. CRISPARKLE, Neville Landless' tutor and friend

The Story:

Mr. Jack Jasper was the choirmaster of the cathedral at Cloisterham. Young as he was, he was also the guardian of his orphan nephew, Edwin Drood, who was only a few years Jasper's junior. Edwin Drood was an apprentice engineer who expected one day to become a partner in the firm that employed him, for his father had been one of the owners. Drood's profession took him all over the world, but he came back at every opportunity to Cloisterham to see his uncle and his fiancée.

Drood's fiancée, Rosa Bud, was attending a finishing school in Cloisterham. She had been there for several years, for both her parents were dead. The fathers of the two young people had been extremely close friends, and both had requested in their will that their two children become engaged and, at the proper time, married. As the years passed, Edwin and Rosa realized that they were not in love and had no desire to marry. During Rosa's last year at the finishing school, they agreed to remain friends but to put aside all ideas of marriage. No one except Rosa realized that Jasper was in love with her. Rosa was very much afraid of Jasper, so much so that she dared not tell anyone of Jasper's infatuation, but she almost gave her secret away when she ceased taking music lessons from him.

During one of Drood's visits to Cloisterham, a young English couple arrived there from Ceylon, where they had been orphaned. The young woman, Helena Landless, who was Rosa Bud's age, entered the finishing school, and the young man, who was the age of Edwin Drood, began studies under one of the minor officials at the cathedral, Mr. Crisparkle. Crisparkle, a friend of Jasper and Drood, introduced his charge, Neville Landless, to Jasper and Edwin, in the hope that they would all become fast friends.

As it turned out, however, young Landless had been immediately smitten with Rosa and became irritated by Drood's casual attitude toward her. The very first evening the three men spent together in Jasper's lodgings, the two quarreled; Jasper claimed that if he had not interceded, Landless would have killed Drood.

Rosa and Helena became close friends, and Rosa confessed to Helena that she was in love with Helena's brother. Jasper soon deduced this fact for himself, and became exceedingly jealous. Jasper, who was addicted to opium, was extremely peculiar and mysterious at times.

He became acquainted with Durdles, a stonemason, who took him about the cathedral and pointed out the various old tombs under the ancient edifice. On one of the visits, which took place in the dead of night, Durdles became very drunk. While he was asleep, Jasper took the key to an underground tomb from Durdles' pocket. What he did with it later on remained a mystery.

During the following Christmas season, Mr. Crisparkle tried to patch up the quarrel between Landless and Drood. He proposed that they meet together at Jasper's lodgings and, after mutual apologies, have a congenial evening together. The two young men agreed. On Christmas morning, however, Drood was reported missing by his uncle, with whom the nephew was staying. Jasper said that late the night before the two young men had walked out of his lodgings and turned toward the river. No one had seen them after that. When Mr. Crisparkle appeared, he reported that young Landless had left earlier that morning on a solitary walking trip. A search party set out after him and brought him back to Cloisterham. Young Landless was unable to convince anyone of his innocence, although there was not enough evidence to convict him of any crime. Indeed, the body of Drood was not found, although Mr. Crisparkle discovered his watch and tiepin in the river.

At first, only Rosa and Helena were convinced of Landless' innocence. They soon won Mr. Crisparkle over to their side, and he helped Landless to leave Cloisterham for a refuge in London. Jasper vowed that he would find evidence to incriminate the murderer. He also intimated that he had some evidence that Landless was the guilty person. Publicly, however, there was no evidence that Edwin Drood had actually been killed.

After a few months, Jasper appeared at the school and requested an interview with Rosa. As they walked in the school gardens, Jasper told her of his love for her and warned her that he had sufficient evidence to send Neville Landless to the gallows. He also implied that he would use his knowledge unless Rosa returned his love. After he had gone, Rosa left the school and went to London, where she sought the protection of her guardian, Mr. Grewgious, an odd man who loved her because he had been in love with her mother years before. Mr. Grewgious arranged for Rosa to remain in safe lodgings in London. Mr. Crisparkle arrived the next day and began to lay plans to extricate Landless and Rosa from their troubles.

One day, a white-haired stranger arrived in Cloisterham. His name was Datchery, and he said he was looking for quiet lodgings where he could end his days in comfort and peace. Looking for a place of residence that would reflect the quaintness of the past, he took a room across from Jasper's home in the old postern gate. Passersby would see him sitting by the hour behind his open door. Every time he heard a remark about Jasper, he made a chalk mark, some long, some short, on the inside of his closet door.

A short time later, Jasper began to be followed about, almost haunted, by a haggard old woman from whom he had in the past bought opium. She apparently had learned something about the choirmaster and suspected a great deal more. Datchery noted her interest in Jasper and followed her to a cheap hotel. The next morning, he and the strange woman attended a service in the cathedral. When the woman told him that she knew Jasper, old Datchery returned home and added another chalk mark to those behind his closet door.

Critical Evaluation:

Charles Dickens died suddenly, leaving the novel incomplete, with no notes among his papers to show how he intended to end the story. Undoubtedly *The Mystery of Edwin Drood* owes some of its popular appeal to the fact that it is unfinished. Dickens had only completed half of the work at the time of his death, and this missing ending has spawned dozens of conclusions, the first four only months after his death, as well as a play in which the audience can choose Drood's murderer. Nevertheless, the existent fragment stands on its own as a good example of Dickens' style and literary technique. An indication of the narrative's power is its invariable inclusion in lists of the best works of mystery and suspense ever written.

Although the titular protagonist is Edwin Drood, the action and psychological drama center on his uncle, John Jasper. There are, in reality, two Jaspers, the seemingly devoted friend and quiet and dedicated choirmaster, and the resentful opium addict who is madly in love with Rosa. This duality does not, however, represent a split personality. Although some critics have seen in Dickens' portrayal of Jasper a precursor to Robert Louis Stevenson's *The Strange Case of Dr. Jekyll and Mr. Hyde* (1886), Jasper the benevolent choirmaster is a conscious façade that enables him to indulge his drug habit in secret. John Jasper's envy of Drood, lust for Rosa, and scorn for his job and environs are never hidden in the narrative. The clues to the choirmaster's true personality, which is uniformly negative, gradually mount. Indeed, there is not much mystery about what happened to Edwin; it is quite clear that he was murdered by Jasper. From Dickens' notes and conversations with friends, family, and artistic collaborators, it is clear that for Dickens the important element of the novel was not the question of guilt but the manner of its disclosure. There is also substantial evidence to indicate that some of the final chapters would have contained Jasper's confession in his prison cell as he awaited execution. In any case, even a superficial reading of the text points rather unmistakably to Jasper.

Although Jasper's true nature is not an enigma to the reader, there are a number of other mysteries, plot intricacies, and personality quirks that fascinate and provide material for speculation. Indeed, the cast of characters of *The Mystery of Edwin Drood* is one of Dickens' finest. Jasper, as villain, stands alone, his portrait being that of a withdrawn, moody man who first releases his inhibitions in his opium dreams and then tries to convert fantasy to fact. The other principal figures can be roughly organized into two groups, the victims and their defenders and protectors, but, as in all of Dickens' best work, there is an infinite variety and psychological detail in their very distinct personalities. The victims—Edwin Drood, Rosa Bud, and the falsely accused, Neville Landless—are all orphans. Their protectors are Mr. Grewgious, Rosa's guardian, and the Canon Crisparkle, Neville's temporary guardian. The betrayal of Jack Jasper, who is Edwin's guardian and responsible for his happiness and well being, is seen as doubly odious for being juxtaposed with the conduct of the other two guardians.

The betrayal and persecution of the innocent is, of course, a common Dickensian theme. In *The Mystery of Edwin Drood*, that theme is emphasized by the sense of fatality that hangs over the first part of the novel. Allusions to Shakespeare's *Macbeth* are frequent (the chapter preceding Drood's disappearance is explicitly entitled "When Shall These Three Meet Again"), and the cold gray dismal landscape positively drips pessimism. Drood's disappearance takes place on Christmas Eve when, instead of being a time of joyous celebration and reunion, Rosa and Edwin break off their engagement and the opium dealer silently stalks Jack Jasper; instead of being a quiet, beautiful night of carols, a fierce shrieking wind scatters everything before it, forcing people inside and leaving the streets empty and echoing.

Much has been made of the fact that Dickens was jealous of Wilkie Collins' success with *The Moonstone* (1868) and that he may have tried to outdo his former close friend on his own terrain, the novel of mystery and suspense (even going so far as to use the effects of opium as a central plot device). Dickens used suspense and mystery, but not in connection with the central action, the disappearance of Drood; any doubt concerning the identity of murderer and victim seems to be wishful thinking on the part of would-be literary detectives. The question of identity is, however, an important theme in the novel. Indeed, the real mystery of *The Mystery of Edwin*

Drood concerns the identities of several of the other major characters. Who are Neville and Helen Landless and what is their past? Who was the Princess Puffer? Why does Jasper seem to be more than just a present client to her? Above all, who is Datchery, the mysterious, obviously disguised stranger, who takes up residence opposite Jasper's lodgings and closely observes the choirmaster? Most close readers of the text believe that Datchery is one of the other characters, Mr. Grewgious, Bazzard, his clerk, Helen Landless, Tartar, or even Edwin Drood himself. In one ingenious suggestion, Datchery is none other than Charles Dickens himself, who enters his own novel not just as omniscient narrator but as main character. In *The Moonstone*, Collins had introduced the figure of the great detective with Sergeant Cuff. Perhaps Dickens was again trying to best the younger man by explicitly introducing himself as the great unraveler of mystery, the better detective, just as implicitly he was trying to prove himself the better novelist. In any case, the appearance of Datchery, who has obviously come to find out the truth, marks a turning point in the novel. The exposition has ended and the denouement begins, but here the fragment ends.

"Critical Evaluation" by Charlene E. Suscavage

Bibliography:

Baker, Richard M. *The Drood Murder*. Berkeley: University of California Press, 1951. Particularly good for its discussion of possible influences on the novel as well as of antecedents in Dickens' own work.

Collins, Philip. *Dickens and Crime*. 2d ed. London: Macmillan, 1965. Interesting attempt to relate Dickens' writings about crime to events in his own life and times. A prime source for the many theories about the personality of Jack Jasper and his role as murderer.

Fruttero, Carlo, and Franco Lucentino. *The D Case, Or, The Truth About the Mystery of Edwin Drood*. Translated by Gregory Dowling. New York: Harcourt, Brace, Jovanovich, 1993. A tour de force, in which the world's most famous fictional detectives try to finish Dickens' novel. The first half contains a good edition of the work, while the second demonstrates an extremely close reading of the text with excellent and witty discussions of current and past theories.

Rowland, Peter. *The Disappearance of Edwin Drood*. New York: St. Martin's Press, 1990. The most recent addition to the honorable scholarly pursuit of finishing the novel.

Symons, Julian. *Mortal Consequences: A History from the Detective Story to the Crime Novel*. New York: Schocken Books, 1973. A history of the suspense genre. Compares and links Dickens' work to that of Collins and Émile Gaboriau.

THE MYTH OF SISYPHUS

Type of work: Essay
Author: Albert Camus (1913-1960)
First published: Le Mythe de Sisyphe, 1942 (English translation, 1955)

Regarded as one of the foremost thinkers and writers of modern France, Albert Camus reached maturity at a time when Hitler came to power; in his writings he expresses the horror of living during Hitler's rise and World War II, and the desire to establish a meaningful life in a meaningless world of war and futile conquest. Not content with the nihilism of his age and unable to ignore the catastrophe of modern life, Camus developed two related concepts, the absurd and revolt, into a significant philosophy of personal life. The concept of revolt he was to examine at length in *The Rebel* (1951), but in *The Myth of Sisyphus* he presents the concept of the absurd and thus outlines the belief that the individual has worth but lives in a world that denies such worth. The absurd is the clash between the order for which the human mind strives and the lack of order that one finds in the world.

Camus begins *The Myth of Sisyphus* by categorically stating that the one truly serious problem of philosophy is suicide, because suicide is the confession that life is not worth living. Why, he asks, do people not commit suicide? From this springboard he goes on to describe the absurdity of existence. People are not logical in the act of killing themselves, but they do believe in the absurdity of their lives. The absurd, Camus explains, forces itself upon one when one desires to find absolutes by which to guide one's life; one searches for absolutes but finds that the world is not reasonable. Once one realizes that existence is absurd, one has two solutions: suicide or recovery. In short, one's experiences bring the necessity of choosing between suicide and life in absurdity. If one chooses life, then one must accept the absurd. This absurdity is neither in the person (who has an internally consistent understanding) nor in the world (which also is consistent), but is the bond uniting them; therefore, physical suicide does not answer the question of absurdity—such an act merely destroys one of the terms.

Having stated this thesis, Camus then considers the alternatives to physical suicide. Philosophical suicide, the existential "leap of faith," is an antirational acceptance of the limits of reason. Reason's limitations are an excuse to transcend to God. Camus calls this attitude an escape; the absurd does not lead to God but only to itself. Hence, to speak of a "leap of faith" is like advocating physical suicide since both are escapes and, therefore, seek to contradict or negate the absurdity of existence. Physical suicide attempts to have value or meaning in a meaningless existence; the existential "leap" tries to evade the condition of life. Rejecting physical and philosophical suicide, Camus reaches the final alternative: One must fully confront the truth of one's existence and accept it. Continually tempted either to kill oneself or to make a "leap," one must live only with the certainty that nothing is certain except the absurd. One must find whether it is possible to live without appeal. Such a person is indifferent to the future but wants to live the now to its fullest; such a person is interested not in the best life but in the most living, realizing that the condition of life is contradictory.

In the second part of this slender volume, Camus treats the ethical implications of life in the absurd. Having chosen absurdity, how does one act positively while consciously aware of the negative character of the choice? Although all systems of morality are based on the idea that every action has consequences, one who recognizes the unpredictable and unreasonable condition of life cannot judge an act by its consequences. Instead, such a person sees action as an end in itself—the value of life being measured by its sterility, indifference, and hopelessness. Don

Juan, for example, goes from one affair to another, not because he searches for total love but merely because he needs the repetition. Yet Don Juan is not melancholy; he knows his condition of life—seducing—and does not hope (the desire to have life other than it is). He can live in neither the past nor the future; he lives entirely in the now. He fully realizes that there is no such thing as eternal love, so he has chosen to be nothing. If he was punished as Christians say, it was because he achieved knowledge without illusion. Like Don Juan, the actor is also an absurd man, because he applies himself wholeheartedly to being nothing—a mask that lives only three or so hours. He seeks the sterile life that accepts the absurd as its basic condition. Finally, Camus describes the conqueror, the third example of the absurd man. Conquerors live completely within time; they are the rebels who shall never succeed, for revolution is always against God and no man can be victorious. Still the conqueror fights on, knowing that conquest is futile. These examples—the seducer, the actor, and the conqueror—represent the extremes of absurd action. The ordinary person, who knows but hides from nothing and who squarely faces life without hope, represents the typical absurd person, but it is the creator who is the most absurd character of all.

Each type of absurd person puts his or her entire effort into a struggle that is doomed from the beginning, but the creator is one who attempts to examine and to enrich the world that is ephemeral and meaningless. Art is the death and propagation of experience, the absurdly passionate repetition of monotonous themes; it is not escape from existence but the portrayal of the blind path of all people. The artist and the art "interlock"; the work of art illustrates the mind's repudiation of itself, the desire of the mind to cover nothing with the appearance of something. Thinking is creating a world of images; the novelist who is philosophical creates the full complexity and paradox of life. Fyodor Dostoevski, for example, was not interested in arguing philosophical problems but rather in illustrating the implications of such speculation. Dostoevski's novels are filled with absurd judgments, the greatest of which is that existence is illusory and eternal. The absurd novelist, then, negates and magnifies at the same time; such a novelist does not preach a thesis but describes the contradictions of life. The absurd novel has no depth beyond human suffering. Thus the creator passionately describes the fleeting, trying to capture the ephemeral that cannot be captured; a human creator, too, is doomed to failure from the beginning.

The closing section of the volume gives the book its title. In the classical myth of Sisyphus' punishment, Camus finds the absurd hero. Sisyphus is condemned to an eternity of futile and hopeless work. He rolls a huge stone up a mountain, a struggle that takes superhuman strength. The moment that the stone reaches the pinnacle, he cannot keep it balanced; it rolls back to the valley. He knows that his strength and effort are hopeless, yet he silences the gods by his determination to do the hopeless. Actually Sisyphus' consciousness of his torment and its hopelessness makes him superior to it—his very act is a revolt because his consciousness makes him happy and happiness negates punishment.

Not until *The Rebel* did Camus analyze the nature and implications of this revolt from the absurd; however, in his lucid, often lyrical *The Myth of Sisyphus* he clearly describes the condition of life that he found in Hitler's Europe. The result of this description, the concept of the absurd, formed the basis for his works and became one of the fundamental essays in modern French philosophy and letters.

Bibliography:
Lazere, Donald. *The Unique Creation of Albert Camus*. New Haven, Conn.: Yale University Press, 1973. This fascinating psychoanalytical study helps readers recognize many new

levels of meaning in Camus' works. Explores the metaphysical dimension and the search for moral values in *The Myth of Sisyphus*.

Lottman, Herbert R. *Albert Camus: A Biography*. Garden City, N.Y.: Doubleday, 1979. This very well-documented biography of Camus enables readers to understand the historical context in which Camus wrote his major works. Explains why *The Myth of Sisyphus* can be read as a philosophical justification of the need to resist the evil of the Nazi occupation of France.

McBride, Joseph. *Albert Camus: Philosopher and Littérateur*. New York: St. Martin's Press, 1992. Contains a thoughtful analysis of the profound influence of Saint Augustine and Friedrich Nietzsche on Camus. Explores the philosophical and theological aspects of *The Myth of Sisyphus*.

Parker, Emmett. *Albert Camus: The Artist in the Arena*. Madison: University of Wisconsin Press, 1965. Discusses the political dimensions of Camus' works written both during the Nazi occupation of France from 1940 to 1944 and after the liberation. Describes Camus' role in the French Resistance.

Rhein, Phillip H. *Albert Camus*. Rev. ed. Boston: Twayne, 1989. Describes the meaning of the absurd as well as the political aspects of *The Myth of Sisyphus*. Contains an excellent annotated bibliography of critical studies in English on Camus.

THE NAKED AND THE DEAD

Type of work: Novel
Author: Norman Mailer (1923-   )
Type of plot: Social realism
Time of plot: World War II
Locale: Anopopei, an island in the South Pacific
First published: 1948

Principal characters:
GENERAL CUMMINGS, commander of the Anopopei campaign
MAJOR DALLESON, an army bureaucrat
LIEUTENANT ROBERT HEARN, Cummings' aide
SERGEANT SAMUEL CROFT, a platoon leader
SERGEANT BROWN,
ROTH,
GOLDSTEIN,
RED VALSEN,
JULIO MARTINEZ,
ROY GALLAGHER,
WOODROW WILSON,
OSSIE RIDGES,
STANLEY,
CASIMIR "POLACK" CZIENWICZ,
MINETTA,
TOGLIO,
WYMAN, and
HENNESSEY, the men in Croft's platoon

The Story:

In the campaign against the Japanese during World War II, United States Army troops commanded by General Cummings landed on the beach of Anopopei, an 150-mile-long South Pacific island held by the Japanese army. The platoon of Sergeant Samuel Croft was assigned to conduct reconnaissance on the beach. Croft's men considered themselves lucky because this duty would keep them busy for a week or so while other troops went on the more dangerous patrols into the interior of the island. Red Valsen, however, resented any duties because of his disdain for authority. Croft could control all the men but Red. Sergeant Brown considered Croft the best and meanest platoon sergeant in the army because he seemed to love combat. Despite Croft's courage and leadership, some of his men were fearful, especially after young Hennessey was killed by a mortar shell. After Croft begged for a replacement for Hennessey, he was given Roth, a pessimistic clerk who resented never getting anywhere in the civilian world despite his education. Of all his men, Croft liked only Julio Martinez, a reliable scout.

Lieutenant Robert Hearn, General Cummings' aide, admired the general's ability to put his thoughts into action but resented his own position, longing for a combat role. A snob who claimed to know everything worth knowing, Cummings picked Hearn as his aide because he considered the lieutenant to be the only officer on his staff with the intellect to understand him. Cummings liked to remind Hearn that Hearn would be nothing without the general.

Croft's platoon grew restless for combat. Most of them instantly disliked Roth, whom Brown considered lazy and shiftless. Moving antitank guns into the jungle after a storm, they dropped one into a muddy creek bed, and Wyman blamed Goldstein. Confronted by a Japanese platoon, Roy Gallagher wanted to surrender, but the enemy troops were repelled, with Toglio slightly wounded. For the first time in combat, Croft was afraid. He ordered Red to shoot four already dead Japanese and then executed a prisoner after being friendly to him, upsetting Red even more. Martinez stole gold teeth from the mouths of Japanese corpses.

Gallagher was told that his wife had died in childbirth, but he could not accept her death. The other men were made uneasy by Gallagher's loss, made even more painful by his continuing, because of the delay of mail from home, to receive letters from Mary for weeks after her death. After the failure of the Japanese attack, Cummings' campaign stalled for no apparent reason, and he felt powerless to change matters. The general began harassing Hearn, who responded by grinding out a cigarette in the middle of Cummings' spotless floor. Cummings forced Hearn to choose between being imprisoned for insubordination and picking up a cigarette the general threw down. Hearn gave in, picking up the cigarette, but asked for a transfer. Cummings refused and sent him to work under Major Dalleson.

The slightly wounded Minetta faked insanity to keep from returning to combat but changed his mind after another patient died of his wounds. Woodrow Wilson agonized over the discomfort of his venereal disease. Cummings decided that sending in a battalion to drive out the enemy without naval support would result in a massacre of his troops. The general devised a plan of attack but decided to send in a reconnaissance patrol first. Based on Dalleson's recommendation, Cummings decided to send Croft's platoon, and he assigned Hearn to lead it just before the mission began. Hearn distrusted the general's motives, and Croft resented giving up his platoon to the untested lieutenant. Croft had always thought that a man was either destined to be killed or not and saw himself as exempt from death, but suddenly he was not so certain. He also disliked Hearn's efforts to make the men like him. Hearn realized how easy it would be to let Croft make all the decisions. Croft thought the best way to accomplish their mission would be to climb Mount Anaka in the center of the island.

When the platoon was ambushed, Wilson was seriously wounded in the stomach. Brown, Stanley, Ridges, and Goldstein were chosen to carry Wilson back to the beach. The remaining men experienced a respite from the shock of battle when Roth discovered an injured bird, but Croft killed it. After Red challenged Croft, Hearn stopped the dispute before blows were struck. Later, the remaining men in the patrol wanted to go back, but Hearn, at first, did not want to seem a failure to the general. When he changed his mind, Croft argued that a successful mission might end the entire campaign. Hearn gave in but decided to resign his commission after the campaign. Sent ahead as a scout, Martinez found Japanese in their path and killed one of them. Croft lied to Hearn about what Martinez had seen, and when the patrol proceeded, the lieutenant was killed. Croft then ordered them to climb the mountain. Meantime, after Brown and Stanley collapsed under the burden of carrying Wilson, Goldstein and Ridges went on with the stretcher on their own.

When Dalleson was left in command after Cummings went away to obtain the support of a destroyer, the situation of the campaign changed suddenly. Not knowing what to do, the major accidentally launched a complete attack. In a few hours, the Japanese were completely routed and Croft's platoon forgotten.

Their sacrifices made pointless by Dalleson's bumbling, the patrol directed their frustration at the weak Roth. Attempting to show them he was as good as they were, Roth jumped awkwardly from a ledge and fell to his death. Wilson also died, but Goldstein and Ridges continued carrying his body until they lost it in a river. Martinez told Croft he would not continue up the mountain, and a rebellion stirred. Croft threatened to shoot Red, and the men gave in again. Shortly afterward, they were attacked by hornets and ran down the mountain. Croft finally gave up on their mission, and all the survivors returned to the beach. Back on their landing craft, they quickly forgot all their hostility toward one another. Cummings was upset that Dalleson had blundered his way to victory and had to be congratulated. As Dalleson planned trivial projects, anonymous soldiers on a mopping-up mission executed some Japanese prisoners.

Critical Evaluation:

Norman Mailer got his career as one of the most highly regarded novelists in the United States off to a resounding start with *The Naked and the Dead*, the first major treatment of World War II in American fiction. It is considered, along with James Jones's *From Here to Eternity* (1951) and Joseph Heller's *Catch-22* (1961), to be one of the few American masterpieces about the war. It is one of the best realistic treatments of combat since Erich Maria Remarque's *Im Westen nichts Neues* (1929; *All Quiet on the Western Front*, 1929). Mailer based the novel on the eighteen months he spent overseas in Leyte, Luzon, and Japan (with the occupation forces) from 1944 to 1946. As is usually the case in a first novel, the influences on the book are fairly clear. Critics cite stylistic echoes of Ernest Hemingway, social concerns like those of John Steinbeck, naïve young men in search of maturity as with the characters of F. Scott Fitzgerald and Thomas Wolfe, and a flashback structure similar to John Dos Passos' *U.S.A.* trilogy (1930-1936). The style of *The Naked and the Dead* is simpler, partly because of the Hemingway influence, than Mailer's later self-conscious, often ornate writing, but the thematic concerns— among them, the conflict of the individual with a hostile, indifferent society—are the same as in his more mature fiction. Mailer intends the Anopopei campaign to be a microcosm not only of the war in the Pacific but of any war at any time or place. In showing how disconnected the worlds of command and combat are, Mailer emphasizes how war creates alienation in all its participants. As represented in figures like Cummings and Croft, the army seems the worst possible version of American society. Not only are the most sensitive, humane, and liberal characters, such as Hearn and Roth, defeated by their experiences; so are their cynical, amoral opposites.

Croft loses control of the patrol and fails to climb the mountain that represents his irrational need for order. Cummings cannot claim credit for the campaign's success and has difficulty in communicating his needs to those above and below him. That only the bureaucratic Dalleson comes out ahead points out how America is a society controlled not by men of action, such as Croft, or thinkers, such as Cummings, but by mere paper pushers, such as Dalleson.

Mailer is concerned with much more than men at war and uses his characters to explore what he considers to be sicknesses within society. The novel's characters are petty, scheming, sensitive to slights, and insensitive to others. They are unable to communicate effectively in any situation. There are huge communication gaps between Cummings and Dalleson, between Hearn and Croft, and between the corporals and privates in Croft's platoon. In Mailer's view of the world, men are at least as dehumanized by their own weaknesses as they are by war.

Neither courage nor education nor religious values seem to count for much. The failure of the latter can be seen in the quest of Ridges, with his traditional, Southern Christianity, and Goldstein, with his struggle to be a good man in an anti-Semitic world, to give Wilson a decent burial. That they fail because of a river points out nature's indifference to people's needs, as do the hornets who end Croft's attempt to conquer the mountain. At least in making the effort to save and then to bury Wilson, Goldstein and Ridges are admirable. In their attempt to find meaning and, possibly, redemption, they try to define themselves while the weaker Brown and Stanley allow the army to determine who they are.

As the flashbacks to their lives before the war indicate, Mailer's protagonists were little different in their peacetime lives. Mailer's civilian America is as chaotic as the war. Throughout *The Naked and the Dead*, Mailer illustrates how humanity's destiny is at the whim of illogical forces over which it is impossible to exert control.

Michael Adams

Bibliography:
Aichinger, Peter. *The American Soldier in Fiction, 1880-1963: A History of Attitudes Toward Warfare and the Military Establishment.* Ames: Iowa State University Press, 1975. Places the novel in the context of other treatments of World War II in American fiction. Complains that Mailer is unable to comprehend the character of the professional officer and that the novel is undermined by turgid ideological discourse.
Gordon, Andrew. *An American Dreamer: A Psychoanalytic Study of the Fiction of Norman Mailer.* Madison, N.J.: Fairleigh Dickinson University Press, 1980. Considers the novel in the context of other Mailer fiction that contrasts weak, liberal, masochistic characters with strong, reactionary, sadistic ones. Says that the novel's central psychological conflict is the doomed struggle for control over the self and outside forces.
Kaufman, Donald L. *Norman Mailer: The Countdown—The First Twenty Years.* Carbondale: Southern Illinois University Press, 1969. Analyzes the contrast between bestial and humane values in the novel and Mailer's depiction of obstacles to the creative urge. Shows how the novel is a commentary on isolation from space, time, and one's fellows.
Leeds, Barry H. *The Structured Vision of Norman Mailer.* New York: New York University Press, 1969. Interprets the novel as a pessimistic examination of the sickness of society and of the flawed nature of the individual. Shows how Mailer is an acerbic social critic.
Solotaroff, Robert. *Down Mailer's Way.* Champaign: University of Illinois Press, 1974. Argues that the novel is an allegory for what Mailer saw as the coming of fascism to America. Says that Mailer loses control of the novel because the values he seemingly endorses go against his deepest beliefs.

NAKED LUNCH

Type of work: Novel
Author: William S. Burroughs (1914-1997)
Type of plot: Fantasy
Time of plot: Mid-twentieth century
Locale: New York, Texas, New Orleans, and "Interzone"
First published: 1959

Principal characters:
WILLIAM LEE, a drug addict
JANE, his companion
DR. BENWAY, a charlatan doctor
A.J., a carnival con man
DOC PARKER, a druggist

The Story:

Bill Lee, a drug addict and hustler, and Jane, his companion, traveled by automobile across the United States to Texas in search of drugs. After picking up a quart of paregoric and a quantity of nembutols they drove on to New Orleans. There they bought some heroin and continued on to Mexico. During this trip, Lee, the narrator, delivered a rambling monologue about drug addicts, addiction, pushers, American cities, the police, narcotics agents, and the drag of life in suburban America where the neighborhoods were all the same and the people all dull and boring. In his monologue Lee concentrated on the terrible agony of need that the drug addict suffers. In Mexico Lee needed to locate a drug supplier, and he found one in Old Ike, a local junkie who received a monthly drug allowance from the government. Jane met a pimp who was a ritual marijuana user and who attempted to put her under his spell. Then Lee went to Interzone, an imaginary city, which was a combination of the Southern United States, South America, Tangier, New York, and Panama. There he met Dr. Benway, a master at controlling human behavior who worked for Islam, Inc. Benway gave Lee a tour of the Reconditioning Center in Freeland, a place where pseudo-science was practiced in bizarre experiments to brainwash human beings. Lee saw the monstrous results of Benway's "science" in creatures called INDs, or humans who had had their minds stripped. INDs were human vegetables who behaved like zombies.

Dr. Benway told Lee about his twisted theories of addiction and described in explicit detail the effects of various drugs, including morphine, LSD, and heroin. Benway showed Lee the criminal ward and gave Lee his opinions concerning homosexuality, specifically that it was a political crime. When a computer malfunctioned, Benway and Lee had to leave the Reconditioning Center. As they departed Lee described the horrible mutants, English colonials, bores, explorers, Arab rioters, hypochondriacs, and rock and roll hoodlums in the streets and at the cafés they passed by.

Interzone, the city, was described as a criss-crossing network of streets that ran through and beneath dwelling cubicles, cafés, and odd-shaped rooms. Merchants sold Black Meat, the addictive flesh of a giant centipede. Mugwumps, subhuman, reptilelike creatures, sat on café stools and dispensed mugwump fluid to addicts. In the hospital, Bill Lee experienced withdrawal from narcotics and told how horribly sick it made him. Dr. Benway explained to the nurses and patients how he practiced surgery. In an insane speech, Benway insulted every standard of medicine and sanitary medical procedure. Lee continued to describe the effects of various addictive drugs, as he tried to take the cure.

In a plushly decorated Interzone bar, a mugwump had perverted sex with a young boy. The boy was tied up and hung from a wooden gallows. He was sodomized by the mugwump. At the point of orgasm the boy's neck snapped. Satyrs, Arab women, Javanese dancers, Aztec priests, and various bizarre inhabitants of Interzone had outrageous sex with boys and with one another. At the campus of Interzone University, a professor lectured on perversions and "The Rime of the Ancient Mariner," by Samuel Taylor Coleridge. A.J. operated as an undercover agent disguised as a playboy and practical joker. At A.J.'s Annual Party, pornographic movies were shown to an audience of depraved sexual perverts who engaged in bizarre acts of sadomasochism.

Lee described Interzone as a Composite city, where all the houses were joined. In the Interzone Market at the Meet Cafe, wanderers, bums, junkies, drug pushers, dwarfs, and black marketeers met to discuss drugs, philosophy, and Dr. Benway's projects. Male prostitutes debated politics with members of the Nationalist Party. Lee recounted a number of short, perversely comic tales. Benway continued his pseudoscientific experiments with the assistance of Dr. Berger and a technician. They tried to "cure" homosexuals by brainwashing them.

Islam Incorporated and several of the political parties of Interzone held meetings at which the delegates and speakers were tortured and put to death. A.J. engaged in disgusting behavior at the restaurant Chez Robert, calling a hundred starving hogs into the restaurant. After he left the restaurant, A.J. took a baboon to the opera.

Bill Lee told the stories of a number of Interzone characters, including Clem and Jody, two vaudeville hoofers, and Salvador, an Italian pimp and drug dealer. Various parties, the Divisionists, Liquefactionists, and the Senders competed for control of the people in Interzone. Lee was forced to file an affidavit to avoid being evicted from his apartment. The County Clerk told Lee about Doc Parker's drugstore, where one could buy drugs. The Clerk also told a story about the vicious murder of a black service station attendant in Texas. Lee told of the lost and unlucky inhabitants of Interzone, who had failed miserably at every enterprise they attempted. Carl Peterson, who lived in Freeland, a welfare state, was summoned by Dr. Benway to undergo tests at the Ministry of Mental Hygiene. Benway told Carl that homosexuality was a sickness and that Carl might need treatment. Carl underwent several tests to determine his sexual orientation. Finally, in disgust, Carl walked out of Benway's clinic.

A sailor, who was in the throes of addiction, described the Exterminator. The Exterminator was actually Bill Lee, and his main job was to poison roaches with pyrethrum powder. Hauser and O'Brien, two narcotics officers, were ordered to arrest Lee at his apartment. After they arrived, Lee tried to take more drugs. Lee ended up murdering the two officers. The road through withdrawal and toward recovery was described by Lee as a horrible nightmare in which the junkie had to face thoughts of suicide to cleanse his "rotting, phosphorescent bones," and silence the "mangled insect screams." Finally, Lee uttered a few desperate words about drug sickness and the pathos of drug commerce and the smells of gasoline and slow, cold fires, burning endlessly.

Critical Evaluation:

Since its first publication in Paris in 1959, *Naked Lunch* has received both praise and censure. While noted authors and critics such as John Ciardi, Norman Mailer, and Mary McCarthy have applauded *Naked Lunch* as a novel of genius and terrible beauty, its publication in the United States in 1962 was met with seizure by the U.S. Postal Service and U.S. Customs on the grounds it was pornographic. *Naked Lunch* was found to be obscene by a Massachusetts Superior Court in 1965, a decision that was later overturned by the Massachusetts Supreme Court.

Naked Lunch is a disjointed account of the horrors of a junkie's addiction, withdrawal, and cure. William Burroughs, one of the original Beat writers, arrived in Tangier, Morocco, in 1953, after spending months in the jungles of South America in search of the hallucinogenic plant, Yage. At that time Burroughs was heavily addicted to narcotics such as morphine and codeine. He was perhaps drawn to Tangier because of its reputation as a zone of permissiveness where drugs were plentiful and expenses were low. Tangier was an International Zone, where there was unregulated free enterprise. It was also known to expatriate writers and artists as a sanctuary where they could live without being scrutinized by the authorities. Once settled in Tangier, Burroughs tried to write but his drug addiction made that process both painful and difficult. As he attempted various cures, his writing slowly progressed. The novel that began to develop would be a narrative based on his addiction and withdrawal and his impressions of Tangier.

Burroughs first compiled a large volume of notes, which contained his travel and drug experiences, hallucinations, dreams, and satirical fantasies about American society. In order to complete the manuscript, Burroughs had to face his addiction and undergo drug treatment. While he made various attempts to withdraw in Tangier, he was finally cured after seeking the help of Dr. John Yerbury Dent of London. His friends Allen Ginsberg, Jack Kerouac, and Alan Ansen visited him in Tangier in 1957, where they helped type, select, and edit the final manuscript and prepare it for publication.

In *Naked Lunch*, Burroughs tells his story metaphorically through a series of episodes, visions, and myths. These fantasies work to describe a state of mind rather than create a traditional narrative. The technique used in *Naked Lunch* is similar to collage or montage. Scenes, episodes, and routines are juxtaposed in a way that makes it possible to read them in almost any order. The episodes are indicated by titles that refer to the subject or theme. The episodes vary from two or three pages in length to more than twenty pages. Within the episode there is usually an introduction in which characters, setting, or a situation is defined, followed by improvisations that may end in a violent or dramatic climax.

The main setting of *Naked Lunch* is Interzone, a city based on a composite of the places where Burroughs had gone in search of drugs: New York, Louisiana, South America, and Tangier. Interzone is inhabited by hustlers, addicts, con men, losers, and petty officials. These inhabitants spend their time taking drugs, having pornographic sex, and engaging in sleazy commerce. There are political and economic conspiracies everywhere, usually made up of groups who are involved in a struggle for power and control over the "consumers." The control the conspirators exercise is based on the consumer's need for drugs, sex, or power. Through the many satirical, hallucinatory scenes, Burroughs exposes the hypocrisy and destructiveness of American society. Doctors, bureaucrats, and politicians are the chief examples of the power elite who manipulate the masses. For example, Dr. Benway and Dr. Berger create "healthy" men by torturing and brainwashing them. The three main political parties are like parasites, seeking to gain control over Interzone through demoniac possession.

In *Naked Lunch* Burroughs uses a variety of literary forms derived from popular culture, including newspapers, advertising, magazines, comics, paperbacks, movies, radio, and television. His characters are all pop-culture types: the crazed doctor, secret agent, private eye, gangster, drug pusher, mad scientist, vampire, and zombie. Bill Lee and A.J. represent Burroughs' alter egos. The episodes are arranged in random order, to create an improvised text that can be entered at any point. While the untraditional, shocking nature of the subject matter and the experimental form of the novel resulted in many negative reviews when *Naked Lunch* was published, there was much praise for its boldness and unrelenting power. Continually in print since 1959, *Naked Lunch* has been vindicated as a work of literary merit that is still capable of artistic and moral revelation.

Francis Poole

Bibliography:
Goodman, Michael Barry. *Contemporary Literary Censorship: The Case History of Burroughs' "Naked Lunch."* Metuchen, N.J.: Scarecrow Press, 1981. A narrative history of the writing, publication, critical reception, and censorship of *Naked Lunch* in the United States. Well documented, it includes much previously unpublished material.

Miles, Barry. *William Burroughs: El Hombre Invisible.* London: Virgin Books, 1992. An entertaining overview of Burroughs' literary and artistic output. Includes chapters devoted specifically to Tangier and to *Naked Lunch*. Offers a personal portrait of Burroughs the man and artist.

Morgan, Ted. *Literary Outlaw: The Life and Times of William S. Burroughs.* New York: Henry Holt, 1988. A detailed biography of William Burroughs which discusses *Naked Lunch*, its style, themes, and organization. Includes interesting photographs of Burroughs taken throughout his life.

Mottram, Eric. *William Burroughs: The Algebra of Need.* Critical Appraisal Series. London: Marion Boyars, 1977. A study of Burroughs' work as a radical critique of Western power structures and the myths that support them. Mottram analyzes *Naked Lunch* and other works of Burroughs' fiction in comparison with other radical thinkers.

Skerl, Jennie. *William S. Burroughs.* Boston: Twayne, 1985. A very good introduction to Burroughs' life and work until 1981 and the publication of *The Cities of the Red Night*. Provides insight into the creation, themes, and techniques of *Naked Lunch*.

THE NAKED YEAR

Type of work: Novel
Author: Boris Pilnyak (Boris Andreyevich Vogau, 1894-1937?)
Type of plot: Regional
Time of plot: Early twentieth century
Locale: Russia
First published: Goly god, 1922 (English translation, 1928)

Principal characters:
DONAT RATCHIN, a merchant's son and a young revolutionist
NASTIA, a chambermaid
ARKHIP, a peasant member of the party
ARKHIPOV, his father
NATALIA ORDYNIN, a young doctor
BORIS,
GLEB, and
EGOR, her brothers
CATHERINE and
LYDIA, her sisters
ANDREY, a fugitive

The Story:

Ordynin Town was a citadel that had existed for years in a normal fashion, where poets, artisans, and merchants dwelt, busy with their tasks. The Ratchin family had been merchants for two hundred years, and for much of that time they had leased the salt trade. Donat, a curly-headed youth, was the youngest son. Already he counted on taking his place in the market, on buying and selling and ruling his clerks.

The monastery held an important place in the lives of the people, for its bells regulated their lives. At nine o'clock the town went to bed; anyone up and about after that hour had to identify himself to the watch. Pranks of boys and dwarfs provided the only excitement, and the stationer's store was the intellectual center of the town.

At the age of fifteen, Donat fell in love with a chambermaid named Nastia. Every evening he went to her kitchen and read church history aloud to her. When Ivan, his father, heard of the attachment, he had both Donat and Nastia whipped; that same night, Ivan sent his housekeeper to Donat's bed. Afterward Donat learned how to get out of the house at night. For a while he clambered out of a window and went to see the persecuted widow of a rich moneylender.

In 1914, war came, and in 1917, revolution. From ancient Ordynin the inhabitants were called up to learn the craft of murder, to kill and die. Donat was sent to the Carpathians. The first casualty of Ordynin was Classic-Spark, a loafer who committed suicide when the vodka ran out. Because the merchants of Ordynin refused to pay a sufficient bribe to the engineers who were laying the railroad tracks, the railway station was put some distance away. Ordynin was doomed to remain in the backwash of progress and change.

The Ratchin house was requisitioned by the Red Guard, and the salt market was broken up. Donat returned from the war full of hatred for the old order. He ordered that the salt building be destroyed and a house for the people erected in its place.

In the monastery, Olly Kuntz printed blank orders for arrest and imprisonment. Arkhip, a peasant unused to writing, was in command, and he frequently laboriously penned orders of execution. Comrade Laitis took Olly to the cinema and saw her home. Later he came back with his soldiers to arrest Andrey, a lodger, but Andrey cleverly gave them the slip and got away. The soldiers broke into Olly's room when they searched the building, and Olly wept out of sympathy for Andrey. Semyon, a bookish man interested in masonry, was much impressed by Andrey's cleverness.

Old Arkhipov, Arkhip's father, went to see the doctor. His fears were confirmed when his doctor, Natalia Ordynin, told him that he had cancer of the stomach. At the moment that Arkhipov decided that he must die, Arkhip was signing an execution warrant. That evening the father asked Arkhip's advice, and upon his son's suggestion, he shot himself in the mouth.

After two years, Gleb returned to the manor. No one could remember whether the town was named for the Ordynin family or whether the family took its name from the town. At any rate the Ordynins had been lords for a long time; now the seal of Cain was on them. In the run-down house no one greeted Gleb, but soon Egor, his brother, half-naked and dirty, came stumbling in with the servant Martha. Martha had found her master in a brothel and brought him home. Egor had paid for the spree by selling his sister Natalia's coat.

Gleb learned that Boris, his older brother, had locked Egor in his room and then raped Martha. Since Egor was half in love with her, the crime seemed particularly serious. When Boris came into Gleb's room, Boris announced gloomily that he was suffering from syphilis, a family disease. Then Gleb thought of his lunatic father, a religious fanatic in his old age, and of the brothers and sisters who had died in infancy.

Arina, the mother, sold clothes and furniture to make ends meet. Natalia, already suspected of being too fond of Arkhip, alienated herself further from the family by going to live at the hospital where she worked. Catherine, the youngest daughter, was pregnant, and the other sister Lydia advised her to have an abortion. To her dismay, Catherine learned that she also had syphilis, but when she ran to Lydia for comfort, her sister, under the influence of morphine, paid little attention to her.

Andrey joined a brotherhood near the Black Streams. The peasant girls called him out to their dances at night, and he was happy for a time. Aganka, the merriest and hardest-working of the girls, attracted him greatly, but she died during the hot summer. Smallpox and typhus broke out, and all Russia suffered from pestilence and famine and war. Andrey became Irina's betrothed, although the comrades frowned on marriage as sentimental nonsense. Donat Ratchin was the unbending leader of their anarchistic commune.

The commune ceased to be a haven when the band of armed strangers arrived. At the instigation of Harry, their English leader, they killed most of the men and then rode on to join an uprising in the Ukraine. Andrey was lucky to get away.

At first, Boris was furious when Ivan, president of the poverty committee, requisitioned the Ordynin manor. He had known Ivan for years and despised him as an unlettered peasant. In a spirit of bravado, Boris left home on foot. A friendly peasant gave him shelter the first night, but the apprehensive peasant made him leave early the next morning. Later that day, Boris found space in a refugee wagon.

The famine became worse. The old men bartered with traveling merchants because there was no money with which to buy anything. There were no young men left to work; they had all gone off with the Reds or the Whites. People did anything they could for bread. At Mar Junction, the railway station, the Red Guards often requisitioned young women who came in on the refugee train.

The Whites occupied Ordynin, and when they left, the Reds swarmed back. Committees and commissions sprang up all over the town. The Moscow functionaries even reopened a mine outside the town. Although the mine, with its antique equipment, was a deathtrap, men were forced to work in it.

Busy with his many duties, Arkhip felt keenly his lack of education. Natalia, the only normal Ordynin, was a doctor under the new government. Arkhip had known Natalia for a long time, and at last, needing an educated partner and wanting children, he asked her to marry him. Natalia thought of her university days, when she had been in love. It was a painful memory. She would welcome this new kind of mating, with neither love nor pain. Despite her resolutions, however, she felt close to Arkhip and talked of the coziness of their union. Arkhip went home and thumbed in vain through his dictionary. He did not know the meaning of the word coziness nor could he find it in the dictionary.

Critical Evaluation:

The "naked year" is 1917, the year of the Bolshevik Revolution, and Boris Pilnyak's attempt to capture its essence in his narrative established him as Russia's first important post-Revolutionary novelist. It can be strongly argued that *The Naked Year* is neither in form a novel, nor in substance a Communistic document. The fragmentary, lyrical, relatively plotless and characterless series of vignettes that make up the book are more like a sequence of random impressions and rhetorical digressions, thinly tied together in time and place, than a controlled, directed narrative. The origins and essence of the revolution, as Pilnyak presents them, do not conform to the tenets of Soviet political dogma.

Despite its narrative difficulties and ideological impurity, *The Naked Year* was generally hailed as a masterpiece upon its publication in 1922. The main character of the book is the Russian people, and the substance of it is their diverse reactions to the civil turmoil that swept across Russia from 1914 to the early 1920's. Although Pilnyak uses a mixture of prose styles and jumps from character to character and event to event with few formal transitions, he does focus most of the action in the town of Ordynin and on characters who represent all levels of Russian society—the Ratchin family belongs to the middle class, the Ordynins are aristocratic, Arkhip represents the rising peasantry—in a fairly complete, if unsystematic fashion. Thus the reader comes away from *The Naked Year* with a coherent impression of life in revolutionary Russia.

The historical vision Pilnyak presents in the novel is that of a spontaneous peasant revolt overthrowing the old order. He sees the conflict not so much in terms of the bourgeoisie versus the proletariat as the "natural" Eastern side of Russian culture, represented by the peasantry, in conflict with the "artificial" European urbanized Russia. The revolution was, in his opinion, the necessary cleansing force, and the Bolsheviks were merely the agents of historical change, not the inevitable culmination of it.

Such unorthodox views displeased the revolutionary hierarchy, but the power and popularity of the novel, coupled with the relative instability of Soviet politics at the time, kept Pilnyak in the ranks of accepted writers. In such later works, however, as "The Tale of the Unextinguished Moon" (1927)—a direct attack on Stalin—and *Mahogany* (1929), he provoked the dictator's wrath. Despite abject disavowals of his works, pitiable recantations, and several orthodox writings, Pilnyak was imprisoned during the Stalinist purges of the mid-1930's and presumably perished in neglect and disgrace.

Bibliography:

Brown, Edward J. "Boris Pilnyak: Biology and History." In *Russian Literature Since the Revolution*. New York: Collier Books, 1963. Considers *The Naked Year* a virtuoso performance both in its symphonic structure of themes and ideas and in being a presentation of the primitive and elemental forces of the Revolution. Good survey of Pilnyak's works.

Maguire, Robert. "The Pioneers: Pil'nyak and Ivanov." In *Red Virgin Soil: Soviet Literature in the 1920's*. Princeton, N.J.: Princeton University Press, 1968. A useful discussion of Pilnyak's role in Russian literature of the 1920's, especially of his iconoclastic approach to literature. Asserts that Pilnyak lacks greatness but was influential in shaping the Russian literature of his time.

Reck, Vera T. *Boris Pil'niak: A Soviet Writer in Conflict with the State*. Montreal: McGill-Queen's University Press, 1975. Extensive account of Pilnyak's celebrated troubles with the authorities, to whom Stalin gave the tone by declaring that Pilnyak expressed his anarchism already in *The Naked Year*.

Slonim, Marc. "Boris Pilnyak: The Untimely Symbolist." In *Soviet Russian Literature: Writers and Problems 1917-1977*. 2d rev. ed. New York: Oxford University Press, 1977. Substantive historical survey of Pilnyak's works and his place in the early Russian literature of the Soviet period.

Struve, Gleb. *Russian Literature Under Lenin and Stalin, 1917-1953*. Norman: University of Oklahoma Press, 1971. Contains a brief but excellent account of Pilnyak's writings, including *The Naked Year*, and of his conflicts with the state that eventually led to his death.

THE NAME OF THE ROSE

Type of work: Novel
Author: Umberto Eco (1932-   )
Type of plot: Detective and mystery
Time of plot: 1327
Locale: An abbey in northern Italy
First published: Il nome della rosa, 1980 (English translation, 1983)

Principal characters:
>WILLIAM OF BASKERVILLE, a Franciscan monk and former inquisitor, now a detective
>ADSO OF MELK, the narrator, a Benedictine novice assigned as William's scribe
>ABO, the abbot of the Benedictine monastery
>JORGE DE BURGOS, an aged, blind monk
>MICHAEL OF CESENA, the leader of the Franciscan order
>BERNARD GUI, a Dominican inquisitor
>THE UNNAMED EDITOR AND TRANSLATOR

The Story:

It was in late November, 1327, that the learned Franciscan William of Baskerville, student of Roger Bacon and friend of William of Occam, arrived at a Benedictine abbey in northern Italy, accompanied by his young Benedictine scribe, Adso of Melk. William had been assigned the difficult task of arranging a meeting between representatives of Pope John XXII and the leader of the Franciscans, Michael of Cesena, at a time of great religious, political, social, and economic upheaval. The Pope held the entire Franciscan order responsible for the extremist position on poverty held by its most radical members. The emperor supported the Franciscans, an odd alliance until one realized his motive: to weaken the Pope's power. The Benedictines also supported the Franciscans, but for a very different reason; they feared that a strong centralized church, especially one located in Avignon, would undermine the spiritual and economic control that individual monasteries had long exerted over surrounding areas.

When William arrived, he was informed by the abbot of a recent event that, although not directly related to William's mission, could threaten both its success and the abbot's sovereignty. The body of a young and handsome monk, a master illustrator named Adelmo, had been found earlier that day. The abbot charged William with clearing up the mystery surrounding Adelmo's death—whether it was murder or suicide—before the arrival of the papal legation. Although allowed considerable latitude in conducting the investigation, William was barred from entering the monastery's great library located on the Aedificium's top floor. The prohibition only piqued William's interest, especially when the body of another monk connected with the library, the Greek Scholar Venantius, was found head down in a great jar filled with pigs' blood the very next day. The old monk Alinardo saw in the two deaths signs of the apocalypse announced in the Book of Revelations. William did not believe that the end was near, but he did believe that the Book of Revelations had something to do with the deaths. As a result, he became even more determined to penetrate the mysteries of the forbidden, labyrinthine library.

Adso found his naïve faith just as challenged as William's wits, first by his master's revelations, then by his own curiosity. The abbey, he learned, was not a world apart from, but a microcosm of, the secular world outside its walls. Divine order and absolute truth gave way to man-made, relativistic pronouncements and interpretations. Adso proved only slightly better at resisting these seeming snares than he did the sexual advances of the young woman he came upon in the kitchen one night after becoming separated from William during one of their forays into the library. After first transmogrifying her into the whore of Babylon, Adso's fevered, book-bound imagination transformed her into the beauty extolled in the Song of Songs.

Adso's post-coital reverie was cut short by the discovery of a third corpse—the second with mysteriously blackened fingers—and the arrival of the papal legation led by the infamous inquisitor Bernard Gui. In the world according to Gui, a man more inquisitorial than inquisitive, all was clear, despite the fog that had descended on the abbey. The girl was not an impoverished peasant but a witch; Remigio was not a lustful cellarer who had his assistant, the grotesque and babbling Salvatore, procure village girls willing to exchange their virtue for bits of meat, but a heretic and the murderer of all four monks, the herbalist Arvenius being his most recent victim. The death of a fifth monk, the illiterate librarian Malachi, provided the most visible proof of the inadequacy of the inquisitor's theory. Much to Adso's dismay, it did not prove the girl's innocence; she was, William claimed, "dead meat" whom Adso would do well to forget.

Adso may not have been able to save the girl, but he did save the day with the chance remark that provided William with the clue he needed to solve yet another of the library's mysteries. Once again, however, solving a mystery did not save a life, that of the abbot sealed in a secret stairway leading to the library. This William learned when he finally reached the library's Finis Africae and confronted his nemesis, the blind monk Jorge de Burgos, mastermind of the murders, although not technically a murderer. Just as William suspected, all the victims had died for lust: in some cases sexual, in others intellectual. Most had died by their own hand, three of them literally so, wetting their fingers before turning the fatal book's poisoned pages. This was the book that Jorge was determined no one else should ever read, the one hidden away in the library's labyrinthine recesses. It was bound with a number of other very different manuscripts, each in a different language: the manuscript "in Greek, made perhaps by an Arab or by a Spaniard, that you found when, as assistant to Paul of Rimini, you arranged to be sent back to your country to collect the finest manuscripts of the apocalypse in Leon and Castile." It was not a manuscript that dealt with the Apocalypse, but one that Jorge feared would bring about a more catastrophic end than the one foretold in the Book of Revelations.

Although his lust for books prevented him from destroying it, Jorge greatly feared the consequences should this "second book of the *Poetics* of Aristotle, the book everyone has believed lost or never written, and of which you hold perhaps the only copy," become known. Jorge believed that Aristotle had, through Thomas Aquinas' writings, already undermined the Church's teachings and authority. What he feared even more was the manuscript's elevating comedy to the level of art, thus giving it a power far greater than the heresies and carnival inversions whose subversive potential the Church could control. In a final act of defiance—at once horrific, childish, and comic—Jorge destroyed the manuscript and himself by eating its poisoned pages and then accidentally starting the fire that destroyed first the library and then the entire abbey: endgame becoming Armageddon in the tale's fiery conclusion.

Critical Evaluation:

The Name of the Rose is that rarest of books: a work that manages to be enjoyable without being escapist, an international bestseller that crosses literary borders as readily as it does national ones, offering something for all its readers and most for those willing to appreciate the playful plural of this inviting yet intricate novelistic labyrinth. Part of its appeal stems from the fullness with which Umberto Eco depicts his medieval world, a world already made appealing by Barbara Tuchman's *A Distant Mirror* (1978) and films such as *Excalibur* (1981). *The Name of the Rose* is not merely a historical novel with gothic shadings. It is also, and more obviously, a detective story (according to Eco, "the most metaphysical and philosophical" kind of plot), although in a parodic, metafictional, postmodern key. As indebted to the great Argentinian writer and national librarian Jorge Luis Borges as to Sherlock Holmes's creator Arthur Conan Doyle, the novel presents "a mystery in which very little is discovered and the detective is defeated."

The novel's impure form constitutes a virtual library of literary echoes, ranging from whole genres to specific authors and works, a towering babel of intertextualized voices in the form of a seamless story, a celebration of narrative on the one hand, a work not without political and pedagogical import on the other. Among its many pleasures is the way the novel, like the essays in Eco's *Travels in Hyperreality* (1986), makes the subject of Eco's scholarly writings, semiotics, accessible to a nonacademic audience. *The Name of the Rose* is not, however, merely a medieval exemplum or detective story dressed up as a *roman à these*. Eco's novel is "a machine for generating meanings," a narrative version of the monastery's labyrinthine library in which one finds "The maximum of confusion achieved with the maximum of order," but a confusion intended to seduce, not repel. In this sense, the novel resembles the rose that figures so prominently in the novel's first words, the title, and its last, where its meaning is both declared and disguised in the unattributed line from Bernard de Cluny's *De contemptu mundi*: "Stat rosa pristina nomine, nomina nuda tenemus" ("Yesterday's rose endures in its name, we hold empty names"). As Eco explains in his postscript, as a symbol, the rose is so full of meanings as to be virtually empty of meaning—a floating signifier.

Such a novel might have proved—like the numerous passages in Latin—too daunting for most readers were it not for Eco's decision "to make everything understood through the words of one who understood nothing." In this way, the reader experiences the shock of the new in much the same way the befuddled Adso does. Because Adso is everything the erudite and ironic William of Baskerville is not—young, naïve, literal-minded, faithful, obedient, credulous—the reader is also allowed, or encouraged, to feel superior to William's scribe and disciple. In this way, the reader comes to experience some of the same doubleness of vision as Adso the eighty-year-old narrator does in trying to reconstruct himself and his world as they existed in 1327 when he was a differently befuddled eighteen-year-old novice.

A similar dualism is at work, and at play, in the novel's overall structure. Adso's manuscript is divided into seven days, or chapters, each chronicling that day's events and subdivided according to the eight canonical hours (matins, lauds, and so on). The structure is apt and easy to follow, but it is also arbitrary. It organizes time and narrative space and orients the reader, but it also serves as a sign of Adso's acceptance of the Benedictine rule and of a divinely ordered universe. The novel is further complicated—denaturalized, made enigmatic and therefore suspect—by the unnamed and, therefore, mysterious editor's untitled preface, dated January 5, 1980. Even as he explains how the manuscript came briefly into his possession, the editor's remarks cast doubt on both the authenticity of Adso's manuscript and the accuracy of the editor's translation. Thus, just as there are two worlds at the abbey—one daytime, one nighttime, with the latter being by far the more intriguing—so too does *The Name of the Rose* comprise a whole succession of stories, one inside another, each requiring a certain kind of sleuthing: there is the one Adso tells and then there are the stories of his telling and the editor's, to which Adso's narrative serves as a five-hundred-page postscript.

The "game of strange alliances" played out in 1327 infects the novel at every level. Absolute truths and univocal utterances give way to ambiguous relations, the meaning of which involves interpretive codes and contexts. "Books," William explains, "are not meant to be believed, but to be subjected to inquiry." Inquiry does not necessarily save or solve, however, as William admits when he finds Jorge at the center of the interpretive web: "There was no plot, and I discovered it by mistake," reaching the right destination by following a series of wrong guesses (abductions). Yet even in failure, there is a certain success of a decidedly humbling kind. As William says and as Eco's apocalyptic yet comic novel reveals, "Perhaps the mission of those who love mankind is to make people laugh at the truth, to make truth laugh, because the only truth lies in learning to free ourselves from insane passion for the truth."

Robert A. Morace

Bibliography:
Coletti, Theresa. *Naming the Rose: Eco, Medieval Signs, and Modern Theory.* Ithaca, N.Y.: Cornell University Press, 1988. Discusses Eco's mingling of medieval and modern and what this means in light of the novel's reception.
Eco, Umberto. *Postscript to "The Name of the Rose."* San Diego: Harcourt Brace Jovanovich, 1984. In the spirit of Poe's "Philosophy of Composition," Eco discusses how the novel came to be written, not how it should be read.
Haft, Adele J., Jane G. White, and Robert J. White. *The Key to "The Name of the Rose."* Harrington Park, N.J.: Ampersand Associates, 1987. A useful source that identifies the novel's literary references and provides translations of all non-English passages.
Inge, M. Thomas. *Naming the Rose: Essays on Eco's "The Name of the Rose."* Jackson: University Press of Mississippi, 1988. Ten essays with a foreword by Eco, a reader-response postscript, and a useful annotated checklist of English-language criticism.
Richter, David H. "Eco's Echoes: Semiotic Theory and Detective Practice in *The Name of the Rose." Studies in Twentieth Century Literature* 10, no. 2 (Spring, 1986): 213-236. Densely detailed and finely argued discussion of the relation between Eco's parodic novel and semiotic theory.

NANA

Type of work: Novel
Author: Émile Zola (1840-1902)
Type of plot: Naturalism
Time of plot: 1860's
Locale: Paris and rural France
First published: 1880 (English translation, 1880)

> *Principal characters:*
> NANA, a beautiful courtesan
> FAUCHERY, a dramatic critic
> STEINER, a wealthy banker
> GEORGE HUGON, a student
> PHILIPPE HUGON, his brother and an officer
> FONTAN, an actor
> COUNT MUFFAT DE BEUVILLE
> SABINE, his wife,
> MARQUIS DE CHOUARD, and
> COUNT XAVIER DE VANDEUVRES, well-known figures of the Parisian
> world of art and fashion

The Story:

Monsieur Fauchery, theatrical reviewer for a Paris paper, was attending the premiere of *The Blonde Venus* at the Variety Theatre because he had heard rumors of Nana, the Venus of the new play. Paris' smart set was well represented at the theater that night, and Fauchery and his cousin Hector de la Faloise noted a few of the more interesting people. In the audience were Steiner, a crooked but very rich banker who was the current lover of Rose Mignon, an actress in *The Blonde Venus*; Mignon, who served as procurer for his own wife; Daguenet, a reckless spender reputed to be Nana's lover for the moment; Count Xavier de Vandeuvres; Count Muffat de Beuville and his wife; and several of the city's well-known courtesans.

The play, a vulgar travesty on the life of the Olympian gods, was becoming boring when Nana finally appeared; with beautiful golden hair floating over her shoulders, she walked confidently toward the footlights for her feature song. When she began to sing, she seemed such a crude amateur that murmurs and hisses were beginning to sound. Suddenly a young student exclaimed loudly that she was stunning. Everyone laughed, including Nana. It was as though she frankly admitted that she had nothing except her voluptuous self to offer. Nana, however, knew that was sufficient for her audience. As she ended her song, she retired to the back of the stage amid a roar of applause. In the last act, Nana's body was veiled only by her golden locks and a transparent gauze. The house grew quiet and tense. Nana smiled confidently, knowing that she had conquered them with her flesh.

Thus Nana, product of the streets of Paris, started her career as mistress of the city. To get money for her scrofulous little son, Louis, and for her own extravagant wants, she sold herself at varying prices to many men. She captivated Steiner, the banker, at an all-night party after her initial success as Venus. He bought her a country place, La Mignotte, a league from Les Fondettes, home of Madame Hugon, whose seventeen-year-old son George had called Nana stunning the opening night of *The Blonde Venus* and who had been enraptured with her at

Nana's party. Nana, making no pretense of belonging exclusively to Steiner, invited a number of friends to visit her at La Mignotte.

Madame Hugon entertained Count Muffat, his wife Sabine, and their daughter Estelle at her home in September. George, who had been expected several times during the summer, suddenly came home. He had invited Fauchery and Daguenet for a visit. Mme Vandeuvres, who had promised for five years to come to Les Fondettes, was likewise expected. Mme Hugon was unaware of any connection between the coming of Nana to La Mignotte and the simultaneous visits of all of these men to Les Fondettes.

George escaped from his doting mother and went in the rain to Nana, who found him soaking wet as she was gathering strawberries in her garden. While his clothes were drying, he dressed in some of Nana's. Despite Nana's feeling that it was wrong to submit to such an innocent boy, she finally gave in to George's entreaties, and she was faithful to him for almost a week. Muffat, who had lived a circumspect life for forty years, became increasingly inflamed by passion as he paid nightly visits to Nana's place, only to be rebuffed each time. He talked with Steiner, who likewise was being put off by Nana with the excuse that she was not feeling well. Meanwhile Muffat's wife attracted the attention of Fauchery, the journalist.

Eleven of Nana's Parisian friends arrived in a group at La Mignotte. George was seen with Nana and her friends by his mother, who later made him promise not to visit the actress, a promise he had no intention of keeping. His brother Philippe, an army officer, threatened to bring him back by his ears if he had anything more to do with Nana.

Being true to George was romantically pleasing, but financially it was unwise, and Nana at last gave herself to the persistent Muffat the night before she returned to Paris to see whether she could recapture the public that had acclaimed her in *The Blonde Venus*.

Three months later Muffat, who had taken the place of castoff George, was involved in financial troubles. During a quarrel with Nana he learned from Nana that his wife Sabine and Fauchery were making a cuckold of him. Nana, by turns irritated or bored by Muffat and then sorry for him, chose this means of avenging herself on Fauchery, who had written a scurrilous article about Nana.

Having now broken with Muffat and Steiner, Nana gave up her place in the Boulevard Haussmann and went to live with the actor Fontan. Fontan, however, became increasingly difficult and even vicious, beating her night after night and taking all of her money. Nana returned to her old profession of streetwalking to pick up a few francs. After a close brush with the police, Nana grew more discreet. She left the brutal Fontan and sought a part as a grand lady in a new play at the Variety Theatre. Given the part, she failed miserably in it; but she began to play the lady in real life in a richly decorated house that Muffat purchased for her. Despite Nana's callous treatment of him, Muffat could not stay away from her.

In her mansion in the Avenue de Villiers, Nana squandered money in great sums. Finding Muffat's gifts insufficient, she added Count Xavier de Vandeuvres as a lover. She planned to get eight or ten thousand francs a month from him for pocket money. George Hugon reappeared, but he was less interesting than he had once been. When Philippe Hugon tried to extricate his young brother from Nana's net, he also was caught. Nana grew bored. From the streets one day she picked up the prostitute Satin, who became her vice.

In a race for the Grand Prize of Paris at Longchamps, Nana won two thousand louis on a horse named for her, but de Vandeuvres, who owned the filly Nana as well as the favorite Lusignan, lost everything through some crooked betting. He set fire to his stable and died with his horses.

Muffat found Nana in George's arms one evening in September; from that time on, he ceased to believe in her sworn fidelity. He became more and more her abject slave, submitting meekly when Nana forced him to play woolly bear, horse, and dog with her and then mocked his ridiculous nudity. Muffat was further degraded when he discovered Nana in bed with his father-in-law, the ancient Marquis de Chouard.

George, jealous of his brother Philippe, stabbed himself in Nana's bedroom when she refused to marry him. He died of his self-inflicted wound, and Nana was briefly sorry for him. Nana also broke Philippe. He was imprisoned for stealing army funds to spend on her.

Nana thrived on those she destroyed. Fate caught up with her at last. Visiting her dying son after his long absence and many conquests in foreign lands, she caught smallpox from him and died horribly in a Paris hospital. The once-beautiful body that had destroyed so many men lay a rotting ruin in a deserted room as outside there sounded the French battle cry. The Franco-Prussian War of 1870 had begun.

Critical Evaluation:

Émile Zola's Rougon-Macquart series (1871-1893), including *Nana*, ran to an aggregate of twenty novels, exploring the naturalistic philosophy of literature. This philosophy was strongly influenced by the scientific method outlined in Claude Bernard's *Introduction to the Study of Experimental Medicine* (1865). Zola himself explained the relationship between science and literature in his theoretical works: *Le Roman experimental* (1880; *The Experimental Novel*, 1894; a direct application of Bernard's principle to literature), *Les Romanciers naturalistes* (1881), and *Le Naturalisme au théâtre* (1881; *Naturalism on the Stage*, 1894). According to Zola, naturalism combines scientific determinism, pessimistic and mechanistic views of human behavior, pathological assumptions about human motivation, and a predilection for examining the life of the lower socioeconomic classes. Thus, Zola's Rougon-Macquart series, designed after the model of Honoré de Balzac's *The Human Comedy*, seeks to portray the society of the Second Empire by "scientifically" describing conditions of life. Zola, however, did not recognize that hereditary (biological) determinants cannot rationalize behavior. His attempt to trace through twenty novels a family epic of neuroses and alcoholism was therefore less than successful. Nevertheless, it did produce some memorable character studies—among them, *Nana*—in the multifaceted collection of one-thousand-odd characters who appear in the series, depicting various social classes, circumstances, and places that Zola knew well.

Indeed, so attentive is Zola to naturalism's scientific principles that he paints in words as vivid a portrait of Nana as could be painted by the most adept realists. Of course, attention to detail as well as to psychological motivation is paramount in the naturalistic canon. Just as scientific experiments require exacting attention to statistical data, so also do naturalistic novels demand factual accounting. Thus, *Nana* satisfies its philosophical imperatives by providing such meticulous details as would be necessary for a laboratory report. These details evolve not only from the physical description of Nana herself but also from the development of the plot. Each twist and turn in Nana's life and fortune, for example, is as carefully documented as a research paper would be. No phenomenon is left unexplained. For Zola's approach to *Nana*— novel and character—is that of a scientist who leaves no possibility unexplored. Hence, in *Nana*, the protagonist is fully explored, fully psychologized.

While Nana is being thoroughly explored, Zola also develops the theme of the novel. Zola presents in the novel an unrelenting account of a fashionable but decadent society. In much the same manner as a twentieth century commentator on the jet-set phenomenon, Zola chronicles the debaucheries of mid-nineteenth century Paris. Money, power, and sex dominate French society, according to Zola: Money buys power, and power gets sex. Thus the central characters, obsessed with the power of money, buy and sell themselves and one another with kaleidoscopic turnover. Monsieur Mignon pimps for his wife; Madame Hugon, wittingly or unwittingly, sets up her son George for seduction by Nana; Nana herself accumulates an incredible number of lovers from Daguenet to Steiner to George Hugon to Count Muffat to Fontan to Count Xavier de Vandeuvres to Philippe Hugon to Satin to the Marquis de Chouard. The moral rot endemic in all of these people reaches its culmination in Nana's literal and symbolic contracting of smallpox from her neglected son.

Zola lays bare the political, social, and ethical bankruptcy of the Second Empire. He does it through plot development and characterization. Nana's sequential—and sometimes simultane-ous—liaisons constitute the thread of plot development. Her fortunes depend not upon her theatrical talents but upon her contacts with monied men who can keep her in style. Her only errors are those that involve sentiment rather than cold analysis and rational evaluation of her prospects for survival. Plot development reveals the theme of the novel as a study in how the economically disadvantaged cope with an inherently inequitable system. Zola's implication is that they do it tenuously and insecurely. For in his characterization of Nana, Zola depicts a woman who is utterly insecure. Nana has no solid resources of her own other than her gorgeous body. She is vulgar; she is cheap; she is sordid. She is all of these degraded things because she has no confidence in her own worth as a human being. Hence, in her view, and in society's view, once she has lost her attractiveness to the debilities of disease, she is worthless.

Still, for all of Zola's professed adherence to naturalistic principles, his work has been judged at its artistic best precisely where he lapses from his systematic method into the natural rhythms of a novelist. The kernel of truth in this judgment certainly applies to *Nana*. Although the protagonist is most often described in great detail, she appears in the mind's eye of the reader at her seductive best when she is limned in only a few bold strokes. Likewise, the inexorable logic of the sordid and predominantly deterministic plot is occasionally softened, and not a little enhanced, by such tender scenes as Nana's meeting with George in the rain-drenched straw-berry patch.

Similarly, Zola's dispassionately analytical language is brightened from time to time with passages of near-poetic prose. Above all, the naturalistic dictum that all characters, including the protagonist, must represent types and not be extraordinary is belied by Nana herself, for Nana is nothing if not extraordinary—in her beauty, in her greed, in her vulgarity. Indeed, these contradictions, the unlikely combination of qualities, render her character atypical. Zola was quite distressed over his romantic tendencies, seeing them as flaws in the naturalistic scheme of things; however, he seemed blind to the flaws of naturalism systematically applied, espe-cially its morbidity, its monotony, and its fundamental mediocrity. Yet in the final analysis, Zola's genius as an artist stems from his inability to follow any one theory undeviatingly, and the best of *Nana* can be attributed to that characteristic.

"Critical Evaluation" by Joanna G. Kashdan

Bibliography:
Baguley, David, ed. *Critical Essays on Émile Zola*. Boston: G. K. Hall, 1986. In "The Man-Eater," Roland Barthes discusses the symbolic movement of *Nana* and the novel's epic scope. He also lauds Zola's comprehensive treatment of the Second Empire. Bibliography.
Grant, Elliott M. *Émile Zola*. New York: Twayne, 1966. Chapter 6 discusses one of Zola's prevalent themes, the destructiveness of love. Grant also explores Zola's knowledge of the world of prostitutes and Nana's symbolic significance. Chronology, notes, and bibliography.

Knapp, Bettina L. *Émile Zola*. New York: Frederick Ungar, 1980. Chapter 4 discusses the role of prostitutes and coquettes in the Second Empire and Zola's handling of them as symbolic characters. Chronology, notes, and bibliography.

Richardson, Joanna. *Zola*. New York: St. Martin's Press, 1978. Chapter 16 discusses the conditions under which Zola wrote *Nana* and the reception of the novel. Analyzes Nana's character and Zola's rich evocation of society. Notes and bibliography.

Walker, Philip. *Zola*. London: Routledge & Kegan Paul, 1985. Chapter 4, "First Great Triumphs," explores the novel's impact on the public, its analysis of society's susceptibility to corruption, Zola's painstaking efforts to make his scenes real and accurate, and Nana's symbolic presence. Bibliography.

THE NARRATIVE OF ARTHUR GORDON PYM

Type of work: Novel
Author: Edgar Allan Poe (1809-1849)
Type of plot: Adventure
Time of plot: Early nineteenth century
Locale: High seas
First published: 1838

> *Principal characters:*
> ARTHUR GORDON PYM, an adventurer
> AUGUSTUS BARNARD, his friend
> DIRK PETERS, a sailor

The Story:

Arthur Gordon Pym was born the son of a respectable trader in Nantucket. While still young, he attended an academy and there met Augustus Barnard, the son of a sea captain, and the two became close friends. One night after a party, Augustus woke Pym from his sleep, and together they set off for the harbor. There, Augustus took charge of a small boat, and they headed out to sea.

Before long, Pym, seeing that his companion was unconscious, realized the sad truth of the escapade. Augustus had been drunk and, now in the cold weather, was lapsing into insensibility. As a result, their boat was run down by a whaler, and the two narrowly escaped with their lives. They were taken aboard the ship which had run them down and returned to port at Nantucket.

The two friends became even more intimate after this escapade. Captain Barnard was at that time preparing to fit out the *Grampus*, an old sailing hulk, for a voyage on which Augustus was to accompany him. Against his father's wishes, Pym planned to sail with his friend. Since Captain Barnard would not willingly allow Pym to sail without his father's permission, the two boys decided to smuggle Pym aboard and hide him in the hold until the ship should be so far at sea that the Captain would not turn back.

At first, everything went according to schedule. Pym was hidden below in a large box with a store of water and food to last him approximately four days. Great was his consternation to discover, at the end of the fourth day, that his way to the main deck was barred. His friend Augustus did not appear to rescue him. He remained in that terrible state for several days, coming each day closer to starvation or death from thirst.

At last, his dog, which had followed Pym aboard the ship, found his way to his master. Tied to the dog's body was a paper containing a strange message concerning blood and a warning to Pym to keep silent if he valued his life. Pym was sick from hunger and fever when Augustus at last appeared. The story he had to tell was a terrible one. Shortly after the ship had put to sea, the crew had mutinied, and Captain Barnard had been set adrift in a small boat. Some of the crew had been killed, and Augustus himself was a prisoner of the mutineers. Pym and Augustus located a place of comparative safety where it was agreed that Pym should hide.

Pym now began to give his attention to the cargo, which seemed not to have been stowed in accordance with the rules for safety. Dirk Peters, a drunken mutineer, helped both Pym and Augustus and provided them with food.

When the ship ran into a storm, some of the mutineers were washed overboard. Augustus was once more given free run of the ship. Augustus, Pym, and Peters planned to overcome the other mutineers and take possession of the ship. To frighten the mutineers during a drunken brawl, Pym disguised himself to resemble a sailor recently killed. The three killed all the mutineers except a sailor named Parker. Meanwhile, a gale had come up, and in a few hours, the vessel was reduced to a hulk by the heavy seas. Because the ship's cargo was made up of empty oil casks, there was no possibility of its sinking from the violence of the heavy seas. When the storm abated, the four survivors found themselves weak and without food or the hope of securing stores from the flooded hold. One day, a vessel was sighted, but as it drew near, those aboard the *Grampus* saw that it was adrift and all of its passengers were dead.

Pym tried to go below by diving, but he brought up nothing of worth. His companions were beginning to go mad from strain and hunger. Pym revived them by immersing each of them in the water for awhile. As their agony increased, a ship came near, but it veered away without coming to their rescue. In desperation, the men considered the possibility of eating one of their number. When they drew lots, Parker was chosen to be eaten. For four days, the other three lived upon his flesh.

At last, they made their way into the stores and secured food. Rain fell, and the supply of fresh water, together with the food, restored their hope. Augustus, who had suffered an arm injury, died. He was devoured by sharks as soon as his body was cast overboard.

A violent lurch of the ship threw Pym overboard, but he regained the ship with Peters' help just in time to be saved from sharks. The floating hulk having overturned at last, the two survivors fed upon barnacles. Finally, when they were nearly dead of thirst, a British ship came to their rescue. It was the *Jane Guy* of Liverpool, bound on a sealing and trading voyage to the South Seas and Pacific. Peters and Pym began to recover. Within two weeks, they were able to look back upon their horrible experiences with almost the same feeling with which one recollects terrible dreams.

The vessel stopped at Christmas Harbor, where some seals and sea elephants were killed for their hides. The captain was anxious to sail his vessel into Antarctica on a voyage of exploration. The weather turned cold. There was an adventure with a huge bear, which Peters killed in time to save his companions. Scurvy afflicted the crew. Once the captain decided to turn northward, but later he foolishly took the advice of Pym to continue on. They sailed until they sighted land and encountered some savages whom they took aboard.

The animals on the island were strange, and the water was of some peculiar composition that Pym could not readily understand. The natives on that strange coast lived in a state of complete savagery. Bartering began. Before the landing party could depart, however, the sailors were trapped in what seemed to be an earthquake, which shut off their passage back to the shore. Only Pym and Peters escaped, to learn that the natives had caused the tremendous landslide by pulling great boulders from the top of a towering cliff. The only white men left on the island, they were faced by the problem of evading the natives, who were now preparing to attack the ship. Unable to warn their comrades, Pym and Peters could only watch helplessly while the savages boarded the *Jane Guy* and overcame the six white men who had remained aboard. The ship was almost demolished. The savages brought about their own destruction, however, for in exploring the ship they set off the ammunition, and the resulting explosion killed about a thousand of them.

In making their escape from the island, Pym and Peters discovered ruins similar in form to those marking the site of Babylon. When they came upon two unguarded canoes, they took possession of one and pushed out to sea. Savages chased them but eventually gave up the pursuit. They began to grow listless and sleepy when their canoe entered a warm sea. Ashy material fell continually around and upon them. At last, the boat rushed rapidly into a cataract, and a human figure, much larger than any man and as white as snow, arose in the pathway of the doomed boat. So ended the journal of Arthur Gordon Pym.

Critical Evaluation:

The reception of Edgar Allan Poe's *The Narrative of Arthur Gordon Pym* after its publication was in no way an unqualified approval. On the contrary, its misreading was the general result. Literal-minded reviewers jumped immediately to the conclusion that the narrative amounted to a fraudulent attempt to bamboozle the unwary. That its author intended to parody the popular voyage literature of the time was not considered. Not all the reviews were hostile. In Great Britain, *The Narrative of Arthur Gordon Pym* went through two editions. Unfortunately it was generally treated as the report of an actual voyage. Therefore, it remained for the French to be the first to recognize *The Narrative of Arthur Gordon Pym* as an extraordinary romance of adventure and as an important work of art. In 1858, the French poet Charles Baudelaire admired *The Narrative of Arthur Gordon Pym* enough to translate it.

Meanwhile, in the United States the work was neglected and practically forgotten, except for Henry James's praise, recorded in his great novel *The Golden Bowl* (1904), of *The Narrative of Arthur Gordon Pym* as "a wonderful tale" fondly remembered by Prince Amerigo. Not until 1950 was *The Narrative of Arthur Gordon Pym* to be taken seriously, when poet and critic W. H. Auden included the romance in his anthology *Edgar Allan Poe: Selected Prose, Poetry, and Eureka.* In his introduction, Auden declares *The Narrative of Arthur Gordon Pym* and *Eureka: A Prose Poem* (1848) to be among Poe's most important works.

Soon even academia woke from its sleep. Patrick F. Quinn, in 1952, emphasized that the narrative is structured by the pattern of deception and revolt. He also discussed the 1933 psychoanalytical interpretation of *The Narrative of Arthur Gordon Pym* by Marie Bonaparte, who saw its central meaning as "the passionate and frenzied search for the Mother." The philosopher Gaston Bachelard held that *The Narrative of Arthur Gordon Pym* derived "from the deepest psychological center of Edgar Poe." Bachelard termed *The Narrative of Arthur Gordon Pym* "one of the great books of the human heart." Edward Davidson viewed *The Narrative of Arthur Gordon Pym* as a philosophical narrative that shows nature to be deceptive, untrustworthy, and destructive. The plot is based on a quest to find the axis of reality on which the world turns. Everything is uncertain and an illusion; to find oneself is to lose one's self and to slip away into nothingness. According to Davis, "terror is the way to a knowledge of the world's primal unity." Quinn's and Davidson's essays proved the launching pads for the many future studies of *The Narrative of Arthur Gordon Pym* and its increasing importance in the Poe canon.

The Narrative of Arthur Gordon Pym reveals Poe's philosophy of the relation of the self to nature, to the world, and to the universe. It also depicts a psychic quest to discover the core of the self. The narrative structure has been explored as have the narrative voices and their tones. The problematics of narrative unity, the use of enclosure, the truncated conclusion, the use of satire, irony, and ways of deception have also been studied. The ideas of the Freudian quest for the mother and of Jungian archetypes, of the roles of dream and wakefulness, of the conscious and the unconscious, of illusion and reality, and of empirical versus intuitive knowledge have been considered as well, in addition to the role of allegory and symbolism. Some critics have been amazed to discover the way Poe calls attention to his textual and narrative space by questioning whether language can ever be clearly understood, whether human life is governed by uncertainty and chance, and whether nature and the universe are completely indifferent to human happiness and welfare. There has been much speculation about the meaning of the great white human figure that appears at the end of the tale, the role of the racial colors of white, black, and red, and whether writing is favored over speech.

"Critical Evaluation" by Richard P. Benton

Bibliography:

Covici, Pascal, Jr. "Toward a Reading of Poe's *The Narrative of Arthur Gordon Pym*." *Mississippi Quarterly* 21 (1968): 111-118. An interpretation of the symbolic role of white, black, and red, especially as racial indicators, with Dirk Peters seen as the mediator between whites and blacks.

Eakin, Paul J. "Poe's Sense of an Ending." *American Literature* 45 (1973): 1-22. Examines the abortive ending relative to the whole and concludes that the narrative is complete.

Irwin, John T. *American Hieroglyphics: The Symbol of the Egyptian Hieroglyphics: The Symbol of the Egyptian Hieroglyphics in the American Renaissance.* Baltimore, Md.: The Johns Hopkins University Press, 1980. Examines the relationships of writing, doubling, and the use of hieroglyphics, including a considerable examination of *The Narrative of Arthur Gordon Pym.* An outstanding study of its subject.

Kennedy, J. Gerald. "Unreadable Books, Unspeakable Truths." In *Poe, Death, and the Life of Writing.* New Haven, Conn.: Yale University Press, 1987. Calls attention to the "self-consciousness" of the text regarding its indefiniteness and insufficiency of language.

Lee, Grace F. "The Quest of Arthur Gordon Pym." *Southern Literary Journal* 4, no. 2 (1972): 22-33. Sees a twofold quest, one "backward in time to the origins of creation" and the other "inward to the depths" of Pym's unconscious.

Peirce, Carol, and Alexander G. Rose III. "The White Vision of Arthur Gordon Pym." In *Poe's Pym: Critical Explorations*, edited by Richard Kopley. Durham, N.C.: Duke University Press, 1992. Seeks to explain Poe's knowledge of Arthurian legend and the myth of the White Goddess.

NARRATIVE OF THE LIFE OF FREDERICK DOUGLASS
An American Slave

Type of work: Autobiography
Author: Frederick Douglass (Frederick Augustus Washington Bailey, 1817?-1895)
First published: 1845

There are about six thousand records in existence of slaves who either wrote their own stories or told them to others. Of these works, commonly known as slave narratives, Frederick Douglass' *Narrative of the Life of Frederick Douglass: An American Slave* is nearly universally considered to be the most compelling and well written. Douglass went on to write two more autobiographies, *My Bondage and My Freedom* (1855) and *The Life and Times of Frederick Douglass* (1881), to found several abolitionist magazines—most notably *North Star*—and to become the greatest African American orator and statesman of his age. Yet he is primarily known for his first book, which he wrote before the age of thirty and despite the fact that he had never gone to school. Douglass' autobiography came to be one of the most frequently taught books at American colleges and universities, where together with *Moby Dick* (1851), *The Scarlet Letter* (1850), and *Uncle Tom's Cabin* (1851-1852) it was regarded as a seminal source for understanding the United States in the antebellum period of the nineteenth century.

Douglass' story began humbly. Douglass describes how, as a young boy growing up as a slave in Talbot County, Maryland, he never knew his age or the identity of his father. Slave owners did not consider it necessary to tell slaves such facts, or to try to keep families together. His mother, Harriet Bailey, was separated from him when he was an infant. Douglass saw her only four or five times during his life, and then only at night when she paid surreptitious visits from the plantation twelve miles away where she had been sold; she always had to leave before her young son woke up, and she died when Douglass was seven.

It is possible that the man who owned Douglass, Captain Anthony, was his father. Owners often took sexual advantage of their slave women, and as a boy, Douglass saw his master beat his Aunt Hester out of jealousy because a slave from a neighboring plantation had paid attention to her. The pain slaves experienced from mistreatment and beatings often led them to sing songs with "words which to many would seem unmeaning jargon" but which conveyed the depths of their hardship. Such songs were their only outlet for expression.

Throughout his childhood on the plantation, Douglass (who did not then have a last name and was simply known as Frederick) witnessed many acts of cruelty, ranging from unjust beatings to unwarranted and unpunished murder of slaves by white owners or their overseers. As a child, he owned only one shirt, had to sleep on the ground, and ate his meals of corn mush from a common trough. It was his good fortune to be sent to Baltimore to the home of Hugh Auld, a relation of Captain Anthony. There, he not only enjoyed better living conditions but was closer to the North. Had he not been sent to Baltimore, Douglass might never have escaped slavery.

In Baltimore, Mrs. Auld began to teach Douglass his ABC's. When Mr. Auld discovered this, he was furious, telling her that teaching a slave how to read was the quickest way to "spoil" him. Deciding that anything his master deemed bad must be good for him, Douglass became determined to teach himself to read. He devised a way to trick other little boys into inadvertently giving him lessons by pretending to know more than they did and making them prove otherwise.

By the age of twelve, Douglass could read essays from a book of famous speeches he had acquired. Reading, however, showed him for the first time the true injustice of his own position.

For the first time, he realized that there were people opposed to slavery and that there were compelling arguments against the practice. He resolved to run away as soon as he was old enough and the right opportunity presented itself.

Along with understanding the potential power inherent in the ability to read—nothing less than "the power of the white man to enslave the black man"—Douglass also began to understand his own condition by reading essays on liberty. The passages in which he describes his awakened understanding are among the most stirring in all of American literature. A succession of metaphors follows the description of his first reading experiences: Slavery is a "horrible pit" with "no ladder upon which to get out"; preferable to his own condition is that of "the meanest reptile." No other work, fiction or nonfiction, so clearly demonstrates the effect of literacy in developing the associative powers of the thinking mind. Hugh Auld was, in a sense, correct when he said that learning to read and write would "spoil" a slave. Once Douglass developed a figurative capacity of language, he was forever unfit to serve slaveholders obediently. Everything in the world reminded him of the injustice of his own enslavement: "It looked from every star, it smiled in every calm, breathed in every wind, and moved in every storm."

Until he became old enough to escape, Douglass did his best to tolerate his condition. As a consequence of his small acts of rebellion, however, he was sent to a slave breaker, Mr. Covey, whose job it was to destroy the will of a slave and create an obedient worker and servant. During his first six months with Mr. Covey, Douglass was subjected to strict discipline and endless work. The slave breaker destroyed wills not just by working the slaves hard but by disorienting them and surrounding them with constant observation and deception. There were various ways in which Mr. Covey created an oppressive atmosphere, as when he told the slaves that he was leaving for town, only to return and spy on them. One day, Douglass fought back when Covey hit him; they fought for two hours, until both men were exhausted, but Douglass held his own. He resolved then that "however long I might remain a slave in form, the day had passed forever when I could be a slave in fact."

The first time he tried to escape, Douglass drew on his ability to write to forge protection papers for himself and several friends. They were caught and jailed, and Douglass was threatened with being sent to Alabama, from where escape was almost impossible. Instead, he was fortunately sent back to Baltimore, and it was determined that he should learn a trade. Douglass worked in a shipyard for one year and became a skilled caulker. When he contracted jobs on his own, earning six or seven dollars a week, he had to give the money to his master.

Douglass eventually escaped to the North. He did not provide details of his flight in the *Narrative of the Life of Frederick Douglass* because he did not wish to create additional obstacles for others who were trying to escape from slavery. He fled first to New York, from where he sent for the woman he planned to marry, a free black woman named Anna. Together, the couple moved to New Bedford, where they sought out the abolitionist Nathan Johnson, who advanced them money and helped them in other ways. Douglass had changed his name to Johnson upon reaching New York, but because there were so many Johnsons in New Bedford, he accepted Nathan Johnson's suggestion that he call himself Frederick Douglass. In New Bedford, Douglass found white abolitionists as well as blacks who abhorred slavery and tried to protect one another from being sent back South.

Moved by the abolitionist cause, Douglass stood up to speak at an antislavery convention in Nantucket. At first, still feeling like a slave, he was abashed at the thought of speaking to white people, but the words soon came more easily. Douglass became an influential abolitionist himself, which eventually led to his writing the story of his life under slavery.

All who read the book are astonished that such a document could have been produced by a man with no formal education less than seven years after escaping from slavery. In Douglass' own time, this remarkable feat led to incredulity among his readership. All slave narratives were subject to charges of fraud from apologists for slavery, for which reason Douglass' book and others open with testament letters from respected white abolitionists. Many of those who heard Douglass speak and found him to be as forceful an orator as he was a writer, found it difficult to credit that he had so lately been a slave. In an era marked by P. T. Barnum's famous hoaxes, an era when even the most well-intentioned Northern whites believed that African Americans were intellectually inferior to whites, Douglass faced skepticism on all sides. A strong motivation for publishing his story was to provide details of his life that could not have been faked. When one early Southern detractor of the book claimed to have been acquainted with Douglass as a slave and to know that he was too uneducated to have written a book, Douglass replied by thanking him for substantiating the book's main claim, that he had indeed been an American slave.

Douglass' accomplishments after escaping slavery fit well into the tradition of American self-sufficiency and success. By rising above the subjugating conditions of his early years, Douglass provided hope for others that through strength and self-reliance they, too, could achieve great things. His later autobiographies and writings testify to the persistence of prejudice as a limiting force on African Americans even after the end of institutionalized slavery, in the North as well as in the South. However, in the argument for the possibility of human achievement and for the liberty for all humans to pursue their potential, there is perhaps no more heroic example in American letters than Douglass provides in his *Narrative of the Life of Frederick Douglass*.

Ted Pelton

Bibliography:
Andrews, William. *To Tell a Free Story: The First Century of Afro-American Autobiography, 1760-1865*. Normal: University of Illinois Press, 1986. A comprehensive account of slave narratives, which includes an extensive interpretation of Douglass' writings.
Douglass, Frederick. *The Life and Times of Frederick Douglass*. 1892. Reprint. New York: Macmillan, 1962. Douglass' last autobiography, which covers his life story through his ambassadorship to Haiti.
Gates, Henry Louis, Jr., ed. *The Classic Slave Narratives*. New York: Penguin, 1987. Contains narratives by Olaudah Equiano, Mary Prince, and Harriet Jacobs, in addition to that of Douglass, as well as an excellent short introduction to the form.
Starling, Marion Wilson. *The Slave Narrative: Its Place in History*. 1947. Reprint. Washington, D.C.: Howard University Press, 1988. The first book about the slave narrative as a form and a good introduction to its historical importance.
Sundquist, Eric L. *Frederick Douglass: New Literary and Historical Essays*. New York: Cambridge University Press, 1990. Scholarly interpretations of Douglass' life and writings.

THE NARROW ROAD TO THE DEEP NORTH

Type of work: Poetry
Author: Matsuo Bashō (Matsuo Munefusa, 1644-1694)
First published: Oku no hosomichi, 1694 (English translation, 1933)

Matsuo Bashō combines his talents as a poet and essayist in the writing of the poetic diary, a form of literature that was prized highly at the time that Bashō lived. Bashō, incidentally, is a nickname meaning "banana tree." He had been called Kinsaku as a child and Matsuo Munefusa when he became an adult. When Bashō first began writing poetry, he called himself Sobo, and later on, for about eight years, he took the name Tosei. However, planted in the garden near one of Bashō's residences was a banana plant whose wide leaves Bashō especially enjoyed. When people sought directions to his house, they were told to go to the house with the banana tree; gradually Bashō came to be referred to as the "banana tree person," and around 1681, he took that name as his pen name. Changing names and taking pen names was not unusual in Japan at that time, especially for a person of samurai, or feudal warrior stock, which Bashō was.

After Bashō moved to Edo, now Tokyo, he became a teacher of *haikai,* a special kind of poem that was at first something of a light-hearted diversion from the more serious *renga,* or linked verse. It is called linked verse because, usually, one person composed the opening stanza and another would continue or finish the poem. Largely because of Bashō's artistry, the *haikai* developed into a serious kind of poem. The word *haiku* developed from the *hokku,* or "starting verse" of a linked verse. A *haiku,* then, is an independent poem derived from the *haikai;* thus, the *haiku* is literally the *hokku* of a *haikai.* This miniature poem has seventeen syllables, which usually follow a pattern of three lines of five, seven, and five syllables, respectively, as in

> a ya me ku sa (blue flag herbage, or iris)
> a shi ni mu su ba n (feet on bind)
> wa ra ji no o (straw sandals of cord)

which can be translated, without following the syllabic pattern, as

> I will bind irises
> Around my feet
> Thongs for my sandals

Bashō felt the need to go beyond traditional *haikai* forms and find fresh ways of writing poetry. He thought that traveling would provide a means of broadening the scope of his life and his poetry, so he made four journeys between 1684 and 1689. These journeys can be considered spiritual pilgrimages as well as physical journeys to seek the ultimate of beauty.

The first journey, westward, began in the fall of 1684 and was completed in the summer of 1685. On returning, he wrote the first of several travel diaries, *Norarashi kikō* (1687; *The Record of a Weather-Exposed Skeleton,* 1966). A second journey westward in 1687 resulted in two more diaries, *Oi no kobumi* (1709; *The Records of a Travel-Worn Satchel,* 1966) and *Sarashina kikō* (1704; *A Visit to Sarashina Village,* 1966). It was Bashō's third journey, his longest, that provided the material for *The Narrow Road to the Deep North.* This time, Bashō went northward into the least developed areas of Japan, the northern part of Japan's largest island, Honshu. The diary in its published form took about four years to complete, although it is only about thirty pages long in English translation.

Oku no hosomichi has been translated in several ways; it is difficult to express in English all that the word oku includes. On the one hand, the name is that of an actual road that Bashō traveled; *oku* is also a short form for Michi-no-Oku (or Michinoku), generally translated as "the road's far recesses." Michi-no-Oku was a popular name for a region called Ōshu, or the "far provinces." Over and above the literal explanations of the word, it carries a sense of an "inner recess" or something "within oneself." Bashō was known for choosing titles such as this that could be interpreted on more than one level, in this case, an actual journey and an inward search.

The Narrow Road of Oku traces Bashō's 1,500-mile route from Edo to Ogaki, describing activities and places he visits or stays during the 156-day trip. The diary is by no means just an ordinary travel journal with a few poems inserted. In fact, Bashō sometimes changes actual facts about the trip—dates, itinerary, and the like—to improve the effect of the work as literature. The *haiku* interspersed with prose passages are some of his finest poems. The diary opens with a prologue that announces Bashō's yearning to travel and reminds the reader that life is a journey. The introduction ends, as many sections do, with a *haiku* that expresses his feeling about his departure.

As he and his companion, Kawai Sora, make their way northward to the well-known temple and mountain at Nikko, and on to Kurobane, Bashō records in his prose commentary on noteworthy sights they visit. Much of the richness of both the prose and the poetry is due to the fact that so many of the places the travelers visit are historical sites that most Japanese have heard of. It is characteristic of Japanese literature, especially of earlier works, to allude to places, sites, and people from ancient classical writing that Japanese people will recognize. The association with the earlier works makes the passage all the more meaningful and evocative of the glory of days long past.

Sometimes Bashō stops only briefly in a village after seeing some famous landmark; at other times he stays several days and visits friends or acquaintances in the area. His *haiku* are evoked by his reaction to or reflection on something associated with what he experiences. At Ashino, for example, going to see a famous willow tree provides his topic; a famous stone at Shinobu inspires another, as does the "tsubo stone," so called because the dimensions of the stone are approximately three by six feet, or one *tsubo* in Japanese measurement of the day. It was near Ichikawa, where the Tsubo Stone was located, that Bashō found the road called Oku-no-hosomichi, which provided the diary's title.

As Bashō advances from one village to another, visiting castles, mountains, and other famous sites or simply noting the natural beauty of a place, he is often overcome with something of awe-inspiring beauty and writes a *haiku* on the spot. Some things were more meaningful than others. At Hiraizumi, on approaching the ruins of the Castle-on-the-Heights, he finds the site now reduced to nothing more than an untended field of grass. Bashō thought of the days long past when the renowned Yoshitsune had fortified himself at this place, glory now reduced to wilderness of grass. He is reminded of a line in a classical Chinese poem by Tu Fu, an eighth-century poet, which says, "Countries may fall, but their rivers and mountains remain." These reflections cause Bashō to sit at the site weeping, oblivious to the passing of time. These strong feelings brought forth one of his often-quoted *haiku*: "Natsugusa ya/ Tsuwamono domo ga/ Yume no ato" (The summer grasses/ Of brave soldiers' dreams/ The aftermath). Since the proper English punctuation is not clearly indicated in the Japanese version, some translations render the last two lines as a question: Are warrior's heroic deeds/ Only dreams that pass? Moving on, Bashō continues to record his impressions, sometimes comparing or contrasting one with another. When he visited Matsushima, a group of many small islands, he was overcome with its beauty and declared that Matsushima was "the most beautiful place in all

Japan!" Later, when he comes to the northernmost point of his journey, Kisakata, he records his visit to a famous lagoon which he describes as having a "sense of desolate loneliness and sorrow of a tormented soul," that is, nevertheless, beautiful, like Matsushima.

Beginning the southwesterly descent from the northern country, Bashō passes through the Etchigo Province. At one point, near present-day Niigata, Sado Island is visible from the mainland, and Bashō writes several *haiku* which are among his best largely because they manifest *sabi*, a kind of loneliness in which the immensity and strength, or even indifference, of the universe is set in contrast to man's finiteness and insignificance. A reader may experience the feeling of being overpowered or dissolved in the face of the infinite. One poem, in which there is no trace of humanity, but only an expression of the primitive universe, illustrates this concept: "Araumi ya/ Sado ni yokotau/ Amanogawa" (The rough sea/ Extending toward Sado Isle,/ The Milky Way). Sometimes "amanogawa" is translated more literally as something like "Heaven's River"; the effect, however, is that of the configuration of the stars in such an arrangement that they look something like a river flowing across the sky, forming what is called the Milky Way in English.

Sometimes Bashō makes associations with older poems in the Japanese tradition. On August 30, 1689, he reaches the castle town of Kanazawa and then makes his way to Daishoji and on to Maruoka. By this time, fall has arrived. His companion Sora becomes ill and returns to relatives in the Ise Province, but Bashō travels on after a student of *haiku* comes to accompany him the rest of the way, arriving in Ogaki around October 18. He comments that, though he has not recovered from the fatigue of the journey, he does not want to miss going to the renowned Ise Shrine to see the ceremony of the Shinto Deity being transferred to a newly built shrine, a special occasion that takes place only once every twenty-one years. Soryū, a scholar-priest who helped prepare the final draft of Bashō's journal, writes a brief epilogue in which he tells readers, "At times you will find yourself rising up to applaud. At other times you will quietly hang your head with emotion." Bashō is said to have had over two thousand students at the time of his death. There is no doubt about his reputation among his contemporaries and later Japanese poets. His work elevated the *haiku* into a mature art form. As a result of the variety of his poems, he appealed to readers of various tastes. The more sophisticated reader liked his early witty verse; rural poets preferred the later poems in a plainer style. The poet Issa is said to have emulated him as a diarist. During the twentieth century, Bashō has been compared by some to England's William Wordsworth because of his seeking a mystic union with nature. Largely because of Matsuo Bashō, there is an interest around the world in the *haiku* as a literary form.

Victoria Price

Bibliography:
Bashō, Matsuo. *A Haiku Journey: Bashō's Narrow Road to a Far Province.* Translated by Dorothy Britton. New York: Kodansha International, 1974. The translator's introduction provides valuable insights into the *haiku* and into Bashō's artistry.
Kato, Shūichi. *A History of Japanese Literature.* 2 vols. Translated by Don Sanderson. New York: Kodansha International, 1979. In addition to placing Bashō in the context of Japanese literature, this treatment discusses Bashō's association with both the *haiku* and the poetic diary as a literary genre.
Martins Janeira, Armando. *Japanese and Western Literature: A Comparative Study.* Rutland, Vt.: Charles E. Tuttle, 1970. Since the Western reader is not always familiar with the *haiku*, this work is insightful in gaining some understanding of the genre.

Ueda, Makoto. *Literary and Art Theories in Japan*. Cleveland: Press of Western Reserve University, 1967. Although this volume treats literary theories of a number of writers, Bashō receives thorough discussion in the light of his contribution to the principles that govern the writing of *haiku*.

_____. *Matsuo Bashō*. New York: Twayne, 1970. One of the most valuable books on Bashō, this work provides substantive discussion of Bashō's life and of his literary development, as well as critical commentary and an evaluation of his place in literature.

NATHAN THE WISE

Type of work: Drama
Author: Gotthold Ephraim Lessing (1729-1781)
Type of plot: Philosophical
Time of plot: Twelfth century
Locale: Jerusalem
First published: Nathan der Weise, 1779 (English translation, 1781); first performed, 1783

Principal characters:
NATHAN, a Jewish merchant
RECHA, his adopted daughter
SULTAN SALADIN, the son of the ruler of all the Saracens
SITTAH, his sister
CONRAD VON STAUFFEN, a Templar who was spared by the sultan
DAJA, a Christian woman and Recha's companion

The Story:

Nathan, a wealthy Jewish merchant, had just returned to Jerusalem from Babylon when Daja, the deeply prejudiced Christian companion to Nathan's adopted daughter, a woman orphaned during the Third Crusade, told him of the dramatic rescue of his beloved Recha from their burning house. Nathan, in spite of the fact that he had suffered severely at the hands of Christians and Saracens alike, wished to reward the young man who had so courageously saved Recha's life. The hero proved to be a young Templar who recently had been pardoned by the sultan.

Each day, at Recha's urging, Daja had attempted to thank and reward the young man as he made a daily visit to Christ's tomb, but each time he rudely repulsed her. Recha, as the result of shock over her narrow escape as much as from gratitude to her benefactor, suffered hallucinations in which she believed that the young Templar was her guardian angel. Nathan thought it miraculous that Sultan Saladin should spare a Christian knight's life or that the Templar would desire to be so spared. The truth was that the Saracen's leniency had been based on the young man's resemblance to his own dead brother Assad.

Daja, told by Nathan to seek out the young man and invite him to their home, found him in a bad mood after he had rejected a friar's request from King Philip that he spy on and murder Saladin. The young man vehemently refused to consider performing such a deed. The knight again told Daja that he had performed his rescue of Recha through happenstance and therefore would accept no reward. Nathan then met with and begged the youth, a penniless stranger in a strange land, to accept aid and friendship. Boorish though the young knight was, he offered to let Nathan buy him a mantle to replace his own, which had burned in the fire. At this suggestion the Jew shed a tear and dissolved the intolerant Templar's disdain and suspicion. They shook hands, friends. Nathan learned that the young man was Conrad von Stauffen, a name somehow associated in the Jew's mind with the name Filneck, but before he could inquire further the Jew received a message demanding his presence at the sultan's palace.

The young knight, in the meantime, called on Recha. Something immediately drew them together, some mutual feeling not unlike romantic love. He hastened off, however, to avert any disaster that might befall Nathan at the hand of Saladin, who had summoned the Jew to obtain from him money to replenish the treasury so that the war against the crusaders might continue.

To put the Jew somewhat at a disadvantage, Saladin asked enlightenment from Nathan, who was called the Wise (which Nathan denied he was), on the paradox of the several "true" religions.

Nathan then told the story of a father who possessed a ring traditionally passed on to the favorite son, who would then be lord of the house. Since he loved his three sons equally well (as the Father in heaven loves all people, said Nathan), the father made exact copies of the ring and gave one to each son. None knew which was the true ring, and after the father's death a controversy arose. The problem of the "true" ring could be resolved no more than the argument over the "true" faith—Jewish, Christian, or Muhammadan. A judge suggested that each son act as if his were the true ring and live and rule as well as he could. Finally, generations hence, it would be decided in a higher, greater court, with religions as with the ring, which was the true one.

When Nathan returned from the palace, young Conrad von Stauffen asked for Recha's hand in marriage. Astounded, Nathan said that he could not consent without due reflection. Daja, on an amorous mission, told the Templar that Recha had been born Christian but had been reared as a Jew, a crime punishable by death. The Templar assumed that Recha had been stolen from her proper parents. Dismayed by Daja's story, the knight guardedly asked counsel of the Patriarch of Jerusalem, who said that in such a case the Jew must die at the stake for holding back salvation from an innocent child. Perplexed and unhappy, the young man went to confer with the sultan.

Saladin, amazed at such accusations, refused to believe ill of Nathan and asked the Christian to exercise prudence and charity. As the young Templar left to save Nathan from the patriarch's wrath, the sultan and his sister remarked the resemblance the young man bore to their long-lost brother, believed dead.

In the meantime, a friar sent to spy on Nathan revealed that eighteen years ago he, the friar, then a squire, delivered Recha to the Jew for his master, Lord Wolf von Filneck, who was later killed in battle; the child's mother, a von Stauffen, was already dead. Nathan confided that his own wife and seven sons had been killed by Christians only shortly before he adopted Recha as his own, an act that saved his sanity and restored his faith in God.

Saladin, who favored the marriage of the two young people, then learned from Nathan that Wolf von Filneck's breviary, turned over to Nathan by the friar, contained a strange story. Crusader Filneck's rightful name was Assad. The sultan's brother, having married a Christian and accepted her faith, had left his son to his deceased wife's brother, Conrad von Stauffen, after whom he was named. The boy's sister he left indirectly to Nathan. The Jewish child and the Christian child both were Muhammadans; their uncle was a sultan, and their godfather was a wise man and a Jew.

Critical Evaluation:

As Gotthold Lessing's final dramatic work, completed only two years before his death, *Nathan the Wise* has invited speculation that it is a summing up of its author's life and thought. Such scrutiny is intensified by Lessing's reputation as possibly the German Enlightenment's most outstanding figure. Confronting fundamental issues in philosophy, literature, and drama at a critical period in Western culture, Lessing's writings have invariably provoked debate.

A theological controversy that embroiled Lessing in 1778 is considered the inspiration for *Nathan the Wise*. After failing in his dream of creating a national theater, Lessing accepted an invitation to head the highly regarded and amply stocked library in Wolfenbuttel. In this position, he undertook a series of publishing projects, which he was assured would escape the censor's desk. Lessing's subsequent publication of a posthumous apologia for the Deist position by Hermann Samuel Reimarus unleashed a series of attacks against him by the religious orthodoxy. Lessing was accused of championing Deism, which challenged religious dogma from the perspective of rationalism. Consequently, the exemption from censorship that his projects had been granted was revoked. Under these conditions, Lessing began reworking an old sketch whose situation, he wrote in a letter to his brother Karl, presented an analogy to his own, that of a man embattled by the forces of prejudice and fanaticism.

As Lessing predicted in another letter to Karl, theaters were reluctant to perform the resulting drama. Censorship was an impediment, but not the only one. The play's length and the demands it made on audiences and on actors posed practical problems. Subtitling his work "a dramatic poem," Lessing invented a form suited to his metaphysical purposes, which unfortunately diminished the play's theatricality. This form consisted of a succession of scenes that prompted the characters to reveal themselves through a dialectical exchange of ideas, rather than through actions.

Consistent with its elevated aim, the play is written in verse, specifically iambic pentameter, or blank verse. This metered, poetic style, along with the poem's philosophic ambitions, mark *Nathan the Wise* as an innovation. Such qualities also distinguish it as a forerunner of classical idea dramas such as Johann Wolfgang von Goethe's *Iphigenie* (1787).

During Lessing's lifetime, the play, which caused a sensation in the literary world, was known primarily in its published form. *Nathan the Wise* finally premiered in Berlin on April 14, 1783, two years after Lessing's death. There were only three performances. The general public became familiar with the work largely through a number of popular parodies. The majority of these satirized Lessing's positive presentation of a Jewish character. *Nathan the Wise*, which was banned from school curricula under Nationalist Socialist rule, became the first play produced in postwar Germany. Presumably, it was revived to demonstrate that a tradition of tolerance existed in German culture.

While the play's advocacy of religious tolerance is universally acknowledged, judgment varies regarding its legacy. Most Jewish critics commend it for allying itself with the cause of emancipation. Others, particularly in the Zionist camp, have assailed the play, contending that it promotes assimilation, which in the long run is destructive to Jewish culture.

Critics also disagree on the nature of Lessing's religious convictions as articulated in the play. The focus of debate is the parable of the rings, which lies at the center of the drama, structurally as well as thematically. The first recorded version of the parable of the rings is found in Spanish Hebrew literature about the time of the Crusades, which Lessing chose for the setting of his play. Lessing's primary source, however, is probably Giovanni Boccaccio's version in his *Decameron* (1348-1353). While Lessing clearly expands the tale, conflict arises over the meaning and import of this development.

Some critics discern in Lessing's account of the parable a utopian religious message. They highlight its mythic qualities and point to Lessing's closing image: a loving circle comprising Jew, Christian, and Moslem. According to this conception, the magic of the ring in the parable parallels the magic that appears to generate Nathan's inexhaustible riches. It is the triumphant power of active, divine love operating through human beings, no matter what faith.

Other critics find in the parable intimations of a modern ambivalence toward faith. They emphasize its implied skepticism toward absolute truth. In this view, the message of the parable is that the power of the ring, apart from any inherent quality of the ring itself, is the power of human beings to believe. Of note is that the father in the tale, who ordered the ring's duplication, is himself unable to discern the original ring—suggesting that it no longer exists. Moreover, these critics point out, judgment in the parable is left open.

Such contradictory inferences are likely the result of the play's absorption in doubts regarding the limits of knowledge, which was endemic to the eighteenth century. *Nathan the Wise* may thereby be anticipating Immanuel Kant's *Critique of Pure Reason* (1781). Belief cannot be knowledge, Lessing apparently argues, so tolerance regarding matters of faith becomes a necessity. Religious faith, his parable demonstrates, is best understood in terms of tradition, which shapes and is shaped by history. Positively understood, the interpretation and application of tradition, which transmits culture and values, is the property of any and all religions. Lessing would appear to illuminate a paradoxical vision that sees unity in diversity.

Lessing's designation of the parable as the kernel from which his play developed suggests the transforming power he intended for *Nathan the Wise*. A parable, while conveying an accessible message, does so indirectly. The listener or reader is thereby challenged to interpret and act on its meaning. Even as the parable in *Nathan the Wise* denies authoritative proof for the primacy of any particular faith, audiences are called upon to authenticate, in acts of beauty and substance, their own traditions.

"Critical Evaluation" by Amy Adelstein

Bibliography:
Brown, Francis. *Gotthold Ephraim Lessing*. New York: Twayne, 1971. Surveys Lessing's accomplishments as dramatist, critic, and theologian. Sees in *Nathan the Wise* his signature emphasis on the virtue of acting with conscious intent. Concludes that Lessing was a product and a prophet of his era.
Eckardt, Jo-Jacqueline. *Lessing's "Nathan the Wise" and the Critics, 1779-1991*. Studies in German Literature, Linguistics, and Culture. Columbia, S.C.: Camden House, 1993. Presents analysis of the work chronologically, revealing the recurrence of motifs and themes as well as the historical development of certain interpretations. Very helpful in shedding light on the idealogical orientation of various critics.
Garland, H. B. *Lessing: The Founder of Modern German Literature*. 2d ed. London: Macmillan, 1962. Determines Lessing's primary role as a dramatist to be that of an innovator. Finds that what matters most in the play is its underlying ethical content.
Graham, Ilse. *Goethe and Lessing: The Wellsprings of Creation*. New York: Barnes and Noble Books, 1973. Analyzes the play's structure in terms of central, unifying symbols. Focuses on poetic elements, such as image patterns and language. Writes passionately if, at times, excessively.
Leventhal, Robert S. "The Parable as Performance: Interpretation, Cultural Transmission, and Political Strategy in Lessing's *Nathan der Weise*." *The German Quarterly* 61, no. 4 (Fall, 1988): 502-527. Argues compellingly that Lessing questioned basic premises of eighteenth century interpretive theory. Stresses Lessing's skepticism of absolute principles.

NATIVE SON

Type of work: Novel
Author: Richard Wright (1908-1960)
Type of plot: Social realism
Time of plot: 1930's
Locale: An American city
First published: 1940

Principal characters:

BIGGER THOMAS, a young African American
MR. DALTON, Bigger's employer
MRS. DALTON, his wife
MARY DALTON, their daughter
JAN ERLONE, Mary's sweetheart
BRITTEN, Dalton's private detective
BESSIE MEARS, Bigger's mistress
BUCKLEY, a state prosecutor
BORIS A. MAX, Bigger's lawyer

The Story:

Bigger Thomas lived in a one-room apartment with his brother, sister, and mother. Always penniless, haunted by a pathological hatred of white people, driven by an indescribable urge to make others cringe before him, Bigger had retreated into an imaginary world of fantasy.

Through the aid of a relief agency, he obtained employment as a chauffeur for a wealthy family. His first assignment was to drive Mary Dalton, his employer's daughter, to the university. Mary, however, was on her way to meet Jan Erlone, her sweetheart. The three of them, Mary and Jan—white people who were crusading with the Communist Party to help the African American people—and Bigger—a reluctant ally—spent the evening driving and drinking. When Bigger brought Mary home, she was too drunk to take herself to bed. With a confused medley of hatred, fear, disgust, and revenge playing within his mind, Bigger helped her to her bedroom. When Mary's blind mother entered the room, Bigger covered the girl's face with a pillow to keep her from making any sound that might arouse Mrs. Dalton's suspicions. The reek of whiskey convinced Mrs. Dalton that Mary was drunk, and she left the room. Then Bigger discovered that he had smothered Mary to death. To delay discovery of his crime, he took the body to the basement and stuffed it into the furnace.

Bigger then began a weird kind of rationalization. The next morning, in his mother's home, he began thinking that he was separated from his family because he had killed a white girl. His plan was to involve Jan in connection with Mary's death.

When Bigger returned to the Dalton home, the family was worrying over Mary's absence. Bigger felt secure from incrimination because he had covered his activities by lying. He decided to send ransom notes to her parents, allowing them to think Mary had been kidnapped. There were too many facts to remember, however, and too many lies to tell. Britten, the detective whom Mr. Dalton had hired, tried to intimidate Bigger, but his methods only made Bigger more determined to frame Jan, who, in his desire to protect Mary, lied just enough to help Bigger's cause. When Britten brought Bigger face to face with Jan for questioning, Bigger's fear mounted. He went to Bessie, his mistress, who wrung from him a confession of murder. Bigger forced her to go with him to hide in an empty building in the slum section of the city. There he instructed her to pick up the ransom money he hoped to receive from Mr. Dalton.

Bigger was eating in the Dalton kitchen when the ransom note arrived. Jan had already been arrested. Bigger clung tenaciously to his lies. It was a cold day. Attempting to build up the fire, Bigger accidentally drew attention to the furnace. When reporters discovered Mary's bones, Bigger fled. Hiding with Bessie in the deserted building, he realized that he could not take her with him. Afraid to leave her behind to be found and questioned by the police, he killed her and threw her body down an air shaft.

When Bigger ventured from his hideout to steal a newspaper, he learned that the city was being combed to find him. He fled from one empty building to another, constantly buying or stealing newspapers so that he could know his chances for escape. Finally, he was trapped on the roof of a penthouse by a searching policeman. Bigger knocked him out with the butt of the gun he had been carrying with him. The police finally captured Bigger after a chase across the rooftops.

In jail, Bigger refused to eat or speak. His mind turned inward, hating the world, but he was satisfied with himself for what he had done. Three days later, Jan Erlone came to see Bigger and promised to help him. Jan introduced Boris A. Max, a lawyer for the Communist front organization for which Jan worked. Buckley, the prosecuting attorney, tried to persuade Bigger not to become involved with the Communists. Bigger said nothing even after the lawyer told him that Bessie's body had been found. When Buckley began listing crimes of rape, murder, and burglary which had been charged against him, Bigger protested, vigorously denying rape and Jan's part in Mary's death. Under a steady fire of questions from Buckley, Bigger broke down and signed a confession.

The opening session of the grand jury began. First, Mrs. Dalton appeared as a witness to identify one of her daughter's earrings, which had been found in the furnace. Next, Jan testified, and, under the slanderous anti-Communist questioning, Max rose in protest against the racial bigotry of the coroner. Max questioned Mr. Dalton about his ownership of the high-rent, rat-infested tenements where Bigger's family lived. Generally, the grand jury session became a trial of the race relations which had led to Bigger's crime rather than a trial of the crime itself. As a climax to the session, the coroner brought Bessie's body into the courtroom in order to produce evidence that Bigger had raped and murdered his sweetheart. Bigger was returned to jail after Max had promised to visit him. Under the quiet questioning of Max, Bigger at last was able to talk about his crime, his feelings, his reasons. He had been thwarted by white people all of his life, he said, until he had killed Mary Dalton; that act had released him.

At the opening session of the trial, Buckley presented witnesses who attested Bigger's sanity and his ruthless character. The murder was dramatized even to the courtroom reconstruction of the furnace in which Mary's body had been burned. Max refused to call any of his own witnesses or to cross-examine, promising to act in Bigger's behalf as sole witness for the defense. The next day, in a long speech, Max outlined an entire social structure, its effect on an individual such as Bigger, and Bigger's inner compulsions when he killed Mary Dalton. Pleading for mitigation on the grounds that Bigger was not totally responsible for his crime, he argued that society was also to blame.

After another race-prejudiced attack by Buckley, the court adjourned for one hour. It reopened to sentence Bigger to death. Max's attempts to delay death by appealing to the governor were unsuccessful.

In the last hours before death, Bigger realized his one hope was to communicate his feelings to Max, to try to have Max explain to him the meaning of his life and his death. Max helped him see that the people who persecute African Americans, poor people or others, are themselves filled with fear. Bigger could forgive them because they were suffering the same urge that he had suffered. He could forgive his enemies because they did not know the guilt of their own social crimes.

Critical Evaluation:

When it appeared in 1940, *Native Son* was without precedent in American literature. Previous African American writing, including Richard Wright's *Uncle Tom's Children* (1938), had treated blacks as passive and innocent victims of racism suffering their lot in dignified silence. As Wright said of his own earlier work, the reading audience could escape into the self-indulgence of pity on reading such work rather than truly face the hard facts of racism. In Bigger Thomas, Wright created a character who was neither a passive sufferer nor an innocent victim. Instead, Wright reminded Americans of the full cost of bigotry in social and human terms by dramatizing the deep anger, hate, and fear that many blacks felt. Years after *Native Son*'s appearance, James Baldwin would assert that every black person carries some degree of Bigger Thomas within himself. Perhaps so, and it is to Wright's credit that he was the first American writer to bring those feelings into the open. Readers are reminded throughout the work that Bigger is a "native son," and his experience is quintessentially a part of the American experience. On the psychological, the sociological, and the philosophical levels, Wright explores the most disturbing implications of what it means to be African American.

The basic tone of Wright's psychological treatment of Bigger is set in the opening scene in which Bigger and Buddy battle the rat. Here is a symbolic paradigm for the entire novel in which Bigger, like the rat, will be hunted and destroyed. The rat, it must be understood, operates entirely at the instinctual level, and its viciousness is in response to fear. Recalling that "Fear" is the title of the first section of the novel, as "Flight" is of the second, suggests that Bigger, too, is a creature motivated by fear and acting instinctively. This is demonstrably true of his killing Mary Dalton while avoiding detection, and it shows up even earlier in the fight with Gus. Fearful of outside forces, particularly white people, Bigger is equally fearful of the repressed anger within himself, as his several comments referring to his concern that he is destined to commit some terrible act indicate. Thus, throughout at least the first two sections of the novel, Bigger, before and after the murder, is operating at the animal level of pure instinct, and it is against this background that his development takes place.

Bigger's psychological state is an obvious result of the sociological conditions prevailing in the novel. As Bigger dramatizes the anger and pain of his race, the Daltons effectively represent the ruling white power structure. It is to Wright's credit that he does not give way to the temptation to create villains, but makes these whites generous, liberal, and humanitarian. It is ironic that even while giving a "chance" to Bigger and helping in ghetto programs, the Daltons are reaping the proceeds of ghetto housing. Appropriately, Wright uses the metaphor of blindness to characterize the attitude of the Daltons here, as he will later, to account for Max's failure to comprehend Bigger. Bigger, too, is described as blind, because, in this world of *Native Son*, there is no real possibility of people seeing one another in clear human perspective. All the characters respond to one another as symbols rather than as people.

Wright's use of the polarities of black and white symbolism is not limited to the literal and racial levels of the novel. The entire world of *Native Son*, as the story unfolds, is increasingly polarized into a symbolic black-white dichotomy. Especially during part 2, the snow which buries the city under a cold and hostile blanket of white becomes a more complicated manifestation of the white symbolism than that limited to the sociological level. At the same time, Bigger not only escapes into the black ghetto in search of safety and security, but he also seeks out the black interiors of abandoned buildings to hide from both the freezing snow and the death-dealing white mob. Finally, Bigger's flight ends with his being spread out against the white snow as though crucified.

It is not probable that Wright had heard of European existentialism when he wrote *Native Son*, so it is all the more remarkable that this novel should so clearly demonstrate concepts that anticipate Wright's embracing of the existentialist philosophy when he went to Europe in the late 1940's. Though Bigger very obviously commits the murder without premeditation, he quickly comes to the realization that somehow the act is the sum of his entire life. Rather than repudiating responsibility for his crime, or seeing himself as a victim of circumstances, either of which would be understandable, Bigger consciously and deliberately affirms the killing as the most creative act of his life. Whereas before he was in the position of constantly reacting— like the rat—he now sees himself as having responsibility for his own fate. Further, the world which before had seemed frighteningly ambiguous is now clearly revealed to him. For the first time in his life, Bigger has a positive sense of his own identity and a concrete knowledge of how he relates to the world around him. Ironically, Max's case that Bigger is a victim of society threatens to deprive Bigger of the identity he has purchased at such terrible cost to himself, but, facing death at the end of the novel, he reaffirms his belief that he killed for something, and he faces death with the courage born of his one creative moment.

Wright's novel is not without faults, particularly the tedious final section in which Max argues a doctrinaire Marxist interpretation of Bigger's crime. Apparently, however, Wright himself could not fully accept this view, since Bigger's reaffirmation of responsibility contradicts Max's deterministic justification. In the final analysis, Bigger's insistence upon responsibility for his act demonstrates the human potential for freedom of act and will and asserts human possibility in contrast to the Marxist vision of people as animals trapped in a world they cannot control.

"Critical Evaluation" by William E. Grant

Bibliography:

Emanuel, James. "Fever and Feeling: Notes on the Imagery in *Native Son*." *Negro Digest* 18, no. 2 (December, 1968): 16-24. Identifies and examines clusters of images and symbols present in the novel. Concludes that Wright uses this sprawling network of images to deepen the reader's understanding of Bigger and Bigger's feelings about himself and his environment.

Felgar, Robert. "The Kingdom of the Beast: The Landscape of *Native Son*." *CLA Journal* 17 (March, 1974): 333-337. Enlightening, important discussion of the novel's depiction of society as a jungle. Convincingly contends that animal imagery pervades the novel and posits that the book's many beast images objectify white society's stereotypical conception of the African American world.

Magistrale, Tony. "From St. Petersburg to Chicago: Wright's *Crime and Punishment*." *Comparative Literature Studies* 23, no. 1 (Spring, 1986): 59-70. Argues that, in composing *Native Son*, Wright was greatly influenced by Fyodor Dostoevski's novel *Crime and Punishment* (1966). Pinpoints and analyzes in detail a number of significant similarities between the two novels. Convincing and informative in its treatment of the novel's debt to the Dostoevski classic.

Nagel, James. "Images of Vision in *Native Son.*" *University Review* 35 (December, 1969): 109-115. Perceptive, highly instructive analysis of Wright's use of sight and blindness in the novel. Argues that blindness is the novel's controlling image and that it functions throughout the book as a metaphor for white America's racial myopia. Remains, even after its initial publication in 1969, one of the most insightful articles ever written on the novel.

Siegel, Paul N. "The Conclusion of Richard Wright's *Native Son.*" *PMLA* 89, no. 3 (May, 1974): 517-523. Detailed, illuminating interpretation of book 3 of the novel. Sets out to refute the frequently advanced criticism that book 3 is the novel's weakest section. Maintains that the lengthy trial that concludes the novel, far from being repetitious and anticlimactic as many critics have claimed, is an integral part of the book's artistry and message.

THE NATURAL

Type of work: Novel
Author: Bernard Malamud (1914-1986)
Type of plot: Fable
Time of plot: 1930's-1940's
Locale: Chicago and New York
First published: 1952

> *Principal characters:*
> ROY HOBBS, nineteen-year-old country bumpkin ballplayer
> POP FISHER, manager of the New York Knights baseball team
> MEMO PARIS, niece of Pop Fisher
> IRIS LEMON, thirty-three-year-old grandmother

The Story:

In section one, "Pre-Game," nineteen-year-old pitcher Roy Hobbs journeyed by train to Chicago for a tryout with the Cubs. He was accompanied by Sam Simpson, an alcoholic former major-league catcher and scout who hoped to use his discovery of Roy to resurrect his scouting career. Roy was a naïve, self-centered, country bumpkin. With his homemade bat, Wonderboy, fashioned from a tree that had been split by lightning and seemed to possess an energy all its own, Roy was, however, a superbly gifted ballplayer.

Also on the train was Walter "the Whammer" Wambold, aging American League batting champion and three-time winner of the Most Valuable Player award. When the train was mysteriously delayed, Roy and the others wandered over to a nearby carnival, where the Whammer displayed his prowess in a batting cage and Roy attracted a crowd by throwing baseballs at milk bottles. As the rivalry built to its confrontation, Sam bet that Roy could strike out the Whammer with three pitches. After the third pitch, the Whammer dropped the bat and returned to the train, "an old man."

Roy's triumph brought him to the attention of Harriet Bird, who guarded a shiny black box as jealously as Roy guarded Wonderboy. Excited by Roy's victory in "the tourney," she told him he was like "David jawboning the Goliath-Whammer, or was it Sir Percy lancing Sir Maldemer, or the first son (with a rock in his paw) ranged against the primitive papa?" Roy responded, "I'll be the best there ever was in the game." "Is that all?" Harriet asked. Harriet turned out to be the mysterious woman Roy had heard about who shot promising young athletes with silver bullets. Soon after, in a Chicago hotel room, Roy reaffirmed his determination to become the best player who ever lived. Harriet reached into her mysterious hatbox, drew out a gun, and shot Roy in the stomach with a silver bullet.

Section two, "Batter Up," takes place fifteen years later. Ashamed of his nearly fatal "accident" in Chicago, Roy was determined to begin a new life after years of wandering and working at odd jobs. As an outfielder, Roy tried out with the New York Knights, a team that had amassed a record number of losses. In order to win a starting spot in the lineup, Roy had to displace the Knight's current left fielder, batting champ Bump Bailey, who looked out solely for himself and whose batting prowess did little to inspire his teammates. The rivalry ended when Bump, trying valiantly to match Roy's flawless fielding, crashed into the left field wall and died of his injuries. With the aid of Roy's superhuman skills, the team began a miraculous drive for the pennant.

Pop Fisher, the aged manager of the Knights and a former major-league player himself, hoped to lead the Knights to the world championship. He became Roy's spiritual father. Pop's ambition, however, was being thwarted by the forces of evil in the form of Judge Banner, a profit seeker who owned sixty percent of the Knights' stock. Pop had sold stock to the judge with the stipulation that the manager would retain control over player deals "as long as he lives." Yet he was slowly losing control. The judge was able to harass the manager in an effort to force Pop to resign so that the judge could seek profits rather than victory. The power behind the judge was Gus, the supreme bookie, who used the magic of statistics and knew that playing the percentages payed off in the long run.

As the team made its final drive for the pennant, Roy became distracted by his fatal attraction to Memo Paris, the niece of Pop Fisher and former girlfriend of Bump Bailey. Pop warned Roy that she will "weaken your strength," but even after Roy discovered that she was in league with Gus and the judge, his passion for her continued unabated. Roy also had an affair with Iris Lemon, a woman in Chicago who brought Roy out of his batting slump by rising up in the stands as an expression of support.

One night Roy ate so much that he became sick and ended up in a maternity hospital. He was told by the doctor that he would recover in time to play in the final game of the season, on whose outcome the elusive pennant rested—but that the game would be his last. Memo told him that she demanded a husband who could provide her with expensive things. To have Memo, Roy accepted a payoff from the judge to throw the crucial playoff game. Near the end of the game, however, Iris' presence in the stands caused Roy to decide that he could not go through with the fix. Wonderboy split in half when Roy swung at the ball with fierce determination. Without Wonderboy, Roy "struck out with a roar" on three pitches and walked away, like the Whammer before him, an old man.

In the final scene, Roy repudiated the betrayal by throwing the bribe money at the judge. On the street outside, Roy, like Shoeless Joe Jackson in 1919, painfully listened as a newsboy, carrying a stack of papers spreading word of the suspected sellout to the world, implored mournfully, "Say it ain't true, Roy."

Critical Evaluation:

The Natural is a fable in which the fortunes of its hero parallel those of Parzival, the medieval knight. Bernard Malamud uses myth and American culture's heroic ritual to explore the psychology of American life. The novel is enriched by drawing on events out of baseball lore and legend, such as the 1949 hotel-room shooting of Philadelphia Phillies infielder Eddie Waitkus by a crazed woman sports fan, the infamous game-fixing scandal of 1919, the many achievements of Babe Ruth, and the fate of Casey at the bat.

Roy Hobbs is a knight and a fool. An aging rookie who comes to play for the hapless New York Knights, he is also a natural baseball player with outstanding talent. After he becomes a knight, Parzival was given the quest of finding and healing the Fisher King of the Wasteland. He failed because he did not ask, rather than answer, the right question. Like Parzival, Roy fails because of his inability to answer Harriet Bird's question about what he hopes to accomplish in his career. His reply is limited and selfish: to be the best there ever was in the game. After Harriet gives him a second chance and he fails again, she discharges a silver bullet into him. It is not enough for the hero to have talent, he must have a purpose in life. Parzival and Roy are heroes that are too wrapped up in their self-image to recognize the responsibility that comes with their great talent.

After fifteen years, Roy returns to baseball, this time, like Babe Ruth, as a home run hitter rather than a pitcher. He joins the Knights, a team so bad that even its field, like the Wasteland, suffers from drought. The team's manager, Pop Fisher, the Fisher King, as spent a career without winning a pennant. In the medieval myth the Wasteland cannot become fertile until the Fisher King is replaced by the young, innocent hero. In *The Natural*, Roy is the mythic hero who can undo the bad luck of his spiritual father, Pop Fisher, and bring relief to the drought. When Roy starts hitting, the team begins winning, torrential rains come down, and the field turns green.

As fertility god, Roy has to choose the proper woman to be his companion. Like other Malamud heroes, he has a choice between a woman who represents life-giving fertility and one whose power lies in her seductive vanity. Iris Lemon, named for a fruit and a flower, is the woman Roy should choose. Roy, however, is attracted to Memo Paris, whose name suggests someone who uses memory rather than imagination and who uses her powers to destroy, as Paris did Achilles, the men in her life. Her condition is symbolized by her sick breast, a sign that she is incapable of either nurturing the hero or of bearing her own offspring.

Iris, on the other hand, is connected with Roy's first selfless act. Roy promises an injured boy, who has given up struggling for his life, that he, Roy, will hit a home run for the boy (the incident is taken from the career of Babe Ruth). Roy understands for the first time that as a hero he has responsibility for another human being. When Iris stands up in the crowd for him, he responds by hitting a home run. Iris urges upon Roy the responsibility inherent in being a hero. A hero must become a moral example for ordinary people, especially for children.

Later, Iris tries to explain to Roy the sacrifice of ego that is required of a hero. The hero is not for himself, but for others. Iris explains to Roy the theory that every person has two lives: One life teaches through experience how to live, and the other life is the life lived out of that knowledge. The life that teaches is always built out of suffering and sacrifice so that the life that is lived can move toward happiness by choosing the right things.

Iris can bring Roy to that life only by freeing him from his fear of mortality. She must make him see that playing baseball with the aim of making himself immortal by setting records is immoral, self-centered, and counterproductive. Roy is not mature enough, however, to accept her wisdom. Malamud believes that redemption lies in the hero's understanding of his own past and his ability to transcend it. Roy's inability to do this is the basis of his failure. A woman laments at the end of the novel, "He coulda been a king." Roy is left only with his self-hatred. As the ballplayer tells himself in the final page, "I never did learn anything out of my past life, now I have to suffer again."

Roy's dismal failure makes *The Natural* a clear introduction to the morality that informs Malamud's later work. Malamud's moral understanding is based upon his insistence that submission to suffering is the only avenue of redemption. Readers see in Roy their own limitations and the possibility that exists to overcome those limitations. Malamud's qualified affirmation comes out of a belief in the resources of the human spirit, with an understanding of the social and economic pressures that can suffocate it. In its use of myth, moral, and symbol, *The Natural* is necessary text for reading Malamud's subsequent fiction.

Milton S. Katz

Bibliography:
Alter, Isaka. "The Good Man's Dilemma: *The Natural*, *The Assistant*, and American Material-
    ism." In *Critical Essays on Bernard Malamud*. Edited by Joel Salzberg. Boston: G. K. Hall,
    1987. Focuses on the social criticism in Malamud's fiction and how in *The Natural*, Roy
    chooses materialism over love and morality.

Helterman, Jeffrey. *Understanding Bernard Malamud*. Columbia: University of South Carolina Press, 1985. A highly readable guide for students and nonacademic readers about what Malamud expresses and the means by which it is conveyed. Chapter 2 discusses mythic dimensions, themes, and symbolism in *The Natural*.

Hershinow, Sheldon. *Bernard Malamud*. New York: Frederick Ungar, 1980. Chapter 2 offers an analysis of *The Natural* as depicting the plight of the mythic hero in the modern world.

Richman, Sidney. *Bernard Malamud*. Boston: Twayne, 1966. Chapter 3 provides an excellent, detailed analysis of *The Natural* as a novel of ideas laced with moral ambiguity and pessimism.

Wasserman, Earl R. "*The Natural*: Malamud's World Ceres." In *Bernard Malamud*. Edited by Harold Bloom. New York: Chelsea House, 1986. Renders a comprehensive analysis of how Malamud weaves historical episodes into an epic.

NAUSEA

Type of work: Novel
Author: Jean-Paul Sartre (1905-1980)
Type of plot: Philosophical realism
Time of plot: 1930's
Locale: France
First published: La Nausée, 1938 (English translation, 1949)

> *Principal characters:*
> ANTOINE ROQUENTIN, a French historian
> ANNY, Roquentin's former sweetheart
> OGIER P., "The Self-Taught Man" and an acquaintance of Roquentin
> FRANÇOISE, the congenial owner of a café and Roquentin's friend

The Story:

After traveling through Central Europe, North Africa, and the Orient, a thirty-year-old Frenchman named Antoine Roquentin settled down in the seaport town of Bouville to finish his historical research on the Marquis de Rollebon, an eighteenth century figure in European politics whose home had been at Bouville. For three years, Roquentin searched the archives of the Bouville library reconstructing the nobleman's life. All Roquentin's energies were concentrated on his task; he knew few people in Bouville except by sight, and he lived more in the imaginary world he was re-creating than in the actual world.

In the third year of his residence in Bouville, during the winter of 1932, Roquentin began to have a series of disturbing psychological experiences that he termed the nausea. He felt there was something new about commonplace articles, and even his hands seemed to take on new aspects, to have an existence all their own. It was then that Roquentin's loneliness became a terrible thing to him, for there was no one to whom he could speak of his experiences. His only acquaintances were Ogier P., whom Roquentin had nicknamed "The Self-Taught Man" because he was instructing himself by reading all the books in the library, and a woman named Françoise, who operated a café called the Rendezvous des Cheminots. Françoise, who had become fond of Roquentin, was the outlet for his physical sexuality, but their acquaintance had not gone beyond that. In his loneliness, Roquentin began to think of Anny, an English girl who had traveled with him some years before and whom he had loved; he had not heard from her in more than three years. The nausea came increasingly often to plague Roquentin; it passed from objects into his body through his hands, and the only way he could describe it was that it seemed like a sweetish sickness.

One evening, shortly after the nausea had first appeared, Roquentin went to the café, only to find that Françoise would be gone for a time. He sat down to listen to music on a battered old phonograph and, for the first time, the nausea crept upon him in a place where there were bright lights and many people; even more horrible, it seemed as if the sickness were outside himself, in other objects.

Strangely enough, as the days passed, The Self-Taught Man made an effort to be friendly with Roquentin. Learning that Roquentin had traveled extensively, The Self-Taught Man asked to see some of the photographs he had collected and to hear some of his adventures. He even went to Roquentin's rooms one evening for that specific purpose. These friendly overtures were not entirely welcome to Roquentin, since he was immersed in his psychological problems, but he acquiesced in setting a date to have dinner with The Self-Taught Man a few days later.

In the interval before the dinner engagement, the book about the Marquis de Rollebon came to a halt. One day, Roquentin suddenly stopped writing in the middle of a paragraph and knew that he would write no more, although he had spent more than three years of his life on the work. Roquentin suddenly felt cheated, as if his very existence had been stolen by the Marquis de Rollebon during those years, as if the marquis had been living in place of himself. The feeling was caused in part as a result of his realization that he would never be able to be certain of the truth about the marquis, who all of his life had used men for his own ends.

Once he realized that he would write no more, Roquentin found that there was little or no purpose in his life. Indeed, there seemed to be no reason for his existence. For three years, Roquentin had not reacted to his own existence because he had been working; now it was thrust on him with disquieting abruptness.

One Wednesday, Roquentin and The Self-Taught Man met for the prearranged dinner, a rather stiff affair, during which The Self-Taught Man tried to convince Roquentin that he, like himself, ought to be a humanist, that in the humanity of the world was to be found the true reason for the universe. Roquentin became so disquieted that the nausea came over him during the discussion, and he abruptly left the restaurant.

A day or two later, Roquentin received an unexpected letter from Anny, which had been forwarded from his old address in Paris. She wrote that she was to be in Paris for a few days and wished to see him. Roquentin looked forward to seeing her and planned to leave Bouville for the first time in three years to visit with her in Paris. When the day arrived, he presented himself at her address.

Anny was no longer the same; she had become fat, but the changes that bothered him the most were those he felt rather than saw. The interview was a dismal failure; Anny accused him of being worthless to her and finally thrust him from the room. Later, he saw Anny getting on a train with the man who kept her, and he went back to Bouville with a sense of numbness. He believed that both he and Anny had outlived themselves. All that was left, he felt, was eating and sleeping, an existence not unlike that of an inanimate object.

Roquentin remained in Bouville only a few days more. Unhappy and lonesome, he sought out The Self-Taught Man and found him in the library. Because The Self-Taught Man was reading to two young boys, Roquentin sat down to read until The Self-Taught Man had finished. He never got a chance to resume his conversation with his acquaintance, for The Self-Taught Man revealed himself to be a homosexual and was brutally ejected from the library by the librarians. The only other person to whom Roquentin wished to say good-bye was the congenial woman who owned the Rendezvous des Cheminots. When he went to see her, however, she could spare him only a moment, for another patron claimed her time.

Roquentin went to the railway station for the train that was to take him to Paris. His only hope was that he might write a book, perhaps a novel, that would make people think of his life as something precious and legendary. He knew, however, that his work on such a book, unlike his attempts at the history of the Marquis de Rollebon, would not be able to keep from him the troublesome problem of existence.

Critical Evaluation:

Throughout Jean-Paul Sartre's *Nausea*, Antoine Roquentin attempts to define the relationship between himself and the world outside himself so that he can understand the powerful sense of nausea that overwhelms him. He hopes that in so doing he can define the meaning of his existence. Roquentin, an existential man, is destined to fail in his search. As Sartre's personification of existentialism, Roquentin cannot but find his own existence abhorrent and ultimately meaningless; in fact, his nausea reflects not only the vertigo of existence but that existence, which is a dispensable element of reality itself, comprises only suffering and despair.

When the novel commences, Roquentin is focused on his historical research in the town library, his frequent visits to cafés, his memory of the past, and occasional sexual trysts with Françoise, the woman who runs one of the cafés he frequents. Other than with Françoise, Roquentin has no contact with anyone except The Self-Taught Man, who "doesn't count." By his own account, Roquentin neither gives nor receives anything from anyone; thus, his existence is isolated.

Through the nausea, Roquentin discovers that all of his pleasures and activities are meaningless. Initially, for example, his trips to cafés provide him with some pleasure, and he is safe from the nausea when he sits in the well-lighted, crowded cafés of Bouville. Eventually, however, the nausea invades the café as well, and he is horrified by the people and objects around him. His sexual encounters with Françoise have little meaning to begin with; they merely serve a need that, according to Roquentin, is "mutual." Yet whatever pleasure Roquentin may have found in these encounters is lost: He is suddenly disgusted by her appearance, her smell, her very existence. The meaninglessness of their relationship is intensified by his final conversation with her before he leaves to board the train for Paris. Françoise barely speaks to him, and she spends Roquentin's final moments in the café doting on another customer.

Another element of Roquentin's life is his walks about town. Yet these walks eventually serve only to reinforce his perception of the futility of existence. He watches people interact with each other and condemns the regularity and predictability of their lives. They are "idiots" with "thick, self-satisfied faces" and empty lives. Occasionally, he focuses on the self-confidence and purpose that he sees in wealthy men, but their world is completely alien to him. In any case, he knows that they too must die, that their lives too are ultimately an illusion. Even the beauty of nature becomes abhorrent to Roquentin when he realizes that the trees "*did not want* to exist, only they could not help themselves." Finally, Roquentin concludes that all that exists, exists "without reason, prolongs itself out of weakness and dies by chance."

As Roquentin realizes the pointlessness of the simple pleasures that he had previously enjoyed, he focuses on the remaining significance of his life: his research on the history of the Marquis de Rollebon and the memory of his own personal history, the highlights of which are adventure and love. The primary difficulty that Roquentin has with searching for meaning in the past is that recollection of the past is subjective. As he explores his personal past, for example, he encounters only "scraps of images"; significantly, he is unsure whether they are "memories or just fiction." In this context, his adventures, which previously held great import, lose their significance. In fact, his sense as to whether or not he has even experienced adventures, in light of his perception of the complexity of truth and memory, begins to waver. Ultimately, he concludes that "things have happened" to him, but that he has had no adventures and that, in fact, he has deceived himself for years. He then turns his attention to the Marquis de Rollebon, to whom he had lent his own life. Yet through his recent discovery of the questionable nature of his own recollection of the past, Roquentin cannot but ask, "How can I, who have not the strength to hold to my own past, hope to save the past of someone else?" Consequently, Roquentin discovers that the past, in fact, cannot exist in the true concept of that term. Only the present can exist, as the subjectivity of memory destroys the possibility of historical truth. Without truth, there can be no existence, just as existence, in its indifference, is truth.

Seeking yet another reason for existence, Roquentin turns not to the memory of his love for Anny but to his hope for the future in the form of his impending meeting with her, which serves as his "sole reason for living." Yet within *Nausea*, as within all of Sartre's works, there is to be no salvation through others. The individual, in his or her own search for meaning, is always let down by the other, much as The Self-Taught Man is ultimately let down by his own belief system, rational humanism, when he is rejected by the librarian and the library's patrons. Anny, reinforcing Roquentin's sense of the inauthenticity of the past, is not as he remembers her. She has grown fat, she talks only about herself, and though her experiences of life seem to parallel Roquentin's, she refuses to acknowledge any correlation between these experiences. Like Françoise and so many of Sartre's women characters, she is self-centered and two-dimensional, incapable of complex thought or tenderness. Again, Roquentin is left with only his existence in all of its futility. In the end, he looks forward to the possibility of writing a novel and to living in Paris, even though he knows that his existence is meaningless. It is this awareness, in fact, that gives him a sense of freedom.

Roquentin serves as the embodiment of Sartre's existential man. Rational humanism, as personified by The Self-Taught Man, serves as a parallel, yet inferior, belief system. Ironically, Roquentin, who never attempts to help anyone throughout the novel, even though he encounters the need of others, reaches out to The Self-Taught Man, as if to reinforce the validity of rational humanism itself. The Self-Taught Man, however, refuses Roquentin's help, choosing instead to face his grief alone. According to Sartre's existentialism, there is no other valid choice.

"Critical Evaluation" by Dana Reece Baylard

Bibliography:

Barnes, Hazel E. *The Literature of Possibility: A Study in Humanistic Existentialism*. Lincoln: University of Nebraska Press, 1959. A philosophical and psychological examination of Sartre's literary output, written by one of his leading translators. Refutes the charge of antihumanism that has been made against Sartre's work.

Danto, Arthur C. *Jean-Paul Sartre*. New York: Viking Press, 1975. The first chapter, "Absurdity: Or, Language and Existence," examines *Nausea* at length and discusses Sartre's views on language, the analytic "philosophy of mind," and the structural representation of reality.

Magny, Claude-Edmonde. "The Duplicity of Being." In *Sartre: A Collection of Critical Essays*, edited by Edith Kern. Englewood Cliffs, N.J.: Prentice-Hall, 1962. Discusses the experience of nausea as "the sudden revelation" of the mutability and impermanence of existence and existing things. Interprets the characters of *Nausea* as "cheaters" who attempt a sequential (and hence "fictitious") narration of their lives. Recommended for more advanced readers.

Murdoch, Iris. *Sartre: Romantic Rationalist*. New Haven, Conn.: Yale University Press, 1959. Includes a well-written introduction to Sartre's thought. Discusses *Nausea* in chapter 1, "The Discovery of Things," and refers to the work throughout. Also contains a bibliography of Sartre's works (French titles) and an updated listing (through 1985) of English translations. An excellent guide to Sartrean themes.

Peyre, Henri. *French Novelists of Today*. New York: Oxford University Press, 1967. An amplified version of Peyre's earlier *The Contemporary French Novel* (1955). Chapter 9 covers *Nausea* and other of Sartre's novels. Also includes a short but helpful bibliography.

A NEST OF SIMPLE FOLK

Type of work: Novel
Author: Seán O'Faoláin (1900-1991)
Type of plot: Regional
Time of plot: 1854-1916
Locale: Ireland
First published: 1933

> *Principal characters:*
> LEO FOXE-DONNELL, an Irish patriot
> JUDITH, his mother
> JULIE, his wife
> JOHNO O'DONNELL, the son of Julie and Leo
> JOHNNY HUSSEY, a policeman
> BID, his wife
> DENIS, the son of Bid and Johnny

The Story:

Foxehall was a bleak, remote manor house, and the family that owned it kept to themselves. Rachel and Anna Foxe were content to live prim maiden lives, poverty-stricken remnants of a landed family. Judith Foxe, however, married Long John O'Donnell, a secretive farmer. Judith was cut off with a dowry of five fields as a punishment for having married beneath her station; for seventeen years, she did not see her sisters. The marriage was a good one for Long John. Poor as he was, he felt that Judith's five fields were good pay for taking an unattractive wife. When their tenth child, Leo, was born, Rachel condescended to sponsor him. Afterward, it seemed to Judith that Leo was her only true son. When her husband was near death, she was determined that Leo should be the heir.

James, the oldest son, worked like a servant for his harsh father. As the oldest, he would inherit the home farm. Phil was next in line; by rights, he should have had the five fields. Long John had obstinately refused to make a will; as he grew weaker, however, Judith harried him into telling a lawyer how the property should be distributed. She also dressed Leo in Phil's clothes and tricked her weak, dying husband into pointing to Leo as the heir to the five fields. By this act, James inherited only the heavily mortgaged home farm and the obligation to find husbands for his numerous sisters. Leo was given the five free fields, with Phil receiving only what James would share with him.

After the funeral, James drove the family home. Young Leo sensed James's state of mind and offered to give him all the land, an offer which infuriated the older brother. James whipped Leo savagely and drove him off the farm. Leo went to live with his maiden aunts. Rachel and Anna did their best to make a genteel aristocrat of their rough and surly nephew. Nicholas, a ne'er-do-well, was his tutor, and Nicholas himself was rough. A long debate ensued over Leo's future as a doctor or a gentleman farmer. Leo had little preference, but when he was sent to Limerick to study with Dicky, his doctor cousin, he went willingly enough.

Nicholas was influential in molding the boy's sympathies and accompanied him on the journey. Because the tutor had told him of the past insults and atrocities by the aristocracy, Leo was angry at the injustices suffered by the poor farmers. In Limerick, the two called on Frankie O'Donnell, Leo's uncle, a tavernkeeper who was a revolutionary at heart. The rough welcome there was in sharp contrast with his treatment at Doctor Dicky's house. The old doctor was a gruff Protestant and a teetotaler. Leo was out of place in his country clothes. After a trial term, Leo was sent home in disgrace; he had no aptitude for medicine.

For years, Leo lived an idle and dissolute life. After his aunts died, he became the owner of Foxehall. Taking no care of the property, he hunted, caroused, and chased girls. One of them, Philly Cashen, was turned out of old Mag Keene's house because of her pregnancy. Distraught, Philly went to Foxehall. Although she knew that Leo was guilty, Judith refused to help the girl. At last, Judith left her youngest son and his fine house and went back to live with James. Philly was not the only girl Leo ruined. Another was Julie Keene, who was too young to resist him successfully.

The Fenian spirit pervaded the countryside. Although a landowner, Mad Leo joined the plotters and led a raid on the police post. By chance, Julie saw them and ran to warn another sweetheart of hers, a detective. The plotters were seized, and Leo was sentenced to fifteen years in jail. While he was in prison, his mother died, but Leo did not know of her death; his family never wrote to him. A change of government brought an amnesty, and after ten years, Leo was released.

Julie was still unmarried. Holding no grudge against her, Leo courted her again, and when she became pregnant, he mortgaged his land to raise money to send her to Dublin. Julie bore her son, gave him away, and returned as happy as ever. Leo continued his shiftless ways and eventually lost his land to his grasping brother James. Finally, with the help of a neighborhood priest, Leo was bullied into marrying Julie, and the strange couple set themselves up in a small paper shop in Rathkeale.

Bid, Julie's pretty youngest sister, came to live with them after a time. Before long, she was walking out with Johnny Hussey, a policeman. After innocent Bid went to visit the police barracks with Johnny, Leo questioned her closely about the visit, for at the age of sixty, he was still an ardent Fenian. Bid assured Leo that the policeman had said nothing about him, but she half guiltily remembered some joking remarks she had heard. Leo was perturbed. Julie was almost hysterical and demanded that Leo bring back their lost son. To quiet her, he found Johno O'Donnell, now a twenty-year-old sailor, and brought him as a nephew to Rathkeale.

After Johnny searched Leo's room and found suspicious letters, the police began to watch Leo carefully. Still a fiery patriot, Leo planned with his son Johno to bring into a river port a shipment of rifles that Johno had smuggled aboard his ship. Leo and a few Fenians were waiting with a skiff to take them off when the police surprised them. Leo fired a warning shot. When an officer was wounded, the conspirators quickly rowed out into the foggy harbor and escaped. Leo landed on the other shore. Returning to Rathkeale, he was arrested and sentenced to five years.

Meanwhile, Johnny had married Bid. When he was transferred to Cork, they took Julie, now old and broken, with them. After Leo's release from prison, the old couple could see nothing to do but to live with Johnny, who had been promoted to the post of acting sergeant. Johno and his wife completed the family circle. Denis, Bid's oldest boy, was always prim. Because Leo and Johno were gusty and loud, Johnny encouraged his son to be different. Bid regarded Denis as a potential scholar and planned for his education. Old Leo had a small shop where he sometimes took bets. As always, he knew what was going on among the revolutionaries.

Bid took in lodgers to get money for the boy's schooling. Although she was always tired, the effort seemed worthwhile. Nevertheless, Denis was a disappointment to her. He had no head for studies and gave up his ambitions after he had failed the civil service examination three times. Worse than that, he quarreled with his father. Rifles were cracking all over Ireland. When an uprising broke out in Dublin, Denis, after helping Leo and Johno to escape arrest, called his father a police spy and went to take shelter with the O'Donnells. Like Ireland, his was a house divided.

Critical Evaluation:

Seán O'Faoláin was the leading Irish man of letters of his generation whose literary reputation rests largely on his short stories. *A Nest of Simple Folk* is the first of his three novels, and the one which draws most directly on his personal and historical experiences. Yet, for various reasons, the work is not to be considered as simply an autobiographical first novel. One reason is that, like many Irish writers of his generation, O'Faoláin was careful to resist the influence of James Joyce, whose *A Portrait of the Artist as a Young Man* (1916) set the standard for Irish first novels in theme, structure, and artistry. O'Faoláin sought his creative model elsewhere, as the title of *A Nest of Simple Folk*—deliberately echoing that of a novel by Ivan Turgenev, *A House of Gentlefolk* (1858)—is intended to suggest.

The invocation of Turgenev does not end with titles. The atmosphere, depiction of the landscape, economic reality, and pace of narrative development all resemble the Russian author's works. O'Faoláin, however, is not merely being a mimic. The clouds and river mists which recur throughout the novel are not just picturesque details. They function as a means of conveying the sense of the recurrent and inescapable conditions of existence. These meteorological and atmospheric features are so prevalent as to constitute the equivalent of a destiny. The view of the landscape, of rural family life, of commercial life in the town of Rathkeale and the city of Limerick, is of such a repetitive and claustrophobic nature as to suggest the title of another nineteenth century Russian novel, N. G. Chernyshevsky's *What Is to Be Done?* (1864). The challenge for the characters is how to resist the destiny inscribed for them by the undramatic but insidious powers of nature, and the powerfully inert forces of custom and social class which are their counterparts. This challenge is presented in terms of the characters, in their various ways, attempting to act as though they had a nature of their own, a life distinct from the one arising from the conditions into which they were born. Inasmuch as such preoccupations constitute the overall narrative interest of *A Nest of Simple Folk*, the novel may be considered a meditation on the origins of the modern, and by virtue of that is a work of more than local Irish interest. It is not coincidental that the work concludes in a setting that, for all its ostensible lack of urban features, is in fact the city of Cork. Unlike his forebears, the landscape which Denis Hussey—heir to his family's two-faced history and to the conflicting tendencies in national history which that family history exemplifies—contemplates in his formative years is one composed entirely of human-made structures.

Although the city and county of Cork were to play a leading role in the violent political events which the rebellion of Easter, 1916, set in motion, the novel quite accurately and tellingly presents the outbreak of Easter, 1916, itself as both a shock, a mere skirmish, and the unlikely culmination of the years of suffering and commitment of the novel's protagonist Leo Foxe-Donnell. The Easter Rising, as it is known in Irish history, accelerated the movement toward political self-determination for the Irish people, whose progress until that juncture had been at best tragically disappointing and at worst stagnantly counterproductive. *A Nest of Simple Folk*, however, is careful not to become the historical novel it easily might have been. The career of Leo Foxe-Donnell is not of great political or historical moment. It represents a reaction against conditions more than an action in favor of alternative conditions. Policy, ideology, strategy, and recruitment play little or no part in Leo's exploits.

On the contrary, he attains his reputation through action—or rather, through abortive action, or through the periods of imprisonment which not only sanctify his efforts in the eyes of the authorities and his fellow nationalists but also confirm the intrinsic historical and political insignificance of those actions. A similar perspective may be applied to those who betray Leo, as his intimate acquaintance and family connection with them suggest. Julie, his wife-to-be, has little thought of the political dimension of her betrayal, nor does her sister Bid. Neither woman's involvement with a policeman alerts her to the political context of her life. They have no particular sense of themselves as members of an Irish nation in the making. They would hardly know what to make of the term "folk" if it were directly applied to them. Such a lack of self-awareness and critical distance is part of what O'Faoláin intends to convey by the term "simple."

It should also be noted, however, that O'Faoláin is also carrying out a complex and sophisticated maneuver in the realm of contemporary cultural ideology. One of the important ideological preconditions of the Easter, 1916, rebellion was the projection of a certain image of essential Irishness, based on a conception of the countryside and its inhabitants. Such an image was intended to make a claim for a pure, long-suffering populace, in whose name the struggle for Irish freedom could justifiably be waged. The hybrid, prefabricated, character of Leo Foxe-Donnell, his siblings' excruciating and embittering demands for land, the complicated morality—or lack of it—which underlies Leo's behavior, and the debatable quality of all the characters' consciousness may be regarded as O'Faoláin's critique of the preceding generation's ideology, and also perhaps of the literature which was that ideology's most important vehicle.

Yet pertinent as O'Faoláin's awareness of cultural and political history is to an appreciation of A *Nest of Simple Folk*, that awareness does not overwhelm the novel. The author's detached but sympathetic manner ensures that the focus remains on his characters' frailty. The significance of their frailty for the themes of attempted change and putative self-realization gives the narrative its dramatic interest. Those themes, in turn, attain a wider, emblematic, significance when seen in the context of Irish political and cultural history.

"Critical Evaluation" by George O'Brien

Bibliography:

Bonaccorso, Richard. *Seán O'Faoláin's Irish Vision*. Albany, N.Y.: State University of New York Press, 1987. A survey of the main phases of O'Faoláin's career. Evaluates A *Nest of Simple Folk* in that career. Analysis of the novel concentrates on its treatment of individuality. Includes a comprehensive bibliography.

Doyle, Paul A. *Seán O'Faoláin*. New York: Twayne, 1968. A general introductory survey of all O'Faoláin's writings. Discussion of A *Nest of Simple Folk* deals with its sense of historical context and its narrative development. Contains a chronology and a bibliography.

Harmon, Maurice. *Seán O'Faoláin: A Critical Introduction*. 2d ed. Dublin: Wolfhound, 1984. An insightful overview of O'Faoláin's career. Discusses his contributions to Irish intellectual life and his major works. Evaluation of A *Nest of Simple Folk* is guided by a sense of the conflict between the individual and society in O'Faoláin's novels. Includes an extensive bibliography.

O'Brien, Conor Cruise. "The Parnellism of Seán O'Faoláin." In *Maria Cross: Imaginative Patterns in a Group of Catholic Writers*. 2d ed. London: Burns and Oates, 1963. Intellectually sophisticated, culturally wide-ranging, critically incisive analysis of certain key features in O'Faoláin's major works, among them history, tradition, and memory. Assesses how these shape the narrative of, and constitute authorial identity in, A *Nest of Simple Folk*.

O'Faoláin, Seán. *Vive Moi!* London: Rupert Hart-Davis, 1965. The author's autobiography. Presents prototypes of the landscape, characters, and rural sensibility featured in *A Nest of Simple Folk*. The contrast between fictional and autobiographical perspectives is critically revealing.

THE NEW ATLANTIS

Type of work: Philosophy
Author: Sir Francis Bacon (1561-1626)
Type of plot: Fable
Time of plot: Early seventeenth century
Locale: Bensalem, South Sea
First published: 1627

> *Principal characters:*
> NARRATOR, visitor to Bensalem
> THE GOVERNOR OF THE HOUSE OF STRANGERS
> JOABIN, a Jew in Bensalem
> A FATHER, from Salomon's House

The Story:

An unidentified narrator, who is a member of a crew of 150 men sailing to China and Japan from Peru, recorded the events that transpired when their ship was blown off course. After some months at sea, they arrived at the port of a large island in an uncharted part of the South Sea. Eight people from the island approached the ship in a small boat and delivered a scroll whose message was repeated in Hebrew, Greek, Latin, and Spanish. The ship, the scroll said, could remain in port for sixteen days. It also extended the islanders' offer to bring whatever supplies were requested and admonished against landing on the island. Three hours after the supplies had been requested another dignitary approached the ship and asked if those on board were Christian. Upon an affirmative answer some of the crew were given permission to land. Six members of the crew were brought to the House of Strangers. Those who were sick aboard the ship were given orange-scarlet fruit to resist infection and small whitish-gray pills to help them sleep.

After three days at the House of Strangers, the six visitors met the Governor of that house. This man, by vocation a priest, welcomed the whole crew to stay for six weeks. Indicating that the island was called Bensalem, he explained that although its existence was relatively unknown, the Bensalemites knew about the rest of the world. Offering to answer any questions, he was first queried about the presence of Christianity on Bensalem. According to the Governor, twenty years after the ascension of Christ, a mysterious pillar of light had appeared off the east coast of the island. After the pillar was acknowledged as a miracle by a wise man from Salomon's House, the light disappeared, leaving a small cedar chest floating on the water. Inside the ark were the canonical and apocalyptic books of the Old and New Testaments and a letter from Bartholomew, who had committed the ark and its contents to water by command of an angel. Similar to the miracle of the preaching at Pentecost, the books and letter were able to be read by all the people of Bensalem, despite the variety of native languages there.

On the next day, the Governor recounted the history of the island. Three thousand years before, Atlantis (identified as America), Mexico, and Peru had been mighty kingdoms, and there had been greater navigation throughout the world. Atlantis had been destroyed by a flood, and, as a result of wars and other factors, navigation had also declined in other kingdoms. The existence of Bensalem had been forgotten. The Governor then described Salamona, the island's famous lawgiver of 1,900 years before. This king was renowned for establishing Salomon's

House, or the "College of the Six Days Works," which was "dedicated to the Study of the Works and Creatures of God." Although visitors to the island were prohibited during his reign and Bensalemites were prevented from visiting other countries, every twelve years six Fellows from Salomon's House were sent abroad to gather information concerning sciences, arts, and inventions in other countries. A week later, the narrator learned more about the island's culture from Joabin, a Jew. The Jews of Bensalem descended from another son of Abraham, Nachoran. Unlike Jews elsewhere, they held the Christian Savior in high regard. Joabin, describing the sexual customs in Bensalem, explained there was no polygamy, prostitution, or homosexuality. The spirit of chastity prevailed, and marriage and family were held in highest honor.

Their discussion was interrupted by news of the arrival of one of the Fathers of Salomon's House. Three days later, the entire crew was admitted into the Father's presence, but a private conference was granted to one member chosen among themselves, the narrator. The Father then discoursed about the area known as Salomon's House. There were caves, high towers, lakes, orchards, and gardens—all for a variety of experiments and for observation. There were parks with birds and beasts, as well as pools of fish, which were used for observation and for scientific purposes. There was a large number of structures and facilities for demonstration of and experimentation with sounds, light, colors, smells, tastes, weather conditions, machines, weapons, foods and beverages, and medicines.

The Father then detailed the variety of offices of the Fellows of Salomon's House. The Merchants of Light sailed to foreign countries and returned with books, reports, and experiments. Each of the following seven offices had three representatives. Depredators collected experiments from books. Mystery Men collected the experiments in mechanical arts and liberal sciences. Pioneers (Miners) tried the new experiments. Dowry-men (Benefactors) devised useful and practical applications from the experiments. Lamps hypothesized new experiments. Innoculators executed the new experiments devised by the Lamps. Interpreters of Nature translated the discoveries from the experiments into general principles and axioms. All of these men took an oath of secrecy and concealed or revealed their discoveries and inventions, both from the government and from the people, as they saw fit. The Father ended by briefly describing two houses called galleries, one for inventions and one for statues of inventors. The narrator then knelt before the Father—who placed his right hand on the narrator's head and blessed him—and was given permission to publish the account related by the Father.

Critical Evaluation:

This unfinished utopian novel, written between 1610 and 1624, was published within a year of Sir Francis Bacon's death by William Rawley, Bacon's chaplain and first biographer. Unlike the other visions of an ideal society to which Bacon indirectly refers (Plato's myth of Atlantis and Thomas More's *Utopia*, 1516), Bacon's vision does not emphasize new governmental and social institutions. In fact, there is only indirect mention, without explanation, of an existing government in Bensalem. The elite ruling class of the peaceful and tolerant Bensalemites consists of a society of scholars and scientists, laboring together and living by the rules of science.

The depiction of this ideal society occurs almost exclusively through monologues or dialogues between the unidentified narrator and the other three main characters (Governor, Joabin, Father). There is very little action in the story. The narrator does not tour the island or visit Salomon's House. There is, likewise, very little description of any of the characters. Apart from the rich costumes worn by the Bensalemites, Bacon offers no physical or psychological details about them. This kind of narrative approach results in flat characters who remain undeveloped and whose only role in the story is to narrate details about Bensalem and its scientific community.

Bacon adds verisimilitude in his narration in a number of ways that are traditional in utopian or science fiction stories. The use of known departure and arrival points on the journey lends credibility to the existence of an unknown island in the South Sea, especially for a seventeenth century audience who was still aware that the earth had many as yet uncharted areas. The Bensalemites have alternate, exotic names for countries: Tyrambel (Mexico) and Coya (Peru). Bacon occasionally describes Bensalemite rituals (the Feast of the Family, which honors fathers of thirty or more living descendants) and cultural customs (the slight lifting of a cane when a command is given). He offered plausible explanations—although chiefly miraculous—for the presence of Christianity on the island and for the absence of language barriers for the narrator.

As the only fictive work in his vast body of writing, Bacon's *New Atlantis* is related to the rest of his work primarily in an ideological way. As early as 1592, Bacon had outlined in a letter to Lord Burleigh, his uncle, his chief interest and desire: "I have taken all knowledge to be my province . . . [and hope to] bring in industrious observations, grounded conclusions, and profitable inventions and discoveries." Interested in reforming the state of human knowledge, Bacon opposed the Aristotelian approach of relying on authority and tradition and of basing its arguments from principles to particulars; he proposed, instead, reliance on observation and experiment as well as reasoning from particulars to general principles. In *The Advancement of Learning* (1605), Bacon surveyed the state of human knowledge in all realms of secular learning, calling attention to the lack of verified and verifiable knowledge. In his *Novum Organum* (1620), Bacon warns against the four categories of the idols of the mind, which can block a mind from arriving at truth. He also presents his new methodology, the inductive method, for philosophical investigation. According to Bacon, those who wish "to examine and dissect the nature of this very world itself . . . must go to the facts themselves for everything."

The New Atlantis, then, embodies Bacon's theories of scientific methodology outlined in his other writings. As the Father tells the narrator, the goal of Salomon's House is "knowledge of Causes and secret motions of things; and the enlarging of the bounds of Human Empire." What Bacon desired—with respect to the reformation of knowledge, the observation of nature and experimentation, and the improvement of conditions in human life—was a reality in Salomon's House. Bacon has been called "the father of modern science." Although he did not invent the inductive method, he was the first to emphasize its use and application in acquiring truth and enlarging the domain of knowledge. The fictive, idealistic scientific society outlined in his *New Atlantis*, however, was not an empty dream. William Rawley had said in the preface that this "fable" had been written "to exhibit therein a model or description of a College instituted for the interpreting of nature." In fact, Bacon's ideas have generally been acknowledged to have been a major factor in prompting the foundation of a "college of philosophy" in 1645, which later grew into the Royal Society of London for Improving Natural Knowledge in 1660. Despite the fact that the novel is an incomplete depiction of the ideal nation, Bacon's highly original vision of scientific research as a collaborative effort has become a reality in modern times.

Marsha A. Daigle-Williamson

Bibliography:
Briggs, John C. *Francis Bacon and the Rhetoric of Nature*. Cambridge, Mass.: Harvard University Press, 1989. Bacon's work seen in the light of the relationship between his scientific reform and his concepts of rhetoric, nature, and religion.

Coquillette, Daniel R. *Francis Bacon*. Stanford, Calif.: Stanford University Press, 1992. Systematic approach to Bacon's legal philosophy with analysis of the inductive method as applied to lawmaking. *The New Atlantis* analyzed from the juristic viewpoint. Thematic bibliography.

Leary, John E., Jr. *Francis Bacon and the Politics of Science*. Ames: Iowa State University Press, 1994. Study of correspondence between Bacon's conservative political ideology and his scheme for organizing science as a collective, collaborative enterprise, organized hierarchically. Most of chapter 6 devoted to political analysis of Salomon's House. Selected bibliography.

Martin, Julian. *Francis Bacon, the State, and the Reform of Natural Philosophy*. New York: Cambridge University Press, 1992. Analysis of interplay between Bacon's legal and political career and the development of his natural philosophy. Chapter 5 includes discussion of Salomon's House as part of Bacon's vision of an imperial state.

Weinberger, Jerry. *Science, Faith, and Politics: Francis Bacon and the Utopian Roots of the Modern Age*. Ithaca, N.Y.: Cornell University Press, 1985. Detailed comparison of Bensalem and Plato's republic.

NEW GRUB STREET

Type of work: Novel
Author: George Gissing (1857-1903)
Type of plot: Naturalism
Time of plot: 1880's
Locale: England
First published: 1891

Principal characters:
JASPER MILVAIN, a writer
ALFRED YULE, a literary hack
MARIAN YULE, Alfred's daughter
AMY REARDON, Alfred's niece
EDWIN REARDON, Amy's husband
DORA MILVAIN and
MAUD MILVAIN, Jasper's sisters

The Story:

There had been three Yule brothers. John, the oldest, had gone into a profitable paper manufacturing business; he abhorred the relatively impoverished state of his brother Alfred, a writer. Edmund Yule, the third brother, died, leaving only a small income to his wife, his daughter Amy, and his son John. Amy married Edwin Reardon, a man with much promise as a writer but who had little success after his first book. Jasper Milvain was Edwin's friend. Jasper spent most of his time writing small pieces for different publications and making friends among people who counted in the world of letters. He believed, as Amy did, that Edwin would some day become financially successful in his work.

Alfred Yule had married a poor woman of a lower class. Her limited education and intelligence made her a drawback to his career. An unfortunate quarrel with an editor named Fadge had caused Alfred to hate Fadge and those associated with him. When Jasper Milvain accepted his first literary appointment from Fadge, Alfred did not want to invite the young man to call at his home in London, although Marian, his daughter, wished him to do so.

Jasper's mother died, leaving his two sisters, Dora and Maud, with no means of support; so Jasper brought the girls to live with him in London. When his sisters arrived in London, Jasper called at Alfred Yule's home to ask Marian if she would become friends with them. Marian was happy to meet Dora and Maud, as she had no close friends of her own.

Because of her calls on his sisters, Jasper was able to see Marian frequently. Dora and Maud were aware of their brother's selfishness, and they viewed their new friend's affection toward Jasper with trepidation. He was looking for a rich wife to support him while he made his way in the world of letters. If Marian suspected Jasper's mercenary motives, she did not admit them to herself. Her great sorrow was that her father hated Jasper along with his enemy, Fadge. Edwin Reardon's personality was such that he succumbed easily to adversity. Amy loved her husband; when he became discouraged, she tried to push him back to work. Edwin became irritable and depended more and more for inspiration on Amy's love. They began to quarrel until they spoke few civil words to each other.

One day, Amy and Edwin realized that they would be starving within a month, for there was no hope that Edwin could produce a profitable story in time to save them. Edwin felt he could no longer write. He had been a clerk in a charitable institution before his marriage and now resumed his former occupation as a means of saving himself from ruin, both spiritual and financial. Amy was furious to think her husband would degrade himself by accepting the position of a mere clerk. She had believed that she had married a clever writer; as a clerk, Edwin did not appeal to her. Finally, they parted. Amy returned to her mother's home, and Edwin assumed his clerical job.

Jasper hesitated to become too much involved with Marian Yule. Although he found her well-suited to himself in temperament and intellect, he could not marry her because she was poor. Suddenly, fortune fell upon all these confused people. John Yule died, leaving a large sum of money to his nieces, Amy and Marian. Jasper immediately proposed to Marian. Convincing herself that Jasper's proposal came from the love he bore her rather than from her new wealth, Marian promised to marry him. Her greatest problem was to reconcile Alfred to his future son-in-law.

Amy was so stunned by the money that John had left her that at first she failed to realize her problems were at an end. The legacy would make it possible for her to return to Edwin, who could now write with no fear of poverty resulting from literary failure. Edwin, however, refused her aid. First, he was sure he had lost his ability to write. Second, his pride would not allow him to accept Amy's kindness, since he felt he had lost her love. His health broke. When he retired at last to his bed because of a serious congestion in his lungs, he would not allow his friends to tell Amy of his condition. He did not want her to come to him out of pity or through a sense of duty.

Marian soon saw Jasper's love put to a test when she learned that because of unfortunate investments she could receive only a small part of the original inheritance. Hearing the news, Jasper said they should not consider marriage until he could establish himself. Meanwhile, Alfred Yule learned his eyesight was failing; in a short while, he would be blind and incapable of earning enough money to support his wife and his daughter. Planning to retire to a small institution with his wife, he called Marian to him and told her that henceforth she must try to earn her own income in anticipation of the time when he could no longer support her.

Edwin received a telegram from Amy, asking him to come to her immediately because their son, Willie, was sick. Edwin went back to his wife. The two, in their sorrow over their son's ill health, were reconciled. Willie died, and Amy went with Edwin to nurse him in his own illness. His last few days were lightened by her cheerfulness and devotion. Jasper's situation became more uncomfortable; without her money, Marian was a luxury impossible for him to contemplate. While his sister Dora disdainfully looked on, Jasper secretly proposed to another woman of his acquaintance, a woman who had both money and connections. When the woman refused his proposal, Jasper went to Marian and insisted that she marry him immediately. Marian's blind father was now totally dependent upon her for support, so Jasper hoped to break the engagement by forcing Marian to make a decision between him and her parents. Marian desperately tried to hold the love she had always imagined that Jasper had for her. At last, however, she saw him as he really was and broke their engagement.

A posthumous publication of the works of Edwin Reardon occasioned a very complimentary criticism from the pen of Jasper Milvain, and a series of grateful letters from Amy Reardon sealed the friendship that had once existed between Jasper and the wife of his former friend. Jasper realized that he must have wealth to attain his goals in the literary world, and Amy recognized that a successful man must know how to use his social and financial advantages. They were married after a very brief courtship.

With Amy's help and with Jasper's wise manipulations, the Milvains soon achieved the success that Jasper had coldly calculated when he had proposed to Marian Yule. Shortly after their marriage, Jasper was appointed to the editorship that Fadge had vacated. With mutual admiration and joy, Jasper and Amy accepted their unexpected success in life together, both satisfied that they were perfectly mated.

Critical Evaluation:

Grub Street was a dismal London street where eighteenth century writers such as Samuel Johnson and Oliver Goldsmith earned meager livings. The name, since changed to Milton Street, came to stand for impoverished, overworked hack writers. By using "Grub Street" in his title, George Gissing implies that the profession had not improved by the late nineteenth century.

During his unhappy lifetime, Gissing produced twenty-two novels. His name was linked with such distinguished contemporaries as George Meredith and Thomas Hardy. Yet if Gissing is remembered at all, it is for his novel about literary life in Victorian England. The reason *New Grub Street* keeps Gissing's reputation aglow is that readers see its parallels with their own times. John Steinbeck said in his 1962 Nobel Prize acceptance speech, "The profession of book-writing makes horse racing seem like a solid, stable business." Gissing displays his intelligence and social awareness by creating characters who all illustrate aspects of his thesis that literary work may seem glamorous to outsiders but is in reality a dog-eat-dog business.

Alfred Yule is an example of men of mediocre talents and unrealistic ambitions who dedicate their lives to literature. Alfred never had any money, so he felt unable to marry a woman of his own class. His kindhearted but hopelessly dull wife is a millstone. They have no social life, which leads to loneliness for their daughter Marian as well. After devoting fourteen hours a day to literature, Alfred goes blind.

Marian's life is blighted by poverty. She is forced to give up any idea of marriage in order to care for her destitute parents. She comes to hate literature. "I don't know how it is in other professions," she tells a friend, "but I hope there is less envy, hatred and malice than in this of ours. The name of literature is often made hateful to me by the things I hear and read."

Dora and Maud Milvain illustrate one persistent problem with writing as a profession. They have no particular talent or great interest in literature, yet on Jasper's advice they begin producing books. The ease with which they become professionals suggests why writers will always be victims of the basic economic law of supply and demand. Too many people flood magazines and book publishers with manuscripts, creating a buyer's market.

Reardon's wife Amy represents the long-suffering wives of many aspiring freelance writers. She has to suffer the same hardships as her husband without the compensatory satisfaction of creative expression. There are still many women who fall in love with artistic men such as Edwin, only to fall out of love during the ensuing years of struggle and disappointment.

Edwin Reardon represents the many writers who fall in love with literature and dream of emulating authors who have inspired them. Like such writers, his sensitivity, introversion, and imagination render him totally "unfitted for the rough and tumble of the world's labour-market." A married man of his time needed three hundred pounds a year to support a family. Jasper shrewdly remarks, "He [Edwin] is absurd enough to be conscientious, likes to be called an 'artist'. . . . He might possibly earn a hundred and fifty a year if his mind were at rest. . . . the quality of his work would be its own reward." Edwin himself admits, "It's unlikely that I should ever have got more than two hundred pounds for a book; and to have kept at my best, I must have been content to publish once every two or three years."

Many creative writers face similar financial problems today. It is not unusual for a contemporary novelist to work one or two years on a book and receive nothing more than the publisher's advance of fifteen hundred dollars. This is why so many writers turn to Hollywood or produce potboilers full of sex and violence. Many dedicated contemporary creative writers are getting academic jobs because they realize it is nearly impossible to make a living writing poetry, short stories, or novels. Another contemporary phenomenon is that of universities' becoming heavily involved in publication of quality literature because commercial houses find it unprofitable. In the times of *New Grub Street*, however, such alternatives were not available.

Jasper Milvain, who resembles the character Mr. Worldly Wiseman in John Bunyan's *The Pilgrim's Progress* (1678), is Edwin Reardon's foil. He says of himself: "It is men of my kind who succeed; the conscientious, and those who really have a high ideal, either perish or struggle on in neglect." Jasper would be right at home in the contemporary literary marketplace, getting invited to the right parties and appearing on all the talk shows.

While Edwin sees literature as a sacred mission and is indifferent to money, Jasper sees success as a sacred mission and is indifferent to literature. Jasper understands public taste. He can turn out an article in one evening that Edwin would labor over for a month. Jasper is a success because the majority are superficial philistines such as himself.

Whelpdale, whose name has canine connotations, is another superficial opportunist who understands the mass mentality. He achieves success when he hits upon the idea of publishing a magazine with no article longer than two column inches. If he were writing in the contemporary marketplace, he would work for one of the tabloids sold at supermarket checkout counters.

Harold Biffen, the hopelessly unrealistic realist, lacks even Edwin Reardon's limited understanding of the marketplace. Gissing uses Biffen to poke mild fun at exponents of pure realism. *New Grub Street* belongs to the school of naturalism, not realism. Realism, represented by Biffen's novel about the life of a grocer, is usually dull because real life is uneventful. Most readers have always preferred romance which typically involves glamorous settings, noble motivations, adventure, and happy endings. Naturalism adds dramatic interest to realism by substituting for interpersonal conflict a sense of destinies shaped by invisible forces.

George Gissing, one of the best writers England ever produced, was overshadowed by Charles Dickens, whose genius has blinded many to the merits of Dickens' contemporaries. Gissing deserves to be better known; *New Grub Street* is an excellent starting place.

"Critical Evaluation" by Bill Delaney

Bibliography:
Coustillas, Pierre, and Colin Partridge, eds. *Gissing: The Critical Heritage*. London: Routledge & Kegan Paul, 1972. Reviews of Gissing's novels by British and American critics of his own time. Contains a generous selection of reviews of *New Grub Street* that offer insight into why Gissing did not achieve popular success.
Halperin, John. *Gissing: A Life in Books*. New York: Oxford University Press, 1982. A biography with many references to *New Grub Street*, including a discussion of its reflections of Gissing's own hardships. Contains a wealth of reference material. Illustrated with rare photographs of Gissing, his relatives, and friends.
Michaux, Jean-Pierre, ed. *George Gissing: Critical Essays*. New York: Barnes & Noble Books, 1981. Fully one-half of the book is devoted to essays about *New Grub Street*, including selections by such prominent authors as Angus Wilson, John Middleton Murry, and Gissing's great admirer and champion, George Orwell.
Selig, Robert L. *George Gissing*. Boston: Twayne, 1983. The best short book on Gissing's life and works. One chapter contains extensive discussion of *New Grub Street*. Bibliography.

Toynton, Evelyn. "The Subversive George Gissing." *American Scholar* 59 (Winter, 1990): 126-138. Discusses Gissing's works, including *New Grub Street*, in relation to Gissing's life. States that Gissing, neither a socialist nor an elitist, presents a picture of Victorian life that makes the reader reevaluate more entertaining but less realistic writers such as Charles Dickens.

THE NEW HÉLOÏSE

Type of work: Novel
Author: Jean-Jacques Rousseau (1712-1778)
Type of plot: Philosophical
Time of plot: Early eighteenth century
Locale: Switzerland
First published: Julie: Ou, La Nouvelle Héloïse, 1761 (*Julie: Or, The New Héloïse*, 1761)

Principal characters:

JULIE D'ÉTANGE, a beautiful and virtuous young woman
BARON D'ÉTANGE, her father
SAINT-PREUX, her tutor
CLAIRE, her cousin
LORD EDWARD BOMSTON, Saint-Preux's patron and benefactor
MONSIEUR DE WOLMAR, Julie's husband

The Story:

Saint-Preux, a young Swiss with unusual talents and sensibilities, was accepted by Madame d'Étange as tutor for her daughter Julie and Claire, Julie's cousin. Under Saint-Preux's instruction the women made excellent progress, until Claire went away to visit her own family, about a year after Saint-Preux had been selected as tutor. During her absence Saint-Preux revealed his love for Julie. After some solicitation, the woman admitted that she, too, was hopelessly in love. The young people viewed their situation as desperate, for the Baron d'Étange, Julie's father, had promised her as the bride of his friend, de Wolmar. In addition, the baron was a lineage-proud man who never would hear of his daughter's marriage to a commoner like Saint-Preux, regardless of the latter's abilities.

Julie feared that she might fall victim to her love for Saint-Preux; she wrote to Claire and asked her to return as a protector. She wrote to her cousin because she was afraid that Madame d'Étange, if she suspected the truth, would immediately send the young man away. Claire returned, and for a time the romance continued to blossom. At last Claire and Julie decided that Saint-Preux ought to leave until the baron returned from an absence which had kept him from home for well over a year. The women feared that he might dismiss Saint-Preux unless the way were paved by someone for the young man's continuation as tutor. Saint-Preux left. The women showed themselves off to the baron when he returned, and he was so pleased with the progress of their education that he had Saint-Preux recalled.

Once again, the love between Saint-Preux and Julie grew. In spite of her virtue, however, Julie fell victim to Saint-Preux's pleas and became his mistress. A short time later Saint-Preux was dismissed because the baron was planning to marry Julie to his friend, de Wolmar. The shock of seeing her lover depart and the news from her father that her marriage day was not far off made Julie very ill. Only a visit from Saint-Preux, smuggled into the sickroom by Claire, saved the woman's life.

After Julie's recovery there followed more than a year of surreptitious meetings between the lovers. As her passion waxed, Julie's fear of her father grew less, until she even had Saint-Preux stay with her throughout the night. Neither of the young people believed that they were committing sin, for they honestly felt that they were already married in the eyes of heaven and that only the father's attitude kept them from living together publicly and with outward virtue.

In the meantime both young people had met Lord Edward Bomston, a British peer living in Switzerland. Saint-Preux and Lord Bomston became friends, even though Lord Bomston sought Julie's hand in marriage. The peer failed, however, in his suit. One night, while he and Saint-Preux were drinking, Bomston charged that someone had already found Julie's favor. Saint-Preux challenged Lord Bomston to a duel, but Julie, mindful of her reputation, sent a letter to Lord Bomston, telling him about Saint-Preux and herself and warning him that her fate and Saint-Preux's rested in his hands. She knew that Saint-Preux would be killed and that the duel would provoke enough scandal to ruin her and drive her to suicide. Lord Bomston was moved by her plea, called off the duel, and publicly apologized to Saint-Preux. Again the two men became the firmest of friends.

Shortly afterward Lord Bomston, interceding on Saint-Preux's behalf with Baron d'Étange, urged that the baron permit a marriage between Julie and Saint-Preux. The baron refused, vowing that he would never break his promise to de Wolmar and that he never would, in any case, permit Julie to marry an adventurer. When the baron refused, Lord Bomston proposed that Julie and Saint-Preux elope to England and spend the rest of their lives as his pensioners on his estate in Oxfordshire. Julie, however, absolutely refused to leave her home without her father's consent.

In the meantime, Claire, Julie's cousin, had married a man friendly with both Lord Bomston and Saint-Preux. The tutor was forced to leave Julie's vicinity after her father had refused to permit their marriage. Through Claire's husband, however, the two lovers managed to maintain a correspondence.

Saint-Preux, after spending some months in France and England, returned to Switzerland to find that Julie was about to marry de Wolmar. He was so overcome that Lord Bomston spirited him away to England and arranged for him to embark with an expedition leaving England to travel around the world. Meanwhile, Julie reconciled herself to her father's will. Her mother, who might have permitted marriage to Saint-Preux, had recently died.

Four years passed before Saint-Preux returned to Europe. By that time Julie and her husband had two children and were settled into domestic tranquillity. De Wolmar, eager to see his wife happy, invited Saint-Preux to visit their home. During the visit it became obvious that the two lovers of years past had become more or less reconciled to their situation. Both seemed so filled with virtue that de Wolmar requested Saint-Preux to remain as tutor to his children. Saint-Preux, anxious to please everyone and to be near Julie, agreed to take on the responsibility, providing Lord Bomston did not need his services elsewhere. Saint-Preux felt that he could never adequately repay the Englishman for keeping him from crime, madness, and possible death at the time of Julie's marriage.

It turned out that Lord Bomston did need Saint-Preux's aid for a short time. The Englishman was traveling to Italy, where he had hopes of marrying a marchioness, and he wished Saint-Preux's aid in the affair. Saint-Preux, however, showed Lord Bomston that the woman was vicious and prevented the marriage; he also prevented a second attempt at marriage between the Englishman and a woman of doubtful reputation. During their absence Julie discovered that Claire, who had been widowed some time before, was in love with Saint-Preux. Hoping to help both Claire and Saint-Preux find happiness, Julie wrote to the tutor and told him of Claire's love. Saint-Preux replied that, although he esteemed Claire, he could not marry her, for he still loved Julie. Julie still hoped that she could arrange the match upon Saint-Preux's return from Italy.

Before his return an accident occurred. One day, while Julie and her family were walking alongside a lake, Julie's little boy fell in. In saving him from death, Julie suffered severe shock and exhaustion. The results were fatal to her. Before dying, however, she wrote a letter to Saint-Preux and asked him to take over the education of her children and Claire's. Her cousin, wrote Julie, would take her own place in making Saint-Preux's life complete.

Critical Evaluation:

The New Héloïse, an epistolary novel written by the most controversial thinker in Europe at the time, was composed at Montmorency, near Paris. Jean-Jacques Rousseau's memories of his passion for Sophie d'Houdetot, a countess, were still fresh in his mind. Together with the author's related dreams and fantasies, these memories became the inspiration for *The New Héloïse*. Upon its publication in 1761, the novel was an immediate success, with seventy-two editions before 1800 (many of them illustrated).

Certain themes emphasized in the novel are part of the French literary tradition. Rousseau calls attention to this fact by his choice of subtitle, *The New Héloïse*. The true story of Héloïse and Abelard is one of the most compelling that has come down from the twelfth century. Pierre (or Peter) Abelard, the most brilliant theologian of his day, was first the tutor and then the lover of Héloïse, an intelligent, highly educated young woman. Though she wished to remain his mistress, Abelard insisted on a secret marriage. When this marriage was discovered by Fulbert, Héloïse's uncle and guardian, he had Abelard castrated; Héloïse entered a nunnery. A famous exchange of letters between the two former lovers followed, in which Héloïse in particular emphasized a kind of love other than physical. Rousseau's readers were familiar with this story and would easily have seen its resemblance to that of Julie and Saint-Preux.

French literature in the Middle Ages was often world-denying and religious, but other traditions within it remained far more secular and permissive. At the time (1277), for example, that the bishop of Paris was condemning allegedly heretical doctrinal errors in a refined book of manners, Andreas Capellanus' *Art of Courtly Love* (c. 1185), a distinctly subversive and very popular erotic poem, *The Romance of the Rose* (c. 1275), was denying the sinfulness of sex between unmarried people.

A series of works in the sixteenth century, many of them reactions to Baldessar Castiglione's *Book of the Courtier* (1528), debated the proper role of women in mixed society. An especially popular long poem of 1542 found love outside of marriage acceptable. Such writings were condemned by contemporary religious writers, including John Calvin, the Protestant moralist. In France at this time, marriages were made for primarily economic, rather than emotional, reasons, with the burden of adjustment placed on the wife. Divorce did not exist until 1792, and was again abolished after the final defeat of Napoleon.

The literary form of the novel emerged in France during the 1670's. Novels quickly became a popular vehicle for the continuing debate about the proper role of the wife and her need for fulfillment. In *The Princess of Cleves* (1678), for example, written by Marie-Madeleine de Lafayette, the heroine confesses to her husband that she loves another man but nevertheless remains faithful to him as a wife. The female author of this work insisted that it was not fictitious. Most novel readers, at this time, were women, and the appropriateness of their taste in subject matter was both defended and attacked.

A more general attack, not on French women alone but on French licentiousness generally, appeared in Charles de Montesquieu's *Persian Letters* (1721), in which a fictitious Parisian visitor from the Middle East contrasts social practices in his chaste country with the habitual wickedness of the French. Like other of Montesquieu's books (his political thinking influenced the founding fathers of the United States), this one was revolutionary in its exposure of the sexual frustration and hypocrisy inherent in French society. Partly because of it, the French would later be strongly attracted to the guiltless eroticism of Tahiti.

Rousseau, then, was writing within a tradition in which the dilemma of woman's fulfillment was well known. The question underlying much of the debate was whether a wife was simply the property of her husband or someone with a destiny and potential of her own. In addition, there are many other themes and topics of importance in the work, especially the central dichotomies of passion versus reason, love versus honor, opportunity versus trust, and pleasure versus duty. Readers will also find Rousseau taking opportunities within the novel to offer opinions on a wide variety of less significant topics.

"Critical Evaluation" by Dennis R. Dean

Bibliography:
Arico, Santo L. *Rousseau's Art of Persuasion in "La Nouvelle Héloïse."* Lanham, Md.: University Press of America, 1994. A study of the novel based upon its rhetorical devices.
Babbitt, Irving. *Rousseau and Romanticism.* New York: Meridian, 1955. This famous attack on Romantic art and attitudes regards Rousseau as their originator.
Ellis, M. B. *"Julie: Ou, La Nouvelle Héloïse": A Synthesis of Rousseau's Thought (1749-1759).* Toronto: University of Toronto Press, 1949. Compares themes in the novel with ideas appearing in other writings by Rousseau.
Jones, James F., Jr. *"La Nouvelle Héloïse": Rousseau and Utopia.* Geneva, Switzerland: Droz, 1977. Concerned primarily with political implications of the novel; interesting for its Swiss perspective.
Miller, Ronald D. *The Beautiful Soul: A Study of Eighteenth-Century Idealism as Exemplified by Rousseau's "La Nouvelle Héloïse" and Goethe's "Die Leiden des Jungen Werthers."* Harrogate: Duchy Press, 1981. Compares two famous European novels of the eighteenth century with aspects of a common theme.
Pickering, Samuel, Jr. *The Moral Tradition in English Fiction, 1785-1850.* Hanover, N.H.: Published for Dartmouth College by the University Press of New England, 1976. Documents the opposition to Rousseau and his novel in England.
Stewart, Philip. *Half-Told Tales: Dilemmas of Meaning in Three French Novels.* Chapel Hill: University of North Carolina Department of Romance Languages, 1987. In English, but primarily for students of French literature.

THE NEW LIFE

Type of work: Poetry with prose comments
Author: Dante Alighieri (1265-1321)
First transcribed: La vita nuova, c. 1292 (English translation, 1861)

> In that part of the book of my mind before which there would be little to read is found a chapter heading which says: "Here begins the new life." It is my intention to copy into this little book the words I find written there; if not all of them, at least their essential doctrine.

So begins Dante Alighieri's *The New Life,* a celebration in prose and poetry of the great poet's love for Beatrice Portinari. Perhaps it is revealing to realize that this love was a poet's love; that is, Dante's love was not ordinary and practical, leading to forthright pursuit, engagement, marriage, and children. When Dante first saw Beatrice he was nine and she was eight. He was so affected by the sight of her that his "vital spirit" trembled, his "animal spirit" was amazed, and his "natural spirit" wept. At least, this is how it was if readers accept *The New Life* literally.

Dante realized that, whatever a poet's passion, such early love could hardly be convincing to anyone save the victim. After a few more sentences of praise *The New Life* proceeds to a description of an encounter nine years after the first, when Beatrice stood between two ladies and greeted Dante. It was the ninth hour of the day, and nine had already become a symbol of their love. Readers will not discover what Beatrice said, and it probably does not matter; the important thing is that her greeting inspired Dante's first poem of love for Beatrice. Readers are told that in a dream after being greeted by Beatrice, Dante had a vision of Love holding Beatrice in his arms "nude except for a scanty, crimson cloth." Holding forth a fiery object, Love said, "Behold your heart," and shortly thereafter persuaded Beatrice to eat the heart. Then Love wept and ascended toward the heavens with the lady in his arms. This dream is the subject of the poem.

We know from other sources that the poem, a sonnet, was sent to Guido Cavalcanti, who wrote a sonnet in return, initiating a strong friendship between the poets. In *The New Life* Dante merely refers to "my first friend" and quotes the beginning of a sonnet by Cavalcanti.

Dante reports that love so weakened him that everyone noticed that he was not himself. When his glances at Beatrice were misinterpreted as being directed at another lady, Dante, seizing upon the opportunity to disguise the true object of his love, pretended that the other lady was his love, and he wrote several "trifles" for her. When the lady who served as his screen left Florence on a journey, Dante knew that he should pretend to be dismayed. In fact, he was, but not from love; he was upset because his lover's scheming had been frustrated. Despite the complications, the resultant sonnet satisfied Dante, and it is included in the collection. The beginning of the sonnet reads:

> O voi che per la via d'Amor passate,
> Attendete e guardate
> S'elli e dolore alcun, quanto 'l mio, grave;
> E prego sol ch'audir mi sofferiate,
> E poi imaginate
> S'io son d'ogni tormento ostale e chiave.

A comparison of this first part of the sonnet with the translation by Mark Musa will give even those ignorant of Italian a sense of Dante's poetic genius:

O you who travel on the road of Love,
Pause here and look about
For any man whose grief surpasses mine.
I ask this only; hear me out, then judge
If I am not indeed
Of every torment keeper and shade.

Despite the attraction of Dante's poetry, it would be a mistake to take *The New Life* as primarily a collection of poems, leaving the prose passages for those interested in biography and the poet's comments on style and intent. The prose passages are charming in themselves, and they reveal an intelligent, sensitive man who is always a poet. Perhaps it is truer to say that Beatrice was for the poems, rather than the poems were for Beatrice. Readers cannot say the same of the prose; it is not merely an instrument to provide a setting for the poetry, but together with the poetry it forms an organic work of art. Dante's account of his love is so clear and ingenuous in style that it is only the cold analysts looking back on what they have read who can say that the entire affair was largely a matter of the poet's imagination extravagantly at work. Although it may have been the imagination or the animal spirit that stirred Dante, the effect created convinces that the passion was genuine (as it probably was, however engendered) and under poetic control.

Upon observing the body of a young lady who had died and was being mourned by weeping ladies, Dante suddenly realized that he had seen her in the company of the lady whom he pretended to love in order to hide his love for Beatrice. Although this knowledge means that the departed lady is two times removed from Beatrice, Dante is moved to write two sonnets about death. The first begins, "If Love himself weep, shall not lovers weep,/ Hearing for what sad cause he pours his tears?" and the second begins, "Brute death, the enemy of tenderness,/ Timeless mother of grief . . . My tongue consumes itself with cursing you."

Since the lady who had served as Dante's screen had left the city, Dante imagined that Love directed him to another lady in order that, pretending to love her, he might hide his love for Beatrice. This device, celebrated in a sonnet, was so effective that Beatrice herself must have believed the stories concerning him—rumors that he himself initiated—and one day she refused to greet him as he passed by. In the midst of Dante's grief, described in long prose passages, Love again appeared to him and told him to write a poem explaining that it was Love's idea, not Dante's, that he pretend to love someone other than Beatrice.

Several poems which follow work out the implications of Beatrice's refusal to greet him. He explains in a sonnet that Love is both good and evil—the poet's way of saying that the lover, especially a poetic one like Dante, has difficulty in staying out of trouble.

A long *canzone*, directed to ladies "refined and sensitive in Love," contains some of Dante's most effective passages. Even Love says of Beatrice, "How can flesh drawn from clay,/ Achieve such purity?" and Dante adds, "She is the highest nature can achieve/ And by her mold all beauty tests itself."

After a *canzone* on the nature of Love ("Love and the gracious heart are but one thing . . ."), Dante includes a sonnet explaining that the power of Love is awakened by Beatrice. This comparatively pleasant and romantic interlude was interrupted by the death of Beatrice's father. Two sonnets recount, with fine poetic elaboration, how Dante wept for her sorrow; but it was only after these poetic tasks and after a serious illness during which Dante realized how frail his own existence was that he finally thought, "Some day the most gracious Beatrice will surely have to die." In his delirium he imagined that Beatrice had died and that he called upon Death to take him; then the ladies at his bedside woke him. The result is a long, dramatic *canzone* in which the events of the dream are told.

One of the most entertaining of the prose sections of *The New Life* is section 25, in which Dante defends his speaking of Love as if it were a thing in itself, a bodily substance. The defense is as charming as it is sophistical. He explains that as a poet writing in the vernacular, not in Latin, it is his duty to make what he writes understandable to ladies. Since the vernacular was invented in order to talk about love, poets using the vernacular to write about love enjoy the same privileges granted to the Latin poets. Also, because Latin poets often spoke of inanimate objects as if they were beings—and Dante gives examples from Vergil, Lucan, Horace, and Ovid—Dante, as a vernacular poet writing of love, has the same right to speak of Love as if it were a human being.

In subsequent poems and prose passages Dante celebrates Beatrice's capacity to delight all persons by her presence; he explains how a word from her revives his spirit when it is overcome by Love; and he argues that her power is such that even remembering her is enough to make one feel her influence.

In section 28 Dante reveals that Beatrice has died. He explains that it would not be proper in this book to discuss the *canzone* he was writing at the time, and he then devotes section 29 to a rather involved discussion of the significance of the number nine in connection with Beatrice. Scholars know that Beatrice—who in 1285 married Simone de' Bardi—died on June 8, 1290. How, then, can Dante read the number nine into the time of her death? He argues that, counting in the Arabian fashion, she departed "during the first hour of the ninth day of the month," and using the Syrian calendar which has a first month corresponding to the Western October, she departed in the ninth month. Other ingenious calculations are used to argue that Beatrice was a miracle since nine was her number and three is its root and the Trinity is the sole factor of all miracles.

A lengthy *canzone* tells of Dante's grief, after which he presents a sonnet cleverly devised to express a brother's sorrow in the first half—for Dante later sent the poem to Beatrice's brother—and the poet's own sorrow in the second half. As he explains in the remarks prefacing the sonnet, only a person examining the sonnet carefully can tell that the dramatic speaker changes.

Dante writes that he was observed while weeping and that the young woman who observed him did so with such compassion that he wrote a sonnet to her. The sonnet was followed by another, and the second by a third, the third a self-chastisement for taking such pleasure in writing poetry for the compassionate lady.

After a few more sonnets Dante decided that he had better cease writing about Beatrice until he could honor her in his writing as no other lady had ever been honored. Readers know that this hope was not mere sentiment or poetic falsehood, for Beatrice appears again as one of the most favored of Heaven, guiding Dante through paradise in *The Divine Comedy* (c. 1320).

The New Life leaves the reader with an impression of Dante the poetic artist, constructing in his walks about Florence the ideas and lines so charmingly used in his book. Although one may be convinced that much of Dante's love was created by the artist for the sake of his poetry, there is so much skill and poetic grace in his work that the distinction between man and artist is not important.

Bibliography:
Foster, Kenelm, and Patrick Boyde, eds. and trans. *Dante's Lyric Poetry*, by Dante Alighieri. 2
  vols. Oxford, England: Clarendon Press, 1967. Includes the poems (but not the prose) of *The*

New Life, accurate English prose translations, and extensive commentary on grammatical, syntactical, thematic, and philosophical points in the poems.

Harrison, Robert Pogue. *The Body of Beatrice*. Baltimore: The Johns Hopkins University Press, 1988. Interprets *The New Life* without recourse to the narrative glosses and interpretive guidlines that Dante embedded in the prose protions of his work. Rejects Charles Singleton's theologized reading of *The New Life* for an approach focusing on the tensions inherent in the mixture of poetry and prose that constitutes Dante's work.

Mazzaro, Jerome. *The Figure of Dante: An Essay on the "Vita Nuova."* Princeton, N.J.: Princeton University Press, 1981. Studies not so much the literary content of *The New Life* as the degree to which Dante's poetry and prose reflect the poet's self-image and the changing society for which he wrote.

Musa, Mark, trans. *Vita Nuova*, by Dante Alighieri. Bloomington: Indiana University Press, 1973. Excellent translation. Musa's essay traces themes and patterns in *The New Life*. Discusses Dante's various roles in the work: narrator, editor, protagonist.

Singleton, Charles S. *An Essay on the "Vita Nuova."* Baltimore: The Johns Hopkins University Press, 1977. The most influential American study of *The New Life* written in the twentieth century. Interprets Dante's work allegorically and as a prelude to his masterpiece, *The Divine Comedy*.

A NEW WAY TO PAY OLD DEBTS

Type of work: Drama
Author: Philip Massinger (1583-1640)
Type of plot: Comedy of manners
Time of plot: Early seventeenth century
Locale: England
First performed: c. 1621-1622?; first published, 1633

Principal characters:
>FRANK WELLBORN, a prodigal young man of good family
>SIR GILES OVERREACH, Wellborn's uncle, a grasping miser
>MARGARET OVERREACH, Sir Giles's beautiful daughter
>LORD LOVELL, Margaret's suitor
>LADY ALLWORTH, a rich young widow
>TOM ALLWORTH, Lady Allworth's stepson and Lord Lovell's page
>MARRALL, a hanger-on of Sir Giles

The Story:

Frank Wellborn, who by his prodigality had gone through a fortune and lost most of his friends, was at a point where even the alehouses refused to give him food or drink. One morning, as he was about to be thrown from an alehouse, he met a young page whom he had once befriended. The boy, Allworth, offered to lend him money, but Wellborn refused, knowing how little the boy had. Allworth confided to Wellborn that he was in love with Margaret, daughter of Sir Giles Overreach, who had despoiled young Wellborn in earlier days.

Later in the morning, Wellborn went to see Allworth's widowed, wealthy young stepmother, Lady Allworth. When the lady promised to help him restore his reputation, his only request was that she receive him as a gentleman in her house. Meanwhile, Sir Giles Overreach was laying plans for his daughter's marriage, and for his own as well. After he had married Margaret to the rich Lord Lovell, he himself planned to marry Lady Allworth.

Overreach was angered to discover that Lady Allworth, who refused to be at home to him, had entertained the prodigal Wellborn as if he were a suitor. His anger was somewhat dissipated, however, by the fact that Lord Lovell was coming to visit. He realized also that if Wellborn got his hands on Lady Allworth's fortune, he, as the young man's uncle and creditor, might take it away.

Lovell, who had promised to visit Overreach's country place, knew of the love between Margaret and his page, Allworth, and he promised the page that he would do all he could to further the affair. Upon his arrival at the Overreach estate, he told Margaret of his plans, and the two pretended to carry on a courtship to deceive her father.

During Lovell's visit, Lady Allworth, accompanied by Wellborn, arrived also. Overreach, who was not in love with Lady Allworth but only desired her money, was pleased by the prospect of marrying his daughter to a nobleman and getting his hands on Lady Allworth's fortune through her possible marriage to his prodigal nephew. He even offered money to Wellborn, so that the latter could pay off his debts and appear once again as a respectable gentleman.

After the party had left Overreach's estate, Lovell released young Allworth from his position and told of further plans to help the page's suit. He intended to send the young man, ostensibly as a letter carrier, every day to the young woman.

Overreach had revealed his true character to Lovell by promising him anything if the nobleman would marry his daughter. The miser had even offered lands belonging to Lady Allworth, who was highly esteemed by Lovell. When Overreach was told that those were not his to give, he explained to Lovell how he had acquired a fortune and would accumulate another. Lovell, indignant at what he heard, promised himself to right the many wrongs Overreach had done and decided to aid young Allworth's suit. Lovell told Lady Allworth that he could never marry into the Overreach family. He added that he had an honorable motive in the pretense she had seen.

Meanwhile, the suspected marriage between Lady Allworth and Wellborn, which had no basis in fact except that she treated him as a friend, had caused Wellborn's debtors to drop their claims against him. Wellborn paid his debts, however, with the money his uncle had lent on the strength of the supposed marriage.

One of Overreach's hangers-on, Marrall, promised to help Wellborn regain his lands, which his uncle had fraudulently taken from him for a fraction of their value. Marrall told Wellborn to ask Overreach to present the deed.

At Overreach's house, young Allworth had supposedly carried a letter to Margaret, which gave him a chance to talk with her. Overreach, reading the letter, learned that Lovell asked Margaret to marry him forthwith. Overjoyed, the miser sent a letter of command to his manor priest, telling the chaplain to marry Margaret to the gentleman who accompanied her with the letter. The young people went off and were immediately married, the letter acting as a means of getting the clergyman to perform the private ceremony.

Lady Allworth told Lovell that she had helped Wellborn to regain his former position because Wellborn had aided her dead husband in years gone by. With that action made clear, Lovell asked her to marry him. Lady Allworth consented. A short time later, Overreach appeared, driving Marrall before him and questioning him about a document that had disappeared. Overreach was also hunting for his daughter, who had failed to return home the night before. In his anger, Overreach asked for the thousand pounds he had lent to Wellborn. Wellborn, in turn, demanded an accounting of his estates. Overreach took his strongbox and removed a parchment that proved to be only a sealed paper with no writing on it. Marrall had removed the true deed.

Overreach realized that he no longer had any legal right to Wellborn's lands. His daughter and young Allworth, married the day before, then arrived to tell of their marriage, in which Overreach had unconsciously aided them by sending a letter to his clergyman.

Overreach, angered beyond measure, would have killed his daughter with his sword, had not Lovell stopped him. Lord Lovell then announced his intended marriage to Lady Allworth and promised to speed the unraveling of Overreach's affairs so that Wellborn could regain his estates, and Margaret and her husband could have their rightful portion of the miser's wealth.

Critical Evaluation:

Although a prolific and workmanlike playwright, Philip Massinger never achieved an outstanding individual style strong enough to distinguish him among his contemporaries or in theatrical history. After studying at Oxford, Massinger wrote plays in collaboration with Cyril Tourneur, John Fletcher, and Thomas Dekker; later he served for fifteen years as the principal playwright for William Shakespeare's old company, the King's Men. *A New Way to Pay Old Debts*, having remained popular over time, is his claim to enduring fame.

The plot, although not particularly original, is lively. The formula of the play, trickery to fool a criminal, was not a new one with Massinger, but he gave his theme dramatic interest and clever satire. The new way to pay old debts is credit, seen in the actions of Lady Allworth, which enables the prodigal Wellborn to establish himself once again in the respectable world after having been cozened by his uncle. The character of Sir Giles Overreach, a favorite with lead actors, was probably based on Sir Giles Mompessen (1584-1651), a famous extortioner of seventeenth century England who had commissions from James I for controlling licenses to innkeepers. His crimes were discovered, and he and his legal associate Francis Michel (Marrall in the play), were prosecuted and convicted a decade before the play appeared.

The themes of this comedy of manners are no more complicated than the plot, but they are valid and convincingly handled. Overreach represents the senseless desire to attain nobility, a desire that is paradoxical when accompanied by his disdain of the nobility's inability to fend successfully for themselves in the mercantile world. Lovell is pitted against Sir Giles; birth and inherited riches are set against wealth won by individual industry. Overreach's complete lack of principle and scruples contrasts him with Lovell, but also makes him a more interesting character. The scene between father and daughter is a clear presentation of the grasping man's willingness to make any means practicable for a determined end: "End me no ends," her father tells Margaret in Act V, scene i, echoing his words in Act III, scene ii, "Virgin me no virgins!" Massinger neatly emphasizes the way in which Overreach—through the complicity of Greedy—sets about corrupting the law he professes, to suit his vicious purpose. The avarice at the heart of the action is a satirical reflection of the central motivation of contemporary society as Massinger views it.

Overreach is the main character, whose forceful personality dominates the stage even when he is not there. Scenes without him pale in dramatic interest by comparison; audiences wait for him to return, to outrage them again. His explanation to Margaret recalls Christopher Marlowe's Barabas (in *The Jew of Malta*, 1633): "Wasn't not to make thee great/ That I have now, and still pursue, those ways/ That hale down curses on me, which I mind not?" Margaret, however, is nothing more to her father than an object, a pawn he can move to his own will. Nobility of blood means nothing to her, but everything to him, who can never know it. He is so vulgar that he has no understanding even of the spiritual nobility Margaret strives to maintain in the face of his demands that she prostitute herself to Lovell: "Stand not on form," he tells her in an echo of Falstaff, "words are no substances." Just as Greedy values only what he can taste, Overreach treasures only what he can touch and reach physically. His relationship with Marrall, as it unfolds, proves that there is not even honor among thieves in their world. His bombastic boorishness is reflected with perfect irony when, expecting Lovell, he asks of Marrall, "Is the loud music I gave order for/ Ready to receive him?" In his uncultured opinion, the louder the music is, the more impressive it is. His brazen, pompous overtures to Lovell in Act IV shock even jaded sensibilities; he and the nobleman clearly are two entirely different kinds of people, and the audience may wonder uneasily who it is more like. The catharsis occurs shortly thereafter, when young Allworth manages to gull Sir Giles with one of his own characteristic legal tricks: "Good Master Allworth,/ This shall be the best night's work you ever made." The play continues with the pathetic spectacle of Overreach's fiscal and mental dissolution, until he is carried away in the outward shambles that finally correspond to his inner moral state.

Not nearly as interesting are the other characters, although Justice Greedy is unforgettably entertaining as a "compleat glutton." Self-styled "arch-president of the boil'd, the roast, the bak'd," he is epitomized by Furnace: "His stomach's as insatiate as the grave." It is one of the most delightful comic ironies of the play that Greedy cannot eat the dinner he prepares with such anxiety lest the fawn not be roasted with "a Norfolk dumpling in its belly." Revolving around Greedy are the uniformly sympathetic ordinary characters of Lady Allworth's cooks, butlers, and household attendants. By comparison with her servants, the lady herself is flat and uninteresting. Her advice to Allworth, in fact an uncannily accurate memory of her husband's dying advice to his son, makes her sound like a latter-day Polonius: "Beware ill company, for often men/ Are like to those with whom they do converse." She, like the nondescript Lovell, is as dramatically superficial as she is morally shallow; she is worried more about appearances than realities, the very opposite of Overreach. In her own subtle way she sells herself to Lovell as Overreach would have Margaret do.

Her son, too, is almost tiresomely virtuous, at his worst when he vows to his mother that he will serve Lovell loyally. She is all too right in calling him "like virgin parchment, capable of any/ Inscription" and one might wish that he were inscribed with more vivid ink. One of the great laughs of the play is Lovell's reaction to Allworth's simpering reception of his commission: "Nay, do not melt." Wellborn has at least a streak of the devil in him to make him interesting, although he does not have the dramatic force one would expect from the pivotal figure in the plot. His undisclosed whispering to Lady Allworth in Act I, scene iii, sets in motion the wheels that lead to the downfall of Overreach by his own trickery. More successful is the character of Marrall, who has the virtue of being a thoroughly despicable parasite without the partially redeeming, intelligent self-irony of Ben Jonson's Mosca. Marrall is a low-class person out of his depth; this is portrayed riotously in Amble's report of his toasting the lady "in white broth" and humbly thanking "my worship" for serving him wine. Marrall ends up as an exaggerated caricature of his own meanness as he offers to let Wellborn ride upon his own back and says, over-elaborately, "an it like your worship,/ I hope Jack Marrall shall not live so long/ To prove himself such an unmannerly beast . . ./ As to be cover'd/ When your worship's present." The audience has no more sympathy for him than Wellborn does and is delighted when Wellborn, having paid his own old debts with credit, cancels Marrall's credit rating as the knave deserves.

"Critical Evaluation" by Kenneth John Atchity

Bibliography:
Ball, Robert Hamilton. *The Amazing Career of Sir Giles Overreach.* New York: Octagon Books, 1968. A detailed stage history. Offers a biography of Sir Giles Mompessen, on whom Overreach is based. Examines the play's production history in Great Britain and the United States.

Clark, Ira. "Massinger's Tragedies and Satiric Tragicomedies in Their Social and Family Settings." In *The Moral Art of Philip Massinger.* Cranbury, N.J.: Bucknell University Press, 1993. Opposes critics who see the play as a conservative attack on social mobility. Finds the play validates a social hierarchy based on gratitude, community service, and ability.

Leonard, Nancy S. "Overreach at Bay: Massinger's *A New Way to Pay Old Debts.*" In *Philip Massinger: A Critical Reassessment*, edited by Douglas Howard. Cambridge, Mass.: Cambridge University Press, 1985. Characterizes the play as a revenge comedy, in which both Overreach and the nobility appeal to ideological positions to rationalize self-serving displays of power.

Neill, Michael. "Massinger's Patriarchy: The Social Vision of *A New Way to Pay Old Debts.*" *Renaissance Drama*, n.s. 10 (1979): 185-213. Argues for a conservative reading of the play, which characterizes the patriarchal hierarchy as a supportive family. Overreach, a combination of biblical patriarch and Renaissance "new man," threatens this ideal by treating social relationships as financial transactions.

Thomson, Patricia. "The Old Way and the New Way in Dekker and Massinger." *The Modern Language Review* 51, no. 2 (April, 1956): 168-178. Contrasts Massinger's play with *The Shoemaker's Holiday* (1600) and finds the difference between them rooted in the sociopolitical developments of Stuart England. Offers valuable background insight into Massinger's life.

THE NEWCOMES
Memoirs of a Most Respectable Family

Type of work: Novel
Author: William Makepeace Thackeray (1811-1863)
Type of plot: Social morality
Time of plot: Early nineteenth century
Locale: England
First published: 1853-1855

> *Principal characters:*
> COLONEL THOMAS NEWCOME, an Anglo-Indian soldier
> CLIVE, his son
> BRIAN and
> HOBSON, his half brothers
> LADY ANN, Brian's wife
> BARNES, Brian's son
> ETHEL, Brian's daughter
> LADY KEW, Lady Ann's mother
> JAMES BINNIE, the colonel's friend
> MRS. MACKENZIE, Binnie's half sister
> ROSEY, Mrs. Mackenzie's daughter
> LADY CLARA, Barnes's wife

The Story:

The elder Thomas Newcome married his childhood sweetheart, who died after bearing their son, who was named after him. Thomas remarried, and his second wife bore two sons, Brian and Hobson. Young Thomas proved to be a trial to his stepmother and when he was old enough was sent to India, where he later became a colonel. He married and had a son, Clive, whom he loved with a passion far beyond the normal devotion of a father. Having lost his mother, little Clive was sent to England to begin his education.

Brian and Hobson Newcome had inherited their mother's wealthy banking house. Brian married Lady Ann, who was well known in London for her lavish parties. When little Clive had spent about seven years in England, his impatient father crossed the ocean to join him. He expected to receive a warm welcome from his two half brothers, Brian and Hobson. Much to his bewilderment, the bankers received him politely but coldly and passed on the responsibility of entertaining him to young Barnes, Brian's son, a social gadfly and a familiar figure in London's clubs.

Colonel Thomas Newcome's late wife had a sister and a brother. The sister, Miss Honeyman, ran a boardinghouse in Brighton, where little Alfred and Ethel came with their mother, Lady Ann, for a vacation; Colonel Newcome and Clive also arrived for a visit. The brother, Mr. Honeyman, also lived in Brighton, where the keeper's young son, John James Ridley, delighted in drawing pictures from the storybooks that he found in Mr. Honeyman's room. Clive, who aspired to be an artist, delighted in Ridley's drawings; Ethel became extremely fond of the colonel and his unaffected manner. The colonel's great love for children caused him to be a favorite with all the Newcome youngsters, but it was fair-haired little Ethel who won his heart with her simple, adoring ways and her sincerity.

Colonel Newcome bought a house in London, where he lived with Clive and Mr. James Binnie, the colonel's friend. Clive was given a tutor, but the young man neglected his studies to sketch. If the colonel was disappointed by Clive's choice of career, he said nothing and allowed Clive to attend art school with his friend Ridley. Clive was becoming a kind, generous, and considerate young man, and the colonel himself was satisfied that his son was growing up to be a fine man. He spent a considerable amount of money setting up a well-lighted studio for Clive in a house not far from his own. Meanwhile, Mr. Binnie had taken a fall from a horse and was laid up in bed. Binnie's widowed half sister, Mrs. Mackenzie, and her daughter, Rosey, came to stay with the bedridden Binnie in the colonel's house.

After a time, the colonel found himself financially embarrassed. Realizing that he could no longer live on his income in London, he planned to return to India until he reached a higher grade in the army. Then with a higher pension he would be able to afford to retire in London.

Ethel Newcome grew into a beautiful and charming young lady, and the colonel dreamed of a match between Ethel and Clive; Lady Ann, however, placed an early prohibition on such a match. She told her brother-in-law that Ethel had been promised to Lord Kew, a relative of Lady Kew, Lady Ann's mother. The other Newcomes thought that Rosey Mackenzie would be a fine wife for Clive.

After Colonel Newcome had returned to India, leaving Clive with a substantial income, Clive and Ridley, now a successful artist, went to Baden. There Clive met Ethel and the other Newcome children, who were vacationing without the dampening presence of Lady Ann or her aristocratic mother. Ethel and Clive enjoyed a short period of companionship and innocent pleasure, and Clive fell in love with his beautiful cousin. When Lady Ann and Lady Kew arrived, Clive was warned that he must not press his suit with Ethel any longer, for Ethel must marry in her own station of life. Clive was reminded that the family had assumed him to have found a woman of his own social level in Miss Rosey Mackenzie. Clive bitterly took his leave and went to Italy with Ridley.

Ethel was beginning to rebel against the little niche that had been assigned to her in society, and she defied social custom and defended Clive against the charges her brother Barnes repeatedly brought against him. Finally, she broke her engagement to young Lord Kew. When Clive heard of it, he returned to England to press his own suit once more.

In London, Clive had little time for his art, for he quickly became a favorite in London society, whose fashionable hostesses thought him the only son of a wealthy officer in India. Against the wishes of her grandmother, Lady Kew, Ethel arranged frequent meetings with Clive. When Clive at last proposed marriage to her, she sadly explained to him that she would not inherit Lady Kew's fortune unless she married properly. Ethel told him that her younger brothers and sisters needed the money, for after her father's death, Barnes Newcome had selfishly kept the family fortune for himself. Meanwhile, Lady Kew was wooing Lord Farintosh for Ethel.

After three years' absence, Colonel Newcome returned to London. During his absence, the colonel had amassed a large fortune for his son. Armed with this wealth, Colonel Newcome went to Barnes with a proposal of marriage between Ethel and Clive. Barnes was polite but noncommittal. Shortly afterward, Lady Kew announced Ethel's engagement to Lord Farintosh. Then, suddenly, Lady Kew died, leaving her immense fortune to Ethel, whose only concern was that the money should go to her younger brothers and sisters.

Barnes's marriage to Lady Clara had never been a happy one. Soon after they were married, he had begun to mistreat his wife, who at last decided that she could no longer stand his bullying treatment and ran off with a lover, leaving her small children behind. The shock of the scandal and the subsequent divorce opened Ethel's eyes to the dangers of loveless marriages. Realizing that she could never be happy with Lord Farintosh because she did not love him, she broke her second engagement.

Ethel retired from her life in society to rear Barnes's children. Clive, meanwhile, had succumbed to the wishes of Mr. Binnie and his own father. Before the news of Ethel's broken engagement with Lord Farintosh had reached the colonel and his son, Clive had married sweet-faced Rosey Mackenzie. Clive's marriage was gentle but bare. The colonel was Rosey's chief protector and her greater admirer. Clive tried to be a good husband, but inwardly he longed for more companionship. Once he admitted to his father that he still loved Ethel.

The colonel had been handling the family income very unwisely since his return from India. Shortly after the birth of Clive's son, Thomas, an Indian company in which the colonel had heavy investments failed, and he went bankrupt. Clive, Rosey, and colonel Newcome were now nearly penniless. Rosey's mother, Mrs. Mackenzie, descended upon them and began ruling them with such tyranny that life became unbearable for the colonel. With the help of some friends, he retired to a poorhouse and lived separated from his beloved son. Clive, who faithfully stayed with Rosey and his abusive mother-in-law, was able to make a meager living by selling his drawings.

When Ethel learned of the pitiful condition of the old colonel, whom she had always loved, and of Clive's distress, she contrived a plan whereby she was able to give them six thousand pounds without their knowing that it came from her. Rosey had been very ill. One night, Ethel visited Clive, and Mrs. Mackenzie raised such an indignant clamor that Rosey was seriously affected. She died the following day. The colonel was broken in spirit and grew weaker by the day; soon afterward, he too died.

Clive had never lost his love for Ethel through all the years of his unfortunate marriage to Rosey. Many months after the death of his wife, he went once more to Baden with little Thomas. There it was said, by observers who knew the Newcomes, that Clive, Ethel, and little Tommy were often seen walking together through the woods.

Critical Evaluation:

"I am about a new story," William Makepeace Thackeray wrote an American friend shortly after his first visit to the United States (1852-1853), "but don't know as yet if it will be any good. It seems to me I am too old for story-telling." At the age of forty-three, with the success of *Vanity Fair* (1847-1848), *The History of Pendennis* (1848-1850), and *The History of Henry Esmond, Esquire, a Colonel in the Service of Her Majesty Q. Anne* (1852) behind him, Thackeray's strength was ebbing, and to his friends he had the physical appearance of an old man broken in health. Because, however, he needed money (his own estimate was the equivalent of twenty thousand dollars), he began writing *The Newcomes*. He wrote while living in various places in Italy, Germany, and Switzerland, and throughout the project he was often in ill health. The novel was published serially between October, 1853, and August, 1855. Extensive even by Victorian standards, *The Newcomes* is a typical mid-nineteenth century family chronicle, replete with cogent observations of manners and morals. Despite its gentle comedy, it satirizes the human follies that Thackeray particularly scorned: snobbery, greed, and misguided romantic idealism.

The chronicle is narrated by Arthur Pendennis, an older friend of Clive Newcome, who purports to "edit" the memoirs of "a most respectable family." At first a mere spokesman for the author, Pendennis gradually becomes a character in his own right, participating in as well as commenting on the action. Prudish, smug, and whimsical, Pendennis provides ironical insight into the other characters. His admiration for Colonel Newcome ("so chivalrous, generous, good looking") is uncritical to the point that it becomes amusing. Moreover, his fulminations on folly, especially in the famous parody of moral anecdotes in chapter 1, ring hollow at last, in view of the narrator's own punctilious regard for class and status, his social snobbery, and his moralizing.

As is typical of Thackeray's fiction, the novel's heroes and heroines (Colonel Thomas Newcome, his son Clive, and Ethel and Rosey) are true-blue, the villains (Barnes Newcome, Lady Kew, and Mrs. Mackenzie) quite dastardly; yet even some of the unpleasant characters are redeemed, if not always completely successfully, by the author's pity. After Barnes Newcome, the colonel's longtime nemesis, is humiliated in the family election, he promises not to mistreat his wife any longer and finally comes to terms with Clive. The coldhearted Lady Kew leaves the bulk of her estate to Ethel. Ethel herself, psychologically the most interesting personality in the book, develops from a charming but calculating young lady to a woman capable of self-sacrifice and deep love. Unlike Rosey, who is simple, innocent, but vacuous, Ethel is sophisticated and clever. Her virtue is tested by life and consequently earned. She becomes a worthy mate for Clive, and the tender-hearted author promises his readers that the couple will be both happy and wealthy.

Clive too must earn the reader's approval. Spoiled by his doting father, he makes the most of his good looks, his modest talents as an artist, and the honorable reputation of his family. His young manhood, however, is spent in prodigality. Thwarted in his desire to marry Ethel, he chooses the sweet but dull Rosey Mackenzie and then chafes at the restraints of wedlock. Nevertheless, like Ethel, he is educated by life, learns his limitations, and grows in self-respect. In chapter 68, the emotional climax of the novel, Clive and his father come to regard each other as equals without recriminations and with mutual respect and affection. Clive comes into his own as a person of worth and a true gentleman.

The Newcomes is a social novel of manners that teaches the Victorian reader how to recognize and, if possible, become a true gentleman or gentlewoman. Colonel Newcome, the epitome of English gentility, is almost too perfect, that is to say, too proper, innocent, and augustly virtuous; his very rectitude becomes a subject for unconscious satire. Some of Thackeray's reviewers detected in the author's creation of the colonel an element of cynicism; one London critic went so far as to attack the book on the grounds of "morality and religion." Thackeray's avowed intention, however, was certainly not to satirize the true gentleman and his outmoded virtues but rather to expose the parvenu, the snob, and the ingrate. He ridicules the upstart middle-class, especially Anglo-Indian, society by revealing it to be ill-bred, vulgarly assertive, and graspingly materialistic.

The thrust of Thackeray's satire is above all toward women. Barnes Newcome is a rascal, to be sure, but not a fool; Thackeray's obnoxious women, however, manipulate their men and lead them into folly, either through aggressiveness or their simpering, smiling domestic tyranny. "Theirs is a life of hypocrisy," concludes Pendennis, speaking for his author, and their chief wile is flattery. Even Ethel, the virtuous and clever heroine, does not wholly escape Thackeray's censure. When he criticizes her for prolonging her romance with Clive, he attributes her weakness to a fault of her sex rather than to a personal folly. Rosey, Clive's unfortunate wife, never transgresses the social prohibitions but is, like Amelia of *Vanity Fair*, a foolish innocent, to be protected and cherished like a pet. Her opposite is her mother, Mrs. Mackenzie, a mean and fearful specimen of womankind.

The reader's final impression of *The Newcomes* is not one of abrasive social satire but rather one of reconciliation. At the end of the novel, Ethel and Clive are reunited and the good Colonel

Newcome dies as nobly as he had lived in a scene that is touching in its restrained dignity. The reader is left hoping that the Newcome family, despite their human folly, will endure. To Thackeray, that hope—"Fable-land"—is the harmless anodyne to the pain of living.

"Critical Evaluation" by Leslie B. Mittleman

Bibliography:

Ferris, Ina. "The Way of the World: *The Newcomes.*" In *William Makepeace Thackeray,* edited by Herbert Sussman. Boston: Twayne, 1983. Includes brief commentaries by Thackeray's contemporaries, as well as one by Thackeray himself. Discusses Thackeray's self-conscious realism and the way in which his fiction responded to the society in which he lived.

Harden, Edgar F. *The Emergence of Thackeray's Serial Fiction.* Athens: University of Georgia Press, 1979. Discussion of the serial structure of five novels, including *The Newcomes,* with particular focus on Thackeray's manuscripts and his compositional process. Explains how the serial installments shaped the forms of the novels.

Hardy, Barbara. *The Exposure of Luxury: Radical Themes in Thackeray.* Pittsburgh, Pa.: University of Pittsburgh Press, 1972. Discusses aspects of Thackeray's social criticism and points out themes that illustrate his preoccupation with the surface manners of his society. Concludes that self-consciousness and lack of moral optimism are closely related as aspects of Thackeray's radical thinking.

Ray, Gordon. *The Buried Life: A Study of the Relation Between Thackeray's Fiction and His Personal History.* Cambridge, Mass.: Harvard University Press, 1952. Comprehensive biocritical study of Thackeray's state of mind while writing the novel. An excellent resource for the serious researcher.

_____. "*The Newcomes.*" In *Thackeray: A Collection of Critical Essays,* edited by Alexander Welsh. Englewood Cliffs, N.J.: Prentice-Hall, 1968. Discusses the structural importance in the novel of the main themes, as well as how Thackeray reflects his disillusionment with his world.

NEWS FROM NOWHERE

Type of work: Novel
Author: William Morris (1834-1896)
Type of plot: Utopian
Time of plot: Late nineteenth century; twenty-first century
Locale: London, along the Thames River
First published: News from Nowhere: Or, An Epoch of Rest, Being Some Chapters from a Utopian Romance, 1891

> *Principal characters:*
> GUEST, the narrator
> RICHARD "DICK" HAMMOND, a boatman
> OLD HAMMOND, Dick's great-grandfather
> CLARA, Dick's fiancée
> ELLEN, a young woman whom Guest finds attractive

The Story:

One evening after a public meeting and political discussion, the narrator returned by train to his home in the London suburb of Hammersmith. When he awoke the next morning from a deep sleep and went to swim in the Thames River, he was amazed to find that the industrial buildings had been transformed into a pastoral landscape. Encountering a boatman named Dick, who was dressed in simple but attractive fourteenth-century-style garb, he began to question him and realized that he had been transported to an England of the twenty-first century.

Dick took the narrator, whom he called Guest, to breakfast in the Guest House at Hammersmith, which resembled a medieval hall. There they met Robert (Bob), the weaver, and Boffin, the dustman, who asked Guest many questions. A pleasant woman named Annie served their food. After breakfast, Guest and Dick went by horse carriage to visit Dick's great-grandfather, Old Hammond, who lived by the British Museum in the Bloomsbury district of London. As they rode through London, Guest marveled at the open-air markets, the attractive architecture, and the wooded areas and gardens that had replaced the tenements and industrial buildings of the nineteenth century.

Guest observed the playful children and Dick told him that they did not attend school but learned as their curiosity led them. Guest and Dick stopped at one of the small shops where Guest received an elaborately carved pipe from two polite children who were tending the shop. As when he had first tried to pay Dick, Guest found that money was not exchanged because it was unnecessary in this society. Guest also discovered that there were no prisons, since everyone was honest and had an occupation.

When they arrived at the square in front of the British Museum, Dick escorted Guest to the living quarters of his great-grandfather, Old Hammond. A young woman named Clara appeared. She and Dick, who were obviously very much attracted to each other, retired to the upstairs room. Old Hammond explained to Guest that the couple had been married, had two children, and had grown apart, but that they were getting back together. In this new England, Nowhere, there was no such thing as divorce since a court was unable to enforce "a contract of passion or sentiment."

Guest and Old Hammond talked for some time. Because of Old Hammond's advanced years, he could answer many of Guest's questions about the striking changes that had occurred in England since the late nineteenth century. He told Guest about the freer and more equal

4460

relationships between men and women, the less structured education of children, and the fresh new appearance of London and its environs after the "big murky places" that were "centres of manufacture" had been removed. Old Hammond explained to Guest how people had left London for country villages that had become peaceful, thriving communities.

Many of Guest's questions related to the way government operated. Old Hammond told him that formal governmental institutions no longer existed because the people lived and worked in harmony with nature and themselves. The two men also spoke about labor, production, and trade. Old Hammond recalled how the new order had come about after an uprising of the people had overthrown the government.

In the evening, Dick and Clara drove Guest back to Hammersmith Guest House, where they had dinner and spent the night. The next morning, the three of them began a journey by boat up the Thames River. Their destination was an area past Oxford where they planned to work at the hay harvest. As they traveled, they observed the beautiful landscape with cottages and people working in the fields, orchards, and forests. They made several stops, first at Hampton Court, the former Tudor royal palace, which was preserved as a museum. The first evening they lodged at Runnymede with an old man who was nostalgic for past times, and his granddaughter, a beautiful, vivacious woman named Ellen.

After a second day observing the sights along the river, the trio spent the night with Walter Allen, one of Dick's friends, who regretfully reported that an unusual altercation between two men had resulted in a murder. On the third day, they stopped to look at a house being built of stone with sculptured reliefs. At Wallingford where they ate lunch, they talked with an old man, Henry Morsom, about arts and handicrafts. As they left again, Ellen caught up with them in a boat. Guest, who found Ellen very attractive, joined Ellen in her boat, while Dick and Clara continued in theirs.

As the two couples continued up the Thames, Guest and Ellen had a chance to observe the beautiful June landscape. Ellen asked many questions about the state of things in the nineteenth century and about the history of the river. When they reached their destination on the upper Thames, the travelers were greeted by a crowd of haymakers. Ellen took Guest to an old stone barn and together they explored the simple beauty of its architecture and sparse furnishings. Guest reflected on the contrasts between the past, present, and future. Ellen rejoiced in her love for the earth, nature, and the seasons.

They went to dinner with the haymakers in a church that was festively decorated with flowers. Suddenly, Guest realized that he had become invisible to Dick, Clara, and Ellen. He walked down the road and encountered a decrepit old man. He himself seemed to be enveloped in a black cloud, and when he awoke he was back in his familiar house in his own century. He concluded that he had experienced a vision rather than a dream, and that he should continue to strive to communicate to others the ideals of the society he had envisioned in his visit to Nowhere.

Critical Evaluation:

A utopian romance is an apt description for this novel; it combines a description of life in "Nowhere"—an ideal England at some future time—with some of the conventions of a medieval romance.

News from Nowhere can be considered an appropriate summation of William Morris' gifts and preoccupations. He was a prolific writer in Victorian England, whose verses, epics, and romances show the influence of medieval literature. He united his literary and design interests when he established Kelmscott Press with the goal of producing well-designed books. He was a staunch advocate of architectural preservation and opposed romantic restoration. Most of his income came from a design firm that produced stained glass, architectural ornaments, furniture, and textiles. Finally, he was a socialist and became actively involved in politics during the later years of his life.

The common thread that joined Morris' diverse activities was his idealism. He believed in good design principles, which he thought were being undermined by mass production and the use of machines. His socialist political views were a protest against the degrading working conditions that industrialization had brought about. He believed in the personal integrity and fulfillment of good craftsmanship. What attracted him to the Middle Ages was his perception that his aesthetic, individual, and communal ideals were embodied in that culture. Morris expressed his convictions in all of the many forms in which he worked.

In *News from Nowhere*, the narrator, who receives the name of Guest, is a thinly disguised self-portrait. When the narrator is asked his name at breakfast at the Guest House at Hammersmith, he replies that he should be called William Guest. The reader first encounters him leaving a political meeting where a socialist agenda had been under discussion. As he returns home he makes a point of noting his distaste for the grimy late nineteenth century surroundings in which he lives.

Guest's utopian dream vision weaves together four main elements of Morris' interests: his socialist politics, his aesthetic sensibilities, his medievalism, and his feeling for the natural environment. He envisions a society where people live in harmony with one another and are free from governmental restrictions. Individuals can pursue occupations that are related to their own interests and talents at the same time that they benefit the larger community. Throughout the book, detailed and vividly drawn descriptions of architecture, clothing, decor, and objects such as Guest's new pipe reveal Morris' admiration for fine design and craftsmanship. The aesthetic models are based on Morris' concept of the Middle Ages, particularly the late medieval period, which began to show the use of natural ornament to enliven the construction of buildings and to decorate furnishings, fabrics, and books. Morris' delight in the natural environment is most fully depicted in the journey along the Thames River. In his descriptions of the city and the countryside, he contrasts the unspoiled beauty of nature with the environmental degradation found in Victorian England.

Critics have pointed out that in *News from Nowhere* Morris fails to clarify many aspects of his utopian community and that he focuses on an idealized reverence for the past instead of on innovative ideas for the future. For example, Morris extols the value of human industry and craftsmanship but uses machine technology where convenient, as in the system of locks that facilitates boat traffic along the Thames. Judging the work by literary criteria, critics have noted that some chapters create abrupt juxtapositions, probably because the work was originally published in serial form in the journal *Commonweal*. The political discussion that occupies much of the first half has a static quality to it, while the description of the journey along the Thames resembles a travelogue.

These drawbacks notwithstanding, *News from Nowhere* remains an eloquent summation of Morris' beliefs and ideals. His utopian vision is not accompanied by completely realized solutions, but he affirms the value and integrity of human endeavor. His respect for nature, which takes the form of evocatively beautiful descriptions, reveals an understanding of the ecological balance between human needs and those of the environment. These qualities give *News from Nowhere* a timeless and universal theme.

Karen Gould

Bibliography:

Aho, Gary L. *William Morris: A Reference Guide*. Boston: G. K. Hall, 1985. A comprehensive guide to studies about William Morris through 1982, with numerous references to *News from Nowhere*.

Faulkner, Peter. *Against the Age: An Introduction to William Morris*. London: George Allen and Unwin, 1980. A concise discussion of the multifaceted work of William Morris. Places *News from Nowhere* in the context of Morris' other writings and activities.

Kirchhoff, Frederick. *William Morris*. Boston: Twayne, 1979. A study of William Morris that concentrates on his literary works. *News from Nowhere* is discussed in the context of Morris' socialism.

Lindsay, Jack. *William Morris: His Life and Work*. London: Constable, 1975. A thorough and readable biography of William Morris.

Silver, Carole. *The Romance of William Morris*. Athens: Ohio University Press, 1982. A study of Morris' prose romances; includes a chapter on *News from Nowhere*.

THE NIBELUNGENLIED

Type of work: Poetry
Author: Unknown
Type of plot: Epic
Time of plot: c. 437
Locale: North-central Europe
First transcribed: c. 1200

Principal characters:
SIEGFRIED, the son of Siegmund and Sieglind
KRIEMHILD, a Burgundian princess and Siegfried's wife
GUNTHER,
GERNOT, and
GISELHER, the brothers of Kriemhild
HAGEN, their retainer
BRUNHILD, the wife of Gunther
ETZEL (ATTILA), Kriemhild's second husband
DANKWART, Hagen's brother

The Story:

In Burgundy there lived a noble family that numbered three brothers and a sister. The sons were Gunther, who wore the crown, Gernot, and Giselher. The daughter was Kriemhild. About them was a splendid court of powerful and righteous knights, including Hagen of Trony, his brother Dankwart, and mighty Hunold. Kriemhild dreamed one night that she reared a falcon that then was slain by two eagles. When she told her dream to Queen Uta, her mother's interpretation was that Kriemhild should have a noble husband but that unless God's protection followed him he might soon die.

Siegfried was born in Niderland, the son of King Siegmund and Queen Sieglind. In his young manhood he heard of the beautiful Kriemhild, and, although he had never seen her, he determined to have her for his wife. Undeterred by reports of her fierce and warlike kinsmen, he made his armor ready for his venture. Friends came from all parts of the country to bid him farewell, and many of them accompanied him as retainers into King Gunther's land. When he arrived at Gunther's court, Hagen, who knew his fame, told the brothers the story of Siegfried's first success, relating how Siegfried had killed great heroes and had won the hoard of the Nibelung, a treasure of so much gold and jewels that five score wagons could not carry all of it. He also told how Siegfried had won the cloak of invisibility from the dwarf Albric and how Siegfried had become invulnerable from having bathed in the blood of a dragon he had slain. Gunther and his brothers admitted Siegfried to their hall after they had heard of his exploits, and the hero stayed with them a year. In all that time, however, he did not once see Kriemhild.

The Saxons, led by King Ludger, threatened to overcome the kingdom of the Burgundians. Siegfried pledged to use his forces in overcoming the Saxons, and in the battle he led his knights and Gunther's troops to a great victory. In the following days there were great celebrations at which Queen Uta and her daughter Kriemhild appeared in public. On one of these occasions Siegfried and Kriemhild met and became betrothed. King Gunther, wanting to marry Brunhild, Wotan's daughter, told Siegfried that if he would help him win Brunhild then he might wed Kriemhild. Gunther set out at the head of a great expedition, all of his knights decked in costly garments in order to impress Brunhild. Her preference for a husband, however, was not a well-dressed prince but a hero. She declared that the man who would win her must surpass her in feats of skill and strength. With Siegfried's aid Gunther overcame Brunhild, and she agreed to go with Gunther as his wife.

Siegfried was sent on ahead to announce a great celebration in honor of the coming marriage of Gunther to Brunhild. A double ceremony took place, with Kriemhild becoming the bride of Siegfried at the same time. At the wedding feast Brunhild burst into tears at the sight of Kriemhild and Siegfried together. Gunther tried to explain away her unhappiness, but once more, Gunther needed Siegfried's aid, for Brunhild had determined never to let Gunther share her bed. Siegfried went to her chamber and there overpowered her. Thinking she had been overcome by Gunther, she was thus subdued. Brunhild bore a son who was named for Siegfried. As time passed she wished once more to see Siegfried, who had returned with Kriemhild to his own country. Therefore, she instructed Gunther to plan a great hunting party to which Siegfried and Kriemhild should be invited.

At the meeting of the two royal families, there was great rivalry between Brunhild and Kriemhild. They vied with each other by overdressing their attendants and then argued as to the place each should have in the royal procession. Finally, Kriemhild took revenge when she told Brunhild the true story of Brunhild's wedding night. Accusing Brunhild of acting the part of a harlot, she said that Brunhild had slept first with Siegfried, then with her husband, Gunther. For proof, she displayed Brunhild's ring and girdle, both of which Siegfried had won from Brunhild the night he had overcome her. Brunhild, furious and desirous of revenge, sought out her husband and confronted him with the story of her humiliation and betrayal. Gunther and Siegfried soon settled to their own satisfaction the quarrel between the two women, but Hagen, the crafty one, stirred up trouble among Gunther's brothers with his claim that Siegfried had stained the honor of their house. They plotted to trap Siegfried and destroy him. When it was reported that the Saxons were to attack Gunther's knights, Kriemhild unwittingly revealed Siegfried's one vulnerable spot. While bathing in the dragon's blood, he had failed to protect a portion of his body the size of a linden leaf because a leaf had fallen down between his shoulders. The villainous Hagen asked her to sew a token on the spot so that he could protect Siegfried during the fighting. Hagen sent men to say that the Saxons had given up the attack. Then, the fear of battle over, Gunther rode out to hunt with all of his knights. There, deep in the forest, as Siegfried was bending over a spring to drink, he was struck in the fatal spot by an arrow from Hagen's bow. Before he died, Siegfried cursed the Burgundians and their tribe forever. Indifferent to the dying man's curse, Hagen carried home the body of the dead hero.

He placed Siegfried's body in the path where Kriemhild would see it on her way to church, but a chamberlain discovered the body before she passed. Kriemhild knew instinctively whose hand had done the deed. A thousand knights headed by Siegmund, his father, mourned the dead hero, and everyone claimed vengeance. The widow gave vast sums of money to the poor in honor of Siegfried. When Siegmund prepared to leave for Niderland, he asked Kriemhild to go with him. She refused but allowed him to take Siegfried's son with him. She was determined to stay with the Burgundians. Queen Brunhild, however, offered no compassion. The Nibelungen hoard was given to Kriemhild because it was her wedding gift. By order of Hagen, who planned to get possession of the treasure, all of it was dropped to the bottom of the Rhine. In the years that followed Kriemhild remained in mourning for Siegfried.

At last the mighty Etzel, King of the Huns, sought to marry Kriemhild. After a long courtship he won Kriemhild and took her to his land to be his wife. Etzel was rich and strong, and after her long years of mourning, Kriemhild again occupied a position of power and honor. Now she began to consider how she might avenge herself for the death of Siegfried. Hoping to get Hagen in her power, she sent a messenger to her brothers, saying that she longed to see all of them again. When they received her message, the brothers and Hagen set out. Old Queen Uta told them that in a dream she had seen a vision of dire foreboding, but the Burgundians refused to heed her warning. Hagen received a token from some mermaids, who said none of the knights would return from Hunland. He disregarded the prediction. Then a quarrel broke out among the Burgundians, and Dankwart slew Gelfrat. Three evil omens now attended the coming journey, but still the brothers refused to turn back. At last the Burgundians came to Etzel's castle. Gunther and his brothers were put into separate apartments. Dankwart and Hagen were sent to other quarters. Warned by Sir Dietrich that Kriemhild still plotted vengeance for Siegfried's death, Hagen urged them all to take precautions. When Kriemhild asked them to give her their weapons, Hagen replied that it could not be. The Burgundians decided to post a guard to prevent a surprise attack while they slept. The court went to mass. At the services the Huns were displeased to see that Gunther and his party jostled Queen Kriemhild.

In honor of the Burgundians, a great tournament was held for all the knights. So bad was the feeling between the Burgundians and the Huns that king Etzel was forced to intervene in order to keep the peace. To appease the brothers, Etzel gave them Kriemhild's small son, Ortlieb, as a hostage. Sir Bloedel, however, pressed into Dankwart's quarters demanding justice for Kriemhild. In a few minutes he had aroused the anger of Dankwart, who rose from his table and killed Bloedel. For this deed the angered Huns killed Dankwart's retainers. Dankwart, at bay, ran to Hagen for help. Hagen, knowing that he would not live to seek his vengeance on Kriemhild later, slaughtered the little prince, Ortlieb. Then a mighty battle followed in which Hagen and Gunther managed to kill most of their adversaries.

Kriemhild now urged her heroes to kill Hagen. The first to take up the challenge was Iring. After he had wounded Hagen, he rushed back to Kriemhild for praise. Hagen recovered quickly and sought Iring to kill him. The battle continued, and many knights from both sides fell in the bloody combat. Outnumbered, the Burgundians fell one by one. Kriemhild herself slew Hagen, the last of the Burgundians to survive. He died without revealing the location of the treasure.

King Etzel grieved to see so many brave knights killed. At a sign from him, Hildebrand, one of his retainers, lifted his sword and ended the life of Kriemhild as well. So died the secret of the new hiding place of the Nibelungen treasure.

Critical Evaluation:

The material that forms the subject matter of the Germanic heroic epics is derived from historical events that became part of an oral tradition and were passed down, sometimes for centuries, in the form of sagas, before being established in written form. The historical events that lie behind the Nibelung saga are to be found in the fifth and sixth centuries, the period of the tribal wanderings at the end of the Roman Empire. The Burgundians, under King Gundahari, whose capital was at Worms, were in fact destroyed by the Huns in 437. The Siegfried figure is probably of Merovingian origin and may derive from an intermarriage between the Burgundian and Frankish royal houses. The record of these events, mingled with purely legendary elements, is preserved in a number of works: Besides *The Nibelungenlied*, the Scandinavian *Poetic Edda* (ninth to twelfth centuries) is the most important. It was upon this latter source rather than the Germanic version that Richard Wagner based his four-part music drama, *The Ring of the Nibelung* (1876). There are four main themes in the work that reflect the saga tradition: the adventures of the young Siegfried, Siegfried's death, the destruction of the Burgundians, and the death of Etzel. These elements occurred as separate works in the early stages of composition. In the present version of the saga, composed by an anonymous German author around the year 1200, the various elements are woven together into a unified plot, linking the death of Siegfried with the destruction of the Burgundians through the motive of revenge. Traces of the older separate versions are evident, however, in such inner inconsistencies as the transformation of the character of Kriemhild, who appears initially as a model courtly figure but becomes the bloodthirsty avenger of her husband's death in the second part. It is a mark of the artistic talent of the anonymous author that he fuses the core episodes with such care and achieves a plausible and aesthetically satisfying work.

The Nibelungenlied is the product of a brilliant period of the Hohenstaufen dynasty of the Holy Roman Empire, a time when the courtly culture of Germany was at its height. The poet was probably of Austrian origin. The importance of the splendid court at Vienna and the noble figure of Bishop Pilgrim of Passau indicate that the poet may have enjoyed the patronage of these courts. That the poet remains anonymous is a tradition of the heroic epic form, evolving from the anonymous court singer of the wandering Germanic tribes. Whereas the writers of Arthurian epics and religious epics name themselves and often discuss their work in a prologue, the composer of the heroic epic remains outside his work, presenting his material more as history and without the self-conscious comments and digressions found in works such as *Parzival* (c. 1200-1210) or *Tristan and Isolde* (c. 1210), both of whose poets name themselves and go into some detail regarding their intentions and artistic conceptions. *The Nibelungenlied*, written in four-line stanzas, bears the signs of its history of oral presentation—frequent repetition of rhyme words, the use of formulaic descriptions and filler lines, and general looseness of composition. The poem was not conceived as a written work. It represents a written record of an oral performance tradition. Even after assuming written form, for centuries the work was read aloud to audiences, books being a scarce and expensive commodity during the Middle Ages.

The purpose of the work, like that of courtly poetry in general, is to mirror courtly society in its splendor, color, and activity. It presents images of an idealized world in which larger-than-life figures act out the social rituals of the time and provide for the audience models of courtly behavior. The work instructs in codes of honor, fortitude, and noble bearing under stress. Repeatedly in the work one observes long passages devoted to description of the court festivities—banquets, tournaments, processions—all filled with details of clothing and jewelry, splendid utensils, and weapons. Questions of etiquette and precedence provide some of the central conflicts of the work, while the lyrical episodes of the love between Siegfried and Kriemhild may be seen as an embodiment of the idealized conception of love. Although the grim events of the old dramatic saga material at times conflict with the more cultivated ideal of the thirteenth century, the poet succeeds even here in transforming the traditional material. Elements related to fairy-tale tradition—the stories of Siegfried's youth, the battle with the dragon, the magic aura surrounding Brunhild on her island—are largely suppressed.

Idealizing elements are, on the other hand, strongly developed. In the first part, Siegfried and Kriemhild stand out against the menacing forces of the Burgundian court, especially Hagen. In the second part, despite the atmosphere of betrayal and carnage, the high points are moments of fortitude and courage and the preservation of ethical integrity. Rudiger, who finds himself torn between feudal loyalty to King Etzel and his loyalty and friendship for the Burgundians, to one of whom his daughter is engaged, is one of the noblest figures. The episode in which he finds himself obliged to fight against the Burgundian Gernot, to whom he has given the sword that now will kill him, is one of the most poignant scenes in the work.

The chain of crime and revenge finds resolution only in the lament for the fallen warriors, and it is in this tragic sense of the inevitable suffering that follows joy that the work preserves its links to the ancient Germanic heroic outlook, establishing its individuality against the more generally optimistic outlook of the Arthurian sagas. Here the fatalistic confrontation with destructive forces is opposed to the affirmation of order and the delight of life. This is typical of much literature of the Hohenstaufen period. The tension between these two attitudes provides much of the power of the work and lifts it into the realm of universal validity.

"Critical Evaluation" by Steven C. Schaber

Bibliography:

Bekker, Hugo. *The Nibelungenlied: A Literary Analysis*. Toronto: University of Toronto Press, 1971. Deals at length with the four main characters and with numerous parallelisms in the epic. Bekker's main point is that Brunhild is offended not because Siegfried overpowers her in bed but because he breaches the rules of kingship by not consummating the sexual act.

Haymes, Edward R. *The Nibelungenlied: History and Interpretation*. Champaign: University of Illinois Press, 1986. Discusses how the epic would have been received around the year 1200, when it was written. Interprets it as an argument for the stability of the old feudal structure and against new elements from chivalric literature.

McConnell, Winder. *The Nibelungenlied*. Boston: Twayne, 1984. An excellent discussion of the epic, with strong historical cultural background information and an interesting overview of the reception of the work in Germany. Well-organized interpretations of the major characters. Emphasizes the anonymous author's style of presenting the events without passing judgment.

Mowatt, D. G., and Hugh Sacker. *The Nibelungenlied: An Interpretative Commentary*. Toronto: University of Toronto Press, 1967. Includes maps and a genealogical diagram. A good general introduction followed by more than one hundred pages of commentary that closely follows the original text. Most useful in conjunction with an English translation that retains the stanza numbers.

The Nibelungenlied. Translated by A. T. Hatto. New York: Penguin Books, 1969. In addition to the translation, Hatto provides more than one hundred pages of information on the epic. He points out many discrepancies in the work. A useful glossary of the characters' names.

NICHOLAS NICKLEBY

Type of work: Novel
Author: Charles Dickens (1812-1870)
Type of plot: Social realism
Time of plot: Early nineteenth century
Locale: England
First published: 1838-1839

Principal characters:

NICHOLAS NICKLEBY, a gentlemanly young Englishman with no money
KATE NICKLEBY, his sister
MRS. NICKLEBY, his mother
RALPH NICKLEBY, his miserly uncle
WACKFORD SQUEERS, a vicious schoolmaster
SMIKE, a young boy befriended by Nicholas
THE CHEERYBLE BROTHERS, Nicholas' benefactors
FRANK CHEERYBLE, their nephew
MADELINE BRAY, their protégée

The Story:

When Nicholas Nickleby was nineteen years old, his father died a bankrupt. A short time after their bereavement, Nicholas, his sister Kate, and their mother set out for London. There they hoped that the late Mr. Nickleby's brother, Ralph, might be willing to do something for them. Ralph Nickleby, a miserly moneylender, grudgingly allowed his sister-in-law and Kate to move into empty lodgings he owned, and he secured a position for Nicholas as assistant to Wackford Squeers, who operated a boys' boarding school in Yorkshire. Nicholas, leaving his mother and sister in Ralph's care, traveled to the school and found it a terrible place where the boys were starved and mistreated almost beyond human imagination. Nicholas was forced to endure the situation, for his uncle had warned him that any help given to his sister and mother depended upon his remaining where he had been placed. A crisis arose, however, when Wackford Squeers unjustly and unmercifully beat an older boy named Smike, who was little better than an idiot. Nicholas intervened, wresting the whip from Squeers and beating the schoolmaster with it instead. Immediately afterward, Smike and Nicholas left the school and started walking toward London.

In London, meanwhile, Ralph Nickleby tried to use Kate to attract young Lord Verisopht into borrowing money at high rates. He also found work for Kate in a dressmaking establishment, where there was a great deal of labor and almost no pay. Kate did not mind the work, but she was deeply distressed at the leers she had to endure when invited to her uncle's home to dine with Lord Verisopht and Sir Mulberry Hawk. Not long afterward, the dressmaker went bankrupt, and Kate found herself a companion to a wealthy but selfish and neurotic woman.

When Nicholas arrived in London, he sought out Newman Noggs, his uncle's clerk, who had promised to help him if it were ever in his power. Newman Noggs helped Nicholas clear himself of the false charges of being a thief that had been brought against him by Wackford Squeers and Ralph Nickleby.

With some notion of becoming sailors, Nicholas and Smike decided to go to Bristol. On the way, they met Vincent Crummles, a theatrical producer, whose troupe they joined. Both Smike and Nicholas were successful as actors. In addition, Nicholas adapted plays for the company to produce. After some weeks, however, Nicholas received a letter from Newman Noggs warning him that his presence was urgently required in London. Nicholas left hurriedly and arrived in London late that night. Not wishing to disturb his family, Nicholas put up at an inn, where he encountered Sir Mulberry Hawk and Lord Verisopht and overheard them speaking in derogatory terms of Kate. Nicholas remonstrated with them and demanded to know their names. In the altercation, Sir Mulberry's horse bolted and the baronet was thrown from his carriage and severely injured.

Newman had asked Nicholas to return because Kate, exposed to the insulting attentions of Sir Mulberry and Lord Verisopht, was increasingly miserable. Both Mrs. Nickleby and the woman to whom Kate was a companion failed to see past the men's titles and were flattered at the acquaintance, and Kate was forced to be often in their company. For Sir Mulberry it had become a point of honor to seduce her.

After Nicholas had thus accidentally learned of the situation, he removed his mother and sister to new and friendlier lodgings, and all intercourse with Ralph Nickleby ceased. Yet the future seemed quite bleak, for Nicholas was long unsuccessful finding work in London. At an employment agency to which he applied, he became acquainted with a kindly gentleman, one of the philanthropic Cheeryble brothers. Hearing that the young man was destitute and believing him to be deserving, the brothers gave Nicholas a job in their countinghouse at a decent salary and made a cottage available to him for himself, Kate, and their mother.

One day, a beautiful young woman came to see the Cheeryble brothers, and Nicholas fell in love with her at first sight. Kate gradually fell in love with the Cheeryble brothers' nephew, Frank. Only Smike seemed unhappy, for he had fallen in love with Kate, yet realized his limitations more than ever before now that he was in cultivated surroundings. Once Wackford Squeers and Ralph Nickleby saw that Nicholas had given a good home to Smike, they began to conspire to kidnap Smike. Apart from the wish for revenge, Squeers was motivated by the fact that Smike had been an immensely valuable, unpaid drudge at the school. Smike was caught twice but escaped, and Nicholas was successful in keeping him out of Squeers's clutches, but the boy's happiness was short-lived. He died of tuberculosis a few months later.

By then, Nicholas had discovered that the young woman with whom he had fallen in love, Madeline Bray, was the daughter of a bankrupt ne'er-do-well who lived off the little income she made by sewing and painting. Unknown to Nicholas, Ralph Nickleby and a fellow miser, Arthur Gride, were planning to force Madeline into a marriage with Gride, who was seventy years old. Fortunately, Madeline's father died an hour before he was to hand his daughter over to the old miser. Nicholas arrived on the scene and took the young woman to his home, where she was cared for by Kate and his mother.

Meanwhile, Gride's old housekeeper left in a fit of jealousy and stole some of her employer's papers. One of the documents was a will which, if known, would have made Madeline Bray a rich woman. Ralph learned of the will and persuaded Squeers to steal it. When he did, however, Frank Cheeryble and Newman Noggs caught him and turned him over to the police. The prisoner confessed his part in the plot and also told about the conspiracy between Ralph and Gride to get Madeline's fortune. An old employee of Ralph appeared and revealed to the Cheeryble brothers that Smike had been Ralph's son; years ago, as a way of revenging himself on his employer, he had told Ralph that his son had died in infancy. Ralph, when given the news, went home and hanged himself.

Thinking that Frank Cheeryble was in love with Madeline, Nicholas asked the Cheeryble brothers that she be taken care of elsewhere. The Cheeryble brothers, in their good-hearted way, took the situation under observation and made it possible for both pairs of lovers, Nicholas and Madeline, as well as Frank and Kate, to be married shortly thereafter.

Years passed, and both couples prospered. Nicholas invested his wife's fortune in the Cheeryble brothers' firm and later became a partner in the house along with Frank Cheeryble. Newman Noggs, who had helped Nicholas so many times, was restored to respectability; he had been a wealthy gentleman before he had fallen into Ralph Nickleby's hands. Old Gride, who had tried to marry Madeline for her money, was murdered by robbers; Lord Verisopht was killed in a duel with his false friend Sir Mulberry Hawk, who subsequently also came to a violent end.

Critical Evaluation:

Although Thomas Arnold, headmaster of Rugby, objected to *Nicholas Nickleby* on the grounds that the novel was insufficiently edifying, most Victorian readers—including Charles Dickens' rival, William Makepeace Thackeray—admired it; from its initial sale of fifty thousand copies, the book was one of Dickens' triumphs. The first of his novels in which the love story is the main subject, *Nicholas Nickleby* still retains many picaresque elements that appeared in *The Pickwick Papers* (1836-1837) and *Oliver Twist* (1837-1838). Dickens' greatest strength in *Nicholas Nickleby* lies in the marvelous descriptions of people and places. The characters still tend to be eccentrics dominated by a single passion (almost in the manner of Ben Jonson's "humors" characters, although lacking Jonson's theory of the psychology of humors); the minor characters in particular seem to be grotesques. Yet there is a vitality in the farcical elements of the novel that is delightful. The influence of Tobias Smollett, both in the comedy and the tendency to realistic detail, is still strong in this early novel. The influence of melodramas also still colors the plot, but Dickens breathes new life into old stock situations.

Even if the melodramatic and episodic structure of *Nicholas Nickleby* is unoriginal, confusing, and improbable, the comedy and vitality of the book are the result of genius. Readers feel the tremendous force of life, of the changing times, of youth and growth, on every page. Tales develop within tales, and countless life stories crowd the chapters. It is a young man's creation, indignant, farcical, and romantic in turn, and it is filled with vivid scenes. At this stage of his career, Dickens was still attempting to provide something for everybody.

Yet because of his complicated, melodramatic plot, Dickens was not wholly successful in working out the psychology of the novel. As critic Douglas Bush has observed, the characters of Dickens' early fiction are given over to self-dramatization. Mrs. Nickleby, in particular, evades the responsibilities of her troubled life by withdrawing into her blissful vision of the past. She sees herself as a romantic heroine, although her admirer is only a lunatic neighbor who throws cucumbers over the wall. Like many other characters of the book—among them Vincent Crummles, Smike, and Nicholas himself—she is isolated in her own imagination, locked in an often inimical world. Her eccentricity, like that of most of the minor characters, is an outward symbol of estrangement from the hostile social mechanisms of convention, order, and mysterious power. Nicholas succeeds in love and fortune, not so much by his own resources but through chance—good luck with the Cheeryble brothers, for example—and through his own amiable disposition. At this point in his development as a novelist, Dickens was unable to create—as he eventually would in David Copperfield, Pip, and other protagonists—a hero who is fully aware of his isolation and confronts his sense of guilt. The reader must accept Nicholas on the level of the author's uncomplicated psychology: as a genial, deserving fellow whose good luck, good friends, and honest nature reward him with happiness, affection, and prosperity.

Bibliography:

Adrian, Arthur A. *Dickens and the Parent-Child Relationship*. Athens: Ohio University Press, 1984. Discusses the status of children in working-class Victorian England and Dickens' own experience as a son and a father. Includes drawings of children at work in a variety of occupations.

Bloom, Harold, ed. *Charles Dickens*. New York: Chelsea House, 1987. A collection of essays on various aspects of Dickens' art. Raymond Williams' contribution is especially illuminating with regard to Dickens' portrayal of urban life in *Nicholas Nickleby*.

Flint, Kate. *Dickens*. Atlantic Highlands, N.J.: Humanities Press International, 1986. Discusses Dickens' works in the context of a newly industrialized society. Flint also calls attention to Dickens' portrayal of women and actors.

Giddings, Robert, ed. *The Changing World of Charles Dickens*. London: Vision Press Limited, 1983. A collection of essays on Dickens' style, generally and in specific works. Loralee MacPike discusses Dickens' influence on Fyodor Dostoevski. David Edgar and Mike Poole discuss stage and film productions of particular novels, including *Nicholas Nickleby*.

Nelson, Harland. *Charles Dickens*. Boston: Twayne, 1981. Explores Dickens' philosophy of writing and his serial publications. Also discusses the structure and narrative of seven of his novels.

NICK OF THE WOODS
Or, The Jibbenainosay, a Tale of Kentucky

Type of work: Novel
Author: Robert Montgomery Bird (1806-1854)
Type of plot: Adventure
Time of plot: 1782
Locale: Kentucky
First published: 1837

Principal characters:
> CAPTAIN ROLAND FORRESTER, a veteran of the Revolutionary War
> EDITH FORRESTER, his cousin
> COLONEL BRUCE, the commander of Bruce's Station
> TOM BRUCE, his son
> NATHAN SLAUGHTER, a Quaker trapper
> ROARING RALPH STACKPOLE, a frontier braggart and horse thief
> PARDON DODGE, a pioneer
> ABEL DOE, a renegade white man
> TELIE DOE, his daughter
> RICHARD BRAXLEY, a Virginia lawyer
> WENONGA, a Shawnee chief

The Story:

The sun was still high on a sultry August afternoon in 1782, when a train of emigrants emerged from the gloom of the forest and rode slowly toward Bruce's Station, one of the principal forts in the District of Kentucky. The travelers, consisting of men, women, children, and slaves, were accompanied by cattle and loaded packhorses, the whole group giving the appearance of a village on the march. In the position of responsibility rode a young man whose five years in the camps and battles of the American Revolution showed in his military bearing and in the mature gravity of his features. The beautiful young woman at his side was sufficiently like him in appearance to suggest their kinship.

Captain Roland Forrester and his cousin Edith were on their way to the Falls of the Ohio. The orphaned children of twin brothers who had died early in the Revolution, they had been reared as wards of their stern, wealthy uncle, Major Roland Forrester. A staunch Tory, the Major had never forgiven his younger brothers for supporting the cause of the American patriots, and to keep them from inheriting his estate, for he was unmarried, he had executed a will in favor of an illegitimate daughter. About the time that his brothers fell in battle, the child burned to death in the home of her foster mother. The Major then adopted his nephew and niece and repeatedly declared his intention of making them his heirs. Young Roland Forrester forfeited his share of the inheritance, however, when he enlisted in a troop of Virginia horsemen. Shortly after the Battle of Yorktown, he returned to find his cousin destitute. On her uncle's death, no will making her his heiress could be found. Richard Braxley, the Major's lawyer and agent, had produced the original will and taken possession of the estate in the name of the Major's daughter, who was, he claimed, still alive and soon to appear and claim her heritage. Having no funds to contest the will, Roland decided to move to Kentucky, his plan being to place Edith in the care of a distant pioneer relative at the Falls while he carved from the wilderness a fortune which would allow him to marry his lovely cousin.

Colonel Bruce, the commander of the station, welcomed the emigrants, greeting the For-resters with special warmth and insisting that they share his cabin. Having served under Major Forrester in earlier Indian wars, he told many stories of those border campaigns. Mrs. Bruce, equally voluble, bustled about giving orders to her daughters and telling them to be as circumspect as Telie Doe, who remained quietly at her loom after a startled glance up from her work when she heard the name of Roland Forrester mentioned. When the others escorted Edith into the cabin, she remained on the porch, where Roland was explaining his intention of pushing on toward the Falls the next day. The Colonel, while deploring his guest's haste, said that there was no danger from Indians on the trace. At last, the Colonel noticed Telie and ordered her into the house. She was, he said, the daughter of a white renegade named Abel Doe. Out of pity, the Bruces had taken her into their own home.

At that moment Tom Bruce, the Colonel's oldest son, appeared with news that the Jibbenai-nosay had been active again; some hunters had found an Indian with a split skull and a slashed cross on his breast. The Jibbenainosay, whom the settlers also called Nick of the Woods, was a mysterious avenger who had killed many Indians and marked them thus. The Shawnees, believing that he was either a ghost or a devil, had given him his name, which meant Spirit-that-walks.

The news of the Jibbenainosay's latest killing had been brought to the station by Roaring Ralph Stackpole, a swaggering braggart. When he challenged anyone in the settlement to a trial of strength, the rough frontiersmen decided to match him with Nathan Slaughter, a Quaker trapper derisively nicknamed Bloody Nathan because of his peaceful ways and gentle speech. Much to the surprise of the crowd, he lifted Roaring Ralph and threw him to the ground. Ralph, admitting that he had been fairly beaten, asked to borrow a horse so that he could continue his journey to Logan's Station. The Quaker trapper told the settlers that the Miami Indians were gathering, but when the others refused to take his news seriously, he exchanged his furs for lead and powder and quietly left the station.

That night, Telie Doe begged Edith to let her go with the emigrants as a servant. When Edith refused, the girl crept away sadly. Roland slept with Bruce's sons on the porch of the cabin. Aroused from sleep during the night, he thought he heard a whispering voice telling him he was to cross Salt River by the lower ford. Only half awake, he decided that he was still dreaming.

The next morning, there was great confusion at the station. Roaring Ralph had sneaked back into the settlement and stolen Roland's horse. Knowing that the fugitive could not get far on the tired animal, Bruce's sons had ridden in pursuit. While the emigrant train started on ahead, Roland, Edith, and one of the slaves stayed at the station to await the return of the horse. The animal was found, wandering loose along the trail, and was brought back by one of the boys. He said that the others were tracking the thief, intending to make him an object of frontier justice. As the travelers were about to set out to overtake the emigrant party, a horseman arrived with word that Indians had attacked Bryant's Station. The need to muster every fighting man in the settlement left Roland and his cousin without an escort; nevertheless, they started out with only one surly frontiersman to guide them. On the way, their guide deserted them to return and join in the fighting. The travelers were relieved from their predicament when Telie Doe appeared and offered to act as their guide.

When they came to the branch to the two fords, Roland insisted on following the road to the upper ford, in spite of Telie Doe's pleadings. On the way, they found Roaring Ralph, his arms bound and a noose around his neck, astride a horse in such fashion that one movement of the animal would hang the rider from a limb overhead. Left to perish in that manner after the pursuers from Bruce's Station had overtaken him, he was grateful to his rescuers and offered to devote his life to Edith's service. Roland curtly sent the braggart and thief on his way.

Not far from the upper ford, they met a fleeing settler named Pardon Dodge, who told them that Indians on the warpath blocked the road ahead. In their attempt to reach the lower ford, they became lost. They then found a dead Indian with a cross gashed on his breast. While they waited for the dread Jibbenainosay to appear, they saw harmless Nathan Slaughter, his faithful hound at his heels, coming through the forest. Hearing that Indians were close, the Quaker became terrified. He promised to guide the party only if he were not called upon to fight.

The travelers took refuge at last in a ruined cabin near the flooded river. Indians attacked the cabin during the night, but they were repulsed. During the lull, it was agreed that Nathan should try to evade the warriors and bring help to the besieged. Shortly before daylight, Roaring Ralph came down the river in a small dugout. The group desperately decided to send Edith, Telie, and Ralph across the flooded stream in the canoe, while Roland, Dodge, and the slave would try to follow on horseback. When Dodge's horse came ashore without his rider, the others decided that he had been drowned.

Later that morning, the fugitives encountered another band of Indians. Edith was captured. Roaring Ralph escaped by rolling down the bank to the river; the slave was killed. Roland, knocked unconscious during the fight, awoke to find himself wounded and tightly bound. While he was wondering what had happened to Edith, a band of Kentuckians, led by young Tom Bruce, appeared and engaged the Indians. When Roaring Ralph climbed the bank and joined in the fight, the Kentuckians, believing that they were seeing the ghost of the man they had hanged, scattered in confusion. Roaring Ralph, throwing wounded Tom Bruce over the saddle, rode away on Roland's horse. The victorious Indians proceeded to divide the spoils of victory under the direction of an old chief by a brave whom Roland thought was of mixed Indian and white blood. He learned the man's identity when Telie ran up to protest the enslavement of Roland to a Piankeshaw warrior. The light-skinned warrior was Abel Doe, the renegade.

His arms bound, Roland was tethered to the Piankeshaw's saddle and forced to make a long, wearying march. Unable to sleep that night, he was startled to hear an explosion close at hand. Horrified when a dead Piankeshaw fell across his prostrate body, Roland lost consciousness. He revived to find Nathan Slaughter bending over him. Another dead Piankeshaw lay nearby.

The Quaker had overheard the renegade and another white man discussing the price to be paid for the capture of Roland and Edith. Convinced by Nathan's account that his cousin had fallen into Braxley's hands, Roland wished to start at once to the main Indian village after the Quaker told him that the old chief must have been Wenonga, a Shawnee chieftain notorious for his brutality. On their way to the Shawnee camp, Roland and the Quaker found five Indians with a white prisoner bound to a tree. While they struggled with the natives, the prisoner, Roaring Ralph, broke his bonds and aided them in killing the warriors.

When they reached the Indian village, the Quaker daubed himself like a brave and went stealthily among the houses to find Edith. Peering through the chinks in one cabin, he saw Braxley and Abel Doe and, from the conversation, learned that Braxley had in his possession Major Forrester's second will. Having disposed of Roland, the lawyer was now planning to marry Edith and get her wealth. While he searched for Edith's place of imprisonment, Nathan found old Chief Wenonga lying drunk in the grass. He was about to plunge his knife in the old man's breast when he heard Edith's voice nearby. Leaving the chief, he went to a skin tent where he found Braxley and his prisoner. Taking the other man by surprise, the Quaker seized and bound him. With the will safe on his own person, Nathan was carrying Edith to safety when a clamor broke out in the Indian encampment.

Roaring Ralph, ordered to steal four horses upon which Edith and her rescuers could make their escape, had attempted to drive off the whole herd, and the stampeding horses ran through the village, arousing the warriors. Unable to escape, the party was captured. Roland and Roaring Ralph were bound and taken to separate wigwams. Nathan, dragged before the drunken old chief, defied Wenonga with such ferocity that the Quaker worked himself into an epileptic fit. The spasm, together with his fantastic disguise, convinced the Shawnee that his white prisoner was a great medicine man.

Doe and Braxley still had not reached an agreement over the renegade's pay. What Braxley did not know was that Doe had taken the will when he had searched the Quaker after his capture. The next day, the renegade went to Roland and offered him his freedom and the estate if he would consent to marry Telie. Roland refused, but offered Doe half the estate if he would save Edith. The man left sullenly.

That night, old Wenonga had the Quaker brought before him. After bragging of the white women and children he had killed and the scalps he had taken, the chief offered the prisoner his freedom if he would use his powers as a medicine man to put the Jibbenainosay in the power of the Shawnee. Nathan promised to do so if his bonds were cut. Freed, he revealed himself as the Jibbenainosay, a friendly settler whose wife and children Wenonga had treacherously killed years previously. Seizing the chief's ax, he sank it into Wenonga's head. Then, after cutting away Wenonga's scalp lock and gashing the dead man's chest, the Quaker retrieved the scalps of his children and with a triumphant cry disappeared into the night.

The next morning, finding the Jibbenainosay's mark on their dead chief, the Shawnees were roused to wild fury. Roland and Roaring Ralph were tied to the stake, timber heaped about them. The fires were lighted, but before the flames could reach them, the sound of gunfire echoed above the yells of the savages, and a band of Kentuckians rode through the smoke to set the prisoners free. Braxley struck spurs into his horse and rode away with Edith in his arms. The resistance ended when Nathan, with Wenonga's scalp at his belt, appeared striking right and left with his steel ax. The Indians scattered and ran, but the rejoicing of the Kentuckians was dimmed by the death of heroic Tom Bruce.

During the confusion, Pardon Dodge rode up with Edith on the saddle before him. He had survived the flooded river and joined the rescue party, saving Edith from Braxley. Doe, mortally wounded, gave Roland the missing will, and the young Virginian promised to look after Telie with a brother's care. Roland and Edith, preparing to return to Virginia to claim her inheritance, assured Nathan that they owed life as well as fortune to his bravery and daring. Although they begged him to return with them, he stoutly refused. The work of the Jibbenainosay was done, and, after a time, the Quaker disappeared quietly into the woods.

Critical Evaluation:

In the tradition of Charles Brockden Brown's *Edgar Huntly* (1799) and James Fenimore Cooper's *Leatherstocking Tales* (1823-1841), Robert Montgomery Bird's *Nick of the Woods* serves as an early milepost in the distinctively American genre of frontier literature. As a number of critics have asserted, Bird reinforces the narrative pattern established by his two literary predecessors: A group of white people ventures into a wilderness setting occupied by Indian antagonists; the virtue of at least one white woman is threatened by some Indian predator or villainous white man; and ultimate tragedy is averted by the intervention of a frontier hero, savvy in the ways of the woods.

During a period of time when Indian warfare was far from a distant memory, Bird used as the subject of his adventure the turning point in the Western colonization of what would eventually become the state of Kentucky: the invasion of Shawnee territory by a citizen army led by George Rogers Clark. Thus, the author's fictional narrative is set against a historical event with which Bird was familiar both as an amateur historian and as a traveler who himself visited the scenes of his novel four years before its publication.

In addition to its place in the canon of wilderness novels, *Nick of the Woods* can be appreciated for its dramatic mode. Much of the novel's exciting, propulsive plot is essentially a direct consequence of Bird's earlier experience as a dramatist. His play *The Gladiator* (1831), for instance, was one of the most popular dramas in nineteenth century America, and *Nick of the Woods* itself was successfully adapted for the stage at various times by a number of authors both in America and in Britain.

As is characteristic of melodrama, the plot of the novel is developed by circumstance and not by character motivation. After seeking shelter in the ruined cabin of a settler family slaughtered by Indians, for example, the Forresters and their companions discover that their Indian foes are also using the spot as a camp. Vigorously besieged and at the point of desperation, the group is offered an escape route by the sudden appearance of Roaring Ralph Stackpole in a canoe. Thus, narrative respites are complicated and difficult situations are temporarily resolved by unexpected and improbable plot twists.

Setting is also used for dramatic effect. As Captain Roland Forrester, for instance, contemplates his predicament at the fort with Indians in front of him and the river behind, the scene is described almost in terms of scenic design. There are "frowning banks," "swollen waters," and "growling thunder." Bird uses setting to underscore incident and to appeal to the emotions of his readers. Repeatedly in the novel, Bird gives indications that he regards the scenes of his novel as stage sets; Wenonga's village, for example, the setting for the last ten chapters, is described as the "theatre in which was to be acted the last scene in the drama of their enterprise."

Besides plot and setting, some of the novel's major characters can be seen as little more than stock figures of the popular stage. Roland Forrester is the romantic and courageous, if not always effectual, gentleman-hero; Edith is the golden-haired damsel in distress; and Braxley is the villain and would-be seducer whose "evil-genius" has been kindled by a lust for possession.

What saves the novel from being largely a product of simple convention, however, is Bird's ability to create a few truly individual characters that play against type. Indeed, the novel's omniscient narrator asserts that frontier life breeds the "strangest contrasts" and the "strangest characters." Thus, the reader is introduced to the joyously larcenous horse thief Ralph Stackpole, the reluctant renegade Abel Doe, and, above all, the schizophrenic Nathan Slaughter.

Nathan, the docile Quaker by day and ferocious Indian hater by night, is the character upon whom most modern critics of the novel focus their attention. It has been pointed out that since Bird himself trained as a physician, this literary use of abnormal psychology is not surprising. Slaughter suffers from a significant post-traumatic disorder, attributable to the fact that, back in Pennsylvania, after he had surrendered his arms to neighboring Indians as a man of peace, he not only was forced to stand helpless while his wife, mother, and five children were murdered before his eyes but also was himself scalped and left for dead.

Some critics believe that Slaughter's personal conflict between the doctrine of Christian pacifism and the requirements of survival in a world of very real evil is a microcosm of the novel's larger thematic issue: the confrontation between the settled, agriculture-based economy of the European American and the nomadic hunter-gatherer society of the Native American. Both ways of life vied for possession of the virgin forests of North America. On the frontier, many a farmer became, of necessity, a fighter; in Bird's novel, many a peaceful settler is forced to become a "wicked Kentucky fighting-man" because of threats posed against him.

In this context, any discussion of Nathan Slaughter would be incomplete without reference to another fictional Nathaniel, the great woodsman created by Bird's contemporary, James Fenimore Cooper. In five novels, Natty Bumppo is forced farther and farther west in order to possess the space and freedom to follow his forest lifestyle. Bumppo and his Indian companion Chingachgook are displaced by the advance of civilization; their combined story is a valedictory of the life led according to the rhythms of nature and the precepts of natural law.

Bird, on the other hand, regarded the hunter lifestyle and the concept of the noble savage as the fantasies of "poets and sentimentalists"; to him, the progress of colonization in the "deserts of the West" was welcome, and the Indians' loss of their land inevitable. To prevent any thematic ambiguity, he demonizes the settlers' Indian adversaries. Yet, no matter how unflattering a picture of Native Americans Bird tries to paint, the Christian settlers, as exemplified by Nathan Slaughter and his satanic sobriquet, "Nick of the Woods," are themselves touched by the evil they try to vanquish.

"Critical Evaluation" by S. Thomas Mack

Bibliography:
Bryant, James C. "The Fallen World in *Nick of the Woods.*" *American Literature* 38 (November, 1966): 352-364. Analyzes the novel's plot as being a struggle between demonic barbarians and civilized Christians with an emphasis on the fact that, in an imperfect world, even the "children of light" are flawed. Discusses three major interpretations for Nathan Slaughter's dual personality.

Cowie, Alexander. *The Rise of the American Novel.* New York: American Book Company, 1948. A good introductory appraisal of Bird's career. Discusses the author's fictional works in the context of other significant contemporaries and followers of James Fenimore Cooper.

Dahl, Curtis. *Robert Montgomery Bird.* New York: Twayne, 1963. The only comprehensive book-length study of Bird's literary canon—poetry, plays, novels, and prose works. Discusses *Nick of the Woods* in the context of the author's other "novels of outlaws and Indians." Features a selective bibliography.

Hall, Joan Joffe. "*Nick of the Woods*: An Interpretation of the American Wilderness." *American Literature* 35 (May, 1963): 173-182. Focuses on the character of Nathan Slaughter and his internal moral conflict. Places *Nick of the Woods* in the context of wilderness novels by James Fenimore Cooper and Herman Melville.

Hoppenstand, Gary. "Justified Bloodshed: Robert Montgomery Bird's *Nick of the Woods* and the Origins of the Vigilante Hero in American Literature and Culture." *Journal of American Culture* 15, no. 2 (Summer, 1992): 51-61. Traces the evolution of the American vigilante hero from Bird's Nathan Slaughter to Clint Eastwood's Dirty Harry. Argues that Bird's negative depiction of the American Indian can be justified in literary terms since a revenge narrative requires that there be villainy to sanction retributive violence.

THE NIGGER OF THE "NARCISSUS"
A Tale of the Sea

Type of work: Novel
Author: Joseph Conrad (Jósef Teodor Konrad Nałęcz Korzeniowski, 1857-1924)
Type of plot: Symbolic realism
Time of plot: Nineteenth century
Locale: Bombay to London
First published: 1897

> *Principal characters:*
> JAMES WAIT, a black sailor on the *Narcissus*
> DONKIN, a fellow sailor
> SINGLETON, another sailor
> MR. BAKER, the first mate
> CAPTAIN ALLISTOUN, the ship's almost godlike leader

The Story:

The British freighter *Narcissus* lay in Bombay harbor on a hot, sticky tropical night in the 1890's. Already loaded, it was to sail the next morning on its homeward voyage. The last crew member to come aboard was a huge black man, James Wait. Wait had a severe cough and asked his shipmates to help him in stowing his gear. A little later, the men were in their bunks, and the only sound was snoring, interrupted at times by Wait's fits of coughing.

At daylight, the *Narcissus* sailed. That evening, as the sailors gathered in little groups about the deck, the laughter and yarn spinning ceased at the sound of a weak rattle in Wait's bunk. It ended with a moan. The black man climbed up on deck, looked about, and made the men miserable by berating them for making so much noise that he, a dying man, could have no rest. It seemed, after a few days, that Wait looked upon his approaching death as a friend. He paraded his trouble to everyone, railing bitterly at the salt meat, biscuits, and tea at mealtime.

All the men in the forecastle were touched by the dying man and his fits of coughing. There was nothing that they would not do for him, even stealing pie for him from the officers' mess. Even Donkin, a Cockney who thought that no one was ever right but him, catered to Wait. Wait did no work after they were a week at sea. The first mate finally ordered him below to his bunk, and the captain upheld the mate's order. Each morning, the men carried the invalid up on deck. Finally, he was put in one of the deckhouse berths. He never let anyone doubt that his death was imminent. He fascinated the officers and tainted the lives of the superstitious sailors, even those who grumbled that his illness was a fraud.

As the *Narcissus* approached the Cape of Good Hope, heavier sails were set, the hatches were checked, and everything loose on deck was securely lashed in place in preparation for the winds that were sure to come. On the thirty-second day out of Bombay, the ship began to put her nose into the heavy waves, instead of riding over. Gear blew loose, and the men were tossed about the deck. At sunset, all sails were shortened in preparation for a terrific gale. That entire night, nothing seemed left in the universe except darkness and the fury of the storm. In the gray morning, half the crew went below to rest. The remainder of them and the officers of the ship stayed on deck. Suddenly, a great wall of water loomed out of the mist. The ship rose with it, as a gust of wind lay the vessel on its side. The watch below decks rushed out of the forecastle and crawled aft on hands and knees to join their comrades already on deck. The ship lay on its side for hours, while the men huddled against the various projections on the deck to which they had lashed themselves. At last, someone asked about Wait. Another man shouted that he was trapped in the deckhouse, now half under water, and had drowned, because the heavy wave had jammed the door.

With five volunteers, the boatswain inched forward along the deck to see if Wait might still be alive. Once above the side of the deckhouse, they let go and slid down to it as the backwash of the heavy seas foamed around them. They crawled into the carpenter's shop next to the deckhouse cabin. One of the sailors drummed on the bulkhead with a piece of iron. When he stopped, they heard someone banging on the opposite side. Wait was still alive. He began to scream for help. Someone on deck found a crowbar and passed it below. The men in the tiny carpenter's shop battered at the planks until there was a hole in the bulkhead. Wait's head appeared in the hole and interrupted the work. Finally, on threat of being brained with the crowbar, he got out of the way. In another minute or two, the men had made a hole large enough to pull him out. With great difficulty, they carried him aft and lashed him tight. When he recovered his breath and began to lose his fear, he began to berate his rescuers for not being more prompt. The men both hated and pitied him.

The day passed and night came. The ship still was afloat but with half her deck under water. An icy wind from the Antarctic began to numb the men who had lain in the open for twenty-four hours without food. At dawn, the captain prepared to bring some order to the ship, for the wind was subsiding. Slowly, the ship began to turn and gather way, with the decks still half under. At every lurch, the crew expected the ship to slide out from under them and sink to the bottom of the sea; but when the wind was directly aft, the ship rose and was no longer at the mercy of wind and pounding seas.

The sailors were put to work, tired though they were, to make sail, to pump out the bilges, and to make the vessel shipshape once again. When they went below, they found the forecastle a ruin. Most of their gear had floated away.

A fair wind pushed the ship northward up the Atlantic under a blue sky and a dancing sea. Wait was again established in the deckhouse. Once more, the doubt that he was really dying pervaded the ship, although no one dared say so. The captain went to interview him because he had to be sure. The crew was in an ugly mood. The captain was certain the man was dying and refused to let him go back to work; the crew, however, were convinced that Wait was well enough to share in their labors, and they threatened mutiny. Sure that Wait would die, the captain wanted to let him die in peace. He persuaded the men that Wait was dying, and their mutterings ended.

As the ship drove northward, Wait seemed to fade. His cheeks fell in, and his skull lost its flesh; his appearance hypnotized the crew. Once again pitying him in his dying, they humored his whims. He was always in their talk and their thoughts. The ship seemed too small to everyone; they could not get away from death.

As the ship approached the Flores islands, Wait seemed better. The older sailors, however, shook their heads; it was common superstition that dying men on shipboard waited until they were in sight of land to breathe their last. Wait died as the Flores islands came over the horizon, and he was buried at sea. As the board on which his body lay was lifted to let the corpse slide into the sea, something caught. The men lifting the board held their breath. Everyone seemed in a trance until the corpse slid slowly downward and then plunged over the rail. The ship suddenly seemed lighter, as though relieved of the burden of Death itself.

Critical Evaluation:

In *The Nigger of the "Narcissus,"* Joseph Conrad constructs a tale that is at once a realistic and a symbolic, even mythic, representation of human life. The sailing ship *Narcissus* serves as a microcosm of society, with its crew forming an isolated cross section of humanity. In this relatively brief novel, Conrad establishes a surprisingly large number of individual characters with fully established personalities which represent the range of human possibilities. Conrad's description of the vessel as "a fragment detached from the earth" accurately summarizes his thematic purpose. The novel implies: These are the basic facts of human existence, and these are the ways in which people respond to their trials and difficulties.

The characters, clearly defined individuals, are also archetypes of personalities and philosophies. Captain Allistoun, the figure at the apex of this narrowly confined nautical society, is described in almost godlike fashion. He appears to see, hear, or notice nothing, but actually he is keenly aware of everything that takes place on the *Narcissus*, and, except for the workings of the inexplicable and unmanageable powers of nature, is responsible for everything that takes place aboard his ship. As is often the case with the divine, the captain is sometimes ambiguous in his purpose and intent, and often apparently absent from the action. Throughout most of the voyage, for example, he fails to resolve the dilemma of Wait, refusing either to confirm the man as dying or condemn him as a malingerer.

Others in the crew play their own particular roles, which often have ironic overtones. Donkin, the master of using language to fool, mislead, and control others, is a lackluster sailor, ultimately despised by his shipmates, but on land he becomes a success among a certain class of society. In contrast, the older man Singleton, an outstanding sailor whose long years of knowledge of the sea have made him almost silent but whose few words are epitomes of wisdom, becomes a sot when ashore.

Undoubtedly the most symbolic figure is that of James Wait, the mysterious black sailor who is the last to board the *Narcissus* and who spends the entire voyage lying in his bunk, awaiting and avoiding death. Wait represents the common fate of humanity; all human lives are a wait, while on a journey, for death. In Conrad's fiction, however, meanings are more ambiguous and expansive. Wait's name is a pun upon his allegorical role. As he waits for death, he is a weight upon the *Narcissus* and its crew. His presence imposes a multiple burden on his shipmates. If he is lying about his illness and is merely a malingerer, then they have become his dupes, tricked into humoring a fraud. Should he actually be dying, however, then their doubts are cynical, undeserved accusations against a suffering fellow human being. The crew's inability to resolve its conflicting feelings about Wait generates much internal tension and gives the novel an additional level of suspense.

Wait is more than a bodiless symbol, and much of his mysterious power over the crew stems from the fact that in him Conrad has created such a realistic and believable individual. This is accomplished most notably with Conrad's careful selection of relevant details in his description of Wait and his ability to provide Wait with a unique, highly distinctive voice. It is largely through the power of Wait's voice that Wait establishes and holds sway over the crew of the *Narcissus*. Throughout much of the novel, as Wait lies unseen, his presence is established and his influence felt through voice alone.

Although a relatively early work (published in 1897), *The Nigger of the "Narcissus"* shows Conrad already possessing considerable artistic abilities, especially in his handling of action and events. The centerpiece of the novel is the dramatic storm scene. The scene flows into the equally compelling rescue of Wait from the wrecked deckhouse. Conrad's sentences, in their syntax and vocabulary, mimic the surging motion and even the sounds of the wind's fierce gusts and the waves' rising and crashing on the *Narcissus*.

This unity of language, action, and theme extends throughout the novel. At the end, when the *Narcissus* docks in London and the paid-off crew leaves, Conrad describes the ship as "dying," the life ebbing out of it with the departure of the men. The imagery, word choice, and sentence structure combine to present an increasing sense of heaviness, slowness, and, finally, stillness. This progression of the prose mimics and emphasizes the slide of the *Narcissus* into its kind of nautical death.

Undoubtedly the most famous part of *The Nigger of the "Narcissus,"* and the one that has had the greatest critical impact, is Conrad's noted preface to the original edition. Originally, Conrad had intended to place this section at the end of the novel, where it would serve as a sort of epilogue, explaining the general meaning and aim of the book. Upon reflection, however, Conrad seems to have concluded that it should prepare the reader for the story that follows.

In his preface, Conrad calls for a community of readers with whom the writer can communicate, and with whom the author can share some understanding of the "sense of mystery surrounding our lives." To accomplish this, Conrad states, requires the writer to be honestly dedicated to achieving, through hard work, the purest possible creation. A work of art, Conrad insists, "should carry its justification in every line." That is the exacting requirement that Conrad imposed upon himself for *The Nigger of the "Narcissus,"* and the artistic success of the novel is proof that he achieved that goal.

"Critical Evaluation" by Michael Witkoski

Bibliography:
Bloom, Harold, ed. *Joseph Conrad.* New York: Chelsea House, 1986. A selection of critical essays that help place *The Nigger of the "Narcissus"* within the framework of Conrad's fictions.
Karl, Frederick R. A. *Reader's Guide to Joseph Conrad.* Rev. ed. New York: Noonday Press, 1969. An introductory volume, especially helpful in guiding the reader through the actions and activities of the novel and relating them to Conrad's thematic and artistic concerns.
Schwarz, Daniel R. *Conrad: "Almayer's Folly" to "Under Western Eyes."* Ithaca, N.Y.: Cornell University Press, 1980. Views *The Nigger of the "Narcissus"* in terms of Conrad's developing style and point of view as an author, relating this growth to his own psychological state.
Watt, Ian. "Conrad Criticism and *The Nigger of the 'Narcissus.'*" *Nineteenth-Century Fiction* 12 (March, 1958): 257-283. Although considerably dated, this is a valuable survey of critical views of the novel from its publication to the mid-twentieth century.
Winner, Anthony. *Culture and Irony: A Study in Conrad's Major Novels.* Charlottesville: University Press of Virgina, 1988. Although the contrast between East and West is not strongly represented in *The Nigger of the "Narcissus,"* the dichotomy between the land-based and sea-based views of life gives Conrad, in the novella, ample material.

NIGHT

Type of work: Novel
Author: Elie Wiesel (1928-   )
Type of plot: Historical
Time of plot: 1941-1945
Locale: Eastern Europe
First published: Un di Velt hot geshvign, 1956; *La Nuit,* 1958 (English translation, 1960)

>   *Principal characters:*
>   ELIEZER, a teenage Jewish boy
>   FATHER of Eliezer
>   MOSHE THE BEADLE, Eliezer's tutor

The Story:

Eliezer lived with his parents and his three sisters in the village of Sighet in Transylvania. He studied the Talmud, the Jewish holy book, under the tutelage of Moshe the Beadle. Late in 1941, the Hungarian police expelled all foreign Jews, including Moshe, from Sighet in cattle cars. Several months later, Moshe returned and informed Eliezer that the deported Jews had been turned over to the German Gestapo and executed in a forest in Poland. Moshe had managed to escape. He had returned to Sighet to warn the Jewish community of what would happen to all Jews if they remained in the area.

Moshe's warning was ignored, and the Jews of Sighet continued with their daily routines. During the Passover celebration of 1944, however, German soldiers arrived in Sighet, arrested Jewish leaders, confiscated the valuables of Jewish townspeople, and forced all Jews to live in a restricted section of town. A short time later, all of Sighet's Jews were forced into cattle cars and transported to Auschwitz, the site of a Nazi concentration camp in Poland. On the train ride to Auschwitz, one woman went mad; in her delirium, she had visions of a huge furnace spewing flames, a foreshadowing of the crematories that would take the lives of many concentration camp inmates.

When they arrived at Auschwitz, Eliezer and his father were separated from his mother and sisters. Many children were led directly toward a crematory, where they were immediately executed. All the men had their heads shaved and a number tattooed on their arms. Eliezer and his fellow captives were forced to live in squalid barracks; they were fed only bread, water, and tasteless broth. Although many of the inmates prayed for strength to survive their horrific ordeal, Eliezer ceased to pray, and he began to doubt God's sense of justice.

A short time later, Eliezer, his father, and hundreds of others were marched to another concentration camp, Buna, where conditions were no better. Eliezer was assigned to work in a warehouse, and he was sometimes beaten by his supervisor. Eliezer's gold-crowned tooth, an article of value to his captors, was removed with a rusty spoon by a concentration camp dentist. Eliezer was whipped after being caught watching his supervisor having sex with a young Polish girl. During Eliezer's stay at Buna, four inmates were hanged for breaking concentration camp rules. At various times, weak and sick inmates were selected for execution in the crematories.

Eliezer lost his faith. He accused God of creating the concentration camps and of running its crematories. He refused to fast on Yom Kippur, the Jewish holy day. Other inmates shared Eliezer's sense of despair. One inmate selected for extermination asked his friends to say the kaddish, the Jewish prayer for the dead, for him, but no one recited the prayer when the man was executed. Eliezer's faith could not sustain him; he survived mainly because of his love and concern for his father, who was weakening with each passing week.

When the Russian army moved toward Buna, Eliezer and his fellow inmates were ordered on a forced march through the snow-covered Polish countryside. The weaker captives who could not maintain the rapid pace fell by the roadside and died or were shot by the German guards. During one rest stop, dozens of inmates fell dead from exhaustion.

After a long trek, the captives arrived at Gleiwitz, another concentration camp. Eliezer met Juliek, a boy whom Eliezer had first seen at Auschwitz. Juliek played the violin, and he had managed to keep the instrument in his possession during his stay in the camps. During Eliezer's first evening at Gleiwitz, Juliek played the Beethoven Violin Concerto, which moved Eliezer. The next morning, Eliezer saw Juliek's corpse lying on the barracks floor.

A few days later, Eliezer, his father, and hundreds of other inmates were packed into open cattle cars and transported to Buchenwald, another concentration camp. En route, many captives died and were unceremoniously thrown from the train cars; their naked corpses were left unburied in open fields. As the train passed through towns, people threw bread into the open cars, then watched as the prisoners beat and killed each other for food.

By the time the train reached Buchenwald, Eliezer's father was seriously ill with dysentery. Eliezer kept a vigil at his father's bedside. A guard hit Eliezer's father in the head when he asked for water. The next day, when Eliezer awoke, his father was gone; he had been taken to the crematory and put to death.

Eliezer lived for about three months at Buchenwald. In April, 1945, as the war neared its end, an evacuation of Buchenwald was announced. An air raid postponed the planned evacuation. Several days later, members of a resistance movement in the camp decided to act. After a brief battle, the German guards departed, leaving the camp in the hands of the resistance leaders. Later that day, an American tank approached the gates of Buchenwald and liberated the camp.

Three days after the liberation of Buchenwald, Eliezer was hospitalized with food poisoning. In the hospital, he looked at a mirror and saw the face of a corpse staring back at him.

Critical Evaluation:

Night, the first novel of Elie Wiesel's trilogy on Holocaust concentration camp survivors, is an autobiographical novel that records the author's own long night of captivity in the Nazi death camps during World War II. Like Eliezer, the novel's narrator, Elie Wiesel was forced from his own village into Auschwitz, became separated from his mother and sisters, witnessed his father's slow demise and death, and was eventually liberated at the end of the war.

Although the powerful tale told in *Night* is deeply personal, Eliezer's narrative can also be viewed as the story of all European Jews who suffered during the reign of Adolf Hitler. When Eliezer admonishes the Jews of Sighet for their refusal to heed the warnings of Moshe the Beadle, when he questions why his fellow Jewish citizens passively follow the orders of their German captors, when he asks why God lets thousands of Jews be put to death Eliezer becomes a Jewish Everyman struggling in anguish to understand the most troubling chapter in his people's history.

The process by which Eliezer begins to doubt God and eventually lose his faith reflects the experience of many Jews during and after the Holocaust. Seeing three concentration camp inmates hanging from a gallows, Eliezer reasons that God, too, has been hanged. During a Rosh Hashanah prayer ceremony, Eliezer asks why he should bless God: "Because He had had thousands of children burned in His pits? Because He kept six crematories working night and day, on Sundays and feast days? Because in his great might He had created Auschwitz?"

Eliezer's story is a cruel reversal of Exodus, the Old Testament epic of liberation and triumph. It is during the feast of Passover, when Jews celebrate the passing of the Angel of Death over their homes and their subsequent liberation from Egypt, that German soldiers begin arresting the Jewish leaders of Sighet. Exodus records the journey of God's chosen people toward a promised land provided by God; *Night* depicts the journey of a people selected for extermination entering into an oppressive captivity in the Nazi death camps. In the face of their trials, the chosen people of Exodus had united; on the other hand, the Jews depicted in *Night* often turn on one another, fighting, and even killing for food. To Wiesel, Hitler's Holocaust nullifies the triumph of Exodus. The Jews of Wiesel's time are faithless, despairing survivors of a long night of captivity; they are not fulfilled travelers who have reached their promised land.

Eliezer's camp is liberated at the end of *Night*, but he does not believe that freedom has been provided by the God of Exodus. Buchenwald is freed only when the camp's resistance movement takes up arms against its Nazi captors. The symbol of freedom is an American tank arriving at Buchenwald's gates. Eliezer is no longer a captive at the end of the novel, but Wiesel offers no hint of any physical or spiritual rebirth. The novel's final image is of Eliezer looking into a mirror and seeing a corpse stare back at him. *Night* is the tale of painful death, not of liberation and rebirth.

The narrating of this harrowing tale undoubtedly presented problems for its author. Wiesel, indeed any writer who tries to depict the horrors of the Holocaust, has to put into words a sequence of terrible events that can never be adequately rendered in language. No description of the Nazi death camps, no matter how skillfully and realistically narrated, can fully depict the terrors that millions of people experienced during World War II. Wiesel and other Holocaust survivors nevertheless felt compelled to record their stories for their contemporaries and for history, and in its plot, characterization, and prose strategies *Night* is a literary work of the highest order.

Wiesel narrates the events of his captivity in a series of vignettes suited to the story of separation, annihilation, and loss. Few of Wiesel's characters are substantially developed; Eliezer and his father are the novel's only well-rounded characters. This strategy is, however, well suited for a book that deals with the marginalization, suppression, and elimination of individuals. Wiesel's prose style is terse and often understated. Eliezer rarely editorializes in *Night*; he prefers to tell his story in lean, taut prose, allowing the events of the novel to speak for themselves.

Wiesel continued to explore the lives of Holocaust survivors in *Dawn* (1960) and *The Accident* (1961), the next two novels in the trilogy begun with *Night*, and in more than a dozen subsequent novels, nonfiction works, and plays. With *Night*, Wiesel became a spokesperson for all those who suffered during Hitler's reign. He was one of the first Holocaust survivors to record his experiences, and he made the rest of the world aware of the horrors that had been perpetrated by Hitler in his campaign to exterminate European Jewry. In 1986, Wiesel received the Nobel Peace Prize for serving as a "messenger to mankind" and as "one of our most important spiritual leaders and guides."

James Tackach

Bibliography:
Cargas, Harry James. *Conversations with Elie Wiesel*. South Bend, Ind.: Justice Books, 1992. A collection of interviews with the author that cover his life, politics, and literary works.

Wiesel speaks frankly and extensively about his childhood in Sighet and of his time in the concentration camps—events that formed the basis for *Night*.

Estess, Ted L. *Elie Wiesel*. New York: Frederick Ungar, 1980. An analysis of Wiesel's key literary works, including *Night*, *Dawn*, and *The Accident*. *Night* receives extended discussion in chapter 2.

Fine, Ellen S. *Legacy of Night: The Literary Universe of Elie Wiesel*. Albany: State University of New York Press, 1982. A critical study of *Night* and Wiesel's other Holocaust works.

Rittner, Carol, ed. *Elie Wiesel: Between Memory and Hope*. New York: New York University Press, 1990. A collection of seventeen essays on Wiesel's life and literary works. *Night* receives an extended discussion in three essays and is mentioned in several others.

Walker, Graham B., Jr. *Elie Wiesel: A Challenge to Theology*. Jefferson, N.C.: McFarland, 1988. Focuses on Wiesel's religious dilemmas as they are reflected in his major literary works.

NIGHT FLIGHT

Type of work: Novel
Author: Antoine de Saint-Exupéry (1900-1944)
Type of plot: Psychological realism
Time of plot: Early 1930's
Locale: South America
First published: Vol de nuit, 1931 (English translation, 1932)

Principal characters:
RIVIÈRE, director of the airmail service
ROBINEAU, the inspector
FABIEN, the lost pilot
MADAME FABIEN
PELLERIN, a pilot
ROBLET, a former pilot
THE WIRELESS OPERATOR

The Story:

Fabien, along with his wireless operator, was flying at sunset, bringing the mail from Patagonia to Buenos Aires. Two other mail planes, one from Chile and one from Paraguay, were also headed for Buenos Aires, where another plane was to take off, at about two in the morning, with a cargo of South American mail intended for Europe. Fabien's wireless operator, hearing reports of storms ahead, urged Fabien to land in San Julian for the night; but Fabien, looking at the clear sky and the first stars, refused and headed for Buenos Aires.

At Buenos Aires, Rivière, the head of the mail service, was pacing the airport. Worried about the safety of his three planes, he was pleased when the plane from Chile landed safely early in the evening. Pellerin, the pilot of the plane from Chile, told of flying through a great storm in the Andes. Although Pellerin had not experienced great difficulty, he was still shaken by his experience. Both men seemed certain, at this point, that the storm would not cross the Andes. Robineau, the inspector at Buenos Aires, somewhat resentful of Rivière's severity and unwillingness to relax discipline, revealed more pity for Pellerin's experience than Rivière had shown. Robineau went out to dinner with Pellerin, a meal over which they could chat about women and domestic concerns, away from the tension of the airfield.

When Robineau returned to the field, Rivière criticized him for making a friend of Pellerin. Rivière went on to point out that supervisors, who had to order men to what might be their deaths, could not become friendly with the men under them; the supervisors had to maintain discipline and impersonality, because the success of the project, the conquest of space at night, depended on firm and immediate control. Rivière, although mastering the pain in his own side only with great difficulty, maintained severe discipline on the airfield at all times. He deprived pilots of bonuses if planes were not on time, no matter what the reason; he disciplined old Roblet severely for any minor infraction, even though Roblet had been the first man in Argentina to assemble a plane; he fired an electrician for some faulty wiring in a plane.

The wife of the pilot who was to fly from Buenos Aires to Europe received a phone call. She awakened her husband, and he prepared for the flight. She was aware, as he was dressing, that he was already part of another world, that he had already lost interest in home, domesticity, herself. He then reported to Rivière, who reprimanded him for turning back on a previous flight. Rivière was severe, although he silently admired the man's skill.

Meanwhile, the plane from Patagonia, piloted by Fabien, entered a violent storm. As the storm became more serious, Fabien tried to find a place to land, for he could see nothing; but all the airfields nearby were completely closed down by the storm. Rivière became more and more concerned. Unable to contact Fabien by radio, he alerted police and emergency services throughout the country. Fabien's wife of only six weeks, accustomed to having him arrive for dinner by a certain hour, telephoned the airfield. Rivière, feeling strong emotion, tried to reassure her that all would be well, but knew he could not honestly say so.

When Fabien, in deep distress and thinking he might try a crash landing, threw out his only landing flare, he found that he had been blown off course by the storm and was now over the ocean. He turned sharply west. After a time, he noticed a clearing above and climbed to it. The storm was still solid beneath him, however, and he could find no airfield open for a landing. He had gas for only thirty minutes. Buenos Aires informed him that the storm covered the whole interior of the country and that no airfield within thirty minutes' flying time was open. Rivière, realizing that Fabien could not fly to safety, could only hope for a lucky crash landing through the storm.

Madame Fabien, distraught, arrived at the airfield. Rivière, knowing that he could not comfort her, was too wise to try, but he sympathized with her distress as he tried to explain the enormous effort it takes to conquer the skies. He did not speak melodramatically to her; rather, he was matter-of-fact in what he said, and they understood each other.

At last, they received a blurred message from Fabien reporting that he was coming down and entering the rain clouds. They did not know whether the fuel had already run out or he was attempting to glide the plane through the storm to some safe spot.

In the meantime, the plane from Paraguay had arrived safely, just skirting the edge of the storm. Robineau watched Rivière closely enough to realize that Rivière was enormously concerned, that his sense of discipline was not callousness but a dedicated sense of the purpose in his mission. Robineau came into Rivière's office with some papers and, for a moment, there was a sense of understanding, of communion, between the two men.

As time passed, everyone realized that Fabien was lost. Although some sign of him might still turn up the next day, there was nothing to do now and little hope that he and his wireless operator could be found alive. The pilot of the plane from Paraguay passed the pilot of the plane going to Europe. They exchanged a few words about Fabien, but there was no sentimentality, for the pilots realized the necessity of carrying on with a minimum of expressed emotion. Rivière felt that this loss might be used as evidence to encourage the government to curtail nighttime flying operations. At the same time, he believed strongly that these operations must continue, that humanity must, in spite of disaster, carry on. He ordered the next plane to take off on schedule.

Critical Evaluation:

Antoine de Saint-Exupéry's *Night Flight* achieved considerable critical praise when it was first published in 1931. The preface by André Gide gave Saint-Exupéry's work the imprimatur of the Parisian literary establishment. Critical reviews of the work were overwhelmingly positive, and Saint-Exupéry was awarded one of France's premier literary awards, the Fémina Prize, for this novel.

Night Flight, Saint-Exupéry's second novel (*Southern Mail* was published in 1929), is the author's most completely realized work of fiction, although, as with all of his writings, there are strong autobiographical elements. It is brief in scope, covering just a few hours in time, and brief in length, less than 150 pages in the original French edition. The author's style and literary technique combine poetic elements, particularly Fabien's struggles in the storm and in the starry skies above the clouds, with a lean, crisp narrative. The story is told in brief chapters which successfully move the narrative along by focusing on the protagonists one at a time and by including flashbacks, brief conversational dialogues, interior monologues, and the use of radio reports and telegrams. The Argentina locale is almost irrelevant; the events could have occurred anywhere.

What Gide admired in *Night Flight* was the heroism exhibited by Fabien and his fellow pilots in the line of duty. Flying was both dangerous and glamorous in the early twentieth century. America's Charles Lindbergh captured the world's attention in 1927 when he flew nonstop from New York to Paris. Saint-Exupéry himself was famous for his exploits in aviation in Africa and South America. The pilots in *Night Flight* rise to what Gide called "superhuman heights of valor." One of the reasons that the work was so highly praised was because of its assertion that humanity could strive to overcome not only nature's challenges in the form of mountains, seas, and storms, but also the weaknesses of human nature, not the least of which are fear and doubt. Fabien could have safely set down in advance of the worst of the storm, but he chose to continue his flight. Civilization in general, and France in particular, had succumbed to cynicism and apathy in the aftermath of the losses—physical, intellectual, and emotional—resulting from World War I. Saint-Exupéry's novel was a reassertion of human nobility.

For all of the pilots' bravery, however, at the center of *Night Flight* is Rivière, the chief operator. Modeled on Saint-Exupéry's first airmail flight supervisor, Didier Daurat, Rivière is the will behind the act. It is he who sends Fabien and the others into the night skies and it is he who keeps them there. He is the one who brings out the superhuman qualities noted by Gide. Fifty years of age and worried about his health, Rivière is the opposite of the clichéd version of the young and handsome hero, but he dominates this novel of heroism.

In brief conversations and in extended internal musings, Rivière ruminates about himself, his power, his responsibilities, and his duty. "For him, a man was a mere lump of wax to be kneaded into shape. . . . Not that his aim was to make slaves of his men; his aim was to raise them above themselves." He loves his men, both pilots and ground staff, but he dares not show that love, or even pity. He questions whether he is too demanding, too critical, but the harder he is, the fewer accidents they have. Rivière's qualities of vision and leadership are brilliantly contrasted with the limitations and inadequacies of Robineau, the self-pitying inspector, who, Rivière claims, lacks even the capacity to think.

Night Flight also poses philosophical questions, most notably why human beings like Fabien must die for a cause, such as proving that flying at night is not only feasible but necessary. The two women in the work, Fabien's wife and the wife of the unnamed pilot who is supposed to continue to carry the mail to Europe, represent the reverse of superhuman striving. Intimate love, personal happiness, and comforting domestic life and values are placed in opposition to the qualities of duty, will, and challenge presented by night flying. Rivière finds it difficult even to meet with Fabien's wife; the gulf between their two realities is too wide. He admits that the ideals she represents might be of equal value to the ones he does, but contends that love and domestic tranquillity are not enough, that there is something higher than individual human life, noting the Incas of Peru who left their monuments of stone as testimony to a vanished world.

It is not even the goal, however, that ultimately matters. It is the progress toward that end, the striving itself, that means the most. Fabien's plane crashes, but the other two planes arrive safely and the European mail is dispatched on time. Due to Rivière's will, death and defeat are overcome, the human spirit is victorious. A momentary transcendence has been achieved.

By the end of the 1930's, Saint-Exupéry's emphasis upon the power of will and the obligations of duty had been perversely achieved in Fascism, and to some readers *Night Flight* prefigured those fascist qualities. In the latter half of the twentieth century, the antihero has become the norm, and traditional heroic qualities have become suspect. In the early 1930's, however, during the height of the Great Depression and in the aftermath of the Great War, qualities of will and duty did not belong only to the fascists but also to democratic leaders such as Franklin D. Roosevelt, who claimed that the only thing to be feared was fear itself, that great deeds could be achieved through the combination of will and act.

Saint-Exupéry's *Night Flight* can be compared to other literary works. Charles Lindbergh's *The Spirit of St. Louis* (1953) concerns his nonstop flight across the Atlantic Ocean. Tom Wolfe's *The Right Stuff* (1979) chronicles the early days of space flight. However, the most apt comparison to *Night Flight* might be with Ernest Hemingway's *The Old Man and the Sea* (1952). Both novels magnificently evoke natural elements, and, in both, the apparent defeat— the loss of the great fish, the death of Fabien—ends in humanity's triumph.

"Critical Evaluation" by Eugene Larson

Bibliography:

Cate, Curtis. *Antoine de Saint-Exupéry: His Life and Times*. New York: G. P. Putnam's Sons, 1970. Born in France and educated in England and America, Cate wrote the first major biography of Saint-Exupéry in English. The author comments extensively on the airman's literary works.

Migeo, Marcel. *Saint-Exupéry*. Translated by Herma Briffault. New York: McGraw-Hill, 1960. Shortly after the end of World War II, in the course of researching the life of Saint-Exupéry, the author interviewed Didier Daurat, the inspiration for Rivière.

Rumbold, Richard, and Lady Margaret Stewart. *The Winged Life: A Portrait of Antoine de Saint-Exupéry, Poet and Airman*. New York: David McKay, 1953. Written by a World War II Royal Air Force pilot and the daughter of a former secretary of air in the British cabinet, the work is a sympathetic study of the famous French pilot.

Schiff, Stacy. *Saint-Exupéry: A Biography*. New York: Knopf, 1994. This well-written biography explores the connection between Saint-Exupéry the pilot and Saint-Exupéry the writer. It includes a comprehensive discussion of the circumstances and influences surrounding *Night Flight*.

Smith, Maxwell A. *Knight of the Air*. London: Cassell, 1959. The author of this work concentrates not only on Saint-Exupéry's life but also, more specifically, on his literary works, including an excellent analysis of *Night Flight*.

'NIGHT, MOTHER

Type of work: Drama
Author: Marsha Norman (1947-   )
Type of plot: Psychological realism
Time of plot: The late twentieth century
Locale: Rural United States
First performed: 1982; first published, 1983

Principal characters:
MAMA (THELMA CATES), the main character
JESSIE CATES, her daughter

The Story:

On Saturday night, while Mama hunted for her sweets, Jessie rummaged for towels and garbage bags and searched the attic for her father's gun. Jessie told Mama that she wanted the gun for protection. Mama, convinced that there were no criminals near the out-of-the-way country house where they lived, thought Jessie was foolish. Jessie eventually told Mama of her plan to commit suicide. At first Mama thought that Jessie, an epileptic, was ill, but Jessie felt fine. Then Mama said that the gun was broken, but Jessie proved that it was in good condition. She had gotten bullets by tricking her brother Dawson into believing that she was watching out for prowlers. Desperate, Mama threatened to call Dawson, but Jessie would shoot herself before he came. Mama suggested calling for the ambulance driver that Jessie liked. Jessie, however, insisted that she wanted the night alone with Mama.

Mama tried to convince Jessie that normal people do not commit suicide, but Jessie wanted to die and escape to a place of quiet nothingness. Unable to convince Jessie that suicide was immoral, Mama tried to gain control by insisting that Jessie could not commit suicide in Mama's house. Trying another tactic, Mama asked Jessie if she did not want to stay around to see what she would get for her birthday. The presents turned out to be predictable and not what Jessie wanted.

Jessie planned the whole evening and made a list of things she wanted to do. Mama thought that Jessie might be trying to escape her family, but Jessie was not committing suicide simply to get away from Dawson, her meddlesome brother, or Ricky, her delinquent son with whom she was unable to communicate. Jessie admitted that she did not like her life with Mama and that going to live with Mama after Cecil (Jessie's husband) left her was a mistake that both Mama and Jessie made. Jessie now felt hurt and used. Her life had come to a dead end. She had been contemplating suicide for about ten years but had started to plan it around Christmas, when she realized how empty her life was.

Mama grasped for reasons to give Jessie to continue living. She suggested getting a dog, planting a garden, shopping at the A&P, and taking up crochet. These activities were unsuitable to Jessie, who saw her life as a meaningless bus ride that she wanted to end now. Mama then accused Jessie of acting like a spoiled brat and blamed Jessie as the cause of her own misery. Jessie retorted that it was time Mama did something about her own miserable life.

Mama continued in vain to urge Jessie to find ways to make herself happy, by buying dishes, moving furniture, or getting a driver's license. Mama even suggested that Jessie get a job, but Jessie had failed at two jobs. She could not sell over the phone, and she made people nervous when she worked at a hospital gift shop. Besides, she could not be around people. Jessie could not make her life better, so she was going to control her destiny and end her life.

After moments of tension, Mama and Jessie settled down to have some cocoa. Jessie wanted a night of truth and sharing. Mama admitted that she never loved Daddy because he resented the fact that he married a plain country woman. He never spoke to Mama, but Jessie loved him. Mama then accused Jessie of being angry that Daddy died and left Jessie with Mama.

When Jessie tried to show Mama where all the pots were, Mama got angry and threw the pots out of the cabinet, saying she would live on sweets. After things settled down, the two women discussed the breakup of Jessie's marriage. Mama had played matchmaker and brought Cecil and Jessie together, but Cecil was the wrong man for Jessie. Cecil was a positive thinker and wanted Jessie to live an active life. She tried to stay outdoors and to get more exercise, but she could not meet his expectations. Cecil felt guilty about the time that Jessie was horseback riding and took a fall that supposedly caused her epilepsy. Jessie also realized that she had taught her son that life was unfair and not to trust anyone. Ricky was Jessie and Cecil battling each other in a small space.

Mama revealed that Jessie did not get epilepsy from a fall but inherited it from her father. Mama then blamed herself for Jessie's problems. She felt that she had failed to convince Jessie not to commit suicide. Jessie tried to show Mama that suicide was a positive solution, a way of saying "No" to everything and everyone. Jessie was tired of waiting around to become the person that she was never going to be.

Outraged, Mama said that people would feel sorry for her, not for Jessie. Jessie helped Mama make funeral plans and instructed Mama in what to do after the suicide. Then Jessie gave gifts for her family, asked Mama to let her go, went into her room, and shot herself. Mama realized that she only thought that she had a right to Jessie's life. Doing what Jessie told her, Mama washed the pan and called Dawson.

Critical Evaluation:

Written in 1981, *'night, Mother* was produced by Robert Brustein at the American Repertory Theatre in Cambridge, Massachusetts, in 1982. The play later moved to the John Golden Theatre on Broadway, where it ran for ten months to mostly favorable reviews. In 1983, the play won a Pulitzer Prize and Marsha Norman was awarded the Susan Smith Blackburn Prize, given annually to a female playwright from an English-speaking country. The drama later played regional repertory theaters and has appeared widely in college anthologies of drama.

'Night, Mother is a tightly crafted drama. Although it has the veneer of realism, there is a classical idealism about it. Norman wants to create real people, yet she divorces them from any set milieu. The house where the drama takes place should not show any character traits. It is neither messy nor quaint. The town is not to be associated with any regional locale or accent. The play holds to the classical unities. There are only two characters, fixed in one location. Narrative time is synchronized to performance time so that all the clocks on stage start at 8:15 P.M., or curtain time, and run throughout the performance. There are no breaks or intermissions. The drama, which moves swiftly and inevitably toward the climax, is based on the unraveling of past events.

Like Norman's other plays, *'night, Mother* treats the frustrations and trials of ordinary women who try to share their lives with each other. From one critical perspective, it is debatable how strong a feminist message the play embodies. The play depicts women's lives as hopeless and futile. The two women in the drama undergo an emotional revelation, but little is done to change their lives. Much of what they do emphasizes the deadly routine of women's lives, but little is done to effect a revolution. Many of the women's problems surround their relations with absent men—fathers, husbands, and brothers. Suicide becomes a tragic gesture but leaves little option for social change.

On the other hand, the play is a powerful one about two women who have endured suffering and try desperately to communicate their pain to each other. Jessie is dependent on her mother even though she is her mother's caretaker. Together the two women undergo an emotional sharing of their lives. In many ways, Jessie has relived her mother's life. Both women married men who accepted them at first, then rejected them for not being someone else. Daddy married a plain country woman, then resented Mama for being one. Cecil wanted to change Jessie into an active outgoing person. Both men escape from their wives. Daddy pretended to go fishing, and Cecil went to the shed with another woman. Neither woman could get her husband to communicate with her. Daddy died without speaking to Mama. Cecil simply left, and Jessie had to write his good-bye note. Both women have been hurt and are having difficulty communicating with their children. At the end, Jessie wants to share her life with her mother, but she wants her mother to let her go. Mama tries, but she has difficulty letting go.

'Night, Mother is a powerful and gripping story of a mother and a daughter trying to communicate the pain in their lives, but it is more than a drama about mothers and daughters—it is a play about family that focuses on the psychological return of the daughter to her father through death. Jessie is her father's daughter. She has inherited not only his epilepsy but also his solitude. Both are reclusive and solitary individuals who seek escape from the world of family and friends. Jessie makes a point of using her father's gun to shoot herself. When she plans her funeral, she wants it to be like her father's. Death to Jessie is quiet and peaceful, an escape to the protected world of the father.

Jessie, who has lost control over the events of her life, consciously seeks to control her destiny by ending her life. By reasserting her power to end her life, Jessie feels that she has found a permanent solution to her alienation and loss of identity. In suicide, she will not only choose what happens to her but will also courageously be able to say no to life and to the false promise that Mama holds out to her for a better future. All of Mama's solutions are ways of getting through life and of passing time. Shopping, rearranging furniture, and learning to drive do not appeal to Jessie, who wants to take a determined action and make a positive statement with her death. Suicide and the right to commit suicide pose a powerful theme in the play. Despite Jessie's protest, suicide is not so much a powerful existential choice, a way to say no to life, as much as it is an escape to a romantic womb-like existence in which no more harm or hurt can come to her.

Paul Rosefeldt

Bibliography:
Burkman, Katherine H. "The Demeter Myth and Doubling in Marsha Norman's *'night, Mother*." In *Modern American Drama: The Female Canon*, edited by June Schlueter. Rutherford, N.J.: Fairleigh Dickinson University Press, 1990. A psychological exploration of the relationship between mother and daughter that traces *'night, Mother* to the ancient Greek myth of Demeter and Kore.
Gross, Amy. "Marsha Norman." *Vogue* 173 (July, 1983): 200-201, 256-258. A general interview article that discusses Norman's views on *'night, Mother*.
Kane, Leslie. "The Way Out, the Way In: Paths to the Self in the Plays of Marsha Norman." In *Feminine Focus: The New Women Playwrights*, edited by Enoch Brater. New York: Oxford

University Press, 1989. A discussion of Norman's plays that focuses on the mother-daughter relationship in *'night, Mother*.

Spencer, Jenny S. "Marsha Norman's She Tragedies." In *Making a Spectacle: Feminist Essays on Contemporary Women's Theatre*, edited by Lynda Hart. Ann Arbor: Michigan University Press, 1989. A feminist reading of Norman's dramas in which *'night, Mother* is seen as a drama of feminine passivity.

Stone, Elizabeth. "Playwright Marsha Norman: An Optimist Writes About Suicide, Confinement, and Despair." *Ms.* 102 (July, 1983): 56-59. An interview of Norman in which she explains Jessie's relationship to her mother, Jessie's suicide, and other aspects of *'night, Mother*.

THE NIGHT OF THE IGUANA

Type of work: Drama
Author: Tennessee Williams (Thomas Lanier Williams, 1911-1983)
Type of plot: Psychological realism
Time of plot: Late summer, 1940
Locale: Puerto Barrio, a Mexican village
First performed: 1961; first published, 1961

Principal characters:
    MAXINE FAULK, a newly widowed hotel keeper
    T. LAWRENCE "LARRY" SHANNON, a defrocked minister, now a tour guide
    HANNAH JELKES, about forty years old, an artist
    JONATHAN "NONNO" COFFIN, a ninety-seven-year-old poet, Hannah's
        grandfather
    MISS FELLOWES, a lesbian voice teacher and tourist
    CHARLOTTE, a young girl whom Shannon seduces
    JAKE LATTA, the tour guide sent to replace Larry

The Story:

Maxine had been a widow for less than a month. Her husband, Fred, snagged himself with a fishhook and died of blood poisoning. She had no real option but to continue running Costa Verde, a small hotel that they owned and managed, perched high above the Pacific near the remote Mexican village of Puerto Barrio. The play is set in the period shortly before the United States entered World War II. The Costa Verde had Nazi guests who cheered at the bombing of London and other German victories.

On the scene came T. Lawrence Shannon, always called Larry, a defrocked minister whose options were running out. He was a tour guide for Blake Tours and, in this instance, was shepherding a group of female Texans through Mexico. Miss Fellowes, seemingly the organizer and mother hen of this group, was agitated because Shannon refused to take them to the hotel for which they had contracted. She was also disturbed by Shannon's attentions to seventeen-year-old Charlotte, the youngest person in the tour group. Fellowes was righteously indignant that Shannon had made a play for Charlotte, but the subtext suggested that she was jealous because she herself had designs on the hapless girl.

Larry came into the hotel to see his old friend Maxine. It soon became evident that Maxine lusted after him and, with her husband recently dead, she hoped for some sort of alliance with him: marriage, or the best she could get short of marriage. Her not insubstantial physical needs were being fulfilled through purely physical acts with her bellboys, a situation that made her fear that she was losing their respect.

On this emotionally charged scene strode Hannah Jelkes, a New England spinster slightly under forty years old, who was wheeling her poet-grandfather, Jonathan Coffin, whom she always called Nonno, around the tropics. Nonno was ninety-seven. The two of them were as bereft of any real future as were Larry and Maxine. They had no money and had been turned away from every hotel in town. The Costa Verde was their last hope.

Maxine assured them that she had room for them and asked for payment in advance. Hannah informed her that they had no money but that they could earn their keep, Nonno by reciting his poetry to the other guests, Hannah by doing charcoal sketches of them and possibly by selling one of her watercolors. Maxine, unimpressed, agreed to let them stay, but for only one night.

Meanwhile, a native boy delivered an iguana that was tied up and left to fatten beneath the veranda. When it reached an appropriate weight, Maxine would cook it for dinner.

It became increasingly clear that Larry Shannon had no reasonable future to which to look forward. He spoke of rejoining the church, but the circumstances of his leaving it were such that he would not likely be welcomed back enthusiastically. His days as a tour guide for Blake Tours were definitely numbered and, when Blake Tours replaced Larry with Jake Latta, tempers ran so high that it seemed reasonable that Larry would be blackballed as a tour guide anywhere.

Larry's problems began when his mother discovered him masturbating when he was an adolescent. She spanked him and told him that God deplored such self-abuse. Resentful of both his mother and God, Larry went on to become an ordained minister who preached atheistic sermons and scandalized his congregations (his vengeance on God) and a lecher who sought out only girls below the age of majority (his vengeance on his mother). Now, with his options narrowing, he considered going back to preach in the church or swimming the Pacific to China, his way of threatening suicide.

Meanwhile, Hannah and Nonno were ensconced in the hotel. Hannah feared that Nonno had suffered a slight stroke as they came through the Sierras. The old man was dying. Hannah said that she tried to persuade her grandfather to return to Nantucket, from which they originally came, but it was clear that she did not have the wherewithal even to get them as far as Laredo. Maxine had made arrangements for Hannah and Nonno to go to another hotel in town, one that would extend them credit. It was clear that Maxine did not appreciate Hannah's presence because she sensed a growing chemistry between Hannah and Larry. Larry had a confrontation with Charlotte during which it became evident that he had seduced her the previous night.

In this exchange, Larry was emotionally bankrupt. He told Charlotte he loved her, but once he had his way with her, he turned mean and rejected any suggestion that the two of them might have more than the few hours of love they had recently experienced. Miss Fellowes, overhearing Charlotte's encounter with Larry, immediately called the authorities in Texas and got them to issue a warrant for his arrest; Larry would have been arrested at once if he crossed the border. One more option thus was closed to him.

Shortly after this encounter, Larry told Hannah the story of how he seduced a young girl in his congregation in Pleasant Valley, Virginia. Hannah remained nonjudgmental, ever trying to see the good in people rather than dwelling on the bad. Larry was becoming intrigued by Hannah because, unlike his mother, she did not judge.

Maxine, sensing this, exploded at Hannah, but she soon realized that jealousy was the reason for her outburst. A storm erupted, with a somewhat cleansing effect on the scene. Then Larry ran to the beach vowing to swim to China. Maxine dispatched her bellboys to drag him back. For his own protection, she had him tied up in a hammock. He had obviously lost his mind. She threatened to admit him to the Casa de Locos the following day.

Hannah came in to comfort Larry and to try to soothe him with poppy seed tea. He begged her to undo his bonds, but she refused. When Nonno called Hannah away for a moment, however, Larry wiggled loose. When Hannah returned, she heard the iguana struggling to break free, at the end of his rope, as many of the play's characters figuratively were at the ends of theirs. Hannah pleaded with Larry to cut the iguana's rope.

Shortly after that, Nonno called Hannah, telling her that he had finally finished his poem, which he dictated to her. As the play ended, Maxine urged Larry to stay with her to help manage the hotel, making it clear that their relationship could only be professional, not sexual. Larry told Hannah that he had cut the iguana's rope. She thanked him. She then turned to put a shawl around her grandfather's shoulders and discovered that the old man was dead.

Critical Evaluation:

In most of Tennessee Williams' major plays, the fear of dispossession looms before the major characters. Even in the affluent setting of *Cat on a Hot Tin Roof* (1955), Brick and Maggie are threatened with disinheritance. In *The Night of the Iguana*, the themes of dispossession and homelessness run high and are sustained throughout the play. Larry Shannon, Hannah Jelkes, and Nonno are all wanderers, wandering without means. One can hardly envision a more hopeless situation than Hannah's: Penniless, she spends her life pushing a ninety-seven-year-old man, a fourth- or fifth-rate poet, around Mexico in his wheelchair.

Despite this, Hannah Jelkes emerges as a unique female character in the Williams canon. She is almost a reverse image of Blanche DuBois in *A Streetcar Named Desire* (1947), although she faces similar problems. Whereas Blanche lives in the shadow of a checkered past, Hannah has always lived within the socially established moral boundaries of her society.

Hannah's celibacy does not make her judgmental of those who do not practice her restraint. In the two romantic episodes of her life that she reveals to Larry Shannon in the play, she has sympathy for the men who tried to have their way with her, the first a youth who pursued her in the balcony of a darkened movie theater, the second, years later, a man who took her out on a sampan one evening when she was in Singapore and, requesting one article of her clothing, used it as his fetish while he masturbated. Hannah averted her eyes and was not disgusted by the encounter because, as she says, nothing human disgusts her.

In *A Streetcar Named Desire*, Blanche's impending homelessness leads her to the desperate state of having to depend upon her sister or public charity. She is a victim of her circumstances. Hannah, on the other hand, is at peace with herself and deplores neither her life nor the circumstances that have caused it to be as it is. When Shannon questions her situation and reminds her that birds build nests because they want at least relative permanence, Hannah replies without rancor that she is a human being, not a bird, and that she is building her nests in her heart.

This bit of dialogue shows not only the reconciliation that Hannah has reached with her lot but also something about Shannon's values: Permanence means more to him than it does to Hannah. When Maxine offers him the opportunity to stay at Costa Verde and help her manage the hotel, hope glimmers that he eventually will find with Maxine the kind of life that will lay his "spooks," as he called them, to rest.

Maxine is a good person, one capable of genuine love. She probably is in love with Shannon, but she realizes that she cannot force him into a situation in which he will feel as trapped as the iguana beneath her veranda. The implication with which Williams leaves his audiences in *The Night of the Iguana* is that things will likely work out for all the principals in the play, a first for a playwright whose previous endings were usually darkly pessimistic.

R. Baird Shuman

Bibliography:

Arnott, Catherine M., comp. *File on Tennessee Williams*. New York: Methuen, 1987. This brief overview is aimed at secondary school students and others who may be unfamiliar with Williams' work. It is easily accessible and, although brief, accurate and well written.

Bigsby, C. W. *Tennessee Williams, Arthur Miller, Edward Albee*. Vol. 2 in *A Critical Introduction to Twentieth-Century American Drama*. New York: Cambridge University Press, 1985. Bigsby is one of the best-informed critics of modern drama. In this volume, he offers sound interpretive insights into Williams' writing career and into his standing among mid-century American dramatists.

Falk, Signi L. *Tennessee Williams*. 2d ed. New York: Twayne, 1978. This revision of Falk's earlier Twayne volume on Williams is very accessible, offering a sound overview of Williams' career and excellent interpretations of his individual plays. The chronological table at the beginning is especially useful.

Spoto, Donald. *The Kindness of Strangers: The Life of Tennessee Williams*. Boston: Little, Brown, 1985. Spoto's excellent biography deals with the man, his background, his demons, and his individual plays and stories, all in accurate detail.

Williams, Tennessee. *Conversations with Tennessee Williams*. Edited by Albert J. Devlin. Oxford: University Press of Mississippi, 1986. This collection of conversations and interviews between Williams and a number of interviewers provides an easy-to-follow overview of what Williams sought to achieve in his plays. A good starting point for those interested in Williams.

NIGHT RIDER

Type of work: Novel
Author: Robert Penn Warren (1905-1989)
Type of plot: Social morality
Time of plot: 1904-1905
Locale: Kentucky
First published: 1939

> *Principal characters:*
> PERCY MUNN, a young Kentucky lawyer and farmer
> MAY MUNN, his wife
> MR. CHRISTIAN, Percy's neighbor and friend
> LUCILLE CHRISTIAN, his daughter
> SENATOR TOLLIVER, a leader in local affairs
> CAPTAIN TODD, a Civil War veteran
> BENTON TODD, his son
> PROFESSOR BALL and
> DR. MACDONALD, the leaders in the association
> BUNK TREVELYAN, a poor tobacco farmer

The Story:

In the summer of 1904, Mr. Munn (as the author calls him throughout the novel) attended a rally of the Association of Growers of Dark Fired Tobacco in Bardsville, Kentucky. After an impromptu speech pleading for the defense of an "idea," he joined the association's board of directors, having been impressed by the leadership of such men as the smooth-talking Senator Tolliver and Captain Todd, a courageous former Confederate officer. He, however, had small success in gaining support for the association.

Curtailing his association activities in order to defend Bunk Trevelyan, accused of murdering a neighbor, Mr. Munn committed the first of a series of lawless deeds in which he convinced himself that an end justifies the means to attain it. Trusting Bunk's protestations of innocence, Munn led an illegal search of the home of an African American in the area in order to find a knife like the one belonging to Bunk, which had been found at the murder scene. When a knife was found and the African American owner told an unlikely story of how he got it, Bunk was released and the innocent man died for the crime.

Two raises in prices paid by the tobacco companies and an association decision to continue holding out brought a public denunciation of the association by Tolliver and a suit to recover his crop. Bitter over Tolliver's betrayal, Munn joined an activist organization, the secret, Ku Klux Klan-like Free Farmers' Brotherhood of Protection and Control, whose bands of night riders scraped the tobacco beds of farmers who refused to join the association. Captain Todd, a man of both courage and probity, disapproved of the new group within the old, and withdrew from the association. Munn inwardly defended his own action because he believed the raids would finally bring "justice" to the farmers. He learned, though, that lawlessness begets lawlessness: Bunk Trevelyan attempted to blackmail a Brotherhood member, and Munn became by lot the leader of a group that shot Bunk after he refused Munn's offer to let him escape. Again Munn defended his deed: Bunk had been the killer, he told himself, of the man for whose death an innocent man died; thus Bunk deserved death. Yet Munn was nauseated at the part he had played, and, returning home, he ravished his wife May, as if to blot out one

4499

violent deed with another. Deserted by May as a result, he soon began a loveless liaison with Lucille Christian, at whose father's home he frequently spent his nights.

Since the companies were still buying tobacco at the prices they set, the Brotherhood members dynamited the company warehouses in Bardsville. Pursuit of the raiders led to the death of young Benton Todd, whose body Mr. Munn delivered to Captain Todd. Troops moved into the area the next day to restore order. New violence, however, developed outside the Brotherhood, with the burning of the homes of planters who used African American laborers instead of white workers. Senator Tolliver's home was burned, and then Mr. Munn's. Munn was roused from bed by Mr. Christian with news of the burning. After Munn's departure, Christian found Lucille hiding in Munn's room and suffered a stroke that left him speechless.

Now homeless and rejected by both his wife and Lucille, Munn moved into the Ball home where, not long afterward, he witnessed the arrest of Dr. Macdonald on a charge of arson. At Macdonald's trial only Al Turpin, a former association member, was in a position to identify Macdonald. When Turpin was killed by a shot fired from Munn's rifle through his law office window, Munn was forced to flee. He later divined that Ball killed Turpin to win an acquittal for Macdonald.

Hiding out at the farm home of Willie Proudfit, one of Macdonald's friends, Munn was visited by Lucille with news of her father's death and the suggestion that flight and marriage would solve their problems. Learning of advances that Senator Tolliver had made to Lucille, however, Munn rejected her offer and determineed instead to kill Tolliver, whom he obsessively identified as the source of the downfall of the association and of himself. For this, Tolliver had to die. When he confronted Tolliver, however, he found he could not shoot, and, learning that troops, informed by a relative of Proudfit's, were coming to arrest him, he fled and was shot down in the dark.

Critical Evaluation:

Among the dominant themes in the novels of Robert Penn Warren are the search for self-identity, the isolation of the individual in society, and the opposition of violence and order in the development of modern America. All three themes appear in Warren's first published novel, *Night Rider*. The principal action of *Night Rider* is based on events that occurred in Kentucky between the years 1905 and 1908. The growers of dark tobacco in Kentucky and Tennessee formed a protective association to combat the tobacco companies and to try to force them to pay higher prices for tobacco. When the companies countered by small increases offered to all who would sell to them, some planters turned to violent action executed by bands of "night riders." This included the destruction of the plant beds of those who refused to join the fight against the companies and finally led to the dynamiting of company warehouses in Hopkinsville, Kentucky. The action of the lawless bands was finally stopped by the sending of troops into the area.

Though most of the events in *Night Rider* are related to the battle of the tobacco planters against the companies and the farmers who refused to join or cooperate with the protective association, the book is not, as Warren warns the reader in a prefatory note, a "historical novel." The tobacco war provides the framework for the story of a young lawyer, Percy Munn, and his degeneration from a man of principle to a man of violence. It is a story of self-realization which comes too late to a man who, though intelligent, lacks the will, moral strength, or clarity of vision to make the right decisions when faced by crises in his life. From one wrong action, he seems to move inevitably to the next, troubled and brooding yet unable to stop the movement toward his certain doom.

Though *Night Rider* is a novel with extensive action and a large cast of characters, Warren has unified it by using Percy Munn as what Henry James called a "central consciousness." People and events are seen primarily through one mind, and introspective Percy Munn seeks cause, meaning, and value in what is done by himself and others. Munn's ambivalence is seen in his alternate revulsion from people and his desire to be a part of a group or to wield power over them. This appears in the opening scene when Mr. Munn resents the crowd on the train and then experiences a moment of near exaltation when he imagines himself being greeted by the even larger crowd at the station. Throughout the novel, he examines his own paradoxes and confusions, his basic coldness opposed to momentary heated involvement in talk and action, and his sense of isolation not only when alone but also with others.

Stylistically, *Night Rider* is marked by recurrent imagery of light and dark. As in the fiction of Nathaniel Hawthorne, Joseph Conrad, and others, this opposition is symbolic. The story opens in brilliant sunshine and ends in the dark. Munn's acts, which show his progress from light into darkness, all occur in the dark: the illegal search of homes, the initiation into the Brotherhood, the night raids, the killing of Bunk, the sexual assault on May, the lust with Lucille, the dynamiting of the warehouses, the death of Benton Todd (the result of Munn's error in judgment), the final confrontation with Tolliver, and Munn's death. The opposed light and dark are sometimes shown as mirroring each other as if one contained the other, and Munn's divided self is often symbolically portrayed, as in the scene in which he reads the account in the morning news of a raid in which he participated and finds it difficult to see himself as a part of it. Such symbolic imagery serves, like the strong focus on Munn's point of view, to unify *Night Rider* and emphasize Warren's intent of writing a novel of moral as well as physical violence, of ethical more than historical significance. *Night Rider* is an important first novel which introduces the themes, style, and structure that Warren was to employ in his later work.

Bibliography:
Burt, John. "Social Realism and Romance: *Night Rider*." In *Robert Penn Warren and American Idealism*. New Haven, Conn.: Yale University Press, 1988. Analysis of Munn as a character caught in the dilemma of "social naturalism": intellectual acceptance of naturalistic philosophy and the antithetical "desire to discover some seat of human integrity and to articulate self-knowledge."
Guttenberg, Barnett. "*Night Rider*." In *Web of Being: The Novels of Robert Penn Warren*. Nashville: Vanderbilt University Press, 1975. Discusssion of Munn as an existential hero attempting to combine quests for personal identity and ideal justice.
Justus, James H. "*Night Rider*: An Adequate Definition of Terror." In *The Achievement of Robert Penn Warren*. Baton Rouge: Louisiana State University Press, 1981. Discussion of the novel's historical roots, themes, and techniques, especially the use of symbolic actions and of the protagonist as the governing point of view.
Law, Richard. "*Night Rider* and the Issue of Naturalism: The 'Nightmare' of Our Age." In *Robert Penn Warren: Critical Perspectives*, edited by Neil Nakadate. Lexington: University Press of Kentucky, 1981. Analysis of *Night Rider* as a philosophical novel portraying the conflict between human will and scientific determinism. Sees the focus upon Munn's consciousness as Warren's technique for demonstrating its limitations.
Ryan, Alvin S. "Robert Penn Warren's *Night Rider*: The Nihilism of the Isolated Temperament." In *Robert Penn Warren: A Collection of Critical Essays*, edited by John Lewis Longley, Jr. New York: New York University Press, 1965. Interpretation of Munn as a man attempting to move from isolation to communion but failing because he lacks self-knowledge and, thus, the means to act.

NIGHTMARE ABBEY

Type of work: Novel
Author: Thomas Love Peacock (1785-1866)
Type of plot: Fiction of manners
Time of plot: Early nineteenth century
Locale: England
First published: 1818

> *Principal characters:*
> CHRISTOPHER GLOWRY, the master of Nightmare Abbey
> SCYTHROP, his son
> MR. FLOSKY, a visitor
> MARIONETTA, Glowry's niece
> MR. TOOBAD, Glowry's friend
> CELINDA, his daughter
> LISTLESS, a dandy

The Story:

Refused by one young lady in his youth, Glowry immediately married another. His wife was cold and gloomy, and Nightmare Abbey was a fitting name for her house. Glowry found relief from his unhappy life in food and drink, and when his lady died, he was easily consoled by increasing his consumption of food and wine. She left one son, Scythrop, who was gloomy enough to suit his father and Nightmare Abbey. A university education had so stripped Scythrop of his thin veneer of social graces that he was rapidly becoming a country boor like his father.

While his father was away in London attending to an important lawsuit, Scythrop amused himself by constructing miniature dungeons, trapdoors, and secret panels. One day, he discovered by chance an apartment in the main wing of the abbey that had no entrance or exit; through an error in construction, the apartment had remained hidden for many years. He imported a dumb carpenter, and together they constructed a cunning secret panel through which one could step from the library into the hidden apartment. Scythrop then had a private refuge for his gloomy meditations.

Miss Emily Girouette declined decidedly to marry Scythrop. In consequence, when his cousin Marionetta came to visit, she rapidly conquered the heart of the sad young man. Marionetta, however, had no fortune, and Glowry refused to hear of the marriage, but Scythrop grew more enamored daily of his coquettish cousin.

Glowry viewed the increasing attachment of Scythrop and Marionetta with great concern. Finally, he told Scythrop that the girl would have to leave. Furious, Scythrop rushed to his tower and filled a human skull with Madeira wine. Confronting his father and holding high the skull, he declared in ringing tones that if Marionetta ever left Nightmare Abbey except of her own free will, he would drink the potion. Convinced that the skull contained poison, his father consented to have Marionetta stay on as a guest. Scythrop drank the wine with gusto.

Glowry confided his troubles to his friend, Toobad, who agreed that marriage with Marionetta was unsuitable in every way. He proposed his own daughter Celinda, a young woman then studying abroad, as a good match for Scythrop. With Glowry's hearty approval, Toobad went to London to meet his daughter and return with her to Nightmare Abbey. Celinda, however, refused to have a husband chosen for her and fled from her domineering father. Toobad appeared at the abbey and left again, vowing to all that he would find his unruly daughter.

The house party at Nightmare Abbey grew larger. Mr. Flosky, a poet of the supernatural, came and spread confusion with his metaphysical paradoxes. Listless, a bored dandy, came with Fatout, his French valet, who was the guardian of his mind and body. Another addition to the party was Mr. Asterias the ichthyologist, engaged in tracing down rumors of mermaids in the vicinity of the abbey. It was not clear what a mermaid would do in the fens around the abbey, but Mr. Asterias had faith. This faith was rewarded one night when Mr. Asterias dimly perceived the form of a woman clad in black. As he rushed across the moat, the mysterious figure disappeared.

Scythrop took as much delight as he could in Marionetta's company; but Listless was the merriest person in the room when Marionetta was present. As far as his languid airs would permit, he followed her about with great eagerness.

Watching Scythrop's affection for Marionetta, Glowry decided that he had been too harsh with his son, and he suddenly announced his approval of their betrothal. To his father's surprise, Scythrop stammered that he did not want to be too precipitate. So the generosity of the father went unrewarded.

There was some mystery about Scythrop. For some time, he had been more distraught than usual; now he practically refused marriage with his beloved. More than that, every time Glowry went to his son's room, he found the door locked and Scythrop slow in answering his knock. A strange, heavy thud always sounded in the room before the door opened.

One evening while the whole company was sitting in the drawing room, a tall and stately figure wearing a bloody turban suddenly appeared. Listless rolled under the sofa. Glowry roared his alarm in Toobad's ear, and Toobad tried to run away. He mistook a window for a door and fell into the moat below. Mr. Asterias, still looking for a mermaid, fished him out with a landing net.

These mysteries went back to the night Mr. Asterias thought he saw the mermaid. Scythrop was sitting alone in his library when the door opened softly and in stepped a beautiful, stately woman. She looked at Scythrop carefully, and reassured by what she saw, she sat down confidently. The bewildered man could only sit and stare. The mysterious stranger gently asked him if he were the illustrious author of the pamphlet, "Philosophical Gas." Flattered, Scythrop acknowledged his authorship of that profound work, only seven copies of which had been sold. Then the girl asked his protection from a marriage that would make her the slave of her sex. Already smitten, Scythrop agreed to hide her in his secret apartment.

Then Scythrop began his dual romance. The serious girl, who called herself Stella, talked night after night of the German metaphysicians and quoted German tragedy. On the other hand, Marionetta was always merry and lively. Scythrop did not know whom to choose.

One night, his father demanded entry into his room while Stella was there. Stella decided to show herself, regardless of consequences. Toobad recognized his long-lost daughter Celinda. Scythrop now had to choose either Celinda or Marionetta; but he hesitated to make a choice, feeling that he could not relinquish either. The next day, however, the decision was made for him. Marionetta had accepted Listless and Celinda would soon be Mrs. Flosky. Stoically, Glowry reminded his son that there were other maidens. Scythrop agreed and ordered the Madeira.

Critical Evaluation:

Thomas Love Peacock, a satirical novelist, never had a wide audience. His ambition was not fame or fortune but merely to please himself. His concerns were not those of most writers within the Romantic movement. Still, the author gained the respect of Percy Bysshe Shelley and George Gordon, Lord Byron in his own times. Peacock's novels are generally set in idyllic country homes in which drinking and flirting seem to be the major activity of the day. Reading between the lines, however, especially in the case of the satirical *Nightmare Abbey*, reveals serious discussions of moral, political, economic, scientific, and aesthetic concerns.

As with most satire, critical evaluations of the writer's work tend to be somewhat negative. Satiric plots, as is true of Peacock's, tend to be insignificant if not implausible. He sketches characters rather than writing rounded characters. Those characters who are more well rounded tend to be polemic in their opinions rather than deep, as they should be in a novel, in their emotions. What Peacock's writing lacks in plot and character he makes up for in wit and epigrams. A classicist at heart, Peacock uses his fine understanding of the contemporary ideas he attacks to show opinion, not ill humor.

Scythrop Glowry, the son of Christopher Glowry, a Lincolnshire landed gentleman of gloomy disposition who presides over the family castle, Nightmare Abbey, is the hero of Peacock's satire, a witty spoof of Gothic fiction and of Romantic attitudes. The reader soon learns that Scythrop was named after an ancestor who committed suicide and whose skull is being used as a punchbowl. A student of Immanuel Kant, Scythrop falls madly in love with Marionetta Celestina O'Carroll, who more or less loves him too. The elder Glowry, however, has in mind a better match: Celinda Toobad, who has been educated abroad and is the heiress to a considerable fortune. Scythrop banishes himself to the tower room of Nightmare Abbey and reads Gothic fiction and dreams of "venerable eleutherarchs"—chiefs of a secret society called The Eleutheri—"and ghastly confederates holding midnight conventions in subterranean caves." The novel ends with a scene that burlesques Johann Wolfgang Goethe's *The Sorrows of Young Werther*: Scythrop, armed with a pistol and an ample supply of Madeira, waits for the fatal hour he has appointed for his death. Before the novel comes to an end, however, a "ghost" and Scythrop yield to reason.

Peacock's targets for his satire are the exalted attitude of the prose and poetry of the Romantic movement (with a special emphasis on Byron) and the coincidences and confusion that are endemic to Gothic fiction. *Nightmare Abbey* is the most literary of Peacock's satires. It targets the gloom affecting contemporary literature, such as Samuel Taylor Coleridge's German transcendentalism, Byron's self-dramatizing, and Shelley's esotericism. The book opens in imitation of William Godwin's novel *Mandeville: A Tale of the Seventeenth Century in England* (1817). Nightmare Abbey is staffed by servants with long, skull-like faces and names like Diggory Deathshead. The senior Glowry gives a party attended by the millenarian pessimist, Mr. Toobad; by Mr. Flosky, who is based on Coleridge; by Mr. Cypress, who is based on Byron; and by Mr. Listless, drawn to represent the common reader. The Younger Scythrop, a writer, is based on Shelley because he cannot decide which hand to take in marriage: that of Marionetta, his frivolous cousin, or that of Stella/Celinda, Mr. Toobad's sibylline daughter. Other guests include the uncommonly cheerful Mr. Asterias, a scientist, and Mr. Hilary, whose literary tastes come from the Greeks. "Peacock seems to have intended to present, in amusing contemporary terms, the dilemma facing the young Milton in 'L'Allegro' and 'Il Penseroso.'" The novel ends with the unfinished Werther-style suicide in a comic denouement.

Nightmare Abbey targets both Gothicism and Romanticism, specifically the Byronic hero. Mr. Flosky, Peacock's portrait of Coleridge, observes the change: "the ghosts . . . have been laid . . . and now the delight of our spirits is to dwell on all the vices and blackest passions of our nature, tricked out in a masquerade dress of heroism and disappointed benevolence." Coleridge is depicted as a philosopher of transcendentalism and as a self-appointed leader of the counter- culture. As represented by Mr. Flosky, Coleridge, according to Peacock, claims rights to divining the taste of the reading public.

The dramatic appearance of Byron (in the guise of Mr. Cypress) in the second half of *Nightmare Abbey* is a tour de force; Peacock uses quotations from *Childe Harold's Pilgrimage* (1812) and mixes them with parody of the fourth canto. When Mr. Cypress departs the abbey, he veers from misanthropic generalization to navel-peering self-observation in a speech about quarreling with his wife, which absolves him of any duty to his country.

The self-destructive Scythrop, caught between two women, is based on Shelley and his elopement with Mary Godwin. Scythrop's estotericism (only seven copies of his pamphlet, "Philosophical Gas," were sold) sheds light on the gap between literary exponents of liberty and the reading public at large. Scythrop's self-immersion in his private dilemma, likely to be judged by the public-at-large as merely scandalous, adds depth to the critique of solipsism, which underlies this literary parody. As the novel comes to an end, Scythrop cannot bring himself to dispose of either lady: "I am doomed to be the victim of eternal disappointment and I have no resource but a pistol." The ladies, however, will have none of this nonsense and reject Scythrop. His disappointment validated and his misanthropy confirmed by both women, Scythrop decides against suicide. His story ends not with a gunshot, but with a cry more familiar in Peacock's world: "Bring some Madeira." With *Nightmare Abbey* as his vehicle, Peacock acts as an active, liberating force, sounding the death knell of self-indulgent Romanticism with his *Nightmare Abbey*.

"*Critical Evaluation*" by Thomas D. Petitjean, Jr.

Bibliography:
Butler, Marilyn. *Peacock Displayed: A Satirist in His Context*. London: Routledge & Keegan Paul, 1979. Makes *Nightmare Abbey* a focal point, positing that as finely drawn as the gentlemen characters are (all of whom are satirically based on real-life personages), the novel is actually the story of two women, Marionetta and Celinda/Stella.
Cunningham, Mark. "'Fatout! Who Am I?' A Model for the Honourable Mr. Listless in Thomas Love Peacock's *Nightmare Abbey*." *English Language Notes* 30, no. 1 (September, 1992): 43-45. Discusses the possibility of who may have been the model for the character of Mr. Listless, who spends whole days on a sofa in perfected ennui.
Schwank, Klaus. "From Satire to Indeterminacy: Thomas Love Peacock's *Nightmare Abbey*." In *Beyond the Suburbs of the Mind: Exploring English Romanticism*, edited by Michael Gassenmeier and Norbert H. Platz. Essen, Germany: Blaue Eule, 1987. Discusses the effectiveness of Peacock's satire, placing Peacock's novel in a category of works that defy satire.
Wolf, Leonard. "Nightmare Abbey." *Horror: A Connoisseur's Guide to Literature and Film*. New York: Facts On File, 1989. Compares Peacock's satirical verse as a precursor to Oscar Wilde's similar style.
Wright, Julia M. "Peacock's Early Parody of Thomas Moore in *Nightmare Abbey*." *English Language Notes* 30, no. 4 (June, 1993): 31-38. Discusses Peacock's use of Thomas Moore as, possibly, a template for a character in *Nightmare Abbey*.

NIGHTWOOD

Type of work: Novel
Author: Djuna Barnes (1892-1982)
Type of plot: Psychological surrealism
Time of plot: 1920's
Locale: Paris and Vienna
First published: 1936

> *Principal characters:*
> FELIX VOLKBEIN, a spurious baron
> DR. MATTHEW O'CONNOR, an aging medical student
> NORA FLOOD, a publicist with a circus
> ROBIN VOTE, Felix's wife and Nora's paramour
> JENNY PETHERBRIDGE, a wealthy multiple widow
> GUIDO VOLKBEIN, Felix and Robin's son

The Story:

Felix Volkbein was no sooner born in Vienna in 1880 than his mother, Hedvig, died. His father, Guido, a descendant of Italian Jews who had tried to overcome the burden of what he took to be an ignoble past by pretending to be of noble birth, had died six months earlier. The orphaned Felix was left with a rather substantial upper-middle-class household and the ficti- tious title of Baron Volkbein.

About thirty years later, Felix, a nominal Christian, owned little more than his spurious title and two "family portraits" that are in fact paintings of long-forgotten actors procured by Guido in his effort to create an aristocratic past for his family line. By 1920, Felix was making a living in international banking in Paris. Here he indulged in his real obsession, the nobility, aristoc- racy, and royalty of "Old Europe." Without legitimate claims to noble blood, he envied the nobility from a discreet distance. To exercise his propensity for make-believe, he became a habitué of the night world of the circus and the theater. Among these "night people," many of whom were also "titled," Felix met a Dr. Matthew O'Connor, an Irishman from San Francisco, and Nora Flood, an American who was in Europe as a publicist for a circus.

O'Connor was a lively and talkative eccentric with an opinion or observation to make on everything and everyone. He and Felix met again in Paris a few weeks later. The doctor was called to assist a young woman who had fainted, and Felix was on hand when O'Connor brought her around. She was Robin Vote, mistress of this world of the night, and in her half-awakened state a beast turning human.

It was in that half-awakened state that she agreed to marry Felix when, in rather short order, he proposed to her to produce an heir to continue the Volkbein line. Felix moved Robin to Vienna, where she sleepwalked through her pregnancy, coming to, as it were, upon the birth of the child. She abandoned Felix and the boy, a sickly baby, and ended up in the company of Nora Flood.

Robin was with a circus in New York in 1923 when she first met Nora, and the two became constant companions. Although Robin was incapable of forming lasting attachments, Nora fell tragically under her spell, rearranging her life to suit Robin's needs and eventually returning with Robin to Europe, where they settled in an apartment in Paris. By 1927, however, the acquisitive Jenny Petherbridge had come into their lives and, much to Nora's mental and emotional pain, stolen Robin away from her.

Jenny was a collector of everyone else's lost dreams and possessions. For a while she made the most of her new catch, but then she too succumbed to the insane jealousy that Robin's insouciant promiscuity and casual animal magnetism inspired in others. During a mad, late-night carriage ride through the streets of Paris, while O'Connor talked about the pains of love, Jenny was distracted by the fear that a young Englishwoman might find Robin attractive, or vice versa. A short time later, Jenny and Robin left Paris for America. For consolation, the heartbroken Nora ventured to O'Connor's apartment at 3 A.M. to find him in bed in a woman's wig, makeup, and nightgown. Nevertheless, she stayed to hear his monologue about the night that is our darkness, our degradation, and our death.

The baron, meanwhile, had been raising his and Robin's son, Guido. By 1931, the boy had grown into a religious idiot of sorts, though O'Connor saw hope in his desire to become a Catholic, whereby he would escape the history that imprisoned Felix. Felix despaired of that possibility but made plans nevertheless to move with the boy to Vienna, where he might be among his own people.

Jenny showed up at his Paris apartment one day, ostensibly to buy a painting but really in search of information about Robin, suggesting that, like Felix and Nora before her, Jenny too had lost Robin to someone else. O'Connor paid another visit to Nora, during which they again discussed, largely through his monologues, the pain of degradation and loss that humans are born for, which for Nora and other characters in the novel was embodied in Robin. Although his ability to articulate the absurd was a source of strength to others, O'Connor was driven to despair when Nora told him the details of her relationship with Robin. O'Connor ended up a broken man, damning all those who had come to him to learn of degradation and the night.

Jenny and Robin returned to New York. Robin, who had become Catholic during her marriage to Felix, still frequented churches, and her devotion, real or feigned, was yet another source of jealousy for Jenny. Robin ended up wandering northward toward Nora's country home. Nora arrived at a chapel near her home in the middle of the night with her dog to find Robin carrying on a quasi-religious ritual, as if to lure her to the spot. Then, in front of the stunned and confused Nora, Robin made love to the dog, simultaneously fulfilling the animal nature she embodies and inflicting further emotional pain on both herself and one of her lovers. The cycle of degradation that flourishes at night promised to continue, nurtured by these kinds of symbiotic relationships between the spirit that is the human and the beast that is also the human.

Critical Evaluation:

If ever a story depended more on its telling than on the tale, Djuna Barnes's *Nightwood* is that story. The plot of *Nightwood* contains traditional elements such as an array of interesting characterizations, narrative twists that are suspenseful if no doubt also puzzling, and a not inconsiderable measure of humor and insight into the human condition. Yet those elements seem to be present only in the most elliptical manner, as if the author's real aim is not to be telling a story at all.

Barnes is, by most definitions of the term, a modernist writer essaying modernist themes and issues. Like other avant-garde literature of the period, *Nightwood* includes confrontations of cultural values; breakdowns in the social order as traditional class structures decay; daring sexual-psychological interpretations of human character and motivation; and a keen, almost morbid attention to eccentric and morally outrageous behavior. Even *Nightwood*'s surrealism, as in O'Connor's monologues, is in keeping with contemporary literary trends and techniques.

Yet *Nightwood* is a rare creation even for an epoch of experimentation in fiction. The novel nags the reader with the suggestion of a meaning that is, like that of the more traditional novel, inherent in the characters and in the way they work out their moral dilemmas. It is possible that *Nightwood*'s real achievement is the almost perfect blending of form and content, so that the story and its telling are inseparable and all enveloping, while at the same time, the vigor of the language belies the paucity of moral imperatives.

Language—both the language of the author's narrative line and the language within that narrative in which the characters communicate their feelings, values, and ideas (and misgivings, confusions, and desires)—is so much a theme of the novel that it is almost a character. It is by and through language that the night, an age-old metaphor for mystery and terror, is given human shape and made a human habitation.

The novel's two ethical poles are Matthew O'Connor, the closet insomniac who cannot stop talking, and Robin Vote, the sleepwalker who hardly seems to be alive except in the most amorally mindless, animalistic way. The other characters are located somewhere between those two extremes and are as surely caught up in this "nightwood" as anyone else. The players can penetrate that darkness to illuminate it momentarily for others, but no one can dissipate or overcome it.

The power to select one's victimhood is all each person has. That is what Felix accepts almost by virtue of circumstance, and it is certainly what O'Connor preaches in his efforts to overcome the darkness. Those in the novel who, either through a stubborn willfulness or a blind disregard, cannot accept this precept, such as Nora Flood and Jenny Petherbridge, become its victim. Robin, meanwhile, the antiprotagonist, appropriately embodies night's mindless power to victimize.

The novel ends with Robin selecting her own victimhood by becoming, in imitation of a dog, the amoral beast nature had made her. She has, however, at least made the moral choice to break free of Jenny, the possessive opportunist, and return to Nora, who is devoted to her. Such an ambiguity of action seems to be the most we can expect from the rich maelstrom of words and ideas that swirl through the pages of *Nightwood*.

Russell Elliott Murphy

Bibliography:
Eliot, T. S. "Introduction" to *Nightwood*, by Djuna Barnes. New York: Harcourt Brace Jovanovich, 1936. Eliot's encomium in his introduction to the first edition of *Nightwood* secured the novel the recognition it deserved but might otherwise never have attained. Brief and to the point, Eliot singles out that one feature of Barnes's prose style, its poetry, that continues to make the novel a classic of modernist technique.

Kannenstine, Louis F. *The Art of Djuna Barnes: Duality and Damnation*. New York: New York University Press, 1977. This scholarly and critically ambitious work on Barnes concludes that Barnes is a transitional writer, difficult to classify and therefore missing the attention her art and work deserve. Defines *Nightwood*, her masterpiece, as a study of mixed being and of the estrangement that results from confused identity.

Plumb, Cheryl J. *Fancy's Craft: Art and Identity in the Early Works of Djuna Barnes*. Selinsgrove, Pennsylvania: Susquehanna University Press, 1986. Points out that Barnes deliberately rebelled against naturalist techniques in her writing, borrowing instead from methods of narrative exposition developed out of symbolist poetry. *Nightwood*, her greatest achievement, presents difficulties for scholars and readers alike precisely because it is the purest realization of these goals.

Scott, James B. *Djuna Barnes*. Boston: Twayne, 1976. A good introduction to Barnes. Points out that the writer as she matured sought to mix and then fuse genres and styles. *Nightwood*, Barnes's one attempt at a "popular" novel, succeeds by fusing elements of a lurid realism with an engagingly poetic style.

Williamson, Alan. "The Divided Image: The Quest for Identity in the Works of Djuna Barnes." *Critique: Studies in Modern Fiction* 7, no. 1 (Spring, 1964): 58-74. Concludes that Barnes is a brilliant if minor writer and that *Nightwood* underscores a recurrent theme of day-night duality, whereby the ordinary truths and values of the daytime world are subverted and exposed as falsehoods.

NINETEEN EIGHTY-FOUR

Type of work: Novel
Author: George Orwell (Eric Arthur Blair, 1903-1950)
Type of plot: Science fiction
Time of plot: 1984
Locale: London
First published: 1949

Principal characters:
WINSTON SMITH, a Party functionary
JULIA, a rebellious girl
O'BRIEN, a member of the Inner Party
MR. CHARRINGTON, one of the thought police

The Story:

Externally, Winston Smith was well adjusted to his world. He drank the bitter victory gin and smoked the vile victory cigarettes. In the morning, he did his exercises in front of the telescreen, and when the instructor spoke to him over the two-way television, he bent with renewed vigor to touch the floor. His flat was dingy and rickety, but at thirty-nine years old, he was scarcely old enough to remember a time when housing had been better. He had a decent job at the Ministry of Truth because he had a good mind and the ability to write newspeak, the official language. He was a member of the outer ring of the Party.

One noon, by giving up his lunch at the ministry, he had a little free time to himself. He went to an alcove out of reach of the telescreen and furtively took out his journal. It was a noble book with paper of fine quality unobtainable at present. It was an antique, bought on an illicit trip to a secondhand store run by old Mr. Charrington. Although it was not illegal to keep a diary, for there were no laws in Oceania, it made him suspect. He wrote ploddingly about a film he had seen of the valiant Oceania forces strafing shipwrecked refugees in the Mediterranean.

Musing over his writing, Winston found to his horror that he had written a slogan against Big Brother several times. He knew his act was a crime, even if the writing was due to gin. Even to think such a slogan was a crime. Everywhere he looked, on stair landings and on storefronts, were posters showing Big Brother's all-seeing face. Citizens were reminded a hundred times a day that Big Brother was watching every move.

At the Ministry of Truth, Winston plunged into his routine. He had the job of rewriting records. If the Party made an inaccurate prediction about the progress of the war or if some aspect of production did not accord with the published goals of the ninth three-year plan, Winston corrected the record. All published material was constantly changed so that all history accorded with the wishes and aims of the Party.

There was a break in the day's routine for a two-minute hate period. The face of Goldstein, the enemy of the Party, appeared on the big telescreen and a government speaker worked up the feelings of the viewers; Goldstein was accused of heading a great conspiracy against Oceania. Winston loudly and dutifully drummed his heels as he took part in the group orgasm of hate.

A bold, dark-haired girl, wearing the red chastity belt, seemed often to be near Winston in the workrooms and in the commissary. He was afraid she might be a member of the thought police. Seeing her outside the ministry, he decided she was following him. For a time, he played with the idea of killing her. One day, she slipped a little note to him in which she confessed that she loved him.

Winston was troubled. He had been married, but his wife belonged to the Anti-Sex League. For her, procreation was a Party duty. When they had not produced any children, his wife had left him. Now this girl, Julia, spoke of love. Winston had a few private words with her in the lunchroom, being careful to make their conversation look like a chance meeting. She quickly named a place in the country for a rendezvous. Winston met her in the woods, where, far from a telescreen, they made love. Julia boasted that she had been the mistress of several Party members and that she had no patience with the Anti-Sex League, although she worked diligently for it. She also bought sweets on the black market.

On another visit to Mr. Charrington's antique shop, the proprietor showed Winston an upstairs bedroom still preserved as it had been before the Revolution. Although it was madness, Winston rented the room and thereafter, he and Julia had a comfortable bed for their brief meetings. Winston felt happy in the old room, which had no telescreen to spy on them.

At work, Winston sometimes saw O'Brien, a kindly looking member of the Inner Party. Winston deduced from a chance remark that O'Brien was not in sympathy with all the aims of the Party. When they could, Winston and Julia went to O'Brien's apartment. He assured them that Goldstein was really the head of a conspiracy and that eventually the Party would be overthrown. Julia told him of her sins against Party discipline, and Winston recounted his evidence that the Party distorted facts in public trials and purges. O'Brien then enrolled them in the conspiracy and gave them Goldstein's book to read.

After an exhausting hate week directed against the current enemy, Eurasia, Winston read aloud to the dozing Julia, both comfortably lying in bed, from Goldstein's treatise. Suddenly, a voice rang out and ordered them to stand in the middle of the room. Winston grew sick when he realized that a hidden telescreen had spied on their actions. Soon the room was filled with truncheon-wielding policemen. Mr. Charrington came in, no longer a kindly member of the simple proletariat, but a keen, determined man. Winston knew then that Mr. Charrington belonged to the thought police. One of the guards hit Julia in the stomach, and the others hurried Winston off to jail.

Winston was tortured for days—beaten, kicked, and clubbed until he confessed his crimes. He willingly admitted to years of conspiracy with the rulers of Eurasia and told everything he knew of Julia. In the later phases of his torture, O'Brien was at his side constantly. O'Brien kept him on a rack with a doctor in attendance to keep him alive. He told Winston that Goldstein's book was a Party production, written in part by O'Brien himself.

Through it all, the tortured man had one small triumph; he still loved Julia. O'Brien knew Winston's fear of rats and brought in a large cage filled with rodents; he fastened it around Winston's head. In his unreasoning terror, Winston begged him to let the rats eat Julia instead. Winston still hated Big Brother and said so. O'Brien patiently explained that the Party wanted no martyrs, for they strengthened opposition, nor did the leaders want only groveling subjection. Winston must think right. The proletariat, happy in their ignorance, must never have a leader to rouse them. All Party members must think and feel as Big Brother directed.

When Winston was finally released, he was bald and his teeth were gone. Because he had been purged and because his crime had not been serious, he was even given a small job on a subcommittee. Mostly he sat solitary in taverns and drank victory gin. He even saw Julia once. She had coarsened in figure, and her face was scarred. They had little to say to each other.

One day, a big celebration took place in the tavern. Oceania had achieved an important victory in Africa. Suddenly, the doddering Winston felt himself purged. He believed. Now he could be shot with a pure soul, for at last he loved Big Brother.

Critical Evaluation:

Nineteen Eighty-Four is one of the keenest pieces of satire to be written in the twentieth century. It was George Orwell's last novel, written between 1946 and 1949 and published less than a year before his death. If took him more than two years to write, considerably more time than he spent on any of his other novels. Orwell was seriously ill with tuberculosis during the writing of this novel. He said that his sickness might have crept into the work and added to the novel's dark and disturbing nature. The protagonist, Winston Smith, does in fact suffer from horrible coughing fits that sometimes leave him paralyzed.

This novel's deepest impact lies in the many Orwellian words and concepts that have entered into the English vocabulary, especially the political vocabulary. "Newspeak," "doublethink," and "Big Brother" were all coined by Orwell. Political commentators often draw from these when they need a negative phrase to describe a government.

Nineteen Eighty-Four is part of a small group of important futuristic novels that use the structure of science fiction to contain political satire. These have been called "anti-Utopia" novels. *Nineteen Eighty-Four* and Aldous Huxley's *Brave New World* (1932) are the best known in English, but both of these draw from an earlier novel, *We* (1924), written by the little-known Russian novelist Yevgeny Zamyatin.

The central theme of *Nineteen Eighty-Four* is the state's imposition of will upon thought and truth. Winston Smith wants to keep the few cubic centimeters inside his skull to himself. He wants to be ruler of his own thoughts, but the state is powerful enough to rule even those. He wants the freedom to believe that two plus two equals four, that the past is fixed, and that love is private.

Orwell saw privacy as one of the most necessary elements in a human's life. The world of *Nineteen Eighty-Four* does not allow privacy for the individual and does not allow the individual to have a personal identity. Everyone must think in the collective way, exactly as everyone else thinks. Thought control is executed through the falsification of history. Winston's job is to falsify history, often rewriting the same event many times, making something different happen each time. Oceania was at war with Eastasia, then Eurasia, and then Eastasia again, and history had to change every time to show that Oceania had always been at war with the present enemy. People learned not to trust their own memories and learned, through "doublethink," not to have memories at all outside of what was told to them.

This depiction of thought control may be Orwell's notice on the concept of history. Different people might recount the same experience in different ways. School books of one country, for example, may reconstruct events differently from history books of another country, each set presenting its country in a positive light.

Another theme came from the propaganda that circulated during the world wars. Enemies were depicted as less than human. This mind manipulation by governments helped their own populations to believe that fighting and killing the enemy was not immoral in any way, because the enemy was a scourge of the planet and should be annihilated. Here again, the futuristic disguise of *Nineteen Eighty-Four* is only a device to magnify a situation that Orwell had witnessed throughout his life, the flagrant deception by governments of their peoples on a regular basis. Orwell gives exemplary cases in mind control, showing how easily a government can divert the attention of its populace by creating an enemy for everyone to hate together.

The severe brutality of *Nineteen Eighty-Four* is a direct link from the post-World War II era to a fierce exaggeration of the possible future. After living through the atrocities of Adolf Hitler and Joseph Stalin, and knowing of concentration camps and of mental and physical tortures, Orwell painted a picture of what the year 1984 could be like if the principles of achieving and retaining power were extended in the same vein as in the past.

The setting for *Nineteen Eighty-Four* is not a contrived high-technology world but instead a World War II-era rotting London with dilapidated nineteenth century buildings, their windows broken and covered with cardboard, insufficient heat, and strictly rationed food. Living conditions are miserable for everyone but the elite. The reason is the war, which does not progress or decrease but continues forever. Because most industry is working toward the war effort, the citizens of Oceania receive few benefits from their work. The proletariat is occupied but is never able to gain even the simplest of luxuries. Citizens are utterly dependent on the small scraps the Party gives them. The "proles" are always wanting, and they are successfully held in a position of servitude and powerlessness.

Orwell undoubtedly did not write *Nineteen Eighty-Four* as a prophecy of that date. It was a warning and an effort to attract people's attention to the atrocities of their own governmental bodies, and the title date was chosen as a partial inversion of 1948, during which he was writing the novel. Orwell knew that most of the people who would read his book would still be alive in 1984. The ideas in this book are overwhelming and incredibly powerful. Although it may not deserve its acclaim as being a masterwork in literature, the novel is a creative effort in leading people to question the power structures and motives behind their governments, war, and economic class distinctions.

"Critical Evaluation" by Beaird Glover

Bibliography:
Atkins, John. *George Orwell: A Literary Study*. London: Calder and Boyars, 1971. A long and detailed account of Orwell's climb to maturity as a political writer. Because it was written in 1954, this book presents a dated perspective on Orwell's work.
Gardner, Averil. *George Orwell*. Boston: Twayne, 1987. Examines Orwell's novels, his longer nonfiction, and his essays for theme, recurrent motifs, and critical response. Includes a chronology, an extended bibliography, and an index.
Hynes, Samuel, ed. *Twentieth Century Interpretations of "1984": A Collection of Critical Essays*. Englewood Cliffs, N.J.: Prentice-Hall, 1971. Offers both favorable and negative criticism and the particular angles of many different critics. The chapters are reviews, essays, and viewpoints; even a letter from Aldous Huxley to Orwell is included.
Lee, Robert A. *Orwell's Fiction*. Notre Dame, Ind.: University of Notre Dame Press, 1969. A chronicle of the development of Orwell's career as a novelist. Themed sections include Orwell's look at poverty and the stricken individual, social strife, and his apocalyptic vision as expressed in *Nineteen Eighty-Four*.
Williams, Raymond, ed. *George Orwell: A Collection of Critical Essays*. Englewood Cliffs, N. J.: Prentice-Hall, 1974. A chronological arrangement of essays on the development of Orwell's writing. A study of not only Orwell's development over time but also the impact of his work over time, with essays from writers of three generations.

NO EXIT

Type of work: Drama
Author: Jean-Paul Sartre (1905-1980)
Type of plot: Existentialism
Time of plot: Twentieth century
Locale: Hell
First performed: 1944; first published, 1945 as *Huis clos* (English translation, 1946)

> *Principal characters:*
> VALET, who escorts the new guests
> GARCIN, a newspaper reporter
> ESTELLE, a young, attractive socialite
> INEZ, a post office clerk

The Story:

Joseph Garcin, a South American newspaper reporter, was ushered into a drawing room by a mysterious Valet. The drawing room itself was decorated with ponderous nineteenth century furniture, and on the mantle stood a massive bronze statue. There were three couches in the room, one blue, one green, and one burgundy. The Valet who showed him into the room answered Garcin's many questions cryptically.

It soon became evident that both Garcin and the Valet knew that they were in a place far removed from the ordinary world. The room was in Hell. Garcin was dead and had recently arrived in the netherworld. The former reporter told the amused Valet that Hell was nothing like it was supposed to be. There were no hot fires nor any instruments of torture. There was only this boring room, with its heavy furnishings and huge bronze sculpture. There were no windows, no mirrors, and no switch to turn off the bright lights or the relentless heat.

Garcin noticed how the Valet never blinked. Garcin surmised that in Hell eyes never closed and concluded that no one ever slept there. When Garcin tried to move the sculpture on the mantle, he could not. He noticed a button to press for calling the Valet, but he was told that the bell worked only some of the time. He asked the Valet the reason why there was a paper knife (the kind used to open envelopes or to separate pages in a book) but received only a shrug in reply. Finally, bored by the servant's taunting indifference, he let the Valet leave, but then, nervously, tried the call button. Although Garcin could not hear it ring, the Valet abruptly returned. With him came another person, a rather drably dressed, plain woman named Inez. The Valet once more departed.

Inez immediately assumed that Garcin must be her torturer. He reassured her that he was no such thing and tried to make polite conversation, but Inez replied testily that she did not believe in good manners. Although they took separate positions in the room, Garcin's facial expressions began to bother Inez. They sat in silence, he on the blue sofa, she on the burgundy one, until once again the door opened.

Now the Valet led in a third guest: Estelle, a pretty, young, well-dressed socialite. Estelle hid her eyes with her hands, afraid that Garcin was someone she knew from her time on earth— someone whose face had somehow been destroyed. When Garcin assured her that he was someone other than this faceless man, she uncovered her eyes and observed how much the room reminded her of her old Aunt Mary's ugly home. Estelle was wearing a pale blue dress, so she begged Garcin to let her sit on the blue sofa instead of the remaining green one. Inez offered hers and flatteringly told Estelle that she wished she might have been able to welcome her with a bouquet of flowers, but Estelle took Garcin's blue couch, and Garcin moved to the green.

The Valet left. Garcin tried to remove his coat, but Estelle was appalled at such informality, asking Inez if she approved of men in their shirtsleeves. Inez replied that she did not care much for men one way or the other. The three began to speculate as to why they were placed together in this room and spoke of the possible reasons each had been sent to Hell. Estelle said that although she had been married she had run off with another man. Garcin said he, during wartime, had worked for a pacifist newspaper. Inez mocked Estelle's excuses about infidelity and Garcin's story about his unpopularity. She said she could now understand that they had been placed together because they would torture one another simply by being there.

In order to prevent this, Garcin decided they should stay on their separate couches and just sit there, in silence—that way, no one could hurt the others. Still, after a time, Inez could not help singing to herself, and Estelle, upset that her handbag mirror had been taken from her, complained that she could not put on her makeup. Garcin remained quiet, but Estelle and Inez talked; Inez convinced Estelle to come over to her sofa, where she would act as Estelle's mirror. Now Estelle, with Inez's guidance, put on her lipstick. Then Inez admitted that she was attracted to Estelle, who was shocked and returned to her own sofa. Estelle told Inez that she would have preferred Garcin to notice her.

Garcin heard their conversation but resisted speaking. Now Inez exhorted him to talk, adding that it was better to choose one's own hell than to try to avoid the inevitable. Exasperated, he joined Estelle and began to kiss her, but he was haunted by images of his wife who, still alive, had suffered from Garcin's mean behavior. Inez recognized that his cruelty to his wife had brought him here, just as her betrayal of her cousin, whose wife she had slept with, had landed her in Hell. The two confronted Estelle, who unwillingly confessed that she had not only deceived her husband but also murdered the illegitimate child she had borne to her lover. As they revealed their horrific acts, the images of the real world began to disappear. They were now really dead—forgotten by the living, alone in a room.

Finally the combined irritation, guilt, and anger in the room made each character unleash the wild rage within. The characters' bitterness and hatred made it impossible for them to find any peace. Inez's scornful and scorned presence made it impossible for Estelle and Garcin to make love. Garcin's masculine presence made it impossible for Inez to find happiness with Estelle. Estelle's presence would forever drive a wedge between Inez and Garcin. Garcin vainly tried to open the locked door to the room. Then, suddenly, the door opened and the three were faced with the possibility of leaving. Yet they could not go—the heat and the uncertainty of what lay beyond the part of Hell they knew frightened them more than the room. They closed the door.

The three attempted yet again to make their time in Hell more reasonable, but the frustration of each having the other two there became more than they could bear. When Garcin pushed Estelle away from him because he could not stand letting Inez watch them together, Estelle took the paper knife and tried to stab Inez. Inez did not die. She merely laughed uproariously because, she reminded them, they were already dead. There was never any chance of leaving their awful, eternal agony. They discovered that Hell is other people.

Critical Evaluation:

Jean-Paul Sartre, professor, philosopher, and author, was internationally known as an existential writer and thinker. His many works explore how the individual is free to act and how such freedom of choice, in an otherwise meaningless universe, can be overwhelming and frightening. In France, Sartre was a leading novelist, having written *Nausea* (1938) and *The Age of Reason* (1945), and playwright, with such credits as *The Flies* (1943) and *The Respectful Prostitute* (1947). He also wrote a number of philosophical works devoted to existentialism; his most famous book on the subject, *Being and Nothingness*, was published in 1943, a year before *No Exit* made its stage debut. In 1964, Sartre's scorn for elitism led him to refuse a Nobel Prize in Literature.

No Exit was written and first produced late in World War II, when France was occupied by Germany. The play therefore had to pass the Nazi censors, who read all scripts that were performed in the private theaters of Paris during the Occupation. Although there is nothing in the play that explicitly challenges German rule, audiences in 1944 regarded *No Exit* as subtly subversive.

For example, Garcin makes references to prewar pacifists, who at the time would have been thought of as collaborators. The three condemned souls repeatedly speak of whoever is in charge of Hell using the pronoun "they," which the French used to refer to the Germans. Moreover, life in Paris during the Occupation, like life in Sartre's drawing room Hell, was at a standstill. Beyond these, there are perhaps other minor, less conscious references that audiences, rather than the playwright, discovered. Simone de Beauvoir recounts how when the Valet ushers Garcin into the room, he tells the new arrival that they have all the electricity and heat that they want, and this made wartime audiences, faced with all kinds of shortages, laugh loudly. *No Exit*, like its author, was identified with the anti-German Resistance and was so successful that after Paris was liberated, the play continued running through the next season.

In part because its author was associated with the Resistance, *No Exit* initially received mixed reviews. Theater critics who collaborated or sympathized with the Germans complained that it was an immoral piece of writing. The crimes committed by Garcin, Inez, and Estelle are serious. During the Occupation, many were outraged by Sartre's frank depiction of such criminal acts. Moreover, Inez's lesbianism was extremely controversial. Although many collaborationist critics condemned *No Exit* and called for its removal from the stage, some reviewers who disagreed with Sartre's political views could not help but praise the brilliance of his concept.

The play has also been viewed as a dramatization of Sartre's existentialist views. Hell for these three people is not a place where torture is assigned them; rather, it is embodied in their inability to alter their lives through choice. As the name of the play implies, there is no escape from the claustrophobic world in which they have been entombed. Nothing will ever change for them, and nothing they can do can ever make things better. This utter lack of freedom, Sartre implies, is for human beings the ultimate dead end—an existential Hell.

Kenneth Krauss

Bibliography:
Bradby, David. *Modern French Drama 1940-1990*. 2d ed. New York: Cambridge University Press, 1991. Looks at Sartre's career and locates *No Exit* as part of Sartre's early period. Presents a significant view of how the dramatist came to regard his own work later in his life.
Champigny, Robert. *Sartre and Drama*. Birmingham, Ala.: French Literature Publications, 1982. An evaluation of Sartre's role as a dramatist that takes the beginnings and end of his career into account. An interesting and comprehensive discussion that features an expansive examination of *No Exit*.
Cohn, Ruby. *From Desire to Godot: Pocket Theater of Postwar Paris*. Berkeley: University of California Press, 1987. An illuminating look at the original production of *No Exit* and how

critics and audiences during the German occupation of France responded. A lively, fascinating interpretation emerges, complete with important details of subsequent productions.

McCall, Dorothy. *The Theatre of Jean-Paul Sartre*. New York: Columbia University Press, 1969. Although somewhat dated, this analysis of how the playwright's works relate to his views on theater still makes for highly informative reading.

Sartre, Jean-Paul. *Sartre on Theater*. Edited by Michel Contat and Michel Rybalka. Translated by Frank Jellinek. New York: Pantheon Books, 1976. In this collection of the playwright's own writings on his own play, the editors compile some pieces that deal directly with *No Exit* and several others that discuss Sartre's views on drama and theater during the time the play was composed and performed.

NO-NO BOY

Type of work: Novel
Author: John Okada (1923-1971)
Type of plot: Historical realism
Time of plot: Shortly after the end of World War II
Locale: Seattle, Washington
First published: 1957

> *Principal characters:*
> ICHIRO YAMADA, a Japanese American "no-no boy"
> KENJI, his friend and a World War II veteran
> MRS. YAMADA, his mother
> MR. YAMADA, his father
> TARO, his brother

The Story:

Ichiro Yamada, a twenty-five-year-old Japanese American, was a "no-no boy" during World War II: That is, he refused to serve in the United States armed services if drafted and to swear unqualified allegiance to the United States. As a result, he spent two years in federal prison. After being released from prison, he returned home to Seattle to live with his mother and father. Like all Japanese aliens and Japanese American citizens, the Yamadas had been forced to spend the war years in American internment camps; only those who were drafted into or joined the armed services were spared the relocation camps. Ichiro's refusal to fight for his country was his protest against this unjust treatment of Japanese Americans. His mother, who spoke very little English and who considered herself Japanese, even though she had lived in the United States for thirty-five years, was proud of Ichiro for going to prison. However, Taro, Ichiro's younger brother, detested him for not serving. Ichiro himself had conflicted feelings about his decision.

After Ichiro returned to Seattle, he met a former friend, Eto, who had fought in the war. When he learned that Ichiro was a "no-no boy," Eto spat on him. Ichiro visited the University of Washington, where he had been an engineering student before the war. He wanted to return to school, but he felt that he had forfeited the right to do so. Ichiro then met Kenji Kanno, his good friend from his university days. Though he shared Ichiro's anger about the internment camps, Kenji had chosen to fight in the war. He was a hero and had lost a leg in battle; his wound had not completely healed and his health was deteriorating. Ichiro envied Kenji and wished he could change places with him. Kenji respected Ichiro for having followed his conscience and gone to prison.

Bull, a Japanese American friend of Kenji, insulted Ichiro; later, two of Taro's friends assaulted Ichiro. Kenji took Ichiro to meet his girlfriend, Emi. She was married to one of Kenji's Japanese American friends in the army, but he had left her. Ichiro and Emi had a brief affair, with Kenji's knowledge; she knew that Kenji was dying. She encouraged Ichiro to put his past behind him and not feel despondent.

Ichiro observed many examples of racial prejudice among all ethnic groups. Hatred and bigotry were everywhere, but there were also many good people, among them Mr. Carrick. He was a white man who had many Japanese American friends and was ashamed of his country for its mistreatment of Japanese American citizens during the war. He offered Ichiro a job, but Ichiro decided not to accept it. Mr. Carrick's kindness gave Ichiro reason to hope that he might be able to resume a normal life.

Kenji's condition grew worse, and he was hospitalized. When Ichiro visited him, Kenji was angry and depressed. He argued that the "melting pot" did not exist; ethnic strife dominated American life. He urged Ichiro to forget that he was Japanese American and to leave Seattle. Kenji died in the hospital and was buried in a section of the community graveyard set aside for Japanese Americans. Ichiro returned from the funeral to find that his mother had committed suicide. He felt pity for her, but he still blamed her for having tried to make him a Japanese rather than an American. Ichiro found his weak-willed father in an alcoholic stupor.

Ichiro met up with Freddie, a fellow "no-no boy" with a hot temper. Ichiro visited Emi again, who informed him that she was getting a divorce. They went dancing. Ichiro began to feel less depressed and more hopeful about the future. A Mr. Morris offered him a job at the Christian Rehabilitation Center, and Ichiro considered taking it. Another "no-no boy," Gary, who worked there, related that he had been harassed by Japanese American veterans at a former job; an African American friend had often defended him against the taunters. Gary eventually was able to make peace with himself, and he started a new life as an artist. The conversation with Gary gave Ichiro further hope that he could renew his life.

Freddie remained filled with self-hatred and was unpredictable. When he and Ichiro went to a bar, they ran into Bull again. Bull and Freddie got into a fight, and Ichiro tried to break it up. Bull chased Freddie to his car, and Freddie wildly sped off; he lost control and died in the crash. Ichiro was upset by the tragic incident, but his experiences with caring people such as Kenji, Emi, Mr. Carrick, and Gary allowed him to face the future with hope for himself and his country.

Critical Evaluation:

A second-generation, or Nisei, Japanese American, John Okada was born and raised in Seattle, where he attended the University of Washington. Shortly after the Japanese bombed Pearl Harbor, President Franklin Delano Roosevelt signed Executive Order 9066, which required that all Japanese aliens and Japanese American citizens be relocated to internment camps, where they were forced to remain for the duration of the war. Despite being imprisoned in their own country, Japanese American men were also subject to the military draft. Thousands of young Japanese Americans enlisted or were drafted into the armed forces, and many gave their lives defending the country that had unjustly imprisoned their relatives and friends. Outraged by the great injustice perpetrated against them, some Japanese Americans refused to serve in the armed forces and to swear allegiance to the United States; they were labeled "no-no boys."

First published in 1957, Okada's first novel, *No-No Boy*, was virtually ignored. A second novel, about "Issei" Japanese Americans, remained unfinished at his death in 1971. Because no one seemed interested in Okada's fiction at the time, his wife burned the manuscript. There was, in fact, growing interest in Okada's work. During the 1960's and early 1970's, Asian Americans, like members of other American racial and ethnic minorities, became increasingly interested in their ethnic heritage and in the literary works that reflected and preserved that heritage. As a result of this increasing interest, *No-No Boy* was reissued by the University of Washington Press in 1976. Since then it has been widely read and is now generally regarded as a classic of Japanese American literature.

No-No Boy is based on fact, but it is not an autobiographical novel. Okada himself was not a "no-no boy"; he served in the army in World War II as an interpreter in the Pacific theater. As Okada explains in the preface to the novel, Ichiro is modeled on a friend of Okada who refused to enter the army unless the government would release his parents from an internment camp. Like the character Kenji, Okada understood and respected his "no-no boy" friend for making his hard decision, a decision which, as is emphasized throughout *No-No Boy*, could bring scorn and even violence from intolerant individuals both inside and outside the Japanese American community. Instead of writing about his personal experiences serving in the war, Okada chose to document the moral issues and turbulent emotions related to the "no-no boy" experience, which had not been explored in literature before.

Okada does not dwell on life in the internment camps or in prison, however. The action of the novel begins after Ichiro has been released from incarceration. There are backward glances at camp and prison life, but the bulk of the narrative centers on Ichiro's attempts to resolve his conflicted feelings about his refusal to serve in the army and about his cultural identity.

The great African American writer W. E. B. Du Bois once stated that African Americans always feel their "twoness," knowing they are both African and American. These two culturally different identities, Du Bois asserted, were ever at war in the individual. Du Bois's observations apply as well to the protagonists of many American ethnic novels, including Ichiro. Ichiro's two selves—his Japanese and American cultural identities—are at war with each other at the start of the narrative. His strong-willed mother never assimilated into American society, and she does not want her sons to assimilate either. Ichiro was born in the United States, however, and was educated in its schools; he therefore feels little connection with traditional Japanese culture. After the Japanese attack on Pearl Harbor, the U.S. government and many "white" Americans treated all Japanese Americans as if they were aliens. It is this that causes the deep psychological conflict in Ichiro: He feels American but his country considers him Japanese. He therefore exists in a cultural no-man's-land at the beginning of the novel.

By the end of the novel, Ichiro's "twoness" is resolved when he reaffirms his faith in America and forgives his country for the great injustice it dealt to Japanese Americans. Ichiro's renewed faith in America is not absolute, however; he has witnessed too much bigotry and injustice to have a naïve view of American race relations. Yet the many good people whom he meets during his journey to self-knowledge—Kenji, Emi, Carrick, and others—save him from sliding into pessimism and despair. He comes to believe that America is like a bruised apple: "Not rotten in the center where it counts, but rotten in spots underneath the skin."

No-No Boy has been criticized for rejecting the Japanese half of Japanese American. The novel contains few positive images of Japanese culture or traditions. Ichiro's mother, the primary representative of Japanese culture, is portrayed as an oppressive force from which Ichiro must liberate himself. Thus, where many ethnic writers celebrate the traditional culture and resolve the "twoness" problem by fusing the ethnic with the American identity, Okada seems to endorse cultural assimilation. Okada's depreciation of Japanese culture, however, must be examined in historical context. *No-No Boy* was written in the 1950's, before the "ethnic revival" of the 1960's. Moreover, though Japan was officially an ally of the United States, anti-Japanese feelings still ran high in the 1950's; and the Korean War (1950-1955) fueled anti-Asian feeling in general. It is therefore not surprising that Okada would emphasize the "Americanness" of Japanese Americans.

Technically, *No-No Boy* is quite conventional. The novel is constructed of a series of scenes and dialogues in which Ichiro is exposed to different ideas and points of view, each of which leads him to new insights and self-awareness. Clearly, Okada was primarily interested in dramatizing the moral dilemma and psychological conflicts that Japanese Americans experienced during and after World War II. Increasing numbers of readers testify that he succeeded in his aim.

Lawrence J. Oliver

Bibliography:

Kim, Elaine H. *Asian American Literature: An Introduction to the Writings and Their Social Context*. Philadelphia: Temple University Press, 1982. An excellent study of Asian American literature, which contains a sound analysis of *No-No Boy* that emphasizes the disintegrating influence of racism on the Japanese American community and psyche.

McDonald, Dorothy Ritsuko. "After Imprisonment: Ichiro's Search for Redemption in *No-No Boy*." *Melus* 6, no. 3 (Fall, 1979): 19-26. Traces Ichiro's psychological journey from guilt and alienation to peace and self-acceptance.

Sato, Gayle K. Fujita. "Momotaro's Exile: John Okada's *No-No Boy*." In *Reading the Literatures of Asian America*, edited by Shirley Geok-lin Lim and Amy Ling. Philadelphia: Temple University Press, 1992. Draws on the Japanese mythic tale "Momotaro" in arguing that *No-No Boy* affirms Japanese American identity by rejecting everything Japanese. Concludes that Japanese culture is portrayed almost entirely in negative terms.

Yeh, William. "To Belong or Not to Belong: The Liminality of John Okada's *No-No-Boy*." *Amerasia Journal* 19, no. 1 (1993): 121-134. Argues that both the novel's central character and historical context represent a state of "betweenness."

NO TRIFLING WITH LOVE

Type of work: Drama
Author: Alfred de Musset (1810-1857)
Type of plot: Tragicomedy
Time of plot: Nineteenth century
Locale: France
First published: On ne badine pac avec Pamour, 1834 (English translation, 1890); first
   performed, 1861

Principal characters:
   THE BARON, a French nobleman
   PERDICAN, his son
   CAMILLE, his niece
   ROSETTE, Camille's foster sister
   MAÎTRE BLAZIUS, Perdican's tutor
   MAÎTRE BRIDAINE, a village priest

The Story:

Maître Blazius, with his three chins and round stomach, was proudly awaiting the arrival of Perdican, whom he had tutored. Perdican had recently received a doctorate at Paris, and Maître Blazius felt that the credit was due to his tutoring. Gulping a huge bowl of wine presented by the chorus of listening peasants, he announced that Camille, niece of the Baron, was also expected home from the convent. The Baron was anxious to see his son Perdican married to Camille; he knew they had been in love since childhood.

Dame Pluche, Camille's chaperon, arrived out of breath. After drinking some vinegar and water, she announced that Camille was on her way. She told of Camille's education in the best convent in France and of the inheritance she was to get that day from her mother's estate. She did not mention the projected marriage.

The Baron brought Maître Bridaine to the house. Since he expected the marriage to take place that day, he wanted the priest to perform the ceremony. To impress Camille, he arranged with Maître Bridaine to speak some Latin to Perdican at dinner; no matter if neither one understood it. Maître Bridaine was agreeable to the plan, but he was hostile at once to Maître Blazius, for he smelled wine on his breath.

When Perdican and Camille met, something seemed amiss. Perdican wanted to embrace his pretty cousin, but Camille spoke formally to her childhood sweetheart and refused a kiss. She was chiefly interested in looking at a portrait of her great-aunt, who had been a nun. At dinner, the two priests, Maître Bridaine and Maître Blazius, vied jealously with each other. Both were gourmets as well as gourmands, and they were apprehensive that there was no place for two priests in the luxurious household. After dinner, Camille again refused a friendly talk with Perdican and even excused herself from walking in the garden. The Baron, upset at her coldness, grew even more indignant when Dame Pluche upheld Camille in her refusals. Perdican, with relief, renewed his acquaintance with Rosette, a pretty peasant who had been Camille's foster sister.

Maître Blazius, attempting to discredit his rival, told the Baron that Maître Bridaine had drunk three bottles of wine at dinner and was now walking about on unsteady feet. The Baron could scarcely listen because Maître Blazius' breath was so strong. Maître Bridaine hurried up to tell the Baron that Perdican was walking with Rosette on his arm and throwing pebbles about wildly.

Perdican was puzzled by Camille's coldness toward him. When Maître Blazius reminded him that the marriage was a project dear to the Baron's heart, the young man was willing to try again, but Camille was resolute. She would not let him hold her hand and refused to talk to him about their childhood. She had come back only to receive her inheritance; the next day, she would return to the convent. After Perdican left her, Camille asked the scandalized Dame Pluche to take a note to him.

Maître Bridaine was very unhappy. His rival was seated next to the Baron at mealtime, and Maître Blazius took all the choice morsels before he passed on the serving plate. In despair, Maître Bridaine felt that he would be forced to give up his frequent visits; although the prospect was repugnant, he would devote his time to parish work. On a friendly walk, Rosette complained to Perdican that women were kissed on the forehead or cheek by their male relatives and on the lips by their lovers; everyone kissed her on the cheek. Perdican was happy to give her a lover's kiss.

Dame Pluche was angry, but she took the note to Perdican. On the way, she was spied on by Maître Blazius, who reported to the Baron that Camille undoubtedly had a secret correspondent. Since Perdican now was romancing a woman who watched the turkeys, surely Camille was looking for a more satisfactory husband.

Invited to meet Camille at the fountain, Perdican found his cousin changed. She willingly kissed him and promised to remain a good friend. Then she frankly asked Perdican if he had had mistresses. Embarrassed, he admitted that he had. When she wanted to know where his latest was, Perdican had to admit he did not know. Camille, acquainted with no men except Perdican, had loved him until recently, when an older nun at the convent had changed her inclinations.

The nun had been rich and beautiful and much in love with her husband. After he took a mistress, she had taken a lover. At last, she had retired to a convent. Her experience had convinced Camille that men were always unfaithful. She forced Perdican to admit that if they were married both of them might be expected to take other lovers. Perdican valiantly defended earthly love, saying that it was worth all the trouble it caused, and that most of the two hundred nuns at the convent probably would be glad to go back to their husbands and lovers. At last, seeing the futility of his argument, he told Camille to return to the nunnery.

Meanwhile, Maître Blazius was unhappy because the servants reported that he was stealing bottles of wine. In addition, the Baron had decided that he had made up the story of Camille's secret correspondent. Disgusted with his second priest, the Baron dismissed him. Not knowing that Maître Bridaine had fallen from favor too, Maître Blazius asked him to intercede with the Baron. Maître Bridaine refused; he thought the Baron would now reinstate him in favor.

Maître Blazius thought he saw a chance to regain lost ground when he met Dame Pluche carrying a letter. While he was trying to take the missive from her by force, Perdican arrived on the scene, took the letter, and read it out of curiosity. It was from Camille to a nun at the convent. In it, Camille said she would soon be back; Perdican was hurt and his pride wounded, just as they had foreseen. Perdican thought the letter meant that the whole affair with Camille had been arranged in advance at the convent, and he resolved to spite her by courting Rosette seriously.

After writing a note to Camille to arrange a rendezvous, he brought Rosette to the fountain. Camille, hiding behind a tree, heard Perdican offer his heart to Rosette. As proof of his love, he gave her a chain to wear around her neck and threw a ring Camille had given him into the water.

Camille retrieved the ring and told Rosette to hide behind a curtain while she talked with Perdican. During the interview, he confessed that he loved Camille. Camille then threw aside the curtain; Rosette had fainted. Perdican decided to go ahead with his marriage to the peasant.

The Baron, told of his son's intention to marry Rosette, was angry. In spite of his father's displeasure, Perdican made arrangements for the ceremony. Camille, in despair, threw herself down before an altar and prayed for help. Perdican came in unexpectedly, and, unnerved by her distress, clasped her in his arms while they confessed their love for each other. Suddenly they heard a cry behind the altar. Investigating, they found Rosette, dead. Camille was the first to realize their guilt in her death. To acknowledge that guilt, she said a final good-bye to Perdican.

Critical Evaluation:

Alfred de Musset did not write his plays for the stage; he used the dramatic form rather as a vehicle for lyric expression. *No Trifling with Love*, reflecting the writer's love affair with George Sand, is a romantic defense of love; considered only as stage drama, it has serious weaknesses. The chorus of peasants is a cumbersome device and extraordinary characters are mingled helter-skelter. The two priests are buffoons, Camille is very stubborn, and Rosette dies in an unconvincing manner.

This piece was classified by Musset as a comedy, but it may better be called a tragicomedy. Earlier examples of the genre include William Shakespeare's *The Merchant of Venice*, 1596-1597. A tragicomedy often includes events associated with tragedy, such as a death of a central character or a grievous situation that is not resolved at the end. The comedic elements of a tragicomedy include jokes and humor, an ending that resolves most or all of the bad situations, and a sense of providence rather than fate. Musset's approach is to dramatize the tragic overtones with comic action: He develops a comedy and resolves it with tragedy.

Most of the action of *No Trifling with Love* is time-honored material for sentimental, romantic, or even cynical comedy. A charming hero and a beautiful heroine, both high-born, go through the dramatic motions of alternately reaching toward and then rejecting each other, while their pride, vanity, and wit entertain the audience through various intrigues and counter-intrigues. In the process of Musset's play, however, the pawn and plaything of their intrigues, a common and impressionable woman, kills herself. Perdican offers a pathetic justification to God: "We are two senseless children, but our hearts are pure." For Musset and for the audience, this is not sufficient: Love is not to be so trifled with. Camille, at least, has the moral fortitude to accept her responsibility for the catastrophe and to renounce the glib Perdican.

What is most interesting about this play is Musset's subtly drawn examination of love. In the first act, his theme appears to be a commonplace one—love is a complex and unpredictable quality. It is not subject to the precise expectations and course of development calculated in advance by the Baron, a man so orderly that he knows to the minute how old his son and niece are, and manages to stage their return, after ten years of absence, at the exact same moment from opposite doors. When things subsequently do not go as he expects, his whole world turns upside down, and he is utterly unable to account for the discrepancy between his planning and human behavior.

In the second act, the theme deepens as Musset turns to an examination of the value of love itself. Camille, who will accept nothing less than an ideal and eternal love, wants desperately to love, but she does not want to suffer. Love always causes suffering and misery, her nuns have assured her; since it involves so much deceit, capriciousness, and betrayal, is it not better to avoid the problem entirely by withdrawing from the world into a cloister, where the maimed and disabled from the battlefields of love can minister to one another? Contrasted to this is

Perdican's more realistic view that love—fickle, temporary, cruel, and imperfect as it is—is nevertheless a part of life, and as such, must be faced and experienced, not avoided.

One is reminded of John Milton, who could not "praise a fugitive and cloistered virtue, unexercised and unbreathed that never sallies out and sees her adversary, but slinks out of the race." One must not slink out of the race by becoming a nun, Musset suggests; having chosen to run the race, one should run it honestly, without pride or intrigue, and, above all, not at the expense of other people.

Bibliography:

Affron, Charles. *A Stage for Poets: Studies in the Theater of Hugo and Musset.* Princeton, N.J.: Princeton University Press, 1971. Extensive analysis of *No Trifling with Love* is included in a volume of essays examining the works of two important French dramatists. Discusses the diction of the play and Musset's handling of the problem of time.

Gochberg, Herbert S. *Stage of Dreams: The Dramatic Art of Alfred de Musset (1828-1834).* Geneva: Librarie Droz, 1967. Devotes a chapter to analysis of the play considered to be Musset's "last theatrical forum for his obsession with dream and reality." Discusses the playwright's handling of the question of love.

Rees, Margaret A. *Alfred de Musset.* New York: Twayne, 1971. Concentrates on characterization of heroes and heroines in *No Trifling with Love*, noting how the playwright contrasts the complex Camille with the admirable but befuddled Perdican to achieve his sober ending.

Sices, David. *Theater of Solitude: The Drama of Alfred de Musset.* Hanover, N.H.: Published for Dartmouth College by the University Press of New England, 1974. One chapter examines the weaknesses of *No Trifling with Love*, but concludes it is a successful endeavor. Believes it best demonstrates "the author's obsession with time and its treachery."

Tilley, Arthur. *Three French Dramatists: Racine, Marivaux, Musset.* New York: Russell & Russell, 1967. Discusses the influence of Pierre Carlet de Chamblain de Marivaux and Shakespeare on this and other of Musset's plays; also comments on the playwright's handling of the element of the fantastic.

THE NORMAL HEART

Type of work: Drama
Author: Larry Kramer (1935-   )
Type of plot: Problem play
Time of plot: Early 1980's
Locale: New York City
First performed: 1985; first published, 1985

Principal characters:
NED WEEKS, an AIDS activist
BRUCE NILES, Ned's friend and rival
BEN WEEKS, Ned's straight brother
FELIX TURNER, Ned's lover
DR. EMMA BROOKNER, a physician
THE EXAMINING DOCTOR, Emma's enemy
HIRAM KEEBLER, the mayor's assistant
TOMMY BOATWRIGHT and
MICKEY MARCUS, volunteers

The Story:

Ned Weeks visited Dr. Emma Brookner's office because he was interested in writing a journalistic story about a strange, new disease called acquired immune deficiency syndrome (AIDS). This disease was responsible for the symptoms experienced by two of Ned's gay associates. While Ned had a physical exam, Emma told him what she knew about the disease: It had already killed some of her patients, it seemed to strike gay men, and the press did not pay much attention to it. She told Ned that he should get the word out and urge gay men to stop having sex, because she thought that might be how the disease was transmitted.

Ned visited Felix Turner's desk at *The New York Times* because he wanted him to inform the public about the disease by writing about it. The request made Felix uncomfortable; he was a homosexual, but was not open about his sexual orientation. Ned also visited his brother, Ben, hoping that Ben's law firm would support an organization Ned had helped to start, which was intended to raise money and spread information about AIDS.

Felix and Ned had their first date at Ned's apartment, where Ned compared the press's lack of interest in AIDS to its lack of interest in Adolf Hitler's extermination of the Jews during World War II. Felix and Ned became lovers.

Several members of Ned's AIDS organization met. Bruce Niles was appointed president of the organization, although Ned was clearly interested in the office. When the members learned about Felix, Ned's new boyfriend, Tommy Boatwright was disappointed because he was romantically interested in Ned; Bruce Niles was relieved because Ned had made unwanted advances toward him.

Ned visited his brother's law office again. This time he wanted to see if Ben would serve on the organization's board of directors. Ben declined, and the brothers parted angrily.

Ned discussed his frustrations about the AIDS organization with Felix. The organization's board of directors thought Ned was creating a panic about the disease and using the disease to make himself into a celebrity. Felix revealed to Ned that he had a purple lesion, one of the symptoms of AIDS, on his foot. Ned met with Emma, who once again told him that gay men must be told to stop having sex in order to stop the spread of AIDS. Ned told her that Felix was sick and she agreed to see him the next day.

Although New York City government officials agreed to meet with officials of Ned's AIDS organization, the mayor's assistant, Hiram Keebler, was two hours late in keeping the appointment. The mayor of New York City refused to help give the organization office space, press the national government to fund research on the disease, or demand that *The New York Times* cover the disease. Ned became angry about the city's slow response to AIDS and verbally attacked Hiram, while Bruce tried to be diplomatic. Ned criticized Bruce for being such a weak leader.

Emma told Felix that he had an early case of AIDS, and she explained to him how she would care for him. She could not answer Felix's questions about whether or not the disease could infect Ned.

Volunteers of the organization were busy answering hot-line phones. The list of gay men who had died from AIDS had grown, yet Mickey Marcus and others were angry with Ned's argument that gay men should stop having sex. Mickey became worried that he might lose his job at the City Department of Health because the gay men's organization had been putting pressure on the mayor's office. Exhausted and angry, he attacked what he considered to be Ned's regressive ideas about gay men's sexuality. Bruce told Ned that Bruce's lover, Albert, had died of AIDS.

Emma became angry with the Examining Doctor after learning that the federal government allotted only five million dollars for AIDS research, a small sum compared to what the government was capable of funding, and that her own funding for research had been denied.

Ned picketed the mayor's office and heard that the mayor finally would meet with members of the organization. Then Bruce read Ned a letter stating that the board of directors wanted Ned to quit the organization he had co-founded. Wishing to remain in the organization, Ned delivered a passionate speech about how gay culture must be recognized for something besides sex.

Felix was very ill and depressed about his illness; he refused to eat. Ned, who had been trying to reason with and care for Felix, finally became angry with his lover. He threw food on the floor. After fighting, the two embraced.

Felix and Ben met for the first time. Ben helped Felix make out a will leaving everything, including a piece of land, to Ned. With Ben present, Emma married Ned and Felix before Felix died. Ned and Ben were reconciled.

Critical Evaluation:

The Normal Heart was one of the first stage productions to deal with acquired immune deficiency syndrome (AIDS). After publishing the novel *Faggots* (1978), which many critics considered an offensive account of the promiscuous sex lives of homosexual men, Larry Kramer's timely and angry play *The Normal Heart*, which urged gay men to stop having sex, earned critical approval and a number of awards. As much a period piece documenting AIDS's rampant spread in the early 1980's as it is a dramatic work of high artistic merit, *The Normal Heart* is partially autobiographical. In 1981, Kramer, like his character Ned Weeks, co-founded an organization to raise money and care for men with AIDS, the Gay Men's Health Crisis. In 1983, Kramer, like his character, was ousted after a meeting with New York City's mayor, Ed Koch. Although critics take umbrage with what they have described as the play's banal script, melodramatic action, and overuse of facts and statistics, *The Normal Heart* is important as an educational tool capable of spurring people to action.

Besides candidly presenting the early outbreak of AIDS and the slow response of the government, the media, and the medical establishment, the play also depicts the gay community, and it does so without relying on stereotypes. Although Kramer acknowledges that some gay men do frequent bath houses some of the time and that some gay men behave as flamboyantly and sexually as does the character Tommy Boatwright, he also depicts relationships between gay men that are based on commitment and caring. "The only way we'll have real pride," Ned says, "is when we demand recognition of a culture that isn't just sexual." One of the themes of the play, in fact, focuses on real love, not just sex, between gay men. As the play's epigraph, stanzas from a poem by W. H. Auden, suggests, everyone wants "Not universal love/ But to be loved alone." This is a normal desire felt by those bearers of "the normal heart," heterosexuals and homosexuals alike.

The Normal Heart is not a subtle play. Kramer's frustration and anger about the disease killing off a whole community comes through loud and clear. His characters are angry, especially Ned, who screams, literally, at almost everyone with whom he comes in contact. Ned is rude, overbearing, ready to throw groceries on the floor to make a point. The play is also notable for its graphic depiction of AIDS symptoms—the purple lesions on one character's face and another's foot, the convulsions experienced by another patient—and for its descriptions of incontinence, cancers, and general weakness. Kramer was interested in publicizing the epidemic that had been hidden for too long.

This is Ned's play, written from his point of view. He dominates all of the scenes except the three in which he does not appear. Of these, two focus on Felix, Ned's lover. The first portrays Felix when he is told by a doctor that he has AIDS; in this scene, Emma is unable to answer his questions about contagion and possible treatments. In the second scene, Felix puts his legal affairs in order before his death. Both scenes are matter-of-fact and unemotional, brief sketches of the medical and legal details thousands of AIDS patients must negotiate each day.

The third scene in which Ned does not appear portrays Emma and the Examining Doctor, a character who personifies the medical establishment. Like Ned, Emma not only understands the horror of AIDS but also knows that in order to fight the epidemic she must get angry at those who have power, even if it means losing her temper, as she does in this scene. Her hurling of folders and papers into space is echoed two scenes later by Ned when he throws food on the floor.

The play ends with Ben Weeks embracing his brother, Ned. Ned and Ben finally reconcile their differences after Felix's death. Not only does this embrace unite feuding family members and suggest that Ben now accepts Ned as a healthy equal but it also depicts the straight world embracing the gay community. It is only by the two working together that the oppression of homosexuality will end and an epidemic such as AIDS can be stopped.

Cassandra Kircher

Bibliography:
Gilbey, Liz. "Being What We Are." *Plays International* 9, no. 2 (October, 1993): 14-15. Discusses *The Destiny of Me* (1992), Kramer's sequel to *The Normal Heart*. In *The Destiny of Me*, Ned Weeks (also the main character in *The Normal Heart*) reflects on his life and family.
Maggenti, Maria. "AIDS Movies: A Swelling Chorus." *Interview* 23, no. 4 (April, 1993): 112. A brief but pointed interview with Kramer in which he talks about the problems he had getting *The Normal Heart* produced. For an early review of *The Normal Heart*, see *The New York Times Book Review*, January 4, 1979.
Shnayerson, Michael. "Kramer vs. Kramer." *Vanity Fair* 55, no. 10 (October, 1992): 228+. An

in-depth portrait of Kramer and his work. Discusses Kramer's relationship to his family and friends, and to the organizations that he founded (Gay Men's Health Crisis and ACT UP).

Winokur, L. A. "An Interview with Larry Kramer." *The Progressive* 58, no. 6 (June, 1994): 32-35. An interview with Kramer in which he criticizes *The New York Times* coverage of AIDS and speaks about Barbara Streisand's film version of *The Normal Heart*.

Zonana, Victor. "Larry Kramer." *The Advocate* 617 (December 1, 1992): 40-48. Extensive interview with Kramer about cultural, political, and medical establishments in the United States. Mentions both *The Normal Heart* and its sequel, *The Destiny of Me*. The second part of the interview, focusing more on personal issues in Kramer's life, such as his own health since being diagnosed as HIV-positive, was published in the December 15, 1992, issue of *The Advocate*.

NORTH & SOUTH

Type of work: Poetry
Author: Elizabeth Bishop (1911-1979)
First published: 1946

North & South, Elizabeth Bishop's first book of poems, is full of waking up and the sea. There are poems set in Paris, others in rural Florida. Some characters are human, some animals, still others are surreal. Poems like "The Man-Moth," "Roosters," and "The Fish" stand powerfully on their own, displaying the mastery that elevated Bishop to the status of a major American poet of the twentieth century. *North & South* as a whole expresses the young Bishop's effort to attune her craft to the world she was encountering.

Although Bishop, unlike other poets of her time, did not use her poems to confess her personal life, the longing and sorrow in them is formidable. Loss characterized her earliest years. Eight months after her birth, her father died suddenly. Five years later, after several breakdowns, Bishop's mother became permanently insane, and Bishop never saw her again. The child lived alternately with family in Massachusetts and Nova Scotia. Illness, especially asthma, kept her from attending school regularly, but she entered Vassar in 1930 and was graduated in 1934, the year that the well-known poet Marianne Moore befriended her and Bishop's mother died. During the decade that Bishop worked on the poems that comprise *North & South*, she lived in New York City and traveled in France and other European countries, and after 1937 (in the hope of relieving her asthma) wintered in Florida.

The first third of *North & South* conveys a sense of starting out and tentativeness. The speaker in the initial poem, "The Map," contemplates much of the Northern Hemisphere and at first playfully considers whether the land "lean[s] down to lift the sea from under." A cautious note sounds when place names run across nearby features, reminding the poet that sometimes "emotion too far exceeds its cause." "The Imaginary Iceberg" emphasizes longing for the fantastical—a condition in which one can feel "artlessly rhetorical" and "rise on finest ropes/ that airy twists of snow provide." On the other hand, "The Gentleman of Shalott" portrays a character content to be incomplete, even indefinite. One element of Bishop's uncertainty is artistic. She organizes several of her poems around conceits—witty, extended metaphors. She demonstrates in "Wading at Wellfleet" that a single image—in this case, the flashing chariot wheels that depict the awesome movement of the sea—can be inadequate. In the final lines, the immensity of the water makes "the wheels/ give way; they will not bear the weight." Another element is emotional. Anxiety pervades "Chemin de Fer" from the "pounding heart" of the second line to the the the hermit's shotgun blast and the challenge he screams, "Love should be put into action!" A similar intimidation underlies "From the Country to the City," as the speaker is drawn irresistibly toward a city consisting of mocking images.

Of the three poems that follow, all making city life fearful, "The Man-Moth" has been most appreciated. Inspired by a newspaper misprint of "mammoth," Bishop created a surreal character—half-human, half-insect—who, ironically, surpasses his human counterpart. "Man" stands passive in the moonlight like an "inverted pin" and seems unable—or unwilling—to comprehend. The Man-Moth, on the other hand, while fearful, "must investigate as high as he can climb." The explanation "what the Man-Moth fears most he must do" characterizes the plight of a number of Bishop's characters. The poem contrasts characters (the first time Bishop does so in *North & South*), but there is no hero to admire. Instead, after the first stanza introduces Man, the next four stanzas emphasize the Man-Moth's uneasiness. Mistaking the moon for a "small hole at the top of the sky," the Man-Moth scales building walls "fearfully," "his shadow dragging like a photographer's cloth behind him." When he returns underground and boards a subway train, he sits "facing the wrong way" and "travels backward." The ride seems endless. In fact, his life is a nightmare; death rides constantly beside him, and he must resist the temptation of suicide. The oppressiveness of the city, nevertheless, allows for hope. In the final stanza, the reader ("you") has the chance to break the Man-Moth's isolation and share his sorrow. Although the tear that slips from Man-Moth's eye is associated with "the bee's sting," empathy permits one to recognize it as "cool" and "pure enough to drink."

Before Bishop goes to new locales, leaving the city, "The Weed," "The Unbeliever," and "The Monument" reiterate the importance of empathy and provide a symbol of the artistic endeavor. "The Weed" dramatizes the invigorating influence of life upon a "cold heart" prone to isolation. The weed eventually splits the heart, releasing "a flood of water." The spillage into the speaker's eyes permit sight; each drop seems to contain "a small, illuminated scene," suggesting that the river has retained "all/ the scenes that it had once reflected." As jolting as the weed's intrusion has seemed, the possibility of insight seems preferable to the self-protective sleep depicted in "The Unbeliever." Understanding this distinction qualifies one to respond in the affirmative to the question that begins the third poem—"Now can you see the monument?" It turns out to be hard even to describe, and Bishop allows for a mocking response ("It's like a stage-set; it is all so flat!"). She defends the contraption: The very carelessness of its appearance "gives it away as having life, and wishing." Such is the "beginning" of art. After this assertion of the importance of the artistic impulse, one may expect an outward movement, aesthetically speaking. Bishop's post-graduation trip to Europe in 1935 yielded several poems set in Paris, but there is little sense of expansiveness. An automobile accident cost her friend Margaret Miller the lower part of the arm with which she painted, and the poems have an intensely melancholy air. However, there is also a technical—and perhaps temperamental—advance evident in "Quai d'Orleans." Rather than impose her ideas, for the first time Bishop lets place and occasion suggest her discovery.

A larger change occurred, as the title *North & South* implies, when Bishop experienced Florida. Exotic tropical details expanded the possibilities for her art, just as they had the poetry of her modernist predecessor Wallace Stevens. The final ten poems in *North & South* contain various voices and embrace much more of physical place. In "Florida," for example, Bishop assembles detail after vivid detail—-in the way that her mentor Marianne Moore had—to suggest the emotion that holds the poems together. In Florida, Bishop took great interest in the lives of Cubans and blacks. While living in Key West in the house she bought with Marjorie Stevens, she also observed signs of American industry preparing for World War II. One finds imagery of warfare and battling in several poems in the latter half of *North & South*, but "Roosters" is Bishop's greatest poetic response to militarism. Like so many poems in the book, this one begins at dawn. The clamorous crowing and the repeated use of "gun-metal blue" prepare us for the appearance of the birds who gloat

> Deep from protruding chests
> in green-gold medals dressed,
> planned to command and terrorize the rest.

The birds fight to the death, "with raging heroism defying/ even the sensation of dying." The three-line stanzas and insistent rhymes mock the martial subject but do not reduce the menace. Such balancing characterizes not only the tone of the poem, but also the commentary in the second section. Bishop recalls the rooster's role in Peter's denial of Christ and suggests that one might find hope in the forgiveness that followed. The serene portrayal of the new morning at the end of the poem perhaps confirms that hope. It is perhaps naïve, however, to miss the sarcasm in the question, "How could the night have come to grief?" Part of the greatness of "Roosters" is that, instead of deciding for the reader, it involves the reader in the emotional turmoil brought on by violence. The poem makes the reader part of the violence he or she may claim to abhor.

The other animal poem in *North & South*, "The Fish," has been, as Bishop herself came to resent, anthologized very often. Her encounter with the "tremendous fish" may remind one of the shocking effect of the weed liberating the "cold heart"; the hooks and lines "Like medals with their ribbons" hanging from the fish's mouth suggest that the fish is another victim of human violence. In this fine poem, the fisher is moved to empathize with the fish to a degree unusual in Bishop's early work. As in "Florida," Bishop adds image to image to narrate the incident. Many of the details are similes that dramatize the struggle to comprehend the unforgettable fish. The description of his eyes indicates some of the difficulty—and challenge in doing so:

> The irises seem backed and packed
> with tarnished tinfoil
> seen through the lenses
> of old scratched isinglass.

In addition, they do not "return my stare." This is no romantic bonding with nature. The fish remains "other" and the poet continues to study hard. After she allows that the hardware in the mouth may be a "beard of wisdom," she is overwhelmed by "victory." Partly, it is her own, having comprehended the immensity of the unlike being; but, in his dignity and survival, the fish shares the triumph. "Anaphora," the concluding poem, harkens back not only to the many poems that recount awaking and the day's beginning but also to the euphoria of setting out in "The Map." In rhetoric, anaphora refers to figures of repetition and renewal. It can also denote the moment in Christian worship that the Eucharistic elements are offered as an oblation. "Anaphora" describes—commemorates and celebrates are better words—the passage of the days, and Bishop skillfully repeats sounds and words and extends repetition to the structure of the poem—two fourteen-line stanzas—their rhymes and thought-patterns reminding one of shrunken sonnets. Morning's "wonder" becomes "mortal/ mortal fatigue," but the poem ends hopefully, the beggar's fire providing "endless/ endless assent." The publication of *North & South* in 1946 finally assured Elizabeth Bishop that she was a poet, that years of preparation, hard work, and doubt had not been wasted. That the book—nominated by the eminent Marianne Moore—had triumphed over eight hundred other entries for the Houghton Mifflin Prize alerted the literary world of an important new presence. Her next book would win a Pulitzer Prize. The poet Robert Lowell's admiring response would begin Bishop's second close friendship with a writer of her own stature. Within five years, she would interrupt a voyage around South America. Ill from an allergic reaction, she would stop in Brazil and remain almost two decades, living with Lota de Macedo Soares and continuing the enlargement of her poetry's embrace of the world around her.

Jay Paul

Bibliography:

Harrison, Victoria. *Elizabeth Bishop's Poetics of Intimacy*. New York: Cambridge University Press, 1993. Studies the evolution of Bishop's poems as vehicles for expression. Chapter 2 discusses intimacy and romance. Chapter 3 emphasizes the effect of events, particularly World War II, on Bishop's imagination. Extensive notes, bibliography, index.

Kalstone, David. *Becoming a Poet: Elizabeth Bishop with Marianne Moore and Robert Lowell*. New York: Farrar, Straus & Giroux, 1989. The probing study of Bishop's complex friendship with Marianne Moore coincides with the making of the poems of *North & South*. Notes, index.

Parker, Robert Dale. *The Unbeliever: The Poetry of Elizabeth Bishop*. Champaign: University of Illinois Press, 1988. Studies the wishful nature of *North & South*—the anxiousness behind her poems, as well as Bishop's readiness to look outside herself for subjects. Notes, index.

Stevenson, Anne. *Elizabeth Bishop*. Boston: Twayne, 1966. The best starting point to study Bishop's life and work. Outlines the period relevant to *North & South* and examines several poems. Helpful primary and secondary bibliographies, notes, and index.

Travisano, Thomas. *Elizabeth Bishop: Her Artistic Development*. Charlottesville: University Press of Virginia, 1988. Relates *North & South* to two phases in Bishop's work—"enclosure" and "history." Detailed but understandable interpretations of many poems. Illuminating explanation of Bishop's interest in Surrealism and the Baroque. Notes, primary and secondary bibliographies, and index.

NORTH AND SOUTH

Type of work: Novel
Author: Elizabeth Gaskell (1810-1865)
Type of plot: Social realism
Time of plot: Mid-nineteenth century
Locale: England
First published: 1854-1855

Principal characters:
MARGARET HALE
THE REV. RICHARD HALE, her father, formerly a Church of England
   minister
MRS. MARIA HALE, her mother
FREDERICK HALE, her brother, a sailor in exile
DIXON, the Hale's family servant
JOHN THORNTON, an industrialist
MRS. THORNTON, his mother
FANNY THORNTON, his sister
EDITH LENNOX (née Shaw), Margaret's cousin, a London socialite
HENRY LENNOX, her brother-in-law, a suitor to Margaret
NICHOLAS HIGGINS, a factory worker
BESSIE HIGGINS, his daughter
MR. BELL, a property owner, Oxford Tutor, and godfather to Frederick

The Story:

Margaret Hale had been living with her Aunt Shaw and her cousin, Edith, in London. The Shaws moved in upper-class society, as did Captain Lennox, Edith's fiancé, and Henry Lennox, his brother, an attorney. After Edith's wedding, Margaret returned to her parents' sheltered home, the vicarage of Helstone, a small village in the south of England. She was surprised by two events: the visit of Henry Lennox to propose marriage, and the resignation of her father from the Church of England because of theological doubts. She refused Lennox, however good his prospects, because she hardly knew him. The resignation meant the family would have to move. Mr. Hale had been offered a tutoring job in Milton Northern by Mr. Bell, his former Oxford professor, who owned property there. They had never lived in the north of England, let alone in an industrial city. Mr. Hale asked Margaret to break the news to her mother, who was distraught.

With the family servant, Dixon, they moved to a rented house, and met John Thornton, a factory owner and leaseholder of Mr. Bell. Thornton was to be one of Margaret's father's students. She was offended by his brusque manner and could not understand why a self-made industrialist should want to study classical languages. Margaret managed to adapt to a city life very different from that of London, as did Dixon. Her mother, however, withdrew into herself, finally suffering a breakdown. Margaret got to know Bessie Higgins, a factory worker, and through her Nicholas Higgins, her father. She visited their home and tried to support Bessie, ill with an industrial disease of the lungs. Bessie was fearful her father would either become alcoholic or get overinvolved in Trades Union agitation. Margaret introduced Nicholas to her father and the two men discussed both industrial and religious matters, coming to like each other.

Margaret was also introduced to the Thornton household, an austere family ruled over by

Mrs. Thornton. Her weak daughter, Fanny, stood in great contract to John, whose tough-minded dealings with his workers brought him into conflict with Margaret. Mr. Hale, as an outsider, could see both sides in the impending industrial dispute. When this dispute broke out, Margaret found herself physically between the two parties, protecting John Thornton when strikers threatened him. John felt she had compromised her honor in doing this and he ought to propose marriage. Margaret angrily rejected him; the feelings of both to each other were very ambivalent at this stage, ranging from admiration to bitterness. Mrs. Thornton was angry over Margaret's rejection.

Both Bessie and Mrs. Hale died soon after. Margaret was persuaded to send for her brother, Frederick, who had previously fled to Spain after a naval mutiny. He managed to return secretly just before his mother died, but in escaping Milton Northern, he was spotted with Margaret by a railway worker. A scuffle ensued in which the worker was accidentally killed. John Thornton, as local magistrate, investigated the death. When asking Margaret for evidence, he was met with less than the truth. He believed Margaret had a lover and yet found it difficult to credit her with such dishonorable behavior, even though his mother did not. Margaret became deeply ashamed of her behavior, and the rift between Margaret and John was at its widest.

Margaret continued to visit Higgins and also the Bouchers, an indigent worker's family now left fatherless by his suicide. Her father went to visit Mr. Bell at Oxford and, suddenly, died there. Margaret, in mourning, was persuaded to return to London to nurse Edith, expecting her first child. While there she pursued the possibility of obtaining a pardon for Frederick, but this proved impossible. Mr. Bell suggested she visit him in Oxford. While on the way, she revisited Helstone, but after Milton Northern it seemed very backward and uninviting. Mr. Bell was able to give her news about Thornton: A recession was hitting him hard. Margaret found herself stirred deeply by talk of him. Shortly after her return to London, Mr. Bell died, too, and Margaret found herself beneficiary of his property—she was now, in fact, Thornton's landlord. He now came to financial ruin himself through the strike and overinvesting at a time of recession. Tables were turned.

Margaret found herself completely unable to settle back to the fashionable life of London, and was much happier when engaged in social action, visiting the poorer parts of the city, although this was much frowned on. Through Henry Lennox's legal work she met Thornton again and discovered he had had a change of heart over the way his workers should be treated. He, too, discovered his misunderstanding over Frederick. Margaret now offered to refinance him. Both at last admitted to themselves they loved each other. Thornton's proposed marriage once again.

Critical Evaluation:

North and South belongs to a group of novels written in the mid-nineteenth century often called "The Condition of England" novels, or more generally, industrial novels. Society as a whole was trying to come to terms with the rapid industrialization and urbanization of Great Britain, the first country to experience such development. Mrs. Elizabeth Gaskell belongs to a group of novelists committed to exposing the social conditions brought about by the industrial revolution, and to suggest ways to go forward and to oppose wrong values and policies. Other novelists of this group include Charles Dickens, Benjamin Disraeli, and Charles Kingsley.

Mrs. Gaskell lived much of her life in Manchester as the wife of a Unitarian minister, and therefore experienced at first hand the living and working conditions of both rich and poor, workers and masters, and had seen the dire results of economic slumps and industrial disputes. She described these conditions in an earlier novel, *Mary Barton* (1848), that is very sympathetic to the working classes, especially her proletarian heroine, Mary. At times, however, it is melodramatic. In *North and South*, Mrs. Gaskell takes a more balanced view and explores the strengths and weaknesses of both sides, allows a good deal more dialogue, and introduces intelligent outsiders (the Hales) who can be relatively impartial. The novel goes at a slower pace, therefore, but its credibility is strengthened, except for such incidents as those involving Frederick.

At a more general level, the novel may also be placed in the category of the provincial novel. This category includes novels that do not take London (or any capital city) as the cultural norm and that explore regional ways of life, speech, values and beliefs in a serious way. Mrs. Gaskell is a provincial novelist through and through.

The title harkens back to Benjamin Disraeli's metaphor of the two nations. He saw Britain divided sharply between rich and poor. His politics sought ways of reconstituting a single nation. Mrs. Gaskell suggests the gap between the north and the south is equally wide, but avoids seeking a solution in politics. Instead, she points toward mutual understanding and intermingling through personal relationships. The marriage of the dynamic, self-made industrialist, Thornton, to Margaret, who stems from the rural home counties and fashionable London, symbolizes this. At the end of the novel, a circle leading back to London is completed to show how much Margaret has changed. She has embraced northern ways of openness and energy, and rejected the artificiality of the capital.

Part of this openness-artificiality dialectic is conveyed through the Victorian theme of what a gentleman is. Thornton is stung by Margaret's accusation at one point that he has not acted as a gentleman. Mrs. Gaskell wished to redefine the concept of the gentleman in terms of inner qualities of sympathy. Industrialists must move away from their own self-images as masters, self-images that are reinforced by the workers. Thornton manages to make the transition. In addition, ironically, Thornton fails financially through trying to do the right thing (invest in a new plant and improve conditions of work). Margaret's wealth is unearned. Mrs. Gaskell's plot demonstrates that men need women, and that women can have and should have responsible financial power to invest in a better society. Women have a readier sympathy to face the suffering and plight of the workers and their families, and for them, this is part of the remaking of society. Men concentrate too much on profit and power alone.

Margaret Hale, however, is more than a symbol for Mrs. Gaskell's wider purposes. She is developed as a complex heroine, expanding traditional gender roles. She has to take over much of the financial decision making from her father. She moves independently into the very masculine Milton society, becoming involved in upper- and lower-class homes and in a strike. She is contrasted to the effete Edith and Fanny, and stands between the domineering Mrs. Thornton and the helpless Mrs. Hale as the ideal Victorian woman for Mrs. Gaskell.

Mrs. Gaskell's style, however, does not allow for careful psychological portrayal. Her descriptions, dialogue, and narrative are realistic, but without show. They do not draw attention to themselves, and avoid not only the melodramatic, but also the symbolic. She can embrace, realistically, a wide variety of speech and locale and can tackle the affairs of the day. An analysis of her style demonstrates real depth, careful arrangement of detail, and subtle insights into observed human behavior.

She refuses both high-flown rhetoric and agendas. Her beliefs, born out by her style, lie in quiet, low-key acts of reconciliation and sympathy that bring human beings together in creative relationships for the good of society as a whole.

David Barratt

Bibliography:

Craik, W. A. *Elizabeth Gaskell and the English Provincial Novel.* New York: Harper & Row, 1975. A major rehabilitation of Mrs. Gaskell as an important novelist, this study sets her five long fictions within the provincial novel tradition. Demonstrates how she expanded the possibilities and universality of the tradition.

Duthie, Enid. *The Themes of Elizabeth Gaskell.* New York: Macmillan, 1980. Despite contrasting settings and plots, there is, according to this book, a unity of thematic material in all of Mrs. Gaskell's fiction. Draws upon Mrs. Gaskell's letters to reconstruct her imaginative world and the themes central to it.

Gerin, Winifred. *Elizabeth Gaskell.* New York: Oxford University Press, 1976. The first biography to make use of the publication in 1966 of Mrs. Gaskell's letters. Although there have been a number of more recent biographies, this is still one of the best, particularly from the point of view of relating fictional material to its background.

Stoneman, Patsy. *Elizabeth Gaskell.* Brighton, England: Harvester Press, 1987. This feminist reading claims that previous accounts of Mrs. Gaskell have seriously misread her, and that the interaction of class and gender must be made central. A condensed but provocative reading of *North and South* is included.

Uglow, Jenny. *Elizabeth Gaskell: A Habit of Stories.* Winchester, Mass.: Faber & Faber, 1993. The chapter on *North and South* expounds the novel fully. A full listing of Mrs. Gaskell's works and an index.

NORTH OF BOSTON

Type of work: Poetry
Author: Robert Frost (1874-1963)
First published: 1914

Like his first book, *A Boy's Will* (1913) Robert Frost's second, *North of Boston*, was first published in England. Despite that irony, it was, and remains, the book that connects the name Robert Frost with America's New England.

Frost began writing poetry in the 1890's while running a small farm in Derry, New Hampshire, but he found few publications that would accept his work. By the time he took his family to England in 1912, he had published a handful of poems in magazines and newspapers. He was a virtually unknown poet approaching the age of forty.

Frost was, and still is, seen as a poet on the fringe of the modernist movement from the 1910's through the 1930's. While others experimented with free verse, jazz rhythms, fragmentation, and other nontraditional methods, Frost chose to stick with conventions such as rhyme and meter. His own experiments had to do with the nuances of human speech organized along a poetic line. Frost theorized that it was possible to understand a sentence's "sound of sense" even if the listener could not make out the individual words spoken. Consequently, his poems sound like talk one might hear between two people—that is, everyday conversation—but talk of uncommon wit and intelligence. Some of the finest examples of that talk appear in the poems of *North of Boston*. *A Boy's Will* presented a speaker who had moved away from the world of people and was observing from a distance. But *North of Boston* is Frost's "book of people."

Most of the poems in this volume are dramatic monologues, where one speaker narrates a story, or dramatic dialogues, in which two speakers act out a conflict. The dialogues depend strongly on tensions to create drama, and Frost presents a great variety of them. "Mending Wall," the opening poem in *North of Boston*, is one of Frost's most famous dramatic dialogues. Two neighbors meet each spring to repair the stone walls that separate their properties. The persona, or narrator, of the poem, observes that "Something there is that doesn't love a wall." His neighbor, on the other hand, quotes his father, saying "Good fences make good neighbors" and thus setting up one of the principal tensions in the poem. The narrator feels that his neighbor is too practical, too old-fashioned in his thinking. He says, "He moves in darkness as it seems to me,/ not of woods only and the shade of trees . . . " He clings to ideas long held by his people, and to the narrator he is "like an old-stone savage armed." Games and work, the mystical and the realistic, humor and seriousness are tensions that combine to make this poem rich in drama and insight into human nature.

"The Death of the Hired Man" is a longer dramatic dialogue that introduces the reader to a husband and wife, Warren and Mary, who have a problem to solve, and two opposing points of view. Silas, a hired hand, has returned to Warren and Mary's farm after having abandoned them to work for someone else at harvest time. Silas is dying. Mary argues for making his last days comfortable and letting bygones be bygones. Warren knows Silas to have a rich brother in a town nearby and wants to send him there.

There is very little action in the story, although the speakers summon up many scenes while talking about the past. Two opposing images form, and the reader is left to choose a side. The use of specific and general language is another source of tension in the poem, as are contrasts of darkness and light, of softness and hardness, and of inside (where Silas sleeps and dies) and outside (where Warren and Mary talk). Each concept is associated with one or the other of the principal characters, but all resolve into a kind of grayness after Silas dies.

Blank verse is Robert Frost's favorite form in *North of Boston*. Blank verse is defined as unrhymed lines of iambic pentameter. (An iamb is a metrical foot of two syllables in which an unstressed syllable is followed by a stressed syllable—for example, the words "about" and "against"; pentameter means there are five feet in the line.) The line "And gave/ him tea/ and tried/ to make/ him smoke" from "The Death of the Hired Man" is regular blank verse. Obviously, not all the lines of a poem are equally regular. Frost was a master at substituting other metrical feet to give his lines variety. Blank verse has been used in English since the sixteenth century, but Frost was influential in establishing it as a twentieth century form.

The poet was also very fond of play in all of its forms, especially word play, which is important for understanding his poems. Metaphors and similes involving games appear often in his poems, as well as in his letters and lectures. "The Mountain" gives good examples of pun, double entendre, contradiction, and other forms of word play. The poem itself provides a clue in the often ignored line "But all the fun's in how you say a thing." From the moment Frost gives the name of the town—Lunenburg or crazy town— until describing a brook that is "cold in summer, warm in winter," the poem is a runaway ride through a verbal landscape that is the equal of Geoffrey Chaucer and William Shakespeare. Verbal tensions are one element that keeps Frost's poems fresh, for new forms of play and meaning can be found even after many readings.

"Home Burial" is a powerful and moving dialogue between a husband and wife who represent the universal conflict between men and women. Like the previous dialogues, this one too presents limited action, and the poem progresses almost entirely through conversation. The wife, Amy, feels that her unnamed husband is cold and unfeeling because his mourning for the death of their child has ended and his thoughts have returned to everyday things. The husband, who feels that Amy is protracting her anguish, says:

> What was it brought you up to think it the thing
> To take your mother-loss of a first child
> So inconsolably—in the face of love.

At a time in history when infant mortality is very low, this might seem harsh and unfeeling. Well into the early years of the twentieth century, however, infant death was a fact of life, and the husband's attitude may be understood to represent the norm, with Amy's grief indeed aberrant for the time. Unlike the situation between Warren and Mary, there seems to be no resolution to the conflict for this couple.

Although Frost's poems can be read as little dramas played out in rural New England, that would be to limit them severely. Nearly all of Frost's characters, settings, and situations can be recognized to be universally true. Names and places and times are merely ways to localize what is ubiquitous and timeless.

For years, critics interpreted the madness and decay in Frost's poems as his comment on the disintegration of the New England society he knew. He was making no such comment but was, rather, simply honest about the characters he portrayed. If there is madness, he seems to say, it is universal.

In the monologue "A Servant to Servants," the speaker is a woman taking time out from her endless domestic duties to talk to people camping on her land. Her talk begins with local matters but quickly turns to other concerns, specifically her own mental health and a history of insanity in her family. It is a dark, distinctly human story.

> My father's brother, he went mad quite young.
> Some thought he had been bitten by a dog,
>
> . . . .
>
> But it's more likely he was crossed in love,
>
> . . . .
>
> Anyway all he talked about was love.

In the hands of a lesser poet, much of the material might have turned sentimental. But Frost's speaker is poignant, not pitiable. She has a clear notion of who she is despite her failing sanity. She is noble and dignified, as Frost's characters tend to be in the hardscrabble world he witnessed and re-created.

"After Apple Picking" breaks the unrelenting sorrow built by "A Servant to Servants." It is a meditation on work. Unlike the other poems so far discussed, this one is not in blank verse, employing instead lines of varying length that rhyme irregularly. The persona of this poem is exhausted after days, perhaps weeks, of work. Read on this level, the work offers images and insights that are completely satisfying. However, the speaker gives a clue early on that the poem also seeks to universalize the experience. The first two lines read "My long two-pointed ladder's sticking through a tree/ toward heaven still." That the speaker says "heaven," not sky, is significant. This is a clue that the speaker does not carry the memory—"the pressure of a ladder round"—in his feet from just this harvest but that he is growing old and tired from a long life of harvests. The poem mentions "sleep" or "dreaming" six times (sleep can be read, as it often is in literature, as death). The speaker is worn out by a lifetime of work and looks forward to his well-deserved rest. This is one of Frost's several masterpieces.

"The Code," too, is about work, but this poem examines the unwritten code of conduct between farmers and their hired hands. In a story within the story, a farmer is nearly killed for driving his men too hard. We learn that "The hand that knows his business won't be told/ to do work better or faster—those two things."

The penultimate poem in *North of Boston* is "The Wood Pile." This is a complex poem that appears on the surface, as do many of Frost's poems, to be terribly simple. It is, however, full of tensions between man and nature, growth and decay, clarity and confusion. The wood pile deep in the woods seems to have been "Cut and split/ and piled" for no reason, but for Frost labor is its own reward. He finds it curious that someone would go to the trouble of cutting wood and piling it neatly only to abandon it, but he also knows the satisfaction of a job well done. The wood pile may appear not to benefit anyone but it benefited the woodsman who did the work. In Frost's world, that is enough.

Robert Frost's reputation continues to grow as critics leave aside the public man he became in his later years to concentrate on the work. In *North of Boston*, Frost presents his narrative voice. That, together with his lyrical voice, demonstrates his unusual balance of vision and ear. Both voices broadened and deepened in the course of the succeeding collections of poetry, to meld finally into one note of exquisite clarity.

H. A. Maxson

Bibliography:
Brower, Reuben A. *The Poetry of Robert Frost: Constellations of Intentions*. New York: Oxford University Press, 1963. Compares Frost's poems with Ralph Waldo Emerson's and William Wordsworth's. Examines prosody and themes.

Lynen, John F. *The Pastoral Art of Robert Frost*. New Haven, Conn.: Yale University Press, 1960. Important examination of Frost as an artist. Discusses adaptations of the pastoral for use in modern poetry.

Poirier, Richard. *Robert Frost: The Work of Knowing*. New York: Oxford University Press, 1977. Reevaluates many of Frost's standards and finds them lacking. Ardent reexamination and reemphasis of Frost's status as a major poet.

Pritchard, William H. *Frost: A Literary Life Reconsidered*. New York: Oxford University Press, 1984. Examines the life through the poems. Balanced, fair appraisal. Shows how inseparable the man and his work were.

Tharpe, Jac, ed. *Frost: Centennial Essays*. 3 vols. Jackson: University Press of Mississippi, 1974-1978. Seventy-six essays on various topics, from analysis and explication to biography.

NORTHANGER ABBEY

Type of work: Novel
Author: Jane Austen (1775-1817)
Type of plot: Domestic realism
Time of plot: Early nineteenth century
Locale: England
First published: 1818

Principal characters:

>CATHERINE MORLAND, an imaginative reader of gothic romances
>MRS. ALLEN, her benefactress
>ISABELLA THORPE, her friend
>JOHN THORPE, Isabella's brother
>JAMES MORLAND, Catherine's brother
>HENRY TILNEY, a young man whom Catherine admires
>GENERAL TILNEY, his father
>CAPTAIN TILNEY, his brother
>ELEANOR TILNEY, his sister

The Story:

Although a plain girl, Catherine Morland thought herself destined to become a heroine like those in her favorite gothic novels. She might, however, have spent her entire life in Fullerton, the small village in which she was born, had not Mrs. Allen, the wife of a wealthy neighbor, invited her to go to Bath. There a whole new world was opened to Catherine, who was delighted with the social life of the colony. At Bath, she met Isabella Thorpe, who was more worldly than Catherine and took it upon herself to instruct Catherine in the ways of society. Isabella also introduced Catherine to her brother, John Thorpe. He and Catherine's brother, James Morland, were friends, and the four young people spent many enjoyable hours together.

Catherine met Henry Tilney, a young clergyman, and his sister Eleanor, with whom she was anxious to become better acquainted. John thwarted her in this desire, and Isabella and James aided him in deceptions aimed at keeping her away from Henry and Eleanor. After Isabella and James became engaged, Isabella doubled her efforts to interest Catherine in her beloved brother. Although Catherine loved her friend dearly, she could not extend this love to John, whom she knew in her heart to be an indolent, undesirable young man.

While James was at home arranging for an allowance so that he and Isabella could be married, Henry Tilney's brother, Captain Tilney, appeared on the scene. He was as worldly as Isabella and, even more important to her, extremely wealthy. Catherine was a little disturbed by the manner in which Isabella conducted herself with Captain Tilney, but she was too loyal to her friend to suspect her of being unfaithful to James.

Shortly after Captain Tilney arrived in Bath, Catherine was invited by Eleanor Tilney and her father, General Tilney, to visit them at Northanger Abbey, their old country home. Catherine was delighted; she had always wanted to visit a real abbey, and she quickly wrote for and received a letter of permission from her parents. Henry aroused her imagination with stories of dark passageways and mysterious chests and closets.

When the party arrived at Northanger Abbey, Catherine was surprised and a little frightened to find that his descriptions had been so exact. When she heard that Mrs. Tilney had died suddenly several years previously, Catherine began to suspect that the general had murdered her. At the first opportunity, she attempted to enter the dead woman's chambers. There Henry found her and assured her that his mother had died a natural death. Catherine was almost disappointed, for this news destroyed many of her romantic imaginings about Northanger Abbey.

For more than a week after this event, Catherine worried because she had received no letter from Isabella. When a letter arrived from her brother James, she learned the reason for Isabella's silence. He wrote that Isabella had become engaged to Captain Tilney. Catherine was almost ill when she read the news, and Henry and Eleanor Tilney were as disturbed as she. They knew that only greed and ambition drew Isabella from James to their wealthier brother, and they feared for his happiness. They thought, however, that the captain was more experienced with such women and would fare better than James had done.

Shortly afterward, Catherine received a letter from Isabella telling the story in an entirely different light. She pretended that she and James had just had a misunderstanding and begged Catherine to write to James in her behalf. Catherine was not taken in. She wasted no time in sympathy for her onetime friend and thought her brother fortunate to be rid of such a schemer.

A short time later, the general had to go to London on business, and Eleanor and Catherine were alone at the abbey. Henry's clerical duties compelled him to spend some time in his nearby parish. One night, soon after the general's departure, Eleanor went to Catherine's room. In a state of great embarrassment and agitation, she told Catherine that the general had returned suddenly from London and had ordered Catherine to leave the abbey early the next morning. Because she loved Catherine and did not want to hurt her, Eleanor would give no reason for the order. In great distress, Catherine departed and returned to her home for the first time in many weeks. She and her family tried to forget the insult to her, but they could not help thinking of it constantly. Most of Catherine's thoughts were of Henry, whom she feared she might never see again.

Soon after her return home, Henry called on her and explained why his father had turned against Catherine. When the Tilney family first met Catherine, John Thorpe had told the general that she was the daughter of a wealthy family and that the Allen money would also be settled on her. He had bragged because at the time he himself had hoped to marry Catherine; when Catherine rebuffed him, and after his sister Isabella was unable to win James again, John spitefully told the general that Catherine had deceived him. Although she had never in any way implied that she was wealthy, the general gave her no chance to defend herself.

After Henry had told his story, he asked Catherine to marry him. Her parents gave their consent with the understanding that the young couple must first win over the general. Henry returned home to wait. Eleanor's marriage to a wealthy peer proved an unexpected aid to the lovers. The general was so pleased at having his daughter become a viscountess that he was persuaded to forgive Catherine. When he also learned that the Morland family, though not wealthy, could give Catherine three thousand pounds, he gladly gave his consent to the marriage. In less than a year after they met and despite many hardships and trials, Catherine Morland married Henry Tilney with every prospect of happiness and comfort for the rest of her life.

Critical Evaluation:

In all the history of the novel, perhaps no genre can claim more popularity than that of the gothic novel of the late eighteenth century. Unfortunately, the gothic fad was all but over when *Northanger Abbey*, Jane Austen's parody of the gothic novel, was published in 1818, a year after her death. Her delightful mockery had actually been written when such works were at their height of popularity, about 1797-1798. The novel had been sold to a publisher in 1803 but was published posthumously. In her early twenties at the time of the composition, the young author lived in the quiet rectory where she was born in the Hampshire village of Steventon; her circumstances resembled those of the young heroine of her novel—even to including such amusements as poring over gothic novels. The reader who has never perused Ann Radcliffe's *The Mysteries of Udolpho* (1794), which occupies so much of Catherine Morland's time and thoughts, will find other reasons to enjoy *Northanger Abbey*, but a knowledge of *The Mysteries of Udolpho* or any other gothic novel will bring special rewards.

At one level, *Northanger Abbey* is an amusing parody of gothic novels, with their mysterious castles and abbeys, gloomy villains, incredibly accomplished heroines, sublime landscapes, and supernatural claptrap. Austen's satire is not, however, pointed only at such novels; the romantic sensibility of the gothic enthusiast is also a target. *Northanger Abbey* is a comic study of the ironic discrepancies between the prosaic world in which Catherine lives and the fantastic shapes that her imagination, fed by gothic novels, gives to that world. Throughout the novel, the author holds up the contrast between the heroine's real situation and the gothic world she fantasizes.

The prevailing irony begins with the first sentence: "No one who had ever seen Catherine Morland in her infancy would have supposed her born to be a heroine." As she grows up, she develops neither the prodigious artistic and intellectual accomplishments nor the requisite beauty necessary for the role. She herself is merely pretty, but once her adventures get underway, she begins to assign stereotyped gothic roles to her new acquaintances. Detecting villainy in General Tilney's haughty demeanor merely because in *The Mysteries of Udolpho* the evil Montoni is haughty, she overlooks the general's real defects of snobbery and materialism, traits that eventually prove far more threatening to her than his hauteur.

Since the central feature of the gothic novel is the sinister, dilapidated castle or abbey, Catherine's most cherished daydreams center on Northanger Abbey and its long, damp passages. In reality, nothing is damp except an ordinary drizzling rain, nor is anything narrow or ruined, the abbey having been thoroughly renovated for modern living. Try as she will, she cannot manufacture genuine gothic horrors. Instead of dark revelations of murder and madness in the Tilney family, she faces self-revelation, her recognition that she has suffered from a delusion in her desire to be frightened.

If the ridicule of gothicism and the exposure of false sensibility compose major themes, another more inclusive theme, common to all Austen's novels, is the problem of limitation. Catherine at age seventeen is "launched into all the difficulties and dangers of six weeks residence at Bath," the fashionable resort, leaving a sheltered life in her village of Fullerton. She immediately discerns, however, a state of artificial confinement as a way of life in Bath:

> Catherine began to feel something of disappointment—she was tired of being continually pressed against by people, the generality of whose faces possessed nothing to interest, and with all of whom she was so wholly unacquainted, that she could not relieve the irksomeness of imprisonment by the exchange of a syllable with any of her fellow captives . . . she felt yet more awkwardness of having no party to join, no acquaintance to claim, no gentleman to assist them.

Throughout the novel, Austen continues to develop this initial image of an empty, fashionable routine in which each day brought its regular duties. Catherine romanticizes this reality, her delusions culminating with the delightful invitation to visit the Tilneys at Northanger Abbey. Thus the gothic parody functions also as a study of a common response—escapism—to a society circumscribed by empty rituals and relationships. This theme is resolved when Catherine's visions of romance are shattered by the mundane discoveries at Northanger Abbey, which compel her to abandon her romantic notions and choose the alternative of acting in the future with common sense.

Nevertheless, in her dismissal of fantasy, she has not yet come to terms with the limitations in reality, the pressures of society that can impose imprisonment. Such experience is melodramatically represented by her expulsion from the abbey. The order is delivered without explanation, the time and manner of departure are determined by General Tilney, and Catherine is denied either friendship or common courtesy. With no alternatives, Catherine is in a situation that resists good sense, and she is reduced to a passive awareness of the reality and substance of life. When she is shut off in her room at the abbey, her mind is so occupied in the contemplation of actual and natural evil that she is numb to the loneliness of her situation. Confined in a hired carriage for the long, unfamiliar journey to Fullerton, she is conscious only of the pressing anxieties of thought. At home, her thought processes are lost in the reflection of her own change of feelings and spirit. She is the opposite of what she had been, an innocent young woman.

Catherine survives the transition from innocence to experience, proving to her mother, at least, that she can shift very well for herself. Catherine's maturity, however, is tested no further. The restoration of her happiness depends less on herself and Henry than it does on General Tilney, and she is finally received by the general on the basis not of personal merit but of money. Only when the Morlands prove to be a family of good financial standing is Catherine free to marry the man of her choice.

Concerning the rapid turn of events in her denouement, Austen wryly observed: "To begin perfect happiness at the respective ages of twenty-six and eighteen, is to do pretty well." Despite the happy ending that concludes the novel, the author leaves Catherine on the threshold only of the reality of life that her experiences have revealed. The area of her testing has already been defined, for example, in the discrepancy between her image of Henry's parsonage and General Tilney's. To Catherine, it is "something like Fullerton, but better: Fullerton had its faults, but Woodston probably had none."

Thus *Northanger Abbey* is a novel of initiation; its heroine ironically discovers in the world not a new freedom, but a new set of restrictions. Once undeceived of her romantic illusions of escape, she is returned with a vengeance to the world as it is, small but decent. As an early novel, *Northanger Abbey* points the way to Austen's mature novels, in which the focus will be on heroines who are constrained to deal with life within defined limitations.

"Critical Evaluation" by Catherine E. Moore

Bibliography:
Dwyer, June. *Jane Austen.* New York: Continuum, 1989. A good basic reference for the general reader. Dwyer suggests that *Northanger Abbey* is the novel that gives the best introduction to Austen's worldview and writing style. Includes a selected bibliography.
Fergus, Jan. *Jane Austen and the Didactic Novel.* London: Macmillan, 1983. Fergus differs from many critics in considering Austen's early novels to be primarily intended to instruct the readers. The chapter on *Northanger Abbey* considers the novel from this perspective.
Jones, Vivien. *How to Study a Jane Austen Novel.* London: Macmillan, 1987. Designed to help students develop their own critical skills, this text offers practical advice about how to read, understand, and analyze literature. Jones uses selected passages from *Northanger Abbey* in her discussion of the power of the authorial voice.

Lauber, John. *Jane Austen*. New York: Twayne, 1993. Discusses *Northanger Abbey* quite extensively. Especially interesting is Lauber's discussion of the connections between *Northanger Abbey* and Austen's juvenilia (works she composed between the ages of twelve and eighteen). Includes a chronology, bibliography, and index.

Monaghan, David. *Jane Austen: Structure and Social Vision*. London: Macmillan, 1980. Monaghan examines the use of and attitude toward formal social ritual in Austen's novels to reveal how Austen viewed her society. He devotes one chapter to *Northanger Abbey*.

NOSTROMO
A Tale of the Seaboard

Type of work: Novel
Author: Joseph Conrad (Jósef Teodor Konrad Nałęcz Korzeniowski, 1857-1924)
Type of plot: Psychological realism
Time of plot: Early twentieth century
Locale: Costaguana, on the north coast of South America
First published: 1904

Principal characters:
> CHARLES GOULD, the manager of the San Tomé silver mine
> EMILIA GOULD, his wife
> GIAN' "NOSTROMO" BATTISTA, the Italian leader of the stevedores
> LINDA VIOLA, the woman to whom he proposed
> GISELLE VIOLA, her sister
> GIORGIO VIOLA, the father of Linda and Giselle
> MARTIN DECOUD, a newspaper editor
> DR. MONYGHAM, the town physician and a friend of the Goulds

The Story:

The Republic of Costaguana was in a state of revolt. Under the leadership of Pedrito Montero, rebel troops had taken control of the eastern part of the country. When news of the revolt reached Sulaco, the principal town of the western section that was separated from the rest of the country by a mountain range, the leaders began to lay defense plans. The chief interest of the town was the San Tomé silver mine in the nearby mountains, a mine managed by Charles Gould, an Englishman who, although educated in England, had been born in Sulaco, his father having been manager before him. Gould had made a great success of the mine. The semiannual shipment of silver had just come down from the mine to the customhouse when the telegraph operator from Esmeralda, on the eastern side of the mountains, sent word that troops had embarked on a transport under command of General Sotillo and that the rebels planned to capture the silver ingots as well as Sulaco.

Gould decided to load the ingots on a lighter and set it afloat in the gulf pending the arrival of a ship that would take the cargo to the United States. The man to guide the boat would be Gian' Battista, known in Sulaco as Nostromo—our man—for he was considered incorruptible. His companion would be Martin Decoud, editor of the local newspaper, who had been drawn from Paris and kept in Sulaco by the European-educated Antonia Avellanos, to whom he had just become engaged. Decoud had incurred the anger of Montero by denouncing the revolutionists in his paper. Decoud also had conceived a plan for making the country around Sulaco an independent state, the Occidental Republic.

When Nostromo and Decoud set out in the black of the night, Sotillo's ship, approaching the port without lights, bumped into their lighter. Nostromo made for a nearby uninhabited island, the Great Isabel, where he cached the treasure. Then, he left Decoud behind and rowed the lighter to the middle of the harbor, pulled a plug, and sank her. He swam the remaining mile to the mainland.

Upon discovering that the silver had been spirited away, Sotillo took possession of the customhouse, where he conducted an inquiry. The next day, Sulaco was seized by Montero, who considered Sotillo of little worth.

When the Europeans and highborn natives who had not fled the town discovered that Nostromo was back, they took it for granted that the silver had been lost in the harbor. They asked Nostromo to take a message to Barrios, who commanded the Loyalist troops on the eastern side of the mountains. In a spectacular engine ride up the side of the mountain and a subsequent six-day horseback journey through the mountain passes, Nostromo succeeded in delivering his message, and Barrios set out with his troops by boat to relieve the town of Sulaco.

Coming into the harbor, Nostromo sighted a boat that he recognized as the small craft attached to the lighter that had carried him and Decoud to Great Isabel. He dived overboard and swam to the boat. Barrios went on to Sulaco and drove the traitors out. Meanwhile, Gould had planted dynamite around the silver mine to destroy it in case of defeat, for he was determined to keep the mine from the revolutionists at any cost.

Nostromo rowed the little boat over to Great Isabel, where he discovered that Decoud was gone and that he had taken four of the ingots with him. He correctly guessed that Decoud had killed himself, for there was a bloodstain on the edge of the boat. Decoud had been left to himself when Nostromo returned to the mainland, and each day he had grown more and more lonely until finally he dug up four of the ingots, tied them to himself, went out into the boat, shot himself, and fell overboard, the weight of the ingots carrying him to the bottom of the harbor. Now Nostromo could not tell Gould where the silver was, for he would himself have been suspected of stealing the four missing ingots. Since everyone thought the treasure was in the bottom of the sea, he decided to let the rumor stand and sell the ingots one by one and so become rich slowly.

In gratitude for his many services to the country, the people provided Nostromo with a boat in which he hauled cargo as far north as California. Sometimes he would be gone for months while he carried out his schemes for disposing of the hidden silver. One day on his return, he saw that a lighthouse was being built on Great Isabel. He was panic-stricken. Then he suggested that the keeper should be old Giorgio Viola, in whose daughter Linda he was interested. He thought that with the Violas on the island no one would suspect his frequent visits. Linda had a younger sister, Giselle, for whom the vagabond Ramirez was desperate. Viola would not allow her to receive his attentions and kept her under close guard. He would not permit Ramirez to come to the island.

To make his comings and goings more secure, one day Nostromo asked Linda to be his wife. Almost at once after that, he realized that he was really in love with Giselle. In secret meetings, he and Giselle confessed their mutual passion. Linda grew suspicious. Giselle begged Nostromo to carry her away, but he said he could not do so for a while. He finally told her about the silver and how he had to convert it into money before he could take her away.

Obsessed by hate of Ramirez, Viola began patrolling the island at night with his gun loaded. One night as Nostromo was approaching Giselle's window, old Viola saw him and shot him. Hearing her father say that he had shot Ramirez, Linda rushed out; but Giselle ran past her and reached Nostromo first. It was she who accompanied him to the mainland. In the hospital, Nostromo asked for the kindly Mrs. Gould, to whom he protested that Giselle was innocent and that he alone knew about the hidden treasure. Mrs. Gould, however, would not let him tell her where he had hidden it. It had caused so much sorrow that she did not want it to be brought to light again. Nostromo refused any aid from Dr. Monygham and died without revealing the location of the ingots.

Dr. Monygham went in the police galley out to Great Isabel, where he informed Linda of Nostromo's death. She was thoroughly moved by the news and whispered that she—and she alone—had loved the man and that she would never forget Nostromo. As Linda in despair cried out Nostromo's name, Dr. Monygham observed that triumphant as Nostromo had been in life, this love of Linda's was the greatest victory of all.

The region about Sulaco finally did become the Occidental Republic. The San Tomé mine prospered under Gould's management, the population increased enormously, and the new country flourished with great vigor. Although Decoud, the country's first planner, and Nostromo, the hero of its inception, were dead, life in the new country went on richly and fully.

Critical Evaluation:

Joseph Conrad has always been known among the mass of readers as a great teller of sea stories. He is also a pertinent, even prophetic, commentator on what he called "land entanglements"—particularly on the subject of political revolution. Conrad's father was an active revolutionary in the cause of Polish independence; he died as the result of prolonged imprisonment for revolutionary "crimes." Three of Conrad's best novels are studies in political behavior: *Nostromo, The Secret Agent* (1907), and *Under Western Eyes* (1911). *Nostromo* is by far the most ambitious and complex of these works. It has a very large international cast of characters of all shapes and sizes, and it employs the typical Conradian device of an intentionally jumbled (and sometimes confusing) chronology. As typical of Conrad, the physical setting is handled superbly; the reader is drawn into the book through the wonderfully tactile descriptions of the land and sea. The setting in South America is also particularly appropriate to Conrad's skeptical consideration of progress achieved either by Capitalism or revolution.

Nostromo is a study in the politics of wealth in an underdeveloped country. The central force in the novel is the silver of the San Tomé mine—a potential of wealth so immense that a humane and cultured civilization can be built upon it. At least this is the view of the idealist Charles Gould, the owner and developer of the mine. There are other views. From the start, Gould is ready to maintain his power by force if necessary. He remembers how the mine destroyed his father. The mine attracts politicians and armed revolutionaries from the interior, but Gould is willing to blow up his treasure and half of Sulaco, the central city, in order to defeat the revolution. He succeeds, but Conrad intends for the reader to regard his success as partial at best. His obsession with the mine separates him from his wife. As with Conrad's other heroes, the demands of public action distort and cancel out his capacity for private affection.

One of the magnificences of the first half of *Nostromo* is that Gould and his silver are seen from so many angles. Readers are given a truly panoramic spectrum of attitude. For old Giorgio Viola, who was once a member of Garibaldi's red shirts, Gould's idealization of material interests is dangerous and wrong because it has the potential of violating a pure and disinterested love of liberty for all humanity. Viola, however, is as ineffectual as the austere and cultured leader of Sulaco's aristocracy, Don José Avellanos, whose unpublished manuscript "Thirty Years of Misrule" is used as gun wadding at the height of the revolution. Ranged against Avellanos and Viola, at the other end of the spectrum, are those sanguinary petty tyrants, Bento, Montero, and Sotillo, who want to run the country entirely for their own personal advantage. Sotillo represents their rapacity and blind lust for Gould's treasure. The most interesting characters, however, are those who occupy a middling position in the spectrum. Of these, two are central to any understanding of the novel. Between them they represent Conrad's own point of view most fully.

The dilettante Parisian boulevardier, Martin Decoud, may be the object of some of Conrad's most scourging irony, but his skeptical pronouncements, as in his letter to his sister, accord well with the facts of Sulaco's politics as Conrad presents them in the early stages of the novel.

Decoud saves the mine by arranging for a new rifle to be used in defense of Gould's material interests, but he does not share Gould's enthusiasm that the mine can act as the chief force in the process of civilizing the new republic. He views the whole business of revolution and counterrevolution as an elaborate charade, a comic opera.

The most trenchant charge against Gould is made by the other deeply skeptical character, Dr. Monygham. His judgment upon material interests is one of the most famous passages in the book:

> There is no peace and rest in the development of material interests. They have their law and their justice. But it is founded on expediency, and is inhuman; it is without the continuity and the force that can be found only in a moral principle. . . . The time approaches when all that the Gould Concession stands for shall weigh as heavily upon the people as the barbarism, cruelty, and misrule of a few years back.

It is clear that Conrad intends for his readers to take Monygham's judgment at face value. The trouble is that the facts of Costaguana's postrevolutionary state do not agree with it. The land is temporarily at peace and is being developed in an orderly fashion by the mine as well as other material interests, and the workers seem better off as a result. Monygham is hinting at the workers' revolt against the suppression of material interests, but this revolt seems so far in the future that his judgment is robbed of much of its power. This surely accounts for part of the hollowness that some critics have found in the novel.

The last section of the novel is concerned with Gould's successful resistance to the attempts of both church and military to take over the mine and the moral degradation of the "incorrupt-ible" man of the people, Nostromo. In this latter case, Conrad abandons the richness and density of his panoramic view of South American society and gives us a semiallegorical dramatization of the taint of the silver within the soul of a single character.

Nostromo's fate is clearly related to the legend of the two gringos that begins the book, for the silver that he has hidden has this same power to curse his soul as the "fatal spell" cast by the treasure on the gringos. ("Their souls cannot tear themselves away from their bodies mount-ing guard over the discovered treasure. They are now rich and hungry and thirsty.") The result of Conrad's absorption with Nostromo at the end of the novel is twofold. First, readers are denied a dramatization of the changing social conditions that would support Monygham's judgment. Second, and more important, the novel loses its superb richness and variety and comes dangerously close to insisting on the thesis that wealth is a universal corruptor, even that "money is the root of all evil."

For roughly two-thirds of its length, *Nostromo* gives readers one of the finest social panoramas in all fiction. The ending, however, suggests that underneath the complex texture of the whole novel lies a rather simplistic idea: that both "material interests" and revolution are doomed to failure. Although set in South America, *Nostromo* suggests a world in which sys-tems and conditions change very little because people do not.

"Critical Evaluation" by Benjamin Nyce

Bibliography:

Bloom, Harold, ed. *Joseph Conrad's "Nostromo."* New York: Chelsea House, 1987. Seven essays discuss irony, Conrad's philosophy of history, and different views of the hero.

Carabine, Keith, Owen Knowles, and Wiesław Krajka, eds. *Contexts for Conrad.* Boulder, Colo.: East European Monographs, 1993. Helpful for understanding *Nostromo* as part of nineteenth century colonialism, capitalism, and frontier exploration. The piece focusing on the novel shows the relationship of *Nostromo* to nineteenth century criticism of capitalism.

Hamner, Robert D., ed. *Joseph Conrad: Third World Perspectives*. Washington, D.C.: Three Continents Press, 1990. Gives the perspective of the colonized on colonialism. Calls *Nostromo* an early conceptualization of a postcolonial world.

Jean-Aubry, Georges. *Joseph Conrad: Life and Letters*. 2 vols. London: Heinemann, 1927. Includes Conrad's notes on the sources for characters and episodes in *Nostromo*.

Watt, Ian. *Joseph Conrad: "Nostromo."* Cambridge, England: Cambridge University Press, 1988. Contains a chronology of Conrad's life and a chronology of events in *Nostromo*. Includes discussion of Conrad's sources, elucidation of the novel's narrative technique, notes on the characters as well as the history and politics in the novel, and a guide to further reading.

NOTES OF A NATIVE SON

Type of work: Essays
Author: James Baldwin (1924-1987)
First published: 1955

James Baldwin's *Notes of a Native Son* is his first collection of essays. Baldwin, generally acclaimed as twentieth century America's greatest essayist, helped cement this reputation with this collection. The book discusses many of Baldwin's central occupations throughout his career: racism, the search for identity, and how African Americans respond to racism. The book is an essential landmark in the thought of James Baldwin.

In examining *Notes of a Native Son*, the reader first should note the structure of the collection, because the essays are organized thematically. Part 1 deals primarily with Baldwin's commentaries on literature, with one essay additionally critiquing the film *Carmen Jones* (1954). Part 2 deals mainly with racial problems in the United States. In part 3 Baldwin examines questions of identity, specifically, African Americans' perceptions of themselves and how they are perceived by others. Baldwin pondered these themes while he traveled in France and Switzerland.

Two of Baldwin's classic essays are contained in part 1: "Everybody's Protest Novel" and "Many Thousands Gone." "Everybody's Protest Novel" has become famous for Baldwin's criticisms of Harriet Beecher Stowe's *Uncle Tom's Cabin* (1852) and Richard Wright's *Native Son* (1940). Baldwin finds Stowe's novel to be ruined by sentimentality, which he feels is a mask for the author's fear of African Americans, especially assertive African Americans. Baldwin questions whether this novel should be thought to champion African Americans' freedom. Furthermore, Baldwin questions the validity of the praise of Wright's *Native Son* as promoting the African American cause. Baldwin's main reservation with Wright's novel is that Baldwin feels the novel hinges on the acceptance by the main character, Bigger, of racists' view of him as subhuman. Baldwin expresses his concern that this ideology itself is, perhaps, Bigger's worst enemy, thus undermining the novel's focus on white racism. Consequently, Baldwin finds fault with two of the novels that had been made into such literary icons that they could have been deemed everybody's protest novels.

Baldwin's critique of the character of Bigger Thomas continues in "Many Thousands Gone," with Baldwin again noting Wright's emphasis on Bigger's self-hatred. Yet, in this essay, it is important to note that Baldwin recognizes the sociological significance of Bigger. Baldwin, for instance, claims that most blacks have an anger inside them against racism that is equivalent to Bigger's rage. Moreover, Baldwin indicts racism for producing such African Americans as Bigger, whose acquiescence to racism entails their own psychological and physical self-annihilation. This essay, therefore, is important in Baldwin's analysis of how racism, in its narcissistic arrogance, demands that African Americans submit their very identity and obey the demands of the dominant society.

Another intriguing aspect of part 1 of *Notes of a Native Son* is that, on the whole, it is a critique of American cultural productions that focus on representations of African Americans. In "*Carmen Jones*: The Dark is Light Enough," for example, Baldwin finds great faults in Otto Preminger's successful film. The film is an all-black production of *Carmen*, starring Dorothy Dandridge and Harry Belafonte. Baldwin is concerned that the film avoids anything that would convey reality in its presentation of life among African Americans, relying instead on such things as songs reworked to fit whites' ideas of black speech and presenting a hero and heroine devoid of real sensuality but who have a dull façade of sanitized sexiness more appropriate to dolls than to people. Baldwin sensed that Hollywood was afraid of presenting African Americans' sensuality because it is so often a subject of racist mythology. Hence, he argues that by divesting the storyline of *Carmen* of sensuality, the film reduces the characters to mere hollow shells. Consequently, as in the two previous essays, Baldwin finds that American cultural productions with African Americans as their subject are not only problematic but also indicative of societal problems in the presentation and treatment of blacks.

In part 2, two essays in particular stand out as major essays in Baldwin's career. "The Harlem Ghetto" and "Notes of a Native Son" examine various aspects of the racial problem and race relations. In "The Harlem Ghetto," Baldwin analyzes a social problem that is still relevant today: tensions between African Americans and Jews. Importantly, Baldwin examines the economic factors at the heart of the maintenance of a racially divided society, and how these economic factors affect relations between the races. The black-Jewish rift, Baldwin felt, had its roots, in part, with the Jewish presence in Harlem as store owners, a position perceived by many blacks as exploitative. Yet, Baldwin points out that the hostility some blacks may feel toward Jews is not a result of the fact that the Jews are Jewish but that the Jews represented, for many blacks in ghettoes, a first contact with white Americans. Jews came to symbolize—rightly or wrongly—the racism of white society. Hence, Baldwin makes a perceptive point: that Jews are caught in the American racial crossfire. The essay does not present solutions to the dilemmas about which Baldwin writes, but it does contain perceptive and important analysis.

Baldwin's essay, "Notes of a Native Son" continues the analysis of race relations. The essay is central in showing Baldwin's own reactions to racism and his ideas on how African Americans should not react to racism. In the essay, Baldwin reminisces about his father, who hated whites and died an embittered man. Baldwin also recounts the racism he met with while working as a young man in New Jersey and how the rude treatment he met with, in particular at a racist restaurant, threatened not only to make him as bitter as his father but even to make him want to kill a white person. Yet, Baldwin came to feel that this urge to violence would mean his own moral death, at the very least, and possibly his physical death, at worst. Baldwin writes of one of his central beliefs, which was to recur throughout his career: that African Americans should never meet hatred with hatred and thus become like their enemy. This moral lesson is what Baldwin emphasizes as he writes of his father's death and of his own experiences with racism.

The final part of the book, part 3 explores another of what was to become a major topic in Baldwin's works: questions of identity as they arise in the lives of African Americans. "Encounter on the Seine: Black Meets Brown," for instance, tells of the relationships between Africans and African Americans. Baldwin states that African Americans are the product of different cultural experiences from Africans and thus cannot be expected to bond instantly with Africans, as some African Americans expect. The African American, Baldwin points out, is a "hybrid": a person of African heritage who is the product of the American experience.

"Stranger in the Village" is another essay that was inspired by Baldwin's travels abroad. A foreign setting yielded Baldwin many important insights into race relations. In "Stranger in the Village," Baldwin recounts the seeming innocence of the people of a Swiss village who looked at him in wonder, as they had never seen a black man before. This innocence prompts Baldwin to ponder the relations between white Americans and African Americans. Baldwin states his belief that white Americans have no such innocence as the Swiss villagers did. White Americans want to claim that they do, however; it would morally be much cozier if African Americans were also visitors to America as Baldwin was to the Swiss village. Thus, Baldwin concludes that whites and blacks in America need to face how deeply entangled they have been in each others' histories. The challenge of how to live with the truth of this fact is the note upon which Baldwin concludes *Notes of a Native Son*.

After examining the thematic structure of the essays in *Notes of a Native Son*, the reader is in a good position to understand further the importance of the book. In fact, the book is significant for several reasons. Baldwin's insights into American literature and film, the racial situation in America, and the perceptions of African American identity are original and incisive. Baldwin's essays give him a unique place in American literature; he is generally hailed as one of America's greatest essayists. *Notes of a Native Son*, therefore, marked the beginning of his career as a premier essayist.

Two of the essays in part 1, "Everybody's Protest Novel" and "Many Thousands Gone" are important in American literary history because they are Baldwin's declaration of independence from Richard Wright. During the 1940's and 1950's, both Wright and Baldwin were living in Paris and came to know each other. Wright was then considered by many, particularly literary critics, to be the elder statesman of African American literature, and his books were sometimes held as an example to other African American writers of the sort of literature they were expected to write: bleak social protest, as in *Native Son*.

Baldwin, then a member of a younger generation of African American writers, did not want to be measured against Wright's themes and literary preoccupations. In fact, Baldwin later admitted that part of the reason for his literary attack on Wright in his essays was to separate himself from any expectations that he would emulate Wright's writings. In fact, he even recalled declaring early in their acquaintance, "The sons must slay their fathers!" Nevertheless, "Everybody's Protest Novel" and "Many Thousands Gone" raise central questions about the protest novel, including whether the genre is obsessed with portraying victims of racism to the point of failing to convey the humanity of the oppressed as anything but defeated victims. There is also the question of whether the novels under discussion, *Native Son* and *Uncle Tom's Cabin*, merely reproduce the prejudices of the society that they intend to criticize. "Everybody's Protest Novel" is an indication of Baldwin's own literary concerns and the problems he finds in two of America's foremost protest novels.

Baldwin's critique of *Uncle Tom's Cabin* is an essay that has gained more relevance as time has gone by. One reason for this relevance is that *Uncle Tom's Cabin* has been lauded by many feminist literary critics as a neglected classic, one of whose chief elements is the power of its sentimentality. In this light, Baldwin's withering attacks on Stowe's sentimentality, which he defines in part as an excessive and gaudy display of artificial emotions, are still important if one wants to debate the merit of Stowe's book. Baldwin's critiques of Stowe's and Wright's novels raise essential questions about these two literary classics that still engage the reader years after the publication of *Notes of a Native Son*.

Equally important to the criticisms of Wright and Stowe in "Everybody's Protest Novel" and "Many Thousands Gone" are the statements that convey inadvertently what were to become consuming interests of Baldwin as his career developed. For example, one of Baldwin's chief attacks on *Native Son* is Wright's portrayal of Bigger's acceptance of how racists label and categorize him. In light of this criticism, it is especially revealing that one of the main themes of Baldwin's novels *Giovanni's Room* (1956) and *Another Country* (1962) is the need for people to reject their internalized prejudices and self-hatred. Furthermore, Baldwin's condemnations of the urge to categorize others and the internalization of such categorization by some people who are targets of prejudice were to be abiding interests in his fiction and later essays. Thus, "Everybody's Protest Novel" and "Many Thousands Gone" are a key to understanding Baldwin's preoccupations as a writer.

Other abiding interests of Baldwin's are evident in the essays in part 2, "The Harlem Ghetto," "Journey to Atlanta," and "Notes of a Native Son." The primary topics in these essays are racism and African Americans' responses to racism. Baldwin's belief in the hypocrisy of some whites who think of themselves as liberals is clear in "Journey to Atlanta," which chronicles his brothers' trip to Atlanta under the auspices of the Progressive Party. Among those self-proclaimed progressive whites of whom Baldwin writes, he notes patronizing and narcissistic attitudes, which to him were the hallmark of hypocritical liberalism. He would return to the subject of hypocritical liberalism in many essays throughout his career, most notably in *The Fire Next Time* (1963). He also writes of this type of person in his drama about the Civil Rights era, *Blues for Mister Charlie* (1964). In addition, on the subject of black-white relations, in "The Harlem Ghetto," Baldwin became one of the first major African American writers to examine tensions between African Americans and Jews. His analysis of the reasons for these tensions— the economic disparity between blacks and Jews in such ghettoes as Harlem and blacks' perception of Jews' insensitivity to fellow members of the oppressed (specifically, African Americans)—are points that many subsequent writers have cited as being accurate descriptions of the black-Jewish rift. Baldwin's analysis is prophetic in that it raises many points made by contemporary analysts of black-Korean tensions in predominantly black areas. Hence, Baldwin's examination of the factors involved in racial tensions and in racism are timely and timeless.

Finally, one of the greatest reasons for the importance of *Notes of a Native Son* is that it announces many of Baldwin's concerns on African Americans' reactions to racism. Reading the essays in *Notes of a Native Son*, one learns of one of Baldwin's lasting beliefs: that the state of African Americans' souls is at stake in how they respond to racism. While this concern is especially clear in "Notes of a Native Son," it is also present in "Everybody's Protest Novel" and "The Harlem Ghetto." Baldwin's main point is his belief that blacks become hopelessly degraded if they respond to white racial hatred with their own racial hatred. He clearly states that such mutual hostility leaves no hope for progress. Baldwin provides no easy solution to reacting to racism, as he frequently admits his own anger. Yet, one of his main beliefs, expressed in *Notes of a Native Son*, is, as he once said, that "all men are brothers." This vision is the alternative and challenge to mutual racial hostility.

One can clearly see that *Notes of a Native Son* has become a classic for many reasons. The quality of the writing, for instance, shows why Baldwin is one of America's most acclaimed writers. The essays consist of complex social commentaries on important issues. For these reasons, *Notes of a Native Son* is a lasting classic of American literature.

Jane Davis

Bibliography:

Bigsby, C. W. E. "The Divided Mind of James Baldwin." In *James Baldwin: A Critical Evaluation*. Edited by Therman B. O'Daniel. Washington, D.C.: Howard University Press, 1977. A lucid discussion of the major themes of some of the essays in *Notes of a Native Son*, including the centrality of love and suffering, and Baldwin's resistance to the protest novel.

Collier, Eugenia W. "Thematic Patterns in Baldwin's Essays." In *James Baldwin: A Critical Evaluation*. Edited by Therman B. O'Daniel. Washington, D.C.: Howard University Press, 1977. A perceptive discussion of Baldwin's concerns with freedom in American life, with problems in relationships, and with the growth of identity.

Hughes, Langston. "From Harlem to Paris." In *James Baldwin: A Collection of Critical Views*. Edited by Kenneth Kinnamon. Englewood Cliffs, N.J.: Prentice-Hall, 1974. A short and pungent review of *Notes of a Native Son* by one of the most important African American writers. Interesting for Hughes's resistance to some of Baldwin's stinging commentary on racism.

Jarrett, Hobart. "*From a Region in My Mind: The Essays of James Baldwin*." In *James Baldwin: A Critical Evaluation*. Edited by Therman B. O'Daniel. Washington, D.C.: Howard University Press, 1977. An insightful thematic discussion of *Notes of a Native Son* in the context of Baldwin's later essays. Creative analysis of Baldwin's rhetoric in "Stranger in the Village."

Stanley, Fred L., and Pratt, Louis H., eds. *Conversations with James Baldwin*. Jackson, Miss.: University Press of Mississippi, 1989. Interviews spanning Baldwin's career that give essential insights into his literary concerns and his views of his works.

THE NOVICE

Type of work: Poetry
Author: Mikhail Lermontov (1814-1841)
Type of plot: Narrative
Time of plot: 1840
Locale: Caucasus mountains, Georgia, Russia
First published: 1840

Principal characters:
THE NOVICE, a novice monk
THE FATHER CONFESSOR
A GEORGIAN GIRL

The Story:

As a boy of six, the young novice was captured by Russians in his native mountains. They wanted to take him to their own country, but he fell ill with a fever and was left with the monks of the monastery. At first, the boy refused food and drink and seemed likely to die. One of the monks, who was to become his father-confessor, took him into his care and nursed him back to health. A Muslim by birth, he was baptized a Christian and became a novice confined within the narrow monastery walls. He found his prisonlike existence intolerable. The memory of his free life in a mountain village constantly haunted him. One night, he escaped. After three days, he was found, starved and exhausted, by his father-confessor. On his deathbed, he offered his confession to the old man. It was an account of what happened to him the night he escaped and during the days that followed before his recapture.

The night he fled, the novice explained, there was a storm so violent that the monks prostrated themselves in fear before the altar. The novice took advantage of the distraction to escape into the surrounding countryside. Trying to reach his village, he wandered in the forest. He felt at home with the wild landscape and the creatures that lived in it. His perception seemed to become heightened so that he clearly heard the many voices of nature. While drinking at a stream, he heard another song; it was that of a beautiful Georgian girl who was fetching water. Unseen, he watched her graceful and sensual movements and saw her go back to her home—an image that brought the uprooted novice much suffering. He longed to head toward her hut, but instead took the path that led into the woods, and, as night fell, he became lost in the dense forest.

For the first time in his life, he cried. Suddenly, he saw two lights shining in the darkness: the eyes of a panther. The novice seized a tree branch as a weapon, the panther pounced, and the novice struck him, inflicting a bloody wound to the animal's head. The panther pounced once more. As they struggled, the novice mystically took on the spirit of the panther, knowing its ways instinctively and echoing its snarls. It was as if the panther's forlorn cry was born deep within him. Eventually, the panther tired and died in the embrace of his opponent.

When the novice emerged from the forest, it was day. With growing despair, he heard the clanging of the monastery bell. He had come in a full circle. He recalled that, since childhood, the noise of the bell had destroyed his beautiful visions of his homeland and family. At that point, he realized that he would never see his birthplace again. He reflected that he was like a plant that had been forced to grow in the dark; it could not survive in the bright daylight, but was scorched by the sun and died. He knew that he too was about to die.

In his delirium, he dreamed that he was at the bottom of a deep stream, being caressed by the cooling waves which quenched his burning thirst. As he watched the fish swimming around him, a fish danced above his head, and, meeting his gaze, sang a song to him. The song invited the novice to come live with the fish in the freedom of the water. Sadness would be driven away, and the centuries would pass quickly and sweetly. The fish ended its song with an affirmation of its love for the novice. He felt himself lured by the bright beauty and calm of the dreamworld.

The novice was found unconscious by his father-confessor and brought back to the monastery. He told his father-confessor that he regretted that his body would lie in alien soil, and that his grave would awake a response in no one. He clasped the old man's hand in farewell, explaining that he did not seek release from worldly chains; on the contrary, he would willingly exchange heaven and eternity for one short hour among the rocks where he played as a child. He thus remained resolute, rebellious and defiant to the end. He asked to be buried in a sunny place in the garden, within view of his beloved Caucasus mountains.

Critical Evaluation:

In his native Russia, Mikhail Yurievich Lermontov is widely considered the greatest poet after Alexander Pushkin and Russia's only true Romantic poet; he also distinguished himself as a playwright and novelist. "The Novice" is one of the finest examples of Romantic poetry in Russian literature. It encompasses a theme which Lermontov had explored in lyric poems such as "The Sail" and "The Angel," and was to re-examine in "The Demon" and the novel *A Hero of Our Time*: the displaced soul, misunderstood and rebellious in nature, which seeks the storm as if calm could be found in storms.

"The Novice" is the impassioned story of an imprisoned soul and its bid for freedom in the form of a lyric monologue. Lermontov found the subject matter for this narrative poem while visiting a monastery in the former Georgian capital Mtskheti on his way to exile in the Caucasus. One of the monks told him how he came to live there. The story provided the substance of "The Novice," although Lermontov made a significant change in his source material. After the monk was recaptured, he lived on in the monastery in resignation, whereas Lermontov's novice dies defiant, asserting his preference for an hour among his childhood haunts over the heaven and eternity espoused by the monks.

The poem thus embodied a spirited bid for freedom at a time when the very word "freedom" was banned in Russia. Contemporaries saw the poem as a political allegory commenting on the repressive regime of Czar Nicholas I. However, it is far more than this. It is a vision of the romantic ideal of the unity of nature and the human spirit. It is this aspect of the poem that gives it a timeless significance beyond the transitory realities of politics.

The imagery of the poem reinforces the contrast between the two opposing worlds: the cold, dark, narrow confines of the monastery and the bright, vivid, and sensually stimulating natural landscape that surrounds it. The novice identifies himself with the natural world in a number of striking and even extravagant images: the novice embracing his brother the storm that helps him escape, the novice catching lightning in his hand, a snake—hiding from human eyes—with whom the novice feels a kinship, the strange whisperings that fill the air and seem to reveal to the novice the secrets of the sky and the earth.

The apotheosis of his unity with nature comes in the fight with the panther. He echoes the panther's snarls, and he suddenly knows the ways of panthers and wolves as if he had spent his whole life in their company. He forgets human language, and within him is born the terrifying and forlorn call of the wounded beast. As the panther dies in his embrace, the novice cannot utter any other sound than this. Such concepts, though they defy the intellect, embody the loftiest spirit of Romanticism. The novice has become part of nature, a companion of the animals, both prey and predator.

In this highly sensual poem, the sense of sound plays a large part. The opposing worlds of cloister and nature, the novice's imprisonment versus his free childhood, are set apart as much by their sounds as by their appearances. The novice recalls the sweet sound of his sisters' singing and the sound of the stream that flowed beside their house. This recollection is echoed after his escape from the monastery when he hears the melodious song of the Georgian girl at the stream. Her voice, he says, had a freedom and an artlessness as if it had been taught to speak only the names of friends. This remark emphasizes the emotionally nurturing quality of the novice's lost life. Finally, the dying novice derives comfort from another song, that of the compassionate fish of his dream who promises to drive the sadness from his eye and the darkness from his heart and offers him freedom and sweet sleep.

The novice's internalization of the wounded panther's cry and his sudden loss of human language is another example of his merging with nature. This wild sound, gained in victory over his opponent, stands in stark contrast with the mechanical sound that tells him of the futility of his bid for freedom—the dull, repetitive tolling of the monastery bell. This sound, like the panther's cry, resonates deeply within him, but it deprives him of power rather than bestowing it. He recalls that this very clanging always destroyed the beautiful visions that came to him of his lost home and family. He likens it to a hand of iron ceaselessly pounding at his heart.

A similar antithesis is drawn between light and dark. As the novice's cell was dark, so was his new world bright—even blindingly so. This world is described in an image of breathtaking beauty. So clear was the sky, says the novice, that an angel's flight could have been perceived. The dream of the fish also has a brightly colored vividness that mesmerizes the novice. This very brightness, however, is too powerful a force for his frail body, weakened by years of darkness, to bear. He compares himself with a plant that grows in the dark between two slabs of stone. It is so weak that when it is transplanted to a garden it cannot survive the scorching sunlight and dies with the dawn. The novice refuses to renounce the world of light, and intends to be reunited with it in death. He asks that he might be buried in a sunny spot in the garden, so that he might forever feast his eyes on the luminous, light-nourished day. The novice's final "confession" thus becomes both a profession of faith and a defiant challenge to physical and spiritual captivity.

Claire J. Robinson

Bibilography:

Eikhenbaum, B. M. *Lermontov*. Translated by Ray Parrott and Harry Weber. Ann Arbor, Mich.: Ardis, 1981. A literary and historical evaluation of Lermontov's works, including "The Novice." Places Lermontov in Russian literary context and offers useful insights into his versification.

Garrard, John. *Mikhail Lermontov*. Boston: Twayne, 1982. Arguably the best overview of Lermontov's life and works for the general reader. Contains a substantial section on "The Novice," examining its background, form, structure, and themes.

Lavrin, Janko. *Lermontov*. New York: Hillary House, 1959. A lucid and intelligent summary of Lermontov's life, major works, and recurrent themes. Includes a short section on "The Novice."

Mersereau, John, Jr. *Mikhail Lermontov*. Carbondale: Southern Illinois University Press, 1962. An extremely useful and readable critical analysis of Lermontov's works, incorporating a valuable discussion of Lermontov's Romanticism and a section on "The Novice."

NUNS AND SOLDIERS

Type of work: Novel
Author: Iris Murdoch (1919-   )
Type of plot: Psychological realism
Time of plot: 1970's
Locale: London and southern France
First published: 1980

> *Principal characters:*
> GUY OPENSHAW, a wealthy man dying of cancer
> GERTRUDE OPENSHAW, his wife
> TIM REEDE, a young, penniless artist
> DAISY BARRETT, his mistress
> ANNE CAVIDGE, a former nun
> PETER SZCZEPANSKI, a Pole called "the Count"

The Story:

Guy Openshaw, an administrator in the British Home Office, lay dying in his luxurious Ebury Street flat. A coterie of friends and relatives dropped in frequently to console his wife, Gertrude. One evening Gertrude received a call from Anne Cavidge, once her best friend at Cambridge, who had been a cloistered nun for fifteen years. Anne had left the order and returned to the world. Gertrude invited Anne to stay with her at Ebury Street. Guy died after telling Gertrude that she might consider the Count for her next husband. In her terrible grief Gertrude elicited Anne's promise to stay with her forever. The Count paid a condolence call, and the two women realized that he was in love with Gertrude.

Meanwhile, the fortunes of young Tim Reede and Daisy Barrett, longtime friends and lovers, had deteriorated. Guy, who had once administered a small trust for Tim, used to give him handouts occasionally. At Daisy's urging Tim went to Gertrude to ask for money. Gertrude, trying to be helpful as Guy would have wished, offered Tim a job repairing her house in France. Tim, overjoyed, accepted the offer and made secret plans to have Daisy join him. He found the house in a beautiful valley crossed by streams and mysterious stone formations. One day he returned from hiking to find that Gertrude had arrived to facilitate the sale of her house. Tim pursued his painting, and Gertrude tried to take care of business. They explored the countryside together and in one night Tim and Gertrude fell passionately in love. Gertrude insisted they must marry, and Tim, overwhelmed by events, neglected to tell Gertrude about Daisy. A few days later, Gertrude's relatives arrived to whisk her home to London.

Tim rushed back to England and told Daisy he was going to marry Gertrude. Daisy insisted it could be only for money, and when Tim denied this, she threw him out in a rage. Gertrude rushed to Tim's shabby studio and declared they must keep the relationship secret until her mourning for Guy ended. Meanwhile, the Count received an anonymous letter, which he shared with Anne, saying that Gertrude was having a love affair with Tim. Confronted by Anne, Gertrude admitted the truth; Anne, horrified and jealous, tried to talk her out of continuing the affair.

Anne moved out of Gertrude's home and Tim moved in. Soon Gertrude, unnerved by Anne's bitter words and confused by her secret double life, told Tim they would have to part and resume their relationship later. Terribly hurt, Tim left and went to Daisy's flat, where they resumed their affair. After a few days, he found living with Daisy intolerable and moved into a hotel, where he longed for Gertrude. She had resumed life with old friends and relatives, but thought obsessively of Tim. When they met accidentally in the British Museum, they were overcome with happiness and married openly soon afterward.

Anne fell in love with the Count, who visited her flat frequently to salve his wounded feelings over Gertrude's marriage. One day he arrived agitated, having heard that Tim had a mistress never mentioned to Gertrude. Worse yet, the Count had heard that Tim and the mistress had plotted for Tim to marry wealth and continue to keep the mistress. Anne, who had never liked Tim, visited Daisy and asked her about the gossip. Angry, Daisy said it was true and threw her visitor out. Anne told Gertrude of her discoveries, and Gertrude asked Tim about Daisy. Tim, embarrassed and confused, admitted it was true but that they had only joked about a rich marriage. Furious, Gertrude left, after ordering Tim to be gone when she returned.

Tim despaired, believing his life with Gertrude was over. He withdrew money from his and Gertrude's account and went to Daisy's flat. As he entered, he saw Anne at the street corner spying on him. Anne moved back to Ebury Street and tried to soothe and comfort Gertrude. Gertrude let herself be comforted, but raged inwardly with pain and jealousy. Tim, suffering intense guilt, gave up hope of reconciliation and continued his tormented life with Daisy.

Gertrude, Anne, and the Count went to Gertrude's house in France for a holiday, where the Count again hoped for a chance with Gertrude. In London, Tim and Daisy came to an understanding that their dissolute lives were not good for either of them, and they parted permanently. Tim was reconciled to his solitary life although he thought constantly of Gertrude. One day a letter from a mutual friend arrived, saying that Gertrude was at her house in France and probably needed and wanted him back.

Tim set out immediately for France. He approached the house from the valley and saw Gertrude holding hands with the Count. He fled, but fell into a canal that swept him through a drainage pipe. He thought he would die until he landed on a sandy shore. Battered, tired, and hungry, Tim crept back to the house, where Gertrude welcomed him joyfully into her arms. Anne finally realized that Gertrude's happiness depended upon him. She snatched the astonished Count off to the village, leaving husband and wife alone for a blissful reconciliation.

Tim and Gertrude returned to London anticipating years of happiness. Gertrude, sorry for the Count's disappointment, declared her new life would include him, and he was comforted. Anne went off to America.

Critical Evaluation:

Iris Murdoch is considered the most influential British novelist to create a major body of work after World War II. A professional philosopher who once taught at St. Anne's College, Oxford, Murdoch is also respected as a literary theorist. Monographs, dissertations, and critical studies have been written about her, and although critics disagree about the strengths and weaknesses of her work, they agree the work is important. *Nuns and Soldiers* (1980), Murdoch's twentieth novel, is a sum of the techniques and philosophical underpinnings of its predecessors.

Religion is one of Murdoch's large themes. In *Nuns and Soldiers*, the opening word of the novel is "Wittgenstein," the name of a philosopher who argued that one cannot prove or disprove the existence of God. Murdoch's novels teem with failed priests, Christ figures, nuns, Greek and Roman gods, and religious symbolism. In *Nuns and Soldiers*, there are hints that Guy Openshaw is a Christ figure. He has been a father to the other characters; he dies on Christmas Eve; he is revered for his wisdom; he is half-Jewish. Anne Cavidge, the former nun, believes she has a vision of the true Christ, from whom she demands answers, solutions, and salvation, only to receive his answer that she must find them in herself. Even Tim, the most openly sinning of the characters, seems to be touched with an ability to see beyond the physical to the miraculous. He sees the sacred quality in the French countryside as well as in the smallest leaves fallen from autumn trees.

The god that drives the plot, however, is the ancient Greek god of love, Eros, striking suddenly and causing endless romantic entanglements. In a typical Murdoch plot device, Tim and Gertrude, indifferent to each other for years, fall in love in seconds. Tim sees Gertrude as a sexual being only after Gertrude swims in a pool of crystal springs, and he undergoes his own ordeal by water when he survives his hazardous journey through a drainpipe. Water is often invoked in Murdoch's work as a symbol of the amorous powers that overcome her characters, and here it is used to wonderful effect. Symmetrical pairings of lovers is another device Murdoch employs. In *Nuns and Soldiers* there are six characters who are paired: Gertrude with Guy, Tim with Daisy, and the Count with Anne Cavidge. Although Guy dies early in the novel, he remains an important character and is often thought of and mentioned, especially by Gertrude. By the end of the novel, however, these neat pairings have been turned around, and one has been blessed while others have been frustrated.

The "nuns" of the title refer to Anne Cavidge and to Daisy Barrett, a woman of loose morals. Anne and Daisy both go off to America. Anne joins a group of religious activists and Daisy joins a female commune, a kind of women's order. America is a favorite place for Murdoch to send her characters when they are no longer needed for her intricate plots. The Count, one of the "soldiers" who has fantasies of fighting for his beloved Poland, accepts his disappointment in love and his role as family retainer in a soldierly way. Tim is a soldier who must undergo several ordeals in order to win his lady. After one of them, a fit of swooning in Hyde Park, Tim is filled with joy as if he has been purified. Nuns and soldiers may also symbolize and contrast cloistered virtue with the embattled goodness acquired by struggling in the real world.

The friends and relatives gathered around Guy and Gertrude, called "*les cousins et les tantes*," form a kind of Greek chorus for the central action. The members comment on and argue about the major characters and predict action to come, although often they are wrong. These minor characters also tie up certain loose threads of plot at the end; one or two step outside their role in the chorus and act in ways that move the story.

Critics have had difficulty classifying Murdoch as a writer because she combines metaphysical themes and unlikely occurrences with an absolutely realistic surface created of precisely observed details. Each character is dressed in perfect accord with his or her class and station in life. Even Daisy's makeup and Anne's haircut are significant in delineating their characters. Interiors are carefully drawn and have a character of their own, creating a solid background for the drama. Gertrude's drawing room reflects seriousness in its arrangement as well as whimsy in the tiny china orchestra on her mantel. One of the triumphs of *Nuns and Soldiers* is the house and surrounding countryside in France, so carefully depicted that the reader could draw a map of it. Sensuous hills and valley lend credence to the romance that occurs there, and the way Murdoch's characters are influenced by their surroundings gives another dimension to her work.

Sheila Golburgh Johnson

Bibliography:
Conradi, Peter J. *Iris Murdoch: The Saint and the Artist.* 2d ed. New York: Macmillan, 1989. Detailed analysis of many of Murdoch's works, including *Nuns and Soldiers.* Chapter 11 traces literary precedents and influences on the novel.

Dipple, Elizabeth. *Iris Murdoch: Work for the Spirit*. Chicago: University of Chicago Press, 1982. Chapter 10 of this comprehensive analysis of Murdoch's novels concerns itself exclusively with *Nuns and Soldiers*. Illuminates many of the philosophical, religious, and literary references in the novel and traces Murdoch's development from her first to her twentieth book of fiction.

Johnson, Deborah. *Iris Murdoch*. Bloomington: Indiana University Press, 1987. A good general overview of the novels, particularly the later ones, including *Nuns and Soldiers*.

Sage, Lorna. *Women in the House of Fiction: Post-War Women Novelists*. New York: Macmillan, 1992. Speculates on what qualities distinguish women writers from men writers. Murdoch's female characters are discussed at length from a feminist viewpoint, and compared with those of Doris Lessing.

Todd, Richard. *Iris Murdoch*. New York: Methuen, 1984. A useful volume that provides information about Murdoch's life as well as her work. Todd attempts to link the novels to Murdoch's philosophical positions, particularly to the existentialism of Jean-Paul Sartre.

O PIONEERS!

Type of work: Novel
Author: Willa Cather (1873-1947)
Type of plot: Regional
Time of plot: 1880-1910
Locale: Nebraska
First published: 1913

Principal characters:
ALEXANDRA BERGSON, a homesteader
OSCAR,
LOU, and
EMIL, her brothers
CARL LINDSTRUM,
MARIE TOVESKY, and
FRANK SHABATA, the neighbors of Alexandra
CRAZY IVAR, a hired man

The Story:

Hanover was a frontier town huddled on the windblown Nebraska prairie. One winter day, young Alexandra Bergson and her small brother Emil went into town from their new homestead. The Bergsons were Swedes. Their life in the new country was one of hardship because their father was sick and the children were too young to do all the work on their prairie acres. Alexandra went to the village doctor's office to get some medicine for her father. The doctor told her there was no hope for Bergson's recovery.

Emil had brought his kitten to town with him. He was crying on the street because it had climbed to the top of the telegraph pole and would not come down. When Alexandra returned, she met their neighbor, Carl Lindstrum, who rescued the cat. The three rode toward home together, and Carl talked of his drawing. When Alexandra and Emil arrived home, their supper was waiting, and their mother and father were anxious for their return. Shortly afterward, Bergson called his family about him and told them to listen to Alexandra, even though she was a girl, for she had proved her abilities to run the farm capably. Above all, they were to keep the land.

Alexandra was still a young girl when her father died, but she immediately assumed the family's domestic and financial troubles; she guided everything the family did, and through her resourcefulness, she gained security and even a measure of wealth for her brothers and herself. Emil, the youngest brother, remained the dreamer of the family, in his mooning over Marie Tovesky, whom he had first loved as a little child. Marie had married Frank Shabata. Frank was wildly possessive and mistrusted everyone who showed the slightest kindness to Marie. Alexandra was in love with Carl Lindstrum, whose father gave up his farm because the new, stubborn land seemed too hard to subdue. He returned to more settled country and took Carl with him to learn the engraver's trade.

Alexandra depended upon Crazy Ivar for many things. He was a hermit, living in a hole dug into the side of a riverbed. The kinder Swedes claimed he had been touched by God. Those who were unsympathetic were sure he was dangerous. Actually, he was a kindhearted mystic who loved animals and birds and who let his beard grow according to the custom of ancient prophets.

Through his lack of concern for worldly matters, he lost his claim, and Alexandra gave him shelter on her own farm, much to the dismay of her brothers and their wives. They demanded that she send Crazy Ivar to an institution, but she refused. She respected Crazy Ivar as she did few other people.

In the same way, Alexandra defended Carl Lindstrum. After the absence of sixteen years, he came back to their settlement. He had studied much, but in the eyes of the thrifty Swedes, his life was a failure because he had not married and he had no property. He seemed willing to marry Alexandra, who was by that time quite wealthy. Her brothers, Oscar and Lou, told Alexandra that she must not marry Carl, and she ordered them from her house. Carl, hearing of the disagreement, set out for the West at once.

Alexandra applied herself to new problems. She paid passage for other Swedes to come to America; she experimented with new farming methods. She became friendlier with Marie Shabata, whose husband was growing more jealous. She saw to it that Emil received an education, and she let him go off to the university despite the criticism of the other brothers. By now Emil knew he loved Marie Shabata, and he went away to study because he felt that if he stayed in the community, something terrible would happen. Even attending the university did not help him. Other girls he met seemed less attractive. His secret thoughts were always about Marie.

Frank Shabata discharged hired hands because he suspected them. He followed Marie everywhere. Even at the Catholic church he was at her heels scowling at everyone to whom she talked. His jealousy was like a disease. At the same time, he treated her coldly and insulted her publicly in front of their friends. She, on her part, was headstrong and defiant. At last, Emil returned from college. His friend Amedee became ill while working in his wheat fields and died shortly afterward. Following the funeral, Emil resolved to see Marie, to say good-bye to her before leaving the neighborhood permanently. He found her in her orchard under the mulberry tree. There for the first time, they became lovers.

Frank returned from town slightly drunk. Finding a Bergson horse in his stable, he took a weapon and went in search of Emil. When he saw the two he fired, killing both. Then Frank, mad with horror, started to run away. Crazy Ivar discovered the dead bodies and ran with the news to Alexandra. For the next few months, Alexandra seemed in a daze and spent much of her time in the cemetery. She was caught there during a terrible storm, and Crazy Ivar had to go after her. She regained her old self-possession during the storm. Frank Shabata, who had been captured soon after the shooting, had been tried and sentenced to prison. Alexandra determined to do what she could to secure his freedom. If she could no longer help her brother, she would help Frank.

While trying to help Frank, she heard that Carl Lindstrum had returned. He had never received her letter telling of the tragedy, but on his return from Alaska he had read of the trial and had hurried to Alexandra. His mine was a promising venture. The two decided that they could now marry and bring their long separation to an end.

Critical Evaluation:

Willa Cather's *O Pioneers!* is one story of the settlement of the American frontier. The title comes from lines written by nineteenth century poet Walt Whitman, who viewed the land as inspirational and a way to commune with God. Likewise, for Cather, the frontier was legendary, almost mythological, in American culture. Cather contributes to the legend of the American frontier in *O Pioneers!*

The frontier is portrayed in the novel as a noble but rugged place where dreams can come true if the characters work hard and believe in the land. *O Pioneers!* reflects the legend of American immigration. It shows the pains, hardships, beauty, and joy of life in the heartland of the United States. One of the novel's great strengths is its careful interplay of the legendary and the realistic.

O Pioneers! emphasizes themes such as the importance of the land, which plays a major role in motivation and plot development. Alexandra, for example, feels she is a part of the land. Through her endurance and ability to farm the land (while others, such as Carl Lindstrum, leave it), she achieves success and riches. In *O Pioneers!*, an American legend, in which the European immigrant comes to the New World to seek his or her fortune through land ownership, figures heavily. The immigrant turns the wilderness along the frontier into a farm or ranch and profits thereby. Alexandra Bergson, the protagonist in *O Pioneers!* lives this American legend. There are other elements of the legendary in the work as well; it is difficult to think of unspoiled land being cultivated by isolated female and male figures without recalling the book of Genesis, and themes of innocence and its loss. To Cather's credit, these powerful themes do not overshadow the book's realism. Alexandra remains a particular woman living in a particular time and place, in spite of the weighty symbolic value that may be placed on her.

O Pioneers! combines two stories, "Alexandra" and "The White Mulberry Tree." Alexandra is what links the two stories, which are separated by sixteen years. The first story tells of a young immigrant woman who must care for a farm; it is about her courage and endurance. Alexandra is a woman who must survive in a man's world. Cather seems to have modeled her protagonist after herself; there are various parallels in the lives of the author and her character. Alexandra's great courage and endurance also have a legendary quality. Alexandra is a female version, or revision, of the hardworking tamer of the land, a figure with origins in the Bible and in the legend of the American immigrant. In the second story, "The White Mulberry Tree," Alexandra is about forty years old, about the age of Willa Cather at the time she published *O Pioneers!* As Alexandra matures, her relationship with the other characters changes. She initially is the proverbial damsel in distress whom Carl Lindstrum helps by rescuing the cat. Later, she is the strong one who is wealthy and who eventually owns the Lindstrum farm.

In "The White Mulberry Tree," characters who were in the background emerge into the foreground. Emil Bergson and Marie Tovesky, who receive brief mention at the beginning of the book, develop into an important subplot. The two ill-fated lovers are murdered under the mulberry tree by Marie's jealous husband, an act whose biblical echoes are apparent. This violent subplot counterbalances the primary story about the development of the farm and the fulfillment of the American legend of the successful immigrant.

The subplot of the failed romance and murder gives Carl a reason to return to the independent Alexandra. She appears weakened by the loss of her brother Emil and close friend Marie. "The White Mulberry Tree" subplot can be interpreted symbolically; murder, deceit, and adultery are the snake in the grass in Cather's pastoral ideal. Additionally, the novel may be read as the story of one woman's psychological development.

O Pioneers! contrasts the peaceful, pastoral world of Alexandra with violence and murder. Yet it ends peacefully as Alexandra tries to rebuild her world. There is much evidence in the novel to support the argument that the novel is a rejection of the American legend of the immigrant's creating an Edenic, not to mention profitable, world. Alexandra's world has been shattered by the death of her beloved Emil and Marie. The novel, however, also ends on a note of hope; Alexandra and Carl may find happiness together.

"Critical Evaluation" by Mary C. Bagley

Bibliography:

Bagley, M. C. *Cather's Myths*. New York: American Heritage, 1994. Discusses *O Pioneers!* in the context of the American myth of the settlement of the land and of the counter-myth of the rejection of the land. Places emphasis on Alexandra's relationship to the land and how this symbolizes the settlement of America.

Bennett, Mildred R. "*O Pioneers!*" In *The World of Willa Cather*. Lincoln: University of Nebraska Press, 1961. Discusses Cather's early life in Nebraska as the setting and inspiration for *O Pioneers!*

Rosowski, Susan J. "*O Pioneers!*: Willa Cather's New World Pastoral." In *The Voyage Perilous: Willa Cather's Romanticism*. Lincoln: University of Nebraska Press, 1986. Discusses how the two stories, "Alexandra" and "The White Mulberry Tree," came to be written and then combined into *O Pioneers!* Says novel is related to the classical tradition of the pastoral.

_____. "Willa Cather—A Pioneer in Art: *O Pioneers!* and *My Ántonia*." *Prairie Schooner* 55 (Spring/Summer, 1981): 141-154. Discusses how Cather's regionalism relates to her skill as an author.

Wiesenthal, C. Susan. "Female Sexuality in Willa Cather's *O Pioneers!* and the Era of Scientific Sexology: A Dialogue Between Frontiers." *Ariel* 21 (January, 1990): 41-63. Emphasizes the relationship between Willa Cather's work and her life. Says that because Alexandra has a career and takes charge of the farm, she has masculine characteristics that may be attributed to Cather as well.

OBASAN

Type of work: Novel
Author: Joy Kogawa (1935-   )
Type of plot: Historical realism
Time of plot: 1972, with flashbacks to the 1940's
Locale: British Columbia and Alberta, Canada; Nagasaki, Japan
First published: 1981

> *Principal characters:*
> NAOMI NAKANE, a thirty-six-year-old elementary teacher
> ISAMU NAKANE, her uncle
> AYAKO NAKANE, her aunt, whom she calls "Obasan"
> EMILY KATO, another aunt, her mother's sister
> STEPHEN NAKANE, Naomi's brother
> SENSEI NAKAYAMA, spiritual leader of Naomi's extended family

The Story:

Naomi Nakane was in the middle of teaching her fifth- and sixth-grade class in the small town of Cecil, Alberta, when she received word that her uncle had died in Granton, 150 miles south. Going home for his funeral meant for her a sad reunion with several family members, notably the quiet widow, the "Obasan" of the book's title, and Stephen, Naomi's older brother. Obasan and Uncle Isamu had actually raised Naomi and her brother from the time that they were young children. Flamboyant Stephen, who had essentially renounced his Japanese heritage and had been involved for a time with a French divorcée, had developed a national reputation as a classical pianist and lived in Montreal. Unmarried Naomi, on the other hand, had been stuck in a dead-end teaching job for the past seven years with no prospects of either romance or fame.

Emily Kato, Naomi's outspoken unmarried aunt living in Toronto, also made the trip to Granton for the memorial service. Politically active, she had hounded Naomi for years to become more interested and involved with exposing the wrongs of the Canadian government in its internment of Japanese citizens during World War II. She had earlier sent Naomi a large box of newspaper clippings, letters, and government documents, which had been stored unread by Obasan under the kitchen table.

The trip home brought back painful memories to Naomi about growing up without her mother. Studying an old family photograph when she arrived in Granton sparked extended reminiscences. In September 1941, Naomi's mother and Naomi's Grandmother Kato went to Japan to care for a relative who was ill, but neither returned, and Naomi, who was five years old at the time, was never told what became of her mother. She and her family and her Japanese neighbors had been forced by the Canadian government to move inland to internment camps and abandon their successful boat-building business near Vancouver. The family members— Naomi, Stephen, Uncle Isamu and Ayaka Obasan—were required to sell off their belongings and leave their comfortable home for an indefinite period of time. They were moved to an abandoned mining settlement inland named Slocan, and were not reunited with Aunt Emily for twelve years. Losing her doll on the train ride was symbolic for Naomi of losing all comfort and vestiges of domestic life. The living conditions in the camp were deplorable, with little food, heat, or sanitation, but at least the family had a small house to themselves, and the children attended school. Led by Sensei Nakayama, the adults constantly reminded one another that they must bond together, help one another, and hide their emotions, for the sake of the children. There were challenges of illness and death: Naomi's Grandmother Nakane died, Stephen developed a bad limp and had to wear a cast on his leg, and her father contracted tuberculosis and later died.

The family, already fractured as were other Japanese families, was forced to relocate a second time, to Granton, near Lethbridge, Alberta, to live in a small hut that had been a chicken coop on the Barker farm. Black flies, contaminated drinking water, and bedbugs were but a few of their daily hardships. Children and adults alike were forced into long hours of backbreaking migrant labor in the blistering heat and dust of beet fields. The government distorted the reality of the harsh situation in newspaper reports that Aunt Emily had kept; one headline jocularly called the Japanese workers "Grinning and Happy." Fifteen-year-old Stephen was given permission to play the piano in the school auditorium, took lessons, and did well in a talent show on the Lethbridge radio station. In 1951, Naomi was a ninth-grader and Stephen was in his final year at Granton High School when the family was able to move from the farm into a two-bedroom house just off Main street. Sensei Nakayama journeyed to Japan to try to find out what had become of Naomi's mother and grandmother, but was unsuccessful. By 1954, Stephen had permanently left Granton, first for Toronto and later Montreal, after winning top marks in a music festival. His international success with music had permanently freed him from the bonds of his Japanese heritage.

By 1972, the year of their Uncle Isamu's funeral, Naomi had not seen her brother for eight years. The Bakers had visited Obasan's house to offer their condolences when Stephen, Aunt Emily, and Sensei Nakayama arrived. With the family united in sadness, love, and prayer, Sensei Nakayama then read the single document that resolved the painful mystery of what happened to Naomi's mother, knowledge that Emily and Obasan had been privy to all along but had shielded from Naomi and Stephen at their mother's request. The document was a letter written from their Grandmother Kato to her niece, Aunt Emily, and reported that she and her daughter (Naomi's mother) were in Nagasaki when the atomic bomb was dropped. It described how Naomi's mother had been horribly disfigured in the bombing and died in terrible and prolonged pain. Her last wish was that her children be spared from knowing how much she had suffered. Naomi was comforted by the fact of learning the terrible secret and finally being able to mourn her mother's death. She recognized that her mother's silence was really borne of a deep love in wanting to spare her daughter and son the truth of her suffering.

Critical Evaluation:

In the United States, many eloquent first-person narratives by Japanese Americans, some more fictionalized than others, document the horrors of internment which Japanese citizens endured during World War II, but in Canada, Joy Kogawa's novel is by far the most significant account. Monica Sone's *Nisei Daughter* (1953) is perhaps the closest to *Obasan* in tone and purpose. Among other compelling accounts are Toshio Mori's *Yokohama, California* (1949), Mine Okubo's *Citizen 13660* (1946), and Yoshiko Uchida's *Desert Exile: The Uprooting of a Japanese-American Family* (1982).

Obasan is a complex and artfully crafted work. It is, in part, autobiography. Kogawa was six years old, one year older than the fictional Naomi Nakane, when Kogawa's family was evacuated from Vancouver to the ghost town of Slocan, in eastern British Columbia. Authentic newspaper clippings, government documents, and real letters of protest written by a Japanese Canadian activist elaborate and enhance her story. Within the framing narrative and the flashback of personal memory, Kogawa infuses rich, deeply layered poetic language, which functions as a keening for the two particular deaths that frame the book, those of her uncle and her mother.

The actual time frame of the story is just a few days, from the phone call that alerts her to her uncle's death to the family gathering in Granton for the funeral. Special emphasis is placed on family unity throughout the novel, described in images of all members being knit together into one blanket. Thus, the migratory saga of both a single family and also an ethnic community evolves. The first eleven chapters are more or less an exposition of Naomi's family history. The following twenty chapters convey the devastation that the family has experienced in being wrenched away from their home. One guiding principal validates the stoicism of the adults throughout the ordeal, the repeated Japanese phrase, "*kodo no tame*—for the sake of the children—*gaman shimasho*—let us endure." The path of the novel is a downward spiral from familial and community harmony into increasing discomfort and pain, until the most painful and intimate secret of all—the demise of Naomi's mother—is revealed.

Important symbols enhance Kogawa's provocative story of belated coming of age and assertion of identity. The dual themes of silence/stone and reporting/acting are separately embodied in the persons of Naomi's two aunts, who represent conflicting family forces, present within Naomi, that she must ultimately choose between. Naomi has been raised by the silent and reticent pair, Ayako and Isamu Nakane. In the narrative frame of the book, Naomi is constantly eating or serving or thinking about her uncle's famous stone bread. It is tough and hard, Stephen does not like it, but it is also nourishing. It symbolizes the hardships endured by the Japanese as well as the community spirit with which they band together for support. Ayako is remarkable in her stasis, constantly referring to herself as "old." Nothing ever changes in her house. Her voice is barely audible, her conversation always oblique. She is forgetful, confused, and bewildered. Vocal Emily Kato is aggressive and opinionated, characterized by vigor and urgency and transformation. She is a relentless attender of conferences and prides herself in sharing with other survivors mutual stories of pain and indignation. She insists that Naomi not only listen to the facts of her ethnic history but act on them.

It is appropriate that Isamu, a man who has nourished his family with his stone bread, should, by his death, be the occasion of Naomi overcoming the ignorance that has rendered her passive. It is even more appropriate that as all the horrors have been revealed and the novel ends, it is Aunt Emily's coat that Naomi pulls on for an early morning walk to clear her head. The strong implication is that Naomi is now braced up with Emily's truth and identity, and will choose life and speech over death and silence.

Kogawa's saga functions on at least three levels. It shows how a woman is empowered and nurtured by her female ancestors. It shows how inner strength can deliver an oppressed people out of the bondage of racism and abuse. Finally, it is an illuminating historical chronicle of the Japanese internment in Canada, told with the objective "facts" of journalism and reportage and with the subjective evocation of poetic language, scripture, and reverie.

Jill B. Gidmark

Bibliography:

Cheung, King-Kok. *Articulate Silences: Hisaye Yamamoto, Maxine Hong Kingston, Joy Kogawa*. Ithaca, N.Y.: Cornell University Press, 1993. Enhances understanding of the writing of three significant Asian American women. The forty-page chapter devoted to *Obasan* examines the negative and positive aspects of silence in the novel.

Chua, Cheng Lok. "Witnessing the Japanese Canadian Experience in World War II: Processual Structure, Symbolism, and Irony in Joy Kogawa's *Obasan*." In *Reading the Literatures of Asian America,* edited by Shirley Geok-lin Lim and Amy Ling. Philadelphia: Temple University Press, 1992. Explores the form and the symbolism in *Obasan*, concentrating on Kogawa's biblical references.

Jones, Manina. "The Avenues of Speech and Silence: Telling Difference in Joy Kogawa's *"Obasan."* In *Theory Between the Disciplines: Authority/Vision/Politics*, edited by Martin Kreiswirth and Mark A. Cheetham. Ann Arbor: University of Michigan Press, 1993. Discusses the power of narrative and the strategies behind storytelling in the novel.

Lim, Shirley Geok-lin. "Japanese American Women's Life Stories: Maternality in Monica Sone's *Nisei Daughter* and Joy Kogawa's *Obasan*." Feminist Studies 16, no. 2 (Summer, 1990): 288-312. A primarily feminist reading of two novels of the Japanese internment experience, focusing on the mother-daughter relationship.

Rose, Marilyn Russell. "Politics into Art: Kogawa's *Obasan* and the Rhetoric of Fiction." *Mosaic* 21, no. 3 (Spring, 1988): 215-226. Discusses *Obasan* in terms of "persuasion" and "history," and explains how the language illuminates the message of the novel.

OBLOMOV

Type of work: Novel
Author: Ivan Alexandrovich Goncharov (1812-1891)
Type of plot: Social realism
Time of plot: First half of the nineteenth century
Locale: Russia
First published: 1859 (English translation, 1915)

Principal characters:
> ILYA ILYITCH OBLOMOV, a slothful Russian landowner
> ANDREY STOLZ, Oblomov's only real friend
> TARANTYEV, a parasitical friend of Oblomov
> OLGA ILYINSKY, the beloved of Oblomov
> ZAKHAR, Oblomov's valet

The Story:

Ilya Ilyitch Oblomov was a Russian landowner brought up to do nothing. As a child he had been pampered by his parents, even to the point where a valet put on and took off his shoes and stockings for him. The elder Oblomovs lived a bovine existence. Their land, maintained by three hundred serfs, provided them with plenty of money. Their days were taken up with eating and sleeping; they did nothing until an absolute necessity arose.

The chief influence on Oblomov during his childhood came from a German, a steward on a neighboring estate, who acted also as a tutor. Young Oblomov went to school at his home and there found his only boyhood friend, the German's son, Andrey Stolz. When the boys grew up, their lives seemed from the first destined to different ends. Stolz was sent off by his father with a few resources to make his way in the world, but among those resources was a great deal of practical experience. Within a few years, Stolz was able to amass considerable wealth for himself and to become a respected, vital businessman.

Oblomov, on the other hand, finished college after doing only enough work to get his diploma. He then became a clerk in a government office, one of the few positions considered an honorable post for a gentleman in Russia. Before three years had elapsed he resigned from his post, ostensibly because of ill health but actually because he could not bring himself to accomplish all his duties; he felt that the work was simply too much trouble for a gentleman. Having retired from the government, he began to do nothing during the daytime. The indolence, spreading like a poison, finally made him extremely inactive.

By his thirtieth birthday Oblomov was no further along in life than he had been at his twentieth; he was, in fact, much worse off than before. His rooms were filthy and unkempt, for he was unable to control his valet, Zakhar. Oblomov had no ambition whatever. He seldom left his rooms, so he had no social life. Even at home, he did nothing but lie around in a dressing gown and eat and sleep. How much money he got from his estates in southern Russia he did not know, for it would have been too much trouble to keep accounts. His bailiff, knowing his master would not stir out of Moscow, cheated Oblomov consistently, as did everyone else. Oblomov did not mind the cheating, so long as people did not disturb him.

At last two misfortunes, as Oblomov saw them, befell him. The bailiff reported by letter that only a few thousand rubles could be sent in the next year, and the landlord sent word that he needed Oblomov's apartment for a relative. Help, in the form of a parasitical friend, Tarantyev, seemed a godsend to Oblomov, for Tarantyev promised to find another apartment and to see what could be done about a new bailiff for the estates.

On the same day Stolz came to visit his boyhood friend and was aghast at the state in which he found Oblomov. His horror was increased when he learned that the doctors had told Oblomov he had only a few years to live unless he began to lead a more active life. Stolz hustled about, taking Oblomov with him everywhere and forcing his friend to become once more interested in life. When Stolz left on a trip to western Europe, he made Oblomov promise to meet him in Paris within a few more weeks.

Fate intervened so that Oblomov never kept his promise. Stolz had introduced him to Olga Ilyinsky, a sensitive, vivacious, and vital young woman. Oblomov had fallen in love with Olga and she with him. Visiting and planning their life together after marriage kept both of them busy throughout the summer, during which Oblomov was partly reclaimed from his apathy, but as winter drew on, the actual wedding was no closer than it had been months before. Even for his marriage, Oblomov could not expend a great deal of effort; the habit of sloth was too deeply ingrained in him. Tarantyev had found an apartment for him in an outlying quarter of Moscow, with a thirty-year-old widow, and Oblomov lived there in comfort. Nor could he have given up the apartment; he had signed the contract without reading it, and he was bound to keep the apartment at an exorbitant price.

Although concerned over his estates, Oblomov was unable to find anyone to set them in order, and he refused to make the journey home. He told himself he was too much in love to leave Olga; actually, he was too apathetic to travel twelve hundred miles to Oblomovka. Olga finally realized that she was still in love with the man that Oblomov could be but that he would never become more than a half-dead idler. In a pathetic scene, she told him good-bye.

Following his dismissal by Olga, Oblomov took to his bed with a fever. His valet, the valet's wife, and the landlady did all they could to help him, and so Oblomov slipped again into the habit of doing nothing. He realized the apathy of his mind and body and called it shameful, giving it a name, Oblomovism. Tarantyev, the parasitical friend, and Mukhoyarov, the landlady's brother, planned to keep Oblomov in his clutches. First, they sent a friend to look after Oblomov's estate, but most of the money went into Tarantyev's pockets. Second, they tried to bring together the cowlike landlady and Oblomov; this second plot was easy, since the lowborn woman was already in love with her gentlemanly tenant.

Meanwhile, Olga had gone with her aunt to France. In Paris they met Stolz, who was there on business. Stolz, observing the great change in Olga, at last learned what had happened in Russia after his departure. Having always loved Olga, he soon won her over, and they were married. Realizing that Olga was still in love with Oblomov, however, Stolz returned to Russia and tried to aid Oblomov by renting the estates and sending the money to Oblomov. Tarantyev was furious and recouped his losses by making Oblomov appear as the seducer of his landlady. The landlady gave a promissory note to Tarantyev and her brother, and they got one on her behalf from Oblomov. Thus Oblomov's income continued to pass into Tarantyev's hands, until Stolz learned of the arrangement and put an end to it.

Years passed. Olga asked her husband to look up Oblomov to find out if he had ever recovered from his terrible apathy. Stolz did so; Oblomov, he learned, had married his landlady and still did nothing. As the doctors had warned, he had suffered a slight stroke. He did ask Stolz to take care of his son, born of the landlady, after his death. Stolz agreed, and not long afterward, he received word that he was to go for the boy. Oblomov had passed away as he had lived much of his life, sleeping.

Critical Evaluation:

"Oblomov's Dream," which Ivan Alexandrovich Goncharov called the overture to the complete novel *Oblomov*, was published in 1849. It took the writer ten years more to finish the whole book. When it appeared in 1859, three years before the emancipation of the serfs, *Oblomov* had an immediate and clamorous success. The period was one of growing political activity in feudal Russia. Progressive democratic forces preached an awakening from inertia and stagnation and expressed general hope for reforms. Although Goncharov had no political goals in mind, his realistic depiction of Russian life of about four decades of the first half of the nineteenth century opened the eyes of those who did not want to see the dangers of serfdom and the necessity of cardinal changes. Goncharov showed how and why the Russian gentry were in gradual decline and proved the necessity of strong, active leaders to rise up and to bring in a new epoch in which the laziness and stagnation would be overcome.

Ilya Ilyitch Oblomov, the main character of the novel, is a product and a victim of a disintegrated Russian culture and primitive natural economy. His life is a terrible process of spiritual and moral degradation. A curious and lively boy, he falls prey to the charms of Oblomovka, his family estate, where work and boredom were synonyms and where food and sleep were all that mattered. There was no need for him to exercise any initiative, since hundreds of servants were always at his call.

By the age of thirty-two he is an inert and apathetic creature wrapped in his dressing-gown and glued to his couch. He has retired from the world and excuses his idleness with the pretence that he is preparing himself for life. His preparations are nothing but vain dreams in which a peaceful and happy childhood is mixed up with an unrealizable future without passions, conflicts, storms, or demands. Lazy, incompetent, clumsy, and good for nothing, Zakhar complements his master and shares his nostalgia for Oblomovka. Oblomov's caprices and way of life are not in the least abnormal for Zakhar; they evoke his respect and admiration. The master and his valet cannot exist without each other and completely depend on each other.

Nothing and nobody can wake Oblomov up and bring him to active and normal life. His friend Andrey Stolz spares no effort to make Oblomov live up to what is best in him and to realize himself as an individual. Stolz introduces Oblomov to the beautiful and vivacious Olga Ilyinsky, who brings some freshness and purpose into Oblomov's life. Although initially carried away by love, Oblomov does not want to have the troubles of this feeling or to take any responsibility for another person. Fear of changing his life routine wins over the feeling of love and leads to separation. Love for Olga and friendship with Stolz are a test of Oblomov's ability to return to life, but Oblomov fails the test because the clutches of his sloth and melancholy are too strong. In the relations and characters of Oblomov and Stolz Goncharov shows the differences and collisions of the old patriarchal Russia and the new European Russia. Intelligent and practical Stolz is the best representative of the capitalist trend that Goncharov thought that Russia could no longer avoid. Lean and muscular, Stolz is the complete opposite of the round, soft Oblomov; Stolz personifies energy, activity, business undertaking, and progress.

There are no complicated intrigues in the novel. The center of attention is the psychology of a person who gradually falls into apathy and the conditions that lead him to this kind of existence. There is not much action in the novel either. Even nature is undisturbed and quiet. The inactivity of nature blends with the inactivity and stagnation prevailing everywhere. The extremely simple plot, thematically based on inaction, develops slowly. This enables the reader to note details which otherwise might escape attention. Goncharov masterfully uses every detail, movement, gesture, posture to thoroughly depict all characters. A true realist in his portraiture, Gorcharov combines concrete physical details with biographical facts and description of the inner world of his characters. Goncharov shows a great talent for fitting every character and every scene into one fully developed, complete picture. Monologues, dialogues, and numerous comical situations bring color and lightness to the novel.

There is a close connection between Goncharov's life and his creation. Goncharov and his protagonist Oblomov spent their childhoods on a provincial estate; both studied at Moscow University; both worked in civil service, and both experienced disappointment in love. Goncharov openly sympathizes with his hero and feels sorry for him. He shows Oblomov as a decent, lovable human being weakened by forces beyond his control. Oblomov, with all his shortcomings, is an intelligent, honest, truthful, and faithful person, who can evoke love and devotion. He understands his personal decline and the reasons for it but has neither power nor courage to do anything about it. He finds a substitute for his Oblomovka in Pshenitsina's house, where he sleeps his life away under the maternal eye of Agafya Matveyevna, his landlady and later his wife. Conflicts between dream and reality, stagnation and striving, tradition and modernization, country and city, true love and sensual toleration bolster the main theme of the novel—the emptiness and inertia of the Russian gentry.

Oblomov is one of the best realistic novels of Russian literature and the height of Goncharov's literary activity. It precipitated much dispute and evoked contradictory interpretations by all major Russian literary critics. Some accused Goncharov of malicious slander on Russian gentry; others praised him for sincerity and authenticity. Nikolay Alexandrovich Dobrolyubov gave the first and most famous treatment of *Oblomov* in his article "What Is Oblomovism?" The article was published in 1859, immediately after the publication of the novel. Dobrolyubov gives a brilliant analysis of the book, demonstrating its significance as a genuine depiction of the disintegration of Russia. "Oblomovism" immediately entered the Russian language, denoting passivity, idleness, apathy, sloppiness, inertia, and lack of self-discipline.

"Critical Evaluation" by Paulina Litvin Bazin

Bibliography:

Andrews, Larry. "The Spatial Imagery of Oblomovism." *Neophilologus* 72, no. 3 (July, 1988): 321-334. Discusses Oblomov's attitude toward himself and toward the outside world. Unfolds the layers Oblomov wraps around himself and explains his immaturity.

Ehre, Milton. *Oblomov and His Creator: The Life and Art of Ivan Goncharov.* Princeton, N.J.: Princeton University Press, 1973. An excellent starting point for the study of *Oblomov,* with a lucid, comprehensive analysis of style, structure, themes, and characters. Draws multiple parallels between Goncharov and his creation.

Hainsworth, J. D. *"Don Quixote, Hamlet* and 'Negative Capability': Aspects of Goncharov's *Oblomov."* AUMLA: *Journal of the Australasian Universities Language and Literature Association* 53 (May, 1980): 42-53. Compares the master-servant relationship of Oblomov and Zakhar with that of Don Quixote and Sancho Panza. Links Oblomov's and Hamlet's rationalizations for inactivity.

Lyngstad, Alexandra, and Sverre Lyngstad. *Ivan Goncharov.* Boston: Twayne, 1971. Focuses on Goncharov's achievement as a novelist. The chapter on *Oblomov* analyzes the novel and demonstrates Goncharov's great artistic versatility in depicting Oblomov.

Wigzell, Faith. "Dream and Fantasy in Goncharov's *Oblomov."* In *From Pushkin to Palisandriia: Essays on the Russian Novel in Honor of Richard Freeborn*, edited by Arnold McMillin. New York: St. Martin's Press, 1990. Examines dreams and daydreams of the main characters of the novel. Analyzes dream and fantasy as key elements of the novel.

THE OBSCENE BIRD OF NIGHT

Type of work: Novel
Author: José Donoso (1924-   )
Type of plot: Magical Realism
Time of plot: Mid-twentieth century
Locale: Chile
First published: El obsceno pájaro de la noche, 1970 (English translation, 1973)

Principal characters:
> JERÓNIMO DE AZCOITÍA, the governor and a local grandee, the father of Boy
> INÉS DE AZCOITÍA, the wife of Jerónimo, called Misiá Inés when in the
>   Casa de Ejercicios Espirituales
> HUMBERTO PEÑALOZA, the main narrator, Jerónimo's secretary and a
>   fledgling writer
> MUDITO, a mute child who lives in the Casa and who is an alter ego of
>   Humberto Peñaloza
> GIANT, a local n'er-do-well believed by some to be the father of Iris
>   Mateluna's illegitimate child
> PETA PONCE, an old ugly witchlike woman, the alter ego of the yellow bitch
> THE YELLOW BITCH, a dog which, by metempsychosis, contains the soul
>   of the nursemaid mentioned in the old wives' tale
> IRIS MATELUNA, the fifteen-year-old girl who is one of the orphans in
>   the Casa de Ejercicios Espirituales and who gives birth to an
>   illegitimate child
> BOY, Jerónimo's deformed son who lives in La Rinconada
> EMPERATRIZ, the woman in charge of La Rinconada
> MOTHER BENITA, the nun in charge of the Casa de Ejercicios Espirituales
> FATHER AZÓCAR, the priest in charge of selling the Casa de Ejercicios
>   Espirituales
> DR. AZULA, the Swiss surgeon responsible for operating on Boy

The Story:

In the Casa de Ejercicios Espirituales there lived thirty-seven female inmates, five orphans, and a nun, Mother Benita, who looked after them. One of the young orphans, a fifteen-year-old girl called Iris Mateluna, became pregnant, and the old women in the Casa became obsessed with the idea that her pregnancy was to be a virgin birth. Halfway through the novel, Inés de Azcoitía, the wife of Jerónimo, arrived to stay at the Casa. As a result of a trip to Rome in which she had unsuccessfully attempted to persuade the bishops that one of her eighteenth century ancestors should be canonized, she had retreated, half-crazed, to a Swiss sanatorium and had then come to stay in the Casa in order to look for the bones of her ancestor, which had never been found. Legend had it that they were hidden somewhere in the Casa. While she had been in Europe, Jerónimo had decided to sell the Casa, which had been a family possession for generations. Inés stopped the sale of the Casa but finally went mad and had to leave. Mother Benita subsequently had a nervous breakdown, at which point the inhabitants of the Casa were moved out by Father Azócar.

Jerónimo's son was born very deformed and was so ugly as to be simply named Boy. Jerónimo took the bizarre decision to have his son brought up in a place in which he would

4576

never become aware of his deformities and, therefore, hired a woman, Emperatriz, to scour the city and find the most deformed people to live in a special residence for Jerónimo's son, La Rinconada. Humberto was hired to be the secretary of Jerónimo and specifically to write an account of Boy's life, but he proved unequal to the task. Boy escaped from La Rinconada, was ridiculed by normal people in the outside world, and decided to take his revenge on the world. He invited his father to stay with him in La Rinconada. Eventually, Jerónimo went mad and was found drowned in the lake in the gardens to the consternation of the general public, who were now without a senator. It was difficult to know whether Boy and the inhabitants of La Rinconada deliberately brought about Jerónimo's downfall, or whether the latter simply went mad through living too long within the walls of La Rinconada.

Critical Evaluation:

The clue to the meaning of the novel appears in the epitaph which is a passage from a letter by the North American author Henry James in which the following sentence appears: "The natural inheritance of everyone who is capable of spiritual life is an unsubdued forest where the wolf howls and the obscene bird of night chatters." The aim of José Donoso's novel is to chart that territory. In exploring the depths of the human mind, one important insight is revealed: Human beings hide from themselves the true realities of things because of their painful nature, just as Jerónimo tries to shield his son from the reality of his ugliness. Since *The Obscene Bird of Night* focuses on the world of the unconscious mind, Donoso deliberately chose to divest his narrative of linear sequentiality, thereby producing a flexible text in which the narrative voice darts quickly and without warning from the mind of one character to that of another. Often the reader is given the bare bones of an event and has to construct probable scenarios for what is being read. Sometimes the narrative swerves unexpectedly as if it were a dream sequence. This is an appropriate device since, as Sigmund Freud once pointed out, dreams are the royal road to the unconscious mind.

There are a number of scenes in the novel which challenge the reader's comprehension and they are good examples of the craftmanship of Donoso's novel. The first narrative is the old wives' tale which is recounted in chapter 2 of the first part of the novel. It tells the spine-chilling tale of a young blonde girl who has nine brothers and, as a result of a bad harvest, is accused of being a witch. The father was reluctant to believe this, but he agreed to investigate. One night, he burst into the room where his daughter was sleeping with her nursemaid and discovered the nursemaid in a strange state between life and death. The father accused the nursemaid of being a witch, and the menfolk took the witch's body, tied it to a log, and sailed it down to the sea. The father sent his daughter away to a monastery, and she was never heard from again. The important detail in the story concerns the description of a yellow bitch, a dog that started baying outside the window when the men seized the nursemaid's body. The implicit suggestion is that the witch's incubus had inhabited the dog and was now unable to return to the nursemaid's body. The yellow bitch subsequently disappeared without a trace. This scene has an impact, like a story within a story, on the narrative being read, since there are many references to a yellow bitch in the narrative proper. Though the novel never spells this out explicitly, the reader is persuaded to interpret the yellow dog as the witch's incubus. At one point of the story, when Humberto is having sex with the old woman Peta (he thought it was Inés but was deceived) the noise of a dog is heard howling outside the window. Likewise, when Iris Mateluna has sex, called "yumyum" in the novel, with her clients, dogs often appear to watch. Thus the novel works by the suggestion of association rather than by explicit metaphor.

A further demonstration of the ways Donoso adds mystery and intrigue to his novel occurs when the narrator of the novel attempts to have sex with Inés. In part 2, chapter 26, the reader is eavesdropping on what is assumed to be the thoughts of Humberto Peñaloza, who managed to get into the room where Inés de Azcoitía was sleeping. The reader is privy to his thoughts as he is thinking about taking revenge on Jerónimo. Suddenly, the narrative changes, Inés screams and Mother Benita rushes into the room and asks what the matter is. At the idea that a man had been in the room, Mother Benita denies that this is possible since there is nobody there. At which point, the reader realizes that to which he or she has been listening are the thoughts of an incubus which was attempting to rape Inés. In this way, by not preparing the reader for what is coming, Donoso is able to shock the reader into believing that he or she has entered the mind of an incubus.

A further degree of mystery is added to this story by the narrator, a diffuse, osmotic consciousness who appears to have several simultaneous identities: Mudito, Humberto, the Seventh Witch, Iris Mateluna's unnamed child, Iris Mateluna's dog, and even a stain on the wall. Mudito is the mute child who lives in the Casa and observes everything. Humberto is Jerónimo's secretary who is intensely jealous of his employer. The narrative voice switches disconcertingly between these identities.

This switching of narrative voice ultimately contributes to the most bizarre scene of the novel. In this scene, the reader is listening to the thoughts of someone being put into a sack and covered with layers and layers of jute. Every time the narrator tries to get out of the sack, some hand outside sews up the hole again. Then, suddenly, the narrative swerves and the reader is presented with the description of a female person who takes a sack out of the house, down to the river, and who then proceeds to burn it. At this point, one is forced to read the previous scene again and to reinterpret it. The unnamed female person who burns the sack is actually burning the person inside the sack who had been expressing his thoughts only a few paragraphs previously. As to the identity of the female person (the reader only knows of her gender because the adjectives reveal it), the reader cannot know for certain, but it is likely to be Peta, the old witch woman who had grown to hate Humberto. The consciousness in the sack is again likely to be an amalgamation of the persons of the Seventh Witch, Mudito, Humberto, and the illegitimate baby of Iris Mateluna, which has now been turned into an "imbunche" which, according to witchcraft legend, is what witches do with children they have stolen (they sew up all their orifices). The last image of the novel, the "imbunche," is an ironic and inverse image of the birth of Christ, since the "imbunche" is wrapped in a material similar to the swaddling clothes in which Christ was wrapped. Fittingly, the narrative consciousness is destroyed as the reader reaches the last page of the book. The novel thereby turns in on itself and destroys itself.

Stephen M. Hart

Bibliography:
Baker, Robert. "José Donoso's *El obsceno pájaro de la noche*: Thoughts on 'Schizophrenic' Form." *Revista de Estudios Hispánicos* 26, no. 1 (1992): 37-60. A clear discussion of the sometimes confusing ways in which characters fuse with each other.
Diamond-Nigh, Lynne. "*El obsceno pájaro de la noche*: An Allegory of Creation." *Hispanófila* 104 (1992): 37-45. Emphasizes the religious metaphors used in the novel.
Donoso, José. "A Small Biography of *The Obscene Bird of Night*." *Review of Contemporary Fiction* 12, no. 2 (1992): 18-31. A fascinating discussion by the author on how the novel came into being, the various rewrites, and the various people and events which inspired their novelistic counterparts.

Rowe, William. "José Donoso: *El obsceno pájaro de la noche* as Test Case for Psychoanalytic Interpretation." *Modern Language Review* 78, no. 3 (1983): 588-96. Focuses on the relationship between Humberto and Jerónimo in the novel and looks at the themes of narcissism and self-destruction.

Swanson, Philip. "José Donoso: *El obsceno pájaro de la noche.*" In *Landmarks in Modern Latin American Fiction.* London: Routledge, 1990. A tightly-argued essay which sets *The Obscene Bird of Night* in the context of Donoso's other novels and concentrates on the different parallels constructed by the novel, such as those between Humberto and Mudito and between the yellow bitch and Peta Ponce.

THE OCTOPUS

Type of work: Novel
Author: Frank Norris (1870-1902)
Type of plot: Naturalism
Time of plot: Late nineteenth century
Locale: San Joaquin Valley, California
First published: 1901

Principal characters:
PRESLEY, a poet
MAGNUS DERRICK, owner of Los Muertos Rancho
HARRAN and
LYMAN, his sons
ANNIXTER, owner of Quien Sabe Rancho
HILMA TREE, his wife, a milkmaid
VANAMEE, a shepherd and ploughman
DYKE, railroad engineer and hop farmer
S. BEHRMAN, railroad agent
CARAHER, saloon-keeper and anarchist
CEDARQUIST, a manufacturer
GENSLINGER, editor of local newspaper
HOOVEN, a ranch worker

The Story:

Trouble had been brewing in the San Joaquin Valley. The Pacific & Southwestern (P & SW) Railroad and the wheat ranchers who leased the railroad's adjacent lands were heading for an economic collision. Presley, an Eastern poet visiting the ranch owned by the powerful and prosperous Magnus Derrick family was caught amid these fierce bickerings. As he cycled toward the town of Bonneville, he met Hooven, a ranch worker who was agitated by the possibility of being fired. Riding on, Presley met Dyke, who told of being dismissed and blacklisted by the P & SW. Feeling uninvolved—even superior to these troubles—Presley continued his journey and encountered Annixter, an abrasive rancher who had been angered by the high-handed railroad "octopus," especially by the agent S. Behrman, who wanted to gain control of the thriving wheat fields. The P & SW had, early on, leased its vacant, unproductive adjacent lands to the ranchers with options for them to buy. With rancher investment and toil, the once worthless lands had become golden. The P & SW was looking for ways to keep the ranchers from winning the deal. Rebellion and warfare were in the air.

As Presley cycled about the properties he met Vanamee, a mystically inclined shepherd, and soon thereafter the poet witnessed the slaughter of a flock of sheep that had wandered innocently onto the railroad tracks. S. Behrman blamed the accident on a broken Annixter fence. Presley became drawn into the intrigue and violence that was seething in the volatile community. Genslinger, a newspaper editor sympathetic to the P & SW, warned the ranchers against fighting the powerful railroad for Shelgrim, its influential president, wielded vast political clout. Annixter exploded against such a timid course and urged an unified rancher front, fighting fire with fire: The ranchers, too, needed to enter the dark arena of bribery and corruption to survive.

While Presley was too deeply concerned with composing an epic poem of the West to immerse himself in these difficulties, Vanamee was too obsessed with the memory of his lost love Angele, who had died eighteen years earlier. He sought "The Answer," a mystical, spiritual response from ineffable forces he sensed pulsating around him and within the mysterious wheat, undulating, it seemed, with a psychic power. In the meantime, Annixter had ridden the same local journey as had Presley. He, too, had meet Hooven and had heard of the man's personal troubles. He had seen freight cars routed from efficient delivery points to more profitable short-haul trips. He had learned of Dyke's misfortune. Nervous and desperate, he made the P & SW an offer for the purchase of the property he now leased. The offer was rejected. He and the others were securely in the tentacles of the octopus. Annixter, nevertheless, finished building a new barn and inaugurated it with a dance to which most Valley families came. That night, with everyone gathered together, they learned that the railroad intended to charge $27 for the ranchers' option on each acre, not the $2.50 expected. Enraged, the ranchers demanded that the aloof, scrupulously honest Magnus Derrick join them in a course of bribery and crooked political machinations. His wife cried out in opposition, but Derrick, reluctantly carried along by mob frenzy, abdicated his principled life and pledged support, even leadership.

Lyman Derrick became the ranchers' choice for commissioner. His secret passion was, unbeknown to the politicking group, to be governor. At a San Francisco meeting, he introduced his Valley constituents to Cedarquist, a manufacturer-tycoon who lectured them on the hard and cruel realities inherent in economic determinism and free-market trade, contrasting such with the superficiality of art in the function of society. Presley wondered about his own role and purpose as an artist. After the conversation ended, the group learned that the legal system had decided in favor of the railroad. Lyman had sold them out.

Dyke tried to escape the arm of the railroad by going into hop farming, but he was ruined when the P & SW quickly raised his shipping costs well beyond his profit margin. Distraught, he went to the saloon of Caraher, a known revolutionary, and after hearing many incendiary tirades against capitalism, Dyke held up a P & SW agency and stole a locomotive. He was chased by a posse and finally trapped. He tried to murder S. Behrman, leader of the pursuers, but the gun unaccountably misfired. In part influenced by the Caraher ambience and rhetoric, Presley at last produced a poem called "The Toilers" in which he identified himself as a man of the people. The work became a huge success among radicals with Presley hailed as a vibrant revolutionary voice. Magnus Derrick was ruined economically and morally as well, his condition exacerbated by the knowledge of his son's duplicity. Senile and weak, he deteriorated into a shell of a person. Vanamee, meanwhile, awash in romance, found "The Answer" to his visions in the daughter of his lost Angele now come, very much alive, to him.

There was a gory rabbit drive to foreshadow the apocalyptic moment of human violence. Armed agents of the railroad and armed ranchers faced off. While neither side looked for bloodshed, fate prevailed. There was slight movement, an accidental brushing of a horse, and both sides fired. Annixter was killed instantly, leaving lovely Hilma Tree a widow. Hooven, whose family had had to take to the streets, was also killed. Harran Derrick, the honest son of the rancher-leader, was also slain. Presley, now totally involved, was so emotionally wrought by the events that he journeyed to confront Shelgrim, president of the P & SW, the ogre behind the pernicious octopus that had caused such massive suffering. Shelgrim, however, proved to be a compassionate, learned man who lectured the poet sternly on the forces of determinism, forces beyond the power of any one person. Presley was perplexed, his purpose unfulfilled, his mission a failure. He went to a dinner at Cedarquist's and enjoyed a table of lavishly expensive foods and imported wines. At the very same time of this feast, the widow and child of Hooven stalked, starving, the streets of the city. At the moment the banquet ended, Mrs. Hooven was pronounced dead.

S. Behrman longed to be Master of the Wheat, whose force was not only economic but also mystical and transcendental. In his passionate desire to control all aspects of its production, transportation, and shipment abroad, Behrman inspected a boat being loaded with overseas-bound grain. He tripped into an open hatch and was first tortured and finally suffocated to death by the continuous, furious avalanche of wheat swirling and tumbling rapidly into the hold. The wheat had been the most vital force in the drama of life: It had beggared, destroyed, killed, inspired, and given life. The seemingly human conflict had actually been one of forces, not of people.

Critical Evaluation:

The Octopus was composed as the first volume of a projected trilogy of wheat. *The Pit* (1903) focused on wheat speculation in Chicago, but *The Wolf*, a planned final volume on wheat distribution, was never written. The trilogy, as planned and partly executed, is of epic dimensions, the type of panoramic novel suggested to Frank Norris by the work of his literary idol Émile Zola. A tale of economic determinism, of social forces caught in Darwinist struggles of the capitalist-monopolist battles characterizing the post-Civil War era, *The Octopus* dramatizes a crucial time in America when industry ran rampant and functioned virtually free from legislative constraint. A critical episode in the tale—the armed battle between ranchers and railroad—was based on a specific historical occurrence. The Mussel Slough Affair of 1878 was an actual bullet-flying conflict. Norris also energized his text by incorporating bizarre real-life incidents he had read about in newspapers. For example, an Oakland, California, train had plunged into and had slaughtered a flock of unattended sheep; in another story, two grain workers had fallen into a great vat of grain and had been smothered to death. Such unusual events became dramatic symbols for the mindless killing of innocents and the incontrovertible force of the wheat.

Norris had once noted that quality fiction examines "whole congeries of forces." In this novel he depicts contemporary antagonistic powers of significant magnitude: railroad and ranchers. The locomotive engine, symbolized as a cold, Cyclopean monster, omnipotent and unassailable, driven by corruption and greed (whose combined energies cannot be opposed), annihilates those who stand against it. The ranchers attempt to engage in the struggle, but they are clearly doomed. The result of their struggle is predictable, despite Norris's sympathetic treatment of their plight. Through their collective suffering, however, one must remember that the ranchers themselves sought merely to exploit the land, to pillage the resources of nature and then move on. Thus, Presley, whose process of education is traced throughout the novel, remains confused by the confluence of events and results. He moves from impersonal, escapist artist to committed radical. He inveighs against the untrammeled power of capitalism manifested by the P & SW, but he is finally made to realize that the railroad itself is simply a gigantic force, impersonally propelled, much like the wheat. Neither force can be controlled by human power. It is ironic, then, that while Norris orchestrates the human actions of S. Behrman, the unmitigated villain of the story, a visible embodiment of absolute evil, the oily, repressive agent can no more manipulate or divert the force of the P & SW than can its president. Nor can anyone control the power inherent in the wheat, with its mysterious, all-pervasive domination.

All of the characters on this large canvas are caught within the confluence of forces impelling their behaviors. No actions indicate complete freedom of the will. The late nineteenth century concept of social Darwinism, therefore, underscores *The Octopus*. The desire for survival dominates the interactions of forces. Norris contrasts the wealth of industrialist Cedarquist, whose guests dine at a table groaning under the weight of exotic viands, with the abject poverty of widowed, homeless Mrs. Hooven, forced to encourage her hungry child to eat a rotting banana peel. The novelist similarly counterpoints the realist Annixter, who plunges wholeheartedly into the struggle and whose life is destroyed, with Vanamee, above and apart from it all, a romantic who eschews the human destruction about him and finds eventual happiness through a meeting with a lost love's daughter. The Vanamee narrative is an apparent appendage to the text, an obvious catering to a *fin de siècle* reading audience that sought romance in fiction. Frank Norris offered no solutions for the problems he presented. His intent was to provide entertaining fiction using such decisive and engaging materials as love and war, force and life.

Norris portrays many of the problems society needed, and still needs, to address. The challenge inherent in maintaining morality in an age of flawed conscience and widespread corruption was dramatized by Magnus Derrick's unhappy strategy to enlist evil in the attempted destruction of evil. The tendency of society to blame powerful individuals for exploitation and poverty was brought into question by the dramas of S. Behrman and Shelgrim. Both men were seemingly in control of the destinies of those afflicted by P & SW repression but were in truth nothing more than pawns in the large game of Force, the true engine driving civilization on all levels. Everyone is a mandatory participant in the vast game. The locomotive slaughters the sheep; the ranch hands massacre the rabbits; prodigal capitalists and poverty-degraded homeless are inevitable by-products of a predatory universe governed by rules of evolutionary Darwinism.

The capricious nature of life is illustrated in the fate of the three educated and thoughtful men who dominate the narrative. Presley discovers the social obligation of the artist, but remains philosophically confused. Vanamee flees from reality but is rewarded with happiness through the fulfillment of a dream. Annixter moves from misanthropy to love, but he leaves a grieving widow. She becomes another victim of the octopus.

Abe C. Ravitz

Bibliography:

Davison, Richard A., ed. *The Merrill Studies in "The Octopus."* Columbus: C. E. Merrill Co., 1969. A collection of essays on the novel. Included are contemporary reviews and personal letters of Norris relevant to the book's composition.

French, Warren. *Frank Norris.* New York: Twayne, 1962. A source for beginning a study of Norris and his literary achievement. Biographical material is accompanied by a scholarly discussion of important texts.

Graham, Don. *The Fiction of Frank Norris: The Aesthetic Context.* Columbia: University of Missouri Press, 1978. An in-depth study of the aesthetic sources and relationships energizing Norris' fiction. An insightful study of *The Octopus* emphasizes the influence of the arts on the novel.

Hochman, Barbara. *The Art of Frank Norris, Storyteller.* Columbia: University of Missouri Press, 1988. A study of the recurrent motifs in Norris's fiction, emphasizing his literary methods. Analyzes use of word and symbol in *The Octopus*.

Pizer, Donald. *The Novels of Frank Norris.* Bloomington: Indiana University Press, 1966. A comprehensive and systematic examination of Norris' novels, with particular attention paid to the author's intellectual backgrounds and the philosophical influences upon him. Analysis and interpretations stress the idea of evolutionary theism and its appearance in various guises in his fictions.

THE ODD COUPLE

Type of work: Drama
Author: Neil Simon (1927-   )
Type of plot: Comedy
Time of plot: Mid-1960's
Locale: New York City
First performed: 1965; first published, 1966

> *Principal characters:*
> OSCAR MADISON, a divorced New York City newspaper sportswriter
> FELIX UNGAR, Oscar's best friend, a television newswriter who is
>   separated from his wife
> SPEED,
> MURRAY,
> ROY, and
> VINNIE, poker-playing buddies of Oscar and Felix
> GWENDOLYN PIGEON, an upstairs neighbor, a British widow
> CECILY PIGEON, Gwendolyn's sister and roommate, a divorcée

The Story:

The regular weekly poker game was under way on a hot summer night in the smoke-filled living room of the once well-kept and fashionable Upper West Side New York City apartment of divorced newspaper sports writer Oscar Madison. In the three months since his wife had divorced him, the easygoing, pleasant, but slovenly Oscar had managed to litter the apartment with dirty dishes, discarded clothes, old newspapers, empty bottles, and other trash. Hosting the poker game, Oscar was serving his friends warm drinks (the refrigerator had been broken for two weeks) and green sandwiches that he declared were made from "either very new cheese or very old meat." The other poker players were Oscar's friends—Murray, Speed, Roy, and Vinnie. Felix Ungar, Oscar's best friend, was uncustomarily late for the game, and all the poker players were worried about him.

A phone call to Felix's wife revealed that Felix and his wife had just separated after twelve years of marriage and that Felix had disappeared, sending his wife a telegram threatening suicide. When Felix finally arrived at the poker game, all the players attempted to calm him by pretending that everything was normal. They steered Felix away from the twelfth-story window of the apartment and waited anxiously as Felix went into the bathroom. Felix eventually confessed that he had swallowed a whole bottle of pills from his wife's medicine cabinet and had then vomited. After the poker players departed, Oscar consoled Felix, who revealed that he did not want a divorce and had stayed up the whole night before in a cheap Times Square hotel room considering a suicidal jump from the window. In an attempt to calm and help his friend, Oscar suggested that Felix move in with him. Felix, a fussy and compulsively neat person, agreed and immediately began to clean up Oscar's apartment.

At the next poker game, two weeks later, the atmosphere was very different because Felix was in charge. The apartment was immaculate and Felix was taking orders for food and drink, serving carefully made sandwiches and ice-cold beer, reminding the poker players to put their glasses on coasters so as not to leave rings on the freshly polished table. A Pure-A-Tron air freshener eliminated the cigar and cigarette smoke, and Felix had even used disinfectant on the playing cards. This fussy behavior unnerved some of the other poker players as much as it had

Oscar during the preceding week, and the game broke up prematurely. Oscar was irritated but felt guilty about his anger and suggested to Felix that they lacked excitement in their lives. Oscar suggested that they take out to dinner two single British women from an upstairs apartment, Gwendolyn and Cecily Pigeon. Felix was not enthusiastic about the plan because he still missed his wife and children and wanted to save his marriage, but Felix finally agreed to give the idea a try if he could cook the meal himself in Oscar's apartment.

A few days later the evening came for the dinner and it was a disaster. Oscar was an hour late coming home from work and Felix was incensed because his carefully planned meal was jeopardized. When Gwendolyn and Cecily arrived, Felix was nervous, morose, and maudlin. Furthermore, he chilled the romantic atmosphere Oscar was trying to create by tearfully sharing with the women snapshots of his wife and children. Nostalgically remembering their own spouses, Gwendolyn and Cecily joined Felix in tears and decided that Felix was sensitive and sweet. Oscar was frustrated and angry that the potentially romantic evening had been ruined until the women suggested that they shift the dinner to their apartment upstairs. Oscar's spirits were lifted until Felix refused to cooperate, citing his loyalty to his wife and children. Before going upstairs alone, Oscar angrily offered the twelfth-story window as a possible place for Felix to jump from.

The next evening Oscar was still not talking to Felix. When Oscar came home from work, Felix was preparing for the night's poker game, cleaning up as usual, but Oscar purposely began to make a mess. He pulled the plug on Felix's vacuum cleaner, threw things on the floor, walked on the couch, and even took from the table the linguini that Felix had fixed himself for supper and threw it onto the walls of the kitchen. In the ensuing argument, Oscar claimed that everything about living with Felix for the last three weeks had irritated him. He then grabbed a suitcase and demanded that Felix move out of his apartment. Felix left, but when the other poker players arrived for the game they joined Oscar in worrying about what Felix would do on his own. Felix then arrived and revealed that he had temporarily moved in upstairs with the Pigeon sisters. He admitted that Oscar had done two wonderful things for him—taking him in and throwing him out—and Oscar and Felix finally shook hands. Felix agreed to return for next week's poker game. After Felix left, the game resumed, with Oscar telling his friends to be a little more careful about their cigarette butts.

Critical Evaluation:

Neil Simon was the most successful commercial playwright in the history of theater and certainly the most recognizable of American playwrights. In creating a steady stream of Broadway hits, starting with *Come Blow Your Horn* (1961), Simon garnered numerous awards, including the Pulitzer Prize in drama in 1991. Though critics often found his work to be sentimental, predictable, and shallow, Simon was consistently popular with Broadway, regional, and community theater audiences. In his most popular period, the mid-1960's and early 1970's, Simon at times had as many as four hits running simultaneously on Broadway.

The Odd Couple is probably the best-known Neil Simon comedy, owing not only to its strikingly comic situation and distinctive main characters but also to the commercially successful spin-offs from the play—a well-received motion picture adaptation in 1968, an enormously popular television series from 1970 to 1975, and a female version sequel in 1985. Simon's plays, and especially his early plays, typically generate belly laughs through carefully orchestrated comic conflict, brisk pace, and extremely witty dialogue freely punctuated with comic one-liners. *The Odd Couple* has all of these.

The theme of *The Odd Couple*, if it has one, involves human incompatibility and the observation that compromise is necessary in any kind of marital-like relationship. Oscar and Felix illustrate that men who do not get along with their wives will probably be incompatible with others in precisely the same way. Regardless of the situation and genders involved, effective compromise in human relationships is rare. To some, however, this description of thematic elements in *The Odd Couple* might seem excessively academic. Do Neil Simon plays really exist to investigate thematic issues? Some find his plays, and especially his later plays, convincing in their treatment of serious thematic issues, while others find nearly all of his plays quite shallow. A large majority however simply assert that Neil Simon plays are just "good entertainment," and that the theme of a Neil Simon play is not intended to be profound.

The comedy of Neil Simon in general and of *The Odd Couple* as a particular example ultimately raise the larger and very important issue of whether craftsmanship, the quality of making a thing well, suffices for literary quality craftsmanship and lasting literary fame. Whatever the answer to that question, there is no question that in terms of comic theater Simon is an adept craftsman. Casual as his style might seem, in *The Odd Couple* Simon leaves nothing to chance. Within the overall architecture of the play, which is amazingly tight and efficient, nearly every word is carefully chosen for its desired effect. For example, the first act of the play, busy as it is, merely establishes what the conflict will be (the "marriage" of an "odd couple"); the second act demonstrates this conflict in action; and the final act resolves the conflict. The success of the play, of course, depends on the intensity and interest generated by the Oscar and Felix relationship, but *The Odd Couple* is theatrically effective because it creates and maintains this focus without appearing too obviously to do so. Nearly the first third of the play features mainly the poker players, who are interesting in themselves but function primarily as a way of introducing the eccentric and conflicting personalities of Oscar and Felix. They characterize Felix before he arrives and react to both Oscar and, once he arrives, Felix. After a brief period with Oscar and Felix onstage alone, the poker players return at the beginning of the second act. Here the reaction of Speed and Roy to Felix's compulsive neatness mirrors Oscar's point of view, while Murray and Vinnie, who like the new atmosphere created by Felix, contrast with Oscar's response. Simon then uses the Pigeon sisters to advance the conflict between Oscar and Felix without reiterating the issue of Felix's obsession with cleanliness. In the scenes with Gwendolyn and Cecily, Felix's eccentricity takes the form of loyalty to his wife and family. This behavior further alienates him from Oscar but for slightly different reasons, which gives variety and texture to the conflict. In the final scenes of the play, Simon brings back the poker players and the Pigeon sisters to create a pleasing symmetry in the resolution of the conflict.

Simon's craftsmanship is even more obvious on the level of comic dialogue, where he is the undisputed master of the witty one-liner. In Act I, for example, Roy says of Oscar's refrigerator, "I saw milk standing in there that wasn't even in the bottle." The image of milk defying gravity surprises at first, then surprise turns to laughter when the exaggeration is seen as in some way appropriate—the milk was left in the refrigerator so long that the container disintegrated and left a sour solid. Simon's skill with such verbal constructions is a testimony to his brilliance with language and to his training in the early fifties as a gag-writer for television. Unsympathetic critics have faulted Simon for his reliance on the humor of one-liners, but there is no denying that he excels at the creation of one-liners.

Terry Nienhuis

Bibliography:
"Divorce Broadway Style." *Newsweek*, March 22, 1965, 90-91. A contemporary review of the

original Broadway production that considered the play limited and predictable, pleasurable but unmemorable and more entertainment than art. Describes the play as "an extended situation with no interior development and with a tacked-on denouement."

"Divorce Is What You Make It." *Time*, March 19, 1965, 66. A contemporary review of the original Broadway production that describes *The Odd Couple* as "an evening of group hysteria" and "an astutely characterized study in incompatibility."

Johnson, Robert K. *Neil Simon*. Boston: Twayne, 1983. A sophisticated book-length treatment of Simon's work. The chapter on *The Odd Couple* argues that in this play Simon was pushing beyond the simpler comedy of earlier plays but that the third act is weaker than the first two.

Kerr, Walter. "What Simon Says." *The New York Times Magazine*, March 22, 1970, 6, 12, 14, 16. A landmark essay on *The Odd Couple*. The only major New York drama critic consistently to champion Simon's work, Kerr considers Simon "to have discovered the exact amount of God's truth a light comedy can properly contain."

McGovern, Edythe M. *Neil Simon: A Critical Study*. 2d ed. New York: Ungar, 1979. The first full-length study of Simon's work. The chapter on *The Odd Couple* asserts that Simon's comedy captures the essence of human incompatibility, irrespective of gender or marital status, and demonstrates that the missing ingredient in such relationships is the inability to compromise.

ODE TO APHRODITE

Type of work: Poetry
Author: Sappho (c. 612-c. 580 B.C.E.)
First published: Sixth century B.C.E.

Although it is possible to read the *Ode to Aphrodite* without extensive knowledge of Sappho and the culture in which she lived and worked, readers familiar with ancient Greece will develop a deeper appreciation for the poet's accomplishments by comparing her works to other classical texts. What may seem like a highly personal poem is actually, on one level, highly derivative and conventional. Clearly designed for public performance, the *Ode to Aphrodite* relies heavily on conventions commonly used by Greek writers whose audiences were expecting to be entertained with familiar subjects and situations.

Specifically, in the *Ode to Aphrodite* the poet makes numerous allusions to Homer and other male writers. Additionally, a careful stylistic and content analysis of the work reveals that it is similar to many religious poems in the Greek tradition. Anne Burnett has called the work "the poetic expression of a personal religious faith," in which Sappho "explores the changes that can be wrought by prayer, in a petitioner and in a divinity."

Deliberate borrowings and conventional themes not only provide a reader with information about the tradition in which Sappho worked, but also reveal something about her strategies for representing the lives of women to her audiences, which were primarily made up of women. What one notices upon careful examination of the *Ode to Aphrodite* is that Sappho does not merely borrow conceits from her predecessors. Instead, she modifies and inverts familiar materials to create entirely new portraits of both the speaker and the goddess she addresses. For example, the scene described in the *Ode to Aphrodite* is reminiscent of one in book 5 of the *Iliad* (c. 800 B.C.E.). Sappho transforms, however, Homer's weak deity into a powerful force on whom women can call for help. Sappho's use of Homeric epithets and situations provides an informed commentary on the values of her culture. Modern readers may discover, as Sappho's original audiences no doubt did, that her poetry is ironic and imaginative, offering a sensitive appreciation of women's experience.

Ode to Aphrodite, a representative introduction to the poetry of Sappho, may be summarized thus: The poet, Sappho, invokes the attention of Aphrodite, goddess of love, and invites her to leave the house of Zeus, mount her chariot, and let her doves bear her to the earth. The poet imagines their meeting: The goddess will ask who it is that troubles Sappho by fleeing from her, by refusing to reciprocate the ardors of love. That person—Sappho imagines the promise of the goddess—will soon suffer as Sappho now suffers. The vision, briefly and movingly expressed, concludes, and in the last lines Sappho takes up the prayer with which the poem begins. It is a prayer to a goddess who may or may not be gracious.

This brilliant specimen from the six hundred lines of Sappho's poetry that remain is characteristic of a body of work very distant from the contemporary age and yet modern. Sappho's poetry once consisted of nine books of some twelve thousand lines, but all except a few fragments are supposed to have been destroyed by Church leaders in Constantinople and Rome. Some of her work survived because it was quoted by grammarians who used her passionate verse to illustrate a syntactical point. Other fragments, written on papyrus, were discovered in 1897 at Oxyrhyncus in Egypt. Also, ancient coffins had been lined with Sappho's verse.

Out of such materials scholars have labored to reconstitute the work of a woman whom the Greeks called "the poetess" just as they called Homer "the poet." Born on the island of Lesbos in the Aegean, Sappho grew up in a civilization that was rich and relaxed, epicurean before the time of Epicurus. The luxury of the life that her class enjoyed stirred the merchants of the island to revolt; they supported a "tyrant" named Pittacus. Sappho was twice exiled from her native town, the second time as far away as Sicily. During her exile she married, bore a daughter, was widowed, and returned to Lesbos. Here, for a time at least, she put masculine affection behind her, even though her fellow exile, Alcaeus, had expressed a warm interest in her. Instead, Sappho set up an academy where she was the mistress and guiding spirit of young women whose self-cultivation and loves she supervised. The charms of the young women were celebrated in Sappho's verse; and their departure to other places or to the marriage altar caused Sappho to lament. Such is one version of her life, necessarily a matter of conjecture in almost all details. There is also a record of Sappho's objection to the marriage her brother made with an Egyptian courtesan. A poetic fragment touchingly describes Sappho pointing to her wrinkles when someone speaks to her of love.

Sappho was certainly "love's creature"; she tells readers that she served a goddess who could make the limbs sweat and tremble as well as stir with joy. When Sappho speaks of a young woman as the sweet apple remaining alone on a high twig, perceived by the gatherer but unreached, or when she tells us of a woman who cannot mind her spinning because her fingers ache with love's desire, Sappho is initiating a tradition of sensual frankness in Western poetry. When Sappho's laments mark the departure of Atthis or some other friend from the charmed and charming circle of young women who used to wander through the gardens of Lesbos, readers can hear in Sappho's lines the authentic voice of passion and desperation. From this poetry comes the current meaning of the word "lesbian." At such moments, Sappho's odes and fragments do not testify to mere convention. They record an experience of life that is as fresh and troubled today as it was six centuries before Christ.

Updated by Laurence W. Mazzeno

Bibliography:
Bowra, C. M. *Greek Lyric Poetry from Alcman to Simonides.* 2d rev. ed. Oxford, England: Clarendon Press, 1961. An important study of major contributions to ancient Greek poetry. Provides a perceptive exploration of Sappho and her influence on other ancient poets. Chapter 6 is exclusively concerned with Sappho, and examines the *Ode to Aphrodite.*
Burnett, Anne Pippin. *Three Archaic Poets: Archilochus, Alcaeus, Sappho.* Cambridge, Mass.: Harvard University Press, 1983. Technical and scholarly, the third section provides close attention to Sappho as a major contributor to ancient Greek poetry and discusses important aspects of Greek society.
Castle, W. "Observations on Sappho's *to Aphrodite." Transactions and Proceedings of the American Philological Association* 89 (1958): 66-76. A brief but concise introduction to the *Ode to Aphrodite* and certain issues of classical scholarship regarding the poem.
Davenport, Guy, trans. Preface to *Sappho: Poems and Fragments,* by Sappho. Ann Arbor: University of Michigan Press, 1965. Provides a useful but brief discussion of Sappho's contribution, her concept of Aphrodite and the poetry's relation to and influence on modern writers. Includes notes on the translation.
Weigall, Arthur. *Sappho of Lesbos: Her Life and Times.* New York: Garden City, 1932. Although a bit antiquated as a general study, chapter 16 provides a superior and exhaustive review of all elements of the ode, from the meter to traditional aspects of the goddess in ancient Greek society. Index.

ODES

Type of work: Poetry
Author: Pindar (c. 518-c. 438 B.C.E.)
First transcribed: Epinikia, 498-446 B.C.E. (English translation, 1656)

By a stroke of luck, Pindar's victory odes have survived almost in their entirety. This is not the case for the author's other works—including hymns, dirges, songs of praise, and processional songs—which have either been lost or are known only from short fragments. Although the victory odes, known as the *epinikia,* were Pindar's most famous and influential works, even in antiquity, they seem typical of their author's general approach and style. Shifting frequently from subject to subject, Pindar's poems have a dreamlike quality. Each line flows logically from what has preceded it but, by the end of the poem, the author often has made so many twists and turns that he sometimes seems to conclude on a radically different note from the one with which he began.

A second element that adds to Pindar's complexity of style is his highly ornate language. Pindar avoids the language of everyday speech; his secular works are modeled on Greek hymns. The religious songs that honored the Olympian gods in the fifth century B.C.E. preserved a reverent tone and exalted style that provided Pindar with a model for his own poems celebrating the glories of human achievement. The complex nature of his poetry also appears to be due to a preference among the archaic Greek poets for elaborate metaphors and difficult allusions. The appreciation of a Pindaric poem often necessitates the reader's knowing much about Greek mythology and athletics. Moreover, it requires the reader to accept each poem as simultaneously having several levels of meaning.

The *epinikia* were originally choral works, sung in celebration of athletic victories at the four Panhellenic games of antiquity: the Olympian games, held in honor of Zeus at the sacred city of Olympia; the Pythian games, held in honor of the god Apollo in his oracular city of Delphi; the Nemean games, held in honor of Zeus near the site where Heracles is said to have slain the Nemean lion; and the Isthmian games, held in honor of Poseidon near the Argive city of Corinth. The title *epinikia* suggests that these poems celebrate victory in an athletic event. The works were occasionally performed at the festival where the victory occurred; more frequently, however, they were commissioned for a later celebration in the victor's home city. The athletic events for which Pindar composed victory odes include boxing, wrestling, the pankration (a combined form of boxing and wrestling in which no holds were barred), the pentathlon (a series of five events featuring running, jumping, throwing the discus, hurling the javelin, and wrestling), running, and chariot racing. Pindar also wrote one ode, *Pythian Ode* 12, for the victor of a musical competition—Midas of Akragas in a flute contest.

The Panhellenic games were religious celebrations as well as athletic competitions; as a result, Pindar's poetry tends to mingle religious and athletic imagery. One theme of these poems is that perfecting the human body and winning an athletic victory are supreme acts of worship. The idea behind this value is that, in seeking physical perfection, people honor the perfect gods by trying to imitate them. For this reason, the athletic victory may be viewed as the winner's sacrifice to the gods. The poet's song is also represented as a religious act in the poem's celebrating the victory and making it immortal. Finally, Pindar thought that the euphoria felt after success in the Panhellenic games was as close as human beings would ever come to the bliss eternally enjoyed by the Olympian gods. Even if only for a moment, therefore, athletic victory elevates humanity to the divine level. Glorification of the victor in these poems aims at glorification of the gods.

These values were shared more frequently by the Greek aristocracy than by the common people. To a large extent, the aristocratic nature of Pindar's poetry reflects the poet's own upbringing. Pindar's family claimed ties to the royal families of Sparta, Cyrene, and Thera. Pindar inherited a priesthood and had clear aristocratic sympathies. As a result of his family's wealth, he was able to travel freely. He studied in Athens under the musicians and poets Apollodorus and Agathocles. When Pindar was a young man, the lyric poetry of Ionia was just beginning to be widely imitated in Athens. Pindar united this lyrical and highly polished style with the Doric taste in choral poems, producing a form of poetry that embodies the intricacy of lyric poetry and the majesty of the choral song. Pindar's language, too, was a mixture of Doric elements (as was nearly all Greek choral poetry), epic forms found in the authors Homer and Hesiod (both eighth century B.C.E.), and his own native dialect.

The poems included in the *epinikia* are either written in strophic form (with the same meter for each verse) or composed of three-verse units. The latter structure is slightly more common and is similar to the choral songs of Greek tragedy. Each three-verse unit consists of a strophe (a "turning," because, as these lines were being sung, the chorus would turn), an antistrophe (a "turning backwards" because the chorus would then reverse its direction), and an epode (an "end song" that brought the unit to a close and was sung by the chorus from its original position). Pindar's epinician poems consist of any number of three-verse units, depending upon the importance of the victory and the nobility of the victor.

The forty-five poems of the *epinikia* vary somewhat in structure, but they have certain organizational similarities to one another. Usually, after a brief introduction on the theme of excellence or human achievement, Pindar quickly mentions the victor, the festival at which he has won his victory, and the event. Praise for the individual's success frequently develops into praise for the victor's family, city, or patron deities. If the victor's family was particularly distinguished, Pindar may introduce legends connected with those gods whom the family claimed as ancestors. Rarely, however, does Pindar ever tell a myth in its entirety. In most cases, he makes only brief, sometimes obscure, allusions to a story that everyone in the audience could have been expected to know. There are a number of moral maxims, scattered through the typical ode; sometimes the maxims were only loosely connected to the subject at hand. On a few occasions, Pindar feels free to discuss his own life and the art of poetry that has produced his ode. In these cases, the patron's triumph may be linked directly to the immortal nature of the poet's song.

A number of themes appear repeatedly throughout the *epinikia*. The most important of these themes deals with the quality of human excellence. In keeping with the poet's aristocratic values, Pindar regarded excellence as an innate quality that could never be learned. For example, in *Olympian Ode* 9, lines 100-104, he says:

> That which is best by nature is best of all.
> Many men have been eager to win glory
> through skills that they have learned. But what
> God has not given is best passed over in silence.

In the *Olympian Ode* 10 (lines 20-21), Pindar speaks of the man who "is born to natural excellence" while, in *Olympian Ode* 13 (line 13), he says that "It is impossible to hide intrinsic character." Inborn excellence, the poet says in *Nemean Ode* 3 (lines 40-42), matters most of all. One who has merely learned a skill is on uncertain ground and will never be sure of success.

To reinforce the theme of innate human excellence, Pindar introduces a variety of images associating humanity's achievement with the gleaming light of the gods. Such images as the sheen of light on rippling water, the warm glow of gold, the flash of a thunderbolt, and the burst of a volcano are introduced by Pindar to provide a visual parallel to his notion of supreme athletic accomplishment. One of the most famous of these images appears at the beginning of *Olympian Ode* 1 (lines 1-6):

> Best of all things is water. But gold, like a fire
> blazing at night, is prized among mortal wealth.
> And so, my heart, if you would sing of games,
> know that there is no star in the empty heavens
> more vibrant than the sun, nor any contest more worthy
> of your song than Olympia.

In this passage, as occurs frequently in Pindar's poetry, the subject seems to shift from line to line. But one unifying theme—the glory of light—holds the poem together and serves to symbolize the human glory that the poet's patron has won through his victory.

A second theme that appears repeatedly in the *epinikia* is Pindar's effort to provide a true account of the gods' deeds. This true account is often set in contrast to the many false and barbaric legends that Pindar has heard. Unlike many of the Greek poets, Pindar views the gods as morally superior to human beings and incapable of the crimes and injustices that others attribute to them. In *Olympian Ode* 1 (lines 41-58), for instance, he rejects the traditional forms of the myth of Pelops, in which that hero was said to have been slaughtered by his own father and his flesh served up in a banquet to the gods. "I cannot attribute such gluttony to the blessed gods," Pindar concludes. "I am repelled." In *Olympian Ode* 9 (lines 35-49), Pindar rejects the ancient myths that depict Heracles as doing battle with the Olympian gods and says:

> Cast away, O lips, such stories from me!
> To insult the gods is mere sophistry—hateful to me!—
> and to boast beyond measure is akin to madness.
> Do not repeat such rumors. Let the gods be seen as
> free of all hostility and discord.

The central goal of a Pindaric poem is to present the true account both of the patron's victory and of the glory of the Olympian gods.

Jeffrey L. Buller

Bibliography:
Greengard, Carola. *The Structure of Pindar's Epinician Odes.* Amsterdam: Hakkert, 1980. Surveys Pindar's literary technique, focusing on organizational structure. Bibliographical references and an index.

Hubbard, Thomas Kent. *The Pindaric Mind: A Study of Logical Structure in Early Greek Poetry.* Leiden, The Netherlands: E. J. Brill, 1985. Provides criticism and interpretation of the *epinicia.* Broadens his discussion to explore the issue of thought and structure in archaic Greek poetry as a whole. Bibliography.

Lefkowitz, Mary R. *First-Person Fictions: Pindar's Poetic "I."* Oxford, England: Clarendon Press, 1991. A rhetorical analysis of the *epinicia,* focusing upon the poet's image of self and how that image is conveyed. Bibliographical references and an index.

Norwood, Gilbert. *Pindar*. Berkeley: University of California Press, 1945. Good general survey of Pindar's poetry. Includes material on Pindar's society, diction, symbolism, and meter. The bibliography contains a number of useful references.

Race, William H. *Pindar*. Boston: Twayne, 1986. A good starting place for study of Pindar's poetry. Contains a summary of all that is known about Pindar's life. Discusses Greek athletics and the legacy of Pindar.

Steiner, Deborah. *The Crown of Song: Metaphor in Pindar*. London: Duckworth, 1986. Studies the imagery in Pindar's poetry. Includes an analysis of metaphors concerning plants and animals and a treatment of Pindar's use of Greek legends. Discusses the athletic metaphor in the *epinicia*.

THE ODYSSEY

Type of work: Poetry
Author: Homer (c. ninth century B.C.E.)
Type of plot: Epic
Time of plot: Years immediately following the Trojan War
Locale: Greece and Mediterranean lands
First transcribed: c. 800 B.C.E. (English translation, 1616)

Principal characters:

ODYSSEUS, the wandering hero of the Trojan War
PENELOPE, his faithful wife
TELEMACHUS, his son

The Story:

Of the Greek heroes who survived the Trojan War only Odysseus had not returned home, for he had been detained by the god of the sea, Poseidon, because of an offense that he had committed against that god. At a conclave of the gods on Olympus, Zeus decreed that Odysseus should at last be allowed to return to his home and family in Ithaca. The goddess Athena was sent to Ithaca where, in disguise, she told Telemachus, Odysseus' son, that his father was alive. She advised the youth to rid his home of the great number of suitors suing for the hand of his mother, Penelope, and to go in search of his father. The suitors refused to leave the house of Odysseus, but they gave ready approval to the suggestion that Telemachus begin a quest for his father, since the venture would take him far from the shores of Ithaca.

The youth and his crew sailed to Pylos, where the prince questioned King Nestor concerning the whereabouts of Odysseus. Nestor, a wartime comrade of Odysseus, advised Telemachus to go to Lacedaemon, where King Menelaus could possibly give him the information he sought. At the palace of Menelaus and Helen, for whom the Trojan War had been waged, Telemachus learned that Odysseus was a prisoner of the nymph Calypso on her island of Ogygia in the Mediterranean Sea.

Zeus had in the meantime sent Hermes, the messenger of the gods, to Ogygia, with orders that Calypso was to release Odysseus. When the nymph reluctantly complied, the hero constructed a boat in four days and sailed away from his island prison. Poseidon, ever the enemy of Odysseus, sent great winds to destroy his boat and to wash him ashore on the coast of the Phaeacians. There he was found by Nausicaa, daughter of King Alcinoüs of the Phaeacians, when she went down to the river mouth with her handmaidens to wash linen. When the naked Odysseus awoke and saw Nausicaa and her maidens, he asked them where he was. Frightened at first by the stranger hiding behind the shrubbery, Nausicaa soon perceived that he was no vulgar person. She told him where he was, supplied him with clothing, and gave him food and drink. Then she conducted him to the palace of King Alcinoüs and Queen Arete. The royal pair welcomed him and promised to provide him with passage to his native land. At a great feast the minstrel Demodocus sang of the Trojan War and of the hardships suffered by the returning Greeks; Alcinoüs saw that the stranger wept during the singing. At the games that followed the banquet and songs, Odysseus was goaded by a young Phaeacian athlete into revealing his great strength. Later, at Alcinoüs' insistence, Odysseus told the following story of his wanderings since the war's end.

When Odysseus left Ilium he had been blown to Ismarus, the Cicones' city, which he and his men sacked. Then they were blown by an ill wind to the land of the Lotus-eaters, where

Odysseus had difficulty in getting his men to leave a slothful life of ease. Arriving in the land of the Cyclops, the one-eyed monsters who herded giant sheep, Odysseus and twelve of his men were caught by a Cyclops, Polyphemus, who ate the men one by one, saving Odysseus until last. That wily hero tricked the giant into a drunken stupor, however, and then blinded him with a sharpened pole and fled back to his ship. On an impulse, Odysseus disclosed his name to the blinded Polyphemus as he sailed away. Polyphemus called upon his father, Poseidon, to avenge him by hindering Odysseus' return to his homeland.

Odysseus' next landfall was Aeolia, where lived Aeolus, the god of the winds. Aeolus gave Odysseus a sealed bag containing all the contrary winds, so that they could not block his homeward voyage. However, the crew, thinking that the bag contained treasure, opened it, releasing all the winds, and the ship was blown back to Aeolia. When he learned what had happened, Aeolus was very angry that Odysseus' men had defied the gods by opening the bag of winds. He ordered them to leave Aeolia at once and denied them any winds for their homeward journey. They rowed for six days and then came to the land of the Laestrigonians, half-men, half-giants, who plucked members of the crew from the ship and devoured them. Most managed to escape, however, and came to Aeaea, the land of the enchantress Circe. Circe changed the crew members into swine, but with the aid of the herb Moly, which Hermes had given him, Odysseus withstood Circe's magic and forced her to change his crew back into men. Reconciled to the great leader, Circe told the hero that he could not get home without first consulting the shade of Teiresias, the blind Theban prophet. In the dark region of the Cimmerians Odysseus sacrificed sheep. Thereupon spirits from Hades appeared, among them the shade of Teiresias, who warned Odysseus to beware of danger in the land of the sun god.

On his homeward journey, Odysseus was forced to sail past the isle of the sirens, maidens who by their beautiful voices drew men to their death on treacherous rocks. By sealing the sailors' ears with wax and by having himself tied to the ship's mast, Odysseus passed the sirens safely. Next, he sailed into a narrow sea passage guarded by the monsters Scylla and Charybdis. Scylla's six horrible heads seized six of the crew, but the ship passed safely through the narrow channel. On the island of the sun god, Hyperion, the starving crew slaughtered some of Hyperion's sacred cows, despite a warning from their leader. The sun god thereupon caused the ship to be wrecked in a storm, all of the crew being lost but Odysseus, who was ultimately washed ashore on Ogygia, the island of Calypso.

When he had concluded his story, Odysseus received many gifts from Alcinoüs and Arete. They accompanied him to a ship they had provided for his voyage to Ithaca and bade him farewell, and the ship brought him at last to his own land.

Odysseus hid in a cave the vast treasure he had received from his Phaeacian hosts. The goddess Athena appeared to him and counseled him on a plan by which he could avenge himself on the rapacious suitors of his wife. The goddess, after changing Odysseus into an old beggar, went to Lacedaemon to arrange the return of Telemachus from the court of Menelaus and Helen.

Odysseus went to the rustic cottage of his old steward, Eumaeus, who welcomed the apparent stranger and offered him hospitality. The faithful servant disclosed the unpardonable behavior of Penelope's suitors and told how Odysseus' estate had been greatly reduced by their greed and love of luxury.

Meanwhile, Athena advised Telemachus to leave the ease of the Lacedaemon court and return home. On his arrival, he went first to the hut of Eumaeus to get information from the old steward. There, Athena having transformed Odysseus back to his heroic self, son and father were reunited. After pledging his son to secrecy, Odysseus described his plan of attack. Eumaeus and Odysseus, again disguised as a beggar, went to Odysseus' house where a meal was in progress. Reviled by the suitors, who had forgotten that hospitality to a stranger was a practice demanded by Zeus himself, Odysseus bided his time, even when arrogant Antinous threw a stool that struck Odysseus on the shoulder.

Odysseus ordered Telemachus to lock up all weapons except a few that were to be used by his own party; the women servants were to be locked in their quarters. Penelope questioned Odysseus concerning his identity but Odysseus deceived her with a fantastic tale. When Eurycleia, ancient servant of the king, washed the beggar's feet and legs, she recognized her master by a scar above the knee, but she did not disclose his identity.

Penelope planned an impossible feat of strength to free herself of her suitors. One day, showing the famous bow of Eurytus, and twelve battle-axes, she said that she would give her hand to the suitor who could shoot an arrow through all twelve ax handles. Telemachus, to prove his worth, attempted, but failed to string the bow. One after another the suitors failed even to string the bow. Finally Odysseus asked if an old beggar might attempt the feat. The suitors laughed scornfully at his presumption. Then Odysseus strung the bow with ease and shot an arrow through the twelve ax hafts. Throwing aside his disguise, he next shot Antinous in the throat. There ensued a furious battle, in which all the suitors were killed by Odysseus and his small party. Twelve women servants who had been sympathetic to the suitors were hanged in the courtyard.When Penelope, in her room, heard what the purported beggar had done, husband and wife were happily reunited.

Critical Evaluation:

The *Odyssey* is undoubtedly the most popular epic of Western culture. Its chief character, Odysseus, or Ulysses, has inspired more literary works than any other legendary hero. From Homer to James Joyce, Nikos Kazantzakis, and after, Odysseus has been a central figure in European literature, and one who has undergone many sea changes. The *Odyssey* has the ingredients of a perennial best-seller: pathos, sexuality, violence; a strong, resourceful hero with a firm purpose braving many dangers and hardships to accomplish it; a romantic account of exploits in strange places; a more or less realistic approach to characterization; a soundly constructed plot; and an author with a gift for description. It is, in fact, one of the greatest adventure stories of all time.

Of the poet, or poets, who wrote the poem there is only conjecture. Tradition says that Homer lived in Chios or Smyrna in Ionia, a part of Asia Minor, and it is probable that he, or whoever composed this epic, did so late in the ninth century B.C.E. The *Odyssey* was originally sung or recited, as is evident from its style and content, and it was based on legend, folk tale, and free invention, forming part of a minstrel tradition similar to that of the Middle Ages.

The style of the poem is visual, explanatory, repetitive, and stately. Like the *Iliad* (c. 800 B.C.E.), the work uses extended similes and repeated epithets, phrases, and sentences. Homer, whoever he was, wanted his audience to visualize and understand everything that happened. He grasped the principles of rhetoric, and he composed in a plain, direct fashion that possesses great eloquence and dignity.

Homer had also mastered certain crucial problems of organization. When the audience knows the story that is going to be told, as Homer's did, it becomes necessary to introduce diversions from the main action, to delay the climax as long as possible. In this manner the leisurely development of the plot stirs anticipation and gives the climactic scene redoubled force. Yet the intervening action must have interest on its own and must have a bearing on the main action. The *Odyssey* shows remarkable ability on all of these counts.

If the subject of the *Iliad* was the wrath of Achilles during the Trojan War, the subject of the

Odyssey is the homecoming of Odysseus ten years after the Trojan War ended. The immediate action of the poem takes place in no more than a few weeks, dramatizing the very end of Odysseus' wanderings and his restoration of order at home. Yet Homer allows Odysseus to narrate his earlier adventures, from the sack of Troy to his confinement on Calypso's island, which extends the magnitude of the poem. Moreover, through Nestor and Menelaus, Homer places Odysseus' homecoming into the wider context of the returns of all the major heroes from Troy, most of which were disastrous. Thus the epic has a sweeping scope condensed into a very brief span of time.

The Telemachy (the first four books dealing with the travels and education of Telemachus) sets the stage for Odysseus' return. The gods make the arrangements, and then the audience is shown the terrible situation in Odysseus' palace, where the suitors are devouring Odysseus' substance, bullying his son, and growing impatient with Penelope. They intend to kill Odysseus if he should ever return, and they arrange an ambush to kill Telemachus. Their radical abuse of hospitality is contrasted with the excellent relations between guest and host when Telemachus goes to visit Nestor and then Menelaus. In an epic whose theme is travel, the auxiliary theme must be the nature of hospitality. In Odysseus' journeyings, his best host is Alcinoüs and his worst is the savage Cyclops.

At first Telemachus is a disheartened young man trying to be hospitable in a house where it is impossible. Then Athena, as Mentes, puts pluck into him with the idea that his long-lost father is alive and detained. Telemachus calls an assembly to state his grievances and then undertakes a hazardous trip to learn of his father. He plainly has the makings of a hero, and he proves himself his father's true son when he helps slay the rapacious suitors, after displaying some tact and cunning of his own.

Odysseus is the model of the worldly, well-traveled, persevering man who overcomes obstacles. He has courage, stamina, and power, but his real strength lies in his brain, which is shrewd, quick-witted, diplomatic, and resourceful. He is also eloquent and persuasive. He needs all of these qualities to survive and make his way home. His mettle is tested at every turn, either by dangers or temptations to remain in a place. Calypso even offers him immortality, but he is steadfast in his desire to return home. Athena may intercede for him with Zeus and aid and advise him, yet the will to return and the valor in doing so are those of Odysseus alone. The one thing Odysseus found truly unbearable in his travels was stasis, being stranded for seven years, even though he had an amorous nymph for company.

However, a good deal of the tale is taken up with Odysseus' preparations, once he has arrived at Ithaca, for killing the suitors. The point is that the suitors are the most formidable enemy Odysseus has encountered, since they number well over a hundred and only he and Telemachus are there to face them. It is here that his true strategic and tactical cunning are truly needed; the previous wanderings were merely a long prologue to this climactic exploit. Coming after nine chapters in which nothing much happens, the killing of the suitors and their henchmen and maids is stunning in its exulting, deliberate violence. The house of Odysseus is at last purged of its predators, and the emotions of the audience are restored to an equilibrium.

"Critical Evaluation" by James Weigel, Jr.

Bibliography:
Camps, W. A. *An Introduction to Homer.* Oxford, England: Clarendon Press, 1980. Excellent source for beginners. Provides an introductory essay that compares *The Odyssey* with the *Iliad.* Includes extensive notes and appendices to each work.

Gaunt, D. M., trans. *Surge and Thunder: Critical Reading in Homer's "Odyssey."* London: Oxford University Press, 1971. Designed for general readers. Gaunt translates selected passages, explaining fine points of language and meaning that are lost in translation. Text includes explication, analysis, and discussion. Has a guide to pronunciation, a list of Greek proper nouns, and an index of literary topics.

Lamberton, Robert. *Homer the Theologian: Neoplatonist Allegorical Reading and the Growth of the Epic Tradition.* Berkeley: University of California Press, 1986. Addresses *The Odyssey* as allegory, presenting a commentary and summary of the work. Supports points with material from Greek scholars. General researchers will find particularly interesting its focus on Homer as theologian. Well-indexed, well-documented, scholarly.

Mason, H. A. *To Homer Through Pope: An Introduction to Homer's "Iliad" and Pope's Translation.* London: Chatto and Windus, 1972. Mason devotes last chapter to *The Odyssey* and major translators of that work. Not recommended for beginning researchers.

Taylor, Charles H., Jr. *Essays on the "Odyssey": Selected Modern Criticism.* Bloomington: Indiana University Press, 1963. Seven selected essays, arranged chronologically. Taylor contends that interest grew in the "emblematic or symbolic implications" at work in events and images in the poem. Extensive notes.

THE ODYSSEY
A Modern Sequel

Type of work: Poetry
Author: Nikos Kazantzakis (1883-1957)
Type of plot: Epic
Time of plot: Antiquity
Locale: Ithaca, Sparta, Crete, Egypt, Africa, and Antarctica
First published: Odysseia, 1938 (English translation, 1958)

Principal character:
ODYSSEUS, king of Ithaca

The Story:
Odysseus, king of Ithaca, subdued a revolt against him soon after his return from the Trojan War. Growing discontent with the routine obligations of lawgiver, husband, and father, he built a ship, formed a crew of similarly individualistic characters, and began another journey—of no return. In Sparta, Odysseus tempted Helen to abandon, once again, her life of sumptuous boredom and accompany him. The shipmates next anchored in Crete, where, outraged by the disparity of wealth between the hedonistic court elite, presided over by the indolent King Idomeneus, and the impoverished kingdom, Odysseus led an uprising of slaves and invading barbarians. Helen became the lover of one of the Dorian invaders and chose to remain in Crete, to rear her child—a symbol for Kazantzakis of the golden age of Greece yet to come—when the conquering shipmates sailed on.

In contrast to the triumphant overthrow of the Cretan court, Odysseus and his crew next joined forces with revolutionaries and barbarians in Egypt to fight against a much larger and stronger army, at whose hands they met bloody defeat, barely surviving. They became prisoners in an Egyptian dungeon. Odysseus eventually managed to terrify the superstitious Pharaoh, who banished him into the desert. Having observed the corruption and injustice of various civilizations, Odysseus determined to create a type of utopian society for the ranks of the lawless and dejected who had followed him into exile, and for his remaining crew. Enduring a slow, painful desert flight, and skirmishes with fierce African tribes, Odysseus formulated plans for an ideal city.

At the moment he concluded the exodus to the sea, Odysseus withdrew from his followers to fast and meditate, commencing an inward, spiritual journey from which he emerged with a new concept of God—the epitome of the evolutionary force present in all life. Great celebrations set to mark the foundation of the city were halted by the sudden occurrence of a devastating earthquake. Odysseus' efforts to create an ideal society were laid waste and, for the first time, he found himself without companionship.

Repudiating his long attempts to clarify a concept of God, Odysseus substituted the creative power of the human mind as the object of his intense religious devotion, and invoked an image of death—anthropomorphized as his identical twin—for his constant companion. Odysseus pressed his journey on toward the southern tip of Africa, as word of Odysseus the ascetic spread across the land.

Before leaving on a last sea voyage, Odysseus met prominent religious figures, unique thinkers, and literary characters, such as Christ, Buddha, Faust, and Don Quixote. Odysseus spent his final moments in human company in an eskimo village (where he was hailed as a god). Although for the humble eskimos hope meant merely clinging to the will to survive until spring, as spring arrived, it brought death and wholesale destruction. As Odysseus paddled away from the village, he watched as once again the sudden, inescapable churning of the earth decimated the society that had nurtured him.

Once alone on the frozen seas, Odysseus paddled toward the unsetting sun, and bid a mystical farewell to life. When his skiff rammed an iceberg, he leapt onto its frigid surface, and hung there. As his life slipped away, Odysseus thanked his five senses for the earthly aid they had provided him, and, in his final moment of life, he shaped a call to his departed comrades, who, both the living and the dead, appeared to join him once again: This moment became a broad and joyful affirmation.

Critical Evaluation:

Nikos Kazantzakis' prolific career included the publication of about thirteen novels, for which he is best known, about twenty dramas, most of them in poetic form, and three philosophical studies, one on Friedrich Nietzsche, one on Henri Bergson, and one on his own vision of life. In addition to these, Kazantzakis published travel books on Spain, Greece, England, China, Japan, Israel, and Russia, hundreds of articles for newspapers and encyclopedias, dozens of books for the public schools of Greece, and several translations, including Homer's *Iliad* (c. 800 B.C.E.) and *Odyssey* (c. 800 B.C.E.), Dante Alighieri's *The Divine Comedy* (c. 1320), Nietzsche's *The Birth of Tragedy* (1872), Bergson's *On Laughter* (1900), and Darwin's *On the Origin of Species by Means of Natural Selection* (1859). Kazantzakis also published two books of poetry. It was *The Odyssey: A Modern Sequel* that Kazantzakis considered his masterpiece, or, in Morton P. Levitt's phrase, "the central document of his life."

The Odyssey: A Modern Sequel is, according to Levitt, "one of the great encyclopedic works of our time," embracing the major themes of Western civilization. It consists of twenty-four books or cantos (one for every letter of the Greek alphabet), comprising 33,333 lines—almost three times the length of the original *Odyssey*. These are in an extremely unusual seventeen-syllable unrhymed iambic measure of eight beats. The poem employs a form of simplified spelling and syntax, eschews the accentual marks that have been part of the Greek language since Byzantine times, and relies upon an idiomatic diction that, at the time of its publication in December, 1938, was more familiar to the shepherds and fishermen throughout the islands and villages of Greece than to Greek scholars. Greatly influenced by the author's work on language reform as it is, *The Odyssey: A Modern Sequel* is by no means an academic work. Pandelis Prevelakis, Kazantzakis' first biographer, said of it, "If read with the attention it deserves, it is capable of changing the reader's soul."

As much as it is a journey through exotic lands and moments of intense experience, *The Odyssey: A Modern Sequel* is a passionate exploration of ideas, with Odysseus threading a path through philosophies of life, adapting and discarding, by turn, sensuality, political engagement, and ascetic detachment. Each new phase provides him with a new perspective from which he can examine life, and, given new insights, re-create himself accordingly. Although each successive phase of his journey rises out of the destruction of the previous one, the whole of Odysseus' journey constitutes a continuum: a single evolutionary flight toward freedom.

Odysseus flees Ithaca to escape the harsh restrictions of a meaningless existence, going off in what Peter Bien describes as "the attempt to gain happiness through sensual gratification." Odysseus becomes an aesthete. Through successive encounters with social injustice, in Sparta, Crete, and Egypt, Odysseus gains an understanding that the aesthetic attitude can lead only to surfeit and indifference, perpetuating misery and human suffering. Recoiling from the isolation of the ego, Odysseus reaches toward an ethical theory that is responsive to a humanitarian concern for the future of the human race. This culminates in his attempt to postulate the Ideal City.

The sudden, unimaginable desolation of the Ideal City plunges Odysseus into despair, from which he emerges as an ascetic. In essence, Kazantzakis exposes the limitations of an ethical self as one dependent upon false polarities of being. In his new state, Odysseus views the inevitable destruction of every human endeavor not as a tragic fact or fate, but as an incentive toward spiritual growth. The struggle between good and evil, or life and death, becomes apparent as a form of disguised collaboration; and the specter of death becomes a tool by which Odysseus may sharpen his perception of the meaning of life—thus, paradoxically, a cause for celebration. Of Odysseus' ascetic insight, translator Kimon Friar has written, "Odysseus . . . sees that through his mind and senses now all creative impulse flows and plunges, laughing, down the abyss: an image of a deathless flowing stream."

Already having forsaken the prison of the self, with this transformation Odysseus achieves an even greater freedom from the loneliness and human estrangement of differentiation. His fundamental mode for organizing life becomes contemplative rather than experiential: Life becomes spectacle for him. In his conversations with other ascetics and unique thinkers—such as Prince Motherth, a type of the Buddha; Captain Sole, a type of Don Quixote; the Hermit, a type of Faust; and the black fisher-lad, a type of Christ—Odysseus reaffirms the oneness of nature, of process, of the woven unity of life, yet honors its particulars. While recognizing the unity of life, Odysseus also accepts the unenlightened aspects of his humanity that constitute part of his existence. In his dialogue with the black fisher-lad, he exclaims that, although the fisher-lad might love the human soul, he, Odysseus, loved the flesh, the stench, and even the death of the individual.

With his death on the iceberg, Odysseus recognizes and embraces his final absolute freedom—escape from the broad concept of ascetic detachment. Odysseus gains freedom from freedom itself.

Although Kazantzakis sought, through *The Odyssey: A Modern Sequel,* to revolutionize the Greek language, his modern epic rose to popularity in the English translation of Kimon Friar. Having been chosen by Kazantzakis for the task, Friar left an academic career and devoted himself to it for four years. Although he did not complete his translation until a year after Kazantzakis' death, the poet read the entire manuscript and approved, according to Friar, "even those few sections with which he did not agree," and declared it to be "not a translation but a recreation" of his poem. James Lea has written that "we will never be able to read this *Odyssey* without thinking also of Friar." It was Friar who completed the title of the poem, by adding *A Modern Sequel* to what Kazantzakis had simply written as *The Odyssey.*

Michael Scott Joseph

Bibliography:
Bien, Peter. *Kazantzakis: Politics of the Spirit.* Princeton, N.J.: Princeton University Press, 1989. First of a two-part study, spanning the start of Kazantzakis' career in 1906 to the publication of *The Odyssey: A Modern Sequel* in 1938.
Kazantzakis, Nikos. *The Odyssey: A Modern Sequel.* Translated by Kimon Friar. New York: Simon & Schuster, 1958. Friar was viewed by Kazantzakis as a collaborator more than a translator, and he bears a major share of the responsibility for the success of *The Odyssey:*

A Modern Sequel in the English-speaking world. Friar's introduction and synopsis are among the clearest and most meaningful available.

Lea, James F. *Kazantzakis: The Politics of Salvation*. Foreword by Helen Kazantzakis. University: University of Alabama Press, 1979. Examines Kazantzakis in the context of his age and culture, provides a general explication of the evolution of Kazantzakis' political thought and his approach to history.

Levitt, Morton. *The Cretan Glance: The World and Art of Nikos Kazantzakis*. Columbus: Ohio State University Press, 1980. Deals with the work of the last two phases of Kazantzakis' long and varied career—with his great epic poem, *The Odyssey: A Modern Sequel*, and with the novels that Kazantzakis wrote afterward.

Prevelakis, Pandelis. *Nikos Kazantzakis and His Odyssey: A Study of the Poet and the Poem*. New York: Simon & Schuster, 1961. First biographical study of Kazantzakis by his longtime friend, which integrates the motifs of *The Odyssey: A Modern Sequel* with the events of the poet's life.

OEDIPUS AT COLONUS

Type of work: Drama
Author: Sophocles (c. 496-406 B.C.E.)
Type of plot: Tragedy
Time of plot: Antiquity
Locale: Colonus, near Athens
First performed: Oidipous epi Kolōnōi, 401 B.C.E. (English translation, 1729)

> *Principal characters:*
> OEDIPUS, the former king of Thebes
> ANTIGONE and
> ISMENE, his daughters
> THESEUS, the king of Athens
> CREON, the former regent of Thebes
> POLYNICES, Oedipus' older son
> ELDERS OF COLONUS

The Story:

Many years had passed since King Oedipus had discovered to his horror that he had murdered his father and married his mother, with whom he had had children. After having blinded himself and given up his royal authority in Thebes, he had been cared for by his faithful daughters, Antigone and Ismene. When internal strife broke out in Thebes, Oedipus was believed to be the cause of the trouble because of the curse the gods had put upon his family, and he was banished from the city.

He and Antigone wandered far. At last, they came to an olive grove at Colonus, a sacred place near Athens. A man of Colonus warned the strangers that the grove in which they had stopped was sacred to the Furies. Oedipus, having known supreme mortal suffering, replied that he knew the Furies well and that he would remain in the grove. Disturbed, the man of Colonus stated that he would have to report this irregularity to Theseus, the king of Athens and overlord of Colonus. Oedipus replied that he would welcome the king, for he had important words to say to Theseus.

The old men of Colonus, who feared the Furies, were upset at Oedipus' calm in the grove. They inquired, from a discreet distance, the identity of the blind stranger and were horror-stricken to learn that he was the infamous king of Thebes whose dreadful story the whole civilized world had heard. Fearing the terrible wrath of the gods, they ordered him and his daughter to be off. Oedipus was able to quiet them, however, by explaining that he had suffered greatly, despite never having consciously sinned against the gods. To the mystification of the old men, he hinted that he had strange powers and would bring good fortune to the land that provided a place of refuge for him.

Ismene, another daughter of Oedipus, arrived in the grove at Colonus after searching throughout all Greece for her father and sister. She brought Oedipus the unhappy news that his two sons, Polynices and Eteocles had fought for supremacy in Thebes. When Polynices was defeated, he had been banished to Argos, where he was now gathering a host to return to Thebes. Ismene also informed her father that the Oracle of Delphi had prophesied that Thebes was doomed to terrible misfortune if Oedipus should be buried anywhere but in that city. With this prophecy in mind, the Thebans hoped that Oedipus would return from his exile. Oedipus, however, mindful of his banishment and of the faithlessness of his sons, declared that he would remain in Colonus and that the land of Attica would be his tomb.

Informed of the arrival of Oedipus, Theseus went to Colonus and welcomed the pitiful old man and his daughters. Oedipus offered his body to Attica and Colonus and prophesied that it would bring good fortune to Attica if he were buried in its soil. Theseus, who had himself known exile, was sympathetic; he promised to care for Oedipus and to protect the old man from seizure by any Theban.

After Theseus had returned to Athens, Creon, the former regent of Thebes, came to the grove with his followers. Deceitfully, he urged Oedipus to return with him to Thebes, but Oedipus was aware of Creon's motives and reviled him for his duplicity. Oedipus cursed Thebes for the way it had disavowed him in his great suffering. Creon's men, at the command of their leader, seized Antigone and Ismene and carried them away. Blind Oedipus and the aged men of Colonus were too old and feeble to prevent their capture. By the time Creon attempted to seize Oedipus, however, the alarm had been sounded, and Theseus returned to confront Creon and to order the return of Antigone and Ismene. Asked to explain his actions, Creon weakly argued that he had come to rid Attica of the taint that Oedipus surely would place on the kingdom if its citizens offered shelter to any of the cursed progeny of Cadmus. Theseus checked Creon and rescued Oedipus' two daughters.

Polynices, Oedipus' older son, had been searching for his father. Hoping to see the prophecy of the Delphic Oracle fulfilled, but also for his own selfish ends, the young man came to the olive grove and with professions of repentance and filial devotion begged Oedipus to return with him to Argos. Oedipus knew that his son wished only to ensure the success of his expedition against his brother Eteocles, who was in authority at Thebes. He heard Polynices out in silence; then he denounced both sons as traitors. Vehemently, he prophesied that Polynices and Eteocles would die by violence. Polynices, impressed by his father's words but still ambitious and arrogant, ignored Antigone's pleas to spare their native city. He departed, convinced that he was going to certain death.

Three rolls of thunder presaged the impending death of old Oedipus. Impatiently, but at the same time with a certain air of resignation, Oedipus called for Theseus. Guiding the king and his two daughters to a nearby grotto, he predicted that as long as his burial place remained a secret known only to Theseus and his male descendants, Attica would successfully resist all invasions. After begging Theseus to protect Antigone and Ismene, he dismissed his daughters. Only Theseus was with Oedipus when he suddenly disappeared. Antigone and Ismene tried to return to their father's tomb, but Theseus, true to his solemn promise, prevented them. He did, however, second them in their desire to return to Thebes, that they might prevent the dreadful bloodshed that threatened their native city because of Polynices and Eteocles.

Critical Evaluation:

Written when Sophocles was about ninety and approaching death, *Oedipus at Colonus* is the dramatist's valedictory to the stage, to Athens, and to life. In its transcendent spiritual power it is reminiscent of William Shakespeare's last great play, *The Tempest* (1611). It was probably inevitable that the great Athenian patriot Sophocles should have written a play based on the story of the legendary past of his birthplace. Indeed, two of the high points of this drama are magnificent odes in praise of Colonus and Attica. *Oedipus at Colonus* represents the culmination of Sophocles' handling of the Cadmean legend, which he had treated earlier in *Antigone* (441 B.C.E.) and *Oedipus Tyrannus* (c. 429 B.C.E.). It is at the same time his last, luminous affirmation of human dignity in the face of an incomprehensible universe.

The theme of the suppliants, or refugees, pleading for protection, was common in Greek tragedy. Both Aeschylus and Euripides had written patriotic dramas on this subject. The plot formula was simple: People threatened with capture sue a powerful but democratic king for aid and receive it. *Oedipus at Colonus* is remarkably similar in its patriotic content to Euripides' *The Suppliants* (423 B.C.E.). Both plays treat the Theban myth and feature an aspect of the War of Seven Against Thebes; both conform to the same plot formula; and both present Theseus and Athens in a heroic light as the defenders of the weak from tyrannical force. When Sophocles wrote his play, Athens was in the final throes of the disastrous Peloponnesian War, which would result in Athens' defeat at the hands of Sparta. In its arrogance of power, the city had become rapacious and morally degenerated. Sophocles' purpose in writing this play, at least from a civic viewpoint, was to remind the Athenians of their legendary respect for the rights of the helpless, a respect that up to that point had kept them safe from invaders. With the Greek tragedians, civic welfare depended directly on moral rectitude. By defending Oedipus and his daughters, Theseus ensures the safety of Athens for generations. Sophocles also shows Theseus acting disinterestedly, however, out of concern for the suppliants and thus as a model ruler. The playwright wished to inspire his fellow citizens with the virtues they had cast aside: piety, courage in a good cause, manliness.

Sophocles' patriotism went beyond state morality. In his two beautiful choral odes on Colonus and Attica there is an intense, wistful passion for the land itself, for the life it supported, and for the people's activities there. Sophocles believed that there was something holy about the place. It is not accidental that the entire action of this play takes place before a sacred grove, for he wanted his audience to feel the presence of divinity. The goddesses here were the hideous and awesome Furies, who judge and punish evildoers. As agents of divine justice they preside invisibly over all that occurs in *Oedipus at Colonus*.

The center of the play, however, is not Theseus or Athens but a frightful beggar who has suffered terribly in his long life—the blind Oedipus. Although he is reconciled to exile, beggary, and blindness, he remains proud and hot-tempered, and he cannot forgive Creon and Polynices, the two men who inflicted exile and penury on him. Oedipus has paid in full for the infamous deeds he committed in ignorance. He rightly insists upon his innocence, not of killing his father, marrying his mother, and having children by her, but of having done these things knowingly. Fate led him into that trap, and the Furies punished him for it. His nobility consists in bearing his suffering with dignity. Even if in his blindness he is the weakest and most pitiful of men, and though he must be led around by a young girl, there is true manliness in him.

By contrast, Creon is a man who lives by expediency, using force when persuasion fails but tamely submitting when Theseus gains the upper hand. In pursuing a reasonable goal, namely the defense of Thebes, he is willing to use any means, including kidnapping Oedipus' only supports, his two daughters. His ruthlessness is distasteful, but even more unpleasant is Polynices' whining plea for Oedipus' aid in attacking Thebes. It stems from selfish ambition rather than concern for his poor father. The curses Oedipus levels at Creon, Polynices, Eteocles, and Thebes are justified and apt. For dishonoring a helpless, blind man they deserve the calamity they have incurred.

In this play, Oedipus is a man preparing for death, as Sophocles must have been as he wrote it. Despite his hard destiny, and despite his power to curse men who have shamed him, Oedipus carries in his breast a profound blessing. In the end, the very Furies who hounded him bestow upon him a tremendous potency in death, the power to protect Athens just as Athens had protected him. The ultimate reason for his suffering remains obscure, but the manhood with which he faced it was the sole blessing he himself received, and that was all he needed. His mysterious and fearsome apotheosis amid flashes of lightning and earth tremors is the tribute the gods pay to Oedipus' supreme courage. Sophocles here offered his last and most sublime testament to a human being's ability to take unmerited pain and transform it into glory.

"Critical Evaluation" by James Weigel, Jr.

Bibliography:
Kirkwood, Gordon MacDonald. *A Study of Sophoclean Drama*. 1958. Reprint. New York: Johnson Reprint, 1967. An examination and analysis of the methods and structures of dramatic composition used by Sophocles. Compares his plays to consider the characters, irony, illustrative forms, and use of diction and oracles in each. Excellent coverage of *Oedipus at Colonus*.

Scodel, Ruth. *Sophocles*. Boston: Twayne, 1984. Includes a synopsis and discussion of the plot of *Oedipus at Colonus*, as well as an analysis of Oedipus and the characters that oppose him. Also provides information on Sophocles' other plays and a chronology of his life, a bibliography, and an index.

Seale, David. *Vision and Stagecraft in Sophocles*. Chicago, Ill.: University of Chicago Press, 1982. Distinguishes Sophocles from other playwrights of his time and demonstrates his influence on later ones. An excellent study for nonspecialists, students, and classicists. Considers the theatrical technicalities in all of Sophocles' plays and contains an extended section on *Oedipus at Colonus*.

Segal, Charles. *Tragedy and Civilization: An Interpretation of Sophocles*. Cambridge, Mass.: Harvard University Press, 1981. Discusses Sophocles' seven plays, including *Oedipus at Colonus*, which is compared to the other works. Also provides background on the figure of Oedipus.

Woodard, Thomas, ed. *Sophocles: A Collection of Critical Essays*. Englewood Cliffs, N.J.: Prentice-Hall, 1966. A fine collection of essays, including writings by Friedrich Nietzsche, Sigmund Freud, and Virginia Woolf. Describes *Oedipus at Colonus* as a play from Sophocles' later years and draws connections between it and his other plays.

OEDIPUS TYRANNUS

Type of work: Drama
Author: Sophocles (c. 496-406 B.C.E.)
Type of plot: Tragedy
Time of plot: Antiquity
Locale: Thebes
First performed: Oidipous Tyrannos, c. 429 B.C.E. (English translation, 1729)

Principal characters:
OEDIPUS, the king of Thebes
JOCASTA, his wife
CREON, Jocasta's brother
TEIRESIAS, a seer

The Story:

When Thebes was struck by a plague, the people asked King Oedipus to deliver them from its horrors. Creon, the brother of Jocasta, Oedipus' queen, returned from the oracle of Apollo and disclosed that the plague was punishment for the murder of King Laius, Oedipus' immediate predecessor, to whom Jocasta had been married. Creon further disclosed that the citizens of Thebes needed to discover and punish the murderer before the plague would be lifted. The people mourned their dead, and Oedipus advised them, in their own interest, to search out and apprehend the murderer of Laius.

Asked to help find the murderer, Teiresias, the ancient, blind seer of Thebes, told Oedipus that it would be better for all if he did not tell what he knew. He said that coming events would reveal themselves. Oedipus raged at the seer's reluctance to tell the secret until he goaded the old man to reveal that Oedipus was the one responsible for Thebes's afflictions because he was the murderer, and that he was living in intimacy with his nearest kin. Oedipus accused the old man of being in league with Creon, whom he suspected of plotting against his throne, but Teiresias answered that Oedipus would be ashamed and horrified when he learned the truth about his true parentage. Oedipus defied the seer, saying he would welcome the truth as long as it freed his kingdom from the plague. Oedipus threatened Creon with death, but Jocasta and the people advised him against doing violence on the strength of rumor or momentary passion. Oedipus yielded, but he did banish Creon.

Jocasta, grieved by the enmity between her brother and Oedipus, told her husband that an oracle had informed King Laius that he would be killed by his own child, the offspring of Laius and Jocasta. Jocasta assured Oedipus that this could not have happened because the child was abandoned on a deserted mountainside soon after birth. When Oedipus heard further that Laius had been killed by robbers at the meeting place of three roads and that the three roads met in Phocis, he was deeply disturbed and began to suspect that he was, after all, the murderer. He hesitated to reveal his suspicion, but he became more and more convinced of his own guilt.

Oedipus told Jocasta that he had believed himself to be the son of Polybus of Corinth and Merope until a drunken man had on one occasion announced that the young Oedipus was not really Polybus' son. Disturbed, Oedipus had consulted the oracle of Apollo, who had told him he would sire children by his own mother and that he would kill his own father. After he left Corinth, at a meeting place of three roads, Oedipus had been offended by a man in a chariot. He killed the man and all of his servants but one. From there he had gone on to Thebes, where he had become the new king by answering the riddle of the Sphinx. The riddle had asked what went on all fours before noon, on two legs at noon, and on three legs after noon. Oedipus had answered, correctly, that human beings walk on all fours as an infant, on two legs in their prime, and with the aid of a stick in their old age. With the kingship, he also won the hand of Jocasta, King Laius' queen.

Oedipus summoned the servant who had reported King Laius' death, but he awaited his arrival fearfully. Jocasta assured her husband that the entire matter was of no great consequence, that surely the prophecies of the oracles would not come true.

A messenger from Corinth announced that King Polybus was dead and that Oedipus was his successor. Polybus had died of natural causes, so Oedipus and Jocasta were relieved for the time being. Oedipus told the messenger he would not go to Corinth for fear of siring children by his mother, Merope.

The messenger went on to reveal that Oedipus was not the son of Polybus and Merope but a foundling whom the messenger, at that time a shepherd, had taken to Polybus. The messenger related how he had received the baby from another shepherd, who was a servant of the house of King Laius. At that point Jocasta realized the dreadful truth. She did not wish to see the old servant who had been summoned, but Oedipus desired clarity regardless of the cost. He again called for the servant. When the servant appeared, the messenger recognized him as the herdsman from whom he had received the child years earlier. The old servant confessed that King Laius had ordered him to destroy the boy but that out of pity he had given the infant to the Corinthian to raise as his foster son.

Oedipus, now all but mad from the realization of what he had done, entered the palace and discovered that Jocasta had hanged herself by her hair. He removed her golden brooches and with them put out his eyes so that he would not be able to see the results of the horrible prophecy. Then, blind and bloody and miserable, he displayed himself to the Thebans and announced himself as the murderer of their king and the defiler of his own mother's bed. He cursed the herdsman who had saved him from death years before.

Creon, having returned, ordered the attendants to lead Oedipus back into the palace. Oedipus asked Creon to have him conducted out of Thebes where no man would ever see him again. He also asked Creon to give Jocasta a proper burial and to see that the sons and daughters of the unnatural marriage should be cared for and not be allowed to live poor and unmarried because of the shame attached to their parentage. Creon led the wretched Oedipus away to his exile of blindness and torment.

Critical Evaluation:

Aristotle considered *Oedipus Tyrannus* the supreme example of tragic drama and modeled his theory of tragedy on it. He mentions the play no less than eleven times in his *Poetics* (334-323 B.C.E.). Sigmund Freud in the twentieth century used the story to name the rivalry of male children with their fathers for the affection of their mothers, and Jean Cocteau adapted the tale to the modern stage in *The Infernal Machine* (1934). Yet no matter what changes the Oedipus myth has undergone in two and a half millennia, the finest expression of it remains this tragedy by Sophocles.

Brilliantly conceived and written, *Oedipus Tyrannus* is a drama of self-discovery. Sophocles achieves an amazing compression and force by limiting the dramatic action to the day on which Oedipus learns the true nature of his birth and destiny. The fact that the audience knows the dark secret that Oedipus has unwittingly slain his true father and married his mother, does nothing to destroy the suspense. Oedipus' search for the truth has all the tautness of a detective tale, and yet because audiences already know the truth they are aware of all the ironies in which Oedipus is enmeshed. That knowledge enables them to fear the final revelation at the same time that they pity the man whose past is gradually and relentlessly uncovered to him.

The plot is thoroughly integrated with the characterization of Oedipus, for it is he who impels the action forward in his concern for Thebes, his personal rashness, and his ignorance of his past. His flaws are a hot temper and impulsiveness, but without those traits his heroic course of self-discovery would never have occurred.

Fate for Sophocles is not something essentially external to human beings but something at once inherent in them and transcendent. Oracles and prophets in this play may show the will of the gods and indicate future events, but it is the individual who gives substance to the prophecies. Moreover, there is an element of freedom granted to human beings, an ability to choose, where the compulsions of character and the compulsions of the gods are powerless. It is in the way individuals meet the necessities of their destiny that freedom lies. They can succumb to fate, pleading extenuating circumstances, or they can shoulder the full responsibility for what they do. In the first case they are merely pitiful, but in the second they are tragic and take on a greatness of soul that nothing can conquer.

A crucial point in the play is that Oedipus is entirely unaware that he has killed his father and wedded his mother. He himself is the cause of the plague on Thebes, and in vowing to find the murderer of Laius and exile him he unconsciously pronounces judgment on himself. Oedipus, the king and the hero who saved Thebes from the Sphinx, believes in his own innocence. He is angry and incredulous when the provoked Teiresias accuses him of the crime, so he naturally jumps to the conclusion that Teiresias and Creon are conspirators against him. As plausible as that explanation may be, Oedipus maintains it with irrational vehemence, not even bothering to investigate it before he decides to have Creon put to death. Every act of his is performed rashly: his hot-tempered killing of Laius, his investigation of the murder, his violent blinding of himself, and his insistence on being exiled. He is a man of great pride and passion who is intent on serving Thebes, but he does not have tragic stature until the evidence of his guilt begins to accumulate.

Ironically, his past is revealed to him by people who wish him well and who want to reassure him. Each time a character tries to comfort him with information, the information serves to damn him more thoroughly. Jocasta, in proving how false oracles can be, first suggests to him that he unknowingly really did kill Laius, thus corroborating the oracles. The messenger from Corinth in reassuring Oedipus about his parentage brings his true parentage into question, but he says enough to convince Jocasta that Oedipus is her son. It is at this point, when he determines to complete the search for the truth, knowing that he killed Laius and knowing that the result of his investigation may be utterly damnable, that Oedipus' true heroism starts to emerge. His rashness at this point is no longer a liability but becomes part of his integrity.

Having learned the full truth of his dark destiny, his last act as king is to blind himself over the dead body of Jocasta, his wife and mother. It is a terrible, agonizing moment, even in description, but in the depths of his pain Oedipus is magnificent. He does not submit passively to his woe or plead that he committed his foul acts in ignorance, though he could be justified in doing so. He blinds himself in a rage of penitence, accepting total responsibility for what he did and determined to take the punishment of exile as well. As piteous as he appears in the final scene with Creon, there is more public spirit and more strength in his fierce grief and his resolution of exile than in any other tragic hero in the history of the theater. Oedipus has unraveled his life to its utmost limits of agony and found there an unsurpassed grandeur of soul.

"Critical Evaluation" by James Weigel, Jr.

Bibliography:

Kirkwood, Gordon MacDonald. *A Study of Sophoclean Drama*. 1958. Reprint. New York: Johnson Reprint, 1967. Examines and analyzes the structures Sophocles uses and his methods of dramatic composition. Compares his plays in considering the characters, irony, illustrative forms, and the use of diction and oracles in each. Excellent coverage of *Oedipus Tyrannus*.

Scodel, Ruth. *Sophocles*. Boston: Twayne, 1984. Provides synopses of the seven Sophoclean plays. Considers works that may have influenced Sophocles. Considers the works' structure and the use of mythological gods and oracles. Includes a chronology of Sophocles, a bibliography, and an index.

Segal, Charles. *Oedipus Tyrannus: Tragic Heroism and the Limits of Knowledge*. New York: Twayne, 1993. Provides an extensive chronology of the life of Sophocles and gives historical and cultural background, as well as a discussion of the design and structure, for *Oedipus Tyrannus*. Refers to influences on the play and its author and discusses interpretation of the Oedipus myth.

_____. *Tragedy and Civilization: An Interpretation of Sophocles*. Cambridge, Mass.: Harvard University Press, 1981. Discusses the seven plays of Sophocles, including *Oedipus Tyrannus*. Extensive interpretation on the identity of Oedipus, including the implications inherent in his name. Breaks down the plot and discusses it with regard to Greek language and English translation.

Woodard, Thomas, ed. *Sophocles: A Collection of Critical Essays*. Englewood Cliffs, N.J.: Prentice-Hall, 1966. A fine collection of essays, including writings by Friedrich Nietzsche, Sigmund Freud, and Virginia Woolf. Contains a thought-provoking section on the character of Oedipus.

OF DRAMATIC POESIE
An Essay

Type of work: Literary criticism
Author: John Dryden (1631-1700)
First published: 1668

> *Principal characters:*
> CRITES, a sharp-tongued gentleman, a staunch classicist
> EUGENIUS, a defender of the English theater of his own time
> LISIDEIUS, a devotee of the French classical drama
> NEANDER, representative of the author, a lover of the great Elizabethans

John Dryden's *Of Dramatic Poesie: An Essay* (also known as *An Essay of Dramatic Poesy*) is an exposition of several of the major critical positions of the time, set out in a semidramatic form that gives life to the abstract theories. *Of Dramatic Poesie* not only offers readers a capsule summary of the status of literary criticism in the late seventeenth century; it also provides them a succinct view of the tastes of cultured men and women of the period. Dryden synthesizes the best of both English and Continental (particularly French) criticism; hence, the essay is a single source for understanding neoclassical attitudes toward dramatic art. Moreover, in his discussion of the ancients versus the moderns, in his defense of the use of rhyme, and in his argument concerning Aristotelian prescripts for drama, Dryden depicts and reflects upon the tastes of literate Europeans who shaped the cultural climate in France and England for a century.

Although it is clear that Dryden uses Neander as a mouthpiece for his own views about drama, he is careful to allow his other characters to present cogent arguments for the literature of the classical period, of France, and of Renaissance England. More significantly, although he was a practitioner of the modern form of writing plays himself, Dryden does not insist that the dramatists of the past are to be faulted simply because they did not adhere to methods of composition which his own age venerated. For example, he does not adopt the views of the more strident critics whose insistence on slavish adherence to the rules derived from Aristotle had led to a narrow definition for greatness among playwrights. Instead, he pleads for common-sensical application of these prescriptions, appealing to a higher standard of judgment: the discriminating sensibility of the reader or playgoer who can recognize greatness even when the rules are not followed.

For this reason, Dryden can champion the works of William Shakespeare over those of many dramatists who were more careful in preserving the unities of time, place, and action. It may be difficult to imagine, after nearly two centuries of veneration, that at one time Shakespeare was not held in high esteem; but in the late seventeenth century, critics reviled him for his disregard for decorum and his seemingly careless attitudes regarding the mixing of genres. Dryden, however, recognized the greatness of Shakespeare's productions; his support for Shakespeare's "natural genius" had a significant impact on the elevation of the Renaissance playwright to a place of preeminence among dramatists.

The period after the restoration of the Stuarts to the throne is notable in English literary history as an age in which criticism flourished, probably in no small part as a result of the emphasis on neoclassical rules of art in seventeenth century France, where many of Charles II's courtiers and literati had passed the years of Cromwell's rule. Dryden sets his discussion in

June, 1665, during a naval battle between England and the Netherlands. Four cultivated gentlemen, Eugenius, Lisideius, Crites, and Neander, have taken a barge down the Thames to observe the combat, and, as guns sound in the background, they comment on the sorry state of modern literature; this naval encounter will inspire hundreds of bad verses commending the victors or consoling the vanquished. Crites laments that his contemporaries will never equal the standard set by the Greeks and the Romans. Eugenius, more optimistic, disagrees and suggests that they pass the remainder of the day debating the relative merits of classical and modern literature. He proposes that Crites choose one literary genre for comparison and initiate the discussion.

As Crites begins his defense of the classical drama, he mentions one point which is accepted by all the others: Drama is, as Aristotle wrote, an imitation of life, and it is successful as it reflects human nature clearly. He also discusses the three unities, rules dear to both the classicist and the neoclassicist, requiring that a play take place in one locale, during one day, and that it encompass one action or plot.

Crites contends that modern playwrights are but pale shadows of Aeschylus, Sophocles, Seneca, and Terence. The classical dramatists not only followed the unities successfully; they also used language more skillfully than their successors. He calls to witness Ben Jonson, the Elizabethan dramatist most highly respected by the neoclassical critics, a writer who borrowed copiously from many of the classical authors and prided himself on being a modern Horace: "I will use no further argument to you than his example: I will produce before you Father Ben, dressed in all the ornaments and colours of the ancients; you will need no other guide to our party, if you follow him."

Eugenius pleads the cause of the modern English dramatists, not by pointing out their virtues, but by criticizing the faults of the classical playwrights. He objects to the absence of division by acts in the works of the latter, as well as to the lack of originality in their plots. Tragedies are based on threadbare myths familiar to the whole audience; comedies revolve around hackneyed intrigues of stolen heiresses and miraculous restorations. A more serious defect is these authors' disregard of poetic justice: "Instead of punishing vice and rewarding virtue, they have often shown a prosperous wickedness, and an unhappy piety."

Pointing to scenes from several plays, Eugenius notes the lack of tenderness in classical drama. Crites grants Eugenius his preference, but he argues that each age has its own modes of behavior; Homer's heroes were "men of great appetites, lovers of beef broiled upon the coals, and good fellows," while the principal characters of modern French romances "neither eat, nor drink, nor sleep, for love."

Lisideius takes up the debate on behalf of the French theater of the early seventeenth century. The French classical dramatists, led by Pierre Corneille, were careful observers of the unities, and they did not attempt to combine tragedy and comedy, an English practice which he finds absurd: "Here a course of mirth, there another of sadness and passion, and a third of honour and a duel: thus, in two hours and a half, we run through all the fits of Bedlam."

The French playwrights are so attentive to poetic justice that, when they base their plots on historical events, they alter the original situations to mete out just reward and punishment. The French dramatist "so interweaves truth with probable fiction that he puts a pleasing fallacy upon us; mends the intrigues of fate, and dispenses with the severity of history, to reward that virtue which has been rendered to us there unfortunate." Plot, as the preceding comments might suggest, is of secondary concern in these plays. The dramatist's chief aim is to express appropriate emotions; violent action always takes place offstage, and it is generally reported by a messenger.

Just as Eugenius devoted much of his discussion to refuting Crites' arguments, Neander, whose views are generally Dryden's own, contradicts Lisideius' claims for the superiority of the French drama. Stating his own preference for the works of English writers, especially of the great Elizabethans, Neander suggests that it is they who best fulfill the primary requirement of drama, that it be "an imitation of life." The beauties of the French stage are, to him, cold; they may "raise perfection higher where it is, but are not sufficient to give it where it is not." He compares these beauties to those of a statue, flawless, but without a soul. Intense human feeling is, Neander feels, an essential part of drama.

Neander argues that tragicomedy is the best form for drama, for it is the closest to life; emotions are heightened by contrast, and both mirth and sadness are more vivid when they are set side by side. He believes, too, that subplots enrich a play; he finds the French drama, with its single action, thin. Like Samuel Johnson, who defended Shakespeare's disregard of the unities, Dryden suggests that close adherence to the rules prevents dramatic depth. Human actions will be more believable if there is time for the characters' emotions to develop. Neander sees no validity in the argument that changes of place and time in plays lessen dramatic credibility; theatergoers know that they are in a world of illusion from the beginning, and they can easily accept leaps in time and place, as well as makeshift battles.

Concluding his comparison of French and English drama, Neander characterizes the best of the Elizabethan playwrights. His judgments have often been quoted for their perceptivity. He calls Shakespeare "the man who of all modern, and perhaps ancient poets, had the largest and most comprehensive soul." Francis Beaumont and John Fletcher are praised for their wit and for their language, whose smoothness and polish Dryden considers their greatest accomplishment: "I am apt to believe the English language in them arrived to its highest perfection."

Dryden commends Ben Jonson for his learning and judgment, for his "correctness," yet he feels that Shakespeare surpassed him in "wit," by which he seems to mean something like natural ability or inspiration. This discussion ends with the familiar comparison: "Shakespeare was the Homer, or father of our dramatic poets; Jonson was the Virgil, the pattern of elaborate writing; I admire him, but I love Shakespeare."

Neander concludes his argument for the superiority of the Elizabethans with a close critical analysis of a play by Jonson, which Neander believes a perfect demonstration that the English were capable of following classical rules triumphantly. Dryden's allegiance to the neoclassical tradition is clear here; Samuel Johnson could disparage the unities in his *Preface to Shakespeare* (1765), but Dryden, even as he refuses to be a slave to the rules, makes Jonson's successful observance of them his decisive argument.

The essay closes with a long discussion of the value of rhyme in plays. Crites feels that blank verse, as the poetic form nearest prose, is most suitable for drama, while Neander favors rhyme, which encourages succinctness and clarity. He believes that the Restoration dramatists can make their one claim to superiority through their development of the heroic couplet. Dryden is very much a man of his time in this argument; the modern reader who has suffered through the often empty declamation of the Restoration hero returns with relief to the blank verse of the Elizabethans.

Dryden ends his work without a real conclusion; the barge reaches its destination, the stairs at Somerset House, and the debate is, of necessity, over. Moving with the digressions and contradictions of a real conversation, the discussion provides a clear, lively picture of many of the literary opinions of Dryden's time.

Updated by Laurence W. Mazzeno

Bibliography:

Hall, James M. *John Dryden: A Reference Guide*. Boston: G. K. Hall, 1984. Extends the work of other bibliographies up to 1981. Summarizes the contents of many secondary works pertinent to Dryden and offers detailed annotations. An index directs the reader to the works that deal specifically with *Of Dramatic Poesie: An Essay*.

Huntley, Frank Livingstone. "On Dryden's *Essay of Dramatic Poesy*." *The University of Michigan Contributions in Modern Philology* 16 (March, 1951): 1-67. This entire volume is devoted to a thorough analysis of Dryden's essay, including its background, argument, and significance in terms of Dryden's theory of drama.

Kramer, David Bruce. *The Imperial Dryden: The Poetics of Appropriation in Seventeenth-Century England*. Athens: The University of Georgia Press, 1994. Examines the French influence on Dryden's thinking; a section focuses on the connection between Dryden and the French critical tradition by way of some contemporary French writers.

Latt, David J., and Samuel Holt Monk. *John Dryden: A Survey and Bibliography of Critical Studies, 1895-1974*. Minneapolis: University of Minnesota Press, 1976. The section on Dryden's critical writings lists a wide array of texts pertinent to seventeenth century criticism in general, Dryden's in particular, most of them published after 1950. Useful annotations accompany many of the entries.

Pechter, Edward. *Dryden's Classical Theory of Literature*. Cambridge, England: Cambridge University Press, 1975. A review of Dryden's classical inheritance. In a chapter discussing *On Dramatic Poesie: An Essay*, Pechter is mainly concerned with the classical structure of the argument in that work.

OF HUMAN BONDAGE

Type of work: Novel
Author: W. Somerset Maugham (1874-1965)
Type of plot: Naturalism
Time of plot: Early twentieth century
Locale: England
First published: 1915

Principal characters:
>PHILIP CAREY, an orphan boy
>WILLIAM CAREY, his uncle
>LOUISA CAREY, his aunt
>MISS WILKINSON, Philip's first love
>MILDRED ROGERS, a waitress
>THORPE ATHELNEY, Philip's friend
>SALLY ATHELNEY, his daughter

The Story:

Philip Carey was nine years old when his mother died and he was sent to live with his aunt and uncle at the vicarage of Blackstable, forty miles outside London. Uncle William Carey was a penny-pinching, smugly religious man who made Philip's life miserable. Having been born with a clubfoot, Philip was extremely sensitive about his deformity, and he grew up bitter and rebellious. The only love he was shown was given to him by his Aunt Louisa, who had never been able to have children of her own.

At school, Philip's clubfoot was a source of much ridicule, for the children were cruel. Philip was so sensitive that any reference to his foot, even a kind reference, caused him to strike out at the speaker.

When he was eighteen years old, Philip, with a small inheritance of his own, went to Berlin to study. He took a room in the home of Professor and Frau Erlin. There he studied German, French, and mathematics with tutors from the University of Heidelberg. He met several young men, among them Weeks, an American, and Hayward, a radical young Englishman. From their serious discussions on religion, Philip decided that he no longer believed in God. This decision made him feel free; for in discarding God, he subconsciously discarded his memories of his cold and bitter youth at the vicarage.

Shortly after his return to Blackstable, Philip became involved with a woman twice his age, Miss Emily Wilkinson, who was a friend of his Aunt Louisa. She was not attractive to him, but he thought a man of twenty years of age should experience love. It was typical of Philip's attitude that even after they became lovers he continued to call the woman Miss Wilkinson. Not long after the affair, Philip went to London to begin a career as a clerk in an accounting firm. Dissatisfied, he worked only a year; then he went to Paris to study art. Two years later, he gave up the idea of becoming an artist and returned to London for his third great start on a career. He had decided to study medicine.

In London, Philip met Mildred Rogers, a waitress. She was really nothing more than a wanton; despite the fact that Philip saw her for what she was, he nevertheless loved her and desired her above all else. He gave her presents that were extravagant for his small income, and he neglected his studies to be with her. She gave him nothing in return. When he asked her to marry him, for it seemed that that was the only way he could ever possess her, she told him bluntly that he did not have enough money for her and that she was marrying someone else. Philip loved her and hated her so much that he was almost consumed by his emotions.

In his affection for another girl, he had begun to forget Mildred when she returned to London. Alone and penniless, she told him that the other man had not married her and that he already had a wife and children. She was pregnant. Philip forgot the other girl and took Mildred back again. He paid her hospital bill and her lodging bills and sent her to the coast to rest. Mildred repaid him by going off for a holiday with a man Philip considered his good friend. They used Philip's money to pay their expenses. Despising himself, he begged Mildred to come back to him after her trip with the other man; he could not overcome his insane desire for her. Mildred, however, did not come back.

Philip then forced himself to study harder than ever. He met Thorpe Athelney, a patient in the hospital where he was studying, and the two men became good friends. Philip visited the Athelney home almost every Sunday. It was a noisy house, filled with happy children, love, and kindness, and the cheerful atmosphere filled an empty place in Philip's heart. One evening, Philip saw Mildred again. She was highly painted and overdressed, and she was sauntering slowly down the street with a vulgar swing of her hips. She had become a common streetwalker. Although Philip knew then that he had lost his desire for her, out of pity he took her and her child into his home. Mildred was to act as his housekeeper. Because Philip's funds were small, they were forced to live frugally. Mildred once again took all that he had to offer and gave him nothing in return. Her only payment was an unknowing one, for Philip loved her child very much, and he had many hours of pleasure holding the baby girl in his arms. Mildred tried again and again to resume their old relationship, but each time, Philip repulsed her. At last, she became insanely angry and left his apartment with her baby. Before she left, however, she completely wrecked the apartment, ripped his clothing and linens with a knife, smashed furniture and dishes, and tore up his pictures.

A short time later, Philip lost what little money he had in a bad investment. The Athelney family took him into their home, and Thorpe obtained work for him as a window dresser in the store where Thorpe himself was employed. Philip had to give up his studies at the hospital because of lack of money. Then, when he was thirty years old, his Uncle William died and left him enough money to finish his medical education. When he walked down the steps with his diploma in his hand, Philip thought that he was ready at last to begin his real life. He planned to sign on as a ship's doctor and sail around the world before he settled down to a permanent practice.

Before he accepted a position, Philip went on a holiday trip with the Athelneys. While on the holiday, he realized with a sudden shock that one of the Athelney girls whom he had always thought of as a child had definitely grown up. As they walked home together one night, he and Sally Athelney became lovers. Back in London a few weeks later, Sally told him that she thought she was pregnant. Philip immediately gave up his dreams of traveling over the world and accepted a small-salaried practice in a little fishing village, so that he and Sally could be married. Sally's fears, however, proved groundless. Free to travel and be his own master, Philip suddenly realized that what he really wanted was a home, a family, and security. He had never been normal because of his deformity, and he had never done what he wanted to do but always what he thought he should do. He had always lived in the future. Now he wanted to live in the present. Therefore, he asked Sally to marry him and to go with him to that little fishing village. He offered her nothing but his love and the fruit of the lessons he had learned from hard teachers, but Sally accepted his proposal. Philip felt that he was his own master after his bleak, bitter years of mortal bondage.

Critical Evaluation:

Almost all of W. Somerset Maugham's writings deal, in one way or another, with the individual's attempt to assert his freedom from "human bondage." Because it is the most direct, thorough, and personal of his works, *Of Human Bondage* is generally considered to be his masterpiece and its hero, Philip Carey, to be a thinly disguised portrait of the author. Like Carey, Maugham lost his beautiful, affectionate mother when he was quite young, was raised in an austere, financially pinched, religiously narrow environment, suffered abuse because of a physical handicap (he stammered), and fled to the Continent as soon as he was able. From that point on, the novel does not follow Maugham's personal life so literally, but it is clear that Philip's education follows Maugham's and that many of the characters and situations had their real-life counterparts. *Of Human Bondage* was, as Maugham himself admitted, an "autobiographical novel."

The first "bondage" that Philip Carey must transcend—outgrow, really—is the oppressive environment of the vicarage. Deprived of his mother's love and thrust into a cold, moralistic milieu, young Philip is starved for affection and approval but finds little of it in his uncle's household. William Carey, a childless, middle-aged parson, is never able to understand or warm up to the boy, and his wife, Aunt Louisa, although well-meaning, lacks the emotional strength necessary to give the boy the needed support. These insecurities are exacerbated by his clubfoot that makes him an object of ridicule at school. The only mitigating factor in these early years is his uncle's library. Books become his only pleasure and excitement and help to mature him; they also provide him with an escape from everyday reality and encourage his natural tendency toward daydreaming and indulging in fantasies. Therefore, his early experiences fix several important character traits: first, his thirst for love; second, his extreme self-consciousness and oversensitivity, especially with regard to his clubfoot; third, his need to dominate and his envy of those who can; fourth, his distaste for social pieties and arbitrary moralities; and finally, his taste for literature and the life of the imagination.

As soon as he is physically capable of it, Philip flees to Germany. There, following closely upon his first experience of personal freedom, Philip has his initial taste of intellectual and spiritual emancipation. Two new friends, Hayward and Weeks, introduce him to the world of ideas. Hayward becomes his mentor and gives him a thorough grounding in the great books of the day, but it is Weeks who supplies him with the one volume, Renan's *Life of Jesus* (1863), which has the most profound effect. It liberates Philip from his unconscious acceptance of Christian dogma and gives him an exultant new sense of personal freedom.

Philip's first intellectual awakening is followed shortly by his first sexual involvement. Back in Blackstable, he seduces Miss Wilkinson, an aging friend of his aunt, and quickly learns the difference between his idealized conception of sexual love and the reality he experiences with this frustrated, demanding, physically unpleasant woman. She satisfies none of his emotional needs and leaves him feeling ridiculous and vulnerable. Miss Wilkinson also introduces him to a second crucial book, Henri Murger's *The Bohemians of the Latin Quarter* (1848). This romanticization of the lives and loves of the bohemian set stimulates Philip to attempt a career as a painter in Paris. At first, he is fascinated by the atmosphere, the activity, and the personalities, especially the degenerate poet Cronshaw, but he soon sees the reality beneath the glamorous surface. From careful observation and repeated exposures, he comes to understand the fakery, pretentiousness, and self-deception that characterizes most of this artistic activity. For the untalented, the life is brutal and destructive. He watches talentless friends like Fanny Price and Miguel Ajuria waste their lives in futile, feverish quest of the impossible. It is Fanny's suicide that finally ends his Paris pilgrimage.

Philip does not regret his Paris sojourn. He knows that he has had important experiences and has learned some valuable lessons; he is not disappointed to discover that he is without real ability. Even the truly talented artist is in a bondage to his discipline and must commit himself completely if he is to realize that talent. Philip has no taste for such total dedication; he would rather live than create. Art study in Paris has taught him how to look at things in a new way, and that is, for him, a sufficient reward.

If Philip's experience with Miss Wilkinson gave him a taste of the reality of sex and love, it did not stifle his need for them. Upon his return from Paris, Philip begins one of the strangest and most intense romantic involvements in modern literature. There is nothing about Mildred Rogers that should logically attract Philip. She is physically unattractive, crude, stupid, and abrasive. Indeed, it is her very insolence that seems initially to interest him, and, once attracted, he becomes obsessed with her. The fact that he rationally knows what Mildred is and consciously rejects her has no effect whatsoever on his passion—a fact that Philip himself clearly recognizes. Given this powerful, irrational need, her continuing arrogance and abuse only excite his desire, and the more unavailable she seems, the more intense it becomes.

Mildred is, finally, like a fever that must be endured until it runs its course. Maugham suggests that such is the nature of romantic love. Once the fever is dissipated, Philip is cured, and Mildred becomes simply an object of charity to him—at least that is Philip's belief. With the situation reversed, however, his adamant rejections of her sexuality must have at least some elements of subconscious revenge, and it is hard to believe that Philip does not, at some level, enjoy her final rage. In any event, the affair with Mildred has two lasting effects: Philip gains control of his passions and, at the same time, comes to understand the limits of rationality in the face of ungovernable emotions.

The last third of the novel has disappointed many readers. Especially disconcerting is the apparent contradiction between the sophisticated bleakness of Philip's final philosophical conclusion and the domestic felicity he expects to attain as a result of his marriage to a simple country girl. A number of events bring Philip to his final intellectual position. Following the end of his affair with Mildred, he meets Thorpe Athelney and his family, endures a short period of economic deprivation, and learns of the meaningless death of two old friends, Cronshaw and Hayward. These circumstances bring him face-to-face with the last bondage. Having emancipated himself from environmental, physical, cultural, religious, aesthetic, and emotional restraints, one final bond remains: Philip's need to understand the meaning of life.

Out of his anguished rumination Philip gains a new and final insight: "suddenly the answer occurred to him. . . . Life had no meaning. . . . Life was insignificant and death without consequence."

Instead of depressing Philip, this revelation, reminiscent of his earlier conversion from Christianity, excites him: "For the first time he was utterly free . . . he was almighty because he had wrenched from chaos the secret of its nothingness." To many, such an insight looks dismal, but to Philip—and Maugham—this view is exhilarating because it frees one to make the most of oneself and one's talents in purely human terms without any need to measure himself against any impossible transcendental absolutes.

It is in this context that Philip's marriage to Sally must be examined. Her father, Thorpe Athelney, is the only truly independent person whom Philip meets during his lifetime. Athelney is free of the religious, cultural, social, and economic pressures that distorted Philip's early environment. On the other hand, he has no need to play any of the false artistic or rebel roles that Philip encountered during his Paris sojourn. Athelney follows no false gods and pursues no impossible dreams. He is, in short, his own man who has lived his life completely in accordance with his own needs, instincts, and desires. The result has been personal satisfaction and happiness.

Since Philip accepts life as it is, he decides to settle for the one kind of happiness and existential meaning that he has seen demonstrated in action, not theory. Sally Athelney may not excite his passion or intellect, but he feels a "loving kindness" toward her and, to him, that promises a more satisfying life than to continue his search for nonexistent absolutes.

Therefore, the resolution of the novel is not inconsistent and can be justified on an intellectual level. These final scenes, however, remain artistically unsatisfying. Maugham himself, in his book of reminiscences, *The Summing Up* (1938), admitted that his final vision of domestic contentment was the one experience in the novel that he did not know personally. "Turning my wishes into fiction," he wrote, "I drew a picture of the marriage I should like to make. Readers on the whole have found it the least satisfactory part of my book." Maugham, who was homosexual, did not find personal felicity in marriage, but he did remain true to the ideas articulated in *Of Human Bondage*. In talking about the importance of the novel to his life, he stated: "It was the kind of effort that one can make once in a lifetime. I put everything into it, everything I knew, everything I experienced."

"Critical Evaluation" by Keith Neilson

Bibliography:

Buckley, Jerome Hamilton. *Season of Youth: The Bildungsroman from Dickens to Golding.* Cambridge, Mass.: Harvard University Press, 1974. Praises *Of Human Bondage* for its theme and "remarkable detachment" considering that it is autobiographical. Discusses freedom realized through the "unfolding of an aesthetic sensibility."

Calder, Robert. *Willie: The Life of W. Somerset Maugham.* New York: St. Martin's Press, 1989. Organized into ten chapters, each delineating approximately one decade. *Of Human Bondage* is most fully related to Maugham's life in the first three chapters (1874-1907). Insightful, sympathetic treatment supported by useful illustrations.

Cordell, Richard A. *Somerset Maugham: A Writer for All Seasons—A Biographical and Critical Study.* Bloomington: Indiana University Press, 1969. The earliest useful critical biography. Offers a separate chapter on *Of Human Bondage* and discusses the novel throughout. Warmer and more sympathetic than Ted Morgan's *Maugham* (see below).

Curtis, Anthony, and John Whitehead, eds. *W. Somerset Maugham: The Critical Heritage.* London: Routledge & Kegan Paul, 1987. An anthology of reviews, including 150 selected items of British and American contemporary criticism, arranged chronologically within genres. Among the five items on *Of Human Bondage* is Theodore Dreiser's landmark review "As a Realist Sees It: *Of Human Bondage*," the first serious critic to praise the novel highly.

Morgan, Ted. *Maugham.* New York: Simon & Schuster, 1980. The standard critical biography, essential for worthwhile study. Establishes correlations between Maugham's life and his works, particularly *Of Human Bondage*. Balanced, perceptive, and carefully documented with extensive notes.

OF MICE AND MEN

Type of work: Novel
Author: John Steinbeck (1902-1968)
Type of plot: Impressionistic realism
Time of plot: Mid-twentieth century
Locale: Salinas Valley, California
First published: 1937

Principal characters:
    LENNIE SMALL, a simpleminded giant
    GEORGE MILTON, his friend
    CANDY, a swamper on the ranch on which George and Lennie worked
    CURLEY, the owner's son
    SLIM, the jerkline skinner on the ranch
    CROOKS, the black stable buck

The Story:

Late one hot afternoon, two men carrying blanket rolls trudged down the path that led to the bank of the Salinas River. One man—his companion called him George—was small and wiry. The other was a large, lumbering fellow whose arms hung loosely at his sides. After they had drunk at the sluggish water and washed their faces, George sat back with his legs drawn up. His friend Lennie imitated him.

The two men were on their way to a ranch where they had been hired to buck barley. Lennie had cost them their jobs at their last stop in Weed, where he had been attracted by a woman's red dress. Grabbing at her clothes, he had been so frightened by her screaming that he had held onto her; George had been forced to hit him over the head to make him let go. They had run away to avoid a lynching.

After George had lectured his companion about letting him talk to their new employer when they were interviewed, Lennie begged for a story he had already heard many times. It was the story of the farm they would own one day. It would have chickens, rabbits, and a vegetable garden, and Lennie would be allowed to feed the rabbits.

The threat that Lennie would not be allowed to care for the rabbits if he did not obey caused him to keep still when they arrived at the ranch the next day. In spite of George's precautions, their new boss was not easy to deal with. He was puzzled because George gave Lennie no chance to talk.

While the men were waiting for the lunch gong, the owner's son Curley came in, ostensibly looking for his father, but actually to examine the new men. After he had gone, Candy, the swamper who swept out the bunkhouse, warned them that Curley was a prizefighter who delighted in picking on the men and that he was extremely jealous of any attention given to his slatternly bride.

Lennie had a foreboding of evil and wanted to leave, but the two men had no money with which to continue their wanderings. By evening, however, Lennie was happy again. The dog belonging to Slim, the jerkline skinner, had had pups the night before, and Slim had given one to simpleminded Lennie.

Slim was easy to talk to. While George played solitaire that evening, he told his new friend of the incident in Weed. He had just finished his confidence when Lennie came in, hiding his puppy inside his coat. George told Lennie to take the pup back to the barn. He said that Lennie would probably spend the night there with the animal.

The bunkhouse had been deserted by all except old Candy when Lennie asked once more to hear the story of the land they would some day buy. At its conclusion, the swamper spoke up. He had three hundred and fifty dollars saved, he said, and he knew he would not be able to work many more years. He wanted to join George and Lennie in their plan. George finally agreed, for with Candy's money they would soon be able to buy the farm they had in mind.

Lennie was still grinning with delighted anticipation when Curley came to the bunkhouse in search of his wife. The men had been taunting him about her wantonness when he spied Lennie's grin. Infuriated with the thought that he was being laughed at, Curley attacked the larger man. Lennie, remembering George's warnings, did nothing to defend himself at first. Finally, he grabbed Curley's hand and squeezed. When he let go, every bone had been crushed.

Curley was driven off to town for treatment, with instructions from Slim to say that he had caught his hand in a machine. Slim warned him that the humiliating truth would soon be known if he failed to tell a convincing story.

After the others had started to town with Curley, Lennie went to talk to Crooks, the black stable buck, who had his quarters in the harness room instead of the bunkhouse. Crooks's coolness quickly melted before Lennie's innocence. While Lennie told the black man about the dream of the farm, Candy joined them. They were deep in discussion when Curley's wife appeared, looking for her husband. The story about her husband and the machine did not deceive her, and she hinted that she was pleased with Lennie for what he had done. Having put an end to the men's talk, she slipped out noiselessly when she heard the others come back from town.

Lennie was in the barn petting his puppy. The other workmen pitched horseshoes outside. Lennie did not realize that the puppy was already dead from the mauling he had innocently given it. As he sat in the straw, Curley's wife came around the corner of the stalls. He would not speak to her at first, afraid that he would not get to feed the rabbits if he did anything wrong, but the woman gradually managed to draw his attention to her and persuaded him to stroke her hair.

When she tried to pull her head away, Lennie held on, growing afraid as she tried to yell. Finally he shook her violently and broke her neck.

Curley's wife was lying half-buried in the hay when Candy came into the barn in search of Lennie. Finding Lennie gone, he called George, and while the latter went off to get a gun, the swamper spread the alarm. The opportunity to catch the murderer was what Curley had been looking for. Carrying a loaded shotgun, he started off with the men, George among them.

It was George who found Lennie hiding in the bushes at the edge of a stream. Hurriedly, for the last time, he told his companion the story of the rabbit farm, and when he had finished, Lennie begged that they go at once to look for the farm. Knowing that Lennie could not escape from Curley and the other men who were searching for him, George put the muzzle of his gun to the back of his friend's head and pulled the trigger. Lennie was dead when the others arrived.

Critical Evaluation:

Throughout John Steinbeck's career, his affinity and compassion for the average person's struggle for autonomy surfaces as a recurrent link among his works. *Of Mice and Men*, set in California's Salinas Valley, depicts the world of the migrant worker, a world in which Steinbeck himself had lived, and the workers' search for independence. Steinbeck was critical of what he perceived as the United States' materialism, and his work echoes his convictions about the land

and its people. Like the characters in his Pulitzer Prize-winning novel *The Grapes of Wrath* (1939), *Of Mice and Men*'s George and Lennie dream of a piece of land to call their own.

Published in 1937, *Of Mice and Men* was Steinbeck's first major success and illustrates his love for both the land and those who worked it. Unlike later novels, *Of Mice and Men* is not a politically motivated protest novel. It does, however, reflect Steinbeck's belief in the interdependence of society, a theme he continues to explore throughout the body of his work.

Of Mice and Men was adapted to the stage the year that it was published. Steinbeck's sympathetic third-person narrator records dialogue and action, thus characterization is built upon external actions rather than internal monologues.

For Steinbeck's characters, the dream of land represents independence and dignity: the American Dream. George and Lennie embody the ordinary man's struggle to grasp the dream, which consists of "a little bit of land, not much. Jus' som'thin that was his." This is one of the central themes that propels the novel's characters and their actions.

As the title suggests, the best laid plans of mice and men can, and do, go awry. They are doomed from the start because of Lennie's fatal flaw—he is developmentally disabled and therefore incapable of bringing the dream to fruition—but his naïveté also allows both him and George to pursue the dream. Lennie's innocence permits George to believe that the dream might be attainable: "George said softly, 'I think I knowed we'd never do her. He usta like to hear about it so much I got to thinking maybe we would.'" Lennie is the keeper of the dream; he does not question its inevitable fulfillment, he simply believes. Without this innocence, George would be like all the other ranch hands, wasting his money on whiskey and women, drifting aimlessly from one job to the next.

George and Lennie are juxtaposed against a group of isolated misfits, to show not only that they need each other, but also that humans cannot live in isolation without consequences. Steinbeck uses characters such as Candy, Crooks, and Curley's wife in order to illustrate the isolation of the human condition. Each of these characters is drawn to George and Lennie and their vision; they, too, want to share in the dream. Their dreams have been systematically destroyed by the insensitivity of the world; as a result, they must appropriate George and Lennie's.

George, Crooks, Candy, and Curley's wife all have the mental capacity to attain the dream, but lack the innocent belief that is needed in order to make it come true. It is their experience that keeps them from attaining the dream. In the world, innocence is inevitably shattered—one must wake from the dream.

Since Lennie can never pass from his state of innocence to that of experience, he must be destroyed. Lennie represents that part in George, possibly in everyone, that remains childlike. It is important that George, himself, must destroy Lennie and that Lennie literally dies with the dream. Before his death, Lennie repeats the dream like a catechism and urges George, "Le's do it now," after which George pulls the trigger. Lennie dies with the dream.

Lennie becomes a metaphor for the death of innocence within a selfish society that cannot comprehend him or his relationship with George. To illustrate this point, Steinbeck allows Carlson the final word, "Now what the hell ya suppose is eatin' them two guys?" Carlson embodies an apathetic society that cannot understand a relationship based upon trust and love rather than avarice. Carlson insists upon killing Candy's dog because "He don't have no fun." Like the society he epitomizes, all of Carlson's judgments deal in the superficial. For Steinbeck, that is a world that cannot sustain innocence.

"Critical Evaluation" by Angela D. Hickey

Bibliography:

Benson, Jackson J., ed. *The Short Novels of John Steinbeck: Critical Essays with a Checklist to Steinbeck Criticism.* Durham, N.C.: Duke University Press, 1990. Contains Anne Loftis' "A Historical Introduction to *Of Mice and Men*," William Goldhurst's "*Of Mice and Men:* John Steinbeck's Parable of the Curse of Cain," and Mark Spilka's "Of George and Lennie and Curley's Wife: Sweet Violence in Steinbeck's Eden."

_____. *The True Adventures of John Steinbeck, Writer.* New York: Viking, 1984. Definitive biography calls *Of Mice and Men*'s popularity the turning point between poverty and success in Steinbeck's career. Traces the novel's composition and its revision into drama.

French, Warren. *John Steinbeck.* Boston: Twayne, 1975. Calls *Of Mice and Men* a naturalistic fable resulting from Steinbeck's fascination with Ed Ricketts' nonteleological belief "that *what* things are matters less than the fact that they *are*." Discusses Steinbeck's deliberate writing of a fiction work that could be easily revised into a play.

Hayashi, Testsumaro, ed. *John Steinbeck: The Years of Greatness, 1936-1939.* Tuscaloosa: University of Alabama Press, 1993. Contains Charlotte Cook Hadella's "The Dialogic Tension in Steinbeck's Portrait of Curley's Wife," Thomas Fensch's "Reflections of Doc: The Persona of Ed Ricketts in *Of Mice and Men*," and Robert E. Morseberger's "Tell Again, George."

Owens, Louis. *John Steinbeck's Re-Vision of America.* Athens: University of Georgia Press, 1985. Discusses the importance of setting to the Eden myth in terms of Lennie's dream of living "off the fatta the lan'." The novel seems pessimistic because Eden cannot be achieved, but commitment between people allows for hope.

OF TIME AND THE RIVER
A Legend of Man's Hunger in His Youth

Type of work: Novel
Author: Thomas Wolfe (1900-1938)
Type of plot: Impressionistic realism
Time of plot: 1920's
Locale: Harvard, New York, and France
First published: 1935

> *Principal characters:*
> EUGENE GANT, a young student and writer
> BASCOM PENTLAND, his uncle
> FRANCIS STARWICK, a friend
> ANN and
> ELINOR, Starwick's friends
> ROBERT WEAVER, Eugene's friend

The Story:

Eugene Gant was leaving Altamont for study at Harvard. His mother and his sister Helen stood on the station platform and waited with him for the train that would take him north. Eugene felt that he was escaping from his strange, unhappy childhood, that the train would take him away from sickness and worry over money, away from his mother's boardinghouse, the Dixieland, away from memories of his gruff yet kind brother Ben, away from all ghosts of the past. While they waited, they met Robert Weaver, who was also on his way to Harvard. Mrs. Gant said that Robert was a fine boy, but that there was insanity in his family. She told Eugene family scandals of the town before the train came puffing in.

Eugene stopped in Baltimore to visit his father, who was slowly dying of cancer. Old Gant spent much of his time on the sunlit hospital porch, dreaming of a former time and of his youth.

At Harvard, Eugene enrolled in Professor Hatcher's drama class. Hungry for knowledge, he browsed in the library, pulling books from the library shelves and reading them as he stood by the open stacks. He wrote plays for the drama workshop. Prowling the streets of Cambridge and Boston, he wondered about the lives of people he met, whose names he would never know.

One day, he received a note from Francis Starwick, Professor Hatcher's assistant, asking Eugene to have dinner with him that night. As Eugene had made no friends at the university, he was surprised by Starwick's invitation. Starwick turned out to be a pleasant young man who welcomed Eugene's confidences but returned none. In Boston, Eugene met his uncle, Bascom Pentland, and his wife. Uncle Bascom had once been a preacher, but he had left the ministry and was now working in a law office.

One day, Eugene received a telegram telling him that his father was dying. He had no money for a ticket home, and so he went to see Wang, a strange, secretive Chinese student who roomed in the same house. Wang gave him money, and Eugene went back to Altamont, but he arrived too late to see his father alive. Old Gant had died painfully and horribly. Only with his death did his wife and children realize how much this ranting, roaring old man had meant in their lives.

Back at Harvard, Eugene and Starwick became close friends. Starwick always confused Eugene when they were together; Eugene had the feeling that everything Starwick did or said was like the surface of a shield, protecting his real thoughts or feelings underneath.

One night, Robert Weaver came to Eugene's room. He was drunk and shouted at the top of his voice. He wanted Eugene to go out with him, but Eugene finally managed to get him to bed on a cot in Wang's room.

Eugene dreamed of becoming a great playwright. After he had completed his course at Harvard, he went back to Altamont and waited to have one of his plays accepted for production on Broadway. That was a summer of unhappiness and suspense. His plays were rejected. While visiting a married sister in South Carolina, he ran into Robert Weaver again. The two got drunk and landed in jail.

In the fall, Eugene went to New York to become an English instructor at a city university. After a time, Robert Weaver appeared. He had been living at a club, but now he insisted that Eugene get him a room at the apartment hotel where Eugene lived. Eugene hesitated, knowing what would happen if Weaver went on one of his sprees. The worst did happen. Weaver smashed furniture and set fire to his room. He also had a mistress, a woman who had married her husband because she knew he was dying and would leave her his money. One night, the husband found his wife and Weaver together. There was a scuffle. The husband pulled a gun and attempted to shoot Weaver before he collapsed. It looked very much as if Eliza Gant's statement about insanity in the Weaver family was true.

Eugene also renewed a college friendship with Joel Pierce, the son of a wealthy family. At Joel's invitation, he went to visit at the magnificent Pierce estate along the Hudson River. Seeing the fabulously rich close at hand for the first time, Eugene was fascinated and disappointed.

At vacation time, Eugene went abroad, first to England, where he lived with the strange Coulson family, and then to France. In Paris, he met Starwick again, standing enraptured upon the steps of the Louvre. Starwick was visiting Europe with two women from Boston, Elinor and Ann. Elinor, who had left her husband, was mistakenly believed by her friends to be Starwick's mistress. Eugene went to see the sights of Paris with them. Ann and Elinor paid all of Starwick's bills. One night, in a cabaret, Starwick got into an argument with a Frenchman and accepted a challenge to duel. Ann, wanting to end the ridiculous affair, paid the Frenchman money to satisfy him for damages to his honor. Eugene attempted to make love to Ann, but when she resisted him he realized that she was in love with Starwick. Eugene then made the discovery that Ann's love was wasted because Starwick was a homosexual.

Disgusted with the three, Eugene went to Chartres by himself. From Chartres, he went to Orleans. There he met an eccentric old countess who believed that Eugene was a correspondent for the New York Times, a journalist planning to write a book of travel impressions. She secured for him an invitation to visit the Marquise de Mornaye, who was under the mistaken impression that Eugene had known her son in America.

Eugene went to Tours. There in that old town of white buildings and narrow, cobblestoned streets, memories of America suddenly came flooding back to him. He remembered the square of Altamont on a summer afternoon, the smell of woodsmoke in the early morning, and the whistle of a train in the mountain passes. He remembered the names of American rivers, the parade of the states that stretched from the rocky New England coastline across the flat plains and the high mountains to the thunder of the Pacific slope and the names of battles fought on American soil. He remembered his family and his own childhood. He felt that he had recaptured the lost dream of time itself. Homesick, he started back to America. One day, he caught sight of Starwick and his two women companions in a Marseilles café, but he went away before they saw him.

He sailed from Cherbourg. On the tender taking passengers out to the ocean liner, he heard an American voice above the babble of the passengers grouped about him. He looked. A woman pointed eagerly toward the ship, her face glowing with an excitement as great as that Eugene himself felt. A woman companion called her Esther. Watching Esther, Eugene knew that she was to be his fate.

Critical Evaluation:

Of Time and the River is the last of Thomas Wolfe's novels to be published before his early death in 1938 (*The Web and the Rock* and *You Can't Go Home Again* were published post-humously in 1939 and 1940). It is furthermore the last work to be completed under the extensive editorial guidance of Maxwell Perkins and is appropriately read as a sequel to *Look Homeward, Angel* (1929), whose hero, Eugene Gant, is clearly Wolfe himself.

As is the case with *Look Homeward, Angel*, the subtitle of *Of Time and the River* is a somewhat useful advertisement for its contents. Wolfe subtitled his first book *A Story of the Buried Life*, and the strain felt by a gifted youth in confined circumstances is a salient theme. Wolfe subtitled his second novel *A Legend of Man's Hunger in His Youth*. This hunger, which is felt for somewhat more than nine hundred pages, traces Eugene Gant's life from his departure for graduate study at Harvard University to his days at Harvard, his return home at the time of his father's death, his first experience of New York City (when he accepts a position to teach college composition there), his growing acquaintance with a more varied circle of people while living in New York, his extended trip to England and then France, and finally his preparations to return to America and resume teaching in New York. As the book concludes he catches sight of a woman who is to be a fellow passenger on the ship home. In this novel she is called only Esther, but through the concluding paragraphs she is made to appear portentous in Eugene's future. She in fact represents Aline Bernstein, an older married woman who was to play a large role in the books published after Wolfe's death, being the great love of his life.

Thomas Wolfe toyed with more than one title for *Of Time and the River* before making his final choice. What these titles had in common was the word "river," which he saw as a suitable metaphor for his task—to drain from experience and memory the enormous variety and complexity of American life, even as a river, particularly the Mississippi, drains the vast continent of America. All of this occurred in time, the dimension that settled events in memory before they are called up by the writer's art.

Wolfe's narratives are close to his life, so a certain amount of form was naturally imposed on his material by virtue of circumstance. Beyond this Wolfe had great difficulty in shaping the things he wanted to say so as to make a coherent story, however close it might be to his own experience. He labored over the manuscript of *Of Time and the River* until Maxwell Perkins simply announced to the writer that the work was done and took it from him.

It seems that *Of Time and the River* improves as it goes along, as if Eugene Gant's hunger becomes increasingly articulate as he removes himself from the familiar things of youth and engages with the larger world. For example, the train ride north, with which the novel opens, is not particularly strong but seems rather an episode wherein Wolfe, in the guise of Eugene Gant, settles scores with people of his home town. At the conclusion of this passage Eugene visits his father in a hospital in Baltimore. Here the author tries to use material he had written earlier— W. O. Gant's recollection of the Battle of Gettysburg—which Wolfe's father did in fact experience as a boy, but again the reader may sense that the material is not presented with the brilliance of which Wolfe is sometimes capable.

Of the characters that emerge during Eugene Gant's Harvard days the most memorable is Uncle Bascom Pentland, modeled on an uncle of Wolfe, curiously educated, who left the ministry to convey property titles in a Boston real estate office. The portrait is memorable, but the exaggerations are improbable and not perfectly flattering (Wolfe's uncle considered a lawsuit).

When Eugene Gant goes to New York City to teach college, three things in his condition are different from the past. First, he is no longer a schoolboy at his studies, even if advanced, but an independent young man. Second, his father has died, which may deprive him of an emotional anchor, but serves adult self-reliance all the same. Third, Eugene begins to incline toward romantic entanglements that may be necessary to complete the psyche, and perhaps the creative energy, of a young man. Eugene first feels himself drawn toward Rosiland Pierce, the daughter in the family of Hudson River gentry that he knows through his friendship with Joel, the son. Then in England Eugene rooms with the Coulson family, whose daughter, Edith, seems attracted to Eugene, as he is later to Ann when he travels in France with her, Elinor, and his Harvard acquaintance Starwick. Finally there is the brief glimpse of Esther with which the novel concludes.

Much of the writing from the time of Eugene's New York City days seems vivid, honest, and effective, as if the writer has learned how to serve his hunger. It may be that the presence of young women renders Eugene Gant a complete person able to encounter experience and forge from it some of the best parts of *Of Time and the River*.

"Critical Evaluation" by John Higby

Bibliography:

Idol, John Lane, Jr. *A Thomas Wolfe Companion*. Westport, Conn.: Greenwood Press, 1987. A reference text for the study of Thomas Wolfe. Useful information not readily available in other sources may be found here, for example, a list of special collections of material on Wolfe, genealogies of major families in Wolfe's fiction, a glossary of people and places in Wolfe, and primary and secondary bibliographies.

Kennedy, Richard S., ed. *Thomas Wolfe: A Harvard Perspective*. Athens, Ohio: Croissant and Company, 1983. A collection of essays in two groupings, "Critical Considerations" and "Texts and Manuscripts." *Of Time and the River* is treated specifically in one essay and incidentally in another.

_____. *The Window of Memory: The Literary Career of Thomas Wolfe*. Chapel Hill: University of North Carolina Press, 1962. A major critical study of Thomas Wolfe, tracing the author's career from his early work to the novels published after his death. *Of Time and the River* receives extended treatment.

Nowell, Elizabeth, ed. *The Letters of Thomas Wolfe*. New York: Charles Scribner's Sons, 1956. A generous collection of the correspondence of Thomas Wolfe by the woman who was his literary agent and later his biographer.

Wolfe, Thomas. *The Story of a Novel*. New York: Charles Scribner's Sons, 1936. This book began as a speech Wolfe gave at the University of Colorado Writer's Conference in August, 1935. It is an account of the creative effort that resulted in *Of Time and the River* and acknowledges Wolfe's debt to his editor, Maxwell Perkins.

THE OLD BACHELOR

Type of work: Drama
Author: William Congreve (1670-1729)
Type of plot: Comedy of manners
Time of plot: Seventeenth century
Locale: London
First performed: 1693; first published, 1693

    Principal characters:
        HEARTWELL, an old bachelor
        BELINDA, a fashionable young woman
        ARAMINTA, her cousin
        BELLMOUR, a young bachelor in love with Belinda
        VAINLOVE, his friend, in love with Araminta
        SILVIA, Vainlove's former mistress
        SIR JOSEPH WITTOL, a fool
        CAPTAIN BLUFFE, his parasite
        FONDLEWIFE, a banker
        LAETITIA, his young wife

The Story:

    Sir Joseph Wittol, a foolish young country knight, returned to the spot in London where he had been attacked by footpads the night before, a fracas from which the gallant Ned Bellmour had rescued him. Bellmour had told his friend Sharper of the incident, whereupon Sharper, encountering Wittol, pretended to be the man who had rescued the country bumpkin. Having ingratiated himself with his false story, Sharper declared that he had lost a hundred pounds in the scuffle, and Wittol promised to make good the loss. Wittol and Sharper were joined by Captain Bluffe, a spurious veteran of campaigns in the Low Countries and Wittol's mentor in the ways of the city. Bluffe's boasting and swaggering ways had deeply impressed the foolish young Wittol.

    In her apartment, Araminta was reproved by her cousin Belinda for being devoted to love. A footman announced that Vainlove and Bellmour had arrived to pay their respects to Araminta. Belinda, who was charmed by Bellmour, declared that she would remain to keep Araminta company, even though she had been preparing to go out. The young men having been admitted, Bellmour and Belinda exchanged amiable insults. Gavot, Araminta's singing-master, enter-tained the group with a song.

    Silvia, a prostitute and Vainlove's discarded mistress, pined for him. Lucy, her maid, suggested that they write a letter filled with foolish protestations of love, sign Araminta's name to it, and send it to Vainlove. This deception, they were sure, would cool Vainlove's ardor for Araminta. Meanwhile, Heartwell, a professed woman-hater and a surly old bachelor, found himself against his will in front of Silvia's door. Bellmour and Vainlove saw him enter.

    The masked Lucy encountered Setter, Vainlove's man. When Setter used abusive language in speaking to her, she unmasked and demanded reparation from her old acquaintance in the form of information about the affair between Vainlove and Araminta. At the same time, Wittol gave Sharper a note of credit for one hundred pounds, to be collected from Fondlewife, a banker. Bluffe rebuked Wittol for his misdirected generosity. When Sharper appeared with the

4628

cash and thanked Wittol, Bluffe intimated to Wittol that Sharper was a trickster. Sharper rejoined by suggesting that Bluffe was a fraud. When he struck Bluffe, the braggart was afraid to retaliate, and Sharper thereupon soundly trounced him and departed. Only then did Bluffe draw his sword and rant brave words.

At Silvia's house, Heartwell entertained the prostitute with hired singers and dancers. When he professed his love for her, she put him off coyly, asserting that she must be married to a man before he could enjoy her favors. Overcome by passion and by Silvia's wiles, he at last agreed to marry her. Saying he would return in the evening, he went to procure a marriage license.

Fondlewife, the banker, arranged to have a Puritan minister visit his young wife, Laetitia, while he was away on business. At the last minute, however, he grew wary and decided not to leave the city. Vainlove, who had been invited to visit Laetitia during the absence of her ancient, doting husband, sent Bellmour in his place. Vainlove received the letter, to which Silvia had signed Araminta's name. The writer pleaded for an end to a slight disagreement between them. Disappointed to find the lady so eager, Vainlove announced that his interest in Araminta had waned.

Bellmour, disguised as the Puritan minister, visited Laetitia and in private revealed his true identity. He explained that he had indiscreetly opened her letter to Vainlove and, the intrigue appealing to him, had come in Vainlove's stead. Laetitia, charmed by Bellmour's gallantry, entertained him in her bedroom.

Vainlove met Araminta in St. James Park and treated her coolly. Araminta failed to understand when he tossed the letter at her feet and stalked away. A few minutes later, Wittol encountered Araminta for the first time and fell in love with her.

Fondlewife, accompanied by Wittol, who had come to get money from the banker, returned home prematurely, and Bellmour hid in the bedroom. Fondlewife went to get cash for Wittol. On his return a frantic Laetitia accused Wittol of having attempted to ravish her. Wittol was asked to leave the house. Laetitia and Bellmour cleverly succeeded in keeping Bellmour's identity from Fondlewife until the cuckolded old gentleman discovered the Scarron novel in the parlor that Bellmour, in his disguise, had carried as a prayer book. Bellmour confessed to evil intentions, but declared that Fondlewife had returned too soon for the couple to have sinned. When Laetitia wept and declared their innocence, Fondlewife reluctantly accepted Bellmour's story.

Bellmour, still in his disguise, passed Silvia's apartment. Lucy, believing him a parson who would marry her mistress and Heartwell, stopped Bellmour. Bellmour revealed his true identity to Lucy and told her that he would provide both her and Silvia with proper husbands if she would agree to no more than a mock marriage of Heartwell and Silvia. Bellmour, practical joker that he was, could not bear to see his friend Heartwell marry a prostitute. He performed the service; then, during Heartwell's momentary absence, he told Silvia of the trick he had played.

Vainlove, meanwhile, learned from Setter that the letter signed by Araminta was probably Lucy's work, since Lucy had made inquiries about the relationship between Araminta and Vainlove. At the same time, Sharper and Setter fooled Wittol into thinking that Araminta had conceived a passion for him. Wittol gave Setter gold to bring Araminta to him. Bluffe privately paid Setter a counterbribe to convey Araminta to him.

Sharper, pretending no knowledge of Heartwell's marriage to Silvia, asked Heartwell to join him in a visit to the prostitute. Heartwell, in a predicament, told of his marriage and warned Sharper not to go near Silvia's house. Vainlove and Bellmour brought Araminta and Belinda, both masked, to Silvia's house. Setter had taken Lucy and Silvia, both also masked, to meet Wittol and Bluffe. Finding Heartwell alone, Vainlove, Bellmour, and the young ladies teased him unmercifully about his marriage. Setter returned with Wittol, Silvia, Bluffe, and Lucy. When the ladies all unmasked, the foolish knight and his roaring companion admitted indulgently that they had been hoodwinked. Heartwell, learning of the mock marriage, thanked Bellmour for his salvation; he vowed that if he were to marry, it would be to an old crone. Vainlove and Araminta, and Bellmour and Belinda, planned their weddings for the next day.

Critical Evaluation:

When the grand old man of Restoration theater, John Dryden, finished reading the manuscript of *The Old Bachelor*, he declared that he had never seen such a first play in his life. Together with several other experienced playwrights, Dryden helped William Congreve put the finishing touches on his play. With the added enhancement of music by England's leading composer, Henry Purcell, Congreve's fledgling dramatic effort propelled the young playwright to fame and fortune. The reasons are not hard to find. *The Old Bachelor* is cast in the tried and tested mold of Restoration comedy, but if the bottle is old, the wine is new. Congreve's dramatic situations are varied and interesting. The plot is not too complicated to follow, the dialogue is sparkling, the characters appealing, and the obligatory Restoration cynicism tempered with just a hint of pathos.

Congreve uses such stock characters as skeptical, witty rakes and reluctant heroines, as well as the cast-off mistress, the braggart soldier, the elderly cuckold, and the old, supposedly woman-hating bachelor. The philosophical assumptions behind the drama are also common Restoration currency: Pursuing women is like pursuing game, the pleasure being in the pursuit more than in the catch (and certainly the game is not expected to pursue the hunter); there is no more ridiculous a sight in nature than the old bachelor taking a young wife; the married state, though it is the goal to which all strive, is by its very nature, an unsatisfying one; the most reprehensible faults of character are dullness, age, and taking oneself seriously.

One of the qualities that distinguishes Congreve from such earlier Restoration masters as William Wycherley and Sir George Etherege (in addition to his more consistently brilliant dialogue) is that he shows a trace of compassion, as well as scorn, for his characters. The cuckold Fondlewife, for instance, and to a greater extent, the old bachelor Heartwell, are figures of pathos as well as fun. The latter is aware of his dangerously intense feelings for Silvia, knows that he should resist them because they will only serve to make him look foolish, and yet is unable to overcome his passion with reason. "O dotage, dotage!" he moans, "that ever that noble passion, lust, should ebb to this degree." We cannot help but sympathize as he writhes in the toils of the old, familiar snake, especially when he is mocked by others (including Belinda) for his folly. Luckily, Bellmour, with a stroke of generosity unusual in a Restoration rake, has taken pity on the poor man: "Heartwell is my friend; and tho he is blind, I must not see him fall into the snare and unwittingly marry a whore." Neither Wycherley nor Etherege would have troubled their heads for a moment about this piece of cruelty; indeed they would have considered it as more fodder for their comic resolutions.

At the end of the play, all of the characters, even the fools, seem reasonably content, though their hopes and expectations have in some cases been thwarted. Congreve intends that the audience arise from its comic repast remembering a good taste, though one that was spiced and sauced with the relieved Heartwell's dour conclusions on the perils of aging: "All coursers the first heat with vigour run; But 'tis with whip and spur the race is won."

Bibliography:
Dobrée, Bonamy. *Restoration Comedy: 1660-1720.* 1946. Reprint. Westport, Conn.: Green-

wood Press, 1981. Essays on Congreve in this collection emphasize the easy flow of language and incidents, the French connection, and the spontaneity of scenes and situations.

Peters, Julie S. *Congreve, the Drama, and the Printed Word*. Stanford, Calif.: Stanford University Press, 1990. Examines the diction, speech patterns, stage conventions, and editorial practices associated with Congreve's plays. Concludes that *The Old Bachelor* is recognized as the culmination of comic routines, philosophical assumptions, and acquired follies.

Thomas, David. *William Congreve*. New York: St. Martin's Press, 1992. Overview of Congreve's career. Reinforces the critical opinion of *The Old Bachelor* as new wine in an old bottle—largely the result of Congreve's brilliant use of repartee. Asserts that the strong conclusion in Act V reorganizes the disparate elements in Acts I through IV, which saves the plot from disintegration.

Van Voris, W. H. *The Cultivated Stance: The Designs of Congreve's Plays*. Chester Springs, Pa.: Dufour, 1967. Analyzes *The Old Bachelor* in the thematic context of time and dialogue in Restoration drama. Examines the relationship between dramatic technique and stage conventions.

Williams, Aubrey L. *An Approach to Congreve*. New Haven, Conn.: Yale University Press, 1979. Accentuates the moralizing effect of Congreve's characterizations and argues against a determinist reading of *The Old Bachelor*. Offers an informative look at the religious background that symbolically frames the play and adds spice to every innuendo.

THE OLD CURIOSITY SHOP

Type of work: Novel
Author: Charles Dickens (1812-1870)
Type of plot: Social realism
Time of plot: Early nineteenth century
Locale: England
First published: serial, 1840-1841; book, 1841

Principal characters:
>LITTLE NELL TRENT, an orphan
>NELL'S GRANDFATHER, a curiosity dealer and gambler
>QUILP, a misanthropic, misshapen dwarf
>KIT NUBBLES, Nell's friend
>DICK SWIVELLER, a profligate young man and Quilp's tool
>SAMPSON BRASS, an attorney and Quilp's aide in crime
>SALLY BRASS, Sampson's sister and fellow criminal
>THE SINGLE GENTLEMAN, Nell's granduncle

The Story:

Little Nell Trent lived alone with her aged grandfather, who ran an old curiosity shop. The grandfather, Little Nell's mother's father, had two obsessions. One was keeping Little Nell away from her brother Fred, a drunken profligate. The other was a burning desire to gamble. Hoping to provide a fortune for the little girl, the old man gambled away every penny he could get. Not content with using the income of the curiosity shop, the old man borrowed money recklessly.

One of his creditors was an ugly, misshapen, cruel dwarf named Quilp. The husband of a pretty but browbeaten young woman, Quilp plotted to ruin the old man and someday marry Little Nell, who was only fourteen years old. Having discovered the old man's passion for gambling by forcing his wife to spy on Little Nell, Quilp was soon able to take over the old curiosity shop by due process of law. Little Nell and her grandfather went away during the night and started an aimless journey from London to western England.

Almost penniless, the old man and the little girl found many friends on their way. For a time, they traveled with a Punch-and-Judy troupe, until the girl became alarmed at the habits of the men connected with the show and persuaded her grandfather to leave them. She and the old man were next befriended by Mrs. Jarley, owner of a waxworks, but the grandfather's passion for gambling caused them to leave their benefactress. At last a schoolmaster, on his way to fill a new post, took them under his wing.

Under the schoolmaster's guidance, the girl and her grandfather were established in a little town as caretakers of a church. Their duties were very light because the church had a regular sexton as well. Meanwhile, the only friend Little Nell and her grandfather had left behind in London was a poor boy named Kit Nubbles. He was attempting to find them but was hampered by the enmity of Quilp and by the fact that he had to help support his widowed mother and two other children. In addition, Quilp, who had an unreasonable hatred for anyone honest, was trying to find Little Nell in order to wed her to one of her brother's worthless companions. This worthless companion, Dick Swiveller, was a clerk in the office of Quilp's unscrupulous lawyer, Sampson Brass.

After Little Nell and her grandfather had disappeared, a strange, Single Gentleman had appeared to rent an apartment from Sampson Brass. It turned out that he also was hunting for Little Nell and her grandfather. Since he was obviously a man of wealth, no one could be certain of the stranger's motives. The Single Gentleman soon proved to Kit and Kit's honest employer that he wanted to aid the two runaways, and Kit tried to help the stranger locate Little Nell and her grandfather. Unfortunately, when they tried to follow the elusive trail of the old man and the girl, they came to a dead end. Their search carried them as far as the woman who ran the waxworks. Afterward, apparently, the two had vanished from the face of the earth.

Quilp was angered that anyone might be willing to help Little Nell and prevent his plans for her marriage; he then tried to circumvent the Single Gentleman's efforts. To do so, he plotted with Sampson Brass and his sister Sally to make it appear that Kit had stolen some money. During one of the boy's visits to the stranger's room, Brass placed a five-pound note in the boy's hat. When the money was discovered a few minutes later, Kit was accused of stealing it. Despite his protestations of innocence and the belief of the Single Gentleman and Kit's employer that the boy had been unjustly accused, he was found guilty and sentenced to be transported to the Colonies.

Dick Swiveller, not a complete rogue, discovered through a little girl he befriended, a girl kept virtually as a slave by the Brasses, that Kit had been falsely accused. With his aid, the Single Gentleman and Kit's employer were able to have the lad released before he was sent out of England. In addition, they discovered evidence that caused Brass to be stripped of his professional status and sent to prison. Sally Brass had been just as guilty in her brother's affairs, and she disappeared. Warned by Sally Brass of the turn his plot had taken, Quilp tried to flee prosecution. He left his riverside retreat late at night, fell into the Thames, and was drowned.

Shortly afterward, the Single Gentleman learned the whereabouts of Little Nell and her grandfather. Kit's employer's brother lived with the vicar of the church, where the girl and her grandfather were caretakers, and the employer's brother had written to tell of the new couple in the village. Accompanied by Kit and his employer, the Single Gentleman started off at once to find Little Nell and her grandfather. During the journey, the Single Gentleman related his reasons for being interested in the pair.

The Single Gentleman was the grandfather's younger brother. Years before, the grandfather and he had both been in love with the same woman. Unsuccessful in his suit, the younger brother had left England. After many years, he had returned to learn that Nell's father and his profligate son, Nell's brother, had wasted the family fortune, leaving Nell and the old man in straitened circumstances from which her grandfather had tried desperately to rescue them. Wealthy in his own right, the Single Gentleman wished to rescue his brother and Little Nell from the plight into which they had fallen.

The rescuers arrived in the village too late. Little Nell had just died, and she was buried the day after their arrival in the churchyard where she had found happiness and employment. Her grandfather, who felt he had nothing to live for after her death, died on her tomb a few days later and was buried beside her.

Kit had been in love with Little Nell as an ideal; he now returned with Nell's granduncle to London. Through his patron's influence and with help from the same men who had judged him guilty of stealing money, only to find him honest and innocent, he found a proper place in society and was married shortly thereafter to a worthy young woman. After Sampson Brass had been released from prison, the Brasses became beggars in and about London. Fortunately, Mrs. Quilp was released by her dwarfish husband's death, and she happily married again. The old curiosity shop was soon destroyed to make way for a new building. Even Kit could not tell exactly where it had stood.

Critical Evaluation:

Considered by many critics to be the best writer of the nineteenth century, Charles Dickens continues to attract readers. *The Old Curiosity Shop*, the author's fourth novel, drew a large audience when it first appeared. In the opening chapter, the narrator who meets Nell and her grandfather is probably Master Humphrey, a persona who was providing a framework for all of the serial's literary selections. The first-person narration later changes to a third-person narration. The third-person narrator provides insightful, ironic, and philosophical commentary.

As in most of his early novels, Dickens criticizes contemporary social, political, and industrial injustices. The ethics of Victorian society allowed the gambling that seduces Nell's grandfather into losing their livelihood and home at the hands of cardsharps. The legal system threatens to imprison Nell's aged, mentally deteriorating grandfather and thus separate him from his beloved grandchild. Economic constraints force people, including children, to work in hellish mills. Also Dickens' Christian society disregards the immoral conditions of poverty and desperation that lead children to steal and then, as the novel illustrates, punishes a youth's petty theft by transporting him over his mother's cries of protest. From such a society, death is the only release. Despite the protests of original readers of the serial novel, Dickens therefore has Little Nell die. Her death before the Single Gentleman can rescue her may be read as Dickens' message that the novel is not intended as mere emotional escapism, but that it is intended as a serious denunciation of his society's moral failings.

Like Dickens' more critically acclaimed works, *The Old Curiosity Shop* is most successful in its characterization. Dickens' typical method is to identify a character, major or minor, with some repetitive speech and mannerism. For example, there are Dick Swiveller's fantastically imaginative diction, the Single Gentleman's abrupt actions, the tiny Marchioness' penchant for looking through keyholes, Tom Scott's standing on his head, and Quilp's shrieks of laughter, to name only a few. Although this repetition tends to flatten the character, the artistic device not only provides humor and variety, it also supports the use of characters to form a moral mosaic.

As do many of Dickens' good characters, the selfless Nell Trent inspires more loving devotion in other characters in the novel than she does in the contemporary reader. Many other thoroughly good characters, such as the Garlands, Kit Nubbles, the poor schoolmaster, and the single gentleman, support the romantic concept, more widely held in Dickens' time, that those who are good are naturally good. One of the few characters who manages to span the gap between the evil and the good characters is Dick Swiveller. Although originally the pawn of Frederick Trent and Quilp, Swiveller switches to the side of goodness by revealing to the police Quilp's part in framing Kit Nubbles because, as the narrator assures the reader, Swiviller is "essentially good-natured."

Daniel Quilp, the dwarf, is the figure of consummate evil who dominates the novel. Quilp possesses such vitality in his evil designs that he enlivens the scenes in which he appears. At one point, his voice interrupts a conversation criticizing him; he seems as omnipresent as the devil. Another set of evil, materialistic characters, Samuel Brass and his "dragon" of a sister Sally also provide examples of moral degeneration. Samuel Brass's subservience in his avowed admiration of Quilp, regardless of that man's outrageous treatment of him, rivals Sally's determined competitiveness. Eventually the greed of these siblings is appropriately rewarded by a life of destitution. Such is the majesty of fiction. They wander through the worst slums of London scavenging for food.

One of the serious weaknesses of the novel lies in the weak connection between the two plot lines. The experiences of Nell and her grandfather as they try to escape the pursuit of Quilp is one plot line, and the events in the lives of those who remain in London is the other. Toward the end of the novel, these two strands meet, but at one point even the narrator apologizes for abandoning one set of characters for an unconscionable period of time while he deals with the other group.

The Old Curiosity Shop contains one of Dickens' favorite recurring themes: the reversal of roles of parent and child. In this novel, granddaughter Nell cares for her gambling-addict grandfather. Amy Dorrit cares for her debt-imprisoned father in *Little Dorrit* (1855-1857), and Jenny Wren supports her alcoholic father in *Our Mutual Friend* (1864-1865). This theme probably originated in Dickens' childhood experience. When his father was put in debtors' prison, the young Dickens was forced to support himself in a blacking factory until an inheritance paid off his father's debt.

Dickens expresses, through the voice of the narrator, some comic and forgiving perceptions of human nature to counterbalance the novel's satiric attacks on social justice. Some examples include the dialogue between the aged sexton and the deaf gravedigger regarding the age of the corpse they are burying. One insists she is their contemporary; the other protests she must be at least ten years their senior. The second estimate gives them ten more years before they need to consider their own deaths. In another scene, in which several friends of Mrs. Quilp come like Job's comforters to criticize her choice of a husband, she astutely observes that if she died, any one of those present would agree to marry him. Another example of the work's ironies is that the pragmatic, materialistic Sally Brass, after years of self-sufficient spinsterhood, is quite smitten with the lazy, improvident Dick Swiveller when he comes to clerk for her brother. Dickens' observations of human inconsistency appeals to readers as much currently as they did to the readers of the nineteenth century. The title of the work suggests a central theme: Only the past contains peace and joy. Nell is looking for such peace when she leaves the curiosity shop, but at the end of her journey she finds only the ultimate peace, death.

"Critical Evaluation" by Agnes A. Shields

Bibliography:

Dyson, A. E. *"The Old Curiosity Shop*: Innocence and the Grotesque." In *Dickens*, edited by A. E. Dyson. Nashville, Tenn.: Aurora, 1970. Argues that justifications of the character of Nell on artistic grounds ordinarily emphasize the ironies that attend her and deny the sentimentality.

Johnson, Edgar. *Charles Dickens: His Tragedy and Triumph*. 2 vols. New York: Simon & Schuster, 1952. Volume 1 of this definitive critical biography includes a criticism of *The Old Curiosity Shop* that defends Dickens' sentimentality over modern cynicism.

Kincaid, James R. *Dickens and the Rhetoric of Laughter*. Oxford, England: Clarendon Press, 1971. Argues that laughter makes the pathos effective in *The Old Curiosity Shop*. Bibliography.

Marcus, Steven. *Dickens, from Pickwick to Dombey*. New York: W. W. Norton, 1985. Provides a lengthy analysis of *The Old Curiosity Shop*, ascribing the inspiration for Nell and Dickens' absorption with death in this novel to the death of Mary Hogarth, his young sister-in-law. Proposes that Nell and Quilp, polar representations of spirituality and carnality respectively, actually represent two sides of one person.

Walder, Dennis. *Dickens and Religion*. Winchester, Mass.: Allen & Unwin, 1981. Shows how Dickens uses death as a moral gauge: Good Nell dies loved and mourned by those who knew her. Evil Quilp, trying to escape the police, drowns alone.

OLD FORTUNATUS

Type of work: Drama
Author: Thomas Dekker (c. 1572-1632)
Type of plot: Allegory
Time of plot: Tenth century
Locale: Cyprus, Babylon, and England
First performed: The Whole History of Fortunatus, commonly known as *Old Fortunatus*,
    1599; first published, 1600

> *Principal characters:*
> FORTUNATUS, a foolish man endowed by Fortune
> ANDELOCIA, his worldly younger son
> AMPEDO, his virtuous older son
> AGRIPYNE, daughter of the king of England
> FORTUNE
> VIRTUE
> VICE

The Story:

    Fortunatus had never assiduously pursued virtue. He had been compelled, however, by his poverty to lead a life of patience and temperance. One day, after wandering for three days in a forest and sustaining himself by eating nuts, he unexpectedly encountered the goddess Fortune. This meeting was to transform his life. The goddess, who enjoyed both the praises and the curses of men as tokens of her power, chose to smile on the old man. Of her six gifts—wisdom, strength, health, beauty, long life, and riches—she offered him one. Believing that all other blessings would naturally flow from it, Fortunatus chose wealth. To effect his wish, she gave to him a magic purse that would always contain ten pieces of gold, no matter how frequently he drew from it. This gift, she told him, would last until he and his sons died. After reproaching him for his foolish choice, she sent him on his way home.

    At home, Fortunatus found his sons, Ampedo and Andelocia, in a despondent mood. Andelocia, the worldly son, had been lamenting his lack of food and money, while his more virtuous brother, Ampedo, had been greatly worried about their father's plight. Fortunatus, returning in rich attire, told them they need sorrow no longer, for he was presenting them with four bags of gold and would give them more when it was gone. Then he announced his intention to travel and associate with the mighty men of the world.

    Meanwhile, Fortune was joined in the forest by Virtue and Vice, goddesses who had come to Cyprus to plant trees of good and evil. Virtue's tree had withered leaves and little fruit, while Vice's flourished. Although Virtue had experienced defeats and was forced to endure the taunts of Vice, she had resolved once again to seek fertile ground for her tree. Fortune, who advanced both the virtuous and the vicious, cared not whose tree flourished, but agreed to judge the contest and declare the winner.

    Fortunatus, once scorned, now found himself honored in every court. Among other rulers, he visited the Soldan of Babylon, who had heard of the purse and wished it for himself. The crafty Fortunatus said that he had given away three of the purses and would make another for him. In gratitude, the soldan proposed to show the old man the wondrous sights of Babylon. He started with his most highly valued possession, a hat that carried its wearer wherever he wished to be. Tricking the soldan into letting him try on the hat, Fortunatus wished himself in Cyprus and disappeared.

Convinced of the supreme value of money, he returned home at the height of his triumph. His self-congratulations were interrupted, however, by a second encounter with Fortune, who, this time, decreed his death. His dying wish that his sons might have wisdom instead of wealth was denied. Bequeathing them the purse and the wishing hat, he asked that the two gifts be kept together and shared equally. No sooner had he died than Andelocia insisted that they be exchanged each year.

Andelocia, in possession of the purse, followed the example of his father by going to court. His first destination was England, where he planned to test the effect of gold on the beautiful Agripyne, daughter of King Athelstane. When Athelstane observed the lavish spending of Andelocia, he advised his daughter to try to discover the source of this wealth. With ease she drew the secret from the foolish young man, then drugged him and took the purse.

Awaking and discovering the theft, Andelocia, discouraged, determined to return home, steal from his brother the hat of Misery, and there make his home. He carried out his resolution to possess the magic hat; but, instead of seeking Misery, he returned to England, abducted Agripyne, and carried her away into the wilderness. She was able to outsmart him, this time accidentally gaining possession of the hat and wishing herself in England.

The hapless Andelocia, after having eaten an apple, discovered that he had grown horns. The goddess Vice stood before him and mocked him, for it was her apple that had caused his deformity. Virtue also stood before him, grieving and offering him apples that would remove the horns. He accepted Virtue's apples and pledged himself to be her minion.

His resolve was short-lived, however, for his love of money was much more compelling than his promise to Virtue. He returned to England, determined to recover the purse and hat. Disguised as Irish costermongers, he and his servant peddled the apples of Vice, which he had brought with him. By falsely representing the effect of eating the apples, he sold them to Agripyne and two courtiers, Longaville and Montrose. While thus employed, he was discovered by his brother Ampedo, who had come to England to find the purse and hat and to burn those sources of grief and shame.

Longaville, Montrose, and Agripyne grew horns; and Agripyne found herself promptly deserted by all but one of her many suitors. After they discovered that the horns grew back after being cut, they sought the help of a French physician, who was, in reality, Andelocia in another disguise. By using a medicine taken from the apples of Virtue, he removed Longaville's horns. As he turned to treat Agripyne, he spied the magic hat. Warning everyone to look the other way so that his cure would work, he grabbed the hat, took Agripyne by the hand, and wished himself with his brother.

After he had recovered the purse, Andelocia removed the horns from Agripyne and released her. He was not destined to enjoy his possessions long. Ampedo, according to his pledge, burned the hat. Soon afterward Longaville and Montrose found Andelocia and took the magic purse. Seeking revenge for the indignities they had suffered, they placed the brothers in the stocks, where Ampedo died of grief and Andelocia was strangled.

Longaville and Montrose then turned to quarreling between themselves over the purse, but were interrupted by the arrival of members of the court and the three goddesses. The purse was reclaimed by Fortune, and the two courtiers were condemned by Vice to spend their lives wandering with tormented consciences.

Again a quarrel broke out between Virtue and Vice. This time Fortune turned to the audience for judgment. For her judge, Virtue singled out Queen Elizabeth. At the sight of this paragon of virtue, Vice fled. Fortune bowed to this superior force, and Virtue admitted that she, by comparison, was a mere counterfeit.

Critical Evaluation:

Thomas Dekker's *Old Fortunatus*, first performed before Queen Elizabeth I on December 27, 1599, is an uneasy combination of morality play and light comedy, combining a serious, allegorical message with a series of highly inventive, fantastic events that propel the characters throughout the world known to the English of the Renaissance, from Turkey to Cyprus to England. Never entirely realistic or completely symbolic, it suffers from internal contradictions and a certain weakness of structure but offers the audience an intensely moral lesson. Moral instruction, aimed at the members of the English court, seems to have been the major intention of the play.

The plot is simple: Fortunatus is confronted by the goddess Fortune, who offers him a choice of strength, health, beauty, long life, riches, or wisdom. Unwisely, Fortunatus chooses wealth, and is given a magical purse that always contained ten gold pieces. Later, through an equally unrealistic turn of events, he obtains the magical hat of the Turkish sultan, which allows him to transport himself from place to place merely by wishing.

Fortunatus dies, and his two sons, Andelocia, the worldly younger boy, and Ampedo, the virtuous older youth, must share the inheritance. Despite their differing ways of using Fortunatus' gifts, they are no better in making use of their legacy than their father, and in the end they, too, come to bitter ends. The theme that this world is a sum of "vanity of vanities," so familiar in Elizabethan literature, is central to *Old Fortunatus*.

The power and capriciousness of Fortune, as the ruling goddess of the world, was a familiar theme during the period. Fortune's wheel, that instrument that causes some to rise and others to fall, and that keeps turning, was a popular image in Dekker's time in poetry and the visual arts. Dekker emphasizes the irrational nature of Fortune and her ways: "This world is Fortune's ball wherewith she sports." The essence of Fortune is that she is fickle, completely devoid of moral sense, arbitrary in her judgments and without regard for the vices and virtues of individual human beings. Given Fortune's arbitrary nature, it is no surprise Old Fortunatus is first blessed, then condemned by Fortune; his sons follow suit in their fashion. Only by embracing virtue (which, at the end of the play, is identified as Queen Elizabeth, the earthly personification of the quality) can human beings rise above the fickle, transitory nature of human life.

This sense of morality—and Dekker's debt to traditional English morality plays such as *Everyman*—has a considerable impact on *Old Fortunatus*. The characters are almost stock figures, representing traditional virtues and vices, rather than complex individuals. Allegorical figures such as Fortune, who embody forces beyond human life, are most representative of this tendency; a number of critics have rightfully noted that Fortune begins as indifferent, even scornful of human beings, only to end the play by announcing her allegiance to Queen Elizabeth as the embodiment of virtue. Again, such a discrepancy was hardly likely to have caused problems during the period when the play was written and first produced.

The source of Dekker's play was almost certainly an old German folktale known as "Old Fortunatus and His Magic Purse and Hat," published in 1509. Dekker adapted the story to fit the conventions of the English stage by emphasizing the spectacular and visual elements of the work and by providing his characters, especially Fortune, with elaborate rhetorical set pieces. It is the sometimes awkward fit between the two elements that has caused some critics to comment on the divided nature of Dekker's drama, which is part fantastic comedy and part moralizing sermon.

It is highly unlikely that Dekker's audience would have been troubled by such a division of purpose and approach. In the context of the dispute between the Puritan culture, which denigrated poetry and popular music, and Renaissance humanism, which endorsed the works of the human imagination, many of the Elizabethans believed that a major purpose of art, especially poetry and the theater, was to serve a didactic purpose. The basis of Sir Philip Sidney's *Defence of Poesie* (1595), the premier apology of poetic art as a worthwhile effort and an answer to Puritan attacks, was that poetry is better able than history or biography to provide a moral lesson to readers; *Old Fortunatus* is a drama that fits precisely into that worldview. The spectacle and romantic elements are to delight the audience, while important moral lessons are being imparted. The classical belief of rhetoric as an art which teaches, delights, and persuades is worked out in the play, and Dekker freely combines the fantastic and the moral to achieve his aim.

Such is the purpose of *Old Fortunatus*, and Dekker was eminently qualified to write such a drama. One of the most productive and popular of Elizabethan and Jacobean playwrights, he claimed an "entire hand" or "at least a major finger" in some 220 plays. He was among the best for tragedy, while the dramatist John Webster ranked Dekker along with William Shakespeare as an example of a playwright of the first order. *Old Fortunatus*, apparently Dekker's first work for the stage, provides an excellent example of what the writers and audiences of Elizabethan London saw in his work: smoothly flowing verse, a strong sense of individual character, and a lively plot that, however fantastic in its individual moments, always provides a moral lesson to courtier and commoner alike.

"Critical Evaluation" by Michael Witkoski

Bibliography:
Champion, Larry S. *Thomas Dekker and the Traditions of English Drama.* New York: Peter Lang, 1985. Situates *Old Fortunatus* at the intersection of the traditions of morality plays and newer, humanist drama.

Hoy, Cyrus. Introduction to *The Dramatic Works of Thomas Dekker*, edited by Fredson Bowers. Cambridge, England: Cambridge University Press, 1980. Places the drama within the context of Dekker's career and in the general literary scene of the period.

Logan, Terence, and Denzell S. Smith, eds. "Thomas Dekker." In *The Popular School: A Survey and Bibliography of Recent Studies in English Renaissance Drama.* Lincoln: University of Nebraska Press, 1975. A sourcebook for additional information about Dekker and his plays.

Price, George. *Thomas Dekker.* New York: Twayne, 1969. A basic study of Dekker's life and work that is especially valuable as a starting place. A helpful discussion of *Old Fortunatus*.

THE OLD MAID

Type of work: Novella
Author: Edith Wharton (1862-1937)
Type of plot: Social realism
Time of plot: 1850's
Locale: New York
First published: 1924

> *Principal characters:*
> DELIA RALSTON, a New York matron
> JAMES RALSTON, her husband
> CHARLOTTE LOVELL, Delia's cousin
> JOE RALSTON, James's cousin
> TINA LOVELL, Delia's ward

The Story:

Among the leading families in New York in the 1850's, none was more correct or more highly regarded than the Ralstons. Their ancestors had come to America not for religious freedom but for wealth. By the time Delia Lovell married James Ralston, the Ralstons considered themselves the ruling class, and all their thoughts and actions were dictated by convention. They shunned new ideas as they did strange people, and the sons and daughters of the numerous branches of the family married only the sons and daughters of similar good families.

Delia was conventional and correct by birth as well as by marriage. Before her marriage, she had been in love with Clement Spender, a penniless young painter; but since he would not give up his proposed trip to Rome and settle down to a disciplined life in New York, it was impossible for a Lovell to marry him. Against her will, Delia often imagined herself married to Clement, but the image was only momentary, for Delia had no place in her life for strong emotions or great passions. Her life with James and their two children was perfect. She was glad, too, that her cousin, Charlotte Lovell, was going to marry James's cousin, Joe Ralston, for at one time she had feared that Charlotte might never have a suitable proposal.

Charlotte was a strange girl who had become quite prudish in the years since she made her debut. At that time, she had been lively and beautiful. Then a sudden illness had caused her to go to Georgia for her health. Since her return, she had been colorless and drab, spending all of her time with the children of the poor. She had set up a little nursery where she cared for the children, and to this nursery had come a baby who had been abandoned by a veiled woman whom no one could identify. Charlotte seemed especially fond of the orphan child and favored her with better toys and clothes than those given the other children.

One day, Charlotte told Delia that she would not marry Joe Ralston. She told Delia that the orphaned baby in the nursery was her own, and that she had gone to Georgia to give birth to the child. Charlotte was ill with a racking cough that often caused a hemorrhage, but it was not her cough that caused her to worry. Joe had insisted that she give up her work with the children after they were married. Since her baby had no known parents, it would have to be placed in an orphanage, and Charlotte could not bear to think of her child in a charity home.

Joe, being a Ralston, would never marry Charlotte and accept her child if he knew the truth. Delia did not know what action to suggest until she learned that the baby's father was Clement

Spender. Charlotte had always loved Clement, who, when he returned from Rome and found Delia married, had turned to Charlotte. When he went back to Rome, Charlotte had not told him of the baby, for she knew that he still loved Delia.

Although Delia thought she no longer cared for Clement, she too could not bring herself to let his child be placed in an orphanage. She persuaded her husband to provide a home for Charlotte and the baby, telling him and the rest of the family that Charlotte and Joe should not marry because of Charlotte's cough. Joe, who wanted healthy children, was not hard to convince.

After Charlotte and the baby, Tina, had been established in a little house, Charlotte's health improved. In fact, she became quite robust, and each day grew more and more into an old maid. After James Ralston was killed by a fall from a horse, Delia took Charlotte and the little girl into her home. Tina grew up with the Ralston children and copied them in calling Delia "Mother" and Charlotte "Aunt."

Delia's children made proper marriages, and at last, she and Charlotte and Tina were left alone in the house. Charlotte often seemed to resent Delia's interest in Tina and the fact that the young girl went to Delia's room for private talks, but she dared not give any hint that Tina owed her love or affection.

When Delia learned that the sons of the good families would not marry Tina because she had no family background, she asked Charlotte to let her adopt the girl and give her the Ralston name. Both women feared that Tina might make the same mistake Charlotte had made if she continued to see the young men who loved her but would not marry her. Soon afterward, Delia made Tina her legal daughter, and the girl became engaged to a correct young man.

Tina was delighted with her new status as Delia's daughter, for she had long thought of her as a mother. The two made endless plans for Tina's wedding. On the night before the wedding, Delia wanted to go up to Tina's room to tell the girl all the things a mother usually tells her daughter on the eve of her wedding, but Charlotte flew into a rage. She accused Delia of having helped her and Tina only because she wanted revenge for Charlotte's affair with Clement. She told Delia that she knew Delia still loved Clement, that she had turned to Delia in her need, years ago, because she knew that Delia would help her for Clement's sake. Charlotte had been carrying hatred for Delia in her heart for many years, thinking always that Delia was trying to take Tina from her real mother. Charlotte declared fiercely that on her wedding eve Tina should talk with her real mother, and she started up to the girl's room.

When Charlotte had gone, Delia realized that there was some truth in what Charlotte had said. She had chosen James and the Ralston life willingly and knowingly, but she had often unconsciously wished for a life filled with love and unpredictable passions. She knew, too, that she had made Tina her own child, leaving Charlotte nothing for herself.

Delia started up to her room. She wanted to see Tina, but she thought that Charlotte deserved this one night with her daughter. Delia met Charlotte coming downstairs. Charlotte had not been with Tina, knowing that the girl would prefer her adopted mother. There was nothing an old maid aunt could say to a bride unless she were to tell her the truth, and that Charlotte could never do. So Delia had her talk with Tina. She did not stay long, for she knew that Charlotte was alone and unhappy. As she kissed Tina goodnight, she asked one favor. On the morrow, for Delia's sake, Tina was to give her last good-bye kiss to her Aunt Charlotte.

Critical Evaluation:

Considered by many critics to be one of the most important American fiction writers of the twentieth century, Edith Wharton in 1921 became the first woman to be awarded the Pulitzer

Prize in fiction. She was then just past the midpoint of a prolific forty-year writing career that included the publication of more than twenty novels and novellas, numerous short stories, travel books, works on interior decoration and gardening, and three volumes of poetry. In the first part of the twentieth century, critics often regarded Wharton as being solely a chronicler of the social mores of the upper classes of old New York. That reductive opinion was later corrected, as many other aspects of her career and works were fruitfully explored and analyzed from various critical angles.

The Old Maid, the second of a quartet of novellas published under the title *Old New York* in 1924, belongs to that phase of Wharton's career after World War I when she focused on the city's aristocracy in the decades prior to her birth. It was written shortly after the publication in 1920 of *The Age of Innocence*, the somewhat nostalgic novel of 1870's New York high society for which Wharton was awarded the Pulitzer Prize. *The Old Maid* is definitely not a nostalgic fictional reminiscence but represents instead a backward glance marked by a keen sense of disappointment, anguish, and loss about the shortcomings of the past. In fact, the topic of illegitimacy, around which the novella revolves, made publishers initially reluctant to accept the work for publication. Despite such prudish fears, the novella turned out to be one of Wharton's most popular and durable successes; it was adapted for the stage by Zoë Atkins and won the Pulitzer Prize in drama in 1935, and a melodramatic film version in 1939 starred Bette Davis and Miriam Hopkins.

The four novellas of *Old New York* are carefully linked and unified through such narrative strategies as chronological sequencing from the 1840's through the 1870's, recurrent family names and characters, and the gradual revelation in each novella of some crucial factors. Such a linking of four novellas under a unified title was an innovation in American literature. In fact, Wharton may have been attempting no less than to emulate a writer she much admired, Honoré de Balzac, and write a short American version of his grand series of interrelated novels of French society, the *Comédie Humaine* (1829-1848). Wharton was also indebted to the work of her friend Henry James, who had written a set of related short stories.

Like the other tales of *Old New York*, *The Old Maid* consists of two short stories linked by the passage of time. The first short story describes how Delia Ralston helps her cousin, Charlotte Lovell, to keep her illegitimate daughter, Tina; the second, set years later, describes her legal adoption of Tina to be able to provide her with the social respectability she needs to find a husband. Both parts revolve around crucial moments in the lives of Delia and Charlotte; both culminate in conversations between Delia and Charlotte in which the two women, despite grave differences, agree to cooperate for the sake of Tina.

The novella's themes—the stifling power of convention, the dubious value of sacrifice, the conflict between passion and social order—reflect common Wharton preoccupations. Meticulously describing the conservative high society of New York of the 1850's in all its variations of stifling uniformity, Wharton explores the problem of finding fulfillment, sexual or emotional, in a society that rigorously ignores and shuts its eyes to such needs. The novella also presents one of Wharton's superb analyses of the mother-daughter relationship, here with the twist that results from the struggle between two women, both of whom claim Tina as a daughter.

The novella's title is rather ironic. On the surface, it seems to refer to Charlotte Lovell who is forced to disavow her own child and who becomes in the eyes of everyone, including her daughter, an old maid with all the accompanying stereotypical character traits. Yet despite being married and having children, Delia is an old maid at heart because she has never given in to passion and remains emotionally unfulfilled and repressed. In an ironic reversion typical of Wharton, it is Charlotte who has known passion but cannot acknowledge the fact because of society's repressive rules, whereas while Delia enjoys all the social privileges of being a wife and mother but remains unfulfilled in her yearnings for an emotionally satisfying relationship.

Delia is the novella's major character, and the entire novella is narrated from her point of view. It is difficult to assess how Charlotte or Tina actually feel, because Delia's losses—in which the reader fully participates—seem greater. Charlotte's loss—giving up her daughter, first by renouncing her relationship with Tina, then by actually consenting to have her adopted by Delia—is not diminished, but Wharton does not describe the full extent of her anguish; it can only be inferred. Through focusing on Delia, Wharton wants the reader to detect yet another loss under the seemingly imperturbable social surface: the fate of a woman who married for security, not for love, and who regrets this choice for the rest of her life. Although the social conventions of the time prevent Charlotte from openly proclaiming to be Tina's mother, Delia can through Tina relive her youthful fantasies about Tina's father, Clement Spender, whom she herself had loved. Delia is successful in imposing her wishes and desires and by manipulating most people around her, but her victory is shallow at best; only in living out her fantasies through Tina can she find satisfaction and fulfillment. Wharton's descriptions of the lives of Delia Ralston and Charlotte Lovell show what it is like, as critic Cynthia Griffin Wolff has written, to "grow old and to be lonely—with all life's options already taken and all life's expectations harshly foreclosed."

"Critical Evaluation" by Ludger Brinker

Bibliography:

Funston, Judith E. "Clocks and Mirrors, Dreams and Destinies: Edith Wharton's *The Old Maid.*" In *Edith Wharton: New Critical Essays*, edited by Alfred Bendixen and Annette Zilversmit. New York: Garland Publishing, 1992. Uses the images of clocks and mirrors to raise larger questions about motherhood and the ways in which women can find their identity in a repressive society.

Lewis, R. W. B. *Edith Wharton: A Biography.* New York: Harper & Row, 1975. Discusses the novella in the context of Wharton's conflict with publishers who initially refused to accept the work because of its theme of illegitimacy.

Rae, Catherine. *Edith Wharton's New York Quartet.* Lanham, Md.: University Press of America, 1984. The only book-length study of the four novellas that make up *Old New York*. Provides analysis and background material.

Raphael, Lev. *Edith Wharton's Prisoners of Shame: A New Perspective on Her Neglected Fiction.* New York: St. Martin's Press, 1991. Discusses shame and its devastating effect on the psyche. Analyzes the novella in the context of jealousy and shame, which distort the relationship between two women and stifle both.

Wolff, Cynthia Griffin. *A Feast of Words: The Triumph of Edith Wharton.* New York: Oxford University Press, 1977. Analyzes the novella in the context of Wharton's look backward at the New York of her youth. Insists that the work is filled with a sense of disappointment and loss. Convincingly claims that the work depicts Wharton's own fear of growing old and lonely.

THE OLD MAN AND THE SEA

Type of work: Novella
Author: Ernest Hemingway (1899-1961)
Type of plot: Symbolic realism
Time of plot: Mid-twentieth century
Locale: Cuba and the Gulf Stream
First published: 1952

> *Principal characters:*
> SANTIAGO, an old Cuban fisherman
> MANOLIN, a young boy

The Story:

For eighty-four days, old Santiago had not caught a single fish. At first a young boy, Manolin, had shared his bad fortune, but after the fortieth luckless day, the boy's father told his son to go in another boat. From that time on, Santiago worked alone. Each morning he rowed his skiff out into the Gulf Stream where the big fish were. Each evening he came in empty-handed.

The boy loved the old fisherman and pitied him. If Manolin had no money of his own, he begged or stole to make sure that Santiago had enough to eat and fresh baits for his lines. The old man accepted his kindness with humility that was like a quiet kind of pride. Over their evening meals of rice or black beans, they would talk about the fish they had taken in luckier times or about American baseball and the great DiMaggio. At night, alone in his shack, Santiago dreamed of lions on the beaches of Africa, where he had gone on a sailing ship years before. He no longer dreamed of his dead wife.

On the eighty-fifth day, Santiago rowed out of the harbor in the cool dark before dawn. After leaving the smell of land behind him, he set his lines. Two of his baits were fresh tunas the boy had given him, as well as sardines to cover his hooks. The lines went straight down into deep dark water. As the sun rose, he saw other boats in toward shore, which was only a low green line on the sea. A hovering man-of-war bird showed him where dolphin were chasing some flying fish, but the school was moving too fast and too far away. The bird circled again. This time Santiago saw tuna leaping in the sunlight. A small one took the hook on his stern line. Hauling the quivering fish aboard, the old man thought it a good omen.

Toward noon, a marlin started nibbling at the bait, which was one hundred fathoms down. Gently the old man played the fish, a big one, as he knew from the weight on the line. At last, he struck to settle the hook. The fish did not surface. Instead, it began to tow the skiff to the northwest. The old man braced himself, the line taut across his shoulders. He had his skill and knew many tricks; he waited patiently for the fish to tire.

The old man shivered in the cold that came after sunset. When something took one of his remaining baits, he cut the line with his sheath knife. Once the fish lurched suddenly, pulling Santiago forward on his face and cutting his cheek. By dawn, his left hand was stiff and cramped. The fish had headed northward; there was no land in sight. Another strong tug on the line sliced Santiago's right hand. Hungry, he cut strips from the tuna and chewed them slowly while he waited for the sun to warm him and ease his cramped fingers.

That morning the fish jumped. Seeing it leap, Santiago knew he had hooked the biggest marlin he had ever seen. Then the fish went under and turned toward the east. Santiago drank sparingly from his water bottle during the hot afternoon. Trying to forget his cut hand and aching back, he remembered the days when men had called him *El Campeón*, and he had wrestled with a giant black man in the tavern at Cienfuegos. Once an airplane droned overhead on its way to Miami.

Close to nightfall, a dolphin took the small hook he had rebaited. He lifted the fish aboard, careful not to jerk the line over his shoulder. After he had rested, he cut fillets from the dolphin and also kept the two flying fish he found in its maw. That night he slept. He awoke to feel the line running through his fingers as the fish jumped. Feeding line slowly, he tried to tire the marlin. After the fish slowed its run, he washed his cut hands in seawater and ate one of the flying fish. At sunrise, the marlin began to circle. Faint and dizzy, he worked to bring the big fish nearer with each turn. Almost exhausted, he finally drew his catch alongside and drove in the harpoon. He drank a little water before he lashed the marlin to the bow and stern of his skiff. The fish was two feet longer than the boat. No catch like it had ever been seen in Havana harbor. It would make his fortune, he thought, as he hoisted his patched sails and set his course toward the southwest.

An hour later, he sighted the first shark. It was a fierce Mako, and it came in fast to slash with raking teeth at the dead marlin. With failing might, the old man struck the shark with his harpoon. The Mako rolled and sank, carrying the harpoon with it and leaving the marlin mutilated and bloody. Santiago knew the scent would spread. Watching, he saw two shovel-nosed sharks closing in. He struck at one with his knife lashed to the end of an oar and watched the scavenger sliding down into deep water. He killed the other while it tore at the flesh of the marlin. When the third appeared, he thrust at it with the knife, only to feel the blade snap as the fish rolled. The other sharks came at sunset. At first, he tried to club them with the tiller from the skiff, but his hands were raw and bleeding and there were too many in the pack. In the darkness, as he steered toward the faint glow of Havana against the sky, he heard them hitting the carcass again and again. Yet the old man thought only of his steering and his great tiredness. He had gone out too far and the sharks had beaten him. He knew they would leave him nothing but the stripped skeleton of his great catch.

All lights were out when he sailed into the little harbor and beached his skiff. In the gloom, he could just make out the white backbone and the upstanding tail of the fish. He started up the shore with the mast and furled sail of his boat. Once he fell under their weight and lay patiently until he could gather his strength. In the shack, he fell on his bed and went to sleep.

There the boy found him later that morning. Meanwhile other fishermen, gathered about the skiff, marveled at the giant marlin, eighteen feet long from nose to tail. When Manolin returned to Santiago's shack with hot coffee, the old man awoke. The boy, he said, could have the spear of his fish. Manolin told him to rest, to make himself fit for the days of fishing they would have together. All that afternoon, the old man slept, the boy sitting by his bed. Santiago was dreaming of lions.

Critical Evaluation:

The publication of the novella *The Old Man and the Sea* near the end of Ernest Hemingway's writing career restored his flagging reputation as a writer. It came at a time when critics thought Hemingway was losing his creative powers. They had panned his previous novel, *Across the River and into the Trees* (1950). The novella earned Hemingway the 1953 Pulitzer Prize and helped him win the Nobel Prize in Literature in 1954. For about fifteen years, the work enjoyed wide critical approval and attention, although it had its detractors. By the late 1960's, critics had begun a reassessment. Only a handful of articles were written about the novella in the 1980's. Whether a revised assessment will be forthcoming remains to be seen.

The Old Man and the Sea works on multiple levels of theme, image, and symbol. It has been compared to Herman Melville's *Moby Dick* (1851) and to Samuel Taylor Coleridge's "The Rime of the Ancient Mariner" (1798)—great tales of sea adventure and the testing of human endurance. The story depicts a world in which the heroic and the mundane intermingle. Hemingway claimed to be writing a story about a real fisherman, the real sea, and a real fish. There is no question, however, that the effort at realism does not mask the metaphorical and symbolic dimensions of the story. The story's lean and spare style focus readers' attention on a timeless drama nearly devoid of contemporary reference, but the modern world is a backdrop to one man's heroic struggle with nature. On one level, the story is a heroic testimony to the endurance and courage of a man in his struggle with nature. This interpretation is based on a reading of the text without recognition of its many ironies. The old man puts up a fierce and superhuman effort to conquer the great marlin, a fish so large and powerful as to remind readers of Moby Dick. In Hemingway's book, the fish is not entirely like Melville's leviathan. The marlin is not malicious or a malignant force of nature. It never attacks its pursuer the way Moby Dick does, but it does put up a fierce and noble fight for its life. The endurance of the old man, and perhaps his intelligence, proves to be superior to that of the fish. The man conquers the fish but, in the end, loses the fish to the sharks.

On one level, the novella is a gripping account of a man in search of meaning and dignity in a world that gives little quarter. To survive in this world and to feel that life has meaning is to struggle. This struggle is not unique to Santiago but rather is typical of the Hemingway hero. The struggle and how it is conducted provides meaning in a man's life. Hemingway puts so much poetic energy into depicting this struggle that it becomes an object of beauty, much as does the perfect pass in the bullring or the swing of Joe DiMaggio. This struggle requires tenacious will, intelligence, and prowess, or, as the old man refers to it, "ability." Readers of Hemingway's greatest works are familiar with his ethos of the graceful struggle. Those that live the struggle and exhibit special prowess are Hemingway's heroes. Such people include bull-fighters, soldiers, or, for that matter, bulls. Those who do not accept that life is a struggle and fail to exhibit prowess in whatever they do are depicted as failures and weaklings.

Hemingway dramatizes this struggle in the sparest of terms. The story presents only two characters, the old man and a boy who is friend and helper. The boy may be seen as the embodiment of the promise of uncorrupted youth. The boy's many kindnesses to the old man reflect a self-effacing and generous spirit that can only be seen as examples of human virtue. Santiago resembles Christ in his sufferings: Readers may note the attention paid to the laceration of Santiago's hands and to his assent up the hill to his hovel while he carries the mast. He falls five times, as did Christ carrying his cross, and finally lies in his bed, arms outstretched and palms turned upward. The spirit of Christ also informs the actions of the boy. Santiago suffers greatly (which is his primary similarity to Christ), but he does nothing to help anyone. He is on the receiving end of help from the boy, who makes sure Santiago has food and care. The owner of the bar also sends the old man food.

Santiago lives an impoverished life. He barely eats, owns almost nothing, reads only yes-terday's newspapers, and lives in a tiny shack with a dirt floor. He owns a small fishing boat, but he has barely enough gear to outfit him as a fisherman. His food and drink are charity.

His inner life is almost as impoverished. He holds a few memories as points of reference. He dreams of the lions on the beach in Africa that he saw as young man and of a titanic arm wrestling match with a powerful black man. These dreams symbolize the power of his youth. Santiago does not speak of his strength, but he credits himself for an ability to triumph over adversity through a combination of will and intelligence. When he is awake, he refers repeatedly to Joe DiMaggio as the epitome of prowess or ability—a model against which Santiago judges himself. His connection to Joe DiMaggio and the world of baseball is indicative of his values. Baseball embodies the values of physical strength and ability. Santiago also refers to Jesus and Mary and seems aware of a higher spiritual realm beyond his present struggle. These symbolic dimensions add depth and complexity to the narrative and contribute the great enjoyment readers continue to derive from this simple, beautifully written tale.

"Critical Evaluation" by Richard Damashek

Bibliography:
Brenner, Gerry. *"The Old Man and the Sea": Story of a Common Man*. New York: Twayne, 1991. Sets the novella's literary and historical contexts and discusses its critical reception. Considers the novella's structure, character, style, psychology, and biographical elements.

Killinger, John. *Hemingway and the Dead Gods: A Study in Existentialism*. Lexington: University Press of Kentucky, 1960. Compares Hemingway's views to those of such European existentialists as Jean Paul Sartre and Albert Camus. Adds much to the understanding of Santiago's character.

Sojka, Gregory S. *Ernest Hemingway: The Angler as Artist*. New York: Peter Lang, 1985. Examines fishing in Hemingway's life and works as "an important exercise in ordering and reinforcing an entire philosophy and style of life." Devotes chapter 5 to *The Old Man and the Sea*.

Waldhorn, Arthur. *A Reader's Guide to Ernest Hemingway*. New York: Farrar, Straus & Giroux, 1972. Sets out explanations of the terms "Hemingway hero" and "Hemingway code" then applies them to the works. Notes that Santiago's humility is an unusual quality in a Hemingway character.

Young, Philip. *Ernest Hemingway: A Reconsideration*. University Park: Pennsylvania State University Press, 1966. Considers the novel's roots in previous Hemingway works and discusses Santiago as a "code hero," as distinct from a "Hemingway hero." Claims simple interpretation of the book's symbols reduces their meanings.

OLD MORTALITY

Type of work: Novel
Author: Sir Walter Scott (1771-1832)
Type of plot: Historical
Time of plot: 1679
Locale: Scotland
First published: 1816

>   *Principal characters:*
>   HENRY MORTON, the heir of Milnwood
>   LADY MARGARET BELLENDEN, the Lady of Tillietudlem
>   EDITH, her granddaughter
>   COLONEL GRAHAME OF CLAVERHOUSE, later Viscount of Dundee
>   LORD EVANDALE, a Royalist
>   JOHN BALFOUR OF BURLEY, a Covenanter
>   BASIL OLIFANT, a renegade Covenanter

The Story:

Henry Morton had the misfortune of being a moderate man, a man who could see both sides of a question. During the rebellion of the Covenanters against the crown in 1679, his position became an exceedingly precarious one. His uncle and guardian was the Squire of Milnwood, by faith a Covenanter and by nature a miser, and Henry's dead father had fought for the Covenanters at Marston Moor. The story of his family was frequently cause for comment among the cavalier gentry of the district, especially at the tower of Tillietudlem, the home of Lady Margaret Bellenden and Edith, her granddaughter.

Henry and Lord Evandale contested as marksmen, and Edith Bellenden was among the spectators when Henry defeated his opponent. Declared the victor at this festival of the popinjay, Henry bowed his respects to Edith Bellenden, who responded with embarrassed courtesy under the watchful eyes of her grandmother.

After the shooting, Henry went with friends to a tavern where some dragoons of Claverhouse's troop, under Sergeant Francis Bothwell, were also carousing. Bothwell, a descendant of the Stuart kings through the bar sinister line, was a man of domineering disposition. Henry and his friends drank a toast to the health of the king; Bothwell, intending to humiliate the Covenanters, resolved that they should drink also to the Archbishop of St. Andrew's. A stranger in the company proposed the toast to the archbishop, ending with the hope that each prelate in Scotland would soon be in the same position as his grace.

Henry and the stranger left the inn; soon afterward, word came that the archbishop had been assassinated. Bothwell realized then that the stranger must have been one of the plotters in the deed, and he ordered a pursuit.

Meanwhile, Henry had learned that his companion was John Balfour of Burley, a Covenanter leader who had saved the life of Henry's father at Marston Moor. That night, Henry gave Balfour lodging at Milnwood without his uncle's knowledge and next morning showed the fugitive a safe path into the hills. Bothwell and his troops arrived shortly afterward. Henry was arrested and taken away.

In company with Henry in his arrest were Mause Headrigg, a staunch Covenanter, and her son Cuddie. The prisoners were taken to Tillietudlem Castle, where Claverhouse sentenced Henry to execution. He was saved, however, by the intercession of Edith and Lord Evandale.

Lord Evandale brought information that a group of Covenanters was gathering in the hills, and Claverhouse gave orders to have his troops advance against them. At a council of war, Lord Evandale, among others, suggested a parley in which both sides could air their grievances. Claverhouse sent his nephew, Cornet Grahame, to carry a flag of truce to the Covenanters. Balfour and a small group met Cornet Grahame, but the Covenanters refused to meet Claverhouse's demands. To the surprise and suppressed indignation of all, Balfour shot Cornet Grahame in cold blood after an interchange of words.

The killing of the young officer was the signal for a general fight. Bothwell and Balfour met beard to beard, and Balfour killed Bothwell with his sword as the dragoon stood defenseless, his sword arm broken by the kick of a horse. In the fray, Henry saved the life of Lord Evandale after the young nobleman's horse had been shot from under him.

Balfour's rebels were victorious and next laid plans to capture Castle Tillietudlem. Claverhouse left a few of his men to defend the place under the command of Major Bellenden, brother-in-law of Lady Margaret. Balfour had taken Henry Morton from the troops of Claverhouse on the battlefield and now wanted Henry to join with the Rebels; Henry, however, still held back. Trying to convince Henry of the righteousness of his cause, Balfour took him to a council of war, where Henry was elected one of a council of six through Balfour's insistence.

Major Bellenden refused to surrender the castle to the insurgents, who then decided to starve out the small garrison. Realizing that Henry wished to remain in the vicinity of the castle because he was concerned for Edith's safety, Balfour sent the young man to Glasgow, the objective of the main Covenanter army. Claverhouse had retreated to Glasgow and laid careful plans for the defense of the city. Henry returned to Milnwood with Cuddie in order to learn what was happening at Tillietudlem. Hearing that Lord Evandale had been captured during a sortie from the castle, Henry once again saved Lord Evandale's life from Balfour's rough justice. Then Henry drew up a document stating the grievances of and the conditions offered by the Covenanters and sent Lord Evandale with the paper to the castle. Edith and Lady Margaret escaped from the castle, and Henry raised the flag of the Covenanters to the castle tower.

The Covenanters were finally defeated at the battle of Bothwell Bridge. In the retreat from the field, Henry was taken prisoner by a party of Covenanter fanatics, who believed him to have deserted their cause. He was sentenced to death. Cuddie Headrigg caught a horse and escaped. He rode to Claverhouse and explained Henry's predicament. Since Henry's death was decreed on a Sabbath day, his captors decided he could not be executed until after midnight. This decision gave Claverhouse and his men time to rescue Henry. With the Covenanters' revolt now broken, Claverhouse agreed to put Henry on a parole of honor. Henry accepted exile from Scotland, promising to remain in banishment until the king's pleasure allowed his return. Henry went to Holland.

There he lived in exile for several years, until William and Mary came to the throne. When he returned to Scotland, he called upon Cuddie, who had married Jenny Dennison, Edith's maid. He learned from Cuddie of all that had occurred during his absence. He was informed that a man named Basil Olifant, a turncoat kinsman of Lady Margaret, had seized Tillietudlem and that Lady Margaret and Edith were forced to depend upon the charity of friends. Henry also learned that Balfour was still alive and that Lord Evandale was soon to marry Edith Bellenden. Henry set out to find Balfour and get a document from him that would place the Bellenden estates in Edith's possession once more. Balfour, however, burned the document and then threatened to fight Henry to the death; but Henry refused to fight with the man who had saved his father's life, and he made his escape from Balfour's fury by leaping across a ravine.

Meanwhile, Edith had refused marriage to Lord Evandale because she had caught a glimpse of Henry Morton as he passed her window. Later, at an inn, Henry overheard a plot to murder Lord Evandale; the murderers hoped to obtain a substantial sum of money from Basil Olifant for so doing. Henry scribbled a note of warning to Lord Evandale and sent his message by Cuddie. Then he went to Glasgow, intending to find Wittenbold, a Dutch commander of dragoons, and to get help from him to protect Lord Evandale. Cuddie, however, tarried too long at an alehouse and forgot that the letter was to be delivered to Lord Evandale. Instead, he asked to see Lady Margaret; when he was refused admittance, he stumbled away bearing the letter with him. Therefore, Lord Evandale was not warned of his danger.

A party of horsemen, led by Basil Olifant, came to kill Lord Evandale. Cuddie knew the danger but warned him too late. Shots were exchanged, and Lord Evandale fell. Olifant ordered Lord Evandale murdered in cold blood just before Henry arrived with a magistrate and a detachment of dragoons.

The troopers quickly dispersed the attackers, and Olifant fell during the charge. Balfour attempted to escape but was swept to his death in a flooded stream. Henry hurried to the side of Lord Evandale, who recognized him and made signs that he wished to be carried into Lady Margaret's house. There he died, surrounded by his weeping friends. His last act was to place Edith's hand in that of Henry Morton. To the great joy of the countryside, Henry married the young heiress of Tillietudlem several months later. In the meantime, Basil Olifant died without a will, and Lady Margaret recovered her castle and her estates.

Critical Evaluation:

Waverley: Or, 'Tis Sixty Years Since, and Sir Walter Scott's second and third novels, *Guy Mannering* (1815) and *The Antiquary* (1816), were successful; Scott, as a result, invested more than he should have in a country estate he called Abbotsford. Needing additional income, Scott changed publishers and invented a second authorial guise for himself.

A series called *Tales of My Landlord* was ostensibly written by the landlord of the Wallace Inn of Gandercleugh, a fictitious Scottish village about halfway between Edinburgh and Glasgow. There, Jedediah Cleishbotham tutored the landlord's six children. When Pattieson died, Cleishbotham found among his papers a parcel called "Tales of My Landlord," which Cleishbotham sold to a bookseller in order to pay Pattieson's funeral expenses. In an introduction to the tales, Cleishbotham insisted that he was not their writer, editor, or compiler. It was Pattieson, Cleishbotham claimed, who had prepared the tales for the press and who was therefore responsible for their departures from historical accuracy.

All this is yarn-spinning, there being no landlord, no Pattieson, and no Cleishbotham other than Scott himself. Why he thought it necessary to adopt such an elaborate disguise has been variously explained. It was common knowledge that "the author of Waverley" and *Tales of My Landlord* were written by the same person. The first of these tales was *The Black Dwarf* (1816), one of Scott's shorter and lesser efforts. The second was *Old Mortality* (1816), which Oliver Elton was first to praise as "the swiftest, the most varied, the least alloyed, the most fully alive of all" of Scott's novels. Critics laud *Old Mortality* as by far the best constructed. Together with *The Heart of Midlothian* (1818) *Old Mortality* is generally regarded as Scott's finest work.

The title of the novel seems at first glance to be another of Scott's subterfuges. *Old Mortality* is ostensibly a narrative by Pattieson, as edited first by Cleisbotham and then by his publishers. The narrative begins with Pattieson's meeting an aged Cameronian sympathizer known only as Old Mortality. The old Cameronian had that name because his sole occupation was to traverse rural Scotland repairing and maintaining the graves of other Cameronians who, like their cause, would otherwise be forgotten. Cameronians were followers of Richard Cameron, who, in opposition to English efforts toward unification, upheld the covenants of 1638 and 1643, which were designed to protect the established Church of Scotland and its rites from governmental interference. The Cameronians were also known as Covenanters.

Old Mortality is a representation of Robert Paterson, who lived from 1715 to 1801. In an introduction to an 1830 reprint of the Waverley novels (when their authorship was no longer denied), Scott claims to have met Paterson. According to the first chapter of the novel, Old Mortality supposedly shared many of his Covenanting memories with the landlord in return for overnight hospitality. Readers learn nothing further of him after that. Old Mortality disappears from the narrative, but he remains a presence in the novel as its title character. His role as title character is symbolic, Old Mortality being intended, with a degree of irony, to personify human transience, the incessant change that history represents, and the futility of attempting to resist the ravages of time. Despite his efforts, the gravestones of the Covenanters will soon erode into nothingness, destroying all memory of them, their cause, and their concerns. In attempting to resuscitate them and their history in his novel, Scott knowingly becomes a kind of Old Mortality himself.

The alleged authenticity of the narrative—which Cleishbotham defends as real history rather than fiction—is compromised by its having supposedly passed through so many hands, from Old Mortality (and other sources) to the landlord to Pattieson to Cleishbotham, with some interference from the publishers after that. The most immediate effects of this fictitious transmission are apparent in the novel and fundamental to it. First, although Old Mortality may have provided the landlord with useful recollections of past events, they could not have been at first hand. The novel proper begins precisely on May 5, 1679, and ends ten years later. Its events therefore take place before Old Mortality was born.

Second, the novel's point of view is not that of the Cameronians, who are represented throughout as overly zealous biblical literalists unfortunately inspired by the harsh retributive ethics of the Old Testament rather than the more accommodating forgiveness of the New. For Scott, Old Mortality is the last of his kind—the sole survivor of a bygone era that we have most fortunately progressed beyond. Scott's understanding of the Cameronians' outdated mentality, however, is remarkable. No writer before Scott recognizes so fully that human awareness of the actual is historically conditioned and that what one generation takes as its eternal verities seems nonsensical or fanatic to later ones. The historicity of mentality is therefore fundamental to *Old Mortality* and many of Scott's other novels.

Just as thought changes through time, so must language. The oldest language in the book would properly belong to Old Mortality, but he never speaks. The Cameronians speak an older, more biblical English than other characters do; one can judge the degree of their religious extremity (and their obsolescence) by their talk. The more moderate Scots, and the English characters uniformly, sound a good deal more modern. As is usually with Scott, the narrator understands and transcribes Scots (most modern editions of the novel include a full glossary) but does not write it.

Third, the alleged origin of the novel's text cannot adequately explain the omniscient knowledge of the narrator, who is privy to the minds not only of the Covenanters but also of all the characters. It is soon apparent that neither Pattieson nor any other of the narrative's supposed transmitters, alone or in combination, could have all the necessary facts at his disposal, if this were indeed true history. In actuality, the novel is not history at all but fiction, and those interested in such things have pointed out how Scott has sometimes altered fact. Scott himself points out, for example, that the Castle of Tillietudlem (together with its siege and all that takes place within) is imaginary.

Old Mortality actually existed but plays no part in the real business of the novel. The several Cameronian preachers, with their highly artificial names, are constructs designed to represent a spectrum of religious fanaticism grading into mania. Monmouth and Claverhouse are both historical, although Scott had to create for each a personality. His Claverhouse has been called the most successful characterization of a historical personage in any of his novels, particularly because Claverhouse strikes readers as both complex and modern. Surprisingly modern too are Scott's low-born characters, including Cuddie Headrigg the plowman, whose ability to survive and to influence events is noteworthy. Jenny, his eventual wife, is similarly likeable and equally successful. Whereas other female characters in the novel feel bound to act in highly constrained and sometimes artificial ways, Jenny is spontaneous and natural.

Recent perspectives on literary study have encouraged closer attention to the roles of women in fiction. Their importance to the society depicted in *Old Mortality* is clear not only from their high social stations but also from their influence on events. Despite Scott's apparent preoccupation with Scottish history, the center of *Old Mortality* is unquestionably the triangular relationship of Edith Bellenden, Lord Evandale, and Henry Morton, in which traditional conflicts between love, friendship, and duty are resolved more by fate than by choice. These three are certainly the most admirable characters in the novel, but readers sense (as perhaps Scott did also) that such scrupulous nobility as theirs was doomed, like the religious fanaticism of the Cameronians, to fail to survive.

"Critical Evaluation" by Dennis R. Dean

Bibliography:
Barrett, Deborah J. "Balfour of Burley: The Evil Energy in Scott's *Old Mortality.*" *Studies in Scottish Literature* 17 (1982): 248-253. Analyzes the character in the novel who, more than any other, fails to affirm a positive code of conduct.
Dickson, Beth. "Sir Walter Scott and the Limits of Toleration." *Scottish Literary Journal* 18, no. 2 (November, 1991): 46-62. Argues that although Scott struggles to understand the Cameronians, it is clear throughout that he also disapproves of them and does not regret their passing.
Fleischner, Jennifer B. "Class, Character and Landscape in *Old Mortality.*" *Scottish Literary Journal* 9, no. 2 (December, 1982): 21-36. Landscape, a prominent element in many of Scott's novels, is often overlooked. Sees landscape in relation to the social and moral standing of major characters.
Humma, John B. "The Narrative Framing Apparatus of Scott's *Old Mortality.*" *Studies in the Novel* 12, no. 4 (Winter, 1980): 301-315. Explores the problem of landlord, Pattieson, Cleishbotham, and editors as commentators upon the narrative.
Whitmore, Daniel. "Bibliolatry and the Rule of the World: A Study of Scott's *Old Mortality.*" *Philological Quarterly* 65, no. 2 (Spring, 1986): 243-262. Bibliolatry is excessive veneration of the Bible, a term the Cameronians would have found objectionable in its presumption. Illuminates the clash within the novel between church and state.

THE OLD WIVES' TALE

Type of work: Novel
Author: Arnold Bennett (1867-1931)
Type of plot: Naturalism
Time of plot: Nineteenth century
Locale: England and Paris
First published: 1908

Principal characters:
> CONSTANCE BAINES POVEY and
> SOPHIA BAINES SCALES, sisters
> JOHN BAINES, their father
> MRS. BAINES, their mother
> SAMUEL POVEY, Constance's husband
> GERALD SCALES, Sophia's husband
> CYRIL POVEY, the son of Constance and Samuel

The Story:

Sixteen-year-old Constance Baines was a plump, pleasant girl with a snub nose. Sophia Baines, aged fifteen, was a handsome girl with imagination and daring. The first symptoms of her rebelliousness and strong individuality came when she announced her desire to be a teacher in 1864. Mr. and Mrs. Baines owned a draper's shop, and their income was adequate. They were most respectable and were therefore horrified at their daughter's unconventional plan, for it had been taken for granted that she as well as Constance would assist in the shop. When Sophia was four years old, John Baines, her father, had suffered a stroke of paralysis that had left him an invalid whose faculties were greatly impaired. Prodded by his capable wife, he joined in forbidding Sophia to think of schoolteaching, but his opposition only strengthened Sophia's resolve.

When Sophia had been left alone to care for her father one day, she saw a handsome young man, representative of a wholesale firm, enter the store. She invented an errand to take her into the shop. She learned that his name was Gerald Scales. When Sophia returned to her father's room, he had slipped off the bed, and, unable to move himself, had died of asphyxia. Mr. Baines's old friend, Mr. Critchlow, was called immediately; having seen Sophia in the shop with Gerald, he instantly accused her of killing her father. Presumably as a gesture of repentance but actually because she hoped for an opportunity to see Gerald again, Sophia offered to give up her plans to teach.

Sophia worked in millinery while Constance assisted Samuel Povey, the clerk, a small quiet man without dignity and without imagination. He and Constance gradually fell in love.

After two years, Gerald returned. By artful contriving, Sophia managed to meet him alone and to initiate a correspondence. Mrs. Baines recognized Sophia's infatuation and sent her off to visit her Aunt Harriet. Several weeks later, Sophia ran off with Gerald Scales. She wrote her mother that they were married and planning to live abroad. A short time later, Constance and Samuel Povey were married. Mrs. Baines turned over the house and shop to them and went to live with her sister.

The married life of Constance held few surprises, and the couple soon settled to a routine tradesman's existence. Nothing further was heard of Sophia except for an occasional Christmas card giving no address. After six years of marriage a son, Cyril, was born. Constance centered her life about the baby, more so since her mother died shortly after his birth. Povey also devoted much attention to the child, but he made his wife miserable by his insistence on discipline. When, after twenty years of marriage, Povey caught pneumonia and left Constance a widow, she devoted herself entirely to Cyril. He was a charming, intelligent boy, but he seemed indifferent to his mother's efforts to please him. When he was eighteen years old, he won a scholarship in art and was sent to London. His mother was left alone.

Life had not dealt so quietly with Sophia. In a London hotel room, after her elopement, she had suffered her first disillusionment when Gerald began to make excuses for delaying their marriage; but after Sophia refused to go to Paris with him except as his wife, he reluctantly agreed to the ceremony. Gerald had inherited twelve thousand pounds. He and Sophia lived lavishly in Paris. Gerald's weakness, his irresponsibility, and lack of any morals or common sense soon became apparent. Realizing that Gerald had little regard for her welfare, Sophia took two hundred pounds in bank notes from his pocket and hid them in case of an emergency. As Gerald lost more money at gambling, they lived in shabbier hotels, wore mended clothes, and ate sparingly. When their funds were nearly exhausted, Gerald suggested that Sophia should write to her family for help. When Sophia refused, Gerald abandoned her.

The next day, she awoke ill and was visited by Gerald's friend, Chirac, who had come to collect money Gerald had borrowed from him. Chirac had risked his own reputation by taking money from the cash box of the newspaper where he was employed. Sophia unhesitatingly used some of the notes she had taken from Gerald to repay Chirac. When she again became ill, Chirac left her in the care of a middle-aged courtesan, Madam Faucault, who treated Sophia kindly during her long illness.

Madame Faucault was deeply in debt. Sophia rented Madame Faucault's flat and took roomers and boarders. At that time, France was at war with Germany, and the siege of Paris soon began. Food was scarce. Only by hard work and the most careful management was Sophia able to feed her boarders. She grew hard and businesslike. When the siege was lifted and Paris returned to normal, Sophia bought the pension Frensham at her own price. This pension was well-known for its excellence and respectability, and under Sophia's management, it prospered. She did not hear from her husband again. By the Exhibition year, she had built up a modest fortune from the two hundred pounds she had taken from Gerald.

One day, Cyril Povey's young English friend came to stay at the pension Frensham. Sophia's beauty and dignity intrigued him, and he learned enough about her to recognize her as his friend's aunt. On his return to England, he hastily informed both Cyril and Constance of Sophia's situation.

Constance immediately wrote Sophia a warm, affectionate letter begging her to come to England for a visit. Meanwhile in Paris, Sophia had suffered a slight stroke; when she was offered a large sum for the pension Frensham, she reluctantly let it go. Soon afterward, she visited England.

Although Sophia had intended to make only a short visit, the sisters lived together for nine years. On the surface, they got along well together, but Sophia had never forgiven her sister for her refusal to move from the ugly, inconvenient old house. Constance, on her part, silently resented Sophia's domineering ways.

Their tranquil existence was interrupted by a telegram to Sophia, informing her that Gerald Scales was very ill in a neighboring town. She went to him at once, but on her arrival, she learned that he was already dead. He was shabby, thin, and old. Sophia was greatly shocked when she saw Gerald; part of her shock was the fact that she no longer had any feeling for the man who had both made and ruined her life. She suffered another stroke while driving home and lived only a few hours. Cyril was left all of Sophia's money. He had continued to live in London on an allowance, completely absorbed in his art, still secretive and indifferent to his mother. When Constance died several years later, he was abroad and did not return in time for the funeral. When the servants went off for Constance's burial, only Sophia's old poodle was left in the house. She waddled into the kitchen to see if any food had been left in her dish.

Critical Evaluation:

Late nineteenth century literary naturalism insists on the determining forces of heredity and environment. Realism concentrates objectively on the social and historical conditions of experience, but it allows for a greater independence in the principal characters. Arnold Bennett's fiction is marked by a blending of these two literary movements. He cultivated detachment and technique in his writing because he felt that the English novel had neglected what he called a "scientific" eye; satire and sentiment, from Henry Fielding to Charles Dickens, had colored the English author's presentation of reality. Bennett turned to France for new models. By absorbing realism and naturalism, he became a master of the "impressions of the moment," but he retained an English sense for the uniqueness of character.

The Old Wives' Tale is his masterpiece. The title is revealing in that, instead of describing a superstitious tale, it dramatizes his objectivity by obliging readers to interpret the phrase literally. The novel is about two women who become old; their story, despite its inevitability, is far more wondrous in its simple reality than any fantastic or "superstitious" tale. What is remarkable about them is that despite their having lived entirely different lives, they emerge, at the end, remarkably similar. This is primarily because of the moral fiber woven into their characters from earliest childhood. Neither woman "has any imagination" (which was Bennett's intention), but each has the stability of a rock. Constance leads a conventional life and never leaves St. Luke's square; Sophia runs off with an attractive salesman, is deserted in Paris, and runs a successful boardinghouse during the siege of Paris and the Commune. (It is no coincidence that Bennett chose to name each symbolically for her main character trait: constancy and wisdom, respectively.) Despite the difference of circumstance in their lives, they remain the self-reliant middle-class daughters of John Baines. Bennett achieves his desired effect of parallelism amid contrast. This pattern is illustrative of what Bennett meant by technique and craftsmanship; it also reveals the interweaving of naturalist and realist techniques in fiction.

The "judicial murder" of Daniel Povey, Samuel's cousin, in the prison at Stafford parallels the public execution of the murderer Rivain, which Sophia and Gerald take in as an unusual "attraction." This and many other parallels in the plot—for example, young Cyril's theft from the till at the shop and Sophia's prudent appropriation of Gerald's two hundred pounds—are done so cleverly that they never seem forced or artificial. Life is simply like this, says Bennett, and the range and sureness of his story vindicate his method.

Bennett's respect for his ordinary characters is intense. He admires their capacity for survival and never underestimates their souls. In the midst of bourgeois contentment, Constance is never free from a strange sadness. She lacks the imaginative power of a Hamlet, but she feels a similar anguish: "The vast inherent melancholy of the universe did not exempt her." Her simple and undistinguished husband, Samuel Povey, dies of toxemia contracted from pneumonia. His death is oddly heroic, because the illness that kills him is a cruelly ironic reward for his selfless dedication to his poor cousin Daniel. Bennett is unequivocal in his praise. He concedes that he thought Povey a "little" man easy to ridicule but that his honesty finally earns a great deal of respect. The end of his life displays a touch of greatness that all souls, insists Bennett, have in common.

It is important that readers understand that Constance's melancholy, Samuel's humility, and Sophia's passionate nature are secondary to what Bennett felt was the mainstream running through all of their natures: the blind will to survive. Fossette, the aged poodle, is the emblem of that instinct at the close of the novel. The great enemy of all is time, and it always wins in the end. Readers may object to assigning Bennett such a cold view of life. To end on a beastly comparison between Fossette and Sophia seems out of keeping with Bennett's fondness and respect for his characters. Nevertheless, readers remember that what Bennett praises the most in Sophia is precisely her pluck, her ability to survive in a totally alien environment. Her emotional life is not a rich one, and the last glimpse of Gerald Scales as an old man does not rekindle her feelings. Unlike Samuel Povey's death, which was senseless but pathetic because of his selflessness, Sophia's death is the result of an unbearable knowledge; she confronts her own death in Gerald's death, which strikes her as overwhelming in its physical meaning. Once a handsome and vital young man who had excited her passions and moved her to abandon respectability, Gerald in the end appears before her as the corpse of a withered and aged man. Sophia is not concerned with his moral weakness or the grief that he caused her. All she can think of is that a young man, once proud and bold, has been reduced to a horribly decimated version of his former self. The cruelty of time, which has made a mockery of all the feelings of love and hatred they shared, shatters her self-confidence. She can no longer separate herself from the mortality around her. When the inevitability of death becomes apparent, even to someone without imagination like Sophia, the will to survive is gone. Suddenly the full weight of her life, the great struggle for survival in Paris, descends with crushing force. It is more than she can stand. Although she fears death, she begs for its deliverance. When she can take no more, she dies. Despite all the pressures and forces that shape *The Old Wives' Tale*, it does not end until the hearts of its protagonists stop beating.

"Critical Evaluation" by Peter A. Brier

Bibliography:
Broomfield, Olga R. Q. *Arnold Bennett*. Boston: Twayne, 1984. Bennett considered *The Old Wives' Tale* a masterpiece. The book demonstrates that in the emotional lives of individuals, the degrees of comedy and tragedy are relative to the characters' perceptions of their experience.
Fromm, Gloria G. "Remythologizing Arnold Bennett." *Novel: A Forum on Fiction* 16, no. 1 (Fall, 1982): 19-34. Discusses Virginia Woolf's criticism, which had a devastating effect on Bennett's reputation. Argues that Woolf missed his assertion that there is no escaping expression of the self, no matter how skillful a writer may be.
Lucas, John. *Arnold Bennett: A Study of His Fiction*. New York: Methuen, 1974. Asserts that Guy de Maupassant's cynicism influenced Bennett's portrayal of Constance. Bennett considered *The Old Wives' Tale* an important demonstration of his seriousness as a writer.
Meckier, Jerome. "Distortion Versus Revaluation: Three Twentieth-Century Responses to Victorian Fiction." *Victorian Newsletter* 73 (Spring, 1988): 3-8. Suggests that *The Old Wives' Tale* is a criticism of the cynicism found in William Makepeace Thackeray's *Vanity Fair* (1847-1848). Bennett drew more joy than Thackeray did from the secular world.
Roby, Kinley E. *A Writer at War: Arnold Bennett, 1914-1918*. Baton Rouge: Louisiana State University Press, 1972. *The Old Wives' Tale*, which shows no meaning in the lives of its characters, anticipates a major theme of twentieth century British and American literature.

THE OLD WIVES' TALE

Type of work: Drama
Author: George Peele (1556-1596?)
Type of plot: Comedy
Time of plot: Indeterminate
Locale: England
First performed: c. 1591-1594; first published, 1595

Principal characters:
ANTIC,
FROLIC, and
FANTASTIC, pages
CLUNCH, a smith
MADGE, his wife
ERESTUS, an enchanted man, called Senex
LAMPRISCUS, a farmer
HUANEBANGO, a braggart
SACRAPANT, a magician
EUMENIDES, a knight
DELIA, a princess of Thessaly
CALYPHA and
THELEA, her brothers
VENELIA, the betrothed of Erestus
ZANTIPPA and
CELANTA, the daughters of Lampriscus

The Story:

Antic, Frolic, and Fantastic, three pages, were lost at night in an English forest. There they encountered Clunch, a blacksmith, who took them to his cottage to spend the night in comfort and safety. When Madge, Clunch's wife, offered them food, they refused it; Antic asked for a story instead. Oddly enough, Antic thereupon went to bed with old Clunch; his companions stayed up to hear Madge's story:

> Once upon a time, a king had a daughter of great beauty. This daughter was stolen away. The king sent men in search of her until there were no men left in the realm except her brothers. Finally they, too, went in search of their sister. It was a magician disguised as a dragon who had kidnapped her. This magician imprisoned her in a great stone castle. The magician also placed at the crossroad a young man who by enchantment appeared by day as an old man, but who by night was changed into a bear.

At that point in Madge's tale two young men appeared and declared dejectedly that they had arrived in England in search of their sister Delia. They had given alms to an old man whom they encountered at a crossroad. In return for their kindness, the old man repeated a verse for them and told them to say to any inquirer about the rhyme that they had learned it from the white bear of England's wood.

After the brothers had left, the old man told aloud his own story. He had been happily married to a beautiful wife in Thessaly. Sacrapant, a sorcerer, had fallen in love with her and had enchanted the husband, Erestus, so that by day he appeared to be an old man and by night a bear. His beloved Venelia, under the influence of Sacrapant, became a lunatic. Distracted, she ran past the crossroad and was recognized by Senex, as Erestus was called in his enchanted form of an old man.

A farmer named Lampriscus, knowing a bear's fondness for sweets, gave Erestus a pot of honey. Lampriscus disclosed that he was twice a widower; by his first wife he had a beautiful daughter who, in her pride and petulance, was a great burden to him; by his second wife he had another daughter who was ugly and deformed. Erestus directed Lampriscus to send his daughters to the well to drink of the water of life; there they would find their fortunes.

Huanebango, a braggart who claimed that he could overpower sorcerers, and Booby, a peasant, came to the crossroad. Both sought to win the favor of the fair lady enchanted by Sacrapant. Huanebango refused to give alms to Erestus; Booby, however, gave him a piece of cake. Erestus predicted that Huanebango would soon be deaf and that Booby would go blind.

In his study, meanwhile, Sacrapant disclosed that he, the son of a witch, had transformed himself into a dragon and had kidnapped Delia, the daughter of the king. Delia entered the study and sat down to a magic feast with her captor. As the pair dined, the two brothers entered. Delia and Sacrapant fled, but Sacrapant soon returned to overcome the brothers with his magic. After they had been taken to a dungeon in the castle, Sacrapant triumphantly revealed aloud that he could die only by a dead man's hand.

When Eumenides, a wandering knight, came also to the crossroad, Erestus forecast his fortune for him in a rhymed riddle. Eumenides lay down to sleep. Before long he was awakened by an argument between two country fellows and a churchwarden; the churchwarden refused to bury their friend, Jack, who had died a pauper. Eumenides, recalling a stipulation of the riddle, paid the churchwarden all of the money he had so that Jack might be properly buried.

Huanebango and Booby came at length to Sacrapant's stronghold. Huanebango was struck down by a flame; Booby was stricken blind and turned loose to wander. Sacrapant then changed Delia's name to Berecynthia and took her to the fields to supervise the labors of her brothers, who were digging in the enchanted ground. Delia, ignorant of her true identity, failed to recognize her brothers.

In the meantime Zantippa, the proud daughter of Lampriscus, and Celanta, the deformed daughter, went to the well of life. Zantippa broke Celanta's waterpot. At the same time two Furies brought Huanebango, in a trance, to the well. As Zantippa dipped her pot into the well, she beheld a head in the water. She impetuously broke her pot on the head; thunder and lightning followed. Huanebango, deaf by enchantment, awoke from his trance. Unable to hear the strident railings of the beautiful Zantippa, he was smitten with love for her. The two left the well together.

Eumenides, continuing his wanderings, arrived at the well, where he was joined by the ghost of Jack, for whose burial he had given all of his money. The ghost declared its intention to serve him, but Eumenides insisted that the ghost should be his equal and share his worldly wealth. The ghost went ahead to an inn to arrange supper for the destitute Eumenides. As he was eating, Eumenides looked into his purse, which he believed completely empty, and discovered that it was full of money. Having dined, Eumenides, followed by the ghost, turned his steps toward Sacrapant's castle.

At the well, in the meantime, Celanta, with a new pot, had returned in the company of the blinded Booby. The peasant, unable to see her deformity, fell in love with her. Celanta, who was a gentle creature, obeyed the dictates of the head in the well and was thereupon rewarded with a pot of gold.

Eumenides and the ghost approached the castle. The ghost, placing wool in the knight's ears, directed him to sit quietly. When Sacrapant came out of his cell and asked Eumenides' identity, the ghost removed Sacrapant's magic wreath and took away his sword. Shorn of his magic powers, Sacrapant died. At the ghost's direction, Eumenides dug into the hillside and discovered a light enclosed in glass, but he was unable to get to the light. The ghost then gave Eumenides a horn to blow. At the sound of the blast, Venelia appeared, broke the glass, and extinguished the magic light to free everyone from the power of Sacrapant.

Eumenides and Delia pledged their troth. Eumenides sounded the horn again, and Venelia, the two brothers, and Erestus appeared. Now that all were together, the ghost demanded, upon the terms of equality with Eumenides, a half of Delia. Eumenides was reluctant; but, true to his word, he prepared to cut Delia in half with his sword. Convinced of Eumenides' good faith, the ghost withheld the stroke of the sword and left the group. All declared their intention of returning immediately to Thessaly.

Fantastic awoke Madge, for day was breaking. The old woman moved toward the kitchen and declared that breakfast would soon be ready.

Critical Evaluation:

Although often mentioned as one of the earlier Elizabethan plays, *The Old Wives' Tale* has not had a very distinguished critical or theatrical history. It was largely ignored in the seventeenth and eighteenth centuries, while nineteenth century critics did little more than compare it contemptuously to John Milton's *Comus* (1637), for which it was probably a partial source. The twentieth century has given the play a more favorable critical reading, but there has been no theatrical revival beyond occasional amateur performances.

The Old Wives' Tale was a highly innovative play when first written and the passage of four hundred years has made it no less uncommon. First, it is a play with a frame; the main action is a play within the play. Unlike in William Shakespeare's *The Taming of the Shrew* (1593-1594), which also uses a frame, in George Peele's play the characters remain on stage and comment from time to time on the action. The result is an unusual intimacy, and at the same time a certain aesthetic distance from the action. A closer and more useful comparison can be made with Shakespeare's *A Midsummer Night's Dream* (1595-1596), in which there is a play within the play, in this case with an audience that comments on the action. In Shakespeare's play, however, the audience is courtly and can only laugh at the foolish efforts of the bumpkin actors to dramatize the story of Pyramis and Thisbe, or at best sympathize with their good intentions. The audience sees the action largely as the court party does. In *The Old Wives' Tale*, however, the audience is drawn into the fantastic fairy-tale world of the story. The old wife who tells the story and her husband are presented as crude rustics, but their speech is not made comic, as is usually the case with Elizabethan rustic characters, and the parental attitude they take toward the three pages the husband has found lost in the woods is accepted by the young men. Clearly the pages belong to a more educated class than their hosts, but their age acts as a bridge for the audience. They are close enough to childhood to make the audience accept their uncritical interest in a fairy story, and yet educated and adult enough that their acceptance leads the audience to accept the fantasy as well.

The frame of the play is well conceived, but the plot is rather harder to judge. Peele has taken a number of folktale plots and motifs and woven them together in a single story that retains all the atmosphere of a fairy story while being far more elaborate in structure. The several story lines, which at first seem independent of each other, all merge ultimately, and every problem and conflict is resolved. The use of multiple interwoven story lines is alien to the folktale and was likely suggested by Medieval romance in general and Ludovico Ariosto's *Orlando Furioso* (1516) in particular. In a play, however, especially one as short as *The Old Wives' Tale*, there is no time for the separate stories to take on a real life of their own, and the continual introduction of new story lines is likely to make the plot seem jumbled and confused. With such a structure, it is also difficult to become involved with any of the numerous characters, even as superficially as one does with the hero or heroine of a fairy tale, or even to know which characters are most worth becoming involved with.

The apparent hero, a wandering knight named Eumenides, does not appear on stage until well into the play, and when he does his importance is not immediately evident. For a hero, Eumenides shows very little initiative. The one thing that he does on his own is provide money for a pauper named Jack to be properly buried. As a result the grateful ghost directs Eumenides' actions, showing him how to destroy the enchanter and to free the princess.

There are two points of convergence in the play. The first is the crossroads presided over by an enchanted bear-man; the second is the castle of the evil sorcerer, Sacrapant. The various characters must first arrive at the crossroads and are there tested. Some then go another way, but most end at the castle. Though the chief unifying factor of the story is the search for the stolen princess, these two geographical points further bring the actions together and help make the plot more coherent than it would be otherwise.

Folktale situations and motifs are a staple of Western literature, but Peele is perhaps the first to use them on their own terms without attempting to disguise them or to transform them into "literature," for although Peele's play is not exactly a folktale it retains all the atmosphere, the sense of magic, and the sense of childhood wonder that are associated with such tales.

Even currently when folk art and literature are taken more seriously than in the past, there is something revolutionary about making an adult play out of fairy-tale material without also making it somehow tongue-in-cheek. For that reason even modern critics, more sympathetic to such material than critics of the past, have tended to read the play as somehow ironic. Otherwise they tend to read it as an appealing, but mindlessly naïve work. It would seem simpler to consider it just what it appears to be—a play that makes unselfconscious and unapologetic use of the situations and motifs of folktale to tell a story that, like dream, is impossibly strange, but strangely compelling because it touches a level deeper than adult cynicism and rationality.

"Critical Evaluation" by Jack Hart

Bibliography:
Boas, Frederick S. *An Introduction to Tudor Drama*. Oxford, England: Clarendon Press, 1933. A useful introduction by a major twentieth century scholar to the beginnings of Elizabethan drama. Not a lot on *The Old Wives' Tale*, but a good introduction to its general context.
Peele, George. *The Dramatic Works of George Peele*. New Haven, Conn.: Yale University Press, 1970. The long introduction provides a good appraisal of *The Old Wives' Tale* that attempts a rational compromise between earlier schools of thought. The first major edition of Pelle since that of A. H. Bullen in 1888.
_____. *The Old Wives' Tale*. Edited by Patricia Binnie. Baltimore: The Johns Hopkins University Press, 1980. This carefully prepared edition has an enthusiastic, but intelligent and readable introduction to the play.
Senn, Werner. *Studies in the Dramatic Construction of Robert Greene and George Peele*. Bern: Francke, 1973. A somewhat specialized work, but helpful, since even the most casual reader is struck by the structural peculiarity of *The Old Wives' Tale*, which this book addresses.

OLDTOWN FOLKS

Type of work: Novel
Author: Harriet Beecher Stowe (1811-1896)
Type of plot: Regional
Time of plot: Late eighteenth century
Locale: Massachusetts
First published: 1869

Principal characters:
HORACE HOLYOKE, the narrator
DEACON BADGER, his grandfather
MRS. BADGER, his grandmother
MR. LOTHROP, the village minister
MRS. LOTHROP, his wife
HARRY PERCIVAL, Horace's friend
EGLANTINE (TINA) PERCIVAL, Harry's sister
MISS MEHITABLE ROSSITER, Tina's adopted mother
ELLERY DAVENPORT, Tina's first husband
ESTHER AVERY, a minister's daughter and later, Harry's wife
SAM LAWSON, the village do-nothing

The Story:

Years later, Horace Holyoke could remember Oldtown as he had known it when he was a boy, a quiet little village beside a tranquil river in Massachusetts. Surrounded by farmhouses deep in green hollows or high on windy hilltops, Oldtown consisted of one rustic street, where the chief landmarks of the community stood. Among these were the meetinghouse with its classic white spire, the schoolhouse, the academy, a tavern, and the general store, which was also the post office. As was common in those days, when New England was changing from a Puritan theocracy of little villages to a group of states under a federal government, the minister was still the leading citizen of the town. Mr. Lothrop, descended from generations of ministers, was an Arminian in his views, a sedate, sensible man whose sermons were examples of elegant Addisonian English. His wife, the daughter of an aristocratic family of Boston, had never forsaken the Church of England, and each Easter, Whitsunday, and Christmas, she traveled in her coach to Boston to attend services in Christ Church. The people of Oldtown called her, without disrespect, Lady Lothrop.

The famous John Eliot had come to Oldtown as an apostle to the Indians. Three generations later, Horace Holyoke's father had arrived in the town to teach in the local academy. There he fell in love with Susy Badger, one of the prettiest of his pupils, and married her. With marriage came responsibilities that dimmed forever his hopes of completing his education at Harvard College. When Horace was a little boy, his father's household was a place of penny-pinching hardships. His mother's beauty faded and his father's health, weakened by his attempts to provide for his family and to continue his studies, broke slowly. Horace was ten and his brother Bill a few years older when their father died of consumption. Horace grieved as only a small boy can over his father's death. His chief comfort in those dark days came from Sam Lawson, the village handyman and do-nothing. Many people called Sam shiftless. A few pitied him because his wife was a scold. A man of good humor and garrulous tongue, he was never too busy to take small boys on fishing or hunting trips and to tell them stories.

After the funeral, Mrs. Holyoke and her sons went to live with her father, Deacon Badger, a leading farmer and miller of Oldtown. He, like Mr. Lothrop, was an Arminian, and a serene, affable man. His wife, on the other hand, was a strict Puritan Calvinist, as fond of theological dispute as she was of cleanliness. Many were the arguments Horace overheard between the two, with scriptural texts flying thick and fast in proof of their contentions. Their unmarried daughters were named Keziah and Lois. Keziah was a romantic-minded woman with a reputation for homeliness throughout the township. Lois was like a chestnut burr, prickly and rough on the outside but soft and smooth within, as her tart tongue and warmhearted nature proved.

Just as the life of the village revolved around the meetinghouse, so the center of the Badger household was the spacious, white-sanded kitchen. There the friends of the family gathered— Miss Mehitable Rossiter, daughter of a former minister of the town, Major Broad, Squire Jones, Sam Lawson, and others. While there, Horace listened to discussions on politics, religion, philosophy, and varied local lore that were to influence him throughout his lifetime. There, too, it was decided that his brother, Bill, who showed very little promise as a scholar, was to work on the farm with Jacob Badger, his mother's brother, while Horace would be allowed to continue his studies in the village school. Horace grew into a dreamy, imaginative boy. Sometimes he felt that auras suggestive of good or evil surrounded people whom he met. Often he dreamed of a silent, lonely lad of about his own age. The boy began to fade from Horace's visions, however, after he found a friend in young Harry Percival.

Harry's father was an English officer, the younger son of a landed family, who had brought his wife to America near the end of the Revolutionary War. The wife was a curate's daughter with whom the officer had eloped and married secretly. The husband proved worthless and dissipated, and at last he deserted his wife and two children when his regiment returned to England. He took his wife's wedding certificate with him and left behind a letter denying the legality of their marriage. Friendless and without funds, the wife set out to walk to Boston with Harry and his sister Eglantine. On the way, the mother fell sick and died in the house of miserly Caleb Smith, called by his neighbors Old Crab Smith. The farmer decided to keep the boy as a field hand. Eglantine, or Tina, as her brother called her, was taken in by Caleb's sister, Miss Asphyxia. The children were treated so harshly, however, that at last they decided to run away. After a night spent with an old Indian woman in the woods, they found a refuge in the Dench mansion, reported to be haunted, on the outskirts of Oldtown. There Sam Lawson and some neighbors found the children after smoke had been seen coming from the chimney of the old house.

Harry and Tina were befriended by Deacon Badger and his wife. Within a few days, it was decided that Harry was to remain with the Badgers, an arrangement made even more satisfactory by Mrs. Lothrop's promise to provide for the boy's clothing and education. Miss Mehitable Rossiter, whose life had been saddened some years before by the mysterious disappearance of her young half sister, Emily, adopted Tina. From that time on, the lives of Horace, Harry, and Tina were to be closely intertwined. As a special Easter treat, Mrs. Lothrop arranged to take the children to Boston with her. They were entertained by Madame Kittery, Mrs. Lothrop's mother, and during their stay, they met Ellery Davenport. Ellery, Mrs. Lothrop's cousin, had served in the Continental army and had held several diplomatic posts abroad. He was handsome and clever. A grandson of the great Jonathan Edwards, he had turned away from the church; his preceptors were the French philosophers of the day. Horace heard that his wife was mad.

Madame Kittery, a kindly old woman, took a great interest in Horace and listened sympathetically while he told of his father's death and of his own desire to attend college. Shortly after the party returned to Oldtown, he was told that money would be provided so that he and Harry could go to Harvard together. Madame Kittery had become his benefactress. Over Thanksgiving, Ellery Davenport and Mrs. Lothrop's sister Deborah came to Oldtown for a visit. At a harvest dance at the Badger homestead, Ellery paid marked attentions to young Tina. He also promised Miss Mehitable that on his return to France he would look for her lost sister, who was believed to have fled to that country.

Tina became more beautiful as she grew older. When the schoolmaster fell in love with her, and Miss Mehitable's cousin Mordecai, hired as her tutor, also succumbed to her charms, it was finally decided that she, with Horace and Harry, would go to Cloudland, where Jonathan Rossiter, Miss Mehitable's half brother, was master of the academy. The boys lived with Mr. Rossiter. Tina boarded with the minister, Mr. Avery, whose daughter Esther became the friend and companion of the three newcomers. Esther and Harry soon fell in love. Under Mr. Avery's influence, Harry decided to study for the ministry. Horace dreamed of a career that would insure his future with Tina, whom he had loved since childhood. When Ellery Davenport returned from England, he had important news for Harry. The boy's father was now Sir Harry Percival. Ellery had also secured possession of the stolen marriage certificate, which he gave to Mr. Lothrop for safekeeping.

Horace and Harry entered Harvard as sophomores. Tina, visiting with the Kitterys in Boston or staying with Miss Mehitable in Oldtown, wrote them letters that were playful, almost mocking in tone. Horace began to worry about Ellery Davenport's influence on the girl. A short time later, he heard that Ellery's insane wife had died. Then word came that Harry's father had died in England. Harry was now Sir Harry Percival. The two friends returned to Oldtown for the spring vacation, to learn on their arrival that Tina was engaged to marry Ellery. Horace, reflecting wryly on the contrast between his own humble position and the high estate to which his friends had been lifted, concealed with stubborn pride the deep hurt he felt. Because Ellery was soon to return to the embassy in London, preparations for the wedding were hurried. After the ceremony, Ellery and his bride planned to spend a short time, before sailing, in the reconditioned Dench mansion. When they arrived, they found a woman dressed in black waiting for them in the parlor of the old house. The caller was Emily Rossiter, whom Ellery had seduced and taken away from her family years before. Emily, spurning the settlement he had provided for her, had followed him to America. To her horror, Tina also learned that he was the father of the unfortunate woman's child.

The course Tina took was both noble and tragic. In spite of the wrong Ellery had done, both to Emily and to his bride, Tina refused to desert him. Instead, she used the fortune she had inherited from her father to establish Miss Mehitable and her sister in a house near Boston. She took the child with her to England when she went there with Ellery. After his graduation, Harry married Esther Avery and left for England with his bride. At first, he planned to return shortly to America, but as time passed, it became apparent that his interests lay abroad and that he intended to make his home there. Horace felt that he had been left alone in the world.

Eight years went by before Ellery and Tina returned to make their home near Boston. By that time, Tina had grown faded and worn. Horace, a successful lawyer, saw her and her husband frequently; as a sympathetic spectator, he watched the course of Ellery's reckless and unprincipled career, which, fed by his ambition, was to bring him close to madness. Ten years after his marriage, Ellery was killed in a political duel. Two more years passed before Horace and Tina were married. Their wedding journey took them to England to see Harry and Esther. Later, as the years came and went softly, Horace and his wife often visited Oldtown and there renewed the familiar associations of earlier days.

Critical Evaluation:

Harriet Beecher Stowe wrote *Oldtown Folks*, a historical novel and an early example of local color fiction, to interpret early New England life and to understand how New England influenced its own people as well as the growing United States. In order to analyze and interpret the small Massachusetts community she re-creates, Stowe focuses on character rather than plot, hypothesizing through her first-person narrator Horace Holyoke that to analyze the life of any given person one must study the society and history that produced that person.

She uses character description and analysis as a means to understand the history of New England, a history that, Stowe believed, profoundly influenced the United States as a whole. In this work, plot takes a lesser importance. The novel may be read as an index of how the New England heritage, which forms certain characters, influences their lives. If readers understand *Oldtown Folks* to be about how culture produces character, and how characters in turn create their lives, readers can see why the book is preoccupied with childhood and child rearing. As the narrator and his friends grow up, the plot is foreshortened, until the final chapters summarize the adult outcomes experienced by the characters. In *Oldtown Folks*, families are created out of difficult circumstances and none of the children whose stories the book tells are raised by mother and father in a nuclear family. Horace's father dies in the opening chapters, and the mother moves back to her parental household along with her children. Horace's Grandmother Badger becomes his dominant motherly influence. Harry and Tina Percival are orphaned; they flee from Crab Smith and his sister Asphyxia Smith, who attempt to rear them to be efficient workers, and happen upon Horace's Grandmother's house. The Badgers take in Harry, while Tina is adopted by village spinster Mehitable Rossiter. The displacement of the children emphasizes how regional culture, rather than simply parental guidance, may play a crucial role in the formation of character.

Stowe discusses at length the theology professed and the religion practiced by the adults involved in the children's upbringing, particularly focusing on Calvinist, Arminian, and Episcopalian faiths, but also pointing out the influence of skepticism. Crab and Asphyxia reject religion altogether, and not coincidentally they lack any compassion for children and are wholly unfit to raise them. Grandmother Badger is a determined Puritan Calvinist, yet she tempers the harsh doctrines of that faith through her own generosity, charity, and love. Her husband, Deacon Badger, is Arminian, and while disagreeing with Grandmother Badger's convictions concerning Original Sin and predestination, he is in accord with her practice of Christian charity. Mehitable Rossiter has long lived in religious doubt, but her faith is renewed when Tina comes to live with her. She has trouble disciplining Tina according to child-rearing advice she reads and hears, and Tina is indulged constantly as she grows up. The children encounter Episcopalian faith, with its tolerant doctrines and aristocratic ritual, when they visit Boston. Harry gravitates toward the Episcopalian church, in which he will eventually be ordained.

Oldtown Folks avoids oversimplifying the characters who ascribe to certain church dogmas; each individual understands and practices faith in complex ways, and Stowe never suggests that personality is simply a product of religious training. Rather, she explores how various temperaments may respond in different ways to a culture whose identity was grounded in religion, and in which religious debate was characteristic of many household discussions.

The plots that the characters eventually live out demonstrate how their New England upbringing influenced them. A harsh Calvinist training unrelieved by compassion taught children that God did not love them and that they were sinful until they experienced conversion. The children raised under this faith struggle in their adult lives, as illustrated by secondary characters Ellery Davenport (the fictional grandson of Puritan theologian Jonathan Edwards) and Emily Rossiter. Ellery rejects the faith of his forefathers, and becomes the clever, charming, and skeptical villain of the novel. His fall is paralleled by the story of Emily Rossiter, Mehitable's half-sister, who, in revulsion from Calvinism, accepted French philosophy and rationalized her decision to become Ellery's mistress. Tina Percival, who was first too harshly, and then too leniently treated, is unable to see Ellery Davenport's moral weakness and marries him. She suffers through ten years of increasingly unhappy marriage until Ellery is killed in a duel, and then marries the narrator Horace, who has always loved her. Harry's simple but strong faith helps rescue Esther Avery, a minister's daughter, from the painful self-doubts created by her Puritan upbringing, and they marry happily. These plots are common in popular fiction: a courtship plot with deserving hero and worthy heroine, and a seduction and betrayal plot with unworthy hero and misguided heroine. Stowe's interest is not in rehashing these narratives, which she briefly summarizes in the final chapters of the novel, but in showing why some characters are more likely than others to establish harmonious domestic lives. Children raised with a balance of discipline and love are inclined to choose a happily resolving courtship plot. Children raised with an excess of either strictness or leniency are more apt to experience an unhappily resolving seduction plot or to enter an unfortunate marriage.

Oldtown Folks contributes to American literature in several ways. It explores conflicting doctrines from the perspective of someone whose life experience and deep reading informed what she wrote. It also portrays with precision and grace many New England characters, customs, and places. Therefore, it is a pioneering work within the local color literary tradition. As a product of the post-Civil War era, *Oldtown Folks* critiques the rapacious capitalism of Reconstruction politics and affirms some claims of the women's rights movement. Within *Oldtown Folks*, Stowe advocates equal education for women, critiques the sexual double standard, and creates a gallery of strong and independent female characters who experience richly complex internal lives.

"Critical Evaluation" by Karen Tracey

Bibliography:

Adams, John R. *Harriet Beecher Stowe.* Boston: Twayne, 1989. Analyzes Stowe's novels according to conventional literary criteria, and argues that *Oldtown Folks,* although flawed by a contrived plot, is the most realistic and imaginative of Stowe's works.

Ammons, Elizabeth, ed. *Critical Essays on Harriet Beecher Stowe.* Boston: G. K. Hall, 1980. Includes early reviews and later critical assessments of Stowe's fiction. Excerpts a reading of *Oldtown Folks* by Charles H. Foster in which he analyzes how Stowe critiques Jonathan Edwards' influence on Puritan New England.

Crozier, Alice C. *The Novels of Harriet Beecher Stowe.* New York: Oxford University Press, 1969. Dated but still useful discussion of Stowe's novels that considers *Oldtown Folks* in the context of her other historical fiction, and argues that Stowe is at times bitingly ironic toward her religious characters.

Donovan, Josephine. *New England Local Color Literature: A Women's Tradition.* New York: Frederick Ungar, 1983. Discusses Stowe's role as a pioneer of the women's tradition of local color realism, asserting that *Oldtown Folks* is the best of Stowe's regional novels.

Hedrick, Joan D. *Harriet Beecher Stowe: A Life.* New York: Oxford University Press, 1994. Tells the story of the inception and writing of *Oldtown Folks.* Discusses how Stowe's awareness of her audience and the changing critical climate might have influenced her writing.

OLIVER TWIST
Or, The Parish Boy's Progress

Type of work: Novel
Author: Charles Dickens (1812-1870)
Type of plot: Social realism
Time of plot: Early nineteenth century
Locale: England, especially London
First published: serial, 1837-1839; book, 1838

Principal characters:
> OLIVER TWIST, a workhouse waif
> MR. BROWNLOW, Oliver's benefactor
> MRS. MAYLIE, a woman who befriends Oliver
> ROSE MAYLIE, her adopted daughter
> FAGIN, a thief-trainer
> BILL SIKES, his confederate
> NANCY, Sikes's beloved
> MONKS (EDWARD LEEFORD), Oliver's half brother
> BUMBLE, a workhouse official

The Story:

Oliver Twist was born in the lying-in room of a parochial workhouse about seventy-five miles north of London. His mother, whose name was unknown, had been found unconscious by the roadside, exhausted by a long journey on foot; she died leaving a locket and a ring as the only tokens of her child's identity. These were stolen by old Sally, a pauper present at her death.

Oliver owed his name to Bumble, the parish beadle and a bullying official of the workhouse, who always named his unknown orphans in the order of an alphabetical system he had devised. Twist was the name between Swubble and Unwin on Bumble's list. An offered reward of ten pounds failed to discover his parentage, and he was sent to a nearby poor farm, where he passed his early childhood in neglect and near starvation. At the age of nine, he was moved back to the workhouse. Always hungry, he asked one day for a second serving of porridge. The scandalized authorities put him in solitary confinement and posted a bill offering five pounds to someone who would take him away from the parish.

Oliver was apprenticed to Sowerberry, a casket maker, to learn a trade. Sowerberry employed little Oliver, dressed in miniature mourning clothing, as an attendant at children's funerals. Another Sowerberry employee, Noah Claypole, often teased Oliver about his parentage. One day, goaded beyond endurance, Oliver fiercely attacked Claypole and was subsequently locked in the cellar by Mrs. Sowerberry. When Sowerberry released Oliver one night, he bundled up his meager belongings and started out for London.

In a London suburb, Oliver, worn out from walking and weak from hunger, met Jack Dawkins, a sharp-witted slum gamin. Known as the Artful Dodger, Dawkins offered Oliver lodgings in the city, and Oliver soon found himself in the midst of a gang of young thieves led by a miserly old Jew, Fagin. Oliver was trained as a pickpocket. On his first mission, he was caught and taken to the police station. There he was rescued by kindly Mr. Brownlow, the man whose pocket Oliver was accused of having picked. Mr. Brownlow, his gruff friend Grimwig, and the old housekeeper, Mrs. Bedwin, cared for the sickly Oliver, marveling at the resemblance of the boy to a portrait of a young lady in Mr. Brownlow's possession. Once he had recuperated, Oliver was one day given some books and money to take to a bookseller. Grimwig wagered that Oliver would not return. Fagin and his gang had been on constant lookout for the boy's appearance. Oliver was intercepted by Nancy, a young street girl associated with the gang, and fell into Fagin's clutches again.

Bumble, in London on parochial business, saw Mr. Brownlow's advertisement for word leading to Oliver's recovery. Hoping to profit, Bumble hastened to Mr. Brownlow and reported that Oliver was incorrigible. Mr. Brownlow thereupon refused to have Oliver's name mentioned in his presence.

During Oliver's absence, Fagin's gang had been studying a house in Chertsey, west of London, in preparation for breaking into it at night. When the time came, Oliver, much to his horror, was forced to participate. He and Bill Sikes, a brutal young member of the gang, met the housebreaker Toby Crackit, and in the dark of early morning they pried open a small window of the house. Oliver, being the smallest, was the first to enter, but he was determined to warn the occupants. The robbers were discovered, and the trio fled; Oliver, however, was wounded by gunshot.

In fleeing, Sikes threw the wounded Oliver into a ditch and covered him with a cape. Toby Crackit returned and reported to Fagin, who, as it turned out, was more interested than ever in Oliver after a conversation he had had with Monks. Nancy had overheard them talking about Oliver's parentage and Monks expressing his wish to have the boy made a felon.

Oliver crawled feebly back to the house into which he had gone the night before, where he was taken in by the owner Mrs. Maylie and Rose, her adopted daughter. Oliver's story aroused their sympathy, and he was saved from police investigation by Dr. Losberne, a friend of the Maylies. Upon his recovery, the boy went with the doctor to find Mr. Brownlow, but it was learned that the old gentleman, his friend Grimwig, and Mrs. Bedwin had gone to the West Indies.

Bumble was meanwhile courting the widow Corney. During one of their conversations, Mrs. Corney was called out to attend the death of old Sally, who had attended the death of Oliver's mother. After old Sally died, Mrs. Corney removed a pawn ticket from her hand. In Mrs. Corney's absence, Bumble appraised her property to his satisfaction, and when she returned, he proposed marriage.

The Maylies moved to the country, where Oliver read and took long walks. During this holiday, Rose Maylie fell sick and nearly died. Harry Maylie, Mrs. Maylie's son, who was in love with Rose, had joined the group. Harry asked Rose to marry him, but Rose refused on the grounds that she could not marry him unless she discovered who she was and unless he mended his ways. One night, Oliver was frightened when he saw Fagin and Monks peering through the study window.

Bumble had discovered that married life with the former Mrs. Corney was not all happiness, for she dominated him completely. When Monks went to the workhouse seeking information about Oliver, he met with Mr. and Mrs. Bumble and learned that Mrs. Bumble had redeemed a locket and a wedding ring with the pawn ticket she had recovered from old Sally. Monks bought the trinkets from Mrs. Bumble and threw them into the river. Nancy overheard Monks telling Fagin that he had disposed of the proofs of Oliver's parentage. After drugging Bill Sikes, whom she had been nursing to recovery from gunshot wounds received in the ill-fated venture at Chertsey, she went to see Rose Maylie, whose name and address she had overheard in the conversation between Fagin and Monks. Nancy told Rose everything she had heard concerning Oliver. Rose was unable to understand fully the various connections of the plot nor could she see Monks's connection with Oliver. She offered the miserable girl the protection of her own home, but Nancy refused; she knew that she could never leave Bill Sikes. The two young women agreed on a time and place for a later meeting. Rose and Oliver went to call on Mr. Brownlow, whom Oliver had glimpsed in the street. The reunion of the boy, Mr. Brownlow, and Mrs. Bedwin was a joyous one. Even old Grimwig gruffly expressed his pleasure at seeing Oliver again. Rose told Mr. Brownlow Nancy's story.

Noah Claypole and Charlotte, the Sowerberrys' maidservant, had run away from the casket maker and arrived in London, where they went to the public house where Fagin and his gang frequently met. Fagin flattered Noah into his employ; his job became to steal small coins from children on household errands.

At the time agreed upon for her appointment with Rose Maylie, Nancy was unable to leave the demanding Bill Sikes. Fagin noticed Nancy's impatience and decided that she had tired of Sikes and had another lover. Fagin hated Sikes because of the younger man's power over the gang, and he saw this situation as an opportunity to rid himself of Sikes. Fagin set Noah on Nancy's trail.

The following week, Nancy was freed with the aid of Fagin. She went to Rose and Mr. Brownlow and revealed to them the haunts of all the gang except Sikes. Noah overheard all this and secretly told Fagin, who in turn told Sikes. In his rage, Sikes brutally murdered Nancy, never knowing that the girl had been faithful to him. He fled, pursued by the vision of Nancy's staring dead eyes. Frantic with fear, he even tried to kill his dog, whose presence might betray him. The dog ran away.

Monks was apprehended and confessed to Mr. Brownlow the plot against Oliver. Oliver's father, Edward Leeford, had married a woman older than himself. Their son, Edward Leeford, was the man now known as Monks. After several years of unhappiness, the couple separated; Monks and his mother remained on the Continent and Mr. Leeford returned to England. Later, Leeford met a retired naval officer with two daughters, one three years old, the other seventeen. Leeford fell in love with the older daughter and contracted to marry the girl, but before the marriage could be performed, he was called to Rome, where an old friend had died. On the way to Rome, he stopped at the house of Mr. Brownlow, his best friend, and left a portrait of his betrothed. He himself fell sick in Rome and died, and his first wife seized his papers. Leeford's young wife-to-be was pregnant; when she heard of Leeford's death, she ran away to hide her condition. Her father died soon afterward, and the younger sister was eventually adopted by Mrs. Maylie. Rose was consequently Oliver's aunt. Monks had gone on to live a dissolute life, going to the West Indies when his mother died. Mr. Brownlow had gone in search of him there, but by then Monks had already returned to England to track down his young half brother, whose part of his father's settlement he wished to keep for himself. It was Monks who had offered the reward at the workhouse for information about Oliver's parentage, and it was Monks who had paid Fagin to see that the boy remained with the gang as a common thief.

After Fagin and the Artful Dodger were seized, Bill Sikes and the remainder of the gang met on Jacob's Island in the Thames River. They intended to stay there in a deserted house until the hunt died down. Sikes's dog, however, led their pursuers to the hideout. Bill Sikes hanged himself accidentally with the rope he was using as a means of escape. The other thieves were captured. Fagin was hanged publicly at Newgate after he had revealed to Oliver the location of papers concerning his heritage, which Monks had entrusted to him for safekeeping.

Harry Maylie became a minister and married Rose Maylie. Mr. Brownlow adopted Oliver and took up residence near the church of the Reverend Harry Maylie. Mr. and Mrs. Bumble lost their parochial positions and became inmates of the workhouse that once had been their domain.

Monks was allowed to retain his share of his father's property and went to America; eventually he died in prison. Oliver's years of hardship and unhappiness were at an end.

Critical Evaluation:

When *Oliver Twist* was published, many people were shocked, and clergymen and magazine editors accused the young novelist of having written an immoral book. In later editions, Charles Dickens defended the book, explaining that one of his purposes had been to take the romance out of crime and show the underworld of London as the sordid, filthy place he knew it to be. Few of his readers ever doubted that he had succeeded in this task.

When Dickens began writing, a popular form of fiction was the so-called "Newgate novel," or the novel dealing in part with prison life and the rogues and highwaymen who ended up in prison. These heroes often resembled Macheath of John Gay's *The Beggar's Opera* (1728). Dickens took this tradition and form and turned it around, making it serve the purposes of his new realism. The subplot concerning Bill Sikes and Nancy contains melodramatic elements, but Sikes is no Macheath and Nancy no Polly Peachum.

The grim birth of the infant who was named Oliver opens the book, immediately plunging the reader into an uncomfortably unromantic world where people are starving to death, children are "accidentally" killed off by their charitable keepers, the innocent suffer, and the cruel and unscrupulous prosper. Dickens does not hesitate to lay the facts out clearly: Nancy is a prostitute, Bill is a murderer, Fagin is a fence, and the boys are pickpockets. The supporting cast includes Bumble and Thingummy and Mrs. Mann, individuals who never hesitate to deprive others of what they themselves could use. Poverty is the great leveler, the universal corruptor; in the pages of *Oliver Twist*, the results of widespread poverty are portrayed with a startling lack of sentimentality. Dickens may become sentimental when dealing with virtue but never when dealing with vice.

The petty villains and small-time corrupt officials, such as Bumble, are treated humorously, but the brutal Bill Sikes is portrayed with complete realism. Although Dickens' contemporaries thought Bill was too relentlessly evil, Dickens challenged them to deny that such men existed in London, products of the foul life forced on them from infancy. He holds up Bill Sikes in all of his blackness, without making any attempt to find redeeming characteristics. Nancy, both immoral and kindhearted, is a more complicated character. She is sentimental because she is basically good, while Bill is entirely practical, a man who will step on anybody who gets in his way and feel no regrets.

In *Oliver Twist*, Dickens attempted a deliberate contrast to his previous work, *The Pickwick Papers* (1836-1837). While there is much humor in *Oliver Twist*, it is seldom like that of its predecessor, and it is woven into a realistic and melodramatic narrative of a particularly grim and dark kind. The readers of Mr. Pickwick's exploits must have been startled when they picked up the magazines containing this new novel by Dickens and discovered old Fagin teaching the innocent Oliver how to pick pockets and children swigging gin like practiced drunkards. Dickens was a man of many talents, however, and in *Oliver Twist*, he exploited for the first time his abilities to invoke both pathos and horror and to combine these qualities in a gripping narrative. United with the vitality that always infused Dickens' prose, these powers guaranteed *Oliver Twist* a wide readership.

The book was the first of Dickens' nightmare stories and the first of his social tracts. A certain amount of social protest could be read into Mr. Pickwick's time in prison, but it is a long distance from the prison depicted there to the almshouse in *Oliver Twist*. The leap from farce to melodrama and social reform was dramatically successful, and Dickens was to continue in the same vein for many years. Some critics called his work vulgar, but his readers loved it. He was accused of exaggeration, but, as he repeatedly emphasized, his readers had only to walk the streets of London to discover the characters and conditions of which he wrote so vividly. If his characterizations of some individuals suggested the "humours" theory of Ben Jonson rather than fully rounded psychological portraits, the total effect of the book was that of an entire society, pulsing with life and energy.

In *Oliver Twist*, Dickens displayed for the first time his amazing gift of entering into the psychology of a pathological individual. He follows Sikes and Fagin closely to their respective ends, and he never flinches from revealing their true natures. The death of the unrepentant Sikes remains one of the most truly horrible scenes in English fiction. (When Dickens performed this passage to audiences in his public readings, it was common for ladies in the audience to scream or faint.) When Fagin is sitting in court, awaiting the verdict of his trial, Dickens describes his thoughts as roaming from one triviality to another, although the fact of his approaching death by hanging is never far away. The combination of the irrelevant and the grimly pertinent was a kind of psychological realism that was completely new in 1838.

Dickens entertained a lifelong fondness for the theater, and this interest in drama had a profound influence on his fiction. He was himself an actor, and he became famous for his readings from his books toward the end of his life. In his novels, the actor in Dickens is also discernible. At times, it is as if the author is impersonating a living individual; at other times, the plots bear the imprint of the popular stage fare of the day, including heavy doses of melodrama, romance, and coincidence. All of these aspects are seen in *Oliver Twist*, particularly the violence of the melodrama and the coincidences that shuffle Oliver in and out of Mr. Brownlow's house. Above all and ultimately much more important, however, stands the realism that Dickens uses to unite the different elements of his story. Perhaps the greatest achievement of the author in this early novel was the giant stride forward he made in the realm of realism. He had not yet perfected his skills, but he knew the direction in which he was moving, and he was taking the novel with him.

"Critical Evaluation" by Bruce D. Reeves

Bibliography:
Anderson, Roland F. "Structure, Myth, and Rite in *Oliver Twist*." *Studies in the Novel* 18, no. 3 (Spring, 1986): 238-257. Anderson explores the rites of passage that the plot of the novel depends on and demonstrates how the narrative structure itself seems to be centered in the myths associated with a rite of passage for a young man.
Dunn, Richard J. *"Oliver Twist": Whole Heart and Soul.* New York: Macmillan, 1993. A thorough reader's companion to the story. Dunn closely examines both the literary and historical context of the novel and includes five critical readings of *Oliver Twist*. This is perhaps the most useful text for beginning readers of the novel.
Ginsburg, Michal Peled. "Truth and Persuasion: The Language of Realism and of Ideology in *Oliver Twist*." *Novel: A Forum on Fiction* 20, no. 3 (Spring, 1987): 220-226. Ginsburg discusses the rhetorical methods that Dickens is using in the narrative voice of the novel to persuade the reader that most commoners in Victorian Britain were living difficult lives because of their low socioeconomic status. He suggests that this novel was Dickens' call for action against the industrialists.
McMaster, Juliet. "Diabolic Trinity in *Oliver Twist*." *Dalhousie Review* 61 (Summer, 1981): 263-277. McMaster believes that the three characters Fagin, Sikes, and Monks are a de-

praved inversion of the holy trinity, representing knowledge, power, and love. Each of these characters takes one of the aspects of the trinity and uses it in an evil way.

Wheeler, Burton M. "The Text and Plan of *Oliver Twist*." *Dickens Studies Annual: Essays on Victorian Fiction* 12 (1983): 41-61. Wheeler discusses unanswered questions and contradictions in the novel. Explains that Dickens did not intend to turn what had begun as a short serial work into a novel and thus did not plan a credible plot.

OMENSETTER'S LUCK

Type of work: Novel
Author: William H. Gass (1924-   )
Type of plot: Symbolic realism
Time of plot: 1890's
Locale: Gilean, Ohio, an imaginary river town
First published: 1966

> *Principal characters:*
> BRACKETT OMENSETTER, a newcomer to Gilean
> HENRY PIMBER, a neighbor of Omensetter's
> JETHRO FURBER, the pastor
> ISRABESTIS TOTT, a storyteller

The Story:

Brackett Omensetter moved his pregnant wife, Lucy, and their two daughters to Gilean, a late nineteenth century town on the Ohio River. After persuading the blacksmith to hire him as an assistant, Omensetter visited Henry Pimber to rent a house. Although the gentle Pimber responded immediately to Omensetter's charismatic ease and self-confidence, he considered Omensetter "a foolish, dirty, careless man." Nevertheless, Omensetter's "carelessness" stirred him, for it seemed to him to be the basis of spiritual grace. Unlike Pimber, who was clumsy and heavy-hearted, Omensetter seemed buoyant: "Shed of his guilty skin, who wouldn't dance?" Pimber asked himself.

When Pimber came by one day to collect the rent, Omensetter took him to see a fox that had fallen into the well and become trapped at the bottom. When Omensetter refused to intervene to save the fox or do anything to put him out of his misery, Pimber shot several rifle shots down into the well. Besides dispatching the fox, Pimber also wounded himself when a bullet ricocheted off a stone wall and penetrated his arm. The wound became badly infected and led to lockjaw, and Doctor Truxton Orcutt, the town doctor, was unable to cure him. As Pimber's life ebbed away, the Reverend Jethro Furber prayed for his soul, but Omensetter prepared a beet root poultice that, to everyone's amazement, saved Pimber's life.

Gilean, already impressed by Omensetter's manner and curious luck, now regarded him with amazement. Pimber healed slowly, his gratitude toward Omensetter deepening into adulation. Having wearied of the routine of life in Gilean and of his wife's habitual demands, Pimber felt the need to possess Omensetter's grace and fluency, his "wide and happy" relation to the natural world around him. Compared with Omensetter, the normal people of Gilean seemed ghostly and unreal to Pimber.

Pimber learned that Omensetter's luck could not be learned or his way of life be imitated. Unable to establish a meaningful relationship with Omensetter, Pimber, weakened and dispirited and swept by a wave of self-pity, hanged himself from one of the topmost branches of a remote oak tree.

Because of the isolated location of the tree Pimber had chosen, the townspeople of Gilean were long unable to find his body. Furber, who disliked Omensetter with fanatical intensity— even to the point of persuading himself that Omensetter might be the devil—exploited Pimber's disappearance to turn the townspeople against the newcomer. Omensetter remained oblivious to Furber's hatred and to being ostracized, just as he had been oblivious to Pimber's love.

When he discovered Pimber's body in the tree, Omensetter went to Furber to ask him to convince the townspeople of his innocence. Confronted by Omensetter's directness, as well as his sheer ordinariness and vulnerability, Furber's hatred vanished. His combativeness took on a new purpose and meaning when he learned that Omensetter's infant son, Amos, had become seriously ill. He strove to convince Omensetter to send for Doctor Orcutt, whom Omensetter distrusted. Omensetter refused, apparently as unable to save his son as he was unwilling to rescue the fox. When Lucy begged him to bring the doctor, Omensetter could only counsel her to trust in his "luck." Having listened to the townspeople of Gilean speak so reverently about it, Omensetter had, at last, come to believe in it, an act of self-consciousness that Furber lamented as a fall from grace.

The crisis of Amos' illness coincided with the removal of Pimber's body from the tree. While Lucy despaired, several of the village men argued intensely among themselves about whether Omensetter was guilty of Pimber's death. Orcutt arrived at Omensetter's house in time to apply the force of common sense and logic to the argument, in favor of Omensetter's innocence, and thus saved his life. Nevertheless, he felt he had arrived too late to save Amos. While Orcutt reasoned with the men, Furber improvised mad, pointless, and obscene limericks.

Furber's illness lifted by the following February, and the Omensetters moved down river. Amos "lingered on alive, an outcome altogether outside science." Omensetter's luck remained a legend on the Ohio River for quite a while, "perhaps forever." With Omensetter and Furber gone, equilibrium and drab normalcy returned to Gilean, as symbolized in the person of the well-balanced, innocuous new minister, Mr. Huffley.

Critical Evaluation:

Although Bracket Omensetter appears to be the protagonist of *Omensetter's Luck,* he functions principally as the catalyst who forces the three articulate character-narrators, Henry Pimber, Israbestis Tott, and Jethro Furber, to confront their dissatisfactions, limitations, and perceptions. In telling contrast with their human foibles, Omensetter is described in natural terms as "a wide and happy man [who] could whistle like the cardinal whistles in the deep snow, or whirr like the shy 'white rising from its cover, or be the lark a-chuckle at the sky.'" By creating in Omensetter a kind of anthropomorphic nature, William Gass sought to examine the painful definitions of the human condition.

Israbestis Tott, who introduces the novel, looks backward at the pivotal events. His impressionistic vision, somewhat blurred and unsynchronized by age, has been likened to Benjy's dreamlike impressions that introduce William Faulkner's *The Sound and the Fury* (1929). The significant details that constitute a part of Tott's miscellaneous stream of meditations serve as intimations that later give the more fully narrated events of the story a sense of familiarity and importance. In contrast to the other character-narrators, Tott remains detached from Omensetter, neither loving him, as Henry Pimber does, nor hating him, as Jethro Furber does. Gass uses Tott's remoteness from Omensetter to delineate his social irrelevance and remoteness from life.

Henry Pimber, whose admiration and love for Omensetter drive him to suicide, is characterized as weak, impressionable, and self-conscious. Omensetter's simple laughter at their first meeting touches Pimber profoundly. "Sweetly merciful God, Henry wondered, sweetly merciful God, what has struck me?" Thereafter, his sensitivity to Omensetter's vitality and "luck" brings home to him his own dissatisfactions and frailties. For him, the human condition signifies ceaseless ineptitude, inferiority, and humiliation, which were the primary colors of his boyhood and of his marriage to Lucy Pimber. Both his wife's physical makeup and her sexual needs repel Pimber, as do the human weaknesses and needs of the townspeople of Gilean. Like the other characters of *Omensetter's Luck,* he interprets Omensetter's power to validate his own preoccupations.

Yearning for escape, Pimber sees Omensetter as the symbol of that escape, the refuge of nature. To Pimber, Omensetter, who "always seemed inhuman as a tree," represents the chance of "losing Henry Pimber" for something larger, richer, and undefined. Yet when Pimber attempts to follow Omensetter, to join him on a remote, wind-swept, hillside, he cannot. The desolation of nature, which so attracted him, is inhospitable to him. He cannot penetrate it. Nature becomes "noise," although Omensetter shrugs happily and asks if he does not love it. Just as Pimber had met failure in his marriage and in childhood, he fails once again when he makes the even harder attempt to overcome the familiar comforts of the self, however wearisome: "No, Henry thought, I don't love the noise; the wind will wash my wits out."

Pimber's dilemma, the dilemma of all human beings, is the conflict between the irresistible need to try to avoid the confines of the human condition and the immovable resistance of the mind to the emptiness of nature. This brings Pinder to the one act open to him. In a gesture ironically combining self-denial and self-aggrandizement, Pimber hangs himself from the highest branch of the tallest oak tree, thus narcissistically exhibiting himself to all and to no one, to admire and, paradoxically, to pity.

Earlier, while meditating on Omensetter's relation to Gilean, Pimber reflects: "Everybody but the preacher stole from him. Furber merely hated." Jethro Furber, modeled on the type of hypocritical clergyman who has flourished in English literature since Geoffrey Chaucer's *Canterbury Tales* (1387-1400), hates Omensetter for reasons that partly correspond to Pimber's for loving him: Whereas Omensetter's natural grace provokes Furber's furious envy, his abundant, sensuous life undermines Furber's torturous asceticism. Unlike Pimber, however, Furber quickly retreats from Omensetter—much as he has retreated into the church, into the remote outpost of Gilean, into the confines of his own small garden, and, finally, into the tricks and traps of language. Furber's withdrawal from nature and from society relegates Omensetter to the margins of the novel, but the mercurial, cultured monologues with which he explains his withdrawal make Furber the dominant force in *Omensetter's Luck.* All subsequent narrators in William Gass's fiction, including the celebrated shorter fiction of *In The Heart of the Heart of the Country* (1966) and *The Tunnel* (1995), are to some degree, reworkings of Jethro Furber.

Furber's few direct confrontations with the implacable Omensetter upset him. When, upon Furber's invitation, Omensetter attends church service, Furber is both dazzled and bewildered by his presence—a reaction that echoes that of Pimber when Omensetter arrived on his doorstep. Like Pimber, who fantasizes that Omensetter can offer him salvation, Furber grasps at the absurd notion that Omensetter represents a supernatural menace and in his charged imagination, the visitor becomes a demon who must be destroyed. In casting Omensetter as personified nature, however, Gass implies that Furber is fighting an invisible foe, a component of his own making.

Just as Furber had almost succeeded in destroying Omensetter—and, at the same time, of immuring himself within the maze of his own bizarre fictions—Omensetter arrives at his door. This final, dead-of-night confrontation is devastating for Furber, for his deviousness is no match for Omensetter's terrible and mysterious innocence. In a dialogue resonant with biblical nuances that underscore his transcendence, Omensetter compels the obstinate Furber to aid him in fending off accusations that he has murdered Pimber. Daunted by Omensetter's inscrutability, by the very intractability of the enigma he has sought both to evade and destroy, Furber meekly agrees. Ironically, although Furber's surrender constitutes intellectual defeat, perhaps even a kind of death, the fruit of his defeat sustains him and, in a final contrast to Pimber, enables him to regenerate human society. Finding himself, at the novel's end, with money Omensetter had used to pay Pimber his last rent, Furber places it in the church's offertory envelope in what Arthur Saltzman has described as "his last, and only sincere, religious gesture."

Michael Scott Joseph

Bibliography:

Brans, Jo. *Listen to the Voices: Conversations with Contemporary Writers.* Dallas, Tex.: Southern Methodist University Press, 1988. Includes an interview with the author that provides interesting anecdotes about the composition of *Omensetter's Luck.*

Holloway, Watson. *William Gass.* Boston: Twayne, 1990. A comprehensive study of Gass, which includes a chapter devoted to the major themes in *Omensetter's Luck.*

McCaffery, Larry. *The Metafictional Muse: The Works of Robert Coover, Donald Barthelme, and William H. Gass.* Pittsburgh: University of Pittsburgh Press, 1982. Includes a chapter on William Gass, which discusses his essays, short stories, and novels, including *Omensetter's Luck.* The author places Gass's work in the context of a "contemporary metasensibility."

Saltzman, Arthur M. *The Fiction of William Gass: The Consolation of Language.* Carbondale: Southern Illinois University Press, 1986. In a separate chapter on *Omensetter's Luck,* Saltzman analyzes the works of William Gass with reference to the author's philosophical beliefs about the insularity of fiction.

Tanner, Tony. *Scenes of Nature, Signs of Men.* Cambridge, England: Cambridge University Press, 1987. An overview of twenty-five years of American fiction. Includes a skillful summary of *Omensetter's Luck.*

OMOO
A Narrative of Adventures in the South Seas

Type of work: Novel
Author: Herman Melville (1819-1891)
Type of plot: Adventure
Time of plot: Early 1840's
Locale: Tahiti and the South Seas
First published: 1847

>   *Principal characters:*
>   HERMAN MELVILLE, an American sailor
>   DOCTOR LONG GHOST, his companion in his adventures
>   CAPTAIN BOB, a jovial Tahitian jailer

The Story:

Rescued from the island of Typee by the crew of a British whaler, Herman Melville agreed to stay on the ship as a deckhand until it reached the next port, where he was to be placed ashore. The *Julia*, however, was not a well-managed vessel. Soon after Melville joined it, several of the men made an attempt to desert. These unfortunates were recovered quickly, however, by the timely aid of the islanders and the crew of a French man-of-war.

In the weeks of cruising that followed this adventure, Melville, relieved from duty because of a lameness in his leg, spent his time playing chess with the ship's doctor and reading the doctor's books. Those were not, however, weeks of pleasure. During that time, two of the men in the forecastle died, and the entire crew lived under the most abominable conditions. The rat-infested, rotten old ship should have been condemned years before. Finally, when the captain himself fell ill, the ship changed its course to Tahiti, the nearest island.

The crew convinced themselves that when the captain left the ship, they would no longer be bound by the agreements they had signed. They intended to leave the ship when it arrived in the harbor at Papeetee. The captain attempted to prevent their desertion by keeping the ship under way just outside the harbor while he went ashore in a small boat. Only Doctor Long Ghost's influence prevented the men from disregarding orders and taking the vessel into the harbor to anchor her. The crew did, however, protest their treatment in a letter sent to the British consul ashore by means of the black cook. Unfortunately, the acting consul in Papeetee and the captain of the *Julia* were old acquaintances, and the official's only action was to inform the men they would have to stay with the ship and cruise for three months under the command of the first mate. The captain himself would remain in Tahiti. After a Mauri harpooner attempted to wreck the ship, the drunken mate decided to take the whaler into the harbor, regardless of the consequences.

In Papeetee, the acting consul had the men, including Melville and Doctor Long Ghost, imprisoned on a French frigate. After five days aboard the French ship, they were removed and were once more given an opportunity to return to their ship. When they refused, the mutineers were taken into custody by a Tahitian native called Captain Bob, who took them to an oval-shaped thatched house, which was to be their jail.

There they were confined in stocks, two timbers about twenty feet long, serving to secure all the prisoners. Each morning, the jailer came to free the men and supervise their baths in a neighboring stream. The natives, in return for hard ship's biscuit from the *Julia*, fed the men baked breadfruit and Indian turnips. Sometimes the kindly jailer led the men to his orange grove, where they gathered fruit for their meals. This fruit diet was precisely what they needed to regain the health they had lost while eating sea rations of salt pork and biscuit.

The prisoners in the thatched hut were in sight of Broom Road, the island's chief thorough-fare. Since the prisoners were easily accessible, the idle, inquisitive Tahitians were constantly visiting, and the prisoners did not lack for company. Within a few days, their jailer freed the sailors from the stocks during the daytime, except when white men were in the vicinity. Once this leniency was granted, the men roamed the neighborhood to take advantage of the natives' hospitality. Doctor Long Ghost always carried salt with him, in case he found some food to flavor.

When the consul sent a doctor to look at the prisoners, all the sailors pretended to be sick. Shortly after the doctor had made his examinations and departed, a native boy appeared with a basket of medicines. The sailors discarded the powders and pills, but eagerly drank the contents of all the bottles which smelled the least bit alcoholic.

British missionaries on the island took no notice of the sailors from the *Julia* other than sending them a handful of tracts. Three French priests, however, came to see the men. The natives, it seemed, looked upon the priests as magicians, and so they had been able to make only a few converts among the islanders. The priests were popular with the sailors because they gave freshly baked wheat bread and liquor to the prisoners. Three weeks after arriving in the port of Papeetee, the captain of the *Julia* sailed away with a new crew recruited from beachcombers idling about the island. After his departure, the mutineers were no longer confined to their jail but continued to live there because the building was as convenient as any other thatched dwelling in the neighborhood. They existed by foraging the surrounding country and by smuggling provisions from visiting ships with the aid of the sailors aboard.

Melville found this life not unpleasant at first, but after a time, he grew bored. He even went to a native church to hear the missionary preach. The theme of the sermon was that all white men except the British were bad and so were the natives, unless they began to contribute more baskets of food to the missionary's larder. Melville did not go to the missionary church again.

Several weeks after the *Julia* had sailed, Melville met two white men who informed him that a plantation on a neighboring island was in need of laborers. Melville and Doctor Long Ghost, introduced to the planters as Peter and Paul, were immediately hired. One moonlit night, the pair boarded the boat belonging to their employers. They left their former shipmates without ceremony, lest the authorities prevent their departure.

The planters lived by themselves in an inland valley on the mosquito-infested island of Imeeo. The prospect of plying a hoe in the heat of the day amid swarms of insects did not appeal to the two sailors, and so at noon of the first day in the fields, Doctor Long Ghost pretended illness. He and Melville agreed to do as little work as possible. After a few days, they gave up farming for good and went on foot to Tamai, an inland village unspoiled by missionaries or other white men. There they saw a dance by native girls, a rite that had been banned as pagan by the missionaries on the island. A day or two later, while the two white men were considering settling permanently at Tamai, the natives forced them to flee, for a reason they were never able to discover.

The next adventure they contemplated was an audience with the queen of Tahiti. Traveling by easy stages from one village to the next on foot or by canoe, they made their way to Partoowye, where the island queen had her residence. They met a runaway ship's carpenter who had settled there and who kept busy building boxes and cabinets for the natives. From him, they learned that a whaler was in the local harbor. When they talked to the crew of the vessel, however, they were told that it was not a good ship on which to sail, and they gave up all thought of shipping away from the islands aboard the whaler.

After five weeks in the village, Doctor Long Ghost and Melville finally obtained admittance to the queen through the good offices of a Marquesan attendant at her court. When they came into the queen's presence, she was eating, and she waved them out of her palace in high-handed fashion, at the same time reprimanding their guide. Disappointed by their reception at court, the two travelers again decided to go to sea. They made friends with the third mate of the whaler, which was still in the harbor. The mate reassured them concerning conditions aboard the ship. The other sailors, knowing the ship could not sail away from the pleasant islands without more men in the crew, had deliberately lied.

Having confidence in the mate, Doctor Long Ghost and Melville then approached the captain and asked to sign on as members of the crew. The captain, however, would not accept Doctor Long Ghost as a deckhand or as the ship's doctor. Reluctantly, Melville shipped out alone on the voyage which would take him to the coast of Japan and, he hoped, eventually home.

Critical Evaluation:

In the language of the Marquesan islanders, *omoo* signifies a rover, one who travels from island to island among the island groups of Polynesia. These islands provide the setting for Herman Melville's first two works. In Melville's day, these islands were still fairly unknown except to missionaries and whalers, and since the latter ships tended to follow known courses through the region, it was still possible to come in contact with islands that had rarely been visited by European or American peoples.

A sequel to Herman Melville's popular first travel novel, *Typee: A Peep at Polynesian Life* (1846), *Omoo* continues the story of Melville's experiences in the region. The question of how factual a reader should consider these experiences has been much debated since the book was first published in 1847. Reviewers objected to various aspects of Melville's first two books, declaring they must be fiction. Melville responded that he had observed "a strict adherence to facts." Research in the twentieth century showed that he had embellished his true experiences— that he had lived one month among the Typee people of Nukuheva, for instance, rather than four as he had claimed. As a result, readers must consider both of these books novels, in which Melville has felt free to alter the details of his experience to deliver a better story.

Omoo stands out among Melville's novels as his most reckless and carefree. Perhaps, for an author associated with darkness, depths of thought, and brooding about the nature of evil, it is Melville at his happiest as well. Like *Typee*, it contains some complaints about missionary activity in Tahiti, but *Omoo* is mostly a light and comical travelogue, as Tommo and his shipboard companion, Doctor Long Ghost, tour and have adventures on Tahiti and neighboring islands. This free spiritedness implies a Melville who has escaped his Puritan demons, a Melville whose narrator can give himself over to pleasure without guilt and to desire without comeuppance. Unlike Melville's other books, there is no dark side to pleasure in *Omoo*, and Tommo and Doctor Long Ghost laze around, a couple of beachcombing slackers, throughout much of the novel, entertaining themselves with various escapades.

Doctor Long Ghost is, like Melville himself was, well read. In the first part of the novel the two play chess and quote poetry from memory to each other aboard their ship, the *Julia*. The two also regale each other with tales of their travels. It was this type of characterization to which British reviewers most objected at the time of *Omoo*'s publication; they argued that no common seaman would have had the breeding to be exposed to literature and the finer pleasures of life. This, Melville countered, was a demonstration of America's democratic, classless society, versus England's more rigid class system. The nineteenth century United States was still new to the world in these respects. In Melville's day, public education allowed the working class to be educated, and learning did not mean that one who had it considered physical labor demeaning.

Democracy is an issue in *Omoo*. Protesting various injustices and the questionable seaworthiness of their captain and ship, several members of the *Julia*'s crew engage in a democratic resistance. Each participant signs the declaration of rebellion, so that no leader may be singled out, with the narrator authoring the document, in effect becoming their Thomas Jefferson. The mutineers are locked up once ashore and for a moment it seems as if all the forces that would seek to restrain American-style democracy are arraigned against them: "four or five Europeans," figures of decadent authority, as well as the ancient ship's articles, "a discolored, musty, bilious affair," are pressed into service far past the age when they might have been relevant. These are more symbols of the forces that once held democracy in check than they are the forces themselves. When the men are not intimidated by them, the men are simply allowed to escape by the native warden, Captain Bob.

In its illustration of the possibilities of democratic organization, then, *Omoo* stands out among Melville's work. Melville is more often obsessed with describing the dangers to democracy in his works. In *Moby Dick: Or, The Whale* (1851), Ahab destroys the possibility of democratic organization among the multicultural crew of the Pequod by ruling them with an iron hand and subjecting the desires of all of his crew to his monomaniacal quest to hunt the white whale. Once at sea, there is nothing that can restrain the tyrannical authority of the captain, and dictatorial sea captains are seen as well in *Typee* and *Redburn: His First Voyage* (1849). A mutiny fails to achieve its desired end in *Moby Dick*'s "Town-Ho's Story," and *Billy Budd, Foretopman* (1924) illustrates the typical severity of justice at sea.

Omoo, one of Melville's most neglected works, reveals much about the young Melville and provides interesting commentaries when viewed in the context of the author's work as a whole. The book provides evidence of his commitment to the American project. Melville abandoned one ship and helped lead a mutiny on another; he was often highly critical of Western influence, in the form of missionaries and armed intrusions, in the South Seas, but he never imagined a life apart from the American ideal. Melville's critique of American abuses of democracy in later works should be viewed as expressions of patriotism, for Melville is an author who examines democracy seriously.

"Critical Evaluation" by Ted Pelton

Bibliography:
Anderson, Charles Roberts. *Melville in the South Seas*. New York: Columbia University Press, 1939. A reliable account of Melville's South Seas voyages, featuring comparisons between the facts of Melville's experience and the fictions of *Moby Dick*, *Typee*, and *Omoo*.
Lawrence, D. H. *Studies in Classic American Literature*. New York: Penguin, 1977. Lawrence was important in the reevaluation of Melville in the 1920's. Lawrence has two essays on him in this book, including one on *Typee* and *Omoo*.
Leyda, Jay. *The Melville Log: The Documentary Life of Herman Melville, 1819-1891*. New York: Harcourt Brace Jovanovich, 1951. Includes excerpts from letters to and from Melville and his family, reviews of his work, and excerpts from his novels that have biographical significance. Good for browsing.

Melville, Herman. *"Omoo": A Narrative of Adventures in the South Seas*. Vol. 2 in *The Writings of Herman Melville*. Evanston, Ill.: Northwestern University Press, 1968. Features an excellent, concise note that places the novel in the context of Melville's career.

Rogin, Michael Paul. *Subversive Genealogy: The Politics and Art of Herman Melville*. Berkeley: University of California Press, 1985. Incisive psychological and Marxist reading of Melville's life and work, arguing that he was one of the leading thinkers of his age. Its reading of Melville's family's place in the historical context of the 1840's is unparalleled.

ON HEROES, HERO-WORSHIP, AND THE HEROIC IN HISTORY

Type of work: Social criticism
Author: Thomas Carlyle (1795-1881)
First published: 1841

Although difficult to read today, Thomas Carlyle's *On Heroes, Hero-Worship, and the Heroic in History* is the best repository in English of that development in late Romanticism that has been called "heroic vitalism." Consisting of a series of six lectures that Carlyle delivered to London audiences in 1840, it represents not so much any soundly based ideas about the making of history as it does Carlyle's view of what the world would be if powerful and inspired people were to have the power he thought they deserved. It thus becomes England's contribution to the nineteenth century cult of the great man, a dream that was most seductively attractive to intellectuals forced to put their ideas in the marketplace with all the other merchants, but closed off from the real power that was being exercised in the newly industrialized world by economic entrepreneurs.

This work has received mixed reviews from readers and critics. Some consider it inferior work; even Carlyle made disparaging remarks about it in his later years. Others, however, find in the volume a clear sense of the values that Carlyle preached consistently in his writings from his earliest sustained social analysis, *Sartor Resartus* (1833-1834), to his later historical writings on Oliver Cromwell and Frederick the Great.

Like most nineteenth century historians and philosophers, Carlyle promotes the notion that progress is good and inevitable; unlike many of his contemporaries, however, he does not believe that the passage of time in and of itself assures progress. Only when persons of heroic temperament step forward to lead the masses can true progress for society occur. The persons featured in *On Heroes, Hero-Worship, and the Heroic in History* were just such people; their actions, and their willingness to live in accordance with the vision of society that motivated them, changed history for the better. Carlyle finds no one around him acting in a way to set his own age right; given to commercialism and self-gratification, the people of nineteenth century Europe lack the will or the leadership to make something worthwhile of their lives. If his work is not totally successful in conveying a portrait of heroism good for all times, it does succeed in showing Carlyle's disenchantment with the nineteenth century and its lack of heroes.

Carlyle's basic idea is that all history is the making of great men, gifted with supreme power of vision or action. It thus becomes our duty to "worship Heroes." "We all of us reverence and must ever reverence Great Men: this is, to me, the living rock amid all the rushings-down whatsoever; the one fixed point in modern revolutionary history, otherwise as if bottomless and shoreless." In the world of onrushing liberalism and industrialism, with the memory of God ever dimming through the growth of science and skepticism, Carlyle needs a faith and develops one based on the worship of great men.

This faith, dubious enough under restrictions of law and order, not to mention the concept of the existence of great women, becomes even more dubious as handled by Carlyle. As the six lectures progress, he moves from myth to history with no clear distinction. He offers leaders of religious movements, great poets, and military conquerors as equally great or heroic. Hero worship not only should be devout; it actually was. In Carlyle's estimation, love of God is virtually identical with loyalty to a leader. Despite his scorn for business activity and its operators, Carlyle's heroes are all men of practical intelligence. He values the same kind of industriousness, resoluteness, and obvious sincerity that could serve to build economic as well as political or clerical empires.

The performance of heroism depends on the interaction of the person with the great social forces of the age; heroes cannot change the course of history alone. In this sense, Carlyle disagrees with his intellectual successor, Friedrich Wilhelm Nietzsche, who argues that the hero can, by sheer force of will, determine the course of events in his or her own life and in society. He is also at odds with his contemporary Karl Marx, whose view of the inevitability of the "march of history" leaves no room for individuals to alter the inexorable course of human events.

Carlyle believes that heroes must use their power in the service of others; all of his heroes are in some fashion selfless. Carlyle expands the notion of heroism to include not only those who lead, but those who serve. Every person is capable of being heroic; hero-worship, the act of recognizing and willingly obeying those who are given the gift to lead, can make heroes of ordinary people. Such a concept may be unacceptable to those who believe in egalitarian societies; for Carlyle, however, the balance of selfless leaders and willing followers was essential to the attainment of the good society.

Carlyle begins his historical survey with the hero as prophet. Mohammed made Islam a historical force through the sword, but history sustained his vision and rewarded him; hence, he is a hero in Carlyle's pantheon. The prophet as hero is a terrifying figure of a bygone age; more in character with the spirit of the time is the poet as hero. After discussing poetry as a romantic vision that makes the poet the spiritual kinsman of the prophet, Carlyle treats Dante Alighieri's *The Divine Comedy* (c. 1320) as the poem of an age of faith. He calls it "genuine song," but it is the Christian message that Carlyle truly values: The literary work is an allegory of the invisible idea. As Dante gave us "Faith, or a soul," so William Shakespeare gave us "Practice, or body." Poet-heroes are born, not made; thus Carlyle labels Shakespeare as a romantic visionary who can be adored, not analyzed. Shakespeare must have suffered heroically himself; otherwise he could not have created Hamlet or Macbeth.

The hero as priest is a spiritual captain, unlike the prophet, who was a spiritual king. Martin Luther and John Knox are Carlyle's subjects—although they were primarily reformers, they become more priestlike than the priests. As are all of Carlyle's heroes, they are visionaries who saw the truth and led their followers forth to battle for it. (Carlyle abounds in military metaphor, whether he writes of peace or war.) Great religious leaders battle idolatry: Idolatry is symbolic, but it is insincere symbolism, and therefore must be destroyed. Carlyle notes that the significant visionary is the man who combats delusion and outworn convention. Every hero, every image breaker, comes to a new sense of reality and brings it to the world. A hero must "stand upon things, not upon the shadow of things."

Protestantism dwindled into factions in Germany, according to Carlyle, but in Scotland, with John Knox, Lutherism found its true home. (Here, and later with James Boswell and Robert Burns, Scottish Carlyle shows a special fondness for his countrymen who found fame and success.) Some may censure Puritanism, but it is fervent faith that brought democracy to England, through Oliver Cromwell, and colonized much of America as well. Knox was intolerant and despotic, but he was a zealot and therefore a hero for Carlyle, who distinguishes between good and bad tyrannies with reasons he never discusses.

The heroes who are closest to Carlyle's audience were Samuel Johnson, Jean-Jacques Rousseau, and Burns. As the priests are less than the prophets, so the heroic men of letters are less than the poets. In Carlyle's opinion, Johann Wolfgang von Goethe is the only heroic poet of the preceding century. Johnson, Rousseau, and Burns were seekers after truth rather than bringers of it. Carlyle delivers a famous paean of praise for learning and publishing, from the

Bible to the newspaper. All ideas are first books; then they become institutions and empires. The eighteenth century was a skeptical age, disbelieving, and therefore unheroic and insincere. Carlyle's three heroes in this section had to struggle against both the climate of opinion and poverty, as all real visionaries should. James Boswell picked his hero well, for Johnson's gospel of moral prudence and practical sense was necessary in an age of cant.

Carlyle was more doubtful about Rousseau. Too complex and introspective to be favored by Carlyle, and French as well, Rousseau stands as an ambiguous hero whom Carlyle acclaims as a zealot but blames for the fanaticism of the French Revolution. Carlyle believes that Rousseau venerated the savage and thus abetted the French lapse into savagery. Robert Burns is a much more engaging figure, and Scottish, as well. Carlyle contradicts himself, however, by admitting that Burns's career was virtually ruined by the lionizing paid him by his hero worshipers in Edinburgh.

The last heroism for Carlyle is kingship—the leadership of people in war and politics. Interestingly, the leaders he specifically presents are not revolutionary heroes, but antirevolutionaries. Heroes seek order, and order, to Carlyle, is discipline and peace, even at the cost of liberty and variety. Napoleon came to equate himself with France, and so fulfilled his ego at the cost of his nation. Carlyle respects Napoleon's practical intelligence, which enabled him to seize the salient factor in a situation and make fools of Europe's conventional generals and statesmen.

Throughout his effusive presentation, Carlyle never analyzes, but exhorts, praises, and condemns. He admires the movers and shakers of the earth; his praise of Dante and Shakespeare is perfunctory compared with his veneration of Cromwell, who could barely speak coherently, but could and did act eloquently. Anti-intellectualism, veneration of power, and love of enthusiasm as an end in itself are everywhere in this work.

Updated by Laurence W. Mazzeno

Bibliography:
Goldberg, Michael K., Joel J. Brattin, and Mark Engel, eds. *On Heroes, Hero-Worship, and the Heroic in History.* Berkeley: University of California Press, 1993. Provides an extensive introduction to Carlyle's text, and more than 170 pages of notes further explain and interpret it.
LaValley, Albert J. *Carlyle and the Idea of the Modern: Studies in Carlyle's Prophetic Literature and Its Relation to Blake, Nietzsche, Marx and Others.* New Haven, Conn.: Yale University Press, 1968. Two chapters place Carlyle's ideas relating to the hero within the historical development of the concept of the prophetic hero. Useful annotated bibliography.
Ralli, Augustus. *Guide to Carlyle.* Vol. 1. Winchester, Mass.: Allen & Unwin, 1920. Two detailed chapters provide a comprehensive introduction to *On Heroes, Hero-Worship, and the Heroic in History.* The first analyzes the contents of the work; the second offers a general interpretation.
Rosenberg, Philip. *The Seventh Hero: Thomas Carlyle and the Theory of Radical Activism.* Cambridge, Mass.: Harvard University Press, 1974. Focusing on the major works that culminate Carlyle's literary career, Rosenberg examines Carlyle's ideas and discusses *On Heroes, Hero-Worship, and the Heroic in History* in detail in the final chapter.
Seigel, Jules Paul, ed. *Thomas Carlyle: The Critical Heritage.* New York: Barnes & Noble Books, 1971. Offers a brief discussion of *On Heroes, Hero-Worship, and the Heroic in History* and other of Carlyle's works in the context of contemporary reaction to his ideas. Reprints many essays by Carlyle's contemporaries, two of which discuss this work specifically, one attacking, the other defending, the work.

ON LIBERTY

Type of work: Philosophy
Author: John Stuart Mill (1806-1873)
First published: 1859

John Stuart Mill, the English utilitarian, concerns himself in this work with the problem of defining the limits of the power of the state to interfere with personal liberty. The result is one of the most important statements in the history of Western democracy. The essay is distinguished by its clarity and the orderly arrangement of its persuasive argument. Throughout the book can be discerned Mill's interest in the happiness and rights of all people and his serious concern that happiness may be threatened by governmental power unwisely used.

Mill states concisely that the purpose of his essay is

> to assert one very simple principle, as entitled to govern absolutely the dealings of society with the individual in the way of compulsion and control, whether the means used be physical force in the form of legal penalties, or the moral coercion of public opinion. That principle is, that the sole end for which mankind are warranted, individually or collectively, in interfering with the liberty of action of any of their number, is self-protection. That the only purpose for which power can be rightfully exercised over any member of a civilized community, against his will, is to prevent harm to others.

Another statement of the author's intention is found in the last chapter, "Applications," in which Mill states that two maxims together form "the entire doctrine" of the essay. The first maxim is "that the individual is not accountable to society for his actions, in so far as these concern the interests of no person but himself," and the second is "that for such actions as are prejudicial to the interests of others, the individual is accountable, and may be subjected either to social or to legal punishment, if society is of the opinion that the one or the other is requisite for its protection."

It would be an error of interpretation of Mill's intention to suppose that he is explicitly objecting to all efforts of government to improve the condition of its citizens. What Mill objects to is the restriction of human liberty for the sake of human welfare; he has nothing against welfare itself. On the contrary, as a utilitarian, he believes that a right act is one which aims at the greatest happiness of the greatest number of persons; and it is precisely because the restriction of human liberty is so destructive to human happiness that he makes a plea for a judicious use of restrictive power, justifying it only when it is used to prevent harm, or unhappiness of whatever sort, to others than the person being restricted.

Restricting personal liberty for one's own good, for one's happiness, is not morally justifiable. Mill permits, even encourages, "remonstrating" and "reasoning" with a person who is determined to act against his or her own best interests; but he does not approve of using force to keep that person from such actions.

After reviewing some of the acts which a person may rightfully be compelled to do—such as to give evidence in court, to bear a fair share of the common defense, and to defend the helpless—Mill asserts that society has no right to interfere when one's acts concern, for the most part, only oneself. This statement means that a person must be free in conscience, thought, and feeling, and that the person must have freedom of opinion and sentiment on all subjects. This latter freedom involves freedom of the press. In addition, people should be free to do what they like and to enjoy what they prefer—provided what they do is not harmful to others. Finally, each should be free to unite with others for any purpose—again, provided no one is harmed by this action.

Certainly this theme is pertinent, for at any time there is either the present or the possible danger of government interference in human affairs. Mill admits that his principal thesis has the "air of a truism," but he goes on to remind the reader that states have often felt justified in using their power to limit the liberty of citizens in areas that Mill regards as sacrosanct. In the context of Mill's philosophic work, *On Liberty* remains one of his most important essays.

In perhaps the most carefully articulated part of his argument, in chapter 2, "On the Liberty of Thought and Discussion," Mill considers what the consequences of suppressing the expression of opinion would be if the suppressed opinion were true; and then, having countered a series of objections to his arguments against suppression, he continues by considering what the consequences of suppressing opinion would be if the opinion were false.

Suppressing true opinion is clearly wrong, particularly if the opinion is suppressed on the claim that it is false. Silencing the expression of opinion on the ground that the opinion is false is a sign of an assumption of infallibility. A moment's thought shows that the assumption may be mistaken, and that suppressing opinion may very well make discovery of error impossible.

In response to the objection that it is permissible to suppress opinion, even true opinion, because the truth always triumphs, Mill answers that the idea that truth always wins out is a "pleasant falsehood" proved false by experience. To the objection that at least in some parts of the world people no longer put others to death for expressing their opinions, Mill counters with the argument that other kinds of persecution continue to be practiced, destroying truth and moral courage.

If the opinion suppressed be false, Mill continues, the prevailing and true opinion, lacking opposition, becomes a dead dogma. When ideas are not continually met by opposing ideas they tend to become either meaningless or groundless. Beliefs that at one time had force and reasons behind them may come to be nothing but empty words.

The argument in favor of freedom of opinion and the press closes with the claim that most opinions are neither wholly true nor wholly false, but mixtures of the two, and that only in free discussion can the difference be made out. In order to reinforce his central contention—that it is always wrong to hinder the freedom of an individual when what the individual does is not harmful to others—Mill devotes a chapter to an argument designed to show that development of individuality is essential to one's happiness. Since there is nothing better than happiness, it follows that individuality should be fostered and guaranteed. Mill supports Baron Wilhelm von Humboldt's injunction that every human being aim at "individuality of power and development," for which there are two prerequisites: "freedom and the variety of situations."

There is a refreshing pertinence to Mill's discussion of the value of individuality, which recalls Ralph Waldo Emerson's defense of nonconformity. Mill states, "Originality is the one thing which unoriginal minds cannot feel the use of," and "He who lets the world, or his own portion of it, choose his plan of life for him, has no need of any other faculty than the ape-like one of imitation." Mill argues that only if uncustomary acts are allowed to show their merits can anyone decide which mode of action should become customary, and, in any case, the differences among people demand that differences of conduct be allowed so that each person may realize what is best within.

In his discussion of the harm that results from a state's interference with the rights of an individual to act in ways that concern only the individual, Mill reviews some of the consequences of religious intolerance, prohibition, and other attempts to restrict liberty for the common good. In each case, he argues, the result is not only failure to achieve the goal of the prohibitive act, but also some damage to the character of the state and its citizens.

Mill closes by saying that "a State which dwarfs its men, in order that they may be more docile instruments in its hands even for beneficial purposes—will find that with small men no great thing can be accomplished."

Bibliography:
Brady, Alexander. Introduction and textual introduction to *On Liberty*. Vol. 18 in *Collected Works of John Stuart Mill*. Buffalo: University of Toronto Press, 1977. Substantial historical and critical introductions to the definitive edition of Mill's works. Contains details of textual variants and extensive annotations.

Cowling, Maurice. *Mill and Liberalism*. Cambridge, England: Cambridge University Press, 1963. Contains the most extended modern criticism of Mill, who is accused of "more than a touch of something resembling moral totalitarianism." *On Liberty*, he argues, is a selective defense of the individuality of the elevated.

Gray, John. *Mill on Liberty: A Defence*. London: Routledge & Kegan Paul, 1983. A spirited defense of Mill's consistency in promoting the right of liberty from a utilitarian point of view. Considers *On Liberty* the most important of philosophical arguments about liberty, utility, and rights.

Rees, John Collwyn. *John Stuart Mill's "On Liberty."* Edited by G. L. Williams. Oxford, England: Clarendon Press, 1985. A valuable blend of historical, philosophical, and textual analysis. Deals substantially with the criticisms of Cowling and Gertrude Himmelfarb's *On Liberty and Liberalism* (1974).

Stephen, James Fitzjames. *Liberty, Equality, Fraternity*. 1873. Reprint. Edited by Stuart D. Warner. Indianapolis, Ind.: Liberty Fund, 1993. The most sustained and trenchant early attack, by an eminent jurist who agreed with Mill that the "minority are wise and the majority foolish," while dissenting from Mill's view that the wise minority has no right to coerce the masses.

ON SEPULCHRES
An Ode to Ippolito Pindemonte

Type of work: Poetry
Author: Ugo Foscolo (1778-1829)
First published: Dei sepolcri: Carme, 1807 (English translation, 1971)

Written in 1806, the poem is also known in English as *Of Tombs, On Tombs*, or *The Sepulchres*. The poem is addressed to Ugo Foscolo's friend, Ippolito Pindemonte, a wealthy, prominent traveler who translated Homer's *Odyssey* (c. 800 B.C.E.). Pindemonte wrote a poem on tombs before Foscolo, but abandoned it to write an epistle responding to his friend's superior verse. Pindemonte inspired *On Sepulchres* by complaining about a Napoleonic government decree regarding interments, which stated that cemeteries should be set some distance away from inhabited areas, that tombstones should follow a uniform design, and that the living should be banned from visiting graves. Like Pindemonte, Foscolo found the decree unreasonable.

Foscolo had explored many of the subjects in *On Sepulchres* in previous, shorter sonnets and odes, forms Foscolo found too limiting. Foscolo wrote that his "hymn" was composed in the style of the Greeks, using the rhetorical device of question and response to give the poem structure. His purpose is political, and he attempts to reach the heart rather than the mind to awaken Italian reverence for its fallen heroes. He treats his subject with a lofty, epic, heroic, and lyrical tone and a civil, moral, and educational spirit.

Throughout the poem, his theme is that the living and dead are united in immortal love, and that tombs communicate the past to the living. Some critics claim the poem says that death is but another country after life, but Foscolo chose the word "sepulchre" carefully, as the term "cemetery" had Christian connotations he wished to avoid. In Catholic Italy, cemeteries were places for bodies to rest before resurrection. For Foscolo, immortality was in the memory of the living, not heaven or hell, and tombs were simply monuments to the dead.

The poem begins with a desolate tone, the dead reflecting on what they have lost under the shade of cypress trees, a symbol of immortality. They remember life as having love, hope, and music now replaced by the oblivion of "melancholy harmony." The poet asks why one living should want to visit the dead, and answers by saying they deserve reverence because the living, dead, and nature are interconnected, nature inspiring serene reflection on the past.

The poet addresses the new law that would deny solace for the living and "the dead their names." He calls on Calliope, the Muse of poetry, to give grieving poets the same spirit she gave previous singers such as Homer, asking her to give him inspiration to justly memorialize past heroes. The poet describes how people have mourned in the past: how graves, altars, and tombs were designed, and how the greatness of past leaders inspires him.

The second part of the poem emphasizes the importance of memory. Speaking to Pindemonte, the poet recalls the glory of Troy, Italian cities including Florence and Tuscany, and famous Italians. He praises fictional and real ancient Romans and Greeks including Plutarch, Plato, Ajax, and Hector. He describes Electra's death, and how she asked for her fame to be immortalized in song. These names, some critics claim, underline Foscolo's antiplebeian, antiegalitarian, and aristocratic point of view. This is possible, but Foscolo is primarily celebrating a pantheon of brave Italian immortals who conquered death in their fame, monuments, and literature.

The poem then prophesies the ruins of contemporary life, warning of dangers to people separated from their past glories. The dead carry secrets and glory the living must embrace and carry on. Part of the popular graveyard school of eighteenth century poetry, *On Sepulchres* is but one of Foscolo's explorations of Italian heroes, myth, and death. On the poem's publication, Foscolo's reputation was elevated into prominence, prompting quick translations into European languages. His detractors, primarily the clergy, objected to his anti-Christian stance and the womanizing in his personal life.

On Sepulchres is now generally regarded as Foscolo's masterpiece. His role as a patriotic bard of Italy's greatness adds much interest into the poem in his mother country. In 1871, the city of Florence had his bones moved to the Church of Santa Croe to be enshrined alongside heroes he had elegized.

Wesley Britton

Bibliography:
Cambon, Glauco. *Ugo Foscolo: Poet of Exile*. Princeton, N.J.: Princeton University Press, 1980. Discusses *On Sepulchres* in passing, but provides a wealth of information on Ippolito Pindemonte's friendship with Foscolo, including a discussion of the two friends writing poems on the same subject, the decree on tombs. Also discussed is the historical setting that helped shape Foscolo's poem.
Cippico, Antonio. "The Poetry of Ugo Foscolo." *Proceedings of the British Academy, 1924-1925*. Vol. 11. London: British Academy Press, 1927. First placing the poem in historical and literary contexts, Cippico evaluates the poem's religious and political nature, emphasizing and explaining in detail the poem's classical allusions.
Foscolo, Ugo. *On Sepulchres: An Ode to Ippolito Pindemonte*. Translated by Thomas C. Bergin. Bethany, Minn.: Bethany Press, 1971. Historical background, explanatory notes, and comments on translating the poem into English. Contains both Italian and English texts of the poem on facing pages.
Pasinetti, P. M. "Notes Toward a Reading of Foscolo's '*Sepolcri*.'" *Italian Quarterly* 3, no. 2. (Winter, 1960): 3-12. Insightful analysis of the poem.
Radcliff-Umstead, Douglas. *Ugo Foscolo*. New York: Twayne, 1970. This literary biography discusses Foscolo's place in the Romantic movement, comparing the poet with other authors and musicians of the era. It discusses Foscolo's interest in and use of classical myth, music, and Italian history and poetic traditions. It describes Foscolo's poetic style and imagery, compares *On Sepulchres* with other Foscolo poems, and briefly evaluates Foscolo's critical reception. This book's explication of *On Sepulchres* is extensive and indispensable.

ON THE NATURE OF THINGS

Type of work: Philosophy
Author: Lucretius (Titus Lucretius Carus, c. 98-55 B.C.E.)
First transcribed: De rerum natura, c. 60 B.C.E. (English translation, 1682)

The staying power of *On the Nature of Things* cannot be questioned. The work has been, over the centuries, widely influential on the greatest writers and has been widely reviled. Quickly dubbed atheistic by early Christian fathers, the book continued to provoke negative reactions from Catholic theologians for nearly a millennium. "Rediscovered" during the Renaissance, it became an oft-quoted source of inspiration for figures as diverse as Giordano Bruno in Italy, Michel de Montaigne in France, and Edmund Spenser in England. British poets John Evelyn and John Dryden translated passages into English; Voltaire found it valuable in his attacks on the Church. The figure of Lucretius, the skeptical scientist struggling to resolve the seemingly random qualities of the natural world with humankind's insistent belief in a controlling deity, served as the source of one of Alfred, Lord Tennyson's finest dramatic monologues. Even in the twentieth century, the work has found its devotees, including noted philosopher Henri Bergson.

Critics of Lucretius most often focus on three major aspects of his work: his investigation of scientific phenomena, his approach to religious issues, and his poetic skills. For the first two, the poet has been alternatively valued and vilified; for the last, however, he has been universally hailed as a master of language, technique, and vision. At the heart of this lengthy analysis of the ways the universe works is a human message that transcends the centuries and speaks to people of all times. Lucretius displays, in his long poem about atoms and gods who are born of the fears and hopes of humans, an appreciation of both humankind and nature that reminds one of the best works of the Romantics.

Often overlooked, especially by those who read *On the Nature of Things* in translation, is Lucretius' contribution to his native Latin. The Latin of the first century B.C.E. was rough and direct (especially when compared to the more sophisticated Greek); hence, Lucretius lacked an adequate vocabulary for philosophic or scientific discussion. The self-imposed demand to transmit his ideas about religion and philosophy in verse rather than prose made his task even more difficult (many words simply would not fit into hexameters, the meter of choice for most serious Latin poetry); hence, his accomplishment is even more significant. The resultant work displays the passion of a sincerely religious man, the scientific insight of a studied practitioner, and the mastery of language characteristic of the most accomplished literary artists; many consider it the finest didactic poem in any language.

On the Nature of Things is also renowned as the greatest poetic monument of Epicurean philosophy. It is outstanding both as a scientific explanation of the poet's atomic theory and as a fine poem. Vergil was much influenced by Lucretius' verse, and echoes passages of *On the Nature of Things* in the *Georgics* (36-29 B.C.E.), a didactic epic modeled on Lucretius' poem, and in the *Aeneid* (30-19 B.C.E.).

Lucretius, following his master Epicurus' doctrine, believed that fear of the gods and fear of death were the greatest obstacles to peace of mind, the object of Epicurean philosophy. He considered that he could dispel these unfounded terrors by explaining the workings of the universe and showing that phenomena interpreted as signs from the deities were simply natural happenings. His goal in *On the Nature of Things* is thus to explain natural events and to expound thereby on Epicurean philosophy.

His scientific speculations are based on Democritus' atomic theory and Epicurus' interpretation of it. Lucretius outlines the fundamental laws of this system in the first book of his poem.

According to Lucretius, everything is composed of small "first bodies," tiny particles made up of a few "minima" or "least parts," which cannot be separated. These "first bodies," atoms, are solid, indestructible, and of infinite number. They are mixed with void to make objects of greater hardness or softness, strength or weakness.

Lucretius "proves" these assertions by calling upon the reader's reason and his or her observation of nature, pointing out absurdities that might come about if his point were not true. For example, he substantiates his statement that nothing can be created from nothing by saying, "For if things came to being from nothing, every kind might be born from all things, nought would need a seed. First men might arise from the sea, and from the land the race of scaly creatures, and birds burst forth from the sky." These proofs, which may fill fifty or one hundred lines of poetry, are often unconvincing, but they reveal the author's knowledge of nature and his imaginative gifts.

The universe is infinite in the Epicurean system. Lucretius would ask one who believed it finite, "If one were to run on to the end . . . and throw a flying dart, would you have it that that dart . . . goes on whither it is sped and flies afar, or do you think that something can check and bar its way?" He ridicules the Stoic theory that all things press toward a center, for the universe, being infinite, can have no center. Lucretius, in his proof that the universe is infinite, does not consider what it would take some two millenia for another thinker to consider; one could go to the "end" of a finite universe, throw a dart from there, and have it sail on unimpeded into another part of the universe, giving the appearance that the universe has no end, if space is curved. He often contradicts what science has since proved true, but he is remarkably accurate for his time.

Book 2 opens with a poetic description of the pleasure of standing apart from the confusion and conflicts of life: "Nothing is more gladdening than to dwell in the calm high places, firmly embattled on the heights by the teaching of the wise, whence you can look down on others, and see them wandering hither and thither." Lucretius is providing this teaching by continuing his discussion of atoms, which he says move continuously downward like dust particles in a sunbeam. They have a form of free will and can swerve to unite with one another to form objects. Lucretius adds that if the atoms could not will motion for themselves, there would be no explanation for the ability of animals to move voluntarily.

The poet outlines other properties of atoms in the latter part of the second book: they are colorless, insensible, and of a variety of shapes which determine properties of the objects the atoms compose. Sweet honey contains round, smooth particles; bitter wormwood, hooked atoms.

While Lucretius scorns superstitious fear of the gods, he worships the creative force of nature, personified as Venus in the invocation to book 1. Nature controls the unending cycle of creation and destruction. There are gods, but they dwell in their tranquil homes in space, unconcerned for the fate of humanity. A passage in praise of Epicurus precedes book 3, the book of the soul. Lucretius says that fear of death arises from superstitions about the soul's afterlife in Hades. This fear is foolish, for the soul is, like the body, mortal. The poet describes the soul as the life force in the body, composed of very fine particles which disperse into the air when the body dies. Since the individual will neither know nor feel anything when the soul has dissolved, fear of death is unnecessary. One should not regret leaving life, even if it has been full and rich. One should die as "a guest sated with the banquet of life and with calm mind embrace . . . a rest that knows no care." If existence has been painful, then an end to it should be welcome.

The introductory lines of book 4 express Lucretius' desire to make philosophy more palatable to his readers by presenting it in poetry. His task is a new one: "I traverse the distant haunts of the Pierides (the Muses), never trodden before by the foot of man."

The poet begins this book on sensation with an explanation of idols, the films of atoms which float from the surfaces of objects and make sense perception possible. People see because idols touch their eyes, taste the bitter salt air because idols of hooked atoms reach their tongues. Idols become blunted when they travel a long distance, causing people to see far-off square towers as round.

Lucretius blames the misconceptions arising from visual phenomena such as refraction and perspective on reason, not sense, for accuracy of sense perceptions is an important part of his theory: "Unless they are true, all reason, too, becomes false."

A second eulogy of Epicurus introduces the fifth book, for some readers the most interesting of all. In it Lucretius discusses the creation of the world and the development of human civilization. Earth was created by a chance conjunction of atoms, which squeezed out sun, moon, and stars as they gathered together to form land. The world, which is constantly disintegrating and being rebuilt, is still young, for human history does not go back beyond the Theban and Trojan wars. The poet gives several explanations for the motion of stars, the causes of night, and eclipses. Since proof can come only from the senses, any theory that does not contradict perception is possible.

Lucretius presents the curious idea that the first animals were born from wombs rooted in the earth. Monsters were created, but only strong animals and those useful to people could survive. A delightful picture of primitive people, hardy creatures living on nuts and berries and living in caves, follows. Lucretius describes the process of civilization as people united for protection, and learned to talk, use metals, weave, and wage war. Problems arose for them with the discovery of wealth and property, breeding envy and discord. It was at this point that Epicurus taught people the highest good, to free them from their cares.

The sixth book continues the explanation of natural phenomena which inspired people to fear the gods: thunder, lightning, clouds, rain, earthquakes. Lucretius rambles over a great many subjects, giving several explanations for many of them. He concludes the poem with a vivid description of the plague of Athens, modeled on Thucydides' account.

Bibliography:
Dudley, D. R., ed. *Lucretius*. London: Routledge & Kegan Paul, 1965. Provides seven important articles on various aspects of Lucretius' life and work. Includes an index of names and important passages from the work.
Hadzsits, George D. *Lucretius and His Influence*. New York: Cooper Square, 1963. A solid analysis of the influence of *On the Nature of Things* from the Roman era through the Middle Ages and Renaissance to modern criticism. The fourth chapter is especially good regarding the work's place in relation to other ancient authors.
Lucretius. *On the Nature of Things*. Edited and translated by Antony M. Esolen. Baltimore: The Johns Hopkins University Press, 1995. A superior translation, skillfully constructed and thoroughly enjoyable to read. A good starting place for those who seek a balance of scholarship and fine translation.
Minadeo, Richard. *The Lyre of Science: Form and Meaning in Lucretius' "De Rerum Natura."* Detroit: Wayne State University Press, 1969. A scholarly study. Thorough discussion of recurrent motifs and the overall design of the work. Provides copious notes, an appendix of Latin words and concepts, and an index.

Sikes, E. E. *Lucretius: Poet and Philosopher*. Cambridge, England: Cambridge University Press, 1936. Addresses all important themes, events in Lucretius' life, and philosophical speculations in relation to other traditions in close detail. Provides the Latin text and a translation. Index and annotated appendix.

ON THE ORIGIN OF SPECIES

Type of work: Nature writing
Author: Charles Darwin (1809-1882)
*First published: On the Origin of Species by Means of Natural Selection: Or, The
Preservation of Favoured Races in the Struggle for Life,*1859

Charles Darwin's *On the Origin of Species* belongs to that category of books that almost every educated person knows by title and subject but has never read. Yet probably few other books have had so powerful an influence on nineteenth and twentieth century thought. Darwin's report on his biological investigations came to have far-reaching importance beyond the field of biology, for the evidence and implications he presented eventually influenced psychology, sociology, law, theology, educational theory, philosophy, literature, and other branches of intellectual endeavor.

The ideas in this work were not entirely new in Western culture, as Darwin himself realized. It was he, however, who gave theory a definitive form that caught the public's attention, so that in the public mind his book and his name came to represent an empirical, positivistic approach to problems and their study.

Scholarly opinion is somewhat divided as to Darwin's contribution to biological science. He built on the researches of his predecessors, as all scientists do, but he brought immense labor of his own to the topic. More than twenty years before the publication of *On the Origin of Species,* he had first contemplated the theory that species were not immutable. He had spent five years in scientific study as a naturalist on the voyage of HMS *Beagle.* During that time he had unprecedented opportunities to observe flora and fauna around the globe. Those observations led him to believe that species did change, and what he observed led him to see the probability of common descent for all living organisms. As early as 1837 he had begun a systematic study to determine whether such hypotheses were correct, and by 1842 he had a rough draft of his theory of evolution. Wishing to secure his data with optimally exhaustive investigations, he postponed publication. In 1858, a manuscript came to him from A. R. Wallace, who, working independently, had come to similar conclusions. Darwin thereupon felt compelled to publish his work, which he began to do in July, 1858, at a meeting of the Linnaean Society. *On the Origin of Species* appeared a little more than a year later. His later books—among them *Variation of Animals and Plants Under Domestication* (1868) and *The Descent of Man* (1871)—elaborated particular aspects of the general theory promulgated in *On the Origin of Species.*

The possibility of evolution of species goes back in the history of thought to classical times; even Aristotle hinted at it in his writings. Darwin opened his book with an account of previous thinking on the theory of evolution in which he outlined earlier statements, beginning with Georges-Louis Leclerc, Georges Buffon, in modern times, and noting such men as Jean-Baptiste Lamarck, Geoffroy Saint-Hilaire, Leopold von Buch, Robert Chambers, the author of *Vestiges of the Natural History of Creation* (1833), and others. In his introduction, Darwin also exercised care in warning the reader what to expect. He wrote:

> I can here give only the general conclusions at which I have arrived, with a few facts in illustration, but which, I hope, in most cases will suffice. No one can feel more sensible than I do of the necessity of hereafter publishing in detail all the facts, with references, on which any conclusions have been grounded.

In his final chapter, entitled "Recapitulation and Conclusion," Darwin declared that the book is "one long argument" in favor of the theory of mutability and evolution of species in the plant and animal worlds. He pointed out that all the evidence had not been gathered and that even the likelihood of someday gathering all the evidence was so slight as to be inconceivable. He pointed out that there have been too many gradations, especially among broken and failing groups of organisms, including those that have in past eras become extinct.

Darwin laid a vast amount of information before the readers of *On the Origin of Species*, of which the chapter headings give an indication. There are chapters on variation in nature and under domestication, on the struggle for existence, on natural selection, on the principles of variation, on instinct, on hybridism, and on the geographical distribution of flora and fauna. There are also chapters on various objections to the general theory of evolution, on the mutual affinities of organic beings, and on the imperfections of the geological record of the succession of organisms. The individual chapters, which are to some extent interdependent and therefore not suited for separate study, cast light on all aspects of the theory of progressive evolution of species. Darwin's organization of his book is as complex as it is lucid, an example of scientific writing at its best.

Bibliography:
Appleman, Philip. *Darwin*. New York: W. W. Norton, 1970. A useful compilation of nineteenth and twentieth century responses to *On the Origin of Species* and to Darwinism as a new intellectual model.
Depew, David J., and Bruce H. Weber, eds. *Darwinism Evolving: Systems Dynamics and the Genealogy of Natural Selection*. Cambridge, Mass.: MIT Press, 1995. Despite the technical terminology of the title, this work compiles a series of general articles on the origin, ideological contexts, and continuing reception of Darwin's theory of natural selection.
Howard, Jonathan. *Darwin*. New York: Hill & Wang, 1982. A concise introduction to Darwin and his work, with chapters on Darwin's biography, pre-evolutionary science, various aspects of Darwin's theory, and an evaluation of Darwin's stature as a scientist.
Weiner, Jonathan. *The Beak of the Finch*. New York: Random House, 1994. A discussion of Darwin's own anxieties over the lack of empirical evidence for the process of natural selection, as a prelude to compelling narrative of later research and the discovery of that evidence. Also includes thoughtful analysis of what natural selection means for the species that discovered it.
Young, Robert M. *Darwin's Metaphor: Nature's Place in Victorian Culture*. Cambridge, England: Cambridge University Press, 1985. A systematic study of Darwin's chief metaphor of "selection." Young explicates Darwinism's place as the main scientific theory successfully to oppose an anthropocentric worldview and establish humanity as a part of nature.

ON THE ROAD

Type of work: Novel
Author: Jack Kerouac (1922-1969)
Type of plot: Autobiographical
Time of plot: 1947-1950
Locale: United States
First published: 1957

Principal characters:
    SAL PARADISE, the narrator, a writer
    DEAN MORIARITY, a young drifter
    CARLO MARX, a poet and intellectual
    OLD BULL LEE, an eccentric and drug addict
    ED DUNKEL, Dean's simple-minded disciple
    GALETA DUNKEL, Ed's wife
    REMI BONCOEUR, a merchant seaman
    MARYLOU, Dean's first wife
    CAMILLE, Dean's second wife
    INEZ, Dean's third wife

The Story:

Sal Paradise was living at his aunt's house in New Jersey while working on his first novel. His "life on the road" began when he read letters written from reform school by Dean Moriarity. When Dean arrived in New York with his new wife Marylou, Sal was impressed with the younger man's enthusiasm and was flattered by Dean's desire to learn to write. He recognized that Dean was a con man who was probably conning him as well, but he enjoyed his company. Sal was sorry when Dean met Carlo Marx, a poet with a "dark mind," for he could not keep up with Dean and Carlo's wild energy.

Sal left New York in the spring of 1947, planning to hitchhike to Denver and continue to San Francisco, where his friend Remi Boncoeur had promised to get him a job on a ship. Sal spent most of his money taking a bus to Chicago. From there, he hitchhiked to Denver and found Carlo and Dean. Dean was divorcing Marylou and planning to marry Camille, a girl he had just met; meanwhile, he was having relations with each in separate hotel rooms. Sal observed as Carlo's and Dean's intellectual pursuits dissolved into drunken parties in town and in the mountains. Depressed, he wired his aunt for money and took a bus to San Francisco.

The seafaring job fell through, but Remi let Sal move into the shack he shared with his girlfriend Lee Ann. Sal attempted to write a screenplay for Remi to sell in Hollywood; meanwhile, Remi got Sal a job as a security guard. After several months, the three thoroughly resented one another, and Sal left. On a bus to Los Angeles he met Terri, a Mexican woman who had abandoned her husband and son. After two weeks of drinking in Los Angeles, they hitchhiked north to Terri's home town. Sal and Terri moved into a tent and Sal got a job picking cotton. Terri's relatives disapproved of Sal, and he knew he had to go. He promised to meet Terri in New York, but both of them knew she would not come.

With money wired from his aunt, Sal took a bus back east, where he worked on his book and went to school on the GI Bill. During Christmas, 1948, he was visiting relatives in Virginia when Dean Moriarity arrived in a new Hudson. Dean had married Camille and settled down to work in San Francisco, but one day he put a down-payment on the Hudson and headed east with his friend Ed Dunkel and Ed's wife Galeta. When Galeta ran out of money, the two men abandoned her in a hotel lobby. Dean picked up Marylou on a detour to Denver, then drove straight to Virginia.

Drawn again into Dean's orbit, Sal abandoned college and a steady girlfriend to take another trip across the country after the usual three-day drunken farewell party in New York. Driving the southern route, Dean stole gas, conned policemen, and talked like a modern mystic all the way to New Orleans. There they visited Old Bull Lee, an iconoclast and drug addict from a rich family. They all took drugs and listened to Bull expound his wild social theories. Sal was the only person actually invited, so the group wore out its welcome quickly. Galeta Dunkel had been waiting for Ed at Bull's; the couple decided to stay in New Orleans while Sal, Dean, and Marylou headed for California. Sal and Marylou came to an understanding that they would be lovers when they reached the coast.

Dean abruptly left Sal and Marylou in San Francisco. They got a room on credit, but were unable to find work. Marylou deserted Sal; Dean found him starving and brought him to Camille's house. He and Dean toured the local jazz clubs, and Dean found Marylou again, but the threesome quickly became disenchanted with one another. Using his next government check, Sal again returned to New York by bus.

In the spring of 1949 Sal wandered back to Denver. A rich girlfriend gave him a hundred dollars and he rushed to San Francisco to find Dean. Though Dean had fathered another child by Camille, he was still obsessed with Marylou. Furious, Camille ordered him to leave the house. Sal proposed that they go first to New York, then to Italy, using the money from his soon-to-be-published book. Dean agreed, but they decided to have "two days of kicks" in San Francisco first. They visited Galeta Dunkel; Ed had abandoned her again, and she and other women friends confronted Dean with his irresponsibility.

Sal defended Dean, and after an all-night party they left for the east in a travel bureau car. Dean took over the wheel and drove at dangerous speeds to Denver. Sal and Dean quarrelled in a restaurant, then made up and went on a two-day drinking binge. Dean stole several cars, but they escaped the police and zoomed east at 110 miles per hour in a new travel bureau Cadillac. By the time they reached Chicago's jazz clubs, the Cadillac was wrecked. Sal and Dean took a bus to Detroit, and then another travel bureau car to New York. Five nights later, Dean met a girl named Inez at a party and proposed marriage. He got a job as a parking lot attendant, and the trip to Italy was canceled.

The next spring, Sal left Dean working in New York and headed for Mexico. Dean bought an old car and caught up with Sal in Denver. Dean, Sal, and a young man from Denver drove through Texas to Mexico. In Gregoria, a Mexican teenager sold them marijuana and led them to the town brothel, where they had a tremendous party with the blessings of the local police. Afterward, they continued south through the jungles and into Mexico City. They caroused until Sal got a bad case of dysentery. Suddenly Dean abandoned him, driving back to Inez with a Mexican divorce from Camille. The night he married Inez, he left her and took a bus bound for San Francisco and Camille.

Sal returned to New York and met Laura, the girl of his dreams. Dean wrote that he would arrive in six weeks to help them move to San Francisco, but he showed up three days later, almost incoherent in his mysticism. Dean visited Inez and suggested that she move to San Francisco and live on the other side of town, but she refused. The last Sal saw of Dean was when he and Laura left for a concert with Remi Boncoeur, who had arrived in New York from an ocean liner cruise. Remi refused to give Dean a ride, and Dean wandered off to take the train back to San Francisco.

Critical Evaluation:

Jack Kerouac coined the term "Beat generation" and he was stereotyped—both positively and negatively—as a "beatnik" writer for most of his short but prolific career. Reaction to *On the Road* has been quite diverse; the novel has been called everything from incoherent blather to pure genius. The final version was not published until six years after Kerouac drafted it in one long paragraph in 1951. In 1957, the Beat poem "Howl" (by Kerouac's friend Allen Ginsberg) had achieved notoriety; the newly published *On the Road* was able to ride the wave of interest in the Beats and make Kerouac an instant celebrity.

On the Road's literary antecedents could include the "road" poetry of Walt Whitman, the mysticism of poets William Butler Yeats, Arthur Rimbaud, and Charles Baudelaire, Marcel Proust's interconnected narratives, the stream-of-consciousness techniques pioneered by James Joyce and John Dos Passos, and the "lost generation" novels of F. Scott Fitzgerald. As with most of Kerouac's work, *On the Road* is largely autobiographical. Dean Moriarity is based on Neal Cassady, later one of Ken Kesey's Merry Pranksters as chronicled in Tom Wolfe's *Electric Kool-Aid Acid Test* (1968); Carlo Marx represents poet Allen Ginsberg; "Old Bull Lee" is novelist William Burroughs; and numerous other real friends of Kerouac appear under pseudonyms.

The book has been criticized for its lack of plot, but while the narrative is episodic, characters do change. *On the Road* can be read as another in a long line of tales in which middle-class lads are exposed to—and finally reject—a lower-class lifestyle. Far from promoting the irresponsibility that Sal chronicles, the underlying mood is restlessness, disillusion, and depression. The road trips are not so much journeys of ecstatic self-expression or even escape as they are mobile drinking binges. *Big Sur* (1962), a later novel featuring renamed versions of Sal and Dean, makes this aspect of Sal's (and Kerouac's) character very clear. Whenever they arrive anywhere, Dean and company quickly alienate their hosts; taking to the road becomes necessary for outcasts who have nowhere to go. In a telling scene after Dean and Sal's debauched trip east, they restlessly walk around the block, symbolically rejecting the fact that they can go no further, that they must change their approach to life or backtrack the tired road again. By the end of the novel, Sal is settled down and off the road, and the split with Dean—the "holy goof"—seems permanent.

Sal's unsparing critique of himself and his friends makes *On the Road* more than the simple-minded "buddy novel" some critics have labeled it. Despite his attraction, Sal is aware of Dean's sociopathic tendencies. Dean and Ed are "cads" when they abandon Galeta; he later labels Dean a "rat" for abandoning him in Mexico. Other characters also come off as less than romantic: Carlo Marx is prissy and paranoid, Bull Lee maniacal. Sal is also unsparing of his own flaws. Between binges, he is usually depressed, and he leaves "the road" with pangs of nostalgia but no real regret.

The novel has survived not because of the subject matter; its real strength is Kerouac's writing: poetic yet lucid, a brilliant mix of detail and compression. Kerouac wrote his first novel, *The Town and the City* (1950), in verbose emulation of Thomas Wolfe, but with *On the Road,* he adopted a spare, rhythmic, driving prose based on the letters of Neal Cassady. Some passages may be too self-consciously lyrical or poetic by contemporary standards, but these elements add to the depth of Sal Paradise as an interestingly unreliable narrator. Whatever one thinks of the characters and their lifestyle, *On the Road* will remain an important American novel that mirrors popular culture at the midpoint of the twentieth century.

Richard A. Hill

Bibliography:

Cassady, Carolyn. *Off the Road: My Years with Cassady, Kerouac, and Ginsberg.* New York: William Morrow, 1990. Background and chronology of *On the Road* from a woman's point of view. See also her 1978 memoir *Heartbeat: My Life with Jack and Neal.*

Charters, Ann. *Kerouac: A Biography.* San Francisco: Straight Arrow Books, 1973. First book by Charters, a tireless Kerouac scholar. Discusses *On the Road*'s biographical underpinnings and connections.

French, Warren. *Jack Kerouac.* Boston: Twayne, 1986. Two chapters analyzing *On the Road* from biographical and critical approaches.

Kerouac, Jack. *Visions of Cody.* New York: McGraw-Hill, 1972. Contains notes, early drafts, and passages expurgated from *On the Road.*

Milewski, Robert J. *Jack Kerouac: An Annotated Bibliography of Secondary Sources, 1944-1979.* Metuchen, N.J.: Scarecrow Press, 1981. Exhaustive bibliography covering primary and secondary works, reviews, theses, dissertations, and related works. Includes a long discussion of *On the Road* with extensive citations and annotations.

ON THE SUBLIME

Type of work: Literary criticism
Author: Unknown; long attributed to Longinus (fl. first century)
First transcribed: Peri hypsous, first century (English translation, 1652)

On the Sublime is one of a number of classical literary treatises that pose the often-considered problem of nature versus art, of the relative contributions of natural genius or inspiration and of acquired skill to great writing. The author of *On the Sublime,* who almost certainly was not Longinus but an anonymous Greek rhetorician of the first century, argues throughout his work that it is a writer's genius that lifts the reader out of himself or herself, above the limitations of reason. The author also points out that it takes great skill, training, and self-discipline to know when to give free rein to one's genius and when to hold it in check.

This treatise is an interesting combination of philosophical speculation about the elevating, moving powers of poetry and oratory, and practical suggestions about the grammatical constructions and figures of speech that contribute to the effectiveness of great or sublime writing. The author, an enthusiastic critic of his literary predecessors, often quotes Homer, Demosthenes, the great Greek dramatists, and even the Book of Genesis to illustrate the powers of literature, and he points out faults with examples from the works of lesser writers and from inferior passages in the works of the masters.

The author begins *On the Sublime* with a definition of the sublime in literature as a "loftiness and excellence in language" that uplifts the reader and makes him or her react as the writer desires. Sublimity may arise from a few words that cast light on a whole subject, or it may be the result of the expansion and development of an idea; the treatise suggests that the former method is generally the more powerful.

The great danger for the writer who seeks to create a sublime passage is the possibility of lapsing into bombast, that what is intended to be majestic will be simply an empty show. Other potential traps are affectation in expression and empty emotionalism, the display of passion that is not sufficiently motivated. The search for novelty, which on occasion can create a striking effect, may also result in inappropriate imagery and diction. The elements of the truly sublime in literature are often hard to distinguish; they are known chiefly by their effect—the reader's sense of exaltation. Too, a great passage will grow in meaning and significance with each rereading.

Five sources of the sublime are outlined. Two of these are results of the natural capacities of the author: grandeur of thought and the vivid portrayal of the passions. The other three are basically rhetorical skills: the appropriate use of figures of speech, suitable diction and metaphors, and the majestic composition or structure of the whole work.

The most important of these sources is the first, which rests upon the sweep of the author's mind. Although a great intellect is innate, it may be enlarged by association with great ideas. Reading the finest works of the past and pondering them is always valuable, although even the greatest minds can sometimes fall below their customary level. The author suggests that Homer's *Odyssey* (c. 800 B.C.E.) is on a lower plane of intensity throughout than his *Iliad* (c. 800 B.C.E.). It is the work of an aging man who dreams, but "he dreams as Zeus might dream."

One of the tormented love lyrics of Sappho, the Greek poet, is analyzed to illustrate the power of emotion to create an impression of sublimity. The tumultuous succession of feelings, burning, shivering, and fainting are described so vividly and follow one another so closely that the reader participates in the emotional crises of the poet. This technique can, however, in the hands of a lesser writer than Sappho, seem contrived, even ridiculous.

The author digresses from this discussion to elaborate on his earlier consideration of the relative merits of succinctness and diffuseness in the creation of sublime literature. He suggests that quickly moving, powerful language can overcome readers or listeners, convincing them in spite of their reason, whereas the more diffuse style tends to hammer an argument in through repetition, if not through logical argument. There are appropriate occasions for the use of each technique; some writers, like Demosthenes, excel in the vehement passionate outburst, while others, including Plato and Cicero, uplift their readers with a majestic flow of language.

The mention of these great masters suggests the next major point: The aspiring writer can learn much by imitating the outstanding writers of the past, by attempting to decide how Plato, Homer, or Thucydides would have expressed the idea with which the writer now is struggling. The helpfulness of such study can be far more than stylistic, because great writing always has the power to inspire, to expand the understanding of the would-be writer.

Moving on to his third source of sublimity, the use of imagery in poetry and oratory, the author notes that the purpose of all figures of speech is to enlighten, to convince, to enrapture, and to overcome all doubt by their emotional power. Many kinds of images can create these effects. Close examination of passages from Demosthenes and others shows how the skillful choice of verbs, the use of an oath at the proper moment, the omission of conjunctions, or rhetorical questions can make the hearer assent, almost unconsciously, to the orator's premises. Again, natural genius must play an important part, for if the figures of speech are not fused into an impressive whole, they will only be an annoyance, convincing the listener that the speaker is trying to dupe her or him.

The writer has many ways of influencing the emotional reactions of readers, and the student of composition would do well to read in full the discussion of the ways in which sentence structure can be varied, or singular and plural interchanged to produce different effects. So simple a device as shifting from the past to the present tense or from the third person to the first can bring a narrative to life.

Appropriate diction is immeasurably important in the creation of great literature. The author notes that the suitable words are not always the most beautiful or elevated ones, and he illustrates the power of commonplace expressions. A writer must depend on taste in order to avoid vulgarity or bombast.

In another important digression, the author considers the relative value of the writer whose work is almost always flawless, polished, and in perfect taste, but never rises to great heights, versus the one whose work has both moments of sublimity and occasional lapses in taste. It is almost impossible for these two virtues to be combined, because the mind that is dwelling on the heights may sometimes overlook details, while the one that is attentive to correctness is never free enough of trivial concerns to achieve greatness. *On the Sublime*'s author gives unqualified approval to the flawed genius, on the grounds that humans are blessed with a wide-ranging intellect that can project them beyond the bounds of individual existence. It is both a duty and a privilege to keep one's eyes focused on heavenly lights, rather than on the tiny flames lit by humans.

Turning to the fifth source of sublimity, the author comments on the power of harmony in writing, as in music, to move people. It is the fusion of thought, diction, and imagery into one harmonious whole that builds up the reader's impression of power. The rhythm of cadence of the language, too, may enhance the almost hypnotic effect of sublime writing.

The final section of *On the Sublime* deals with the lack of great writing and oratory in the age in which the treatise was written. The author argues that the benevolent despotism of the age has curtailed humans' creative spirit, but he contends that it is rather people's greed and their search for pleasure that enervate them. When humans' minds are bound to earth by their quest for wealth, they no longer reach out to achieve that magnitude of mind and spirit that is essential for the great writer. People's apathy and indifference to all but their own immediate interests prevent them from achieving the greatness of their predecessors. On this discouraged and discouragingly modern note, the treatise ends, as its author states his intention to begin another work, enlarging on what he has said here about the place of the passions in great writing.

Bibliography:

Blamires, Harry. *A History of Literary Criticism*. New York: St. Martin's Press, 1991. Summarizes the place of *On the Sublime* in the development of critical ideas; explains relevant issues. Notes and bibliography.

Kennedy, George A., ed. *Classical Criticism*. Vol. 1 in *The Cambridge History of Literary Criticism*. Cambridge, England: Cambridge University Press, 1989. The section covering *On the Sublime* summarizes its content, its significance, and relevant questions. Notes, bibliography, and index.

On the Sublime. Edited and translated by James A. Arieti and John M. Crossett. Vol. 21 in *Texts and Studies in Religion*. New York: Edwin Mellen Press, 1985. Gives a line-by-line commentary on the work and its critics. Includes bibliography.

Roberts, W. Rhys, ed. *Longinus: On the Sublime*. New York: AMS Press, 1979. This definitive textual, critical, and historical study by an eminent nineteenth century classical scholar forms the basis for subsequent studies of Longinus. Includes introduction, facsimiles, appendices, notes, indices, and bibliography of seventeenth, eighteenth, and nineteenth century scholarship.

Wimsatt, William K., and Cleanth Brooks. *Classical and Neo-Classical Criticism*. Vol. 1 in *Literary Criticism: A Short History*. Chicago: University of Chicago Press, 1978. The analysis of *On the Sublime* in chapter 6 is especially useful for the student, as it distinguishes between the "sublime" of Longinus and that of Immanuel Kant.

THE ONCE AND FUTURE KING

Type of work: Novel
Author: T. H. White (1906-1964)
Type of plot: Arthurian romance
Time of plot: Middle Ages
Locale: England
First published: 1958 (as tetralogy): *The Sword in the Stone*, 1938; *The Witch in the Wood*, 1939 (also known as *The Queen of Air and Darkness*); *The Ill-Made Knight*, 1940; *The Candle in the Wind*, 1958

Principal characters:
> KING ARTHUR, earlier known as WART, king of Gramarye
> SIR KAY, Arthur's childhood playmate
> SIR ECTOR, Arthur's guardian and the father of Sir Kay
> SIR CRUMMORE GRUMMURSUM, a friend of Sir Ector
> KING PELLIMORE, a gentle and absentminded knight
> MERLYN, a magician and Arthur's tutor
> ROBIN WOOD, a robber who lives in the forest
> MORGAN LE FAY, a wicked sorceress
> UTHER PENDRAGON, Arthur's father and his predecessor on the throne
> QUEEN MORGAUSE, the sister of Morgan le Fay and wife of King Lot of Orkney
> GAWAINE,
> AGRAVAINE,
> GARETH, and
> GAHERIS, the sons of King Lot and Queen Morgause, referred to as "the Orkney faction"
> ST. TOIRDEALBLACH, a Pelagian heretic from Cornwall
> LANCELOT, an ugly boy who becomes Arthur's chief knight and Guenever's lover
> GUENEVER, Arthur's adulterous queen
> UNCLE DAP, Lancelot's tutor
> ELAINE, a girl who seduces Lancelot and bears him a son
> GALAHAD, Lancelot's son
> KING PELLES, Elaine's father
> MODRED, the son of Arthur and Morgause, who hates his father
> SIR MADOR DE LA PORTE, a knight who accuses Guenever of adultery
> SIR MELIAGRANCE, a knight who kidnaps Guenever

The Story:
    In educating the Wart, as Arthur was called, to understand the world and its moral and ethical values, Merlyn allowed him to assume the forms of various animals so that he could view life in different social orders. When he became a fish and swam in the castle moat, the great pike told him that "Might is Right," demonstrating how the most powerful fish can rule the moat. From falcons, he learned about the rigors of military life; from ants, about societies that demand total conformity; from wild geese, about heroism; and from the badger, about the potential

greatness of humans. Arthur's childhood was filled with the wonders of the universe as revealed by Merlyn and with adventures of the sort all boys dream about.

Arthur received his education with no knowledge that he was being prepared for a throne. Rather, as the mere ward of Sir Ector, he expected to see Ector's son Kay reap whatever success was to be attained. When word came that Uther Pendragon, ruler of Gramarye, had died and that his successor would be the person who could pull a sword out of an anvil, it was as much a surprise to Arthur as to Sir Ector and Sir Kay when it was he, the Wart, who accomplished that feat and became king. The tone of Arthur's rule was foreshadowed by the fact that he performed the deed that put him on the throne without knowing that that was how the new king was to be chosen; the boy had merely been trying to find a sword for Sir Kay to use in the tournament. Arthur's reign represented the establishment of a new order. In defending his right to the throne, Arthur first had to abandon the polite forms of chivalric warfare for other tactics. Then, announcing that he would use might only to accomplish right, he established the Round Table.

The first test to his reign as a just king was the enmity of Queen Morgause, wife of King Lot and sister of Morgan le Fay. Morgause hated anyone who sat on the throne of Uther Pendragon because he had murdered her father and raped her mother, but she did not realize that Arthur was the child of Uther and her mother. When she seduced Arthur in an attempt to gain power over him, she unknowingly committed incest with her half brother. She taught the child of this union, Modred, along with her other sons—Gawaine, Gareth, Gaheris, and Agravaine—to hate Arthur. Modred became the embodiment of the ultimate destruction of the Round Table.

The second test of Arthur's reign came from the love that Lancelot, despite his worship of Arthur, bore for Arthur's queen, Guenever. Lancelot fought his attraction to Guenever by spending most of his time on quests, but he eventually succumbed to temptation and was seduced by Elaine, whom he had rescued from Morgan le Fay, when she pretended to be Guenever. After this union, which produced Galahad, Lancelot gave up his resistance and began an adulterous relationship with Guenever. Plagued by the loss of his virginity and purity, he broke off with Guenever and was even insane for a time. His unsuccessful fight against temptation became a kind of microcosmic representation of Arthur's ultimately unsuccessful attempt to establish a kingdom of justice.

Arthur attempted to find ways to control and use wisely the might at his command, but his troubles increased. The "Orkney faction," the sons of Morgause, stirred up discontent. Arthur initiated the quest for the Holy Grail to provide a healthy outlet for the energies of the knights of the Round Table; although Galahad eventually found the Grail, the best knights were lost in the search, and the other knights became quarrelsome and decadent. Lancelot and Guenever were twice accused of adultery, and Lancelot had to face two trials by combat, in the second of which he murdered Sir Meliagrance to keep him from revealing the truth.

Faced with the spiritual and physical disintegration of his kingdom, Arthur turned to the idea of justice under law as a last resort. As he did, he set the stage for the final blow to be struck against his dream. Modred now had the means to turn his father's own concept of justice against him. When Modred and Agravaine accused Guenever of adultery and demanded that she be tried in a court of law, Arthur's failure was assured because he found that he could not accept the burden of his principles; he indirectly warned Lancelot and Guenever of danger, and he confessed to having tried to murder Modred as an infant in a vain attempt to escape the prophecy that his son would become his enemy.

Arthur was unable to stem the tide of forces moving irrevocably toward the destruction of his kingdom. While Arthur was away on a hunting trip, Lancelot went to Guenever's bedroom, whereby he unknowingly gave Modred the evidence needed to convict Guenever of adultery. When Guenever was sentenced to be burned at the stake, Arthur was unable to intervene and yet remain true to his ideal of justice. When his hope was fulfilled and Lancelot rescued Guenever, Arthur had to go to France to lay siege to Lancelot's castle. Even an appeal to the Church in the form of the pope could not reconcile the forces of destruction. Although the pope ordered Arthur to take Guenever back and Lancelot to go into exile, Arthur was forced to return to his siege of Lancelot's castle to obtain justice for the murder of Gareth and Gaheris.

In the end, Arthur was forced to fight for what was left of his once glorious kingdom. In his absence, Modred had proclaimed himself king and announced that he would marry Guenever. Arthur thereupon prepared to go into battle against Modred. Even when faced with the possibility of failure, however, Arthur recalled the noble ideals Merlyn had taught him. He realized that although he had been unsuccessful in putting those ideals into action, his having been able to make the attempt boded well for the future. At last, he could face the future with a peaceful heart.

Critical Evaluation:

At the end of book 2 of *The Once and Future King*, T. H. White states that the story of King Arthur is a tragedy in the true Aristotelian sense, according to which most tragic heroes have an inherent flaw that contributes to their "reversal of fortune." The hero's tragic flaw is not necessarily a bad quality. Arthur's flaw, in fact, is his belief in the decency and perfectibility of humanity.

Arthur's flaw is revealed as the novel moves from descriptions of his innocent childhood to the imperfect, even corrupt world of his adulthood and, finally, to the loss of his kingdom; this movement is the "reversal of fortune" that results from Arthur's tragic flaw. It is the movement that unites the four narrative strands of the novel. The stories of Gawaine (book 2), Lancelot (book 3), and Mordred (book 4), considered within the framework of Arthur's own story, illustrate the theme that while some people may be decent, there will always be those who make Arthur's dreams of a better civilization impossible.

Believing people to be basically good, Arthur establishes the Round Table to destroy the authority of those who rule through brutal force and to impose on humanity the notion of decency. Arthur remains blind, however, to reminders that his vision will fail. He willfully overlooks the affair between Lancelot and Guenever, the murderous depth of Gawaine's rage, and the evil madness of his son Modred. If he were to acknowledge deception, rage, and evil in those closest to him, he would have to deny humanity's perfectibility. Lancelot and Gawaine do turn out to be good and honorable men, however, thus reinforcing Arthur's convictions.

By nature, Lancelot is not deceptive, but he is weak. As a medieval Christian, he knows that his sinful nature stands in the way of one of his greatest ambitions: to perform a miracle. Lured by Guenever and encouraged by Arthur's blindness, he can never resist the queen's seduction and he remains, at least in his own eyes, a weak man. Yet, as he tells Guenever, his awareness of his own flawed nature drives him to be the best knight in the world. Significantly, when he fully accepts his own imperfect nature, he is allowed to perform a miracle by healing Sir Urre of his bleeding wounds.

Gawaine, too, reinforces Arthur's belief in the goodness of humanity. Gawaine has learned rage, even hatred from his mother Morgause, who is consumed by hatred for Uther Pendragon, Arthur's father, who killed Cornwall, the husband of her mother Igraine. She passes her hatred for the Pendragons on to her sons, and Gawaine pledges to get revenge. Gawaine has an inclination to do good, however. Thus, once he is a knight of the Round Table, Gawaine transfers much of his loyalty to the king. Gawaine knows that Arthur is not an evil man, but he experiences tremendous conflict when Lancelot kills his two brothers while rescuing Guenever. Gawaine vows revenge but eventually overcomes his vindictiveness, forgiving Lancelot and so performing an act nearly as miraculous as Lancelot's healing of Sir Urre.

The political machinations of Modred reveal Arthur's tragic flaw clearly. An extraordinarily bright young man, Modred is both insane and evil. His mother, Morgause, has taught him to hate Arthur, and, unlike Gawaine, Modred never relinquishes this hatred. Knowing Arthur's belief in the decency of humanity and realizing that his father is fond of him, Modred easily takes the kingdom from Arthur and shatters Arthur's world. Indeed, White's point seems to be that as long as there are Modreds, the human race will never reach perfection or even decency, and will continue to perpetuate its greatest evil, war.

Beyond its contribution to Arthurian literature and its tragic plot structure, *The Once and Future King* is a novel about war and evil and thus deserves a place alongside *The Red Badge of Courage* (1895), *All Quiet on the Western Front* (1929), *Lord of the Flies* (1954), and *Catch-22* (1961). Certainly, it is significant that White lived in England and, little more than a decade before the publication of this novel, witnessed a terrible war and terrible evil waged by humans. The novel suggests that wars are not started by the Arthurs of the world but by the Mordreds who take advantage of the goodness of others and abuse power to maintain power. Indeed, according to White's novel, if there is hope for humanity, it lies not in its innate goodness (for it is neither innately good nor innately evil) but in the existence of people like Arthur, who devote their lives to decency and justice.

"Critical Evaluation" by Richard Logsdon

Bibliography:

Lacey, Norris J., and Geofrey Ashe. *The Arthurian Handbook*. New York: Garland, 1988. A critical survey of Arthurian legend from the fifth century to the late twentieth century.

Logario, Valerie M., and Mildred Leake Day, eds. *King Arthur Through the Ages*. Vol 2. New York: Garland, 1990. A study of contributions to Arthurian literature from the Victorian period into the twentieth century. *The Once and Future King* is acknowledged as the "most influential and enduringly popular of modern Arthurian fiction."

Owen, D. D. R., ed. *Arthurian Romance: Seven Essays*. New York: Barnes & Noble Books, 1971. Collection of essays reflecting late twentieth century interest in Arthurian romance that range from close textual scrutiny to overviews of artistic purposes.

Sandler, Florence Field. "Family Romance in *The Once and Future King*." *Quondom et Futuris: A Journal of Arthurian Interpretations* 2, no. 2 (Summer, 1992): 73-80. An examination of the medieval concept of family and romance as applied to White's novel.

Tanner, William E. "Tangled Web of Time in T. H. White's *The Once and Future King*." *Arthurian Myth of Quest and Magic: A Festschrift in Honor of Lavon Fulwiler*. Dallas: Caxton Moern Arts, 1993. Considers White's treatment of historical time in relation to his concern for war.

ONE DAY IN THE LIFE OF IVAN DENISOVICH

Type of work: Novel
Author: Aleksandr Solzhenitsyn (1918-   )
Type of plot: Historical realism
Time of plot: 1951
Locale: Siberia, northern Soviet Union
First published: Odin den Ivana Denisovicha, 1962 (English translation, 1963)

Principal characters:
IVAN DENISOVICH SHUKOV, a prisoner in a Soviet labor camp
TIURIN, Shukov's squad leader
TSEZAR,
ALYOSHA,
PAVLO,
FETIKOV,
SENKA,
KILGAS, and
BUINOVSKY, members of Shukov's work squad

The Story:
Reveille began the day for Ivan Denisovich Shukov, a victim of the mass imprisonments that took place in the Soviet Union during the Stalin era. He had been unjustly sentenced to ten years in a labor camp and was serving out his term in a remote corner of Siberia. It was the dead of winter, and Ivan woke up feeling ill. He intended to report for sick call.

His plan to report for sick call was apparently thwarted when one of the camp guards arrested him for violating a rule: not getting up at reveille. Ivan was told he would be sentenced to ten days in the guardhouse but soon discovered the prison guard only wanted someone to mop the guardhouse floor. Having been thus "let off," Ivan adroitly managed to get out of the work he was assigned as punishment and returned to his barracks. The sort of adroitness he demonstrated in this incident was a necessary characteristic for survival in the brutal environment of the camp.

Ivan then began the routine of his day. After a trip to the mess hall, he still had time to go to the infirmary and try to get on sick call. At the infirmary, he was turned down because the daily quota of two prisoners exempted from work because of sickness had already been filled. As with many of the episodes in *One Day in the Life of Ivan Denisovich*, this trip to the infirmary was illustrative of the bureaucratic culture that ruled the camp. In contrast to the filth of the barracks and the mess hall, the infirmary was clean. It was quiet and orderly and warm. When Ivan went in, the doctors were still asleep. An orderly was on duty. He was writing not a medical report but poetry for the doctor in charge. The orderly was one of the prisoners who was "better off"—who had an easy job and some privilege—because of his educational level. There was a definite hierarchy in the camp, even among the prisoners or "zeks."

After this, the squad moved out to the work site. As they began their work, they started telling the stories of their lives. The prison camp was a microcosm of Russia. Besides Shukov, there was Tiurin, the squad leader, imprisoned because his father was a kulak, a group persecuted by Stalin. There was Senka, a deaf former soldier who had survived Buchenwald; Fetikov, a former high-ranking Communist arrested in one of Stalin's purges; Captain Buinovsky, also a loyal Communist and a Soviet naval captain unjustly accused of spying; Alyosha, a Baptist imprisoned for his religion; and Tsezar, an intellectual. These, together with others, struggled through the day with Ivan, sharing the victories, harassment, tragedies, and triumphs of prison life.

After breakfast, the squad was sent to work at an outpost where a power station was being built. The disorganization, ruin, and waste seen at the building site were illustrative of the Soviet government's overall management of society. Ivan's squad went to work on the building, Ivan's task being that of mason. As the squad continued working, the building of the wall became a heroic task; the dignity of work preserved Ivan's humanity.

Adroitness carried with it additional benefits. Ivan, who by camp standards was "poor" and did not receive money or food packets from home, was able to survive and live a bit better because of his abilities. Ample opportunities to use his skills arose throughout the day. He had his own trowel, which he hid in different places so it would not be confiscated by the authorities; at the noon meal, he was able to steal two extra bowls of oatmeal. Such things, though small, were incidents that empowered the inmates of the camp and created a sense of independence that the authorities there could not crush.

After the meal, the job of building continued. One of the prisoners who was an "overseer" for the camp authorities, Der, came to the site and noticed that Ivan's squad had pilfered some building material to seal windows. He threatened to report Tiurin and his squad, but the squad surrounded him and threatened to kill him. Der was reduced to passivity and promised not to say anything about the pilfering. This incident was a great moral victory for Ivan's squad.

The workday ended and the men were lined up to return to the prison compound. For some reason, there came a delay. Since time was a precious commodity to the prisoners, they deeply resented being kept waiting half an hour in the freezing cold. The trouble was finally revealed to be a missing Moldavian prisoner who had fallen asleep in one of the buildings. He was charged with attempted escape, and the column finally returned to the prison compound.

Once in the compound, Ivan helped Tsezar get his food parcel from home and managed to fight his way into the mess hall afterward. While in the mess hall, he took the time to notice a legendary prisoner, an old man who was eating near him. Despite decades in prison camps and many physical infirmities, the old man ate with irrepressible dignity, a symbol of the unconquerable humanity demonstrated again and again by Ivan Denisovich and the other camp inmates.

As the day drew to an end, there was more harassment by the camp authorities. The men were called out for a final assembly. Captain Buinovsky was sent for ten days of solitary confinement for an infraction committed that morning. Ivan lay down for the night, thankful for the many good things that had happened that day, and uttered a prayer. His prayer was overheard by Alyosha, the Baptist, and the two engaged in a discussion of the reasons they were in the prison camp. Alyosha believed that he was there because God had willed it to be so, and thus he could fully accept his lack of freedom. Ivan, however, thought he was suffering only because his country was unprepared for war. He only wanted to return to his home and could not accept his incarceration as Alyosha did. After another assembly, Ivan was able to go to sleep. It had been, the narrator commented, an "almost happy day."

Critical Evaluation:

Aleksandr Solzhenitsyn is considered by many to be the greatest Russian author of the twentieth century. His writing has attracted worldwide attention, and he has been the recipient of numerous awards and honors, including the Nobel Prize in Literature in 1970.

Solzhenitsyn's own experience as a prisoner in a Siberian labor camp is the basis for *One Day in the Life of Ivan Denisovich*. Solzhenitsyn was born in 1918, received a degree in mathematics and physics in 1941, and began teaching high school. He served with distinction as an artillery officer in World War II but was arrested in 1945 for allegedly making a derogatory remark about Stalin in a letter to a friend. Sentenced to eight years' imprisonment, he was incarcerated in a camp similar to the one described in the novel. He survived and was released in 1953, but he was exiled to live in Central Asia until Stalin was denounced by the new Soviet Premier, Nikita Khrushchev, in 1956, and restrictions upon those who had suffered during Stalin's political purges were eased.

Solzhenitsyn moved to a small Russian town near Moscow and began to teach mathematics and to render some of his experiences in fictional form. It was the anti-Stalinist mood of the day that enabled him to get his first novel published. *One Day in the Life of Ivan Denisovich* appeared in the November 20, 1962, issue of *Novy Mir*, the official literary journal of the Communist Party. It was published largely because the editors of the journal thought it represented a specifically anti-Stalinist piece of literature. The work's success was immediate. The entire November run of *Novy Mir* sold out in a day, and Solzhenitsyn was catapulted to international fame.

The officials of the Soviet Communist Party soon realized they had made a mistake. *One Day in the Life of Ivan Denisovich* was not, as they had assumed, a piece of literature denouncing Stalin, but an indictment of the Soviet system as a whole, a denunciation of the repression and totalitarianism that was Communist Russia. Solzhenitsyn had become a symbol of freedom for the persecuted artistic community of the Soviet Union and of courage and individualism to all who read him around the world.

The government soon moved against him. He was denounced, dismissed from his teaching position, and exiled from Moscow. In 1974 he was arrested, charged with treason, and imprisoned; he was exiled from the Soviet Union that same year. Solzhenitsyn resided in the United States until returning to Russia in 1993, after the collapse of Communism.

Solzhenitsyn's output as a writer is tremendous. Some of his more important works of fiction include *The Cancer Ward* (1968), *The First Circle* (1968), and *August 1914* (1971). He is also well known for his massive nonfictional chronicle of the repressive activities of the Stalin era, *The Gulag Archipelago* (1973-1975). Like *One Day in the Life of Ivan Denisovich*, these works champion human rights and denounce the totalitarian nature of the Soviet regime. Solzhenitsyn has attempted to set Russian literature back on course after the hiatus of Socialist Realism that stultified Russian arts and letters during the years of Communist domination. His historical novels recall the rich Russian literary heritage of the nineteenth century, an influence that almost disappeared during the years of Soviet realism.

One Day in the Life of Ivan Denisovich is a prime example of Solzhenitsyn's art; it makes political statements but never falls to the level of a mere tract or manifesto. The story of Ivan Denisovich and his companions creates feelings of fellowship, empathy, and admiration in the reader, but it does not force or impose such reactions—unlike Socialist Realism, which tends to impel the reader toward approved conclusions and to demand certain reactions to politically approved story lines. Solzhenitsyn's approach is indirect, ironic, even humorous.

At times, the novel seems almost allegorical. Ivan Denisovich represents an Everyman figure, the average Russian peasant persecuted by larger forces he does not understand. The other characters in the book fill similar symbolic slots: Tsezar represents the persecuted artist; Fetikov, who is called "the jackal" or the "scavenger," symbolizes the Party opportunist who has no morals or scruples and has ironically landed in the bottom end of a system he helped to create; Captain Buinovsky is a loyal Communist officer imprisoned by Stalinist paranoia and completely bewildered by this turn of events; Tiurin, the squad leader, is another innocent Russian persecuted merely because his father was a kulak; Alyosha, representing all those who experienced religious persecution, has been sentenced to twenty-five years merely because of his Baptist religion. All these are "types," figures of the groups who suffered under Soviet totalitarianism.

One Day in the Life of Ivan Denisovich, unlike many other Russian novels, is rather short and moves quickly. Its crisp, fast-paced narrative enables the author to sketch his characters quickly and to involve the reader in the thoughts of Ivan Denisovich, through whose perspective the action is often reported (though there is an unidentified third-person narrator telling the story). The chronicle of the day is told in the racy slang of the camp, often profane, always colorful and rich, giving the reader a further sense of participation.

Overall, the reader comes away from *One Day in the Life of Ivan Denisovich* with a sense of triumph. Though the conditions in the camp are brutal, though the prisoners have been stripped of all human rights and are harassed and badgered throughout the day, it is clear that life in the concentration camp has not broken them. An implicit theme lodged strongly in the story is that the rulers of the Soviet regime which created the camp will no more succeed at stifling the spirit of freedom in the Russian people than the local camp officials have succeeded in stamping it out of Ivan Denisovich and his fellow prisoners. The human spirit, which always craves freedom, will ultimately triumph.

David W. Landrum

Bibliography:

Barker, Francis. *Solzhenitsyn: Politics and Form*. New York: Barnes & Noble Books, 1977. A study of Solzhenitsyn's various works, with emphasis on their very important political aspects and on the way political considerations shape his works.

Curtis, James M. *Solzhenitsyn's Traditional Imagination*. Athens: University of Georgia Press, 1984. Examines the currents of imaginative thought in Solzhenitsyn and emphasizes his transformation of traditional material into new, creative forms.

Ericson, Edward. *Solzhenitsyn and the Modern World*. Washington, D.C.: Regnery Gateway, 1993. Recent book that examines Solzhenitsyn in light of the collapse of Communism in Russia. Answers some of the common criticisms that are leveled at his writing.

_____. *Solzhenitsyn, the Moral Vision*. Grand Rapids, Mich.: Eerdmans, 1980. Excellent overview of Solzhenitsyn's works with an eye to their sources, origins, and relationship to modern political and social reality.

Nielsen, Niels Christian. *Solzhenitsyn's Religion*. Nashville: Nelson, 1975. A discussion of the very important religious aspect in Solzhenitsyn's writing, tracing it through all his early works.

ONE FLEW OVER THE CUCKOO'S NEST

Type of work: Novel
Author: Ken Kesey (1935-   )
Type of plot: Psychological realism
Time of plot: Fall, 1960
Locale: An asylum in Oregon
First published: 1962

Principal characters:
    CHIEF BROMDEN, a big Indian patient
    RANDLE P. MCMURPHY, a new patient
    NURSE RATCHED, the ward boss, also known as Big Nurse
    BILLY BIBBIT and
    CHARLES CHESWICK, longtime patients

The Story:

Chief Bromden, thought by all to be deaf and dumb, heard the booming voice of a new patient. He was Randle Patrick McMurphy, a big, red-headed Irishman with scarred hands and a free laugh, who resisted the aides' pushing him around. McMurphy came from prison, having been banished for fighting. When McMurphy shook the Chief's hand it seemed to swell and become big again, the first small step in McMurphy's rescue of the Chief from his fog.

The Chief saw the ward as a repair shop for the Combine, the nationwide conspiracy that turned people into machines run by remote control. The asylum was the repair shop populated by two kinds of broken-down machines: the chronics and the acutes. The chronics were considered hopelessly insane; the acutes were considered to have hope of recovery. Nurse Ratched sought to make her ward a smoothly running repair shop, so when McMurphy arrived, free from the controls of the Combine, he upset the mechanistic routine. On his first day on the ward, McMurphy urged the patients to stand up against the Big Nurse, to show their guts by voting for something. He bet that he could make her crack within a week.

That week, McMurphy was eager to see the World Series on television; to do so required a change in ward policy. Eventually he got the patients to vote for the change, the deciding vote coming from the Chief, but the Big Nurse vetoed the result on a technicality. At game time, McMurphy and the other acutes sat down in front of a blank television and had a party, making believe they were watching the game. When the Big Nurse could not get them to move, she lost control of herself. McMurphy had won his bet, showing that she was beatable.

Shortly thereafter, McMurphy discovered that as a committed patient he could be held indefinitely. To prevent that, he began to cooperate, no longer standing up for the other patients. One day Cheswick looked to McMurphy for support in an argument, but the Irishman stayed silent. The next day Cheswick drowned himself. McMurphy felt responsible for Cheswick's death. The decisive blow against McMurphy's self-interested stance came when he learned that most of the acutes were not committed, but were voluntary inmates. Their problems had more to do with how they saw themselves than with clinical insanity. This realization changed McMurphy, bringing him back into the battle against the Big Nurse. First, he "accidentally" punched through her window to get his cigarettes, then, after it had been replaced he did it again, apologizing profusely. After a month had passed, McMurphy got the Chief to speak again, bringing him closer to health and freedom. They talked about the Combine, how it had turned the Chief's father into an alcoholic by buying out their fishing village to make a dam. When his father shriveled, the Chief did too.

The first of three final dramatic episodes in the story was the fishing trip, on which McMurphy and his twelve friends caught several huge fish. They came to see that they could be free, that a trip outside the machinelike asylum into the world of nature could be successful. The biggest step was their laughing binge, led by McMurphy, because laughter shows people are free. All the men became stronger, except McMurphy, because he was bearing the weight of their burdens, doling out his life for the others.

The next day, when the aides bullied one of the fishing crew, McMurphy went to his defense. That started a fight in which the Chief joined. Later both were taken to the shock shop and blasted into unconsciousness by a jolt of electricity. Unlike on previous occasions, the Chief came quickly out of the fog of the shock treatment. Since McMurphy had made him big again, he did not need to hide from the world. After giving McMurphy three more shock treatments, the Big Nurse brought him back to the ward, threatening a lobotomy. All of McMurphy's friends urged him to escape the next weekend when McMurphy's friend Candy was coming for a visit. She brought another whore with her, helping the patients have an uproarious party filled with games, drunkenness, and sex. The orgy was a victory to the Chief; it showed that even at the center of the Combine people could be free.

McMurphy was supposed to escape at dawn but overslept. In the morning, the Big Nurse found Billy Bibbit in bed with Candy. In front of all the other patients, the Big Nurse shamed Billy, threatening to tell his possessive mother about his sexual experience. That drove Billy to kill himself, and Nurse Ratched blamed McMurphy for it. Outraged by the accusation, McMurphy attacked the Big Nurse, tearing her dress open to expose her breasts, showing that she was really a woman, not a machine. The terror that the inmates saw in her eyes forever diminished her power over them. She had finally lost the war.

Over the next few weeks, almost all the acutes left the ward. The Chief stayed, to counter the Big Nurse's final move. Her gambit was a body on a gurney, a vegetable with black eyes (indicating that a lobotomy had been performed), with the name Randle P. McMurphy attached to it. The Chief decided that McMurphy would never have allowed such proof of the nurse's power to lie around the ward. So he smothered the vegetable. Then he lifted a huge control panel and threw it through the reinforced window screen. Escaping finally from the cuckoo's nest, he returned to his free life, ready to tell McMurphy's story.

Critical Evaluation:

The central theme of the story is how Chief Bromden becomes strong, self-confident, and sane again. This rescue and transformation succeeds because McMurphy treats him as a worthwhile, intelligent, and sane individual. In addition, McMurphy gives him the example of standing up to and occasionally beating the apparently all-powerful Combine.

That machine is the central symbol of evil in the story. The Chief accurately sees that the powerful in society subtly and unsubtly coerce people into becoming cogs in the machine. The Chief imagines the ruling part of the mechanistic society as a combine, which is a huge harvesting machine. It chews up the growing plants in the field and spits them out as identical products for sale. Thus, the Combine is the machinelike conspiracy that sucks people in, turns them into robots, and spits them out to carry out the Combine's will in society. In the cuckoo's nest, the repair shop for the Combine, the same kind of oppression continues. The shop symbolizes the hidden oppression operating in the outside world. The patients are broken-down machines that the asylum seeks to adjust. The Big Nurse's basic method is to destroy the patients' self-confidence by making them admit their guilt, shame, and uselessness.

Into that repair shop McMurphy comes, a man free from the controls of the Combine because he has never stayed in one place long enough for the controls to be installed. He is an outsider, like the three geese flying overhead in the song: One flew east, one flew west, one flew over the cuckoo's nest. The last goose came and rescued the singer, just as McMurphy rescues the Chief, who is the singer of this novel-length song. The Chief, the narrator of the story, provides a central source of its power. Readers initially see the ward through the Chief's psychotic haze. His fantastic visions show both his paranoia and how oppressive the asylum really is. Then as McMurphy brings him back to sanity, the picture gradually clears, the fantastic visions becoming realistic. The Chief comes to see that his slavery is due not only to the Combine but also to his own capitulation. McMurphy's refusal to give in provides the example the Chief needs to give him confidence in his own ability to live freely.

The Chief sees McMurphy as not only the goose who rescued the slaves from a cuckoo's nest but also as other popular culture heroes. He speaks of him as a superman, calling him a giant come out of the sky to rescue them. Often the Chief describes him as a cowboy hero coming into town to gun down the bad guys. In particular, one of the patients identifies McMurphy as the Lone Ranger. The allusion that the Chief uses most to place McMurphy in the pantheon of heroes is that of Jesus, the self-sacrificing savior. On the fishing trip, for example, the group is called "McMurphy and his twelve," and one patient tells them to be fishers of men. On the way back, the Chief sees McMurphy as a Man of Sorrows, doling out his life for his friends. The shock treatment takes place on a table shaped like a cross, with McMurphy referring to their anointing his head and asking if he will get a crown of thorns. A patient speaks like Pilate, saying he washes his hands of the whole affair. The ward party is a Last Supper parody. In the end the powers destroy McMurphy by lobotomy, just as Jesus was killed by the Combine of his day. After that, the Chief (a big fisherman) escapes to tell his story, just as Jesus' disciples escaped.

Though the Chief's portrait of McMurphy in some central ways alludes to Jesus, in a variety of other ways it provides a contrast. McMurphy is not simply a selfless savior but is also the fabled western American fighter, sexual braggart, and con man, which contrasts with Jesus' nonviolence, chastity, and honesty. In particular McMurphy promotes sexual indulgence as a saving activity. In the story, however, the Chief realizes that sexual indulgence is what led to Billy's death, thereby portraying his savior as far from perfect. That imperfection has led some critics to object to the novel as promoting immorality. Whether one considers that the novel promotes immorality or not depends on whether one takes McMurphy as a model for all that is good. The Chief does not. He sees the good and the bad in his rescuer. An even stronger criticism made of the novel is that it is misogynistic. The women in the novel are either tyrannical emasculators or sweet-natured whores. Certainly it offers no example of an ideal woman. It offers no model men either; McMurphy's considerable weaknesses lead to his destruction.

The great value of the novel is that it provides a picture of a universal fact of human life. Oppression of the weak by the strong is a constant reality. Rebellion by the weak is occasionally successful and can appropriately be celebrated and encouraged by stories such as this. In the end, the two chief opponents, Big Nurse and McMurphy, do not provide the only two choices available to readers. Instead, the model is the Chief, for he gains his free life again and lives to tell the tale.

Peter W. Macky

Bibliography:

Carnes, Bruce. *Ken Kesey*. Boise, Idaho: Boise State University Press, 1974. A short summary of the author's two novels with emphasis on imagery.

Kesey, Ken. *One Flew over the Cuckoo's Nest: Text and Criticism*. Edited by John Clark Pratt. New York: Viking Press, 1973. Contains the text of the novel, articles on the author, and literary criticism of the novel.

Leeds, Barry H. *Ken Kesey*. New York: Frederick Ungar, 1981. A discussion of the author and his works. Beginning with a brief biography, it continues with summaries and evaluations of each of the author's published works.

Porter, M. Gilbert. *The Art of Grit: Ken Kesey's Fiction*. Columbia: University of Missouri Press, 1982. An analysis of Kesey's published works, emphasizing their affirmation of traditional American values, especially optimism and heroism. The chapter on *One Flew over the Cuckoo's Nest* also emphasizes the significance of Chief Bromden as the narrator.

Tanner, Stephen L. *Ken Kesey*. Boston: Twayne, 1983. A short introduction to the author and his works. The chapter on *One Flew over the Cuckoo's Nest* emphasizes the frontier values of self-reliance and independence.

ONE HUNDRED YEARS OF SOLITUDE

Type of work: Novel
Author: Gabriel García Márquez (1928-   )
Type of plot: Magical Realism
Time of plot: 1820's to 1920's
Locale: Macondo, a town in Latin America
First published: Cien años de soledad, 1967 (English translation, 1970)

> *Principal characters:*
> José Arcadio Buendía, the Buendía family patriarch and founder
>   of Macondo
> Úrsula Iguarán, the Buendía family matriarch and wife of José
> Melquíades, a gypsy
> Colonel Aureliano Buendía, the younger son of José and Úrsula
> José Arcadio Buendía, the older son of José and Úrsula
> Amaranta, the daughter of José and Úrsula
> Rebeca, the adopted daughter of José and Úrsula
> Pietro Crespi, suitor to both Rebeca and Amaranta
> Aureliano Segundo and
> José Arcadio Segundo, twin great-grandchildren of José and Úrsula
> Remedios the Beauty, sister of the twins
> Aureliano, a sixth-generation Buendía who deciphers family history
>   and fathers the last Buendía
> Aureliano, the last Buendía, born with a pig's tail

The Story:

Standing before a firing squad, Colonel Aureliano Buendía remembered the day that his father, José Arcadio Buendía, had taken him to see ice for the first time. This had taken place in the early years of Macondo, the town that the elder Buendía, his wife Úrsula, and others had founded after José Arcadio and Úrsula had sought to escape the ghost of a man that José Arcadio had killed. The dead man had accused José Arcadio of impotence, when the real reason that the Buendías had avoided sex for so long after marriage was that they were afraid of producing a child with a pig's tail, something that had already happened between their two inbred families. Soon after the founding of Macondo, gypsies began to visit the town with incredible inventions, the wonder of which ignited the scientific curiosity of José Arcadio. Through these visits the Buendías met Melquíades, a wise and magical gypsy and author of a mysterious manuscript. On one particular visit by the gypsies, right after the town learned of Melquíades' death in a far-off land, José Arcadio Buendía and his sons were introduced to ice, which the elder Buendía called "the great invention of our time."

José Arcadio and Úrsula Buendía had two sons, Aureliano and José Arcadio, and two daughters, Amaranta and Rebeca, the latter of whom they had adopted after she had shown up on their doorstep, orphaned and with her parents' bones in a canvas sack. The two sons both fathered illegitimate children by Pilar Ternera, and the older son, José Arcadio, soon ran off with the gypsies. An insomnia plague attacked the town and brought with it a temporary but severe loss of memory. Melquíades, who had died "but could not bear the solitude," returned to Macondo. A Conservative magistrate, the peaceful town's first, settled in shortly thereafter. An

Italian dance teacher, Pietro Crespi, arrived to tune the pianola and to teach the Buendía girls the latest steps. He began to court Rebeca, which touched off a life-long jealousy and bitterness in Amaranta. Meanwhile, Melquíades continued to be a presence (as would his manuscript) in the Buendía house. José Arcadio (the elder) attempted to photograph God, began having visits from the ghost of Prudencio Aguilar (the man he had killed years before), started speaking a strange language (later identified as Latin), and was tethered to a chestnut tree in the backyard. Aureliano fell in love with and married Remedios, the magistrate's barely pubescent daughter, who would die, pregnant with twins, just days before Rebeca's scheduled marriage to Pietro Crespi.

José Arcadio (the son) returned, enormous and tattooed, and married his adopted sister (Rebeca), and Pietro Crespi turned his affections to Amaranta. Aureliano became Colonel Aureliano Buendía and led an uprising against the Conservatives. He would lead thirty-two uprisings and all would end in failure before an embittered Aureliano returned home to live out his days making little fish of gold, melting them down, and making them again, over and over. He would also father seventeen illegitimate sons with seventeen different women. While Aureliano was off fighting the government, Amaranta rejected Pietro Crespi, who committed suicide, brother José Arcadio was killed mysteriously, his blood flowing in a stream from his house across town to the Buendía house, José Arcadio (the father) died, initiating a rain of yellow flowers from the sky, and Arcadio (José Arcadio's illegitimate son) became the town dictator and was executed. This was not before, however, he and wife Santa Sofía de la Piedad had three children: twin sons Aureliano Segundo and José Arcadio Segundo (whose identities were accidentally switched), and one daughter, Remedios the Beauty.

Aureliano Segundo spent most of his time with Petra Cotes, but he married Fernanda del Carpio, who would never quite fit in with the Buendías, and with whom Aureliano Segundo too had three children: José Arcadio, who was sent to seminary in Rome; Renata Remedios, or "Meme," who had an illegitimate child by auto mechanic Mauricio Babilonia, who was always accompanied by a swarm of yellow butterflies; and Amaranta Úrsula, who was sent to school in Belgium. Colonel Aureliano Buendía's seventeen bastard sons suddenly showed up in Macondo. One of them, Aureliano Triste, eventually brought a train to town, and with it came inventions every bit as wondrous as those the gypsies had brought years before: electric light bulbs, moving pictures, and phonographs. The intrusion from the outside world also brought something else, a North American banana company. Meanwhile, Remedios the Beauty, whose physical perfection drove men mad, ascended to heaven while hanging laundry on the line. Soon thereafter, sixteen of Colonel Aureliano Buendía's illegitimate sons were hunted down and killed; the seventeenth would be killed later. Amaranta began sewing her own shroud, soon after which Colonel Aureliano Buendía died. Amaranta continued to sew her shroud with the intention of dying on the day that she finished it, which she did. It was at this time that Meme bore Mauricio Babilonia's illegitimate son (Aureliano).

Relations between the banana company and Macondo gradually worsened, and soon there was a strike. José Arcadio Segundo, who had become a union leader, was in a crowd of demonstrators when the army fired on it and killed three thousand people. José Arcadio Segundo was not killed but was unable thereafter to find anyone else who would say that the massacre had occurred. It, officially at least, simply did not happen. A continuous five-year rainstorm followed. Úrsula, now well over one hundred years old, died, as did Rebeca, Aureliano Segundo, and José Arcadio Segundo. Santa Sofía soon moved out and Fernanda died as well. Meanwhile, Aureliano (son of Meme and Mauricio Babilonia) became obsessed with Melquíades' mysterious manuscript. José Arcadio returned home from Rome and opened the house to children he picked up and brought to the house, some of whom came back later, murdered him, and made off with a stash of gold. Amaranta Úrsula returned from Belgium with her husband and soon engaged in an incestuous relationship with her nephew Aureliano. Their child was born with a pig's tail. Amaranta Úrsula died, and the baby was eaten by an army of ants. Suddenly Melquíades' mysterious manuscript became clear to Aureliano. The manuscript contained the history of Macondo and the Buendías, written before it actually happened, and that history would be complete, with Aureliano's death and the destruction of Macondo, as soon as Aureliano finished deciphering the manuscript.

Critical Evaluation:

One Hundred Years of Solitude is considered by most critics to be, quite simply, the most important, and certainly the most internationally famous, Latin American novel of the twentieth century and the most important and most famous Spanish-language novel since Miguel de Cervantes' *Don Quixote de la Mancha* (1605, 1615). Written during the "Boom" in the Spanish American novel, the period in the 1960's during which writers such as Carlos Fuentes and Mario Vargas Llosa wrote their masterpieces, *One Hundred Years of Solitude* contributed greatly to putting the Latin American novel on the world literary map.

Like many Latin American novels, and certainly the most acclaimed ones published in the latter half of the twentieth century, *One Hundred Years of Solitude* is what is known as a New Novel. It is "new," or nontraditional (particularly when compared to the Latin American novels of the 1920's and 1930's) in many ways, not the least of which has to do with the version of reality it presents. Macondo, with its characters who die but return as ghosts, its clairvoyant residents, its stream of blood with a mind of its own, its flowers falling from the sky, its young woman ascending to heaven, and its five-year-long rainstorm, for example, presents a reality that is anything but the one to be found in realistic fiction. The book does not slip into pure fantasy, however, but remains in the domain of what has been labeled Magical Realism. Instead of presenting nonrealistic elements side-by-side with realistic ones in such a way that the nonrealistic stands out as odd, the author frequently describes the normal as if it were fantastic (the description of ice in the first chapter, for example) and the fantastic as if it were normal (Remedios the Beauty's ascension, for example). The reader's reaction is to take a new perspective on what is real versus what is not real. This technique, along with the fact that Gabriel García Márquez bombards the reader with characters and events (the book is approximately four hundred pages long but contains the plot of a much longer book), pulls the reader into the world of Macondo, where the outside rules of what is real and what is not do not apply. *One Hundred Years of Solitude* is a New Novel as well in that although it deals with Latin American themes, such as political strife from within (the Liberals versus the Conservatives) and exploitation from without (the banana company), it also deals with universal themes, most notably solitude—the solitude of power, language, envy, insanity, death, blindness, and other types, including the act of reading. The book's enormous popularity outside Latin America is vivid testament to the story's universal reach.

This enormous popularity, however, separates *One Hundred Years of Solitude* from other Latin American New Novels. While novels such as Fuentes' *La muerte de Artemio Cruz* (1962; *The Death of Artemio Cruz*, 1964) and Vargas Llosa's *La casa verde* (1966; *The Green House*, 1968), for example, clearly contributed to the Latin American novel's international reputation, novels such as these remain largely the interest of the intellectual reader. *One Hundred Years of Solitude*, however, is readable; except for keeping track of the repetitive names and the numerous events, one does not have to work nearly as hard to read the work as one does for most other New Novels. It is, moreover, an entertaining, and even spellbinding story of biblical proportions (with numerous biblical parallels), and it has reached audiences of all kinds and interests. It is one of the few books appreciated by literary critics and taken to the beach by those simply looking for a "good read." Few books have ever been able to accomplish such a feat.

Keith H. Brower

Bibliography:
Bell-Villada, Gene H. *Gabriel García Márquez: The Man and His Work*. Chapel Hill: University of North Carolina Press, 1990. Definitive book-length study of García Márquez and his work for the North American reader. Contains a twenty-eight-page chapter about *One Hundred Years of Solitude*.
Gallagher, D. P. "Gabriel García Márquez (Colombia, 1928-   )." In *Modern Latin American Literature*. New York: Oxford University Press, 1973. Gallagher covers several aspects of the work and in the process presents a fine and very readable overview of the novel.
McMurray, George R. *Gabriel García Márquez*. New York: Frederick Ungar, 1977. *One Hundred Years of Solitude* is the subject of a forty-page chapter discussing diverse topics, including the story's connection to Colombian history, the use of cyclical and mythical time, humor, and the significance of the novel's final three pages.
Vázquez Amaral, José. *The Contemporary Latin American Narrative*. New York: Las Américas, 1970. Topics covered in the chapter on *One Hundred Years of Solitude* include the novel's focus on the subject of revolution, the theme of the "solitude of the warrior" once he has attained power, and the possible influence on García Márquez of Mexican writers Elena Garro and Juan Rulfo.
Williams, Raymond L. *Gabriel García Márquez*. Boston: Twayne, 1984. A twenty-three-page chapter on *One Hundred Years of Solitude* presents an excellent overview of García Márquez's masterpiece.

ORATION ON THE DIGNITY OF MAN

Type of work: Philosophical
Author: Giovanni Pico della Mirandola (1463-1494)
First published: Oratio de hominis dignitate, 1496 (English translation, 1940)

Giovanni Pico della Mirandola's *Oration on the Dignity of Man* is a remarkable document, but not for the reason that is sometimes thought. Even though it is an important statement by an influential early Renaissance humanist, the *Oration on the Dignity of Man* is neither a proclamation of the worth and glory of worldly life and achievement nor an attack on the medieval worldview as such. Pico was, in fact, a man of his time, and he was willing to defend the medieval theologians and philosophers from the attacks of his humanist friends. Yet in his statement he does go beyond what was then the traditional view of human nature.

Pico was a scholar whose erudition included a familiarity not only with Italian, Latin, and Greek but also with Hebrew, Chaldean, and Arabic. He had read widely in several non-Christian traditions of philosophy, and he had come to the conclusion that all philosophy, whether written by Christians, Jews, or pagans, was in basic agreement. In Rome, in December, 1486, Pico published nine hundred theses and invited all interested scholars to dispute them with him the following month. The *Oration on the Dignity of Man* was to have been the introduction to his defense. Pope Innocent VIII forbade the disputation, however, and appointed a papal commission to investigate the theses; the commission found some of them heretical. Pico tried to defend himself in a published *Apologia*, but this made matters worse, and for several years he remained in conflict with the Church. Pico had not expected this state of affairs and, being no conscious rebel, he was very much disturbed by it. As a result he became increasingly religious and finally joined the Dominican order. The *Oration on the Dignity of Man* was never published in Pico's lifetime, though part of it was used in his *Apologia* to the papal commission.

In form, the *Oration on the Dignity of Man* follows the then-standard academic, humanistic, rhetorical pattern. The piece is divided into two parts. The first part presents and deals with the philosophical basis of the speaker; the second part announces and justifies the topics to be disputed. The philosophical first part of the *Oration on the Dignity of Man* begins by praising human beings; this, as Pico points out, is a common topic. However, he immediately rejects the traditional bases for praise, that is, the medieval view that the distinction of human beings is a function of their unique place at the center of creation, in other words that each individual is a microcosm.

Pico accepted the premise that human beings are the most wonderful of all creations, but he inquired into the reasons why this should be so. Some, he said, believed that human beings are wonderful because they can reason and are close to God. Yet the same qualities, he pointed out, may be found among the angels. Pico's view was that God was ready to create human beings only after he had created the world and everything in it, which are the objects of human contemplation in the divine scheme of things. Everything, including the angels, had been given a fixed and immutable form, but human beings, created with no definite abode or form, were given both free will and the use of all of God's creatures. Pico claimed that human beings were neither heaven nor earth, mortal nor immortal, but free to choose between sinking to the level of animals or rising to the divine.

God's great gift to humankind was free choice. Individuals can be what they will to be. If they choose to be vegetables, then they will act like plants; if they choose to be sensual, they will act like animals; if they choose to be rational, they will be saintlike; if they choose to be intellectual, they will appear like angels; and if they reject the lot of all created things, they will draw into the center of their own beings and thus unite their spirits with the divine. Human beings have this capability of becoming either an animal or more than an angel, and their inconstant nature is their greatest blessing. It is, therefore, their duty to seek out the highest level they can obtain, striving to rise above the angels who, fixed in form, cannot surpass themselves and reach the godhead.

Pico's is an exalted idea of human nature. Though it is otherworldly in focus and thus resembles what is considered as the worldly view of the Renaissance, it is also Renaissance in embracing the position that human beings are limitless by their very nature. Pico sees as a great human strength that inconstancy of being that had so long been the despair of Christian dogmatists.

In the second part of his *Oration on the Dignity of Man*, Pico points out that human beings are assisted in their attempt to achieve the highest form of existence by philosophy. This view explains Pico's own interest in philosophy and also the plan of the disputation that was to follow the *Oration on the Dignity of Man*. Pico says that he must undertake to defend so great a number of theses because he is not an adherent of any one philosopher or school of philosophy. He feels the need to argue for positions drawn from a great variety of sources. He very broadly surveys his nine hundred theses, commenting on the various writers from whom they are drawn. In so doing he displays the full extent of his learning in both Christian and non-Christian writings. As he concludes this longer and more involved part of his *Oration on the Dignity of Man*, he challenges his readers to plunge joyfully into argument with him as if joining in battle to the sound of a war trumpet.

In this second part of the *Oration on the Dignity of Man*, Pico rejects the idea that any one philosopher may have a monopoly on final truth. He proclaims instead the idea of the unity of truth. He adopts this position in an attempt to solve the ancient problem of reconciling the great multiplicity and many contradictions of varying philosophical schools. Ancient thinkers as well as later ones have tended to adopt a relativistic position and to use the idea of philosophical multiplicity to prove there can be no truth or absolute. Pico, writing in the tradition of the ancient eclectics and neo-Platonists, assumes that opposing philosophical doctrines share both in error and in insight into universal truth. For him, truth is a collection of true statements drawn from various sources. He recognizes some error but also some truth in all the different philosophers.

In his work Pico hoped to winnow out error, to extract various aspects of truth, and to combine them eclectically into a unified statement of truth that would help human beings take advantage of their freedom to seek the highest form of existence. Although this is not an original position, it is humanistic and thus a justification for the typically Renaissance humanistic desire to study all ancient writings rather than just those that were thought to support the medieval Christian tradition of philosophy and theology.

Bibliography:
Cassirer, Ernst. "Giovanni Pico della Mirandola." *Journal of the History of Ideas* 3 (1942): 123-144. The second part of this article analyzes Pico's philosophy as it is outlined specifically in the *Oration on the Dignity of Man*. Remains an important source on the work.
Kristeller, Paul Oskar. "Introduction to *Oration on the Dignity of Man*. In *Renaissance Philosophy of Man*, edited by Ernst Cassirer et al. An excellent survey of the treatise, written by a preeminent scholar of Renaissance philosophy who places it within its historical and intellectual context.

Pico della Mirandola, Giovanni. "*Oration on the Dignity of Man.*" Translated by Elizabeth Livermore Forbes. In *Renaissance Philosophy of Man*, edited by Ernst Cassirer et al. Chicago: University of Chicago Press, 1948. The standard English translation, which has generally been used in subsequent Renaissance anthologies.

Trinkaus, Charles Edward. *In Our Image and Likeness: Humanity and Divinity in Italian Humanist Thought*. 2 vols. London: Constable, 1970. Chapter 10 of this important study focuses on Pico and the *Oration on the Dignity of Man*, relating them to other Renaissance humanists' conceptions of the essence of human existence.

Vasoli, Cesare. "The Renaissance Concept of Philosophy." In *The Cambridge History of Renaissance Philosophy*, edited by Quentin Skinner and Eckhard Kessler. Cambridge, England: Cambridge University Press, 1988. Places the *Oration on the Dignity of Man* in its philosophical context. Other articles in this volume provide information on the intellectual heritage upon which the *Oration on the Dignity of Man* drew.

ORATIONS

Type of work: Political
Author: Cicero (106-43 B.C.E.)
First transcribed: 81-43 B.C.E. (English translation, 1741-1743)

Thoughts of the greatness of Rome, and especially of its government, are likely to bring to mind the name of Cicero. Whereas a figure like Julius Caesar may symbolize the military greatness of imperial Rome, the figure of Cicero is a symbol of Roman justice and law, of the Roman senate and its traditions, and of landmark strides in philosophy and literature. Cicero is important in literature primarily for his orations and his many writings about oratory and rhetoric. Through his writings Cicero set a pattern in public speaking that is still alive in Western culture. Moreover, on the bases of what he wrote and said and of the viewpoints he held and defended to the point of dying for them, Cicero became historically one of the great advocates of culture and conservatism.

Cicero took ten years to prepare himself as a lawyer before he appeared on behalf of a client in public. He believed that a thorough education is necessary for success in any activity. There have been exponents of oratory who averred that manner is everything; Cicero disagreed, believing that matter is as inescapably a factor in oratorical success as manner. In the *Orator* (46 B.C.E.), one of his most mature pieces of writing on the art of oratory, Cicero wrote that his own success, like that of any orator, was more to be credited to his study of the philosophers than to his study of earlier rhetoricians, and that no one can express wide views, or speak fluently on many and various subjects, without philosophy. Although Cicero tried to make a science of rhetoric and saw profit in his own attempts at its systemization, he also realized that no simple set of formulas could ever make a great orator. As he put it, an eloquent man should be able to speak "of small things in a lowly manner, of moderate things in a temperate manner, and of great things with dignity."

In Cicero's time there were two prevalent styles in oratory, the Attic and the Asian. In the Asian type, Cicero himself discerned two subtypes, the one epigrammatic and euphuistic, dependent upon artful structure rather than importance of content, and the other characterized by a swift and passionate flow of speech in which choice of words for precise and elegant effect was a dominant factor. Cicero found both styles wanting in some degree and built his own style on an eclectic combination of the two.

Fifty-eight speeches by Cicero are still extant, although not all are complete. The number of his speeches is unknown, but more than forty are known to have been lost. Not all the speeches Cicero wrote were delivered; sometimes he wrote them for an occasion that did not occur. His second *Philippic* (44-43 B.C.E.) is an example of such a speech. Marcus Antonius had been so enraged by Cicero's first speech against him after the death of Julius Caesar that Cicero's friends persuaded the orator to leave the city of Rome temporarily. While absent from Rome, living at a villa near Naples, Cicero wrote the second *Philippic*, which was not spoken in the senate or even published immediately. A copy was, however, sent to Brutus and Cassius, who enjoyed its invective against their enemy.

Not all of Cicero's speeches are of equal interest to later readers. His earliest extant oration, containing relatively little of interest, was delivered in a law court on behalf of Publius Quinctius. Cicero appeared for the defense, as he usually did, and spoke against Quintus Hortensius, the greatest lawyer in Rome at the time. Cicero won his case, but it may be difficult to retain interest in a case decided two thousand years ago when the stuff of the argument is largely points of law. This speech, however, along with other early efforts, provided Cicero the opportunity to prove himself. He made such a reputation that he was chosen to prosecute Caius Verres, who had been accused of tyranny and maladministration in Sicily. Once again the famous Hortensius was Cicero's legal opponent. In the second oration he made against Verres, Cicero managed to produce such overwhelming evidence against the defendant that he went voluntarily into banishment. The evidence included chicanery designed to prevent the case from coming to trial, and even Hortensius could find little to say for the defendant. Although Cicero had no occasion to deliver five additional speeches he had written for the trial, scholars have judged that they are among Cicero's best and have found them excellent sources for material about Sicilian government, history, and art. Another of Cicero's noteworthy speeches is the one given in defense of Aulus Cluentius, who was tried and acquitted on a charge of having poisoned his father-in-law, who had in turn tried a few years earlier to poison Cluentius.

Cicero's intent was to move his hearers, and his devices to ensure victory in court were not always above reproach, as his speech in defense of Lucius Flaccus indicates. That defendant had been accused of extortion while he was an administrator in Asia, and apparently Cicero could find little to say in his client's defense beyond impugning the Jews and Greeks who were witnesses against him, members of groups not much in favor in Rome. Also of great interest is Cicero's defense of Aulus Licinius Archias, a poet of Greek descent whose status as a Roman citizen had been questioned. In this oration Cicero developed a long passage in praise of literature, saying that literature and its creators are of paramount interest to a nation because they afford excellent material for speeches, because they make great deeds immortal by preserving them in writing, and because they give readers a useful and refreshing pastime.

Not all of Cicero's speeches were intended for courtroom presentation. Some were written for delivery in the senate and some with a view to Cicero's own benefit. In 58 B.C.E., Cicero was exiled temporarily as a result of his activities in crushing the conspiracy of Catiline. When Pompey recalled him to Rome a year later, he thanked the Roman senate in one speech for his recall; in another he thanked the Roman people generally; and in a third he made a request to the senate for the return of his home, which had been taken over by Clodius for the state.

The most famous of Cicero's speeches are those he wrote against Marcus Antonius after the death of Julius Caesar. Cicero, a conservative, had not been favorable to the autocracy of Caesar, and he rejoiced when Caesar was assassinated. During an eight-month period in 44-43 B.C.E., when Marcus Antonius presumed to try to succeed Caesar, Cicero directed fourteen orations against him. These orations, passionate and sincere, are called the *Philippics* after the famous speeches of Demosthenes against Philip, the father of Alexander the Great. In his first speech Cicero spoke with some moderation, referring only to Antonius' public life and appealing to his sense of patriotism. In later speeches, especially the second *Philippic*, he made various attacks on Antonius' private life, accusing him of almost every conceivable type of immorality. Eventually Antonius had his revenge: When he, Lepidus, and Octavianus formed their triumvirate, Cicero was put to death.

Bibliography:
Dorey, Thomas Alan, ed. *Cicero*. London: Routledge & Kegan Paul, 1965. A collection of essays on Roman politics, Cicero's political career, speeches, poetry, philosophy, and character. Includes a detailed chapter on orations, which evaluates Cicero's style, form, and oratorical devices. The breadth and detail of this work makes it a useful study of Cicero and his speeches.
Haskell, Henry Joseph. *This Was Cicero: Modern Politics in a Roman Toga*. New York: Al-

fred A. Knopf, 1942. Focuses on Cicero's political career and discusses his major speeches in their historical context. A helpful source for a student of Roman history and for studying the influence of Cicero's orations.

Martyn, John, ed. *Cicero and Virgil: Studies in Honour of Harold Hunt*. Amsterdam: Adolf M. Hakkert, 1972. Contains six useful, detailed essays on the style, techniques, influence, and philosophy of Cicero's writings and speeches. Important for in-depth study of Cicero's work.

Petersson, Torsten. *Cicero: A Biography*. Berkeley: University of California Press, 1920. Still the best general biography of Cicero, a comprehensive and detailed analysis of the orator's life, career, orations, and treatises. Also includes a thorough and insightful discussion of Cicero's philosophy and speeches. An important and useful work for both students and serious scholars.

Richards, George Chatterton. *Cicero: A Study*. Boston: Houghton Mifflin, 1935. A brief work that includes two chapters specifically on Cicero's speeches and rhetorical treatises. Discusses the character and technique of Cicero's speeches in a concise survey. A useful and accessible introduction to Cicero's orations.

THE ORDEAL OF RICHARD FEVEREL
A History of Father and Son

Type of work: Novel
Author: George Meredith (1828-1909)
Type of plot: Tragicomedy
Time of plot: Mid-nineteenth century
Locale: England
First published: 1859

> *Principal characters:*
> RICHARD FEVEREL, the young heir to Raynham Abbey
> SIR AUSTIN FEVEREL, his father
> ADRIAN HARLEY, Sir Austin's nephew
> RIPTON THOMPSON, Richard's playmate and friend
> BLAIZE, a neighboring farmer
> LUCY DESBOROUGH, Blaize's niece
> CLARE, Richard's cousin and his beloved

The Story:

Richard Feverel was the only son of Sir Austin Feverel of Raynham Abbey. After Sir Austin's wife left him, the baronet became a misogynist who was determined to rear his son according to a system that, among other things, virtually excluded females from the boy's life until he was twenty-five years old. At that time, Sir Austin thought, his son might marry, so long as a girl good enough for the young man could be found.

Because of his father's system, Richard's early life was carefully controlled. The boy was kept from lakes and rivers so that he would not drown; from firecrackers so that he would not be burned; and from cricket fields so that he would not be bruised. Adrian Harley, Sir Austin's nephew, was entrusted with Richard's education.

When he was fourteen years old, the Hope of Raynham, as Adrian called his charge, became restless. It was decided that he needed a companion of his own age, and his father chose young Ripton Thompson, the none-too-brilliant son of Sir Austin's lawyer. In their escapades around Raynham Abbey together, Richard led and Ripton followed.

Despite Ripton's subordinate position, he apparently had much to do with corrupting his companion and weakening Sir Austin's system. Soon after Ripton arrived at Raynham, the two boys decided to go shooting. A quarrel arose between them when Ripton, not a sportsman by nature, cried out as Richard was aiming his piece at a bird. Richard called his companion a fool, and a fight ensued. Richard won because he was a scientific boxer. The two boys soon made up their differences, but the state of harmony was short-lived. The same afternoon, they trespassed on the farm of a neighbor named Blaize, who came upon them after they had shot a pheasant on his property. Blaize ordered the boys off his land; when they refused to go, he horsewhipped them. Richard and Ripton were compelled to retreat. Ripton suggested that he stone the farmer, but Richard refused to let his companion use such ungentlemanly tactics. The two boys did, however, speculate on ways to get even with farmer Blaize.

Richard was in disgrace when he returned to Raynham because his father knew of his fight with Ripton. Sir Austin ordered his son to go to bed immediately after supper; he later discovered that Richard had disobeyed and had gone to meet Ripton, and the boys were overheard talking mysteriously about setting something on fire. Shortly afterward, when Sir Austin discovered that farmer Blaize's hayricks were on fire, he suspected Richard. Sir Austin was chagrined, but he did not try to make his son confess. Adrian Harley suspected both Richard and Ripton, who was soon sent home to his father.

The next day a laborer named Tom Bakewell was arrested on suspicion of having committed arson. Tom had indeed set fire to Blaize's property, but he had been bribed by Richard to do so. Nevertheless, Tom refused to implicate Richard. Conscience-stricken and aware of the fact that a commoner was shielding him, Richard went to Blaize and confessed that he was responsible for Tom's action.

Blaize was not surprised by Richard's visit, for Sir Austin had already called and paid the damages. Richard was humiliated by the necessity of apologizing to a farmer. He told Blaize that he had set fire to the farmer's grain stacks; Blaize, however, implied that Richard was a liar because the farmer had a witness, a dull-witted fellow, who said that Tom Bakewell had done the deed. Richard insisted that he himself was responsible, and he succeeded in confusing Blaize's star witness. Richard, however, left the farmer's place in an irritated frame of mind, so much so that he did not even notice the farmer's pretty thirteen-year-old niece, Lucy Desborough, who had let the young man in and out of Blaize's house. At Tom's trial, Blaize's witness was so uncertain about the identity of the arsonist that the accused was released. Thereafter, Tom became Richard's devoted servant.

When Richard reached the age of eighteen, Sir Austin set about finding a prospective wife for the Hope of Raynham, a girl who could be trained for seven years to be a fit mate for Sir Austin's perfect son. Richard, however, could not wait seven years before beginning at least to show an interest in women. He was first attracted to his cousin Clare, who adored him and dreamed of marrying the handsome young man. In a single afternoon, however, Richard completely forgot Clare. When, while boating on the weir, he came upon a young lady in distress and saved her boat from capsizing, the system in an instant collapsed completely. She introduced herself as farmer Blaize's niece, Lucy Desborough. Richard and Lucy were immediately attracted to each other, and they met every day in the meadow by the weir.

Meanwhile, Sir Austin had found in London someone he thought would be the perfect mate for his son, a young woman named Carola Grandison. Informed by Adrian and his butler that Richard was secretly meeting Lucy, Sir Austin ordered his son to come to London immediately to meet Carola. At first, Richard refused to obey his father, but Adrian tricked Richard into going to London by saying that Sir Austin had apoplexy.

Richard found his father physically well but mentally disturbed by the young man's interest in Lucy. He told Richard that women were the ordeal of all men, and although he hoped for a confession of Richard's affair with Lucy, he received none. Sir Austin, however, refused to let the young man return to Raynham as soon as Richard would have liked. Richard met the Grandisons, listened to his father's lectures on the folly of young men who imagined themselves in love, and moped when, after two weeks, Lucy mysteriously stopped writing.

When Sir Austin and his son finally returned to Raynham Abbey, Richard found that Lucy had been sent away to school against her will by her uncle so that she would not interfere with Sir Austin's system. Although the farmer did not object to Richard, he refused to have his niece brought back. After his unsuccessful attempt to have his sweetheart returned to him, Richard decided upon drastic measures. Sir Austin unwittingly aided his son's designs when he sent Richard to London to see the Grandisons. Tom Blaize was destined by Sir Austin and her uncle to be Lucy's husband, and he went to London by the same train. Richard got in touch with his old friend, Ripton Thompson, and asked him to get lodgings for a lady. While in London,

Richard came upon Adrian Harley, Clare's mother, and Clare, who had picked up a wedding ring that Richard had dropped. Tom Blaize was tricked into going to the wrong station to find Lucy, and Richard met her instead. He installed her with Mrs. Berry in lodgings in Kensington and married her soon afterward. Good-hearted Mrs. Berry gave them her own wedding ring to replace the one Richard had lost.

When Adrian learned of Richard's marriage, he admitted that the system had failed. Ripton broke the news to Sir Austin, who remarked bitterly that he was mistaken to believe that any system could be based on a human being. Actually, Sir Austin objected not so much to his son's marriage as to the deception involved.

Efforts were made to reconcile Richard and his father, but they were unsuccessful. Richard was uneasy because he had not heard from his father, and Sir Austin was too proud to take the first step. While Richard and Lucy were honeymooning in the Isle of Wight, he was introduced to a fast yachting crowd, including Lord Mountfalcon, a man of doubtful reputation. Richard naïvely asked him to watch over Lucy while Richard himself went to London to see his father and ask his forgiveness.

In London he met a woman Lord Mountfalcon had bribed to bring about Richard's downfall; Mountfalcon's plan was to win Lucy for himself by convincing her of Richard's infidelity. Richard did not know that Mrs. Mount, as she was called, was being bribed to detain him and that while she kept him in London, Lord Mountfalcon was attempting to seduce Lucy.

Because he could not bear separation from his son any longer, Sir Austin consented to see Richard. Relations between Richard and his father were still strained, however, for Sir Austin had not yet accepted Lucy. Since she could not have Richard, Clare, meanwhile, had married a man much older than she. Shortly after her marriage, she died and was buried with her own wedding ring and Richard's lost one on her finger.

The death of Clare and the realization that she had loved him deeply shocked Richard. Moreover, his past indiscretions with Mrs. Mount made him ashamed of himself; unworthy, he thought to touch Lucy's hand. He did not know that Mrs. Berry had gone to the Isle of Wight and had brought Lucy back to live with her in Kensington. Richard himself had gone to the Continent; there he traveled aimlessly, unaware that Lucy had borne him a son. Then an uncle who disbelieved in all systems returned to London. Learning of Lucy and her child, he bundled them off to Raynham Abbey and prevailed on Sir Austin to receive them. Then he went to the Continent, found Richard, and broke the news that he was a father. Richard rushed back to Raynham to be with Lucy and to reconcile completely with his father.

The reunion between Lucy and Richard was brief. Richard saw his son and received complete forgiveness for his past misdeeds from his wife. A letter from Mrs. Mount to Richard had revealed how Lord Mountfalcon had schemed so that his lordship could see Lucy and separate her from Richard. Knowing Lucy's innocence and Mountfalcon's villainy, Richard went immediately to France; there he was slightly wounded in a duel with Lord Mountfalcon. The news of the duel, however, was fatal for Lucy. She became ill of brain fever and died of shock, crying for her husband. Richard was heartbroken. Sir Austin was also grieved, but his closest friend often wondered whether he had ever perceived any flaws in his system.

Critical Evaluation:

The Ordeal of Richard Feverel was George Meredith's first novel, although he had by that time published poetry, journalism, and two entertaining prose fantasies. George Eliot praised the novel, but other critics found it unconvincing and excessively intellectualized. Later critics have generally agreed that it is somewhat thesis-ridden, but they find its flaws counterbalanced by wit and emotional force, and it has remained probably the most popular if not the most admired of Meredith's novels.

There is no denying that at times Meredith's concern for his thesis acts to the detriment of the novel; in this the novel serves as a kind of unintentional exemplification of the thesis that life is too various, too rich, too spontaneous to conform to even the most admirable system. Few readers can quite believe that Richard would remain separated from Lucy for as long as the plot requires, and the deaths of both Lucy and Clare seem less from natural than from authorial causes. These events are necessary to Meredith's design, but he is unable to give them the quality of inevitability that characterize other elements of the plot.

The novel nevertheless works remarkably well. Meredith may have intended to keep Sir Austin Feverel at center stage, demonstrating the fatuity of high intelligence and lofty ideals without the precious leaven of humor and common sense. The message is effectively conveyed, and Meredith's comic purpose is served by the reader's last sight of Sir Austin still blindly clinging to his theories in the shipwreck of his beloved son's life. It is the romantic pathos of the love of Richard and Lucy, however, that most fully engages the reader and is most vivid at the conclusion. Meredith's later revisions for a new edition suggest that he recognized what had happened to his original intention and concluded that the gain in emotional power was worth preserving. To value intense feeling about strict adherence to a preconceived system was thoroughly Meredithian.

Bibliography:

Horne, Lewis. "Sir Austin, His Devil, and the Well-designed World." *Studies in the Novel* 24, no. 1 (Spring, 1992): 35-48. Argues that Richard Feverel's ordeal is also to a great extent that of his father, Sir Austin. Analyzes the novel's metaphors and classical references.

Muendel, Renate. *George Meredith*. New York: Twayne, 1986. Good introduction to the Victorian writer and his works, with broad, insightful analyses. Includes bibliography and a concordance to Meredith's poetry.

Shaheen, Mohammad. *George Meredith: A Reappraisal of the Novels*. Totowa, N.J.: Barnes & Noble Books, 1981. Suggests that traditional Meredith criticism has viewed his fiction too much in the light of *The Egoist*. Concentrates on the writer's other major works as being more representative of his truly independent mind. Specifically explores how character expresses theme in Meredith's novels.

Stone, James Stuart. *George Meredith's Politics: As Seen in His Life, Friendships, and Works*. Port Credit, Canada: P. D. Meany, 1986. Attempts to expound what Stone calls Meredith's "evolutionary radicalism" and the complex and interesting ways in which this suffuses his greatest novels. Useful for beginning students.

Williams, Joan, ed. *Meredith: The Critical Heritage*. London: Routledge & Kegan Paul, 1971. A collection of reviews and essays showing the critical reception of Meredith's work from 1851 through 1911.

THE ORESTEIA

Type of work: Drama
Author: Aeschylus (525/524-456/455 B.C.E.)
Type of plot: Tragedy
Time of plot: After the fall of Troy
Locale: Argos, Delphi, and Athens
First performed: Agamemnōn (Agamemnon), Choēphoroi (Libation Bearers), and
   Eumenides, 458 B.C.E. (English translation, 1777)

Principal characters:
Agamemnon:
WATCHMAN
CLYTEMNESTRA, queen of Argos
HERALD
AGAMEMNON, king of Argos, son of Atreus
CASSANDRA, the captured visionary princess of Troy
AEGISTHUS, Agamemnon's cousin, Clytemnestra's lover
CHORUS, old men of Argos

Libation Bearers:
ORESTES, son of Agamemnon and Clytemnestra
PYLADES, Orestes' friend
ELECTRA, Orestes' sister
CHORUS, foreign slave-women
SERVANT, the doorkeeper
CLYTEMNESTRA
CILISSA, the nurse
AEGISTHUS
SERVANT, loyal to Aegisthus

Eumenides:
PYTHIAN PRIESTESS of Apollo
APOLLO, the god of prophesy and light, son of Zeus and Leto
GHOST OF CLYTEMNESTRA
ORESTES
ATHENE, the goddess of wisdom, war, and crafts; daughter of Zeus, from
   whose head she sprang
CHORUS, the Furies, who become the Eumenides
SECOND CHORUS, Athenian women
JURORS, Athenian men

The Story:
   Agamemnon. Clytemnestra's Watchman spied a beacon signaling victory at Troy. Hoping
that Agamemnon would right the wrongs in Argos, the Watchman left to inform Clytemnestra.
   The Chorus lamented the unjustified ten-year war. It was fought for Helen, Clytemnestra's
sluttish sister, wife of Agamemnon's brother, Menalaus, and paramour of Trojan Paris. Al-

though Paris violated a guest's obligations in stealing Helen, she was unworthy of the anguish. The brothers' attack wedded Greeks and Trojans in spilled blood, first sacrifice being Clytemnestra's innocent daughter, Iphigenia. Beached at Aulis, a prophet, Calacas, said the goddess Artemis demanded Iphigenia as the price of reaching Troy. Agamemnon complied. Now, as Clytemnestra laid offerings at her altars, the chorus, anticipating trouble, prayed to Zeus for guidance.

Clytemnestra reported Agamemnon's victory, fearing the victors, glorying excessively, might offend the gods. The chorus, considering the suffering the brothers caused and the curses that might bring divine wrath upon them, hoped the beacons lied. A herald confirmed that Troy was leveled; basking in victory, they could ignore the dead.

Agamemnon, accompanied by Cassandra, credited the gods with his victory. Clytemnestra claimed their son, Orestes, was sent away because, after rumors that Agamemnon had been killed, she had tried to commit suicide. She laid out crimson tapestries for him. Agamemnon feared stepping on them would show pride, but Clytemnestra goaded him into doing so.

Alone with Cassandra, the chorus wanted to be joyous but sang a dirge. Returning, Clytemnestra invited Cassandra in, but, perceiving herself entangled in a net, she remained outside. She bewailed her fate after Clytemnestra left, predicting slaughter in Agamemnon's house.

The chorus was perplexed because, after promising Apollo love, Cassandra had reneged, for which he punished her with visions that could not be communicated. They knew well that Aegisthus, whose father had been deceived by Agamemnon's into eating his own children, had used Agamemnon's absence to seduce Clytemnestra. The prediction that the two would slay Cassandra and Agamemnon left them mystified. Despairing, Cassandra entered the palace.

Agamemnon cried out from within. Clytemnestra attributed her deceptions to necessity, delighting in stabbing Agamemnon so viciously that his blood drenched her. His lust for Cassandra rankled, but she attributed his death to the curse on Atreus and guilt for Iphigenia's death. Revenged, Clytemnestra said she would relinquish power.

Aegisthus, however, had grand plans. Intending to use Agamemnon's wealth to consolidate power, he took credit for plotting this "justice bringing day." Clytemnestra wanted to end bloodshed, but the chorus opposed them. Disdainful, the two entered the palace, buoyed by the helplessness of their enemies.

Libation Bearers. Orestes, a man now, returned with Pylades and placed a lock of hair at Agamemnon's tomb. When Electra arrived with a chorus of servingwomen, the two hid.

The chorus mentioned Clytemnestra's nightmare, which led her to send offerings to the tomb. Electra wondered how to supplicate. Should she ask good for her mother or spill the libations on the ground? The chorus suggested blessings for those who hated Aegisthus. Urged to ask for vengeance, Electra thought that might be impious, but the chorus claimed that violence earned violence.

While following their advice, Electra found Orestes' hair. They wondered if Orestes sent it because he could not return, but Electra found footprints like hers. Thus discovered, Orestes identified himself. Electra welcomed him with four loves: love of their father; love she wished to bestow on Clytemnestra; love of Iphigenia; and love for him. Orestes prayed for Zeus's aid. Apollo had ordered him to avenge Agamemnon. Both he and Electra wanted it otherwise: Orestes wished Agamemnon had died nobly at Troy; Electra, that his murderers had been killed by their friends. The chorus invoked the law—blood for blood—but killing placed Orestes in the chain of those killed. Spurred on, he claimed a willingness to pay with his life for vengeance, in a battle of right against right. Electra saw only their side as right and prayed for justice.

Both ultimately hoped to kill and survive. When Orestes asked why Clytemnestra sent offerings, Electra recounted Clytemnestra's dream—that she gave birth to a snake, gave it her breast, and, as it sucked, was bitten, spilling blood and milk into its mouth. Orestes, claiming to be that snake, laid out his plan for vengeance, and left.

After the chorus recalled treacheries of past women, Orestes returned, disguised, and reported his own death to Clytemnestra. She seemed saddened, averring that she relinquished Orestes to save him. They entered the palace, and Cilissa, once Orestes' nurse, sought out Aegisthus with what was, for her, heartbreaking news: Orestes was dead. The chorus, having convinced her to have Aegisthus come to the palace alone, anticipated success.

Aegisthus, lamenting Orestes' death, entered the palace to learn whether the strangers actually had seen the body. His scream informed the chorus that assassination was underway, and, to avoid complicity, they moved off.

Aegisthus' servant stumbled out, horrified by the murder of his master, to warn Clytemnestra. She sought to arm herself, but Orestes and Pylades stopped her. Clytemnestra mourned her dead lover, reinforcing Orestes' desire to kill her, but she appealed to him as the child that had suckled at her breast. Shaken, Orestes was advised by Pylades to be loyal first to the gods. The advice carried Orestes through both pleading and threats. He slew Clytemnestra in the palace, returning to claim right on his side.

The chorus expected trouble, however, and almost immediately Orestes felt stained by matricide. Convinced that Clytemnestra's Furies were attacking him, he rushed off to seek Apollo's aid.

Eumenides. At Delphi, Apollo's Pythian priestess honored Earth, Themis, and Phoebe, who gave the gift of prophesy to Apollo, enshrined as fourth prophet by Zeus. She honored many gods, including Athene, before entering the temple, but soon rushed out again. Within, she saw Orestes, dripping blood, surrounded by Gorgon-like women, and abandoned the problem to Apollo.

Inside, Apollo and Hermes protected Orestes, for Apollo had demanded Clytemnestra's death. The shade of Clytemnestra, seeking vengeance, awakened the sleeping Furies, who accused Apollo of stealing power from older gods, inspiring matricide, being stained with blood, and dependent upon force. Apollo thought killing the murderess of a husband just, but the Furies saw no kindred bloodshed in Clytemnestra's deed.

Shifting the case to Athene, Apollo sent Orestes as suppliant to Athens, where he claimed to have been cleansed of pollution by Apollo's sacrifice of a pig. The Furies rejected such acts. Their subterranean powers preceded and repelled Olympians.

When Athene arrived, she found the Furies interesting rather than terrifying. Valuing justice, she decided to hear both sides, but, after preliminary inquiry, ruled herself unqualified to adjudicate. She empowered a jury of citizens to decide the case. The Furies saw this as a threat to their order, which employed fear to ward off evil, punish misdeeds, and reward pain with wisdom. If the new order's first decision freed a matricide, it would be useless from the start. The trial proceeded, with the Furies arguing for blood guilt and Apollo for the fulfillment of Zeus's demand that Agamemnon be avenged. Mothers are only vessels, he said; fathers alone are blood relatives of offspring.

Aware that the jury might be divided, Athene cast an anticipatory tie-breaking vote—not guilty, because, as daughter of Zeus, who gave birth to her, she was partial to men. The jury deadlocked and her vote proved decisive. Orestes vowed allegiance to Athene and Athens.

Athene wisely placated the outraged Furies, claiming the jury's decision aimed at justice, not their defeat. As an inducement to peace, she offered honor among Athenians as Eumenides, "kindly ones." Patiently, she convinced them, and, accepting veneration, they blessed Athens and embraced peace between old and new gods.

Critical Evaluation:

Aeschylus created what we call drama, conceiving of a second actor and, thus, the possibility of dialogue between individuals. The *Oresteia*, his last triumph at Athens' festival of Dionysus (he wrote more than seventy plays and won thirteen times during his lifetime), is the only extant trilogy, a unit of three related plays performed on one day.

Although interested in characterization and individual motivation, Aeschylus' concerns are larger than individuals or even human character generally. He explores relationships among gods and humanity; the roles of power, hatred, and love in the creation of human values; the transformation of divinity from a rigid threat to a generous force for good; and the creation of justice out of a chaos of sexual aggression and brute rage. *Oresteia* explores all of these issues.

What passes for justice in *Agamemnon* demands the abandonment of personal values. Outrage merits retribution through outrage, which starts the cycle again. Agamemnon's sacrifice of his daughter to reach Troy was wrong, but Trojan Paris was wrong to violate laws of hospitality, stealing Helen from his host. Clytemnestra was right to kill her daughter's murderer but wrong to kill her husband, who was the murderer. Although complicated by adultery and lust for power, her slaughter of Agamemnon falls into the primitive pattern of evil begetting evil. The chain of guilt and retribution, begetting more guilt and retribution, traces back to primordial humanity and past them into the brutal histories of Titans and gods—Cronos castrating his father, Uranus, to escape imprisonment; Zeus's conquest of his father, Cronos, who was consuming his own children in an effort to retain power.

Libation Bearers continues the pattern, with this difference: Unlike self-motivated Clytemnestra, Orestes murders his father's murderers because, knowingly or in ignorance, Apollo enjoined it for a reason greater than blood guilt. The issue is larger than filial or political fealty and betrayal: Orestes' history is the mythological instrumentality by which civilized justice is born. When the tragic double bind of individual motives becomes clear—he is both right and wrong; his mother was both right and wrong; so, too, his father—there can be no escape from slaughter unless governing principles change. As Aeschylus understands the problem, such fundamental changes cannot occur justly or unjustly. Means, for him, are not justified by ends; injustice will not lead to justice, but neither will old justice lead to change. Initially, there must be recourse to an intermediate justice, an arbitrary severance of past practices, for change to occur.

Under the beneficent guidance of Athene, wisest of the gods, the action of *Eumemides* accomplishes just that. Her capriciously determined vote of not guilty amounts to a confession: justice in the case of Orestes is impossible because both sides are right and wrong. Through her genius, the anguish of the past has ended. Blood vengeance is replaced by disinterested justice, trial by jury, in a state controlled by and devoted to the good of its citizens. The net in which Clytemnestra caught Agamemnon metaphorically invoked nets of serial injustice in which humanity and gods were caught. The *Oresteia* traces a route by which such nets were severed, to the benefit of all.

Albert Wachtel

Bibliography:

Gagarin, Michael. *Aeschylean Drama.* Berkeley: University of California Press, 1976. An accessible and worthwhile source for the nonspecialist. Clearly written and argued, with helpful notes and a bibliography. Includes two excellent chapters devoted to *The Oresteia*.

Goldhill, Simon. *Aeschylus: "The Oresteia."* Cambridge, England: Cambridge University Press, 1992. A short but highly informative book by a leading scholar in the field of Greek drama. An ideal introduction to the *Oresteia*. Especially good discussion of the social contexts for the plays.

Herrington, John. *Aeschylus*. New Haven, Conn.: Yale University Press, 1986. Designed for the nonspecialist. Part 1 provides background for Aeschylus' plays, and part 2 discusses the seven existing plays in detail. Discusses the *Oresteia* as the reconciliation of male and female principles.

Rosenmeyer, Thomas G. *The Art of Aeschylus*. Berkeley: University of California Press, 1982. Intended for the somewhat advanced student of Greek drama, but includes an excellent discussion of Aeschylus' stagecraft which is accessible to the general reader as well. Includes a useful selected bibliography.

Spatz, Lois. *Aeschylus*. Boston: Twayne, 1982. A serviceable introduction to the plays of Aeschylus. Includes a fifty-page discussion of the *Oresteia* and a useful annotated bibliography.

ORFEO

Type of work: Drama
Author: Poliziano (Angelo Ambrogini, 1454-1494)
Type of plot: Pastoral
Time of plot: Antiquity
Locale: Sicily
First performed: 1480; first published, 1863 (English translation, 1879)

> *Principal characters:*
> ORPHEUS,
> EURYDICE,
> ARISTAEUS,
> MOPSUS, and
> THYRSIS, shepherds
> PLUTO
> PROSERPINA
> TISIPHONE, one of the Furies

The Story:

While looking for a lost calf, old Mopsus came upon Aristaeus and his servant Thyrsis. They had not seen the animal, but Aristaeus sent the young man in search of it. Meanwhile, he told Mopsus that he had seen a nymph more beautiful than Diana in the woods. Although she had been accompanied by a youthful sweetheart, Aristaeus declared that either he must win her love or he would die. Mopsus tried to warn him of the desolation and unhappiness caused by love, but without success; the return of Thyrsis with word that the girl was still in the woods sent Aristaeus hurrying to find her. The shepherds were convinced that he was mad and that some evil would result from his actions.

After finding the nymph, Aristaeus tried to woo her, but she fled. A moment later another nymph appeared with news that the lovely Eurydice had just died of a serpent bite by the riverside. She called on her sister dryads to join in a dirge "to set the air ringing with the sound of wailing." As they sang, they saw Orpheus, her sweetheart, approaching with his lyre. The dryad took it upon herself to break to him the sad news of Eurydice's death.

When Orpheus' song about the exploits of Hercules was interrupted by the nymph bearing "crushing tidings," the desolate poet called on sky and sea to hear him lament his bitter fate. At last he vowed to go to the gates of Tartarus in an attempt to win back his dead love—perhaps the magic of his lyre would move even Death to pity. The satyr Mnesillus, who had been listening, had his doubts.

In Tartarus, Orpheus' lyre of gold and his beautiful voice "moved the gates immovable." In fact, Pluto acknowledged that everything stood still at his melody. Proserpina was so charmed by it that she seconded Orpheus' request that Eurydice should be returned to him. Pluto agreed on condition that the poet return to earth without looking behind. In spite of Orpheus' promise not to look back, his doubts betrayed him. Orpheus looked back and saw Eurydice drawn again toward Tartarus. When he tried to follow her, Tisiphone refused to let him pass.

While he was lamenting his woes and expressing his determination never again to desire a woman's love, Orpheus was overheard by a chorus of Maenads. One of the Bacchantes, angered that a man should scorn love, exhorted the others to take revenge, and the fierce creatures tore him to pieces in their rage, so that every twig close by was soaked with his blood.

Critical Evaluation:

Orfeo, by Poliziano, also known as Politan, holds several distinctions. Literary scholars consider it the first modern pastoral drama, that is, one set in the countryside; it is the first modern drama drawing on a classical, or ancient, theme and on classical authors, and also the first Italian play with a nonreligious theme. In addition, musicologists consider it the first modern opera, or at least opera's precursor, since it was intended to be accompanied by music in its public performance.

Above all, *Orfeo* is a testament to the poetic talents of its author. When he was still a relatively young man, Poliziano wrote the entire drama in the span of only two days. The drama was a part of the festivities, in 1480, celebrating a visit by the child duke of Milan, Giangaleazzo Sforza, to Mantua; the drama had been commissioned by the Mantuan cardinal Franceso Gonzaga. The Sforza dukes were delighted with music, and they sponsored the Milanese choir and individual composers. Lorenzo de' Médici, Poliziano's patron for most of his life, also cultivated music in his city, Florence. Poliziano's drama emerged from an historical setting that encouraged his natural poetic and musical talents.

In composing *Orfeo*, Poliziano employed his vast knowledge of classical literature to produce elegant poetry in several languages (Italian, Latin, and Greek). He adopted his theme from Greek mythology, recounting a tale that would have been well known among his audience. The challenge was to weave together an entertaining presentation. Although the legend of Orpheus concerns his journey to the underworld in order to retrieve his wife, Eurydice, Poliziano begins the story at an earlier point, before her untimely death. It seems that he almost shifted the traditional plot line from Orpheus' endeavors to those of Aristaeus, who first sought to make Eurydice his lover.

Set in a pastoral scene, *Orfeo* gives freedom to the audience to enjoy all the warmth and the instinctive emotions of their earthy existence. Although the story itself is tragic (Orpheus loses Eurydice), the tone of the play is light and lyrical, a tone in which audiences can revel. Listeners can participate, cheering on Orpheus in his efforts to regain his wife. They can join in his excitement when he sings, "Eurydice is won—my life restored. . . . Triumph, by my skill achieved." When he, in his careless pride, however, loses her on the way back, they can just as eagerly enjoy condemning him. Poliziano succeeds in turning the classical tragedy into a Renaissance sport, as passionately entertaining as any joust. Indeed, the gaiety of the drama and of its occasion is reinforced in *Orfeo*'s ending, in which a chorus of bacchants urges everyone to "drink down the wine."

The theme may have been classical and the circumstances festive, but *Orfeo* stands also in the tradition of medieval religious dramas. From the eleventh century, mystery plays—called mystery plays because they dealt with the wonders of Christian history and beliefs—had been presented publicly as entertainment and as tools of instruction. Audience members would have already been familiar with the stories, such as Noah's flood, but they nevertheless enjoyed the performances. Poliziano succeeds in drawing upon this tradition for the basic form of his play, but he created for it a wholly new content with *Orfeo*. The ancient legend of Orpheus was well known, but Poliziano gives it new life in this festive setting.

The structure of *Orfeo* reflects the rapidity with which Poliziano composed it. The play begins with shepherds discovering the beauty of Eurydice, and Aristaeus' desire to make her his lover. There is dramatic potential in that portion alone of the story for Poliziano to develop, but he does not do so. Instead, he uses the pretext of Orpheus singing to insert public praise of Cardinal Gonzaga, whom he applauds as a great patron. From there, Poliziano quickly moves to Orpheus' resolve to journey to the underworld. The audience, therefore, receives a seemingly new principal character, in place of Aristaeus. Finally, after Orpheus' unsuccessful endeavors to be reunited with Eurydice, a chorus of women overhears him complaining of the futility of loving women. In response, they decapitate him, and so the play's structure takes another, seemingly illogical turn before culminating with the call to drink. Despite these structural inconsistencies, the play's purpose is entertainment, for which such discrepancies are minor.

Orfeo serves two purposes. First, it expresses a celebration for the young duke and the cardinal and anticipation for their future leadership of their cities. Second, it serves as a harbinger of Poliziano's talents and of the presumably glorious literary achievements that he will produce for all Italians. Orpheus is so charming that his music is able to calm the savage beast and even to cause rocks to sway. Be implication, Poliziano's music must surely inspire comparable responses among his human listeners.

"Critical Evaluation" by Alan Cottrell

Bibliography:
Bolgar, R. R. "Imitation in the Vernaculars." 1954. Reprint. In *The Classical Heritage and Its Beneficiaries*. Cambridge, England: Cambridge University Press, 1977. Places *Orfeo* in its literary framework as the first contemporary drama with a classical theme and drawing on classical authors.
Haar, James. *Essays on Italian Poetry and Music in the Renaissance, 1350-1600*. Berkeley: University of California Press, 1986. Analyzes the relationship between poetry and music. Provides much information for persons interested in the historical context of Poliziano's work.
Pirrotta, Nino. "Music and Cultural Tendencies in Fifteenth-Century Italy." *Journal of the American Musicological Society* 19 (1966): 139-146. Indicates Poliziano's interest in music.
Pirrotta, Nino, and Elena Povoledo. *Music and Theatre from Poliziano to Monteverdi*. Translated by Karen Eales. Cambridge, England: Cambridge University Press, 1982. Places Poliziano's poetic work within the historical framework of Italian Renaissance musical performance.
Poliziano, Angelo. *A Translation of the Orpheus of Angelo Politian and the Aminta of Torquato Tasso*. Translated by Louis E. Lord. London: Humphrey Milford, 1931. The only readily available translation; the English is archaic. Contains translations of Poliziano's original edition and of an expanded edition published in the late eighteenth century. Includes a lengthy (about seventy pages) introduction to pastoral drama, the form that *Orfeo* takes.

ORLANDO
A Biography

Type of work: Novel
Author: Virginia Woolf (1882-1941)
Type of plot: Phantasmagoric
Time of plot: 1588-1928
Locale: England
First published: 1928

> *Principal characters:*
> ORLANDO, first a man, then a woman
> SASHA, a Russian princess loved by Orlando
> NICHOLAS GREENE, a poet pensioned by Orlando
> ARCHDUCHESS HARRIET OF RUMANIA, an admirer of Orlando
> MARMADUKE BONTHROP SHELMERDINE, ESQUIRE, Orlando's husband

The Story:

One day in 1588, young Orlando was slashing at the head of a Moor tied to the rafters in his ancestral castle. His forefathers had been of noble rank for centuries and had lived out their lives in action, but Orlando was inclined toward writing. Bored by his play in the attic, he went to his room and wrote for a while on his poetic drama, "Aethelbert: A Tragedy in Five Acts." Tiring of poetry before long, he ran outdoors and up a nearby hill, where he threw himself down under his favorite oak tree and let himself fall into a contemplative revery.

He was still lying there when he heard trumpet calls announcing the arrival of Queen Elizabeth. He hurried to the castle to dress in his finest clothes to serve Her Majesty. He dressed and dashed toward the banquet hall. On the way, he noticed a shabbily dressed man in the servant's quarters, a man who looked like a poet, but he had no time to stop. The man's image was to haunt him the rest of his life. Reaching the banquet hall, he knelt before the queen and offered a bowl of rose water for her to wash her hands after her journey. Elizabeth was so impressed with the boy that she deeded a great house to his father. Two years later, she summoned Orlando to court, where in time he was made her treasurer and steward. One day, however, she saw Orlando kissing a lady of the court and became so angry that Orlando lost her royal favor.

Orlando had many adventures with women. He decided to marry at the time of the Great Frost in 1604. That year, the Thames was frozen so deeply that King James had the court hold carnival on the ice. There Orlando met and fell in love with Sasha, a Russian princess, with whom he skated far down the river. They went aboard a Russian ship to get something for Sasha, who remained below so long that Orlando went to investigate. He found her sitting on the knee of a common seaman. Sasha was able to reconcile with Orlando, however, and the two planned to elope. While waiting for her that night, Orlando began to feel raindrops; the thaw had set in. After waiting two hours, he dashed down to the riverbank, where he saw great pieces of ice crashing down the flooded waters. Far out to sea, he saw the Russian ship sailing for home. Sasha had betrayed him.

For six months, Orlando lived in grief. One morning in June, he failed to get out of bed as usual. He slept for seven days. When he awoke at last, he seemed to have forgotten much of the past. He began to think a great deal about the subject of death, and he enjoyed reading from Sir Thomas Browne's *Urn Burial* (1658). He read, thought, and wrote.

He summoned Mr. Nicholas Greene, a poet, to visit him. Greene talked to him almost incessantly about the poets, about life, and about literature. Orlando was so grateful to Greene that he settled a generous pension on the poet. Greene could not, however, endure the quiet country. One morning, he went back to his beloved London.

Still pondering the meaning of life, Orlando decided to try filling his life with material achievement. First, he set about refurbishing his house. He spent a substantial part of his fortune and traveled into distant countries in his search for precious ornaments. The time was that of the Restoration, when Charles II was king.

One day while Orlando was working on a long poem, "The Oak Tree," he was interrupted by a tall, bold woman, the Archduchess Harriet of Rumania. She had heard of Orlando and wanted to meet him. She stayed so long in his vicinity that Orlando asked King Charles to send him to Constantinople as Ambassador Extraordinary.

His duties in the Turkish capital were formal and arid, and he became extremely bored and began to wander about the city in disguise. While he was abroad, the king of England made him a member of the Order of the Bath and granted him a dukedom by proxy.

The next morning, Orlando could not be awakened; for seven days, he slept soundly. When at last he did rouse himself, he was no longer a man. He had become a beautiful woman. In confusion, Orlando left Constantinople and joined a nomadic tribe. Although Orlando spent many happy days in their camp, she could not bring herself to settle down among them. Selling some of the pearls she had brought with her from Constantinople, she set sail for England.

She noticed a difference in attitudes while on the ship. She who had been a man now received courteous attention from the captain, and she saw that her new role would require new responsibilities and bring new privileges. Back in England, she learned that all of her estates were in chancery, for she was considered legally dead. At her country house, she was received courteously by her servants. Again, she was haunted by the Archduchess Harriet, who now, however, had become a man, the Archduke Harry; at last, however, she managed to rid herself of his attentions.

Orlando went to London to get a taste of society. The reign of Queen Anne was a brilliant one. Conversation flowed freely, and dinners and receptions were entertaining affairs. Joseph Addison, John Dryden, and Alexander Pope were the great names of the age. After a time, however, intercourse with the great wits began to pall, and Orlando went looking for adventure. She began to associate with women of the streets and pubs and found their earthiness a welcome change from the formalities of the drawing room. The company of women without men, however, soon grew dull and repetitive.

At last came the darkness and doubt of the Victorian era. Orlando saw that marriage, under Victoria's influence, was the career toward which most women were striving. Orlando married a man named Marmaduke Bonthrop Shelmerdine, Esquire, who took off immediately on a sea voyage. A wedding ring on her left hand, however, was Orlando's emblem of belonging to accepted society. Orlando's lawsuits had been settled in her favor, but they had been so expensive that she was no longer a rich woman.

She went to London, where she saw her old friend Greene, now a prominent literary critic. He offered to find a publisher for her poem "The Oak Tree." London had become a roaring metropolis. It was October 11, 1928. Orlando began to muse over her long heritage. She recalled Sasha, the Archduchess, Constantinople, the Archduke, and the eighteenth and nineteenth centuries. She saw herself now as the culmination of many influences.

She drove back to her country house and walked out to the great oak tree where, more than three hundred years before, she had watched the arrival of Queen Elizabeth. The stable clock began to strike twelve. She heard a roar in the heavens. Shelmerdine, now a sea captain of renown, was arriving home by plane.

Critical Evaluation:

One of the most prolific and influential modernist writers, Virginia Woolf wrote *Orlando* as a radically different response to the literary genre of biography. Her father, Leslie Stephen, had begun editing the massive *Dictionary of Literary Biography* when Woolf was born; in her diaries, she wrote that his serious immersion in that work had the effect of making her more clever but less stable. In *Orlando,* her response to the previously serious business of writing biographies, Woolf consciously uses exaggeration and fictitious sources to create the half-serious biography of a nonexistent person.

Yet the work is based on the life of a real person. Vita Sackville-West, who came from an aristocratic family and was a writer and intellectual, was also Woolf's friend and lover. Like Woolf, she and her husband, Harold Nicolson, belonged to the Bloomsbury group, that loose association of English artists, writers, and intellectuals in the early twentieth century that included the economist John Maynard Keynes, the artists Roger Fry and Duncan Grant, Vanessa Bell (Woolf's sister) and her husband Clive Bell, and another writer of a new kind of biography, Lytton Strachey, who wrote *Eminent Victorians* (1918). Strachey's book departed from traditional biography by painting subjective and critical portraits of four representatives of the Victorian age, Cardinal Henry Edward Manning, Florence Nightingale, Thomas Arnold, and General Charles George Gordon. Strachey did not, however, cross the line into fiction, as Woolf does in *Orlando.* By doing so, Woolf tacitly acknowledges that any biography is necessarily subjective and biased and that it includes fictional elements although pretending to be factual. Woolf's work, too, pretends to be factual while wildly violating facts of time and gender. By breaking with the traditions of biography, she was also breaking with the tradition that was the basis of her father's work.

Sackville-West had grown up in the ancient castle at Knole, which had belonged to her family for many centuries. Much of Woolf's description of the young Orlando is based on what she knew of Sackville-West's early life. The pseudobiography provides many parallels to her life, but because the character lives for more than three hundred years—Orlando is a sixteen-year-old boy in 1588 during the reign of Queen Elizabeth and a woman of thirty-six in 1928—Woolf at the same time describes the fictional character's entire family heritage. In Orlando's romantic involvement with various women and men, Woolf explores the attitudes and experiences of any two people involved in a physical and spiritual relationship; through Orlando's gender-changing character, Woolf is able to examine how social roles and expectations are based on gender and in turn how these values affect personal attitudes and experiences. Orlando's romantic life, based as it is on the relationship between Woolf and Sackville-West, illustrates a romance that existed in fact yet did not conform to the prescribed gender roles of Victorian society.

The gender switch from male to female is the most important aspect of this new kind of biography. Woolf wrote a fictional work that claims to be an actual biography as part of her analysis of how gender affects a person's true biography. Woolf comments on this by showing how the character is treated differently in social and legal situations depending on his gender. These observations, disguised as a fanciful biography, allow Woolf to deliver a social and political critique in a satirical form. While the work therefore mocks the contemporary seriousness of Victorian English literature and society, it resides firmly in the English literary tradition of satire represented by such writers as Jonathan Swift and Daniel Defoe.

Woolf also wrote serious social and political essays on the inequality of women and men.

Her most influential feminist work, *A Room of One's Own* (1929), was written at the same time she was writing *Orlando* and is therefore often considered to be a companion piece to *Orlando*. Both works examine how gender affects literature, social roles, and financial opportunities, especially for women living in the strongly patriarchal Victorian society. In both works, Woolf elaborates on the set of values accepted by men and women and believed to be universal and genderless. She suggests that the accepted social and political norms are inherently masculine and patriarchal; in her 1938 essay, *Three Guineas*, she elaborates on the different way in which women would handle issues such as education and war.

Woolf's portrait of her friend and lover Vita Sackville-West has been described by Sackville-West's son, Nigel Nicolson, as the longest love letter in English literature. More important, Woolf continues in *Orlando* the rebellion against the standard forms of English literature on which she had embarked in her earlier novels. She challenges female writers to create a different style, a "woman's sentence" that would capture an androgynous picture of the world rather than the prevailing masculine one. *Orlando* is both part of Woolf's long and articulate analysis of gender and a lighthearted argument in favor of androgyny, where a person, especially an artist, can be either "woman-manly" or "man-womanly." The work has been difficult for readers and critics to categorize—as biography or fiction, as social criticism or fantasy—and has therefore perhaps not been as influential as Woolf's other works. The book continues, however, to challenge accepted notions of the role gender plays in literature and society, and it provides a whimsical look at gender inequality in recent English history.

"Critical Evaluation" by Bradley R. Bowers

Bibliography:
Harper, Howard. *Between Language and Silence: The Novels of Virginia Woolf.* Baton Rouge: Louisiana State University Press, 1982. Provides details of the biographical correspondences between the character of Orlando and Vita Sackville-West. Includes citations from Sackville-West's son Nigel Nicolson's *Portrait of a Marriage* and Sackville-West's own *Knole and the Sackvilles.*
Hussey, Mark, and Vara Neverow, eds. *Virginia Woolf: Emerging Perspectives.* New York: Pace University Press, 1994. Contains essays that address *Orlando*, as well as Woolf's sexual identity and her attitude toward gender. Also examines her writing techniques, providing feminist interpretations.
Raitt, Suzanne. *Vita and Virginia: The Work and Friendship of V. Sackville-West and Virginia Woolf.* Oxford, England: Clarendon Press, 1993. An analysis of the relationship, both personal and professional, of Woolf and Sackville-West based on sources such as Woolf's Diaries.
Sackville-West, Vita. *The Letters of Vita Sackville-West to Virginia Woolf.* Edited by Louise De-Salvo and Mitchell A. Leaska. New York: Morrow, 1985. Highlights the sometimes intimate correspondence between two fascinating women whose romance was the basis for *Orlando.*
Woolf, Virginia. *The Diary of Virginia Woolf.* 5 vols. Edited by Anne Olivier Bell. New York: Harcourt Brace Jovanovich, 1977-1984. The diaries provide a wealth of detail and insight into the relationship of Woolf and Sackville-West, especially volumes 2 and 3. Also includes Woolf's discussion of writing *Orlando.*
_____. *A Room of One's Own.* New York: Harcourt Brace, 1929. Written as an essay for students at a women's college, Woolf in this work explores the same social and political aspects of gender roles as she did in *Orlando.* Includes the passage known as "Shakespeare's Sister."

ORLANDO FURIOSO

Type of work: Poetry
Author: Ludovico Ariosto (1474-1533)
Type of plot: Romance
Time of plot: Eighth century
Locale: France, Spain, and Africa
First published: 1516; second revised edition, 1521; third revised edition, 1532

> *Principal characters:*
> CHARLEMAGNE, the king of France
> ORLANDO, his nephew, a paladin of France
> RINALDO, another nephew, a paladin of France
> BRADAMANT, Rinaldo's sister, a maiden knight
> ROGERO, a noble Saracen, in love with Bradamant
> AGRAMANT, the king of Africa
> ANGELICA, the princess of Cathay
> RODOMONT, the king of Algiers
> LEO, the prince of Greece
> ASTOLPHO, an English knight
> ATLANTES, a magician

The Story:

As Charlemagne and his paladins battled against the Saracens, the great press of their enemies scattered the Christians and drove them back toward Paris. Angelica, the damsel whose beauty and deceit had caused so much dissension among her lovers, Christian and Saracen alike, escaped during the confusion and fled into a nearby wood.

As she rode deeper into the forest, her desire being to reach the nearest seaport, from which she could take a ship to return to her own land of Cathay, she saw walking toward her Rinaldo of France, the lover whom she hated. Straightaway she fled from him as fast as she could ride and in her flight came upon Ferrau, a Saracen knight, weary after the battle. While Rinaldo and Ferrau fought for the maid, she rode away. They followed, both upon the Saracen's horse, until they came to a fork in the path, where they parted. A short time later Rinaldo saw his own lost horse, Bayardo, but the animal ran from him in the direction Angelica had taken, the knight in pursuit.

Angelica rode for a day and a night, until at last from weariness she lay down and slept. While she rested, Sacripant, Circassia's king, came riding through the forest. Awaking, Angelica pretended love for him and begged his aid. Before they had traveled far, Rinaldo overtook them. The two knights fought with fury until Sacripant's shield was splintered.

Seeing her champion overthrown, Angelica fled again until she met a white-bearded hermit, a magician, who put a spell upon her, so that she fell down in a deep sleep upon the seashore. There some travelers saw her and carried her by boat to the dread island of Ebuda, where each day a beautiful maiden was sacrificed to a monstrous orc sent by an angry sea god to harry the island. When the day came for Angelica to be the orc's victim, the islanders stripped her of all ornaments except one bracelet before they tied her to a rock on the sands.

The unhappy lovers who would have died for Angelica knew nothing of her plight. Orlando, paladin of France, dreamed an evil dream as he lay behind the walls of Paris after that city had been besieged by the Saracens. Forgetful of his duties to King Charlemagne, he arose and passed at night through enemy lines to begin his search for Angelica, a quest that took him into many lands and that finally drove him mad.

Meanwhile Bradamant, the maiden knight, Rinaldo's sister, rode through the land in search of Rogero, the gallant Saracen whom she loved. During her travels she met Count Pinabel, who told her that Rogero had been imprisoned, along with many other brave knights, in the enchanted castle of old Atlantes, high in the Pyrenees. Pinabel proved a treacherous knight intent on killing Bradamant. Leading her to the entrance of a cave, he pushed her headlong into the deep cavern.

Luckily, a tree broke her fall. Regaining consciousness, she found herself in the wizard Merlin's cave. There Melissa, a seer, foretold a happy life for Bradamant and Rogero and related the history of the noble house they would found. The next day Melissa led Bradamant from the cave after telling the maiden that she could free Rogero with the aid of a magic ring given by Agramant, the king of Africa, to Brunello, his faithful dwarf.

Bradamant found Brunello, as Melissa had directed, and obtained the ring. Armed with the ring, she caused the disenchantment of Rogero and all the other knights whom Atlantes held in his power. Released, the knights tried to capture the flying hippogryph, the old magician's steed. Rogero was successful in the chase, but when he mounted upon its back the creature soared high into the air. Bradamant grieved to see her lover carried skyward from her sight.

The hippogryph flew with Rogero to the realm of Alcina, a sorceress. There he saw Astolpho, a daring English knight, whom Alcina had enchanted. Later he slew Eriphilia, a giantess. Bradamant encountered Melissa again and from her learned that Rogero had yielded to Alcina's evil beauty. Melissa had herself conveyed to that strange land. There she reproved Rogero and gave him a magic ring by which he was able to break Alcina's spell. Mounting the hippogryph, he passed over many lands and came at last to the island of Ebuda, where he saw a beautiful maiden chained to a rock beside the sea.

The damsel was Angelica. She saw him check his flying steed and watched him as he prepared to battle the dreadful orc rising from the waves. Rogero put upon her finger the magic ring to keep her from all harm. Then he blinded the monster with the dazzling brightness of his shield. Leaving Ebuda, they rode away on the flying steed until they came to lesser Britain. By that time Rogero had forgotten Bradamant; he swore he would be Angelica's true knight forever.

Faithless Angelica made herself invisible by means of the magic ring and fled from him. Disconsolate, Rogero prepared to mount the hippogryph but found that the beast had flown back to its master. While he was returning to his own land, he saw Bradamant in the power of a giant. Following that false vision, conjured up by old Atlantes, he was lured to another enchanted palace in which the magician held captive many noble knights and ladies. Atlantes had been Rogero's tutor; he wished to keep the young knight safe from hurt in battle.

At Paris, meanwhile, the Saracens under fierce Rodomont had been defeated by the Christian champions. Rinaldo himself had killed in hand-to-hand combat Dardinello, the king of Zumara. While Charlemagne's knights celebrated their victory, two Saracen youths mourned beside the body of Dardinello, their dead lord. One was Cloridan, a brave hunter; the other was Medoro, his brother. That night, like silent angels of death, they killed many Christian warriors to avenge their king. At daybreak they met Prince Zerbino of Scotland and his men. The Scottish knights killed Cloridan and left Medoro for dead upon the field.

There Angelica, journeying under the protection of the magic ring, found him. Taking him to a herdsman's hut nearby, she nursed him until his wounds had healed, for she who had been wooed by the most famous of knights had fallen in love with that young Saracen of humble birth. When they left the hut to continue their travels, Angelica had only the bracelet left from her perilous experience on Ebuda with which to reward the herdsman. She and Medoro finally reached Cathay, and Angelica made him a king in that far land.

In his search for Angelica, Orlando came one day to the herdsman's hut. When the peasant told him the story of Medoro and Angelica, and displayed the bracelet, Orlando, recognizing the jewel, thought his heart would break. That night, in sudden madness, he saddled his horse and rode away. At last he threw away his armor, tore his clothes, and raged naked through the forest. There was great grief when it was known that Orlando, greatest of knights, lived like the wild beasts he fought with his bare hands.

Once more the Saracens besieged Paris, but as good fortune would have it dissension broke out in the attackers' camp between Rodomont and Mandricardo, a prince of Tartary, over Doralice, the Spanish princess. Doralice chose Mandricardo as her knight, so Rodomont left King Agramant's camp and traveled until he met Isabella, a princess of Galicia, who was mourning her dead lover, Zerbino, whom Mandricardo had slain. While drunk, Rodomont killed Isabella. Grief-stricken, he built a bridge across a river near her tomb and there challenged all passing knights in honor of the dead woman. Twice, however, he was overthrown, once by a naked madman, Orlando, and again by Bradamant.

Bradamant fought with Rodomont on the plea of Flordelice, whose husband, Brandimart, had been imprisoned by the Saracens. Defeated, Rodomont promised to release all his Christian prisoners, including Brandimart. Bradamant took Rodomont's horse, Frontino, which had once been Rogero's property, and asked Flordelice to deliver it to Rogero.

For, in the meantime, Rogero had been freed from the enchantment of Atlantes. His deliverer was Astolpho, whom Melissa had released from Alcina's power. By the blast of a magic horn, Astolpho put Atlantes to flight. Then, mounting the wizard's hippogryph, he flew to the land of Prester John. From there he journeyed to the regions of the moon, where St. John showed him many wonders, including some mysterious vials containing the senses lost by poets, lovers, and philosophers. Among the vials Astolpho saw one containing Orlando's lost wits. With that vial he flew down to Nubia, where, after proper ceremonies, he held the vial to Orlando's nose and the madman's senses returned to his head. Orlando and Astolpho thereafter led a Nubian army against Biserta and sacked that city.

Rogero, returning to the Saracen camp, quarreled with Mandricardo over the Tartar's right to wear the escutcheon of Trojan Hector, and Rogero killed Mandricardo in single combat. As dissension continued in the Saracen camp, Agramant withdrew his army from the walls of Paris. Then it was decided to settle the war by a battle between champions. Rinaldo was named defender of the Christians. Agramant chose Rogero as his bravest knight. In the midst of the combat Agramant broke his oath and attacked Charlemagne's knights. Although he had promised Bradamant that he would accept Christianity after the combat, Rogero, seeing the rout of the Saracens, chose to follow his defeated king. After many adventures, separated from his comrades, he was cast away on a desert isle. There a holy man baptized him, and there he lived while Orlando, Oliver, and Brandimart fought with the Saracen kings—Agramant, Gradasso, Sobrino—and overcame them at Lipadusa. Agramant, Gradasso, and Brandimart were killed in the fight. Old Sobrino survived to turn Christian.

On his return voyage, Orlando stopped at the desert isle and rescued Rogero. Great was the rejoicing when the knights learned that Rogero had been baptized. Rinaldo, who was among the paladins, gladly promised his sister to Rogero. Bradamant's parents, however, wished her to marry Leo, son of the Emperor Constantine of Greece, and to force her to their will they shut her up in a strong castle. Separated from his love, Rogero decided that Leo should die. On his way to challenge his rival, he joined an army of Bulgarians and fought with them against Constantine's troops. When the Greeks fled, he pursued them until he found himself alone in enemy country. Captured, he was imprisoned by Theodora, the emperor's sister, whose son he had slain. When Leo, a courteous knight, heard what had happened, he rescued Rogero and hid him in his own house.

Word came that Bradamant had vowed to wed only a knight who could withstand her in combat. Leo, unaware of Rogero's true name but impressed by the Saracen's valor, asked him to be the prince's champion. Bradamant and Rogero fought, and Rogero was the victor. Then the sad knight went off into the forest alone. Leo found him there, almost dead from grief. When he learned who the strange knight really was, Leo gave up his own claim to Bradamant's hand and returned with Rogero to Charlemagne's court. There Bradamant and Rogero were reunited.

At a feast to celebrate their betrothal Rodomont appeared to accuse Rogero of apostasy, and Rogero slew the haughty Saracen in single combat. So the Christian knights celebrated the wedding of Rogero and Bradamant with all goodwill. There was even greater cause for rejoicing when ambassadors from Bulgaria appeared to announce that the grateful Bulgarians had named gallant Rogero as their king.

Critical Evaluation:

Son of a minor Lombardian military official, Ludovico Ariosto was initially encouraged to study law but was finally allowed to pursue his preference for literature by studying the classics. As the eldest of ten children, he was obliged in his mid-twenties to undertake the management of family affairs upon the death of his father. Shortly thereafter, although it grated against his independent spirit, he accepted an appointment to serve Cardinal Ippolito d'Este, and some years later entered the service of the cardinal's brother Alphonso, the duke of Ferrara, who assigned Ariosto, among other tasks, to a brief (1522-1525) governorship of a lawless mountain province. These experiences, particularly the latter, did much to undermine Ariosto's health, yet he survived until his fifty-ninth year, when he succumbed to tuberculosis.

As for literary output, early translations of Plautus and Terence—from Latin to Italian—were followed by Ariosto's own Italian comedies, modeled after his classical mentors: *La cassaria* (1508), *I suppositi* (1509), *Il negromante* (1520), *La lena* (1529), and the unfinished *I studenti*. In addition to his letters and some rather undistinguished Latin poems—posthumously edited for publication by his illegitimate son Virginio—Ariosto also wrote a number of pungent satires that rank not far behind his monumental *Orlando furioso* for literary merit.

Orlando furioso is Ariosto's complement to Matteo Maria Boiardo's *Orlando innamorato* (1483), but Ariosto's version differs greatly from Boiardo's. In its first edition (1516), *Orlando furioso* contains forty cantos; the final edition (1532) contains forty-six. In between those editions, much polishing, revising, and improving took place. Ariosto's artistic instincts would not rest until he was satisfied with the nuance of each word, the sound of each rhyme, the beat of each metrical foot, and the synthesis of all into exactly the right action, character, or setting which he was striving to describe. Ariosto's dedication to artistic perfection was coupled with a certain independence of mind which enabled the poet to portray knightly adventures from a more realistic point of view than Boiardo's fabular tale did. It is these qualities that make *Orlando furioso* superior to *Orlando innamorato*.

One of Ariosto's motives in composing his epic was to glorify the noble house of Este, rulers of Ferrara and Modena, under whose patronage Ariosto served. Hence, the main plot line of *Orlando furioso* deals with the troubled romance between the pagan Saracen Rogero and the Christian French Bradamant. When at last they marry—having overcome many obstacles, not the least of which were Rogero's several infidelities—they found, so the story goes, the ancestral line of the Este family. One intriguing aspect of the Rogero-Bradamant union is its implication of marriage between pagan and Christian, despite the merely ceremonial ritual of Rogero's baptism and his killing of the Saracen Rodomont. Even more interesting is Bradamant's skill, resourcefulness, and courage as a warrior. She is no maiden in distress but a strong-minded and strong-armed knight who takes the initiative in finding her beloved Rogero, who takes part in wars, who defeats men in single combat, and who defiantly declares she will marry none but the man who can match her or best her in battle. Stereotypes crumble in the face of Rogero and Bradamant, singly or united. Stereotypes of epic behavior and stereotypes of real behavior alike cannot stand up under Ariosto's skillful characterization, for the poet—indeed, the artist—convinces us of the plausibility of Rogero's and Bradamant's actions. In doing so, Ariosto demonstrates his consummate facility for imaginatively transforming incredible magic into verisimilitude.

Orlando's story, although his name lends itself to the title of the poem, is secondary. To be sure, Orlando's quest for Angelica, begun in Boiardo's work, provides Ariosto's point of departure. The thrust of Ariosto's title, however, is that Orlando—under the dual stress of searching for Angelica and fulfilling his knightly obligations—temporarily parts company with his rational faculties. Orlando is thus *furioso*. In the story, Orlando's psychiatric problems are of far less import than the empirical and pragmatic problems of, say, Agramant and Charlemagne or of Rogero and Bradamant. Thus, Orlando's anguish over Angelica's liaison with Medoro and Orlando's subsequent shedding of human appurtenances is merely a personal tragedy without cosmic or global significance. For all of the emphasis that Renaissance thinkers placed on the individual, society was still paramount; not until the Romantic Age did thoughtful people consider the plight of the individual seriously. Consequently, Orlando and his aberrations are simply not matters of overriding importance, and Ariosto does not give them undue attention.

Ariosto was thoroughly a product of the Renaissance and reflected its values and priorities in his writings. His calculated demotion of Orlando's role in the epic signals another aspect of Renaissance attitudes. This aspect pertains to the Renaissance view of history, a view that differs considerably from the more modern ones. Ariosto, like virtually all other Renaissance writers, felt no compelling obligation to strict historical accuracy. For example, Ariosto depicts the Saracen Rodomont as killing Isabella in a fit of drunkenness. Saracens, as devout Muslims, were and are prohibited by the Koran from consuming any alcoholic beverage. A Saracen Muslim such as Rodomont, battling Christian crusaders, would honor the proscriptions of the religion that he was defending. This proscription and its implications are disregarded by Ariosto as a Christian, Western European, Renaissance poet. This is to say nothing of the poem's many fanciful elements. For example, Ariosto portrays, only half-skeptically, events influenced by Merlin, the seer Melissa, a magic ring, a hippogryph, the giantess Eriphilia, the conjurer Atlantes, and various supernaturally endowed herdsmen and hermits, among others. Although an apparent contradiction to the modern reader, this combination of historical factuality and a credulity about magic marks both Ariosto and *Orlando furioso* as genuine products of the Renaissance and, in turn, a key to the study of Renaissance culture.

"Critical Evaluation" by Joanne G. Kashdan

Bibliography:
Brand, C. P. *Ludovico Ariosto: A Preface to the "Orlando Furioso."* Edinburgh, Scotland: Edinburgh University Press, 1974. A general introduction to Ariosto and his work. Includes

a biography; a survey of literary forms that influenced *Orlando furioso*; a discussion of the poem's major themes, a review of important criticism, and a bibliography.

Craig, D. H. *Sir John Harington*. Boston: Twayne, 1985. Harington wrote the first important English translation of *Orlando furioso* in the 1580's. This critical study of Harington's work, focusing especially on canto 10, sheds light on the themes and images of Ariosto's poem. Also examines Harington's illustrations, critical comments, and notes.

Giamatti, A. Bartlett. *The Earthly Paradise and the Renaissance Epic*. Princeton, N.J.: Princeton University Press, 1966. A scholarly but lively examination of images of a blessed landscape in European literature. Illuminating chapter on *Orlando furioso* as an early Renaissance epic. Annotated bibliography.

Griffin, Robert. *Ludovico Ariosto*. New York: Twayne, 1974. Offers accessible criticism and analysis of Ariosto's major and minor work, as well as biographical and historical material to place the work in context. Includes a chronology and suggestions for further reading. A good source for the student.

Pavlock, Barbara. "Ariosto and Roman Epic Values." In *Eros, Imitation, and the Epic Tradition*. Ithaca, N.Y.: Cornell University Press, 1990. Traces the forces of love and piety as they act on the work's two protagonists. Also takes up the centuries-old question of whether *Orlando furioso* is an epic or a romance, and finds the influence of both.

ORLANDO INNAMORATO

Type of work: Poetry
Author: Matteo Maria Boiardo (c. 1441-1494)
Type of plot: Romance
Time of plot: Eighth century
Locale: France, India, and Africa
First transcribed: 1483-1495 (English translation, 1823)

> *Principal characters:*
> CHARLEMAGNE, the king of France
> ORLANDO, his nephew, a paladin of France
> ANGELICA, a princess of Cathay
> UBERTO, in reality Argalia, her brother
> RINALDO, a paladin of France
> MALAGIGI, a magician, Rinaldo's brother
> BRADAMANT, a maiden knight, Rinaldo's sister
> ROGERO, a noble young Saracen
> FERRAÙ, a Spanish knight
> ASTOLPHO, an English knight
> AGRAMANT, the king of Africa

The Story:

King Charlemagne summoned all his paladins and vassal barons to a court plenary meeting in Paris, an occasion to be celebrated with magnificent tournaments and great feasts. Christians and Saracens, friend and foe alike, were invited to take part. To the banquet on the opening night of this fete came an unknown knight, a beautiful damsel, and four giants serving as bodyguards. The knight, who called himself Uberto, offered his lovely sister Angelica as the prize to any man who could defeat him in the jousts to be held the next day. He, in turn, would claim as his prisoner any knight whom he unhorsed. When he saw the beautiful damsel, Orlando, the greatest paladin of Charlemagne's court, immediately fell in love. Only respect for the monarch kept Ferraù, a Spanish knight, from snatching her up and carrying her away in his arms. Even the great Charlemagne was affected by her charms. The only person who remained unmoved was Malagigi, a magician, who sensed in the visitors some purpose quite different from that which they claimed.

After the damsel and her brother had retired, Malagigi summoned a fiend who informed him that Uberto was in reality Argalia, the son of King Galaphron of Cathay, who had been sent with his sister to demoralize the Christian knights. With Angelica as his lure, protected by a magic ring that would ward off all enchantment or make him invisible if placed in the mouth, Argalia planned to overcome the Christian knights and dispatch them as prisoners to distant Cathay. Armed with this knowledge, Malagigi mounted a magic steed and flew through the air to the stair of Merlin, where Argalia and Angelica were asleep. There he cast a spell over the watchers that caused them to fall into a deep slumber. The magician approached Angelica with the intention of killing her, for she was as false as she was fair, but he himself became enslaved by her beauty and clasped her in his arms. Angelica awoke with a shriek. Argalia, aroused by her scream, ran to her assistance and together they overcame Malagigi. Angelica summoned fiends and ordered them to carry the magician to Cathay. There King Galaphron confined him in a dungeon beneath the sea.

Dissension had meanwhile broken out among the knights of Charlemagne's court, for all wished to try their skill against the strange knight in order to win such an enchanting prize. At length lots were cast to determine the order of combat. The first fell to Astolpho, the second to Ferraù, and the third to the giant Grandonio. Next in order came Berlinghier, Otho, and Charlemagne himself. Orlando, much to his indignation, was thirty-seventh on the list.

At the running of the first course, Astolpho was jolted from his saddle. Ferraù, who followed, was also unhorsed, but, contrary to the rules of the joust, he leaped to his feet and continued the fight on foot. After he had slain the giants who attempted to restrain him, he bore himself so fiercely that Argalia, even though he was protected by enchanted armor, finally called a brief truce. When the combat was renewed, Angelica suddenly disappeared, followed by Argalia. Ferraù pursued them into Arden forest but found no trace of the knight or the damsel. Rinaldo and Orlando also set off in pursuit of the fleeing maiden. Meanwhile, Astolpho had taken up the magic spear that Argalia had left behind; with this weapon he performed great feats of valor until, carried away by the excitement of the combat, he felled friends and foes alike. Finally, Charlemagne commanded that he be subdued.

Rinaldo, Ferraù, and Orlando wandered through the forest in search of Angelica. Rinaldo had a rather ironic success in his quest. After drinking from a fountain that Merlin had created years before to relieve the love pangs of Tristram and Isolde, the knight's love for Angelica turned to hate. A short time later he fell asleep beside a nearby stream. Angelica, coming upon the stream, drank from its magic waters and immediately became enamored of the sleeping knight. When she pulled a handful of flowers and threw them over him, Rinaldo awoke and, in spite of her piteous pleas and avowals of love, fled from her in loathing.

Ferraù, riding through the forest, came upon Argalia asleep beneath a tree. The two engaged in fierce combat. Ferraù, finding a chink in his enemy's magic armor, struck him to the heart. Dying, Argalia asked that his body and armor be thrown into the stream. Ferraù agreed, keeping only the helmet of his adversary. As he rode on through the wood, he came upon Angelica and Orlando, who, having chanced upon the sleeping maiden, had thrown himself down by her side. Supposing that Orlando was her protector, Ferraù awoke the sleeping man with taunts and insults. Orlando, starting up, revealed himself, but Ferraù, although surprised, stood his ground. A duel followed, in the midst of which Angelica again fled. The combat of champions ended only when a strange maiden, Flordespina, appeared with news that Gradasso, the king of Sericane, was ravaging the Spanish dominions. Ferraù, torn between love and duty, departed for Spain with Flordespina.

Gradasso, a mighty monarch who coveted whatever he did not possess, had invaded Europe in order to obtain possession of Durindana, the famed sword of Orlando, and Bayardo, Rinaldo's horse. Charlemagne, assembling all the knights summoned to the tournament, dispatched a mighty army under Rinaldo to aid King Marsilius against the pagans. During a battle fought near Barcelona, Gradasso and Rinaldo engaged in single combat. Neither prevailing, they agreed to fight again on the following day; if Rinaldo were the victor, Gradasso would release all the prisoners he had taken, but if the victory went to Gradasso, Rinaldo would surrender Bayardo to the king.

Angelica had meanwhile returned to Cathay. Deciding to use Malagigi as the mediator in her pursuit of the disdainful Rinaldo, she released the magician and promised to give him his complete liberty if he would bring Rinaldo to her. Deceived by his own brother, Rinaldo was decoyed away from his encounter with Gradasso. His troops, left leaderless, returned home, whereupon Gradasso invaded France and took Charlemagne and his knights prisoner. When Charlemagne was offered his liberty and the restoration of his lands if he surrendered Durindana and Bayardo to the conqueror, he agreed. He sent to Paris for the horse, which had been returned from Spain, but Astolpho refused to give up the animal and challenged Gradasso to a duel. Using the enchanted lance, Astolpho overthrew the king. Gradasso, true to his promise, released his prisoners and returned to Sericane.

Orlando, continuing his wanderings, learned that Agrican, the king of Tartary, had sought the hand of Angelica in marriage. Angered by the girl's refusal, Agrican besieged Albracca, the capital of Cathay; he had sworn to raze the city, if need be, to possess the princess. Because news of the war had spread far and wide, Orlando, Astolpho, and Rinaldo journeyed by different routes to the kingdom of Cathay. There Orlando and Astolpho joined the side of the defenders, while Rinaldo, still filled with loathing for Angelica, joined the forces of King Agrican. Orlando, riding to the defense of King Galaphron, met Agrican in single combat and slew the Tartar king. Later Orlando and Rinaldo engaged in furious combat. When night fell, each withdrew in expectation of resuming the struggle on the following day; that night, however, lovesick Angelica, scheming to save Rinaldo from his kinsman's fury, sent Orlando on a quest to destroy the garden of Falerina in the kingdom of Orgagna.

Agramant, the young king of Africa, prepared to lay siege to Paris in revenge for the killing of his father. One of his advisers prophesied failure in his efforts, however, unless he could obtain the help of Rogero, a gallant young knight held prisoner by the magician Atlantes on the mountain of Carena.

After Orlando had set out on his quest, Rinaldo and several of his companions left the camp near Albracca and started in pursuit because Rinaldo was still eager to settle the quarrel. On the way, Rinaldo encountered a ruffian with whom he fought until both plunged into a lake and disappeared beneath the waves. While these events were taking place, the messenger of Agramant returned with word that he had been unable to find Rogero. Irked by the delay, Rodomont, a vassal king, decided to embark with his forces on the invasion of France. Agramant was told that the garden of Atlantes was invisible and that the young knight could be freed only by possession of Angelica's magic ring. A dwarf, Brunello, offered to obtain the prize for his master.

Orlando, having accomplished his quest, arrived at the lake where Rinaldo had been carried under the waves. Seeing his kinsman's arms stacked by the shore, Orlando determined to avenge his former companion in arms. He and the guardian of the place fought a mighty battle in which Orlando was victorious. From the enchanted garden beneath the lake he freed all the prisoners held there by Morgana, the sorceress. All the knights except Orlando then returned to France to aid in the defense of Christendom. Orlando, now reconciled with Rinaldo, turned back toward Albracca. On the way he encountered Brunello, who had in the meantime stolen Angelica's magic ring.

In possession of the ring to dispel the mists of enchantment, Agramant came at last to the castle where Atlantes held Rogero. At Brunello's suggestion, the king announced a tournament. Joining in the tourney, Rogero was wounded but revenged himself on his assailant. When his wounds were miraculously healed and he returned to the tourney, Agramant recognized him and made him his knight. Rinaldo and Rodomont had meanwhile engaged in single combat in a great battle between Christians and pagans. When they were separated during the fighting, Rinaldo, in pursuit of his enemy, rode once more into the forest of Arden.

On his arrival in Albracca after his perilous quest, Angelica prevailed upon Orlando to help her in her escape from the beleaguered city and to escort her into France. Orlando did not suspect that her real purpose was the pursuit of Rinaldo, and he immediately agreed. After many adventures they embarked for France and at length arrived, hot and tired, in the forest of Arden. There, Angelica drank from the waters of hate; at the same time Rinaldo drank from the waters of love. When they met a short time later, the circumstances of their love had become reversed. Angelica now fled from Rinaldo in disgust, while he pursued her with passionate avowals. Again Orlando and Rinaldo fought, and in the midst of their struggle, Angelica fled. When she took refuge in Charlemagne's camp, the king, hearing her story, gave her into the keeping of Namus, the duke of Bavaria.

Agramant, joined by Gradasso, began the siege of Paris. In the ensuing battle, Bradamant, a maiden warrior and the sister of Rinaldo, became enamored of Rogero and went over to the side of the Saracens. When she removed her helmet and allowed her hair to fall down, Rogero fell in love with the valiant maiden. They were attacked from ambush and Bradamant, unhelmeted, was wounded slightly in the head, but Rogero avenged her hurt by routing their enemies. When Rogero pursued the enemy, he and Bradamant were separated, but she would later become his wife and the mother of the illustrious line of Este.

Critical Evaluation:

Matteo Maria Boiardo's *Orlando innamorato* (Orlando in love) is a romance epic whose first part was published in the early 1480's during the Italian Renaissance. The humanist poet Ludovico Ariosto (1474-1533) composed a sequel, *Orlando furioso* (Orlando in a Frenzy), which reinforced Boiardo's fame and, together with *Orlando innamorato*, influenced the composition of the famous English epic *The Faerie Queene* (1590/1596) by Edmund Spenser. Other later poets also drew on *Orlando innamorato*, among them Miguel de Cervantes in his *Don Quixote de la Mancha*, and John Milton in his *Paradise Lost* (1667) and *Paradise Regained* (1671).

Boiardo lived in Ferrara, a minor but influential center of Renaissance humanistic culture under the ruling Este family. Because the Ferrarese regional dialect of the poem's verse limited the appeal of the original, the work was popularized through a version by Francesco Berni (c. 1497-1535), who recast it in the Tuscan dialect. The Renaissance's cultural center, Florence, was in the region of Tuscany, and this dialect became the dominant form of the Italian language.

Orlando innamorato consists of sixty-nine cantos or chapters, grouped in three books, or divisions. Even though unfinished when Boiardo died in 1494, the work contains more than four thousand ottava rima stanzas, groups of eight lines of heroic verse with a rhyme scheme of *abababcc*. The epic relates a series of military adventures motivated principally by love, which provides the unifying element to the work. It is Orlando's infatuation for Angelica that inspires his actions, and the epic revolves around his subsequent pursuit of his love from France to distant India and back. The work's intriguing quality is found not so much in its combination of romance and militaristic glory as it is in the opposition of the values of those pursuits.

Love inspires the warrior to great deeds, motivating him to set off in quest of a lady or even causing him to risk death in defending a lady in his charge. Yet love is also capable of urging on a knight excessively and without reason, leading him to his ultimate destruction. Individual episodes in *Orlando innamorato* hold specific allegorical lessons that contribute to the underlying moral lesson of the entire epic.

The multiple interpretations that are possible for the epic and its scenes have led to doubt as to Boiardo's purpose. The delightful tales of *Orlando innamorato* were, to be sure, intended as entertainment for the Ferrarese courtly audience, and they continued to be enjoyed since then. The work also had didactic aims, however, for Boiardo incorporated a moral vision in the work.

The goal of Renaissance humanistic education was to mold character, that is, to instruct on how to act virtuously in a way that would advance the good of society as a whole. The stories of Orlando, Rinaldo, Angelica, and the other characters all contribute to such ethical instruction for Boiardo's audience. Boiardo mocks Orlando, for example, for his inability to perceive the deeper meanings in fables that he reads, yet Boiardo implies that Orlando has the capacity to become enlightened, or educated. *Orlando innamorato* offers insight into human character and into human motivation, and it depicts natural hierarchy of emotions, actions, and subsequent consequences, both fortunate and punitive.

Boiardo drew on three fundamental intellectual heritages. The structure and setting of his epic reflect the early twelfth century French epic *Song of Roland*, an account of the eighth century struggle by the Christian emperor Charlemagne against the incursion of Muslim forces from the Iberian peninsula into the heart of Europe. That epic concerns the exploits of Charlemagne's ideal knight, Count Roland (Orlando), who fought for the honor of his feudal lord and the Christian god in the Battle of Roncesvalles in 778.

Boiardo also incorporated the medieval legends of the English king Arthur and the chivalric deeds of his knights of the Round Table, popularized by the northern French writer Chrétien de Troyes. Specific adventures are included in *Orlando innamorato*, among them the appearance of Uberto and his challenge to the other knights in the beginning of the epic. Even more important was the moral ideal underlying the legendary world of Arthur.

Finally, classical Roman authors inspired elements of *Orlando innamorato*. The influence of Ovid's *Metamorphoses* (1-8 C.E.), in particular, added the spirit of fantasy and a fairy-tale element to the epic; Ovid, too, had in his other poetic works asserted the ideal that romantic love conquers all misfortunes. Boiardo composed his epic in the cultural context of Renaissance humanism, which emphasized classical literature as its basis of learning.

An important aspect of *Orlando innamorato* is the way in which Boiardo interlaces his episodes, many of which occur simultaneously. The narrative often jumps from one adventure to an unrelated one, creating an intricate pattern that does not unfold in a sequential manner. Also interwoven into this structure are features of Boiardo's own historical context, for he makes many references to Renaissance court life and specific individuals and events. Moreover, he uses the epic's eighth century narrative to herald the future glory of the Este family in the fifteenth century. The poem concludes with a description of the turmoil that the invasion of the French king Charles VIII had brought upon Italy shortly before Boiardo's death.

"Critical Evaluation" by Alan Cottrell

Bibliography:
Boiardo, Matteo Maria. *Orlando innamorato*. Translated by Charles Stanley Ross. Berkeley: University of California Press, 1989. The first complete modern English verse translation, with an excellent thirty-page introduction by the translator. Also contains the Italian text for a comparison of the intricacies of the two languages.
Cavallo, Jo Ann. *Boiardo's "Orlando innamorato": An Ethics of Desire*. Madison, N.J.: Fairleigh Dickinson University Press, 1993. Analyzes the epic in terms of Ferrara's status as a center of humanistic education. Argues that the work forms a coherent argument for classical ethics based on the traditionally moralistic interpretation of ancient texts.
Di Tommaso, Andrea. *Structure and Ideology in Boiardo's "Orlando innamorato."* Chapel Hill: University of North Carolina Press, 1972. A brief but perceptive work. Regards *Orlando innamorato* as an independent work rather than as an inspiration for Ludovico

Ariosto's sequel, *Orlando furioso*. Reveals how courtly ideology emerges in contrast to the epic's warrior features.

Durling, R. M. *The Figure of the Poet in Renaissance Epic*. Cambridge, Mass.: Harvard University Press, 1965. In chapter 4, Durling analyzes the poet's function as narrator in *Orlando furioso*, tracing this authorial role from other major epics, including *Orlando innamorato*.

Marinelli, Peter V. *Ariosto and Boiardo: The Origins of "Orlando Furioso."* Columbia: University of Missouri Press, 1987. Analyzes *Orlando innamorato* as a source of literary capital that Ariosto consciously drew upon while he manipulated and re-created it in his *Orlando furioso*.

ORLEY FARM

Type of work: Novel
Author: Anthony Trollope (1815-1882)
Type of plot: Domestic realism
Time of plot: Mid-nineteenth century
Locale: England
First published: serial, 1861-1862; book, 1862

Principal characters:

> LADY MASON, the mistress of Orley Farm
> LUCIUS MASON, her son
> JOSEPH MASON, ESQ., the owner of Groby Park
> SIR PEREGRINE ORME, a gallant old gentleman
> MRS. ORME, his daughter-in-law
> PEREGRINE ORME, his grandson
> SAMUEL DOCKWRATH, a rascally attorney
> MIRIAM, his wife
> MR. FURNIVAL, a London attorney
> SOPHIA, his daughter, loved by Lucius
> MR. CHAFFANBRASS, a celebrated lawyer
> FELIX GRAHAM, a penniless young barrister
> MADELINE STAVELY, Graham's beloved

The Story:

Sir Joseph Mason was nearing seventy years of age when he married a second wife forty-five years his junior. Having been in turn merchant, alderman, mayor, and knight, he had by that time amassed a large fortune, out of which he purchased Groby Park, a landed estate in Yorkshire. He turned over this property to the son of his first marriage, Joseph Mason, Esq., who under his father's generous provision was able to lead the life of a country gentleman with as much magnificence as his mean, grasping nature would allow. Sir Joseph himself made his home at Orley Farm, a country residence not far from London. Joseph Mason had always been assured that the farm would go to him, as head of the family, at his father's death.

The baronet's second marriage was little more than an old man's attempt to find companionship and comfort in his declining years, and young Lady Mason, a quiet, sensible, clever woman, cheerfully accepted it as such. One son, Lucius, was born to them. Then Sir Joseph died suddenly; when the time came to read his will, it was discovered that in an attached codicil he had bequeathed Orley Farm to his infant son. Joseph Mason felt that he had been deprived of property rightfully his, and he contested the codicil.

The Orley Farm Case, as it was called, had many complications. The will had been drawn up by Jonathan Usbech, Sir Joseph's attorney, but it, like the codicil, was in Lady Mason's handwriting, since old Usbech had suffered from a gouty hand at the time. It had been witnessed by John Kennerby, Sir Joseph's clerk, and by Bridget Bolster, a housemaid. At the trial, both swore that they had been called to their master's bedside and there, in the presence of Usbech and Lady Mason, had signed a document that all assumed had been the codicil. Lady Mason readily admitted that while she had asked nothing for herself, she had wanted much for her child. She also contested that before Usbech and Mr. Furnival, a barrister, she had often urged her husband to leave Orley Farm to little Lucius. Old Usbech having died in the meantime, she was unable to have her statement confirmed by him, but Mr. Furnival testified to the truth of her assertion.

Joseph Mason lost his case. The will and codicil were upheld, and Lady Mason and her son continued to live at Orley Farm and to enjoy its yearly income of eight hundred pounds. Joseph Mason retired to sulk at Groby Park. Miriam Usbech, old Jonathan's daughter, also benefited under the terms of the codicil to the extent of two thousand pounds, an inheritance she lost when she entrusted it to her husband, Samuel Dockwrath, a shady young attorney from the neighboring town of Hamworth. Relations between Usbech's daughter and the mistress of Orley Farm were always friendly. Thanks to Lady Mason, Dockwrath held two outlying fields on the estate at low rental.

Sir Peregrine Orme of The Cleeve was among the neighbors who had stood by Lady Mason during the trial. Other members of his household were his daughter-in-law, Mrs. Orme, who was Lady Mason's best friend, and his grandson, namesake, and heir. Young Peregrine Orme and Lucius Mason were the same age but had little else in common. Peregrine had been educated at Harrow and Oxford and was heir to a great estate. A well-meaning but somewhat wild young man, Peregrine's chief interests were fox hunting and rat-baiting. He was also in love with Madeline Stavely, the lovely daughter of Judge Stavely of Noningsby. After a term at a German university, Lucius Mason returned to Orley Farm with the plan of putting into practice methods of scientific farming he had learned abroad.

One of his first acts was to serve notice of his intention to repossess the fields leased to Dockwrath. An unpleasant interview between Lady Mason and the angry attorney followed. Concerned over Dockwrath's vague threats, she went to Sir Peregrine for advice, as she had gone on many occasions during the past twenty years. Sir Peregrine snorted with disgust over Lucius' agricultural theories and announced that he would bring the young man to his senses. Lucius went to dine at The Cleeve but refused to give up his plans. Sir Peregrine decided that the earnest young man was as conceited as he was stubborn.

In the meantime, Dockwrath had been busy. He went through his father-in-law's papers and learned that on the date carried by the codicil, Sir Joseph had signed a deed of separation dissolving a business partnership between him and a man named Mr. Martock. Either two documents had been signed on that day, a possibility that the evidence at the trial made unlikely, or the codicil was a forgery. Armed with this information, Dockwrath went to Groby Park to confer with Joseph Mason. The upshot of that conference was Mason's decision to reopen the Orley Farm Case.

Dockwrath hoped to advance himself in his profession and begged for an opportunity to handle the case, but the squire, aware of Dockwrath's reputation, told him to take his information to the firm of Round and Crook, reputable London lawyers who would be above suspicion. Mason, however, did promise that Dockwrath would be rewarded if Lady Mason were convicted and Orley Farm returned to its rightful owner. The Hamworth lawyer then went to London and offered his services to Round and Crook. They were willing to use him, but only to collect information that might prove useful.

When Miriam Dockwrath carried an account of her husband's activities to Orley Farm, Lady Mason appealed to Sir Peregrine, her good friend, and Mr. Furnival, her attorney, for advice and help. With the passing of time, Mr. Furnival had changed from a hardworking young barrister into a fashionable attorney with a weakness for port wine and lovely women. Lady Mason was still attractive, and so he comforted her more as a woman than as a client, assuring her that the Orley Farm Case, unappealed at the time, was not likely to be reviewed. Chivalrous Sir Peregrine was stirred to great indignation by what he considered the dastardly conduct of Joseph Mason, whom he had always disliked. Hearing the news, Lucius was equally indignant and told his mother to leave the matter in his hands. Sir Peregrine and Mr. Furnival had difficulty in restraining him from acting rashly.

The outcome of the suit was more important to Lucius than he realized. He was in love with Sophia Furnival, daughter of his mother's attorney, but the prudent young woman intended to choose her husband with discretion. Another of her suitors was Adolphus Stavely, son of the distinguished jurist. She could afford to wait for the present time.

Meanwhile, Peregrine's wooing of Madeline Stavely had fared badly, for Madeline had no interest in anyone except Felix Graham, a penniless young barrister. The judge, convinced that Graham would make his way in the world, silently approved his daughter's choice, but her mother, eager to see her daughter mistress of The Cleeve, grew impatient with her husband because of his refusal to speak up for young Orme.

There was some delay in determining grounds for a suit. The will had been upheld years before, so it was felt that a charge of forgery was impossible after such a long time. Finally, Round and Crook decided to prosecute for perjury; they charged that in the previous trial Lady Mason had sworn falsely to the execution of the will. When word came that Lady Mason would have to stand trial, Mrs. Orme invited her to stay at The Cleeve. Dictated by Sir Peregrine, this invitation was intended to show to the county the Ormes's confidence in their neighbor's innocence. Sir Peregrine's chivalry, however, did not stop there. At last, he offered Lady Mason the protection of his name as well as his house, and she, almost overwhelmed by the prospect of the coming trial, promised to marry him.

Lucius and Peregrine were both opposed to the marriage, although Sir Peregrine reconciled his grandson in part by encouraging the young man in his own unsuccessful suit. Mr. Furnival became less gallant. Lady Mason's conscience, however, would not allow her to accept Sir Peregrine's offer. One night she went to him and confessed that she had forged the codicil in a desperate effort to keep the property for her son. Sir Peregrine was shocked by the news but was still determined to stand by her during the trial.

Mr. Furnival was shrewd. When he heard that his client was not to marry Sir Peregrine after all, he was convinced that the whole story had not been told. Suspecting her possible guilt, he hired the famous Mr. Chaffanbrass and his associate, Mr. Solomon Aram, noted criminal lawyers, to defend Lady Mason at the trial. Felix Graham was to act as a junior counsel for the defense.

The trial lasted for two days and part of another. The heckling attorneys so confused John Kennerby that his testimony was worthless. Bridget Bolster insisted, however, that she had signed only one document on that particular day. Even Mr. Chaffanbrass was unable to break down her story; the most damaging admission she made was that she liked an occasional glass of liquor. Dockwrath, however, was completely discredited, especially after Mr. Chaffanbrass forced him to admit his revengeful motives and Joseph Mason's promise to reward him for his services. At the end of the second day, Lady Mason confessed her guilt to her son. He was not in court with her the next morning when the verdict was announced. Lady Mason was acquitted.

The jury's verdict was legal but not moral. A few days later, Mr. Furnival notified Joseph Mason that Lucius was transferring Orley Farm to his half brother. Lucius was returning to Germany with his mother; later, he hoped to become a farmer in Australia. Sir Peregrine went to see Lady Mason in London. Their farewell was gentle and sad on his part, final on hers.

Dockwrath sued Joseph Mason to collect payment for his help and was completely ruined in the suit. Sophia Furnival decided that she could never be anything but a sister to Lucius. Madeline Stavely married her penniless barrister and lived more happily than her mother thought she deserved. Young Peregrine Orme eased his broken heart by shooting lions and elephants in central Africa.

Critical Evaluation:

Anthony Trollope considered his lengthy novel *Orley Farm* to be one of his most ambitious undertakings. *Orley Farm* incorporates more central characters than Trollope's previous novels, individually, do, and has a more complicated plot and deeper insights into social and legal hierarchies. It was met with praise from novelist George Eliot and critic G. H. Lewes. In its day *Orley Farm* was a popular work, one that Trollope considered possibly his finest.

Orley Farm depends largely upon irony: Often, characters are not as they seem to be, and the plot frequently takes an unexpected turn of events. For example, Lady Mason seems to be a model of fragile innocence, and is found innocent of the charges brought against her by Samuel Dockwrath and Sir Joseph Mason, but she is unquestionably guilty of the crime for which she is accused and displays incredible strength, rather than ladylike fragility, in the midst of the adversities that she has brought upon herself. Twenty years before, she forged a codicil to her late husband's will in order to provide for their son, Lucius. Although she has committed a crime, Trollope would have the reader consider Lady Mason to be anything but a criminal, because she forged the codicil only out of love for her son. Furthermore, although she is guilty and is acknowledged as being so by most of those attorneys involved in her trial, she is treated far more sympathetically than her accusers, Dockwrath and Joseph Mason. Although they are clearly in the right concerning the charges they bring against Lady Mason, they prove to be two of the most contemptible characters of the novel. In a final ironic twist, after she is found innocent, Lady Mason agrees with Lucius' decision that she should follow her conscience and turns Orley Farm over to its rightful heir, Joseph Mason.

The fact that the courts ultimately find for Lady Mason is not merely an ironic defense of the woman's character; it is also an indictment of the corruption and inefficacy of the English legal system. Trollope's purpose in writing *Orley Farm* goes beyond the telling of a story of guilt and innocence. The ultimate ironic point of the novel is that the execution of justice in the English courts of the early-to-middle nineteenth century bore little relationship to the Christian world-view upon which the laws of those courts are supposedly based.

Trollope's belief in the working out of divine justice, and in the importance of the related virtues of repentance and forgiveness, is made clear throughout the novel. For example, Mrs. Orme quickly forgives Lady Mason after she learns of her sin. Mrs. Orme becomes Lady Mason's best friend during the trial and repeatedly encourages Lady Mason to repent and ask forgiveness from God. Other examples of forgiveness are provided by Mrs. Furnival, who forgives Mrs. Mason for becoming too familiar with her husband, and Sir Peregrine, who at one point asks Lady Mason to marry him and is devastated when he learns that Lady Mason is guilty of the crime of which she is accused. When the trial is over, Sir Peregrine forgives Lady Mason and makes a statement regarding the adversities Lady Mason has had to suffer that the narrator reinforces: "No lesson is truer than that which teaches us to believe that God does temper the wind to the shorn lamb." In other words, the trials that Lady Mason has had to endure have been allowed by God for the spiritual strengthening of her character and have brought her to a point at which she asks God's forgiveness and forgives those who took her to court. At this point, and even earlier in the novel, the narrator asks the reader to sympathize with—and therefore forgive—Lady Mason, comparing her to the biblical character of Rebekah, the wife of Isaac, who deceived her husband—as did Lady Mason—to secure a blessing for her son Jacob.

Trollope emphasizes the importance of forgiveness again in the final scene of the novel, as Felix Graham and young Peregrine Orme nearly part from each other as enemies, because Graham has won the heart of Madeline Stavely, whom Peregrine also loves. In a movement away from the animosity that has characterized many of the relationships in the novel, Peregrine overcomes his bitterness toward Graham, acknowledges his wrong, and shakes his friend's hand. Then the two young men separate on a note of reconciliation.

Trollope's belief in a system of justice, in a code of ethics that transcends the dealings of the English court, is made clear through the characters of Felix Graham and Madeline Stavely. An attorney, Felix conducts his career in line with the Ten Commandments of the Bible. The point is made early in the novel that Felix Graham, in his determination to be guided by his conscience, is not following the standards of most attorneys and therefore, monetarily at least, will not be rewarded in this world. For conducting himself during Lady Mason's trial according to the dictates of his conscience and of the Bible, for sympathizing with witnesses who, attempting simply to tell the truth about the Orley case, have their characters assassinated, Felix Graham earns only the scorn of the top criminal defense lawyer, Mr. Chaffanbrass. Felix, however, does receive a reward of sorts: He is to be married to Madeline Stavely, the woman whom the narrator extols as the most interesting of the novel. Madeline Stavely spends her spare time caring for the poor, is not at all concerned about wealth or associating with the rich and famous, and, in her relationship with Felix Graham, goes beyond the rather plain surface to discern a truly noble and moral character. Part of Felix and Madeline's reward is that Judge Stavely will provide his daughter and her husband with an income sufficient to support them in a lifestyle to which they are accustomed.

One should not conclude that *Orley Farm* is simply an eight-hundred-page novel about the rewards for good behavior. Trollope's vision is more complicated than this, for he makes it clear that almost no one involved in this trial is concerned with carrying out justice. Most of the characters—from the most base to the most seemingly noble—act primarily out of self-interest. For example, Joseph Mason agrees to proceed with the trial against his half sister not to right a wrong but chiefly to get even. Ironically, when Lucius offers him the lands of which he has been deprived, Joseph first rejects the offer and seeks legal help to sue the lawyers who represented him as well as those standing for Mrs. Mason. He simply wants to see Lady Mason—and everyone else associated with her defense—punished. The lawyer Dockwrath, initially deprived of his land when Lucius reaches legal age, is a small, mean-spirited man who derives far more enjoyment out of bullying others than he does in seeing the carrying out of justice. Mr. Furnival initially agrees to represent Lady Mason not because he is concerned that justice be done—indeed, he deduces that Lady Mason is guilty of the crime with which she is charged—but because he is attracted to her. To emphasize that the English courts are not at all about the carrying out of justice, Trollope introduces the characters of two criminal defense attorneys, Aram and Chaffanbrass, whose reputations are built upon their ability to destroy witnesses and gain a verdict of not guilty for people who are unquestionably guilty.

Orley Farm is a good, possibly great, novel. Unity of design as well as shrewd and ironic conceptualization of character and plot enable Trollope to depict an English court system that protects the guilty and punishes the innocent. Trollope's indictment of the English courts and his revelation of the types of characters that the court sustains emphasizes the need for change.

"Critical Evaluation" by Richard Logsdon

Bibliography:

Adams, Robert Martin. "*Orley Farm* and Real Fiction." *Nineteenth Century Fiction* 8, no. 1 (June, 1953): 27-41. Argues that, in *Orley Farm*, Trollope strives for the kind of realism expounded by Victorian critic G. H. Lewes.

Booth, Bradford A. "Trollope's *Orley Farm*: Artistry Manqué." In *Victorian Literature: Modern Essays in Criticism*, edited by Austin Wright. New York: Oxford University Press, 1961. Pages 358-371 discuss *Orley Farm* in terms of its adherence to literary standards.

King, Margaret F. "Trollope's *Orley Farm*: Chivalry Versus Commercialism." *Essays in Literature* 3, no. 2 (Fall, 1976): 181-193. Explores the novel's conflict between characters who act out of a sense of honor and integrity, and those who are motivated by their pocketbooks.

Polhemus, Robert. *The Changing World of Anthony Trollope*. Berkeley: University of California Press, 1968. Examines Trollope's novels as the author's expression of the need for reform.

Sadleir, Michael. *Trollope: A Commentary*. 3d ed. New York: Oxford University Press, 1961. A helpful biography, focusing on Trollope's life and commercial and political career as reflected in his novels.

OROONOKO
Or, The Royal Slave, a True History

Type of work: Novel
Author: Aphra Behn (1640-1689)
Type of plot: Didactic
Time of plot: Seventeenth century
Locale: Africa and Surinam
First published: c. 1678

> *Principal characters:*
> OROONOKO, an African prince
> IMOINDA, his wife
> ABOAN, a friend of Oroonoko
> THE KING, Oroonoko's grandfather

The Story:

In the African kingdom of Coromantien, the ruler was an old man more than one hundred years of age. His grandson, Prince Oroonoko, was the bravest, most beloved young man in all the land. When the commanding general was killed in battle, Oroonoko was chosen to take his place, even though the prince was only seventeen years old. After a great victory in battle, Prince Oroonoko presented himself at the court of his grandfather, the king. His noble and martial bearing made him an instant favorite with lords and ladies alike.

Oroonoko also visited Imoinda, the daughter of his dead general, a girl as beautiful and modest as he was handsome and brave. The two noble young people immediately fell in love. She became his wife, but before the marriage could be consummated, Oroonoko made known his plans to his grandfather the king. Although the old man already possessed many wives, he had heard of the loveliness of Imoinda and wanted her for his own. When Oroonoko was absent one day, the king sent his veil to Imoinda, a royal command that she was to join his harem. Since it was against the law for even a king to take another man's wife, the old man made her forswear her marriage and acknowledge him as her husband.

When Oroonoko returned and learned of the old man's treachery, he renounced all pleasures in longing for his lost wife. The lovers dared not let the king know their true feelings, for to do so would have meant death or worse for both of them, although Oroonoko was of the king's own blood. While pretending not to care for his lost Imoinda, Oroonoko was again invited to the royal palace. There he learned from some of the king's women that Imoinda was still a virgin. Oroonoko planned to rescue her. With the help of his friend Aboan and one of the older wives of the king, Oroonoko entered the apartment of Imoinda and took her as his true wife. Spied upon by the king's orders, Oroonoko was apprehended and forced to flee back to his army camp, leaving Imoinda to the mercies of the king. Enraged because he had been betrayed by his own blood, the old man determined to kill the girl and then punish Oroonoko. In order to save her life, Imoinda told the king that Oroonoko had ravished her against her will. The king then declared that she must be punished with worse than death; he sold her into slavery.

The king gave up his intent to punish his grandson, for Oroonoko controlled the soldiers and the king feared they might be turned against him. Instead, he took Oroonoko back into his favor after telling the boy that Imoinda had been given an honorable death for her betrayal of the king. Oroonoko held no grudge against the king and did not act against him; for a long time, however, he pined for his lost wife. At last, his grief grew less, and he once more took his place at the royal court.

Soon afterward, an English merchant ship came to the port of Coromantien. When her master, well known to Oroonoko, invited the Prince and his friends to a party on board, Oroonoko, Aboan, and others gladly accepted the invitation. Once on board, all were seized and made prisoners and later sold as slaves in Surinam on the coast of South America. The man who bought Oroonoko, seeing the nobility of his slave, immediately felt great esteem for him. Indeed, except for the fact that he had been bought, Oroonoko was not a slave at all, but rather a friend to his master. In the colony as in his own homeland, Oroonoko was loved, admired, and respected by all who saw him. His name was changed to Caesar.

In a short time Oroonoko, now known as Caesar, heard of a lovely young girl whom all the men wanted for their own. It was believed, however, that she pined for a lost love. When Oroonoko saw her, he found that she was his wife Imoinda, whom he had thought dead. Reunited with great joy, the lovers were allowed to live together and were promised their freedom and passage to their own country as soon as the governor arrived to make the arrangements.

Oroonoko, however, began to fear that he and his wife were never going to be set free, that the promise would not be kept. Imoinda was pregnant and they feared that they were to be kept until the child was born, another slave. When the masters were gone one day, Oroonoko tried to persuade the slaves to revolt against their bondage; he promised to lead them to his own country and there give them liberty. Although most of the slaves followed him, they quickly deserted him when they were overtaken by their masters; Oroonoko was left with Imoinda and one man. The governor, who was with the pursuers, promised Oroonoko that if he would surrender, there would be no punishment. Again, Oroonoko was betrayed. No sooner had he surrendered than he was seized and tied to a stake. There he was whipped until the flesh fell from his bones. Oroonoko endured his punishment with great courage, but he vowed revenge on his captors even if it meant his death. His own master, still his friend, had also been betrayed into believing the promises made to Oroonoko. He took the sick and feeble man back to his own plantation and nursed him. There he refused to let anyone near Oroonoko except his friends, and he posted a guard to see that no harm came to the sick man.

Oroonoko was resolved to have his revenge on his tormentors, and he conceived a grim plan. Fearing that Imoinda would suffer ravishings and a shameful death, he told her that she must die at his hand so that he would be free to accomplish his revenge. Imoinda blessed her husband for his thoughtfulness; after many caresses and words of love, Oroonoko severed her head from her body. Then he lay down beside her and did not eat or drink for many days while he grieved for his beloved.

Found by the side of his dead wife by those who had come to beat him again, he took his knife, cut off his own flesh, and ripped his own bowels, all the while vowing that he would never be whipped a second time. Again, friends took him home and cared for him with love and kindness. Then the governor tricked his friends once more, and Oroonoko was tied to a stake and whipped publicly. After the beating, the executioner cut off his arms, legs, nose, and ears. Because of his enemies' treachery, Oroonoko died a cruel and shameful death.

Critical Evaluation:

Aphra Behn was the first woman in the history of English literature to earn her living as a writer. While earlier women writers had left important works in varied genres, none had achieved commercial success. Her primary significance to literary history lies in her prose fiction. She is an important figure in the transition between the prose romances of the Renaissance and the novel in the early eighteenth century. Her narrative art assures her place in literature, and the humanitarian themes of her works endow them with enduring relevance.

Through its narrative techniques and extensive use of specific details to promote verisimilitude, *Oroonoko: Or, The Royal Slave, a True History*, the most significant and best known of Behn's seventeen prose romances, represents an important work in the development of the English novel. Ostensibly narrating from the authorial point of view, Behn asserts at the outset that the story is factual and claims to have known the characters and witnessed much of the action. She injects numerous details to enhance the realism, foreshadowing the narrative techniques of Daniel Defoe and Jonathan Swift. Like her successors in prose fiction, she selects details calculated to appeal to the interest of the English in exotic places like the New World. She describes, for example, South American creatures like the armadillo and the anaconda, and her account of the indigenous peoples idealizes their primitive and simple lives in the wilderness. The numerous descriptive details are highly specific, though sometimes inaccurate, as when Behn describes a serpent thirty-six yards long or discusses tigers in Surinam.

The narrator persona assures the reader that all of the account is true and claims periodically to have encountered Oroonoko personally at specified points in the action. Also, the narrative incorporates names of actual people known to have been officials in Surinam at the time of the plot, and at one point Behn leads the reader to assume that she was sent to gather information from the hero by colonists who feared a slave uprising. This detail is in accord with her previous work as an intelligence agent for Charles II in Holland. In 1664, she may have actually traveled to Surinam, as she claims. Other details relevant to her own experiences and life include references to her writings, especially her dramatic works. Collectively, these details support her assurances to the reader that she had been a witness to many of the episodes.

Yet the most important parts of her book, like its themes and characters, make it evident that she is following not a real life, but a literary convention. Measured against a hero who is larger than life in the narrative, many details must be regarded as conscious art, not truth, even though they effectively lend the narrative a strong air of authenticity.

The primary interest of the work lies in the depiction of its protagonist, who is also shaped by literary convention and contemporary taste. Oroonoko is a Restoration hero, capable of intense passions and modeled more on the protagonists of the heroic dramas of the period than on a living person. In love, he knows no half measures, for Behn embraces the assumption that great love implies a great soul. A man of natural nobility, Oroonoko embodies both the Achilles type of active hero and the Oedipus type of suffering, contemplative hero.

Though his character owes something to the literary concept of the noble savage, he is more than this. Despite his origin in tribal Africa, he is not a primitive man, but a well-educated, charismatic youth who has learned to read Latin and French and who speaks fluent English. An admirer of Roman virtues, he becomes known as Caesar when he arrives in Surinam because he is invincible in warfare, eloquent and inspiring in speech, and triumphant in the daunting challenges posed by nature.

His first obstacle in love is his own grandfather, the king of his country, who wants Oroonoko's beloved Imoinda for himself. Once he has overcome this challenge, he must confront the evils of slavery. While he will endure servitude for himself, he is unwilling to accept it for his unborn child. His struggle against institutional slavery, however, is doomed to failure. Behn depicts her hero as the epitome of honor and dignity whose happiness is destroyed by evils brought to Africa and the New World by Europeans. Ironically, he represents the ideals professed by Europeans, ideals which they themselves have disregarded.

Thematically the work touches on values typical in Behn's fiction, including the right of women to select their spouses and the paramount value of romantic love. The two dominant themes, however, are opposition to slavery and the celebration of primitivism. In terms of modern understanding, both themes must be severely qualified. The celebration of primitive tribal life is calculated to appeal to a contemporaneous audience fascinated with the New World. Although she develops the theme in both Africa and Surinam, her most extensive depiction of primitive nobility relates to the New World. The natives of Surinam demonstrate the superiority of the primitive over the more complex European civilization. A people guided by modesty, simplicity, and innocence, they have no concept of sin, no natural sense of guilt, no words for falsehood and deception. They have no need of complex laws to govern their behavior, but are guided by a natural sense of right and wrong. Admirably adjusted to their environment, they live a life of basic virtue and do little harm. Behn cautions that European mores and religion could only harm their idyllic lives.

As for its antislavery message, the approach is less clear. Slavery is depicted as endemic in Africa, though a clear evil. Even Oroonoko and his grandfather sell their low-ranking captives into slavery, though Oroonoko attempts to protect his noble captives. Those who are enslaved think first and foremost of regaining their liberty and attempt this whenever an opportunity arises. The narrative exposes the violence done to family units under slavery. Europeans involved in the slave trade are portrayed as treacherous and evil, yet once the slaves have reached plantations, not all masters are unkind to them. The supervisor of Oroonoko's plantation, Trefrey, treats him as an equal and attempts to intercede on his behalf and to offer protection. By portraying Oroonoko as a noble savage, unjustly and treacherously enslaved, Behn contributed to the growing antislavery sentiment in England. The story of Oroonoko gained further public exposure after the dramatist Thomas Southerne used the romance as the source for his popular drama *Oroonoko* (1695).

"Critical Evaluation" by Stanley Archer

Bibliography:
Duffy, Maureen. *The Passionate Shepherdess*. London: Jonathan Cape, 1977. Duffy's sympathetic biography scrutinizes the known details of Behn's life. She also offers a comprehensive treatment of Behn's London literary career.
Hunter, Heidi, ed. *Rereading Aphra Behn: History, Theory, and Criticism*. Charlottesville: University Press of Virginia, 1993. The book offers a selection of previously unpublished essays on aspects of Behn's works. It includes an essay by Charlotte Sussman that centers on the character Imoinda and explores the plight of women under polygamy and slavery.
Link, Frederick M. *Aphra Behn*. New York: Twayne, 1968. Link's readable study offers a comprehensive account of the life and works of Behn. He provides a concise critical evaluation for each of the prose romances.
Rogers, Katharine M. "Fact and Fiction in Aphra Behn's *Oroonoko*." *Studies in the Novel* 20 (Spring, 1988): 1-15. Rogers examines the accuracy of numerous details cited by Behn in *Oroonoko*. The article finds the book generally accurate in its portrayal of Africa and Surinam but mistaken in some details.
Sypher, Wylie. *Guinea's Captive Kings*. Chapel Hill: University of North Carolina Press, 1942. Sypher places *Oroonoko* within the context of eighteenth century antislavery literature. His analysis shows that, by combining the antislavery theme with that of the noble savage, Behn swayed sentiment against slavery.

ORPHEUS

Type of work: Drama
Author: Jean Cocteau (1889-1963)
Type of plot: Tragicomedy
Time of plot: Early twentieth century
Locale: Thrace, Greece
First performed: 1926; first published, 1927 (English translation, 1933)

> *Principal characters:*
> ORPHEUS, a poet
> EURYDICE, his wife
> HEURTEBISE, their guardian angel, a glazier in appearance
> ALGAONICE, leader of the Bacchantes
> DEATH, an elegantly dressed woman
> THE COMMISSIONER OF POLICE, a bumbling bureaucrat

The Story:

Seated across from his wife, Eurydice, in their villa in Thrace, the poet Orpheus concentrated on the tapping of a white horse, housed in a niche in the center of the room. Orpheus believed this would indicate the next letter in an inspired message. Eventually, the horse tapped out "hell," and finally, "hello" (in the original French, *mer* became *merci*). Orpheus had submitted a previous message, "Orpheus hunts Eurydice's lost life" to the Thracian poetry competition. Eurydice's complaints of neglect, compounded by her doubts regarding these messages, began to provoke Orpheus. In response to her warnings regarding the jealousy of the Bacchantes, a cult of women to whom Eurydice used to belong, Orpheus accused her of disloyalty. He went on to insist that Eurydice broke a windowpane each day so that the glazier, Heurtebise, would come to their villa. To deny his jealousy, he broke a pane himself and summoned Heurtebise.

Upon Heurtebise's entrance, Orpheus departed for town to prepare for the competition. In exchange for some poison-laced sugar from the Bacchante leader, Algaonice, Eurydice handed Heurtebise an incriminating letter in her possession. Heurtebise also gave Eurydice an envelope from Algaonice in which to place the letter to eliminate any trace of Eurydice's involvement. Shrinking from giving the poison to the horse herself, Eurydice convinced Heurtebise to do the deed. Heurtebise, however, interrupted by Orpheus' reappearance, stood on a chair at the window, pretending to take measurements. Orpheus had forgotten his birth certificate for the competition. To retrieve the document from the top of the bookcase, Orpheus grabbed the chair upon which Heurtebise stood. Heurtebise remained suspended in air. Orpheus, oblivious, left with the certificate. Eurydice, however, demanded an explanation from Heurtebise, who refused to acknowledge anything unusual. Eurydice hastily sealed Algaonice's envelope with her tongue in order to give the letter to Heurtebise before dismissing him. She remarked on its peculiar taste and, calling Heurtebise back, revealed that she was dying; the envelope had been poisoned. She sent Heurtebise after Orpheus.

Death then came onto the stage through a mirror. Two attendants, dressed in surgeon's uniforms, followed her. Death herself entered, dressed in evening dress and cloak, which she exchanged for a white tunic. Before beginning her "operation" on Eurydice, Death ordered the horse to take the sugar Heurtebise had tossed on the table. The horse disappeared. An elaborate procedure to obtain Eurydice's soul began. It involved calculations, measurements, mechanical devices, and a watch supplied by an audience member. Following a drum roll, a dove attached to a thread emerged from Eurydice's room; once the thread was cut, the dove—Eurydice's soul—flew off. Death and her attendants left the way they had come. Death, however, had forgotten her gloves.

Orpheus and Heurtebise entered to find Eurydice dead. Heurtebise counseled Orpheus to put on Death's gloves and return them to her for a reward. Heurtebise led Orpheus to the mirror, revealing it to be the door through which Death had traveled. Orpheus sank into the mirror, Eurydice's name on his lips. A postman came to deliver a letter, which Heurtebise instructed him to slip under the door. The scene repeated, implying the arbitrariness of time. Orpheus reappeared through the mirror, Eurydice behind him. As explained by Orpheus, Death made a pact that Eurydice could remain with him as long as he never looked at her. Their initial bliss at reunion degenerated into bickering. Having avoided looking at Eurydice several times, Orpheus, careless in his anger, lost his balance, and found himself gazing at her. She disappeared.

Orpheus insisted that his look was deliberate, Eurydice having stifled his artistry. He spied the delivered letter and held it up to the mirror to read it, as it was written backward. The letter warned Orpheus that his entry to the competition was denounced by Algaonice as an offense. The initial letters of the sentence he had submitted spelled out "O Hell!" The jury considered the entry a hoax. A mob, led by the Bacchantes, was on its way for revenge. Orpheus acknowledged that the horse, as Eurydice feared, had tricked him. He walked out on the balcony to meet his fate. Following clamoring and drums, something flew through the window: Orpheus' head. It called out to Eurydice, who came through the mirror to take Orpheus' invisible body by the hand. Together, they sank into the mirror.

A knock on the door was heard, followed by a voice demanding entrance. Before opening the door, Heurtebise placed Orpheus' head on a pedestal. The Commissioner of Police entered, with a scrivener. The Commissioner announced a reversal in public opinion in Orpheus' favor. An eclipse of the sun that day was interpreted as a sign of anger at Orpheus' humiliation, the poet being a priest of the sun god. The Commissioner was sent to investigate Orpheus' murder and also to obtain a bust of Orpheus for a celebration in his honor. Orpheus' head began to speak to distract the Commissioner from Heurtebise, now the prime suspect. Heurtebise fled into the mirror. To the Commissioner's questioning, the head gave Cocteau's place of birth, name, and current address. Having noticed Heurtebise's absence, the Commissioner and scrivener exited in search of him, rushing back later for the "bust."

Orpheus, Eurydice, and Heurtebise—revealed to be the couple's guardian angel—appeared together in Paradise. They smiled and leisurely prepared to take lunch, prayed over by Orpheus.

Critical Evaluation:

Jean Cocteau began his career during one of the most fertile periods in French cultural and artistic history: the 1920's. His work was conspicuously avant-garde. *Orpheus* shares characteristics of the theater of the absurd, particularly its grim delight in the twisting of language. Attention is drawn to the fact that language is a construct, that is, a purely arbitrary system of signs and symbols. Meaning itself may therefore be unstable. The language of *Orpheus* is replete with puns and wordplay. Structurally, the course of the play is determined more by the ambiguities of language than by the twists and turns of conventional plotting. The protagonist's fate, for example, depends on the interpretation (or misinterpretation) of a phrase. Nevertheless, *Orpheus* cannot truly be categorized as absurdist theater. Its resolution lacks the rigor of absurdism.

In fact, Cocteau remained aloof from any particular "school" of dramatic thought, despite the fact that his work at times appeared Dadaist, Surrealist, or Futurist in style if not in substance. Cocteau was even denounced by the Surrealists, who judged him a "dabbler," unable to fully appreciate the movement's profound and radical intent. Indeed, the play's mockery of Orpheus' attempts to extract poetry from the tapping of a horse ridiculed Surrealism's attachment to automatic writing, a system in which people attempted to ascertain meaning from words written without conscious thought. While Cocteau, like the Surrealists and Dadaists, created art to shock the public, his use of surprise was determinedly conscious. Cocteau's detailed production notes, which, unprecedentedly, he published, show the tight rein he kept on theatrical effects.

The myth of Orpheus provided a vehicle for Cocteau to explore themes relating to the creative imagination and the destiny of the artist, ideas which obsessed him throughout his career. Orpheus was the paradigmatic poet and musician; his songs charmed any creature who heard them. His gifts softened the hearts of the god of the underworld and his consort, to the point that they allowed Orpheus' dead bride to accompany him back to the world of the living. The Orphic myth had inspired numerous musical and literary works before Cocteau addressed it. Starting with the Latin poet Vergil, the love story between Orpheus and Eurydice had moved to the forefront, obscuring the myth's original focus on the transformative power of poetry and art. Cocteau's burlesquing of the marriage not only contributed to the play's collage effect of Greek tragedy, melodrama, spectacle, and music hall magic show, it also allowed him to shift the myth's thematic weight back to the eternally regenerative power of art. Cocteau saw creativity, death, and immortality as interrelated, convinced that the true artist would be vindicated despite the persecution he suffered in his time. Tellingly, Cocteau never used his full first name, Jean-Maurice, and later derived satisfaction from sharing the initials, "JC," of the martyred Christian god.

Notably, the figure of Orpheus appeared in early Christian tomb paintings in Rome, indicating a link in Greek and Christian myth via the theme of resurrection. *Orpheus* itself was written when Cocteau was under the influence of the Catholic poet Jacques Maritain. A one-act play in nine scenes, it began as a five-act theatrical work about the Incarnation, featuring Mary, Joseph, and Gabriel, the angel of the Annunciation. The character of Heurtebise remains from Cocteau's original intent to explore the Christian myth. When Heurtebise first enters, he kneels and crosses his arms in the pose of Gabriel. He is forced to reveal his angelic nature when he must remain suspended in air at one point in the play. Significantly, as the couple's guardian angel, it is Heurtebise who suggests a way for Orpheus to win over Death and also reveals to him Death's passageway to and from this world. Cocteau evidences the religious conversion he was undergoing at the time by associating the horse/medium with the devil, and ending the play with a prayer that affirms to God, "thou art poetry."

Another myth that Cocteau incorporates in *Orpheus* is that of the machine. Processes in the play operate mechanistically and with the mystique surrounding technology and its promise of precision. The horse appears to function as a kind of "poetry machine." Death's procedures are a blend of magic show theatrics and mechanical wizardry. The machinery of the state, degenerated into bureaucracy, is personified in the Commissioner of Police. In *Orpheus*, the machine behaves like fate in modern dress. It proceeds as inescapably and as mercilessly.

The author himself claimed that the play was "half farce, half meditation upon death." Whether a pastiche or a serious attempt to dramatize the various mythologies informing twentieth century life, *Orpheus* is historically significant as one of the first in a series of modernizations of Greek myths by French playwrights. This trend also includes Jean Giraudoux's *Amphitryon 38* (1929), Jean-Paul Sartre's *Les Mouches* (1943), and Jean Anouilh's *Antigone* (1944). Most critics agree that the dramatists used the myths as a shared point of reference from which to examine Western culture in a state of crisis and doubt. Ever an intuitive artist, Cocteau appears to have grasped early their vestigial power.

Amy Adelstein

Bibliography:
Crowson, Lydia. *The Esthetic of Jean Cocteau*. Hanover, N.H.: University Press of New England, 1978. Crowson's insights rest on her research of structuralism and analytical philosophy. The clarity of her writing belies an elusive thesis: On a certain level, *Orpheus* reflects Cocteau's personal conflicts regarding sex and gender.

Fowlie, Wallace. *Jean Cocteau: The History of a Poet's Age*. Bloomington: Indiana University Press, 1966. Fowlie approaches Cocteau's life and artistry with great seriousness. A distinctive element of this work is an epilogue describing a meeting between Fowlie and Cocteau shortly before the latter's death.

Freeman, E. Introduction to *Orphée/Jean Cocteau*. Oxford, England: Basil Blackwell, 1976. Freeman's introduction to both the play and the film, and his notes to the play, offer a wealth of background information as well as details about the production. The reader's understanding of the work is broadened by Freeman's investigation of its mythological matrix. A French/English dictionary may be needed, as Freeman does not translate French quotations for the reader.

Knapp, Bettina Liebowitz. *Jean Cocteau*. Updated ed. Boston: Twayne, 1989. Knapp acknowledges paradoxes that inform her understanding of Cocteau, paradoxes that she then attempts to analyze. Her analysis resembles Crowsen's as it draws on psychological points of view to find the reality in the legend.

Oxenhandler, Neal. *Scandal and Parade: The Theatre of Jean Cocteau*. New Brunswick, N.J.: Rutgers University Press, 1957. This first American study of Cocteau focuses on his work in the theater. Oxenhandler takes a philosophical approach to his subject. He finds Cocteau's inability to "engage" in the world around him a kind of tragedy for the modern age.

ORPHEUS AND EURYDICE

Type of work: Short fiction
Author: Unknown
Type of plot: Mythic
Time of plot: Antiquity
Locale: Thrace and the Underworld
First published: Unknown

> *Principal characters:*
> ORPHEUS, a musician
> EURYDICE, his wife

The Story:

Orpheus, son of Apollo and the Muse Calliope, grew up in Thrace, a land long noted for the purity and richness of its divine gift of song. His father presented him with a lyre and taught him to play it. So lovely were the songs of Orpheus that the wild beasts followed him when he played, and even the trees, the rocks, and the hills gathered near him. It was said his music softened the composition of stones.

Orpheus charmed Eurydice with his music, but Hymen brought no happy omens to their wedding. His torch smoked so that tears came to their eyes. Passionately in love with his wife, Orpheus became mad with grief when Eurydice died. Fleeing from a shepherd who desired her, she had stepped upon a snake and died from its bite.

Heartbroken, Orpheus wandered over the hills composing and singing melancholy songs of memory for the lost Eurydice. Finally he descended into the Underworld and made his way past the sentries by means of his music. Approaching the throne of Proserpine and Hades, he sang a lovely song in which he said that love had brought him to the Underworld. He complained that Eurydice had been taken from him before her time and if they would not release her, he would not leave Hades. Proserpine and Hades could not resist his pleas. They agreed to set Eurydice free if Orpheus would promise not to look upon her until they should safely reach the Upperworld.

The music of Orpheus was so tender that even the ghosts shed tears. Tantalus forgot his search for water; Ixion's wheel stopped; the vulture stopped feeding on the giant's liver; the daughters of Danaus stopped drawing water; and Sisyphus himself stopped to listen. Tears streamed from the eyes of the Furies. Eurydice then appeared, limping. The two walked the long and dismal passageway to the Upperworld, and Orpheus did not look back toward Eurydice. At last, forgetting his vow, he turned, and, as they reached out their arms to embrace, Eurydice disappeared.

Orpheus tried to follow her, but the stern ferryman refused him passage across the River Styx. Declining food and drink, he sat by the River Strymon and sang his twice-felt grief. As he sang his melancholy songs, so sad that oaks moved and tigers grieved, a group of Thracian maidens attempted to console him, but he repulsed them. One day, while they were observing the sacred rites of Bacchus, they began to stone him. At first, the stones fell without harm when they came within the sound of the lyre. As the frenzy of the maidens increased, however, their shouting drowned out the notes of the lyre so that it no longer protected Orpheus. Soon he was covered with blood.

Then the savage women tore his limbs from his body and hurled his head and his lyre into the river. Both continued singing sad songs as they floated downstream. The fragments of Orpheus' body were buried at Libethra, and it is said that nightingales sang more sweetly over his grave than in any other part of Greece. Jupiter made his lyre a constellation of stars in the heavens. Orpheus joined Eurydice in the Underworld, and there, happy at last, they wandered through the fields together.

Critical Evaluation:

The longest and most familiar version of this myth is found in Ovid's *Metamorphoses* (c. 8 c.e.), and Ovid may well have been inspired by Vergil's less florid account, carefully placed at the dramatic end of his *Georgics* (c. 37-29 b.c.e.). In Vergil's work, Eurydice is bitten by a snake as she flees the lustful rustic deity, Aristaeus. There, the Orpheus-Eurydice theme was most appropriate to Vergil's subject of rebirth and fruitfulness through sacrifice and discipline; indeed, this myth, perhaps more than any other, illustrates that humanity can never achieve vic- tory over death without divine aid and that human immortality can be gained only through art.

Through extraordinary powers of music, Orpheus was able to perform unnatural feats, such as moving beasts, trees, even rocks, and ultimately to obtain a rare favor from the rulers of the dead; yet his lack of discipline, that is, his inability to obey the command of Proserpine and Hades to the letter, resulted in his failure to achieve victory over death for Eurydice. (Even if he had won, however, one must assume that death would have eventually come again for them both.) Nevertheless, there is a hopeful side to the myth: Eventually the two lovers are permanently united in death.

This may be satisfying romantically, but it is less important than Orpheus' literary legacy, symbolized by his severed head continuing to sing his beloved's name, harmoniously echoed by sympathetic nature. Orpheus, therefore, has achieved ultimate victory over death: His art has given him the life after death he sought for Eurydice. This is further symbolized in his burial by the Muses near Olympus, in Apollo's petrifying his head on Lesbos (an island renowned for its poets), and finally by the transformation of Orpheus' lyre into a constellation of stars. Certainly Vergil, if not Ovid, had this victory in mind, since their versions broke with the tradition in which Orpheus succeeded in rescuing Eurydice from death.

Both parts of the original myth—the retrieval of Eurydice and the death of Orpheus— probably originated in preclassical poetry, perhaps in cultic Orphism. Orpheus himself was believed to be the earliest of poets, along with Musaeus (his son), Homer, and Hesiod. He is given a place among Jason's Argonauts. His remote Thracian origins lend mystery to his myth, and no doubt this had a bearing on the relatively restricted popularity of Orphism, which seems to have been more of a philosophy than a religion. The aim of the Orphics was to lead a life of purity and purification, so that eventually the successively reincarnated soul, having purged itself of the Titanic (or earthly) element, would be pure spirit divinely born of Zeus through his son Dionysus and thus would be released from the cycle, eternally to wander the Elysian fields.

Exactly how Orpheus is connected with this cult is unclear and indeed confusing. In Ovid's version, Orpheus refuses to love any woman other than Eurydice; furthermore, he turns his attention to boys, which is why the Thracian women murder him. Yet, these women are bacchants, that is, Dionysian orgiasts, and, in other versions, Dionysus himself directs them to kill Orpheus because the bard, in his devotion to Apollo the sun-god, has prevented the wine-god's acceptance in Thrace. On the other hand, the oracle established in Lesbos in honor of Orpheus was suppressed by Apollo. If Orpheus was the poet-priest-prophet of Apollo who refused the frenzy of Dionysus, it may well be that he became the cultic model whose sacrifice ironically inspired others to accept Dionysus. Orphic mysteries seem to have resembled the orgies of Dionysus, but whereas the Dionysiac is striving for that momentary ecstatic union with the god, the Orphic is striving for eternal peace.

The descent of Orpheus into the Underworld obviously symbolizes an Orphic's death, which will be followed by a new life, repeated until the cycle is complete. Other symbolic interpretations aside, the descent and return would be frightening were they not so entertaining. Having given readers a whirlwind classic tour of the Underworld, including introductions to the king and queen, Ovid slowly leads readers back along the murky upward path until suddenly Orpheus' concern for Eurydice outstrips his easy promise. The pathos of this second separation is intensified by its swiftness and by Orpheus' inability even to regain passage across the Styx, much less to see or hear his love again.

Few love stories from classical antiquity have made such an impression on succeeding ages. This myth became the subject of the first secular drama in vernacular, *Orfeo* (1480), composed in the era of the Medici family by Angelo Poliziano (Politian). In 1600, the first Italian opera, *Euridice*, was composed. Christoph Gluck's *Orfeo ed Eurydice* (1762) is considered the first "modern" opera for its balance of music and tragic drama, although a happy ending was supplied: Amore (Love) brings Eurydice back to prevent Orfeo's suicide. Twentieth century playwrights have adapted the story to their own settings and purposes, among them, Jean Anouilh and Tennessee Williams. Composers such as Jacques Offenbach, Darius Milhaud, and Igor Stravinsky have borrowed the theme. In film, Vinicius de Moraes' Brazilian masterpiece, *Black Orpheus* (1957), takes place in Rio de Janeiro during Carnival and deftly uses the primitive color of the celebration to heighten the frenzy of Orpheus' search for his love, who vainly tries to elude her stalking killer costumed as Death.

Bibliography:
Anouilh, Jean. *Eurydice and Medée*. Edited by E. Freeman. New York: Basil Blackwell, 1984. A modern analysis of the Orpheus/Eurydice story and the story of Medea as dramatized by modern writers. Compares the two women as opposites, while exploring the loss of love as it relates to one's view of the world.
Cotterell, Arthur. *The Macmillan Illustrated Encyclopedia of Myths and Legends*. New York: Macmillan, 1989. Associates Orpheus with the doctrines of Orphism, a mystery cult derived from Orpheus' poetry to his lost love, Eurydice.
Graves, Robert. *The Greek Myths*. New York: Penguin Books, 1960. Retells the story of Orpheus, father of music, and his beloved Eurydice, who dies and is held in the Underworld. Orpheus is seen both as a hero and as one who spreads the culture of music throughout the world.
Guthrie, W. K. C. *Orpheus and Greek Religion: A Study of the Orphic Movement*. Princeton, N.J.: Princeton University Press, 1993. Analyzes Orpheus and Dionysus as the catalysts for the Orphic religion. Places emphasis on the mysteries of the cult and their attraction for women.
Warden, John, ed. *Orpheus: The Metamorphoses of a Myth*. Buffalo, N.Y.: University of Toronto Press, 1982. An in-depth analysis of the uses to which ancient Greek, Roman, and more recent Western European poets, playwrights, musicians, and composers have put the Orpheus legend. Includes a look at the songs of Orpheus compared to the songs of Christ. Since Orpheus, like Christ, was killed as a sacrifice, the mythic implications of the two stories are of major significance.

OTHELLO
The Moor of Venice

Type of work: Drama
Author: William Shakespeare (1564-1616)
Type of plot: Tragedy
Time of plot: Early sixteenth century
Locale: Venice and Cyprus
First performed: 1604; first published, 1622; revised, 1623

> *Principal characters:*
> OTHELLO, the Moor of Venice
> DESDEMONA, his wife
> IAGO, a villain
> CASSIO, Othello's lieutenant
> EMILIA, Iago's wife

The Story:

Iago, an ensign serving under Othello, Moorish commander of the armed forces of Venice, was passed over in promotion when Othello chose Cassio to be his chief of staff. In revenge, Iago and his follower, Roderigo, aroused from his sleep Brabantio, senator of Venice, to tell him that his daughter Desdemona had stolen away and married Othello. Brabantio, incensed that his daughter would marry a Moor, led his servants to Othello's quarters.

Meanwhile, the duke of Venice had learned that armed Turkish galleys were preparing to attack the island of Cyprus, and in this emergency he had summoned Othello to the senate chambers. Brabantio and Othello met in the streets but postponed any violence in the national interest. Othello, upon arriving at the senate, was commanded by the duke to lead the Venetian forces to Cyprus. Then Brabantio told the duke that Othello had beguiled his daughter into marriage without her father's consent. When Brabantio asked the duke for redress, Othello vigorously defended his honor and reputation; he was seconded by Desdemona, who appeared during the proceedings. Othello, cleared of all suspicion, prepared to sail for Cyprus immediately. For the time being, he placed Desdemona in the care of Iago; Iago's wife, Emilia, was to be her attendant during the voyage to Cyprus.

A great storm destroyed the Turkish fleet and scattered the Venetians. One by one, the ships under Othello's command put into Cyprus until all were safely ashore and Othello and Desdemona once again united. Still intent on revenge, Iago told Roderigo that Desdemona was in love with Cassio. Roderigo, himself in love with Desdemona, was promised all of his desires by Iago if he would engage Cassio, who did not know him, in a personal brawl while Cassio was officer of the guard.

Othello declared the night dedicated to celebrating the destruction of the enemy, but he cautioned Cassio to keep a careful watch on Venetian troops in the city. Iago talked Cassio into drinking too much, so that when provoked by Roderigo, Cassio lost control of himself and fought with Roderigo. Cries of riot and mutiny spread through the streets. Othello, aroused by the commotion, demoted Cassio for permitting a fight to start. Cassio, his reputation all but ruined, welcomed Iago's promise to secure Desdemona's goodwill and through her have Othello restore Cassio's rank.

Cassio importuned Iago to arrange a meeting between him and Desdemona. While Cassio and Desdemona were talking, Iago enticed Othello into view of the pair, and spoke vague innuendoes. Afterward, Iago from time to time asked Othello questions in such a manner as to lead Othello to think there might have been something between Cassio and Desdemona before Desdemona married him. Once Iago had sown these seeds of jealousy, Othello began to doubt his wife.

When Othello complained to Desdemona of a headache, she offered to bind his head with the handkerchief that had been Othello's first gift to her. She dropped the handkerchief inadvertently, and Emilia picked it up. Iago, seeing an opportunity to further his scheme, took the handkerchief from his wife and hid it in Cassio's room. When Othello asked Iago for proof that Desdemona was untrue to him, threatening his life if he could not produce any evidence, Iago said that he had slept in Cassio's room and had heard Cassio speak sweet words in his sleep to Desdemona. He reminded Othello of the handkerchief and said that he had seen Cassio wipe his beard that day with that very handkerchief. Othello, completely overcome by passion, vowed revenge. He ordered Iago to kill Cassio, and he appointed the ensign his new lieutenant.

Othello asked Desdemona to account for the loss of the handkerchief, but she was unable to explain its disappearance. She was mystified by Othello's shortness of speech, and his dark moods. Goaded by Iago's continuing innuendoes, the Moor succumbed to mad rages of jealousy in which he fell into fits resembling epilepsy. In the presence of an envoy from Venice, Othello struck Desdemona, to the consternation of all. Emilia swore that her mistress was honest and true, but Othello, who in his madness could no longer believe anything good of Desdemona, reviled and insulted her with harsh words.

One night, Othello ordered Desdemona to dismiss her attendant and to go to bed immediately. That same night Iago persuaded Roderigo to waylay Cassio. When Roderigo was wounded by Cassio, Iago, who had been standing nearby, stabbed Cassio. In the scuffle Iago stabbed Roderigo to death as well, so as to be rid of his dupe, who might talk. Then a strumpet friend of Cassio came upon the scene of the killing and revealed to the assembled crowd her relationship with Cassio. Although Cassio was not dead, Iago hoped to use this woman to defame Cassio beyond all hope of regaining his former reputation. Pretending friendship, he assisted the wounded Cassio back to Othello's house. They were accompanied by Venetian noblemen who had gathered after the fight.

Othello entered his wife's bedchamber and smothered her, after telling her, mistakenly, that Cassio had confessed his love for her and had been killed. Then Emilia entered the bedchamber and reported that Roderigo had been killed, but not Cassio. This information made doubly bitter for Othello his murder of his wife. Othello told Emilia that he had learned of Desdemona's guilt from Iago. Emilia could not believe that Iago had made such charges.

When Iago and other Venetians arrived at Othello's house, Emilia asked Iago to refute Othello's statement. Then the great wickedness of Iago came to light, and Othello learned how the handkerchief had come into Cassio's possession. When Emilia gave further proof of her husband's villainy, Iago stabbed her. Othello lunged at Iago and managed to wound him before the Venetian gentlemen could seize the Moor. Emilia died, still protesting the innocence of Desdemona. Mad with grief, Othello plunged a dagger into his own heart. The Venetian envoy promised that Iago would be tortured to death at the hands of the governor general of Cyprus.

Critical Evaluation:

Although *Othello* has frequently been praised as William Shakespeare's most unified tragedy, many critics have found the central character to be the most unheroic of William Shakespeare's heroes. Some have found him stupid beyond redemption; others have described him as a passionate being overwhelmed by powerful emotion; still others have found him self-pitying and insensitive to the enormity of his actions. Yet all of these denigrations pale before the excitement and sympathy generated for the noble soldier in the course of the play.

As a "Moor," or black man, Othello is an exotic, a foreigner from a fascinating and mysterious land. Certainly he is a passionate man, but he is not devoid of sensitivity. Rather, his problem is that he is thrust into the sophisticated and highly cultivated context of Renaissance Italy, a land that had a reputation in the England of Shakespeare's time for connivance and intrigue. Shakespeare uses the racial difference to many effects: most obviously, to emphasize Othello's difference from the society in which he finds himself and to which he allies himself through marriage; more subtly and ironically to heighten his tragic stance against the white Iago, the embodiment of evil in the play. More than anything, Othello is natural man confronted with the machinations and contrivances of an overly civilized society. His instincts are to be loving and trusting, but he is cast into a society where these natural virtues would have made him extremely vulnerable.

The prime source of that vulnerability is personified in the figure of Iago, perhaps Shakespeare's consummate villain. Iago is so evil by nature that he does not even need any motivation for his antagonism toward Othello. He has been passed over for promotion, but that is clearly a pretext for a malignant nature whose hatred for Othello needs no specific grounds. It is Othello's candor, openness, and spontaneous, generous love that Iago finds offensive. His suggestion that Othello has seduced his own wife is an even flimsier fabrication to cover the essential corruption of his nature.

Iago sees other human beings only as victims or tools. He is the classical Renaissance atheist—an intelligent man, beyond moral scruple, who finds pleasure in the corruption of the virtuous and the abuse of the pliable. That he brings himself into danger is of no consequence, because he relies on his wit and believes that all can be duped and destroyed. There is no further purpose to his life. For such a manipulator, Othello, a good man out of his cultural element, is the perfect target.

More so than in any other Shakespeare play, one character, Iago, is the stage manager of the whole action. Once he sets out to destroy Othello, he proceeds by plot and by innuendo to achieve his goal. He tells others just what he wishes them to know, sets one character against another, and develops an elaborate web of circumstantial evidence to dupe the vulnerable Moor. Edgar Stoll has argued that the extraordinary success of Iago in convincing other characters of his fabrications is simply a matter of the conventional ability of the Renaissance villain. Yet there is more to the conflict than Iago's abilities, conventional or natural. Othello is the perfect victim because he bases his opinions and his human relationships on intuition rather than reason. His courtship of Desdemona is brief and his devotion absolute, as is his trust of his comrades, including Iago. It is not simply that Iago is universally believed. Ironically, he is able to fool everyone about everything except the subject of Desdemona's chastity. On that subject it is only Othello whom he is able to deceive. Roderigo, Cassio, and Emilia all reject Iago's allegations that Desdemona has been unfaithful. Only Othello is deceived, but that is because Iago is able to make him play a game with unfamiliar rules.

Iago entices Othello to use Venetian criteria of truth rather than the intuition on which he should rely. Iago plants doubts in Othello's mind, but his decisive success comes when he gets Othello to demand "ocular proof." Although it seems that Othello is demanding conclusive evidence before jumping to the conclusion that his wife has been unfaithful, it is more important that he has accepted Iago's idea of concrete evidence. From that point on, it is easy for Iago to falsify evidence and create appearances that will lead to erroneous judgments. Othello betrays hyperemotional behavior in his rantings and his fits, but these are the result of his acceptance of what seems indisputable proof. It takes a long time, and a lot of falsifications, before Othello finally abandons his intuitive perception of the truth of his domestic situation. As Othello himself recognizes, he is not quick to anger, but, once angered, his natural passion takes over.

The crime that Othello commits is made to appear all the more heinous because of Desdemona's utter loyalty. It is not that she is naïve—indeed, her conversation reflects that she is sophisticated—but there is no question of her total fidelity to her husband. The evil represented by the murder is intensified by the audience's perception of the contrast between the victim's virtue and Othello's conviction that he is an instrument of justice. His chilling conviction reminds us of the essential probity of a man deranged by confrontation with an evil he cannot comprehend.

Critics such as T. S. Eliot have argued that Othello never comes to an understanding of the gravity of his crime—that he realizes his error but consoles himself in his final speech with cheering reminders of his own virtue. That does not, however, seem consistent with the valiant and honest military character who has thus far been depicted. Othello may have been grossly deceived, and he may be responsible for not clinging to the truth of his mutual love with Desdemona, but, in his final speech, he does face up to his error with the same passion with which he had followed his earlier misconception. Just as he had believed that his murder of Desdemona was divine retribution, he now believes that his suicide is a just act. His passionate nature believes it is meting out justice for the earlier transgression. There is a reference to punishment for Iago, but Shakespeare dismisses the obvious villain so as to focus on Othello's final act of expiation.

Edward E. Foster

Bibliography:
Bloom, Harold, ed. *William Shakespeare's "Othello."* New York: Chelsea House, 1987. Seven essays that explore the issues of power and the difference between male and female roles and occupations. Holds that the play is at once tragic and comic. Includes helpful bibliography and Shakespeare chronology.
Calderwood, James L. *The Properties of "Othello."* Amherst: University of Massachusetts Press, 1989. Takes the theme of ownership as a starting point and provides an overview of Elizabethan property lines to set the stage for argument. Stretches the term property to include not only material and territorial possessions but racial, social, and personal identity.
Heilman, Robert B. *Magic in the Web: Action and Language in "Othello."* Lexington: University of Kentucky Press, 1956. Extensive discussion of Iago's manipulative rhetoric. Argues against Othello as a "victim," presenting him as responsible, if only in part, for his own actions. A good resource for both general readers and students.
Nevo, Ruth. *Tragic Form in Shakespeare*. Princeton, N.J.: Princeton University Press, 1972. Chapter on *Othello* describes the two primary ways of looking at the Moor of Venice: as a man blinded by love, and as a man blinded by his tainted vision of that love. Chronicles the events leading to the protagonist's downfall.
Vaughan, Virginia Mason, and Kent Cartwright, eds. *"Othello": New Perspectives*. Teaneck, N.J.: Fairleigh Dickinson University Press, 1991. A collection of twelve essays that examine different theoretical approaches. Goes beyond a discussion of good versus evil to reveal a variety of nuances in the play. Traces readings and misreadings from the first quarto to the present.

THE OTHER ONE

Type of work: Novel
Author: Colette (Sidonie-Gabrielle Colette, 1873-1954)
Type of plot: Psychological
Time of plot: 1920's
Locale: Franche-Comté and Paris
First published: La Seconde, 1929 (English translation, 1931)

> *Principal characters:*
> FAROU, a playwright
> FANNY, his wife
> JANE, their secretary-companion and Farou's mistress
> JEAN FAROU, Farou's son by a former mistress

The Story:

The difference in the way Fanny and Jane waited for a letter from Farou, who was in Paris, pointed up the contrast between their personalities. The beautiful, heavy Fanny, whose dark Mediterranean beauty had long ago won Farou's devotion, slept on the sofa, while Jane, a thin, nervous, ash-blond woman of nearly thirty, stood weeping quietly on the veranda. Fanny's stepson, Jean, awoke her when the letter arrived. Farou wrote enthusiastically about a young lady who was obviously his new mistress. Fanny was amazed at Jane's violent reaction to this news and wondered why, despite her companion's affection and indispensability, she did not regard Jane as a close friend.

Their lives quickened with Farou's return. Jane was happy, busy taking dictation as Farou worked on his play. To Fanny, Farou's roaring voice and the murmur of the bees sounded in the heat like the office of the Mass. Farou's immense presence completely absorbed them. When Fanny was alone with him, it was clear that she both depended upon him and supported him. He was her one love, and in this knowledge she was proud. Farou and his son were uneasy when together. Jean had developed an unhappy passion for Jane, and he watched her and Farou very closely. When Jane went for a walk, he climbed into the lime tree to see where she went.

Farou's establishment dated from a time before his plays had become successful. At one point, Jean had contracted typhus, Farou's last play had failed, and the secretary had left. Then Jane arrived, who nursed Jean, worked for Farou, and established an easy relationship of affection and respect with Fanny. After the crisis passed, Jane begged to stay, and the Farous were glad to keep her on as a secretary for Farou and a companion for Fanny.

Soon afterward, the family left for their first summer in the Franche-Comté, and they were now spending their second summer there. During the hot days, Fanny, whose intelligence was more that of emotional awareness than of intellectual penetration, found herself unable to consider Jean and his father objectively. The household revolved around Farou, and they all rejoiced when he sold a play. Their practical dependence on Jane continued. Jean's restlessness increased, and at last he won Farou's unwilling permission to leave France for South America after the summer.

Once, when Jean and Fanny were on the balcony and heard Jane and Farou talking in the garden, Jean leaped to the wall to watch them. Fanny joined him. Both were suddenly aware of the intimate nature of Jane's relationship with Farou. When Farou returned to the balcony, Fanny felt nothing but unaltered devotion toward him. Only later did she feel vulnerable, even indignant that she should have been pulled into one of Farou's affairs. This realization, however, did not significantly alter her feelings for Jane.

Fanny slept little that night. At dawn she heard Jane moving about. Fanny realized that she was disturbed by the fact that Jane, too, suffered over Farou and that no longer did she alone, as it were, possess his unfaithfulness. The sight of Farou sleeping intensified her emotions of hurt and tenderness and emphasized her need for self-control.

One morning, Fanny found Jean lying on the path leading from the village where she had been to shop. He had fainted from the heat and from his agony over Jane and Farou's relationship. He was scornful of the telegram Fanny was bringing, a message that summoned Farou to Paris, and he mocked its theatricality. Farou, meeting them, called Jane to arrange their return to Paris. Fanny became convinced that her moral duty was to feel wounded, but instead she was afraid of the possible disruption in their lives. Jean was angered by her obvious lack of pride and emotion.

Surprisingly, Fanny was regretful when they left the house the next day. Farou teased Jane, who immediately told him to help Fanny. Suddenly, Fanny remembered how often Jane had done that. In the train, Jane tried to persuade Fanny to read or sleep, but Fanny declared that she was managing very well. Then she was surprised to find that what she had said was true.

In Paris, Fanny entertained the friends that gathered around toward the end of rehearsals for Farou's new play. Farou was harsh and demanding with Jane. Fanny scolded him and defended Jane—terrified that their relationship would somehow be exposed. The women dined together after Farou had left for the theater. When Jean found them amicably reading, he taunted Jane for her endless companionship with Fanny, a relationship he despised because he thought it hypocritical.

Farou's nervousness and Fanny's jealousy and feeling of responsibility increased as the confusions of the rehearsals continued. One day, upon returning from her dressmaker, Fanny saw Farou kiss Jane. She realized then that she would have to face the fear of desertion within her own home, which had previously been inviolate. Hoping that they had not seen her, Fanny pretended to be ill. Jane and Farou were solicitous, but Jean, because of his own obsession with Jane, was anxious only to learn what exactly had upset Fanny. When Farou returned home exhausted from the rehearsal, Fanny pretended to be asleep instead of soothing him; her loss was at least as great as his.

By the time of the dress rehearsal, Fanny was utterly exhausted, and Jane and Jean were tense. Farou was approaching the state of boredom from which he always suffered when a new play was finally out of his hands. After the rehearsal, critics pronounced the play strong, direct, and dynamic. Fanny wondered whether Farou's reputation, if he had been small and wiry instead of being massive and having the head of a pagan god, would have been for subtlety and insight instead of force and power. On the way home, Fanny feared that the relaxation after weeks of strain might precipitate a crisis in the taxi. She dreaded the prospect that this might happen before she had had time to prepare herself for it or while she was not protected by the familiarities of her home.

The next day, Fanny reluctantly told Jane that she knew that Farou was her lover. She was discomposed when Jane saw the matter as a joint problem. They kept reasonably calm. Jane appealed to her friendship, explaining that she was no longer Farou's mistress and reproaching herself because she had helped to create the situation by disregarding Farou's infidelities in the past. Farou interrupted them and, discovering the situation, wondered why Fanny had spoken at all. He reminded her that it was she who had always commanded his greatest passion and devotion. This fact made him confident that Fanny would reorder their lives satisfactorily.

Fanny and Jane spent the rest of that evening together. As Jane prepared to leave, Fanny realized that she could not bear to be alone, abandoned to Farou's moods, absences, and frequent inarticulateness. Gently, and with only a few words, it was arranged that Jane should stay and that in this solution would lie a measure of security for them all.

Critical Evaluation:

Sidonie-Gabrielle Colette, considered the premier French woman novelist of the early twentieth century, began her career by writing stories of her girlhood in the Claudine novels. She went on to produce other novels, novellas, short stories, sketches, and memoirs. Among her most famous works were *Chéri* (1920) and *Gigi* (1943), a collection of four short stories, the title story of which was made into a play and a popular film.

In *The Other One*, one of her last major novels, Colette explores a theme that appeared in many of her works: the relationship between a woman and her unfaithful husband. Colette, who was fascinated with the effect of infidelity on a marriage, examines the tensions created by such situations. In a variation on the theme of jealousy, Colette focuses on the relationship between Farou's wife, Fanny, and Jane, his secretary and occasional mistress. Instead of dealing with themes of hatred or revenge, Colette shows the strength and endurance of the women, who bond together for survival.

The autobiographical nature of Colette's writing is evident in the novel. At the age of twenty, Colette had married Henri Gauthier-Villars, who wrote under the pen name Willy and remained a strong influence in her life. Like Farou, Willy, a well-known figure in literary and theatrical circles, engaged in extramarital affairs, one of which bore a resemblance to the situation in the novel. When she learned of Willy's affair with Charlotte Kinceler, Colette befriended the other woman and occasionally met with Willy and Charlotte.

The other strong influence in Colette's life was Sido, her mother. As Willy was the symbol of male sexuality, Sido became the symbol of female strength. In *The Other One*, the two women emerge as stronger than the male, and Colette seems to imply that women's basic identity is found in relationships with other women.

The relationship between a wife and her husband's mistress lies at the heart of the novel. Fanny has long accepted her husband's other women, but Jane has a difficult time dealing with his infidelities. Fanny is secure in her role as wife and as the most important woman in Farou's life, but Jane plays an increasingly minor part in his life. Jane, like many of Colette's characters, exists on the fringe of society. Unlike Fanny, who is defined by her attachment to her husband, Jane is the unmarried secretary; she is replaceable, and she depends on Farou for her livelihood and on Fanny for her emotional support. Fanny looks to Jane for companionship, realizing that Farou can easily find another mistress but that she would have trouble finding a friend like Jane. Each woman depends on the other for support and friendship and for a way of filling in the empty space caused by Farou's absences and affairs.

Colette provides little in the way of descriptions of scenes or actions, relying instead on dialogue to further the plot. The story is told from the third-person point of view and develops in conversations between the two women. Dialogue between Fanny and Farou is brief, signaling their lack of communication.

Conversation between Farou and Jane is even more rare, for Jane does not speak in front of Farou but only when she and Fanny are alone. Both women speak more openly when Farou is absent.

In addition to dialogue, Colette shows the strength of the relationship through the small, ordinary gestures of everyday life. Jane performs small acts for Fanny's comfort, placing a pillow under her head, covering her with a blanket, or combing her hair. Yet early in the novel Colette shows that it is Jane who looks to Fanny for support and contact. In one scene, as Jane takes Fanny's arm, she asks why Fanny never takes her arm. Later in the story, when Farou interrupts the conversation between the two women, Jane "advanced on Farou with an aggressive movement," revealing the desire to protect her relationship with Fanny. After Farou leaves the room, Jane "let her arms fall down, along her sides" in a gesture that signaled a more relaxed atmosphere. The novel ends with a tranquil scene, one woman reading and the other sewing, each comfortable in the security of the bond between them.

The novel opens with the women discussing Farou's play, *The House Without Women*, a title that echoes themes of the novel. As Farou enters his house, he greets his women heartily with this phrase, "Aha, all my fine women! I have women in my house!" Drawing energy from the admiration of the women around him, Farou is young at the age of forty-eight, "like all men who surround themselves, in the course of life, only with women." When Fanny confronts Jane about the affair, Jane stresses the importance of her relationship with Fanny, saying, "For four years I have thought so much more of you than of Farou." She shows her admiration for Fanny who, she says, is "a much finer person" than Farou. At the end of the novel, when Farou walks in on the scene between his "fine women," his presence seems extraneous and indicates that the relationship between wife and mistress is at center stage.

The resolution of the novel is similar to the end of Charlotte Perkins Gilman's short story "Turned" (1911), in which a husband's affair with the maid leaves the girl pregnant; once she recovers from the initial shock, the wife leaves her husband, resumes her teaching career, and sets up a new household with the maid and her baby. In both stories, the women work together to create a bond that promotes healing and renewal.

Colette resolves the conflict in *The Other One* in favor of the women. The female rivals come to an understanding, deciding to share the man and continue their relationship rather than jeopardize their friendship. In doing so, they establish a refuge for each other. A relationship that begins in jealousy ends in a bond that goes beyond the women's relationship as rivals. Colette shows that the women's maturity allows them to make constructive choices during a crisis in their lives.

"Critical Evaluation" by Judith Barton Williamson

Bibliography:

Cottrell, Robert. *Colette*. New York: Frederick Ungar, 1974. Discusses the theme of feminine adaptability and endurance in *The Other One*. Compares Farou to Colette's first husband, Willy, and refers to Willy's affair with Charlotte Kinceler, whom Colette befriended. Includes chronology, biographical information, and discussion of major novels.

Flieger, Jerry. *Colette and the Fantom Subject of Autobiography*. Ithaca, N.Y.: Cornell University Press, 1992. Points out that the resolution between female rivals is a common theme for Colette.

McCarty, Mari. "Possessing Female Space: *The Tender Shoot*." *Women's Studies* 8 (1981): 367-374. Special issue devoted exclusively to Colette's works. McCarty claims that Fanny and Jane escape from male shallowness by cultivating their own inner resources.

Spencer, Sharon. "The Lady of the Beasts: Eros and Transformation in Colette." *Women's Studies* 8 (1981): 299-312. Discusses Colette's fascination with the impact of chronic adultery on a marriage.

Stewart, Joan Hinde. *Colette*. Boston: Twayne, 1983. Points out that victory and revenge, typical themes in stories of triangles, are not the issues in *The Other One*. Colette chose instead to focus on the role and meaning of female friendships.

Wescott, Glenway. Introduction to *Short Novels of Colette*. New York: Dial Press, 1951. Claims that Colette wrote *The Other One* because she was dissatisfied with an earlier novel, *The Indulgent Husband*, which dealt with a similar theme.

OTHER VOICES, OTHER ROOMS

Type of work: Novel
Author: Truman Capote (Truman Streckfus Persons, 1924-1984)
Type of plot: Psychological realism
Time of plot: Mid-twentieth century
Locale: Mississippi
First published: 1948

> *Principal characters:*
> JOEL KNOX, thirteen-year-old protagonist
> COUSIN RANDOLPH, the antagonist
> AMY SANSOM, Randolph's cousin
> ZOO FEVER, the cook at the Landing
> IDABEL, Joel's tomboy friend
> LITTLE SUNSHINE, a hermit
> ELLEN KENDALL, Joel's aunt
> ED SANSOM, Joel's father

The Story:

Joel Knox was traveling to his father's at Skully's Landing. He had never met the man, and after his mother died, had lived with his Aunt Ellen in New Orleans. She treated him kindly, but he felt abandoned. When a letter came from his father asking Joel to come live with him, he wanted to go. Ellen allowed it, saying she loved him and to come back if he became unhappy. On his eventful trip, he met the twin adolescents Idabel and Florabel Thompkins, neighbors to his father.

Joel's father was ill, and Joel had to wait to meet him. He met Amy, his stepmother, and Zoo, who nurtured him. Exploring the grounds, he saw a "queer lady" staring down at him from a window. At dinner with Cousin Randolph and Amy, he mentioned the lady. Randolph said that to Joel she was a ghost. While Amy played the pianola, Randolph held Joel's hand. He found that distasteful.

Joel wrote Ellen, telling her he hated the Landing. As he put stamp money in the mailbox with the letter, he noticed Little Sunshine giving Zoo a charm. Joel, headed for the twins', asked the hermit for a protective charm. Little Sunshine told him to come to the Cloud Hotel for one. At the twins' house, Idabel and Florabel began brawling, and Joel left. Back home, the mail had come; he assumed his letter to Ellen went off, though he found his coins spilled on the ground.

Joel finally met his partially paralyzed father who, seemingly, had lidless eyes. He began feeding and reading to him, but felt nothing for him. By then, Joel and Idabel had become friends. One day as they fished and talked, Joel learned she yearned to be male. Feeling tender, he kissed her cheek. She beat him up, but he forgave her. One day in Randolph's room, Joel noticed a snapshot of Randolph, Ed, another man, and a woman. Randolph told a sordid story about the group's relationships, which explained how he realized his homosexuality, how he happened to shoot Ed, how his cousin Amy, a nurse, came to help him with Ed, and brought him to the Landing.

Idabel asked Joel to run away with her. She and Florabel had fought, and Idabel had broken her twin's teeth and nose. Joel agreed to go, but got a sword Zoo had given him and said they first had to go to Little Sunshine's and get his charm. As they crossed Drownin' Creek on a rotting log, Joel spied a cottonmouth staring at him, and froze. Already, he felt stung with the snake's poison, seeing in it the adults who had betrayed him, especially Ed's staring eyes. Idabel grabbed his sword, stepped past him, and killed the snake. Having survived the snake, Joel refused to go after the charm, saying he no longer needed it.

After dinner, Randolph sent Joel to his room for a bottle of wine. There, he saw a letter Randolph was writing and realized that Randolph, not Ed, had sent for him. He told his father good-bye, and ran off with Idabel. They planned to stop, in their flight, at the fair in town. On their way to town, Idabel and Joel saw a black couple tenderly making love. Instinctively, Joel knew such union defined "making love": It meant "withness." Idabel fled, hating the sight. Joel wanted to tell her he loved her, but knew not to.

At the fair, they met Miss Wisteria, a twenty-four-old midget who looked like Shirley Temple. Joel watched Idabel fall in love with her. The three rode the ferris wheel. On Joel's turn riding with Wisteria, a thunderstorm came and rains descended. From high above, he watched as Idabel fled for cover. Lightning outlined a man whom Joel thought was Randolph. On the ground, Joel ran, searching for Idabel. He finally fell asleep in an old house. He became ill, delirious.

He awakened, in his room at the Landing, with Randolph nursing him. As he gained strength, Joel decided he liked being dependent. He felt Randolph was the only person who cared for him. Ellen, he thought, had rejected him. He wanted to stop the calendar and stay forever in Randolph's room. Then one day, Randolph rushed in saying Little Sunshine wanted them, and they had to go. Joel argued, but fruitlessly.

When they reached Cloud Hotel, it was obvious Little Sunshine had not sent for them. They spent the night, and the next day walked home. When they reached home, Amy told Randolph she had followed his instructions. She had told the people from New Orleans that he and Joel were on a hunting trip. Randolph and Amy went inside, and Joel asked Zoo about the people. She told him a lady with a deaf girl had come. Joel said he had a deaf cousin in New Orleans. He yearned for New Orleans, wondering why Ellen had rejected him.

Joel sat a long while in the garden, finally looking toward the house. The "queer lady" was staring down at him from Randolph's window. She beckoned. Joel, with a brief backward glance, went into the house.

Critical Evaluation:

Truman Capote's first novel, *Other Voices, Other Rooms*, quickly drew literary acclaim. Its pathos and psychological realism are starkly drawn in the simple language of its thirteen-year-old protagonist. The novel's central theme is that the elemental need for "withness" drives people to any lengths to acquire it. The setting, replete with grotesques and mystical overtones, is the legendary deep South. Capote intermingles the physical and the psychological to weave his story. That story is a boy's effort to maneuver himself, unguided—and often misguided—from childhood into adulthood. Such rites of passage stories are often the choice of beginning novelists.

Capote builds tension by weaving two plots together: Randolph manipulates events so that Joel will be driven to fulfill his elemental need through Randolph. Tension multiplies when Capote creates a Randolph who not only wants Joel at the Landing to satisfy his homosexual drives, but also wants Joel to choose to satisfy and enjoy those drives, himself. By creating a Joel at the beginning of puberty as the character whose choice provides the plot's resolution, Capote compels audiences to invest abundant emotional energy in the novel. Randolph, using his knowledge of human needs, sets the action in motion. He manipulates events to get Joel to the Landing, monitors events to keep him there, takes advantage of events to make himself the boy's only dependable friend, and averts Ellen's effort to visit him. This effectively closes all other doors of fulfillment, erases all other voices of love which might speak to the boy, leaving Joel but one room and one voice to satisfy his elemental need. Joel, after visiting that room, finds he must visit others—hence the title.

Capote mirrors Randolph in Joel. For example, when Randolph holds Joel's hand, whispering, "Try to like me, will you?" the lonely Joel thinks Randolph is mocking him, "so he questioned the round innocent eyes, and saw his own boy-face focused as in double camera lenses."

Randolph's definition of love mirrors the definition Joel later stumbles upon for himself. Telling Joel his story, Randolph says, "few of us learn that love is tenderness." Later, just prior to his illness, recovery, and surrender, Joel discovers this truth in the crucial scene in which he watches the black lovers and learns in a deeply personal and psychological way that love is tender. Joel would have turned to Idabel, but she wanted to be a male. They met Wisteria, and Joel watched Idabel fall in love. Capote uses Joel's stifled yearnings to foreshadow his surrender to Randolph after the fair.

At the fair, lonely Wisteria makes advances to Joel, so he hides as she searches the old house for him. His hiding fills him with self-contempt; he thinks, "What . . . terror compared with" hers? When he awakens from feverish delirium later, he is in that bed, that room, and Randolph is there.

Seeing himself as both a child to leave behind and a man to become, Joel examines his face, and the handglass affirms his approaching manhood. This passage makes it clearer that Joel and Randolph mirror each other. Joel notes the ageless quality of his own face, clearly connecting himself with Randolph's "impeccably young," still-hairless face.

As the implication becomes clearer, Joel's decision draws nearer. Capote makes believable Joel's willingness to surrender. Joel moves beyond a victimlike dependency on Randolph (which developed, briefly, during Joel's recovery) and wonders if he should tell Randolph he loves him. Joel decides no, because he realizes Randolph is "neither man nor woman, an X, an outline to be colored in." This passage reveals that Joel is now no innocent being led to slaughter. Further evidence of lost innocence comes at Little Sunshine's, where Randolph claims they were expected. At the hotel, Joel knows Randolph lied, but he asks no questions; more significant, he does not even wonder why Randolph lied. He simply stares into the fire, drifting toward sleep, hearing the old hotel's whispers of other voices, other rooms, wondering who will love him.

His answer comes when, with morning, he and Randolph, of one accord, feel it is a new day, "a slate clean for any future . . . as though an end had come." Joel is elated by this, not regretful. He asks who he is. Randolph does not answer, so Joel whoops, "I am Joel, we are the same people." Gladly, it seems, Joel identifies completely with Randolph. Later in the day, when Joel takes that last poignant look at "the boy he had left behind," and moves toward the beckoning figure, he goes unhesitatingly.

Jo Culbertson Davis

Bibliography:
Capote, Truman. Preface to *Other Voices, Other Rooms*. New York: Random House, 1968. Reflects on his first novel, explaining the source of its inspiration and discussing its autobiographical nature. Reading Capote's insights into his own work enriches the reading of the novel.

Clarke, Gerald. *Capote: A Biography*. New York: Ballantine, 1989. Well-documented from primary sources, including seven years of interviews with Capote. *Other Voices, Other Rooms* gets extensive coverage, from publication to theme to the novel's symbolism. Gives Capote's view on the homosexuality in the novel. Bibliography, notes, and an annotated index.

Moates, Marianne M. *A Bridge of Childhood: Truman Capote's Southern Years*. 1st ed. New York: Henry Holt, 1989. A compilation of stories about Capote's childhood, giving background on Joel Knox as an autobiographical character. The pathos in Joel Knox comes from Capote's investing his adult sense of abandonment in the child character.

Nance, William L. *The Worlds of Truman Capote*. Briarcliff Manor, N.Y.: Stein and Day, 1970. Illuminates Capote's insight on his use of imagination. A full chapter on *Other Voices, Other Rooms*. Provides a plot summary and thorough analysis of themes in the novel.

Reed, Kenneth T. *Truman Capote*. Boston: Twayne: 1981. Gives extensive plot summary and analysis of *Other Voices, Other Rooms*.

OTHER WOMEN

Type of work: Novel
Author: Lisa Alther (1944-   )
Type of plot: Social realism
Time of plot: Early 1980's
Locale: A city in New Hampshire
First published: 1984

Principal characters:

CAROLINE KELLY, emergency room nurse, weaver, mother of two boys
HANNAH BURKE, psychotherapist
JASON and
JACKIE, Caroline's sons
DIANA, Caroline's housemate and sometime lover
JACKSON, physician, Caroline's former husband
RICHARD DEAN, Caroline's onetime hippie lover
BRIAN STONE, physician and Caroline's suitor
ARTHUR BURKE, Hannah's husband

The Story:

Caroline Kelly was a thoroughly and helplessly divided woman. She had been married and divorced. She had left her husband for a hippie and his commune only to find that she was strongly attracted to a woman with whom she shared her lover. She currently lived with another woman in a downstairs apartment with her two sons, while Diana lived upstairs with her adolescent daughter Sharon. The two women had been physically involved, but their relationship was under great strain; Caroline decided she must have help. She went to Hannah Burke for therapy.

Caroline's divided nature displayed itself as soon as Hannah asked her to think of words that defined her. When Caroline thought of a positive quality, such as kindness, it was immediately negated by recollections of times when she had been cruel to someone she loved. When she came up with generosity, she remembered occasions of parsimony in her dealings with others. Her problems were deeply personal, but she felt that to focus on them was pointless when there was so much pain and agony in the world. Her sexual nature, in which she preferred women but also enjoyed sex with men and looked to men for security, was a further manifestation of the division in her psyche. So was her choice of profession. She not only chose to be a nurse, but she also worked in situations in which human pain and misery were constantly and immediately present, although that pain hurt her deeply.

As Caroline's therapy proceeded, the stories of her life and of Hannah's were gradually revealed. Some of their experiences were similar. Hannah's mother had died when Hannah was very young and her father had taken her from Australia to England, leaving her to be raised by a grandmother. Caroline's father was gone for years during World War II, and her parents always maintained an emotional distance from her and their other children. Hannah was distinctly heterosexual, an orientation that Caroline, for a time, took as implying a criticism of her own divided nature and less conventional lifestyle. Hannah was considerably older than her patient but like Caroline had to wrestle with depression and misery. For years after two of her

4782

four children had been killed in a freak accident, she alternated periods of rage and of despair. The equanimity that Caroline envied was hard-won.

Caroline's troubles were traceable to her childhood. Both of her parents were heavily involved in charitable work of one kind or another, and they continually reminded their children that they were much more fortunate than the objects of the parents' charities. Having given themselves so completely to their good works, the parents had no warmth left for Caroline or her younger brother. At an early age, Caroline was charged with becoming a surrogate mother for her brother and with much of the responsibility for running the household. She also was made to feel somehow responsible for all the starving children, the victims of wars and oppression, and all the poor and downtrodden. Any attempt to claim attention for herself was met by reminders of how lucky she was to have a roof over her head and food on the table.

In the course of the novel, Caroline received a forceful reminder of this upbringing and of the damage it had done her when she and her sons went to her parents' house for a Thanksgiving dinner. As usual, the family was joined by unhappy, poverty-stricken, and half-mad acquaintances of her parents. There were too many guests for the amount of food that had been prepared and the family, including Caroline's small sons, were warned not to ask for more food than they were given. Jackie, the younger son, received very little to eat and no dessert. When the company was gone, Jackie complained that he was hungry, only to be reminded by his grandparents how lucky he was to have been given anything. He left the house, and Caroline had to search for him to find him half-frozen, several blocks away. The episode created a breakthrough in Caroline's struggle to come to terms with her strong sense of guilt.

During the course of her therapy, significant changes were taking place in Caroline's life. The relationship with Diana went through several phases. Habituated to rivaling each other in making gifts and adjustments to the other's needs, they swore to break this pattern only to fall back into it whenever they tried to renew their physical intimacy. Caroline made one final attempt to find happiness in the financial and psychological security of a heterosexual relationship, experiencing a brief affair with Brian Stone, a doctor she met at the hospital where she was an emergency room nurse. When she recognized how similar she was to Brian's first wife and how Brian, despite appearances, would grow to be much like Jackson, Caroline's first spouse, she broke off the affair.

While she was guiding Caroline through a difficult process, the therapist, Hannah Burke, was also going through a similar period of growth. The deaths of two of her children had caused her years of guilt and grief, although the accident had been in no way her fault. She emerged from her depression in part through determining to become a psychotherapist in order to help others who were similarly afflicted. She succeeded in part by shutting off her own emotions in her contacts with those she advised. In coming to know Caroline and her problems, Hannah was forced to respond on a more personal level to the emotions of the other woman. The experience enabled Hannah to come to a fuller recognition of her own needs and a stronger sense of commitment to those she loved. In the end, the patient-therapist relationship was transformed into close friendship.

Caroline was able to confront her personal problems, including the growing pains of her children, by recognizing that she could not be responsible for all of the world's miseries or even all of the problems that confronted those she loved. She could be of service to others only if she accepted herself and those others as independent beings who must take responsibility for their own actions. She had not solved all of her problems, but she was able to face new experiences with an open mind. Hannah's experience with Caroline's therapy made her a more effective healer and helped renew the warmth of her solid marriage.

Critical Evaluation:

Other Women is a realistic novel whose intention is to convince the reader that the two principal characters represent real people with the problems of the real world, and these characters live with other real people in real circumstances and locations. Lisa Alther is dealing with what she regards as serious problems in a serious manner, so *Other Women* lacks the satiric bite and comic dimension of *Kinflicks* (1976) and *Original Sins* (1981). There is some humor in the novel, for example, in the jokes Caroline and Hannah tell each other when the therapeutic sessions become too intense. There is also satire in the depiction of Caroline's grotesque parents: They are so extreme in their do-gooding that they are nearly caricatures. Still, the tone of the novel is serious.

In *Other Women*, Alther explores the therapeutic relationship in two ways that break new ground. In the first place, the novel is entirely sympathetic to the role of psychotherapy in assisting troubled women to face life without fear. Hannah Burke is no Freudian, but she certainly uses many of the techniques in general use in psychiatry and in some psychoanalysis. In the second place, Alther portrays the patient-therapist relationship as very much a two-way street. The therapy that Hannah supplies for Caroline is affected directly and indirectly by events, memories, and changes in Hannah's personal life. At the same time, Caroline's experiences and the emotions she shows during sessions of therapy have their own effect on Hannah's life.

There have been critical objections to the considerable length of *Other Women*. It is a very detailed account of the lives of its characters. Caroline's experiences and her emotional and psychological changes add genuine depth to Alther's pictures of her protagonist. In a realistic novel like this one, a lack of supporting detail would be a considerable deficiency.

Other critics, comparing *Other Women* to Alther's other novels, especially to *Kinflicks*, have raised the objection that Alther loads the scales against men, too didactically favoring lesbian relationships. It is true that none of the three men with whom Caroline has had relationships is an admirable person, and that all of her heterosexual connections have turned sour. Jackson became so thoroughly involved in his medical practice that he totally neglected his wife and children. Richard Dean, after seemingly rescuing Caroline from a failed marriage, almost immediately was flagrantly unfaithful to her and showed little regard for her well-being. Brian Stone, as already noted, was on the road to becoming another Jackson.

It is also true, however, that Caroline's affairs with other women are neither emotionally secure nor permanent. At the end of the novel she recognizes that her life with Diana will soon be at an end. The relationships Caroline has had with women have been warmer and more supportive than those with men, but they also have been troubled. In *Other Women* the single important relationship between two adults that persists to the satisfaction of both is the marriage of Hannah and Arthur Burke. They have provided a home for each other and their children; they have survived by supporting each other through the trauma of losing two of those children; and they have sustained a nurturing physical and emotional relationship.

Other Women lacks some of the variety and other ingratiating qualities that attracted popular attention to Alther's earlier novels. It is not only a serious novel but one in which, unfortunately, the resolutions of its protagonists' problems are too cut-and-dried and in some senses too neatly achieved. Caroline Kelly and Hannah Burke are, nevertheless, believable and memorable characters, and the novel makes a real contribution to the understanding of how psychotherapy can work successfully.

John M. Muste

Bibliography:

Evans, Nancy. "Lives of Caroline." *The New York Times Book Review*, November 11, 1984, 26. Points to a lack of humor and originality, but with praise for the characterization.

King, Francis. "Hannah and Caroline." *The Spectator* 254, no. 8174 (March 9, 1985): 23. A friendly reading of *Other Women*, pointing out the solidity of Alther's depiction of psychotherapy and lamenting the novel's lack of humor.

Lehmann-Haupt, Christopher. Review of *Other Women*, by Lisa Alther. *The New York Times*, December 10, 1984, C16. Takes issue with Alther's negative depiction of the men in her heroine's life and argues that the case for psychotherapy is overstated.

Oktenberg, Adrian. "Odd Couple." *New Directions for Women* 14, no. 1 (January/February, 1985): 17-20. Regards *Other Women* as the most successful of Alther's novels, praising it for its reverberations and accuracy in depicting a successful relationship between women.

Peel, Ellen. "Subject, Object, and the Alternation of First- and Third-Person Narration in Novels by Alther, Atwood, and Drabble." *Critique* 30, no. 2 (1989): 107-122. Places Alther in the company of other distinguished women novelists and discusses the techniques of her fiction.

OUR ANCESTORS

Type of work: Novel
Author: Italo Calvino (1923-1985)
Type of plot: Satire
Time of plot: Middle Ages to early nineteenth century
Locale: Europe
First published: Il nostri antenati, 1960 (English translation, 1980); *Il visconte dimezzato,*
1952 (*The Cloven Viscount,* 1962); *Il barone rampante,* 1957 (*The Baron in the Trees,*
1959); *Il cavaliere inesistente,* 1959 (*The Non-existent Knight,* 1962)

> *Principal characters:*
> *The Cloven Viscount:*
> VISCOUNT MEDARDO OF TERRALBA, a Christian knight
> DOCTOR TRELAWNEY, his nephew's tutor
> PAMELA, a goatherd
>
> *The Baron in the Trees:*
> COSIMO PIOVASCO DI RONDO, the son of the Baron of Rondò
> ENEA SILVIO CARREGA, his father's illegitimate brother
> VIOLANTE, daughter of the Marchese of Ondariva
> GIAN DEI BRUGHI, a bandit
> URSULA, daughter of Don Frederico Alonso Sanchez y Tobasco
>
> *The Non-existent Knight:*
> AGILULF, a nonexistent knight in the army of Charlemagne
> RAIMBAUD OF ROUSILLON, a young recruit taken under Agilulf's wing
> BRADAMANTE, a warrior maid
> TORRISMUND OF CORNWALL, another knight
> SOPHRONIA, the woman whose rescue from brigands qualified Agilulf
> for knighthood

The Story:
The Cloven Viscount. The idealistic Viscount Medardo went to fight for Christendom against the Turks in Bohemia and was awarded the rank of lieutenant by the Holy Roman Emperor. In his first battle, he charged a cannon and was blown apart; the surgeons managed to save the right half of his body and sent him home, but he soon became deeply embittered and was increasingly disposed to terrible acts of cruelty. He placed traps on his estate, nearly causing the deaths of his nephew (the story's narrator) and his nephew's tutor, the amiable Dr. Trelawney. The Viscount fell in love with a goatgirl named Pamela, but she was understandably reluctant to marry him.

The Viscount's other half, which had been saved and nursed back to health by monks, reappeared in Terralba. Unlike his counterpart, the left side of Medardo had been infused with such sympathy for his fellow man that he became a virtual saint. The right half would not admit him to the castle, but he set about undoing much of the evil his other half had done. He, too, fell in love with Pamela, and the two halves fought a duel over her. Because neither of them was properly equipped for combat, they only succeeded in ripping open each other's wounds, and

Dr. Trelawney took advantage of the opportunity to sew them up as a single individual. The resultant whole man combined the characteristics of the two halves, but he had obtained considerable wisdom from his disjunct experience.

The Baron in the Trees. In 1767, when he was twelve years old, Cosimo quarreled with his father, an Italian baron in the province of Ombrosa, over a basket of snails. After being ordered to leave the table, he climbed a tree in the garden and swore never to set foot on the ground again. He resisted all attempts at capture and lived for fifty-three years in the canopy of the heavily wooded estates, which he eventually inherited, occasionally undertaking arboreal journeys much further afield.

Cosimo was able to strike up an acquaintance with Violante (called Viola for short), the daughter of a neighboring family. He formed a firm friendship with the Cavalier Carrega, his father's illegitimate brother, until the latter was killed in a fight against Muslim pirates. He also made friends with the notorious bandit Gian dei Brughi, after saving him from pursuing constables, and the two of them collaborated in educating themselves from books until Gian was captured and executed. Cosimo continued his studies alone, constructing an arboreal library in which he accumulated all the volumes of Denis Diderot and Jean D'Alembert's *Encyclopedia* (1751-1752) and many other volumes.

On one of his expeditions, Cosimo visited Olivabassa in Spain, where he fell in love with Ursula, the daughter of a grandee exiled by the Inquisition. Ursula joined him in the trees for a while, but she was eventually reclaimed by her family when they became reconciled with the church. After that, Cosimo was reputed to have had many brief liaisons before being reunited with Viola; unfortunately, their love affair was soon broken off, and Cosimo went mad for a while.

Cosimo had many adventures during the Napoleonic Wars. He once encountered the emperor himself and briefly exchanged words with a Russian nobleman (Prince Bolkonsky, from Leo Tolstoy's *War and Peace*). Eventually, Cosimo died, but even then he refused to descend to the ground. He was carried out to sea by a hot air balloon.

The Non-existent Knight. During a roll call of his army, Charlemagne discovered that it included a knight named Agilulf who did not exist but who, nevertheless, contrived to animate an empty suit of armor by sheer willpower and faith in the king's holy cause. Although he presented the outward appearance of the ideal knight—noble, brave, and utterly chaste— Agilulf was constantly beset by worries about the way other men saw and thought of him.

The legendary warrior-maid Bradamante (borrowed, along with the entire background of the story, from Ludovico Ariosto's *Orlando furioso* 1516-1532) was disdainful of all existing men, but she passionately loved Agilulf. Agilulf's infallible memory enabled him to correct the exaggerations that his fellow knights incorporated into their own accounts of their exploits. This caused such bad feelings that Torrismund of Cornwall was led to challenge the legitimacy of Agilulf's knighthood, alleging that the supposed virgin that Agilulf had saved from rape was, in fact, Torrismund's mother. Agilulf set out to find Sophronia, the lady in question, and he eventually recovered her from the harem of a Moroccan sultan, into which she had been sold as a slave. He hid her in a cave while he fetched Charlemagne to investigate her virginity. Unfortunately, by the time they returned, Torrismund, recently returned from a grail quest, had found her and—without having any inkling of her identity—had made love to her.

The distraught Torrismund was able to confirm that Sophronia had been a virgin, but it was too late; all that remained of poor Agilulf was his scattered armor. Agilulf's armor was recovered by his protégé, Raimbaud of Rousillon, who was then fortunate enough to be mistaken for its previous owner by Bradamante. Charlemagne made Torrismund a count, but

Torrismund had difficulty exerting his authority over the serfs he had previously saved from the villainous Knights of the Holy Grail; the serfs were now beginning to absorb the lesson that they, too, were not mere nonentities.

Critical Evaluation:

In combining his three comic fantasies into an eccentric trilogy, Italo Calvino contended that they made up "a family tree for contemporary man" cast in the mold of the *contes philoso- phiques* of Voltaire. In his introduction to the omnibus edition, the author informs readers that each fantasy contains allegorical references to the period in which it was written: *The Cloven Viscount* is, in part, a commentary on the Cold War. *The Baron in the Trees* is partly about the problem of ideological commitment in a world of rapidly shifting values; and the *The Non-ex- istent Knight* includes an investigation of the psychology of fitting into large bureaucratic organizations. Calvino's observations are obviously as studiously ironic as the stories them- selves.

The Cloven Viscount carries forward a long tradition of *Doppelgänger* stories, which Calvino's introduction traces back to the German writers Adalbert von Chamisso and E. T. A. Hoffmann, although *The Cloven Viscount* is actually closest in form and spirit to Théophile Gautier's "Le Chevalier Double." Its moral is simple enough: that there is good and bad in all human beings, and that a healthy person is one who can reconcile contrary impulses into a coherent whole. The book relates to the Cold War by insisting that division and opposition inflame and exaggerate contrary tendencies to the point at which conflict becomes inevitable— but the final confrontation in the story occurs because both halves of the unfortunate viscount have the same ideal in the humble but lovely Pamela.

The Baron in the Trees is a more original work, although it discovers its central motif simply by literalizing the common saying that idealistic intellectuals are not sufficiently "down to earth." Cosimo has a good heart, and his sympathies are all of the right kind—he is as whole and complete, in his own way, as the reunited Medardo—but he can never get fully involved in the affairs of his fellow human beings. He loses both his close friends and both his lovers because he cannot join in their adventures. He wins the respect of great men (and the enmity of some who are not great) for his nobility of spirit, but they are the doers, while he remains an observer. Although he remains true to his reckless promise to the very end, his is not an example that can or should be followed. By the time he has lived through the Enlightenment, the French Revolution, and the Napoleonic Wars, a quieter evolution of folkways has devastated the great forests which had allowed him such freedom as he had; in the final paragraph, the anonymous brother who has told his story observes that Ombrosa itself no longer exists.

On one level, *The Baron in the Trees* is a forthright assault on that kind of idealism that refuses all material anchorage, arguing that such an attitude of mind is ultimately futile. The work is, however, a sympathetic commentary that deftly develops a great fondness for Cosimo, to the extent that his fate seems authentically tragic. What, after all, do the earthbound doers actually achieve? Their deaths are, for the most part, ignominious—Cosimo learns that Ursula eventually died in a convent. The titles of the Utopian tracts that Cosimo writes in later life—but that hardly anyone reads—are pompously overblown, but so was the empire that Napoleon tried to build. When Tolstoy's borrowed hero tells Cosimo about his quest to understand the appalling phenomenon of war, and Cosimo replies that his own equally problematic devotion to trees has been "entirely good," the reader is entitled to wonder which of them has pursued the nobler cause. Such open-mindedness is typical of Calvino; the politeness of his satire is remarkable, and it is almost without parallel.

Although it encompasses less than one hundred pages, *The Non-existent Knight* is the most complicated and the most eventful of the three tales. It is humorous, and fully deserves to be ranked as one of the comedic masterpieces of world literature. Like Miguel de Cervantes Saavedra's *Don Quixote*, it looks with a coolly cynical eye at the tradition of chivalric romance, taking as its primary model the greatest Italian contribution to that tradition, Ariosto's fifteenth century epic poem, *Orlando furioso*.

On a superficial level, *The Non-existent Knight* performs much the same deflationary task as Cervantes' novel, revealing the perfect knight of romance as a phantom unsustainable in confrontation with a more down-to-earth view of reality. Even though Calvino wrote three and a half centuries after Cervantes, it cannot be said that the puncturing of such illusions was no longer necessary; many of the myths of "romance" have proved astonishingly resilient, surviving into the present in degraded but nevertheless powerful versions. The story is, however, more evidently multilayered than its predecessors; the passive narrators are by no means disinterested in the events they report, but the hypothetical reporter of this tale—a nun named Sister Theodora, who is writing it as a penance—turns out to have been much more intimately involved in it than is first apparent. This adds a further twist to an already convoluted plot.

Calvino may well have been justified in claiming a particularly timeliness for *The Non-existent Knight* because the problem of facelessness and lack of identity became particularly marked in the era of bureaucratization, but the text itself claims a much wider relevance. The unwillingness of the serfs to accept Torrismund as their appointed overlord provides a reminder that chivalric romance and real history have been equally culpable in ignoring the vast majority of the people who lived in the past, tacitly pretending that progress is the work of the few rather than of the many.

While he is correcting the self-congratulatory exaggerations of braggarts, Agilulf becomes a spokesman for all those who have been excluded from the many-stranded story of our ancestors. When he uses his expertise to obtain a place in the line of battle where Raimbaud might take reprisals against the slayer of his father, but, instead, only succeeds in enabling him to kill his enemy's spectacle-bearer, he stands in the place of anyone who has ever seen well-laid plans go awry. His anxieties regarding his own nonexistence and his consequent problems of self-image are the anxieties of everyone who feels that the social self presented to the world is not a true self at all. This is nowhere more evident than in Agilulf's amours; on the one hand, Bradamante only loves him because he does not exist, and on the other, the lovely Priscilla only spends one unforgettable night with him because she is under the misapprehension that he does exist.

Agilulf's adventure, however impossible and nonsensical it may be, compels people to consider the extent and nature of their own existence, and perhaps to find it tragically lacking in some intangible but vital respect. People all obtain their identities from their roles—their suits of armor—and they are all in danger of seeing those roles fall apart, only to be reassembled and redefined by others luckier than themselves.

Some readers may be puzzled by the non-chronological order of the three stories, but they are not arranged as they are simply because that is the order in which Calvino wrote them. The cloven viscount is, indeed, the most remote of our ancestors, crudely separated into good and evil halves, without a great deal of philosophical sophistication residing in either. The baron in the trees is much more contemporary, possessed of an encyclopedic education that he really ought to be able to put to practical use but, somehow, cannot. The nonexistent knight may belong to a distant era (an era that had never been, save in the literary imagination), but he is the closest of all to the kind of person people actually are; he is people as they were the last time they turned to look at themselves with a sadly critical and contemplative eye, and he is a caricature more apt than the most carefully detailed character of any mundane novel.

Brian Stableford

Bibliography:
Cannon, JoAnn. *Italo Calvino: Writer and Critic*. Ravenna, Italy: Longo, 1981. A brief, comprehensive survey of the writer and his work.
Carter, Albert Howard III. *Italo Calvino: Metamorphoses of Fantasy*. Ann Arbor: University of Michigan Press, 1987. A comprehensive study focusing on uses of fantasy in the author's works.
Hume, Kathryn. *Calvino's Fictions: Cogito and Cosmos*. Oxford, England: Clarendon Press, 1992. The most comprehensive study of Calvino's works. The main discussion of the trilogy is in the chapter "Identifying the Labyrinth."
Woodhouse, J. R. "From Italo Calvino to Tonio Cavilla: The First Twenty Years." In *Calvino Revisited*, edited by Franco Ricci. Ottawa, Canada: Dovehouse Editions, 1989. A compact overview of the writer's earlier work, including a commentary on the trilogy.
_____. *Italo Calvino: A Reappraisal and an Appreciation of the Trilogy*. Hull, England: University of Hull Publications, 1968. A long essay on the trilogy.

OUR HOUSE IN THE LAST WORLD

Type of work: Novel
Author: Oscar Hijuelos (1951-   )
Type of plot: Bildungsroman
Time of plot: 1920's-1970's
Locale: Cuba and the United States
First published: 1983

Principal characters:
ALEJO SANTINIO, an immigrant from Cuba in New York
MERCEDES SANTINIO, his wife
HORACIO and
HECTOR, their sons

The Story:

The aristocratic Sorrea family lived in Holguín, a prosperous old city in eastern Cuba. Their immense house had to be sold when the patriarch, Teodoro Sorrea, died in 1929. Mercedes, the second of three daughters, saw the ghost of her father frequently and dreamed about the happy life she had lived in the house. She married Alejo Santinio, a well-dressed dandy from the small town of San Pedro, ten miles away from Holguín. He was the youngest of two brothers and nine sisters. His family owned farmland, but he wanted a more exciting life away from rural Cuba and decided to emigrate with his wife Mercedes to the United States.

Alejo sent his wife and children to visit their relatives in Cuba. The three-year-old Hector loved Cuba, but his other brother Horacio was only impressed by the sight of Teodoro Sorrea's ghost. They met Alejo's great-grandmother Concepción O'Connors; she had married an Irish sailor, which explained the light skin and European looks of the two brothers.

Upon their return to New York, Hector had to be hospitalized for almost a year because he had contracted an infection in Cuba. The nurses ridiculed him for not speaking English and made him afraid of speaking Spanish. Hector became sickly and obese. His brother tried to make him tougher so that other children would not treat him like a freak. Horacio was very talented and hardworking; he was a choirboy and held several jobs to help the family. Frustrated by his family and failed love relationships, he joined the Air Force.

Alejo had a heart attack because he worked too much and stayed out too late, and Mercedes had to get a job scrubbing floors. She had two sisters in Cuba, Rina and Luisa. The latter came to America with her family in the 1960's, escaping from the government of Fidel Castro. The arrival of Hector's relatives made him remember the smells and tastes of Cuban things. Mercedes realized that, after twenty years of life in America, her family did not have anything, while her relatives who had recently arrived had established themselves quickly and prospered in a short time.

Two of Alejo's sisters, Lolita and Margarita, lived in America. Margarita had been living in New York City since 1932 with her husband Eduardo Delgado, a Cuban tobacco exporter. They welcomed the new immigrants who settled in as boarders in their apartment in Spanish Harlem. Alejo enjoyed having fun with his friends while Mercedes worried about the expenses. He spent their savings on gifts, worthless business investments, and gambling. After several jobs, he became a cook in a hotel restaurant.

Horacio had been named after his maternal great-grandfather, and Hector was named after Alejo's older brother who had died in Cuba. Buita, Alejo's eldest sister, had come to visit from

Cuba with her husband Alberto Piñón, a musician who was the leader of a popular band. She hated Mercedes and made life unbearable for her. Mercedes dreamed about Buita coming at her with a knife. Margarita and Eduardo also had a son and moved back to Cuba. When her husband died, Margarita returned to America. She, her son, Buita, and Alberto settled in Miami, where many other Cubans lived.

Alejo started drinking heavily after the news of his brother's death. Influenced by Buita, he was treating Mercedes badly and responding with physical abuse when she complained about their poverty. He hit his wife and children to show them that he was the man of the house. He spent many nights away from home; Mercedes was afraid that he would abandon her and that she would be thrown out of the country.

When Horacio came back from service in Europe, he criticized his family, not wanting their life of poverty. He moved out of the house and got married. Hector did not listen to his parents, got drunk often, and dreamed of escaping to a better life; he visited his aunt Buita and her rich husband in Miami. Hector admired the Cubans who lived well, wanting to be like them. He was enjoying himself when he suddenly heard about his father's death and had to return home.

For a few years, Alejo had been holding two jobs. While Hector was in Miami, he suffered an injury at work and died. Mercedes became oblivious to everything, kept the apartment dark, walked in circles, went off into trances, imitated the voices of the dead, and talked to herself. Hector, who had not been able to cry for his father, was afraid to see his ghost at night. He could not sleep because of the strange noises around him; ghosts seemed to inhabit the house.

Hector graduated from high school and college; he also traveled throughout the country. After he moved out, he lived near his mother's apartment, helping her with shopping and household chores. At the age of twenty-five, he worked a few blocks from where his father used to work. He wrote thoughts down, dreaming about writing a book. He often heard the voices of his family members; by writing down his dreams and theirs, he felt closer to them.

Critical Evaluation:

Oscar Hijuelos, a native New Yorker of Cuban parentage, graduated from the City College of New York. He was awarded the Rome Fellowship in Literature of the American Academy and Institute of Arts and Letters for *Our House in the Last World*. He won the 1990 Pulitzer Prize, the first given to a Latino, for his second novel, *The Mambo Kings Play Songs of Love* (1989), which became a major motion picture. He published *The Fourteen Sisters of Emilio Montez O'Brien* in 1993. The first novel illustrates the experience of immigrant life and coming of age in America.

Narrated in the third person, the novel is divided into fifteen sections, each headed by a title and, except for the last one, with years indicating the time of plot covered. The last section, entitled "Voices from the Last World," includes the first-person memories of the dreams of the principal characters. Several literary techniques are used successfully; flashbacks, anticipation, monologues, and dialogues enliven the narrative. Familiar incidents are seen from different points of view. The use of Spanish words, with a fluid transition from that language to English, represents the sociocultural dualism of bilingual texts.

Just as their ancestors had emigrated from Spain to Cuba, Alejo and Mercedes Santinio move to the United States in search of more opportunity. They remain attached to memories of the old country while their children, born in the new country, struggle to achieve an identity within the two cultures. Horacio and Hector provide an account of the experience of growing up in a Hispanic immigrant family, one in which the tension between generations allows the author to portray the cross-cultural differences between two worlds.

The nostalgia for the warm and sunny island clashes with the cold reality of life in a crowded inner-city neighborhood. The parents have moved from a privileged position in Cuba to become an underprivileged ethnic minority in America. They compensate for their feelings of powerlessness by committing violent acts against each other and their sons. Life in the urban barrio gives them all a sense of alienation, fear, and bitterness. While other Cubans prosper, they allow circumstances to destroy their self-confidence and self-respect; they feel isolated because they cannot communicate in English and do not take advantage of sound opportunities. They scream, cry, and fight, making the lives of their sons miserable.

Horacio and Hector encounter street violence and discrimination; they are called "Whitey" or "Pinky" because of their light skin and are told: "Why don't you go back to where you came from." Kids shout at the sickly Hector, "Look at the little queer," and make fun of his Spanish. For Hector, to be "americanized" means to be fearful and lonely, and yet Spanish represents "the language of memory, of violence and sadness" which his parents use. Hector, "tired of being a Cuban cook's son," reacts by refusing to talk to his father, not wanting to be like him. He admires the Cubans who did not despair and "did not fall down."

Hector's identity crisis is revealed when the reader is told that he feels "Part 'Pop,' part Mercedes; part Cuban, part American—all wrapped tightly inside a skin in which he sometimes could not move." He questions what it is to be "Cuban" since he is considered American by the Hispanics. He is not sure whether Cuba is a paradise, and his sense of marginality prevails. Horacio decides to leave his drunken father, his lunatic mother, and his troubled brother; he escapes from the world of ghosts.

In the novel, the island becomes a poetic motif. Recollections and nostalgic remembrances are the driving force for poetic creation. In the end, we listen to the voices of the protagonists telling us their dreams. Horacio imagines Alejo visiting him, his wife Marilyn, and his son Stevie; he realizes that, after all, the father gave them the ability to love and survive. Hector imagines a house which is "memory," where he finds love, respect, and happiness. He feels transported by a light into "another world before awareness of problems" and is mesmerized by images of Cuba.

Hector understands that his parents never had the chance to get what they wanted out of life. His mother used to write poetry and was a singer but never achieved her dreams; she searched for the lost house of her father and was surrounded by ghosts in her own house. Their future was destroyed by fear, worries, and memories; they were not strong enough to face social injustice, racism, and economic suffering. Hector realizes that writing is a form of survival and that it will help him succeed in the future. Alejo's words to Mercedes in a dream will guide him: "Do not be afraid." With this message, Hijuelos' novel represents a valuable contribution to the Latino narrative that has been integrated into American mainstream fiction.

Ludmila Kapschutschenko-Schmitt

Bibliography:
Augenbraum, Harold, and Ilan Stavans, eds. *Growing up Latino: Memoirs and Stories.* Boston: Houghton Mifflin, 1993. This collection of Latino fiction and nonfiction, discusses the coming-of-age and memoir literary tradition which helps to understand Hijuelos' works; a selection from his second novel is included.
Fein, Esther B. "Oscar Hijuelos's Unease, Wordly and Otherwise." *The New York Times* (April 1, 1993): 19. Excellent article about Hijuelos, his life and works, including his personal observations. Confirms the autobiographical nature of his first novel.

Foster, David William. *Handbook of Latin American Literature*. New York: Garland, 1992. Includes Latino writing in America. Discusses Hijuelos' works in the context of the cultural history and cultural contributions of Cuban Americans in the United States.

Kanellos, Nicolás. *Biographical Dictionary of Hispanic Literature in the United States*. Westport, Conn.: Greenwood Press, 1989. Each entry provides a biography, the literary genres, themes and analyses of the works by each author, and a bibliography. Hijuelos' novel is discussed for its treatment of Cuban assimilation in America.

Perez Firmat, Gustavo. *Life on the Hyphen: The Cuban-American Way*. Austin: University of Texas Press, 1994. Focuses on Cuban American performers and writers. Hijuelos is presented as a cultural figure whose work exemplifies a bilingual, bicultural identity in search of a collective identity.

OUR MUTUAL FRIEND

Type of work: Novel
Author: Charles Dickens (1812-1870)
Type of plot: Domestic realism
Time of plot: Mid-nineteenth century
Locale: London
First published: serial, 1864-1865; book, 1865

> *Principal characters:*
>> JOHN HARMON, alias JULIUS HANDFORD, alias JOHN ROKESMITH, the son
>> of Old John Harmon
>> MR. BOFFIN and
>> MRS. BOFFIN, Old John Harmon's employees and heirs
>> BELLA WILFER, the young woman betrothed to John Harmon
>> WEGG, a scheming street peddler with a wooden leg
>> MR. VENUS, a taxidermist and Wegg's compatriot
>> MORTIMER LIGHTWOOD, an indolent lawyer hired by Mr. Boffin
>> EUGENE WRAYBURN, his friend
>> GAFFER HEXAM, a man who gets his living from the river
>> LIZZIE HEXAM, his daughter
>> ROGUE RIDERHOOD, another waterfront character

The Story:

Upon his return to England to marry Bella Wilfer in compliance with the conditions of his father's will, John Harmon was thought to have been murdered soon after having left the ship; a body found by Gaffer Hexam was identified as his. Actually, Harmon had not died; fearing for his life and shrinking from the enforced marriage, he assumed the name first of Julius Handford, then of John Rokesmith.

As Rokesmith, Harmon became a secretary to Mr. Boffin, who had inherited the estate of Harmon's father after young John Harmon was pronounced dead. Before that, Mr. Boffin, who had never learned to read, had begun to employ a street peddler named Wegg to read to him such books as took his fancy. Mr. and Mrs. Boffin enjoyed their new wealth and leisure, but they both regretted that the son and disinherited daughter of old Harmon should not have lived to enjoy the fortune that had come to them. They tried to find a little orphan whom they could raise, hoping that the boy could have some of the advantages little John Harmon had not had. The Boffins also brought Bella Wilfer to live with them in their grand new house, wishing to provide her with the kind of life she might have had as John Harmon's wife.

Bella Wilfer, who was beautiful but mercenary, intended to make a good match. When Harmon, in his role as Rokesmith, declared his love, she rejected him with disdain. When, much later, Mr. Boffin heard that Rokesmith had aspired to her hand, there was a bitter scene, in which he charged Rokesmith with impudence and discharged him. By that time, however, Bella had become wiser, having seen how money and wealth had apparently changed the easygoing Mr. Boffin into an ill-tempered, avaricious miser. She refused to stay any longer with the Boffins and returned to the modest life of her father's home.

Mr. Boffin began to have trouble with Wegg, whom he had established in the comfortable house in which the Boffins and old Harmon had lived. Not satisfied with his good fortune, Wegg had become increasingly avaricious and spent all his time searching for possible items of value that old Harmon might have secreted in his house or in the dustheaps in the yard, on which his fortune had been based. In his searches, Wegg found a will dated after the will from which the Boffins had profited, in which most of the money was to go to the Crown.

With the assistance of an acquaintance, the taxidermist named Venus, Wegg blackmailed Mr. Boffin, telling him that unless he shared the fortune equally with them, they would make known the existence of the later will. Mr. Boffin pretended to agree.

Mr. Boffin had offered a reward to anyone giving information about the murderer of young Harmon and had placed the matter in the hands of Mortimer Lightwood, a lawyer. Lightwood's only clue was Handford, who had been present when the body was identified as young Harmon's. For a time, Lightwood thought that the murderer might have been Gaffer Hexam, who was known to make a living from finding corpses in the river. Hearing that the Hexam's daughter suffered under the suspicion attached to her father, Harmon, in his role as Rokesmith, secured an affidavit from Rogue Riderhood, who had informed against Hexam; in the affidavit Riderhood admitted to having given false information.

When Bella Wilfer returned to her father's home, she was much improved; she had realized that she could only marry a man she loved, and that she loved Rokesmith, who had been unjustly discharged on her account. When Rokesmith, apparently penniless and without a job, came to her she joyfully accepted his suit. Their marriage proved a happy one, for Rokesmith told her that he had found a job that kept them in modest comfort. Both were happy when their child was born.

One day, Lightwood accidentally met Rokesmith and Bella on the street and immediately recognized Rokesmith as Handford. That evening, a policeman came to arrest Rokesmith, who was forced to admit his real identity as John Harmon. As it turned out, the corpse identified as Harmon's had really been that of his would-be murderer, who had been killed by thieves. The mistake had occurred because the man had changed into Harmon's clothes after drugging him. Harmon had to admit his real identity to his wife, and more besides. Mrs. Boffin had early guessed who he really was, and Mr. Boffin had only pretended to become an unpleasant miser for the purpose of showing Bella the kind of person she might become if she continued in her mercenary ways. The success of their scheme was proved when she defended Rokesmith to Mr. Boffin and returned to her father's home. Anxious for Harmon to inherit his father's fortune, the Boffins turned over the estate to him; Bella thus became the rich woman she had at one time wished to be.

The situation with Wegg and Venus was easily settled because there, too, Mr. Boffin had only pretended when he agreed to the terms of their blackmail. Mr. Boffin actually possessed an even later will, which he had kept secret only because of its insulting language about Harmon and his dead sister. This later will, too, left the fortune to the Boffins, but they returned it to Harmon and his family. Wegg was taken out of the house by a servant and dropped into a wagon piled high with garbage.

Critical Evaluation:

Charles Dickens' last completed novel, *Our Mutual Friend*, is certainly among his greatest novels, containing perhaps the most mature expression of his artistic abilities. The novel, which reflects many of his major concerns as a writer and social critic, is a complicated one, with a very intricately constructed and elaborate plot. The first two chapters of the novel provide a stark contrast. In the first, Gaffer Hexam, the "bird of prey," is in a boat on the Thames with his daughter Lizzie, on the lookout for the drowned bodies that are the source of his livelihood; in the second, the newly rich Veneerings are giving a dinner party. The unexpected link between the two worlds is provided in the third chapter.

By revealing the real links between people and classes that suspect no connection at all (this culminates in the wedding of Eugene Wrayburn and Lizzie Hexam at the end), Dickens shows that these two worlds, separated from each other in thought, are physically close, each involved with the other.

In holding a mirror up to the cumbersome structure of society, Dickens used the idea of depth and surface to reflect the polite world on top and the seething, half-known world of misery and crime below. Dickens also implies that the sophisticated few are often stupid and easy to understand, while the unlettered many can be complex and intriguing.

This inversion of the expected is one of the book's dominating features. Other reversions include the scene in which misguided charity hounds Betty Higden, the reversed parent-child relationship of Jenny Wren and her father (to some extent, though in a more benign sense, this is also true of Bella Wilfer and her father), and the unequal relationship between the morally upright Riah and the scoundrel Fledgeby. These reversals indicate something of a new-found flexibility in Dickens' treatment of moral problems. As the problems came to seem more doubtful and difficult, his literary treatment of them became that much more clear and intense.

Also central to the novel is the relationship between marriage, money, and societal values. This theme is worked out in the three important marriages in the novel, those between Harmon and Bella, Eugene and Lizzie, and Alfred and Sophronia Lammle. In each of these marriages, money is an important issue. Harmon, though he is or could be rich, must pretend to be poor to be certain that Bella is not marrying him for his money. Eugene must marry Lizzie in the face of pressures from his family and society that he marry a woman with money. When the Lammles marry, each is motivated solely by the delusion that the other has money.

Money destroys and corrupts in a wide variety of ways. Old Harmon was the ruined victim of his own money. His son, too, is nearly ruined by this money. Boffin pretends to be corrupted by money in order to show its corruptive force, and is so harassed by his money that he can scarcely wait to get rid of it. Bella begins to be corrupted by money and is saved.

The two major symbols in *Our Mutual Friend*, the river and the dustheap, show Dickens at the height of his abilities. The river cuts across all inflated, unreal social distinctions in much the same way that the epidemic cuts across these same boundaries in *Bleak House* (1853). At times, the river—its motion, mystery, swell, and obscurity—is used quite overtly as a symbol for the passage of life itself. It is also hard to resist the idea that the river has a sacramental, baptismal character. It is a source of mystery, bringing salvation or damnation. In the course of the narrative, many of the characters fall into the river. Either they are drowned or they emerge as new men. John Harmon emerges as John Rokesmith, a guise he can abandon only when he has been assured that Bella Wilfer loves him and not his money. Eugene Wrayburn's narrow escape from drowning comes at a time when he has at last overcome the view natural to a man of his class that someone like Lizzie is not a suitable marriage partner. For characters such as Headstone and Riderhood, however, the river is a source of death. Riderhood, a man to whom the river means nothing more than a criminal livelihood, almost drowned once before. Others expect him to change after he is rescued, but he refuses the gift of a second chance and eventually really drowns, locked in the murderous grasp of the schoolmaster Headstone.

The novel's other dominant symbol is the dustheap. The image of the dustheap is, in fact, less fantastic than it may at first appear. Dust, dustheaps, and dust contractors were all common in Dickens' time. The dust collected from the streets was piled in huge heaps, which came to have great value, and were often the source of great fortunes in early Victorian times.

Frequently, the dustheaps contained buried treasures along with the wastes. Thus, there is an obvious connection between money and dirt. Money equals dust. The dustheaps were filth, ordure, excrement—and money. Money is also linked with dirt in the tales from the book about misers, all of whom are physically unclean and squalid. This equation of money with dirt and the quest of money with the sifting of rubbish pervades the work. The comical figure Wegg cuts in his lantern-lit scavenging on the dustheap finds a sinister echo in Lizzie Hexam's father at his grisly occupation on the river, and a refined, although equally precise, reverberation in the economic maneuvering of the Lammles and the Veneerings. At every level of society, people of all ages are shown in the act of hunting for money. The heroine herself does so in the beginning. The force of the dustheaps as a symbol resides in its absurdity, the high ironic comedy that clings to the surreptitious activity of digging through refuse to find nonexistent gold. It is as if the whole society were being not chastised but made to appear mad. Few novelists deal better with the fascination money exerts on people than Dickens does in *Our Mutual Friend*.

"Critical Evaluation" by Craig A. Larson

Bibliography:
Ackroyd, Peter. *Dickens*. New York: HarperCollins, 1990. An exhaustive, critical coverage of Dickens' life and work.
Cockshut, A. O. J. *The Imagination of Charles Dickens*. New York: New York University Press, 1962. Contains an insightful chapter on *Our Mutual Friend*, which focuses on the symbolic meanings of the river and the dustheaps.
Cotsell, Michael. *The Companion to "Our Mutual Friend."* London: Allen and Unwin, 1986. Contains factual annotations on every aspect of the text and notes on historical allusions to current events, and intellectual and social issues and customs, etc. An excellent accompaniment to the novel.
Herst, Beth F. *The Dickens Hero: Selfhood and Alienation in the Dickens World*. New York: St. Martin's Press, 1990. A good study of Dickens' protagonists. Views John Harmon as one who moves "from alienation through self-discovery to a new sort of alienation."
Romano, John. *Dickens and Reality*. New York: Columbia University Press, 1978. Discusses realism in Dickens, using *Our Mutual Friend* as one of the primary examples. Despite its realist nature, the novel makes no effort to conform to our "real" world, which contributes to its overall success.

OUR TOWN

Type of work: Drama
Author: Thornton Wilder (1897-1975)
Type of plot: Symbolism
Time of plot: 1901-1913
Locale: New Hampshire
First performed: 1938; first published, 1938

> *Principal characters:*
> DR. GIBBS, a physician
> MRS. GIBBS, his wife
> GEORGE and
> REBECCA, their children
> MR. WEBB, a newspaper editor
> MRS. WEBB, his wife
> EMILY and
> WALLY, their children
> SIMON STIMSON, director of the choir

The Story:

Early one morning in 1901, Dr. Gibbs returned to his home in Grover's Corners, New Hampshire. He had just been across the tracks to Polish Town to deliver Mrs. Goruslowski's twins. On the street he met Joe Crowell, the morning paperboy, and Howie Newsome, the milkman. The day's work was beginning in Grover's Corners. Mrs. Gibbs had breakfast ready when her husband arrived, and she called the children, George and Rebecca, to the table. After breakfast the children left for school in the company of the Webb children, Wally and Emily, who were neighbors.

After the children had gone, Mrs. Gibbs stepped out to feed her chickens. Seeing Mrs. Webb stringing beans in her back yard, she crossed over to talk with her. Mrs. Gibbs had been offered three hundred and fifty dollars for some antique furniture; she would sell the furniture, she had decided, if she could get Dr. Gibbs to take a vacation with her. Dr. Gibbs had no wish to take a vacation, however; if he could visit the Civil War battlegrounds every other year, he was satisfied.

The warm day passed, and the children began to come home from school. Emily Webb walked home alone, pretending she was a great lady. George Gibbs, on his way to play baseball, stopped to talk to Emily and told her how much he admired her success at school. He could not, he insisted, imagine how anyone could spend so much time over homework as she did. Flattered, Emily promised to help George with his algebra. He said that he did not really need school work, because he was going to be a farmer as soon as he was graduated from high school. When George had gone, Emily ran to her mother and asked if she were pretty enough to make boys notice her. Grudgingly, her mother admitted that she was, but Mrs. Webb tried to turn Emily's mind to other subjects.

That evening, while Mrs. Webb and Mrs. Gibbs were at choir practice, George and Emily sat upstairs studying. Their windows faced each other, and George called to Emily for some advice on his algebra. Emily helped him, but she was more interested in the moonlight. When she called George's attention to the beautiful night, he seemed only mildly interested.

The ladies coming home from choir practice gossiped about their leader, Simon Stimson. He drank most of the time, and for some reason he could not adjust himself to small-town life. The ladies wondered how it would all end. Mr. Webb also wondered. He was the editor of the local paper; as he came home, he met Simon roaming the deserted streets. When Mr. Webb reached his home, he found Emily still gazing out of her window at the moon—and dreaming.

At the end of his junior year in high school George was elected president of his class, and Emily was elected secretary-treasurer. When George walked home with Emily after the election, she seemed so cold and indifferent that George asked for an explanation. She told him that all the girls thought him conceited and stuck-up because he cared more for baseball than he did for his friends. She expected men to be perfect, like her father and his.

George said that men could not be perfect, but that women could—like Emily. Then Emily began to cry, insisting that she was far from perfect. George offered to buy her a soda. As they drank their sodas, they found that they really had liked each other for a long time. George said he thought he would not go away to agricultural school, after all. When he graduated from high school, he would start right in working on the farm.

After a time Dr. and Mrs. Gibbs learned that George wanted to marry Emily as soon as he left high school At first it was a shock to them, for they could not imagine that George was anything but a child. They wondered how he could provide for a wife, and whether Emily could take care of a house. Then Dr. and Mrs. Gibbs remembered their own first years of married life. They had had troubles, but now they felt that the troubles had been overshadowed by their joys. They decided that George could marry Emily if he wished.

On the morning of his wedding day George dropped in on Mr. and Mrs. Webb, and Mrs. Webb left the men alone so that her husband could advise George. All that Mr. Webb had to say, however, was that no one could advise anyone else on matters as personal as marriage.

When George had gone, Emily came down to her last breakfast in her parents' home. Both she and Mrs. Webb cried. Mrs. Webb had meant to give her daughter some advice on marriage, but she was unable to bring herself to it.

At the church, just before the ceremony, both Emily and George felt as if they were making a mistake; they did not want to get married. By the time the music started, however, both of them were calm. The wedding ceremony was soon over. Grover's Corners had lost one of its best baseball players. Nine years passed; it was the summer of 1913. Up in the graveyard above the town the dead lay, resting from the cares of their lives on earth. Now there was a new grave; Emily had died in childbirth and George was left alone with his four-year-old son.

It was raining as the funeral procession wound its way up the hill to the new grave. Then Emily appeared shyly before the other dead. Solemnly they welcomed her to her rest—but she did not want to rest; she wanted to live over again the joys of her life. It was possible to do so, but the others warned her against trying to relive a day in her mortal life.

Emily chose to relive her twelfth birthday. At first it was exciting to be young again, but the excitement wore off quickly. The day held no joy, now that Emily knew what was in store for the future. It was unbearably painful to realize how unaware she had been of the meaning and wonder of life while she was alive. Simon Stimson, a suicide, told her that life was like that, a time of ignorance and blindness and folly. He was still bitter in death.

Emily returned to her resting place. When night had fallen, George approached, full of grief, and threw himself on Emily's grave. She felt pity for him and for all the rest of the living. For now she knew how little they really understood of the wonderful gift that is life itself.

Critical Evaluation:

Thornton Wilder won a Pulitzer Prize in fiction in 1928 for his second novel, *The Bridge of*

San Luis Rey, and then won Pulitzers for drama in 1938 and 1943 for *Our Town* and *The Skin of Our Teeth*, thus making him the only writer ever to win Pulitzers for fiction and for drama. Wilder is most remembered and admired for *Our Town*, perhaps the most popular and frequently produced of all American plays, given the great number of high school and community theater productions it has generated. The popularity and simplicity of *Our Town* frequently obscure its fundamentally radical style and theme.

In a period when realism was the common style of the American theater, Wilder's dramatic style was militantly antirealistic. In *The Happy Journey to Trenton and Camden* (1931), Wilder uses a bare stage and four kitchen chairs to represent a family making a journey of seventy miles by automobile. In *Our Town*, the Act I stage directions insist on "No curtain. No scenery. The audience, arriving, sees an empty stage in half-light." In the earliest productions of *Our Town*, many audience members were uncomfortable with the Stage Manager, who comments on the action, and actors who pantomime to create the illusion of set and props. In his preface to *Three Plays* (1957), Wilder asserts that by the 1930's in American theater, stage realism had undermined the audience's capacity for a full emotional and intellectual response to plays. According to Wilder, when the stage set is filled with scenery, furniture, and props designed to trick the audience into believing that the present moment is "real," the audience's imagination is also chained to the particularity of that play's time and place. Wilder wanted to communicate general ideas that transcended the particularity of individual experience, so he created characters who were types rather than psychologically complex individuals, and he placed these characters in bare stage environments, avoiding particulars of time and place. Thus, George and Emily have little depth as characters, but as types they can represent all young people who court one another, marry, and encounter catastrophic loss. The town Emily and George live in is also not simply Grover's Corners, New Hampshire, but a little New England town that is part of "the United States of America; Continent of North America; Western Hemisphere; the Earth; the Solar System; the Universe; the Mind of God," as Rebecca Gibbs puts it in Act II. When George and Emily talk to each other from their upper-story bedroom windows, they do so from the tops of stepladders rather than from realistically represented rooms. Thus, the audience focuses on George and Emily's conversation rather than on particulars of place and time.

Thematically, Wilder asserts that a sensitivity to human sadness and failure does not have to lead to despair. Awareness of human pain can coexist with a belief in an essentially benevolent universe. In Wilder's plays, human lives are disappointingly brief and their actions seem small when measured against the cosmic scale, yet Wilder insists that humans and their lives are not insignificant. Humans may suffer profoundly or survive by the skin of their teeth, but life remains worth living. The glory of existence resides in the mundane and particular moment—in the birth of a child, the singing of a hymn, or even in the clanking of Howie Newsome's milk bottles as he delivers milk on his morning route. In Act III of *Our Town* Emily discovers that human beings are generally blind to the joys of life and do not "ever realize life while they live it—every, every minute." Wilder's plays exhort their audiences to rediscover their zest for life.

Our Town is most important in the history of American drama for its innovations in dramatic style. Wilder brought to prominence in America the possibilities of nonrealistic staging. These possibilities were also developed in the revolutionary modern dramas of the Italian playwright Luigi Pirandello and of the German playwright Bertolt Brecht. Wilder is also important because he confronts the pain and disappointment of human life yet maintains an optimistic vision. Measuring human lives against a cosmic scale, without the comfort of God, led many writers in the twentieth century to various forms of despair. For Wilder, however, the prevalence of human pain, frustration, and failure meant that people could rediscover the simple joys of existence. Human beings can face life's pain and live with hope because, as the Stage Manager says, there is "something way down deep that's eternal about every human being." Ironically, Wilder is perhaps more respected in Europe, especially in Germany, than he is in the United States. European dramatists as important as Brecht, Max Frisch, and Eugène Ionesco have acknowledged their debt to Wilder's stylistic innovations and profound themes.

"Critical Evaluation" by Terry Nienhuis

Bibliography:
Castronovo, David. "The Major Full-Length Plays: Visions of Survival." In *Thornton Wilder*. New York: Frederick Ungar, 1986. A striking, intelligent, and convincing reading of *Our Town* as "American folk art."
Corrigan, Robert W. "Thornton Wilder and the Tragic Sense of Life." In *The Theater in Search of a Fix*. New York: Delacorte Press, 1973. Finds that Wilder's plays "fall short of tragedy" but argues that "no other American dramatist more fully affirms that miracle of life which so much modern drama would deny."
Fergusson, Francis. "Three Allegorists: Brecht, Wilder, and Eliot." In *The Human Image in Dramatic Literature*. New York: Doubleday, 1957. Still one of the best discussions of Wilder's unusual dramatic technique and its relationship to the themes of his plays.
Haberman, Donald C. *Our Town: An American Play*. Boston: Twayne, 1989. A thorough examination of the play and its place in literary history. Attempts "to recover the play's intellectual respectability and to demonstrate how solid and at the same time how revolutionary its stagecraft is."
Wixon, Douglas Charles, Jr. "The Dramatic Techniques of Thornton Wilder and Bertolt Brecht: A Study in Comparison." *Modern Drama* 15 (September, 1972): 112-124. A thorough analysis of the devices Wilder uses to subordinate the theatrical illusion of reality and to emphasize the examination of ideas.

OUT OF AFRICA

Type of work: Autobiography
Author: Isak Dinesen (Baroness Karen Blixen-Finecke, 1885-1962)
First published: Den afrikanske Farm, 1937 (English translation, 1937)

> *Principal characters:*
> KAREN BLIXEN, a passionate, courageous Danish woman
> DENYS FINCH-HATTON, a British trader and hunter
> FARAH ADEN, Karen's Somali servant
> KAMANTE GATURA, a young Kikuyu boy
> BERKELEY COLE and
> INGRID LINDSTROM, friends and neighboring landowners
> BROR BLIXEN, Karen's husband

The Story:

Karen Blixen owned a coffee farm in Africa, at the foot of the Ngong Hills. As she sat at home in Rungstedlund, Denmark, many years later, she remembered her seventeen years in Kenya. Captivated by the beauty of the African landscape and its people, she was struck by the feeling of having lived for a time up in the air. Nairobi was the closest town, twelve miles away, and when Karen and her husband, Bror, first came to Africa, there were no cars. She traveled to and from the farm, Mbogani House, by mule cart. Her able overseer, Farah Aden, helped her make the adjustment to her new life. From her first weeks in Africa, she felt a great affection for the East African tribes: the Somali, the Kikuyu, and the Masai.

Karen met Kamante Gatura when he came to the small medical clinic she operated for the people on the farm. He looked as if he were dying. Open sores covered his legs, and he seemed to face death with passionless resignation. In spite of her best efforts, Karen's treatment failed. The disease was beyond her. She decided to send the nine-year-old boy to the Scotch Mission hospital, where he remained for three months. Kamante returned to the farm on Easter Sunday, his legs completely healed. He said, "I am like you," meaning that now he, too, was a Christian.

In time, Kamante was trained as Blixen's chef. A genius in the kitchen, he could pick out the plumpest hen in the poultry yard, and his egg whites towered up like clouds. He rarely tasted his own dishes, preferring the food of his fathers, yet he grew famous preparing meals for Karen's friends and guests, including the prince of Wales.

Following a year-long drought, when it seemed the universe was turning away from her, Karen Blixen began to write. Her workers asked what she was doing. When she said she was trying to write a book, they viewed it as an attempt to save the farm. Comparing her scattered loose-leaf pages to Homer's *Odyssey* (c. 800 B.C.E.), a book pulled from her library shelves, Kamante expressed doubt that she would ever be able to write a book. He asked what she would write about; she replied that she might write of him. He looked down at himself and in a low voice asked, "Which part?" It was many years before she published her reflections of Africa, but when she finally did, Kamante was an important part of her story.

Karen Blixen did not understand the various African dialects, but the regal and intelligent Farah served as interpreter throughout her sojourn in Kenya. Many of the tribes looked to Blixen to settle their disputes. On one occasion, when she was asked to judge a shooting accident, she turned to her friend Chief Kinanjui, who ruled over more than a hundred thousand Kikuyus. By this time, the automobile had come to Africa, and when Chief Kinanjui arrived in his new car, he did not want to get out until she had seen him sitting in it. Finally alighting, he took his seat next to Karen and Farah, and together they agreed upon a fair restitution for the parties in the case: One man must give the other a cow with a heifer calf. Blixen never shied away from such disputes. Eventually she crusaded for the rights of all East Africans to each successive governor of the colony and to any wealthy or influential settlers who would listen.

After Karen and Bror divorced, the farm had many visitors, from large groups of Africans who came for the Ngomas (social dances) to European friends. Berkeley Cole called Mbogani House his sylvan retreat. He brought leopard and cheetah skins to be made into fur coats and fine wines to serve with dinner. He reminded Karen of a cat, a constant source of heat and fun. His stories of the old days would make even the Masai chiefs laugh, and they were prepared to travel many miles to hear them. When Berkeley died young, Karen felt a tremendous sense of loss.

Karen's friend Ingrid Lindstrom had come to Africa with her husband and children to operate a flax farm. Like Karen, Ingrid worked passionately to save her farm during the hard times. They wept together at the thought of losing their land. As the years passed and one bad harvest followed another, Karen's chances of keeping the farm grew slimmer.

Denys Finch-Hatton gave Karen a powerful reason to stay in Africa, and thanks to his love and encouragement, she fought to stay as long as she could. Although he owned land in another part of the continent, Denys made her farm his home. He lived there between safaris, returning unexpectedly after weeks or months away. His visits were like sparkling jewels. Denys taught her Latin and introduced her to the Greek poets; he brought her a gramophone and classical music. In the evenings, he spread cushions on the floor, and she would sit and spin long tales she had made up while he had been away. Karen and Denys, whenever they were together, had great luck hunting lions. One spring, two lions came to the farm and killed two of the oxen. That night, Denys was determined to get the pair before they could strike again. With Karen holding a torch, they tracked the lions and killed them near the edge of the property.

One of Karen's greatest pleasures was flying in Denys's airplane over Africa. His moth machine, as she called it, could land on her farm only a few minutes from the house, and the two often made short flights over the Ngong Hills at sunset. Other times, they traveled farther to find huge herds of buffalo or to soar with the eagles. These happy days did not last, because the coffee plantation was rapidly failing. Too little rain produced poor yields. When the price of coffee fell, Karen Blixen's investors said she would have to sell.

She was making plans to dispose of her belongings and to find suitable land for her workers when the news came that Denys had been killed in the crash of his plane. Heartbroken, Karen searched in the rain to find an appropriate burial site. Finally she chose a narrow, natural terrace in the hillside behind the farm. At the grave, she and Farah erected a tall white flag so that from her window she could look to the hills and see a small white star. After she left Africa, the Masai reported to the district commissioner that many times at sunrise and sunset they had seen a lion and lioness standing on the grave.

In the dark days following the funeral, Ingrid stayed with Karen. They did not talk of the past or the future. They walked together on the farm taking stock of Karen's losses, naming each item and lingering fondly at the animal pens and the beautiful flower gardens. Blixen's last months in Africa took her on a beggar's journey from one government official to the next. Her goal was to find enough land for her workers to settle on together. Finally, the government agreed to give them a piece of the Dagoretti Forest Reserve where they could preserve their community. In the end, Farah drove Karen to the train station. She could see the Ngong Hills to the southwest, but as the train moved farther from her home, the hand of distance slowly smoothed and leveled the outline of the mountain.

Critical Evaluation:

Only things at a distance can be seen clearly. Although it was several years before Isak Dinesen published her African experience, her early formal training at the Royal Academy of Fine Arts helped form her sense of what it meant to be a writer. The notes for her book had been written in times of great weariness and anger. Distanced from those conflicts, she became essentially a modernist artist, attempting to replace the real with the ideal. Critics have said that there are no real Africans in her writing, only mythical representations of a lost era. *Out of Africa* was written for and well received by Europeans and Americans. It is Dinesen's vision of the African's vision of her. With her widely read book, Dinesen participated in the construction of Africa and Africans in the Western consciousness. At the same time, she constructed her own identity.

Taking a line from philosopher Friedrich Nietzsche as the epigraph for *Out of Africa*— "Equitare, arcem tendere, veritatem dicere: To ride, to shoot with a bow, to tell the truth"— Dinesen echoes many of his ideas. An important theme, well illustrated by Blixen's character as well as by the Africans, is Nietzsche's belief that fate, rather than guilt or sin, is the cause of suffering, and that fate should be courageously accepted. Denys Finch-Hatton, who clearly emerges as a hero in the work, represents Nietzsche's call for a new nobility, individuals who have learned to know life through action and who, therefore, have a use for history. In essence, he teaches Karen Blixen how to become herself. Before knowing Finch-Hatton, she had found her teachers in the library and become herself only in her imagination, while her false self acquiesced to society's demands. As she constructs her new life in Africa, both in the living and in the remembering, those restraints are lifted and she truly soars. Much of the book's appeal rests with its power to allow readers to find themselves through their imagination.

Dinesen's philosophical flights were grounded, however, in very real cultural concerns: the relations between the colonizers and the oppressed; the encroachment upon Africa of modern life; and the implications of a sexist, racist, and classist society. Her writing is full of paradox. Although she sympathizes with the problems of Africans under colonization, she frequently refers to them as primitive children and sees the ideal situation as that of colonial settler and African working harmoniously side by side, as she and Farah had. Although she supported Denys' beloved safaris, she portrayed the lion hunts as efforts by wealthy Europeans to play at being self-sufficient by hunting their own food. Finally, in spite of her efforts to cultivate an independent woman's life, her relationship with Denys, and indeed with the land, placed her in a variation of the African mythic figure of suffering woman. Yet the notion of a paradise lost dominates *Out of Africa*. Perhaps Dinesen's greatest gift is her assurance that the most tragic losses, whether real or imagined, can be overcome.

Carol F. Bender

Bibliography:

Dinesen, Isak. *Letters from Africa, 1914-1931.* Translated by Anne Born and edited by Frans Lasson. Chicago, Ill.: University of Chicago Press, 1981. Excellent collection of correspondence. Illuminates the reality of Dinesen's African experience.

_____. *Shadows on the Grass.* New York: Random House, 1960. Written much later in her life, this book is an epilogue to *Out of Africa*. Brings the reader up to date on the individuals mentioned in the first book.

Donelson, Linda. *Out of Isak Dinesen in Africa: The Untold Story.* Iowa City: Coulsong List, 1995. A thoughtful analysis of existing correspondence. Medical doctor Donelson gives special attention to Dinesen's persistent ill health and the myths surrounding it.

Horton, Susan. *Difficult Women, Artful Lives: Olive Shreiner and Isak Dinesen In and Out of Africa*. Baltimore: The Johns Hopkins University Press, 1995. Outstanding analysis of how Dinesen journeyed to Africa to discover her own interior.

Thurman, Judith. *Isak Dinesen: The Life of a Storyteller*. New York: St. Martin's Press, 1982. Critically acclaimed biography. Begins with Dinesen's ancestors and scrupulously traces the development and the personality of Isak Dinesen. Essential reading.

OUT OF THE SILENT PLANET

Type of work: Novel
Author: C. S. Lewis (1898-1963)
Type of plot: Science fiction
Time of plot: Early 1900's
Locale: England and Mars
First published: 1938

Principal characters:
>ELWIN RANSOM, a Cambridge philologist
>WESTON, a renowned physicist
>DEVINE, a greedy academic
>SORNS, tall, intellectual Martians
>HROSSA, friendly, otterlike Martians
>HYOI, a hross who befriends Ransom
>HNAKRA, a ferocious water beast
>PFIFLTRIGGI, dwarflike Martians
>ELDILS, translucent spirit beings
>OYARSA, the ruling spirit of Mars

The Story:

Elwin Ransom was on vacation, taking a walking tour alone through the English countryside. Seeking shelter from the rain and lodging for the night, he met a farm woman, frantic that her retarded son, Harry, had not yet come home from his job at a neighboring professor's home. Hoping this professor might provide lodging, he promised to find Harry. The professor's house was dark and locked. Ransom squeezed through the hedge and came upon Professor Weston and his friend Devine in a scuffle with young Harry. Startled, they let Harry go. Devine recognized Ransom as an old schoolmate, and introduced him to Weston, a renowned physicist. They offered Ransom a drink, and Ransom realized too late that he had been drugged.

Ransom regained consciousness aboard a spaceship. He overheard Weston and Devine say they were returning to Malacandra, where aliens called sorns had ordered them to bring a human sacrifice. Ransom realized he was that sacrifice.

As they traveled, Ransom found that space was not black, cold, or vacant but flooded with invigorating light. A month later, they landed on Malacandra. The ground was covered by a rubbery pink vegetation, the sky was pale blue, the distant mountains were lavender: It was a bright, pastel world. Since the gravity was so low, everything (mountains, trees, ocean waves) was thinner and taller than on earth.

The three men set up camp. Six sorns approached, each one fourteen feet tall, pale, and spidery thin. Devine and Weston grabbed Ransom and pulled him toward the sorns, but as they stepped into a lake, a large sea monster with crocodile-like jaws attacked them. As Devine and Weston shot at it, Ransom escaped. The next day Ransom encountered an alien that looked like a tall otter. They stared curiously at each other and tried to communicate. It was a hross, and Ransom became eager to learn its language. After a long, choppy boat ride and a short walk, they came to the hross village.

Ransom lived peacefully among the hrossa for about five weeks, studying the language and becoming close friends with Hyoi, the hross who first found him. He learned that in addition to sorns and hrossa, there was a third intelligent species on the planet called pfifltriggi, craftsmen who made articles out of gold. The three species, or hnau, lived in harmony.

He was also instructed in their religion: Maleldil the Young created all things, and now lived with the Old One. A spirit called Oyarsa ruled the whole planet, and lesser spirit beings named eldil frequently visited the planet and talked to its inhabitants. The hrossa insisted that Ransom should go to Oyarsa. Ransom told the hrossa about the sea monster with the crocodile jaws. They became intensely excited: The hnakra had not been seen for many years. The greatest honor in their culture was to kill the hnakra. The entire village began to prepare their boats and spears for the great hunt. Ransom was honored by an invitation to fight alongside Hyoi and Whin. As they sought the hnakra, an eldil appeared and commanded Ransom to go to Oyarsa. Ransom refused. Immediately the hnakra appeared. After a furious fight, Ransom, Hyoi, and Whin killed it. As they rested on the shore, jubilant in their victory, Hyoi was suddenly shot and killed by Weston, who had been hiding in the forest. As he died, Hyoi called Ransom his eternal brother because they had slain the hnakra together.

Whin told Ransom that Hyoi had died because Ransom had disobeyed the eldil. Ransom left immediately to seek Oyarsa. He climbed a steep mountain where he met Augray, a sorn. Augray gave him oxygen and food, and showed him Earth through his telescope. Augray called Earth Thulcandra, which means the silent planet. The next day, Ransom climbed onto Augray's shoulder, and Augray carried him to Meldilorn, an island covered with huge golden flowers and filled with eldils. While exploring the island, Ransom saw a row of stone monoliths, each one bearing an intricate relief carving of significant events. One showed the solar system, and by studying it, Ransom realized Malacandra was Mars. A pfifltrigg named Kanakaberaka carved a likeness of Ransom, Weston, Devine, and their spaceship into a monolith.

The next morning, Ransom was awakened by an eldil who announced, "Oyarsa sends for you." Ransom walked between two long rows of hrossa, sorns, and pfifltriggi to where Oyarsa appeared as a shimmer of light hovering over the water. Oyarsa said that he sent for Ransom in order to learn about Earth. He explained that each planet has its own Oyarsa, but that long ago the Oyarsa of Earth had rebelled against the Old One. Since then, no word had come from the silent planet. Weston and Devine were also brought before Oyarsa. They could not see Oyarsa and suspected a trick. Weston bellowed, in his broken version of the Martian language, "Everyone who no do all we say pouff! bang! we kill him." Then Weston tried to bribe them with cheap beads. They burst out laughing: Weston was making a fool of himself.

Oyarsa ordered Weston to be taken away and doused with cold water, hoping to bring him to his senses. Meanwhile, the Malacandrians sang a beautiful, elaborate funeral song to honor Hyoi and the two other hrossa that Weston had murdered. Then, with blinding light, Oyarsa disintegrated the three bodies. Weston returned dripping wet, and answered Oyarsa's questions, with Ransom acting as interpreter. Weston said he wanted to perpetuate the human race onto other planets. He expected Oyarsa to be impressed, but instead Oyarsa became convinced that Weston was utterly corrupt. Oyarsa ordered Weston and Devine to return to Earth. He gave them exactly ninety days' worth of air and food.

Oyarsa dismissed Weston and Devine, and talked with Ransom about Earth. He gave Ransom the choice to remain on Malacandra or to return to Thulcandra. Ransom chose to return. On the trip back, the spaceship passed dangerously close to the sun. Then the moon cut in front of them, and they were forced to turn the ship away from Earth. Realizing they were almost out of air and food, Ransom returned to his cabin to prepare for death. He fell asleep, and when he woke, he heard rain. The ship had somehow landed on Earth.

He emerged from the ship and walked half an hour through the English countryside. Suddenly he heard a loud noise as the ship disintegrated. He walked into a pub and ordered a pint of bitter. Ransom fell ill and feared that the trip had been a delusion. Then he received a letter from Lewis asking about the word "Oyarses," found in an ancient book. Ransom told Lewis the whole story. They agreed no one would believe it, so they decided to write the novel. The postscript is a letter from Ransom to Lewis criticizing the "mistakes" in the book.

Critical Evaluation:

Out of the Silent Planet is the first of three books that tell the story of Elwin Ransom. In the second book, *Perelandra* (1943), Ransom is transported to Venus, where he prevents the king and queen of that world from falling to temptation. In the third book, *That Hideous Strength* (1945), the focus shifts to Earth, where a team of scientists threaten England. In *Out of the Silent Planet*, C. S. Lewis writes a fairly straightforward narrative. What gives the book its unusual power is its mythic quality. The complexity of the Martian cultures, the sensitivity of the description, and the themes of courage, friendship, and charity all combine to create a cosmic vision that is moving, poetic, and uniquely beautiful.

Lewis intends his space trilogy to be a criticism of typical space operas and an answer to the scientific materialism of writers such as H. G. Wells, Olaf Stapledon, and J. B. S. Haldane. Lewis mocks science-fiction conventions such as aliens that are insects or bug-eyed monsters, the need for page after page of pseudoscientific explanation, and constant conflict and adventure. Lewis addresses each of these conventions by contrasting Ransom's expectations with the reality he finds on Malacandra. Ransom expects cold, dark space; instead, as he travels he is flooded with light, "totally immersed in a bath of pure ethereal colour and of unrelenting though unwounding brightness." Ransom expects Martians to be characterized by "twitching feelers, rasping wings, slimy coils, curling tentacles"; instead, he meets aliens who are thoughtful, not physically repulsive, and civilized. Ransom expects science to be central to advanced cultures; instead, he finds a superior culture in which art, music, and poetry are integral to survival. Ransom expects nonstop, hair-raising adventure; instead, he is most moved by his experience as part of the ordinary, decent, daily life of the hrossa.

Lewis also uses the novel as a platform to condemn the notion of progress for its own sake, progress without any regard for the worth of the individual. This is seen most clearly in the discussion between Weston and Oyarsa toward the end of the book. Ransom must act as interpreter between them, and through this ingenious device, Lewis shows that Weston's high-sounding goals—more technology, human progress, greater space exploration—are motivated by selfish ambition. Oyarsa emphasizes that it is impossible to love humanity as an abstract concept; one can only love each individual person. It is clear from everything Weston has said and done that he does not know how to do that.

In his letters, Lewis also makes clear that he intended his novels to elaborate Christian truths without using typical Christian symbols. In his description of Maleldil the Younger, for example, Lewis is making reference to Jesus Christ. In discussing the rebellion of the Oyarsa of Earth, Lewis is making reference to the rebellion of Satan. The silence that has come to the planet as a result of this great rebellion has separated Earth from the other planets, and has separated Earth's people from knowledge of their creator. Throughout the novel, Lewis is arguing that the peace, charity, artistry, and productivity of the hnau of Malacandra are the direct result of their harmony with God.

Diana Pavlac Glyer

Bibliography:

Downing, David C. *Planets in Peril: A Critical Study of C. S. Lewis's Ransom Trilogy.* Amherst: University of Massachusetts Press, 1992. The only book-length study of the space trilogy. Exceptionally insightful, helpful, and complete. Begins with a discussion of Lewis' life, showing how Lewis' values and Christian faith influenced these books.

Gibson, Evan K. *C. S. Lewis: Spinner of Tales: A Guide to His Fiction.* Washington, D.C.: Christian University Press, 1980. *Out of the Silent Planet* receives a rather brief chapter; a good introduction to Lewis' fiction.

Howard, Thomas. *C. S. Lewis: Man of Letters: A Reading of His Fiction.* San Francisco: Ignatius Press, 1987. Contains a lengthy chapter about *Out of the Silent Planet.* A highly personal and energetic discussion.

Manlove, Colin N. *C. S. Lewis: His Literary Achievement.* New York: St. Martin's Press, 1987. Analyzes each of Lewis' novels, with careful attention to the underlying themes of each.

Walsh, Chad. *The Literary Legacy of C. S. Lewis.* New York: Harcourt Brace Jovanovich, 1979. Evaluates the strengths and weaknesses of Lewis' works, concluding that Lewis' best work is his fiction. Praises Lewis' ability to combine great literary skill with a distinctly Christian worldview.

THE OVERCOAT

Type of work: Short fiction
Author: Nikolai Gogol (1809-1852)
Type of plot: Social realism
Time of plot: Early nineteenth century
Locale: St. Petersburg, Russia
First published: "Shinel," 1842 (English translation, 1923)

Principal characters:
> AKAKII AKAKIIEVICH BASHMACHKIN, a government clerk
> PETROVICH, a tailor
> A CERTAIN IMPORTANT PERSONAGE, a bureaucrat

The Story:

In one of the bureaus of the government, there was a clerk named Akakii Akakiievich Bashmachkin. He was a short, pockmarked man with dim, watery eyes and reddish hair beginning to show spots of baldness. His grade in the service was that of perpetual titular councilor, a resounding title for his humble clerkship. He had been in the bureau for so many years that no one remembered when he had entered it or who had appointed him to the post. Directors and other officials came and went, but Akakii Akakiievich was always to be seen in the same place, in the same position, doing the same work, which was the copying of documents. No one ever treated him with respect. His superiors regarded him with disdain. His fellow clerks made him the butt of their rude jokes and horseplay.

Akakii Akakiievich lived only for his work, without thought for pleasure or his dress. His frock coat was no longer the prescribed green but a faded rusty color. Usually it had sticking to it wisps of hay or thread or bits of litter someone had thrown into the street as he was passing by, for he walked to and from work in complete oblivion of his surroundings. Reaching home, he would gulp his cabbage soup and perhaps a bit of beef, in a hurry to begin transcribing papers he had brought with him from the office. His labors finished, he would go to bed. Such was the life of Akakii Akakiievich, satisfied with his pittance of four hundred rubles a year.

Even clerks on four hundred a year, however, must protect themselves against the harsh cold of northern winters. Akakii Akakiievich owned an overcoat so old and threadbare that over the back and shoulders one could see through the material to the torn lining beneath. At last he decided to take it to Petrovich, a tailor who did a large business repairing the garments of petty bureaucrats. Petrovich shook his head over the worn overcoat and announced that it was beyond mending, fit only for footcloths. For one hundred and fifty rubles, he said, he would make Akakii Akakiievich a new overcoat, but he would not touch the old one.

When he left the tailor's shop, the clerk was in a sad predicament. He had no money for an overcoat and little prospect of raising so large a sum. Walking blindly down the street, he failed to notice the sooty chimney sweep who jostled him, blacking one shoulder, or the lime that fell on him from a building under construction. The next Sunday he went to see Petrovich again and begged the tailor to mend his old garment. The tailor surlily refused. Then Akakii Akakiievich realized that he must yield to the inevitable. He knew that Petrovich would do the work for eighty rubles. Half of that amount he could pay with money he saved, one kopeck at a time, over a period of years. Perhaps in another year he could put aside a like amount by doing without tea and candles at night and by walking as carefully as possible to save his shoe leather. He began that very day to go without the small comforts he had previously allowed himself.

In the next year Akakii Akakiievich had some unexpected luck when he received a holiday bonus of sixty rubles instead of the expected forty which he had already budgeted for other necessities. With the extra twenty rubles and his meager savings, he and Petrovich bought the cloth for the new overcoat—good, durable stuff with calico for the lining and catskin for the collar. After some haggling it was decided that Petrovich was to get twelve rubles for his labor.

At last the overcoat was finished. Petrovich delivered it early one morning, and opportunely, for the season of hard frosts had already begun. Akakii Akakiievich wore the garment triumphantly to work. Hearing of his new finery, the other clerks ran into the vestibule to inspect it. Some suggested that the owner ought to give a party to celebrate the event. Akakii Akakiievich hesitated but was saved from embarrassment when a minor official invited the clerks, including Akakii, to drink tea with him that evening.

Wrapped in his warm coat, Akakii Akakiievich started off to the party. It had been years since he had walked out at night, and he enjoyed the novelty of seeing the strollers on the streets and looking into lighted shop windows.

The hour was past midnight when he left the party; the streets were deserted. His way took him into a desolate square, with only the flickering light of a police sentry box visible in the distance. Suddenly two strangers confronted him and with threats of violence snatched off his overcoat. When he came to himself, in the snowbank where they had kicked him, the clerk ran to the policeman's box to denounce the thieves. The policeman merely told him to report the theft to the district inspector the next morning. Almost out of his mind with worry, Akakii Akakiievich ran all the way home.

His landlady advised him not to go to the police but to lay the matter before a justice of the peace whom she knew. That official gave him little satisfaction. The next day his fellow clerks took up a collection for him, but the amount was so small that they decided to give him advice instead. They told him to go to a certain important personage who would speed up the efforts of the police. Finally Akakii Akakiievich secured an interview, but the very important person was so outraged by the clerk's unimportance that he never gave the caller an opportunity to explain his errand. Akakii Akakiievich walked sadly home through a blizzard which gave him a quinsy and put him to bed. After several days of delirium, in which he babbled about his lost overcoat and a certain important person, he died. A few days later another clerk sat in his place and did the same work at the bureau.

Before long rumors began to spread through the city that a dead government clerk seeking a stolen overcoat had been seen near Kalinkin Bridge. One night a clerk from the bureau saw him and almost died of fright. After Akakii Akakiievich began stripping overcoats from passersby, the police were ordered to capture the dead man. Once the police came near arresting him, but the ghost vanished so miraculously that thereafter the police were afraid to lay hands on any malefactors, living or dead.

One night, after a sociable evening, a certain important personage was on his way to visit a lady friend about whom his wife knew nothing. As he relaxed comfortably in his sleigh, he felt a firm grip on his collar. Turning, he found himself eye to eye with a wan Akakii Akakiievich. In his fright he threw off his overcoat and ordered his coachman to drive him home at once. The ghost of Akakii Akakiievich must have liked the important person's warm greatcoat. From that time on he never molested passersby or snatched away their overcoats again.

Critical Evaluation:

Nikolai Gogol's "The Overcoat" was the inspiration for many major nineteenth century Russian authors. The impact of this work was summarized by Fyodor Dostoevski in a now-famous statement: "We all come from under Gogol's 'Overcoat.'" Gogol's fiction, Gogol's life (particularly in his social origins), his orientation toward Russian society, and his literary aspirations anticipated experiences common to many of his literary followers.

Gogol's life was aristocratic to the core, containing at the same time many of the most venerable and lackluster elements of this dominant Russian social class. He was the son of a Ukrainian noble who enjoyed some prestige and little wealth. Gogol early abandoned any thought of leading a bucolic life. Instead, he moved to St. Petersburg, the capital of czarist Russia, and attended a school designed to prepare him for a profession in the Department of Justice. A career in the Russian civil service was entirely in keeping with one of the most esteemed values of the nobility, service to society. Gogol hoped to achieve this goal as a bureaucrat rather than as an agronomist. After less than a year, however, he became intolerant of the tedium of the bureaucratic life and began to write. He led a dissident, cavalier life, wrote an epic poem and, after borrowing money from his mother that she could ill afford to lend, published his own work. The poem was unsuccessful. Distraught, Gogol purchased all the copies he could locate and burned them. Ironically, Gogol framed his literary life with the burning of his work. Shortly before his death, Gogol spent an entire evening casually tossing a manuscript of the second part of *Dead Souls* into a stove.

Disenchanted with St. Petersburg, with his literature, and with his career, Gogol again borrowed from his nearly penniless mother and left Russia for Western Europe. Like other Russian writers who followed, Gogol spent most of his productive life in Western Europe. He died in Russia in 1852. At the time of his death, he had become a religious fanatic, and his death was the result of a grotesque religious fast. Even in his death, he was a model for future writers, such as Fyodor Dostoevski and Leo Tolstoy, both of whom became religious zealots in their later lives.

Gogol's published works are relatively few in number. He is best remembered for *Dead Souls* (1842, 1855) and for the comedic drama *The Inspector General* (1836). The latter was Gogol's most successful work to appear during his lifetime. Spoofing the Russian bureaucracy, it brought cascades of laughter from the otherwise sober Czar Nicholas I. Of his shorter works, "The Overcoat" is the best known. Although Gogol rejected a career as a Russian bureaucrat, he never deviated from his commitment to the aristocratic ideal of service to society. In fact, age intensified his desire to better Russia, and he became convinced that he was chosen to deliver a great message to his countrymen.

In "The Overcoat," Gogol tailored a trenchant and unmistakable, and often repeated, statement. The Russian bureaucracy, once the agent and symbol of enlightenment and change in Russia, had become in Gogol's time the instrument of oppression and sterility for both those whom it purported to serve and those who functioned within it. Akakii Akakiievich, possessing neither an inclination toward agriculture nor an ability therein, was a model bureaucrat: loyal and conscientious. He was faceless too; his days were spent as a copier of government documents, each day exactly like all the others. Underpaid and unpraised, Akakii was like all of his bureaucratic contemporaries, the foundation on which the nineteenth century Russian state stood. He rarely came in contact with the public. His vapid, tedious, and impersonal professional existence eradicated his personal life. Akakii was virtually isolated from society and from his own humanity. When his overcoat was stolen, he was forced into the role of Ivan Q. Public, confronting an irritated and disinterested police magistrate who scolded him for his lack of respect and sent him unaided on his way. In the end, Akakii's death can be attributed as much to the newly acquired knowledge that the Russian bureaucracy is cold and unfeeling as to the loss of his coat.

It was precisely bureaucracy's icy inability to serve Russian society that forced Gogol to forsake a life as a civil servant. Yet, he could not divorce himself from his own, however poorly practiced, aristocratic ideal to serve society. Unable to serve from within the state, Gogol left Russia for Western Europe; unable to serve as a bureaucrat, Gogol left justice for literature. Service through literature was difficult, and Gogol knew it. This perhaps irreconcilable problem accounts for an aspect of Gogol's literature which is unique—his humor. Gogol fashioned in "The Overcoat" a literary pattern ideally suited to the needs of Russian writers. The unique Gogolian technique is a mix of scathing satire and gentle humor; such a combination was conspicuously missing in Russian literature. While *Dead Souls* remains the author's humorous magnum opus, "The Overcoat" contains ample evidence of Gogol's gift of satire. Dostoevski's dictum is correct—Russian literature did come from Gogol's "The Overcoat." No Russian writer ever duplicated Gogol's sense of humor. Maybe other Russian authors did not need to, but when Gogol lined his works with humor, he was shielding himself from what he considered to be the insanities and the difficulties of his literary mission.

The difficulty, or even the impossibility, of service to Russia is one message contained in "The Overcoat." Gogol, like all premier writers, identified a social problem the resolution of which became a mission for future Russian authors. After Gogol, writers did not hesitate to challenge the inadequacy of the Russian state and society even when, as was frequently the case, they were censored or incarcerated for doing so.

"Critical Evaluation" by John G. Tomlinson, Jr.

Bibliography:
Alissandratos, Julia. "Filling in Some Holes in Gogol's Not Wholly Unholy 'Overcoat.'" *The Slavonic and East European Review* 68, no. 1 (January, 1990): 22-40. Examines the patterns and allusions relating to religious texts in Gogol's story. Argues that Gogol parodies Russian religious tradition.
Chizhevsky, Dmitry. "About Gogol's 'Overcoat.'" In *Gogol from the Twentieth Century*, compiled by Robert A. Maguire. Princeton, N.J.: Princeton University Press, 1976. An insightful essay that shows how Gogol's seemingly humorous story points to a serious moral vision: The devil ensnares humans into obsession not only with exalted things in life, but also with trivia.
Eichenbaum, Boris. "How Gogol's 'Overcoat' Is Made." In *Gogol from the Twentieth Century*, compiled by Robert A. Maguire. Princeton, N.J.: Princeton University Press, 1976. Analyzes Gogol's stylistic technique, highlighting the performative nature of the narrative by focusing on its puns, hyperbole, and abrupt shifts in tone.
Fanger, Donald. *The Creation of Nikolai Gogol.* Cambridge, Mass.: The Belknap Press of Harvard University Press, 1979. Underscores the problematic nature of Gogol's text. Noting the presence of discrete elements of several thematic patterns, this analysis concludes that "The Overcoat" remains elusive, pointing always to movement rather than resolution.
Nabokov, Vladimir. *Nikolai Gogol.* New York: New Directions, 1944. A dazzling evocation of the stylistic and verbal idiosyncrasies of Gogol's text. Nabokov's commentary identifies the salient features of Gogol's style and suggests what kind of worldview this stylistic display reveals.

THE OX-BOW INCIDENT

Type of work: Novel
Author: Walter Van Tilburg Clark (1909-1971)
Type of plot: Regional
Time of plot: 1885
Locale: Nevada
First published: 1940

Principal characters:
> GIL CARTER, a ranch hand
> CROFT, his friend
> CANBY, a saloon keeper
> TETLEY, a rancher
> GERALD, his son
> DAVIES, an old storekeeper
> MARTIN, a young rancher

The Story:

Gil Carter, a cowpuncher, and his friend Croft rode into the little frontier town of Bridger's Wells. At Canby's saloon, they reined in their horses. Canby was alone at the bar. He served Gil and Croft with silent glumness and told them that Rose Mapen, the girl Gil sought, had gone to Frisco. He also told the two cowboys that all the local cowhands and their employers were on the lookout for rustlers who were raiding the ranches in the valley. More than six hundred head of cattle had been stolen, and the ranchers were regarding one another with suspicion. Gil and Croft felt suspicion leveled at them when a group of riders and townsmen came into the bar.

Gil began to play poker and won one hand after another. The stakes and the bad feeling grew higher and finally erupted in a rough confrontation between Gil and a man named Farnley. Gil downed his opponent but was knocked unconscious when Canby hit his head with a bottle.

A rider rode up to the saloon with the word that rustlers had killed Kinkaid, Farnley's friend. Farnley did not want to wait for a posse to be formed, but cooler heads prevailed, among them old Davies, a storekeeper, and Osgood, the Baptist minister. Everyone there joined in the argument for and against immediate action. Davies sent Croft and a young cowboy named Joyce to ask Judge Tyler to swear in a posse before a lawless manhunt began. The judge was not eager to do so in the absence of Risley, the sheriff, but Mapes, a loud, swaggering, newly appointed deputy, demanded that he be allowed to lead the posse.

Meanwhile the temper of the crowd had begun to grow sullen. Ma Grier, who kept a boardinghouse, joined the mob. When Judge Tyler arrived, his long-winded oration against a posse stirred the men up more than anything else could have done. Davies took over again and almost convinced the men they should disband. At that moment, however, Tetley, a former Confederate officer and an important rancher, rode up with the news that his Mexican herder had seen the rustlers.

Mob spirit flared up once again. Mapes deputized the men in spite of Judge Tyler's assertion that a deputy could not deputize others. The mob rode off in the direction of Drew's ranch, where Kinkaid had been killed. There the riders found the first trace of their quarry. Tracks showed that three riders were driving forty head of cattle toward a pass through the range. Along the way, Croft talked to Tetley's sullen son, Gerald, who was not cut out to be a rancher, a fact ignored by his stern, domineering father. Croft thought the boy appeared emotional and unmanly.

The stagecoach suddenly appeared over a rise. In the darkness and confusion, the driver thought that the riders were attempting a holdup. He fired, hitting Croft high in the chest. When he learned his mistake, he pulled up his horses and stopped. One of the passengers was Rose Mapen, the girl Gil had hoped to find in Bridger's Wells. She introduced the man with her as her husband. Gil was furious.

Croft had his wound tended and continued with the posse. On a tip from the passengers, the posse headed for the Ox-Bow, a small valley high up in the range. Snow was falling by the time the riders came to the Ox-Bow. Through the darkness, they saw the flicker of a campfire and heard the sound of cattle. Surrounding the campfire, they surprised the three men sleeping there—an old man, a young, dark-looking man, and a Mexican—and seized and tied them.

The dark-looking young man insisted that there was some mistake. He said that he was Donald Martin and that he had moved into Pike's Hole three days earlier. One of the members of the posse, however, a man from Pike's Hole, claimed he did not know Martin or anything about him. Martin began to grow desperate. He demanded to be taken to Pike's Hole, where his wife and two children were. The members of the posse were contemptuous. Only Davies tried to defend Martin, but Mapes soon silenced the old storekeeper. The cattle were proof enough. Besides, Martin had no bill of sale. He claimed that Drew, who had sold him the cattle, had promised to mail a bill of sale later.

The posse was for an immediate hanging. Tetley wanted to force a confession, but most of the riders said it was no kindness to make the three wait to die. Martin told them that the Mexican was only his rider and that he knew little about him because the man spoke no English. The old man was a simpleminded fellow who had agreed to work for Martin for very little pay. Martin was permitted to write a letter to his wife. Shortly afterward, when it was discovered that he possessed Kinkaid's gun, the Mexican began to speak English, claiming that he had found the gun.

Tetley appointed three of the posse—his milksop son, Farnley, and Ma Grier—to lead the horses away from the men, whose necks would then be caught in the nooses of the ropes tied to the overhanging limb of a tree. Martin, despairing, made Davies promise to look after his wife, and he gave Davies the letter he had written and a ring.

A fine snow continued to fall as the three were executed. The Mexican and the old man died cleanly. Martin, whose horse had been started slowly by Gerald, had to be shot by Farnley. Tetley felled his son with the butt of his pistol for bungling the hanging. Then the posse rode away. As they rode out of the Ox-Bow, they met Sheriff Risley, Judge Tyler, Drew, and Kinkaid, who was not dead after all. The judge shouted that every member of the posse would be tried for murder. The sheriff, however, said that he could not arrest a single man present for the murders because identity was uncertain in the swirling snow. He asked for ten volunteers to continue the search for the real rustlers.

Only old Davies seemed moved by the affair, more so after he learned that Martin's story was true and that the cattle had been bought from Drew without a bill of sale. Nearly maddened, he gave the ring and letter to Drew, who promised to look after Martin's widow. After Croft and Gil had returned to Canby's saloon, Davies began to moan to Croft. Davies convinced himself that he himself had caused the hanging of the three men. Gil got drunk. Later that day, Gerald Tetley hanged himself, and a few hours later his father also committed suicide. The cowhands took up a collection for Martin's widow. In their room at Canby's, Gil and Croft could hear Rose laughing and talking in the bar. They decided to leave town.

Critical Evaluation:

The Ox-Bow Incident begins as a Western horse-opera with all the stage settings and characters of a cowboy thriller, but it ends as a saga of human misery. The novel has the action and pace of a classic drama. The mob assumes the nature of a Greek chorus, now on one side, now on the other. The story rises toward an inevitable climax and, as it does so, forcibly states the harsh truth: The law of survival is linked to the curse of relentless cruelty. Walter Van Tilburg Clark made the Western thriller a novel of art.

Although set against a Nevada landscape in 1885, the novel's portrayal of mob justice is timeless. The tragedy in the novel involves not only the theme of innocent people wrongly punished but also the theme that unjust and cruel acts can be carried out by intelligent, moral men who allow their sense of social duty to corrupt their sense of justice.

Bridger's Wells, Nevada, the initial setting for the novel's development, offered its citizens recreational diversions limited to eating, sleeping, drinking, playing cards, and fighting. Into that frontier setting stepped Gil Carter and Art Croft, who learn that rustlers had provided the place with an exciting alternative, lynching. Osgood, the Baptist minister from the only "working church" in town, realized early on that hot mob temper could subdue individual reason and sense of justice. In times of despair, reason and justice seem less attractive than immediate action. Bartlett, a rancher who found rustling a particularly vile threat, argued that "justice" often proved ineffective and worked too slowly to guarantee that guilty men would pay the penalties for their crimes. He was able to persuade twenty townspeople to form an illegal posse, even though none of the men he exhorted owned any cattle and only a few of them even knew the allegedly murdered man. One man, physically weak and unsound, won over the rest by deriding those among his listeners who opposed his argument. Notwithstanding their thoughtfulness, the words or reason spoken by the storekeeper Davies proved unsuccessful, especially against the renewed harangues of the self-important Major Tetley.

Major Tetley's son Gerald, whom his father forces to take part in the posse, painfully realized the weakness of individuals who were afraid to challenge the mob and felt that to resist would be to admit weakness. "How many of us do you think are really here because there have been cattle stolen, or because Kinkaid was shot?" he asks. In the absence of Sheriff Risley, who as the legally constituted police authority might have stopped the lynching, the formation of the illegal posse, the manhunt, and the lynchings all went ahead with the inevitability of a Shakespearean tragedy.

In the eleventh hour, no gesture suggesting innocence could spare the doomed men. When Davies, in an effort to save the life of a man he believed was innocent, wanted to communicate Martin's emotional letter to his wife to the posse, Martin himself objected. He used the incident to make another point, that even an initial promise to preserve the integrity of his letter would have proved futile among men in whom conscience had failed as a measure of just conduct. In a moment where bravery might understandably have failed among men about to be hanged, the Mexican removed a bullet from his own leg, washed the wound and dressed it with a fire-heated knife. He tossed the knife into the ground within an inch of where its owner's foot would have been had he not, in fear, drawn quickly away. The Mexican, who smiled often at the proceedings, did so again, seeing in the posse the absence of the very bravery they thought they all possessed. The sympathy that Martin's letter and the Mexican's courage might otherwise have elicited never materialized either because most of the posse had simply made up their minds about the prisoners' fate or because they believed that the rest had.

Davies, the one man who had had least to do with the hangings, and perhaps did most to prevent them, was himself plagued with guilt, which he felt did not apply to those such as Tetley, for "a beast is not to blame." Davies' sense of guilt and justice make him realize, as no one else did, how little he had actually done to prevent the hangings from taking place. He faces the realization that he let the three men hang because he was afraid and lacked the "only thing Tetley had, guts, plain guts." The sensitive man, lacking the brute convictions of his opposite, is rendered impotent. Davies' final confession is accompanied by laughter in the background.

The Ox-Bow Incident has no hero yet cries out for one in a world where the lessons of the Ox-Bow may not be remembered, much less learned. Inasmuch as the novel was written in 1937 and 1938, while Nazism bullied a world into submission, the novel presented a theme in step with domestic as well as world developments. Clark once said of *The Ox-Bow Incident*, "What I wanted to say was 'It can happen here.' It has happened here, in minor but sufficiently indicative ways, a great many times."

"Critical Evaluation" by Frank Joseph Mazzi

Bibliography:
Andersen, Kenneth. "Form in Walter Van Tilburg Clark's *The Ox-Bow Incident*." *Western Review* 6 (Spring, 1969): 19-25. Discusses literary devices Clark uses to give *The Ox-Bow Incident* its "clean, ordered, classical" structure. Analyzes the novel's proportions, dramatic sequencing of events, unified tone, and use of irony, nature imagery, and contrasting sounds.
Bates, Barclay W. "Clark's Man for All Seasons: The Achievement of Wholeness in *The Ox-Bow Incident*." *Western American Literature* 3 (Spring, 1968): 37-49. Finds a serious flaw in every character in *The Ox-Bow Incident* except Swanson, Rose Mapen's husband, who alone is free, guiltless, rational, eloquent, and in control.
Laird, Charlton, ed. *Walter Van Tilburg Clark: Critiques*. Reno: University of Nevada Press, 1983. A collection of original material by Clark and evaluations of his work by several critics, most notably Wallace Stegner (on "Clark's Frontier") and Robert B. Heilman (on justice, male camaraderie, communities in opposition, and artistic techniques in *The Ox-Bow Incident*).
Lee, L. L. *Walter Van Tilburg Clark*. Boise, Idaho: Boise State University, 1973. Regards *The Ox-Bow Incident* as more than an anti-Western novel. Analyzes ambiguities and compares and contrasts major characters in *The Ox-Bow Incident* and their complex responses to physical and moral courage, the limits of nature as a force for good, and justice.
Westbrook, Max. *Walter Van Tilburg Clark*. New York: Twayne, 1969. Analyzes *The Ox-Bow Incident* not as an antilynching novel but as a tragedy of those who willingly alienate themselves from the "grace of archetypal reality."

THE PAINTED BIRD

Type of work: Novel
Author: Jerzy Nikodem Kosinski (1933-1991)
Type of plot: Social morality
Time of plot: 1939-1945
Locale: Eastern Europe
First published: 1965

Principal characters:

THE YOUNG BOY, an unnamed war refugee
MARTA, an old woman with whom the young boy first lives
OLGA, a wise old woman who saves the young boy
LEKH, a peasant who traps and sells birds
GARBOS, a sadistic farmer who tries to kill the boy
EWKA, a young woman who introduces the boy to sex
GAVRILA, a political officer in the Soviet army who teaches the boy to read
MITKA, a Russian sniper who teaches the boy self-reliance
THE SILENT ONE, a resident of the orphanage where the young boy is
placed after the war

The Story:

In fear of Nazi reprisals, the parents of the six-year-old narrator sent the young boy to a distant village. The parents lost touch with the man who placed the child in the village, and when the boy's foster mother died, the young boy, left on his own, began a series of travels from village to village. Considered to be either a Jew or a Gypsy because of his dark hair and olive skin, the boy was treated horribly by the brutal and ignorant peasants met in his travels.

He first lived in the hut of Marta, a crippled and superstitious old woman. When she died of natural causes, the boy accidentally burned down her house. He was saved from villagers, who sought to kill him, by Olga, a woman called "the Wise" for her knowledge of folk medicine. After being tossed into the river by the villagers and carried downstream on an inflated catfish bladder, the young boy came to live with a miller and his wife, and witnessed a scene of unspeakable brutality. Jealous of a young farmhand's attraction to his wife, the miller gouged out his eyes with a spoon. The boy ran away and found refuge with Lekh, who trapped and sold birds, and who was in love with Stupid Ludmila. When villagers killed Ludmila, Lekh was heartbroken, and the young boy was forced to flee again.

He next stayed with a carpenter and his wife who were afraid that the boy's black hair would attract lightning to their farm. Whenever there was as storm, the carpenter dragged the boy out to a field and chained him to a heavy harness. When the carpenter threatened to kill him, the boy led his master to an abandoned bunker and pushed him into a sea of rats. Next, the young boy stayed with a blacksmith who was helping the partisans; when the blacksmith was killed, the boy was turned over to German soldiers, but the one charged with his execution let him escape into the woods. The young boy found a horse with a broken leg and returned it to a farmer, who briefly sheltered the boy, but he was forced to escape again when he witnessed a murder at a wedding celebration.

The terror was unrelenting. He was staying with a giant farmer when he first witnessed the trains carrying Jews to the death camps. When a Jewish girl was found along the tracks, she was kept at the house next door, and the boy witnessed her gang rape and murder. When Germans searched the village for more Jews, he fled, but was captured and given to an old priest, who delivered him to Garbos, a sadistic farmer with a huge and vicious dog named Judas. Garbos beat the boy daily and then hung him from two hooks over Judas, hoping that he would fall and that the dog would kill him. Garbos was afraid of killing the boy himself, for religious reasons. Meanwhile, the boy had been taking religious instruction from the old priest, but one day, as an acolyte, he tripped and dropped the missal during a service. The enraged congregation threw the boy into a large manure pit. At this point, the boy lost his voice.

He escaped again and came to live with another cruel farmer named Makar and his family. The daughter Ewka initiated the boy into sex, and what he thought was love, but when he witnessed Makar forcing the girl into sexual acts with her brother and a goat, he lost his love for Ewka. He escaped on skates he had made, but a gang of boys captured him and threw him into a hole in the frozen river. He was saved by a woman named Labina, but she died. The eastern front of the war was pushing closer, and the boy witnessed another gruesome scene. A band of Kalmuks—mostly Soviet deserters aligned with the Germans—took over a village and wantonly raped and slaughtered its inhabitants. The boy's first moment of stability came when the advancing Soviet army captured and executed the Kalmuks and adopted the boy. He became a kind of mascot to Gavrila, the political officer of the regiment, and Mitka, a crack sniper. Gavrila taught the boy to read and explained socialism to him, while Mitka taught the boy revenge. When several Soviet soldiers were killed by drunken villagers, Mitka enacted his own vengeance with his high-powered rifle.

World War II ended, and the boy reluctantly left his Russian friends to be placed in an orphanage in the city from which he was first exiled. Six years passed; the boy was now twelve. The city had been damaged in the war, but not more severely than the children in the orphanages. The narrator befriended another orphan named the Silent One, and together they wandered the city. When the Silent One saw the boy humiliated by a peasant merchant, he caused a terrible train wreck in a failed attempt to kill the man. The boy was finally located by his parents, but he was not ready for the reconciliation, and he was still mute. He was taken to the mountains for his health, and he learned to ski. He awoke in a hospital room after a skiing accident, and picked up the phone and began to speak. His speech convinced the boy that he was alive, and able to communicate.

Critical Evaluation:

The Painted Bird has emerged as one of the most powerful novels about World War II and about the Holocaust. Since it only obliquely deals with both events, the novel is a kind of allegory for the senseless cruelty and brutality of any war. Jerzy Kosinski claimed, falsely, that the novel was based on experiences that he went through. Kosinski was not averse to creating fiction in more than one realm; he was candid about this practice. The point of Kosinski's claim, it may be argued, is that the book's unspeakable brutalities are realistic—indeed, they are much less than what happened.

Characterization is notably thin in *The Painted Bird*, and even the narrator is two-dimensional. The scenes that he narrates are, however, often overwhelming, and the power of the novel comes in large part from its simple language and imagery. The point of view and sentence structure are remarkably simple. (Kosinski once claimed that he learned English writing the novel, which may explain some of its directness.) Such simple language only makes the horror greater: There is no complex linguistic shield that protects readers from the violence. What makes the events of the narrative even starker and more horrible is that there is no adult moral perspective to condemn the primitive or animalistic behavior of the characters. The narrator is a young boy with little understanding of what is happening to him, and Kosinski does not provide readers with an intermediary. At one level, this short, episodic novel is an allegory. Kosinski has written that the novel is a fairy tale experienced by a child rather than told to him, and this is an apt description. Each incident in *The Painted Bird* can be considered as a stepping stone in an allegorical *Bildungsroman*, or novel of education. In each encounter, the boy learns another lesson, only to discard it for a new lesson in the following chapter or incident—religion from the priest, politics from Gavrila, vengeance from Mitka and the Silent One, and so on. The final answer with which Kosinski leaves readers is ambiguous. At the end, the boy is losing the muteness that the horror of the world forced him into. There is evil in the world, surely, and, as the boy has seen, neither the religious nor the political solution cancels it—in fact, they often exacerbate it. The only thing that is certain is the individual.

At another level the novel is about not merely an individual boy but also the Holocaust of World War II. *The Painted Bird* can be read as one of the most powerful indictments of the madness and terror of the Holocaust in literature. Although the horrors depicted in *The Painted Bird* are much less brutal than the actuality—no death camps or gas ovens are in the novel— they are horrible for their starkness and immediacy; they are the concrete and individual horrors of one alien child in a world gone mad.

The major thematic question the novel raises is the one at the center of the Book of Job and other classic pieces of literature: What is one to make of the evil of the world? Kosinski has no clear answer—except that the novel, with all its horror, is its own answer. The boy begins to speak again; the novel is testimony to what he has witnessed—the powerful communication is that *The Painted Bird* is.

For all its realistic detail, the novel also has a symbolic meaning. There are a number of incidents in the novel that have this symbolic quality—the story to which the title makes reference, for example. The painted bird is an apt symbol for the boy himself. Lekh captures a bird, paints it, and releases it. The bird's own flock, not recognizing it, pecks the bird to death. This bird also represents all of those who are marked as aliens and who thus are destroyed— including the millions in the death camps of World War II.

Animal imagery pervades the story. In chapter 1 alone, for example, there are stories of a pigeon among the chickens, a snake crawling out of its skin, and a squirrel set on fire by village boys. This imagery conveys the proximity of animal and human life. Kosinski's novel, in language and theme, forces readers to confront the potential horror of human behavior, without recourse to easy answers.

David Peck

Bibliography:
Everman, Welch D. *Jerzy Kosinski: The Literature of Violation.* San Bernardino, Calif.: Borgo Press, 1991. "The author's point is that the boy's experience is not unique; what happened to him also happened to many others and could happen again to anyone."
Kosinski, Jerzy. *Notes of the Author on "The Painted Bird."* 3d ed. New York: Scientia-Factum, 1967. In this pamphlet, Kosinski explains the novel as "fairy tales *experienced* by the child, rather than *told* to him."
Lavers, Norman. *Jerzy Kosinski.* Boston: Twayne, 1982. Lavers identifies the themes of freedom, revenge, and education, identifying the novel as a picaresque *Bildungsroman*.
Lilly, Paul R. *Words in Search of Victims: The Achievement of Jerzy Kosinski.* Kent, Ohio: The

Kent State University Press, 1988. Kosinski's fiction "is about the art of writing fiction"; *The Painted Bird* is "primarily a book about language testing."

Sherwin, Byron L. *Jerzy Kosinski: Literary Alarmclock*. Chicago: Cabala Press, 1981. "Kosinski prefers to convey the horror of the Holocaust by shocking us into feeling the terror of a single individual rather than by asking us to try abstractly to comprehend the pain, death and suffering of . . . millions."

PALE FIRE

Type of work: Novel
Author: Vladimir Nabokov (1899-1977)
Type of plot: Parody
Time of plot: Late 1950's, early 1960's
Locale: Northeastern United States and Zembla
First published: 1962

> *Principal characters:*
> DR. CHARLES KINBOTE, a scholar
> JOHN FRANCIS SHADE, a poet
> SYBIL SHADE, John Shade's wife
> GERALD EMERALD, a university instructor
> JACK GREY or JACOB GRADUS, a madman and assassin

The Story:

Pale Fire purports to be a scholarly edition of the poem *Pale Fire* by the American poet, John Shade. There is, as part of the novel, an editor's foreword, then the poem itself, followed by five times as many pages of editorial commentary as there are pages to the poem, and finally an index. The editor, Charles Kinbote, was a one-time colleague of Shade at Wordsmith University in New Wye, which is in Appalachia. Kinbote told a story, or rather a number of stories, all by indirection—for there is no simple "and then" of events in the novel.

The primary story is realistic, introduced by Kinbote in the foreword and carried on in the rest of the editorial apparatus and in Shade's poem. In the poem, an autobiographical meditation written in loose, rhymed couplets, Shade recounted not only his own life and his love for his wife, Sybil, but his daughter's life and death. His daughter was an unattractive, intelligent girl, too sensitive for the world, who ended up, probably, killing herself. Kinbote may actually have been named V. Botkin—and he probably was quite mad. Newly arrived as a teacher at Wordsmith, he rented the house of Judge Goldsworth, next to Shade's house. Kinbote did not fit well into the academic world. Most of his colleagues, especially a young teacher named Gerald Emerald, made fun of his appearance and his manners. Moreover, Kinbote, a homosexual, had a series of unfortunate love affairs. An admirer of Shade's work, Kinbote forced himself upon Shade and his wife Sybil. Shade was working on his new poem; Kinbote believed that he had given Shade the major subject for the poem. He was to be cruelly disappointed.

Another madman, Jack Grey, once sentenced to prison by Judge Goldsworth but having escaped from an asylum for the criminally insane, arrived in New Wye, intent upon revenge. Grey mistook Shade for the judge and shot him. Kinbote believed, and Mrs. Shade accepted as truth, that Kinbote had tried to save Shade. She gave Kinbote permission to edit the poem. Grey committed suicide in prison. Kinbote fled, going to the western United States, taking the poem with him. There he wrote the notes and the index.

The most fascinating, fantastic, and perhaps "real" story in the novel is the one that Kinbote told in his foreword, commentary, and index. This story is the subject that Kinbote thought that Shade was writing about. Kinbote used his scholarly apparatus (the foreword, commentary, and so on) to give his autobiography or, at least, what he believed was his autobiography. Disappointed to find that the great story he had given Shade is not the obvious matter of Shade's poem, Kinbote, as an artist-reader himself, "re-wrote" or rather interpreted the poem to say what it should have said. Shade's poem is warped into something monstrous.

Gradually it is revealed that Kinbote was "Charles Xavier the Beloved," deposed king of Zembla, a "distant northern land," somewhere in Europe. Zembla was a happy, romantic place, indeed a dream place, with a comfortably rigid social hierarchy, that is, a king, nobles, a small, efficient middle class, a happy peasantry, and the usual malcontents, the stirrers-up of whatever trouble there was. Charles Xavier pretended to be merely an American academic in order to escape the far left, totalitarian revolutionaries who brought about the revolution in Zembla. They feared the king's return and were intent upon his assassination. Jack Grey, furthermore, was no madman but a man of many disguises and names, among them Jacob Gradus and de Grey, a committed believer in the revolution, an assassin sent by the revolutionaries and who accidentally killed Shade while trying to kill Charles.

Charles Xavier (or Charles Kinbote), telling his life before he came to be at Wordsmith, asserted that he was truly beloved by most of his people but regretfully unsuccessful in his personal life, especially as a husband, because of his homosexuality. Charles Xavier was a clever, attractive, learned man, but harassed by continual palace intrigues. He was brought to marry in hopes of fathering an heir but could not consummate the marriage. The revolutionists, unsupported of course by the Zemblan people but backed by a giant neighboring state, dethroned and imprisoned the king.

The king, with the aid of friends and courtiers, escaped in a marvelous, operatic fashion, leaving everything behind, including his identity. After he arrived in America, other friends helped him to this new identity, that of Charles Kinbote, a scholarly authority on Zemblan literature. The Shadows, a secret group inside the Zemblan revolutionaries, sent Grey (Jacob Gradus), and the fate of Shade is intertwined with that of Charles Xavier. One of these Shadows, the one who gives Gradus the American address of Charles Xavier, is named Izumrudov, which is a Russian word for "emerald," linking Izumrudov with Gerald Emerald.

Critical Evaluation:

Many of the first critical studies of Vladimir Nabokov concentrated upon the form of his work, to the neglect of its human content. Nabokov himself contributed to this approach. His work seems to argue that art is a kind of magnificent play, denying that there was a "human interest" story to be found in good art. Nabokov personally was deeply caring about other human beings; his wife was of Jewish descent, and he was bitterly opposed to all racism, not just anti-Semitism. Politically, he was antifascist, and, because he had been forced into exile and in a sense deprived of his beloved Russian language by the Communist revolution in Russia, anticommunist. Extremes of the political spectrum are what he regarded with distaste. They were, to Nabokov, not opposites but mirrors of each other, external controls over human beings.

Pale Fire is, at bottom, humanist and even realistic. Although ludic, it is more than mere form. The characters, despite their many qualities that call attention to the novel's satiric and ludic design, also exemplify differing points of view on the human condition. Nabokov also never denies the reality of the world. It exists and can be talked about. In his art there is no distinction between form and content; the way a story is told is necessarily a way of understanding and examining human existence. *Pale Fire* is a complex, experimental work and its messages are not simple. It can be read as a case study, as a parody of academic criticism (for example, of Nabokov's own editing of Alexander Pushkin's *Eugene Onegin* of 1825-1833, or of critical evaluations in general), or a prefiguring of modern deconstructionist criticism. All of these readings are correct, but they are also limiting.

The novel is constructive rather than deconstructive. Language and the structure find and create connections, uncovering and discovering reality and making order of that reality. At the same time, the novel shows that language cannot grasp all the complexities of existence. If Charles Kinbote is only a madman, the novel is merely a case study and says little about other human beings. Granted, the story Kinbote tells is too fantastic to be accepted as that of a sane person. *Pale Fire* is a madman's story, as far as the everyday world is concerned. It is not "story," however, with which Nabokov is concerned. The novel is a fiction: All of its stories are made up; it is through the imagination, which deals in fictions, that one understands. The book eschews nihilism and the absurd, despite its game-playing and craziness. Ultimately, it is about how the human imagination creates. For this reason, it is a humanistic novel.

Kinbote, in rewriting Shade's work, makes sense of Kinbote's life. Nabokov, in turn, hints that he wrote the novel in order to make sense out of his own life. He and Kinbote both create their own fictive worlds. The name V. Botkin recalls the name Vladimir Nabokov. In a sense, Botkin (and so, Kinbote) is also Nabokov, Nabokov the European American, the exile. Nabokov is suggesting that everyone creates worlds out of the details of life. Everyone who imagines, tells stories, has fantasies, goes crazy, is an artist.

Pale Fire is about the order that the imagination tries to impose on reality. Some kind of personal order is absolutely necessary for people to live. *Pale Fire* is also about disorder, which is what the world is. A major theme of the novel is the interplay between order and disorder, between good and evil. Although there are absolutes of good and evil, the human world is gray rather than black or white. *Pale Fire* is, then, art making and commenting on reality. Art is controlled but not controlling. Art acknowledges multiple interpretations and multiple possibilities. In the novel, this is reflected in the variable nature of some of the characters' identities. Their names vary, their stories vary, the reader's reaction to the stories may vary. The implicit political comment of the novel is that externally imposed "reality," or authorized interpretations of reality, do not allow for doubt and for ambiguity. The novel implicitly supports the individual's right to find irony.

For instance, Shade's poem is in iambic pentameter couplets, loose ones perhaps, but they echo, in the twentieth century, the couplets of the eighteenth century English poets. Shade's choice of form recalls a time when intellectuals could believe that humanity might soon order the world through reason; art as order was a foremost value. In Nabokov's time, art was at best what Robert Frost (who is possibly the model for Shade) has said of the art of poetry—it is a momentary stay against confusion. This example shows how Nabokov weaves form (iambic pentameter) and content (the theme of reason and order versus madness and disorder) together. He does so, furthermore, in a playful way; play and serious work are also themes of the novel.

Another theme of the work is the patterns of two views of time, cyclic and linear. Kinbote's story is linear; he has moved through madness to a kind of death; his time will come to a stop. The time of art, however, is cyclic. The two stories echo each other, echo within themselves, and make connections. Gerald Emerald is Izumrudov, Izumrudov is Gerald Emerald, Grey is de Grey. Shade, perhaps, is half a Shadow. The characters and time repeat themselves, in a slightly different way each time. Time stops for the individual, but life and its forms continue.

L. L. Lee

Bibliography:
Bader, Julia. *Crystal Land: Artifice in Nabokov's English Novels.* Berkeley: University of California Press, 1972. The discussion of *Pale Fire* is extensive and insightful, concentrating upon the novel as imaginative experience.

Boyd, Brian. *Vladimir Nabokov: The Russian Years* and *Vladimir Nabokov: The American Years*. Princeton, N.J.: Princeton University Press, 1990, 1991. This two-volume biography is absolutely essential not only for its information about Nabokov's life but about his life's relation to his art.

Dembo, L. S., ed. *Nabokov: The Man and His Work*. Madison: University of Wisconsin Press, 1967. This early collection of articles on Nabokov introduced many of the ideas that later critics would continue to discuss. Excellent article by John O. Lyons on *Pale Fire*.

Rampton, David. *Vladimir Nabokov: A Critical Study of the Novels*. New York: Cambridge University Press, 1984. Although Rampton limits his discussion to a few novels, his concentration upon content is a good antidote to the many formal approaches to Nabokov.

Roth, Phyllis A., ed. *Critical Essays on Vladimir Nabokov*. Boston: G. K. Hall, 1984. Comprehensive, very helpful selection of articles on Nabokov. *Pale Fire* is treated in several of the essays.

PALE HORSE, PALE RIDER
Three Short Novels

Type of work: Novellas
Author: Katherine Anne Porter (1890-1980)
Type of plot: Psychological realism
Time of plot: Old Mortality, 1885-1912; *Noon Wine*, 1836-1905; *Pale Horse, Pale Rider*, 1918
Locale: New Orleans, Texas, and Colorado
First published: 1939

> *Principal characters:*
> MIRANDA
> MARIA, her sister
> GABRIEL, her uncle
> ADAM BARCLAY, an officer whom Miranda loves
> ROYAL EARLE THOMPSON, a farmer with a weak character
> MRS. THOMPSON, his wife
> OLAF HELTON, a strange farmhand who works for Mr. Thompson

The Story:

Old Mortality. Miranda and her sister Maria, aged eight and twelve, respectively, lived after the death of their mother with their father and grandmother. Legends of the family's past surrounded them in the house, especially tales of their dead Aunt Amy, whose melancholy photograph hung on the wall. According to the story, Amy toyed with the affections of her fiancé Gabriel by appearing scantily dressed at the Mardi Gras with another man. Harry, Amy's father, defended her honor by shooting the man. Amy and Gabriel married, and six weeks later, Amy died of consumption. Although the two young sisters understood that some details were untrue, they went on believing the story.

Two years later, after their grandmother died, the girls were sent to a convent school where, to relieve the sedate life, they read romantic novels. Except for Saturday afternoons, when their father sometimes appeared, they were cut off from life. One Saturday, their father took them to the racetrack, where their Uncle Gabriel's beautiful horse was entered in a race. Instead of the romantic figure of the family's legends, Miranda saw that Gabriel was an alcoholic who lived in a slum hotel with his second wife. The horse, rather than winning elegantly, ended the race trembling and bleeding at the nose.

Eight years later, Miranda, now married, returned to Texas to attend Gabriel's funeral. On the train, she met her cousin Eva, who told her about Gabriel and Amy. Eva refuted every romantic family legend with realistic details of Amy's scandalous behavior and death from tuberculosis. When they arrived, Miranda found herself distanced from her father. When Eva and he began to speak of the past, Miranda vowed she would face the truth and leave her fictions behind.

Noon Wine. As Royal Earle Thompson churned milk on the porch one day, a stranger arrived and, in an English unfamiliar to the Texas farmland, asked for work. Thinking the man would work cheaply and do all the nasty chores on the small dairy farm, Thompson hired him. Olaf Helton spoke almost not at all, even at dinner with Thompson, his wife, and two sons. All he revealed was that he was a Swede from North Dakota and that he knew how to make butter and cheese. He also played the harmonica, the same tune over and over.

After a while, the farmhand's strangeness ceased to bother the Thompsons, especially Mr. Thompson, who saw his farm prosper with Helton's work. The cows and chickens were cared for, the yards cleaned up, and the income from dairy products increased. He and his wife tried repeatedly to make conversation with Helton, but it was no use. He remained silent, even when the two boys teased him. In the second year, an incident occurred that made Mrs. Thompson uneasy. One day she came upon Helton shaking her sons ferociously by the shoulders. When her husband questioned Helton, he replied that the boys had entered his shack and damaged his harmonicas. Mr. Thompson threatened his sons with a beating if they ever did that again, and that was the end of the incident.

Nine years passed, and Helton continued to work and play the harmonica. The boys grew into responsible young men, the farm made a profit, and Mrs. Thompson's health got no worse. One day another stranger appeared in the hot dusty yard and introduced himself as Mr. Homer T. Hatch. Hatch was looking for Helton whom, he said, had escaped from a mental hospital in North Dakota, where he had been committed after killing his brother in a fight over a harmonica. Hearing the tune of the harmonica, Hatch realized that Helton was on the farm and got out a pair of handcuffs. In the scuffle that ensued, Mr. Thompson, thinking Hatch was going to harm his hired man, killed Hatch with an ax. Helton fled the farm, but was caught by the sheriff's patrol and killed by a mob.

A jury acquitted Mr. Thompson, but he kept trying to explain to his neighbors exactly what had happened. Day after day, he made the rounds of the small farms, telling his story. The boys took over the task of farming. One night, unable to sleep, and realizing that no one, not even his own family, believed him, he took his gun and killed himself.

Pale Horse, Pale Rider. Miranda dreamed of riding a horse with a stranger. When he beckoned her to ride further with him, she demurred because she felt there would be another ride and another time. She awoke to face the world of World War I and the deadly influenza epidemic that was sweeping the country. Her job at a newspaper required her to work late hours reviewing plays and vaudeville acts and putting up with complaining fellow employees. The war and its rumors took their toll. She made the rounds of the veterans' hospital to bring flowers and cheer to wounded soldiers. They rejected her offers. Professional patriots tried to force her to buy bonds with money she did not have. Miranda found peace and stability with Adam Barclay, a Texas-born officer who lived at the same rooming house as she did. He accompanied her to the shows she had to review, and afterward they went to cafés, where they talked of their past lives and of the war.

Miranda was infected with the influenza virus, and as she got sicker and sicker, affairs at work became too hard to handle. Other reporters dealt with her reviews. Her dreams continued, now full of torturous images of childhood memories mixed with jungles and icy mountains. She became more and more ill, but the hospitals were full. Adam appeared at her bedside to care for her as the influenza progressed, and the two confessed their love for each other. Soon afterward, Miranda dreamed of singers who were swept away by death and, finally, that Adam had died. When at last she was taken to a hospital in a half-conscious state, she mistook the doctor for a German murderer. Dreams continued to haunt her. On Armistice Day, she regained consciousness fully, only to learn that although the war had ended, Adam had died in the epidemic.

Gradually, with the help of friends, Miranda's health returned. She was able to read Adam's letters and cope with the fact that she had been the agent of his death. After a period of mourning, Miranda emerged as a stronger person.

"The Story" by Louise M. Stone

Critical Evaluation:

Pale Horse, Pale Rider is an important book in the literary career of Katherine Anne Porter. Following, as it did, her highly esteemed first collection of short stories, *Flowering Judas* (1930), this collection composed of three short novels marks an advance in technical interest and resources. It demonstrates clearly the artist's ability to handle the expansive complexity of forms larger than the conventional short story. The artistic success of the forms in Pale Horse, Pale Rider is complete; Porter is one of the few American masters of the short novel. She matches the weight and density of many fine conventional novels in her shorter form.

One should begin by acknowledging the real daring of *Pale Horse, Pale Rider*. When it was written, the short story of conventional length was difficult enough to place and publish, and a collection of short stories was, in fact, a rare thing. It was easier to publish a collection of poems than a book of stories. There were many reasons for that condition, some of them economic, others the whimsical rationale of publishers. In view of these facts, it is quite remarkable that *Pale Horse, Pale Rider* ever appeared. There could have been small encouragement for Porter to produce anything except a novel. Moreover, the short novel as a form was even more rare in the United States than a collection of short stories, for its difficulties began at the common marketplace. The magazines would from time to time publish a serious short story among their lighter and more conventional fiction, never willing to surrender the space necessary for the long story or short novel. The choice of the form, then, whether at the outset or as a result of the demands of the material in the process of making, represented a major decision on the part of the artist. In the face of such pressure and such an element of risk, it is a wonder and a triumph that Porter not only created exemplary models of the form but also managed to overcome all the odds so that these stories are now simply and beautifully a part of the American literary heritage.

From the beginning, Porter has been accepted and acknowledged as a master stylist. While this view may be true, it has certainly been misleading. Taxonomy, the name of the human game of classification, seems to be an essential part of the human consciousness. It is a great strength that permits people to think and relate; yet it is also a dangerous weakness in that the rigid and unquestioning exercise of this power can quickly lead to nonthinking, to the comfortable, narcotic illusion that a label has a life of its own as valid as the thing which is so named and tagged. The arts are difficult enough to think about and have not been spared from this kind of danger. To call attention to Porter's style is a useful observation, but it is rather like describing an oak tree exclusively in terms of the shape and color of its leaves. Moreover, associatively, emphasis on style tends to imply virtuosity for its own sake and a certain absence of content, with the result that the critic need not come to terms with content at all. In the case of Porter, this habit or cliché of critics is particularly disappointing. She writes very well indeed, sentence by sentence, but it is the supreme virtue of her style that it is designed not to call attention to itself but to fit hand-in-glove the matter and content of her stories, to carry the weight and to suggest the depth of complexity without once interrupting the magic spell which gives fiction its reality. All her virtuosity is at the service of her story and her characters. It is easy enough for a writer to divert the reader away from content and character by dazzling and intriguing verbal performance. Porter has never chosen that way. Her method has been the more difficult one; clearly, the reader is intended to weigh the story in a total and meaningful sense and not to stop short with admiration for its surface and decoration. What she has to say is important, and it is a critical mistake to ignore this fact.

The three short novels of *Pale Horse, Pale Rider* are arranged in a structure to make a larger, single statement and effect, and each demonstrates a different way of handling the short novel.

The first, *Old Mortality*, is in three parts and is, in a sense, a smaller version of the whole book. It is superficially a romantic tale of turn-of-the-century America. Part 1 is set in the shifting, complex world of a large family, gossip and the tall tales of the past being its imitative form. The point of view is of the two young sisters, Maria and Miranda, and the thematic concern is the romance and tragedy of their beautiful Aunt Amy. A great deal, the whole substance of what might have been a romantic novel of the period, is packed into a few pages, filtered through the consciousness of the two young girls. Somehow it all seems leisurely, even digressive, as it should. Describing the way the family passed on its own history, Porter is able to give simultaneously a clue to her own method in this section and to indicate the flaw at the heart of her family's, and the reader's, history, a romantic commitment of the heart and the imagination to the past.

In part 2, Maria and Miranda are young schoolgirls in a New Orleans convent. They are now characterized as quite different from the unquestioning girls they were. There is a single, central event—their meeting with Uncle Gabriel—the dashing figure of the tragic legend of Aunt Amy. The girls have a confrontation with the reality of the family story. Here, beautifully executing her chosen point of view, Porter avoids the easy way out—of letting this event have a shattering and instant impact on the two young girls. The impact is implied. Readers see what the girls see and feel what the girls feel; however, readers are not invited, as they might be in the much more conventional story of youthful disillusionment, to greater and false intimacy. Nor is the romantic past neatly (and falsely) discredited. It is modified. In part 2, the center of conscious-ness is Miranda, a young woman now, going home to the funeral of Uncle Gabriel and sharing her train ride by coincidence with the practical and worldly Cousin Eva, who had always been the antithesis of Aunt Amy. Miranda is capable, up to a point, of judging and evaluating the events of the past and able to decide to break with it. Yet the story, which has evolved and emerged as the story of Miranda growing up, is subtly and carefully shown to be incomplete. For Porter, unlike many contemporary writers, is not willing to settle for the simplistic truth of young idealism. Miranda's resolution at the end changes nothing as finally as she imagines, yet is in itself an inevitable change.

In *Old Mortality*, certain basic conditions are firmly established that inform the character of the whole book. The subjects, the conflicts, are the past and the present, "romance" and "reality," a history of how the times and the world changed and became what they are. The larger theme is change and mutability. All these things are shown through character. Characters grow and change credibly and with ever-increasing dimension. The framework is within the terms of the conventional serious story, but these conventions will be given renewed vigor and life; for precisely at the point at which the conventional response or reaction could end the story and be a solution, the author will give the story an unexpected resonance. Her stories do not "end," then, but project a sense of life going on and echo afterward in the reader's mind, an effect which is artistically consistent with her theme and subject of change.

The second of the short novels, *Noon Wine*, stands in apparently sharp contrast to *Old Mortality*. In time, it parallels the first two parts of the other and, in fact, stands in relation to *Old Mortality* much as the second part of that story does to its first part. It is a rural tragedy, plain and harshly realistic, the other side of the coin, so to speak, of a family's romantic legends. There are two young people who grow up, too—grubby, small, towheaded—but they are not involved in the consciousness of the story. Told from an omniscient point of view, the story settles into the tragedy of Mr. Thompson, as unlikely a tragic figure as can be imagined, one who for a large part of the story is tagged with characteristics which are conventionally unsympathetic in modern writing. In the end, he changes in the reader's view and estimation, his awful suicide becoming tragic, but not through the usual trick of the revelation of something new or unknown about his character. His character evolves, grows as things happen to him cumulatively, just as the character of Miranda grows and changes in *Old Mortality*, although in a rude and realistic setting and without the benefits of great intelligence or sensibility. Taken together, the two short novels say: From these roots the living have grown to maturity. Both are part of the American heritage. The stories are related in such areas as theme, structure, and contrast, not in the areas of shared characters and plot. *Noon Wine*, like the other novellas, is about the mutability of understanding; what one sees is what one understands.

Pale Horse, Pale Rider combines elements of both the previous stories. There is a real, tragic romance, the love of Adam and Miranda, in many ways a parallel of the grand romance of Gabriel and Amy, in part a retelling of the Adam and Eve legend. There is the harsh reality of a country at war, in the closing days of World War I, and in the midst of the raging influenza epidemic that marked the end of that war. That sickness takes the life of Adam and almost kills Miranda as well. The story ends with the end of the war and Miranda leaving the hospital "cured." The final image projects a future, but now a strangely bleak and bitter one. All things have changed. Part of the subtlety of this story lies in the author's ability to use the war, conventionally, as the end of something of the old order and the loss of something indefinable from the American spirit, and yet to do this within the context of the home front. The raging epidemic, at first as seemingly remote as the bloody fields of France, gradually becomes part of the whole sickness that inflamed the world and destroyed so much. Miranda emerges as much a war casualty as any shell-shocked veteran.

The three short novels of *Pale Horse, Pale Rider* are related and designed to give a rich and complex social history. Porter is not often credited with being a social historian as well as a fine crafter of prose. Perhaps the reason is that she is only indirectly concerned with politics and so those critics whose social vision is conditioned by their political views cannot grant the truth of her grand theme. Politics, however, is a two-dimensional enterprise, a game of "the image." Porter's fictional art is based upon the flesh and spirit of character, and none of her characters remains an "image" for long. The social history of *Ship of Fools* (1962) or *The Leaning Tower and Other Stories* (1944), for example, is evident, and it is equally present in *Pale Horse, Pale Rider*; but in a larger sense, social history is, however complex, merely part of her design. Social history becomes, by the examples of recurring and parallel events, much more than chronology. It becomes a stage on which human beings act out their lives. The scenes change, but the human heart and all its mystery does not. Mutability is a fact of life, but it is not life. Her deepest concern is with people, with character, and in this compassionate and always honest concern, she joins the ranks of the very few great artists of fiction. *Pale Horse, Pale Rider*, her three short and related novels, would guarantee her that place among the few had she never written another line.

In Porter's rhetoric, there is great respect for the reader. She engages the reader's imagination and lets it work too. The result is a highly condensed fiction which does not seem so because of the richness of echo she has managed to suggest and evoke. There is nothing small about her work. Its aims are the grandest to which a writer can aspire. Its glory is the remarkable and daring achievement of those aims.

Bibliography:
Bloom, Harold, ed. *Katherine Anne Porter*. New York: Chelsea House, 1986. Explains Porter's complex use of symbolism and irony. Asserts that the dream sequences of the Miranda stories reveal the unexpressed causes of her discontent.

Givner, Joan. *Katherine Anne Porter: A Life*. New York: Simon & Schuster, 1982. Explores key events that affected Porter's work. Explains the connection, for example, between Porter's near death experience and *Pale Horse, Pale Rider*.

Hendrick, George. *Katherine Anne Porter*. Boston: Twayne, 1965. Details Porter's life and works. Explores the theme of innocence and experience in the stories in which Miranda appears.

Unrue, Darlene Harbour. *Truth and Vision in Katherine Anne Porter's Fiction*. Athens: University of Georgia Press, 1985. Lists criticial sources. Studies the themes of Porter's fiction, asserting that her works have a thematic unity built around Porter's understanding of truth.

West, Ray. *Katherine Anne Porter*. Minneapolis: University of Minnesota Press, 1963. Sets the novellas in the context of Porter's Southern background. Develops the idea that historic memory uses myths to portray truths.

THE PALM-WINE DRINKARD

Type of work: Novel
Author: Amos Tutuola (1920-1997)
Type of plot: Folktale
Time of plot: Indeterminate
Locale: Nigeria
First published: 1952

> *Principal characters:*
> THE NARRATOR, a young man
> HIS WIFE
> HIS PALM-WINE TAPSTER
> THE CURIOUS CREATURE, a skull in disguise
> THE FAITHFUL MOTHER, helper of those in trouble
> DANCE, the Red-Lady of Red-Town
> THE RED-KING, her father
> THE INVISIBLE PAWN, chief of all bush creatures

The Story:

The narrator lived contentedly as the son of a rich man who retained a palm-wine tapster for his son's exclusive use. Each day, the tapster drew enormous amounts of palm-wine for the narrator, who drank it, together with his friends. One day, after the narrator's father had died, the tapster fell from a palm tree and was killed. The narrator missed his supply of palm-wine, and his friends no longer came to see him, so he decided to go to Deads' Town to find his tapster.

His journey led him from his town to various parts of the bush—that place outside civilization that is the habitation of all sorts of inhuman creatures. He had many adventures. For instance, he stayed with a man who promised to give directions to Deads' Town if the narrator would find Death and bring him to the town. The narrator tricked Death into coming along to the town. After that, Death could not return to his former home, and so Death entered the world. The narrator asked again for directions to Deads' Town, but his host said that he must first rescue his daughter, who had been attracted to a handsome gentleman and followed him into the bush. The gentleman was really a creature of the bush. As he went, he gave back each bodily part that he had rented from a human being, until he was nothing but a skull, and then he held the young woman captive. The narrator found the daughter and escaped with her.

They married and stayed in her town until the day when a child was born from her thumb, and was instantly able to speak, move, and eat and drink everything in sight. Driven from town because of this insatiable child, they wandered into the bush, where they met three persons named Drum, Dance, and Song. The child was so attracted by their music that he followed them. Released from their terrible companion, the narrator and his wife wandered on until they came to Wraith-Island. The beautiful creatures who lived here had nothing to do but plant their magic seeds and then dance all day long. After encounters with a huge creature that demanded a sacrifice for the narrator to use its field and with a tiny creature that could undo the work of all other creatures, the narrator and his wife left Wraith-Island with some of the magic seeds.

In Unreturnable Heaven's Town, they encountered people who called themselves the enemies of God, and did everything exactly the opposite from the normal world. The narrator and his wife were beaten, stoned, scraped by rocks and broken bottles, and finally buried up to their necks in the ground. With the help of a friendly eagle, they escaped from the town and, after a short recuperation, went on their way. As they passed a huge, white tree, two hands reached out of an opening in the tree and drew them inside. This was the land of the Faithful Mother, whose sole task was to solace and care for those who had experienced great difficulties in the world. As they entered this land they rented their fear and sold their death. When they left, after staying the maximum allowable three months, they took back their fear, but could no longer be killed, since they had sold their death. This led to the odd circumstance that they could feel fear in the face of danger, even though the danger could not kill them.

In Red-Town, the narrator's wife spoke in riddles for the first time, and it developed that she had the gift of prophecy. Everything and everyone in this town was red because of a mistake the Red-King had made years ago. By facing fearful creatures, the narrator freed them from their curse and settled down to use his magic seeds, soon becoming a rich man. While there, they met the Red-Lady, daughter of the king and also the person who had been called Dance in an earlier adventure. She and her two companions played together in Red-Town until they had played themselves right out of this world, so only their names remained. When the narrator hired a farm laborer called the Invisible Pawn, who was really the chief of all bush-creatures, the Pawn's overenthusiastic completion of his labors angered the townspeople, so again they moved on.

After passing through the town of the Wise-King, they reached Deads' Town and found the tapster, but could not stay, because "alives" were not allowed to live with "deads." With a marvelous egg from the tapster, they returned to the narrator's town, where they used the egg to feed people during a famine, until someone broke the egg. Finally, the narrator ended a cosmic war between Heaven and Earth and the people prospered again.

Critical Evaluation:

Amos Tutuola's early life consisted of living as a servant away from his own family, attempting to advance his schooling, and experiencing distant kindness from his master but cruelty from his master's cook. After leaving his master, he persisted in his studies and finally found an unsatisfactory job. Some of this determination in the face of life's vicissitudes appears in his narrators, who seem to undergo the most terrible trials without losing sight of their ultimate goals.

The effect of his unsettled education is apparent in his use of English, which is not his native tongue. His style has been called naïve, but might also be called grotesque, fantastic, magical, or charming. Long, run-on sentences, filled with unusual combinations and forms of words, paint pictures alien to the Western imagination, yet strangely compelling and familiar. The titles of Tutuola's best-known works—the novels *The Palm-Wine Drinkard* and *My Life in the Bush of Ghosts* (1954)—are exemplary of one aspect of his style. "Drinkard" appears in no dictionary of the English language, but the meaning is clear. The "ghosts" of the second title are not ghosts as that word is understood by the average American or European. Tutuola's English is eccentric—sometimes a word-for-word translation from Yoruba—but never inaccurate. If the narrator might be envious of a man, he says, "I would jealous him." If he means 2:00 A.M., he says, "two o'clock in the mid-night." The combination of flamboyance and uncomplicated innocence conveyed by his style is at first annoying, but eventually captivating, as his story unfolds.

In *The Palm-Wine Drinkard*, Tutuola's unusual style is the framework for motifs and figures from the folklore of his native Nigeria, strung together like the episodes in a picaresque novel, and connected by nothing more than the character of the narrator. Despite this literary form,

Tutuola's novelistic writings (as remarked by the noted mythologist Geoffrey Parrinder in his foreword to *My Life in the Bush of Ghosts*) are truly African. That is, they reflect the tales Tutuola heard from childhood. They are distinguished from many recorded folktales by their descriptive technique. Folktales, as they have been collected in Africa and elsewhere, tend to describe briefly, using character types. The emphasis is on action and on confrontation, especially between human beings and creatures outside the human sphere. Tutuola does for the African folktale, in a very different way, what Evangeline Walton does for Welsh mythology: He fleshes it out, offering a vivid description of actions that might have been taken for granted in a recorded tale. He makes use of what Robert P. Armstrong calls "precise hyperbole" and "visual hyperbole." The narrator's captivity in Unreturnable Heaven's Town would no doubt be disposed of in a standard, recorded tale with a few brief sentences. Tutuola spares no verb in describing the horrors that are visited upon him and his wife. The "barbing" of their hair by unsuitable implements like flat stones and broken bottles gains much of its effect from the typical Tutuolan technique of accretion—the repetition and variation of an activity until it overwhelms the reader with a descriptive barrage. It is quite possible that this aspect of Tutuola's style reflects the oral tradition directly, not in the same way as collected folktales.

As is shown in recorded performances, the oral tradition encourages drama, hyperbole, repetition, and what might be called "joy in storytelling." Some of this spirit is evident in *The Palm-Wine Drinkard*. Some critics have seen Tutuola as a poet of the past, because he adapts folkloric material rather than pursuing the "mythopoetic" direction of some of his contemporaries, who are searching for a new African identity. Others, apparently unaware of the source of his material, have praised his Kafkaesque originality. The significance of Tutuola's work lies in combining these two characteristics: creating a narrative fabric in which old motifs and figures are juxtaposed to human beings in a new frame of reference. He begins with certain givens of folk belief: that the dead are not dead in a Western sense of the word but have gone somewhere to "live" with other "deads"; that the areas of forest or savannah lying outside the influence of town or city—called "the bush"—contain a variety of spirits and powers that may endanger or enrich the human being who ventures into them. To these assumptions, he adds another assumption that is also standard to many bush tales: Bush creatures may be dangerous and hostile but in the end their magic powers are no match for the cunning and determination of a human being.

The situations and figures in Tutuola's episodes range from those which seem to be peculiar to African folklore, like the Curious Creature who has rented his body parts to come to town and returns them on the way back into the bush, to universally recognizable motifs like "how Death came into the world." Tutuola's narrator is a person of Tutuola's present, bringing with him the beliefs and thought patterns of the modern world. He is a Christian who may encounter the very enemies of God, but is never persuaded—or expected—to change his beliefs or his ideas. He enters a world in which time seems to change according to the situation, and yet, as one critic points out, he always notes the time in terms of a twenty-four-hour clock. He adapts to his surroundings, but does not yield to them. Because his vigorous, eccentric style and command of local lore newly validate both the form and the substance of an old genre, Tutuola has emerged as a significant figure in African literature.

James L. Hodge

Bibliography:
Asagba, O. A. "The Folklore Structure in Amos Tutuola's *The Palm-Wine Drinkard.*" *Lore and*

Language 4, no. 1 (January, 1985): 31-39. Builds on earlier studies to analyze the novel's use of folklore motifs and to examine claims that it is a "quest" novel.

Coates, John. "The Inward Journey of the Palm-Wine Drinkard." In *African Literature Today*, compiled by Eldred D. Jones and edited by Eldred Durosimi Jones. New York: African Publishing, 1973. Examines the novel as a psychological development with allegorical overtones.

Collins, Harold R. *Amos Tutuola*. Boston: Twayne, 1969. In-depth treatment of Tutuola's writings, using his life and environment as background. Workmanlike survey of aspects and critiques of his work.

Lindfors, Bernth. "Amos Tutuola's *The Palm-Wine Drinkard* and Oral Tradition." *Critique* 11, no. 1 (1969): 42-50. By a pioneer student of Tutuola's work, solid in its analysis of folklore structure in the novel.

_____. *Critical Perspectives on Amos Tutuola*. Washington, D.C.: Three Continents Press, 1975. Useful collection of critical comment on all of Tutuola's works, divided into early reactions, reappraisals, and later criticism.

PAMELA
Or, Virtue Rewarded

Type of work: Novel
Author: Samuel Richardson (1689-1761)
Type of plot: Epistolary
Time of plot: Early eighteenth century
Locale: England
First published: 1740-1741

> *Principal characters:*
> PAMELA ANDREWS, a servant girl
> MR. B——, her master
> MRS. JERVIS, Mr. B——'s housekeeper
> MRS. JEWKES, the caretaker of Mr. B——'s country home
> LADY DAVERS, Mr. B——'s sister

The Story:

Pamela Andrews had been employed from a very young age as the servant girl of Lady B—— at her estate in Bedfordshire. She had grown very fond of her mistress, so the letter to her parents telling of her ladyship's death expressed her deep sorrow. Her own plans were uncertain, but it soon became clear that Lady B——'s son wanted her to remain in his household. Taking her hand before all the other servants, he had said that he would be a good master to Pamela for his dear mother's sake if she continued faithful and diligent. Mrs. Jervis, the housekeeper, put in a friendly word as well, and Pamela, not wishing to be a burden upon her poor parents, decided to remain in the service of Mr. B——. Shortly, however, she began to doubt that his intentions toward her were honorable. When he kissed her one day, while she sat sewing in a summerhouse, she found herself in a quandary as to what to do.

Once again, she discussed the situation with the good Mrs. Jervis, and she decided to stay if she could share the housekeeper's bed. Mr. B—— was extremely annoyed at this turn of affairs. He tried to persuade Mrs. Jervis that Pamela was a very designing creature who should be carefully watched. When he learned that she was writing long letters to her parents, telling them in great detail of his false proposals and repeating her determination to keep her virtue, he had as many of her letters intercepted as possible.

In a frightening interview between Mr. B——, Pamela, and Mrs. Jervis, he intimidated the housekeeper by his terrifying manner and told Pamela to return to her former poverty. After talking the matter over with her friend, however, Pamela decided that Mr. B—— had given up his plan to ruin her and that there was no longer any reason for her to leave. Another interview with Mr. B——, however, convinced her that she should return to her parents upon the completion of some household duties entrusted to her. When Mr. B—— discovered that she was indeed planning to leave, a furious scene followed, in which he accused her of pride beyond her station. That night he concealed himself in the closet of her room. When she discovered him, Pamela threw herself on the bed and fell into a fit. Pamela and Mrs. Jervis served notice. Despite Mr. B——'s threats on the one hand and his cajolings on the other, Pamela remained firm in her decision to return home. The housekeeper was reinstated in her position, but Pamela set out by herself in the coach Mr. B—— had ordered for her to return to her parents.

What she had thought was Mr. B——'s kindness was but designing trickery. Instead of

4837

arriving at her parents' humble home, Pamela now found herself a prisoner at Mr. B——'s country estate, where the coachman had driven her. Mrs. Jewkes, the caretaker, had none of Mrs. Jervis' kindness of heart, and Pamela found herself cruelly confined. It was only by clever scheming that she was able to continue sending letters to her parents. She was aided by Mr. Williams, the village minister, who smuggled her mail out of the house. The young man soon confessed his love for Pamela and his desire to marry her. Pamela refused his offer, but she devised a plan to escape with his help. Unfortunately, Mrs. Jewkes was too wily a jailer. When she suspected that the two were secretly planning Pamela's escape, she wrote to Mr. B——, who was still in London. Pamela's persecutor, aided by his agents, contrived to have Mr. Williams thrown into jail on a trumped-up charge.

Although her plot had been discovered, Pamela did not allow herself to be discouraged. That night, she dropped from her window into the garden. When she tried to escape from the garden, however, she found the gate padlocked. Mrs. Jewkes discovered her cringing in the woodshed. From that time on, her warder's vigilance and cruelty increased. At length, Mr. B—— arrived and frightened Pamela still further with his threats. With the help of Mrs. Jewkes, he attempted to force himself upon her, but opportunely Pamela was seized by fits. Mr. B—— expressed his remorse and promised never to attempt to molest her again. Pamela now began to suspect that her virtue would soon be rewarded, for Mr. B—— proposed marriage to her. Just as she was enjoying the thought of becoming Mrs. B——, an anonymous warning arrived, suggesting that she beware of a sham marriage. Pamela was greatly upset. At her request, a coach was called, and she set out to visit her parents. On the way, however, letters arrived from Mr. B—— entreating her to return to him and offering an honorable proposal of marriage.

Pamela returned immediately to Mr. B——'s hall; despite all that had passed, she found that she was in love with Mr. B——. He, in turn, was delighted with her beauty and goodness. She and Mr. B—— were married by Mr. Williams before a few witnesses. Mr. Andrews, Pamela's father, was present. There was great rejoicing in the Andrews household when Mr. Andrews returned and told of his daughter's virtue and of the happiness it had brought her.

Pamela readily adapted herself to her new role as the wife of a gentleman. With typical virtue, she quickly forgave Mrs. Jewkes for her former ill treatment. The only flaw in her married state was the fact that Lady Davers, Mr. B——'s sister, was angry with her brother because of his marriage to a servant girl. Pamela was alone when Lady Davers arrived. She insulted Pamela, who fled to her husband for consolation. A terrible scene took place between Mr. B—— and Lady Davers, but Pamela soon won the love and respect of the good woman when she showed her the letters she had written about her earlier sufferings.

One day, Mr. B—— told Pamela of a previous love affair with Miss Sally Godfrey and took her to see his daughter, who had been placed in a boarding school in the neighborhood. Pamela liked the little girl and asked to have the pretty child under her care at a future time. Mr. and Mrs. Andrews were pleased with Pamela's accounts of her happiness and of Mr. B——'s goodness to her. He gave the old people a substantial gift of money and thus enabled them to set themselves up in a small but comfortable business.

Lady Davers' correspondence with Pamela continued at great length, and she increasingly expressed her approval of Pamela's virtue and her disgust with her brother's attempts to dishonor her. During a visit she paid the young couple, Mr. B—— expressed his regret for his earlier unmannerly conduct toward the one who had become his dearly beloved wife. Mr. B——'s uncle, Sir Jacob Swynford, paid his nephew a visit; he was prepared to detest the inferior creature Mr. B—— had married. Pamela's charm, beauty, and virtue, however, won his heart completely, and the grumpy old man left full of praises for his lovely niece.

At last, Mr. B—— and Pamela decided to leave the country and return to London. Although her husband was still as attentive and thoughtful as ever, Pamela began to suspect that he might be having an affair with another woman. She was particularly distressed that she could not accompany him to the theater and other places of amusement, as she was about to bear a child. The scene of the christening of their son was joyful; in addition to the family, tenants from the estate arrived to express their joy that Mr. B—— now had a son and heir.

Nevertheless, Pamela's suspicions after all had been justified. An anonymous note informed her that the business trip which Mr. B—— had taken was in reality a journey to a neighboring city with a countess with whom he was having an affair. Pamela controlled her passions, and when Mr. B—— returned, he was so overcome by this further evidence of her kindness and understanding that he begged her forgiveness and promised to remain faithful to her from that day on. Pamela made good use of the letters she had written to Lady Davers during this trying period by sending them to the countess, hoping that she might learn from them and turn away from the path of license.

True to her earlier wish, Pamela decided to take in Sally Godfrey's child and bring her up as a sister for her own son, Billy. Mr. B—— was faithful to his resolve to devote himself only to his wife, and he spent the remainder of his days admiring and praising her virtue.

Critical Evaluation:

Samuel Richardson has often been awarded the title "Father of the English Novel." Like most such titles, this one is an oversimplification of a complex issue and one that has been particularly disputed by students of Richardson's contemporary Daniel Defoe, who is also justly noted for his important contributions to the genre. The importance of Richardson's position in the tradition of the novel, however, is undeniable and is based on his redefinition of the form, through his success in *Pamela* in dealing with several of the major formal problems that Defoe and others had left unsolved.

The most significant of these problems was that of plot. Prior to the publication of *Pamela*, a novel was commonly defined as "a small tale, generally of love." Although this definition has more recently been applied to the novella, most of the sources in Richardson's era, notably Dr. Johnson's dictionary, construed it as referring to the novel. When *Pamela* appeared, it was considered a "dilated novel" because its subject matter was basically the single amorous episode that the short novels had previously emphasized. Nevertheless, its treatment was on a scale much closer to the romances of Defoe and Henry Fielding, two authors who did not confront the definition problem in most of their works, which tended to deal with many episodes within a larger context. Works such as *Moll Flanders* (1722) and *Tom Jones* (1749) fit more easily into the romance category (with the word "romance" understood to mean adventure more than love). Richardson combined the large scale of the romance and the intimate scope of the traditional novel to form the basis of the novel as readers have come to know it. Richardson's use of the epistolary style—a style of which he was perhaps literature's foremost practitioner—facilitated the birth of the new form, although it causes some problems for modern readers.

Pamela's plot structure was based on a radically new concept in the novel form. This innovative plot structure is the work's major strength and its major weakness. Viewed in context with later novels, it appears awkward, contrived, and lacking in realism. Indeed, a major criticism of Richardson's novel concerns the question of how the major characters found the time in the midst of all of their adventures to be writing lengthy letters to one another. In a purely technical sense, perhaps the worst defect in the plot is that it is too long for its essential purpose, causing it to be static in movement and lacking in tension; it reaches a climax and resolution midway through the book, thus leaving hundreds of pages of dull and uneventful narrative. The account of Pamela's married life, serving as it does only to confirm her virtue in the eyes of the world, could have been trimmed considerably, thus enhancing the overall effect of the novel. As it is, the falling action of the novel, consisting of Mr. B——'s adultery and Pamela's forgiveness as well as the growing appreciation on the part of Mr. B—— of his wife's virtue, is unconvincing and sentimental.

The strength of the plot structure lies in Richardson's epistolary form; notwithstanding its shortcomings, the author's form does convey a degree of realism. Letters are normally a means for the relation of one's doings, and they presuppose an actual writer and an actual reader. Preconceived notions concerning the normal functions of the mode make believable an actual maiden, an actual seducer, and an actual marriage. Richardson's manipulation of the machinery governing the epistles—the hidden pens and ink, the evasions and discoveries, and the secreting of letters in bosoms and underlinens—causes the effect to grow. The realism is further enhanced by the clustering and lingering effect that comes to surround each incident. An incident occurs and is reflected on, committed to paper, entrusted to a porter, and spied upon; it is either intercepted or received, reflected upon, and responded to. Although it slows down the action, the whole complex, repetitious effect lends great credibility to the original incident.

Richardson's epistolary form, after establishing the necessary suspension of disbelief in readers regarding a servant girl who can read and write, also logically excuses much of Pamela's smooth and affected rhetoric; since a letter is an editing of life rather than life itself, the writer has an editorial option to tailor and refurbish experience. By positing a servant girl with a certain flair for writing, Richardson can justify a further suspension of disbelief, although sometimes not as much as the circumstances demand.

The weakest part of the plot's structure in terms of realism is Richardson's handling of the sequence of incidents. While perhaps the incidents in *Pamela* do not disappoint the reader's preconceived notions of drawing-room and boudoir reality, they are little more than interesting fits of manners and rarely reveal any depth of character or morals. These incidents are little more than stylistically balanced situations; outrages in the summerhouse are followed by contrition and tearful farewells by triumphant reunions.

The same shallowness applies to some of Richardson's characters, who, being allegorical as demanded by the instructional premise of the novel, offer little depth of personality. The heroine herself, however, presents an interesting study: Pamela begins as the most fully allegorical figure and concludes by being the most fully human. Beginning in ignorance, she presents the prospect, particularly to readers used to the less sentimental Fielding, of becoming a satirical figure; yet she never does. Pamela is an incorruptibly good woman. What is interesting about her characterization is how the author converts readers to accept the reality of his protagonist and her maidenly dilemma. He manages this by placing her in a crisis that is inherently genuine and appropriate to her way of life. He supplies her with neatly counterpoised groups of friends and enemies and fleshes out her vulnerability with an impressive strength and a striking ability to cope—a believable middle-class trait. The implied spectacle of her parents nervously hanging on from letter to letter adds further believability to the picture. Richardson also imbues Pamela with little vices which she realizes she has. Pamela, for example, knows that she is long-winded, prone to construe motives to her own advantage, and inclined to cling to praise and flattery. This realization of some of her own faults makes Pamela much more credible than a character who is merely symbolic and displays no insight into herself.

Despite Richardson's virtues and faults as a writer, it is his redefinition of the form of the novel that most makes him worth reading. *Pamela* was a radical departure from accepted concepts. While subsequent novelists learned from and modified Richardson's techniques, they for the most part drifted away from his epistolary form; while keeping his idea of treating a simple episode on a larger scale, they tended to follow the techniques developed by Fielding and Defoe. *Pamela* is thus as much of an anomaly today as it was in the eighteenth century. Nevertheless, it is a vital part of literary tradition and was instrumental in creating the novel as it is now known.

"Critical Evaluation" by Patricia Ann King

Bibliography:

Brissenden, R. F. *Samuel Richardson.* New York: Longmans, Green, 1965. Emphasizes Richardson's work over his biography. Provides a useful starting point for readers unfamiliar with *Pamela.*

Day, Martin S. *History of English Literature, 1660-1837.* Garden City, N.Y.: Doubleday, 1963. Compares *Pamela* to the Cinderella story, claiming Pamela Andrews as "the first great character creation in English prose fiction."

Eaves, T. C. Duncan, and Ben D. Kimpel. *Samuel Richardson: A Biography.* Oxford, England: Clarendon Press, 1971. Although the authors' chief attention is to Richardson's life, they consistently connect his life and writing, offering extensive commentary on *Pamela*'s evolution.

Flynn, Carol Houlihan. *Samuel Richardson: A Man of Letters.* Princeton, N.J.: Princeton University Press, 1982. Approximately one-third of this carefully researched, splendidly reasoned assessment of Richardson and his work is devoted to *Pamela.*

Keymer, Tom. *Richardson's Clarissa and the Eighteenth Century Reader.* Cambridge, England: Cambridge University Press, 1992. Although Keymer's major focus is on *Clarissa,* he makes cogent comparisons to *Pamela* and helps readers to understand the cultural milieu Richardson addressed.

McKillop, Alan Dugald. *Samuel Richardson, Printer and Novelist.* Chapel Hill: University of North Carolina Press, 1936. McKillop focuses on Richardson's later years, 1739-1754, during which his significant writing was accomplished. Detailed, biographically oriented commentary on *Pamela.*

Watt, Ian. *The Rise of the Novel: Studies in Defoe, Richardson, and Fielding.* Berkeley: University of California Press, 1957. Watt assesses *Pamela* in a chapter emphasizing Richardson's initiation of the novel as a genre.

PARADE'S END

Type of work: Novel
Author: Ford Madox Ford (Ford Madox Hueffer, 1873-1939)
Type of plot: Impressionism
Time of plot: World War I and after
Locale: England and France
First published: 1950: *Some Do Not . . .* , 1924; *No More Parades*, 1925; *A Man Could Stand Up*, 1926; *The Last Post*, 1928

Principal characters:
> CHRISTOPHER TIETJENS, the "last English Tory"
> SYLVIA, his wife
> MARK, his brother
> MACMASTER, his friend
> GENERAL CAMPION, his godfather
> VALENTINE WANNOP, his mistress

The Story:

Christopher Tietjens was probably the last real eighteenth century Tory in the England of pre-World War I. A thoroughly good man, he was so much a gentleman that he would not divorce his wife Sylvia, even though she was flagrantly unfaithful to him. It was even doubtful that the child she had borne was his own, and she had gone off for several weeks with another man; Christopher, however, held that no gentleman should ever publicly disgrace a woman by divorcing her or even by admitting her infidelities. Sylvia Tietjens hated her husband blindly because she could never break down his reserve, and all of her plots and meanness were for that purpose alone. She detested the various men she lived with, but she hated Christopher's virtue more.

Christopher's old-fashioned type of virtue had grown out of his family background. His oldest brother, Mark, who had inherited the estate of Groby and its vast income, lived with a Frenchwoman whom he would probably never marry and who would certainly bear no children, and the estate would one day belong to Christopher. The brothers feared that their father had committed suicide, for Sylvia had manipulated the old man into believing that Christopher lived off the earnings of immoral women and that he had sold her, his wife, to influential friends. Christopher thought his father's suicide was a sign that the family was weakening; consequently, he would not accept one penny of the estate for himself. Mark therefore proposed to set Sylvia up at Groby, with arrangements for the estate to go to her son. Even if the boy were not Christopher's, he must be treated as if he were a Tietjens. The plan suited Christopher, who had no interest in anything except protecting his wife's name and his son's future. Knowing that war was imminent, he wanted to gather up the loose ends of his life before he left.

Christopher was one of the most brilliant men in the government service, but, strangely, his brilliance coupled with his goodness made everyone want to hurt him. His only real friend was Macmaster, a Scotsman and a Whig, who was also in the service. Perhaps their friendship was due primarily to the fact that Macmaster owed Christopher a great deal of money. Christopher had also lent money to other men who, although they admired him, seemed bent on ruining him.

Christopher often wished to make Valentine Wannop his mistress. Valentine was a young suffragist, the daughter of his father's best friend, and a woman novelist whom Christopher admired greatly. Valentine was willing to accept Christopher as her lover, but they seemed destined to have their plans obstructed by someone bent on hurting Christopher. Although no word of their desire was ever spoken between them, their feelings were obvious to others, who believed that Valentine was already Christopher's mistress. On the night before his departure for the army, Christopher asked Valentine to spend the night with him. She consented, but again they were kept apart. Later, they both agreed that it was for the best, as neither seemed suited for an affair.

In France, unjustified troubles continued to haunt Christopher. Sylvia was at the bottom of most of them. Because she seemed to think he would soon be killed and out of her reach, she seemed compelled to hurt him as much as possible while he still lived. Christopher's godfather, General Campion, was his highest ranking officer. Convinced by Sylvia that she was an abused wife, the general constantly berated Christopher for his brutality as a husband. He also berated him for getting dirty, mixing with his men, and helping them with their personal troubles; it was not fitting for an English officer to get into the dregs of war.

Christopher often thought that he was surrounded by people with troubles. One of his fellow officers, almost insane over an unfaithful wife, often had fits of madness that threatened to destroy company morale. The first in command was a drunken colonel whom Christopher tried to shield, thus getting himself into trouble with General Campion. On one occasion, Christopher refused leave to a Canadian because he knew his wife's lover would kill the man if he went home. When the Canadian was killed in battle later on, it preyed on Christopher's mind that he had saved the soldier from one death only to lead him into another. Christopher's good intentions constantly brought discredit on him.

To his distress, Sylvia went to France to see him. Having accepted at last the fact that no matter what she did, she could not upset him emotionally, she remained true to her character in her determination to make him return to her in body. Her scheme failed. After she had maneuvered him into her room, one of her former lovers and the drunken colonel opened the door that she had left unlocked for them but that she had forgotten to lock when Christopher went in with her. Christopher was forced to throw out the two men in order to protect his wife's honor. Having decided it was Christopher's fault that his wife wanted to entertain other men, General Campion again berated him.

It seemed to Christopher that the whole war campaign bogged down because of lack of effective communications between various parts of the army. To him, the failure was symbolic. Life, too, bogged down into beastly messes because of lack of communication between people. To him, the horror of the war was not his physical suffering and inconvenience but rather the fact that the conflict was the end of everything that mattered. Believing that England was not prepared either for victory or for defeat, that this was the end of everything that was good no matter who won the battles, he found it almost impossible to remember anything of his old creed or his way of life at home. With Valentine so far away, she too seemed unreal to him. Like the others, General Campion admired and liked Christopher but could not understand him and wanted to make him suffer. Because Christopher had thrown the men out of Sylvia's bedroom, General Campion sent him to the front.

At the front, Christopher found himself second in command to hopelessly outnumbered troops under the leadership of the drunken colonel. Finally forced into assuming command, he tried to sustain the shattered morale of his troops. The only thing that kept his mind in balance was a dream of standing on a hilltop in peace, serenity, and privacy. Privacy was what he desired above all else. The army gave a man no chance to be alone or to keep his life and thoughts to himself. Because of his reticent nature, the lack of privacy was the worst hardship for Christopher. When an exploding shell buried him and two of his men under a pile of dirt, he dug out one of the soldiers and carried the other to safety through enemy fire. On his return, General Campion sent for him and relieved him of his command because his uniform was not spotless and flawless and because he had been reported away from headquarters. His heroism and disgrace marked the physical end of the war for Christopher.

Valentine Wannop received a telephone call from Macmaster's wife, who said that Christopher was home and almost out of his mind. Ready to give up everything to live with him and care for him, Valentine went to him at once. She did not know or care about the story of his mental deterioration. The fact that he had never written to her was also of no importance. She intended to become his mistress, although she realized she might first have to be his nurse. Back home in Valentine's company on Armistice Night, Christopher was about to declare his love when they were interrupted by celebrating members of Christopher's old company. His mind fuzzy, he found nothing sad in their being thwarted again or in the obvious hate he saw in the eyes of a wife whose husband's life he had saved in the trenches.

There were changes at Groby, too. Mark had married his Frenchwoman and made her Lady Tietjens, partly to spite Sylvia, who had let the estate to an obnoxious rich American woman and her husband. It was said that Mark, having suffered a stroke just after the Armistice, could not speak or move. The truth was that, partially paralyzed, he had simply withdrawn from the world. Like Christopher, he belonged to another era. Mark believed that the last of the Tietjens were misfits. Truth had given way to confusion and untruth, and the brothers were likely to be swallowed up in this mad new world to which neither belonged. Avoiding the rest of the world, he waited quietly for death. Christopher and Valentine went to live in a cottage close by. Having refused to go back into government service or to accept help from his brother, Christopher had become a dealer in antique furniture.

Sylvia finally decided to divorce Christopher so as to marry General Campion and go with him to India. Although she had given up all hope of getting Christopher to notice her again, she had continued her petty attempts to make his life miserable. When she learned that Valentine was to have a baby, however, she became afraid that her attacks on Christopher and Valentine would harm the unborn child. She also began to regret her last and cruelest act against Christopher and Mark: She had persuaded the American woman to cut down the Groby Great Tree, an immense cedar that had guarded the manor house for generations; for a time, she feared the wrath of the brothers because of her deed. Both felt, however, that the Groby Great Tree had symbolized the curse hanging over the family and that its removal might take away part of that curse. When they ignored her spite, she stopped her vicious tricks and decided to let Christopher marry Valentine. Sylvia hated General Campion, too, but she wanted to become a great official's wife and be resplendent in a tiara.

Dying, Mark rationalized his father's death and knew that the old gentleman had not committed suicide but had died as a result of a hunting accident. He also realized that the appearance and actions of Sylvia's son proved that Christopher was his father, and that the boy was the rightful heir to Groby. It seemed to Mark that he could at last understand and love his brother, and he believed that the tales he had heard about Christopher were really lies told by people who could not understand Christopher or him because the Tietjens did not belong to this century of deceit, confusion, and untruth. Before he died, Mark spoke once more, assuring Valentine that Christopher was a good man and asking her to be kind to him.

Critical Evaluation:

During his long life, Ford Madox Ford published eighty-one books, of which thirty-two were novels, but of these only *The Good Soldier* (1915) and the tetralogy with the collective title *Parade's End* are generally regarded as having the status of major works. *Parade's End* is many things: a portrait of an English country gentleman before the cataclysm of World War I; an individual's experience of the hardships of that war; a vivid picture of a terrible marriage; and a romantic story with a happy ending.

Each of the four novels composing *Parade's End* makes use of impressionistic methods. Critical scenes carry most of the narrative burden, as the action moves with little transition from one scene to another, while the narrative moves backward and forward in time. An episode that concludes the sixth chapter of part 2 in the first novel, *Some Do Not . . .* , is, for example, not explained until part 1, chapter 3, of the second novel, *No More Parades*; the aftermath of that scene is not resolved until the final chapter of the third novel, *A Man Could Stand Up*. Jumps in time include that between the 1916 beginning of part 1 of *Some Do Not . . .* , when Tietjens, his memory shattered by his combat experiences, is preparing to return to the front from London, and the end of the same part four years earlier.

Ford's style in these novels also includes experiments with point of view, and the narrative voice switches from Tietjens to the object of his love, Valentine Wannop, to Sylvia, with brief stops along the way to the minds of other characters. In the final novel, *The Last Post*, Christopher Tietjens' older brother Mark becomes the central character and most of that novel takes place in Mark's mind. Each of the main characters is portrayed not only by a third-person narrator but also through interior monologues in a stream-of-consciousness style. Contemporaries, including James Joyce and Virginia Woolf, were using similar techniques, but Ford created an idiosyncratic combination of narrative stream of consciousness and time shifts.

The four novels of *Parade's End* cover most of the adult life of Christopher Tietjens. It is a life filled with frustration over the end of the world as he had known it, a world in which he seems to be the only man left upholding moral standards. His wife, who both hates and loves him, treats him dreadfully. A classic shrew, she lies to Tietjens, lies to others to blacken his name, seduces anyone who catches her fancy, and fights to secure her son's rights as heir to the Tietjens' estates. Tietjens, in love with Valentine Wannop, refuses for years to consummate their love because of his marital vows. He endures much pain, not only from Sylvia but from his experiences in the war and the sorrow he feels for the men under his command who are being slaughtered in the mire of trench warfare. The first three novels paint a bitter picture of England's destruction. Only in *The Last Post*, in which Christopher does not appear at all but is reported to be happily engaged in the antique business while Valentine is pregnant with his child, does the life of this character attain peace and happiness.

Parade's End is simultaneously a series of very funny novels and a bitterly accurate description of the destruction of a generation. Tietjens and Sylvia are not only victims and victimizers, they are superbly drawn comic figures, and the attempts of both to get their own way provide a wealth of comic scenes. In one scene of *Some Do Not . . .* , Sylvia accuses her husband of adultery, reminds him that she has blackened his name with lies to his parents and his bank, and finally shies crockery at him in the attempt to break through his self-possession. Ford lightens even the bleak tone of the grimmest of the four novels, *No More Parades*, with a kind of French bedroom farce involving Sylvia and several officers in a French hotel. Valentine's protracted conversation with the headmistress of the school where she teaches introduces a new tone in the opening of *A Man Could Stand Up*, which shifts to the end of the war and provides the information that Tietjens has survived the war. Finally, *The Last Post* includes a hilarious scene in which all the main characters except Christopher gather at Groby, the Tietjens' ancestral home, to fight over Christopher and the heritage of Groby.

Characterization is a major reason for the success of these novels, for all of the characters are sharply drawn. From Valentine Wannop and her novelist mother to General Campion, Mark Tietjens with his longtime French mistress, and Father Consett, who functions as whatever conscience Sylvia has, the characters who populate these novels are individualized and memorable.

In the end, it is beyond question Christopher Tietjens who carries the heaviest significance in *Parade's End*. It is clear that he is based on Ford Madox Ford's own character and experience and that his highly individual sense of values is very much Ford's own. The nostalgia for an earlier and more moral society is obviously an important element in the novels. Ford saw himself and his ideals clearly enough, however, to realize that they were anachronistic in the aftermath of World War I and to portray them as comic in the context of postwar society. *Parade's End* is a superb achievement.

"Critical Evaluation" by John M. Muste

Bibliography:
Agenda 27, no. 4, and 28, no. 1 (Winter, 1989; Spring, 1990). A double issue devoted to essays on Ford's fiction by twenty-eight different critics.
Cassell, Richard A., ed. *Critical Essays on Ford Madox Ford*. Boston: G. K. Hall, 1987. An excellent collection of essays, most focusing on *The Good Soldier* but with significant attention paid to *Parade's End*.
Mizener, Arthur. *The Saddest Story*. New York: World Publishing, 1971. The definitive biography of Ford, a long and thorough study that includes an appendix with a separate discussion of *Parade's End*.
Moore, Gene M. "The Tory in a Time of Change: Social Aspects of Ford Madox Ford's *Parade's End*." *Twentieth Century Literature* 28 (Spring, 1982): 48-69. A discussion of the ways in which the novel reflects Ford's views of the dramatic changes inflicted on English society by World War I.
Sniton, Ann Barr. *Ford Madox Ford and the Voice of Uncertainty*. Baton Rouge: Louisiana State University Press, 1984. Studies Ford's style in detail, showing how its hesitancy and ambiguity reflect Ford's ambivalent attitude toward his times.

PARADISE LOST

Type of work: Poetry
Author: John Milton (1608-1674)
Type of plot: Epic
Time of plot: Creation of the world
Locale: Heaven, Hell, and Earth
First published: 1667

Principal characters:
GOD THE FATHER
CHRIST THE SON
LUCIFER, later Satan
ADAM
EVE

The Story:

In Heaven, Lucifer, unable to abide the supremacy of God, led a revolt against divine authority. Defeated, he and his followers were cast into Hell, where they lay nine days on a burning lake. Lucifer, now called Satan, arose from the flaming pitch and vowed that all was not lost, that he would have revenge for his downfall. Arousing his legions, he reviewed them under the canopy of Hell and decided his purposes could be achieved by guile rather than by force.

Under the direction of Mulciber, the forces of evil built an elaborate palace, Pandemonium, in which Satan convened a congress to decide on immediate action. At the meeting, Satan reasserted the unity of those fallen, and opened the floor to a debate on what measures to take. Moloch advised war. Belial recommended a slothful existence in Hell. Mammon proposed peacefully improving Hell so that it might rival Heaven in splendor. His motion was received with great favor until Beelzebub, second in command, arose and informed the conclave that God had created Earth, which he had peopled with good creatures called humans. It was Beelzebub's proposal to investigate this new creation, seize it, and seduce its inhabitants to the cause of the fallen angels.

Announcing that he would journey to Earth to learn for himself how matters were there, Satan flew to the gate of Hell. There he encountered his daughter, Sin, and his son, Death. They opened the gate and Satan winged his way toward Earth.

God, in his omniscience, beheld the meeting in Hell, knew the intents of the evil angels, and saw Satan approaching Earth. Disguised as various beasts, Satan acquainted himself with Adam and Eve and with the Tree of Knowledge, which God had forbidden to them.

Uriel, learning that an evil angel had broken through to Eden, warned Gabriel, who appointed two angels to hover about the bower of Adam and Eve. The guardian angels arrived too late to prevent Satan, in the form of a toad, from beginning his evil work. He had influenced Eve's dreams.

Upon awaking, Eve told Adam that in her strange dream she had been tempted to taste of the fruit of the Tree of Knowledge. God, seeing danger to Adam and Eve was imminent, sent the angel Raphael to the garden to warn them. At Adam's insistence, Raphael related in detail the story of the great war between the good and the bad angels and of the fall of the bad angels to eternal misery in Hell. At Adam's further inquiries, Raphael told of the creation of the world and of how Earth was created in six days, an angelic choir singing the praises of God on the seventh day. He cautioned Adam not to be too curious, that there were many things done by God which were not for humans to understand or to attempt to understand. Adam then told how he had been warned against the Tree of Knowledge of Good and Evil, how he had asked God for fellowship in his loneliness, and how Eve was created from his rib.

After the departure of Raphael, Satan returned as a mist to the garden and entered the body of a sleeping serpent. In the morning, as Adam and Eve proceeded to their day's occupation, Eve proposed that they work apart. Adam, remembering the warning of Raphael, opposed her wishes, but Eve prevailed, and the couple parted. Alone, Eve was accosted by the serpent, which flattered her into tasting the fruit of the Tree of Knowledge. Eve, liking what she tasted, took the fruit to Adam, who was horrified when he saw what Eve had done. In his love for Eve, however, he also ate the fruit.

Having eaten, the couple knew lust for the first time, and after their dalliance they knew sickening shame. They also ate many apples, adding gluttony to their list, which they were rapidly completing, of the seven deadly sins. The guardian angels now deserted the transgressors and returned to God, who approved them, saying they could not have prevented Satan from succeeding in his mission.

Christ descended to Earth to pass judgment. Before Adam and Eve, who had been reluctant, in their shame, to come out of their bower to face him, Christ sentenced the serpent to be forever a hated enemy of mankind. He told Eve that her sorrow would be multiplied by the bearing of children and that she would be the servant of Adam to the end of time. Adam, said Christ, would eat in sorrow; his ground would be cursed and he would eat bread only by toiling and sweating.

Meanwhile, Death and Sin, having divined Satan's success, left the gates of Hell to join their father on Earth. Within sight of Earth, they met Satan, who delegated Sin and Death as his ambassadors on Earth. Back in Hell, Satan proudly reported his accomplishments to his followers. He was acclaimed, however, by hisses as his cohorts became serpents, and Satan himself was transformed into a serpent before their reptilian eyes. Trees similar to the Tree of Knowledge appeared in Hell, but when the evil angels tasted the fruit, they found their mouths full of ashes.

God, angered at the disaffection of Adam and Eve, brought about great changes on Earth. He created the seasons to replace eternal spring, and the violence and misery of storms, winds, hail, ice, floods, and earthquakes. He caused all Earth's creatures to prey upon one another. Adam and Eve argued bitterly (adding anger to their sins) until they realized they had to face their common plight together. Repenting their sins, they prayed to God for relief. Although Christ interceded for them, God sentenced them to expulsion from Eden and sent the angel Michael to Earth to carry out the sentence. Adam and Eve, lamenting their misfortune, contemplated suicide, but Michael gave them new hope when he brought to Adam a vision of life and death; of the rise and fall of kingdoms and empires; of the activities of Adam and Eve's progeny through their evil days to the flood, when God destroyed all life except that preserved by Noah in the ark; and of the subsequent return to evil days and Christ's incarnation, death, resurrection, and ascension as the redeemer. Despite the violence and evil and bloodshed in the vision, Adam and Eve were pacified when they saw that their children would be saved. They walked hand in hand from the heights of Paradise to the barren plains below.

Critical Evaluation:

John Milton prepared himself for many years for the creation of an epic poem in English that would rank with the epics of Homer and Vergil. *Paradise Lost* is nothing less than the Christian epic of humanity. One of Milton's models for *Paradise Lost* was the *Iliad* (c. 800 B.C.E.), an epic poem of the oral tradition, which evolved as the composition of a number of poets, but is commonly attributed to Homer. The *Iliad* celebrates heroes. A model of even greater influence was the *Aeneid* (c. 29-19 B.C.E.), an epic poem written by a single poet, Vergil, whose intent was to celebrate the national glory of Rome. Milton's original intent was to follow Vergil's lead and write a patriotic epic poem of England, but he changed his mind, espousing an even greater enterprise. In retelling the story of the Fall of Man, he attempts to do nothing less than "justify the ways of God to men."

To emphasize the importance of his subject matter, Vergil chose to write in solemn tone using heightened language, and Milton adopted the same policy. Much of the difficulty of *Paradise Lost* lies in the language. The poem uses uncommon words put together in long sentences containing multiple clauses constructed and ordered in peculiar ways. This convoluted syntax and unfamiliar language give the poem its distinctive cadences, its majestic rhythm, and its ceremonial atmosphere. The many classical, biblical, and geographical references add authority, pointing to the learning of the poet. In such ways, Milton brings grandeur to his poem.

The background to the poem is from the Bible and follows the teaching of St. Augustine. Although Milton was involved in religious controversy in his life, this great poem, in its adherence to basic Christian doctrine, largely stands outside the issues of Milton's time. The cosmos as it is described in the poem conforms to the popular view of Milton's day. Chaos is bounded above by Heaven and beneath by Hell. Earth, at the center of a spherical "solar system," is suspended into chaos from the floor of Heaven. Above all is God, who is dazzling light. Hell, at the other extreme, is absolute lack of light. Within the cosmos, all beings exist in a hierarchy under God, and all beings owe obedience to their hierarchical superiors. The hierarchy, the Great Chain of Being, is of central importance, as is the doctrine of obedience. Satan and his followers rebel against the authority of God and are thrown out of Heaven, and Adam and Eve disobey God and are ejected from the garden of Eden.

The characterizations of God and Satan are problematic, not the least because neither is human. Milton's readers, being human, however, understand character in anthropomorphic terms. God is invisible and can be defined by people only in terms of attributes, such as "Immortal" or "Almighty." God thus tends to seem abstract and distant rather than real. God is absolute authority. In addition, God is omniscient, knowing all that happens and all that will happen, but has given the lower orders free will. Consequently, God can be seen as tyrannical and cruel in not preventing evil. Easier to understand is the reflection of God, as seen in the Son of God, superior to all but the Creator:

> Beyond compare the Son of God was seen
> Most glorious, in him all his Father shone
> Substantially expressed.

Satan, with his fallen nature, is easier to understand. Before his fall Satan was Lucifer, an archangel. In the early part of Milton's poem readers see his magnificent qualities, then follow the progress of his self-destruction caused by pride and envy. The danger in the characterization of Satan is that readers tend to find him attractive, sympathize with his resentment, and admire his passionate determination. The strength of the characterization lies in these qualities. His gradual degeneration, however, is convincing; awareness of his sinfulness grows in the readers' consciousness. At first Satan longs for good; finally Satan embraces evil. Readers observe Satan metamorphose in a series of disguises, each a lower life form than before, a continuum, recalling the Great Chain of Being, from archangel to serpent.

The problem of presenting Adam and Eve is that they must at first be innocent, free of sin, yet they must be intelligent and aware enough to be capable of choosing sin, and strong enough to resist. Milton shows how the potential for their fall is present from the start. Satan is there in the garden of Eden, observing, plotting, beginning to work at undermining Eve's integrity. Reaching her through a dream, he acquaints her with temptation. She ultimately succumbs to the temptation of surpassing her true place in the hierarchy, and the sin of pride accompanies her disobedience in eating the forbidden fruit. She tempts Adam to follow her into sin because she cannot bear to lose him, and Adam succumbs because he cannot bear to lose her. His sin also goes beyond disobedience. He violates the hierarchical order in putting Eve, who, the poem makes clear, is inferior to him, above himself and his power of reason, and therefore above God.

Adam and Eve and the world itself are incomparably diminished by the Fall, but it is also to be seen as the opportunity for a new hope, and for the occasion of their later redemption. It affords them the chance to develop for themselves virtues such as repentance, humility, and understanding.

Milton is considered the greatest poet after Shakespeare, and *Paradise Lost* is his greatest poem. Yet this huge work has not received universal acclaim. Critics have objected to implications they see in the characterizations. It is hard to imagine that Milton could have better fit such a story into the form of an epic, but nevertheless critics have complained of what may be perceived as God's tyranny and Satan's heroism. Milton's portrayal of Eve also has generated much criticism. There have also been objections to the style of the poem: overuse of abstractions, too little visual imagery, unnatural syntax. Many critics have also found *Paradise Lost* fascinating and satisfying, one of the truly great and enduring works of literature of all time.

"Critical Evaluation" by Susan Henthorne

Bibliography:
Broadbent, John Barclay. *Some Graver Subject: An Essay on "Paradise Lost."* New York: Barnes & Noble Books, 1960. Serves as an excellent introduction to *Paradise Lost*. Acknowledging the difficulties of reading the poem, Broadbent systematically analyzes and explains Milton's meanings.

Gardner, Helen. *A Reading of "Paradise Lost."* New York: Oxford University Press, 1965. Focuses on reading the poem with a twentieth century sensibility, including discussion of twentieth century Milton criticism.

Kranidas, Thomas, ed. *New Essays on "Paradise Lost."* Berkeley: University of California Press, 1969. Essays by American scholars examine such topics as form, style, genre, and theme. Links the poem with its biblical sources.

Lewis, C. S. *A Preface to "Paradise Lost."* New York: Oxford University Press, 1961. Considers epic form in general and continues with a discussion of Milton's epic, based on a specifically Christian interpretation. Rather dogmatic, this is nevertheless a lucid, enormously helpful analysis of form and doctrinal issues.

Patrides, C. A., ed. *Approaches to "Paradise Lost."* London: Edward Arnold, 1968. Contains a series of lectures offering a wide variety of approaches, such as literary, doctrinal, musical, and iconographical. Illustrations. The broad range of this book is an aid to appreciating the complexity of the poem and the vast array of Milton criticism that is available.

PARADISE REGAINED

Type of work: Poetry
Author: John Milton (1608-1674)
Type of plot: Epic
Time of plot: First century
Locale: The Holy Land
First published: 1671

Principal characters:
JESUS OF NAZARETH
SATAN

The Story:

Jesus was baptized by John the Baptist. This rite was attended by Satan, the Adversary, cloaked in invisibility. Thunderstruck by the pronouncement from Heaven that Jesus was the beloved Son of God, Satan hastily assembled a council of his peers. They chose "their great Dictator" to attempt the overthrow of this new and terrible enemy. God, watching Satan set out on his evil mission, foretold the failure of the mission to the angel Gabriel. The angels sang a triumphant hymn.

Led by the Spirit, Jesus entered the desert and pursued holy meditations. In retrospect, he examined his life, considered his destiny, but did not wish for revelation of his future until God chose to give it. For forty days he wandered unharmed through the perils of the desert; then for the first time he felt hunger. Just at that moment, he met an aged man in rural clothing. The old man explained that he was present at the baptism, then expressed amazement at the lost and perilous situation of the wanderer. Jesus replied: "Who brought me hither will bring me hence, no other Guide I seek." The old man then suggested that if Jesus were really the Son of God, he should command the stones to become bread. In his refusal Jesus asked: "Why dost thou then suggest to me distrust, knowing who I am, as I know who thou art?" At this discovery, Satan abandoned his disguise and entered a dispute attempting self-justification. Overcome in the argument, he vanished as night fell. The other newly baptized people and Mary the mother of Jesus were distressed at his absence, but did not allow themselves to despair.

Satan called a fresh council of war. He dismissed Belial's suggestion, "Set women in his eye and in his walk," and received a vote of confidence for his own plan of using honor, glory, and popular praise combined with relief from the suffering of physical hunger.

Jesus dreamed of the ravens who fed Elijah by Cherith's Brook and of the angel who fed him in the desert. Awakening, he looked for a cottage, a sheepcote, or a herd, but found nothing. Suddenly Satan appeared again in a new form, but did not attempt to conceal his identity. He disclosed a table loaded with delicious food and invited Jesus to eat. Jesus refused the food, not because the food itself was unlawful but because it was the offering of Satan. Disgruntled, Satan caused the food to vanish and returned to the attack, offering wealth with which to buy power. When this was declined as an unworthy aim for life, Satan proposed the career of a glorious conqueror. Jesus retorted with references to Job and Socrates, as justly famous as the proudest conquerors, and he declared that desire for glory, which belonged to God, not humanity, was sacrilege. Satan then attempted to relate conquest to the freeing of the Jews from their Roman oppressors. Jesus replied that if his destiny were to free his people from bondage it would come about when God chose. He then asked another of his penetrating questions: Why did Satan hasten to overthrow himself by trying to found Christ's everlasting kingdom? This question tortured Satan internally, but he took refuge in hypocritical assurances that he had lost hope of his own triumph. Then, remarking that Jesus had seen little of the world, he took him to the top of a mountain and showed him the terrestrial kingdoms, in particular the empires of Rome and Parthia, one of which he advised him to choose and to destroy the other with it. Jesus, however, refused earthly empire. Then Satan tried a particularly Miltonic temptation. He offered the empire of the mind: philosophy, learning, poetry, particularly those of Greece and Rome. Against these, Jesus placed the sacred literature of the Hebrews. Satan, baffled again, returned Jesus to the desert and pretended to depart. When Jesus slept again, Satan disturbed him with ugly dreams and raised a fearful storm. With morning and the return of calm weather, Satan appeared for a last, desperate effort, no longer so much in hope of victory as in desire for revenge. He seized Jesus, flew with him to Jerusalem, placed him on the highest pinnacle of the Temple, and cried:

> There stand, if thou wilt stand; to stand upright
> Will ask thee skill. . . .
> Now show thy Progeny; if not to stand,
> Cast thyself down; safely if Son of God:
> For it is written, He will give command
> Concerning thee to his Angels, in their hands
> They shall uplift thee, lest at any time
> Thou chance to dash thy foot against a stone.
> To whom thus Jesus. Also it is written,
> Tempt not the Lord thy God; he said and stood.
> But Satan smitten with amazement fell.

After Satan's second fall, a host of angels flew to the temple, took Jesus to a fertile valley, and spread before him a table of celestial food. After they sang another hymn of triumph, Jesus returned home to his mother's house.

Critical Evaluation:

Paradise Regained is composed of four books averaging about five hundred lines of blank verse each; the poem, therefore, contains more than two thousand lines. The Gospel of Luke, John Milton's principal source, is contained in seventeen verses spread over two chapters. Although Milton regarded this "brief epic" as his greatest masterpiece, that evaluation has not generally been shared by his critical or popular readership. Unlike his internationally acclaimed epic, *Paradise Lost* (1667), *Paradise Regained* lacks both an intense conflict between worthy moral antagonists and the narrative action such conflicts afford. To many, its Satan seems to have been pathetically reduced to an incompetent schemer who is no match for the stoical Jesus of Nazareth, who dominates the extended debates occupying most of the epic. Yet if Milton was not wholly wrong about his final work, in what does its greatness consist?

Although lacking some of the complexity of its forerunner, *Paradise Regained* can be breathtaking in its stark poetic simplicity and in its profound narrative expansion of Luke's brief account of Jesus' three temptations in the wilderness. To appreciate its narrative "action" is thus to understand how Milton uses a dialogical form of conflict drawn from the Book of Job to illuminate and expand these three themes. Yet it is also to understand how Job-like this Jesus is, who is not merely an omniscient being who must "inevitably" triumph over Satan but a man undergoing extreme trial without any assistance from friends or family, including his heavenly father. Confronted by the most powerful opponent he or any human will ever face, his success becomes a virtual summa of the virtues of the rational Christian, the person who diligently employs well-disciplined mental energies in conjunction with a well-grounded faith in divine providence. The temptations which Jesus is required to face are lack of faith, hunger, desire for glory, desire to overthrow the enemies of his people by violence, and pride in being declared the beloved Son of God. Milton's anti-Trinitarianism allows him to present Jesus as the highest type of human being, the true Son of God whose example has something to teach all people, a being divine only in being fully and perfectly human. Like the rest of humankind, he can demonstrate his love of God only by maintaining his faith, hope, and integrity, which in turn empower his love of others and of self.

The contrast to this all-embracing love is the all-enslaving hate of Satan and his cohorts, who have by now become less like the mighty archangels of *Paradise Lost* and more like the spirits of worldly ambition, pride, and greed who deceive the faithful and the wicked alike. What they lack in epic splendor is compensated for in psychological realism, which portrays in them all the qualities of those who would achieve earthly glory only for the purposes of domination and exploitation. As he himself gradually realizes, Jesus is their moral opposite, the man who would subdue the world by first subduing himself and his passions, the egoistic cravings which would render his rule despotic rather than liberating. The more compassionate and less stoical aspect of Jesus' refusal to yield to any of Satan's temptations is dramatically highlighted by scenes which portray his devastated followers sadly "missing him thir joy so lately found," who they "began to doubt, and doubted many days." Even Mary begins to doubt, but as the maternal equivalent of her son, she "with thoughts/ Meekly compos'd awaited the fulfilling." This behavior was rewarded once Jesus "unobserv'd/ Home to his Mother's house private return'd." Such success depends upon a heroism which is neither military nor tragic but fundamentally individual and lyric—something available to anyone who sees personal ethics as the clue to social responsibility.

In a sense, then, Milton challenges the reader to reject mainstream heroic values in favor of the humble ethos with which Jesus conquered. Although primarily a Christian message, this epic "trial" of the worldly principles of leadership and learning can challenge anyone to examine how best to exercise them. Confronted with the imminent collapse of the great social programs inherited from Enlightenment—-confidence in the universal progress of knowledge, education, and democracy as solutions to all human ills—the postmodern reader can gain a rare opportunity to examine an earlier and ultimately quite different solution to the problems of the individual in society, a moral synthesis of classical and Christian values grounded in Milton's staunchly libertarian belief in the inalienable freedoms of conscience and action. Just as his epic debates refuse to separate individual action from social consequences, they also refuse to privilege any single side of those debates. Both the "high Authority" of God's prophets and the "inspired Oracles" of Delphi can cause doubt, disbelief, or self-promotion in those who fail to understand them correctly. The alternative is to realize that "so much bounty is in God, such grace,/ That who advance his glory, not thir own,/ Them he himself to glory will advance."

Yet what, ultimately, is divine glory? This goodness beyond thought is revealed in the fourth book, which, if read otherwise, appears anticlimactic. Here Jesus' temptation is not all the kingdoms and accomplishments of the world offered by Satan but his means of gaining them. Urging that ends justify means, he sees the successful leader as seizing any occasion to achieve his destiny. In reply, Jesus redefines that destiny as the individual's own ability to observe proper proportion, ignoring not only the "false portents" of success but any unearned or premature fame, which in the much earlier poem, "Lycidas" (1645), Milton had described as "that last infirmity of Noble mind." By demonstrating the process whereby that last infirmity is overcome, *Paradise Regained* can be read as a worthy testament to a poet whose entire life was a struggle to balance the temptations of literary and political power.

"Critical Evaluation" by Catherine Gimelli Martin

Bibliography:
Fixler, Michael. *Milton and the Kingdoms of God*. Evanston, Ill.: Northwestern University Press, 1964. Examines *Paradise Regained* in the historical, religious, political, and literary contexts of Milton's life and works. It is particularly valuable in exploring the Puritan dilemma after the failure of their revolution.
Lewalski, Barbara K. *Milton's Brief Epic*. Providence, R.I.: Brown University Press, 1966. The single most comprehensive exploration of Milton's use of the literary and biblical traditions invoked in the poem, particularly the story of Job and its varying interpretations.
Pope, Elizabeth M. *"Paradise Regained": The Tradition and the Poem*. New York: Russell and Russell, 1962. A good beginner's introduction to the text and its theological implications, less perceptive on the textual subtlety of Milton's innovations.
Stein, Arnold. *Heroic Knowledge*. Minneapolis: University of Minnesota Press, 1957. A classic study of the dramatic aspects of *Paradise Regained*, especially in relation to the other major works of the mature Milton.
Wittreich, Joseph. *Calm of Mind*. Cleveland, Ohio: Case Western University Press, 1971. An important collection of essays centered on *Paradise Regained* and *Samson Agonistes* (1671), considering the dominant literary and interpretive problems raised by the poems.

PARADOX, KING

Type of work: Novel
Author: Pío Baroja (1872-1956)
Type of plot: Social satire
Time of plot: Early twentieth century
Locale: Spain, Tangier, and the imaginary Bu-Tata, in Uganga, Africa
First published: Paradox, rey, 1906 (English translation, 1931)

> *Principal characters:*
> SILVESTRE PARADOX, a modern adventurer
> AVELINO DIZ, his skeptical friend
> ARTHUR SIPSOM, an English manufacturer of needles
> EICHTHAL THONELGEBEN, a scientist
> HARDIBRÁS, a crippled soldier
> UGÚ, a friendly black man
> BAGÚ, a jealous medicine man

The Story:

After many adventures, Dr. Silvestre Paradox, a short, chubby man of about forty-five years, settled in a small Valencian town. Tiring at last of his quiet life, he announced one morning to his friend, Avelino Diz, his intention of taking a trip to Cananí, on the Gulf of Guinea. A British banker, Abraham Wolf, was setting out on his yacht *Cornucopia* with a party of scientists and explorers for the purpose of establishing a Jewish colony in Africa, and he had invited Paradox to go with him. Paradox suggested that Diz join the expedition.

In Tangier they met several other members of the party, including General Pérez and his daughter Dora, and a crippled, scarred soldier named Hardibrás. They drank to the success of the venture with whiskey. When one of the company fed whiskey to a rooster, the fowl broke into human speech and deplored what humans drink. Paradox declared that only Nature is just and honorable. He was eager to go where people lived naturally.

They boarded the yacht, Hardibrás swinging himself aboard by the hook he wore in place of his lost hand. There Paradox and Diz met others of the expedition: Mingote, a revolutionist who had tried to assassinate the king of Portugal; Pelayo, who had been Paradox's secretary until his employer fired him for crooked dealings; Sipsom, an English manufacturer; Miss Pich, a feminist writer and former ballet dancer, and "The Cheese Kid," a former French cancan dancer. Wolf himself was not on board. He was conferring with Monsieur Chabouly, a French chocolate king who was also emperor of Western Nigritia, in an attempt to establish peaceful diplomatic relations between Chabouly's domain and the new state of Cananí.

The yacht put out to sea. On the third day, stormy waves washed the captain overboard. The mate and the crew were drunk, so Paradox and two others were forced to take over the yacht. Paradox, alone at the wheel, conversed with the wind and the sea, who told him that they had wills of their own. Yock, his dog, admired his master's resolution and strength and declared that he was almost worthy of being a dog.

As the storm increased in fury, the mast broke and crashed upon the deck. Paradox called the passengers together and suggested that one of them, Goizueta, be appointed captain because of the maritime experience he had had. Goizueta was elected. His first act, after saving one bottle of brandy for medicine, was to throw the rest overboard.

For a week they sailed through heavy fog that never lifted to reveal their position. At last the coal gave out, and they drifted. One night some of the passengers and crew, Miss Pich, Mingote, and Pelayo among them, stole the only lifeboat and deserted the ship.

When the fog lifted, the passengers saw a beach not far away. The yacht struck a rock, but all were able to save themselves on rafts which they loaded with supplies from the ship. The next morning the yacht broke up, leaving the party marooned on an island. It was then proposed that Paradox be put in charge. After modestly protesting, he accepted and assigned jobs to all the survivors. Nevertheless, he failed to make provisions for their defense. The next night a band of blacks came in two canoes, surprised the sleepers, and took them bound to Bu-Tata.

The first demand Prime Minister Funangue made was for rum. One of the party, Sipsom, explained that they could provide rum only if they were allowed to return to their base of supplies. In his greed, Funangue decided to ignore the advice of Bagú, the medicine man, who wanted all the whites slain. A friendly native, Ugú, was assigned to instruct the prisoners in tribal language and customs. From Ugú the captives learned Bagú's prejudices and superstitions. When the witch doctor later appeared, Sipsom declared that one of the prisoners was a wizard fated to die on the same day as Bagú. If Bagú sided with them, however, the white magician would help the medicine man to marry Princess Mahu, King Kiri's daughter. Bagú accepted the proposal.

King Kiri, engaged in his favorite pastime of killing subjects whom he disliked, paused in his diversion long enough to receive the prisoners. After a conversation about vested interests, he ordered that their lives be spared. Giving them permission to get supplies from their camp, he dispatched them under guard in two canoes. During the trip, the prisoners, having lulled the suspicions of the guards, were about to take their guns and free themselves, but Paradox objected. He said that he had other plans. Diz scoffed at the way his friend put on airs.

After damaging one canoe, the prisoners used the delay to impress the blacks with their white superiority by working magic tricks. A Frenchman in the party led a discussion on the rights of individuals. The scheme worked. After two weeks, the blacks agreed to desert their king and accompany the whites to Fortunate Island, a defensible plateau suggested by Ugú. Although Paradox preached the virtues of life out of doors, the others built Fortune House, a communal dwelling.

When King Kiri's army appeared, Paradox's machine gun quickly repulsed them, and a searchlight finally put the natives to flight. Peace had finally come to Fortune House. The blacks constructed huts and spent their evenings at magic lantern shows. The Fortune House Herald began publication.

Prime Minister Funangue and two attendants, appearing under a flag of truce, brought King Kiri's appeal for help. The Fulani were attacking Bu-Tata. Paradox and Thonelgeben, the engineer, returned to the capital with the blacks. At Paradox's suggestion, the river was dynamited to turn Bu-Tata into an island. Bagú objected to such interference with nature and discussed the change with fish, serpents, and frogs. Only the bat refused to voice an opinion.

One day warriors from Bu-Tata appeared at Fortune House with the head of King Kiri and begged one of the whites to become their ruler. At a meeting, all debated monarchial theories. When they failed to agree, Sipsom showed Paradox to the natives and announced that he had been chosen by popular vote. All the natives then returned to Bu-Tata for a coronation feast.

By that time Paradox, reconciled to the advantages of civilization over life close to nature, was tired of Africa. At a session of Congress he argued against state support of art and criticized formal education. Pelayo and Mingote, captured by Moors after the storm, arrived in Bu-Tata. Miss Pich had been violated by savages, and the others had been eaten.

Political life continued. Two white couples got married. Sipsom held law court and gave judgment in complicated cases. Then the French captured Bu-Tata and burned it. The whites were released at the request of "The Cheese Kid." Bagú was shot.

Three years later an epidemic filled the Bu-Tata Hospital. French doctors declared the outbreak the result of civilization, for one of the doctors had unknowingly taken smallpox to a native village while fighting another epidemic. Civilization had also driven Princess Mahu to dancing nude in a nightclub. As an enterprising journalist stated regarding Bu-Tata, the French army had brought civilization to that backward country.

Critical Evaluation:

The most prominent writer in the Generation of '98, Pío Baroja has been accused of pessimism, even misanthropy, for his scathing portraits of modern society. His satires were rendered with great detail in the dozens of novels he produced during the early decades of the twentieth century. Like other Spanish novelists of his time, Baroja reacted strongly against the social and political complacency he saw around him in Spain and the evils that those attitudes inflicted on the poor in the country, especially those in his native Basque region. It is not surprising, therefore, to learn that *Paradox, King*, the third novel in a trilogy that Baroja titled "The Fantastic Life," has been called by one critic "a catalog of human flaws and life's pitfalls." The hero, a likable optimist who wants only to make life better for himself and his friends, continually stumbles into one depressing situation after another, and his efforts at remedying the ills of the people he encounters are met with only minimal success.

Fast paced and filled with action, *Paradox, King* holds readers' attention by moving quickly from scene to scene, highlighting the bumblings of the title character in his efforts to establish a perfect society in the outer regions of Africa. The presence of talking animals and supernatural events give the work a quality of fantasy similar to that found in travel literature dating as far back as the Middle Ages. Loosely plotted and episodic in nature, the novel shares many qualities with the picaresque tradition, although Baroja's hero, Silvestre Paradox, is no rogue. The central motif of his journey to strange lands provides links with a number of important satires in the European canon, most notably François Rabelais' *Gargantua and Pantagruel* (1532-1564) and Jonathan Swift's *Gulliver's Travels* (1726). There are similarities, too, between the hero and his sidekick Avelino Diz and that more famous traveling duo from Miguel de Cervantes' *Don Quixote de la Mancha* (1605-1615).

The novel is a biting satire on the evils of modern society. Through his assemblage of an international cast of characters thrown together in the isolated African terrain, Baroja creates a microcosm of humanity, closed off from European society and able to start over in creating a political system based on different principles of human interaction. Through his portrait of Paradox and his companions' attempts to deal justly with the natives in Bu-Tata, the novelist offers a view of the decadence brought on by blind reliance on authority, represented chiefly by the political leadership and by the clergy. The kingdom Paradox establishes among the natives is free from such authority and decidedly antiprogressive. The protagonist proclaims himself against art, science, or any authority. "Let us live the free life," he demands, "without restraints, without schools, without laws, without teachers." He commands that any schools established in the land be devoid of faculty, and that any training for the useful trades be voluntary. Naturally, the small successes he enjoys during his brief reign are quickly brought to an end when the French come to "civilize" the land; with them they bring disease and authoritarian rule, two components of "civilization" that Baroja singles out for special condemnation.

Perhaps the most stinging condemnation, however, is reserved for technology, the sign of progress for Baroja's contemporaries in the nineteenth and early twentieth centuries. A useful comparison may serve to highlight the Spanish novelist's aim in this respect. Readers familiar with American literature will see in *Paradox, King* parallels to another novel which highlights the evils of technology: Mark Twain's *A Connecticut Yankee in King Arthur's Court* (1889). Both novels rely on the motif of the journey—in Baroja's, a sojourn to a foreign land; in Twain's, a trip back in time. In both instances, the protagonists find themselves in a primitive civilization, and the possession of advanced technology gives them power. Both Paradox and Twain's Harry Morgan initially use their knowledge for good, establishing Utopian societies in which people benefit from an increased standard of living, and in which communications are improved (both rely on the press as an agent for increasing people's awareness of and participation in social and political activities). Eventually, however, the possibility of consolidating power or overcoming enemies forces them to use the same technology for destructive purposes. While Paradox's decision to isolate his kingdom by dynamiting the river and forming an island may not be motivated by evil intent, the action is nevertheless futile. More telling yet is the hero's decision at the end of the work to return to civilization; even he becomes tired of the idyllic life, opting instead for the civilized cesspool he has tried so hard to escape.

Unquestionably, the harshness of the novel's ending has led many critics to condemn Baroja as a nihilist. As do his other novels, *Paradox, King* offers little hope for the human race; instead, it seems to be only an angry cry against the evils the novelist sees around him. Like his forebears in the satiric tradition, he is able to bear the terrible burden of reality only by masking it in the face of comedy. Seen in this light, *Paradox, King* is a decided achievement in literary art.

"Critical Evaluation" by Laurence W. Mazzeno

Bibliography:
Barrow, Leo L. *Negation in Baroja: A Key to His Novelistic Creativity*. Tucson: University of Arizona Press, 1971. Explores the novelist's technique of "creating by destroying," an approach he shares with other modern writers who rebel against conventional Western values. Discusses the style, dialogue, atmosphere, characterization, and landscape in *Paradox, King* and other novels to explain how Baroja uses fiction to express his philosophical, political, and social attitudes.

Devlin, John. *Spanish Anticlericalism: A Study in Modern Alienation*. New York: Las Americas, 1966. Links Baroja with other pre-Republican writers whose works exhibit strong anticlerical bias. Locates the source of his disdain for religion in the agnosticism that underlies *Paradox, King* and his other novels.

Landeira, Ricardo. *The Modern Spanish Novel 1898-1936*. Boston: Twayne, 1985. A chapter on Baroja surveys the novelist's achievement and discusses *Paradox, King* and the other novels in the trilogy dealing with "The Fantastic Life." Calls the novel the bitterest of the three in attacking social ills.

Patt, Beatrice P. *Pío Baroja*. New York: Twayne, 1971. Excellent introduction to the writer and his works. Briefly discusses Baroja's attitudes toward the church and state. Reviews Baroja's use of extended dialogue in *Paradox, King*; points out how it permits him to introduce personal prejudices into a work he considered "half-fantasy, half-satirical poem."

Reid, John T. *Modern Spain and Liberalism*. Stanford, Calif.: Stanford University Press, 1937. Extensive study of Baroja's novels as documents chronicling the social and political climate in his country. Claims the novelist intends that *Paradox, King* and other works serve as statements of the principles of liberalism that counter the fascist tendencies of his homeland.

PARALLEL LIVES

Type of work: Biography
Author: Plutarch (c. 46-after 120)
First transcribed: Bioi parallēloi, c. 105-115 (English translation, 1579)

Principal personages:
JULIUS CAESAR, Roman general and statesman
ALEXANDER THE GREAT, King of Macedon
MARC ANTONY, Roman statesman
DEMETRIUS, Macedonian king
MARCUS BRUTUS, Roman statesman
DION, statesman of Syracuse
DEMOSTHENES, Greek orator and statesman
CICERO, Roman orator and statesman
ALCIBIADES, Athenian general
CORIOLANUS, Roman leader
SOLON, Athenian lawgiver
POPLICOLA, Roman lawgiver
THESEUS, legendary Athenian hero
ROMULUS, legendary founder of Rome

The collection that is today known simply as Plutarch's *Lives* is derived from the *Parallel Lives,* a work in which Plutarch presented a large number of biographies (of which forty-six survive), alternating the lives of eminent Greeks with comparable lives of eminent Romans. A number of shorter essays compared the lives accorded biographical treatment. The collection as it survives includes some biographies written independently of the *Parallel Lives,* such as the biographies of Otho, Galba, Artaxerxes, and Aratus.

Plutarch considered the lives of famous men important for their moral implications, and his treatment shows his concern to apply the ethics of Aristotle to the judgment of those whose lives he reports. His treatment is more personal than political; like the biographer Suetonius, whose *Lives of the Caesars* (c. 120) lacks the moral emphasis of Plutarch's work, Plutarch was interested in great figures as human beings liable to the errors and inevitable temptations that confront all human beings. Also, like Suetonius, Plutarch delights in anecdote and uses various tales concerning the Greeks and Romans partly for their intrinsic interest and partly to suit his moral intention. Although there are inaccuracies in the *Lives,* the charm and liveliness of Plutarch's style give the biographies a convincing appeal that more than compensates for errors in fact. In any case, all history is the result of an attempt to make an intelligible statement about a past that must be reconstructed from the perspective of its writer. If one says that in the *Lives* readers see the famous Greeks and Romans only as they appeared to Plutarch, then one must say of any history or biography that it is the past only as it appears to its author. The conclusion might be that since biographies are sensible only relative to their authors, the character and the ability of the author are of paramount importance. If the *Lives* are judged in this manner, then again Plutarch emerges as an excellent historian, for his work expresses the active concerns of a sensitive, conscientious, and educated Greek writer.

The comparisons that Plutarch makes between his Greeks and Romans have sometimes been dismissed as of minor historical importance. The error behind such judgment is that of regarding the comparisons as only biographical and historical. Plutarch's comparisons are attempts not only to recover the past, but moreover to judge. In the comparisons a moralist is at work, and whatever the truth of the biographies, readers come close to the truth about the moral climate of Plutarch's day. Another way of putting it is that in his biographical essays Plutarch defines men of the past; but in the comparisons he defines himself and the men of his age.

Thus, in comparing Romulus, the legendary founder of Rome, with Theseus, the Athenian hero of Greek mythology, Plutarch first considers which of the two was the more valiant and the more aggressive for a worthy cause. The decision is given to Theseus, who voluntarily sought out the oppressors of Greece—Sciron, Sinnis, Procrustes, and Corynetes—and who offered himself as part of the tribute to Crete. Plutarch then finds both heroes wanting. "Both Theseus and Romulus were by nature meant for governors," he writes, "yet neither lived up to the true character of a king, but fell off, and ran, the one into popularity, the other into tyranny, falling both into the same fault out of different passions." Plutarch then goes on to criticize both men for unreasonable anger, Theseus against his son, Romulus against his brother. Finally, he severely takes Theseus to task for parricide and for the rapes he committed.

Even from this brief comparison readers learn a great deal about Plutarch. Although he has an inclination to favor the Greeks, he gives the Romans their due, achieving a near balance of virtues and vices. He honored courageous action provided it was motivated by a love of country and of humanity; he approved the ancient morality that called for respect toward parents and faithfulness to friends and brothers.

Plutarch was aware of the difficulty and the dangers of the biographical tasks he undertook, and he gives the impression that the presence of the comparisons is intended both to unify and to justify the book as a whole. At the outset of his biographical survey of the adventures of Theseus he compares those biographies of men closer to his own time with biographies such as that of Theseus, in which he is forced to deal with fictions and fables. He writes, "Let us hope that Fable may, in what shall follow, so submit to the purifying processes of Reason as to take the character of exact history"; but he recognizes the possibility that the purifying process might not occur, and so begs the indulgence of the reader. He then compares Theseus and Romulus briefly, showing parallels of position and fortune in their lives, in order to justify his having decided to place their biographies side by side and to undertake a comparison of their moral characters.

Other comparisons that survive are those of Numa Pompilius, Romulus' successor as king of Rome and originator of Roman religious law, with Lycurgus, the Spartan lawgiver; of Poplicola, or Publius Valerius, the Roman ruler who converted a despotic command to a popular one, thus winning the name "Poplicola" or "lover of the people," with Solon, the Athenian lawgiver; of Fabius, the Roman leader who was five times consul and then dictator, who harassed Hannibal with his delaying tactics, with Pericles, the Athenian soldier and statesman who brought Athens to the height of its power; of Alcibiades, the Athenian general, with Coriolanus, the Roman leader; of Timoleon, the Corinthian, the opponent of Dionysius and other Sicilian tyrants, with Aemilius Paulus, the Roman who warred against the Macedonians; of Pelopidas, the Theban general who recovered Thebes from the Spartans, with Marcellus, the Roman consul who captured Syracuse; of Aristides, the Athenian general who fought at Marathon, Salamis, and Plataea, with Marcus Cato, the Roman statesman who disapproved of Carthage and destroyed the city in the third Punic war; of Philopoemen, the Greek commander of the Achaeans who defeated the Spartan tyrants Machanidas and Nabis, with Flamininus, the Roman general and consul who freed Greece from Philip V of Macedon; of Lysander, the Spartan who defeated the Athenians and planned the government of Athens, with Sylla, the Roman general who defeated Mithridates VI, sacked Athens, and became tyrant of Rome; of Lucullus, who continued Sulla's (or Sylla's) campaign against Mithridates and pursued him into

Armenia, with Cimon, the Greek who defeated the Persians on both land and sea at Pamphylia; of Crassus, one of the First Triumvirate with Pompey and Caesar, with Nicias, the Athenian who was captured by the Syracuse forces which repelled the Athenians; of Sertorius, a Roman general who fought in rebellion against Pompey in Spain, with Eumenes, the Greek general and statesman who was opposed by Antigones; of Pompey, the Roman general who became Caesar's enemy after the formation of the First Triumvirate, with Agesilaus, the Spartan king who fought the Persians and the Thebans without preventing the downfall of Sparta; of Tiberius and Caius Gracchus, the Roman statesmen and brothers who fought and died for social reform in the effort to assist the poor landowners, with Agis and Cleomenes, the Spartan reformer kings; of Demosthenes, the Greek orator and statesman, with Cicero, the Roman orator and statesman; of Demetrius, the Macedonian who became king after numerous campaigns and after murdering Cassander's sons, with Antony, Caesar's defender and the lover of Cleopatra; and of Dion of Syracuse, who attempted to introduce Dionysius and his son to Plato, with Brutus, the slayer of Caesar.

The most important of the biographies are those of Alexander the Great and Julius Caesar. Acknowledging the difficulty of his task, Plutarch declares his intention to write "the most celebrated parts," and he adds that "It must be borne in mind that my design is not to write histories, but lives. The most glorious exploits do not always furnish us with the clearest discoveries of virtue or vice in men; sometimes a matter of less moment, an expression or a jest, informs us better of their characters and inclinations."

Plutarch wrote at the beginning of his biography of Timoleon that he had come to take a personal interest in his biographies, and he explained that "the virtues of these great men" had come to serve him "as a sort of looking-glass, in which I may see how to adjust and adorn my own life." Over the centuries readers have responded with respect to Plutarch's moral seriousness, thus testifying to his power both as biographer and commentator.

Bibliography:
Barrow, R. H. *Plutarch and His Times.* Bloomington: Indiana University Press, 1967. A comprehensive introduction for the beginner to Plutarch's life, times, and works. Contains two chapters on the *Lives,* in which they are examined primarily in terms of their purpose, digressions, and historical sources.
Gossage, A. J. "Plutarch." In *Latin Biography,* edited by T. A. Dorey. New York: Basic Books, 1967. An excellent concise introduction to the *Lives.* Includes discussion of their influence on English writers of the sixteenth through the nineteenth centuries. Valuable endnotes list passages that illustrate Plutarch's biographical methods.
Plutarch. *Shakespeare's Plutarch.* Edited by T. J. B. Spencer. New York: Penguin Books, 1964. An edition, with introduction, of Thomas North's 1579 translation of the four *Lives* from which the Elizabethan playwright William Shakespeare drew the plots of his Roman tragedies. Abundant quotation of parallel passages from the plays. Invaluable for an understanding of Shakespeare's literary debt to Plutarch.
Russell, D. A. *Plutarch.* New York: Charles Scribner's Sons, 1973. An introduction to Plutarch's thought and writings from a literary perspective; for the general reader. In the three chapters devoted to the *Lives,* that of Alcibiades receives the greatest emphasis.
Wardman, Alan. *Plutarch's Lives.* Berkeley: University of California Press, 1974. A sophisticated study that ranges broadly throughout the fifty extant *Lives.* Analyzes their form and nature, Plutarch's concept of the ideal political leader, his means of depicting character, and the influence of philosophy and rhetoric on his biographical methods.

PARLEMENT OF FOULES

Type of work: Poetry
Author: Geoffrey Chaucer (c. 1343-1400)
Type of plot: Allegory
Time of plot: Fourteenth century
Locale: A dream world
First published: c. 1380

> *Principal characters:*
> CHAUCER, the dreamer and narrator
> SCIPIO AFRICANUS, his guide
> DAME NATURE
> THE FORMEL EAGLE
> THREE TERCEL EAGLES, the highest-ranking birds

The Story:

Parlement of Foules opened with comments on the hardships of love, which, the poet and narrator assured his reader, he knew only through his books; and books, he said, were the source of all people's new discoveries. The narrator, Chaucer, had read Cicero's *Somnium Scipionis*, one of the most popular stories during the Middle Ages. Chaucer told the reader how, in this story, Scipio Africanus appeared to the younger Scipio in a dream and showed him all the universe, pointing out how small the earth was in comparison with the rest. He advised the younger man to live virtuously and with knowledge that he was immortal, so that he might come swiftly to heaven after death.

Darkness forced the narrator to put his book aside; and, falling asleep, he dreamed that the same Scipio Africanus came to him and led him to the gate of a beautiful garden. Over one half of the gate was a message promising happiness to those who entered; above the other half was a warning of pain and sorrow. As the dreamer deliberated, his guide pushed him through the gates, explaining that neither motto applied to him since he was not a lover but adding that he might discover there something about which to write.

The two men found themselves in a garden filled with every kind of tree and bird. Deer, squirrels, and other small beasts were playing there. Music and fragrant breezes permeated the atmosphere. Around the garden were familiar personifications: Cupid, tempering his arrows, Pleasure, Beauty, Youth, Jollity, Flattery, and many others. Nearby stood a temple of brass upon pillars of jasper. Women were dancing around it, and doves sat on the roof. Before the doors sat Dame Peace and Dame Patience "on a hill of sand."

When he entered the temple, the dreamer saw the goddess Jealousy, the cause of the great sighing he heard around him, Venus and the youth Richess, Bacchus, god of wine, and Ceres, who relieved hunger. Along the walls were painted the stories of many unhappy lovers.

Returning to the garden, the dreamer noticed Dame Nature, so fair that she surpassed all others as much as the sunlight does the stars. Around her were all the birds, ready to choose their mates, for it was St. Valentine's Day. Dame Nature decreed that the tercel eagle, the bird of highest rank, should have the first choice.

He asked for the lovely formel eagle who sat on Dame Nature's own hand, but immediately two other high-ranking fowls interrupted; they, too, loved the formel eagle. A lengthy debate followed. One had loved her longest; another said that he had loved as deeply, if not for so long.

(This kind of discussion was popular in court circles in Chaucer's day.) The other birds, thought by scholars to represent different levels of English society, the clergy, peasants, and the bourgeoisie, soon wearied of the debate, since they wanted to pick their own mates. They decided that each group should elect a spokesperson to give its opinion of the "cursed pleading."

The birds of prey chose the tercelet falcon, who suggested that the formel wed the worthiest knight, the bird of gentlest blood. The goose, speaking for the water fowls, said simply, "If she won't love him, let him love another." The gentle turtledove dissented, and the seed fowls held that a lover should serve his lady until he dies, whether or not she loves him in return.

The duck offered a saucy retort: "There are more stars, God wot, than a pair." The tercel chided him for having no idea of love. Then the cuckoo gave the verdict of the worm fowls: Give us our mates in peace, and let the eagles argue as long as they wish. Let them be single all their lives if they can reach no decision. One of the noble birds insulted the cuckoo, calling him a murderer because of his usual diet, and Dame Nature had to intervene to keep peace.

Since none of the birds' opinions had provided a solution, Dame Nature ordered the formel eagle to choose the one she loved best. Although she advised the formel to wed the royal tercel, since he seemed noblest, she said that the bird herself must make a choice. The formel pleaded that she was still too young to marry; she wanted to wait a year to decide. Dame Nature agreed, and at last all the birds were permitted to choose their own mates. Before they departed, they sang a charming roundel. The noise the birds made as they flew away awakened the poet, who immediately picked up other books, hoping that some day he would read something that would give him a dream to make him fare better.

Critical Evaluation:

The occasion of *Parlement of Foules* was the marriage of King Richard II of England to Anne of Bohemia. Since the convocation of the birds in the story takes place in the spring, it is possible that in selecting Valentine's Day—the day on which lovers traditionally choose mates—Geoffrey Chaucer was referring not to the customary date of February 14 but to May 3, the date of Richard and Anne's betrothal. This was also the feast day of Saint Valentine of Genoa. Although this saint was generally known only in the vicinity of his hometown, Chaucer had visited Genoa and may have heard his name. While the poem primarily celebrates the royal nuptials, it seems to serve a secondary function. Through the contention of the birds, Chaucer very subtly and gently questions the wisdom of certain practices and ideologies among the nobility.

In 1376, Chaucer, an emissary for the royal family, traveled to France to negotiate a marriage contract between King Richard (then ten years of age) and Marie, the five-year-old daughter of King Charles V of France. By means of this alliance, England hoped to end the Hundred Years' War that had raged between the two countries. Unfortunately, Marie died suddenly in 1377; nevertheless, England resumed negotiations the following year, proposing that Charles's younger daughter, Isabel, be the bride. When Isabel also died, a proposal was made for the hand of Catherine, Charles's one remaining daughter, who was then an infant. These negotiations were interrupted by political events, but, in 1380, Richard married Anne, the sister of Wenceslas, king of Bohemia. This alliance had been proposed and partly executed by the Vatican. At the time of the wedding, Richard was fourteen, and his wife was about thirteen years of age. Although the young monarchs reputedly enjoyed a compatible marriage, it is doubtful that either of them had much, if any, power to make decisions regarding their union. Thus, when Chaucer has Nature decree that the eagle's must "agre to his elecciou, whoso he be that shulde be hire feere," he may be implying that, even in noble families, individuals should be allowed some measure of control regarding marriage partners. Later, the formel herself asks Nature for a year's respite in which to make her decision, even though she is under the goddess' "yerde," just as noble children are under the control of their parents, the state, and, in some cases, the Church.

Throughout the poem, Chaucer questions not only the establishment of marriage contracts between nonconsenting children but also the principles of courtly love, a mystique of the noble class. In this context, it is important to note the symbolism of his personified birds. Chaucer draws on a long literary tradition of using animals to portray human attributes. His use of birds, in particular, stems from the influence of several French poets who associated them with various types of passion. The eagles, associated in nearly all ancient cultures with divinity, majesty, and power, obviously represent gentlemen of the nobility. High soaring birds, these suitors hold lofty ideals of pairing and love.

The falcon, or hawk, the spokesperson for the "noble" birds, was the breed most closely associated with the aristocracy, being both a pet and a medium of sport. Noblemen and noblewomen often carried falcons and engaged in frequent hawking expeditions. Moreover, elaborate rituals defined the steps in teaching a falcon to attack its prey. Since these birds were so closely bound to their noble masters, it is fitting that Chaucer's falcon should voice the sentiments of the aristocracy concerning the choice of a mate.

> Me wolde thynk how that the worthieste
> Of knyghthod, and lengest had used it,
>
> Most of estat, of blod the gentileste,
> Were sittyngest for hire, if that hir leste.

Some of the "lower-class" birds, however, offer opinions that counter and challenge the romantic ideals of the nobles. When the turtledove, associated with lifelong fidelity even after the death of a mate, says on behalf of the seed fowl, or country gentry, that a gentleman should love his lady until his own demise, the duck retorts that this mandate is ridiculous. In this scenario, the duck may be seen in two lights. It is possible that Chaucer was drawing on the bird's usual medieval association with persons of low social standing. In this light, the tercel's reference to the duck as "cherl" is appropriate. Among the ancient Chinese, however, the mandarin duck was said to couple for life; the strength of its fidelity to a deceased mate supposedly surpassed even that of the medieval turtledove. If Chaucer was familiar with the alleged character of the mandarin, his duck may represent a member of the nobility who questions the social strictures of his own group.

The goose speaks on behalf of the waterfowl. According to some critics, these birds represent the merchant class; according to others, they represent the lowest segment of society. In either case, the goose is not an aristocrat. She therefore is bold enough to counter the courtly principle that women should hold their suitors in disdain in order that they might be "won over," by stating that a lover should not choose a partner who does not love him in return. Rather than considering this a piece of practical wisdom, the sparrowhawk (a bird of the nobility) dismisses it as "a parfit resoun of a goose."

Through the "lower" birds' mundane views of love and the "noble" birds' rude rejoinders, Chaucer may have been warning his young monarch of a growing spirit of rebellion among the common people. Unfortunately, King Richard did not perceive the meaning of the avian allegory until it was too late. On June 12, an army of peasants and artisans invaded London, protesting their poverty, their high taxes, and their lack of economic autonomy—situations that had been ignored or dismissed by the nobility. Richard was able to quell the crowd's agitation with false promises, but the aura of their unrest remained.

On the surface, *Parlement of Foules* is a poem of lighthearted banter, written to celebrate a wedding. A close reading, however, reveals that it is also a work of social criticism and prophecy.

"Critical Evaluation" by Rebecca Stingley Hinton

Bibliography:

Bennett, J. A. W. *"The Parlement of Fouls": An Interpretation.* Oxford, England: Clarendon Press, 1957. Compares Chaucer's style to that of various poets in both antiquity and his own time. Contains several plates of illustrations, including a medieval representation of birds.

Braddy, Haldeen. *Chaucer's "Parlement of Foules," in Its Relation to Contemporary Events.* New York: Octagon Books, 1969. Discusses the poem as a retrospective account of Chaucer's attempts to negotiate a marriage contract between the king of England and a princess of France. Although more recent scholars maintain that it celebrates Richard II's marriage to Anne of Bohemia in 1380, Braddy nevertheless offers a thorough piece of research on the international nuptial negotiations, which began in 1376. He also provides chapters discussing Chaucer's view of various social classes and his use of personified birds.

Howard, Donald R. *Chaucer: His Life, His Works, His World.* New York: Dutton, 1987. Discusses in detail several of Chaucer's major poems, including *Parlement of Foules.* It also offers a glimpse into the milieu of fourteenth century England, with chapters on such topics as the Black Death, the Peasants' Revolt, and life in a royal court.

Rowland, Beryl. *Birds with Human Souls.* Knoxville: University of Tennessee Press, 1978. Contains detailed analyses of sixty birds, discussing their symbolic significance throughout the ages. Includes many black-and-white illustrations from medieval manuscripts, mostly of birds in their symbolic forms.

_____. *Blind Beasts: Chaucer's Animal World.* Kent, Ohio: Kent State University Press, 1971. Discusses Chaucer's use of personified animals, including birds. Also contains chapters on the medieval and ancient symbolic significance of the boar, hare, wolf, horse, sheep, and dog.

PARZIVAL

Type of work: Poetry
Author: Wolfram von Eschenbach (c. 1170-c. 1217)
Type of plot: Arthurian romance
Time of plot: Age of chivalry
Locale: Western Europe
First published: c. 1200-1210 (English translation, 1894)

Principal characters:

GAMURET, prince of Anjou
PARZIVAL, Gamuret's son
GAWAIN, knight of King Arthur's court
KING ARTHUR
FEIREFIS, Parzival's half brother
LOHENGRIN, Parzival's son

The Story:

Gamuret, younger son of King Gandein of Anjou, refused to live as a vassal in the kingdom of his older brother, notwithstanding the brother's love for Gamuret. The young man, given gifts of gold by his king brother, as well as horses and equipment and men-at-arms, left Anjou to seek his fortune. Hoping to find for himself fame and love, Gamuret went first to battle for Baruch at Alexandria; from there he went to the aid of the Moorish Queen Belakane. Belakane had been falsely accused of causing the death of her lover, Eisenhart, and was besieged in her castle by two armies under the command of Friedebrand, king of Scotland and Eisenhart's uncle.

Gamuret, after raising the siege, became the husband of Belakane, who bore him a son named Feirefis. Gamuret tired of being king of Assagog and Zassamank, and so he journeyed abroad again in search of fame. Passing into Spain, Gamuret sought King Kailet and found him near Kanvoleis. The two entered a tournament sponsored by the queen of Waleis. Gamuret did valiant deeds and carried off all the honors of that tournament, thereby winning a great deal of fame as the victor. Two queens who had watched the lists during the tournament fell in love with Gamuret, but Queen Herzeleide won his heart and married him. They loved each other greatly, but once again the call of honor was too great to let Gamuret remain a housed husband. Receiving a summons from Baruch, he went once more to Alexandria. In the fighting there he was treacherously killed and given a great tomb by Baruch. When news of his death reached the land of Waleis, Queen Herzeleide sorrowed greatly, but her sorrow was in part dissipated by the birth of a child by Gamuret. Herzeleide named the boy Parzival.

Parzival was reared by his mother with all tenderness and love. As he grew older he met knights who fared through the world seeking honor. Parzival, stimulated by tales of their deeds, left his homeland in search of King Arthur of Britain. He hoped to become one of Arthur's knights and a member of the order of the Round Table. During his absence his mother, Queen Herzeleide, died. On his way to Arthur's court Parzival took a token from Jeschute and thus aroused the jealous anger of her husband, Orilus. Further along on his journey he met a woman named Sigune and from her learned of his lineage and his kinship with the house of Anjou. Still later Parzival met the Red Knight and carried that knight's challenge with him to King Arthur.

Having been knighted by the king, Parzival set forth again in quest of knightly honor. Finding himself in the land of Graharz, he sought out Gurnemanz, prince of the land, who taught the young knight the courtesy and the ethics of knighthood.

From Graharz, Parzival journeyed to Pelrapar, which he found besieged by enemies. He raised the siege by overthrowing Kingron. After this adventure Parzival fell in love with Queen Kondwiramur, and the two were married. Parzival, like his father before him, soon tired of the quiet life and parted from his home and queen to seek further adventures.

Parzival journeyed to the land of the Fisher King and became the king's guest. In that land he first beheld the fabulous bleeding spear and all the marvels of the Holy Grail. One morning he awoke to find the castle deserted. Parzival, mocked by a squire, rode away. Later he met Orilus, who had vowed to battle the young knight for taking Jeschute's token. They fought and Parzival was the victor, but he was able to reconcile Orilus to Jeschute once again and sent the couple to find a welcome at the court of King Arthur.

Arthur, meanwhile, had gone in search of the Red Knight, whose challenge Parzival had carried. Journeying in search of King Arthur, Parzival had the misfortune to fall into a love-trance, during which he overthrew Gagramor and took vengeance on Sir Kay. He met Gawain, who took him back again to Arthur's court. There Parzival was inducted into the company of the Round Table. At Arthur's court both Gawain and Parzival were put to shame by two other knights. When in his anger and despair Parzival set out to seek the Holy Grail and Gawain rode off to Askalon, the whole company of the Round Table was dispersed.

While Parzival sought the Grail, Gawain had many adventures. He joined the knights of King Meljanz of Lys, who sought vengeance on Duke Lippaut. When the fighting was over, Gawain rode to Schamfanzon, where he was committed by the king to the care of his daughter Antikonie. Gawain wooed the maiden and thus aroused the wrath of the people of Schamfan-zon. Gawain was aided, however, by the woman and by Kingrimursel. After Gawain swore to the king that he would ask Scherules to send back some kinsmen to him, Gawain left, also to search for the Holy Grail.

Parzival, meanwhile, had traveled for many days in doubt and despair. In the forest of Monsalvasch he fought with a knight of the Holy Grail and passed on. Then, on Good Friday, he met a pilgrim knight who told him he should not bear arms during the holy season. The knight bade him seek out Trevrezent, a hermit who showed Parzival how he had sinned in being wrathful with God and indicated to Parzival that he was a nephew to Amfortas, one of the Grail kings. The two parted in sorrow and Parzival resumed his search for the Grail.

Gawain, continuing his adventures, had married Orgeluse. When Gawain decided to battle Gramoflanz, King Arthur and Queen Guinevere agreed to ride to see the joust. Before the joust could take place Gawain and Parzival met and did battle, each unknown to his opponent. Gawain was defeated and severely injured by Parzival, who was filled with grief when he learned with whom he had fought. Parzival vowed to take Gawain's place in the combat with Gramoflanz, but the latter refused to do battle with anyone but Gawain himself.

Parzival, released from his vow, longed to return once again to his wife. One morning before dawn he secretly left the camp of King Arthur. On his way back to his wife Parzival met a great pagan warrior who almost vanquished him. After the battle he learned the pagan knight was Feirefis, Parzival's half brother, the son of Gamuret and Belakane. The two rode back to King Arthur's court, where both were made welcome by the king. In company the half brothers went into the lists and won many honors together. At a feast of the Round Table Kondrie entered the great hall to announce Parzival's election to the Grail kingdom. Summoned to Monsalvasch, Parzival, his wife, and Lohengrin, Parzival's son, were guided there by Kondrie. Feirefis, although he failed to see the Grail, was baptized and married to Repanse de Schoie. With her he returned to his kingdom, which was held later by his son, Prester John.

"The Story" by Walter E. Meyers

Critical Evaluation:

Parzival is the masterpiece of Germany's greatest medieval poet. It is, moreover, the groundwork of the great body of Richard Wagner's operas on knightly themes. Despite its place in German literature and its influence on modern opera, *Parzival* is little known to English-reading people. Wolfram von Eschenbach's influence on the legends of the Arthurian cycle is also important. The Arthurian legends had a relatively low moral tone prior to their treatment by this poet who, upholding the knightly virtues of fidelity to the plighted word, of charity, and of a true reverence toward God, lifted the moral tone of the Arthurian romances. Most interesting is the identity of the Grail in *Parzival*. Here it is not the chalice used at the Last Supper, as it is in other versions, but a precious stone of supernatural powers.

Written at the beginning of the thirteenth century, *Parzival* is the most famous German tribute to the Arthurian legends, a celebration of the high nobility of knighthood. This masterpiece is a panoramic vision of chivalric deeds, loosely centered on its hero, Sir Parzival, and the quest for the Holy Grail. It is a tale of magnificence and splendor, where the spectacle of one astonishing battle is soon eclipsed by another. There is little of the farce or sly comedy of the French or Celtic traditions. In sixteen books of verses, Wolfram introduces close to two hundred characters, with the birth of Parzival not coming until the very close of book 2. The first two books concern themselves with the exploits of Parzival's father, the gallant Gamuret, and many of the succeeding ones relate the adventures of Sir Gawain, one of King Arthur's nephews.

In many respects *Parzival* is best seen against the tradition it represents and with which it is at odds. Its primary source is Chrétien de Troyes's *Perceval: Ou, Le Conte du Graal* (c. 1180), but Wolfram also mentions a "master Kyot" whose identity remains problematic to scholars. Wolfram's version is probably most familiar to contemporary audiences through Richard Wagner's opera *Parsifal* (1882). The quest for the Holy Grail is one of the most ambitious adventures of the Arthurian court; American readers are probably most familiar with the tradition as it is recounted in T. H. White's popular novel, *The Once and Future King* (1939-1958). White's novel is based, in turn, on Sir Thomas Malory's *Le Morte d'Arthur* (1485). *Parzival* departs from Arthurian tradition in several significant respects, the most important being a general secularization of the legend. In Christian tradition, the Holy Grail is the vessel from which Christ drank during the Last Supper. In *Parzival*, it is something on the order of a magic rock, which furnishes each baptized beholder with whatever he desires in the way of food or drink. Another important deviation from Malory's account is that Percival is permitted to see the Grail only because he is sexually pure, whereas Wolfram's Parzival is not only happily married to Kondwiramur but is the father of the twins Kardeiz and Lohengrin.

What matters most in Wolfram's story is knightly honor, by which is understood one's repute in battle and the riches one displays. These riches include fine silken clothing, beautiful, gem-studded armor, lands, kingdoms, and women. In Wolfram's world women offered themselves as prizes, in order to secure, not diminish, their honor. A woman's prestige was measured by the renown of her knight and protector, and her beauty was the means she had of enticing the ablest to her side. There was no taint of impropriety in such offerings; Herzeleide, Parzival's mother, and Orgeluse, Gawain's lady, offer themselves in this way.

Wealth was the visible proof of honor, since a knight's riches would frequently consist of things he had won by conquering other knights. Wolfram describes repeatedly the fabulous wealth (and corresponding generosity) of Feirefis, Parzival's half brother by a pagan queen. Since Parzival, the hero, must be the most honorable knight in this tale, it falls to his nearest kin to be the wealthiest. Since wealth is so nearly equivalent, however, with honor, Feirefis, although a pagan, is allowed to accompany Parzival to Monsalvasch, the Grail Castle, as his only companion.

While Feirefis can neither win the woman of his heart—Repanse de Schoie, the only one permitted to carry the Grail—nor even have the sight to see the Grail until he is baptized, this is not perceived as a serious obstacle. The baptismal ceremony is quickly performed, Feirefis showing no reluctance to renounce his religion in order to win Repanse de Schoie. Although it would be a mistake to read *Parzival* as a strictly secular tale, the energy that infuses it is not religious. The Christian core is respected, but Wolfram is much more interested in the noble tradition of knighthood.

This kind of secularization makes for some disjunctions in the narrative. For example, when Parzival fails at first to ask the suffering Grail King, Anfortas, the question that would have healed him of his long-festering wound, he does so out of politeness. He was taught not to ask nosy questions. This leads, however, to his failure and shame, a burden that he carries for years. By one set of standards his behavior was impeccable, but, unbeknown to him, in this instance the rules changed on him. His return to grace and power is equally arbitrary, as he is given a second chance to return to Munsalvaesche to ask the question.

The religious element to this part of the story is at odds with the story's generally secular orientation. It is not because Parzival has expiated himself in any meaningful way that he is chosen to heal and later succeed Anfortas, but because he has been faithful to knightly conduct.

Unlike other Arthurian tales, in which knightly encounters are depicted frequently as contests between good and evil, *Parzival* reveals a world in which greatness tests greatness. There are none of the traditional villains of medieval romance: no evil knights, no ogres, no lecherous abductors. Everyone, to some degree, is noble, and all the battles seem to be fought to establish a hierarchy of nobility. In this context, the battles between Parzival and Gawain, and later Parzival and Feirefis (in which each knight is ignorant of the identity of his adversary), become emblematic of Wolfram's chivalric vision. Nobility strives with nobility, until it is finally reconciled in harmony. *Parzival* is a salute to that knightly ideal.

"Critical Evaluation" by Linda J. Turzynski

Bibliography:

Blamires, David. *Characterization and Individuality in Wolfram's "Parzival."* Cambridge, England: Cambridge University Press, 1966. Devotes a chapter to each of the nine major characters in his exploration of the technique of individualization in Wolfram's romance, demonstrating that *Parzival* fits within the trend toward individuality in twelfth century literature.

Green, Dennis Howard. *The Art of Recognition in Wolfram's "Parzival."* Cambridge, England: Cambridge University Press, 1982. Posits that much of the difficulty in reading *Parzival* lies in Wolfram's style of revealing while concealing. The audience is invited to cooperate in the process of recognition: "Penetrating the mysteries of the Grail thus becomes for the listeners what the attainment of Grail kingship is for Parzival."

Loomis, R. S. "Wolfram von Eschenbach's *Parzival*." In *The Development of Arthurian Ro-*

mance. New York: W. W. Norton, 1970. Introduction to the themes and origins of *Parzival*. Places the romance within the context of the growth of Arthurian literature from its beginnings to Malory.

Poag, James F. *Wolfram von Eschenbach*. Boston: Twayne, 1972. Chapters on Wolfram's life, his literary outlook, his other works, and *Parzival*. Bibliography.

Weigand, Hermann John. *Wolfram's "Parzival": Five Essays with an Introduction*. Edited by Ursula Hoffmann. Ithaca, N.Y.: Cornell University Press, 1969. Examines such topics as Wolfram's originality versus his dependence on sources and the nature of Parzival's misadventures during his first visit to the Grail Castle.

A PASSAGE TO INDIA

Type of work: Novel
Author: E. M. Forster (1879-1970)
Type of plot: Social realism
Time of plot: c. 1920
Locale: India
First published: 1924

Principal characters:
>DR. AZIZ, a young Indian surgeon
>MRS. MOORE, a visiting Englishwoman and Dr. Aziz's friend
>RONALD HEASLOP, the city magistrate and Mrs. Moore's son
>ADELA QUESTED, Ronald's fiancée, visiting India with Mrs. Moore
>CECIL FIELDING, principal of the Government College and Dr. Aziz's
>friend

The Story:

Dr. Aziz had been doubly snubbed that evening. He had been summoned to the civil surgeon's house while he was at supper, but when he arrived, he found that his superior had departed for his club without bothering to leave any message. In addition, two Englishwomen emerged from the house and took their departure in his hired tonga without even thanking him.

The doctor started back toward the city of Chandrapore afoot. Tired, he stopped at a mosque to rest and was furiously angry when he saw an Englishwoman emerge from behind its pillars with, as he thought, her shoes on. Mrs. Moore, however, had gone barefoot to the mosque, and in a surge of friendly feelings, Dr. Aziz engaged her in conversation.

Mrs. Moore had recently arrived from England to visit her son, Ronald Heaslop, the city magistrate. Dr. Aziz found they had common ground when he learned that she did not care for the civil surgeon's wife. Her disclosure prompted him to tell of the usurpation of his carriage. The doctor walked back to the club with her, although as an Indian, he himself could not be admitted.

At the club, Adela Quested, Heaslop's prospective fiancée, declared she wanted to see the real India, not the India seen through the rarified atmosphere of the British colony. To please the ladies, one of the members offered to hold what he whimsically termed a bridge party and invite some native guests. The bridge party was a miserable affair. The Indians retreated to one side of the lawn, and although the conspicuously reluctant group of Anglo-Indian ladies went over to visit the natives, an awkward tension prevailed.

There was, however, one promising result of the party. The principal of the Government College, Mr. Fielding, a man who apparently felt neither rancor nor arrogance toward the Indians, invited Mrs. Moore and Adela to a tea at his house. Upon Adela's request, Mr. Fielding also invited Professor Godbole, a teacher at his school, and Dr. Aziz. At the tea, Dr. Aziz charmed Fielding and the guests with the elegance and fine intensity of his manner. The gathering, however, broke up on a discordant note when the priggish and suspicious Heaslop arrived to claim the ladies. Fielding had taken Mrs. Moore on a tour of his school, and Heaslop was furious at him for having left Dr. Aziz alone with his prospective fiancée.

Adela was irritated by Heaslop's callous priggishness during her visit and informed him that she did not wish to become his wife. Later that evening, during a drive into the countryside, a mysterious figure, perhaps an animal, loomed out of the darkness and nearly upset the car in which they were riding. Their mutual loneliness and a sense of the unknown drew them together, and Adela asked Heaslop to disregard her earlier rejection.

One extraordinary aspect of the city of Chandrapore was a natural formation known as the Marabar Caves, located several miles outside the city. Mrs. Moore and Adela accepted Dr. Aziz's offer to escort them to the caves. The visit proved catastrophic for all. Entering one of the caves, Mrs. Moore realized that no matter what was said, the walls returned only a prolonged booming, hollow echo. Pondering that echo while she rested, and pondering the distance that separated her from Dr. Aziz, from Adela, and from her own children, Mrs. Moore saw that all her Christianity, all her ideas of moral good and bad, in short, all her ideas of life, amounted only to what was made of them by the hollow, booming echo of the Marabar Caves. Adela entered one of the caves alone. A few minutes later she rushed out in a terrified state and claimed she had been nearly attacked in the gloom. She also claimed that Dr. Aziz was the attacker, and the doctor was arrested.

There always had been a clear division between the natives and the Anglo-Indian community, but as the trial of Dr. Aziz drew nearer, the division sharpened and each group demanded strict loyalty from its members. When Mrs. Moore casually intimated to her son that she was perfectly certain Dr. Aziz was not capable of the alleged crime, he immediately shipped her off to a coastal port of embarkation. After Fielding expressed the same opinion at the club, he was ostracized.

At the trial opening, a sensational incident occurred when one of Dr. Aziz's friends pushed into the courtroom and shouted that Heaslop had smuggled his mother out of the country because she would have testified to the doctor's innocence. Hearing the name of Mrs. Moore, the restless body of Indian spectators worked it into a kind of chant as though she had become a deity. The English colony was not to learn until later that Mrs. Moore had already died aboard ship.

Adela's testimony concluded the trial. The tense atmosphere of the courtroom, the reiteration of Mrs. Moore's name, and the buzzing sound in her ears that had persisted since the time she left the caves combined to produce a trancelike effect upon Adela. She relived the whole of the crucial day as she recollected its events under the interrogation of the prosecuting attorney. When she reached the moment of her lingering in the cave, she faltered, changed her mind, and withdrew all charges.

For several hours afterward, Chandrapore experienced a great bedlam. The Anglo-Indians sulked while Indians exulted. As far as the British were concerned, Adela had crossed the line. Heaslop carefully explained to her that he could no longer be associated with her. After accepting Fielding's hospitality for a few weeks, she returned home. Dr. Aziz's anglophobia had increased, but Fielding persuaded him not to press for legal damages from Adela.

Two years later, the Muhammadan Dr. Aziz was court physician to an aged Hindu potentate who died on the night of the Krishna Festival. The feast was a frantic celebration, and the whole town was under its spell when Fielding arrived on an official visit. In the intervening time he had married again, and Dr. Aziz, assuming he had married Adela Quested, tried to avoid his old friend. When he ran into him accidentally, however, he found that it was Mrs. Moore's daughter, Stella, whom Fielding had married. The doctor's shame at his mistake only caused him to become more distant.

Before they parted for the last time, Dr. Aziz and Fielding went riding through the jungles. The misunderstanding between them had been resolved, but they had no social ground on which to meet. Fielding had cast his lot with his countrymen by marrying an Englishwoman. The rocks that suddenly reared up before them, forcing their horses to pass in single file on either side, were symbolic of the different paths they would travel from then on. The affection of two men, however sincere, was not sufficient to bridge the vast gap between their races.

Critical Evaluation:

E. M. Forster was a member of the intellectual Bloomsbury group, which flourished in London just before and after World War I. Educated at Cambridge, as were many of the group, Forster became one of England's leading novelists during the prewar Edwardian period. His Bloomsbury friends included Lytton Strachey, the biographer; Virginia Woolf, the novelist; Clive Bell, the art critic; Roger Fry, a painter; John Maynard Keynes, the economist; and G. E. Moore, the philosopher. The group rejected convention and authority and placed great faith in its own intellect and good taste.

Forster wrote several acclaimed novels between 1905 and 1910: *Where Angels Fear to Tread* (1905), *The Longest Journey* (1907), *A Room with a View* (1908), and *Howards End* (1910). Then after a hiatus of fourteen years came *A Passage to India* in 1924, the last work he published during his lifetime. (The early novel *Maurice* was published posthumously in 1970.) He once confessed that he did not understand the post-World War I values and had nothing more to say. *A Passage to India*, however, belies this statement, for it is a novel for all times.

Forster took his title from the Walt Whitman poem by the same name, an odd choice, since Whitman's vision is of the total unity of all people while in the novel the attempt to unite people fails at all levels. The book is divided into three sections: Mosque, Cave, Temple. These divisions correspond to the three divisions of the Indian year: cool spring, hot summer, and wet monsoon. Each section is dominated by its concomitant weather. Each section also focuses on one of the three ethnic groups involved: Muslim, Anglo-Indian, Hindu. The Cave could also have been called "The Club." Just as the Mosque and the Temple are the Muslim and Hindu shrines, so is the Club the true Anglo-Indian shrine. Forster realizes that religious-ethnic divisions control social modes of activity. The Muslims are emotional; the British rely on intellect. Only the Hindus, in the person of Godbole, have the capacity to love.

Yet the novel is much more than merely a social or political commentary. Forster belittles social forms on all sides of the conflict and favors neither the Indians nor the British. The bridge party, Fielding's tea party, and Aziz's cave party are all failures. More important than social forms are the relationships among individuals. The novel's theme is the search for love and friendship. Forster presents primarily male-male relationships with the capacity for mutual understanding, and his male characters are the most clearly defined. The females— Mrs. Moore and Adela Quested—have no real possibility of finding friendship across ethnic lines. Mrs. Moore is too old, Adela too British. Both women want to see the "real" India, but they are unprepared for it when the experience comes. Mrs. Moore at the mosque and the first cave, and Adela at the cave and the courtroom, discover the real India, and both suffer an almost catatonic withdrawal.

The male characters are more complex. With his Muslim sensitivity, Aziz is determined to find humiliation no matter what the experience. He tries to be both physician and poet—healer of body and soul—but he is inept in both attempts. In the last section, readers see him abandoning both. Aziz needs love and friendship, but ultimately he is incapable of establishing a satisfying relationship among his own people, with the Hindus, or, more important, with Fielding. Muslim sensitivity prevents him from accepting friendship when it is offered.

Out of the multiple failures of the first two sections of the novel there is only the relationship between Aziz and Fielding that holds any promise of reconciliation. Muslim and Anglo-Indian, they meet in the final section in the Hindu province. Both men desire friendship and understanding, but in the final scene the very land seems to separate them. They are not in tune with nature, which is renewing itself in the monsoon downpour, and neither man has come to accept the irrational. They are not ready, in the Hindu sense of love, to accept things as they are. Only Godbole, a Hindu, can fully accept India and her people. The nothingness of the caves and the apparent chaos of the people do not disturb the Hindu.

The most crucial scene in *A Passage to India* is the visit to the Marabar Caves. These caves puzzle and terrify both Muslims and Anglo-Indians and form the center of the novel. Only Godbole instinctively understands them. The Hindus possessed India before either the Muslims or British came. The caves are elemental; they have been there from the beginnings of the earth. They are not Hindu holy places, but Godbole can respect them without fear. Cave worship is the cult of the female principle, the Sacred Womb, Mother Earth. The Marabar Caves, both womb and grave, demand total effacing of ego. The individual loses identity; whatever is said returns as Ommm, the holy word.

The caves are terrifying and chaotic to those who rely on the intellect. The trip itself emphasizes the chaos that is India. Godbole can eat no meat; Aziz can eat no pork; the British must have their whisky and port. The confusion of the departure epitomizes the confusion that pervades the novel. Significantly, it is Godbole, the one man who might have helped, who is left out. Once in the caves, the party encounters the Nothingness that terrifies. Only Mrs. Moore seems to accept it on a limited scale, but the caves have reduced her will to live. She retreats from the world of experience. She came to India seeking peace; she finds it in death. Ironically, as her body is being lowered into the Indian Ocean, she is being mythified into the cult of Emiss Emoore.

The conclusion of the novel emphasizes the chaos of India, but it also hints at a pattern that the outsider, Muslim or British, cannot understand. Drenched in water and religion, the last chapters portray the rebirth of the God Shri Krishna. It is the recycling of the seasons, the rebirth and renewal of the earth that signals the renewal of the Hindu religious cycle. Godbole shows that humans may choose to accept and participate in the seeming chaos, or they can fight against it. They must, however, be in tune with the natural rhythms of the universe to receive true love and friendship. Neither Fielding nor Aziz, products of Western civilization, can accept the confusion without attempting to impose order. Although they have moved toward the irrational in the course of the novel, they have not moved far enough.

"Critical Evaluation" by Michael S. Reynolds

Bibliography:
Bradbury, Malcolm, ed. *E. M. Forster, "A Passage to India": A Casebook*. London: Macmillan, 1970. Nineteen essays about every aspect of the novel. Particularly interesting are an interview with Forster in which he discusses his writing of *A Passage to India* and a selection of early reviews and reactions to his novel.
Furbank, P. N. *E. M. Forster: A Life*. New York: Harcourt Brace Jovanovich, 1978. Provides many details about Forster's travels in India. Explains Forster's struggles to write his masterpiece and how he coped with its critical and financial success.
Godfrey, Denis. *E. M. Forster's Other Kingdom*. New York: Barnes & Noble, 1968. Focuses on the mystical themes in the novel. Shows how Mrs. Moore—a symbol of good—influences the other characters and the plot even after her death.
Herz, Judith Scherer. *"A Passage to India": Nation and Narration*. New York: Twayne, 1993.

Overview of the novel with a section explaining the historical background of the British Raj. Detailed discussion of Forster's style and use of symbolism; also addresses the problem of narrative voice.

Shahane, V. A., ed. *Perspectives on E. M. Forster's "A Passage to India": A Collection of Critical Essays*. New York: Barnes & Noble, 1968. Fourteen essays about *A Passage to India*, many of which discuss its symbolic qualities. Insights include those from Indian literary critics.

PASSING

Type of work: Novel
Author: Nella Larsen (1891-1964)
Type of plot: Social realism
Time of plot: Early twentieth century
Locale: New York
First published: 1929

> *Principal characters:*
> IRENE REDFIELD, a black socialite
> CLARE KENDRY, a black socialite who is "passing"
> BRIAN REDFIELD, Irene's husband
> JOHN ("JACK") BELLEW, Clare's husband

The Story:

Irene Redfield received a letter from Clare Kendry that she considered dangerous, since she knew that Clare had been passing for white and that Clare's association with any black person was dangerous. Irene recalled that Clare had always been different, sneaky, and clever, as well as independent, selfish, and self-centered; she remembered Clare's poise as a teenager when her drunken father bellowed at her for disobeying him. When Clare's father was killed in a saloon fight, Clare had been angry with him for abandoning her.

Irene read the letter from Clare, who was in New York and wanted to see her. Irene was determined not to see Clare, recalling the last time she had accidentally run into Clare. Two summers earlier, Irene had been in Chicago, shopping for her sons, Brian, Jr., and Theodore. Feeling very warm and thirsty, she had stopped at the Drayton Hotel for tea. She noticed a woman staring at her and thought it was because she was black. The woman approached Irene and claimed to know her, but Irene had not remembered her until she laughed, when she recognized the laugh as belonging to Clare Kendry. There had been rumors about Clare's sudden disappearance from the black community twelve years earlier. Irene and Clare talked about what they had been doing over the years. Irene invited Clare to her house but immediately regretted it. Irene questioned Clare about passing for white but Clare, noting that they were both drinking tea at the all-white Drayton Hotel, turned the question back. Irene became angry and left, vowing to have nothing more to do with Clare.

A few days later, Clare had repeatedly called the Redfield residence but Irene refused to speak with her, letting her maid, Liza, answer the phone. Finally, exasperated by the constant ringing of the phone, she had answered the phone and had let Clare badger her into visiting her. At Clare's home, Irene and another woman, Gertrude Martin, exchanged cool greetings. Irene did not like Gertrude who, like Clare, was passing for white and who had married a white man. Irene's opinion of Gertrude did not improve when Gertrude told her and Clare that she did not want to have any "dark" children. Irene's temper flared and she reminded Gertrude that her children—Brian, Jr., and Theodore—were dark. At that moment, John "Jack" Bellew, Clare's husband, walked in and greeted Clare with the nickname "Nig." Amid tense silence, when Clare told Jack to explain why he called her that, Jack said that when he had met Clare she was "white as a lily," but that she appeared to be getting darker. "Nig" was his affectionate way of telling her that one morning she would wake up a "nigger." Prompted by an angry but subdued Irene,

Jack went on to say that he hated black people. Suppressing both laughter and anger, Irene left, followed by Gertrude.

Just before she returned to New York, Irene received a note from Clare, begging for understanding and forgiveness. Irene tore up the note and turned her thoughts to the situation at home. Her main concern was whether Brian, her husband, was still discontent and restless.

That had all occurred two years earlier in Chicago, and until that morning, Irene had not heard from Clare. Irene was suspicious of Clare's alleged love for her own people. She brought up the subject of Clare with Brian at breakfast. Brian expressed admiration of Clare's sense of adventure and went on to talk of his desire to go to Brazil. Irene became angry, telling him that he had made the right decision when he set up his race philanthropy charities in New York. They parted angrily from each other, and Irene felt uneasy about the security of her marriage.

Still upset over her fight with Brian, Irene tore up the letter from Clare and determined not to contact her. Days went by and Irene forgot about Clare. Instead, she continued to worry about Brian's restlessness and unhappiness. Several days later, Irene was shocked to answer her doorbell and find Clare standing there. To her own surprise, Irene was happy to see Clare, yet she warned Clare that it was not safe for them to be friends, given John Bellew's beliefs about blacks. Clare found Irene's concern humorous and told her that she wanted to be invited to the Negro Welfare Dance that Brian had organized. Irene gave in despite her own premonitions of disaster, but once Clare had left she was angry with herself for giving in to Clare. Irene then became angry with Clare, realizing that she was as selfish as she had always been.

Clare became a regular visitor to the Redfield household. Irene began to notice how well Brian and Clare got along and gradually began to suspect that Clare had designs on her husband. When Clare admitted to Irene that she was bad and not to be trusted, Irene's suspicions flared into terror, especially since Brian seemed even more distant and withdrawn. Irene began to consider how she could rid herself of Clare, and she began to wish horrible afflictions on Clare's family. Meeting Jack Bellew on the street, she told him she was black and was pleased to see his distress and hatred. For a moment, she considered destroying Clare, too, by revealing her race, but she could not go through with it. As a black woman she felt loyalty to Clare even if only because of their sex and race.

Just before leaving for a party, Irene and Brian argued over how to raise their sons. Afterward, Irene admitted to herself that the only thing she wanted from Brian was security. She was shocked to realize that she had never loved Brian and never would. Yet she was determined to keep him, no matter what the cost. They went to the party with Clare. Shortly after they arrived at the party, a loud knock was heard at the door and John Bellew rushed in, demanding his wife. When he called her a nigger, Clare began to laugh. Bellew seized her arm and Irene tried to stop—or help—him. In the next instant Clare fell or jumped—or was pushed—out of the open window. Everyone except Irene rushed downstairs to the sidewalk. Irene was in shock, but she was also relieved that Clare was dead. A policeman came upstairs and asked Irene if she was sure Clare jumped. Brian had told him that Bellew had pushed Clare, but Irene refuted her husband. The policeman decided that Clare's death had probably been an accident.

Critical Evaluation:

With the publication of *An Intimation of Things Distant: The Collected Fiction of Nella Larsen* in 1992, the resurrection of Nella Larsen's reputation as an important figure of the Harlem Renaissance continued. Like her contemporary Jesse Redmon Fauset, Larsen was a victim of the literary skirmishes between the champions of the "new negro" and those who saw the aestheticization of lower-class African American life as pandering to the negrophilia of white Manhattanites. Larsen's subject matter was the light-skinned middle-class African American woman who was afflicted and endowed with means, taste, and ambition. Larsen's self-imposed limitations were decidedly unfashionable among the critics of the period, though popular with the general readership, but her works became anachronisms with the appearance of the works of Langston Hughes, Countée Cullen, and Claude McKay. Against the rough-hewn world depicted by these writers, Larsen's genteel angst fared badly, not least because her concerns seemed mostly those of middle-class African American women with too much time on their hands.

While some, like James Weldon Johnson, George Schuyler, and Jean Toomer, returned again and again to the peculiarly African American phenomenon of "passing" for white, only Larsen conflated the problem of racial and class boundaries with the problem of gender in asking what it meant to be a middle-class African American woman in the first half of the twentieth century. In *Passing*, Larsen simultaneously treats three seemingly intractable issues in a provocative, if melodramatic, narrative. For that reason alone, the book represents a significant landmark in the history of American literature. Beyond its important subject matter, however, *Passing* provides a concise, unelaborated story. Larsen's prose is sparse but effective. With a few deft strokes, characters become believable humans with vices and virtues. The plot moves swiftly, and the dialogue fleshes out characters and propels the narrative forward.

The principal theme of *Passing* is the social and cultural nexus in which light-skinned African American women find themselves. Though she never deals with it explicitly in her fiction, Larsen's work implies, even more ominously, that if African American women whose skin is so light they can pass for white cannot make it, darker-skinned African American women have no chance at all. By "making it," Larsen meant indirect but proximate access to economic, social, and cultural power. *Passing* takes for granted the hierarchies of race, class, and gender in American life. The three main female characters—Clare Kendry, Irene Redfield, and Gertrude Martin—understand that the best they can hope to do is to imitate white women. Both Clare and Gertrude have married white men, which is as close to real power—white male power—as they will ever get. Irene, from whose point of view the story is told, disdains her female peers for their treason to their race, yet she too desires the proximity to power that Clare and Gertrude have by virtue of their marriages. This explains Irene's hostility to Gertrude, a mere acquaintance, and her ambivalence in her relations with Clare, her friend. Irene envies their "passing" even as she detests it. When Irene believes Clare to be a threat to her marriage, she wishes Clare were dead. Yet, loyal to her race, she refuses to betray Clare to her husband when she has the opportunity to do so, knowing that he hates "niggers," even though that same loyalty to race drives her to reveal her own race to him.

Passing also concerns the problem of class, which is at least as important to Irene as race, although the issue is raised explicitly only once when Irene thinks about Gertrude, who has married a white butcher. Marriage to this man has destroyed Gertrude's adolescent beauty and charm. Of the two light-skinned women married to white men, one is married to a rich bigot and forced to pass for white while the other is married to a man who accepts her for what she is but who is, the novel implies, only a butcher. The moral is clear: Only a lower-class white man, "white trash," would knowingly marry an African American woman. The irony of Irene's marriage to Brian Redfield is that he, though from the same middle class as she, would much prefer working with the poor in Brazil. Throughout the novel, Irene worries because Brian's dissatisfaction with sponsoring chic parties for the Negro Welfare League draws him further and further from her. By novel's end, Irene admits to herself that she has never loved Brian, though she remains desperate to save her marriage. She married him for his social and cultural connections, limited as they are by his being an African American. Small wonder that Irene feels superior to both Gertrude and Clare, for she married a man from a higher class than Gertrude's husband yet, unlike both Gertrude's and Clare's husbands, someone from her own race.

Tyrone Williams

Bibliography:

Blackmore, David L. "'That Unreasonable Restless Feeling': The Homosexual Subtexts of Nella Larsen's *Passing*." *African American Review* 26, no. 3 (Fall, 1992): 475-484. Offers a complementary reading to Deborah McDowell's essay (see below). Blackmore focuses on Irene's husband's enchantment with Brazil as a symptom of his homosexual desire; Brazil is portrayed as an idealized locus of sexual and racial experimentation and freedom.

McDowell, Deborah E. Introduction to *Quicksand* and *Passing*, by Nella Larsen. New Brunswick, N.J.: Rutgers University Press, 1986. Explores the sexually charged relationship between Irene and Clare and its eventual suffocation by the reigning black bourgeois ideology of the period.

Madigan, Mark J. "Miscegenation and 'the Dicta of Race and Class': The Rhinelander Case and Nella Larsen's *Passing*." *Modern Fiction Studies* 36, no. 4 (Winter, 1990): 523-529. Argues that the one reference to the Rhinelander case in Larsen's novel suggests that the work may have been inspired by it. Leonard Rhinelander was a young man from a prominent New York family, who had married a black woman light enough to pass for white. When his family discovered her race, they forced him to divorce her, and a public uproar resulted.

THE PASSION FLOWER

Type of work: Drama
Author: Jacinto Benavente y Martínez (1866-1954)
Type of plot: Tragedy
Time of plot: Early twentieth century
Locale: Castile, Spain
First performed: La malquerida, 1913 (English translation, 1917)

Principal characters:
> ESTEBAN, a well-to-do Spanish peasant
> RAIMUNDA, his second wife
> ACACIA, her daughter
> RUBIO, a family servant
> JULIANA, another servant
> NORBERT, Acacia's former fiancé
> FAUSTINO, engaged to Acacia

The Story:

There was much excitement in the home of Esteban, a wealthy peasant living in an outlying section of a small town in Castile, Spain. The engagement of his stepdaughter Acacia to Faustino, son of Tio Eusebio, a friend of Esteban, had just been announced, and friends of Raimunda, Acacia's mother, were calling to talk over the event. Acacia, after turning down several suitors, had finally consented to Faustino's suit. The women were wondering whether she still thought about Norbert, who some time before had broken off his engagement to her without explanation.

Fidelia, one of the callers, said that she had seen Norbert leaving angrily with his gun after the engagement was announced that afternoon. Another, Engracia, shrewdly suspected that the young woman had accepted Faustino to get away from Esteban, against whom she had borne a grudge for marrying Raimunda so soon after the death of her first husband. Raimunda assured her friends that she had seen no signs of ill feeling except in Acacia's unwillingness to call him father. Certainly Esteban had been most generous to both of them.

Night was coming on. Faustino and his father, who lived in the next village, would have no moonlight for their journey, and hungry husbands would soon be demanding suppers; so the party ended. Esteban offered to accompany his friends to the edge of the village.

Raimunda, still not certain how her daughter felt about the coming marriage, began questioning her, but she was reassured by her daughter's replies. Only the servant, Juliana, struck a sour note as she began to tidy the house after the party, declaring that she wished that Acacia's real father had lived to see this day. Milagros, a friend who had stayed to see Acacia's hope chest, also asked the girl how she felt toward Norbert. When she suggested that Acacia was still in love with him, Acacia's answer was to tear his last letter to her into bits and throw it out the window into the darkness.

At that moment, a gunshot was heard outside. Raimunda sent Juliana to investigate. The servant returned with villagers carrying the body of Faustino. None had seen the shot fired, but the women were sure Norbert was the assassin. At the court trial, however, unbiased witnesses gave Norbert an unbreakable alibi. Weeks later, the village was still arguing about the affair. Esteban moped about the house and talked so much about the killing that Acacia was almost frantic. Raimunda finally decided to send Juliana after Norbert. She was sure she could learn the truth from him.

Rubio, the servant, who was becoming increasingly drunk and impudent, tried to keep Eusebio from calling on Esteban to discuss the murder. Eusebio's other sons, disgusted with what they regarded as a miscarriage of justice, were threatening to shoot Norbert. Their father hinted that even if the young man was innocent, rogues can be hired to assassinate or family servants can act through loyalty. Raimunda told him she prayed every day that God would reveal and punish the murderer.

After Eusebio left, Juliana sneaked Norbert into the house. He assured Raimunda that he was completely innocent of the crime. Bernabe, another servant, arrived with accounts of Rubio's drunken boasting that he was now master in Esteban's house. The servant also repeated a song, heard in the tavern, which called Acacia the Passion Flower because she inspired an unholy love in men. Norbert confessed that he had broken off his engagement to her because he had been threatened and had not been courageous enough to resist.

When Acacia appeared, Raimunda, to test her suspicions, accused her of being in love with her stepfather. The girl replied that her father was in the cemetery and that she hated the man who had taken his place. The arrival of Esteban brought further denunciation from Raimunda. Let him get Rubio's help to murder Acacia and her, if he wished, but she would kill him if he approached her daughter. Norbert, trying to leave the house in spite of Bernabe's warning, was shot by Eusebio's boys.

Norbert began to recover, but an atmosphere of hatred hung over all that was said or done. Raimunda and Juliana discussed the time when Esteban had come courting; now they wondered whether he had loved Acacia then. Juliana warned that great hatred like Acacia's might contain the germ of great love.

Rubio, becoming insolent in his demands, proved that Esteban had never actually told him to murder Faustino. He had only audibly hoped that no one would take Acacia from his house. There was still love between Esteban and Raimunda, however, and to preserve it they decided that it would be wise to send Acacia briefly to a convent and then try to find a husband for her. Acacia, who had been listening outside the door, burst in with the announcement that she would not leave the house. Esteban acquiesced; since he was the cause of all the trouble, he should be the one to go. At that Acacia broke down. Esteban must not go; she loved him.

Raimunda's screams denouncing him brought the neighbors to the scene. The trapped Esteban shot Raimunda, who died happy because Acacia had turned to her at the end as she lay dying, and not to Esteban. With her death, Raimunda had saved her daughter. Esteban would never have her now.

Critical Evaluation:

The Passion Flower is the rather cinematographic title given to the English-language version of Jacinto Benavente y Martínez's *La malquerida*, the drama upon which Benavente's British and American reputation largely rests. Its production by Nance O'Neil in 1920 met with huge success and was in part responsible for the author's receiving the Nobel Prize in Literature in 1922.

Some critics have referred to the play as a classical drama, but scholars attempting to analyze the play according to Aristotelian principles would find it difficult to discover unity of action. The protagonist is at one juncture Raimunda, at another Esteban, and at yet another Acacia. It is impossible to designate any one of the three as the hero or heroine of the tragedy. Indeed, it would be more realistic to call the play's real protagonist the people, and the chief theme of the drama the gradual awakening of public consciousness in this village of the Castilian uplands. In each successive act, public opinion in favor of punishing the guilty sinner increases in strength. Initially, the innocent Norbert is considered guilty, but after public opinion has sifted the evidence, he is led home in triumph by large crowds. Though the people of the village do not actually appear on stage, they function like an invisible chorus, constantly commenting on the tragic fatality of human beings.

More than any of the author's other works, *The Passion Flower* shows the strength of Benavente's female characters. Indeed, it is difficult to visualize the traditional character of the proud Castilian male in Esteban, who becomes a whimpering coward by the end of the play. Esteban, who can hardly face the glance of his wife, is far removed from the proud heroes of Spanish chivalry. In the early acts of the play, Esteban appears but little and never utters any but evasive words. After the murder has been committed, he crumbles and has not even the spirit to face his servant Rubio. In the great scene with Raimunda, her strength and courage contrast with his cowardice. He is the most inglorious antihero ever created by Benavente.

Acacia is, from the beginning, a rather strange character. Ever since her mother's marriage to Esteban she has shown a reserve toward her stepfather in spite of his kindness and obvious affection. By subtle touches that give an impression of gloomy sadness, Benavente instills increasing amounts of mystery into Acacia's characterization. One of these touches is the use of cleverly written dialogue that indicates either that a peculiar sexual hatred exists between Acacia and Esteban, or that Acacia is an unbalanced neurotic. This mystery continues through-out the drama. By contrast, Raimunda is a character who is essentially submissive in tempera-ment. She has lived blandly unconscious of the tragedy near at hand. It takes a great shock to cause the scales to fall from her eyes and make her see her husband as he really is. When the crisis does come, she is torn by conflicting emotions: She still loves her husband passionately but wants him to suffer for his sin. Benavente develops this conflict by postponing the great scene of recrimination between husband and wife until the third act, by which time her feelings of horror have softened and pity for him has weakened her resolve. No scene in Benavente's works provides a greater example of antithesis. Being both an honorable and a religious woman, Raimunda wishes Esteban to suffer to the fullest extent as an atonement to God for his sin—a spirit of justice characteristic of the Castilian mind. Yet the soft, womanly side of her character causes her to feel compassion for him, seeing him trapped on all sides like a wild beast.

The first performances of this play aroused a great deal of criticism. Some considered the tragedy too rough, the story that of too monstrous a sin; others speculated as to possible real models for the story of the love of a stepfather for his stepdaughter. Yet most of the criticism gave way eventually to the public enthusiasm engendered by the play. *The Passion Flower* marked the summit of Benavente's literary career, and he became a leading influence for an entire generation of Spanish playwrights.

"Critical Evaluation" by Stephen Hanson

Bibliography:

Goldberg, Isaac. *The Drama of Transition.* Cincinnati: Stewart Kidd, 1922. Lengthy discussion of Benavente's achievement; provides insight into the critical reception of *The Passion Flower* both in Spain and throughout Europe. Also includes summaries of critical commen-taries on Benavente by several early twentieth century scholars and artists.

Jameson, Storm. "The Drama of Italy and Spain." In *Modern Drama in Europe.* London: Collins, 1920. Places Benavente in the context of twentieth century Spanish drama; links him with the earlier dramatist Lope de Vega Carpio as one of the country's major playwrights. Discusses formal qualities of the plays and provides insight into the dramatist's method for re-creating the pathos of human existence.

Peñuelas, Marcelino C. *Jacinto Benavente*. Translated by Kay Engler. New York: Twayne, 1968. Introductory summary of a writer Peñuelas considers the most popular Spanish playwright of the first half of the twentieth century. Establishes the relationship of this play to the social and literary climate in which it was written.

Starkie, Walter. *Jacinto Benavente*. London: H. Milford, 1924. Includes commentary on *The Passion Flower* in a general discussion of Benavente's dialect plays; analyzes character development and compares the work to similar dramas by other European playwrights.

Underhill, John Garrett. Introduction to *The Plays of Jacinto Benavente*. Vol. 1. New York: Charles Scribner's Sons, 1921. Discusses the work as one of Benavente's "peasant dramas," in which the playwright dramatizes "the struggle of the individual conscience against the conscience of the masses."

PASSIONS AND ANCIENT DAYS

Type of work: Poetry
Author: Constantine P. Cavafy (Kōnstantionos Petrou Kabaphēs, 1863-1933)
First published: English translation with original Greek, 1971

The works of Constantine Cavafy were not published during the poet's lifetime. At least, they cannot be said to have been published in the conventional sense. Frequently revising his early poems and suppressing those that he thought were inferior, Cavafy shared much of his poetry with only his closest friends, often distributing his works in the form of privately printed broadsides, pamphlets, or small volumes. At the time of his death of cancer at the age of seventy, the poet left behind sixty-eight poems arranged thematically in two small books, a folder of sixty-nine additional poems printed on broadsides, and a large number of poetic drafts in various stages of completion. Two years after Cavafy's death, his literary executor, Alexander Singopoulos, issued a volume containing 153 of Cavafy's poems, all that the poet himself considered to be his finest work.

Passions and Ancient Days is an edition of twenty-one additional poems that the editors, Cavafy scholars Edmund Keeley and George Savidis, have judged to be of quality equal or superior to those appearing in Singopoulos' edition. At times, Cavafy seems to have suppressed these poems because they were dramatically different in tone and subject matter from his other work. (This seems to have been the case, for instance, with "King Claudius," Cavafy's only surviving poem on a Shakespearean theme.) At times, reading this book of rejected work, one thinks that the poet appears to have been excessively critical of his own work. In any case, the poems that Keeley and Savidis have selected develop themes and images already introduced in the 153 canonical poems. For example, "Julian at the Mysteries" closely resembles six poems dealing with the historical figure of Julian the Apostate (c. 331-363 C.E.) such as "Julian in Nicomedia" (1924) and "On the Outskirts of Antioch" (1933). "The End of Antony" completes a cycle of earlier poems about the Roman politician and soldier Marc Antony (c. 83-30 B.C.E.), including "The Gods Abandon Antony" (1918) and "In a Township of Asia Minor" (1926). "September, 1903" and "December, 1903" are works that capture the erotic sensation of a single moment, similar to "Days of 1903" (1917) and "Days of 1896" (1927) among Cavafy's works in the Singopoulos edition.

The title *Passions and Ancient Days* is derived from a thematic structure that Cavafy himself once used for his poetry. In a commentary on his work, Cavafy said that all of his poems could be divided into three categories: the historical, the philosophical, and the erotic. In *Passions and Ancient Days*, "passions" refer to Cavafy's erotic poems and "ancient days" to his historical poems. Cavafy's philosophical poems are largely unrepresented among the twenty-one works included in this volume. *Passions and Ancient Days* reproduces each poem in the original Greek on the left-hand page, with an English translation by Keeley and Savidis on the right-hand page.

The erotic poems contain many of the same themes appearing in Cavafy's other work: passionate homosexuality; brief, often furtive, encounters with strangers; and the shame and secrecy imposed upon homosexuals by an intolerant society. For example, "September, 1903" addresses the poet's own fears of admitting his feelings to others. He chides himself for his cowardice, wondering why he could not speak even the few words that may have ended his loneliness. He is grieved by the number of times he was near someone whom he could have loved if only he had had the courage to speak. Now, all he wants to do is to console himself by recalling the comforting illusion of what might have been.

Keeley and Savidis note that the conflict between illusion and reality is a repeated theme in all of Cavafy's erotic poems. For instance, in "December, 1903," a companion piece to "September, 1903," Cavafy observes that, while he can never speak of the love that he once felt, his lover's memory haunts him still. Imagining the sound of this person's voice adds a hidden level of meaning to each of the poet's thoughts and words. In both of Cavafy's "1903" poems—as well as in "Days of 1903" in the earlier collection—the lasting effects of a lost love or a chance encounter provide the incident that the author uses to develop the poem. Moments that may seem insignificant to others, even to certain persons involved in them, can sometimes be of profound significance to someone in love. The cherished memory, replayed in one's mind or altered by fantasy, can provide a level of meaning far more satisfying than that derived from everyday life. For Cavafy, who was often reluctant to initiate encounters through fear of how others might respond to his homosexuality, these moments give his erotic or romantic poems a wistful air of regret.

In "At the Theatre," the encounter itself is imaginary. While bored at a play, the poet glances around the audience and notices a young man whom other people had been mentioning that very afternoon. The poet imagines the stranger (not as the poet sees him there, elegantly dressed and world-weary in one of the seats of the box circle) as he had been described earlier— exciting, corrupt, and possessing a "strange beauty." The two of them never meet but Cavafy finds himself aroused far more than he ever has been before. In a nearly contemporary poem, "On the Stairs," he describes a brief encounter between himself and another patron at a house of prostitution. For a split second, their eyes meet and the poet is aware—he is convinced that they are both aware—that these two men are capable of a love far more meaningful than the sheer physical pleasures of this "disgraceful house." In shame, however, the two of them avert their eyes. Their opportunity is lost and they each rush away from the other, both of them still strangers.

The objects of Cavafy's passions are never named in the poems. (In their notes to the works, Keeley and Savidis do occasionally attempt to identify certain people from the poet's notes and unpublished prose.) Cavafy's lovers are faceless strangers whose brief appearance in the author's life have left an unexpected void. Little information is provided about these anonymous figures, so readers will find it easy to identify with the narrator of the poem. Even the sex of Cavafy's lover is often left unspecified, with the result that both heterosexual and homosexual readers will find that they are able to relate to many of these works.

Unlike Cavafy's erotic poems, his historical poems are quite specific in both setting and focus. They usually derive from some incident that the author encountered in his wide reading of classical and Byzantine history. The themes explored by Cavafy's historical poems include the nature of Greek nationalism, the relationship between Christianity and paganism, and the author's surprising (and almost certainly ironic) interpretations of historical events. "Theophilos Palaiologos," for instance, deals with an incident that occurred during the conquest of Constantinople by the Ottoman Turks in 1453. The title character, a relative of the last Byzantine emperor, Constantine Palaiologos, is reported to been in despair before the Turkish onslaught. His brief comment "Better to die than live" is quoted in a historical chronicle. Those five words, Cavafy says, are filled with all the weariness and sorrow of the Greek people, a nation that has been worn down by centuries of injustice and persecution. As in his erotic poems where Cavafy finds meaning and deep passion in what appear to be insignificant moments, so does the poet in this work see the entire heritage of the Greek race reflected in a forgotten line of a forgotten work of history.

In "Return from Greece," Cavafy imagines a conversation between two Greek philosophers living in an unnamed eastern country sometime during the Hellenistic period (323-27 B.C.E.). One of them, named Hermippus, has grown silent and nostalgic as a ship carries them farther and farther from Greece on their voyage home to Asia. The other, the anonymous narrator of the poem, admonishes Hermippus that his hypocrisy is inappropriate to the Greek spirit. Hermippus should admit, the narrator continues, that they are relieved to be returning home. The two of them, he says, display a Hellenism that is tinged with the cultures of Asia, Arabia, and Persia; this fusion should be a cause of celebration. True Greeks do not try to conceal their origins, but exult in their rich diversity.

"Poseidonians" explores the mixed heritage of modern Greeks from a slightly different perspective. Beginning with an incident described by the Alexandrian author Athenaeus (third century B.C.E.) in the *Deipnosophistai*, Cavafy portrays an ancient festival celebrated by the Greek inhabitants of Paestum, a city in southwestern Italy. Once a year, these citizens would put on their Greek garments and engage in rituals that few of them understood, speaking a language that none of them still spoke. Then, lamenting the loss of their heritage, they would drift away to their homes. Cut off from the society that once gave meaning to their lives, the Greek citizens of Paestum seemed a people without a culture: no longer Greek, not yet Italian, they were forever lost because they were too foolish to preserve the identity that would have sustained them.

Preserving his Greek heritage was of great importance to Cavafy, a Greek poet who lived and worked in the Egyptian city of Alexandria. Cavafy's historical poems explore the many threads—classical, Byzantine, Christian, Egyptian, Asiatic—that compose his culture. To Cavafy, Hellenism was a living tradition that absorbed much from the cultures with which it had come into contact, but which had also imbued those cultures with something of the Greek spirit. Through his poetry, Cavafy attempts to define both his culture and himself. The author's identity that emerges from *Passions and Ancient Days* is that of a poet, a Christian, a lover, a Greek living in a world that is not Greek, and a man whose regret for lost opportunities gives his works a melancholy flavor but also great meaning.

Jeffrey L. Buller

Bibliography:
Bien, Peter. *Constantine Cavafy*. New York: Columbia University Press, 1964. A brief but informative introduction to Cavafy's life and poetry. Bien's essay is probably the best place for anyone who is unfamiliar with Cavafy's work to begin. The short bibliography provides suggestions for continued study.
Jusdanis, Gregory. *The Poetics of Cavafy: Textuality, Eroticism, History*. Princeton, N.J.: Princeton University Press, 1987. Contains a detailed thematic interpretation of Cavafy's poetry. Individual poems are explored in great depth as are themes that appear repeatedly throughout the poet's work. With an introduction, index, and extensive bibliography.
Kapre-Karka, K. *Love and the Symbolic Journey in the Poetry of Cavafy, Eliot, and Seferis*. New York: Pella, 1982. A poem-by-poem analysis of Cavafy's erotic poetry, viewed alongside the works of T. S. Eliot (1888-1965) and George Seferis (1900-1971). Also examines the theme of the journey or pilgrimage in the poetry of all three authors.
Keeley, Edmund. *Cavafy's Alexandria: Study of a Myth in Progress*. Cambridge, Mass.: Harvard University Press, 1976. Written by one of the editors and translators of *Passions and Ancient Days*, this work explores Cavafy's Hellenism and its relationship to the city of Alexandria, the setting for many of Cavafy's poems.

Liddell, Robert. *Cavafy: A Critical Biography*. London: Duckworth, 1974. The most readable biography of Cavafy available and a good introduction to his poetry. Liddell explores the relationship between Cavafy's poetry and his life, scholarship, and religious beliefs. Contains an index and a good general bibliography.

Pinchin, Jane Lagoudis. *Alexandria Still*. Princeton, N.J.: Princeton University Press, 1977. Relates Cavafy's poetry to the writing of E. M. Forster (1879-1970) and Laurence Durrell (1912-1990) as authors who explored the landscape and meaning of Alexandria. Provides a valuable insight into Cavafy's historical poems.

PAST AND PRESENT

Type of work: Essays
Author: Thomas Carlyle (1795-1881)
First published: 1843

In *Past and Present*, Thomas Carlyle brings to the task of social commentary the same searching, tenacious, and idiosyncratic analysis that characterized his *Sartor Resartus* (1835). In the earlier work, Carlyle explores his crisis of faith; in *Past and Present*, however, he analyzes the problems of newly industrialized England both by invoking historical events and by dissecting contemporary issues. Carlyle offers his assessment in four books: "Proem," "The Ancient Monk," "The Modern Worker," and "Horoscope." While his method may at first appear haphazard, Carlyle weaves striking examples, blistering caricatures, and shrewd political analyses into a memorable pattern, closing with a stern warning about England's future.

Born into a family of resolute Scottish Calvinists, Carlyle was never shy about offering opinions, advice, criticism, and even insults in his essays. While he no longer accepted the tenets of the faith, Carlyle never shed its didactic approach. For this reason, some Victorian critics considered his style indecorous, even grotesque. Readers, however, will find his unpredictability and exaggeration surprisingly modern. Carlyle also inherited from his family an abiding respect for and insistence upon work. Throughout *Past and Present*, he demands constructive efforts from all persons "each in their degree" and lambastes the idle gentry, whom he calls "enchanted dilettantes."

Despite his admiration for the worker and emphasis on solid, practical accomplishment, Carlyle remained scornful of the prevailing Victorian doctrine of utilitarianism. Expounded by Victorian optimists, including Jeremy Bentham and John Stuart Mill, utilitarianism sought to achieve "the greatest happiness of the greatest number." Its method required assessing every act, belief, or idea for its usefulness or "utility." Like the utilitarians, Carlyle had little use for existing religious and social institutions; however, he found their emphasis upon happiness infantile and their confidence in utility exaggerated and mechanistic. To Carlyle, the utilitarians wasted energy in endlessly classifying and codifying human efforts. By contrast, he claimed that, given the appropriate conditions, a genuine "Aristocracy of Talent" would arise to lead society. Such "heroes" deserved to be worshiped; they possessed a vital energy capable of reinventing and ordering society. Later generations have deemed such views authoritarian, even fascistic, but Carlyle's defense of his position in *Past and Present* defies easy labeling.

In "Proem," Carlyle introduces most of the major themes of his work as well as his characteristic rhetorical strategies. In Carlyle's opinion, England in 1843 was burdened by a huge surplus of wealth and activity, improperly managed and frivolously expended. Able working men languished "enchanted" in poorhouses or were daily exploited by profiteering and callous employers. Early in the discussion, Carlyle takes a stand on one of the most controversial economic issues of his day: the infamous Corn Laws (repealed in 1846). These tariffs on imported grains were established to eliminate foreign competition and to keep the price of English farm products high; they also effectively robbed working people of their daily bread. Carlyle defends an early popular movement against the Corn Laws, the Manchester Insurrection of 1819, arguing that the agitators "put their huge inarticulate question, 'What do you mean to do with us?' in a manner audible to every reflective soul in this kingdom." Those who labor deserve to be responsibly and actively governed, rather than enduring the laissez-faire neglect of the political system. To achieve this organic, vital government, Carlyle urges his readers to "put away all Flunkyism, Baseness, Unveracity from us." Only a heroic nation of "faithful, discerning souls" will be capable of electing a heroic government, of discerning the "Aristocracy of Talent" crucial to England's future.

Also in "Proem," Carlyle creates the first of his imaginary characters, who appear periodically throughout the work to serve as "straw men," ludicrous proponents of the arguments he despises. Bobus Higgins, for example, typifies the fatuous, greedy middle classes, incapable both of self-rule and of choosing worthy leadership. In the following book, "The Ancient Monk," Carlyle turns to an actual historical figure to dramatize the diminished stature of profit-minded Victorians. The book presents a biography of Samson, abbot of the medieval monastery of St. Edmundsbury, whose deeds are recorded by his faithful biographer Jocelin of Brakelond. Given Carlyle's distaste for the social machine conceived by utilitarians, it is not surprising that he looked to an age of faith for his heroes. Throughout the essay, however, Carlyle emphasizes that it is Samson's works, rather than his faith alone, that make him heroic. Abbot Samson, Jocelin assures the reader, made all "the Earth's business a kind of worship." The model for Carlyle's practical man, Samson "had a talent; he had learned to judge better than Lawyers, to manage better than bred Bailiffs." Medieval social vitality is expressed not only by Samson's stature but also by the monks' capacity to elect him without benefit of ballot box or bribery. Casting a critical eye on Victorian religious fads, Carlyle contrasts Abbot Samson's quiet efficiency with the "noisy theoretic demonstrations" of Tractarianism, or the Oxford Movement (beginning in 1833), which sought to enhance ceremony and ritual in the Church of England. He entreats his audience to dispose of "blockhead quacks" and acknowledge instead England's "real conquerors, creators, and eternal proprietors," "those who ever cut a thistle, drained a puddle out of England, contrived a wise scheme in England, did or said a true and valiant thing in England."

Having offered both a definition and an exemplar of heroism, Carlyle's analysis continues in "The Modern Worker." In these chapters, Carlyle's language becomes the most militant and his arguments the most prescient. Lacking Samson's insight and distracted by the "Shows and Shams of things," Victorian society adheres only to the false gospels of "Mammonism" and "Dilettantism." Carlyle exposes what he terms "Social Gangrene" by citing some unforgettable cases, including that of a poor Irish widow and mother of three whose appeals to various charitable institutions are repeatedly denied. Eventually, the widow contracts typhus and dies, but not before she spreads the contagion so that seventeen of her fellow laborers die with her. Carlyle asks "with a heart too full for speaking, Would it not have been economy to help this poor Widow?" To Carlyle, society's studied neglect of the poorer classes is not only inhumane but also foolish. He remarks (with some irony) that, despite being rejected, the dying widow "proved her sisterhood" in the end; disease underscores the biological link between classes, the organic relationship of all humankind.

Though he defends honest labor, Carlyle repudiates profit as a motive for human endeavor. He foresees the rise and impact of advertising, impatiently dismissing the "Puffery" of an English hatter who "has not attempted to make better hats . . . but his whole industry is turned to persuade us that he has made such!" Things made only for profit are, to Carlyle, "no-things." Recalling his Calvinist roots, he insists that work must not be profaned by notions of economic gain; nor should it be trivialized by fantasies of happiness. Utilitarians such as Bentham and Mill degrade the dignity of labor, just as surely as do profiteers, by making happiness its goal. Both happiness and profit are ephemeral, irrelevant. Only work provides an index of human worth to Carlyle, a means of recognizing an "Aristocracy of Talent." Society is not held together by cash payments or by supply and demand. In demanding "let us see thy work," Carlyle seeks a more organic social structure than economic class and a less arbitrary measure of success than a full purse.

In "The Modern Worker," Carlyle also makes it clear that democracy (at least as he defines it) does not represent the climax of political evolution. Liberty, he claims, "requires new definitions." He has little faith in the capacity of representative government to secure genuine liberty, nor can he tolerate that liberty which measures human relationships only in terms of cash flow. At its worst, democracy becomes the pursuit of economic liberty by hypocrites eager to enslave themselves anew by gratifying their most "brutal appetites." Carlyle expresses his belief that democracy is merely a transitional phase when he states, "The Toiling Millions of Mankind, in most vital need and passionate instinctive desire of Guidance, shall cast away False Guidance; and hope, for an hour, that no-Guidance will suffice them: but it can be for an hour only." Espousing his own brand of radicalism, Carlyle supports the people's right to topple inept or self-interested governments, but he does not extend to them the right to govern themselves. He sees genuine liberty only in an integrated society, one in which individuals perform appropriate work and coexist with inferiors, equals, and superiors. In closing, Carlyle returns to history for an example of such right governance, contrasting the talent of Oliver Cromwell with the empty platitudes of Sir Jabesh Windbag (another of Carlyle's symbolic characters).

In book IV, entitled "Horoscope," Carlyle returns to the subject of true aristocracy, reiterating that it is "at once indispensable and not easily attained." He implores his readers to use the continuity between past and present to instruct the future. The nineteenth century has a new epic to write, "Tools and the Man" (in contrast to Vergil's "Arms and the Man"), which must address unprecedented social forces such as industry and democracy. Carlyle warns that the present parliamentary system, rife with corruption and ineptitude, is incapable of organizing labor and managing the working classes. Characteristically, he asserts that these problems can only be solved "by those who themselves work and preside over work," in other words, a "Chivalry of Labor." Carlyle's manifesto replaces a feudal aristocracy with an industrial aristocracy. He exhorts them to abandon an economics of supply and demand and to offer in its place "noble guidance" in return for "noble loyalty." He stresses that this must be a permanent bond. The "freedom" afforded by monthlong (vs. lifelong) contracts is comparable to the "liberty" guaranteed by democracy; for Carlyle, it is a worthless commodity. While the bond between laborer and master is sacred to Carlyle, the worker is no mere serf. Carlyle raises the possibility of jointly owned ventures in which the worker's interests, as well as his efforts, are permanently represented. The landed gentry remain relevant in Carlyle's scheme only to the extent that they exert themselves and use their accumulated resources on behalf of their fellow beings. Otherwise, they are scarcely human; they are "living statues" who are pampered, isolated, and absurd. Similarly, the "gifted"—writers, artists, and thinkers—cannot be segregated from those who haul timber or dig ditches; their position in a "Chivalry of Labor" depends upon active contribution and is no more or less honorable than any other.

For Carlyle, these are the prerequisites for an epic future. Though he has been accused of fascism, Carlyle seeks, ultimately, to reawaken and to recover the connections between persons. (In this respect, his ideas heavily influenced Ralph Waldo Emerson and American Transcendentalism.) *Past and Present* closes with a memorable avowal of this human interdependence: "Men cannot live isolated: we are all bound together, for mutual good or else for mutual misery, as living nerves in the same body."

Sarah A. Boris

Bibliography:

Calder, Grace J. *The Writing of Past and Present: A Study of Carlyle's Manuscripts.* New Haven, Conn.: Yale University Press, 1949. Contains valuable information on Carlyle's composing process and stylistic eccentricities.

Fielding, K. J., and Roger L. Tarr, eds. *Carlyle Past and Present: A Collection of New Essays.* New York: Barnes & Noble Books, 1976. Presents a variety of approaches to the work and its author.

Holloway, John. *The Victorian Sage: Studies in Argument.* London: Macmillan, 1953. A landmark study of Carlyle's rhetorical strategies and persuasive tactics.

Levine, George. *The Boundaries of Fiction: Carlyle, Macauley, Newman.* Princeton, N.J.: Princeton University Press, 1968. Learned discussion of Carlyle's style in the larger context of Victorian prose.

Waring, Walter. *Thomas Carlyle.* Boston: Twayne, 1978. An excellent introduction to Carlyle's ideas. Helps explain the philosophical tensions and social conditions of the early Victorian period.

PATERSON

Type of work: Poetry
Author: William Carlos Williams (1883-1963)
First published: 1946-1958

A hasty reading of William Carlos Williams' *Paterson* may leave the reader at the end of the poem with a feeling not unlike that of the country bumpkin on his first trip to the big city: There are so many different things to look at, in so many different shapes and sizes, and all the people seem to be rushing about so haphazardly that the poor rustic winds up his day bemused but happy. Such a reaction to *Paterson* is part of Williams' purpose. The poem interweaves the story of a city with the story of a man so that the two become interchangeable, and the jumbled kaleidoscope of city life turns and glitters like the conflicting ideas, dreams, loves, and hates that assail the minds of twentieth century human beings.

Looked at more closely, the poem can be seen to take on shape, like a city coming out from under a rolling fog or a person walking out of the shadows of trees in a park. Williams unifies his poem by letting the river that flows through the city serve as a symbol of life, both that of the city and that of the man. Life equated to a river flowing somewhere safe to sea is an image as old as poetry itself, but the ways in which Williams uses this image are so fresh and individual in style and presentation that it seems as if he had discovered the idea.

The poem is divided into four books, which correspond to four parts of the river: the portion above the falls; the falls themselves; the river below the falls; and the river's exit into the sea. Williams opens the first book, called "The Delineaments of the Giants," with these lines:

> Paterson lies in the valley under the Passaic Falls
> its spent waters forming the outline of his back. He
> lies on his right side, head near the thunder
> of the water filling his dreams!

Having presented the blended image of city and man, the poet goes on to present symbols for women—a flower, a cliff, the falls—and to introduce one of the main concerns of Paterson: the search for a language by which human beings may "redeem" the tragedies of life. To counterbalance this somewhat abstract and nebulous idea, Williams intersperses his poem with many concrete passages, some in prose, which serve as an entrancing documentation of the backgrounds of the city and the man. In book 1, for instance, historical notes and newspaper clippings tell us of the finding of pearls in mussels taken from Notch Brook, near the city; of General Washington's encounter with "a monster in human form"; of the accidental drowning of a Mrs. Cumming at the falls; of the death there of a stunt man named Sam Patch; and of a great catch of eels made by the local people when a lake was drained. Paterson the man is represented by letters written to him, one from a misunderstood lady poet. Williams rounds off book 1 with a quotation from John Addington Symonds' *Studies of the Greek Poets* (1873, 1876). Such diversity of material seems to call for a prestidigitator to make it all seem a part of the whole; Williams does it easily, for he is a master juggler who never quite lets his readers see all of the act that makes them fill in some of the parts from their own imagination.

Book 2, entitled "Sunday in the Park," concerns itself chiefly with love, including the many kinds of lovemaking found in a city park, and with poetry, for *Paterson* is as much a tribute to language as it is to a city or a man. Fittingly, this section ends with another long passage from a letter written by the lady poet who is struggling to fit together her work, her life, and her friendship with the "dear doctor" to whom she writes.

Book 3, "The Library," continues to probe the inarticulateness of tragedy and death, searching for some way that language may assuage, even prevent those things we accept as a part of existence. Williams describes poetry in these lines:

> The province of the poem is the world.
> When the sun rises, it rises in the poem
> and when it sets darkness comes down
> and the poem is dark

Book 3 also describes a great fire that sweeps the city and destroys the library. Williams continues to insert prose passages, one of which recounts the story of Merselis Van Giesen, whose wife was tormented by a witch that appeared to her nightly in the form of a black cat. In telling the story, Williams throws in several humorous comments. When the witch is revealed to be a Mrs. B., "who lived in the gorge in the hill beyond," he comments, "Happy souls! whose devils lived so near." Interspersing the tale with other witty remarks, the poet concludes with the husband shooting the cat with a silver bullet made from his cuff links. The shot is a difficult one because the cat is visible only to his wife, who must locate the target for him and direct his aim. He kills the cat and, in the best tradition of witch stories, Mrs. B. suffers for some time with a sore on her leg.

The last book, "The Run to the Sea," opens with an idyll involving Corydon, Phyllis, and Paterson. This section also introduces the image of the bomb. The poem concludes when Paterson the man reaches the sea, but he, along with a dog found swimming there, is able to escape from this symbol of death and to head inland.

Paterson, which appeared in segments between 1946 and 1958, has been compared with Walt Whitman's *Leaves of Grass* (1855-1892), Archibald MacLeish's *Conquistador* (1932), and Hart Crane's *The Bridge* (1930). Admittedly the work lacks the eloquent brilliance of *Conquistador*, and to compare Williams with Whitman is to stretch the superlatives until they become tenuous. Whitman writes like a great wind, whereas Williams wafts with far gentler breezes.

Paterson is a poem filled with variety and surprises. There are times when Williams turns his kaleidoscope so quickly that the reader becomes dizzy and would like to quote back to the poet the line: "Geeze, Doc, I guess it's all right but what the hell does it mean?" On the other hand, there are many passages of great lyrical beauty in *Paterson*, and a careful reading of the poem creates a feeling in the reader of having visited a typical American city and been taken on a tour of it by someone who tells its history as they walk along. More important, the reader becomes acquainted with the man himself, who is clever, witty, sensitive, wise, and deeply concerned with the people of his city and their problems. Thus does *Paterson* achieve its purpose and forge a bond between the reader of the poem and the poem's man and city.

Bibliography:

Duffey, Bernard. *A Poetry of Presence: The Writing of William Carlos Williams.* Madison: University of Wisconsin Press, 1986. Considers Williams' epic as a lyrical dramatization of his descent into the ambiguities of his concept of himself as an American poet. Williams, who was a doctor, wanted to reenact the facts of human misery in a new and healing speech.

Mariani, Paul L. "Putting Paterson on the Map: 1946-1961." In *William Carlos Williams: The*

Poet and His Critics. Chicago: American Library Association, 1975. Chronicles the struggle of critics and reviewers, including many notable poets, to come to grips with the meaning and importance of a strangely structured but major new work.

Markos, Donald W. *Ideas in Things: The Poems of William Carlos Williams*. Rutherford, N.J.: Fairleigh Dickinson University Press, 1994. Interprets *Paterson* in the context of Williams' idealist belief in beauty as the emanation of a universal, ideal reality through the particular world of things. This Platonism links him to Ralph Waldo Emerson and Jonathan Edwards in the American tradition of individual perception and creative imagination.

Sankey, Benjamin. *A Companion to William Carlos Williams's "Paterson."* Berkeley: University of California Press, 1971. Interpretive guide to the text, with pertinent information and comments by Williams. An introductory chapter presents Williams' philosophy, design, and methodology.

Schmidt, Peter. *William Carlos Williams, the Arts, and Literary Tradition*. Baton Rouge: Louisiana State University Press, 1988. The relationship of Williams' poetry to precisionist, cubist, and Dadaist aesthetics and to the literary tradition that preceded modernism. Williams used a variety of approaches to collage, while both critiquing and renewing epic form.

THE PATHFINDER
Or, The Inland Sea

Type of work: Novel
Author: James Fenimore Cooper (1789-1851)
Type of plot: Adventure
Time of plot: 1756
Locale: Lake Ontario and environs
First published: 1840

Principal characters:
> SERGEANT DUNHAM, an officer at the Oswego garrison
> MABEL DUNHAM, his daughter
> CHARLES CAP, Mabel's uncle
> NATTY BUMPPO (PATHFINDER), a frontier scout
> JASPER WESTERN, Pathfinder's friend
> LIEUTENANT DAVY MUIR, the garrison quartermaster

The Story:

Mabel Dunham and Charles Cap, her seaman uncle, were on their way to the home of her father, Sergeant Dunham. They were accompanied by Arrowhead, a Tuscarora Indian, and his wife, Dew-of-June. When they reached the Oswego River, they were met by Jasper Western and Natty Bumppo, the wilderness scout known as Pathfinder among the English and as Hawkeye among the Mohicans. Pathfinder led the party down the Oswego on the first step of the journey under his guidance. Chingachgook, Pathfinder's Mohican friend, warned the party of the presence of hostile Indians in the neighborhood. They hid but were discovered and had a narrow escape. Arrowhead and Dew-of-June disappeared, and Pathfinder's group feared they had been taken captive. Chingachgook was captured by the Iroquois, but he escaped. On the lookout for more hostile war parties, they continued their journey to the fort, where Mabel was joyfully welcomed by her father.

The sergeant tried to promote a romantic attachment between Mabel and Pathfinder, which was his real purpose in having brought Mabel to the frontier. Actually Mabel had already fallen in love with Jasper. When the commander of the post, Major Duncan, proposed Lieutenant Davy Muir as a possible mate for Mabel, the sergeant informed the major that Mabel was already betrothed to Pathfinder. Muir learned that he had been refused, but he did not give up hope.

A passage of arms was proposed to test the shooting ability of the men at the post. Jasper scored a bull's-eye. Muir shot from a strange position, and it was believed by all that he had missed, but he said he had hit Jasper's bullet. Pathfinder used Jasper's rifle and also struck the bullet in the bull's-eye. The next test of marksmanship was to drive a nail into a tree with a bullet. Jasper almost drove the nail into the tree; Pathfinder did. In the next test, shooting at a potato tossed into the air, Muir failed, but Jasper hit the potato in the center. A silken calash was the prize, and Jasper desired it greatly as a present for Mabel. He mentioned this to Pathfinder, who thereupon did no more than cut the skin of the potato. After he had lost the match, Pathfinder could not resist killing two gulls with one bullet, which allowed Mabel to understand how Jasper had won the calash. In appreciation, she gave Pathfinder a silver brooch.

An expedition was sent to one of the Thousand Islands to relieve the garrison there. The party was to leave in the *Scud*, a boat captured by Jasper. Before the party had departed, however, Major Duncan received a letter that caused him to suspect Jasper of being a French spy. Pathfinder refused to believe the charge against his friend, but when the *Scud* sailed under the command of Jasper, he was kept under strict surveillance by Sergeant Dunham and Charles Cap. On the way the *Scud* overtook Arrowhead and his wife, who were taken aboard. When Pathfinder began to question the Tuscarora, Arrowhead escaped in a canoe that the *Scud* was towing astern. Becoming suspicious, Sergeant Dunham removed Jasper from his command and sent him below. Charles Cap took over the management of the boat, but Cap, being a saltwater sailor, was unfamiliar with freshwater navigation. When a storm came up, it was necessary to call upon Jasper to save the ship. The *Scud* escaped from *Le Montcalm*, a French ship, and Jasper brought the *Scud* safely to port.

Pathfinder had fallen in love with Mabel, but when he proposed to her, she refused him. Muir had not given up his own suit. He admitted to Mabel that he had had three previous wives.

Sergeant Dunham decided to take some of his men and harass a French supply boat. Starting out with his detachment, he left six men at the post, Muir among them, with orders to look after the women. Soon after her father's departure, Mabel went for a walk and met Dew-of-June, who warned her of danger from Indians led by white men. Muir was unmoved by the intelligence when Mabel told him. Mabel then went to Corporal MacNab with her story, but he too treated Dew-of-June's warning lightly. While they talked, a rifle cracked in the nearby forest, and MacNab fell dead at her feet. Mabel ran to the blockhouse. The attacking party was composed of twenty Indians led by the Tuscarora renegade Arrowhead. Mabel, Cap, and Muir survived the ambush through the help of Dew-of-June, but Cap and Muir were captured a little later. Mabel discovered Chingachgook, who had been spying about the fort. She acquainted him with the details of the situation.

Pathfinder arrived secretly at the blockhouse. He had not been fooled by the dead bodies of the massacred people that the Indians had placed in lifelike poses along the riverbank. The relief party of soldiers under Sergeant Dunham was ambushed, but the sergeant, seriously wounded, managed to reach the blockhouse. Cap escaped from the Indians and also gained the protection of the blockhouse. The small group fought off the Indians during the night. Jasper arrived with men in time to relieve the situation. Muir, however, still believing Jasper to be a spy, ordered him bound. Arrowhead stabbed Muir and disappeared into the bushes, hotly pursued by Chingachgook, who later killed him. Muir died, and Captain Sanglier, the white leader of the Indians, admitted that the French spy had been Muir, not Jasper. On his deathbed Sergeant Dunham, thinking Jasper to be Pathfinder, took Jasper's hand, placed it in that of Mabel, and gave the two his blessing. He died before the surprised witnesses could correct his error. Deciding that Mabel really loved Jasper, Pathfinder relinquished his claim to her. Pathfinder disappeared into the wilderness with his Indian friend Chingachgook and was seen no more by Jasper and Mabel. From time to time, Indian messengers came to the settlement with gifts of furs for Mrs. Jasper Western, but no name ever accompanied these gifts.

Critical Evaluation:

Of the five novels in James Fenimore Cooper's Leatherstocking series, *The Pathfinder: Or, The Inland Sea* was the fourth. In the chronology of the hero Natty Bumppo's life, it is, however, the third tale. It finds Natty resurrected from the death described in *The Prairie*, which had been written thirteen years earlier. *The Pathfinder* is distinguished by being the first and only Leatherstocking story in which the celibate and thoroughly independent frontier scout falls in love with a woman.

Cooper was an essentially romantic writer, and although as a thorough and competent historian he was easily able to back up his fictional narrative with factual information, his primary purpose was to stir the reader's imagination through idealized portraits of frontier life. Cooper's most lasting appeal lies in his gift for storytelling. Working with even the simplest and least original plot, he was able to sustain the reader's interest by employing ambushes and chases, hairbreadth escapes, and harrowing violence, as well as sentiment, chivalry, and romance. Linked inextricably with such a colorful and adventure-filled story line is the familiar Cooper setting: The primal beauty of forest and sea and the grandeur and rich abundance of unspoiled nature provide an appropriate backdrop for courageous and manly deeds. The author was intimately familiar with the area around the mouth of the Oswego River, having spent the winter of 1808 there as a midshipman in the American Navy, and both his knowledge and love of the land are apparent in the descriptive passages of *The Pathfinder*.

Yet Cooper's talents as a storyteller and descriptive writer have obscured his merits as a serious artist whose works illustrate important social and religious concerns. One recurrent theme, for example, which is strongly apparent in *The Pathfinder*, is the idea that to achieve happiness and self-fulfillment, human beings must live according to their "gifts," or talents, be they great or limited. Cooper believed strongly in democracy but in a conservative way. He felt that the American continent was the perfect environment in which people could develop fresh and individualistic forms of society, but he feared that some frontierspeople were moving too close to anarchy. The key to success was that all individuals recognize and accept their separate places within the scheme of things, places determined not by heredity but by natural talent that located each person in a "class." Much of the interest in *The Pathfinder* stems from the question of Mabel Dunham's marriage, since it involves discoveries about talent and appropriate courses of action on the part not only of Mabel but also of Natty, Lieutenant Muir, Jasper Western, and Sergeant Dunham.

In addition to being aware of his true talents and calling and of his proper relationship to society, Natty Bumppo in *The Pathfinder* has also reached a high level of consciousness in the religious area, another crucial Cooper theme. Through this self-sufficient hero, the author conveys his conviction, which grew stronger with age, that Divine Providence was involved in human destiny. Natty's is a natural piety, a faith taught him by nature, which he calls "the temple of the Lord"; as he explains simply, "It is not easy to dwell always in the presence of God, and not feel the power of his goodness."

Bibliography:

Blakemore, Steven. "Language and World in *The Pathfinder*." *Modern Language Studies* 16, no. 3 (Summer, 1986): 237-246. Examines Cooper's treatment of his major characters through an examination of the differentiated language he uses and creates for them.

Darnell, Donald. "Manners on a Frontier: *The Pioneers*, *The Pathfinder*, and *The Deerslayer*." In *James Fenimore Cooper: Novelist of Manners*. Newark: University of Delaware Press, 1993. Explores the role of social class on the frontier. The main characters, Darnell claims, are fully aware and respectful of their own lower rank.

Kolodny, Annette. "Love and Sexuality in *The Pathfinder*." In *James Fenimore Cooper: A Collection of Critical Essays*, edited by Wayne Fields. Englewood Cliffs, N.J.: Prentice-Hall, 1979. Discusses Cooper's need to show the possibility of love for Natty Bumppo in order to make him a whole human being. Natty faces a choice between love of the forest and love of a woman.

Rans, Geoffrey. *Cooper's Leather-Stocking Novels: A Secular Reading*. Chapel Hill: University of North Carolina Press, 1991. Good introductory overview. The chapter "A Matter of Choice" shows how *The Pathfinder* focuses more on the mythical character of Natty Bumppo and less on the Indians and the wilderness than do the other Leatherstocking novels.

Walker, Warren S. "The Tragic Wilderness." In *James Fenimore Cooper: An Introduction and Interpretation*, by Warren S. Walker. New York: Holt, Rinehart and Winston, 1962. Places the work in the context of the Leatherstocking series and explores common themes and images. *The Pathfinder* carries Natty Bumppo through early middle age and through his last attempt at love.

PATIENCE
Or, Bunthorne's Bride

Type of work: Drama
Author: W. S. Gilbert (1836-1911)
Type of plot: Operetta
Time of plot: Nineteenth century
Locale: England
First performed: 1881; first published, 1881

> *Principal characters:*
> REGINALD BUNTHORNE, a fleshly poet
> ARCHIBALD GROSVENOR, an idyllic poet
> THE LADY JANE, a rapturous maiden
> PATIENCE, a dairymaid

The Story:

At Castle Bunthorne, twenty lovesick maidens pined and wilted for love of Reginald Bunthorne, a fleshly poet. Reginald, however, loved only Patience, the village milkmaid. Patience did not know what love was and thus did not know that the utmost happiness came from being miserable over unrequited love. The lovesick maidens set her straight, however, by showing her that to be in agony, weeping incessantly, was to be truly happy in love. Patience tried to remind them that just a year ago they had all been in love with dragoon guards, but they scorned her for being so ignorant about real love. A year ago they had not known Reginald, the poet.

The dragoon guards, billeted in the village, saw Reginald approaching, followed by the lovesick maidens, singing and playing love songs directed to the fleshly poet. The maidens ignored their former loves, having eyes only for Reginald. Reginald himself had eyes only for Patience, the milkmaid. At the insistence of the maidens, he read them his latest poem, into which he had poured his whole soul—as he did three times a day. The maidens swooned in ecstasy at the poetry, but Patience said it was just nonsense, which it was.

Later, alone, Reginald confessed that he was a sham, that he hated poetry and all other forms of aesthetic pleasure. When Patience came upon him, he made the same confession to her, telling her again that he loved only her, not poetry. However, Patience knew nothing of the love of which he spoke, for she had loved only her great-aunt and that love did not count. After Reginald had left her, one of the maidens told Patience that to love was to feel unselfish passion. Patience, ashamed that she had never been unselfish enough to love, promised that before she went to bed that night she would fall head over heels in love with somebody. In fact, she remembered that when she was a little girl she had liked a little boy of five. Now she was sorry that she had not loved him. It was her duty to love someone. If necessary, she would love a stranger.

Archibald Grosvenor appeared unexpectedly upon the scene. He was an idyllic poet who grieved because he was completely perfect. Since he had no rival on earth in perfection, it was his lot to be loved madly by everyone who saw him. Recognizing Patience, he told her that he was the little boy she had known when he was five. When he asked her to marry him, she refused. He was perfect; therefore she would not be acting unselfishly in loving him. If he had only one small imperfection, she said, she could marry him in good conscience. Candor forced him to admit that such was not the case. Patience told him, however, that he could love her even if she could not return his love, for she had faults. Grosvenor agreed, and they sadly parted.

Reginald Bunthorne prepared to raffle himself to the rapturous maidens, but before they could draw for him Patience entered and begged his forgiveness for not loving him sooner. Certainly to love such a creature would be unselfish; she would do her duty. As they left together, the lovesick maidens turned back to the dragoon guards, prepared to fall in love with them once more.

Before their embraces were over, Grosvenor entered, and the fickle maidens left the guards to follow Grosvenor. They loved him madly. All deserted Reginald but Lady Jane, one of the unattractive older women. She hoped her faithfulness would be rewarded, but she knew her beauty was too far gone ever to lure Reginald away from Patience.

Grosvenor would not stop loving Patience in order to love the rapturous maidens. He pitied them for not being able to receive his love and was annoyed by their attentions. They had followed him since Monday, with no half-holiday on Saturday. Then he read them one of his poems. It told of a little girl who put mice in the clock and vivisected her best doll and of a little boy who punched his little sisters' heads and put hot pennies down their backs. The maidens nearly swooned with admiration of his lyric beauty.

Patience continued to love Reginald, even though she found the matter difficult. He had no good habits and was not attractive, but it was her duty to love him and she did, shunning the perfect Grosvenor who loved her. None of the rapturous maidens except plain Lady Jane still loved Reginald, the others having taken their allegiance to Grosvenor. Reginald, resentful because the other maidens had forsaken him, decided to change his character; he would be as insipid as Grosvenor. Lady Jane promised her help.

The dragoon guards returned to the maidens, dressed as foppishly as even Grosvenor could dress. They acted insipidly and stupidly, and the lovesick maidens were impressed by this proof of their devotion. Reginald also became a changed man. He was mild and kind, even handsome. He told Grosvenor that he must change, that he had too long had the devotion that once was Reginald's. On the threat of a curse from Reginald, Grosvenor changed his nature and became a cad, admitting that he had long wished for a reasonable pretext for getting rid of his perfection.

When Patience saw that Reginald was now perfect and Grosvenor was not, she was happy, for she could now unselfishly love Grosvenor. The lovesick maidens, seeing Grosvenor forsake aestheticism, knew that since he was perfect he must be right. They, too, gave up the arts and returned to the dragoon guards. The duke of Dunstable, a dragoon officer, took plain Lady Jane, leaving the now perfect Reginald quite alone, without a bride.

Critical Evaluation:

William Schwenk Gilbert collaborated with the composer Arthur Seymour Sullivan on many highly successful comic operettas between 1875 and 1896, of which *Patience: Or, Bunthorne's Bride* is a major work. It satirizes both the mainstream and the avant-garde of British Victorian culture. These specific targets, however, are also manifestations of such universal human foibles as the desire to impress the opposite sex, jealousy of rivals in love and publicity, and the fickle nature of fame. *Patience* was one of the first literary works to recognize and satirize the cultural faddishness made possible by improved communication in the nineteenth century. *Patience* remains a favorite because of its essentially timeless conflicts and characters, and its highly polished lyrics matched with one of Sullivan's most accomplished scores.

Gilbert incorporates contemporary debates about art and artists in his libretto. By the 1870's, an artistic counterculture was challenging the established culture of Victorian England by emphasizing an otherworldly beauty at odds with everyday life. With its roots in the Oxford Movement to respiritualize the Anglican church in the 1840's and in the Pre-Raphaelite movement among artists to separate themselves from realistic and popular art in the 1850's, this counterculture tried to reject everything modern, middle class, and commercial, in favor of whatever seemed ancient, aristocratic, and spiritual. Through newspapers and magazines such as the humorous *Punch*, these intellectual currents were made familiar to many people beyond the artistic and academic worlds of London and the universities. Medieval art, loose, flowing clothing, and an overly refined distaste for the crude ordinary world became popular among not only a few artists and students but also a wide range of people who wished to identify with the avant-garde. Playing upon ordinary people's interest in these debates as well as their suspicion of artists in general and resentment of the counterculture's attacks on middle-class sensibilities, Gilbert's libretto parodies avant-garde ideas while ensuring that down-to-earth virtue ultimately triumphs. The central character, the outrageously dressed, hypersensitive artist Reginald Bunthorne, is a composite of several persons who were famous in the 1870's, including painter James A. McNeill Whistler, painter-poet Dante Gabriel Rossetti, poet Algernon Charles Swinburne, and the playwright and media star Oscar Wilde (whose lecture tour of the United States in 1882 was arranged by Gilbert and Sullivan's theater manager Richard D'Oyly Carte in part to educate American audiences about aestheticism so that they would attend *Patience*).

Within this specifically nineteenth century context, Gilbert's complex, farcical plot turns on the most traditional of themes: the many complications of love (requited and unrequited) and the rivalry between suitors of maidens and fame. In the first of the operetta's two acts, the major conflicts in love are neatly paralleled. On the female side, twenty lovesick maidens swooning for Bunthorne are set against the individual character Patience the milkmaid, who insists that she has no idea what love is. On the male side, the individual character Bunthorne, who loves only Patience (the one woman not infatuated with him), is set against the mainstream dragoon guards, stereotypical soldiers who expect that "every beauty will feel it her duty" to fall in love with a man in a uniform. Bunthorne and the maidens are satirized for their artificial ultrapoetical pose, and Patience and the soldiers for their literal-minded inability to comprehend the pose.

In the second act, the conflicts focus the satire more directly on the masks the characters put on as they try to impress one another. Beneath the humorous surface lie not only tensions between appearance and reality, as Gilbert calls attention to the absurd traps the characters set for themselves, but also a need to disparage any commitment to anti-middle-class values as hypocritical. Thus Bunthorne, who in his patter song directly admits "I'm an aesthetic sham," does not really admire the aesthetic women or believe in the values he pretends to personify, but maintains his pose to keep the fawning devotion of the female chorus. The lovesick maidens play a version of the same game, pretending to be aesthetic and, ironically, driving Bunthorne and Grosvenor away by their efforts to win them. Grosvenor feels oppressed by the devotion Bunthorne craves, but tolerates the lovesick maidens because of a misplaced sense of duty until he is given the chance to become commonplace. Even the soldiers, with equal insincerity and the funniest results of all, mimic Bunthorne's dress and manner in the hope of winning back the love of the maidens.

Only two characters, both women, are not hypocrites: Patience and Lady Jane. In satirizing Patience, Gilbert makes fun of her unsophisticated ignorance of the aesthetic fad and of her naïve willingness to accept at face value the other characters' overblown puffings about poetry, true love, and duty. In satirizing Lady Jane, however, Gilbert is less playful and shows a strain of mean-spiritedness. The audience is invited to laugh at Lady Jane for being a plain, middle-aged woman in love, and for maintaining her loyalty to Bunthorne and aestheticism when everyone else deserts them. Despite a poignant song in which she laments the inevitable depredations of aging, Jane is more ridiculed than sympathized with.

As is always the case in Gilbert's librettos, mainstream values triumph in the end. In *Patience*, that triumph involves Grosvenor's self-transformation into a perfect representative of the consuming middle class, "a steady and stolid-y, jolly Bank-holiday . . . matter-of-fact young man." All of the lovesick maidens except Lady Jane similarly reenter the middle class, declaring devotion to the exclusive department store Swears & Wells and pairing off with the soldiers. When the curtain falls with Bunthorne the only character not happily paired off with a member of the opposite sex, the cult of art and beauty has been tamed.

"Critical Evaluation" by Julia Whitsitt

Bibliography:

Baily, Leslie. *Gilbert and Sullivan and Their World*. London: Thames and Hudson, 1973. Examines the original production of *Patience* and considers the play as a satire on Pre-Raphaelite poets and aesthetes such as Rossetti and Oscar Wilde. Contains photographs and sketches of early productions of the opera.

Dunn, George E. *A Gilbert and Sullivan Dictionary*. New York: Da Capo Press, 1971. Goes beyond the mere listing of characters to include allusions to Greek and Roman mythology; Latin, French, German, and Italian languages; mathematics; rhetoric; and other topics. Shows correlations between various Gilbert and Sullivan plays.

Godwin, A. H. *Gilbert and Sullivan: A Critical Appreciation of the Savoy Operas*. Port Washington, N.Y.: Kennikat Press, 1969. Includes a consideration of *Patience* as a satirical gust of common sense in the midst of the aesthetic movement. Shows antecedents of characters in the opera.

Jones, John Bush, ed. *W. S. Gilbert: A Century of Scholarship and Commentary*. New York: New York University Press, 1970. Includes a study of the sources Gilbert drew on in writing *Patience*, a consideration of the character of Archibald Grosvenor, and two pieces on the opera's place in the tradition of the Greek comic drama.

Moore, Frank Ledlie. *Handbook of Gilbert and Sullivan*. New York: Schocken Books, 1975. Gives a good overview and synopsis of *Patience* and examines its satire of the aesthetic movement. Considers the role of Richard D'Oyly Carte in the success of the play and in Gilbert and Sullivan's other work.

PATIENCE AND SARAH

Type of work: Novel
Author: Isabel Miller (Alma Routsong, 1924-　　)
Type of plot: Love
Time of plot: Early 1880's
Locale: Connecticut and New York
First published: 1969, as *A Place for Us*

Principal characters:
>MA and PA DOWLING
>RACHEL, their second daughter
>SARAH, their oldest daughter
>PARSON DANIEL PEEL, a bookseller who befriends Sarah
>PATIENCE WHITE, a young woman who falls in love with Sarah
>EDWARD, Patience's brother
>MARTHA, his wife

The Story:

Patience White lived with her brother Edward, his wife Martha, and their children. As Patience and Martha sat inhospitably doing their winter chores, Sarah Dowling delivered firewood. Intrigued with this young woman, Patience invited her to dinner, later telling Sarah that she would go homesteading with her.

On the Sabbath, Patience skipped a religious meeting to make plans with Sarah. Sarah confessed her feelings of love for Patience, and they kissed. Later, Sarah told her sister Rachel that she had "found her mate" in Patience, so Rachel could not go homesteading with her. This angered Rachel greatly.

The next day, Patience could barely suppress her happiness. Her mood changed when Edward told her Pa Dowling had come to their house demanding that Patience be kept off his land. Meanwhile, Pa told Sarah that Rachel had told him everything. For ten days, whenever Sarah headed for Patience's house, Pa beat her.

After Rachel told Sarah to lie so that Pa would let her see Patience, Sarah and Pa went together to ask Patience if she wanted to go away with Sarah. Patience said she could not. Back home, Sarah announced that she would leave as soon as possible. Being supportive, Ma told her Patience was probably frightened. After cutting her hair to "look like a boy," Sarah became Sam, and, in April, with a few possessions in a bedroll, she stopped by Patience's house, but Patience was not home.

Sarah/Sam headed north, exchanging chores for room and board. Everyone tried to detain her, thinking she was a runaway apprentice until she met Parson Daniel Peel in his wagon. He hired her to help with his bookselling.

Traveling with Parson, Sarah/Sam learned to read and learned about the world. When she expressed her pleasure in his company, Parson made advances, saying men have always loved one another; Sam replied that she was really Sarah. He began treating her like a woman. As summer was ending, Parson headed to New York, and Sarah started for home.

Sarah wanted to go directly to Patience but went instead to her family. When Rachel spoke of Patience, Sarah pretended to have feelings for Parson. The next morning, Sarah worked bringing in corn; Patience came to welcome her.

Sunday afternoon, Sarah went to Patience's house. When Patience arrived, she took Sarah to bed for kisses. They were apart Monday through Saturday and together on Sunday afternoons. One Sunday, Patience showed Sarah that they could do more than kiss. Later, Patience again mentioned homesteading. With Sarah reluctant, Patience compromised, insisting Sarah see her every day for lessons. The first time, Sarah brought her mother, and the three enjoyed playing cards.

The next day, during a storm, Sarah did not come, so Patience went to her. After lessons, despite urgings to stay the night, Patience returned home. Every day after Sarah came to her lessons with a sister.

One Sunday, Martha found Patience and Sarah kissing. They prepared to meet Edward, who decided to pray over the matter. Patience told Sarah that he would probably ask her to leave, but it would not happen until Sarah was ready.

Martha brought Patience St. Paul's passage forbidding such behavior; the passage equally rebuked those who judge. Martha described how she had thought life would be with the three of them together and left. Edward returned; his solution was that Patience must leave; he would buy her portion of the house and provide for her. She told Sarah when she arrived with Ma, and, with Ma's support, Sarah agreed to go.

In March, Edward sleighed the women to the coastal trader; it felt like their wedding day. Arranging passage to New York, Edward blessed them and hugged both good-bye.

Sarah watched as the ship set sail; Patience stayed below deck. Going below, Sarah was grabbed by a man who only released her when Patience appeared. For protection, they began training Sarah to be a lady.

On the way to shore, the captain told them of safe lodgings; he admitted that Edward had asked him to look after them. After supper, they were at last alone in their own room.

Fellow boarders warned the women that the area where they wanted to live, Genesee, was expensive—a problem echoed by Parson during a visit with his family and by a banker the women consulted. Walking to the theater, Parson suggested Sarah consider Greene County; she did not tell Patience.

The next morning, while Patience made plans, Sarah lied to justify waiting, the lie ruining her day. That night, Sarah woke Patience and confessed. Patience forgave her, and they made love and slept contentedly.

They took a steamboat to Greene County, landed in Hudson, and took a ferry to Kaatskill, where they began their search. Sarah explored farms; Patience sewed and painted. While boarders speculated about the women, they liked Patience. This admiration led to the sale of her first painting.

In mid-May, Sarah and Patience found their farm and moved. After the seller left, they hugged and kissed in the open. That first night, they made a comfortable camp and began work. A dog adopted them; they named him George. One night, he woke them with his barking, warning them of a wolf. Sarah shot the wolf, and the bounty for it paid for the roof.

A week later, they moved inside. While Patience baked and painted, Sarah built a bed. When the bed was made, they attempted to initiate it but loosened its webbing. Working until late, they bedded on the floor, where love returned.

Critical Evaluation:

In 1969, when *Patience and Sarah* was first published as *A Place for Us*, few works dealt positively with love between women. Isabel Miller wrote this work and three others, *The Love of Good Women* (1986), *Side by Side* (1990), and *A Dooryard Full of Flowers* (1993), because she felt the world did not understand lesbianism. She made it her purpose to help educate the world, hoping to make being a lesbian easier for others. She set *Patience and Sarah* in the early 1880's (at a time before the word *lesbian* was used) to show that this love was not new; it had a history. While the novel was originally designed to appeal to a broad audience, some suggest a younger audience, it has been a classic with all ages in the gay sector of the women's movement since its publication, partly because its publication coincided with the beginning of the gay liberation movement.

The story draws on the life of Mary Ann Willson, a painter, and Miss Brundidge, her companion; the couple lived on a farm in Greene County, New York, in the early 1800's. The voice of the story alternates between Sarah's and Patience's—each having equal time, representing the equality of the relationship, and each speaking in the first person, drawing the reader into the woman's view of the relationship and the conflicts experienced as she feels her way in this new world. Miller also uses this device to illustrate differences between the women, their styles of upbringing, and their social class. When Patience is talking, her grammar and vocabulary follow a generally standardized dialect of English, peppered with biblical references. When Sarah speaks, her word choice is associated more with working-class individuals or with those living in rural communities.

As compared with other works available at its publication, Regina Minudri wrote in *Library Journal* that *Patience and Sarah* provided a better introduction to lesbianism than either Radclyffe Hall's *The Well of Loneliness* (1928), with its speculation on causes of lesbianism, or Lillian Hellman's *The Children's Hour* (1934), and its guilt-driven plot.

In her examination of lesbian fiction published from 1969 to 1989, *The Safe Sea of Women*, Bonnie Zimmerman outlined characteristics that can be applied to *Patience and Sarah*. Lesbians are often cast as outsiders or as different and unique individuals given their time and place. In the early 1880's, Patience is educated, a painter, and financially independent; Sarah, the oldest of seven daughters, is physically strong and has been trained to be the boy in the family, so she wears men's clothes and does men's work. Neither is devout in the Puritan religion of the New England of their time. The author begs the question whether they are lesbians because of these differences or whether their differences open them to nontraditional sexual expressions.

Joy is the emotion exhibited by many characters in novels from this period. Sarah and Patience know there were women like them because the Bible complains about them. Even though they have no living models, they are not confused in their love for each other; it is easy and natural. Their conflict arises in discovering a safe environment in which to express their love and sexuality away from society's conventions and censure. Hence, they want to have their own farm.

Authors of this time supply their characters with this freedom through pastoralism, an escape from the confining, civilized world into an idealistic, freeing frontier. Patience and Sarah move from the land of their families in Connecticut (referred to as "frosty" and lacking passion supposedly because of the Puritan religion) to Greene County, New York, where everyone seems open and friendly and where they establish a secluded farm, becoming amazingly self-sufficient. In this idyllic setting, the land cares for them, giving them gifts—first a dog becomes their protector, then a wolf gives his life to pay for their roof. Despite this escape, the author presents the women characters as yearning for community and role models. Sarah in particular wishes to meet others like them with whom to share their happiness.

Another theme involves lesbian feminist fiction's general rejection of the religious definition of homosexuality as a sin beyond others. When Martha quotes St. Paul to Patience, the passage equates the sin of engaging in homosexual activity with judging those who participate in it.

It has also been suggested that lesbian characters often lack a mother or are unlikely to become mothers. Though Sarah's mother is very much present and supportive, Patience never mentions hers. Patience's brother believes the women can succeed together because there will be no children.

Overall, the work has established itself as an enduring classic of love between women and provides excellent material for discussion of stereotypes about lesbians.

Su A. Cutler

Bibliography:

Juhasz, Suzanne. *Reading from the Heart: Women, Literature, and the Search for True Love.* New York: Viking, 1994. After examining twentieth century women authors' writings and the theme of the search for love, Juhasz examines works by Isabel Miller and Louisa May Alcott in case studies.

"Routsong, Alma." In *Contemporary Authors: A Bio-Bibliographical Guide to Current Authors and Their Works*, edited by Clare D. Kinsman. Detroit, Mich.: Gale Research, 1975. The article contains an introduction to the author and a list of her early works.

"Routsong, Alma." In *Gay and Lesbian Literature*, edited by Sharon Malinowski. Detroit: St. James Press, 1994. The article provides a biography of Routsong and a list of critical sources and reviews of works, exploring ways particular works such as *Patience and Sarah* reflect Routsong's personal growth and change.

Wavle, Elizabeth M. "Isabel Miller, pseud. (1924-   )." In *Contemporary Lesbian Writers of the U.S.: A Bio-Bibliographical Critical Sourcebook*, edited by Sandra Pollack and Denise D. Knight. Westport, Conn.: Greenwood Press, 1993. In addition to a biography, major works, including *Patience and Sarah*, and their themes are discussed. Most helpful is the section on the critical reception of Miller's works.

Zimmerman, Bonnie. *The Safe Sea of Women: Lesbian Fiction 1969-1989.* Boston: Beacon Press, 1990. While Zimmerman does not provide in-depth analysis of *Patience and Sarah*, she uses the novel to illustrate general trends in lesbian fiction: pastoralism, the longing for home, and the lack of religious definitions of homosexuality as sin in lesbian fiction.

PEACE

Type of work: Drama
Author: Aristophanes (c. 450-c. 385 B.C.E.)
Type of plot: Satire
Time of plot: Peloponnesian War
Locale: Athens
First performed: *Eirēnē*, 421 B.C.E. (English translation 1837)

Principal characters:
TRYGAEUS, a citizen of Athens
HERMES
WAR
HIEROCLES, a soothsayer from Areus

The Story:

Being tired of the wars and hungry, Trygaeus, like most Athenian citizens, called upon the gods for aid. Unlike the others, however, Trygaeus searched for a way to gain entrance to the heavens so that he might make a personal plea to Zeus and thus save himself, his family, and his country. He had tried climbing ladders but had succeeded only in falling and breaking his head. He decided to ride to heaven on the back of a dung beetle, in the manner of Bellerophon on Pegasus.

This attempt to make his way to heaven succeeded, but when Trygaeus arrived at the house of Zeus he found that the gods had moved to that point farthest away from Greece so that they need see no more of the fighting among those peoples and hear no more prayers from them. Having afforded the Greeks an opportunity for peace, which they had ignored, the gods had now abandoned them and given the god War, aided by his slave Tumult, full power to do with them as he pleased.

Trygaeus soon found out that War had already begun to carry out his plans. He had cast Peace into a deep pit and was now preparing to pound up all the cities of Greece in a mortar. Trygaeus watched him as he threw in leeks representing the Laconians, garlic for the Megarians, cheese for the Sicilians, and honey for the Athenians. Fortunately, this deed of destruction was momentarily postponed because War could not find a pestle. After several unsuccessful attempts on the part of Tumult to find one for him, War himself had to leave the mortar and go make one.

His departure gave Trygaeus the chance he needed to save Peace, and immediately he called on all the states of Greece to come to his aid. All came, but with noise enough to bring Zeus himself back from his retreat. Hermes, who had been left in the house of Zeus, was aroused and angered by the noise, and could only be cajoled into allowing them to go on with their work after many promises of future glorification.

Even at such a crucial moment the people refused to work together. The Boeotians only pretended to work; Lamachus was in the way of everyone; the Argives laughed at the others but profited from their mistakes; the Megarians tried hard but had not enough strength to do very much. The Laconians and the Athenians worked earnestly and seriously, but it was primarily through the efforts of the farmers that Peace was finally freed. With her in the pit were Opora and Theoria. Everyone was now apparently happy, and to ensure the peace Opora was given to Trygaeus as a wife and Theoria was sent to the Senate. All then descended to earth, where preparations for the wedding were begun.

Before going on with the wedding, Trygaeus decided to make a sacrifice to Peace. During his preparations he was interrupted by Hierocles, a prophet from Areus. Trygaeus and his servant both tried to ignore the prophet because they felt he had been attracted only by the smell of cooking meat, but he was not to be put off so easily. When Hierocles learned to whom the sacrifice was being made, he began to berate them and gave them many oracles to show that this was not a lasting peace and that such could not be achieved. When they were ready to eat the meat, however, he was prepared to agree with anything they said in order that he might satisfy his own hunger. Trygaeus, wishing to have nothing to do with the soothsayer, beat Hierocles and drove him away.

With peace newly restored to the country, the people of Athens seemed to enjoy the feasting and mirth before the wedding. A sickle-maker approached Trygaeus and praised him for bringing back peace and prosperity, but he was followed by an armorer and various other personages representing those trades which had profited by the war. These people were unable to join in the festivities; theirs was not so happy a lot. Trygaeus, however, had no sympathy for them and offered only scorn. When they asked what they could do with their wares in order to regain at least the cost of manufacturing them, he mocked them. He offered to buy their crests and use them to dust the tables, and he offered to buy their breastplates for use as privies. He told them to sell their helmets to the Egyptians who could use them for measuring laxatives, and he told them to sell their spears as vine-props. When Opora appeared, the whole party went off to the wedding singing the *Hymen Hymenaeus*.

Critical Evaluation:

After a decade of fighting, Sparta and Athens were ready to make some kind of peace between themselves, and the peace of Nicias was nearly complete. In this play Aristophanes joyfully looks forward to a successful conclusion of the negotiations, although it was not to be achieved as quickly as he expected. In the play he anticipates some of the difficulties to be overcome within the various Greek states, and he shows that the farmers of the country will be most instrumental in bringing about the peace.

Peace is distinct from many of the plays of Aristophanes in representing not a bitter or frustrated complaint about contemporary politics, but a kind of celebration in advance of an actual peace treaty, which was signed only ten days after the play was performed. Produced in 421 B.C.E., *Peace* was written with every expectation that the Peace of Nicias, which temporarily halted the conflict between Athens and Sparta, would soon become official and permanently put an end to the Peloponnesian War. Another cause for hope was that the Athenian general Cleon, one of the great obstacles to peace (at least in Aristophanes' opinion), had fallen during the previous summer in the same battle in which the leading Spartan general, Brasidas, had also been killed. Aristophanes' comic fantasy expresses an impatient longing for an end to the war, and one of its most remarkable features is an elaborate anticipatory celebration of the conclusion of actual negotiations.

The character Trygaeus reflects the play's topicality. Like many protagonists in the plays of Aristophanes, he is stubborn and self-assertive in achieving his goal. He flies up to heaven and finds out directly from Zeus himself what is preventing Peace, who is personified as a beautiful goddess, from returning as soon as possible to the earth. Trygaeus undertakes his fantastic mission not merely for himself or for the Athenians, but on behalf of all the Greeks. The play acknowledges that all of the Greeks are probably weary of the conflict, whatever private disputes they still may have. Although the identity of the chorus seems to change in the course of the play, at one point the play's Panhellenic aspect is emphasized by an indication that the chorus is composed of elements from all cities and all classes of Greece. Trygaeus' fantastic plan, or great idea as it is sometimes called, therefore seems nobler than the notions concocted by other Aristophanic protagonists. Moreover, Trygaeus, an elderly Athenian farmer, is rather pleasant and likable, despite the play's typical emphasis on obscenity, which was probably a traditional feature of the comic genre.

Mounted on his giant dung beetle, a grotesque comic parody of the winged horse Pegasus, Trygaeus ascends to heaven only to discover that most of the Olympian gods have vacated Olympus in disgust with the bellicose ways of human beings. Their departure is an Aristophanic refutation of the traditional Greek concept of heroism, which asserted that the gods delighted in the martial prowess of mortals. Trygaeus' beetle is also more than a comic prop. In Aesop's fable of the beetle and the eagle, which is mentioned in several of Aristophanes' plays, an avenging beetle who pursues an eagle right up to the throne of Zeus is a symbol of the righteous vengeance of the lowly on the mighty. This image is appropriate to the bold plan of an elderly Athenian peasant. The first half of the play depicts the determined hero's encounters with those few gods who remain: the Olympian Hermes and the personified abstractions War, Peace, Opora ("late harvest"), and Theoria ("sacred festival").

When Trygaeus discovers that an audience with Zeus on the matter of peace is impossible, he encounters only token resistance from Hermes to his new plan to bring Peace back to earth himself. As befits a play about peace, *Peace* contains no real contest in which the protagonist defends his or her plan against vigorous opponents and ultimately emerges the victor. As threatening as he seems, the good War is quickly dispatched. After Peace is retrieved from the place where she is buried—by a cooperative effort of the Greeks who form the chorus— and Trygaeus returns to earth, all that remains to do is celebrate and enjoy the benefits of peace. There is, again, only token resistance to the enjoyment of Trygaeus' success. Characters such as Hierocles, the arms-dealer, and the sons of Lamachus offer comic foils but no real challenge to Trygaeus, who busily prepares for the celebratory sacrifice and his marriage to Opora.

The wedding of the peasant Trygaeus and the goddess Opora, a literal marriage of heaven and earth, is symbolic of the new state of peace that has been achieved. The extravagant enjoyment of food, wine, and love appears also in other plays of Aristophanes, especially when the protagonist overcomes all opposition to his or her plan. What makes *Peace* unusual is that the celebration is an event in which all Greeks are implicitly invited to participate, as spectators of a comic fantasy and in reality as the peace negotiations come to their conclusion. It should be noted that the celebratory mood of the play is also captured in some of the most beautiful and engaging lyrics of Aristophanes, choral songs that capture the essence of the longing for peace and the eager anticipation of its realization.

The celebration marked by *Peace*, which won second prize at the dramatic competition, was to be short-lived. The next few years were tense and open hostilities broke out again between Athens and Sparta in 411 B.C.E. with part of Athenian territory occupied by a Spartan garrison. Aristophanes' message of peace and Panhellenism was lost in the renewed fighting of the Peloponnesian War.

"Critical Evaluation" by John M. Lawless

Bibliography:
Aristophanes. *Acharnians.* Edited and translated by Alan H. Sommerstein. 2d ed. Warminster, Wiltshire, England: Aris & Phillips, 1984. Provides scholarly introduction, bibliography,

Greek text, facing English translation, and commentary keyed to the translation. Sommerstein's translation supersedes most earlier versions.

Dover, K. J. *Aristophanic Comedy*. Berkeley: University of California Press, 1972. Useful and authoritative study of the plays of Aristophanes. Chapter 10 gives a synopsis of the play, discusses problems in production, and comments on the play's themes of peace and Panhellenism. An essential starting point for study of the play.

Harriott, Rosemary M. *Aristophanes: Poet and Dramatist*. Baltimore: The Johns Hopkins University Press, 1986. A recent study of Aristophanes. The plays are discussed not in individual chapters but as each illustrates the central themes and techniques of Aristophanes' work.

Spatz, Lois. *Aristophanes*. Boston: Twayne, 1978. A reliable introduction to the comedy of Aristophanes for the general reader. Chapter 2 summarizes the problems of the play and offers a good discussion of imagery.

Whitman, Cedric. *Aristophanes and the Comic Hero*. Cambridge, Mass.: Harvard University Press, 1964. A standard work on the characterization of the Aristophanic protagonist. Chapter 3, "City and Individual," contains an excellent discussion of themes and offers valuable comments on the special characteristics of the play.

THE PEASANTS

Type of work: Novel
Author: Władysław Reymont (1867-1925)
Type of plot: Social
Time of plot: Late nineteenth century
Locale: Poland
First published: Chłopi, 1904-1909 (English translation, 1924-1925)

Principal characters:
MATTHIAS BORYNA, a well-to-do peasant
ANTEK, Matthias' son
DOMINIKOVA, a widow
YAGNA, her daughter
HANKA, Antek's wife

The Story:

It was autumn, and the peasants of Lipka village were hurrying to finish the harvest before winter. In Matthias Boryna's barnyard, the villagers gathered to see a cow that had been chased from manor lands and was now dying of colic. Hanka, Matthias' daughter-in-law, took the loss most to heart when old Kuba, the lame stableman, said that he could do nothing for the stricken cow.

That night Matthias, charged with having fathered a servant girl's child, went to visit the *voyt*, the headman of the village, to ask about his trial. The *voyt*, after assuring Matthias that he would get off easily in court, flattered Matthias and told him he should marry again, now that his second wife was dead. Matthias pretended he was too old, but he was hopeful of marrying Yagna, the daughter of Dominikova. Yagna would some day inherit three acres of land.

The next morning, the case against Matthias was dismissed. After the trial, Matthias met Dominikova and tried to sound her out on her plans for her daughter.

On the day of the autumn sale, Matthias went off to sell some hogs, and Hanka her geese. Old Matthias, pleased when Yagna accepted some bright ribbons, asked her hand in marriage. He did not know that his son Antek, Hanka's husband, was secretly in love with Yagna. When Matthias settled six acres upon Yagna in return for the three she brought with her marriage portion, Antek and his father fought, and Matthias ordered his son off the farm. Antek and Hanka moved with their children into the miserable cabin of Hanka's father.

The wedding of Matthias and Yagna was a hilarious affair. In the midst of the merriment, Kuba, poaching on manor lands, was shot in the leg by a gamekeeper. Fearing the hospital, he cut off his own leg and died from loss of blood.

Winter came swiftly, and wolves lurked near the peasants' stock barns. That winter, Hanka and Antek had to sell their cow to keep themselves in food. Antek took work with men building a new sawmill. Matthew, the foreman, was his enemy, for Matthew also loved Yagna. One day, Antek overheard Matthew bragging that he had been with Yagna in her bedroom. In a great fury, Antek struck Matthew so hard that the carpenter broke several ribs when he fell over the railing and into the river.

At Christmas, there was great rejoicing in Matthias' house, for Yagna was pregnant. At the midnight mass on Christmas Eve, Yagna and Antek saw each other for a moment. Antek asked her to meet him behind the haystack. That winter, the peasants of the village came to Matthias to report that a part of the forest that the peasants used for gathering wood had been sold by the manor people. Unhappily, Matthias allowed himself to be dragged into the dispute. While Matthias was away, Antek went to his father's farm to see Yagna. Returning, Matthias nearly caught them together.

One night at the inn, Antek became drunk, ignored his wife, and asked Yagna to dance with him. Matthias arrived, seized Yagna, and took her away. On his way home, Antek found his wife almost dead in the snow. From that time on, Matthias treated Yagna like a servant.

Antek lost his job, and Hanka was forced to go with the paupers seeking firewood in the forest. Walking home through the storm, Hanka was given a ride by Matthias. He insisted that Hanka come back to his farm the next day. That night, Antek took Yagna into the orchard. Coming upon them, Matthias lit up a straw stack in order to see them. Antek and the old man fought. Then Antek fled and the fire spread, threatening the whole village. Yagna fled to her family. Everyone avoided Antek and refused to speak to him.

At last, Matthias took Yagna back, but only as a hired servant. Hanka was with him much of the time. When Yagna began to see Antek again, the old man took no notice.

Word came that the squire was cutting timber on land the peasants claimed. The next morning, a fight took place in the forest as the villagers tried to protect their trees. Antek thought he might kill his own father in the confusion, but when he saw Matthias struck down, he killed the woodcutter who had wounded his father. Antek walked alongside as Matthias was carried home.

When spring came, many of the villagers, Antek among them, were in jail after the fight in the forest. Fields went unplowed. Old Matthias lay insensible. Yagna had now begun to consort with the *voyt*. It seemed as if the devil himself had possessed the village. Easter was a sad season, because the men were still in prison. Word went around that the squire, who had been ordered to stop the sale of his land, was in desperate straits for money and vowing revenge upon the peasants. Shortly after Easter, Hanka gave birth to a boy, who was named Roch. Although gifts were given out in Antek's absence, the christening did not seem complete.

At last, the peasants were set free. Their homecoming was a happy occasion in every cabin but that of Matthias, for Antek had not been released. Yagna was also unhappy. Even Matthew, the carpenter who had once loved her, now ignored her for the younger Teresa. One night, Matthias arose from his stupor. For hours, he wandered the fields as if about to sow his land. In the morning, he fell over and died.

Summer brought additional woes to the peasants. There were quarrels over Matthias' land. Some Germans came to occupy the squire's land, but the peasants threatened them and they went away. The squire made arrangements to parcel out the land to the peasants, and some of them bought new land for homesteading.

Old Dominikova and Simon, one of her sons, had quarreled, and Simon bought his own land from the squire. Simon and his wife, Nastka, received many gifts from the villagers who wanted to spite old Dominikova. When the *voyt*'s accounts were found to be short, the villagers blamed Yagna. Antek was released from prison and returned to work on the farm. He was still attracted to Yagna, but the duties of his farm and the possibility that he still might be sent to Siberia pressed even harder upon him. That summer, the organist's son, Yanek, came home from school. In a short time, he and Yagna were seen together. At last, the peasants put Yagna on a manure cart and told her never to return to the village.

The summer was dry and the harvest scanty. One day a wandering beggar stopped at Nastka's house. He gave her some balm for Yagna, who had taken refuge there. As the sound of the

Angelus rose up through the evening air, he strode away. For the food Nastka had given him, he called down God's blessing on her peasant home.

Critical Evaluation:

Although *The Peasants* was not translated into English until 1924, when its author was awarded the Nobel Prize for Literature, the Germans had already recognized its worth. It has been rumored that during the German occupation of Poland in World War I, German officers were required to read and study the novel as a text to enable them to understand the Polish customs and mores and, thus, have more success in controlling the stubborn and proud peasants than did the previous occupiers, the Russians.

The Peasants is epic in the sweep and significance of its story. The problems of Europe are contained in this novel: overpopulation, poor and overworked soil, ignorance, imperialism. The novel is at once a text on the subject of mass sociology and a human, heartwarming narrative. In keeping with the seasonal movement of its story, Władysław Reymont's masterpiece is divided into four volumes: *Autumn, Winter, Spring,* and *Summer.*

As an intimate, detailed picture of the Polish peasant, the book is magnificent. Using a naturalistic approach, Reymont gives an unbiased account of both the sordidness and the beauty of the peasants' lives. Between these extremes, there seems to be no middle ground. Life is filled either with animal joy and lustiness (as is shown in the elaborate details of the three-day celebration of Matthias and Yagna's wedding) or with intimate details of poverty, despair, and illness. Yet the peasants never surrender; they all accept their fate.

The novel is more than a sociological analysis of Polish life, however, for Reymont creates characters who are individual and vital. He explores in detail the universal struggles of society: the poor who produce against the rich who exploit; the young who struggle for what is legally theirs against the old who desperately try to hold on to their hard-earned land. He examines the eternal conflicts between the sexes, between humans and nature, between religion and super-stition, and the lonely struggle of one asserting and defending oneself in a harsh, unyielding, threatening world.

Reymont never allows himself to abandon the basic standard of naturalism: objectivity. Although the reader becomes more involved with some characters than others, the involvement is never caused by Reymont's intervention.

Yagna is perhaps the most interesting character in the novel. She is one of the few villagers not motivated by greed; true, she delightedly accepts a scarf and ribbons Matthias buys for her at the fair, but she is completely uninterested in the marriage settlement, which is handled by her greedy mother, Dominikova. The mother realizes the problems that may arise from the May-December marriage, but she is eager to obtain the six acres Matthias offers. The mother does not force Yagna to marry; Yagna is motivated solely by animal spirit and does not really care. Married to an old man, her health and vitality drive her into the younger arms of Antek and Matthew, but it is this same animalism that initially attracts Matthias to her. She lets her mother handle such things as marriage settlements; her own interests are more physical.

Yagna is driven by sexual passions she cannot begin to understand. She neither appears concerned about the quarrel she has caused between Antek and his father, nor does she worry about the rupture she has caused between Antek and Hanka. She sees only Antek's youth, and that is sufficient for her. She has the same intensity of sexual attraction for Matthew and is unable to control her passion. When he creeps into her darkened cottage before the wedding, she defends herself before her mother by pleading that she could not keep him off.

Yagna cannot transfer her passionate feelings to old Matthias Boryna, which he, a deeply proud man, resents. Although he has heard rumors about Yagna with Antek and Matthew, he ignores them until he sees her creeping into the warm protection of the straw stack with Antek. He then shows no mercy and blocks the entrance to the stack before he sets fire to the rick, hoping that both will be burned alive.

When Matthias takes Yagna back as a serving girl, the young woman accepts it stoically and does not beg for mercy. Like the true peasant, she accepts her lot with resignation and spends no time in self-recrimination. Her position is essentially tragic in the naturalistic sense. Young, attractive, and full of natural self-interest, she allows herself to be controlled by forces she cannot understand.

It is hard to visualize Antek as a sympathetic character, because all of his actions are motivated by jealousy or greed. He abuses Hanka, his wife, and defies both her and his father when he makes no secret of his affair with Yagna. After being expelled from his father's house, he finally gets a job at the mill but spends all of his wages at the tavern so that Hanka and her children are completely dependent upon Hanka's destitute, sick old father. During the harsh winter, when Hanka is nearly frozen while gathering forest wood in a raging snowstorm, it is old Boryna, not Antek, who comes to her aid. Yet, in spite of the hatred Antek bears his father, he instinctively kills the squire's woodcutter who attacks Matthias. Thus, through Antek, the author indicates that underneath the hardness and materialism of the villagers, a vestige of mutual concern remains. It is this element that keeps the book from depicting total despair. Despite the bitter environment, all the peasants retain a zest for life revealed in their delight in celebrations and in their love for food, drink, dance, and brightly colored clothes and ribbons. The dignity of humanity is described as the peasants stop their individual bickering to join forces against the squire and his men who attempt to overtake the ancestral forests of the peasants.

The book is an amazing portrait of common life in a Polish village. Reymont presents all details of daily life—sowing and harvesting the cabbage crops, house life, clothing, furniture, and food. The notes of the translator are invaluable, for without them, the reader might not understand the importance of certain ceremonies, traditions, and superstitions, which are so much a part of the Polish culture.

When the four-volume work appeared, many reviewers criticized it for redundancy, but, in a work more prose epic than novel, each detail enhances the rest. It becomes more than simply a narrative of Polish life; its universal aspect describes the emotions and impulses alive in the peasant everywhere. The work must be read as a whole, beginning with *Autumn* and ending with the harvest scenes of *Summer*, for then the reader may view a splendid picture of life in all aspects.

"Critical Evaluation" by Vina Nickels Oldach

Bibliography:

Kridl, Manfred. *A Survey of Polish Literature and Culture*. Translated by Olga Sherer-Virski. New York: Columbia University Press, 1956. Claims *The Peasants* is universally acknowledged as "the richest and artistically the most perfect picture of peasant life in world literature." Excellent description of Reymont's ability to endow characters with individual traits while preserving the general impression of peasant life in Poland.

Krzyżanowski, Jerzy R. *Władysław Stanisław Reymont*. New York: Twayne, 1972. A chapter on *The Peasants* discusses Reymont's interest in rural peoples. Asserts that it is inappropriate to consider the novel simply a political tract; claims the novelist is adept at portraying the psychological dimensions of his characters.

Krzyżanowski, Julian. *A History of Polish Literature*. Translated by Doris Ronowicz. Warsaw: Polish Scientific Publishers, 1972. Places *The Peasants* in the context of a larger tradition of Polish novels depicting the life of rural folk. Highlights the struggle between traditional values and the changes wrought by the introduction of foreign elements into the society.

Miłosz, Czesław. *The History of Polish Literature*. New York: Macmillan, 1969. Describes Reymont's plan to write the epic of the Polish peasantry. Explains how *The Peasants* presents traditional Polish values through a story that has more universal significance.

Pietrkiewicz, Jerzy. *Polish Prose and Verse*. London: Athlone Press, 1956. Insightful comments about *The Peasants*, highlighting the use of the seasons as a unifying device and citing the psychological complexity Reymont achieves with both major and minor characters.

PEDER VICTORIOUS

Type of work: Novel
Author: O. E. Rölvaag (1876-1931)
Type of plot: Regional
Time of plot: Late nineteenth century
Locale: Dakota Territory
First published: Peder Seier, 1928 (English translation, 1929)

Principal characters:
>>BERET HOLM, a pioneer woman
>>PEDER VICTORIOUS, her youngest child
>>OLE,
>>STORE-HANS, and
>>ANNA MARIE, her other children
>>MR. GABRIELSEN, their minister
>>CHARLIE DOHENY, Peder's friend
>>SUSIE, Charlie's sister

The Story:

When Peder Holm was growing up, he lived in three rooms. In one, he lived everything in English; here there was a magic touch. In the second, where he lived everything in Norwegian, things were more difficult. In the third room, only he and God were allowed. Before he was born, his mother had dedicated him to God, and God had become a very real person to the boy.

As he grew up, however, he was not always sure that God was the kind of being that his mother and the minister, Mr. Gabrielsen, talked about. Peder had been taught that God was love, and yet God was blamed for the death of Per Hansa, his father, the destruction of the crops, and the bleakness of the land. To Peder, such calamities could not be reconciled with his God of love; he read his Bible assiduously in an attempt to straighten out his thoughts.

Mr. Gabrielsen was sure that once Peder had gone to seminary, he would be the right person to minister to the Norwegian settlement. The preacher expected English to supplant Norwegian as the common language there in the next twenty years, and Peder's English was fluent, though still tinged with an accent.

The whole community was in a fever of change. After a long argument in church about disciplining a girl whose shame had caused her to hang herself, one group broke away and established a second church. There were two schools, one strictly Norwegian and one taught in English, to which the Irish came as well. An imminent problem was the division of the territory before it entered the union. Such matters aroused the people nearly to fighting pitch, and the meetings in which they were discussed were sources of fine entertainment to all within riding distance.

Peder's mother, Beret, wanted everything Norwegian kept intact; she tried to ensure that the children spoke Norwegian to her at home, though that became hard after the children went to school. Most particularly, she wanted Peder to enter the ministry. Often, though, she could not understand him when he spoke English at school and church affairs. His voice was fine and loud, and he spoke often and entered into every kind of entertainment. He might become a minister, but he was certainly having fun beforehand. As a matter of fact, he found considerable entertainment and satisfaction right on the farm.

After a political meeting at the schoolhouse that Beret and her whole family attended and at which Peder recited Lincoln's Gettysburg Address in English, his teacher spoke at length to Beret about letting him speak English all the time so that he would lose his Norwegian accent. Beret was so disturbed that she spoke to her husband's picture that night. Although he seemed to smile at her anxiety, she decided that Peder should go to the school that was attended only by Norwegians.

The change of schools did not help much. Beret asked a widowed friend about moving both their families back to Norway, but Sorine questioned the wisdom of taking their children into a strange land. Beret could not understand what Sorine could be talking about. Were not their children Norwegian? Sorine assured her that their children were American.

One thing helped Beret to keep her mind off her troubles. She could plan for the farm. Everyone in the settlement admitted that she was prosperous. Soon she had a windmill and a fine big barn for both horses and cows. She never knew quite how she did that job; usually she felt overcome by her problems and tried a solution out of desperation, but her solutions tended to be the right ones.

With her farm going so well, Beret liked to give the minister donations for the missions. Her generosity gave her satisfaction until, just before Peder was to be confirmed, the preacher asked him at a meeting to read a part of the Bible in English. Beret objected to that, but she was even more incensed sometime later when he asked the blessing in English in her own house. She still wanted Peder to be a minister, however.

Peder was beginning to have ideas of his own. In the first place, he began to resent being kept at home, away from dances and parties. The Irish were great for parties, and Peder liked a great many of them, especially the Dohenys. He began to go out at night without telling his mother where he was going. He could not prevent her knowing that he was out, however, because she stayed awake until he came in. She began to hear rumors about him, but he refused to confide in her. When the minister heard that Peder was running around with girls, he begged Peder to go to the seminary immediately, but the young man refused.

Instead, he began to take part in rehearsals for a play, the first to be put on in the settlement. He had the role of the hero and Susie Doheny that of the heroine. To him, the lines in the play became real and Susie his true love. He was happier than he had ever been and he sang all day and was tireless in his work. When the minister heard about the play, he came to Beret and begged her to remove Peder from that kind of temptation. Beret thought it was up to the minister himself to restrain Peder. She was confused. Perhaps Peder was going astray, but lately he had been kinder than he had ever been before. She questioned him and was relieved when she heard that some of her old friends were also in the cast.

When the next rehearsal took place, she went through the fields to the schoolhouse and peered in. There she saw Peder with the Irish girl Susie in his arms.

Beret hid in the shadows until the players left. Her mind went blank, then she began to pick up small sticks that she piled close to the school. When a storm came up and the heavy rain and wind prevented the sticks from burning, she crept home. She was so tired that she merely looked at her husband's picture and fell on her bed. Hearing a noise, she looked around and there was her husband, Per Hansa, standing by her bed and telling her to let Peder have that girl that he was so fond of. The next day, Peder thought Beret seemed preoccupied. It was a shock and then a delight to him to hear her say they must hurry to the Dohenys' to arrange for his and Susie's wedding.

Critical Evaluation:

O. E. Rölvaag, perhaps the best-known Norwegian American author, interpreted the immigrant experience and depicted the human cost, as well as the material benefits, of becoming an American. Rölvaag himself immigrated from Norway in 1896 when he was twenty years old. In the United States, he was able to obtain the education he had always desired, but he experienced the pain of separation from home and family and he knew that immigrants continue to feel like outsiders in their new country while at the same time they become estranged from the old.

The myth of the American frontier as a second Eden where people could start a new, more prosperous life lured many immigrants to settle there. This myth included the necessity of being reborn as a new person, of cutting all ties with the past. Rölvaag believed that this results in rootlessness and spiritual disintegration. Rather than a melting-pot society of bland uniformity, he advocated the preservation of the Norwegian language and culture to provide a sense of continuity for the immigrants and their descendants. This philosophy is everywhere apparent in his fiction.

Peder Victorious is the second novel in Rölvaag's trilogy chronicling the Holm family. *Giants in the Earth* (1927), which covers events from 1873 to 1881, describes the struggles of Per and Beret Hansa, who are among the first to settle in Spring Creek in Dakota Territory. That novel concludes with Per's death in a snowstorm. *Peder Victorious* picks up the story in 1885 and takes it through 1895, covering Peder's childhood and youth. Peder is the youngest child of Per and Beret and the first child born in the Spring Creek settlement. By 1885, Spring Creek is no longer a frontier but an established community with churches and schools; more mundane cultural, social, and psychological conflicts have replaced the dramatic, mythical struggles of the first book. *Their Fathers' God* (1931), which follows Peder into young adulthood, continues these themes.

Polarity and division are recurring images in *Peder Victorious*. During the time of the novel, Dakota Territory is divided into the states of South Dakota and North Dakota. St. Luke's Lutheran Church is split and Bethel Congregation formed; the Holm family is separated when one son and his wife leave Spring Creek for Montana. The main emphasis, however, is on the internal conflicts of Peder and Beret, especially those that result from the Americanization process. Much of the book is told from Peder's point of view, but Beret's is also considered; in fact, some critics contend that it is as much her story as his.

Beret has always been torn between sexuality and spirituality. She had felt a strong physical attraction for her husband and regrets not having taken advantage of the opportunities for a more active sexual relationship when he was alive. At the same time, she is devout and has never resolved her guilt about having become pregnant before they were married. Not only does she repress this part of her personality, but she is also extremely uncomfortable with Peder's developing sexuality.

Beret is well aware that she is caught between the Old World and the New and belongs to neither. For her, Norway represents civilization and established values, while the United States represents materialism and the potential loss of one's soul. She considers returning to Norway but realizes that her children would be strangers there and that even she would no longer fit in. Instead, she tries to pass her cultural values on to them. She is concerned with the preservation of the Norwegian language and is baffled when her children prefer to speak English. Unable to communicate intimately with her children, she becomes a stranger to them. Ironically, she achieves the American Dream of material prosperity: After Per's death, she becomes one of the most successful farmers in the area.

Peder thinks that Norway is all in the past; he considers himself an American and is clearly in rebellion against his mother and her values. The three rooms described in the beginning of the book symbolize the segmentation of his life into an English-speaking, a Norwegian-speaking, and a spiritual world. When he is young, he moves easily from one room to another, but as he grows older, he becomes increasingly comfortable only in the English-speaking world. As a small child, Peder had felt a close, personal relationship with God. His father's tragic death, however, and the congregation's harsh treatment of an unmarried young woman who had become pregnant result in a distrust of God in general and Lutheranism in particular. The pastor thinks Peder should study for the ministry, but Peder rejects religion and concentrates on a secular life.

Although the Holm family speaks only Norwegian at home, once Peder starts school he is drawn to the English-speaking world. Everything interesting to him, everything that concerns the future, has to do with that world rather than with the Norwegian-speaking one, and he starts to speak English at home too. Beret tries to teach him to read and write Norwegian, but he refuses to cooperate.

Peder, having revolted against Lutheranism, the Norwegian language and culture, and even his own family, considers himself to be completely Americanized, but there is evidence that his heart, too, is divided. When Pastor Gabrielsen, speaking English, urges him to enter the seminary, a prospect Peder does not welcome, Peder forgets himself and answers in Norwegian. Although he denies it, something deep inside is still identifiably Norwegian.

Peder dates two Norwegian girls, but it is Susie, the twin sister of his Irish friend, Charlie, who attracts him. Norwegian or Irish, Lutheran or Catholic, it does not matter—Peder believes in the great ideal of a mixed society where everyone is an American, and he wants to marry Susie. Beret feels it is morally wrong for them to marry, but she acquiesces. These conflicts are not, however, entirely resolved at the end of *Peder Victorious*. Peder gets his way and will marry Susie, but there is an ominous sense that his future will not be happy.

"Critical Evaluation" by Eunice Pedersen Johnston

Bibliography:
Haugen, Einar. *Ole Edvart Rölvaag*. Boston: Twayne, 1983. A detailed discussion of all Rölvaag's works from a Norwegian American perspective. Haugen, a former student of Rölvaag, is an expert on Norwegian American dialects, and he has studied Rölvaag's writing in the original Norwegian as well as the English translations.

Moseley, Ann. *Ole Edvart Rölvaag*. Boise, Idaho: Boise State University, 1987. A brief, general introduction to Rölvaag's life and writings. Focuses on the importance of Rölvaag's work to the general student of American literature. Includes a useful bibliography.

Paulson, Kristoffer F. "Rölvaag as Prophet: The Tragedy of Americanization." In *Ole Rölvaag: Artist and Cultural Leader*, edited by Gerald Thorson. Northfield, Minn.: St. Olaf College Press, 1975. Discusses the physical and spiritual dangers that Rölvaag saw confronting immigrants.

Reigstad, Paul. *Rölvaag: His Life and Art*. Lincoln: University of Nebraska Press, 1972. An extensive discussion of Rölvaag's novels. Emphasizes the artistic merits of Rölvaag's work, rather than the social history aspects.

Simonson, Harold P. *Prairies Within: The Tragic Trilogy of Ole Rölvaag*. Seattle: University of Washington Press, 1987. Emphasizes Beret's role in all three novels of Rölvaag's trilogy of the Holm family. Argues that Beret is Rölvaag's most important character and the one who best represents his views.

PEDRO PÁRAMO

Type of work: Novel
Author: Juan Rulfo (1918-1986)
Type of plot: Psychological symbolism
Time of plot: Late nineteenth and early twentieth centuries
Locale: Comala, Jalisco, Mexico
First published: 1955 (English translation, 1959)

> *Principal characters:*
> PEDRO PÁRAMO, a rural boss and landowner
> JUAN PRECIADO, one of his many sons and the main narrator of the story
> DOÑA EDUVIGES DYADA, the friend of Juan's dead mother
> SUSANA SAN JUAN, Páramo's childhood sweetheart and, later, his wife
> FATHER RENTERÍA, the priest of Comala
> ANA, Father Rentería's niece
> ABUNDIO MARTÍNEZ, another of Páramo's sons and his killer
> MIGUEL PÁRAMO, the son whom Páramo acknowledged
> DAMIANA CISNEROS, Páramo's housekeeper
> FULGO SEDANO, Páramo's man of business
> DOROTEA, an old procuress
> DAMASIO (EL TILCUATE), a revolutionary in the hire of Páramo

The Story:

Juan Preciado, a peasant and Pedro Páramo's son, in fulfillment of the last will of his mother, arrived on foot to Comala looking for his father. During his journey, another man had joined him; the traveler turned out to be another of Páramo's sons. He told Juan Preciado that their father was a "kindled rancor" and that he was dead. Preciado found only one other person in Comala, Eduviges Dyada, an old friend of his mother, and she gave him shelter. The woman was dead, as was the companion of Preciado during the journey.

Pedro Páramo appeared as a boy, dreaming of his childhood sweetheart, Susana San Juan, and doing some domestic chores. Susana was the only true, deep love of Páramo, in contrast to the many other women whom he seduced or raped. Eduviges Dyada told Preciado that she should have been his mother, for on her nuptial night his true mother, advised by a soothsayer, asked Eduviges to take her place beside Pedro Páramo. Little by little, Pedro Páramo's moral profile was drawn by Eduviges. She continued to tell Preciado what kind of man his father was. She told of Miguel Páramo—the only son whom Pedro acknowledged—a violent, sexually predatory young man who died in an accident. Father Rentería, the local priest, entered the plot. His brother had been murdered and his niece raped by Miguel Páramo, but he had to celebrate a funeral mass and perform the last Catholic rites for the soul of Miguel. To add to this conflict of emotions, he also believed that he had betrayed his priestly state because he had not taken a firm stand against the abuses committed by wealthy people, Pedro Páramo in particular. The priest also had not given true hope and consolation to the poor. Once, when he went to confess to the parish priest of Contla, he was reprimanded for this and denied the absolution because he had allowed his parishioners to live lives of superstition and fear.

Pedro Páramo appeared again, as an adult. He had grown, as Father Rentería said, as weeds do. He had obtained all that he ever wanted—women, children, lands—by such unscrupulous means as unfulfilled promises, money, threats, violence, and death. His only redeeming trait was his love for Susana San Juan, who was previously married to Florencio and who, after becoming a widow, agreed to become Páramo's wife. She went insane and a change began to transform Pedro's soul. He felt old, sad, and impotent, and his situation became worse after Susana died in his hacienda, Media Luna. On her deathbed, she believed herself to be with her dead husband. Páramo's life began to disintegrate; he suspected that death would come soon. One morning a son, Abundio Martínez, grief stricken because of his wife's death, got drunk and went to his father to ask for money for the burial. Blinded by wine, Abundio stabbed his father to death. Páramo fell as if he were a pile of stones.

Critical Evaluation:

In *Pedro Páramo*, Juan Rulfo delves, as no Mexican writer of fiction had done before, into the complex, atavistic, desolate, and fatalistic world of the Indians of Mexico. *Pedro Páramo* is a book of voices—voices of people, voices of nature, and voices of circumstance, morality, and passion. All of its characters are dead; they are only voices, murmurs, who live in a town, Comala, a village of echoes. All of these dead people, souls in pain, are presented as if they were living in another world, in a strange limbo of memory.

A mixture of fantasy and reality, *Pedro Páramo* contains thematic threads that express Rulfo's pessimistic vision of life. Each inhabitant of Comala relives a single moment of pain or guilt over and over again, but the experience never brings any increased self-awareness, any insight into the causes of behavior, or any suggestion of possible remedies for dilemmas. The characters are symbolic figures; they stand for the individual as a powerless victim of both external and internal forces. Rulfo's men and women are helpless in the face both of outside circumstances and of their own psychic problems. Comala is a microcosm in a state of irremediable chaos and inescapable disintegration. The despair of this situation is conveyed powerfully through the author's style, which is based on the basic rhythms of common speech.

Pedro Páramo stands as a landmark work in the evolution of the twentieth century Spanish American novel in that it represents, for many critics and other readers, the first example of the Spanish American New Novel. After the 1920's and 1930's, in which Spanish American fiction sought to paint realistic and detailed pictures of external Spanish American (and often national or even regional) reality, in which description often ruled over action, environment over character, types over the individual, and social message over artistic subtlety, and in which the understanding of the story required little attention on the part of the reader, the nature of Spanish American fiction began to change radically. In the 1940's, as a result of internal and external influences (chiefly of Argentine short story writer Jorge Luis Borges and of William Faulkner, respectively), Spanish American fiction developed a new narrative that, unlike its predecessor, treated the fictional world as just that—fiction. This new narrative presented various, and often alternative, versions of reality, entered the inner worlds of its characters, and expressed universal as well as regional and national themes. In doing so, it broke with tradition. The new Latin American narrative also was unafraid of unconventional modes of telling the story, of subtle presentation of theme, and of requiring the reader's participation at all levels of the narration. Though numerous Spanish American novels of the late 1940's and early 1950's possessed characteristics of Spanish America's new narrative, *Pedro Páramo* can be considered Spanish America's first New Novel.

The world it depicts, for example, is anything but the realistic world presented in the Spanish American novel of the 1920's and 1930's. The characters in the book are dead and their stories come from voices from the grave. Juan Preciado, for example, the character whose narration opens the book, the reader eventually learns, is dead as he narrates, and his narratee is not the reader, but the woman (Dorotea) with whom he shares his tomb. Likewise, the narration of other stories floats out from the tombs of other characters, and the living, what few there are in the story's present, communicate freely with the dead, and the dead themselves communicate with one another (as is the case with Preciado and Dorotea). Even beyond the specter of the dead, the story seems to be pervaded by an otherworldliness, all of which together places *Pedro Páramo* well outside the parameters of what anyone might consider realistic fiction.

Rulfo's novel paints a vivid realistic picture, however, of the relationship between the local despot (cacique) and those in his influence. The novel departs from tradition by not making this picture the novel's explicit moral message. Rather, the novel explores the inner workings of its characters, all of whom suffer from frustration, guilt, and obsessive desires. These misfortunes of the human condition are universal concerns and not at all limited to the Indians of the Jalisco region of Mexico.

While the novel's many departures from tradition help place *Pedro Páramo* within the rubric of the Spanish American New Novel, the aspect of Rulfo's work that most earns it classification as a New Novel and that which has inspired the most critical commentary and acclaim, as well as reader frustration, is the novel's unconventional presentation of its story. The relatively short novel is told in sixty-eight (or sixty-four, depending on the edition) sections that frequently shift in narrative voice and narrative focus. Different sections initiate, resume, and drop story lines and subplots with virtually no predictability. The sections present new characters with no introduction or context, and seem to be arranged in no logical order. So confusing is *Pedro Páramo* to first-time readers, and particularly to its first readers in 1955, that many might agree with one of the novel's first critics, who accused Rulfo of writing the novel in chronological order and then cutting it into pieces and rearranging it at random. A close reading of the text reveals, however, that Rulfo could not have first written the novel in chronological order. Even reconstructed into chronological order, the novel has numerous gaps in the story, and the story and its many subplots are like, in chronological order or not, snapshots taken over many years and many lives. Furthermore, the novel's structure is not nearly so chaotic as it may first appear. Rereading reveals its associative construction.

The unconventional presentation of the story in *Pedro Páramo*, therefore, characterizes the Spanish American New Novel. The New Novel demands an active, participatory reader, who not only must read the novel carefully, but also must strive to make connections, work to identify changing narrative voices, seek to establish who is who, and attempt to assess the significance of the events, with little or no help from the author. The fact that the reader may have to read and reread to understand what he or she is reading is a major and defining characteristic of the Spanish American New Novel in general and of *Pedro Páramo* in particular.

One final common characteristic of the New Novel, which is found in Rulfo's work, is that because the presentation of the story is so challenging, the presentation itself may overshadow the story, and the reader may be more concerned with how the story is told than with the story itself. The New Novel may actually be of more interest for how it tells what it tells than for what it actually tells.

The timing of Rulfo's novel has made it a landmark novel in Spanish American literature. Its haunting story and its challenging presentation have won it enduring fame with its many readers. Few novels, in any literature, present the reader with so compelling a reading experience as that found in *Pedro Páramo*.

"Critical Evaluation" by Keith H. Brower

Bibliography:

Brotherston, Gordon. *The Emergence of the Latin American Novel*. Cambridge, England: Cambridge University Press, 1977. Discusses the plot of *Pedro Páramo*, the nature of its narrative, its themes, its atmosphere, and its place within the context of literature concerned with the Mexican Revolution. Good introduction to Rulfo's fictional world.

Harss, Luis, and Barbara Dohmann. *Into the Mainstream: Conversations with Latin-American Writers*. New York: Harper & Row, 1967. Provides interview-based overview of Rulfo and his works. Discussion of works punctuated by comments from Rulfo himself. Excellent starting point for further study.

Leal, Luis. *Juan Rulfo*. Boston: Twayne, 1983. This solid study of Rulfo's life and career contains two chapters dedicated to *Pedro Páramo*. Topics covered include the place of Rulfo's novel within the context of the novel of the Mexican Revolution, the novel's roots in Rulfo's short stories, its structure, initial critical reaction, the work's multiple narrative threads, and the role of imagery.

McMurray, George R. *Spanish American Writing Since 1941: A Critical Survey*. New York: Frederick Ungar, 1987. Offers concise commentary on *Pedro Páramo* before discussing Rulfo's contribution to Spanish American fiction. Brief but good introduction.

Sommers, Joseph. *After the Storm: Landmarks of the Modern Mexican Novel*. Albuquerque: University of New Mexico Press, 1968. Discusses the narrative perspective of *Pedro Páramo*, its structure, its characters, and, as Sommers puts it, the work's "mythic underpinnings."

PEDRO SÁNCHEZ

Type of work: Novel
Author: José María de Pereda (1833-1906)
Type of plot: Picaresque
Time of plot: 1852-1879
Locale: Santander and Madrid
First published: 1883

Principal characters:

PEDRO SÁNCHEZ, a provincial from the Cantabrian Mountains
AUGUSTO VALENZUELA, a politician from Madrid
CLARA, his daughter
SERAFÍN BALDUQUE, a former state employee
CARMEN, his daughter
MATA or MATICA, a student in Madrid
REDONDO, the editor of *El Clarín* of Madrid
BARRIENTOS, Governor Pedro Sánchez's secretary

The Story:

Pedro Sánchez, a young provincial proud of his descent from Sancho Abarco, a tenth century king of Navarre, had seen little of Spain when he left his father and three sisters to go to Madrid. Augusto Valenzuela, a visiting politician, had promised to look after Pedro's future in the capital. It was October, 1852, when Pedro took the coach from Santander. Among the passengers were a down-at-heels bureaucrat, Serafín Balduque, and his attractive daughter Carmen. From a student in the coach, Pedro learned of a cheap boardinghouse where he hoped to stay until he could contact Valenzuela.

The politician proved hard to find. After settling in his lodgings, Pedro called at Valenzuela's house, where Pilita, his wife, and his daughter Clara gave the young man a cool reception. The politician, finally tracked down after a dozen visits to his office, vaguely promised to keep Pedro in mind if anything should turn up. The boy, however, wrote his father an optimistic letter in which he lied about his reception by the Valenzuela family.

Pedro's acquaintances at the boardinghouse were more helpful. Matica showed him around Madrid and, when Pedro's money gave out and he was about to return home, found him a job on the antigovernment newspaper, *El Clarín*, at twenty-five *duros* a month. Pedro learned from the staff of the crookedness of Valenzuela. Occasionally Pedro saw Balduque. Mostly he spent his free time in efforts to become a writer.

In the autumn, when one of the *El Clarín* contributors entered government service, Pedro was advanced to writing reviews under his own name, which was announced as the pseudonym of a famous literary man. Redondo, the editor, hinted that plays and novels by friends in the party were to get preferential treatment, while literary works by members of the opposition were to be severely criticized. One of Pedro's first tasks was to criticize *Clemencia*, by Pardo Bazán.

Pedro's success went to his head. He abandoned his old friends, even Matica. He saw Clara, and in spite of his disdain he found himself falling in love with her. Valenzuela, however, did nothing to help the young man get ahead in Madrid. Since all *El Clarín* employees were revolution-minded, Pedro caught the fever and wrote a fable attacking the government.

Featured on the front page, it brought him much attention. Valenzuela sent for Pedro and offered him a meager job on a government publication, but he refused it. Warned by Balduque that his refusal would put the police on his trail, Pedro took refuge with Balduque and Carmen.

After the overthrow of the government in the revolution of July 17, 1854, there was no longer any reason for Pedro to stay in hiding. On his way from the Balduque house to the office of *El Clarín*, he saw a mob burning government buildings. When they began shouting against Valenzuela, he diverted the rioters to the palace of Cristina, the queen mother, and rushed to save Clara. He was unwilling to admit, however, that he acted out of love for her.

Street fighting broke out, with Pedro in command of a barricade. He was joined by Balduque, who was eager to get revenge for the wrongs committed against him. When Balduque was killed, Pedro and Matica were forced to break the news to Carmen. She refused their offers of help.

Finally Baldomero Fernández Espartero imposed peace on the troubled country. Valenzuela fled, and his family accepted an invitation to the country estate of the Duchess of Pico. Pedro was rewarded with a provincial governorship. Going to tell Clara good-bye, he found himself proposing to her. A fall marriage was arranged. Through Pedro's efforts the government granted a pension to Carmen, but when he went to tell her the news and to announce his approaching marriage, her lack of approval puzzled him. Matica was also unenthusiastic. Redondo was downright angry. The marriage was performed after Pedro had visited his father for the first time in three years.

Clara, her mother, her brother, and Barrientos, a secretary whom Pedro disliked from the first, accompanied him to the seat of his government. There everything went wrong. Clara's family was extravagant and snobbish. Pedro's secretary sneered at him and so did the citizens. Finally, from a friendly editor, Pedro got an explanation: His secretary was collecting bribes, and his wife was exploiting her husband's political position. Returning home unexpectedly, Pedro surprised Barrientos in his wife's bedroom. When Pedro and Barrientos met in the street, they fought with sabers, and Pedro was wounded.

At last a change of government cost Pedro his governorship. Ashamed to return to Madrid, he got Matica's promise to look after Carmen, and he gave up his political life. The passing years brought many changes in Pedro's affairs. Valenzuela soon died, as did his wife. Barrientos was killed in a duel. Clara had several protectors and eventually died, leaving Pedro free to return to Madrid and marry Carmen, but evil luck still plagued him. His new wife and their small son died during an epidemic. When he tried to squander his money, Pedro became rich. Homesick for the mountains, he sold his business and returned to Santander, but there he found no happiness. His father was dead; the countryside and the people seemed strange. Unhappy, Pedro wrote his autobiography, ending it in true picaresque style, with the hope that the example of his disillusionment would serve as a warning to his readers.

Critical Evaluation:

Essentially a realist, José María de Pereda attempted to express his moral convictions through his novels, while portraying honestly the conditions of life in Spain as he saw them. *Pedro Sánchez* is one of his most successful explorations of the character of the Spanish people, despite its essentially pessimistic political message. By the time he wrote *Pedro Sánchez*, he had come to feel that the revolution was not working, and he also felt scorn for the newly rich who exploited liberalism for their personal ends. The novel shows the sincere disillusion of an enthusiast who left the provinces and plunged into the political life of the capital. Perhaps Pereda's didactic tendency injures his effects, and his grim satire occasionally degenerates into caricature, but Pereda understands character, and it is for this reason that *Pedro Sánchez* endures.

In treatment of subject matter and in composition, *Pedro Sánchez* is one of Pereda's most finished works. It is a modern picaresque novel, an autobiography satirizing all the phases of the protagonist's life as office seeker, journalist, political agitator, revolutionist, social lion, and governor. Pedro's opinions of life and politics in Madrid doubtless reflect those of the author, who had followed a somewhat similar career in the capital before he yielded to homesickness and returned disillusioned to his native region. There is nothing heroic about Pedro. He is an ordinary mortal with a weak moral sense, yet he arouses sympathy and pity when viewed in contrast to the snobbery and villainy of the people about him.

Pereda's keen sense of the ridiculous is everywhere evident in *Pedro Sánchez*; the novel displays a broad range of humor, from gentle irony to biting satire. Pereda excels in his ability to portray common people and to reproduce the popular vernacular with all of its lusty humor. In this regard, although the novel is essentially picaresque, *Pedro Sánchez* does advance realism in the Spanish novel. The characters in the book are real human beings, flawed and foolish, and intrinsically human. The author does not condescend to his lowly born characters; he understands them and portrays them with zest. Above all, he is never sentimental about his characters. Pedro is one of the great characters of Spanish literature, never idealized, but sympathetic and understandable. Women are relegated to secondary roles in the novel and in the author's view of society.

The narrative centers on the revolution of 1854, which Pereda witnessed as a student in Madrid. With great skill, the author moves Pedro through the stages of success, from journalist to revolutionary leader and official, always looking out for his own interests. Pedro, however, pays a price for his opportunism, the price of ultimate disillusionment. It is significant that he finally returns to his own native village, after his years of political intrigue. If the book has any message, it is that one should distrust the claims of would-be political saviors; a healthy skepticism should greet the birth of any new movement. Revolutions come and go, but the people endure.

Bibliography:
Eoff, Sherman. "A Fatherly World According to Design." In *The Modern Spanish Novel: Comparative Essays Examining the Philosophical Impact of Science on Fiction.* New York: New York University Press, 1961. Pages 21 to 50 speculate on the influence of scientific discovery on Pereda. Stimulating discussion of cultural history.
_____. "Pereda's Conception of Realism as Related to His Epoch." *Hispanic Review* 14 (1946): 281-303. Reassessment of Pereda's contributions to Spain's literature and of Pereda's politics.
_____. "Pereda's Realism: His Style." *Washington University Studies: New Series Language and Literature* 14 (1942): 131-157. Argues that Pereda's style is realistic and influenced by the author's own interpretations of realism and by other traditions in the Spanish novel.
Glascock, Clyde. "Modern Spanish Novelists: José María de Pereda." *Southwest Review* 8 (1923): 329-353. Discusses Pereda's appreciation for the mountains of Spain.
Klibbe, Lawrence Hadfield. *José María de Pereda.* Boston: Twayne, 1975. A good starting place in the study of Pereda. Bibliography.

PEER GYNT

Type of work: Drama
Author: Henrik Ibsen (1828-1906)
Type of plot: Satire
Time of plot: Mid-nineteenth century
Locale: Norway
First published: 1867 (English translation, 1892); first performed, 1876

>*Principal characters:*
>PEER GYNT, a Norwegian farmer
>ASE, his mother
>SOLVEIG, a Norwegian woman whose love for Peer remains constant
>THE GREAT BOYG, a troll monster
>THE BUTTON MOULDER, who threatens to melt Peer in his ladle

The Story:

Peer Gynt, a young Norwegian farmer with a penchant for laziness and bragging, idled away his hours in brawling and dreaming. Upbraided by his mother, Ase, for his willingness to waste his time, he answered that she was perfectly right. She ridiculed him further by pointing out that had he been an honest farmer, Hegstad's daughter would have had him, and he would have been a happy bridegroom. He told her that he intended to break the marriage of Hegstad's daughter, a wedding planned for that night. When his mother protested, he seized her in his arms and set her on the roof of their house, from where her unheeded cries followed him up the road to Hegstad's home.

At the wedding he was scorned by everyone present except Solveig, a girl unknown to him. Even she, however, avoided him as soon as she heard of his base reputation. Peer became drunk and began to tell fantastic tales of adventure, stories that bridged an embarrassing gap in the marriage ceremony when the bride locked herself in the storeroom and refused to come out. In desperation, the bridegroom appealed to Peer for help. As Peer left for the storeroom, his mother, who had been released from the roof, arrived. Suddenly the bridegroom cried out and pointed toward the hillside. Rushing to the door, the guests saw Peer scrambling up the mountain with the bride over his shoulder.

Peer quickly abandoned the bride and penetrated into the wilderness. Eluding the pursuit of Hegstad and his neighbors, he married and deserted the daughter of the elf-king of the mountains. He encountered the Great Boyg, the riddle of existence in the figure of a shapeless, grim, unconquerable monster. Peer tried repeatedly to force his way up the mountain, but the Boyg blocked his way. When Peer challenged the Boyg to a battle, the creature replied that though he conquered everyone he did not fight.

Exhausted, Peer sank to the ground. The sky was dark with carnivorous birds that were about to swoop down upon him. Suddenly he heard the sound of church bells and women's voices in the distance. The Boyg withdrew, admitting defeat because Peer had the support of women in his fight. An outlaw for having carried off Hegstad's daughter, Peer built himself a hut in the forest, to which Solveig came to keep him company. Their happiness was brief, however, for one day Peer met the elf-king's daughter, whom he had deserted. With her was an ugly troll, Peer's son; unable to drive them off, he himself went away after telling Solveig that she must wait for him a little while.

Before leaving the country, he paid a farewell visit to his dying mother. With his arms around her, Peer lulled her into her last sleep. Over her dead body he uttered thanks for all his days, all his lullabies, all his beatings.

He went adventuring over the world. In America he sold slaves; in China, sacred idols. He did a thriving business in rum and Bibles. After being robbed of his earthly goods, he went to the African desert and became a prophet. Prosperous once more, he set himself up in Oriental luxury. One day he rode into the desert with Anitra, a dancing girl. Stopping to rest, he could not resist the urge to show off by proving to Anitra that he was still young in spirit and body. While he was performing, she stole his moneybag and horse and galloped away. Solveig had grown middle-aged while she waited for Peer Gynt's return. Peer Gynt, on the other hand, still struggled on with his planless life, still drifted around the all-consuming Boyg of life without any apparent purpose in mind.

On his way back to Norway at last, his ship was wrecked. Peer clung to a spar that could hold only one man. When the ship's cook attempted to grasp the spar also, Peer thrust him into the ocean. He had saved his own life, but he doubted whether he had been successful in saving himself from his aimless existence.

On his return to Norway, he decided, however, that he was through with wandering, and he was willing to settle down to the staid life of a retired old man. One day on the heath he met a Button Moulder, who refused to let the aged Peer realize his dream of peace and contentment. Informed that he was to go into the Button Moulder's ladle to be melted, Peer became frantic. To lose his soul, his identity, was an end he had not divined for himself despite his aimless and self-centered life. He pleaded with the Button Moulder to relent. He was at worst a bungler, he cried, never an exceptional sinner. The Button Moulder answered that Peer, not bad enough for hell nor good enough for heaven, was fit only for the ladle. Peer protested, but the Button Moulder remained adamant. Peer was to be melted into the ladle of nonentity unless he could prove himself a sinner worthy of hell. Hell being a more lenient punishment than nothingness, Peer desperately enlarged upon his sins. He had trafficked in slaves, had cheated people and deceived them, and had saved his life at the expense of another. The Button Moulder ironically maintained that these iniquities were mere trifles.

While they argued, the Button Moulder and Peer came to a house where Solveig stood in the doorway ready for church, a psalmbook under her arm. Peer flung himself at her feet, begging her to cry out his sins and trespasses, but she answered that he was with her again, and that was all that mattered. She was shocked when Peer asked her to cry out his crime to her; she said that it was he who had made life beautiful for her. Hearing her words, the Button Moulder disappeared, prophesying that he and Peer would meet again. Peer Gynt buried his face in Solveig's lap, safe and secure with her arms to hold him and her heart to warm him. Solveig's own face was bathed in sunlight.

Critical Evaluation:

A satire on a man, one of those contradictory creatures with an upright body and groveling soul, *Peer Gynt* is an example of Henrik's Ibsen's symbolic treatment of the theme of individualism. This drama is a long episodic fantasy, with a picaresque, jaunty, boastful, yet lovable sinner. Ibsen combines folklore and satire with a symbolism that imparts a rich emotional impact to the drama. The unorthodox and untheatrical elements of the play, however, make stage presentation difficult. The play deals with the degeneration of the human soul, yet the triumphant note at the end regarding the redeeming power of love keeps the play from being tragic.

Peer Gynt was Ibsen's last verse play; his later dramas were written in prose, in keeping with his shift to more realistic themes. *Peer Gynt* is a masterpiece of fantasy and surreal effects, which, in combination with Ibsen's delicately graceful eloquence, makes the play difficult to stage, especially in a realistically oriented theater. In some ways, the play resembles a picaresque novel more than it does a play. It is episodic and involves a journey filled with disparate adventures. *Peer Gynt* has been faulted by some critics for being overloaded with "spectacle": too many rapid changes of exotic scene. It is just such qualities, however, that lend the play its greatest strength.

In fact, such inspiration prompted Ibsen himself in 1874 to request that his famous contemporary, the Norwegian composer Edvard Grieg, compose incidental music for *Peer Gynt*. Grieg undertook the project with reluctance, having personal and artistic reservations about its feasibility. After two years of strenuous work, he completed the job, and in 1876, Ibsen's *Peer Gynt* was performed with Grieg's *Peer Gynt*, two orchestral suites of unsurpassing beauty including "Anitra's Dance," "In the Hall of the Mountain King," and "Solveig's Song," among others. To a large extent, this artistic collaboration proved fruitful because both Ibsen and Grieg intuitively agreed about the uniquely and distinctively Norwegian qualities of *Peer Gynt*. The protagonist, as drawn by the playwright, could have no other ethnic identity; the music, as composed by the musician, could have no other cultural origin, for Grieg was a master at absorbing and utilizing peasant and folkloric themes. Indeed, it has been somewhat acerbically observed that *Peer Gynt* will be remembered not as Ibsen's play but as Grieg's music.

The play describes the adventures of an egocentric but imaginative opportunist. To be sure, Peer is a lovable rogue, but a self-obsessed one. His preoccupation with himself—his own gratification—is his egocentricity; his upwardly mobile changes of locality and women constitute his opportunism; his exotic tastes suggest his imaginative approach toward coping with life. Still, his final return to native hearth and native woman—as he buries his head in Solveig's waiting lap—indicates the limits of adventuring.

Finally, it is this inevitable return to the home territory that makes *Peer Gynt* irrevocably, unavoidably, categorically a play about home, in this case Norway. Such a concept of territoriality is concisely expressed in a line from Mikhail Bulgakov's Russian play, *The Days of the Turbins* (1926), in which one character flatly asserts, "Homeland is homeland," implying an influence of national identity which transcends egocentricity and opportunism as well as political affiliation and religious preference. Peer returns to the land of his origin in a denouement that shows his own as well as Ibsen's ultimate commitments, and those commitments lend the play its compelling force.

Bibliography:

Fjelde, Rolf. "Peer Gynt, Naturalism, and the Dissolving Self." *The Drama Review* 13, no. 2 (Winter, 1968): 28-43. Explores a rhetorical perspective on Peer's identity, concluding that Peer is an example of the uncentered self who can achieve wholeness only through a relationship with others.

Groddeck, Georg. "*Peer Gynt.*" In *Ibsen: A Collection of Critical Essays*, edited by Rolf Fjelde. Englewood Cliffs, N.J.: Prentice-Hall, 1965. A psychoanalytical exploration of *Peer Gynt*, this book chapter emphasizes Peer's relationships to the women in his life.

Johnston, Brian. *To the Third Empire: Ibsen's Early Drama*. Minneapolis: University of Minnesota Press, 1980. A detailed and insightful survey of Ibsen's early dramatic production, the volume includes a major section devoted to *Peer Gynt*. Points out that the drama, which has a moral purpose, owes its appeal to the same playful strategies for dealing with reality that Ibsen argues against.

McFarlane, James. *Ibsen and Meaning: Studies, Essays and Prefaces, 1953-87*. Norwich, England: Norvik Press, 1989. In a major contribution to Ibsen criticism, his play *Brand* (1866) is compared to and contrasted with *Peer Gynt*. Unlike the protagonist of *Brand*, says McFarlane, Peer Gynt is a man who lives entirely in his illusions.

Shapiro, Bruce G. *Divine Madness and the Absurd Paradox: Ibsen's "Peer Gynt" and the Philosophy of Kierkegaard*. Westview, Conn.: Greenwood Press, 1990. An in-depth discussion of the relationship between the character of Peer Gynt and Kierkegaardian philosophy, particularly his theory of the contrast between the aesthetic and the ethical spheres of existence.

PELLE THE CONQUEROR

Type of work: Novel
Author: Martin Andersen Nexø (Martin Andersen, 1869-1954)
Type of plot: Social realism
Time of plot: Late nineteenth century
Locale: Denmark
First published: Pelle erobreren, 1906-1910 (English translation, 1913-1916)

> *Principal characters:*
> PELLE KARLSSON, a young Swede
> LASSE KARLSSON, his father
> RUD PIHL, his playmate
> ELLEN STOLPE, his wife
> MASTER ANDRES, his master
> MR. BRUN, his friend

The Story:

Among a shipload of migrant workers traveling from Sweden to the Danish island of Bornholm in the spring of 1877 were Lasse Karlsson, a Swedish farmhand who was old before his time, and his eight-year-old son, Pelle. Like other Swedes who went to Bornholm, Lasse Karlsson was enticed from his homeland by the relatively high wages paid on the Danish island. Lasse and his son were hired to look after cattle on a large farm on the island. Their life there was neither pleasant nor unpleasant. The farm was a dreary one. The owner left the management of the place to a bailiff, drank heavily, and sought after women. Pelle's greatest happiness was going out to look after the cattle in the common pastures. After a time, he found a playmate in Rud Pihl, the farmer's illegitimate son, who lived in a shack with his mother near the edge of the farm. For the elder Karlsson, life was not easy; he was old and weak, and the rest of the laborers made him the butt of all their jokes. Even so, the man and his son stayed at Stone Farm for several years, since it was easier to remain there than to look for a new location.

The second winter found Pelle in school, for the authorities insisted that he attend. Though he was nine years old, he had had no formal education. He was the only Swede among more than twenty Danish children. Gradually, however, Pelle made a place for himself and even became a leader among his schoolmates.

After two years, Pelle was confirmed. Everyone now considered him capable of taking care of himself. Realizing that his father was content where he was, the boy decided to leave the farm by himself. Early one morning, he set his face toward the little town that was the chief city of the island. While trudging along the road, Pelle met a farmer who had known him for some time and who gave him a ride into town. When Pelle confided to him that he was on his way to look for work, the farmer introduced him to a shoemaker who accepted Pelle as an apprentice.

Master Andres was an easy master but, even so, the six-year apprenticeship was not easy. The journeyman under whom Pelle worked was a grouchy person who taunted Pelle for his rural upbringing. Pelle was not sure what he would do once his apprenticeship was over, for he saw that many shoemakers had no work and that machine-made shoes were slowly taking the place of the handmade variety.

In the last year of his apprenticeship, Master Andres died and the business was sold. Rather than finish out his time with a new master, Pelle ran away from the shop. For several months, he simply drifted, picking up odds and ends of work of any kind. The only thing that saved him from becoming a ne'er-do-well was the friendship of Marie Nielsen, a dancer. She made him keep looking for work, patched his clothes, and bolstered his self-esteem so that he did not become a mere tramp. Finally, a traveling shoemaker named Sort asked Pelle to join him for a time. The two traveled about the country and were very successful. One day, they met Pelle's father, who had just been evicted from the farm he had purchased during Pelle's apprenticeship. The sight of his father, broken and miserable, convinced Pelle that he ought to leave Bornholm for Copenhagen, where he hoped to make his fortune.

In Copenhagen, Pelle soon found work, but the pay was slight. Finally he joined a newly organized trade union. He quickly became interested in the activity of the union and became a leader in the labor movement. He met many people, among them Ellen Stolpe, the daughter of a leader in the stonemasons' union. Pelle fell in love with her, and she with him. They were married on the day Pelle became president of the shoemakers' union.

After his marriage, Pelle lost interest in the union; he spent as much time as possible with his wife and eventually with his two children. Then a very bad winter came. All the workmen were hard-pressed by lack of work. The hardships he and others suffered aroused Pelle once again to work with the union. His private life, too, had become miserable, for he discovered that his wife had turned prostitute to keep the family fed and sheltered. When he discovered this, Pelle left his wife.

The workmen were successful in a general strike against their employers, but Pelle, who was recognized as a ringleader, was thrown into prison on charges of having been a counterfeiter; the police had discovered in his house a block of wood that was a crude plate for a banknote. Pelle had made it just for something to do while unemployed. For six years, Pelle languished in prison. When he was released, he became reconciled with his wife. He also discovered that the lot of the workingmen had become considerably better during his period of imprisonment, although in his own trade machinery had taken the place of the shoemaker-craftsman. Pelle took a job in a factory that specialized in metal fabrications, but he left the job, although he had become a salaried employee, when the management tried to use him as a strikebreaker.

Again Pelle was out of work for quite a time. He picked up odd jobs wherever he could find them, and he spent a great deal of time in a public library reading everything he could find about the labor movement and about ways of improving the lot of the workingmen. He became a friend of the librarian, Mr. Brun, and the two of them started a cooperative shoe factory. Their experiment was successful, even though rival companies opposed them, and they prospered to the point where they could open their own leather factory and buy a large tract of land on which to build model homes for their employees.

Pelle had become convinced that it was by such peaceful measures that the lot of the working class could be improved. The former firebrand addressed meetings, urging workers to take constitutional means to make their work conditions and wages better rather than to use the more combative and costly means of the strike.

Critical Evaluation:

Pelle the Conqueror resembles much other successful radical and socialist literature in being basically autobiographical. Like Martin Andersen Nexø, who was born in one of the poorest slums of Copenhagen, Denmark, the central character of *Pelle the Conqueror* was a member of the working class. While he follows his own particular destiny, Pelle also represents choices for the working-class movement as a whole, and there can be no doubt that, beyond telling an interesting story, Nexø intended his book to help transform the life of working people. Lasse,

Pelle, Kalle, and Erik are all meant to serve as social types and as indicators of working-class responses.

The background of *Pelle the Conqueror* is the struggle between workers and employers during the rise of the labor movement in Denmark in the last half of the nineteenth century. At no time, however, does social criticism overwhelm the narrative. Obviously the book was written to expose the struggles of working people, but the maturing of a young man from direst poverty is always foremost. The author's love for so-called common people and their problems is perhaps best illustrated in the insight with which he depicts small incidents of life. The many digressions from the main story to customs and experiences of other characters in whom Nexø was interested are anything but boring because of the sympathy and warmheartedness with which they are presented.

Lasse, Pelle's father, is already an old widower when the novel opens; he is conservative, unwilling to rebel, and resigned to his fate. Pelle dreams of being like Erik, a fighter and rebel, but Erik's problem is that he is subject to rages; he is meant to suggest a certain type of rural worker who rebels blindly but without plans or organization. One day, goaded beyond endurance, Erik assaults the bailiff and is smashed on the head and reduced to near idiocy. Kalle, at the other extreme, is good-naturedly willing to accept everything. Erik and Kalle represent opposite aspects of the rural working poor who, as a group, vacillate between blind rebellion and passive acceptance.

Pelle's youth, described in book 1 of the novel, represents the experience of the rural working class that, at the onset of industrialization, was attracted to the city and became the urban proletariat. The adolescence of the working class, corresponding to the stage of handicraft industry, is pictured in *Apprenticeship*, the second book, and Pelle's maturity as a workingman is portrayed in *The Great Struggle*, the third volume, which takes place during a time of trade union activity on a mass scale. The final book, *Daybreak*, contains Nexø's ideas for the future: profit sharing, communal living near nature, and human solidarity. Nexø rejects more radical solutions, such as revolutionary Communism, and in the end Pelle is shown at rest.

Nexø's novel, which influenced proletarian, socialist, and communist writers around the world, stands as a monumental vision of class history and struggle summarized and dramatized in the life of a single, interesting man. Nexø is a competent novelist who does an excellent job of dramatizing, individualizing, and organizing his vast subject.

Bibliography:

Ingwersen, Faith, and Niels Ingwersen. *Quests for a Promised Land: The Works of Martin Andersen Nexø*. Westport, Conn.: Greenwood Press, 1984. The primary reference on Nexø and his works. Discusses *Pelle the Conqueror* as a realistic work with a mythical dimension that tells an optimistic tale of a worker who is also a mythical liberator. Discusses the political, heroic, and ambiguous facets of the novel.

Ingwersen, Niels. "The Rural Rebellion." In *A History of Danish Literature*, edited by Sven H. Rossel. Lincoln: University of Nebraska Press, 1992. A brief article showing the novel's symbolism and stark realism and describing it as a socialistic *Bildungsroman*.

Johanson, Joel M. "*Pelle, the Conqueror:* An Epic of Labor." *The Sewanee Review Quarterly* 27 (April, 1919): 218-226. Describes the novel as a true epic of labor, in which the worker emerges as the self-sufficient hero. Argues that the work anticipates the positive effects of unionism when Pelle makes his own "promised land" at home.

Moritzen, Julius. "Martin Andersen Nexø." In *Literary Stars on the Scandinavian Firmament*. Girard, Kans.: Haldeman-Julius, 1923. A brief introduction to Nexø's work showing the autobiographical aspects of *Pelle the Conqueror*. Credits Nexø's novels with having brought about the improvement of workers' lives in Denmark.

Slochower, Harry. "Socialist Humanism: Martin Andersen Nexø's *Pelle the Conqueror*." In *Three Ways of Modern Man*. 1937. Reprint. New York: Kraus Reprint, 1969. An excellent discussion of *Pelle the Conqueror* as the classic proletarian novel. Shows how the major characters and four parts reflect all facets of the rise of the workers' movement.

PELLÉAS AND MÉLISANDE

Type of work: Drama
Author: Maurice Maeterlinck (1862-1949)
Type of plot: Symbolism
Time of plot: Middle Ages
Locale: The mythical kingdom Allemonde
First published: Pelléas et Mélisande, 1892 (English translation, 1894); first performed, 1893

> *Principal characters:*
> ARKËL, the king of Allemonde
> GENEVIÈVE, the mother of Pelléas and Golaud
> PELLÉAS and
> GOLAUD, Arkël's grandsons
> MÉLISANDE, Golaud's wife
> LITTLE YNIOLD, the son of Golaud by a former marriage

The Story:

Golaud, Arkël's grandson, became lost while hunting, and as he wandered through the forest he came upon Mélisande weeping beside a spring. She too was lost, her beautiful clothes torn by the briars and her golden crown fallen into the spring. She was like a little girl when she wept. Golaud tried to comfort her. Although she would not let him touch her or reach for her crown, which he could have retrieved easily, she followed him out of the forest.

Afraid of Arkël, who wanted his grandson to marry the daughter of an enemy in order to bring peace to the land, Golaud wrote his half brother Pelléas that he had married Mélisande and wished to bring her home if Arkël would forgive him. He would wait near the castle for Pelléas to signal that he and Mélisande might enter. Their mother, Geneviève, persuaded Arkël, who was now too old to resist, to give his permission. Pelléas wanted to visit a dying friend before Mélisande came, but Arkël persuaded him to stay for the sake of his own sick father.

When Pelléas took Mélisande to see Blind Man's Spring, a delightfully cool place on a stifling day, he realized that Golaud had found Mélisande beside a spring. As he asked her about that meeting, Mélisande, playing with her wedding ring, let it fall into the water. As the ring fell, the clock in the castle grounds struck twelve.

Golaud had been hunting. When the clock struck twelve, his horse bolted and ran into a tree, throwing Golaud. He was recovering from his accident when Mélisande came to tell him that she wanted to go away because the castle was too gloomy. He noticed that her ring was gone. She said that she had lost it in the grotto by the sea while picking up shells for Little Yniold. Golaud sent her back immediately to find the ring before the tide came in.

Pelléas took Mélisande to the grotto so that she would be able to describe the place where she claimed to have lost Golaud's wedding ring.

Whenever Golaud was away, Pelléas spent as much time as he could with Mélisande. Usually Little Yniold was with them. Once, when the little boy was unable to sleep because he said Mélisande would go away, Pelléas took him to the window to see the swans chasing the dogs. Little Yniold saw his father crossing the courtyard and ran downstairs to meet him. Returning to the room, Little Yniold noticed that both Pelléas and Mélisande had been crying.

One night, Mélisande leaned from a tower while she combed her beautiful, long hair. Pelléas, coming into the courtyard below, entwined his hands in her hair and praised her beauty. When

Golaud came by shortly afterward, Pelléas could not let go of Mélisande's hair. Golaud scolded them for playing at night like children.

On some days, the castle had a smell of death. Golaud, convinced that an underground lake in one of the crypts beneath the castle was responsible for the smell, led Pelléas down into the crypts the next morning to see the lake and smell the overpowering scent of death there. As Golaud swung the lantern around, Pelléas would have fallen into the lake if Golaud had not caught his arm.

When the half brothers came out on the terrace, Golaud told Pelléas that Mélisande was young and impressionable and that she must be treated more circumspectly than Pelléas had treated her the night before, because she was with child.

Golaud tried to find out from Yniold how Pelléas and Mélisande acted when the child was with them, what they said and what they did. When he could not get the child to answer any of his questions satisfactorily, he lifted him so that the boy could look through the window of the room in which Pelléas and Mélisande were standing. Even then he could not learn from Yniold what Pelléas and Mélisande were doing.

A short time later, Pelléas' father was so much better that the prince decided to start on his delayed journey the next day. He asked Mélisande to meet him that night near Blind Man's Spring.

Arkël told Mélisande that happiness ought to enter the castle now that Pelléas' father had recovered. He wondered why she had changed from the joyous creature she was when she entered the castle to the unhappy one she now seemed to be. Although Mélisande disclaimed being unhappy, Arkël sensed her sadness. Golaud, coming to look for his sword, suddenly began raging at Mélisande, and he dragged her on her knees until Arkël intervened.

That night, Mélisande went to meet Pelléas, and as they made love in the shadows Pelléas felt that the stars were falling. When they went into the moonlight, their shadows stretched the length of the garden. Pelléas thought Mélisande's beauty unearthly, as if she were about to die. As the gates clanged shut, they realized that they were locked out of the castle for the night. Suddenly Mélisande saw Golaud. Knowing they could not flee from his sword, Mélisande and Pelléas kissed desperately. When Golaud struck Pelléas at the brink of the fountain, Pelléas fell. Golaud pursued Mélisande into the darkness.

An old servant found Mélisande and Golaud at the gates early the next morning. Mélisande had a slight cut under her breast, not enough to harm a bird. She was delivered of a tiny, premature daughter. Golaud had tried without success to kill himself.

Golaud dragged himself to Mélisande's room, where Arkël and the physician were attending her. The physician tried to convince Golaud that Mélisande was not dying of the sword wound, that she had been born without reason to die, and that she was dying without reason. Golaud could not be convinced. He felt that he had killed both Pelléas and Mélisande without cause—that they were both children and had kissed simply as children do—but he was not sure.

When Mélisande awoke, she seemed to have forgotten her hurt and Golaud's pursuit, and she thought her husband had grown old. Hoping to hear her confess to a forbidden love for Pelléas, Golaud asked the physician and Arkël to leave him alone with her for a moment. When he questioned her, however, Mélisande innocently exclaimed that she and Pelléas were never guilty. She asked where Pelléas was. Because Golaud begged her to speak the truth at the moment of death, she asked who was to die. She could not answer his questions any better than Little Yniold had done when Golaud lifted him to the window to spy for him.

Arkël showed Mélisande her tiny daughter. Mélisande pitied the child because she looked sad. While Mélisande was looking at the baby, a group of women servants came into the room.

Mélisande stretched out her arms and then lay as if weeping in her sleep. Suddenly the servants knelt. The physician looked at Mélisande and saw that she was dead.

Critical Evaluation:

Maurice Maeterlinck wrote *Pelléas and Mélisande* and other symbolic plays as a reaction to the late nineteenth century positivistic belief in rationalistic solutions to all social and scientific problems. He felt that naturalistic, well-made plays that portrayed life realistically left little room in the reader's or spectator's mind for imaginative, mystical responses. By setting his play in the distant Middle Ages in a mysterious kingdom called Allemonde, which literally means "all the world" (from the German *alle* and the French *monde*), he established a time and place very different from those used in the traditional drama of his era.

During the 1880's, Maeterlinck read medieval literature such as works by the Flemish mystic Jan van Ruysbroeck and many modern symbolical texts, including poems and stories by the French authors Phillipe-Auguste de Villiers de L'Isle-Adam, Stéphane Mallarmé, Charles Baudelaire, and Joris-Karl Huysmans. He also appreciated the writings of the German Romanticist writer Novalis and the American writer Edgar Allan Poe. William Shakespeare's plays and European fairy tales fascinated him. He wanted to express in his art a language that was purer and simpler than adult, scientific prose, one that would somehow suggest primitive peoples and deep emotions.

Born and raised in Ghent, Belgium, a city of canals and medieval buildings, Maeterlinck grew up surrounded by artifacts from the Middle Ages. He often felt haunted by death, and a foreboding atmosphere pervades most of his plays. An audience often feels as if something awful, but unknown, is about to strike and cause the death of one or more of the characters. To portray both this sense of dark oppression and the simplicity of primitive peoples, Maeterlinck's characters often repeat certain words or phrases, a practice he had noticed in Flemish peasants when they told stories. Maeterlinck's goal was not to evoke a rational understanding of the events that occur in his plays but rather to help the reader or spectator feel the emotions of suspense, anxiety, fear, and occasionally joy.

Pelléas and Mélisande, more mystical and emotional than rational, subsequently attracted several composers, among them Gabriel Fauré, Claude Debussy, Arnold Schoenberg, and Jean Sibelius, all of whom composed works based on the play in the first decade of the twentieth century. When it was staged in London in 1898, the play used sets designed from paintings by the pre-Raphaelite artists Dante Gabriel Rossetti and Edward Burne-Jones, who portrayed slender, mysterious young women in medieval surroundings. The combination of the play's text with impressionistic music and beautiful art transported the spectators into the Allemonde of their and Maeterlinck's imaginations.

Allemonde is a place of degeneration, pending death, and fleeting hopes of happiness through love. Despite the political marriage arranged for him by his father, Golaud chooses to wed Mélisande, a fairylike creature without family relations, a lost soul he has found in a dark forest. Golaud hopes to find joy in his new relationship, and Mélisande does indeed seem to bring temporary happiness into the gloomy castle. Golaud, a widower, is renewed by her apparent love. His dying father, never named, temporarily recovers so that the family believes the physicians' optimistic reports. Pelléas thereupon resolves to leave Allemonde to visit Marcellus, his dying friend, and invites Mélisande to meet him by the Blind Man's Spring so that they may bid each other adieu. If they had not been discovered that night by the jealous Golaud, the tragedy of a murdered brother and fatally wounded wife would perhaps have been avoided. The brief, passionate moment between Pelléas and Mélisande is destroyed by

Golaud's violence. The themes of passionate love and hovering death prevail throughout, and in the end death conquers in this very enclosed world.

In some ways, Allemonde resembles the realm of the legendary Fisher King. According to this myth, the king's wounds and sickness are reflected in the infertility of his realm. The fetid smells from beneath the palace in Allemonde suggest decay and the possible collapse of the structure and destruction of its inhabitants at any moment. In contrast to the Fisher King story, however, no Galahad arrives in Allemonde to free the king and restore fertility to his realm; instead, he remains ill, and his son Golaud kills his own brother Pelléas and wounds Mélisande.

Unlike an indestructible fairy, Mélisande, despite her mysterious past, is a mortal creature. She can survive neither her husband's attack nor giving birth to a premature daughter. She has no magical powers to prevent destruction and death. Although Maeterlinck wanted to escape the naturalistic style of his contemporaries, which realistically portrayed the dark moments of life, he succumbed to his own fascination with death by transforming into tragedy the optimistic medieval legends of a Fisher King who is healed and fairies who have power to grant wishes. The expectations aroused in the reader and spectator that magical events will occur in this strange, isolated, medieval setting are disappointed at the conclusion when death reigns. The wise grandfather Arkël's final words suggest that the tragedy will continue: "Come; the child must not stay here, in this room. . . . It must live now, in her stead. . . . The poor little one's turn has come."

The first production of *Pelléas and Mélisande* in Paris in 1893 accentuated the mystical tension between the opposing forces of love and death. It emphasized an unrealistic setting where emotions were more important than a concrete time and place. The set was extremely simple with overhead lighting casting shadows everywhere. The characters, who wore apparel similar to that of figures in paintings by the Pre-Raphaelite artists, performed behind a gauze curtain, suggesting to the spectator a realm of mystery divorced from the real world. Both the drama and the set differed from the furnished sitting rooms of many contemporary naturalistic plays of the time.

Symbolism had been recognized as a poetic movement in reaction to more concrete types of poetry, but Maurice Maeterlinck was the first to introduce it so fully into the theater. He became honored internationally for his innovative works, and when he was awarded the Nobel Prize in Literature in 1911, he was commended for "his diverse literary activity and especially his dramatic works . . . which sometimes in the dim form of the play of legend display a deep intimacy of feeling, and also in a mysterious way appeal to the reader's sentiment and sense of foreboding." He wrote prolifically throughout his life, including plays such as *The Blue Bird* (1908) and several books of essays on insects and parapsychology, but his popularity gradually waned. Maeterlinck is now most remembered and honored for innovative symbolist plays like *Pelléas and Mélisande*.

"Critical Evaluation" by Carole J. Lambert

Bibliography:
Delevoy, Robert L. *Symbolists and Symbolism*. New York: Rizzoli, 1982. A beautifully illustrated chronicle of the Symbolist movement. Describes the cultural events of the era and the aesthetic theories of the Symbolist pictorial and literary artists. Includes an analysis of *Pelléas and Mélisande*.
Halls, W. D. *Maurice Maeterlinck: A Study of His Life and Thought*. Oxford, England: Clarendon Press, 1960. This brief biography is based on the author's research into Maeter-

linck's letters and interviews of his acquaintances. Includes concise critical summaries of each work. A good scholarly starting point for Maeterlinck studies.

Knapp, Bettina. *Maurice Maeterlinck*. Boston: Twayne, 1975. Discusses the writer's life and works with particular emphasis on his use of archetypes and symbols.

Lambert, Carole J. *The Empty Cross: Medieval Hopes, Modern Futility in the Theater of Maurice Maeterlinck, Paul Claudel, August Strindberg, and Georg Kaiser*. New York: Garland, 1990. The introduction and conclusion describe the cultural environment that stimulated Maeterlinck to write symbolic plays. Chapter 2 provides a detailed analysis of *Pelléas and Mélisande*. Includes an extensive bibliography, with references to unpublished texts and works about Maeterlinck in several languages.

Mahony, Patrick. *Maurice Maeterlinck, Mystic and Dramatist*. 2d ed. Washington, D.C.: The Institute for the Study of Man, 1984. The author, a friend and editor for Maeterlinck during his travels in the United States, relates personal anecdotes and gives a summary of his life. Also discusses some of the plays and prose works, as well as his interest in psychic phenomena.

PENGUIN ISLAND

Type of work: Novel
Author: Anatole France (Jacques-Anatole-François Thibault, 1844-1924)
Type of plot: Satire
Time of plot: Ancient to modern times
Locale: Mythical Alca
First published: L'Île des pingouins, 1908 (English translation, 1914)

>   *Principal characters:*
>   MAEL, a missionary monk
>   KRAKEN, an opportunist penguin
>   ORBEROSIA, Kraken's mistress
>   TRINCO, a conqueror
>   PYROT, a scapegoat
>   MONSIEUR CERES, a cabinet minister
>   EVELINE, his wife
>   MONSIEUR VISIRE, Prime Minister of Penguinia

The Story:

In ancient times Mael, a Breton monk, was diligent in gathering converts to the Church. One day the devil caused Mael to be transported in a boat to the North Pole, where the priest landed on an island inhabited by penguins. Being somewhat snow-blind, he mistook the birds for people, preached to them, and, taking their silence as a sign of willingness, baptized them into the Christian faith.

This error of the pious Mael caused great consternation in paradise. God called all the saints together, and they argued whether the baptisms were valid. At last they decided that the only way out of the dilemma was to change the penguins into people. After this transformation took place, Mael towed the island back to the Breton coast so that he could keep an eye on his converts.

Thus began the history of Penguinia on the island of Alca. At first the penguins were without clothes, but before long the holy Mael put clothes on the females. The novelty of covering excited the males, and sexual promiscuity was enormously increased. The penguins began to establish the rights of property by knocking one another over the head. Greatauk, the largest and strongest penguin, became the founder of power and wealth. A taxation system was established by which all penguins were taxed equally. This system was favored by the rich, who kept their money intended to benefit the poor.

Kraken, a clever penguin, withdrew to a lonely part of the island and lived alone in a cave. Finally he took as his mistress Orberosia, the most beautiful of penguin women. Kraken gained great wealth by dressing up as a dragon and carrying off the wealth of the peaceful penguins. When the citizens banded together to protect their property, Kraken became frightened. It was predicted by Mael that a virgin would come to conquer the dragon. Kraken and Orberosia fashioned an imitation monster. Orberosia appeared to Mael and announced herself as the destined virgin. At an appointed time she revealed the imitation monster. Kraken sprang from a hiding place and pretended to kill it. The people rejoiced and thenceforth paid annual tribute to Kraken. His son, Draco, founded the first royal family of Penguinia.

Thus began the Middle Ages on the island of Alca. Draco the Great, a descendant of the original Draco, had a monastery established in the cave of Kraken in honor of Orberosia, who was now a saint. There were great wars between the penguins and the porpoises at that time, but the Christian faith was preserved by the simple expedient of burning all heretics at the stake.

The history of the penguins in that far time was chronicled by a learned monk named Johannes Talpa. Even though the battles raged about his ears, he was able to continue writing in his dry and simple style. Little record was left of the primitive paintings on the isle of Alca, but later historians believed that the painters were careful to represent nature as unlike nature as possible.

Marbodius, a literary monk, left a record of a descent into hell similar to the experience of Dante. Marbodius interviewed Vergil and was told by the great poet that Dante had misrepresented him. Vergil was perfectly happy with his own mythology and wanted nothing to do with the God of the Christians.

The next recorded part of Penguinian history treated modern times, when rationalistic philosophers began to appear. In the succeeding generation their teachings took root. The king was put to death, nobility was abolished, and a republic was founded. The shrine of Saint Orberosia was destroyed. The republic, however, did not last long. Trinco, a great soldier, took command of the country; with his armies he conquered and lost all the known world. The penguins were left at last with nothing but their glory.

Then a new republic was established. It pretended to be ruled by the people, but the real rulers were the wealthy financiers. Another republic of a similar nature, New Atlantis, had grown up across the sea at the same time. It was even more advanced in the worship of wealth.

Father Agaric and Prince des Boscenos, as members of the clergy and nobility, were interested in restoring the kings of Alca to the throne. They decided to destroy the republic by taking advantage of the weakness of Chatillon, the admiral of the navy. Chatillon was seduced by the charms of the clever Viscountess Olive, who was able to control his actions for the benefit of the royalists. An immense popular antirepublican movement was begun with Chatillon as its hero; the royalists hoped to reinstate the king in the midst of the uproar. The revolution, however, was stopped in its infancy, and Chatillon fled the country.

Eveline, the beautiful daughter of Madame Clarence, rejected the love of Viscount Clena, after she had learned that he had no fortune. She then accepted the attentions of Monsieur Ceres, a rising politician. After a short time they were married. Monsieur Ceres received a portfolio in the cabinet of Monsieur Visire, and Eveline became a favorite in the social gatherings of the politicians. M. Visire was attracted by her, and she became his mistress. M. Ceres learned of the affair, but he was afraid to say anything to M. Visire, the prime minister. Instead, he did his best to ruin M. Visire politically, but with little success at first. Finally M. Visire was put out of office on the eve of a war with a neighboring empire. Eveline lived to a respectable old age and at her death left all of her property to the Charity of Saint Orberosia.

As Penguinia developed into an industrial civilization ruled by the wealthy class, the one purpose of life became the gathering of riches; art and all other nonprofit activities ceased to be. Finally the downtrodden workers revolted, and a wave of anarchy swept over the nation. All the great industries were demolished. Order was established at last, and the government reformed many of the social institutions, but the country continued to decline. Where before there had been great cities, wild animals now lived.

Then came hunters seeking the wild animals. Later shepherds appeared, and after a time farming became the chief occupation. Great lords built castles. The people made roads; villages appeared. The villages combined into large cities. The cities grew rich. An industrial civilization developed, ruled by the wealthy class. History was beginning to repeat itself.

Critical Evaluation:

With its mixture of satire, burlesque, and fantasy, *Penguin Island* resembles Voltaire's *Candide* (1759) and Thornton Wilder's play *The Skin of Our Teeth* (1942). Like *Candide*, Anatole France's episodic novel is a reasoned attack upon unreason. Unlike Voltaire's work, which ridicules philosophical error for the most part, *Penguin Island* attacks the absurdities that have fastened onto human customs and institutions. For its flights into fantasy and its ambitious attempt to explain the course of civilization in terms of a burlesque of history—past, present, and future—*Penguin Island* also may be compared to Wilder's *The Skin of Our Teeth*. Both works turn history into myth, comment with tolerance upon human follies, and suggest that a dim, ambiguous purpose ultimately controls human destiny. Wilder's comedy, however, is essentially optimistic and melioristic; in spite of natural and social disasters, his message is that the human animal will not only survive but also actually improve its lot in the universe. France, on the other hand, is pessimistic. He believes that humanity's course is cyclical, not linear. By the conclusion of *Penguin Island*, the human race has reached the apex of its scientific and technological advance, after which point it retreats into barbarism. The future of Penguinia is not much brighter than its past; every movement forward is succeeded by a step backward, until the cycle is repeated endlessly. Whatever divine force operates in the universe, France seems to believe, its machinery—just as its intelligence—is beyond understanding.

Yet the author, always amiable, treats a doomed humankind with kindly tolerance instead of scorn. Although his satire occasionally has a cutting edge, he is more often the gentle ironist than the stern moralist. France exposes folly but does not castigate the foolish. The two great subjects for his satire are the follies of human customs and institutions. Throughout history—or mythologized French history, France's particular field of investigation—the author analyzes the conventions of woman's role as opposed to her biological nature. Her real nature, France believes, is that of sexual temptress, concerned only, or mostly, with the satisfaction of her physical needs. The blessed Mael, for example, creator (so to speak) of the race of Alca, describes woman as a "cleverly constructed snare" by which a man is taken before he suspects the trap. Moreover, Mael opines that, for vulnerable man, the imagined sexual lure of a woman is more powerful than her real body. As proof of this idea, Orberosia is more attractive to the male pseudopenguins when she is clothed than when she is nude. An Eve-figure, Orberosia is flagrantly promiscuous (among her many lovers is a hunchbacked neatherd), is unfaithful to her husband Kraken, yet maintains the necessary social fiction of chastity. She even pretends to be the sole virgin among the Alcas. Similarly, Queen Glamorgan tempts the pure monk Oddoul, who repulses her lascivious advances; for his chastity, he is disgraced; the "angel" Gudrune derides him as impotent; and a woman empties a chamber pot upon his head. So long as Glamorgan pretends to be chaste she is socially accepted, no matter what may be her true morality. Other licentious women are safe from censure so long as they perform a role of conventional virtue. Examples include Queen Crucha, the fickle Viscountess Olive, and the adulterous Eveline Ceres. The appearance, not the fact, of virtue is important for women to maintain.

Just as France contrasts the pretended with the actual condition of women's chastity, so he contrasts ideal with real social institutions. Ideally, the state is intended to protect the weak, but in fact it protects the powerful. To conceal abuses of power, social institutions employ fictions that make them appear benevolent. Even in heaven, among a council of the blessed, Saint Augustine argues that it is form, not substance, that matters. Saint Gal agrees that in the signs of religion and the laws of salvation, "form necessarily prevails over essence." Among people, the national state, created by brute force, employs laws to formularize its power. The monk Bullock interprets the actions of a madman who bites the nose of his adversary as a sign of the creation of law; the murderer of a farmer, similarly, he condones as one who establishes the right of property. Taxes take money from the poor but never a proportionate share from the rich. The modern national state, according to France, is nothing more than an institution to consolidate wealth and, through warfare, to extend its influence. Trinco (Napoleon) is the great hero of Penguinia because he creates an empire, no matter at what cost. "Glory never costs too much," says a patriotic guide to young Djambi. Patriotism itself becomes formularized. As Colonel Marchand observes, the armies of all nations are "the finest in the world"; so every nation must use its military force to test its strength. The Prince des Boscenos cynically argues that just causes, in order to triumph, need force. Thus, the national powers mobilize not to protect the weak but to support the mighty.

In the celebrated book 6, "The Affair of the Eighty Thousand Trusses of Hay," France shows how the Dreyfus case demonstrates in microcosm the abuses of institutional power. All the institutions of the state and of society—the government bureaucracy, the army, the Church—oppose Pyrot (Dreyfus). At first, only his Jewish relatives, seven hundred strong, dare to support his just cause. Later, the courageous writer Colomban (Émile Zola), along with liberals of different persuasions, join the battle as Pyrotists. They fight not only against falsehood (the Count de Maubec has never delivered the eighty thousand trusses of hay, so Pyrot could not have stolen the lot), but also against prejudice and tradition. As Father Cornemuse puts the matter, Pyrot must be guilty, because he has been convicted; and the courts must be defended even if they are corrupt. Only after Justice Chaussepied examines the so-called evidence against the defendant—732 square yards of debris containing not a shred of proof, not a single word about the accused—does he declare the case a farce. Yet Justice Chaussepied's correct ruling results not so much from a recognition of the truth as from expediency; if he had allowed the folly to continue, the Pyrot case would have destroyed the political institutions of the state. Thus, the author once again drives home his point: People are slaves to customs and conventions. In *Penguin Island*, France shows how little headway reason, honesty, and justice make against these ancient stumbling blocks to progress.

"Critical Evaluation" by Leslie B. Mittleman

Bibliography:

Bresky, Dushan. *The Art of Anatole France.* The Hague: Mouton, 1969. A critical overview of France's work, with discussion of France's place within the French literary tradition. Sections on humor and utopianism, and great sensitivity to questions of aesthetics.

Kennett, W. T. E. "The Theme of *Penguin Island.*" *Romanic Review* 33, no. 3 (October, 1942): 275-289. Traces the theme of an imaginary island populated by penguins in romantic European travelogue literature since the Renaissance, concluding with a critical examination of France's *Penguin Island.*

May, James Lewis. *Anatole France: The Man and His Work, an Essay in Critical Biography.* 1924. Reprint. Port Washington, N.Y.: Kennikat Press, 1970. Profiles France's formative influences in the first half of the book, followed by critical discussions of France's works.

Stewart, Herbert Leslie. *Anatole France, the Parisian.* 1927. Reprint. Freeport, N.Y.: Books for Libraries Press, 1972. Correlates elements in France's works to specific personal, cultural, and philosophical influences. Many anecdotes and pertinent quotations. Emphasizes France's humanism and its effect on his work.

Virtanen, Reino. *Anatole France.* New York: Twayne, 1968. A chronologically arranged critical perspective on France's body of work. Traces France's debts to earlier satirists.

PENSÉES

Type of work: Philosophical
Author: Blaise Pascal (1623-1662)
First published: 1670 (English translation, 1688)

Blaise Pascal, scientist and mathematician, became a member of the society of Port Royal after his conversion as the result of a mystical experience in 1654. He was actively involved in the bitter debate between the Jansenists, with whom he allied himself, and the Jesuits; the series of polemical letters titled *The Provincial Letters* (1656-1657) is the result of that great quarrel. Wanting to write a defense of Catholic Christianity that would appeal to people of reason and sensibility, Pascal, about 1660, began to prepare his defense of the Catholic faith.

Like many other great thinkers whose concern was more with the subject of their compositions than with the external order and completeness of the presentation, he failed to complete a continuous and unified apology. When he died at thirty-nine he left little more than his notes for the projected work, a series of philosophical fragments reflecting his religious meditations. These form the *Pensées*. Despite its fragmentary character, the book is a classic of French literature, charming and effective in its style, powerful and sincere in its philosophic and religious protestations.

Philosophers distinguish themselves either by the insight of their claims or by the power of their justification. Paradoxically, Pascal distinguishes himself in his defense by the power of his claims. This quality is partly a matter of style and partly a matter of conviction. It was Pascal, in the *Pensées*, who wrote, "The heart has its reasons, which reason does not know," by which he meant not that emotion is superior to reason, but that in being compelled by a moving experience one submits to a superior kind of reason. Pascal also wrote that "All our reasoning reduces itself to yielding to feeling," but he admitted that it is sometimes difficult to distinguish between feeling and fancy. Pascal believed that the way to truth is by the heart, the feeling, and that the intuitive way of knowledge is the most important, not only because feeling or intuition is what leads the mind regarding the most important matters but also because it is essential to all reasoning, providing the first principles of thought. Much of the value of the *Pensées* results from the clarity with which Pascal presented his intuitive thoughts.

A considerable portion of the *Pensées* is taken up with a discussion of philosophical method, particularly in relation to religious reflection. The book begins with an analysis of the difference between mathematical and intuitive thinking and continues the discussion, in later sections, by considering the value of skepticism, of contradictions, of feeling, memory, and imagination. A number of passages remind the reader of the fact that a proposition that seems true from one perspective may seem false from another, but Pascal insists that "essential" truth is "altogether pure and altogether true." The power of skepticism and the use of contradictions in reasoning depend upon a conception of human thinking that ignores the importance of perspective in determining one's belief. Thus, from the skeptic's point of view nothing is known because people can be sure of nothing. The skeptic forgets, however, that "It is good to be tired and wearied by the vain search after the true good, that we may stretch out our arms to the Redeemer." Contradiction, according to Pascal, "is a bad sign of truth" since there are some certainties that have been contradicted and some false ideas that have not. Contradiction nevertheless has its use: "All these contradictions, which seem most to keep me from the knowledge of religion, have led me most quickly to the true one."

Pascal had the gift of responding critically in a way that added value to both his own discourse and that of his opponent. Criticizing Montaigne's skepticism, he came to recognize the truth—a partial truth, to be sure—of much that Montaigne wrote. His acknowledgment of this is grudging; he writes that "It is not in Montaigne, but in myself, that I find all that I see in him," and also "What good there is in Montaigne can only have been acquired with difficulty." As T. S. Eliot has pointed out in an introduction to the *Pensées*, however, Pascal uses many of Montaigne's ideas, phrases, and terms.

Perhaps the most controversial part of the *Pensées* is Pascal's section on miracles. He quotes Saint Augustine as saying that he would not have been a Christian but for the miracles, and he argues that there are three marks of religion: perpetuity, a good life, and miracles. He writes, "If the cooling of love leaves the Church almost without believers, miracles will rouse them," and "Miracles are more important than you think. They have served for the foundation, and will serve for the continuation of the Church till Anti-christ, till the end." Although there are other passages that assert the importance of faith and that are in no way dependent upon miracles for their assertions (for example, "That we must love one God only is a thing so evident, that it does not require miracles to prove it"), Pascal seems unambiguously to assert that miracles are a way to faith. This idea is opposed by those who insist that belief in miracles presupposes a belief in God and the Gospel. Pascal had been profoundly affected by a miracle at Port Royal, but his defense of the importance of miracles goes beyond that immediate reference, using appeals to reason and authority as well as to feeling.

Pascal's "Proofs of Jesus Christ" is interesting not only because it pretends to offer demonstrations to appeal to unbelievers, but also because it uses persuasive references that throw light on the question of Jesus' historical status. He argues that it is because of the actions of unbelievers at the time of Christ that the faithful have witnesses to Him. If Jesus had made His nature so evident that none could mistake it, the proof of His nature and existence would not have been as convincing as it is when reported by unbelievers. Pascal emphasizes the function of the Jews as unbelievers when he writes: "The Jews, in slaying Him in order not to receive Him as the Messiah, have given Him the final proof of being the Messiah. And in continuing not to recognize Him, they made themselves irreproachable witnesses."

Pascal's famous wager is presented in the *Pensées*. He makes an appeal to "natural lights"— ordinary human intelligence and good sense. God either exists or He does not. How shall you decide? This is a game with infinitely serious consequences. You must wager, but how shall you wager? Reason is of no use here. Suppose you decide to wager that God exists. "If you gain, you gain all; if you lose, you lose nothing." Pascal concludes that there is everything to be said in favor of committing oneself to a belief in God and strong reasons against denying God. To the objection that one cannot come to believe simply by recognizing that one will be extremely fortunate if one is right and no worse off if one is wrong, Pascal replies by saying that if an unbeliever will act as if he believes, and if he wants to believe, belief will come to him. This wager later inspired William James's *The Will to Believe and Other Essays in Popular Philosophy* (1897), in which the American pragmatist argued that Pascal's method is essentially pragmatic. James's objection to Pascal's wager is that the wager alone presents no momentous issue; unless one can relate the particular issue being considered to a person's great concerns, the appeal of the wager is empty. If such proof would work for Pascal's God, it would work for any god whatsoever. James's use of the wager to justify passional decisions, however, is much like Pascal's.

In a section titled "The Fundamentals of the Christian Religion," Pascal writes that the Christian religion teaches two truths: that there is a God whom people can know and that because of their corruption people are unworthy of Him. Pascal rejected cold conceptions of

God that reduce Him to the author of mathematical truths or of the order of the elements. For Pascal, the God of salvation has to be conceived as He is known through Jesus Christ. The Christian God can be known, according to Pascal, but since people are corrupt they do not always know God. Nature assists God to hide Himself from corrupt people, although it also contains perfections to show that nature is the image of God.

In considering "The Philosophers," Pascal emphasizes thought as distinguishing people from brutes and making the greatness of humanity possible. "Man is neither angel nor brute," he writes, "and the unfortunate thing is that he who would act the angel acts the brute."

Pascal was a man who was on the one hand eager to defend the Christian faith and on the other determined to indicate the shortcomings of humanity. He is remorselessly critical in his attacks on skeptics, atheists, and other critics of the Church, not simply because they err, but because they do so without respect for the possibilities of human understanding or the values of religion. In regard to skepticism he wrote that his thoughts were intentionally without order in order to be true to the disorderly character of his subject.

It is not Pascal the bitter critic who prevails in the *Pensées*; it is, rather, the impassioned and inspired defender of the faith. Even those who do not share his convictions admire his style and the ingenuity of his thought, and much that is true of all humanity has never been better said than in the *Pensées*.

Bibliography:
Hammond, Nicholas. *Playing with Truth: Language and the Human Condition in Pascal's "Pensées."* Oxford, England: Clarendon Press, 1994. Scholarly yet readable discussion of the role that human language plays in argumentation, especially as it relates to the human condition as addressed by Pascal. Thorough bibliography and index.
Melzer, Sara E. *Discourses of the Fall: A Study of Pascal's "Pensées."* Berkeley: University of California Press, 1986. Critical discussion of the major dilemma in *Pensées*, that is, a strong claim for belief in a transcendent God (although limited by human language and under-standing) set against an element of uncertainty.
Nelson, Robert J. *Pascal: Adversary and Advocate.* Cambridge, Mass.: Harvard University Press, 1981. A critical study of Pascal's works, including a valuable section on "the thoughts" in relation to the "advocate" position. Focuses on the ultimate question that chiefly concerned Pascal. Includes notes, index, and bibliography.
Steinmann, Jean. *Pascal.* Translated by Martin Turnell. New York: Harcourt, Brace & World, 1966. A critical biography following the life of Pascal in connection with his works. Includes a major section on *Pensées*. A valuable study showing the human context that gave birth to Pascal's thoughts. Helpful illustrations; well indexed.
Topliss, Patricia. *The Rhetoric of Pascal: A Study of His Art of Persuasion in the "Provinciales" and the "Pensées."* Leicester, England: Leicester University Press, 1966. Part 2 of this work focuses on *Pensées*, including discussion on the relationship between argumentation and style. Bibliography.

THE PEOPLE, YES

Type of work: Poetry
Author: Carl Sandburg (1878-1967)
First published: 1936

Although Carl Sandburg wrote *The People, Yes* during the Depression of the 1930's, his strong voice remained as cheerful and reassuring to later ages as it was in the time of bread lines and soup kitchens. Yet Sandburg does not raise his voice to shout down the pessimists, he does not sing hymns to America out of a sense of duty. His book arises from a genuine love of the plain people who will somehow survive their blunders, somehow find the answers to "Where to?" and "What next?"

Sandburg asks these questions in the opening in the voices of children of workers who come to build the Tower of Babel, and the questions are still unanswered at the end, when the poet looks forward to the "Family of Man" and the time when "brother may yet line up with brother." Between those two points, the poet pays his tribute to people, the American people in particular, as he presents the legends, sayings, slang, tall tales, and dreams of twentieth century America.

Among the best and most quoted sections of the work are the one that deals with Abraham Lincoln and the one about tall tales, beginning "They have yarns. . . ." Sandburg gained a solid reputation as an authority on Lincoln, having written a great biography and many poems, speeches, and articles about Lincoln, but nowhere is he more successful than in this short poem. Here Sandburg presents the many talents of a great man by asking such questions as "Lincoln? was he a poet?" and "Lincoln? was he a historian?," to which he supplies answers from speeches, letters, and conversations of the man himself. The tall-tales poem is an encyclopedia of laughs that range from the familiar "man who drove a swarm of bees across the Rocky Mountains and the Desert 'and didn't lose a bee'" to the less familiar story of a shipwrecked sailor who has caught hold of a stateroom door and floated in near the coast; when his would-be rescuers tell him he is off the coast of New Jersey, he takes a fresh hold on the door and calls back "half-wearily, 'I guess I'll float a little farther.'"

Much of *The People, Yes* is in this same light-hearted tone, for Sandburg loves the American language and the twists of its sayings. For irony, he quotes from a memorial stone:

> We, near whose bones you stand, were Iroquois.
> The wide land which is now yours, was ours.
> Friendly hands have given us back enough for a tomb.

He offers such homespun wisdom as "Sell the buffalo hide after you have killed the buffalo," and he throws in: "The coat and the pants do the work but the vest gets the gravy." There are scores of other wisecracks and jokes, some new and some that wink at the reader like old friends from childhood.

Sandburg filled his book with American people—the real, the legendary, and the anonymous. Among the real ones are John Brown, "who was buried deep and didn't stay so"; Mr. Eastman, "the kodak king," who at the age of seventy-seven shot himself to avoid the childishness of senility; and the Wright brothers, who "wanted to fly for the sake of flying." The legends include Mike Fink, John Henry, and Paul Bunyan, to whom Sandburg devotes a whole section, explaining how the people created this Master Lumberjack, his Seven Axmen, and his Little Blue Ox. Of the anonymous, there are hundreds, and Sandburg pays tribute to them all, from the person who first said, "Wedlock is a padlock" to the one who first remarked, "No peace on earth with the women, no life anywhere without them."

By no means does Sandburg consistently handle the American people with kid gloves of gentleness and affection. When he feels so inclined, Sandburg puts on the six-ounce mitts of a prizefighter (as he often did since his *Chicago Poems* first appeared in 1916) and flails away at what he hates: the liars who do not care what they do to their customers so long as they make a sale; the torturers and the wielders of the rubber hose; the cynics who shrug off the unemployed; the crooked lawyers; the judges who can be bought and the men who boast that they can buy them; and, most of all, the mis-leaders who spit out the word "peepul" as if it were scum hocked from their throats.

Of Sandburg's many books, both prose and poetry, *The People, Yes* comes closest to being his coda, the summing up of what he tried to say in a lifetime. As if to indicate as much, he includes echoes from earlier poems. There is the hyacinths-biscuits combination that appeared first in one of his most famous definitions of poetry; he mentions the Unknown Soldier, "the boy nobody knows the name of"; and he includes the refrain from his "Four Preludes on Playthings of the Wind": "We are the greatest city, the greatest people. Nothing like us ever was." Certainly the themes in this book are the same as those that run through all of Sandburg's poetry, his love of America and its democracy, the mystery of human beings and where they are going, the hope that people everywhere will someday blunder through the fogs of injustice, hypocrisy, and skulduggery into a bright world of peace. Sandburg put it all in *The People, Yes*, and expressed it there in the fluent style that is so very much his own. No American poet had a better ear for the right combination of words, and certainly none ever matched his ability at writing dialogue, at putting on paper the way Americans really talk.

As in all books, there are caution signs for the reader to observe. No one should try to read *The People, Yes* at one sitting. It is not a narrative poem with suspense enough to carry the reader breathless to the end. Some sections are repetitious, and in places the Whitmanesque cataloging drones on monotonously. Instead, this is writing to be dipped into, savored for a time, put aside, and taken up again when one's sense of humor is drooping or faith in humanity needs restoring.

Bibliography:
Benét, William Rose. "Memoranda on Americans." *Saturday Review of Literature* 14, no. 17 (August 22, 1936): 6. Written at the time of the publication of *The People, Yes*, this review discusses the work as a mélange and criticizes a lack of cohesiveness and depth. Provides a starting point for a comparison of the early criticisms of Sandburg's works with later discussions.
Crowder, Richard. "The People and the Union." In *Carl Sandburg*. New York: Twayne, 1964. Discusses Sandburg's skill as a writer, the development of the concept of the work and how it exemplifies the culmination of the poet's career. Focuses on the importance of the book to sociologists and historians as an enchiridion of folk literature.
Duffey, Bernard. "Carl Sandburg and the Undetermined Land." *The Centennial Review* 23 (Summer, 1979): 295-303. A reevaluation of Sandburg as being more than merely a sentimental or populist poet. Discusses Sandburg's poetry as an authentic voice with a wholeness of perception rooted in identification with the American people.
Golden, Harry. *Carl Sandburg*. Cleveland: World Publishing, 1961. Examines Sandburg's personality and how it related to his writing. Includes a discussion of *The People, Yes* as a poetic definition of the elemental forces love, death, life, and work.

Hoffman, Dan G. "Sandburg and 'The People': His Literary Populism Reappraised." *The Antioch Review* 10 (June, 1950): 265-278. Examines the limitations in Sandburg's efforts to exemplify communal rather than individual emotion. Contains a thorough discussion of the theme and motifs of *The People, Yes.*

PEPITA JIMÉNEZ

Type of work: Novel
Author: Juan Valera (Juan Valera y Alcalá Galiano, 1824-1905)
Type of plot: Psychological realism
Time of plot: c. 1870
Locale: Andalusia, Spain
First published: Pepita Ximenez, 1874 (English translation, 1886)

> *Principal characters:*
> LUIS DE VARGAS, a student for the priesthood
> DON PEDRO DE VARGAS, his father
> PEPITA JIMÉNEZ, a young widow
> ANTOÑONA, her housekeeper and duenna
> COUNT DE GENAZAHAR, a designing nobleman

The Story:

On March 22, four days after returning to his home in Andalusia, Luis de Vargas wrote the first of his letters to his uncle and favorite professor at the seminary. He reported that his father intended to fatten him up during his vacation, to have him ready to return in the fall to finish his training for the priesthood. He mentioned in passing that his father was courting a young and attractive widow, Pepita Jiménez, twenty years old to his father's fifty-five. Pepita had been married for only a short time to an eighty-year-old moneylender named Gumersindo. Luis was not eager to see his father married again, but he promised his uncle not to judge Pepita before he knew her.

His next letter, dated six days later, reported that he was already tired of the little town and anxious to get back to school. In the meantime he had met Pepita. Having decided that she paid too much attention to the body and not enough to the spirit, he could not understand why the local vicar held so high an opinion of her. He hoped, however, that she would have a good effect on his somewhat unsettled father.

In his next letter, Luis continued to criticize Pepita for her coquetry toward his father. He tried to forgive her vanity about her pretty hands by remarking that Saint Teresa had exhibited the same fault. In closing, he apologized for not at once fleeing the life that seemed to be making a materialist of him, but his father had begged him to stay on a while longer.

In a letter dated April 14, Luis expressed concern over Pepita's diabolic power, shown by the manner in which she charmed both his father and the vicar, and made him write more about her than about others in the town. Meanwhile, his time was so occupied that it was May 4 before he wrote again to describe a picnic his father had given for Pepita. Luis had ridden a mule. While the others rode or played games, he stayed behind to chat with the vicar and an old lady, an experience more boring than he had believed possible, but when he took a walk and came upon Pepita alone, he could not understand his strange excitement. She reproved him for being too serious for his age and remarked that only very old people like the vicar traveled on muleback. That night Luis told his father that he wanted to learn to ride a horse.

In later letters he described his embarrassment during evening gatherings at Pepita's house, where he always felt out of place. Nevertheless, he did enjoy his riding lessons and the thrill of riding past her balcony on the day his father decided he could ride well enough to do so. He later confessed to his uncle that he was disturbed in his feelings over Pepita, and as a result he had stopped going to her house. He thought that he would be wise to return to the seminary at once.

He was still more perplexed when Antoñona, Pepita's housekeeper, scolded him for making her mistress unhappy. When Luis called to apologize and explain, the sight of tears in Pepita's eyes upset him, and before he knew it he kissed her. Certain that he must leave as soon as possible, he told his father that he intended to depart on June 25, immediately after the Midsummer Eve celebration. He ended his letter with assurances that his uncle would be seeing him within a week.

Five days after Luis' last letter, Pepita summoned the vicar to her house. She wanted to confess that she no longer loved Don Pedro because she had fallen in love with his son. Convinced that Luis loved her also without knowing it, she intended to keep him from carrying out his plans to become a priest. The scandalized vicar ordered her to remain engaged to the father and let Luis go away as he had planned. Pepita promised. No one, however, could force Antoñona to keep such a promise. She determined to take a hand in the situation.

In the Vargas household, meanwhile, Don Pedro worried about his moping son and at last urged the boy's young cousin, Currito, to engage Luis in some activity. Luis went with his cousin to the casino, where the Count de Genazahar was among the gamblers. Having borrowed five thousand pesetas from Gumersindo, he had tried, after the old man's death, to cancel the debt by marrying Pepita. Her curt refusal had made him hate her. At the casino that night, Luis overheard some of his slighting remarks about the young widow.

Antoñona went to see Luis again and accused him of behaving discourteously toward her mistress. Luis protested that he, too, was unhappy but that it was his duty to return to the seminary. Antoñona insisted that he must first set things right with Pepita, so he promised to go to her house at ten o'clock that night. The streets would be full of Midsummer Eve revelers, and no one would notice him.

After Antoñona's departure he regretted his promise, but it had been given and he went. His talk with Pepita was long and difficult. Each made self-accusations. At last, sobbing, Pepita ran to her bedroom. Luis followed her. When he came out, he was convinced that he was not among the men of whom priests are made. On his way home, seeing the Count de Genazahar in the casino, he stopped. Declaring that he no longer wore his religious robe, he announced that he had come to beat the count at cards.

During a long run of luck he won all the count's money. When the Count de Genazahar wished to continue, Luis insultingly answered his promise to pay later by reminding him that he had failed to pay his debt to Gumersindo's widow. The count challenged him to a duel and called for sabers. The fight was brief and bloody, and both men were wounded. Currito and a friend took Luis home to his worried father.

Alone with Don Pedro, Luis tried to confess that he had become his father's rival for Pepita's affections. Don Pedro merely laughed, and from his pocket he took two letters. One from his brother in the seminary said that he felt Luis had no calling for the priesthood and would do better to remain at home. The other was Don Pedro's answer. Having realized that Pepita's affection had shifted to Luis, he would be happy in watching their happiness. He invited his brother the dean to come and marry the young lovers.

The dean refused the invitation, but a month later, after Luis' wounds had healed, the village vicar married them. Don Pedro gave a splendid reception. Although it was the local custom to serenade with cowbells anyone marrying a second time, the town thought so highly of Luis and his bride that they were allowed to steal away without the embarrassing celebration.

Recovering after five months in bed, the count paid part of his debt and arranged to pay the remainder. After the birth of their son, Luis and Pepita took a trip abroad. For many years they and their farms prospered, and all went well with them.

Critical Evaluation:

Naturalism and realism were the two literary currents in vogue when Juan Valera decided to write his first novel. Valera felt a profound antipathy for naturalism, with its emphasis on what he considered the gross and the vulgar, and he disliked realism for its lack of imagination. He believed that a good novel must be both inventive and amusing. Searching for an alternative to either naturalism or realism, he decided on a new form, the psychological novel. His work remains within the general framework of realism, but unlike his contemporaries, Valera describes an interior reality rather than the objective reality.

Valera, considered to be one of the three most important novelists of nineteenth century Spain (along with José María de Pereda and Benito Pérez Galdós), was also one of the major literary critics of that period. He was born into Spanish aristocracy, studied law and religion, was an elected deputy in Congress, and had a long career as a diplomat, serving as minister in Lisbon, Washington, and Brussels, and as an ambassador to Vienna. Valera first received critical acclaim for his essays, which covered a wide array of subjects. His most important literary contribution was his psychological analysis of his characters. Although Valera attempted earlier novels (some of which appeared in serial form in newspapers), *Pepita Jiménez* is his first completed novel, and is regarded as his best.

Valera was an elegant and refined author. He is acknowledged as the foremost stylist in his language of the nineteenth century. He was a keen observer who studied human passions and feelings, and a master of the understated emotion. In general he created well-developed characters, using balanced, artificial language to add depth to his novels and draw out the relationship between the characters. A writer who used a contemporary setting to address the problems existing in his society, he believed that a novel could be credible and true to life without portraying the vulgar things common in the works of naturalistic authors. He was an admirer of form and beauty and believed that the purpose of art was to inspire and create beauty. These views, along with his opposition to didactic literature, set him apart from his contemporaries, who followed the tenets of naturalism and realism. Unlike many of his contemporaries who wrote for a living and had to follow the established trends, Valera's wealth enabled him to formulate and try out his own literary theories.

One example of Valera's literary independence is his use of local color. In his novels, the description of the beautiful Andalusian landscape often enhances the story line, while allowing the author to focus his attention on the psyche and to explore the emotions of his characters. In *Pepita Jiménez* Valera uses his favorite theme of love in his psychological analysis of the main character, seminary student Luis de Vargas. This novel, which is written in the form of a series of letters, reveals Luis' inner thoughts and feelings through his correspondence with his uncle, the dean of a cathedral. Valera incorporates other perspectives into *Pepita Jiménez* too. In the introduction to the novel, the author claims to have found this manuscript among the personal papers of the dean of an unnamed cathedral. This is followed by letters written by Luis, his uncle, and his father. Taken together, these letters provide an analysis of Luis' growing attraction to the young widowed Pepita Jiménez and his resulting internal conflict between physical love and spiritual duty. The combination of the different perspectives is particularly important since they provide a more complete picture by which an accurate evaluation of Luis' situation may be made when Luis is incapable of discerning the truth about himself. The frame of the preliminary letters underscores the contrast between true mysticism and the main character's perception of it.

Valera draws heavily upon his knowledge about sixteenth century ascetic and mystical literature to expose Luis' false mysticism and to criticize the preparation of candidates for service in the priesthood. To do this, the author uses irony and parody of the mystical experience to show how Luis has misinterpreted his calling. The young seminary student rationalizes and employs mystical language to hide his true feelings, confusing religious devotion and human passion. Believing himself to be blessed by God (an error of pride) and uplifted to the mystical experience, he is unprepared for life outside the safety of the seminary walls. Instead of experiencing the truth and goodness of God and the absorption into God's love, Luis gradually abandons his soul to Pepita, whose beauty has captivated him. Torn between his growing love for the young widowed Pepita and his vows to enter the priesthood, Luis is forced to evaluate his feelings and finally realizes that he has not, in truth, been called to the priesthood. At first Luis intends to follow through with his original plans to take up his vows rather than to admit his mistake and marry Pepita. Eventually, however, Luis acknowledges his error and, enchanted by Pepita and the sensual happiness of the Andalusian landscape, renounces his vows in order to marry the woman he loves.

"Critical Evaluation" by Pamela Peek

Bibliography:
Bianchini, Andreina. "*Pepita Jiménez:* Ideology and Realism." *Hispanofila* 33, no. 2 (January, 1990): 33-51. An examination of the novel's relationship to ideology and idealism. Discusses the three-part structure of the work.
DeCoster, Cyrus C. *Juan Valera.* New York: Twayne, 1974. A very good resource for study of Valera's works. Contains an overview of Juan Valera's life and literary career and analyzes his literary characters and themes. There is a chapter devoted to *Pepita Jiménez.*
Lott, Robert. *Language and Psychology in "Pepita Jiménez."* Champaign: University of Illinois Press, 1970. A well-regarded study of the language and psychology found in *Pepita Jiménez.* The first part is an analysis of language, style, and rhetorical devices. The second section is a psychological examination of characters.
MacCurdy, G. Grant. "Mysticism, Love and Illumination in *Pepita Jiménez.*" *Revista de Estudios Hispanicos* 17, no. 3 (October, 1983): 323-334. This article is an original approach to studying Valera's treatment of mysticism, love, and illumination.
Turner, Harriet S. "Nescit Labi Virtus: Authorial Self-Critique in *Pepita Jiménez.*" *Kentucky Romance Quarterly* 35, no. 3 (August, 1988): 347-357. Examines the omniscient narrator, the writer, the use of irony, and the relationship to virtue.

PÈRE GORIOT

Type of work: Novel
Author: Honoré de Balzac (1799-1850)
Type of plot: Naturalism
Time of plot: c. 1819
Locale: Paris
First published: Le Père Goriot, 1834-1835 (English translation, 1860)

Principal characters:
　　PÈRE GORIOT, a boarder at the Maison Vauquer
　　COUNTESS ANASTASIE DE RESTAUD and
　　BARONESS DELPHINE DE NUCINGEN, Goriot's daughters
　　EUGÈNE DE RASTIGNAC, a young law student
　　MADAME DE BEAUSÉANT, Rastignac's cousin
　　MONSIEUR VAUTRIN and
　　VICTORINE TAILLEFER, Rastignac's fellow boarders

The Story:

There were many conjectures at Madame Vauquer's boardinghouse about the mysterious Monsieur Goriot. He had taken the choice rooms on the first floor when he first retired from his vermicelli business, and for a time his landlady had eyed him as a prospective husband. When, at the end of his second year at the Maison Vauquer, he had asked to move to a cheap room on the second floor, rumor had it that he was an unsuccessful speculator, a miser, and a money-lender. The mysterious young women who flitted up to his rooms from time to time were said to be his mistresses, although he protested that they were his two daughters. The other boarders called him Père Goriot. At the end of the third year, Goriot moved to a still cheaper room on the third floor. By that time, he was the common butt of jokes at the boardinghouse table, and his daughters visited him only rarely.

One evening, the impoverished law student, Eugène de Rastignac, came home late from the ball his wealthy cousin, Madame de Beauséant, had given. Peeking through the keyhole of Goriot's door, he saw the old man molding silver plate into ingots. The next day, he heard his fellow boarder, Monsieur Vautrin, say that early in the morning he had seen Père Goriot selling a piece of silver to an old moneylender. What Vautrin did not know was that the money thus obtained was intended for Goriot's daughter, Countess Anastasie de Restaud, whom Eugène had met at the dance the night before.

That afternoon Eugène paid his respects to the countess. Père Goriot was leaving the drawing room when he arrived. The countess, her lover, and her husband received Eugène graciously because of his connections with Madame de Beauséant, but when he mentioned that they had the acquaintance of Père Goriot in common, he was quickly shown to the door, the count leaving word with his servant that he was not to be at home if Monsieur de Rastignac called again.

After this rebuff, Eugène went to call on Madame de Beauséant, to ask her aid in unraveling the mystery. She explained that de Restaud's house would be barred to him because both of Goriot's daughters, having been given sizable dowries, were gradually severing all connection with their father and therefore would not tolerate anyone who had knowledge of Goriot's shabby circumstances. She suggested that Eugène send word through Goriot to his other daughter, Delphine de Nucingen, that Madame de Beauséant would receive her. She knew that Delphine would welcome the invitation and would become Eugène's sponsor out of gratitude.

Vautrin had another suggestion for the young man. Under Madame Vauquer's roof lived Victorine Taillefer, who had been disinherited by her wealthy father in favor of her brother. Eugène had already found favor in her eyes, and Vautrin suggested that for two hundred thousand francs he would have the brother murdered, so that Eugène might marry the heiress. Vautrin gave him two weeks to consider the offer.

The next evening, Eugène escorted Madame de Beauséant to the theater, where he was presented to Delphine de Nucingen, who received him graciously. The next day he received an invitation to dine with the de Nucingens and to accompany them to the theater. Before dinner, he and Delphine drove to a gambling house where, at her request, he gambled and won six thousand francs. She explained that her husband would give her no money, and she needed it to pay a debt she owed to an old lover.

Before long, Eugène learned that it cost money to keep the company of his new friends. Unable to press his own family for funds, he would not stoop to impose on Delphine. Finally, as Vautrin had foreseen, he was forced to take his fellow boarder's offer. The tempter had just finished explaining the duel between Victorine's brother and his confederate, which was to take place the following morning, when Père Goriot came in with the news that he and Delphine had taken an apartment for Eugène.

Eugène wavered once more at the thought of the crime that was about to be committed in his name. He attempted to send a warning to the victim through Père Goriot, but Vautrin, suspicious of his accomplice, thwarted the plan and drugged their wine at supper so that both slept soundly that night.

At breakfast, Eugène's fears were realized. A messenger burst in with the news that Victorine's brother had been fatally wounded in a duel. After the girl hurried off to see him, another singular event occurred. After drinking his coffee, Vautrin fell to the ground as if he had suffered a stroke. When he was carried to his room and undressed, it became clear from marks on his back that he must be the famous criminal Trompe-la-Mort. One of the boarders, an old maid, had been acting as an agent for the police; she had drugged Vautrin's coffee so that his criminal brand could be exposed. Shortly afterward the police appeared to claim their victim.

Eugène and Père Goriot prepared to move to their new quarters, for Goriot was to have a room over the young man's apartment. Delphine arrived to interrupt Goriot's packing. She was in distress. Père Goriot had arranged with his lawyer to force de Nucingen to make a settlement so that Delphine would have an independent income on which to draw; now she brought the news that her money had been so tied up by investments it would be impossible for her husband to withdraw any of it without bringing about his own ruin.

Hardly had Delphine told her father of her predicament when Anastasie de Restaud drove up. She had sold the de Restaud diamonds to help her lover pay off his debts, and she had been discovered by her husband. De Restaud had bought them back, but as punishment, he demanded control of her dowry.

Eugène could not help overhearing the conversation through the thin partition between the rooms; when Anastasie said that she still needed twelve thousand francs for her lover, he forged one of Vautrin's drafts for that amount and took it to Père Goriot's room. Anastasie's reaction was to berate him for eavesdropping.

The financial difficulties of his daughters and the hatred and jealousy they had shown proved too much for Père Goriot. At the dinner table, he looked as if he were about to have a stroke, and when Eugène returned from an afternoon spent with Delphine, the old man was in bed, too ill to be moved to his new home. He had gone out that morning to sell his last few possessions, so that Anastasie might pay her dressmaker for an evening gown.

In spite of their father's serious condition, both daughters attended Madame de Beauséant's ball that evening, and Eugène was too much under his mistress' influence to refuse to accompany her. The next day, Goriot was worse. Eugène tried to summon the daughters, but Delphine was still in bed and refused to be hurried over her morning toilet. Anastasie arrived at Père Goriot's bedside only after he had lapsed into a coma and no longer recognized her.

Père Goriot was buried in a pauper's grave the next day. Eugène tried to borrow burial money from the daughters, but each sent word that they were in deep grief over their loss and could not be seen. He and a poor medical student from the boardinghouse were the only mourners at the funeral. Anastasie and Delphine sent their empty carriages to follow the coffin, their final tribute to their indulgent father.

Critical Evaluation:

Honoré de Balzac's writing career spanned thirty years, from the decisive point in 1819 when he elected to abandon the study of law until his untimely death in 1850. His work until 1829 consisted of novels, stories, and sketches on a variety of philosophical and social themes. They are, on the whole, undistinguished; Balzac later averred that the decade from 1819 until he began work on *The Chouans* in 1829 constituted his apprenticeship in the art of fiction. Certainly, the works of the last twenty years of his life show the benefits of that long period of development, both in stylistic and tonal precision and in general weight and narrative direction.

Many critics contend that the generative idea for *The Human Comedy* (1829-1848) came to Balzac as he was writing *Père Goriot*, because in the manuscript the name of the young student is Massiac, until, in the scene of the afternoon call at Madame de Beauséant's house, "Massiac" is abruptly scratched out and "Rastignac" inserted. The character Eugène de Rastignac had appeared in a minor role in *The Wild Ass's Skin* (1831), and the assumption is that the decision to reintroduce him at an earlier stage of his life in *Père Goriot* betokens a flash of inspiration that gave the author the idea of creating a cycle of interconnected novels depicting every aspect of society and having many characters in common. That the idea came to him quite so suddenly is doubtful, since, as Henry Reed has pointed out, he had already decided to bring in Madame de Langeais and Madame de Beauséant and the moneylender Gobseck, all of whom had appeared in previous works. It is certain, however, that *Père Goriot* is the first work in which the device of repetition occurs and in which the uncertain fates of two main characters, Eugène and Vautrin, point so obviously to other stories.

The novel began as a short story about parental obsession and filial ingratitude. The title is most often translated into English as *Père Goriot* or *Father Goriot*, whereby the significance of the definite article is lost, which, because it is not grammatically necessary in French, is all the more pointed; the sense is more truly rendered as Goriot the Father. The point is that the condition of fatherhood absorbs the whole life and personality of old Goriot. At one time a husband and a businessman, he has lost or given up these roles and now lives only in the paternal relation; at other times, he exists, in the boarders' neat phrase, as "an anthropomorphous mollusc." He seems at first glance horribly victimized, so betrayed and ill-repaid by his harpy daughters that his situation excites the silent sympathy of even such hard gems of the *haute monde* as the Duchesse de Langeais and Madame de Beauséant. His gratitude to his offspring for their least notice, ungraciously bestowed as it may be, and his joyful self-sacrifice and boundless self-delusion fill the reader with pity. Was there ever, Balzac seems to ask, a parent so ill-used?

Ultimately, Balzac leaves no doubt that Goriot reared the two girls in such a way as to ensure that they would be stupid, vain, idle, and grasping women. "The upbringing he gave his daughters was of course preposterous." As he lies dying, his outburst of impotent rage reminds one of Lear; their situations are similar in that each in the folly of his heart causes his own ruin. Lear's abasement leads to self-recognition and moral rebirth, but Goriot clings to his delusion with a mad tenacity to the end, demanding that reality conform to his dream of the rewards due to a devoted father. In fact, he is properly rewarded, for he has been the worst of fathers. Parenthood is both a privilege and a trust. Goriot has enjoyed the first and betrayed the latter, as he himself recognizes in a brief interval of lucidity: "The finest nature, the best soul on earth would have succumbed to the corruption of such weakness on a father's part." Indulging himself in the warmth of their goodwill, he has failed in his duty to their moral sense; as adults, they are mirror images of his own monumental selfishness, made, as it were, of the very stuff of it: "It was I who made them, they belong to me."

To this "obscure but dreadful Parisian tragedy" is added the separate tales of Rastignac and Vautrin, each quite self-contained and yet bound to the other tales by the most subtle bonds. One of these links is the recurrent reference to parenthood. At every turn, some facet of the parent-child relation is held up to the reader's notice: the wretchedness of the cast-off child Victorine Taillefer, for example, which so resembles Goriot's wretchedness; Madame de Langeais' disquisition on sons-in-law, later echoed by Goriot; the parental tone taken with Eugène both by Madame de Beauséant ("Why you poor simple child!") and, in a different way, by Vautrin ("You're a good little lad"), who give him wicked worldly advice in contrast to the good but dull counsel of his own mother; the filial relationship that develops between Eugène and Goriot; even Vautrin's enormously ironic nicknames for his landlady ("Mamma Vauquer") and the police ("Father Cop").

Another element linking the *haute monde*, the Maison Vauquer, and the underworld is the fact that they are all partners in crime. Goriot made his original fortune in criminal collusion with members of the de Langeais family. Vautrin neatly arranges the death of Mademoiselle Taillefer's brother for the benefit of the half-willing Rastignac. The Baron de Nucingen invests Delphine's dowry in an illegal building scheme. Vautrin, Goriot, and Anastasie all resort to "Papa Gobseck" the moneylender. The reader hears a precept uttered by Madame de Beauséant ("In Paris, success is everything, it's the key to power") enunciated a few pages later by Vautrin ("Succeed! . . . succeed at all costs"). The reader is clearly meant to see that whatever differences exist among the various levels of society, they are differences not of kind but of degree. Corruption is universal.

"Critical Evaluation" by Jan Kennedy Foster

Bibliography:
Bellos, David. *Honoré de Balzac: "Old Goriot."* Cambridge, England: Cambridge University Press, 1987. Provides a brief general overview of the relevant cultural contexts and major interpretive traditions of the work. Specifically intended as an introductory text for high school and college students.
McCarthy, Mary Susan. *Balzac and His Reader: A Study of the Creation of Meaning in "La Comédie humaine."* Columbia: University of Missouri Press, 1982. Includes a long chapter on *Père Goriot*, in which McCarthy relies on reader-response theory to examine the ways in which Balzac uses his recurring characters to focus the reader's interpretation of the novel.
Maurois, André. *Prometheus: The Life of Balzac.* Translated by Norman Denny. Harmonds-

worth, England: Penguin Books, 1971. A thorough, generally objective, and highly readable account of Balzac's life. Provides detailed context for and some commentary on all of the major works, including *Père Goriot*.

Prendergast, Christopher. *Balzac: Fiction and Melodrama*. New York: Holmes & Meier, 1978. Argues for the importance of the stock conventions and devices of melodrama for the interpretation of Balzac's analyses of French society. Contains a detailed analysis of *Père Goriot* as well as an overview of previous critical work on the book.

Stowe, William W. *Balzac, James, and the Realistic Novel*. Princeton, N.J.: Princeton University Press, 1983. Discusses the solutions Balzac and Henry James adopted in solving various problems of realistic fictional representation. Includes a comparative study of issues of interpretation in *Père Goriot* and James's *The American*.

PEREGRINE PICKLE

Type of work: Novel
Author: Tobias Smollett (1721-1771)
Type of plot: Picaresque
Time of plot: Early eighteenth century
Locale: England and the Continent
First published: The Adventures of Peregrine Pickle, in Which Are Included Memories of a Lady of Quality, 1751

Principal characters:
PEREGRINE PICKLE, a reckless young man
GAMALIEL PICKLE, his father
GRIZZLE PICKLE, his aunt, later Mrs. Trunnion
COMMODORE HAWSER TRUNNION, an old sea dog and Peregrine's godfather
LIEUTENANT HATCHWAY, the Commodore's companion
TOM PIPES, a companion and servant
EMILIA GAUNTLET, Peregrine's sweetheart

The Story:
Mr. Gamaliel Pickle was the son of a prosperous London merchant who had bequeathed his son a fortune of no small degree. Later, having lost a part of his inheritance in several unsuccessful ventures of his own, Mr. Pickle prudently decided to retire from business and to live on the interest of his fortune rather than risk his principal in the uncertainties of trade. With his sister Grizzle, who had kept his house for him since his father's death, he went to live in a mansion in the country.

In the region to which he retired, Mr. Pickle's nearest neighbor was Commodore Hawser Trunnion, an old sea dog who kept his house like a seagoing ship, and who possessed an endless list of quarterdeck oaths he used on any occasion against anyone who offended him. Other members of his household were Lieutenant Hatchway, a one-legged veteran, and a seaman named Tom Pipes.

Shortly after he had settled in his new home, Mr. Pickle met Miss Sally Appleby, the daughter of a gentleman in a nearby parish. After a brief courtship, the two were married. Before long, Mr. Pickle discovered that his wife was determined to dominate him completely. Peregrine was the oldest son of the ill-starred union. During her pregnancy, Mrs. Pickle took such a dislike to Grizzle that she tried in every way possible to embarrass and humiliate her sister-in-law. Grizzle realized that she was no longer wanted in her brother's household, and she began a campaign to win the heart of old Commodore Trunnion.

Ignoring his distrust of women in general, she won out at last over his obstinacy. The wedding was not without humor; on his way to the church, the Commodore's horse ran away with him and carried him eleven miles with a hunting party. Upset by his experience, he insisted that the postponed ceremony be performed in his own house. The wedding night was also not without excitement: The ship's hammocks, in which the bride and groom were to sleep, collapsed and dropped them to the floor. The next morning, wholly indifferent to her husband's displeasure, Mrs. Trunnion proceeded to refurnish and reorganize the Commodore's house according to her own notions.

In order to silence his protests, Mrs. Trunnion pretended to be pregnant. The Commodore's hopes for an heir, however, were short-lived; his wife employed her ruse only to make herself absolute mistress of the Trunnion household. Lacking an heir of his own, the gruff but kindly old seaman turned his attention to young Peregrine Pickle, his nephew and godson. Peregrine was an unfortunate child. While he was still very young, his mother had taken an unnatural and profound dislike to him, and the boy was often wretched from the harsh treatment he received. Under the influence of his wife, weak-willed Mr. Pickle did little to improve the unhappy situation. As a result, Peregrine grew into a headstrong, rebellious boy who showed his high spirits in all kinds of pranks that mortified and irritated his parents. He was sent away to school, and he rebelled against his foolish and hypocritical teachers; at last, he wrote to the Commodore to request removal from the school. The Commodore felt pity for the boy and admired his spirit of independence, so he took him out of school and adopted him as his son and heir.

When Peregrine's pranks and escapades became more than his indulgent uncle could stand, the boy was sent to Winchester School. Pipes accompanied him as his servant. Mindful of his uncle's kindness, Peregrine studied and made steady progress until he met Miss Emilia Gauntlet and fell in love with her. Emilia was visiting in Winchester; her own home was in a village about a day's journey away. Peregrine's infatuation was so great that soon after she had returned home, he ran away from school and took lodgings in the village in order to be near her. His absence had been reported by the school authorities, and Hatchway was sent to look for him. The boy was summoned to visit his uncle, who was alarmed by his heir's interest in a penniless young woman. Peregrine's mother grew even more spiteful, and his father disowned him for his youthful folly. Indignant at the parents' harsh treatment of their son, the Commodore sent Peregrine to Oxford to continue his studies. There he encountered Emilia again and renewed his courtship. Hoping to make a good match for his nephew, the Commodore attempted to end the affair by sending Peregrine on a tour of the Continent. Aware of his uncle's purpose in sending him abroad, Peregrine visited Emilia before his departure and vowed eternal devotion.

Shortly thereafter, warned by the Commodore that his reckless behavior would lead only to disaster, Peregrine set out for France. Peregrine was accompanied by Pipes, as his servant, and a mentor who was supposed to keep a check on Peregrine's behavior. All efforts in that direction were fruitless. Peregrine had barely set foot on French soil before he made gallant advances to Mrs. Hornbeck, the wife of a traveling Englishman. In Paris, he encountered the lady again and eloped with her, an escapade that ended when the British ambassador intervened to send the lady back to her husband. On one occasion, Peregrine was imprisoned by the city guard. At another time, he fought a duel with a musketeer as the result of an amorous adventure. He quarreled with a nobleman at a masked ball and was sent to the Bastille in company with an artist friend. After Pipes had discovered his whereabouts and had secured his release, Peregrine was ordered to leave France within three days.

On his way back to England, Peregrine became embroiled with a knight of Malta, quarreled with Pipes, and was captivated by a lady he met in a carriage. Shortly afterward, he lost his carriage companion and resumed his earlier affair with Mrs. Hornbeck. Her husband interposed, and Peregrine was thrown into prison once more. After his release, the travelers proceeded to Antwerp and then to England. His uncle, who still retained his affection for his wayward nephew, received him with great joy.

On his return, Peregrine called on Emilia, but he found her indifferent to his attentions. He wasted no time in pining over a lost love, but continued to disport himself in London and Bath, until he was called home by the final illness of his uncle. The old Commodore was buried according to his own directions, and he was remembered with great affection and respect by his nephew. His uncle willed a fortune of thirty thousand pounds and his house to Peregrine. After a vain attempt to reach a friendly understanding with his parents, Peregrine left the house to the tenancy of Hatchway and returned to London.

As a handsome, wealthy young bachelor, he indulged in extravagance and dissipation of all kinds. After exaggerated reports of his wealth had been circulated, he was pursued by match-making mothers. Their efforts merely amused him, but their designs gave him entrance into the houses of the fashionable and the great.

Peregrine met Emilia again and began the same campaign to win her that had been successful with his other light and casual loves. Disappointed in his attempts to seduce her, he took advantage of the confusion attending a masquerade ball to try to overcome her by force. He was vigorously repulsed, and her uncle forbade him to see Emilia again.

He became the friend of a notorious lady who gave him a copy of her memoirs. The woman was Lady Vane, whose affairs with many lovers had created a great scandal in London. Peregrine's friend Cadwallader had assumed the character of a fortune-teller and magician. In that way Peregrine was able to learn the secrets of the women who came to consult Cadwallader. Peregrine had acquired a reputation as a clever man and a wit and used his knowledge to advance his own position.

Grizzle Trunnion died, and Peregrine attended her funeral. On the road, he met a vulgar young female beggar whom he dressed in fashionable clothes and taught a set of polite phrases. It amused him to introduce the beggar into his own fashionable world. When his contemptuous joke was at last exposed, he lost many of his fine friends. Peregrine decided to retrench. He cut down his foolish expenses and made loans at a good rate of interest. He was persuaded to stand for Parliament. This decision was taken after he had met Emilia at her sister's wedding, and he had begged the sister to intercede for him. His political venture, however, cost more money than he had expected. After he lost the election, he was, for the first time in his life, faced with the need for mature reflection on himself and his world.

His affairs went from bad to worse. A mortgage that he held proved worthless. A friend for whom he had endorsed a note defaulted. Reduced at last to complete ruin, he tried to earn money by writing translations and satires. He was again thrown into jail after the publication of a satire directed against an influential politician.

His old friends, Hatchway and Pipes, remained loyal to him in his adversity. Each brought his savings to the Fleet prison and offered them to Peregrine, but he refused to accept their aid. It was his intention to earn money for his release by his writing or else starve in the attempt.

Emilia's brother, Captain Gauntlet, learned that he had been promoted to his rank largely through Peregrine's services in the days of his prosperity. Discovering Peregrine's plight, he set about to relieve his benefactor. Peregrine had an unexpected bit of luck when one of his debtors repaid a loan of seven hundred pounds. Emilia had inherited ten thousand pounds and offered the money and her hand to Peregrine. Although he was touched by her generosity and forgiveness, he reluctantly refused to burden her with his debts and degradation.

Peregrine was saved by the death of his father, who died intestate. Legal heir to his father's fortune, he was able to leave Fleet prison and take immediate possession of his estate. Having settled an allowance upon his mother, who had gone to live in another part of the country, Peregrine hastened to ask for Emilia's hand in marriage. With his bride, he settled down to lead the life of a country squire.

Critical Evaluation:

Peregrine Pickle, Tobias Smollett's second novel, has never been as popular as his first,

Roderick Random (1748), or his last, *Humphry Clinker* (1771). He wished it to be a more polished and panoramic work, with wider appeal, but a variety of circumstances flowed together to frustrate that hope. It met with a mixed reception when it was published in 1751, a response that has persisted.

Smollett was the most prolific and venturesome of the eighteenth century's novelists. After 1754, when Henry Fielding died and Samuel Richardson published his last work, he was often praised as the most talented novelist in the language. At the same time, he was one of England's foremost political journalists, serving as defender of both prime minister and monarch, and directing two major reviews. He also came to be regarded as the most influential historian after David Hume, and was easily the most productive, publishing three dozen volumes within a decade. In the 1750's and 1760's, he wrote or edited more than seventy volumes of nonfiction. These interests and the quarrels they fostered help explain the peculiar flavor of *Peregrine Pickle*.

Controversy became his forte, as a conservative, pugnacious Scot making his way in Whiggish London. For his fiction, he chose two forms that made contention not only possible but also inevitable. The first was a modification of the picaresque—the journey of a roguish outsider through contemporary places and manners. The second was satire—the relentless exposure of fools and knaves. In each new novel, he seeks a different mixture of exotic adventure and harsh ridicule. In *Peregrine Pickle* he creates twice as many characters—226— and covers nearly three times as many pages as he did in the earlier *Roderick Random*, and balances exotic adventure and contemporary scandal. Peregrine Pickle passes through a three-part series of peregrinations that reveals his hot blood, his thirst for adventure, and his sympathy for the downtrodden. First comes his youth, with ribald stories of life at sea and at school; then the panorama of the Grand Tour; finally, life as a fortune hunter in London.

What distinguishes the novel, then and now, are the three long, interpolated narratives of contemporary scandal that make up a third of the novel, more than those of any earlier English novel. These insert stories may have been evoked by the growing taste for journalistic narrative. As long as a novel in itself, "Memoirs of Lady Vane"—Frances Vane, a prominent socialite with a taste for the sensual—echoes parts of Peregrine's story, especially his jousts with the money-hungry, and follows John Cleland's tale of Fanny Hill, *Memoirs of a Woman of Pleasure* (1748-1749). The others are those of Daniel Mackercher, who assisted James Annesley in a legal battle with the Earl of Anglesey, and the Count d'Alvarez, captured and found in bondage in Bohemia. Critics can appreciate these digressions in themselves, yet doubt their contribution to the novel. Similarly, critics have applauded the gusto and originality of the opening part, with its theme of home, family, and surrogates, and its gallery of unforgettable characters: Pipes, Grizzle, Keypstick, Hatchway, and Trunnion. This section is notable for many reasons, but especially for the more than fifty pages Smollett uses to introduce the major characters other than Peregrine. Such a modernist device provides a prehistory of the title character, a foretaste of the social and emotional world into which he will grow. Historians of child rearing and education have studied it to advantage.

The second part of the novel, which takes place on the Continent, disappointed many. Neither originality nor precision is as apparent, as Smollett resorts to a lamer form of satire. He surely knew the territory, for during the summer of 1750 he had traveled to Paris and the Low Countries, probably gathering material to be used in the novel. There is a Swiftian quality to the relentless exposure of stupidity in this section. Yet Peregrine cannot be as successful a moral vehicle as Gulliver, for he is too proud and venal to be a proper judge. He does not long remain an amused spectator of French affectation, for example, but soon becomes an active participant.

Part three regains some of the opening vigor, however, as Peregrine endures the trial by adversity. He is scalded by misfortune and despair, then recuperates by the generosity of friends, the love of Emilia, and the inheritance of his father's estate. Many readers have doubted Peregrine's deserts; he is granted such rewards, rather than earning them. The novel provides more of a dazzling world to examine than a sympathetic hero to admire. Even those who admire the exuberance of that world find their admiration impeded by the length of the interpolated stories that bulk so large in this section. Although they upset the symmetry of the novel, these stories do support its theme. Long and now shorn of their original scandal, Lady Vane's memoirs prove that the behavior of the upper classes can be brutal and immoral. All of the inset pieces reveal the fate of those who would be ruled by their passions, rather than the dictates of moral common sense.

So too with their creator. In this novel, Smollett is more troubled and troubling than he was in his first and last fictions. Little is known of his life while composing the novel, but one can presume a measure of disquiet never fully removed. Smollett never possessed the gift of repose and, in this period, seems more irascible than ever. Hence his quarrels with more than a dozen contemporary figures whom he would challenge for at least a short while, until he found other opponents. He wanted a direct and unmediated outlet for his antagonisms and soon found one in his work in political reviews.

"Critical Evaluation" by John Sekora

Bibliography:
Buck, Howard S. *A Study in Smollett, Chiefly "Peregrine Pickle."* New Haven, Conn.: Yale University Press, 1925. The earliest scholarly study of the novel, still valuable. It collates the first and second editions of the novel and explains the many quarrels Smollett included in it.
Evans, David L. "Peregrine Pickle: The Complete Satirist." *Studies in the Novel* 3, no. 3 (Fall, 1971): 258-274. A favorable view, arguing that the novel is not only a satire but also a study of satire, combining the conventions of both forms.
Putney, Rufus. "The Plan of *Peregrine Pickle*." *PMLA* 60, no. 4 (December, 1945): 1051-1065. An argument for the careful and harmonious structure of the novel, focusing upon Peregrine's moral journey.
Smollett, Tobias. *The Adventures of Peregrine Pickle*. Edited by James L. Clifford. New York: Oxford University Press, 1964. Unexpurgated text of the first edition, with good introduction, notes, and bibliography. The supporting text is an excellent starting point.
Weinsheimer, Joel. "Defects and Difficulties in Smollett's *Peregrine Pickle*." *Ariel: A Review of International English Literature* 9, no. 3 (July, 1978): 49-62. An unfavorable estimate, arguing that the novel fails as satire, as a *Bildungsroman*, and as a combination of the two.

PERICLES, PRINCE OF TYRE

Type of work: Drama
Author: William Shakespeare (1564-1616)
Type of plot: Comedy
Time of plot: Hellenistic period
Locale: Eastern Mediterranean Sea and its littorals
First performed: c. 1607-1608; first published, 1609

> *Principal characters:*
> PERICLES, Prince of Tyre
> THAISA, his wife
> MARINA, their daughter
> CLEON, governor of Tarsus
> DIONYZA, his wife
> LYSIMACHUS, governor of Mytilene
> ANTIOCHUS, King of Antioch

The Story:

In Syria, King Antiochus' wife died in giving birth to a daughter. When the child grew to lovely womanhood, King Antiochus conceived an unnatural passion for her. Her beauty attracted suitors to Antioch from far and wide, but King Antiochus, reluctant to give up his daughter, posed a riddle to each suitor. If the riddle went unanswered, the suitor was executed. Many men, hoping to win the princess, lost their lives in this way. Prince Pericles of Tyre went to Antioch to seek the hand of the beautiful princess. Having declared that he would willingly risk his life for the hand of the king's daughter, he read the riddle, the solution to which disclosed an incestuous relationship between King Antiochus and his daughter. Pericles understood but hesitated, prudently, to reveal his knowledge. Pressed by King Antiochus, he hinted that he had fathomed the riddle. King Antiochus, unnerved and determined to kill Pericles, invited the young prince to stay at the court for forty days, in which time he could decide whether he would forthrightly give the solution to the riddle. Pericles, convinced that his life was in great danger, fled. King Antiochus sent agents after him with orders to kill the prince on sight.

Pericles, back in Tyre, was fearful that King Antiochus would ravage Tyre in an attempt to take Pericles' life. After consulting with his lords, he decided that he could save Tyre by going on a journey to last until King Antiochus died. Thaliard, a Syrian lord who had come to Tyre to take Pericles' life, learned of Pericles' departure and returned to Antioch to report the prince's intention. Meanwhile, in the remote Greek province of Tarsus, Cleon, the governor, and his wife Dionyza grieved because there was famine in the land. As they despaired, it was reported that a fleet of ships stood off the coast. Cleon was sure that Tarsus was about to be invaded. Actually, the ships were those of Pericles, who had come to Tarsus with grain to succor the starving populace. Cleon welcomed the Tyrians, and his people invoked the Greek gods to protect their saviors from all harm.

Pericles received word from Tyre that King Antiochus' agents were relentlessly pursuing him, so that he was no longer safe in Tarsus. He thereupon took leave of Cleon and set sail. On the high seas the Tyrians met disaster in a storm. The fleet was lost; Pericles was the only survivor. Washed ashore in Greece, he was helped by simple fishermen. Fortunately, too, the fishermen took Pericles' suit of armor from the sea. With the help of the fishermen, Pericles went to Pentapolis, the court of King Simonides.

There a tournament was held to honor the birthday of Thaisa, the lovely daughter of King Simonides. Among the gallant knights he met, Pericles presented a wretched sight in his rusted armor. Even so, he defeated all antagonists and was crowned king of the tournament by Thaisa. At the banquet following the tourney Pericles, reminded of his own father's splendid court, lapsed into melancholy. Seeing his dejection, King Simonides drank a toast to him and asked him who he was. He disclosed that he was Pericles of Tyre, a castaway. His modesty and courteous deportment made an excellent impression on King Simonides and Thaisa.

Meanwhile, in Antioch, King Antiochus and his daughter, riding together in a chariot, were struck dead by a bolt of lightning. In Tyre, Pericles had been given up for dead, and the lords proposed that Helicanus, Pericles' deputy, take the crown. The old lord, confident that his prince was still alive, directed them to spend a year in search of Pericles. In Pentapolis, Thaisa, having lost her heart to Pericles, tricked her suitors into leaving by reporting that she would remain a maid for another year. Then she and Pericles were married.

A short time before Thaisa was to give birth to a child, Pericles was told that King Antiochus was dead and that Helicanus had been importuned to take the crown of Tyre. Free to go home, Pericles, with Thaisa and Lychorida, a nurse, took ship for Tyre. During the voyage the ship was overtaken by storms. Thaisa, seemingly dead after giving birth to a daughter, was placed in a watertight casket which was thrown into the raging sea. Pericles, fearful for the safety of his child, directed the seamen to take the ship into Tarsus, which was not far off.

The casket containing Thaisa having drifted ashore in Ephesus, the body was taken to Cerimon, a skilled physician. Cerimon, suspecting that Thaisa was not really dead, discovered by his skill that she was actually quite alive. Pericles, having reached Tarsus safely, remained there a year, at the end of which time he declared that Tyre had need of him. Placing little Marina, as he had named his daughter, in the care of Cleon and Dionyza, he set out for Tyre. In the meantime Thaisa, believing that her husband and child had been lost at sea, took the veil of a votaress to the goddess Diana. Years passed, while Pericles ruled in Tyre. As Marina grew, it was clear that she was superior in every respect to her companion, the daughter of Cleon and Dionyza. When Marina's nurse Lychorida died, Dionyza, jealous of the daughter of Pericles, plotted to have Marina's life, and she commissioned a servant to take Marina to a deserted place on the coast and kill her. As the servant threatened to take the girl's life, pirates frightened away the servant and took Marina aboard their ship. Taking her to Mytilene, they sold her to a brothel owner.

In Tarsus, meanwhile, Dionyza persuaded the horrified Cleon that for their own safety against the rage of Pericles they must mourn the loss of Marina and erect a monument in her memory. When Pericles, accompanied by old Helicanus, went to Tarsus to reclaim his daughter, his grief on seeing the monument was so great that he exchanged his royal robes for rags, vowed never again to wash himself or to cut his hair, and left Tarsus.

In Mytilene, in the meantime, Marina confounded both the owners of the brothel and the customers by preaching the heavenly virtues instead of deporting herself wantonly. Lysimachus, the governor of Mytilene, went in disguise to the brothel. When Marina was brought to him, he quickly discerned her gentle birth, gave her gold, and assured her that she would soon be freed from her vile bondage. Alarmed, the bawd put Marina in the hands of the doorkeeper. Marina shamed him, gave him gold, and persuaded him to place her as a teacher of the gentle arts. The money she earned by teaching singing, dancing, and needlework she gave to her owner, the bawd.

When Pericles, now a distracted wanderer, came to Mytilene, Lysimachus took a barge out to the Tyrian ship, but he was told that Pericles, grieved by the loss of both wife and daughter, would not speak to anyone. A Mytilene lord suggested that Marina, famous for her graciousness and charm, be brought. Marina came and revealed to Pericles that she knew a grief similar to his, for she had lost her father and mother. It soon became apparent to bewildered Pericles that his daughter stood before him. Rejoicing, he put aside his rags and dressed in regal robes. The goddess Diana then put him into a deep sleep, in which she directed him in a dream to go to Ephesus and to tell in the temple of Diana the loss of his wife.

Pericles hastened to Ephesus, where, in the temple, he revealed his identity to the votaries in attendance. Thaisa, overhearing him, fainted. Cerimon, who was also present, disclosed to Pericles that the votaress who had fainted was his wife. Pericles and Thaisa were joyfully reunited. Since Thaisa's father had died, Pericles proclaimed that he and Thaisa would reign in Pentapolis and that Lysimachus and Marina, as man and wife, would rule over Tyre. When the people of Tarsus learned of the evil done by Cleon and Dionyza, they burned the governor and his family alive in their palace.

Critical Evaluation:

By scholarly consensus, it appears that in the case of *Pericles, Prince of Tyre*, William Shakespeare finished a play that someone else had been commissioned to write. Recent scholarship indicates that Shakespeare revised the entire play of *Pericles, Prince of Tyre* from an earlier version by another playwright, probably Thomas Heywood. The play was tremendously popular in its day and was the basis of a prose version by George Wilkins. *Pericles, Prince of Tyre* is now considered to have been the first of the tragicomedies, or dark romances, that became so popular on the Jacobean stage. The play disregards consideration of time and place, delights in romantic improbabilities, and employs the obscure, compact style of Shakespeare's late plays. Probably it paved the way not only for *Cymbeline* (c. 1609-1610), *The Winter's Tale* (c. 1610-1611), and *The Tempest* (1611), but also for the plays of Francis Beaumont and John Fletcher.

Although seldom performed, *Pericles, Prince of Tyre* does possess an interesting, romantic story and a certain sentimental beauty. It abounds in situations and surprises, although parts of its theme might be considered unpleasant. The similarities between it and Shakespeare's other late plays are striking. The likeness between Marina in *Pericles, Prince of Tyre* and Perdita in *The Winter's Tale* is clear. The meeting between father and daughter, long separated, is suggestive of *Cymbeline*, and the reunion of Pericles and Thaisa anticipates that of Leontes and Hermione. Pericles and Cerimon are wise and superior men in the manner of Prospero. The themes of reunion after long division, reconciliation, and forgiveness seem to recur in all of these late plays, beginning with *Pericles, Prince of Tyre*. Storms appear twice in the play, perhaps as a symbol of the storms of life; this resembles *The Tempest*. In Shakespeare's last plays, there are children lost and found again, parents divided and reunited, a wife rejected and ill-used and restored again. The recurring myth of royalty lost and recovered apparently had some special significance for Shakespeare and his audience.

The play is heavy with symbols and is particularly concerned with the concept of lost authority or control, without which life cannot properly be conducted. It is possible that some allusion to the late queen is intended, but the meaning may have been more personal to Shakespeare, and may reflect a change or confusion in his life. The atmosphere, like that of *The Tempest*, is all sea and music. The brothel scenes are decidedly Shakespearean, with their joking references to disease. There is a hint of the attitudes of *Timon of Athens* (c. 1607-1608), namely, a certain anger and disgust with humanity in the midst of the poetry and music. Up to the third act, Shakespeare's revisions apparently were mostly confined to style, but comparison to the prose story based on the earlier version of the play suggests that with the fourth act he began to make extensive revisions in the plot as well. Certainly, the later scenes are superior in quality to the earlier ones. There is a subtlety and delicacy in the handling of certain scenes—such as when Pericles strikes Marina when she reproves him for his stubborn grief—that mark them as clearly from the hand of Shakespeare. *Pericles, Prince of Tyre*, because of its uncertain place in the canon, has long been underrated as a play. Its importance, however, as the beginning of a new style for Shakespeare and other Jacobean playwrights cannot be overestimated.

Bibliography:

Bergeron, David M. *Shakespeare's Romances and the Royal Family.* Lawrence: University Press of Kansas, 1985. Emphasizes the relationship of the masquelike elements of the play to the ceremonial forms predominant at the court of James I. One of the best historical analyses of *Pericles, Prince of Tyre.*

Fawkner, H. W. *Shakespeare's Miracle Plays.* Madison, N.J.: Fairleigh Dickinson University Press, 1992. This fascinating book does not condescend to *Pericles, Prince of Tyre* as so many Shakespeare studies do. Considers the play as a mature, complex, and achieved work of art.

Frye, Northrop. *A Natural Perspective: The Development of Shakespearean Comedy and Romance.* New York: Columbia University Press, 1965. In this work and in his earlier *Anatomy of Criticism,* Frye establishes a critical model of the Hellenistic romance by which the reader may better understand the plot and genre of *Pericles, Prince of Tyre.*

Knight, G. Wilson. *The Crown of Life.* New York: Oxford University Press, 1947. Knight was the first modern critic to take *Pericles, Prince of Tyre* seriously. Discusses the play's verbal beauty, its adventure, and its spiritual richness.

Neely, Carol Thomas. *Broken Nuptials in Shakespeare's Plays.* New Haven, Conn.: Yale University Press, 1985. The most important feminist analysis of *Pericles, Prince of Tyre.* Argues that the play affirms and subverts the conventional marriage plot of comedies.

THE PERSIANS

Type of work: Drama
Author: Aeschylus (525/524-456/455 B.C.E.)
Type of plot: Tragedy
Time of plot: 480 B.C.E.
Locale: Susa, the capital of Persia
First performed: Persai, 472 B.C.E. (English translation, 1777)

Principal characters:
    XERXES, the King of Persia
    ATOSSA, his mother
    PERSIAN ELDERS
    GHOST OF DARIUS, Xerxes' father

The Story:

Xerxes, son of the late King Darius of Persia, was a man of overwhelming ambition, who, eager to add more countries to his tremendous empire, had led a great army against the Greek states. During his absence, he had left only the Persian elders to maintain authority in Susa, the capital. The old men waited apprehensively for some word of the invasion forces, and their fears grew as time passed and no message came from Xerxes. They lamented that the land had been emptied of the young men who had marched valiantly to war, leaving their wives and mothers to wait anxiously for their return.

Atossa, widow of Darius and mother of Xerxes, was also filled with vague fears. One night she saw in a dream two women, one in Persian dress, the other in Greek robes, and both tall and beautiful. When they began to quarrel, King Xerxes appeared and yoked them to his chariot. The woman in Asian costume submitted meekly enough, but the other broke the reins, overturned the chariot, and threw young Xerxes to the ground. Then, in her dream, Darius came and, seeing his son on the ground, tore his robes with grief. Later, awakening, Atossa went to pray for her son's safety. While she was sacrificing before the altar, she saw an eagle pursued and plucked by a hawk. To her these visions seemed to portend catastrophe for the Persians.

The elders, after hearing her story, advised her to pray to the gods and to beg great Darius to intercede, from the realm of the dead, to bring success to the Persian expedition. Atossa, her thoughts far across the sea with her son, asked the elders where Athens was. The elders told her that it was in Attica, in Greece, and that the citizens of Athens were a free people who derived great strength from their freedom. Their words did little to reassure the troubled mother.

A messenger arrived and announced that the Persian host had been defeated in a great battle fought at Salamis, but that Xerxes, to Atossa's relief, had been spared. His news threw the elders into sad confusion. Atossa told them that men must learn to bear the sorrows put upon them by the gods. Quieted, the elders listened while the messenger related the story of the defeat.

At Salamis, more than twelve hundred Persian ships had been arrayed against three hundred and ten vessels of the Greeks. The defenders, however, proved themselves craftier than their enemies. Deceitfully, a Greek from the Athenian fleet informed Xerxes that at nightfall the far outnumbered Greek ships would leave their battle stations and fly, under cover of darkness, to escape the impending sea fight. Xerxes immediately gave orders that his fleet was to close in about the bay of Salamis and to be on the alert that night to prevent the escape of the Athenian vessels. The wily Greeks kept their places in the bay. When morning came, the light showed the Persian ships crowded so closely into the outlet of the bay that they were unable to maneuver. The Greeks thereupon moved against the Persians and destroyed them.

Meanwhile, the messenger continued, Xerxes had sent troops to the island of Salamis, where he planned to cut off all Greeks who sought refuge on land. The Greeks, having destroyed the Persian fleet, put their own soldiers ashore. In the fierce fighting that followed, the Persians, unable to escape by water, were slain. Seeing his great army scattered and killed, Xerxes ordered the survivors to retreat. As the Persians, now without ships, marched overland through hostile Greek territory, many of them perished of hardships or were slain by enraged men of the lands through which they traveled. The elders of Susa bewailed the terrible misfortune brought upon Persia by the king's desire to avenge his father, who had been defeated years before by the Greeks at Marathon.

Having heard the story of her son's defeat, Atossa retired to make offerings to the gods and to pray for the warriors who had lost their lives in the war with Athens. In mourning, she invoked the spirit of Darius, for whom she and the old men had great need at this most depressing time.

The shade of Darius appeared and asked what dire event had occurred in Persia to make necessary his summons from the lower regions. The elders were struck speechless with fear and respect by his august appearance, but Atossa bravely confronted the ghost of her dead husband and told him that Persia had met disaster, not by plague or by internal strife, but by defeat at the hands of the Athenians.

Darius was shocked to hear of the losses Xerxes had suffered and to learn of the ambitious scope of his enterprise. He lamented his son's god-offending pride in bridging the sacred Hellespont and in gambling away all the power and wealth of Persia upon the success of his ill-fated expedition. Atossa tried to defend Xerxes by saying that he had been influenced by evil advisers. Darius reminded his listeners that he and his forebears had never jeopardized the welfare of the country to such an extent.

In despair, the old men asked Darius how Persia could redeem her great defeat. The dead king replied that the Persians must never again attack Greece, for the gods unquestionably favored those free people. He urged the elders to teach the Persian youths to restrain all god-provoking pride, and he advised Atossa to welcome Xerxes and to comfort him on his return. With these words, the shade of Darius disappeared into his tomb.

Xerxes returned, sorrowing that he had not perished on the field of battle. Filled with remorse at the catastrophe he had brought upon his people, he blamed only himself for his defeat. The old men sang a dirge, asking what had befallen various great Persian warriors. Xerxes replied that some had drowned in the sea battle and that others had been slaughtered on the beach. Many, he said, were killed and buried without final rites. Xerxes, in the deepest despair, joined the elders in their grief. Even though his greatest ambition had been dashed, he praised the bravery and virtues of the Greeks whom he had tried in vain to conquer.

Critical Evaluation:

The Persians is the only surviving example of a Greek drama based entirely on an actual historical event. Although other extant Greek tragedies allude to contemporary Greek history, they transfer the action of the play to a mythical time or faraway place. In a sense, *The Persians* also moves the locale of its action to the exotic court of the Persians; however, the poet was interested in portraying the specific aftermath of the Battle of Salamis, a naval battle in which the Persians were decisively defeated. The play is therefore to be understood in part as an extraordinary celebration of this astonishing victory of Greek over barbarian. *The Persians* is also unique as the only extant example of a monodrama, that is, a play that was complete in itself and not presented as part of a dramatic trilogy. All elements of the story are explored by the end of the play, and none is left to be explored in a sequel. On the dramatic level, however, the only real event in the course of the play is the arrival of news of the Persian defeat and the effect that this announcement has on the court of Xerxes. Scene after scene explores the unfolding of horror at the calamity that has already taken place. The appearance of the ghost of Darius, who acts as a semidivine interpreter, adds a new moral and even theological dimension to this work. Aeschylus incorporates this element to emphasize that the defeat of the Persians was no ordinary victory of one political entity over another. The stunning defeat was the work of Zeus, the supreme god of the Greeks, and a punishment for the excessive arrogance of the Persians.

Other Greek plays, which are now lost, took their subjects from contemporary history. Yet as the only surviving example of such historical tragedy, *The Persians* occupies a special place in literary history. Instead of presenting a myth and exploring its moral implications for his audience, Aeschylus struggled with the considerable challenge of making a living person (Xerxes died in 465 B.C.E.) the tragic hero of a drama. Virtually everyone in Aeschylus' audience had had firsthand experience of the Persian threat, and it is believed that Aeschylus was himself an eyewitness to the Battle of Salamis, which he describes in an exciting messenger's speech. This account of the battle constitutes the only version by an eyewitness of any event from the Persian wars. Beyond this historical connection, the play may have had some role in contemporary politics as political propaganda glorifying the recent victory over the Persians. Implied praise of Themistocles' grand naval strategy, by which the Persians were defeated, may have been intended to influence contemporary debates about the extension and development of Athenian naval power.

The Persians is, after all, a dramatic work. Aeschylus focuses entirely on the arrival of a messenger announcing the defeat at Salamis and the reaction of the Persians who are attached to the royal court. In this depiction, history gives way to fantasy about an exotic people whose private habits and characters were known to the Greeks, if at all, only through hearsay. Catalogs of fallen Persians are recited, many of whose names were clearly concocted by the dramatist, and the entire Persian court turns to mourning. Although, in its broad outline, the story of the Persian defeat is one of a fall from prosperity to adversity, the play itself concentrates almost entirely on the effects of defeat. Elaborate and moving passages of ritual lamentation are a central feature. It is interesting that among the ancient dramatists, Aeschylus was famous for his elaborate use of spectacle. Certainly, production of *The Persians* permitted Aeschylus to give full expression to dramatic display and fantasy as exotically dressed members of the Persian royal court lamented the disaster that befell them.

Aeschylus is careful to express no open contempt for the defeated Persians. The fear and grief of Queen Atossa are as moving as the despair of any heroine from Greek tragedy. Even Xerxes, whose arrogant acts are depicted as the obvious cause of the calamity, is not singled out for condemnation. Instead, the disaster of Salamis is represented as a disaster for all of Persia, and the entire people share in the blame. At the crucial moment, as the Persians seek to understand the ultimate causes of their downfall, the ghost of Darius appears. Darius, with whose name the growth of Persian power and the prosperity of the empire were synonymous, acts as an interpreter for all that has happened. In his extraordinary commentary, one detects Aeschylus' search for the ultimate nature of guilt and punishment which reaches well beyond the immediate circumstances of the defeated Persians. Darius makes it clear that Xerxes is indeed guilty, but that a calamity of this magnitude must exceed the limits of individual responsibility. Beyond the specific crimes of Xerxes or of other Persians, the dramatist explores the implications of an age-old law of fate: Ultimately, disaster strikes anything that has grown too great.

As a dramatist deeply interested in ideas, Aeschylus especially wanted to communicate the moral implications of his stories. The probable first reaction of his audience was satisfaction at this representation of the humiliation of barbarian might by Greek courage and ingenuity. Yet the drama of the Persian defeat also engaged their minds and even their sympathies. Poised on the verge of developing their own empire, the Athenians were invited to consider the fate of the Persians as a warning for their own future. Seen in its broadest context, *The Persians* is a model for the human condition and what appears to be the inevitable cycle of prosperity and adversity.

"Critical Evaluation" by John M. Lawless

Bibliography:
Aeschylus. *The Persians*. Translated by Janet Lembke and C. J. Herington. New York: Oxford University Press, 1981. A happy collaboration between a practicing poet and a classical scholar. Lembke's translation captures lyric qualities of this seemingly prosaic play, while Herington's informative introduction provides an excellent orientation for the reader new to the drama of Aeschylus.

Gagarin, Michael. *Aeschylean Drama*. Berkeley: University of California Press, 1976. Chapter 2 presents a detailed analysis of *The Persians*. Gagarin shows that presentation of political propaganda is not inconsistent with tragic practice. Also explores the moral theme of calamity brought on by excessive pride.

Podlecki, Anthony J. *The Political Background of Aeschylean Tragedy*. Ann Arbor: University of Michigan Press, 1966. Chapter 2 still presents the most succinct introduction to the historical and political background. Podlecki has an excellent understanding of Themistocles, the Athenian general whose plan to encounter the Persians at Salamis saved the Greeks.

Spatz, Lois. *Aeschylus*. Boston: Twayne, 1982. Chapter 2 presents a detailed analysis of the historical and political significance of the play. Spatz is particularly good in her discussion of *The Persians* as simultaneously alien to Greek audiences and yet a paradigm for the human condition.

Winnington-Ingram, R. P. *Studies in Aeschylus*. Cambridge, England: Cambridge University Press, 1983. Chapter 1 offers an excellent discussion of the theological aspects of the play, concentrating on the figure of Zeus. Though not actually present in the play, Zeus is mentioned repeatedly as the cause of the Persian disaster.

PERSONAE AND OTHER POEMS

Type of work: Poetry
Author: Ezra Pound (1885-1972)
First published: 1926

From the beginning, Ezra Pound's problem was to re-create what he found meaningful in the past and yet sound new to his contemporaries. He solved the problem partially in *Hugh Selwyn Mauberley* (1920), completely in *The Cantos* (1948). That he did solve it is attested by the enormous influence of his poetry and criticism on the poetic idiom, an influence felt even by those who find it difficult to understand his works. The solution to what was essentially a problem of form meant, inevitably, any number of false starts that the later Pound sought, quite humanly, to ignore.

In *Personae*, his 1926 collection of shorter poems, Ezra Pound notes that it contains all of his poems up to that date except for the unfinished *Cantos*. The statement is misleading. The volume contains a relatively small selection of the very early Pound, the poet who, without any difficulty, had two of his poems published in *The Oxford Book of Victorian Verse* ("Ballad for Gloom" and "The Portrait," neither reprinted in *Personae*), and the Pound who bears such clear resemblances to the Pre-Raphaelites, Algernon Charles Swinburne, the poetry of the 1890's, William Butler Yeats, and Robert Browning. Of the 145 poems printed in Pound's first volumes—*A Lume Spento* (1908), *A Quinzaine for This Yule* (1908), *Personae*, *Exultations* (1909), and *Canzoni* (1911)—only forty-two survive in the *Personae* volume of 1926. Basically, this is the Pound concerned with medieval themes, Provençal forms, and the tradition of the aesthetes generally.

In both imagery and idea, "Grace Before Song," from *A Lume Spento*, bespeaks the aesthetic ideal of the 1890's. Concern with fleeting moods, lack of concern with society—these attitudes describe at least one aspect of that era's decadence. In line with the English decadence, Pound, too, drew heavily on Swinburne and the Pre-Raphaelites. The medieval atmosphere of the Pre-Raphaelite ballad is also to be found in his "Ballad Rosalind."

The Pre-Raphaelite ideal of feminine beauty is never absent from these early poems; indeed, it never quite seems to have left Pound. As for the impact of Swinburne, it is defined by Pound himself in the reverential "Salve O Pontifex—for Swinburne; an hemi-chaunt." Of the early Yeats, Pound was almost a disciple. One critic has pointed out that "the Tree" is a compendium of Yeatsian influences. Pound clearly echoes Yeats's opening lines from "He Thinks of His Past Greatness When a Part of the Constellations of Heaven," with their references to the hazel tree and grief for all things known.

The central fact of these early volumes is the tremendous variety of influences and modes they reveal. Pound shows himself to be a seeker who is willing to try anything at least once. These early volumes also reflect Pound's concern with translation as a means of providing techniques for the developing poet and insight into earlier states of mind. At this time, Pound's translations, mainly from Provençal and early Italian, were unfortunately colored by Pre-Raphaelite diction and turns of phrase. Thus he not only failed to "make it new," to quote a favorite phrase of Pound but produced obfuscated translations.

Ripostes, published in 1912, is generally taken to mark a turning point in his poetry, but there is still a good deal of the old preciosity in "A Virginal" and "Silet." The best poems (and some of the worst) are translations and adaptations. As always, Pound is concerned not with literal translation but with a revival of the spirit of the poet and his time; ultimately, the translation is as much Pound's work as the original poet's. The volume contains Pound's famous version of "The Seafarer," for it was inevitable that Pound should attempt at least one example of Anglo-Saxon form. (He repeated it later in "Canto I.")

The volume also contains "The Return," modeled on a poem by Henri de Régnier. The poem deals with the return of the Greek gods, who, to Pound, represent eternally recurrent states of mind that he later defines again in *The Cantos*. It stands as a metaphor of Pound's efforts to make what is still alive in the past speak to and help salvage the present. It also suggests a shift in allegiance away from the poets of the English decadence to the French Symbolists.

By the time he published *Ripostes*, Pound had begun to teach others, becoming a propagandist for the Imagist movement with its stress on compactness and concreteness. In 1914, he edited the anthology *Des Imagistes*, and in the following year he published what was essentially a set of variations on the Imagist mode in *Cathay*, a book of translations from the Chinese, based on notes left by the expert on Japanese art, Ernest Fenollosa. Inaccurate as they are, these translations are still considered the best introduction to Chinese poetry available to Westerners. Pound knew not a word of Chinese; clearly his ability to work with Fenollosa's notes was the result of a deeply felt affinity with the nature of Chinese poetry, its avoidance of abstract statement, and its reliance on concrete imagery to suggest mood and idea. In the famous "River-Merchant's Wife: A Letter," the wife's sense of loss and desire for her absent husband are suggested not by direct assertions, but by indirect description.

In 1916, again working from Fenollosa's notes, Pound, who knew no more Japanese than he did Chinese, published *Noh or Accomplishment*. Again inaccurate in many ways, the work made Japanese drama available to the Western mind. In the same year, Pound published *Lustra*, which presented the work of Pound's Imagist period, a Pound free of clutter. Certainly Pound seemed to think so, as can be noted in "Salutation the Second."

The sardonic attitude toward his audience is repeated in a number of poems: "Tenzone," "The Condolence," "Salutation," "Causa," "Commission," "Further Instructions," and "Salvationists." The satiric muse has taken possession of Pound, and it is employed to pillory many of the states of mind later satirized in *The Cantos* as useless, confused, uncreative. Among these satiric poems are "The Garden," "Les Millwin," "The Bellaires," and "Our Contemporaries." Seeking hardness and directness, Pound had turned to the Latin and Greek epigrammatists, and a number of the poems reflect this study. Though scarcely Imagistic, the epigrams—"The New Cake of Soap," "Epitaph," "Arides," "The Bath Tub," and a number of others—are concentrated and in this way reflect one of the major concerns of the Imagistic movement. The translations, too, have shed their Pre-Raphaelite haze, a fact exhibited in the translation from the Provençal of Bertrans de Born. Imagist poems proper, as well as adaptations from the Chinese, appear, including what has become the archetype of the Imagist poem, "In a Station of the Metro."

The relatively bald statements of the satires, the sharp pictures of the Imagist poems, are mingled with poems that show the astonishing qualities of Pound's ear in such lyrics as "The Spring," an adaptation of Ibycus, and "Dance Figure," which is apparently based on the mood of "The Song of Songs."

Lustra gives the impression of an author testing his technical skills in preparation for a major work. That work came in 1920 with *Hugh Selwyn Mauberley*, which a number of critics consider Pound's "break-through," the poem in which he became, finally, modern. Other long poems of the period are the culminations of earlier developments: Translations as a means of re-creating an earlier poetic mood may be seen in "Homage to Sextus Propertius," satire in "Moeurs Contemporaines" and "Villanelle: The Psychological Hour." A sequence rather than a single poem, *Hugh Selwyn Mauberley* was new in its tight juxtaposition of disparate moods and images, in its containment of a complex of attitudes and experiences, and in its careful, often ironic, control of tone. The poem maintains a duality and a deliberate ambivalence that can be confusing. It mocks, at the same time that it bids farewell to, the aesthete in Pound.

If the aesthete is out of step with his time, the time itself was not much to be proud of, and several poems deal with its pervasive tawdriness. World War I, the ultimate shock to the aesthete, raised the question of the relevance of art and culture in a period of confusion and change. Neither the Pre-Raphaelites nor the aesthetes seemed to have very much to say in such a time because they failed to reflect the mood of the decade. Such successful writers as the pseudonymous "Mr. Nixon" (who probably represents Arnold Bennett) were seen to be as tawdry as their age. In the tenth poem of Pound's sequence he states that in an age of cheapness and insincerity that is impatient of craftsmanship or indifferent to the heroic example of the artist, the stylist has sought shelter from the world. In the second part of *Hugh Selwyn Mauberley*, the poet drifts toward death, unable to create what "The Age Demanded," and also unable to provide what the age needed, poetry that would relate his private passions to the society around him. The ultimate confrontation of poet and society took place in *The Cantos*, the long, major poem on which Pound was already then at work.

Bibliography:
Bloom, Harold, ed. *Ezra Pound*. New York: Chelsea House, 1987. A collection of essays by major Pound scholars that address the politics, prejudices, and obscurity of language in Pound's poetry. In his essay, Louis L. Martz declares that *Personae* is Pound's definitive collection of poetry. The essay by Max Nänny deals with such aspects of Pound's use of language as context, contiguity, contact, and tropes.
Durent, Alan. *Ezra Pound, Identity in Crisis: A Fundamental Reassessment of the Poet and His Work*. Totowa, N.J.: Barnes & Noble Books, 1981. A reassessment that addresses Pound's representation of the American experience as one that does not please Americans, but must be acknowledged.
Kenner, Hugh. *The Poetry of Ezra Pound*. 1951. Reprint. Millwood, N.Y.: Kraus, 1974. Overview of Pound's work by the world's leading Pound scholar. Discusses how Pound helped shape the poetry of his contemporaries.
Knapp, James F. *Ezra Pound*. Boston: Twayne, 1979. A useful, general introduction to Pound's work and life. Offers readings of the poet's often obscure use of language.
Nänny, Max. *Ezra Pound: Poetics for an Electric Age*. Bern: Francke Verlag, 1973. An assessment of Pound's poetics. Discusses Pound's use of Roman Jakobson's theory of the bipolar nature of language, what he termed the metaphoric and metonymic function of discourse.

PERSUASION

Type of work: Novel
Author: Jane Austen (1775-1817)
Type of plot: Domestic realism
Time of plot: Early nineteenth century
Locale: Somersetshire and Bath, England
First published: 1818

Principal characters:

SIR WALTER ELLIOT, the owner of Kellynch Hall
ELIZABETH ELLIOT, his oldest daughter
ANNE ELLIOT, his second daughter
MARY MUSGROVE, his youngest daughter
CHARLES MUSGROVE, her husband
HENRIETTA and
LOUISA, Charles Musgrove's sisters
CAPTAIN FREDERICK WENTWORTH, a naval officer
MRS. CLAY, Elizabeth Elliot's friend
WILLIAM ELLIOT, Sir Walter's cousin and heir to Kellynch Hall

The Story:

Sir Walter Elliot was a conceited man, vain of both his good looks and his title. He lived at his country seat, Kellynch Hall, with two of his daughters, Elizabeth and Anne. Elizabeth, handsome and much like her father, was the oldest and her father's favorite. Anne, sweet, self-effacing, and quietly intelligent, was ignored and underrated by both. Mary, the youngest daughter, was married to an agreeable young man named Charles Musgrove; they lived in an untidy house at Uppercross, three miles from Kellynch Hall.

Living beyond his means had brought financial disaster to Sir Walter. On the advice of his solicitor and of a family friend, Lady Russell, he was persuaded to rent Kellynch Hall and take a smaller house in Bath. Anne would have preferred to take a modest house near home, but as usual, her father and sister had their way in the matter.

Reluctantly, Sir Walter let his beloved country seat to Admiral Croft and his wife, who was the sister of a former suitor of Anne, Captain Frederick Wentworth. Anne and Captain Wentworth had fallen in love when they were both very young, but the match had been discouraged. Anne's father felt that the young man's family was not good enough for his own, and Lady Russell considered the engagement unwise because Captain Wentworth had no financial means beyond his navy pay. Anne had followed their advice and broken the engagement, but Wentworth had advanced and had become rich in the navy, just as he had said he would. Anne, now twenty-seven years old, had not forgotten her love at age nineteen, and no one else had taken Captain Wentworth's place in her affection.

With all arrangements completed for the renting of Kellynch Hall, Sir Walter, Elizabeth, and her friend, Mrs. Clay, were off to Bath. Before they departed, Anne warned Elizabeth that Mrs. Clay's was not a disinterested friendship and that she was scheming to marry Sir Walter if she could. Elizabeth would not believe such an idea nor would she agree to dismiss Mrs. Clay.

Anne was to divide her time between her married sister, Mary Musgrove, and Lady Russell until Christmas. Mary and her family also lived near her husband's father and mother and their two daughters, Henrietta and Louisa. During her visit to the Musgroves, Anne met Captain Wentworth again while he was staying with his sister at Kellynch Hall. She found him little changed in eight years.

Because the Musgroves took the Crofts and Captain Wentworth into their circle immediately, the captain and Anne met frequently. He was coldly polite to Anne, but his attentions to the Musgrove sisters caused Mary to begin matchmaking. She could not decide, however, whether he preferred Henrietta or Louisa. When Louisa encouraged Henrietta to resume a former romance with a cousin, Charles Hayter, it seemed plain that Louisa was destined for Captain Wentworth.

Further events increased the likelihood of such a match. During a visit to friends of Captain Wentworth at Lyme Regis, Louisa suffered an injury while the captain was assisting her to jump down a steep flight of steps. The accident was not his fault, for he had cautioned Louisa against jumping, but he blamed himself for not refusing her firmly. Louisa was taken to the home of Captain Wentworth's friends, Captain and Mrs. Harville and Captain Benwick. Quiet, practical, and capable during the emergency, Anne had the pleasure of knowing that Captain Wentworth relied on her strength and good judgment, but she felt that a match between him and the slowly recovering Louisa was certain.

Anne reluctantly joined her family and the designing Mrs. Clay at Bath. She was surprised to find that they were glad to see her. After showing her the house, they told her the news—mainly how much in demand they were and about the presence of a cousin, Mr. William Elliot, who had suddenly appeared to make his peace with the family. Mr. Elliot was the heir to Sir Walter's title and estate, but he had become estranged from the family years before because he did not marry Elizabeth as Sir Walter and Elizabeth felt he should have. Also, he had affronted Sir Walter's pride by speaking disrespectfully of his Kellynch connections.

Now, however, these matters were explained away, and both Sir Walter and Elizabeth were charmed with him. Anne, who had seen Mr. Elliot at Lyme Regis, wondered why he chose to renew a relationship so long neglected. She thought it might be that he was thinking of marrying Elizabeth, now that his first wife was dead; Lady Russell thought Anne was the attraction.

News shortly came of Louisa Musgrove's engagement to Captain Benwick. Joy, surprise, and a hope that Captain Wentworth had lost his partiality for Louisa were mingled in Anne's first reaction. Shortly after she had heard the news, Captain Wentworth arrived in Bath. After a few meetings, Anne knew that he had not forgotten her. She also had the pleasure of knowing that he was jealous of Mr. Elliot, although his jealousy was groundless.

Even if Anne had felt any inclination to become Lady Elliot, the ambition would have been short-lived, for Mr. Elliot's true character now came to light. Anne learned from a former schoolmate, who had been friendly with Mr. Elliot before he basely ruined her husband, that his first design in renewing acquaintance with Sir Walter's family was to prevent Sir Walter from marrying Mrs. Clay and thus having a son who would inherit the title and estate. Later, when he met Anne, he had been genuinely attracted to her. This information was not news to Anne, since Mr. Elliot had proposed to her at a concert the night before. She gave him no encouragement.

Convinced that Anne still loved him as he did her, Captain Wentworth poured out his heart to her in a letter. Soon all was settled happily between them. Both Musgrove girls were also married shortly afterward, but, much to Mary's satisfaction, neither of their husbands was as rich as Wentworth. Mrs. Clay, sacrificing ambition for love, left Bath with Mr. William Elliot, and went to live under his protection in London. Perhaps she hoped some day to be Lady Elliot, though as the wife of a different baronet.

Critical Evaluation:

Completed a year before Jane Austen's death but published posthumously in 1818, *Persuasion* is the novelist's last long work. The novel completes her study of English country families begun in *Sense and Sensibility* (1811) and *Pride and Prejudice* (1813). The story begins with a description of Sir Walter Elliot of Kellynch Hall in Somersetshire, who because he is egotistical, improvident, and idle, has managed to fritter away much of his patrimony. When his extravagance necessitates the letting of Kellynch Hall and the renting of a smaller house in Bath, his capable daughter Anne must make most of the provisions, while her father pouts like a spoiled child. Austen uses Sir Walter as well as his deceitful and scheming cousin and heir William Elliot to criticize the indolent, debilitated gentry of her era.

Like Jane Austen's earlier novels, *Persuasion* articulates and criticizes late eighteenth century English views of courtship and marriage. While marriage is clearly the greatest good achievable by a young woman, the path to this achievement is not a smooth one for Anne Elliot. She must defy her family in order to marry the man she loves. Austen shows the reader that she leaves very little behind when she does marry. Prior to marriage she had cared for her selfish father and elder sister, as well as aiding her hypochondriac younger sister and her children. Since Anne had no status in her family, becoming Mrs. Wentworth would in any case have been a distinct improvement.

Because Anne has previously rejected Captain Wentworth, the normal slow pace of courtship slows to a snail's pace. As in all of Austen's novels, much time is given over to reading and interpreting the sentiments of others. The reader is allowed greater knowledge of Anne Elliot's views than of Wentworth's. The courtship proceeds to some extent by negation, for whereas at first Anne dreads seeing Captain Wentworth again, later she is convinced he loves Louisa rather than herself. Eighteenth century politeness leads to this false conclusion, since Wentworth must be gracious to all but effusive toward none, especially not toward Anne, who had previously rejected him.

Other courtship rituals in *Persuasion* are instructive as well. The Reverend Charles Haytor is initially thought unsuitable for Henrietta Musgrove because he is a simple curate, but once he secures a better living he becomes the perfect match. William Elliot renews his acquaintance with his cousin Sir Walter when he hears that the latter is courting Mrs. Clay; he is afraid Sir Walter will have a male heir thus cutting him out of his inheritance. Money is at the root of these courtship considerations, not love. Even Captain Wentworth is more palatable to Sir Walter and Elizabeth and more defensible as a lover for Anne because he has risen in the world in the intervening eight years.

Jane Austen employs several interesting new devices in *Persuasion*. Although she describes Sir Walter and a number of other characters, Anne Elliot's appearance and demeanor are never described directly but allowed to be gleaned from the reactions of other characters. At the beginning of the novel, her whole family thinks she is drab, and even Captain Wentworth opines that she has altered for the worse in eight years. As the book progresses, Anne comes to be considered more attractive by the other characters, and in the end both William Elliot and Captain Wentworth judge her to be a beauty. Certainly Mrs. Musgrove and Lady Russell have commented on her excellent character throughout the story, but love and appreciation apparently cause Anne's appearance to improve and blossom.

Austen achieves another interesting effect in the denouement of the story when Captain Wentworth writes a letter in the same room in which Anne is talking to Captain Harville about his dead sister Fanny, who was engaged to Captain Benwick, who has since then become engaged to Louisa Musgrove. Harville is not critical of Benwick but wonders why he was not eternally loyal to his dead sister. A conversation ensues between Anne and Harville about men and women and which sex is the most steadfast in love. Anne defends her sex, while Harville defends his. The conversation is just barely audible to Captain Wentworth and Anne is not speaking in order to be heard by him, yet the exchange could easily be between Anne and Wentworth. As Wentworth writes his letter pouring out his love for her, he hears her defending the constancy of women in love and can deduce from what she says that she will accept him. Several previous small instances of indirect discourse between Anne and Wentworth culminate in this final exchange that seals their love for each other. As in all of her work, Jane Austen in her final novel *Persuasion* continues to examine courtship, marriage, the family, and the gentry, as well as the first impressions, last impressions, pride, prejudice, and persuasion that go into changing those central aspects of life.

"Critical Evaluation" by Isabel B. Stanley

Bibliography:

Kirkham, Margaret. *Jane Austen, Feminism and Fiction.* Totowa, N.J.: Barnes and Noble Books, 1983. Connects Jane Austen to earlier feminist writers such as Mary Wollstonecraft and Fanny Burney, as well as to Samuel Richardson's novel *Sir Charles Grandison* (1753-1754). Places Anne Elliot of *Persuasion* in the tradition of feminist heroines.

Paris, Bernard J. *Character and Conflict in Jane Austen's Novels: A Psychological Approach.* Detroit, Mich.: Wayne State University Press, 1978. Analyzes the characters of Anne Elliot and Captain Frederick Wentworth and makes a case for *Persuasion* as Austen's most romantic novel. Evaluates the roles played in the novel by such secondary characters as Lady Russell, Mrs. Musgrove, and Mrs. Croft.

Scott, P. J. M. *Jane Austen: A Reassessment.* Totowa, N.J.: Barnes and Noble Books, 1982. Contains a full assessment of *Persuasion*, which the author sees as the culmination of Austen's work. Examines the egotism and idleness of the entire Elliot family save Anne.

Tanner, Tony. *Jane Austen.* Cambridge, Mass.: Harvard University Press, 1986. Examines Austen's novels in relationship to society, education, and language. Shows *Persuasion* to be a new form of novel for Austen in that it is a negation of her previous works; the action arises from Anne Elliot's denial of her love for Wentworth.

Thompson, James. *Between Self and World: The Novels of Jane Austen.* University Park: The Pennsylvania State University Press, 1988. Considers late eighteenth century views of courtship and marriage in Austen's novels. Shows *Persuasion*'s place in the Austen canon which, as a whole, revolves around reading or interpreting the sentiments of others.